Lecture Notes in Computer Science 11961

More information about this series at http://www.springer.com/series/7409

Yong Man Ro · Wen-Huang Cheng ·
Junmo Kim · Wei-Ta Chu ·
Peng Cui · Jung-Woo Choi ·
Min-Chun Hu · Wesley De Neve (Eds.)

MultiMedia Modeling

26th International Conference, MMM 2020
Daejeon, South Korea, January 5–8, 2020
Proceedings, Part I

Springer

Editors
Yong Man Ro
Korea Advanced Institute of Science and Technology
Daejeon, Korea (Republic of)

Junmo Kim
Korea Advanced Institute of Science and Technology
Daejeon, Korea (Republic of)

Peng Cui
Tsinghua University
Beijing, China

Min-Chun Hu
National Tsing Hua University
Hsinchu, Taiwan

Wen-Huang Cheng
National Chiao Tung University
Hsinchu, Taiwan

Wei-Ta Chu
National Cheng Kung University
Tainan City, Taiwan

Jung-Woo Choi
Korea Advanced Institute of Science and Technology
Daejeon, Korea (Republic of)

Wesley De Neve
Ghent University
Ghent, Belgium

ISSN 0302-9743 ISSN 1611-3349 (electronic)
Lecture Notes in Computer Science
ISBN 978-3-030-37730-4 ISBN 978-3-030-37731-1 (eBook)
https://doi.org/10.1007/978-3-030-37731-1

LNCS Sublibrary: SL3 – Information Systems and Applications, incl. Internet/Web, and HCI

This Springer imprint is published by the registered company Springer Nature Switzerland AG
The registered company address is: Gewerbestrasse 11, 6330 Cham, Switzerland

Preface

These proceedings contain the papers presented at MMM 2020, the 26th International Conference on MultiMedia Modeling, held in Daejeon, South Korea, during January 5–8, 2020. MMM is a leading international conference for researchers and industry practitioners to share new ideas, original research results, and practical development experiences from all MMM-related areas, broadly falling into three categories: multimedia content analysis; multimedia signal processing and communications; and multimedia applications and services. MMM 2020 received 241 paper submissions across 4 categories: 171 full research paper submissions, 49 special session paper submissions, 11 demonstration submissions, and 10 submissions to the Video Browser Showdown (VBS 2020). Of the 171 full papers submitted, 40 were selected for oral presentation and 46 for poster presentation. Of the 49 special session papers submitted, 28 were selected for oral presentation and 8 for poster presentation. In addition, 9 demonstrations and 10 VBS submissions were accepted. The overall acceptance percentage across the conference was thus 58.51%, but 50.29% for full papers and 23.39% of full papers for oral presentation. The submission and review process was coordinated using the EasyChair conference management system. All full-paper submissions were assigned for review to at least three members of the Program Committee. We owe a debt of gratitude to all these reviewers for providing their valuable time to MMM 2020. We would like to thank our invited keynote speakers for their stimulating contributions to the conference. We also wish to thank our organizational team: Special Session chairs Changick Kim and Benoit Huet; Demonstration Chairs Munchurl Kim and Kai-Lung Hua; Video Browser Showdown Chairs Klaus Schoeffmann, Werner Bailer, and Jakub Lokoč; Publicity Chairs Phoebe Chen, Kiyoharu Aizawa, Yo-Sung Ho, Björn ór Jónsson, Yan-Ying Chen, and Bing-Kun Bao; Finance Chair Hoirin Kim; Tutorial Chairs Jitao Sang and Jinah Park; Industrial Chair Young Bok Lee; Panel Chairs Shin'ichi Satoh and Guo-Jun Qi; Web Chair Seung Ho Lee; Conference Secretariat Seul Lee, Minjeong Lee, and A-Young Kim. We would like to thank KAIST for hosting MMM 2020. Special thanks go to the Steering Committee for timely support and advice. In addition, we wish to thank all authors who spent time and effort submitting their work to MMM 2020, and all of the participants and student volunteers for their contributions and valuable support.

October 2019

Yong Man Ro
Wen-Huang Cheng
Junmo Kim
Wei-Ta Chu
Peng Cui
Jung-Woo Choi
Min-Chun Hu
Wesley De Neve

The original version of the book was revised: the first volume editor was added. The correction to the book is available at https://doi.org/10.1007/978-3-030-37731-1_68

Organization

Organizing Committee

General Chairs

Yong Man Ro	Korea Advanced Institute of Science and Technology, South Korea
Wen-Huang Cheng	National Chiao Tung University, Taiwan

Program Chairs

Junmo Kim	Korea Advanced Institute of Science and Technology, South Korea
Wei-Ta Chu	National Cheng Kung University, Taiwan
Peng Cui	Tsinghua University, China

Organizing Chair

Jung-Woo Choi	Korea Advanced Institute of Science and Technology, South Korea

Special Session Chairs

Changick Kim	Korea Advanced Institute of Science and Technology, South Korea
Benoit Huet	Eurecom, France

Panel Chairs

Shin'ichi Satoh	National Institute of Informatics, Japan
Guo-Jun Qi	University of Central Florida, USA

Tutorial Chairs

Jitao Sang	Beijing Jiaotong University, China
Jinah Park	Korea Advanced Institute of Science and Technology, South Korea

Demo Chairs

Munchurl Kim	Korea Advanced Institute of Science and Technology, South Korea
Kai-Lung Hua	National Taiwan University of Science and Technology, Taiwan

Video Browser Showdown Chairs

Klaus Schoeffmann	University of Klagenfurt, Austria
Werner Bailer	Joanneum Research, Austria
Jakub Lokoč	Charles University in Prague, Czech Republic

Publicity Chairs

Phoebe Chen	La Trobe University, Australia
Kiyoharu Aizawa	University of Tokyo, Japan
Yo-Sung Ho	Gwangju Institute of Science and Technology, South Korea
Björn Þór Jónsson	IT University of Copenhagen, Denmark
Yan-Ying Chen	FXPAL, Taiwan
Bing-Kun Bao	Nanjing University of Posts and Telecommunications, China

Publication Chairs

Min-Chun Hu	National Tsing Hua University, Taiwan
Wesley De Neve	Ghent University, Belgium

Industrial Chair

Young Bok Lee	Genesis Lab, South Korea

Financial Chair

Hoirin Kim	Korea Advanced Institute of Science and Technology, South Korea

Web Chair

Seung Ho Lee	Korea University of Technology and Education, South Korea

Steering Committee

Phoebe Chen	La Trobe University, Australia
Tat-Seng Chua	National University of Singapore, Singapore
Kiyoharu Aizawa	University of Tokyo, Japan
Cathal Gurrin	Dublin City University, Ireland
Benoit Huet	Eurecom, France
Klaus Schoeffmann	University of Klagenfurt, Austria
Richang Hong	Hefei University of Technology, China
Björn Þór Jónsson	IT University of Copenhagen, Denmark
Guo-Jun Qi	University of Central Florida, USA
Wen-Huang Cheng	National Chiao Tung University, Taiwan
Peng Cui	Tsinghua University, China

Special Sessions Organizers

SS1: AI-Powered 3D Vision

You Yang	Huazhong University of Science and Technology, China
Qifei Wang	Google Inc., USA

SS2: Multimedia Analytics: Perspectives, Tools and Applications

Björn Þór Jónsson	IT University of Copenhagen, Denmark
Laurent Amsaleg	CNRS-IRISA, France
Cathal Gurrin	Dublin City University, Ireland
Stevan Rudinac	University of Amsterdam, The Netherlands
Xirong Li	Renmin University of China, China

SS3: MDRE: Multimedia Datasets for Repeatable Experimentation

Cathal Gurrin	Dublin City University, Ireland
Duc-Tien Dang-Nguyen	Dublin City University, Ireland
Klaus Schoeffmann	University of Klagenfurt, Austria
Björn Þór Jónsson	IT University of Copenhagen, Denmark

SS4: MMAC: Multi-modal Affective Computing of Large-Scale Multimedia Data

Sicheng Zhao	University of California, USA
Jufeng Yang	Nankai University, China
Hatice Gunes	University of Cambridge, UK

SS5: MULTIMED: Multimedia and Multimodal Analytics in the Medical Domain and Pervasive Environments

Georgios Meditskos	Centre for Research and Technology Hellas, Greece
Klaus Schoeffmann	University of Klagenfurt, Austria
Leo Wanner	ICREA, Universitat Pompeu Fabra, Spain
Kunwadee Sripanidkulchai	Chulalongkorn University, Thailand
Stefanos Vrochidis	Centre for Research and Technology Hellas, Greece

SS6: Intelligent Multimedia Security

Youliang Tian	Guizhou University, China
Hongtao Xie	University of Science and Technology of China, China
Bing-Kun Bao	Nanjing University of Posts and Telecommunications, China
Zhineng Chen	Institute of Automation, Chinese Academy of Sciences, China
Changgen Peng	Guizhou University, China

Tutorial Organizers

Tutorial 1: Introduction to Biometrics and Anti-Spoofing

Wonjun Kim	Konkuk University, South Korea

Tutorial 2: Recent Advances in Deep Novelty Detection for Medical Imaging

Jaeil Kim	Kyungpook National University, South Korea

Tutorial 3: Haptic Interaction with Multimedia Data

Sang-Youn Kim	Korea University of Technology and Education, South Korea

Program Committee

Aaron Duane	Insight, Ireland
Adam Jatowt	Kyoto University, Japan
Adrian Muscat	University of Malta, Malta
Alan Smeaton	Dublin City University, Ireland
Amon Rapp	University of Turin, Italy
Anastasios Karakostas	Aristotle University of Thessaloniki, Greece
Andreas Leibetseder	University of Klagenfurt, Austria
Antonino Furnari	Università degli Studi di Catania, Italy
Athina Tsanousa	Centre for Research and Technology Hellas, Greece
Benjamin Bustos	University of Chile, Chile
Benoit Huet	Eurecom, France
Bing-Kun Bao	Nanjing University of Posts and Telecommunications, China
Björn Jónsson	IT University of Copenhagen, Denmark
Björn Thor Jonsson	IT University of Copenhagen, Denmark
Bogdan Ionescu	Politehnica University of Bucharest, Romania
Borja Sanz	University of Deusto, Spain
Byoung Tae Oh	Korea Aerospace University, South Korea
Cathal Gurrin	Dublin City University, Ireland
Cem Direkoglu	Middle East Technical University, Turkey
Changick Kim	Korea Advanced Institute of Science and Technology, South Korea
Chong-Wah Ngo	City University of Hong Kong, Hong Kong, China
Christian Timmerer	University of Klagenfurt, Austria
Claudiu Cobarzan	University of Klagenfurt, Austria
Cong-Thang Truong	University of Aizu, Japan
Daniel Stanley Tan	De La Salle University, Philippines
Debesh Jha	Simula Research Laboratory, Norway
Dongyu She	Nankai University, China
Duc Tien Dang Nguyen	University of Bergen, Norway
Edgar Chavez	Ensenada Center for Scientific Research and Higher Education, Mexico

Esra Açar	Middle East Technical University, Turkey
Estefania Talavera	University of Groningen, The Netherlands
François Destelle	Dublin City University, Ireland
Frank Hopfgartner	The University of Sheffield, UK
Fuli Feng	National University of Singapore, Singapore
Georges Quénot	Laboratoire d'Informatique de Grenoble, CNRS, France
Georgios Meditskos	Centre for Research and Technology Hellas, Greece
Gylfi Gudmundsson	Reykjavik University, Iceland
Henning Müller	HES-SO, Switzerland
Hong Wu	University of Science and Technology of China, China
Hong-Han Shuai	National Chiao Tung University, Taiwan
Hongtao Xie	University of Science and Technology of China, China
Hyowon Lee	Singapore University of Technology and Design, Singapore
Ichiro Ide	Nagoya University, Japan
Ioannis Kompatsiaris	Centre for Research and Technology Hellas, Greece
Jakub Lokoč	Charles University in Prague, Czech Republic
Jan Zahálka	Czech Technical University in Prague, Czech Republic
Jean-Marc Ogier	University of La Rochelle, France
Jenny Benois-Pineau	University of Bordeaux, France
Jen-Wei Huang	National Cheng Kung University, Taiwan
Jianjun Qian	Nanjing University of Science and Technology, China
Jie Shao	University of Science and Technology of China, China
Jiro Katto	Waseda University, Japan
Jochen Laubrock	University of Potsdam, Germany
Jochen Meyer	OFFIS Institute for Information Technology, Germany
John See	Multimedia University, Malaysia
John Virtusio	National Taiwan University of Science and Technology, Taiwan
Josep Blat	Universitat Pompeu Fabra, Spain
Jun Shi	Harbin Institute of Technology, China
Jung-Woo Choi	Korea Advanced Institute of Science and Technology, South Korea
Junmo Kim	Korea Advanced Institute of Science and Technology, South Korea
Jun-Wei Hsieh	National Taiwan Ocean University, Taiwan
K. Selcuk Candan	Arizona State University, USA
Kai-Lung Hua	National Taiwan University of Science and Technology, Taiwan
Kathy Clawson	University of Sunderland, UK
Keiji Yanai	The University of Electro-Communications, Japan
Kevin Mcguinness	Dublin City University, Ireland
Klaus Schöffmann	University of Klagenfurt, Austria
Koichi Shinoda	Tokyo Institute of Technology, Japan
Konstantin Pogorelov	Simula Research Laboratory, Norway

Konstantinos Avgerinakis	Centre for Research and Technology Hellas, Greece
Ladislav Peska	Charles University in Prague, Czech Republic
Lai-Kuan Wong	Multimedia University, Malaysia
Laurent Amsaleg	CNRS-IRISA, France
Lei Huang	Ocean University of China, China
Li Su	Chinese Academy of Sciences, China
Lianli Gao	University of Science and Technology of China, China
Lifeng Sun	Tsinghua University, China
Linjun Zhou	Tsinghua University, China
Marcel Worring	University of Amsterdam, The Netherlands
Marco A. Hudelist	University of Klagenfurt, Austria
Mariana Damova	Mozaika, Bulgaria
Mario Taschwer	University of Klagenfurt, Austria
Markus Koskela	CSC - IT Center for Science Ltd., Finland
Martin Winter	Joanneum Research, Austria
Mathias Lux	University of Klagenfurt, Austria
Mathieu Delalandre	Laboratoire d'Informatique, France
Matthias Zeppelzauer	University of Applied Sciences St. Pölten, Austria
Mei-Ling Shyu	University of Miami, USA
Michael E. Houle	National Institute of Informatics, Japan
Michael Lew	Leiden University, The Netherlands
Miloš Radovanović	University of Novi Sad, Serbia
Min H. Kim	Korea Advanced Institute of Science and Technology, South Korea
Min-Chun Hu	National Tsing Hua University, Taiwan
Ming Sun	SenseTime, Hong Kong, China
Minh-Son Dao	National Institute of Information and Communications Technology, Japan
Mitsunori Matsushita	Kansai University, Japan
Mohan Kankanhalli	National University of Singapore, Singapore
Monica Dominguez	Universitat Pompeu Fabra, Spain
Munchrl Kim	Korea Advanced Institute of Science and Technology, South Korea
Mylene Farias	University of Brasília, Brazil
Naoko Nitta	Osaka University, Japan
Neil O'Hare	Yahoo Research, Spain
Ognjen Arandjelovic	University of St Andrews, UK
Olfa Ben Ahmed	Eurecom, France
Panagiotis Sidiropoulos	Cortexica, UK
Peiguang Jing	Tianjin University, China
Peng Cui	Tsinghua University, China
Pengming Feng	China Aerospace Science and Technology Corporation, China
Petros Alvanitopoulos	Centre for Research and Technology Hellas, Greece
Phivos Mylonas	National Technical University of Athens, Greece

Pyunghwan Ahn	Korea Advanced Institute of Science and Technology, South Korea
Qi Dai	Microsoft, China
Qiao Wang	Southeast University, China
Qifei Wang	Google, USA
Qiong Liu	Huazhong University of Science and Technology, China
Richang Hong	Hefei University of Technology, China
Robert Mertens	HSW University of Applied Sciences, Germany
Roger Zimmermann	National University of Singapore, Singapore
Sabrina Kletz	University of Klagenfurt, Austria
Sanghoon Lee	Yonsei University, South Korea
Savvas Chatzichristofis	Neapolis University, Cyprus
Seiji Hotta	Tokyo University of Agricultural and Technology, Japan
Sen Xiang	Wuhan University of Science and Technology, China
Seong Tae Kim	Technical University of Munich, Germany
Shaoyi Du	Xi'an Jiaotong University, China
Shijie Hao	Hefei University of Technology, China
Shingo Uchihashi	Fuji Xerox Co., Ltd., Japan
Shin'Ichi Satoh	National Institute of Informatics, Japan
Shintami Hidayati	Institute of Technology Sepuluh Nopember, Indonesia
Sicheng Zhao	University of California, Berkeley, USA
Silvio Guimaraes	Pontifícia Universidade Católica de Minas Gerais, Brazil
Simon Mille	Universitat Pompeu Fabra, Spain
Stefan Petscharnig	AIT Austrian Institute of Technology, Austria
Stefanos Vrochidis	Center for Research and Technology Hellas, Greece
Stevan Rudinac	University of Amsterdam, The Netherlands
Thanos Stavropoulos	Aristotle University of Thessaloniki, Greece
Thomas Koehler	TU Dresden, Germany
Tianzhu Zhang	University of Science and Technology of China, China
Tien-Tsin Wong	The Chinese University of Hong Kong, Hong Kong, China
Tomas Grosup	Charles University in Prague, Czech Republic
Tongwqei Ren	Nanjing University, China
Tong-Yee Lee	National Cheng Kung University, Taiwan
Toshihiko Yamasaki	The University of Tokyo, Japan
Tse-Yu Pan	National Tsing Hua University, Taiwan
Vasileios Mezaris	Centre for Research and Technology Hellas, Greece
Vincent Oria	New Jersey Institute of Technology, USA
Weiming Dong	Chinese Academy of Sciences, China
Weiqing Min	Chinese Academy of Sciences, China
Wei-Ta Chu	National Cheng Kung University, Taiwan
Wen-Huang Cheng	National Chiao Tung University, Taiwan

Wen-Ze Shao	Nanjing University of Posts and Telecommunications, China
Werner Bailer	Joanneum Research, Austria
Wolfgang Minker	University of Ulm, Germany
Wolfgang Weiss	Joanneum Research, Austria
Wu Liu	JD AI Research of JD.com, China
Xi Shao	Nanjing University of Posts and Telecommunications, China
Xiang Wang	National University of Singapore, Singapore
Xiangjun Shen	Jiangsu University, China
Xiao Wu	Southwest Jiaotong University, China
Xiaofeng Zhu	Guangxi Normal University, China
Xiaoqing Luo	Jiangnan University, China
Xiaoxiao Sun	Nankai University, China
Xirong Li	Renmin University of China, China
Xu Wang	Shenzhen University, China
Xueting Liu	The Chinese University of Hong Kong, Hong Kong, China
Yang Yang	University of Science and Technology of China, China
Yannick Prié	University of Nantes, France
Yanwei Fu	Fudan University, China
Ying Cao	City University of Hong Kong, Hong Kong, China
Yingbo Li	Eurecom, France
Ying-Qing Xu	Tsinghua University, China
Yong Man Ro	Korea Advanced Institute of Science and Technology, South Korea
Yongju Jung	Gachon University, South Korea
Yo-Sung Ho	Gwangju Institute of Science and Technology, South Korea
You Yang	Huazhong University of Science and Technology, China
Yue Gao	Tsinghua University, China
Yue He	Tsinghua University, China
Yu-Kun Lai	Cardiff University, UK
Zan Gao	Tianjin University of Technology, China
Zhaoquan Yuan	Southwest Jiaotong University, China
Zhe-Cheng Fan	Academia Sinica, Taiwan
Zhenzhen Hu	Nanyang Technological University, Singapore
Zhineng Chen	Chinese Academy of Sciences, China
Zhiyong Cheng	Shandong Artificial Intelligence Institute, China
Zhongyuan Wang	Wuhan University, China
Zhu Li	University of Missouri, USA
Zhuangzhi Yan	Shanghai University, China
Ziyu Guan	Northwest University of China, China

Additional Reviewers

Ahn, Jaesung
Alvanitopoulos, Petros
Avgerinakis, Konstantinos
Chatzilari, Elisavet
Ding, Yujuan
Giannakeris, Panagiotis
Gkountakos, Konstantinos
Guo, Yangyang
Healy, Graham
Hu, Wenbo
Hu, Xinghong
Huang, Tianchi
Huyen, Tran Thi Thanh
Kim, Hyungmin
Krestenitis, Marios
Le Capitaine, Hoel
Liu, Fan
Lu, Jian
Lu, Steve
Lu, Yu
MacFarlane, Kate
Michail, Manos
Mouchère, Harold
Orfanidis, Georgios
Ortego, Diego
Park, Byeongseon
Patrocínio Jr., Zenilton K. G.
Rudinac, Stevan
Ruiz, Ubaldo
Sadallah, Madjid
Shimoda, Wataru
Vystrcilova, Michaela
Wang, Wenxuan
Xia, Menghan
Xiao, Junbin
Xu, Pengfei
Yang, Juyoung
Yao, Xin
Yu, Jaemyung
Yu, Sha
Zhang, Haoran
Zhang, Ruixiao
Zhang, Zhuming
Zhao, Wanqing
Zhou, Liting
Zhou, Yuan
Zhu, Haichao
Ètefan, Liviu-Daniel

Contents – Part I

Oral Session 1A: Audio and Signal Processing

Oral Session 2A: Coding and HVS

Oral Session 3A: Color Processing and Art

Oral Session 4A: Detection and Classification

Oral Session 5A: Face

Contents – Part II

Poster Papers

Special Session Papers SS1: AI-Powered 3D Vision

SS3: MDRE: Multimedia Datasets for Repeatable Experimentation

SS4: MMAC: Multi-modal Affective Computing of Large-Scale Multimedia Data

SS5: MULTIMED: Multimedia and Multimodal Analytics in the Medical Domain and Pervasive Environments

SS6: Intelligent Multimedia Security

VBS Papers

Oral Session 1A: Audio and Signal Processing

Light Field Reconstruction Using Dynamically Generated Filters

Xiuxiu Jing[1,2], Yike Ma[1], Qiang Zhao[1(✉)], Ke Lyu[2], and Feng Dai[1]

[1] Key Laboratory of Intelligent Information Processing, Institute of Computing Technology, Chinese Academy of Sciences, Beijing, China
zhaoqiang@ict.ac.cn

[2] University of Chinese Academy of Sciences, Beijing, China

Abstract. Densely-sampled light fields have already show unique advantages in applications such as depth estimation, refocusing, and 3D presentation. But it is difficult and expensive to access. Commodity portable light field cameras, such as Lytro and Raytrix, are easy to carry and easy to operate. However, due to the camera design, there is a trade-off between spatial and angular resolution, which can not be sampled intensively at the same time. In this paper, we present a novel learning-based light field reconstruction approach to increase the angular resolution of a sparsely-sample light field image. Our approach treats the reconstruction problem as the filtering operation on the sub-aperture images of input light field and uses a deep neural network to estimate the filtering kernels for each sub-aperture image. Our network adopts a U-Net structure to extract feature maps from input sub-aperture images and angular coordinate of novel view, then a filter-generating component is designed for kernel estimation. We compare our method with existing light field reconstruction methods with and without depth information. Experiments show that our method can get much better results both visually and quantitatively.

Keywords: Light field reconstruction · Angular super-resolution · CNN · Kernel estimation

1 Introduction

Compared with traditional 2D images, which only measure the total amount of light at each point on the photosensor, light field (LF) images record the amount of light traveling along each ray that intersects the sensor. Thus they store radiance information in both spatial and angular dimensions. Due to the capture of the additional two dimensions of data, light field imaging [10] has become one of the research hotspots in the field of computational photography, and has been widely used in many applications. In particular, densely-sampled LF images record a richer range of visual information in natural scenes, and

Y. M. Ro et al. (Eds.): MMM 2020, LNCS 11961, pp. 3–13, 2020.
https://doi.org/10.1007/978-3-030-37731-1_1

have demonstrated unique advantages in areas such as multi-perspective rendering [15], refocusing [16,27], depth estimation [11,20,21], 3D display and virtual reality.

Early approaches to capture LF images involve the use of camera arrays [23], which contain a large number of cameras. Although these systems can capture LF images with both high spatial and angular resolution, they are bulky and expensive. Nowadays, commodity portable LF cameras, such as Lytro [1] and Raytrix [2], are introduced to the market. These cameras are more compact than the camera array systems and provide an effective ways to obtain LF images. However, due to the design of using 2D sensors to capture 4D LF images, they must make a trade-off between spatial and angular resolution, which means these cameras sample sparsely in either spatial or angular domain. To fully exploit the advantages of LF images, we need to reconstruct densely-sampled LF images from sparsely-sampled ones.

LF reconstruction that effectively increases the number of sub-aperture images (SAIs) of sparsely-sampled LF[1] is an on-going problem. A variety of solutions have been proposed. Recently developed methods based on deep learning [13,24] have far outperformed traditional methods [22]. In particular, Kalantari et al. [13] used two sequential convolutional neural networks (CNNs) to synthesize new SAIs from sparsely-sampled LF image, with the first CNN estimating the disparity and the second CNN estimating the final pixel colors. However the quality of new SAIs synthesized by this approach relies heavily on the quality of estimated disparity. Inspired by the idea of single image super-resolution [8], Wu et al. [24] proposed a CNN to map the epipolar-plane images (EPIs) from low to high resolution, and then presented a blur-deblur scheme to solve the problem of angular and spatial information asymmetry caused by angular sparse sampling. However, this approach requires complex preprocessing and postprocessing steps.

In this paper, we treat LF reconstruction as filtering operations on SAIs of input sparsely-sampled LF image, and propose a deep CNN to dynamically generate these filters [12,17]. The network contains two components: an U-Net component is used to extract features and a filter-generating component is used to estimate filters. For a pixel in the SAI to be synthesized, the network takes patches from sparse SAIs and the position of new SAI as input and estimates filtering kernels that will be used to filter the input patches for output pixel synthesis. As our method does not need to estimate the disparity, it has better quantitative and visual reconstruction results as shown by the experiments. Since our method processes the original SAIs instead of EPIs, it also does not need complex preprocessing and postprocessing steps.

The rest of this paper is organized as follows. Section 2 reviews the most related work. We describe the problem in Sect. 3, and introduce structure and training details of the network in Sects. 4 and 5 respectively. After discussing the experimental results in Sects. 6, 7 concludes the paper.

[1] We use sparsely-sampled LF to refer light field sampled sparsely in *angular* domain.

2 Related Work

For the problem of LF reconstruction in spatial or angular dimension, many researchers have proposed a variety of methods. This work focuses on improving angular resolution of LF images, which effectively increases the number of SAIs of sparsely-sampled LF images. According to whether or not the depth information is used, the mainstream LF angular super-resolution methods can be classified into two categories.

2.1 Light Field Reconstruction with Depth

Most of these methods are based on the idea of warping the input SAIs to novel new SAIs guided by an estimated disparity map. Bishop et al. [5] first proposed LF reconstruction in super-resolution. By using accurate camera internal parameters and estimated depth map, they built an imaging model of microlens array camera, then reconstructed the LF through blind deconvolution. Wanner et al. [22] described a variational method for disparity estimation as well as spatial and angular super-resolution. They obtained disparity map by computing the structure tensor of 2D EPI slices. The quality of such methods depends heavily on the quality of disparity estimation. Although there are many excellent subsequent disparity estimation methods [6,11,21] being proposed, ghosting and tearing effects in novel SAIs appears when input SAIs are sparse.

With the wide application of deep learning in computer vision field, Kalantari et al. [13] trained two sequential CNN to estimate disparity and color. According to a series of disparity levels, they wrapped sparse SAIs of the LF and input them to the first CNN to obtain the disparity. Then they warpped the input SAIs with the estimated disparity to novel views. This approach alleviates the deficiency of the method in [22] by minimizing the error between novel SAIs and ground truth rather than optimizing disparity map. However, it still relies on the intermediate disparity estimation step, and can not deal with occlusion very well.

2.2 Light Field Reconstruction Without Depth

Shi et al. [19] reconstructed LF using the sparsity in the continuous Fourier domain. They transformed the densely-sampled LF to discrete Fourier domain, then recovered the coefficient values and continuous position to obtain the angular frequency. And the reconstructed densely-sampled LFs are obtained by applying inverse Fourier transform. This method is sophisticated but requires the acquisition of light fields in a specific mode, which limits its use.

Cho et al. [7] proposed a learning-based sparse coding method, which uses raw data to train a dictionary that encodes natural image structures, and generates image pairs through Barycentric interpolation. Yoon et al. [26] trained a CNN to solve the problem of spatial and angular super-resolution of the LF, which was inspired by the 2D image super-resolution method [8]. However these two above methods do not make full use of the information of LF images.

Wu et al. [24] proposed a CNN model that inherits the basic architecture of the network in [8] and added the residual learning component. They utilized the idea of single image super-resolution to restore the detail of the EPI in the angular domain after it has been upsampled to the desired angular resolution using bicubic interpolation. They also presented a blur-deblur scheme to solve the problem of angular and spatial information asymmetry caused by angular sparse sampling. However, this approach requires complex preprocessing and postprocessing steps, and works well just when at least 3 views are provided in each angular dimension.

3 4D Light Field and Problem Formulation

According to 4D light field model $L(u, v, s, t)$ [15], the light field can be described by the light rays passing through two parallel planes. For light field cameras, the *st* plane and *uv* plane represents the plane formed by camera main lens and microlens array respectively. After decoding and extracting the SAIs, the LF is represented by the SAIs array. The *uv* plane determines the camera plane, which gives the angular coordinates of LF. And the *st* plane determines the image plane, which gives the spatial coordinates of LF.

Our goal is to reconstruct a densely-sampled LF image from a sparsely-sampled one, whose angular resolution is low, i.e. 2×2 in this paper. Our method takes the sparse 4 SAIs and an angular coordinate (u, v) as input, and synthesizes a novel SAI at the specified position. The main idea of our method is to treat LF reconstruction as filtering operations on input SAIs. To be specific, for a pixel (x, y) in the novel SAI I_n to be synthesized, we assign its color as the sum of filtered patches extracted from the SAIs of input sparsely-sampled LF image, i.e.

$$I_n(x, y) = \sum_{i=1}^{4} K_i(x, y) * P_i(x, y), \tag{1}$$

where K_i is the filtering kernel to be estimated, $P_i(x, y)$ is the patch centered at (x, y) in input SAI I_i, $*$ is the filtering operation. We design a deep CNN f, which takes four patches $\mathcal{P} = \{P_1(x, y), P_2(x, y), P_3(x, y), P_4(x, y)\}$ and coordinate (u, v) as input, and dynamically generate input-specific filters $\mathcal{K} = \{K_1(x, y), K_2(x, y), K_3(x, y), K_4(x, y)\}$, i.e.

$$\mathcal{K} = f(\mathcal{P}, u, v). \tag{2}$$

4 Proposed Framework

In this section, we introduced the proposed neural network. We first describe the integral structure of the neural network and the role of each component, and then describe the characteristics of the network designed for LF reconstruction. Combined with the characteristics of LF, we proposed a deep CNN based on pixel-level generation, which is designed for the angular super-resolution task of sparsely-sampled LF images. The architecture of the network is illustrated in Fig. 1. It contains two components: a U-Net component and a filter-generating component. The former one is used to extract features and is composed of encoding, decoding and local concatenation parts. The latter one estimates the filtering kernels $\mathcal{K}$ and contains eight sibling sub-networks.

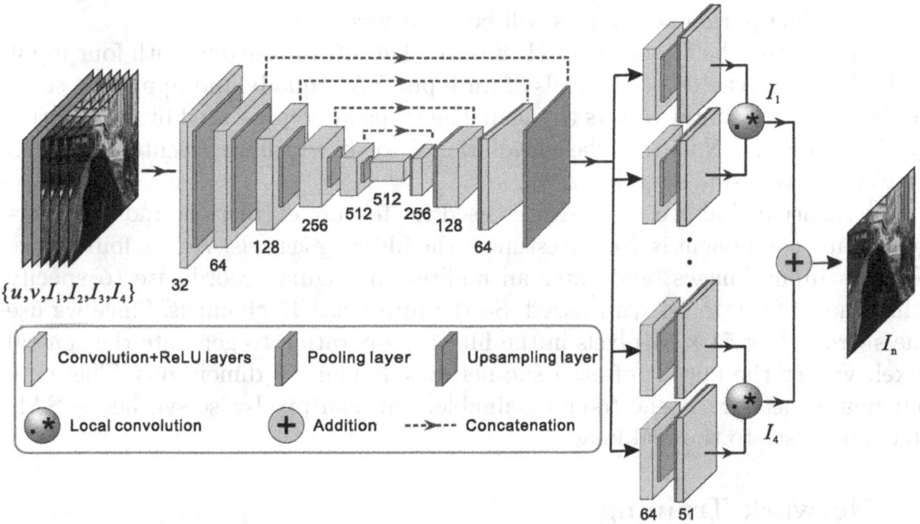

Fig. 1. The integral structure of the adaptive separable convolution network.

The encoding part of the U-Net contains 5 basic blocks and 5 pooling layers. Each basic block contains 3 convolutional and ReLU layers. The encoding part is used to extract feature maps from the input patches and angular coordinate. The decoding part contains 4 same basic blocks as encoding part and 4 up-sampling layers. Each up-sampling layer contains a bilinear up-sampling layer, a convolutional layer and a ReLU layer. The decoding part is used to increase the size of the feature maps through up-sampling, and perform the dense prediction. In order to better extract features and prevent the degradation of the weight matrix, skip connections are added between the convolutional layers in encoding part and the up-sampling layers in decoding part. Skip connections are the concatenations in Fig. 1.

The filter-generating component consists of eight identical sub-networks in parallel and four dynamic filter layers [12]. Each sub-network contains a same basic block as encoding part and a same up-sampling layer as decoding part. Instead of directly estimating filters $\mathcal{K}$ to convolve with input patches $\mathcal{P}$ to synthesize pixels of novel SAI, eight identical sub-networks, which paired up, are used to estimate four pairs of 1D filters $\{(K_i^h, K_i^v)|i = 1, \ldots, 4\}$ to approximate the four 2D filters [18]. Then the filter K_i can be represented as $K_i = K_i^h * K_i^v$, which can reduces parameters of each K_i from N^2 to $2N$.

For clarity, we make a distinction between model parameters and filter parameters. In general, model parameters are the weights of channels at each layer, which are initialized in advance and updated only during training. And once the training is complete, they are same for each input sample. Filter parameters are the estimated contributions of $P_i(x, y)$ to each pixel in the synthesized patch, which does not need to be initialized and will change according to different input patches. The closer between pixels of input and output images are, the greater corresponding parameters values will be. And vice versa.

Then we use the four pairs of 1D filtering kernels to convolve with four input SAIs. We treat the three channels of an input SAI equally and apply the same vertical and horizontal vectors to them. The steps are represented by the asterisk symbols in Fig. 1. Note that the convolution is local, which we execute it through a network layer similar to [9,12,25].

As mentioned above, the U-Net is used for feature extraction, and the filter-generating component is used to estimate the filtering kernels. We use four sparse SAIs as input images, and enter an additional angular coordinate to specify which novel view to be synthesized. So the input has 12 channels. Since we use the surrounding 51×51 pixels in the filtering operation to generate the central pixel, we set the output of each sub-network having 51 dimensions. Therefore our neural network is end-to-end trainable, and can pixel-wise synthesize SAIs that are closer to the real images.

5 Network Training

This section explains the details of the network training. We first describe the characteristics and acquisition method of the training dataset. Then we mainly introduce the implementation details, including the software and hardware that we use, the optimization method and loss function, the processing of input image boundaries, and several important hyper-parameters, ect.

5.1 Training Dataset

We train the network using 100 LF images provided by Kalantari et al. [13], and use other 30 LF images as test data. All of these LF images are captured using a Lytro Illum camera, and include a variety of indoor and outdoor scenes such as bicycles, cars, trees, people, etc. Each LF can be compiled into a 14×14 array of SAIs, each of which has resolution 376×541. Because the three SAIs from each side are usually black, we use only the central 8×8 SAIs in the experiment. During training, we randomly selected a SAI as ground truth and send its angular coordinate (u, v) together with four corner SAIs to the network.

In order to ensure the diversity and validity of training data, and to solve the problem of not enough training data, we extract patches of size 150×150 from SAIs and perform data augmentation to the patches including inversion, rotation, scaling, etc. Then we random crop sub-patches with size 128×128 for training. Ultimately, we get approximately 71500 training sample for each LF image in the dataset at a specific angular coordinate (u, v).

5.2 Implementation Details

We implemented our method with pytorch and trained it with two GeForce GTX 1080 Ti GPUs. To train our neural network, we initialized its parameters using a convolution aware initialization method [3] and applied AdaMax solver [14] with $\beta_1 = 0.9$, $\beta_2 = 0.999$. And a learning rate between 0.001 to 0.0001 was applied without weight decay. Due to the large number of network parameters and memory pressure, we selected a mini-batch size of 32 samples, and sub-batch size was 4. And we used MSE loss to minimize the error between the synthesized SAI and the ground truth.

Hyper-parameter Selection. In addition to the normal parameters in training, several hyper-parameters play an important role during the training. We reasonably selected the hyper-parameters through the validation dataset. This validation dataset are identical with training dataset, but mutually exclusive with training dataset. We used patches of size 128×128 instead of training on entire sub-aperture images. As described by Bansal et al. [4], this can help us avoid patches that contain no useful information and leads to diverse mini-batches. Through prior knowledge and experimental results, we discovered using patches of size 51×51 in filtering operation gives the best performance.

Angular Coordinate. Another choice we should make is how to represent the angular coordinate (u, v) of the novel SAI to be synthesized. Assume we want to reconstruct a densely-sampled LF, whose angular resolution is 8×8, from a sparsely-sample LF. The angular coordinate (u, v), which is taken as the input of the network, of novel SAI satisfies $1 \leq u \leq 8, 1 \leq v \leq 8$. Since the pixel values of the four input patches are normalized to $[0, 1]$, we also input the normalized (u, v) to the network. For example, for $(u, v) = (3, 5)$, its normalized coordinate is $(\frac{3}{8}, \frac{5}{8})$. We convert u and v to matrices, whose sizes are the same as the input image patches, i.e. 128×128 in our implementation. Then the network takes a tenser with size $128 \times 128 \times 14$ as input.

Boundary Processing. When generating pixel (x, y) of novel SAI, due to disparity, occlusion and other phenomena, the neighborhood of (x, y) on the input SAIs should be considered. We used the surrounding 51×51 pixels in the filtering operation and generate the central pixel. Thus the input patches needs to be expanded 25 pixels all around the patches by padding, such that boundary pixels can be processed. We tried reflective padding, zero padding, and padding by repetition. And we found padding by repetition works well.

6 Experimental Result

In this section, we evaluated the proposed framework on 30 real-scenes provided by [13]. This test dataset mostly includes trees, flowers, vehicles, buildings, etc.

The objects in the SAIs of the LFs are complex and the boundaries are not easy to distinguish. We compared our approach with representative state-of-the-art methods for LF reconstruction. And our method showed good results in both qualitative and visual evaluation.

Table 1. Quantitative performance of different methods for 8 × 8 light field reconstruction over 30 real-world scenes.

Metrics	Wang el al. [21]	Jeon el al. [11]	Kalantari el al. [13]	Ours
PSNR	32.78	34.02	37.50	**38.54**
SSIM	0.946	0.952	0.970	**0.973**

6.1 8 × 8 Light Field Reconstruction

We first reconstruct densely-sampled LFs with angular resolution 8 × 8. We compare our method with previous algorithms with and without depth information. For algorithms with depth information, we adopt several light field disparity

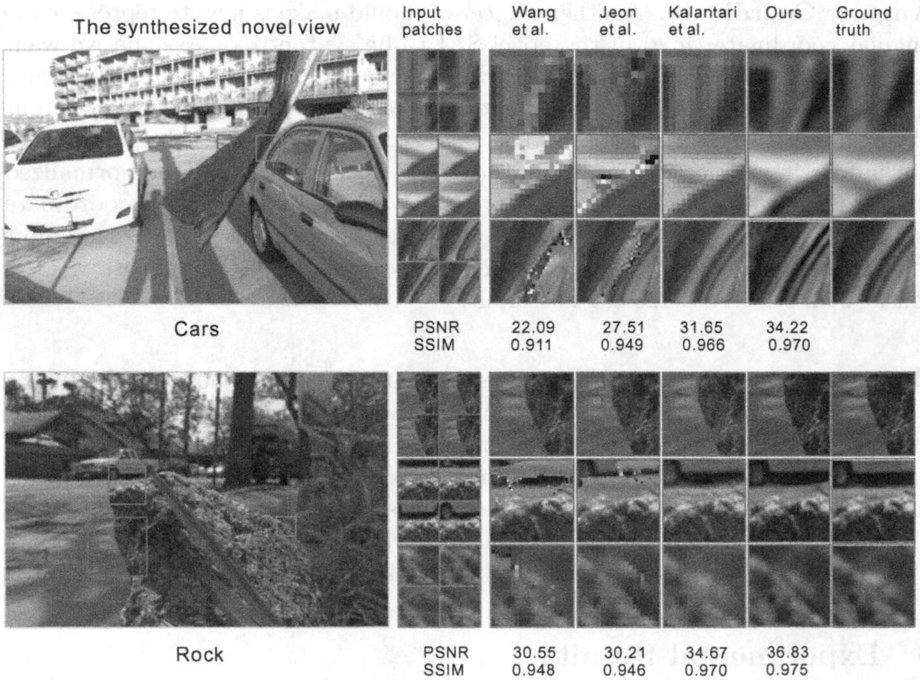

Fig. 2. Visual comparison among LF reconstruction methods.

estimation methods [11,21] to generate the disparities and use them in an light field angular super-resolution method [22]. After reconstruction, we compute the PSNR and SSIM between the ground truth and the synthesized SAIs. The quantitative performance of different methods are given in Table 1. We can see that our method achieves the best performance.

In order to more intuitively illustrate the advantage of our method, we give two reconstructed light fields in Fig. 2. The foregrounds of these two scenes are simple, but the backgrounds are complex. The car scene contains a branch in front of the street, cars and buildings, and the disparity of the four input SAIs is small. The rock scene contains mainly grass, cars and stones, and the disparity of the four input SAIs is large. Although we choose some simple patches in the foreground of the cars scene, the compared algorithms are not very good at reconstructing the details. Their results contain tearing and the chessboard artifacts. The result of Kalantari el al. [13] is relatively well, but still can not deal with the occlusion problem well and has the effect of boundary ambiguity in the red inset. For the patches in the complex background of the rock scene, this is difficult for the baseline methods. They can not reconstruct the details of the car very well. For the blue inset of the rock scene, the result of Kalantari el al. [13] also have the effect of boundary blurring. In general, the baseline methods show ghosting, tearing, boundary blurring and other effects. Only our method can reconstruct details of the novel SAIs well, and the results of our method are closer to the ground truth than others.

6.2 7×7 Light Field Reconstruction

We also compare our method with the approach proposed by Wu et al. [24]. As our method accepts a sparsely-sampled light field with angular resolution 2×2 as input, we run their code for 2×2 to 7×7 light field reconstruction task. We also estimate the disparities using the method in [11] and take a depth based reconstruction method as baseline. The PSNR and SSIM computed between ground truth and the reconstructed results by different methods are given in Table 2. Again, our method can achieve the best quantitative performance.

Table 2. Quantitative performance of different methods for 7×7 light field reconstruction over 30 real-world scenes.

Metrics	Jeon el al. [11]	Wu el al. [24]	Ours
PSNR	32.95	38.69	**38.92**
SSIM	0.942	0.958	**0.975**

Another fact we can get from the table is that when reconstructing 7×7 light field from a 2×2 one, the performance of depth based reconstruction method is worse than that when reconstructing a 8×8 light field. This is because the method in [11] can not give good depth estimation when the baseline is too small. In contrast, our method can get better result when reconstructing 7×7 light field, as it does not reply on the result of depth estimation.

7 Conclusion

In this paper, in view of the handheld LF camera cannot simultaneously sample the angular and spatial resolution of the LF, we combined with the current state-of-the-arts methods for LF reconstruction, and proposed a method to synthesize arbitrary in-between SAIs through learning the contributions four input images made. Our neural network does not directly estimate depth or disparity, and does not require complex pre- and post-processing steps. The SAIs produced by our method, which takes into account the influence of surrounding pixels on each pixel generation, are closer to the real SAIs.

However, our approach also has inherent flaws. Because the method synthesize images one pixel by one, it has the problem of large computation and slow processing speed, although we have used separable sub-networks to reduce the number of parameters.

Acknowledgements. This work was supported by National Key R&D Program of China (2018YFB0804203), National Natural Science Foundation of China (U153124, 61702479,61771458), the Science and Technology Service Network Initiative of the Chinese Academy of Sciences (KFJ-STS-ZDTP-070), and Beijing Municipal Natural Science Foundation Cooperation Beijing Education Committee: No. KZ 201810005002.

References

1. Lytro illum. https://www.lytro.com
2. Raytrix. https://raytrix.de
3. Aghajanyan, A.: Convolution aware initialization. arXiv:1702.06295v3 (2017)
4. Bansal, A., Chen, X., Russell, B.C., Gupta, A., Ramanan, D.: Pixelnet: Representation of the pixels, by the pixels, and for the pixels. arXiv: 1702.06506v1 (2017)
5. Bishop, T.E., Zanetti, S., Favaro, P.: Light field superresolution. In: Proceedings of the IEEE International Conference on Computational Photography, pp. 1–9 (2009)
6. Chen, J., Hou, J., Ni, Y., Chau, L.: Accurate light field depth estimation with superpixel regularization over partially occluded regions. IEEE Trans. Image Process. **27**(10), 4889–4900 (2018)
7. Cho, D., Lee, M., Kim, S., Tai, Y.W.: Modeling the calibration pipeline of the Lytro camera for high quality light-field image reconstruction. In: Proceedings of the IEEE International Conference on Computer Vision, pp. 3280–3287 (2013)
8. Dong, C., Loy, C.C., He, K., Tang, X.: Learning a deep convolutional network for image super-resolution. In: Fleet, D., Pajdla, T., Schiele, B., Tuytelaars, T. (eds.) ECCV 2014. LNCS, vol. 8692, pp. 184–199. Springer, Cham (2014). https://doi.org/10.1007/978-3-319-10593-2_13
9. Finn, C., Goodfellow, I., Levine, S.: Unsupervised learning for physical interaction through video prediction. In: Advances in Neural Information Processing Systems, pp. 64–72 (2016)

10. Ihrke, I., Restrepo, J., Mignarddebise, L.: Principles of light field imaging: briefly revisiting 25 years of research. IEEE Signal Process. Mag. **33**(5), 59–69 (2016)
11. Jeon, H., et al.: Accurate depth map estimation from a lenslet light field camera. In: Proceedings of the IEEE Conference on Computer Vision and Pattern Recognition, pp. 1547–1555 (2015)
12. Jia, X., De Brabandere, B., Tuytelaars, T., Gool, L.V.: Dynamic filter networks. In: Advances in Neural Information Processing Systems, pp. 667–675 (2016)
13. Kalantari, N.K., Wang, T.C., Ramamoorthi, R.: Learning-based view synthesis for light field cameras. ACM Trans. Graph. **35**(6), 193:1–193:10 (2016)
14. Kingma, D.P., Ba, J.: Adam: a method for stochastic optimization. arXiv:1412.6980 (2014)
15. Levoy, M., Hanrahan, P.: Light field rendering. In: Proceedings of the 23rd Annual Conference on Computer Graphics and Interactive Techniques, pp. 31–42 (1996)
16. Ng, R., Levoy, M., Brédif, M., Duval, G., Horowitz, M., Hanrahan, P.: Light field photography with a hand-held plenoptic camera. Computer Science Technical Report CTSR 2005-02, Stanford Univ. (2005)
17. Niklaus, S., Mai, L., Liu, F.: Video frame interpolation via adaptive separable convolution. In: Proceedings of the IEEE International Conference on Computer Vision, pp. 261–270 (2017)
18. Rigamonti, R., Sironi, A., Lepetit, V., Fua, P.: Learning separable filters. In: Proceedings of the IEEE Conference on Computer Vision and Pattern Recognition, pp. 2754–2761 (2013)
19. Shi, L., Hassanieh, H., Davis, A., Katabi, D., Durand, F.: Light field reconstruction using sparsity in the continuous fourier domain. ACM Trans. Graph. **34**(1), 12 (2014)
20. Tao, M.W., Hadap, S., Malik, J., Ramamoorthi, R.: Depth from combining defocus and correspondence using light-field cameras. In: Proceedings of the IEEE International Conference on Computer Vision, pp. 673–680 (2013)
21. Wang, T., Efros, A.A., Ramamoorthi, R.: Occlusion-aware depth estimation using light-field cameras. In: Proceedings of the IEEE International Conference on Computer Vision, pp. 3487–3495 (2015)
22. Wanner, S., Goldluecke, B.: Variational light field analysis for disparity estimation and super-resolution. IEEE Trans. Pattern Anal. Mach. Intell. **36**(3), 606–619 (2014)
23. Wilburn, B., et al.: High performance imaging using large camera arrays. ACM Trans. Graph. **24**(3), 765–776 (2005)
24. Wu, G., Zhao, M., Wang, L., Dai, Q., Chai, T., Liu, Y.: Light field reconstruction using deep convolutional network on EPI. In: Proceedings of the IEEE Conference on Computer Vision and Pattern Recognition, pp. 1638–1646 (2017)
25. Xue, T., Wu, J., Bouman, K., Freeman, B.: Visual dynamics: probabilistic future frame synthesis via cross convolutional networks. In: Advances in Neural Information Processing Systems, pp. 91–99 (2016)
26. Yoon, Y., Jeon, H., Yoo, D., Lee, J., Kweon, I.S.: Light-field image super-resolution using convolutional neural network. IEEE Signal Process. Lett. **24**(6), 848–852 (2017)
27. Zhao, Q., Dai, F., Lv, J., Ma, Y., Zhang, Y.: Panoramic light fieldfrom hand-held video and its sampling for real-time rendering. IEEE Trans. Circuits Syst. Video Technol. (2019). https://doi.org/10.1109/TCSVT.2019.2900051

Speaker-Aware Speech Emotion Recognition by Fusing Amplitude and Phase Information

Lili Guo[1], Longbiao Wang[1(✉)], Jianwu Dang[1,2(✉)], Zhilei Liu[1], and Haotian Guan[3]

[1] Tianjin Key Laboratory of Cognitive Computing and Application, College of Intelligence and Computing, Tianjin University, Tianjin, China
{liliguo,longbiao_wang,zhileiliu}@tju.edu.cn

[2] Japan Advanced Institute of Science and Technology, Nomi, Ishikawa, Japan
jdang@jaist.ac.jp

[3] Huiyan Technology (Tianjin) Co., Ltd., Tianjin, China
htguan@huiyan-tech.com

Abstract. The use of a convolutional neural network (CNN) for extracting deep acoustic features from spectrograms has become one of the most commonly used methods for speech emotion recognition. In those studies, however, common amplitude information is chosen as input with no special attention to phase-related or speaker-related information. In this paper, we propose a multi-channel method employing amplitude and phase channels for speech emotion recognition. Two separate CNN channels are adopted to extract deep features from amplitude spectrograms and modified group delay (MGD) spectrograms. Then a concatenate layer is used to fuse the features. Furthermore, to gain more robust features, speaker information is considered in the stage of emotional feature extraction. Finally, the fusion features that considering speaker-related information are fed into the extreme learning machine (ELM) to distinguish emotions. Experiments are conducted on the Emo-DB database to evaluate the proposed model. Results demonstrate the recognition performance of average F1 in 94.82%, which significantly outperforms the baseline CNN-ELM model based on amplitude only spectrograms by 39.27% relative error reduction.

Keywords: Speech emotion recognition · Amplitude spectrogram · Phase information · Modified group delay · Speaker information

1 Introduction

Speech emotion recognition has attracted continually increasing attentions from researchers partly due to the rapid growth of human-computer interactions including automated call centers, intelligent voice assistants, etc. The key issues of speech emotion recognition are how to extract effective emotional representations [1] and how to build models with augmented emotional generalization

Y. M. Ro et al. (Eds.): MMM 2020, LNCS 11961, pp. 14–25, 2020.
https://doi.org/10.1007/978-3-030-37731-1_2

ability [2]. However, it is so far unclear what types of features and models are most effective for speech emotion recognition task. This is because emotional expressions are complicated as they vary from speaker to speaker [3]. Thus, speech emotion recognition is still a challenging task.

Traditional studies work on extracting auditory-based features (such as F0, energy, and voice probability) from speech signals followed by a classifier to predict emotions [4]. For example, Luengo et al. [5] selected the auditory-based features firstly, and then trained the support vector machine (SVM) as the classifier. With the development of deep learning, Wang et al. [6] adopted the deep neural network (DNN) to learn high-level representations from the auditory-based features, and then trained the extreme learning machine (ELM) to recognize emotion. Furthermore, models based on the recurrent neural network (RNN) have shown good performance as seen in the RNN-ELM model [7]. However, these auditory-based features may not be optimal as emotional representations because it is difficult to choose adequate features manually.

As the convolutional neural network (CNN) is adept at extracting local features from raw input, CNN-based models have been proposed to extract features automatically [8]. Satt et al. [9] trained a CNN to extract deep amplitude-based features from amplitude spectrograms, and then the bidirectional long short term memory (BLSTM) [10] was trained to recognize emotions. The CNN-BLSTM model has become the most commonly used method for speech emotion recognition. Later on, Guo et al. [11] presented the CNN-ELM model, which obviously improved the accuracy of speech emotion recognition. Although above models achieved a good success, they all ignored phase information that is another component to comprise speech spectra. Some studies have proven the effect of the phase information for different tasks including speech recognition [12] and speaker recognition [13–15], whereas there are few studies on speech emotion recognition.

Furthermore, there are some models that improve emotion recognition by considering other types of information. Zhang et al. [16] proposed a multi-task learning method for the joint domain (speech or song) with gender classification in an emotion recognition system. Zhang et al. [17] proposed a speech emotion recognition method with gender-related information. Tao et al. [18] introduced the advanced LSTM for a joint method for emotion, speaker, and gender classifications. However, most previous studies only used the traditional auditory-based features, while abundant features available in spectrograms were not incorporated. As there is no unified way to express emotions for humans [3], individuality features should contribute strong robustness to different emotional expressions, while few work is done to explore this benefit using spectrogram information.

To address above issues, we propose a speaker-aware speech emotion recognition model by fusing amplitude and phase information. This paper focuses on exploring the effect of phase information on the performance of speech emotion recognition. To take full advantage of the complementarity of the amplitude and phase features, we propose a multi-channel model based on these two types of features. Firstly, two separate CNN channels are used to extract amplitude-based and phase-based features from amplitude and MGD spectrograms, respectively. Then a concatenate layer is adopted to fuse these two types of features. The multi-channel model can set up constraints between amplitude and phase channels by using the error back propagation (BP) so as to improve the contributions of the fusion features. To enhance the robustness of features to different emotional expressions, we take special attention to the impact of speaker information during feature extraction. Speech emotion recognition and speaker recognition tasks are trained together by using a multi-task learning method. Finally, the ELM is used as the classifier to distinguish emotions because previous studies [6,11,19] have demonstrated that the ELM performs better on speech emotion recognition task. To the best of our knowledge, it is the first work for speech emotion recognition that use amplitude and MGD spectrograms. In addition, during the stage of fusion feature extraction, we consider the speaker-related information toward the more robust performance.

The rest of this paper is organized as follows. Section 2 describes the proposed speaker-aware speech emotion recognition model based on amplitude and phase information. The experimental results and discussions are reported in Sect. 3. Finally, Sect. 4 gives the conclusions.

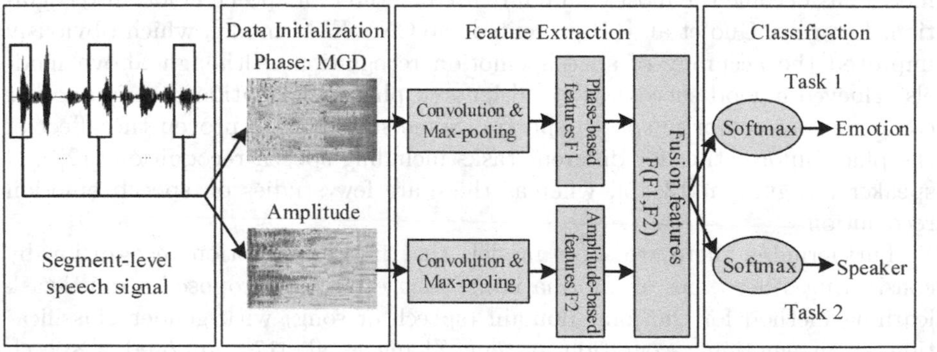

Fig. 1. Diagram of fusion feature extraction with speaker-related information.

2 The Proposed Speaker-Aware Multi-channel Model

This paper proposes a speaker-aware model using amplitude and phase information for speech emotion recognition. Figure 1 shows the block diagram of the fusion feature extraction with considering speaker-related information by fusing amplitude and MGD information. To explore the effect of phase information on speech emotion recognition and take advantage of the complementarity of the amplitude and phase information, we propose a multi-channel network based on amplitude and MGD information. As there is no sufficiently labeled public corpus of emotional speech at present [3], to obtain more training samples, the speech signals are divided into several segments with a fixed length firstly. In the stage of data preprocessing, MGD and amplitude spectrograms are extracted from segment-level speech signal. Then amplitude-based and phase-based features are extracted by two separate CNN channels followed by a concatenate layer to combine these two types of features. In addition, to improve the robustness of features to different speakers, this model takes account of the effect of speaker-related information for speech emotion recognition. In the course of fusion feature extraction, we train a joint model for emotion and speaker recognition. The input and hidden layers are shared across all the tasks, while the output layer contains both emotion and speaker labels.

In this work, the ELM is used as the classifier. Because ELM is a static method, while the extracted fusion features are segment-level, we calculate certain mean values to all the segments of one utterance to obtain utterance-level emotional representations, which is similar to previous studies [6,11,19]. Finally, the fusion features with utterance-level representations are fed into the ELM to distinguish emotions.

2.1 Extraction and Analysis of MGD

The most commonly used phase related information is the group delay based features [20]. The extraction of MGD is as follows.

The spectrum $X(\omega)$ is obtained by the discrete Fourier transform (DFT) from an input speech signal $x(n)$ as following:

$$X(\omega) = |X(\omega)|\, e^{j\theta(\omega)}, \tag{1}$$

where $|X(\omega)|$ and $\theta(\omega)$ are the amplitude and phase information at frequency ω.

The group delay is the most popular method to manipulate phase information, which is defined as the negative derivative of the Fourier transform phase for frequency, as shown in formula (2):

$$\tau(\omega) = -\frac{d(\theta(\omega))}{d\omega}. \tag{2}$$

The group delay function can be calculated directly from the speech spectrum using formula (3):

$$\tau_x(\omega) = \frac{X_R(\omega)Y_R(\omega) + X_I(\omega)Y_I(\omega)}{|X(\omega)|^2}, \tag{3}$$

where, $X(\omega)$ and $Y(\omega)$ are the Fourier transforms of signal $x(n)$ and $nx(n)$, respectively. Subscripts R and I denote the real and imaginary parts of the Fourier transform.

Hegde et al. proposed the modified group delay function which has proved better than the original group delay in many studies [21]. The modified group delay function τ_m can be defined as

$$\tau_m(\omega) = \left(\frac{\tau(\omega)}{|\tau(\omega)|}\right) (|\tau\,(\omega)|)^{\alpha}, \tag{4}$$

$$\tau(\omega) = \frac{X_R(\omega)Y_R(\omega) + X_I(\omega)Y_I(\omega)}{|S(\omega)|^{2\gamma}}, \tag{5}$$

where $S(\omega)$ is the cepstrally smoothed $X(\omega)$, and the range of α and γ are $(0 < \alpha < 1)$ and $(0 < \gamma < 1)$.

To analyze the difference between amplitude and MGD representations, we present their spectrograms as shown in Fig. 2. From the figures, we can observe that the MGD spectrogram can weaken some noise in marking 2 compared with amplitude spectrogram in circle 1. In addition, the MGD spectrogram can highlight some regions with rich information as shown in marking 3. Meanwhile, some important regions with higher energy may be weakened as seen in marking 4, while the amplitude spectrogram can still retain these important features in marking 5. To sum up, there is a complementary relationship between amplitude spectrogram and MGD spectrogram to some extent. Therefore, this paper proposes a multi-channel model to utilize the potential advantage of complementarity between the amplitude and phase information for speech emotion recognition.

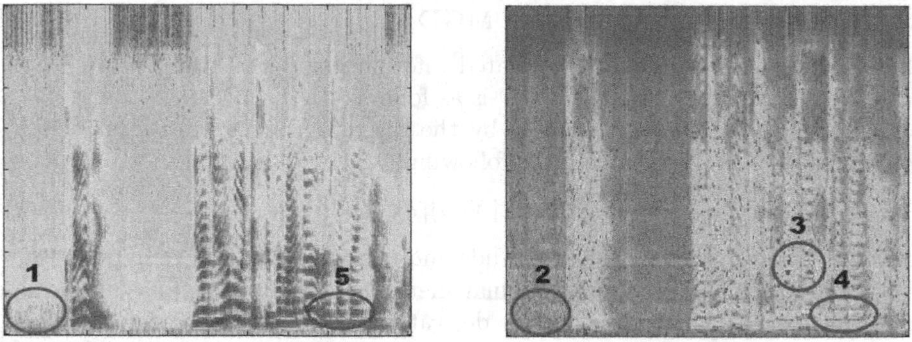

(a) Amplitude (b) Phase: MGD

Fig. 2. Spectrograms of amplitude and MGD.

2.2 Feature Extraction by Considering Speaker-Related Information

To extract more robust features, speaker-related information is considered in the stage of feature extraction. As it is an effective way to enhance the interrelated tasks by multi-task learning [22,23], we train emotion recognition and speaker recognition tasks together by using a multi-task learning method. In this work, speech emotion recognition is the main task, and the auxiliary task is speaker recognition. The speaker-aware speech emotion recognition model can be trained by minimizing the cost function:

$$L = \lambda L_e + (1 - \lambda) L_s, \tag{6}$$

where $\lambda \epsilon (0, 1)$ is a weighting parameter that uses to adjust the contribution of those two tasks. L_e and L_s are the costs generated by speech emotion recognition and speaker recognition tasks, respectively.

In this work we use the cross-entropy function which is a commonly used function for classification tasks [24]. The cost function L can be expressed in detail as following:

$$\begin{aligned} L = & -\frac{\lambda}{m}\left[\sum_{i=1}^{m} t_e^i log(y_e^i) + (1 - t_e^i) log(1 - y_e^i)\right] \\ & - \frac{1-\lambda}{m}\left[\sum_{i=1}^{m} t_s^i log(y_s^i) + (1 - t_s^i) log(1 - y_s^i)\right], \end{aligned} \tag{7}$$

where m is the number of training samples, t_e and t_s are the targeted labels of emotion and speaker, respectively, y_e and y_s are the detected labels of emotion and speaker, respectively.

Then gradient descent algorithm is used to update all the parameters in the model as Fig. 1. Finally, we can obtain the fusion features F that considering speaker-related information.

2.3 ELM for Classification

The fusion features are fed into the ELM to distinguish emotions. The ELM is proposed by Huang et al., which is a single-hidden layer neural network [25]. The training process of the ELM only needs to set the number of hidden layer units and finishes in a single iteration without using the error back propagation (BP), which leads to faster computation than conventional BP-based methods [26] such as the BLSTM. The ELM has been used for many classification tasks and achieved better results than some of the traditional classifiers such as the SVM [27]. Furthermore, the ELM can perform well on small database, being superior under the situation where sufficiently labeled speech emotion data are unavailable [3].

3 Experiments

3.1 Experimental Setup

To evaluate the proposed model, we conduct experiments on the Berlin Emotional Database (Emo-DB) [28]. This corpus consists of 535 utterances with seven emotions that were produced by 10 speakers including 5 males and 5 females. All the sentences are sampled at 16 kHz in approximately 2–3 s. Table 1 shows the emotion distribution of this corpus. As it is a small database, to obtain more training data, we transform an utterance into several segments with a fixed length, and all segments in the same utterance share the same label. However, it is a challenging problem to set the length of a segment. Researchers have found that the segment longer than 250 ms contains sufficient emotional information [29]. Therefore, we adopt 265 ms as a segment size and 25 ms as a segment-shift length in this work, which is similar to [27]. In addition, we adopt 10-fold cross-validation in experiments.

Table 1. Emotion distribution of the Emo-DB database.

Emotion	Number of utterances	Percentage
Fear	69	12.90%
Disgust	46	8.60%
Happiness	71	13.27%
Boredom	81	15.14%
Neutral	79	14.77%
Sadness	62	11.59%
Anger	127	23.74%

In this paper, the short-time Fourier transform (STFT) with 256 FFT points, 256 points window and 50% overlap is utilized to generate spectrograms. In the stage of MGD extraction, $\alpha = 0.1$ and $\gamma = 0.2$ are used. To choose the optimal parameters, we evaluated with different numbers of layers and hidden units, etc. The selected CNN contains two convolutional layers with a size of 5 $\times$ 5 and two max-pooling layers with a size of 2 $\times$ 2. The numbers of filters in two convolutional layers are 32 and 64. Then a flattened layer followed by a full connected layer with 1024 units is utilized. Finally, to avoid over-fitting, a dropout layer with 0.5 factor is used.

To make the experimental results more convincing, for all the comparison methods, we attempted many times to choose the optimal parameters under the same conditions. All the methods are listed as follows.

Amplitude (CNN-ELM) [11]: It is the baseline model, which uses the CNN to extract deep amplitude-based features from amplitude spectrograms, and then the ELM is adopted as a classifier to recognize emotions. The optimal hidden units of ELM is set to 2100.

MGD (CNN-ELM): This model uses the CNN to extract phase-based features from MGD spectrograms, and then the phase-based features are fed into the ELM. The hidden layer of the ELM adopts 2000 units.

The single-channel model (Amplitude + MGD (CNN-ELM)): To compare with the proposed multi-channel model, we also consider the single channel model based on the amplitude and phase information. First, we make a combination of amplitude and MGD spectrograms in the way of the time-domain alignment. Then the CNN is adopted to extract deep features from the fusion data. Finally, the ELM is used as the classifier, and the hidden unit number of the ELM is set to 2000.

The multi-channel model: This model uses two CNN channels to extract amplitude-based and phase-based features from amplitude and MGD spectrograms, respectively. Then these two types of features are combined by a concatenate layer. Finally, the fusion features are fed into the ELM to distinguish emotions. The hidden unit number of the ELM is set to 2800.

The speaker-aware multi-channel model: To improve the robustness of features to different emotional expressions, speech emotion recognition and speaker recognition tasks are trained together using multi-task learning in the stage of feature extraction. The parameter λ that is used to adjust the contribution of two tasks is set to 0.8. In addition, the hidden unit number of the ELM is set to 4400.

3.2 Results and Discussions

In this paper, we use two common assessment criteria including weighted accuracy (WA) and unweighted accuracy (UA) to evaluate the overall performance of the proposed method [9]. WA is the classification accuracy for the entire test data. UA is the average value for each emotion's accuracy. Table 2 lists the comparison of the results of our methods and other state-of-the-art methods in recent years. Wang et al. [6] proposed the DNN-ELM model which firstly extracted the deep representations from the amplitude-related features (such as F0, energy, and voice probability) using DNN and used an ELM to identify emotions. Satt et al. [9] adopted the CNN to extract features from amplitude spectrograms followed by the BLSTM to distinguish emotions. The CNN-ELM [11] that uses only amplitude spectrogram is the baseline model.

Table 2. Comparison results of the proposed method and other methods.

Model	WA (%)	UA (%)	Year
Amplitude (DNN-ELM) [6]	84.67	84.09	2017
Amplitude (CNN-BLSTM) [9]	87.66	86.66	2017
Amplitude (CNN-ELM) [11]	91.21	90.83	2018
MGD (CNN-ELM)	91.59	90.80	
The single-channel model: Amplitude + MGD (CNN-ELM)	92.52	91.97	
The multi-channel model	93.46	92.99	
The speaker-aware multi-channel model	**94.58**	**94.38**	

From Table 2, some conclusions can be drawn as following: (1) The results of MGD demonstrate that the phase has the same amount of information as the amplitude for speech emotion recognition. (2) The single-channel model that integrate amplitude spectrogram with MGD spectrogram outperforms the models that use only amplitude or MGD spectrogram. This means that the amplitude and phase spectrograms are supplementary one to another to some extent. (3) The proposed multi-channel model outperforms the single-channel model

'Amplitude + MGD (CNN-ELM)' by over 12% relative error reduction in terms of WA and UA, which indicates that the proposed multi-channel model using amplitude and phase information is better than the single-channel model for speech emotion recognition. A possible reason is that the multi-channel model can capture the mutual correlation among amplitude and phase. (4) When considering speaker-related information, the model outperforms the multi-channel model by over 17% relative error reduction in terms of WA and UA, indicating that emotion recognition can be enhanced by considering speaker-related information. It is reasonable to assume that after training emotion recognition and speaker recognition systems together, the model does not only learn emotion-related information but also learn some speaker-related information (such as speaking style and characteristics), which has been proven useful to speech emotion recognition [30]. Therefore, this model can extract features with high robustness to different expressions. (5) Overall, the proposed speaker-aware multi-channel model outperforms the other comparative methods. The proposed model significantly outperforms the baseline 'Amplitude (CNN-ELM)' model by relative error reduction of 38.34% and 38.71% in terms of WA and UA, respectively. It is reasonable to assume that the proposed multi-channel model can make good use of amplitude-based and phase-based information.

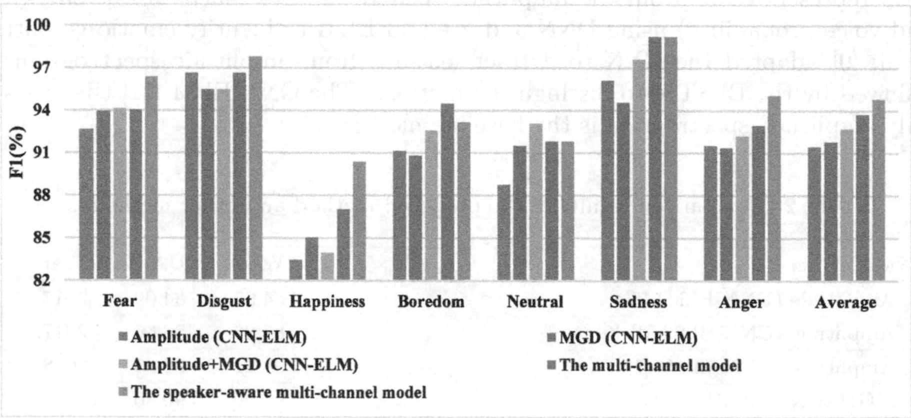

Fig. 3. F1(%) of each emotion.

To analyze the contribution of our models on classifying different types of emotion, Fig. 3 gives F1-score of the baseline CNN-ELM model that uses only amplitude spectrograms and the proposed models. F1-score is the most commonly used evaluation criterion for testing accuracy because it can keep balance between recall (R) and precision (P). From Fig. 3 we can observe that the MGD is slightly better than amplitude in term of the average F1. We can also see that the proposed speaker-aware multi-channel model performs best in most classes including fear, disgust, happiness, sadness and anger, and performs the second in classes of boredom and neutral. For average F1, our models ('MGD (CNN-ELM)', 'Amplitude + MGD', 'The multi-channel model', 'The speaker-aware multi-channel model') precede the baseline model, and the proposed speaker-aware model outperforms the baseline model by 39.27% (F1 from 91.47% to 94.82%) relative error reduction.

4 Conclusions

This paper aimed to improve speech emotion recognition by using phase information. We proposed a multi-channel model by fusing amplitude and phase information. In addition, in the process of feature extraction, we considered the speaker-related information to extract more robust features. Experiments were conducted on the Emo-DB database to validate the proposed method. Experimental results reveal that phase data has the same amount of information as the amplitude in speech emotion recognition. Two types of information are supplementary one to another to some extent. Furthermore, when using amplitude and MGD information together, the proposed multi-channel model outperforms the single channel model. The results also show that the performance of emotion recognition can be enhanced by considering speaker-related information. In the future work, we will make detailed analysis about how speaker-related information affects emotion recognition.

Acknowledgements. This work was supported by the National Natural Science Foundation of China under Grant 61771333, by the Tianjin Municipal Science and Technology Project under Grant 18ZXZNGX00330, and by the China Scholarship Council (CSC).

References

1. Schuller, B., Steidl, S., Batliner, A., Burkhardt, F., Devillers, L.: The INTERSPEECH 2010 paralinguistic challenge. In: Eleventh Annual Conference of the International Speech Communication Association (INTERSPEECH), pp. 2794–2797 (2010)
2. El Ayadi, M., Kamel, M.S., Karray, F.: Survey on speech emotion recognition: features, classification schemes, and databases. Pattern Recognit. **44**(3), 572–587 (2011)
3. Schuller, B., Batliner, A., Steidl, S., Seppi, D.: Recognising realistic emotions and affect in speech: state of the art and lessons learnt from the first challenge. Speech Commun. **53**(9–10), 1062–1087 (2011)
4. Slaney, M., McRoberts, G.: Baby ears: a recognition system for affective vocalizations. In: 1998 IEEE International Conference on Acoustics, Speech and Signal Processing (ICASSP), vol. 2, pp. 985–988 (1998)
5. Luengo, I., Navas, E., Hernáez, I., Sánchez, J.: Automatic emotion recognition using prosodic parameters. In: Ninth European Conference on Speech Communication and Technology, pp. 493–496 (2005)

6. Wang, Z., Tashev, I.: Learning utterance-level representations for speech emotion and age/gender recognition using deep neural networks. In: 2017 IEEE International Conference on Acoustics, Speech and Signal Processing (ICASSP), pp. 5150–5154 (2017)
7. Lee, J., Tashev, I.: High-level feature representation using recurrent neural network for speech emotion recognition. In: Sixteenth Annual Conference of the International Speech Communication Association (INTERSPEECH), pp. 1537–1540 (2015)
8. Bertero, D., Fung, P.: A first look into a convolutional neural network for speech emotion detection. In: 2017 IEEE International Conference on Acoustics, Speech and Signal Processing (ICASSP), pp. 5115–5119 (2017)
9. Satt, A., Rozenberg, S., Hoory, R.: Efficient emotion recognition from speech using deep learning on spectrograms. In: Eighteenth Annual Conference of the International Speech Communication Association (INTERSPEECH), pp. 1089–1093 (2017)
10. Keren, G., Schuller, B.: Convolutional RNN: an enhanced model for extracting features from sequential data. In: International Joint Conference on Neural Networks, pp. 3412–3419 (2016)
11. Guo, L., Wang, L., Dang, J., Zhang, L., Guan, H.: A feature fusion method based on extreme learning machine for speech emotion recognition. In: 2018 IEEE International Conference on Acoustics, Speech and Signal Processing (ICASSP), pp. 2666–2670 (2018)
12. Hegde, R., Murthy, H., Gadde, V.: Significance of the modified group delay feature in speech recognition. IEEE Trans. Audio Speech Lang. Process. **15**(1), 190–202 (2007)
13. Nakagawa, S., Wang, L., Ohtsuka, S.: Speaker identification and verification by combining MFCC and phase information. IEEE Trans. Audio Speech Lang. Process. **20**(4), 1085–1095 (2012)
14. Oo, Z., Kawakami, Y., Wang, L., Nakagawa, S., Xiao, X., Iwahashi, M.: DNN-based amplitude and phase feature enhancement for noise robust speaker identification. In: Seventeenth Annual Conference of the International Speech Communication Association (INTERSPEECH), pp. 2204–2208 (2016)
15. Wang, L., Nakagawa, S., Zhang, Z., Yoshida, Y., Kawakami, Y.: Spoofing speech detection using modified relative phase information. IEEE J. Sel. Top. Signal Process. **11**(4), 660–670 (2017)
16. Zhang, B., Provost, E.M., Essi, G.: Cross-corpus acoustic emotion recognition from singing and speaking: a multi-task learning approach. In: 2016 IEEE International Conference on Acoustics, Speech and Signal Processing (ICASSP), pp. 5805–5809 (2016)
17. Zhang, L., Wang, L., Dang, J., Guo, L., Yu, Q.: Gender-aware CNN-BLSTM for speech emotion recognition. In: Kůrková, V., Manolopoulos, Y., Hammer, B., Iliadis, L., Maglogiannis, I. (eds.) ICANN 2018. LNCS, vol. 11139, pp. 782–790. Springer, Cham (2018). https://doi.org/10.1007/978-3-030-01418-6_76
18. Tao, F., Liu, G.: Advanced LSTM: a study about better time dependency modeling in emotion recognition. In: 2018 IEEE International Conference on Acoustics, Speech and Signal Processing (ICASSP), pp. 2906–2910 (2018)
19. Guo, L., Wang, L., Dang, J., et al.: Exploration of complementary features for speech emotion recognition based on kernel extreme learning machine. IEEE Access **7**, 75798–75809 (2019)

20. Kua, J., Epps, J., Ambikairajah, E., Choi, E.: LS regularization of group delay features for speaker recognition. In: Tenth Annual Conference of the International Speech Communication Association (INTERSPEECH), pp. 2887–2890 (2009)
21. Hegde, R., Murthy, H., Rao, G.: Application of the modified group delay function to speaker identification and discrimination. In: 2004 IEEE International Conference on Acoustics, Speech and Signal Processing (ICASSP), vol. 1, pp. 517–520 (2004)
22. Chen, Y., Chen, Y., Wang, X., Tang, X.: Deep learning face representation by joint identification-verification. In: Advances in Neural Information Processing Systems, pp. 1988–1996 (2014)
23. Zhang, Z., Luo, P., Loy, C.C., Tang, X.: Facial landmark detection by deep multi-task learning. In: Fleet, D., Pajdla, T., Schiele, B., Tuytelaars, T. (eds.) ECCV 2014. LNCS, vol. 8694, pp. 94–108. Springer, Cham (2014). https://doi.org/10.1007/978-3-319-10599-4_7
24. Foody, G.M.: Cross-entropy for the evaluation of the accuracy of a fuzzy land cover classification with fuzzy ground data. ISPRS J. Photogramm. Remote. Sens. **50**(5), 2–12 (1995)
25. Huang, G.B., Zhu, Q.Y., Siew, C.K.: Extreme learning machine: theory and applications. Neurocomputing **70**(1), 489–501 (2006)
26. Zhu, Q.Y., Qin, A.K., Suganthan, P.N., Huang, G.B.: Evolutionary extreme learning machine. Pattern Recognit. **38**(10), 1759–1763 (2005)
27. Han, K., Yu, D., Tashev, I.: Speech emotion recognition using deep neural network and extreme learning machine. In: Fifteenth Annual Conference of the International Speech Communication Association (INTERSPEECH), pp. 223–227 (2014)
28. Burkhardt, F., Paeschke, A., Rolfes, M.: A database of German emotional speech. In: Ninth European Conference on Speech Communication and Technology, pp. 1517–1520 (2005)
29. Provost, E.: Identifying salient sub-utterance emotion dynamics using flexible units and estimates of affective flow. In: 2013 IEEE International Conference on Acoustics, Speech and Signal Processing (ICASSP), pp. 3682–3686 (2013)
30. Busso, C., Metallinou, A., Narayanan, S.S.: Iterative feature normalization for emotional speech detection. In: 2011 IEEE International Conference on Acoustics, Speech and Signal Processing (ICASSP), pp. 5692–5695 (2011)

Gen-Res-Net: A Novel Generative Model for Singing Voice Separation

Congzhou Tian[1(✉)], Hangyu Li[2], Deshun Yang[1], and Xiaoou Chen[1]

[1] Peking University, Beijing, China
{tcz,yangdeshun,chenxiaoou}@pku.com
[2] Beihang University, Beijing, China
lhy1623@buaa.edu.cn

Abstract. In most cases, modeling in the time-frequency domain is the most common method to solve the problem of singing voice separation since frequency characteristics differ between different sources. During the past few years, applying recurrent neural network (RNN) to series of split spectrograms has been mostly adopted by researchers to tackle this problem. Recently, however, the U-net's success has drawn the focus to treating the spectrogram as a 2-dimensional image with an auto-encoder structure, which indicates that some useful methods in image analysis may help solve this problem. Under this scenario, we propose a novel spectrogram-generative model to separate the two sources in the time-frequency domain inspired by Residual blocks, Squeeze and Excitation blocks and WaveNet. We apply none-reduce-sized Residual blocks together with Squeeze and Excitation blocks in the main stream to extract features of the input spectrogram while gathering the output layers in a skip-connection structure used in WaveNet. Experimental results on two datasets (MUSDB18 and CCMixer) have shown that our proposed network performs better than the current state-of-the-art approach working on spectrograms of mixtures – the deep U-net structure.

Keywords: Singing voice separation · Spectrogram · Residual blocks · Squeeze and Excitation Blocks · WaveNet

1 Introduction

Generally, modern pop music mainly consists of two tracks: the singing track which forms the melody of a song and the backing track which provides the rhythmic and harmonic support for the melody of a song [1]. The singing voice itself can provide useful information, for instance, the lyrics, the emotion and singing skills of the song. Applications developed on these information are common in many music information retrieval (MIR) tasks such as the lyric recognition and alignment [2], the music emotion recognition [3] and the singer identification [4]. However, although a great number of songs are available around the world, they cannot provide direct information for these tasks since they are mixtures

Y. M. Ro et al. (Eds.): MMM 2020, LNCS 11961, pp. 26–36, 2020.
https://doi.org/10.1007/978-3-030-37731-1_3

of the singing voice and the accompaniment. Identifying the singing voice from the mixture in monaural recordings seems to be an easy task for human beings [5], but is extremely difficult for computers. Thus singing voice separation is the key step to filter the interfering accompaniment and to obtain the clean singing voice for the subsequent process.

Most separation models work in the time-frequency domain, whose aims are to reconstruct the singing voice spectrogram and accompaniment spectrogram from the mixed spectrogram separately. They usually employ short-time Fourier transform (STFT) with time-shifting filters to convert the 1-dimension waveform to spectrograms in the time-frequency domain. After the predicted spectrogram is obtained, ISTFT (inversed STFT) is implemented to obtain the predicted singing voice track and accompaniment track. Several approaches have been proposed for the singing voice separation task based on this framework. In [6], Raffii et al. uses the repetitive pattern in the mixed music source to separate singing track and accompaniment track. Jeong et al. [7] extracts spectrograms in a form of low-rank and sparse matrices to improve the separation performance. During these days, with the advancement of deep learning, the singing voice separation task has attained its state-of-the-art results. Huang et al. [8] reconstruct the source spectrogram with predicting the mask through the optimization of a DRNN architecture. Mimilakis et al. [9] first introduced the RNN network in an auto-encoder structure to compute the mask and the predicted spectrogram. In Luo et al.'s work [10], bidirectional-LSTM is adopted to both cluster the TF bins in the spectrogram as well as predict the corresponding mask. While the models above show the prevalence of RNN's structure, Jansson et al.'s U-net [11] indicates that performing singing voice separation by treating the input spectrogram as a time-frequency image and using convolution neural network (CNN) is also a possible solution for this task. The U-net architecture is originally derived from image segmentation [21] which contains skip connections between the encoding stages and the decoding stages to extract low-level information and directly transmit them from the high-resolution input to the high-resolution output. Besides U-net architecture, there are some other CNN networks explored by researchers [12,13] to help solve the singing voice separation task.

In this paper, we explore the effectiveness of using Residual blocks (RB) in ResNet [14] to compute spectrogram masks to solve the singing voice separation problem by treating spectrograms of the mixed audio as 2d images. We further refine the model by two methods, Squeeze and Excitation Blocks (SEB) [15] and WaveNet [16]'s skip-connection output layers. The SEB, which was proposed by Jie He et al., aims to strengthen the representational power of a CNN architecture with its adaptively recalibrational channel-wise feature by explicitly modeling interdependencies between channels. In the WaveNet structure, when computing the final output of the network, WaveNet gathers all the output layers of each residual block to predict the final output waveform. Based on the ResNet, our model integrates the advantages mentioned above. First, after applying STFT to the segmented source audio and passing them through a convolutional layer, we feed them to the main stream – the stacked SE-Res blocks (SERESB) to rectify the layers' and channels' relationship when extracting the source feature. Then all the output of SERESBs are added together and the final predicted mask is obtained after a simple deconvolutional layer. The predicted singing voice mask and accompaniment mask are trained separately in two networks.

The rest of this paper is organized as follows. In Sect. 2, we describe the design of the proposed Gen-Res-Net method and the training procedure. In Sect. 3, we describe the dataset and the data augmentation, the evaluation metrics and compare our experimental results with the baseline U-net structure. Finally, we summarize this paper in Sect. 4.

2 Methodology

2.1 Model Architecture

Input Data. Due to the heavy computational requirements of training such a model, we first downsample the input audio to 16000 Hz in order to accelerate the training process. Then we compute the Short-Time-Fourier-Transform of the mixed audio with a window size of 1024 and a hop size of 256 frames. We extract 256 steps (roughly 4 s) for each batch and feed them to our network. The magnitude spectrograms are normalized to range [0, 1].

SE-Residual Block. We derive bottleneck's structure [14] with the implementation of SEB(SERESB). In the SERESB. The input is duplicated and divided into two branches - the identical branch and the residual branch. In the identical branch, the input passes through a (1×1) filter with stride 1. The channel numbers may double depending on the tuning parameter. The residual block consists of three convolution blocks. The first and third filter is (1×1) filter with stride 1. The second filter is (3×3) and the stride is a parameter to be set to adjust the output size of the feature map. The channel number is doubled in the third filter. The SE block is placed after the bottleneck block. The SE block takes $(H \times W \times C)$ pictures as its input(neglecting the batch dimension). It first implements a global average pooling on the input picture at the dim of $(H \times W)$. As a result, the picture turns to $(1 \times 1 \times C)$. Then it is fed into two fully-connected layers with a LeakyReLU and a sigmoid activation function, which first squeeze the channel dimension $(1 \times 1 \times \frac{C}{r})$ and then excite it to its original channel dimension $(1 \times 1 \times C)$. Finally, it serves as a kind of weight and is channel-wisely multiplied by the output of the bottleneck block. Finally, the output of the identical branch and SE block are elementwise added to form the output. Figure 1 shows the overall structure of SE-Residual Block.

Bypass Branch. The idea of Bypass Branch derives from the WaveNet's skip-connection layers except that the feature in WaveNet is a 1-dimensional vector while in our model it turns to 2-dimensional pictures. Through the summation of all the bypass layers generating from different depths of the network,

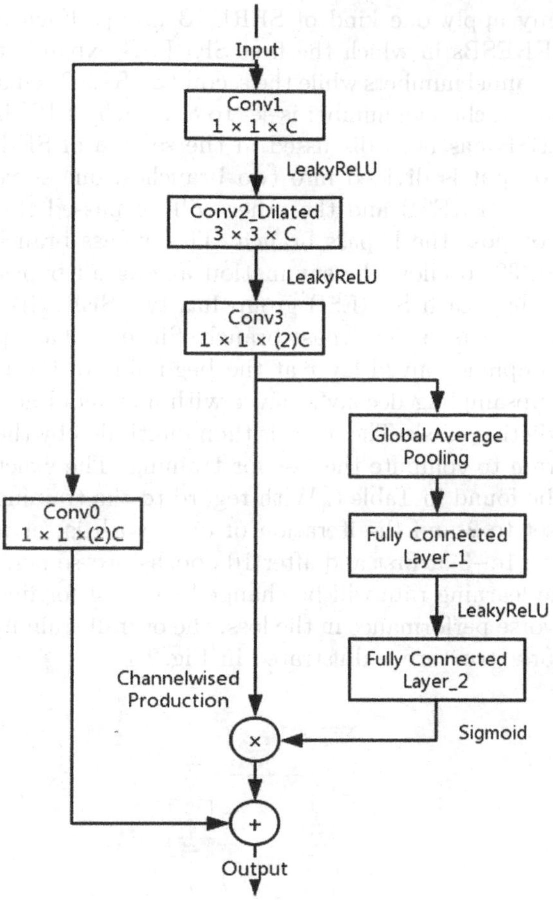

Fig. 1. Overview of the SE-Residual block

our model can greatly maintain both high-level information and low-level information in the same size. During the backpropagation process, the gradient can be transmitted back to the main stream to update its value for better prediction. This explicit data integrating between low-level and high-level information can greatly contribute to the increase in the performance of our network.

Training. We have referred to Res-Net50 [14]'s structure in our task. First, we inherit the original (7 × 7) conv2d layer with stride 2 and 64 channels to reduce the convolution filters' dimension in view of the large memory consumption and map the 1-channel spectrogram to a higher dimensional space. Since the input spectrogram is (256 × 512 × 1), it will be reduced to (128 × 256 × 64). The following (3 × 3) max pooling is abandoned in our model because we hope to capture as much feature information as possible from the original spectrogram.

After that, we only apply one kind of SERESB group. Each SERESB group consists of two SERESBs in which the first SERESB expands the channels to twice of its input channel numbers while the second SERESB remains the channel number. The squeezed channel number is set to 8 in each SERESB. The detailed structure of SERESB has been discussed in the section of SE-Residual Block. Each SERESB's output is divided into two branches, one serves as the input features to the next SERESB and the other will be passed through a (1×1) conv2d layer to compose the bypass branch. The bypass branch has the same channel number of 32 to allow the summation among all bypass layers. There is one point that since each SERESB group has two SERESBs, both of them contribute one layer each to the bypass branch. Since we have passed the data through a downsampling conv2d layer at the beginning of the network, we use a (9×9) conv2d upsampling deconv2d layer with a sigmoid activation layer to construct the predicting mask. The mask is then multiplied by the corresponding original spectrogram to compute the loss for training. The exact parameters of the network can be found in Table 1. With regard to the training configuration, the batchsize is set to 2 and the iteration of one epoch is set to 1400. We set the learning rate to 1e−3 at first and after 10 epochs' worse performance on the validation set, the learning rate will be changed to 1e−4 for fine-tuning. Again after 10 epochs' worse performance in the loss, the overall training process stops. The overall network structure is illustrated in Fig. 2.

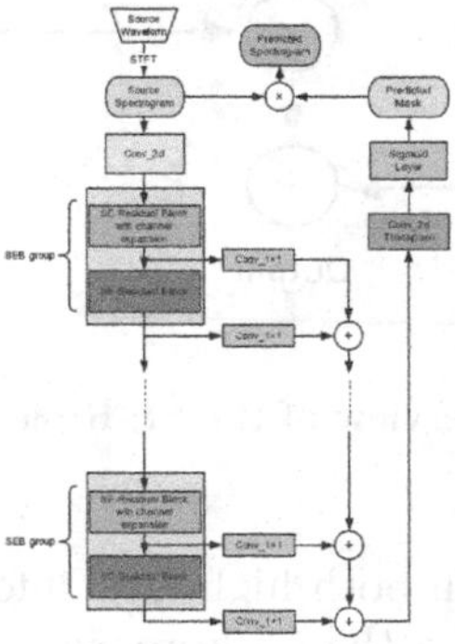

Fig. 2. The whole structure of Gen-Res-Net

2.2 Loss Function

The loss function is a standard $L1, 1$ norm of the difference between the clean singing voice($sing$)/accompaniment(acc) source spectrogram and the predicted spectrogram which is the production of the original mixed spectrogram and the predicted mask. The formulas are noted below:

$$L(X, Y_N, \Theta_N) = \|f(X, \Theta_N) \odot X - Y_N\|_{1,1} \tag{1}$$

Table 1. Network configuration

Bypass model summary		
The input/output data with size (256 × 512 × 1) samples		
Layer	Main Stream	Bypass branch
1	(DATA IN) conv2d (7 × 7 × 64) stride = 2	-
2, 3	SERESB IC[a] = 12 OC[b] = 48	conv2d (1 × 1 × 32) stride = 1
4, 5	SERESB IC = 24 OC = 96	conv2d (1 × 1 × 32) stride = 1
6, 7	SERESB IC = 48 OC = 192	conv2d (1 × 1 × 32) stride = 1
8, 9	SERESB IC = 96 OC = 384	conv2d (1 × 1 × 32) stride = 1
10	–	conv2d + sigmoid (DATA OUT) (9 × 9 × 1) stride = 1

[a]In channels [b]Out channels

$$Y_N \in \{Y_{sing}, Y_{acc}\} \tag{2}$$

$$\Theta_N \in \{\Theta_{sing}, \Theta_{acc}\} \tag{3}$$

where L represents the loss function for *sing*/*acc*, $f(X, \Theta_N)$ represents the output of the network and $\odot$ means element-wise production. The Y_N and Θ_N are the clean source *sing*/*acc* and network parameter for singing/acc network separately.

3 Experiment

3.1 Dataset and Data Augmentation

The training data is selected from the MUSDB18 [17] and the CCMixer [18] dataset under the framework of Wave-U-Net [19]. In the training process, we select 70 songs in the training set of MUSDB18 and the whole set of CCMixer as our training set. The remaining 30 songs in the MUSDB18 training set are selected as the validation set. The whole 50 songs in the MUSDB18 test set are used as our test set. Considering the data flow, the overall dataset is reset from 44100 Hz to 16000 Hz to accelerate the training process. Due to the silent parts' tremendous impact on the *SDR*'s rate, we first cut down the songs into 16 s segments without silent parts. Under this circumstance, for training set and validation set, we simply match each 16 s singing voice track with a randomly chosen accompaniment track to increase the variety of training samples [8] while for the test set, the segmented singing tracks and accompaniment tracks are corresponded. Let us make some clarification, if the number of the segmented singing voice track is N^i_{sing} and the number of segmented accompaniment track is N^i_{acc}, where i denotes the training or test set, *sing* denotes the singing voice track and *acc* denotes the accompaniment track, we will first compute all $(N^i_{acc} \times N^i_{sing})$ possible track pairs and take 2500 16 s pairs from the MUSDB training set and the CCMixer dataset. Then they are divided into two parts: 2250 pairs for training and 250 pairs for validation. There are 330 matched pairs in the test set so the total time for training, validation and testing are 10 h, 1.11 h and 1.47 h, respectively.

3.2 Evaluation Metrics

We use Global Signal-to-Distortion Ratio (GSDR), Global Signal-to-Artifact Ratio (GSAR) and Global Signal-to-Interference Ratio (GSIR) [20] for evaluation. Since the mean is dramatically influenced by the worst cases, which is quite common in the singing voice separation task, we compute both the mean and median of the selected evaluation parameters (Mean-GSI-SDR, Mean-GSAR, Mean-GSIR, Med-GSI-SDR, Med-GSAR, Med-GSIR) to describe the results in a more robust and unbiased way.

3.3 Results

In order to prove our model's capability, we compare the Plain-Res model (with output flowing from the main stream instead of the bypass branch), Bypass-Res model (proposed model without SEB) and Gen-Res model (proposed model) with the baseline U-net model. The configuration of the baseline U-net model is set as the U7 in Wave-U-Net [19]. Table 2 shows the evaluation result on the test dataset of MUSDB18. The number of RB/SERESB group is set to 4 due to the memory limitation. In the second experiment, we compare the impact of the SERESB's depth on the separation ability. In the second experiment, in order to prove our model's strong learning ability when the depth of the network increases, we choose the SERESB groups of 2 as a contrast test and the results are listed in Table 3.

In Table 2, barely the Plain-Res model outperforms U-net's structure in most experiments except for the GSIR, which proves the correctness of applying ResNet structure in singing voice separation task. According to the table, the Bypass structure and the SEB are both effective ways to improve the experimental performance. The Bypass structure gains an enhancement of 0.31 dB in the singing voice's Mean-GSDR and 0.30 dB in the accompaniment's Mean-GSDR over Plain-Res while the SERESBs improve the results by approximately 0.44 dB and 0.33 dB in singing track and accompaniment track respectively based on Bypass-Res. Our proposed model (Gen-Res) obtains best scores on all evaluation items, specifically with nearly 30 percent's improvement in singing voice's GSDR, roughly an increment of 1.3 dB compared with the U-net structure. All the performances above show that our proposed model works well in tackling singing voice separation task in the time-frequency domain.

Table 3 indicates that as the number of SERESB increases, the proposed model performs better on the MUSDB18 test set, suggesting that deeper SERESB can extract and store more information from the original spectrogram.

Table 2. Singing voice and accompaniment separation results on MUSDB18 augmented test set

Models	Singing					
	Mean			Median		
	GSDR	GSIR	GSAR	GSDR	GSIR	GSAR
U-net (Baseline)	4.532	9.364	6.174	4.777	10.245	6.205
Plain-Res	4.974	8.616	7.659	5.629	9.600	7.644
Bypass-Res	5.284	10.508	7.341	5.862	10.683	7.243
Gen-Res	5.729	10.945	7.419	5.902	11.016	7.306
Models	Accompaniment					
	Mean			Median		
	GSDR	GSIR	GSAR	GSDR	GSIR	GSAR
U-net (Baseline)	10.044	14.091	12.984	9.984	13.979	12.752
Plain-Res	10.712	15.052	13.016	10.785	15.800	13.110
Bypass-Res	10.666	15.290	13.188	10.588	14.920	13.188
Gen-Res	10.996	14.810	13.826	10.790	14.600	13.743

Table 3. Effects of SERESB's number on MUSDB18 test set

Blocks	Singing					
	Mean			Median		
	GSDR	GSIR	GSAR	GSDR	GSIR	GSAR
2	5.187	10.759	6.429	5.507	11.157	6.462
4	5.729	10.945	7.419	5.902	11.016	7.306
Block numbers	Accompaniment					
	Mean			Median		
	GSDR	GSIR	GSAR	GSDR	GSIR	GSAR
2	10.498	14.088	12.670	10.488	13.820	12.756
4	10.996	14.810	13.826	10.790	14.600	13.743

These improvements can be attributed to the SERESB's great ability to rectify the data flowing between channels and layers, which allows us to stack more blocks to improve the network's performance.

With the aim of assessing the mask predicted by our Gen-Res model, we visualize the ideal mask and the predicted mask of our proposed model. The ideal mask is obtained by simply divide clean singing voice spectrograms with mixed spectrograms. We choose 203_mix.wav, 203_vocals.wav and 203_acc.wav in our test set to achieve the results. Figure 3 shows predicted singing voice and accompaniment mask and their corresponding ideal masks. If the color of time-frequency bins is close to red, the mask values are close to 1, while for blue ones, they locate near 0. It can be observed that our model successfully characterize

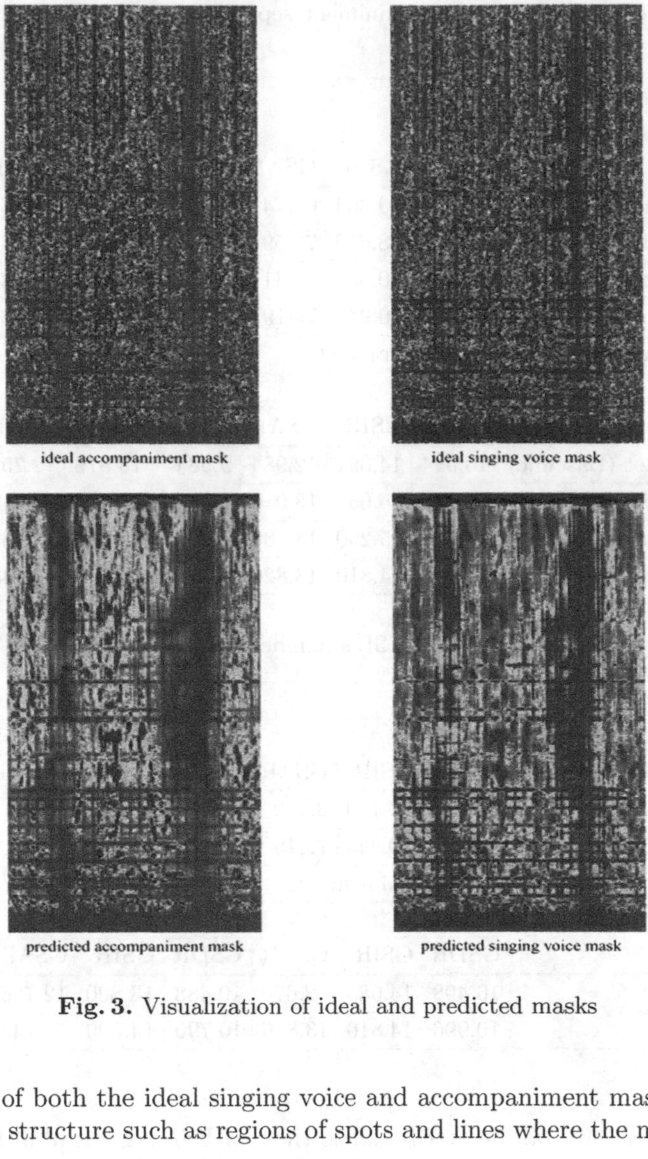

Fig. 3. Visualization of ideal and predicted masks

the outline of both the ideal singing voice and accompaniment mask as well as the delicate structure such as regions of spots and lines where the mask value is close to 1.

4 Conclusion and Future Work

In this paper, we try to potentially enhance singing voice separation performance based on a generative ResNet structure. Experiments show that the single Plain-Res model produces results exceeding U-net's model. Then we explore several methods to improve our model. We apply the Bypass branch and SEB to our basic ResNet model and experiments show that each improvement contributes to our model's separation ability. Our final proposed model which integrates the structure above greatly outperforms U-net – the baseline model by approximately 30% in singing voice's GSDR, which is able to show the great effectiveness of our model. In our future work, we will first collect a larger dataset to investigate our model's generalization ability. The second trial will be to refine our model together with Sound Event Detection. With regrad to the singing voice, singers inevitably breathe between sentences, which brings about near-zero magnitudes in spectrograms and these silent regions considerably deteriorate evaluation indexes. Therefore, we will try to train our model to detect these silent regions and separate singing voice and accompaniment where their magnitudes are not close to zero. Performance increases can be expected as silence boundaries may help our model focus on the useful mixture where actual singing voice and accompaniment are audible.

References

1. van der Merwe, P.: Origins of the Popular Style: The Antecedents of Twentieth-Century Popular Music, p. 320. Clarendon Press, Oxford (1989). ISBN 0-19-316121-4
2. Fujihara, H., Goto, M., Ogata, J., Komatani, K., Ogata, T., Okuno, H.G.: Automatic synchronization between lyrics and music CD recordings based on Viterbi alignment of segregated vocal signals. In: Proceedings of ISM, pp. 257–264, December 2006
3. Yang, Y.-H., Chen, H.H.: Machine recognition of music emotion: a review. ACM Trans. Intell. Syst. Technol **40**, 1–30 (2012)
4. Berenzweig, A., Ellis, D.P.W., Lawrence, S.: Using voice segments to improve artist classification of music. In: AES 22nd International Conference: Virtual, Synthetic, and Entertainment Audio (2002)
5. Li, Y., Wang, D.: Separation of singing voice from music accompaniment for monaural recordings. IEEE Trans. Audio Speech Lang. Process. **15**(4), 1475–1487 (2007)
6. Rafii, Z., Pardo, B.: Repeating pattern extraction technique (REPET): a simple method for music/voice separation. IEEE Trans. Audio Speech Lang. Process. **21**(1), 73–84 (2013)
7. Jeong, I.-Y., Lee, K.: Singing voice separation using RPCA with weighted l_1-norm. In: Tichavský, P., Babaie-Zadeh, M., Michel, O.J.J., Thirion-Moreau, N. (eds.) LVA/ICA 2017. LNCS, vol. 10169, pp. 553–562. Springer, Cham (2017). https://doi.org/10.1007/978-3-319-53547-0_52
8. Huang, P., Kim, M., Hasegawa-Johnson, M., Smaragdis, P.: Joint optimization of masks and deep recurrent neural networks for monaural source separation. IEEE/ACM Trans. Audio Speech Lang. Process. **23**(12), 2136–2147 (2015)
9. Mimilakis, S.I., Drossos, K., Virtanen, T., Schuller, G.: A recurrent encoder-decoder approach with skip-filtering connections for monaural singing voice separation. In: 2017 IEEE 27th International Workshop on Machine Learning for Signal Processing (MLSP), Tokyo, pp. 1–6 (2017)
10. Luo, Y., Chen, Z., Hershey, J.R., Le Roux, J., Mesgarani, N.: Deep clustering and conventional networks for music separation: stronger together. In: 2017 IEEE International Conference on Acoustics, Speech and Signal Processing (ICASSP), New Orleans, LA, pp. 61–65 (2017)

11. Jansson, A., Humphrey, E., Montecchio, N., Bittner, R., Kumar, A., Weyde, T.: Singing voice separation with deep U-net convolutional networks (2017)
12. Chandna, P., Miron, M., Janer, J., Gómez, E.: Monoaural audio source separation using deep convolutional neural networks. In: Tichavský, P., Babaie-Zadeh, M., Michel, O.J.J., Thirion-Moreau, N. (eds.) LVA/ICA 2017. LNCS, vol. 10169, pp. 258–266. Springer, Cham (2017). https://doi.org/10.1007/978-3-319-53547-0_25
13. Grais, E.M., Ward, D., Plumbley, M.D.: Raw multi-channel audio source separation using multi-resolution convolutional auto-encoders. In: 2018 26th European Signal Processing Conference (EUSIPCO), pp. 1577–1581. IEEE (2018)
14. He, K., Zhang, X., Ren, S., Sun, J.: Deep residual learning for image recognition. In: CVPR (2016)
15. Hu, J., Shen, L., Sun, G.: The IEEE Conference on Computer Vision and Pattern Recognition (CVPR), pp. 7132–7141 (2018)
16. van den Oord, A., et al.: WaveNet: a generative model for raw audio. http://arxiv.org/abs/1609.03499 (2016)
17. Rafii, Z., Liutkus, A., Stter, F.-R., Mimilakis, S.I., Bittner, R.: The MUSDB18 corpus for music separation (2017)
18. Liutkus, A., Fitzgerald, D., Rafii, Z.: Scalable audio separation with light kernel additive modelling. In: 2015 IEEE International Conference on Acoustics, Speech and Signal Processing (ICASSP), pp. 76–80. IEEE (2015)
19. Stoller, D., Ewert, S., Dixon, S.: Wave-U-Net: a multi-scale neural network for end-to-end audio source separation. arXiv preprint arXiv:1806.03185 (2018)
20. Vincent, E., Gribonval, R., Fevotte, C.: Performance measurement in blind audio source separation. IEEE Trans. Audio Speech Lang. Process. **14**(4), 1462–1469 (2006)
21. Ronneberger, O., Fischer, P., Brox, T.: U-Net: convolutional networks for biomedical image segmentation. In: Navab, N., Hornegger, J., Wells, W.M., Frangi, A.F. (eds.) MICCAI 2015. LNCS, vol. 9351, pp. 234–241. Springer, Cham (2015). https://doi.org/10.1007/978-3-319-24574-4_28

A Distinct Synthesizer Convolutional TasNet for Singing Voice Separation

Congzhou Tian(✉), Deshun Yang, and Xiaoou Chen

Peking University, Beijing, China
{tcz,yangdeshun,chenxiaoou}@pku.com

Abstract. Deep learning methods have already been used for music source separation for several years and proved to be very effective. Most of them choose Fourier Transform as the front-end process to get a spectrogram representation, which has its drawback though. Perhaps the spectrogram representation is just suitable for human to understand sounds, but not the best representation used by powerful neural networks for singing voice separation. TasNet (Time Audio Separation Network) has been proposed recently to solve monaural speech separation in the time domain by modeling each source as a weighted sum of a common set of basis signals. Then the fully-convolutional TasNet raised recently achieves great improvements in speech separation. In this paper, we first show convolutional TasNet can also be used in singing voice separation and bring about improvements on the dataset DSD100 in the singing voice separation task. Then based on the fact that in singing voice separation, the difference between the singing voice and the accompaniment is far more remarkable than the difference between the voices of two different people in speech separation, we employ separate sets of basis signals and separate encoder outputs for the singing voice and the accompaniment respectively, which makes a further improved model, distinct synthesizer convolutional TasNet (ds-cTasNet).

Keywords: Sing voice separation · TasNet · Distinct synthesizer · Monaural source · Time domain

1 Introduction

Singing voice separation is a task to separate the singing voice from the accompaniment given the mixture of both. It can be helpful for many music information retrieval missions. For example, it could be much easier to solve problems like music transcription, melody extraction with the separated sources. Singing voice correction mission also needs clean singing voice to be the label of training data. Singing voice separation has its commercial usages too. Karaoke would like to pay well to get tons of clean accompaniments of pop songs.

With the development of deep learning, several deep learning methods for monaural audio separation working in the frequency domain [5,10,11] have been

Y. M. Ro et al. (Eds.): MMM 2020, LNCS 11961, pp. 37–48, 2020.
https://doi.org/10.1007/978-3-030-37731-1_4

proposed and show great superiority over conventional solutions. These methods usually use short time Fourier Transform to transform original song signals into spectrograms and obtain time-frequency masks of target sources through a nerual network with the input mixture spectrograms, and then let the Hadamard product of the mask and original spectrograms to be the spectrograms of sources, which are the singing voice and accompaniment in this task. In one of the earliest works [2], DRNN is used to estimate source frequency masks and show its gain compared with NMF models. The hybrid system [7] of deep clustering [3] and conventional RNN has been proposed to show better effects than both components. Jansson et al. [4] shows a different way to directly predict separated spectrograms with U-net, which doesn't need the RNN or LSTM as the time series model to consider the relationship between adjacent t-f bins.

Recently, more and more researchers focus on the question that whether the spectrogram is the best representation of the audio signal in monaural source separation. Because we can't take the phase information into consideration while just magnitude information matters in the time-frequency representations and the IBM or soft mask ranged from 0 to 1 can't restore the magnitude of target source from the mixture perfectly either. Shrikant and Jonah [12] show that there could be adaptive front-ends instead of Fourier Transform in end-to-end audio separation. And a time-domain audio separation network [8] has been proposed to solve the blind speech separation problem in the time domain. In this method, an encoder first transforms the mixture signal into the weighted summation of a group of basis signals and then a separator separates the mixture to get weights of basis signals for each speaker. At last, a decoder resynthesizes the estimated source signals from the separated results with basis signals. This method performs well in blind speech separation and is a great innovation compared with the old frequency-based methods. After the former paper, Luo et al. [9] proposes convolutional TasNet with TCN [6] as the separator instead of LSTM and find it surpasses all the past methods of monaural speech separation.

In this paper, we first explore the use of convolutional TasNet to separate the singing voice and accompaniment in songs. Our system is an end-to-end system which directly produces the waveform of the singing voice from the mixture so that the system can learn not only how to separate sound sources based on their own characteristics, but also how to directly generate natural source waveforms. We advance the performance of singing voice separation by just using the convolutional TasNet. Furthermore, it's easy to spot that in singing voice separation, the two sources (i.e. the singing voice and accompaniment) are much more different from each other than in speech separation, where a common set of basis signals and the same encoder output are for all speakers. So for singing voice separation, we need different outputs from the front-end encoder and different synthesizers for the singing voice and accompaniment. Considering this, we redesign our system to adapt to the task of singing voice separation by letting the encoder produce different features and using two different sets of basis signals for synthesizing the singing voice and accompaniment. Better separation results are obtained after our improvements.

2 Methodology

2.1 Fully Convolutional TasNet

Because our work is mainly based on the Fully Convolutional TasNet [9], this model is first introduced here before we describe our model.

There are three major components in TasNet, which are encoder, separator and decoder respectively [8]. Because TasNet is an end-to-end system in the time domain, a convolution layer is first used to transform all analyzed segments of the input signal into the weight vectors of basis signals of these segments, $\mathrm{w}_{1,...,n}$, which form the input mixture together. After the convolution operation, the weight vectors are passed through a RELU activation function to make sure they are non-negative.

The separator plays an important role in separating while considering time series. In the former time-frequency mask methods, one analyzed segment is a short-time window, which is at least long enough to analyze the short time frequency information, but in TasNet, the length of analyzed segment is far more shorter (1.25 ms in our experiment), which makes it more important to concatenate neighboring audio information to separate. Considering this situation, the separator takes more segments of the input segment to predict. The separator gives the basis signal weight masks for two sources so that we can obtain two time series of sources by calculating the multiplication of weight vectors of two sources and the basis signal group:

$$w^1 = m^1 \odot w_n^{en} \tag{1}$$

$$w^2 = m^2 \odot w_n^{en} \tag{2}$$

where w_n^{en} represents the weight vector produced by the encoder, w_n^1 and w_n^2 represent the weight vector of source 1 and source 2 respectively. $n = 1, ..., N$ is the index of basis signals. Since TasNet considers its front-end and back-end as an autoencoder, the sum of weight vectors of two sources must be equal to the weight vector produced by encoder:

$$w_n^{en} = w_n^1 + w_n^2 \tag{3}$$

To assure Eq. 3, softmax is used as the activation function of the output of separator to make sure the produced masks' sum is one.

And the decoder defined in TasNet is a group of basis signals. The estimated source signal can be reconstructed with the basis signals and signals' weights.

2.2 Our System

Considering the property of the task of singing voice separation, we give the singing voice and accompaniment different encoders to extract suitable separation features and use different synthesizers to reconstruct sources in our distinct synthesizer convolutional TasNet. We expect the network can figure out the best encoders and synthesizers for two different types of sources to separate. The entire system is shown in Fig. 1.

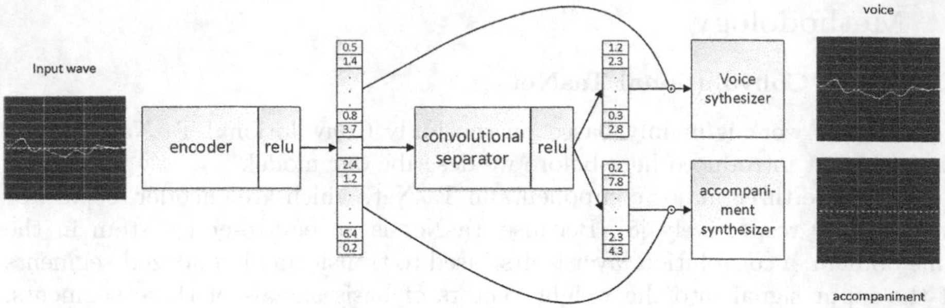

Fig. 1. The entire system of our distinct synthesizer convolutional TaseNet. The encoder extracts the separation feature vectors from the input mixture. Then the convolutional separator uses the feature vectors to generate feature masks. The weight vectors of the voice synthesizer and the accompaniment synthesizer are calculated with the separation features and feature masks. At last, the synthesizers generate different source signals respectively.

Problem Formulation. The mixture signal of a song can be formulated as the sum of two components, the singing voice $s^v(t)$ and accompaniment $s^a(t)$, which is the mixture of all instruments:

$$x(t) = s^v(t) + s^a(t) \tag{4}$$

We assume that the singing voice and accompaniment are composed of different sets of basis signals respectively:

$$s^v(t) = \sum_{n=1}^{N} w_n^v \odot B_n^v(t) \tag{5}$$

$$s^a(t) = \sum_{n=1}^{N} w_n^a \odot B_n^a(t) \tag{6}$$

where $B_n(t)$ and w_n are the n-th basis signal and the weight factor to the corresponding basis signal respectively.

Encoder. A piece of input mixture signal $x(t) \in R^{1\times L}$ is first split into segments $x_k(t) \in R^{1\times \hat{L}}$, where k $= 1, ..., L/\hat{L}$ and then we transform each of the segments into a higher dimensional feature $f \in R^{1\times N}$ by a 1-D convolution operation:

$$f = Relu(x \circledast U) \tag{7}$$

where $U \in R^{N\times \hat{L}}$ denotes the convolution layer, and x denotes the input mixture signal. By this step, it is intended that a high dimensional feature suitable for source separation will be obtained. We call this feature the separation feature. This separation feature is then fed to the separator. At the same time, the feature, skipping the separator, is multiplied by the output of the separator to obtain weights to the basis signals for the singing voice and the accompaniment. The output of the separator is called the feature mask. We designate half of the components of the separation feature to voice estimation, which will be multiplied by the voice feature mask to get the voice weight vector, and the other half for the accompaniment estimation, which will be multiplied by the accompaniment feature mask to get the accompaniment weight vector.

Separator and Synthesizer. The goal of the separator is to obtain the weight vectors to the sets of basis signals for the singing voice and accompaniment respectively. The separator produces separate masks for the singing voice and the accompaniment. We first denote the mask for the singing voice by $m^v \in R^{1\times\hat{N}}$, where $\hat{N}$ = N/2(N is the number of encoder output). We denote the mask for the accompaniment by $m^a \in R^{1\times\hat{N}}$. These two masks are then multiplied by the corresponding half of the separation features $f \in R^{1\times N}$ i.e. either the separation features of the singing voice or the accompaniment to obtain the weight vectors to the respective sets of basis signals:

$$w^v(t) = m^v \odot f[0 : \hat{N} - 1] \tag{8}$$

$$w^a(t) = m^a \odot f[\hat{N} : N - 1] \tag{9}$$

We no longer make the explanation of the autoencoder in TasNet so we don't have to satisfy Eq. 3 to let the sum of w^v and w^a be equal to the encoder output. There is no explicit restriction to the feature masks and we use RELU as the activation function of the separator output instead of softmax. We choose to multiply the separation features by the masks to get the weight vectors rather than predicting weight vectors directly. This can be thought of as a kind of bypass, to constrain the output of later layers with the initial features to make network training converge faster.

The separation module in our model is similar to the one used in [9]. Because the size of segments in TasNet is very small, it takes more time to train a recurrent neural network model. In contrast, the temporal convolutional network [6], which is supposed to be an alternative to RNN, needs less amount of computation by using dilated convolution layers to model time series. So a TCN is used as the separator in TasNet instead of LSTM. The main idea is to use a dilated convolutional network to model all the separation features of segments over the receptive field. The network can be seen as composed of a few convolution groups. Each convolution group consists of several dilated convolutional blocks and the dilation factors of respective blocks increase as the depth of layer grows. The convolutional separator is consisted of a few of this kind of convolution groups by connecting them tail to head. It is worth noting that paddings are added to the input of each convolution layer to make sure the convolution layer's output has the same size as its input. All convolutional layers have skip-connections to the end and we sum the results up to form the feature masks. Figure 2 illustrates the main structure of the convolutional separator.

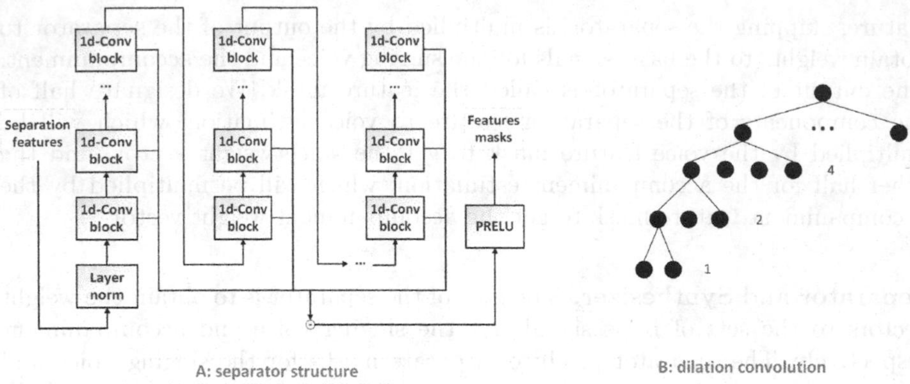

Fig. 2. A: The separator consists of several convolution blocks, and the input is normalized before fed to the separator. The output of a current block is the input to the next block. B: the dilated convolutional layers of a separator convolution group. The first layer's dilation factor is 1, the second layer's dilation factor is 2, the third layers's dilation factor is 4, and so on.

Since we designate different sets of basis signals for the singing voice and the accompaniment, we need two different synthesizers to reconstruct two sources as weighted sums of the respective set of basis signals, as in Eqs. 5, 6. The separator has to produce two masks, one for the singing voice and the other for the accompaniment. It's easy to be accomplished by putting the separator's output through two separate full-connected layers.

Loss Function. We use scale invariant SDR (SI-SDR), which is called SI-SNR in [8,9] as our loss function to evaluate the similarity between the estimated sources and the ground truth. Scale invariance is assured by normalizing the estimated sources and the ground-truth clean sources before loss calculation. It's called SI-SNR in speech separation because interference from sources other than the interest source is simply thought of as noise as well in speech separation. But here we call it SI-SDR in our task. The equation to calculate SDR [13] is:

$$\begin{aligned} SDR &= 10log_{10}\frac{||s_{target}||^2}{||e_{interf}+e_{artif}||^2} \\ &= 10log_{10}\frac{||s_{target}||^2}{||\hat{s}-s_{target}||^2} \end{aligned} \tag{10}$$

And the s_{target}, e_{interf}, e_{artif} [13] in Eq. 10 are defined by:

$$s_{target} = P_{s_j}\hat{s}_j \tag{11}$$

$$e_{interf} = P_{\mathbf{s}}\hat{s}_j - P_{s_j}\hat{s}_j \tag{12}$$

$$e_{artif} = \hat{s}_j - P_{\mathbf{s}}\hat{s}_j \tag{13}$$

where $P_a b$ denotes the orthogonal projection of estimated b onto the ground truth source a.

It's reasonable to use SDR as our loss function instead of MSE often used in source separation task because SDR represents the projection of the estimated source onto the corresponding target source. If we optimize the ratio of the projections of both estimated voice and accompaniment onto their targets i.e. s_{target} to the difference between estimated source $\hat{s}$ and s_{target} respectively, the projection of the estimated source onto the ground truth sources other than the interest one i.e. e_{interf} and the difference between estimated source and the orthogonal projection of this estimated source onto the subspace spanned by all ground truth sources i.e. e_{artif} will be both optimized to some extent, which concerns SIR and SAR. That means we can consider all the three terms of criteria, SDR, SIR and SAR, in the singing voice separation by just optimizing SDR. We will prove it's workable through our experiment in the following part.

To sum up, our loss function of the network is the negative mean value of both SDR of the estimated singing voice and accompaniment:

$$loss = -(SDR_v + SDR_a)/2 \tag{14}$$

3 Experiment

3.1 Dataset

For the convenience to be compared with the Chimera model [7], which is the best model in the 2016 MIREX Source Separation campaign using deep clustering and improved by combining conventional network, we follow the same procedure in [7] to create dataset DSD100-remix, derived from DSD100 dataset to train and evaluate. It's a shame that we can't evaluate on iKala dataset to test our model's power because the it's no longer available.

The DSD100 dataset consists of a total of 100 songs of different styles, half of which (50 songs) is for training and the other half is for evaluation, with the mixture and clean separated sources. We detect and remove the silent segments in both voice and accompaniment tracks at first. Then we get 15 h training set and 0.5 h validation set and evaluation set consisted of 50 clips of 32 s length. All the segments are mixed with 0 dB SNR. We always generate different mixtures by mixing different voice and accompaniment in random order when training while the mixed segments in validation and evaluation sets are fixed and cut directly from original songs. All the tracks are downsampled from 44100 Hz to 16000 Hz to reduce the amount of calculation. We also evaluate our model in the mir1k dataset [1] to test model's generalization ability. There are 1000 clips in mir1k dataset, extracted from 110 Chinese karaoke songs performed by both male and female singers. The sampling rate of all clips is 16000 Hz, which can be tested in our model directly.

3.2 Metrics

We report our experiment results with Global Signal-to-Distortion Ratio (GSDR), Global Signal-to-Artifact Ratio (GSAR) and Global Signal-to-Interference Ratio (GSIR), which are introduced in the MIREX singing voice separation task as the criterion. 'global' means we calculate the mean metrics over all the clips of evaluation dataset.

3.3 Results

We train a fully convolutional TasNet (conv-TasNet) model proposed in [9] and our distinct synthesizer convolutional TasNet (ds-cTasNet) with the training set of DSD100-remix. To compare these two models fairly, we keep the complexity of models nearly unchanged. We compare our models with Chimera at first. The result is shown in Table 1. It's obvious that TasNet models outperform Chimera a lot.

Table 1. The results of SDR of conv-TasNet, ds-cTasNet. The three columns are average SDR, voice SDR, accompaniment SDR respectively.

	SDR		
	Average	Voice	Acc
Chimera	6.7	5.5	7.8
conv-TasNet	10.48	9.19	11.76
ds-cTasNet	10.7	9.42	11.97

Table 2 shows the detailed results of ds-cTasNet and conv-TasNet. We can see that ds-cTasNet is better than original conv-TasNet. It's reasonable because conv-TasNet is proposed as a speech separation model and in speech separation, all sources are the same type of sounds, sharing many similar properties with each other. But in the task of singing voice separation, greater differences between voice and instruments bring more troubles. If we still use the only autoencoder for separation, the goal to get better basis signals to separate will be influenced by both sides harmfully. By giving accompaniment and singing voice different separation features and basis signals to resynthesize them separately, we have different and better ways to express two sources in separation while we still consider them together as a whole in the network by sharing these two sources' characteristics inside. This result also prove that only using GSI-SDR as the loss function can assure all the criteria including GSAR and GSIR in singing voice separation.

Because our model works and is evaluated in time domain directly. We also wonder about the performance of frequency information. An example of spectrograms of our estimated results and target sources is shown in Fig. 3. The figure shows that our model also works well in the frequency domain.

Table 2. The GSDR, GSIR, GSAR of estimated voices and accompaniment of conv-TasNet and ds-cTasNet in DSD100-remix test dataset.

	GSDR		GSIR		GSAR	
	v	a	v	a	v	a
conv-TasNet	9.19	11.76	17.56	17.94	10.2	13.5
ds-cTasNet	9.42	11.97	17.8	18.54	10.53	13.56

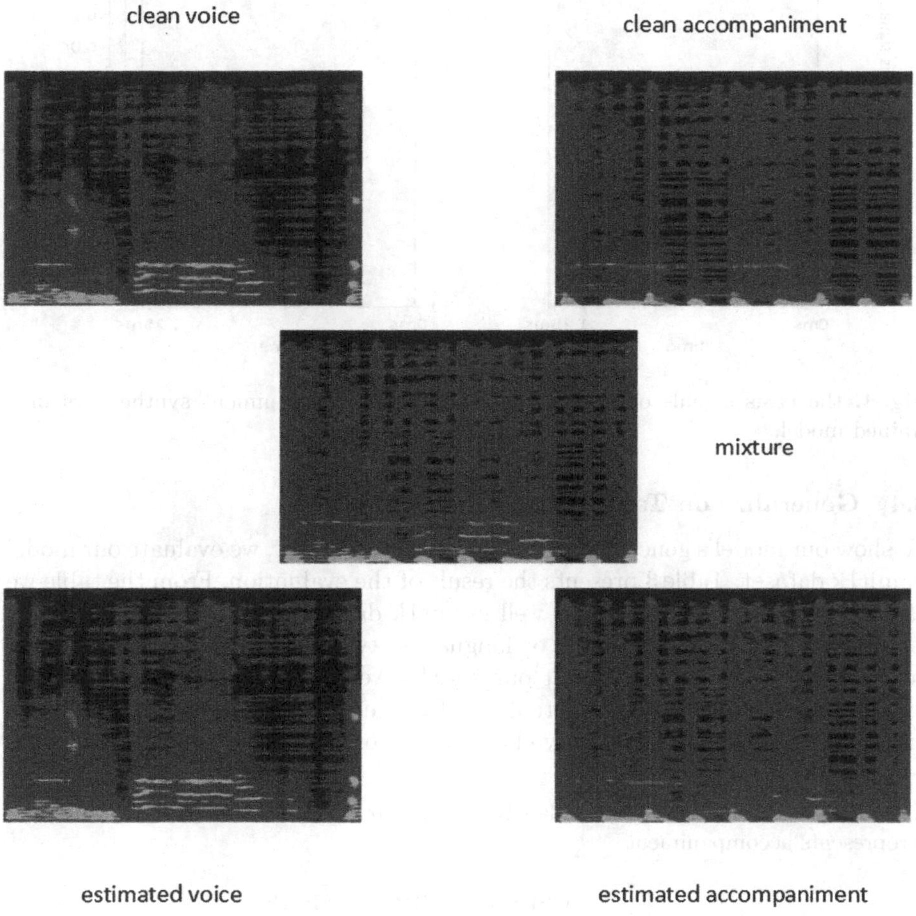

Fig. 3. An example of spectrograms of separated results

To visualize the basis signals in the decoders, we extract an example from a trained model. The distinct basis signals of the singing voice and accompaniment are shown in Fig. 4. It's obvious that they differ from each other, which proves the improvement to have distinct decoders in our model is reasonable in another way.

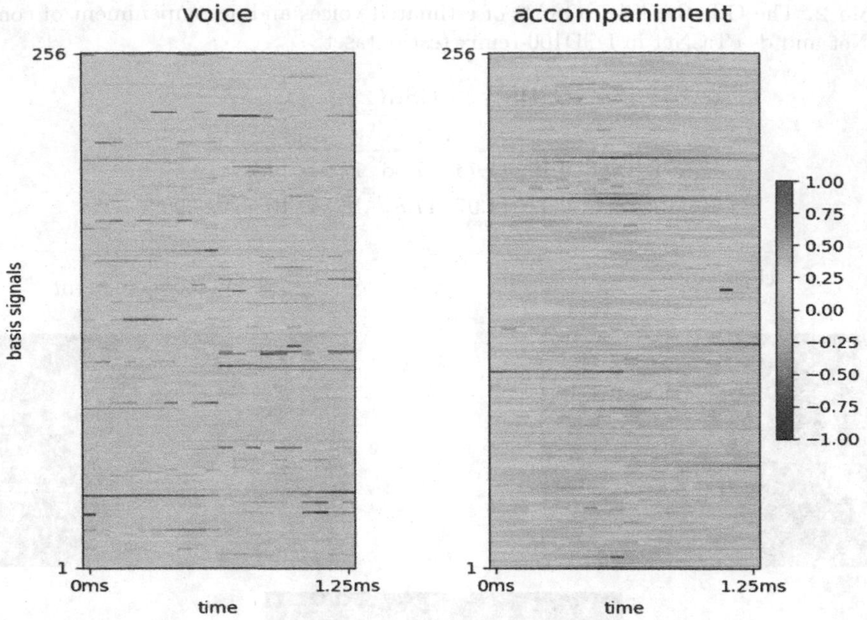

Fig. 4. the basis signals of the singing voice and accompaniment synthesizers in a trained model.

3.4 Generalizaion Test

To show our model's generalization and robustness ability, we evaluate our model in mir1k dataset. Table 3 presents the result of the evaluation. From the table we can see that our model performs well in mir1k dataset, which means our model is robust to the different kinds of languages, types of songs, SNR of singing voice. This result also show that our da-cTasNet can model the singing voice and accompaniment without mutual interference because the GSI-SDR of voice and accompaniment are still very close to each other.

Table 3. The evaluation result of da-cTasNet in mir1k dataset. v represents voice and a represents accompaniment

	GSI-SDR		GSIR		GSAR	
	v	a	v	a	v	a
da-cTasNet	10	10	22.1	22.6	10.8	10.7

4 Conclusion and Future Work

In this paper, we first try the conv-TasNet in singing voice separation and find it surpasses one of the best separation model in the frequency domain. We then propose the distinct sythesizer convolutional TasNet to adapt to the singing voice separation task and improve the capacity of the original model in the singing voice separation task. Because we want to compare two models fairly, we haven't changed the complexity of ds-cTasNet a lot. We think that because the process of mixing different voice sources together loses a lot of information of different sources at the beginning, the effects of separation must have its upper limits. The time-domain model, TasNet inspires us an another way to synthesize the waveforms of different sources given the mixture signal. That means we can use a time-domain network to synthesis different sources instead of simply requiring the estimated and ground truth signals are exactly same with each other. The future work should be to explore how to resynthesize singing voice and accompaniment given the separation results.

References

1. Hsu, C., Jang, J.R.: On the improvement of singing voice separation for monaural recordings using the MIR-1K dataset. IEEE Trans. Audio Speech Lang. Process. **18**(2), 310–319 (2010). https://doi.org/10.1109/TASL.2009.2026503
2. Huang, P., Kim, M., Hasegawa-Johnson, M., Smaragdis, P.: Joint optimization of masks and deep recurrent neural networks for monaural source separation. IEEE/ACM Trans. Audio, Speech, Lang. Process. **23**(12), 2136–2147 (2015). https://doi.org/10.1109/TASLP.2015.2468583
3. Isik, Y., Roux, J.L., Chen, Z., Watanabe, S., Hershey, J.R.: Single-channel multi-speaker separation using deep clustering. In: Interspeech 2016, 17th Annual Conference of the International Speech Communication Association, San Francisco, CA, USA, 8–12 September 2016, pp. 545–549 (2016). https://doi.org/10.21437/Interspeech.2016-1176
4. Jansson, A., Humphrey, E.J., Montecchio, N., Bittner, R.M., Kumar, A., Weyde, T.: Singing voice separation with deep U-Net convolutional networks. In: Proceedings of the 18th International Society for Music Information Retrieval Conference, ISMIR 2017, Suzhou, China, 23–27 October 2017, pp. 745–751 (2017). https://ismir2017.smcnus.org/wp-content/uploads/2017/10/171_Paper.pdf
5. Kolbæk, M., Yu, D., Tan, Z., Jensen, J.: Multitalker speech separation with utterance-level permutation invariant training of deep recurrent neural networks. IEEE/ACM Trans. Audio Speech Lang. Process. **25**(10), 1901–1913 (2017). https://doi.org/10.1109/TASLP.2017.2726762
6. Lea, C., Flynn, M.D., Vidal, R., Reiter, A., Hager, G.D.: Temporal convolutional networks for action segmentation and detection. In: 2017 IEEE Conference on Computer Vision and Pattern Recognition (CVPR), pp. 1003–1012, July 2017. https://doi.org/10.1109/CVPR.2017.113
7. Luo, Y., Chen, Z., Hershey, J.R., Le Roux, J., Mesgarani, N.: Deep clustering and conventional networks for music separation: stronger together. In: 2017 IEEE International Conference on Acoustics, Speech and Signal Processing (ICASSP), pp. 61–65, March 2017. https://doi.org/10.1109/ICASSP.2017.7952118
8. Luo, Y., Mesgarani, N.: Tasnet: Time-domain audio separation network for real-time, single-channel speech separation. In: 2018 IEEE International Conference on Acoustics, Speech and Signal Processing (ICASSP), pp. 696–700, April 2018. https://doi.org/10.1109/ICASSP.2018.8462116

9. Luo, Y., Mesgarani, N.: Conv-TasNet: surpassing ideal time-frequency magnitude masking for speech separation. IEEE/ACM Trans. Audio Speech Lang. Process. **27**(8), 1256–1266 (2019). https://doi.org/10.1109/TASLP.2019.2915167
10. Nugraha, A.A., Liutkus, A., Vincent, E.: Multichannel audio source separation with deep neural networks. IEEE/ACM Trans. Audio Speech Lang. Process. **24**(9), 1652–1664 (2016). https://doi.org/10.1109/TASLP.2016.2580946
11. Simpson, A.J.R., Roma, G., Plumbley, M.D.: Deep Karaoke: extracting vocals from musical mixtures using a convolutional deep neural network. In: Vincent, E., Yeredor, A., Koldovský, Z., Tichavský, P. (eds.) LVA/ICA 2015. LNCS, vol. 9237, pp. 429–436. Springer, Cham (2015). https://doi.org/10.1007/978-3-319-22482-4_50
12. Venkataramani, S., Casebeer, J., Smaragdis, P.: End-to-end source separation with adaptive front-ends. In: 2018 52nd Asilomar Conference on Signals, Systems, and Computers, pp. 684–688, October 2018. https://doi.org/10.1109/ACSSC.2018.8645535
13. Vincent, E., Gribonval, R., Fevotte, C.: Performance measurement in blind audio source separation. IEEE Trans. Audio Speech Lang. Process. **14**(4), 1462–1469 (2006). https://doi.org/10.1109/TSA.2005.858005

Exploiting the Importance of Personalization When Selecting Music for Relaxation

Daniel Mélo(✉) and Nazareno Andrade

Federal University of Campina Grande, Campina Grande, Brazil
danielgondim@copin.ufcg.edu.br, nazareno@computacao.ufcg.edu.br

Abstract. Listening to music is not just a hobby or a leisure activity, but rather a way to achieve a specific emotional or psychological state, or even to better perform an activity, e.g., relaxation. Therefore, making the right choice of music for this purpose is fundamental. In the area of Music Information Retrieval (MIR), many works try to classify, in a general way, songs that are better suited to certain activities/contexts, but there is a lack of works that seek first to answer if personalization is an essential criterion for the selection of songs in this context. Thus, in order to investigate whether personalization plays a vital role in this context, more specifically in relaxation, we: (i) analyze more than 60 thousand playlists created by more than 5 thousand users from the 8tracks platform; (ii) extract high and low-level features from the songs of these playlists; (iii) create a user perception based on these features; (iv) identify users groups by their perceptions; (v) analyze the contrasts between these groups, comparing their most relevant features. Our results help to understand how personalization is essential in the context of relaxing music, paving the way for more informed MIR systems.

Keywords: Personalization · Relaxing music · Music features · Context-aware music recommendation

1 Introduction

Listening to music is a daily habit of many people, but more than a habit or leisure activity, it can be seen as a way to achieve a particular emotional or physiological state, and even assist in performing other tasks. People listen to music to exercise, to relax after a day at work, to study, sleep, that is, music is often used to improve moods for certain activities [1,5].

For each different activity, the same person may have different musical preferences. For sleeping, for example, a relaxing song is probably better, while for physical exercise, energizing music may be preferable. Besides, different people may have distinct musical preferences for the same activity. In this way, it is necessary to search for songs that are appropriate for certain situations according to user preferences. However, due to the number of streaming services like Spotify, 8tracks, Youtube, Deezer, Soundcloud, among others, where users have access to millions of songs, this task has become very costly for users.

Y. M. Ro et al. (Eds.): MMM 2020, LNCS 11961, pp. 49–61, 2020.
https://doi.org/10.1007/978-3-030-37731-1_5

Therefore, understanding the musical preferences of the users for certain contexts, such as performing specific activities, allows the development of tools that help them in the process of choosing songs that are relevant to what is desired. For example, recommendation systems can be built precisely for this purpose.

Among the many everyday activities people perform when listening to music, is relaxation. According to the area of music therapy [2], personalizing music choices for relaxation is essential for a better user experience.

To expand the findings of music therapy, taking into account aspects of musicology and a large amount of data, and to fill the gap in current works in this area, this paper verifies and better analyzes the importance of personalization, taking into account different perceptions of users about relaxing music. To do this, we use a corpus of playlists manually created by thousands of users from 8tracks[1].

Using this corpus, our objective, in summary, was to answer the following research question and then analyze the result of the answer:

1. *RQ: Is there any difference in perceptions of relaxing music among users?*

To this end, we identified the existence of different user groups with similar musical tastes, and from these groups, we analyzed their set of playlists, more explicitly taking into account 33 features of the songs. High and low-level features, such as energy, valence, danceability, MFCC-like (segments timbre [3]), were analyzed.

In these analyses, we created the representation of users' perceptions and then built a logistic regression model (with all users) to identify the most relevant musical features that determine their preferences for relaxing music. After this, to investigate if there are different user perception groups, we apply the k-means clustering algorithm. Subsequently, for each of the 5 clusters found, we built a regression model and verified that they indeed have different relevant musical features. Thus, it was possible to realize that there are differences between users' preferences when creating playlists for relaxation; thus, personalization is something that matters in this context.

This paper is structured as follows: in Sect. 2, we do a review of related works in the fields of music as technology and context-aware music recommendation. In the third section, we describe the data we collected for use in our analysis. In Sect. 4, we present the steps and results of the analysis carried out. Finally, in Sect. 5, we discuss some conclusions of this work and list some future steps.

2 Related Work

As commented in the previous section of this paper, listening to music has become a way to facilitate the listener to reach a specific emotional or physiological state, and even to assist in performing specific activities.

[1] https://8tracks.com/.

In this way, [4] suggests that we also analyze music as a technology. To better understand the use of the term *music as technology*, it is first necessary to understand the meaning of the word technology. In this context, it refers to *a manner of accomplishing a task especially using technical processes, methods, or knowledge*[2]. That is, it is suggested that there are some cases in which listeners use music as a direct tool to reach a particular goal, for example, to improve their performance when doing some physical exercise, or just to perform some daily/specific activity [2,5,6], such as: chill out, study, work, etc.

Although the use of this term has been suggested in recent work in the MIR area, this notion of music as technology is older and already used in works from the sociology area, as in [7] in 1999. In this work, music is characterized as part of a continuous process of self-development, and also indicated that people use music to maintain a social identity as well as regulate their emotions, moods, energy levels, and conditions of their well-being.

The increase in the consumption of music that accompanies other activities also brought together the belief that specific musical selections can potentiate its use as a technology [5]. Thus, it becomes essential to select songs according to the goal that one wants to achieve because, as shown in [8], users reported that music plays different roles in different situations.

Therefore, understanding the context of the user when listening to music is currently a significant trend in the research area of music recommendation systems [9], including becoming a specific research line, known as Context-aware recommender systems [10]. In this new perspective of recommendation, we have a new dimension to be considered: the context (see Eq. 1), unlike collaborative and content-based filtering approaches, where the only dimensions considered are the users and the items (see Eq. 2).

$$Users \times Items \times Contexts \rightarrow Recommendations \quad (1)$$

$$Users \times Items \rightarrow Recommendations \quad (2)$$

It is within this scope of context-aware music recommendation that this work is inserted. More specifically, the context under consideration is the activity that the user is performing or wishes to perform while listening to music. In this area, researches were developed to identify the general characteristics of the songs to perform certain everyday activities, such as: relax, study and exercise, making use of a set of low and high-level acoustic features [1,11,12]. However, none considers personalization as an essential criterion for a better music recommendation to perform specific activities. For these reasons, in this work, we investigate the existence, or not, of different perceptions of the users when creating playlists for relaxation, foreseeing a possible improvement in recommender systems, using the personalization as an essential criterion.

[2] https://www.merriam-webster.com/dictionary/technology.

3 Data Used in Analysis

We will describe the process of data acquisition in two parts: (i) obtaining all the playlists and (ii) adding high and low-level acoustic features from the songs in these playlists. All data were collected from the 8tracks platform. At the end of this section, we show the process used to represent the musical perception of each user.

3.1 8tracks

8tracks is an internet radio and social network where users can share and discover music in a free, simple, and legal way. A fundamental characteristic to note is that in 8tracks playlists are created manually, without the interference of mechanisms for automatic playlists generation, which makes the lists created and shared represent the musical preferences of their creators. Playlists created must have at least eight songs, which can be uploaded by the user, or browsed in the 8tracks library.

Playlists Acquisition. To obtain the 8tracks playlists, a dump of their database was used, provided by the platform administrators themselves. This dump includes data from September 2007 to June 2012. This data has information about the users of the platform, songs, and obviously about playlists created and shared.

For each playlist, it is possible to retrieve its name, description, the number of songs, tags, creator, among other information. Thus, as we wanted to verify the existence or not of different user profiles regarding their musical perception of relaxing songs, and also which the most relevant features that define a song to be relaxing or not, we perform a query to return users who had created at least one relaxing playlist and one not relaxing (a general playlist). With this filtering, we get 5,886 users and thousands of playlists and songs, as we can see in Table 1.

Table 1. Number of filtered songs and playlists

	8tracks
# users	5,886
# relaxing playlists	8,068
# non-relaxing playlists	52,316
# average songs per playlist	8.3
# relaxing musics	53,444
# non-relaxing musics	448,484

3.2 Adding Musical Features

To identify the perceptions of users when creating playlists, considering that their perceptions are linked with the song's features in their playlists, it was necessary to extract from each song some information that characterized it.

To do so, we made use of some of the services provided by the Spotify API[3], which returns a series of high and low-level acoustic features of a song. That way, for every song we had in our data set, we looked for its features.

These features describe various aspects of music, such as rhythm, timbre, how danceable a song is, its energy, valence. In Table 2, it is possible to identify each of the features extracted, their dimensionality (in parentheses), and their meaning (retrieved from Spotify API reference).

Table 2. Features extracted from songs

Feature	Feature description
Acousticness (1)	A confidence measure from 0.0 to 1.0 of whether the track is acoustic. 1.0 represents high confidence the track is acoustic
Danceability (1)	Danceability describes how suitable a track is for dancing based on a combination of musical elements including tempo, rhythm stability, beat strength, and overall regularity. A value of 0.0 is least danceable and 1.0 is most danceable
Energy (1)	Energy is a measure from 0.0 to 1.0 and represents a perceptual measure of intensity and activity. Typically, energetic tracks feel fast, loud, and noisy
Instrumentalness (1)	Predicts whether a track contains no vocals. The closer the instrumentalness value is to 1.0, the greater the likelihood the track contains no vocal content
Liveness (1)	Detects the presence of an audience in the recording. Higher liveness values represent an increased probability that the track was performed live
Speechiness (1)	Speechiness detects the presence of spoken words in a track. The more exclusively speech-like the recording, the closer to 1.0 the attribute value
Tempo (1)	The overall estimated tempo of a track in beats per minute (BPM)
Valence (1)	A measure from 0.0 to 1.0 describing the musical positiveness conveyed by a track. Tracks with high valence sound more positive (e.g. happy, cheerful, euphoric), while tracks with low valence sound more negative
Loudness (1)	The overall loudness of a track in decibels (dB)
MFCC-like - Mean (12)	The mean value of each of the 12 coefficients extracted from each segment of the song
MFCC-like - Variance (12)	The mean value of the variance of each of the 12 coefficients extracted from the segments of the song

[3] https://developer.spotify.com/documentation/web-api/.

Thus, after adding the high and low-level features of each song, our data set was enriched, as we can see in Table 3, where a small portion of a user's playlist information is represented, allowing us to, from that moment on, analyze users profiles according to their perceptions when creating playlists. All analyses performed are described in Sect. 4.

Table 3. User playlist excerpt

spotify_id	*energy*	*liveness*	...	*loudness*	*valence*	*MFCC-like - mean*					*MFCC-like - variance*				
3pJ5IvPXsmpj7DrkxFTZpc	0.555	0.083	...	-8.333	0.705	47.128	33.248	...	-9.660	-1.737	40.834	2082.043	...	168.146	183.848
5yMQERKmNx6ajo4qHi1KT2	0.498	0.059	...	-9.856	0.212	47.023	34.178	...	-6.608	-0.603	35.805	2422.681	...	193.786	183.390

3.3 Representing the Perception of Each User

Since we had information on several songs that each user added to their playlists, more specifically thirty-three features for each song, we summarized the user's profile (what we call "perception" in this work) as being the average values of each of these features, as evidenced by Table 4.

Table 4. Generating user perception

Songs Added by a User

	energy	*liveness*	...	*loudness*	*valence*	*MFCC-like - mean*					*MFCC-like - variance*				
Music 1	0.515	0.111	...	-12.643	0.435	43.886	-10.345	...	-9.110	-3.459	29.209	1420.853	...	164.514	130.962
Music 2	0.166	0.152	...	-20.402	0.583	31.316	-40.567	...	-12.563	20.695	46.672	2629.858	...	313.778	228.478
Music 3	0.166	0.0919	...	-15.443	0.178	38.555	5.210	...	-13.396	2.966	26.346	4907.772	...	289.418	217.203
Music 4	0.13	0.178	...	-9.821	0.304	42.448	-32.217	...	-10.966	-4.103	59.371	3255.888	...	474.255	178.428
Music 5	0.25	0.107	...	-15.588	0.0734	39.016	-8.551	...	-10.823	8.617	36.750	3275.406	...	259.682	295.683
Music 6	0.136	0.0995	...	-20.063	0.275	34.987	-4.773	...	-14.446	3.175	19.564	5993.859	...	356.067	262.748
Music 7	0.148	0.116	...	-15.287	0.381	36.209	-49.319	...	-15.648	5.125	54.560	3357.988	...	542.875	248.857
Music 8	0.269	0.0871	...	-14.892	0.506	40.560	40.532	...	-9.632	-1.975	33.780	2069.288	...	284.228	213.213

The User Perception

	energy	*liveness*	...	*loudness*	*valence*	*MFCC-like - mean*					*MFCC-like - variance*				
Perception	0.222	0.117	...	-15.517	0.341	38.372	-12.503	...	-12.073	3.880	38.282	3363.864	...	335.602	221.947

Thus, after representing the perception of each user, it was possible to begin a descriptive analysis of these data to find regression models that would indicate the features that best characterize the user preferences for relaxing songs. Besides, we also perform an analysis to find possible distinct groups of users who have similar preferences for relaxing songs, and for each of these groups, we also sought to identify the most relevant features.

4 Data Analysis

After collecting, filtering, enriching, and summarizing the data, as described in Sect. 3, we scaled it and try to identify, in a general way, the most relevant features that define the users' perceptions about relaxing songs.

To perform this analysis, we used the perceptions of all the 5,886 users. Each user has two types of perception: that of relaxing songs and that of non-relaxing songs. Thus, a logistic regression model [16] was developed, consisting initially of thirty-three independent variables and a dependent one - which represents the type of user perception.

After fitting the logistic regression model, it was possible to identify that of the thirty-three features eighteen were statistically significant to define the user's perception as relaxing or not. Table 5 presents these features with their coefficients and p-value.

Table 5. Most relevant features to the general user model.

Feature	Coefficient	p-value ($\alpha = 0.05$)
energy	−0.6394738	2.72e−12
tempo	−0.0464791	0.048381
acousticness	−0.2083381	0.001309
instrumentalness	0.1503535	0.000119
valence	−0.1656396	4.54e−05
mfcc3.mean	−4.2449813	2.40e−05
mfcc5.mean	0.1599303	2.03e−06
mfcc6.mean	0.2097834	0.000161
mfcc7.mean	0.1163353	0.000738
mfcc8.mean	−0.3260760	2e−16
mfcc10.mean	−0.2422519	3.58e−06
mfcc11.mean	0.1818077	0.003156
mfcc1.variance	0.1056258	0.000645
mfcc3.variance	−0.0847946	0.017829
mfcc5.variance	0.1138786	0.000790
mfcc6.variance	0.2027986	0.010342
mfcc11.variance	−0.6320118	5.02e−15
mfcc12.variance	0.1397304	4.98e−06

Observing Table 5, analyzing the p-value, we can see that some features have a higher association with the dependent variable (the type of perception), such as energy, mfcc8.mean, and mfcc11.variance.

It is worth explaining that the MFCCs features are responsible for describing characteristics of the timbre of the songs. Timbre is the quality of a musical note or sound that distinguishes different types of musical instruments or voices. In the Spotify API, the timbre is represented by a vector of 12 dimensions (for each music segment), where each of these dimensions is a high-level abstraction of the song spectral surface. For our analysis, we used the mean and variance of each of these dimensions in the songs added by 8tracks users in their playlists.

Since our research question seeks to verify if there are differences in users' perceptions about relaxing music and that until now we had only a general regression model, we tried to find distinct groups of users that have similar perceptions and create regression models for each one of these groups, analyzing the existence of differences between the most relevant features among them and the general model.

4.1 Clustering the Users

A non-hierarchical clustering algorithm, k-means [15], was used to group the users by their perception of relaxing music. The methodology used in the choice of the algorithm was based on [14]. The basic idea of this algorithm is to find similarities between the data and to group them according to a number K of clusters. This algorithm uses the criteria of the distance between two points to calculate the similarity. We used the Euclidean distance [17] in our clustering.

To estimate the number of groups to be identified in our data, we first standardized it and then used the gap statistic method [13]. The gap statistic compares the total within intra-cluster variation for different values of K with their expected values under the null reference distribution of the data. The estimate of the optimal number of clusters will be the value that maximizes the gap statistic (i.e., that yields the largest gap statistic) before any decrease in its value.

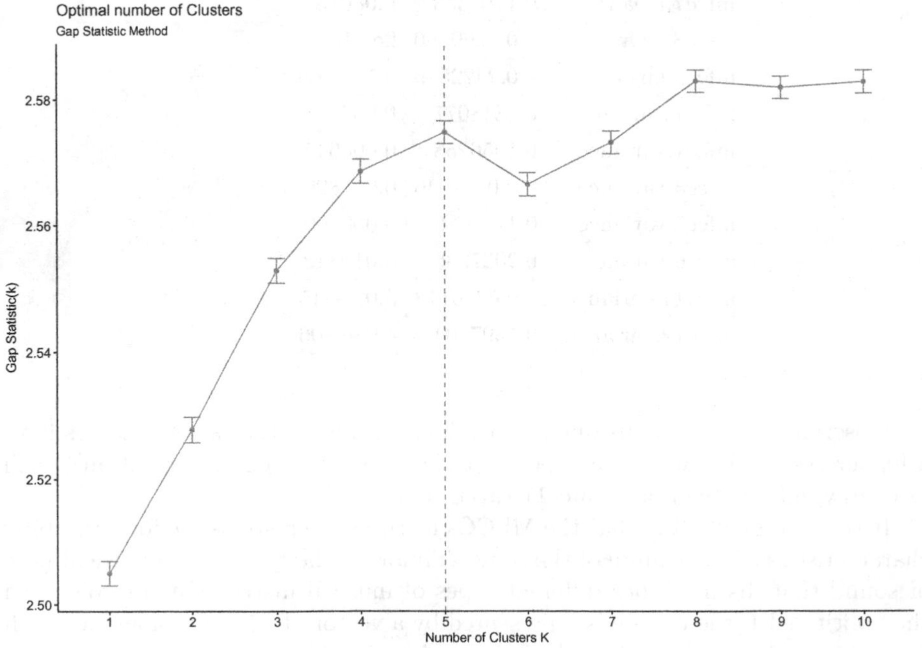

Fig. 1. Optimal number of clusters.

It means that the clustering structure is far away from the random uniform distribution of points. By this method, as we can see in Fig. 1, the optimal number of clusters was five.

In Table 6, we can see the size of the groups identified by the k-means algorithm.

Table 6. Number of users per cluster

	Cluster 1	Cluster 2	Cluster 3	Cluster 4	Cluster 5
# users	503	591	1961	2221	610

4.2 Analyzing Clusters

After grouping the users into 5 clusters, we analyzed each of them. A regression model was developed for each cluster, identifying the statistically significant features.

To summarize all the results found, we created Table 7, where it is possible to distinguish for each cluster, which features are relevant. A feature is considered relevant when its value is associated (has statistical significance) to the classification of the perception type from the group users.

It is possible to identify, looking at Table 7, that each cluster has different sets of relevant features, suggesting that users in each group have different perceptions when choosing songs for relaxation.

To describe the identified clusters to understand their differences better, we analyze the centroids of each one and discuss the most relevant features of them. In Fig. 2, we can see the scaled centroid values of each cluster about each of the 33 features considered in this study.

- Cluster 1: The smallest of all, it is made up of users who have added to their relaxing playlists, songs with high instrumentalness and acousticness values, and low danceability, loudness, and valence values compared to the other groups. Also, it can be seen that the means values of MFCC are not as relevant as the variances in determining the perception of relaxing music for the members of this group.
- Cluster 2: In this group, as we can see in Table 7, the MFCC variances play a crucial role in defining the perception of relaxing music, where 8 of the 12 coefficients were statistically significant for this purpose. As in Cluster 1, in this group, the MFCC means were not so relevant.
- Cluster 3: As we can see in Fig. 2, analyzing the cluster centroids, songs with higher energy values were added to the relaxing playlists of the users of this group compared to the other groups. It is also possible to observe that the values of the MFCC play a significant role in defining the perception of relaxing music for users in this group.

Table 7. Relevant features in each cluster.

Feature	Cluster 1	Cluster 2	Cluster 3	Cluster 4	Cluster 5
energy			✔	✔	
liveness		✔		✔	
tempo				✔	
speechiness		✔	✔	✔	
acousticness	✔	✔	✔	✔	
instrumentalness				✔	
danceability			✔		✔
loudness		✔	✔		
valence	✔				✔
mfcc1.mean		✔			
mfcc2.mean		✔			
mfcc3.mean			✔	✔	
mfcc4.mean				✔	✔
mfcc5.mean			✔		
mfcc6.mean			✔		✔
mfcc7.mean			✔	✔	
mfcc8.mean		✔	✔	✔	
mfcc9.mean				✔	✔
mfcc10.mean	✔		✔	✔	✔
mfcc11.mean			✔		
mfcc12.mean					
mfcc1.variance	✔	✔		✔	
mfcc2.variance			✔		
mfcc3.variance		✔	✔		
mfcc4.variance			✔		✔
mfcc5.variance	✔	✔			
mfcc6.variance		✔	✔		✔
mfcc7.variance		✔			
mfcc8.variance					
mfcc9.variance		✔	✔		
mfcc10.variance		✔			✔
mfcc11.variance	✔		✔	✔	
mfcc12.variance	✔	✔	✔	✔	

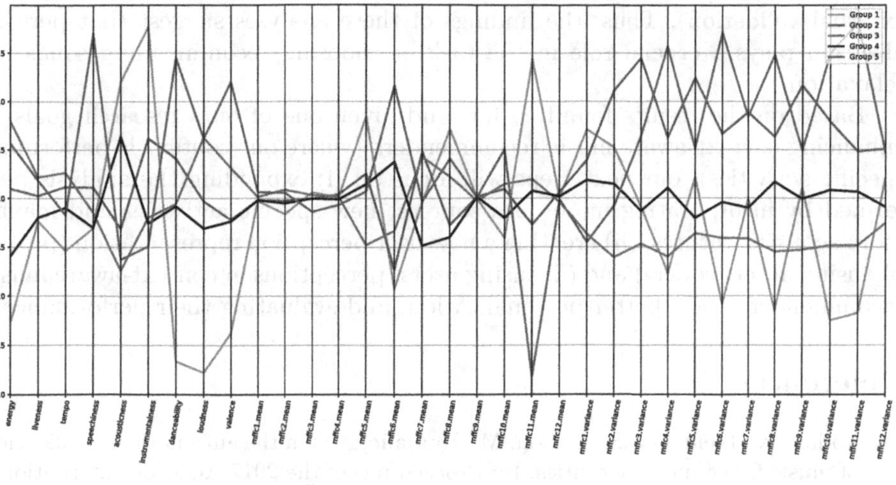

Fig. 2. Scaled values of group centroids.

- Cluster 4: The biggest group, consisting of users who mostly have relaxing songs with feature values very close to the average feature values of all users studied, as we can identify by analyzing Fig. 2 since their values are close to 0 and the data is scaled.
- Cluster 5: Finally, this cluster includes users who have added to their relaxing playlists, songs with higher values of speechiness, danceability, and valence, suggesting that this group comprises people who relax listening to happy and dancing songs.

Thus, we can see that there are several differences between the clusters identified in our analysis. These differences suggest that treating personalization as a significant criterion when choosing songs to relax is extremely important.

5 Conclusion and Future Work

In this work, we propose the exploiting and analysis of the importance of personalization for context-aware music recommendation [10], more specifically, recommendations to perform specific activities. For this analysis, we investigated a corpus of relaxing and non-relaxing playlists from thousands of users from the 8tracks platform. We come up with the use of high and low-level acoustic features to identify the existence or not of different perceptions of users when creating relaxing playlists.

To accomplish this task, we initially searched for a database of playlists created manually by users, and with that data, we performed some analysis, described in Sect. 4, to verify the importance of personalization in this context. The results of these analyses showed that, in the data used, there are different perceptions of the users when creating relaxing playlists (we found five different groups), which partially answers our research question positively (needs an external validation). Thus, the findings of these analyses suggest that personalization plays a crucial role in the task of choosing/recommending songs for relaxation.

Based on the results found so far, and given one of ours research goals of enhancing context-aware music recommenders (where our context is performing specific activities), our next steps will focus on (i) expanding the analysis performed by incorporating more data sources, new specific activities and maybe more acoustic features; (ii) creating a new user perception representation (probably using autoencoders) and (iii) using users' perceptions in context-aware music recommenders, for a better personalization, and evaluating their performance.

References

1. Yadati, K., Liem, C.C.S., Larson, M., Hanjalic, A.: On the automatic identification of music for common activities. In: Proceedings of the 2017 ACM on International Conference on Multimedia Retrieval, ICMR 2017, Bucharest, Romania, 6–9 June 2017, pp. 192–200 (2017). https://doi.org/10.1145/3078971.3078997
2. Rentfrow, P.J., Gosling, S.D.: The do re mi's of everyday life: the structure and personality correlates of music preferences. J. Pers. Soc. Psychol. **84**(6), 1236 (2003)
3. Schindler, A., Rauber, A.: Capturing the temporal domain in echonest features for improved classification effectiveness. In: Nürnberger, A., Stober, S., Larsen, B., Detyniecki, M. (eds.) AMR 2012. LNCS, vol. 8382, pp. 214–227. Springer, Cham (2014). https://doi.org/10.1007/978-3-319-12093-5_13
4. Demetriou, A., Larson, M., Liem, C.C.S.: Go with the flow: when listeners use music as technology. In: Proceedings of the 17th International Society for Music Information Retrieval Conference, ISMIR 2016, New York City, United States, 7–11 August 2016, pp. 292–298 (2016)
5. North, A.C., Hargreaves, D.J., Hargreaves, J.J.: Uses of music in everyday life. Music Percept. Interdiscip. J. **22**(1), 41–77 (2004)
6. Sloboda, J.A., O'Neill, S.A., Ivaldi, A.: Functions of music in everyday life: an exploratory study using the experience sampling method. Musicae Scientiae **5**(1), 9–32 (2001)
7. DeNora, T.: Music as a technology of the self. Poetics **27**(1), 31–56 (1999)
8. North, A.C., Hargreaves, D.J.: Situational influences on reported musical preference. Psychomusicol. J. Res. Music. Cogn. **15**(1–2), 30 (1996)
9. Schedl, M., Zamani, H., Chen, C.W., Deldjoo, Y., Elahi, M.: Current challenges and visions in music recommender systems research. Int. J. Multimed. Inf. Retr. **7**(2), 95–116 (2018)
10. Adomavicius, G., Tuzhilin, A.: Context-aware recommender systems. In: Ricci, F., Rokach, L., Shapira, B. (eds.) Recommender Systems Handbook, pp. 191–226. Springer, Boston (2015). https://doi.org/10.1007/978-1-4899-7637-6_6
11. Dias, R., Fonseca, M.J., Cunha, R.: A user-centered music recommendation approach for daily activities. In: CBRecSys@ RecSys, pp. 26–33 (2014)
12. Wang, X., Rosenblum, D., Wang, Y.: Context-aware mobile music recommendation for daily activities. In: Proceedings of the 20th ACM International Conference on Multimedia, pp. 99–108. ACM (2012)
13. Tibshirani, R., Walther, G., Hastie, T.: Estimating the number of clusters in a data set via the gap statistic. J. R. Stat. Soc. Ser. B **63**, 411–423 (2001). https://doi.org/10.1111/1467-9868.00293

14. Furtado, A.A.: Perfis de contribuidores em sites de perguntas e respostas. Mestrado, Universidade Federal de Campina Grande (2013)
15. Hartigan, J.A., Wong, M.A.: Algorithm AS 136: a k-means clustering algorithm. J. R. Stat. Soc. Ser. C (Appl. Stat.) **28**(1), 100–108 (1979). https://doi.org/10.2307/2346830
16. Menard, S.: Applied Logistic Regression Analysis, vol. 106. Sage, Thousand Oaks (2002)
17. Moita Neto, J., Ciaramella, Moita.: Uma introdução à análise exploratória de dados multivariados. Química Nova. **21** (1998). https://doi.org/10.1590/S0100-40421998000400016

Oral Session 2A: Coding and HVS

An Efficient Encoding Method for Video Compositing in HEVC

Yunchang Li, Zhijie Huang, and Jun Sun(✉)

Wangxuan Institute of Computer Technology, Peking University, Beijing, China
{liyunchang,zhijiehuang,jsun}@pku.edu.cn

Abstract. Video compositing for compressed HEVC streams is highly demanded in instant communication applications such as video chat. As a flexible scheme, pixel domain compositing involves the processes of completely decoding the streams, inserting the decoded video, and finally re-encoding the new composite video. The time consumption of the whole scheme comes almost entirely from the re-encoding process. In this paper, we propose an efficient encoding method to speedup the re-encoding process and improve encoding efficiency. The proposed method separately designs encoding for blocks inside the frame region covered by inserted video and blocks in non-inserted region, which overcomes numerous difficulties of utilizing information from the decoding process. Experimental results show that the proposed method achieves a PSNR increase of 0.33 dB, or a bit rate saving of 10.11% on average compared with normal encoding using unmodified HM software. Furthermore, the encoding speed is 7.04 times that of normal encoding method, equivalent to an average reduction of 85.8% in computational complexity.

Keywords: Video compositing · High Efficiency Video Coding (HEVC) · Encoding optimization · Information reuse

1 Introduction

Picture-in-picture (PiP), i.e., one primary video is displayed on the full screen while one or more other videos are displayed in inset windows, is widely used in today's instant communication scenarios, such as video chat and video conference. As depicted in Fig. 1, for a common conference scenario, one of the incoming streams transmitted from different sources is chosen as the primary video stream. Then the central server is responsible for inserting videos of other streams into the primary video side by side and generating a composite video stream. Obviously, the time it takes for compositing will have an impact on communication latency. Furthermore, compared with the previous video coding standard H.264/AVC, the successor High Efficiency Video Coding (HEVC) saves nearly 50% bit rate consuming with the equal perceptual quality [10]. However, the encoding complexity of HEVC has increased several times [3]. Such increase in computational complexity makes video compositing more difficult to meet the requirements of real-time scenarios.

Y. M. Ro et al. (Eds.): MMM 2020, LNCS 11961, pp. 65–76, 2020.
https://doi.org/10.1007/978-3-030-37731-1_6

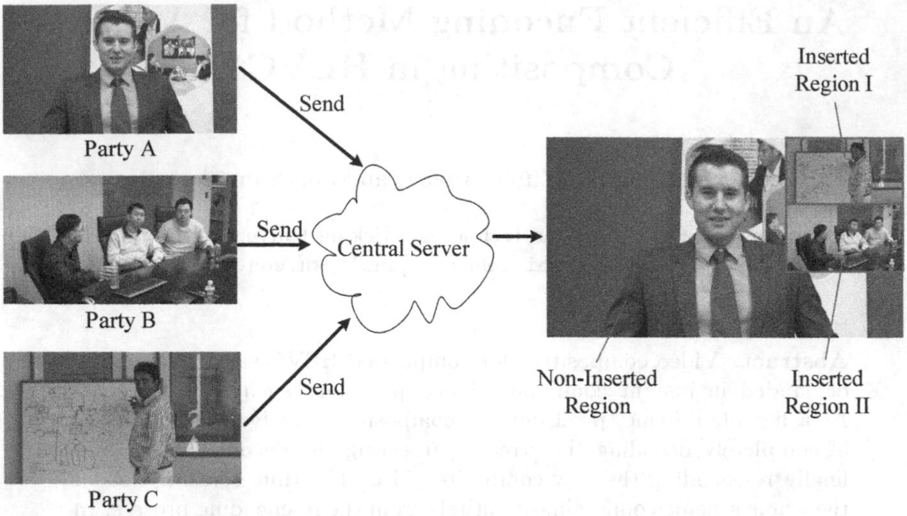

Fig. 1. Example of a three-party video conference scenario. Stream of party A is chosen as the primary video stream.

To reduce computational cost of video compositing, there are already some related works producing a PiP video stream in compressed domain. Amon *et al.* [1] proposed a tile-based compositing method, which directly re-groups the entropy encoded data of input streams using tiles as the basic unit and modifies the slice header and parameter sets to generate a new video stream. Later, Sanchez *et al.* [9] proposed a similar tile-based method without modifying the original definition of tiles, guaranteeing that the mixed streams can be correctly decoded by a standard HEVC decoder. Since the real encoding process is not performed, computational cost is significantly reduced by these methods. However, the size and location of inserted videos must be multiples of the largest coding units (LCUs) due to the limitations of tiles, which greatly reduces the diversity of the PiP video. Besides, since the compositing is performed in compressed domain, the resolution of inserted video is unchangeable.

As a more flexible scheme, pixel domain compositing of HEVC video streams is chosen to overcome the above disadvantages. In this scheme, the incoming video streams are completely decoded at first, and then the down-scaling process is performed for the videos to be inserted. Finally, these down-scaled videos are inserted into the primary video and the encoder re-encodes the new PiP video. Since re-encoding is the most time consuming process in the whole scheme, in this paper, we design an efficient encoding method that utilizes information from the decoding process. Experimental results show that compared with normal encoding method, the proposed method can achieve an average PSNR increase of 0.33 dB, or a bit rate saving of 10.11%. At the same time, computational complexity is significantly reduced by 85.8%.

The remainder of the paper is structured as follows: Sect. 2 introduces the encoding method for blocks inside inserted region (i.e., the frame region covered by inserted video), while Sect. 3 introduces the encoding method for blocks in non-inserted region. Experimental results of the proposed method are presented in Sect. 4, and conclusion is drawn in Sect. 5.

2 Encoding in Inserted Region

Although inserted region is usually a small part of the entire frame, its encoding complexity overhead still accounts for a large portion, especially when the encoding process for non-inserted region has been optimized. For a coding unit (CU) located inside inserted region, the region having the same content can be matched in the video of original size. As the temporal and spatial characteristics are preserved after down-scaling, the proposed method reuses the decoding information of the matched region to speedup the encoding. However, misalignment, i.e., the CUs inside inserted region can't be aligned with CUs in the matched region, may occur in the following two circumstances: the down-scaled ratio is not an integer power of two, or the left and upper boundary of inserted region is misaligned with LCUs. This is clearly depicted in Fig. 2. Obviously, reusing information is not easy in this situation.

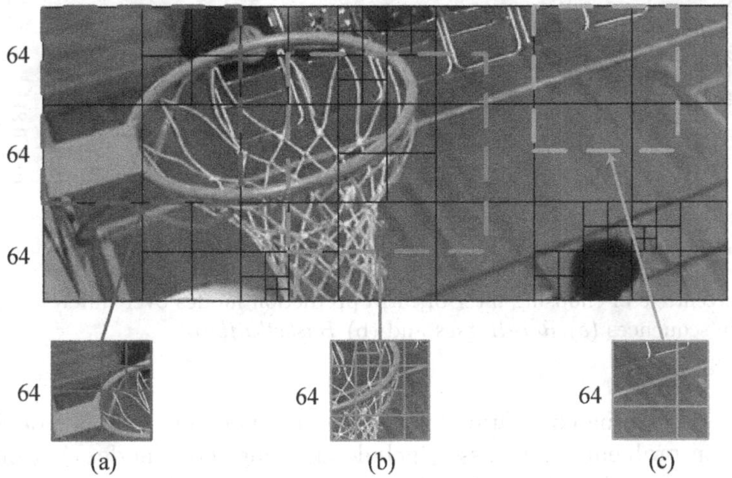

Fig. 2. Examples of the matched region for a 64 × 64 CU, indicated by the dotted box. (a) Aligned matching. (b) Misaligned matching, inserted location is misaligned with LCUs. (c) Misaligned matching, down-scaled ratio is 3:2.

Nevertheless, a prediction mode decision model which avoids unnecessary searches for intra or inter mode is built for inter frames. In another model, the partition types of prediction units are estimated by analyzing the consistency of motion vectors. The following two subsections describe these models in detail.

2.1 Prediction Mode Decision Model

It can be inferred that there is a strong correlation of prediction mode between the down-scaled video and the original video. Hence, for each CU in inserted region, the model calculates the area ratio of CUs using inter prediction in the corresponding matched region based on the decoding information of splitting and prediction modes. Note that considering the case of misalignment, only the overlapping part with the matched region participates in the area calculation.

Figure 3 shows the percentage of choosing inter or intra prediction modes over different area ratio intervals, which is summarized from the statistics of the original and the triple down-scaled sequences *RaceHorses* and *BasketballDrill*. As can be seen, the percentage of choosing inter modes increases gradually as the area ratio increases. Particularly, when the area ratio exceeds 0.9 or is lower than 0.1, the percentage of choosing inter or intra prediction mode is over 95%, no matter whether in the motion intense sequence *RaceHorses* or the motion smooth sequence *BasketballDrill*.

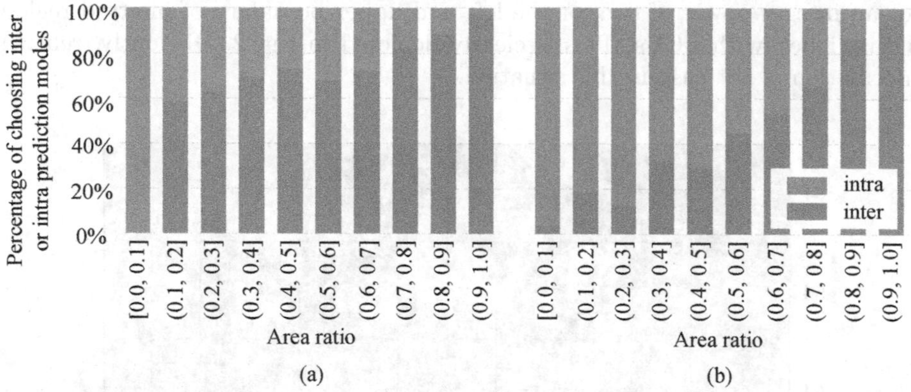

Fig. 3. Percentage of choosing inter or intra prediction modes over different area ratio intervals in sequences (a) *RaceHorses* and (b) *BasketballDrill*.

Due to this strong correlation, the prediction mode decision is modeled as a classification problem. The classes include choosing inter mode, choosing intra mode, and performing the normal mode search, denoted as c_{inter}, c_{intra}, and $c_{pending}$, respectively. The classification decision rule can be written as

$$\begin{cases} c_{inter}, & if\ r > \alpha \\ c_{intra}, & if\ r < \beta \\ c_{pending}, & otherwise \end{cases} \tag{1}$$

where r is the aforementioned area ratio, α and β are thresholds determined by experiments. It's worth mentioning that class $c_{pending}$ in otherwise condition is set to reduce bit rate loss in the dilemma of choosing inter or intra mode.

To determine the threshold parameters, the posterior probability $p(c_{inter}| r > \alpha)$ that indicates the probability of correct decision on inter mode is given by Bayes rule [5] as

$$p(c_{inter}|r > \alpha) = \frac{p(r > \alpha|c_{inter}) \cdot p(c_{inter})}{p(r > \alpha)} \tag{2}$$

$$p(r > \alpha) = \sum_{x}^{\{inter,intra\}} p(r > \alpha|c_x) \cdot p(c_x) \tag{3}$$

where $p(r > \alpha|c_x)$ and $p(c_x)$ are the conditional probability densities of $r > \alpha$ and the prior probability of class c_x, respectively. These probability values can be estimated from the statistics of the above sequences. In a similar manner, we calculate the posterior probability $p(c_{intra}|r < \beta)$ that indicates the probability of correct decision on intra mode.

Table 1 gives the calculation results of the posterior probability for the different thresholds α and β. In principle, the thresholds could be adjusted to the desired behavior of the encoding, i.e., used to balance time saving and model accuracy. To ensure bit rate loss within an acceptable range, the thresholds α and β are set to 0.9 and 0.1, respectively, providing an average model accuracy of 0.98.

Table 1. Posterior probability with different α and β values

Sequence	$p(c_{inter}\|r > \alpha)$			$p(c_{intra}\|r < \beta)$		
	$\alpha = 0.95$	$\alpha = 0.90$	$\alpha = 0.85$	$\beta = 0.10$	$\beta = 0.13$	$\beta = 0.15$
RaceHorses	0.979	0.976	0.968	0.996	0.971	0.912
BasketBallDrill	0.983	0.981	0.978	0.958	0.936	0.914

2.2 Partition Type Decision Model

Prediction unit (PU) is the basic unit of prediction in HEVC. If the prediction mode is selected to be inter, at most 8 ways will be applicable to split the CU into one, two or four PUs [10]. For each PU, either one or two motion vectors (MVs) can be used for unidirectional or bidirectional inter prediction. In order to find the partition with the minimal rate-distortion cost, the normal method checks them one by one during encoding. However, some unnecessary checks can be skipped by analyzing the consistency of the motion. This is based on the observation that the partition is closely related to the motion in the CU, e.g., CU with different motions on the left and right sides is most likely to be split vertically into two PUs.

According to the property of linear transformation, the pixel located at the PiP video coordinate (x, y) is considered to be a mapping of the pixel located at the original video coordinate $(x^{'}, y^{'})$ if the following conditions are satisfied

$$\begin{cases} x = x_{ir} + \text{round}(x^{'}/sr_x) \\ y = y_{ir} + \text{round}(y^{'}/sr_y) \end{cases} \tag{4}$$

where $(x_{ir},\ y_{ir})$ is the coordinate of the top-left corner of inserted region, sr_x and sr_y are the down-scaled ratios of the x-axis and the y-axis, respectively.

To explore the correlation of MVs between the down-scaled video and the original video, we calculate the absolute MV difference d_{mv} between each pair of mapped pixels, which is formulated as

$$d_{mv} = \text{abs}(mv_x - \text{round}(mv_x^{'}/sr_x)) + \text{abs}(mv_y - \text{round}(mv_y^{'}/sr_y)) \tag{5}$$

where (mv_x, mv_y) is the MV of pixel in inserted region, $(mv_x^{'}, mv_y^{'})$ is the MV of mapped pixel in the original video. Note that the scaling for the MV in formula (5) is used to align the metrics. The histograms of d_{mv} between the original and the triple down-scaled sequences *RaceHorses* and *BasketballDrill* are depicted in Fig. 4. It can be observed that for both sequences, the cumulative frequency of d_{mv} less than 8 (i.e., 2 pixels) is nearly 90%. The average values of d_{mv} of two sequences is 3.47 and 2.39, respectively, meaning the vertical and horizontal MV differences are within half a pixel on average. This MV difference is expected to be even smaller when using a better down-scaled interpolation method than the currently used bilinear interpolation.

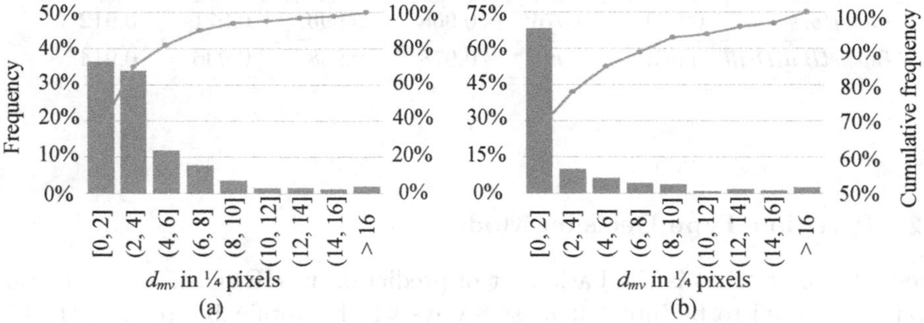

Fig. 4. Histograms of absolute MV difference d_{mv} of sequences (a) *RaceHorses* and (b) *BasketballDrill*.

Therefore, MV information of the original video is utilized to estimate the motion in inserted region during encoding. Specifically, for pixels in a particular PU, if all the mapped pixels in the original video use the same MV, we consider the motion in the PU to be consistent. However, when there are some mapped pixels using intra prediction or using a reference picture different from the others, the analysis of motion consistency becomes complicated. Moreover, in general, pixels in the original video may refer to the pixels outside the picture boundary generated by the border extension. This isn't applicable to the PU in inserted region because the region boundary is not necessarily the picture boundary, which does not guarantee the execution of the border extension. As a result, we consider the motion to be unanalyzable in these cases.

Subsequently, considering a CU to encode, the actual procedure whether to include a certain partition type or not reads as follows. First, it is assumed that the CU has been split into PUs according to the partition type. Then, the motion consistency is analyzed for each PU. As long as there is a PU whose motion is unanalyzable, the partition type will be directly included in the check candidate to keep encoding efficiency. Besides, if the motions of all PUs are consistent, the partition type will also be included. Otherwise, the check for the partition type will be skipped.

To improve the performance of the model, we point out some special rules. First, the prediction type 2N × 2N is always included because *Skip Mode* and *Merge Mode* are widely used for inter prediction, which have low bit rate overhead and low computational complexity. Second, when the motion of the partition type 2N × 2N is consistent, then all the partition types will be included in the check candidate since no matter how the CU is split, the motion of each PU will also be consistent. To remedy the defect in this case, we specifically skip the checks for all partition types except 2N × 2N.

3 Encoding in Non-inserted Region

Since the down-scaled video can be inserted into any position of the primary video, there is inevitably a problem that the boundary of inserted region may not be aligned with CUs. Considering that the aforementioned methods cannot be applied to the CUs crossing the boundary of inserted region, we choose to encode them using the normal encoding method. Despite the increase in computational cost, it is a good choice to maintain encoding efficiency.

The remaining CUs to be optimized for encoding are all located inside non-inserted region, where the pixel values are exactly the same as the original primary video. The most intuitive optimization method is to utilize the decoding information of the primary video to guide the encoding. In HEVC, the quadtree search process allows the CU to be split into four smaller CUs. The leaf node CU can be further split into PUs and transform units (TUs) for prediction and residual coding. In order to reduce computational cost of the search process, we reuse the splitting information of CU, PU, and TU. Although the way of splitting may not be the most appropriate due to the effects of inserted video, encoding quality is guaranteed by re-encoding the CUs whose distortion exceeds the limit. This will be described in detail at the end of the section.

The next step is to determine prediction parameters for each PU. In luma intra prediction, a set containing three most probable modes is derived based on the modes of two neighboring PUs, one above and one to the left of the current PU [7]. During encoding, if the luma intra prediction mode to be reused is equal to one of the most probable modes, we only encode the index in the set. Otherwise, the luma mode is explicitly coded. Since the chroma mode derivation is only related to the current luma mode, no information adjustment is needed for chroma intra prediction. However, the reference samples may contain pixels inside inserted region, resulting in unexpected prediction values. To keep encoding quality, we have to discard the reused information and re-encode the CUs containing these PUs.

In inter prediction, the challenge of reusing MV information comes from the high dependency on the neighboring PUs. This is because the actual MV is not directly coded. Instead, it is derived from the MV prediction or merging candidate list built from the available MVs of the neighboring PUs [8]. Affected by inserted video and re-encoding of some CUs, the MV changes of neighboring PUs may lead to the change of the candidate list. To mitigate the effects and prevent the propagation of MV changes, we consider modifying the information of PUs. Specifically, for PUs using normal inter mode, the MV to be reused can be restored by selecting a MV predictor from the candidate list and re-encoding the MV difference. For PUs using *Skip* and *Merge Mode*, we check whether the MV is included in the merging candidate list. If the MV is included, then we only encode the merge index of the MV in the list. Otherwise, a modification is performed, which changes the *Skip* or *Merge Mode* to normal inter mode and restores the MV with the method of normal inter mode described above. Besides, since residual coding is bypassed in *Skip Mode*, it is necessary to explicitly set all coded block flags to zero. Similar to intra prediction, in the case that the MVs of some PUs point to inserted region, the corresponding CU needs to be re-encoded.

For the CUs that are not re-encoded, modes of intra prediction and MVs of inter prediction remain the same as the original primary video. In addition, even if the reconstructed pixels used for prediction may have been changed, they are not expected to be significantly different from the original pixels. For these reasons, the prediction residuals should be similar to the residuals of the original primary video. Therefore, we directly copy the residual coefficients to skip the time-consuming transform and quantization process. Note that when the transform block has no non-zero residual coefficients, the corresponding coded block flag is set to zero.

Finally, some issues need to be addressed. Pixel error, i.e., the difference in the reconstructed pixel between the current video and the original primary video, is generated in inserted region and re-encoded CUs. Since reusing information makes the encoder lose the ability of error correction, such pixel error can be propagated to the subsequent CUs by prediction, sub-pixel interpolation, and in-loop filtering. As the number of encoded CUs increases, pixel error is accumulated and amplified, resulting in a gradual decline in encoding quality. To compensate pixel error, we choose to re-encode the CUs whose distortion exceeds an empirical threshold. Here, the sum of squared difference (SSD) is used as a measure of distortion, and the threshold value is set to be positively correlated with the size of CU and the quantization step. By doing so, we can keep the loss of encoding quality within an acceptable range.

4 Experimental Results

In this section, we simulate a video compositing scenario to evaluate the performance of the proposed method in terms of encoding efficiency and computational complexity.

4.1 Experiment Setup

The proposed encoding method has been implemented in the HEVC reference software HM–16.20 [6]. The test platform is a workstation with Intel Xeon(R) E5-1680 CPU @ 3.40 GHz and RAM 64 GB. Video sequences employed in the experiments are commonly used HEVC standard testing sequences, including Class A, B, C, D, and E [4].

To simulate the video chat scenario, the input streams are generated first by encoding all testing sequences with *lowdelayP* configuration and intra period equal to 32. For each class, one sequence is selected to be triple down-scaled using bilinear interpolation and then inserted into the upper right corner of the other sequences. Details of the inserted sequences are given in Table 2. The output is the compressed streams of these composite PiP sequences with the same quantization parameter and picture structure as the input. Computational complexity of the method is evaluated by time consumption from the stream input to the stream output. The ratio of the time consumption between two comparable methods is denoted as speedup ratio SR.

Table 2. Settings of the inserted sequence for each class.

Class	Resolution	Inserted sequence	Inserted resolution
A	2560 × 1600	*Traffic*	854 × 532
B	1920 × 1080	*ParkScene*	640 × 360
C	832 × 480	*RaceHorses*	276 × 160
D	416 × 240	*RaceHorses*	140 × 80
E	1280 × 720	*Vidyo1*	428 × 240

To evaluate encoding efficiency, Bjøntegaard delta bit rates ΔBR and delta PSNR values ΔPSNR with piece-wise cubic interpolation [2] are computed by setting the quantization parameter values to 22, 27, 32, and 37. The PSNR of encoded sequence is the average value of the PSNR_{YUV} of each frame, which is calculated as $\text{PSNR}_{\text{YUV}} = (6 \cdot \text{PSNR}_{\text{Y}} + \text{PSNR}_{\text{U}} + \text{PSNR}_{\text{V}})/8$, where PSNR_{Y}, PSNR_{U}, and PSNR_{V} are the peak signal to noise ratio of three color components, respectively. The reference for PSNR calculation is the corresponding original uncompressed PiP sequence.

4.2 Performance Evaluation on Encoding Efficiency and Complexity

The previous works that focus on compressed domain video compositing are not applicable to the application scenario of this paper due to the limitations of tiles. Therefore, the traditional normal encoding method using unmodified HM software is taken as a comparison in the experiment.

In the following, the proposed encoding methods in inserted region and non-inserted region are denoted as EMIR and EMNIR, respectively. The results are summarized in Table 3, subdivided into two parts.

Table 3. Performances comparison between the proposed method and the traditional normal encoding method. The ΔPSNR is given in dB and the ΔBR is given in %.

Class	Sequence	EMNIR			EMNIR+EMIR		
		ΔPSNR	ΔBR	SR	ΔPSNR	ΔBR	SR
A	*PeopleOnStreet*	0.48	−11.52	8.59x	0.48	−11.48	9.96x
	Traffic	0.35	−10.84	6.55x	0.34	−10.74	7.61x
B	*BasketballDrive*	0.28	−11.42	6.70x	0.28	−11.27	8.16x
	BQTerrace	0.24	−13.21	6.01x	0.24	−13.06	7.28x
	Cactus	0.27	−11.82	6.50x	0.27	−11.68	8.01x
	Kimono	0.25	−9.07	6.46x	0.25	−8.88	7.88x
C	*BasketballDrill*	0.41	−10.76	4.21x	0.39	−10.33	5.02x
	BQMall	0.39	−10.75	4.25x	0.38	−10.25	5.09x
	PartyScene	0.36	−9.10	4.98x	0.35	−8.83	5.98x
D	*BasketballPass*	0.39	−8.92	4.29x	0.39	−8.78	4.74x
	BlowingBubbles	0.35	−9.22	4.24x	0.35	−9.14	4.66x
	BQSquare	0.30	−7.78	4.39x	0.30	−7.67	4.76x
E	*FourPeople*	0.41	−10.52	6.73x	0.40	−10.47	8.94x
	Johnny	0.28	−9.68	6.47x	0.28	−9.61	8.69x
	KristenAndSara	0.33	−9.58	6.55x	0.33	−9.52	8.86x
Average		**0.34**	**−10.28**	**5.79x**	**0.33**	**−10.11**	**7.04x**

The left part lists the performance employing the EMNIR only. It can be observed that for the same bit rate, the EMNIR outperforms the traditional method by 0.34 dB on average in terms of PSNR. For the same PSNR, an average of 10.28% bit rate saving is achieved. This encoding efficiency improvement is mainly due to the reuse of the original video information. The EMNIR preserves more high-frequency component of the original sequence, while the traditional method loses the video details. More importantly, the average speedup ratio of the EMNIR is close to 5.8 times, reducing computational complexity significantly.

The right part of the table shows the performance of the proposed EMNIR together with the EMIR. Compared with using the EMNIR only, the impact on encoding efficiency is negligible while the average speedup ratio is improved by at least one fifth. Note that the performance of the EMIR is expected to be better when the proportion of inserted region area becomes larger. We also observe that the worst performance is given by Class D, whose resolution is the lowest. This is mainly because there are fewer LCUs in low resolution video frames, making pixel errors be easily propagated to larger areas. The encoding speed is affected by the re-encoding process that compensates for pixel errors. Overall, compared with the traditional method, the proposed method can achieve a speedup ratio by 7.04 times, or a 85.8% computational complexity reduction on average.

It's worth mentioning that the experiments are based on a two-party video chat scenario. This can be extended to a multi-party video conference scenario with just inserting more down-scaled videos into the primary video. Since the EMIR and the EMNIR both perform well for encoding in inserted region and non-inserted region, we expect that the proposed method still performs much better than the traditional method in the video conference scenario.

5 Conclusion

In this paper, we propose an efficient encoding method for pixel domain video compositing in HEVC. The proposed method overcomes numerous difficulties of utilizing information from the decoding process. For encoding in video inserted region, prediction mode and partition type decision models are built to properly handle the misalignment problem and avoid some unnecessary searches. For encoding in non-inserted region, the proposed method reuses the decoding information of splitting, prediction modes, motion vectors and residual coefficients, which improves encoding efficiency and reduces lots of computational cost. Pixel error propagation that has a poor impact on encoding quality is mitigated by re-encoding the quality-loss blocks. Experimental results show that compared with the traditional normal encoding method using unmodified HM software, the proposed method achieves an average PSNR increase of 0.33 dB, or a bit rate saving of 10.11%. Furthermore, computational complexity is significantly reduced by 85.8% on average. Such a convincing result implies that the proposed method can be well applied to instant communication scenarios such as video chat and video conference.

Acknowledgment. This work was supported by National Natural Science Foundation of China under contract No. 61671025.

References

1. Amon, P., Sapre, M., Hutter, A.: Compressed domain stitching of HEVC streams for video conferencing applications. In: 2012 19th International Packet Video Workshop (PV), pp. 36–40, May 2012
2. Bjøntegaard, G.: Calculation of average PSNR differences between RD-curves. In: Document VCEG-M33, Video Coding Experts Group (VCEG) (2001)

3. Bossen, F., Bross, B., Suhring, K., Flynn, D.: HEVC complexity and implementation analysis. IEEE Trans. Circ. Syst. Video Technol. **22**(12), 1685–1696 (2012)
4. Bossen, F.: Common test conditions and software reference configurations. In: Document JCTVC-L1100, ITUT VCEG and ISO/IEC MPEG (JCT-VC) (2013)
5. Duda, R.O., Hart, P.E., Stork, D.G.: Pattern Classification, 2nd edn. Wiley, New York (2001)
6. HEVC Reference Software HM-16.20. http://hevc.hhi.fraunhofer.de/svn/svn_HEVCSoftware. Accessed 10 Oct 2019
7. Lainema, J., Bossen, F., Han, W., Min, J., Ugur, K.: Intra coding of the HEVC standard. IEEE Trans. Circ. Syst. Video Technol. **22**(12), 1792–1801 (2012)
8. Lin, J., Chen, Y., Huang, Y., Lei, S.: Motion vector coding in the HEVC standard. IEEE J. Sel. Top. Signal Process. **7**(6), 957–968 (2013)
9. Sanchez, Y., Globisch, R., Schierl, T., Wiegand, T.: Low complexity cloud-video-mixing using HEVC. In: 2014 IEEE 11th Consumer Communications and Networking Conference (CCNC), pp. 213–218, January 2014
10. Sullivan, G.J., Ohm, J., Han, W., Wiegand, T.: Overview of the High Efficiency Video Coding (HEVC) standard. IEEE Trans. Circ. Syst. Video Technol. **22**(12), 1649–1668 (2012)

VHS to HDTV Video Translation Using Multi-task Adversarial Learning

Hongming Luo[1,2,3,4], Guangsen Liao[1,2,3,4], Xianxu Hou[1,2,3,4], Bozhi Liu[1,2,3,4], Fei Zhou[1,2,3,4](✉), and Guoping Qiu[1,2,3,4,5]

[1] College of Electronics and Information Engineering, Shenzhen University, Shenzhen, China
flying.zhou@163.com

[2] Guangdong Key Laboratory of Intelligent Information Processing, Shenzhen, China

[3] Guangdong Laboratory of Artificial Intelligence and Digital Economy (SZ), Shenzhen, China

[4] Shenzhen Institute of Artificial Intelligence and Robotics for Society, Shenzhen, China

[5] School of Computer Science, University of Nottingham, Nottingham, UK

Abstract. There are large amount of valuable video archives in Video Home System (VHS) format. However, due to the analog nature, their quality is often poor. Compared to High-definition television (HDTV), VHS video not only has a dull color appearance but also has a lower resolution and often appears blurry. In this paper, we focus on the problem of translating VHS video to HDTV video and have developed a solution based on a novel unsupervised multi-task adversarial learning model. Inspired by the success of generative adversarial network (GAN) and CycleGAN, we employ cycle consistency loss, adversarial loss and perceptual loss together to learn a translation model. An important innovation of our work is the incorporation of super-resolution model and color transfer model that can solve unsupervised multi-task problem. To our knowledge, this is the first work that dedicated to the study of the relation between VHS and HDTV and the first computational solution to translate VHS to HDTV. We present experimental results to demonstrate the effectiveness of our solution qualitatively and quantitatively.

Keywords: VHS · HDTV · Video translation · Multi-task learning · Unsupervised · GAN

1 Introduction

With the rapid development of electronic technology, especially video display technology, the resolution of television and display is higher and higher as well as the expanding of color space. Nowadays, high-definition television is widespread and 4K television, even HDR television is gradually available. Compared with the development of video display technology, video resources that can suitable for such high-resolution display are very scarce. Massive video resources have been

Y. M. Ro et al. (Eds.): MMM 2020, LNCS 11961, pp. 77–86, 2020.
https://doi.org/10.1007/978-3-030-37731-1_7

generated in the long-term accumulation. Some classic old movies, programmes as well as some important events and moments are recorded through a large amount of video or image data, but these precious old resources can't reach the level of 4K or HDR display. If these resources are not processed, playing on the above display device will result in very poor visual experience.

In addition, the original imaging equipment and storage methods not only determine the low resolution of these video resources, but also their poor color performance. For example, Video Home System (VHS) was the dominant video format widely used across the world since 1970s before it was replaced by high-definition television (HDTV) in the new millennium. Due to the analog nature of VHS recording medium and limited storage memory, the visual quality of VHS video is inferior. As shown in Fig. 1(a), VHS frame has low resolution and low color contrast. Hence, it is very important to effectively process these resources to give users a better visual experience on existing high-definition television.

(a) VHS frame (b) HDTV frame

Fig. 1. Illustration of VHS and HDTV frames.

The most perfect video enhancement and restoration technology is transforming shaky, blurry, color-distorted, noisy, overly dark or bright and low resolution video footage into sharper, clearer and visually pleasing videos. However, most of existing technology only focus on single problem mentioned above and there are corresponding training pairs, which is to say that there are ground truth. But in reality, we sometimes can't reach that situation. To translate the video frames like Fig. 1(a) to the video frames like Fig. 1(b), we need video frames with high resolution and high color contrast corresponding to VHS video frames. Although we can get HDTV video frames, they are not pixel-wise corresponding to VHS video frames which means we lack of ground truth for training (More details are introduced in Sect. 3). Based on this problem, we propose a method that settle unsupervised multi-task problem. Our goal is learning a mapping from the video frames like Fig. 1(a) to the video frames like Fig. 1(b). Firstly, we use generative adversarial network to translate VHS video frames to HDTV video frames. At the same time, the cycle consistency loss is needed to keep the contents of video frames. Only HDTV video frames can be used for training super-resolution model due to the lack of VHS paired training samples from low resolution to high resolution. But the discrepancy between VHS video frames and HDTV video frames makes the model trained on HDTV video frames not applicable for VHS video frames. Therefore, we need a method to make the model have better applicability to both training samples. The most simple way to achieve that is sharing weights of models training for two kinds of samples, so as to achieve the effect of the model to complete the color conversion and super-resolution with single model. Our contribution can be summarized as:

- As far as we known, this is the first work to focus on translating VHS video to HDTV video which is a unsupervised multi-task problem.
- We propose a novel multi-task adversarial learning model for translating VHS to HDTV video and set up a framework that can solved unsupervised multi-task problem. Our experimental results to demonstrate our approach's effectiveness.

2 Related Works

Style Transfer. After Gatys et al. [4] successfully apply convolutional neural networks (CNN) in style transfer, many work based on CNN emerge. Gatys et al. [4] use pre-trained model to extract features of content and style, then train a generative network to synthesize stylized images through iterative optimization. The speed of this strategy is slow because one network is trained for one image. Subsequently, Johnson et al. [6] propose a feed-forward network to generate styled image by decreasing both style and content features losses, which increase the speed a lot. However, all these works are kept the features unchanged between generated image and content image. Even though the style image is natural image, the generated image has some non-photorealistic artifacts. Hence, there are some work focusing on photorealistic style transfer. Deep photo style transfer, proposed by Luan et al. [10], augments style loss with semantic segmentation and adds photorealism regularization to make generated image look more photorealistic. After that, photoWCT [9], uses photorealistic variant of WCT to replace VGG network's upsampling module and applies additional post-processing to reduce artifacts. In addition, generative adversarial network (GAN) is used in CycleGAN [18] to transfer image style, and cycle consistency loss is used to constrain the content information.

Super Resolution. Recently, deep neural networks have achieved great success in the field of super resolution. Deep network cascade for super resolution [1] uses multi-level autoencoder to achieve super resolution. And Dong et al. [2] use convolutional neural network (CNN) simulate each module in traditional super resolution task with different convolutional layers: low-resolution feature extraction, low-resolution to high-resolution feature mapping and high-resolution image reconstruction. But when the network gets deeper, the performance is not further improved. In order to improve the efficiency of network, Dong et al. [3] take low-resolution image instead of bilinearly interpolated image as input, and design a deconvolutional layer at the end of network to complete the upsampling of image features. To achieve deeper network, Kim et al. [7] propose VDSR (very deep super resolution) model with a skip-connection to transmit low frequent signal. DRRN [14] (deep recursive residual network) recursively calls the same residual module whose parameters are shared, so it makes the network deeper without increasing number of parameters. RDN [17] (residual dense network) utilizes both residual block and dense block, which is more complex skip-connection to achieve super resolution. From these cases, deeper networks, better performance. As the development of generative adversarial network, Ledig et al. [8] define adversarial loss, and acquire better perceptual results using adversarial training strategy.

3 Adversarial Learning for VHS to HDTV

As shown in Fig. 2, our goal is to learn a mapping function from the domain of VHS videos like Fig. 2(a) with low color contrast and low resolution to the domain of target videos like Fig. 2(b) with high color contrast and high resolution. And Fig. 2(b) should be similar with HDTV videos like Fig. 2(d). We can obtain high color contrast and high resolution HDTV frames like Fig. 2(d) and downsample HDTV frames to low resolution frames like Fig. 2(c). Using Fig. 2(a), (c) and (d), we can learn a mapping from Fig. 2(a) to (c), which is only enhance color contrast, and a mapping from Fig. 2(c) to (d), which is only enhance resolution. However, the target frames like Fig. 2(b) corresponding to VHS frames are unavailable, so that there is no way to learning a mapping from Fig. 2(a) to (b) directly. Hence, this problem is divided into an unsupervised multi-task problem category, which we need to address not only the color style but also the resolution of videos without ground truth. Our multi-task adversarial learning model for translating VHS video to HDTV video will be introduced below.

We use x and y to represent the VHS (Fig. 2(a)) and HDTV frames (Fig. 2(d)) respectively, and z is the low-resolution counterpart (Fig. 2(c)) of y. The distributions of x and y are denoted as $x \sim p_{data}(x)$ and $y \sim p_{data}(y)$ respectively.

3.1 Model Architecture

The architecture of our model is given in Fig. 3, which consists of two parts. Each part is denoted by a dashed box in Fig. 3. The top part is the same as CycleGAN [18], where we define two generators $G : x \rightarrow Y_x$ and $F : Y_x \rightarrow x$ as two mappings as well as two discriminators D_Y and D_X. D_Y aims to distinguish images generated by G and HDTV frames while D_X aims to distinguish images generated by F and VHS frames. The generator in the bottom part, i.e., the Enhance Net, shares weights with the generator G above. And we add a perceptual loss between y and generated Y_z, which is computed via features extracted by the pre-trained (and fixed) VGG19 [13]. In addition, we also define another discriminator D_Z, which aims at distinguishing images generated by G

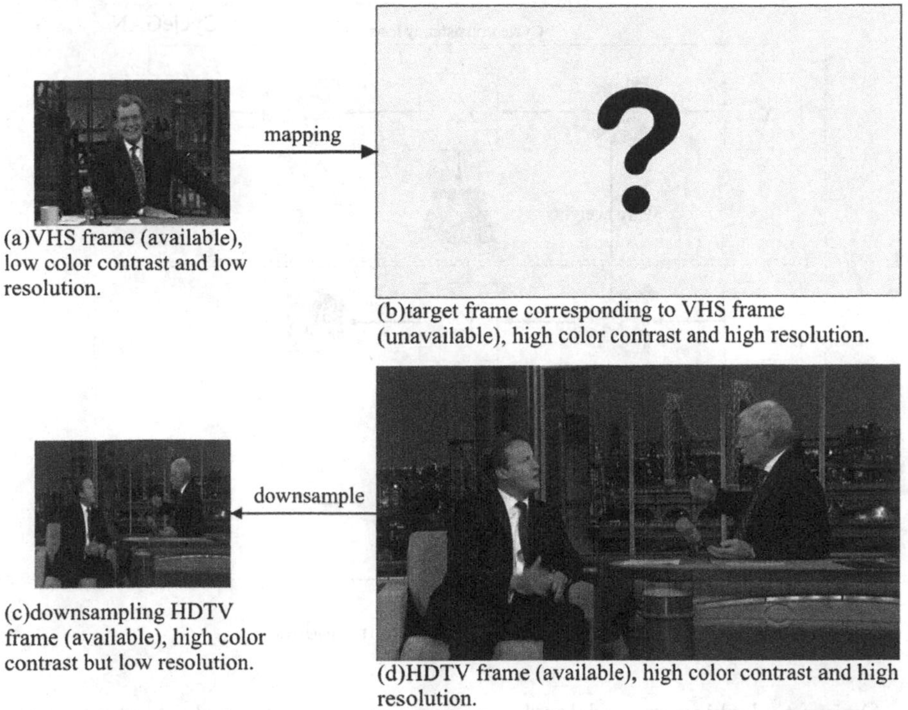

Fig. 2. Problem description.

and HDTV frames. The difference of the generated images and the ground truth lies in spatial resolution only. Y_x is image that contains the content of x with Y style while Y_z contains the content of z with Y style. We use U-net [12] as the architecture of all the generators and PixelGAN [5] for the discriminators.

3.2 Cycle-Adversarial Loss

The basic adversarial loss is expressed as:

$$\begin{aligned}\mathcal{L}_{GAN}(G, D_Y, X, Y) = &\mathbb{E}_{y\sim p_{data}(y)}[logD_Y(y)] \\ &+ \mathbb{E}_{x\sim p_{data}(x)}[1 - D_Y(G(x))]\end{aligned} \tag{1}$$

After defining the loss function, we optimize it as

$$min_G max_{D_Y} \mathcal{L}_{GAN}(G, D_Y, X, Y),$$

which means that we maximize the distance between the generated images and HDTV frames by training D_Y and then minimize the distance between them by training G to generate images look similar to HDTV frames. Using the same training strategy, we optimize the other adversarial loss,

$$min_F max_{D_X} \mathcal{L}_{GAN}(F, D_X, Y, X).$$

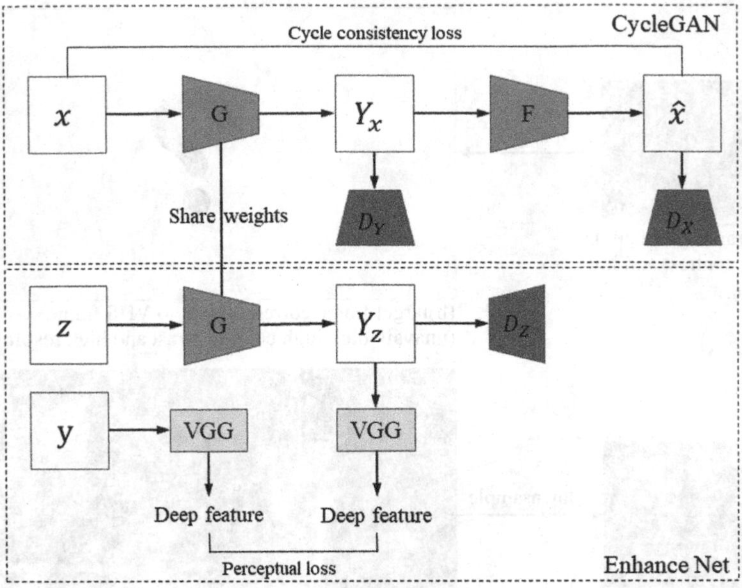

Fig. 3. Architecture of our model.

Owing to lacking ground truth, it is no guarantee that the content of the input is unchanged after translating. If we train the model long enough with adversarial loss, the generated image would become an image that is independent of input. Hence, a cycle consistency loss is essential to keep the information of input. The cycle consistency loss can be formulated as

$$\mathcal{L}_{cyc}(G,F) = \mathbb{E}_{x\sim p_{data}(x)}[\|F(G(x)) - x\|_1] + \mathbb{E}_{y\sim p_{data}(y)}[\|G(F(y)) - y\|_1], \quad (2)$$

where $\| * \|_1$ denotes L_1 norm.

3.3 Resolution Loss

CycleGAN [18] does not consider the change of resolution during the translation but in our problem, the change of resolution cannot be ignored. However, VHS frames have no corresponding high-resolution or clear images as ground truth. Thus we synthesize data Z by blurring and downscaling HDTV frames with the purpose of making them close to the resolution of VHS frames. In order to fuse data from X and Z, we train them with the same generator G by sharing their weights. In addition, we use perceptual loss to constrain the perceptual quality between output and target by reducing their distances of deep features extracted by a pre-trained VGG19 [13] network. The perceptual loss can be expressed as:

$$\mathcal{L}_{perc}(G) = \mathbb{E}_{y\sim p_{data}(y)}[\|VGG(G(z)) - VGG(y)\|_2] \quad (3)$$

where $|| * ||_2$ denotes L_2 norm.

Similar to the adversarial loss in Eq. 1, we define another adversarial loss, which distinguishes the generated images and HDTV frames in resolution. As input is blurred HDTV frames, the difference between output and target is only the resolution that D_Z need to capture. Our goal is just like above:

$$min_G max_{D_Z} \mathcal{L}_{GAN}(G, D_Z, Z, Y),$$

which makes translated images look more like high-resolution ones.

3.4 Overall Objective

The overall objective function of our multi-task learning model is

$$\begin{aligned} \mathcal{L}(G, F, D_X, D_Y, D_Z) = & \mathcal{L}_{GAN}(G, D_Y, X, Y) \\ & + \mathcal{L}_{GAN}(F, D_X, Y, X) + \lambda \mathcal{L}_{cyc}(G, F) \\ & + \mathcal{L}_{GAN}(G, D_Z, Z, Y) + \kappa \mathcal{L}_{perc}(G) \end{aligned} \tag{4}$$

where $\mathcal{L}_{GAN}(G, D_Y, X, Y)$, $\mathcal{L}_{GAN}(F, D_X, Y, X)$ and $\mathcal{L}_{cyc}(G, F)$ are the losses that constrain the image style while the remaining losses constrain the image resolution. We aim at optimizing the following:

$$\{G^*, F^*\} = arg \min_{G,F} \max_{D_X, D_Y, D_Z} \mathcal{L}(G, F, D_X, D_Y, D_Z) \tag{5}$$

4 Results and Evaluation

4.1 Training Details

We collected a dataset from the Internet. The VHS frames were taken from a 1990s program of the show "Late Show with David Letterman" and the HDTV frames were taken from a 2010s program of the same show. We also collected VHS frames from the 1995 production of 'Toy Story' and HDTV frames of the 2010 production of the same title. There are around 8000 VHS frames and around 8000 HDTV frames, 95% were used as training data and the rest as testing data.

Since the improvement of resolution is more difficult than that of colors, for each training iteration of the cycle-adversarial loss, we train the resolution loss several iterations (5 in the experiment). Our learning rate is 0.0001 and we use Adam to optimize the model while momentums are set as 0.5 and 0.999. And the parameters in Eq. 4 is set as $\lambda = 0.1$ and $\kappa = 0.05$.

4.2 Visual Results

To show the superiority of the proposed model, we compare it with CycleGAN [18], DRRN [14], and Johnson et al. [6]. In Fig. 4, the results demonstrate that CycleGAN [18] and Johnson's [6] method can improve color contrast, but CycleGAN [18] fails to improve the resolution of images and Johnson's [6] method causes some artifacts and the color seems strange. On the other hand, DRRN [14] enhances image resolution but the color remains unchanged. Our method performs better both in color and resolution.

(a)
(b)
(c)
(d)
(e)

Fig. 4. Visual examples of translating input (VHS) to HDTV by various methods. These five rows represent (a) input, (b) CycleGAN [18], (c) DRRN [14], (d) Johnson et al. [6], (e) ours respectively.

4.3 Quantitative Evaluation

Because our problem is lack of ground truth, we can only use some No-Reference Image Quality Assessment (NRIQA) methods to evaluate our results quantitatively. There are two common methods called BRISQUE [11] (blind/referenceless image spatial quality evaluator) and PIQUE [15] (perception-based image quality evaluator). Comparison of various methods is shown in Table 1. The lower the score, the better the quality.

Table 1. Comparison of several methods in BRISQUE and PIQUE score.

Evaluation methods	Input	CycleGAN	DRRN	Johnson et al.	Ours
BRISQUE	31.4105	30.43	29.34	26.03	**24.70**
PIQUE	62.1714	59.91	52.96	51.29	**48.55**

Table 2. Comparison of several methods in human preferred score.

	Input	CycleGAN	DRRN	Johnson et al.	Ours
Human preferred	0%	7.94%	9.99%	13.52%	**68.55%**

In addition, subjective evaluation is another important evaluation for no-reference image quality assessment. In the subjective evaluation procedure, we show 5 images, input and four generated images by four methods, to 50 participants, and let them select their preferred image under unified environment. Collect their selection and compute the preference percentage of 5 kinds of images. Table 2 shows the voting results. We can see that there is an obvious preference for our method against all other methods for the translating task.

5 Concluding Remarks

In this paper, we focus on an unsupervised multi-task problem, VHS video to HDTV video translation, which takes color contrast as well as spatial resolution into account. In order to incorporate multiple tasks into a single model and handle the unsupervised problem, we propose a multi-task adversarial learning model, which learns not only on color contrast but also image resolution. Taking advantage of cycle-adversarial loss and resolution loss, we fuse two kinds of input images by sharing weights between two networks. Experimental results demonstrate the effectiveness of our method.

6 Future Works

So far, our work focus on video translation frame by frame. This can be limited in that neighboring frames might not be consistent in terms of colors and contrast after translation, which would lead to a not very enjoyable video. For this reason, we will take into account the continuity of video, just like how Wang et al. [16] have done on video-to-video synthesis.

Acknowledgement. This work was supported by initial funding of newly-introduced teacher in Shenzhen University with No. 2019121. The authors would like to thank the editors and reviewers for their constructive suggestions on our work. The corresponding author of this paper is Fei Zhou.

References

1. Cui, Z., Chang, H., Shan, S., Zhong, B., Chen, X.: Deep network cascade for image super-resolution. In: Fleet, D., Pajdla, T., Schiele, B., Tuytelaars, T. (eds.) ECCV 2014. LNCS, vol. 8693, pp. 49–64. Springer, Cham (2014). https://doi.org/10.1007/978-3-319-10602-1_4

2. Dong, C., Loy, C.C., He, K., Tang, X.: Image super-resolution using deep convolutional networks. IEEE Trans. Pattern Anal. Mach. Intell. **38**(2), 295–307 (2015)
3. Dong, C., Loy, C.C., Tang, X.: Accelerating the super-resolution convolutional neural network. In: Leibe, B., Matas, J., Sebe, N., Welling, M. (eds.) ECCV 2016. LNCS, vol. 9906, pp. 391–407. Springer, Cham (2016). https://doi.org/10.1007/978-3-319-46475-6_25
4. Gatys, L.A., Ecker, A.S., Bethge, M.: Image style transfer using convolutional neural networks. In: Proceedings of the IEEE Conference on Computer Vision and Pattern Recognition, pp. 2414–2423 (2016)
5. Isola, P., Zhu, J.Y., Zhou, T., Efros, A.A.: Image-to-image translation with conditional adversarial networks. In: Proceedings of the IEEE Conference on Computer Vision and Pattern Recognition, pp. 1125–1134 (2017)
6. Johnson, J., Alahi, A., Fei-Fei, L.: Perceptual losses for real-time style transfer and super-resolution. In: Leibe, B., Matas, J., Sebe, N., Welling, M. (eds.) ECCV 2016. LNCS, vol. 9906, pp. 694–711. Springer, Cham (2016). https://doi.org/10.1007/978-3-319-46475-6_43
7. Kim, J., Kwon Lee, J., Mu Lee, K.: Accurate image super-resolution using very deep convolutional networks. In: Proceedings of the IEEE Conference on Computer Vision and Pattern Recognition, pp. 1646–1654 (2016)
8. Ledig, C., et al.: Photo-realistic single image super-resolution using a generative adversarial network. In: Proceedings of the IEEE Conference on Computer Vision and Pattern Recognition, pp. 4681–4690 (2017)
9. Li, Y., Liu, M.-Y., Li, X., Yang, M.-H., Kautz, J.: A closed-form solution to photorealistic image stylization. In: Ferrari, V., Hebert, M., Sminchisescu, C., Weiss, Y. (eds.) ECCV 2018. LNCS, vol. 11207, pp. 468–483. Springer, Cham (2018). https://doi.org/10.1007/978-3-030-01219-9_28
10. Luan, F., Paris, S., Shechtman, E., Bala, K.: Deep photo style transfer. In: Proceedings of the IEEE Conference on Computer Vision and Pattern Recognition, pp. 4990–4998 (2017)
11. Mittal, A., Moorthy, A.K., Bovik, A.C.: No-reference image quality assessment in the spatial domain. IEEE Trans. Image Process. **21**(12), 4695–4708 (2012)
12. Ronneberger, O., Fischer, P., Brox, T.: U-Net: convolutional networks for biomedical image segmentation. In: Navab, N., Hornegger, J., Wells, W.M., Frangi, A.F. (eds.) MICCAI 2015. LNCS, vol. 9351, pp. 234–241. Springer, Cham (2015). https://doi.org/10.1007/978-3-319-24574-4_28
13. Simonyan, K., Zisserman, A.: Very deep convolutional networks for large-scale image recognition. arXiv preprint arXiv:1409.1556 (2014)
14. Tai, Y., Yang, J., Liu, X.: Image super-resolution via deep recursive residual network. In: Proceedings of the IEEE Conference on Computer Vision and Pattern Recognition, pp. 3147–3155 (2017)
15. Venkatanath, N., Praneeth, D., Bh, M.C., Channappayya, S.S., Medasani, S.S.: Blind image quality evaluation using perception based features. In: 2015 Twenty First National Conference on Communications (NCC), pp. 1–6. IEEE (2015)
16. Wang, T.C., et al.: Video-to-video synthesis. arXiv preprint arXiv:1808.06601 (2018)
17. Zhang, Y., Tian, Y., Kong, Y., Zhong, B., Fu, Y.: Residual dense network for image super-resolution. In: Proceedings of the IEEE Conference on Computer Vision and Pattern Recognition, pp. 2472–2481 (2018)
18. Zhu, J.Y., Park, T., Isola, P., Efros, A.A.: Unpaired image-to-image translation using cycle-consistent adversarial networks. In: Proceedings of the IEEE International Conference On Computer Vision, pp. 2223–2232 (2017)

Improving Just Noticeable Difference Model by Leveraging Temporal HVS Perception Characteristics

Haibing Yin[1(✉)], Yafen Xing[1], Guangjing Xia[2], Xiaofeng Huang[1], and Chenggang Yan[1]

[1] Hangzhou Dianzi University, Hangzhou, China
yhb@hdu.edu.cn
[2] China Jiliang University, Hangzhou, China

Abstract. Temporal HVS characteristics are not fully exploited in conventional JND models. In this paper, we improve the spatio-temporal JND model by fully leveraging the temporal HVS characteristics. From the viewpoint of visual attention, we investigate two related factors, positive stimulus saliency and negative uncertainty. This paper measures the stimulus saliency according to two stimulus-driven parameters, relative motion and duration along the motion trajectory, and measures the uncertainty according to two uncertainty-driven parameters, global motion and residue intensity fluctuation. These four different parameters are measured with self-information and information entropy, and unified for fusion with homogeneity. As a result, a novel temporal JND adjustment weight model is proposed. Finally, we fuse the spatial JND model and temporal JND weight to form the spatio-temporal JND model. The experiment results verify that the proposed JND model yields significant performance improvement with much higher capability of distortion concealment compared to state-of-the-art JND profiles.

Keywords: Just Noticeable Difference (JND) · HVS characteristics · Self-Information · Information entropy

1 Introduction

Just noticeable difference (JND) refers to the minimum visibility threshold of the human visual system (HVS) [8]. The computational JND models have been widely applied for perceptual video coding, video quality assessment, watermarking. JND models are supposed to be built by fully utilizing the spatio-temporal HVS perception characteristics, such as masking, foveation, contrast sensitivity function (CSF) etc.

JND models are often categorized into two groups: transform domain and pixel-domain JND models. Several transform JND models were proposed by considering the spatial contrast sensitivity function (CSF), temporal masking,

Y. M. Ro et al. (Eds.): MMM 2020, LNCS 11961, pp. 87–98, 2020.
https://doi.org/10.1007/978-3-030-37731-1_8

foveated masking [1]. The pixel-domain JND models were built using luminance adaptation [8], luminance contrast [4], and pattern masking [5] etc.

Although the existing models can hide quantization noise more or less by utilizing the HVS characteristics. There are still deficiencies in above two kinds of models. Transform domain models suffer from accuracy imperfection due to that block transform splits the correlation between image blocks and blocks, resulting in insufficient utilization of spatial masking. Pixel-domain JND models also suffer from model accuracy inconsistence with HVS due to that temporal masking is not fully considered in the reported models.

Focusing on complicated temporal masking effect, this paper proposes a pixel level JND model, in which spatio-temporal HVS characteristics are both fully taken into consideration. Distortion perception capacity of HVS, equivalently JND, depends adaptively on visual attention, which is determined by positive stimulus saliency and negative uncertainty driven by the input video in terms of attention surprisal and masking degree. This paper measures the stimulus saliency according to two crucial stimulus-driven parameters, the foreground relative motion and the temporal duration along the motion trajectory in video. Comparatively, we measure the uncertainty according to two uncertainty-driven parameters, the background global motion and the intensity fluctuation of inter-frame prediction residue along the motion trajectory. In addition, we use self-information and information entropy to quantitatively measure the stimulus saliency and uncertainty, aiming at homogenizing the heterogeneous stimulus-driven and uncertainty-driven perceptual parameters. With the homogenized parameters, we build the computational temporal JND adjustment weight model, and finally propose the spatio-temporal JND model by fusing the temporal JND weight and spatial JND threshold together.

The rest of this paper is organized as follows. The homogenization method of temporal perceptual parameters is illustrated in Sect. 2. The proposed spatio-temporal JND model is proposed in Sect. 3. The experimental results are given in Sect. 4. Finally, conclusions are drawn in Sect. 5.

2 Parameter Homogenization

2.1 Temporal Domain Perceptual Parameters

This paper investigates three types of motion: absolute motion, global motion, and relative motion. Absolute motion $\overrightarrow{v_a}$ is the displacement of pixels between two adjacent frames, using optical flow method [2]. The global motion $\overrightarrow{v_g}$ is determined by estimating the peak value of the absolute motion histogram. Finally, the relative motion $\overrightarrow{v_r}$ is the difference between the absolute and global motion. The relationship can be formulated as follows:

$$\overrightarrow{v_r} = \overrightarrow{v_a} - \overrightarrow{v_g}. \tag{1}$$

The speed of motion can be computed as the length of the motion vector, which, for convenience, we denote as $v = \| \overrightarrow{v} \|_2$. Thus, v_a, v_g and v_r represent the speed of the absolute motion, the global motion, and the relative motion, respectively.

We assume that the t-th frame and (t−1)-th frame are the current and reference frames respectively. Suppose that the current pixel is located at (i, j) of the t-th frame, its most matched pixel is located at (p, q) of the (t−1)-th frame, and the inter-frame prediction residue is e. This frame employs forward motion estimation for each frame, and the motion trajectory is described the forward horizontal and vertical components $f_x(t,i,j)$, $f_y(t,i,j)$, as well as the prediction error $e_f(t,i,j)$. Then, the backward motion trajectory are deduced, and the corresponding components and prediction error, $b_x(t-1,p,q)$, $b_y(t-1,p,q)$ and $e_b(t-1,p,q)$, are given as follows:

$$f_x(t,i,j) = p, f_y(t,i,j) = q, e_f(t,i,j) = e, \tag{2}$$

$$b_x(t-1,p,q) = i, b_y(t-1,p,q) = j, e_b(t-1,p,q) = e. \tag{3}$$

Based on the arrays of f and b, motion trajectory of a pixel (i,j) is shown as the blue line in Fig. 1, where trajectory is paused at the frame (t+4)-th for example. Temporal duration τ is the number of adjacent frames covering the trajectory, and τ is equal to 5 here in Fig. 1. The residue intensity fluctuation δ is measured by the residue standard deviation along the motion trajectory.

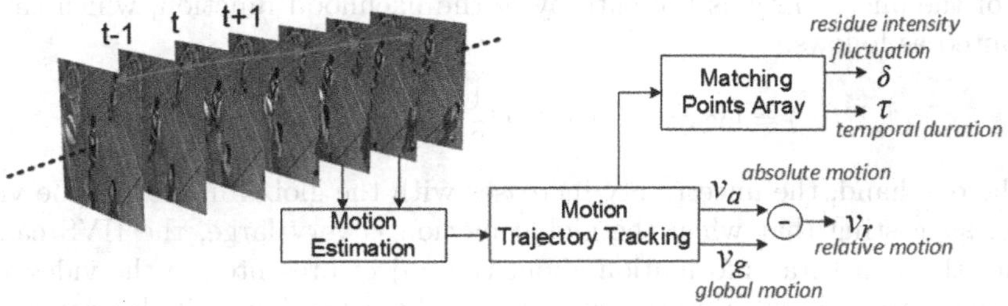

Fig. 1. Relative motion, global motion, temporal duration and residue intensity fluctuation (Color figure online)

2.2 Parameter Homogenization for Relative Motion

Targets with relatively larger motion generally attract more human attention and correspond to greater stimulus saliency. This intuitive idea inspires us a quantitative method to measure the stimulus saliency, providing that the prior probability distribution function (PDF) of motion in the sense of human perception is known [6]. The PDF of relative motion can be expressed by a power function [10]:

$$p(v_r) = \frac{\beta}{{v_r}^{\alpha}}, \tag{4}$$

where α and β are two positive constants. Using the self-information criterion, we can estimate the stimulus saliency for a given v_r as follows

$$I(v_r) = -\log_2 p(v_r) = \alpha \log_2 v_r - \log_2 \beta. \tag{5}$$

Equation (5) suggests that the motion stimulus saliency increases with the speed of relative motion, which is consistent with our intuition discussed earlier.

2.3 Parameter Homogenization for Global Motion

When a video have nonzero background motion, the global motion will decrease the HVS perception ability to discern the video details and small distortions. This phenomenon can be equivalently formulated as adding noise into video in the sense of detail information perception. We use a likelihood function to formulate the "equivalent" noise or uncertainty. Following the prevailing work in the literature [6], we employ the log-normal distribution to represent this likelihood function as follows:

$$p(m_1|v_g) = \frac{1}{\sqrt{2\pi}\sigma_1 m_1}\exp[\frac{-(\log_2 m_1 - \log_2 v_g)^2}{2\sigma_1^2}], \tag{6}$$

where v_g and m_1 are the stimulus and the generated noise, respectively. Furthermore, the width parameter σ_1 in the log-normal distribution is roughly constant for the stimulus v_g and inversely dependent on the contrast c [10].

$$\sigma_1 = \frac{\varepsilon}{c^\gamma}, \tag{7}$$

where ε and γ are both positive control constants. A nature way to quantify the level of the uncertainty, is the entropy of the likelihood function, which can be computed as follows:

$$U(v_g) = \log_2 v_g - \gamma \log_2 c + \frac{1}{2} + \frac{1}{2}\log_2(2\pi) + \log_2 \varepsilon. \tag{8}$$

On the one hand, the uncertainty increases with the global motion of the video frame, suggesting that when the global motion is very large, the HVS cannot extract the structural information about the object presented in the video with the same accuracy as in static images. On the other hand, it decreases with the contrast, implying that higher contrast objects are perceived with lower uncertainty.

2.4 Parameter Homogenization for Duration

The recency effect is an inherent nature of HVS, and it reveals that there is a transient memory effect in HVS. Videos with longer temporal duration result in stronger transient memory effect, and impose relatively higher stimulus saliency on the human perception system. Therefore, the duration along motion trajectory has an important influence on video perception. The stimulus saliency is quantitatively measured providing that the prior probability distribution of the temporal duration is known [9]. Following the inherent recency effect, we formulate the prior probability distribution of temporal duration as follows:

$$p(\tau) = 1 - \lambda \ln(\tau + 1), \tag{9}$$

where λ is a positive constant. For any observed duration τ, we can then estimate the duration-driven stimulus saliency by computing its self-information as follows:

$$I(\tau) = -\log_2 p(\tau) = -\log_2(1 - \lambda \ln(\tau + 1)), \tag{10}$$

Equation (10) suggests that the stimulus saliency increases with the duration, which is consistent with the HVS characteristics.

2.5 Homogenization for Residue Intensity Fluctuation

Given identical temporal duration, different video sequence with different motion characteristics have different inter-frame prediction accuracy characterized by temporal uncertainty, which result in varying temporal masking. We evaluate the temporal uncertainty with the residue intensity fluctuation δ along motion trajectory. In this paper, pixel-level δ is measured with the pixel-level standard deviation of the prediction errors along the motion trajectory during pixel duration. The larger fluctuation δ is, the stronger perception uncertainty in terms of temporal masking. How to formulate the likelihood function for fluctuation δ quantitatively is vital for mathematic modeling. Inter-frame prediction intensity fluctuation result in negative stimulus, perception uncertainty. This negative stimulus can be equivalently formulated as adding noise m_2 into video. Inspired by the temporal masking effect of HVS, we formulate the likelihood function for fluctuation-driven noise with log-normal distribution in the sense of perception as follows:

$$p(m_2|\delta) = \frac{1}{\sqrt{2\pi}\sigma_2 m_2}\exp[\frac{-(\log_2 m_2 - \log_2\delta)^2}{2\sigma_2^2}], \tag{11}$$

where m_2 is the equivalently generated noise. Furthermore, inspired by Stocker and Simoncelli [6], and the width parameter σ_2 in the log-normal distribution is roughly constant for the stimulus δ and inversely dependent on the background luminance adaptation threshold (LA) described as follows:

$$\sigma_2 = \frac{\xi}{LA^\eta}, \tag{12}$$

where ξ and η are two positive control constants, and the LA is formulated similar with [8] as follows:

$$LA(x) = \begin{cases} 17 \times (1 - \sqrt{\frac{B(x)}{127}}) + 3, & \text{If} \quad B(x) \le 127 \\ \frac{3}{128} \times (B(x) - 127) + 3, & \textit{else} \end{cases} \tag{13}$$

where $B(x)$ is the background luminance of pixel x. We measure the fluctuation-driven uncertainty with the information entropy according to the likelihood function shown as follows:

$$U(\delta) = \log_2\delta - \eta\log_2 LA + \frac{1}{2} + \frac{1}{2}\log_2(2\pi) + \log_2\xi. \tag{14}$$

Equation (14) shows that the uncertainty increases with the intensity fluctuation of residue and decreases with the luminance adaptation.

The parameters are handpicked and we find that the following parameters give reasonable results and use them in all experiments reported later in this paper: $\alpha = 0.8$, $\beta = 0.2$, $\varepsilon = 1.34$, $\gamma = 2.5$, $\lambda = 0.12$, $\eta = 0.5$, and $\xi = 8$.

The illustrative results of the stimulus saliency and perception uncertainty are demonstrated in Fig. 2, here the sequence "Backetball Drill". Figures 2(a) and (b) show the stimulus saliency maps of relative motion an temporal duration, where the brighter regions correspond to higher saliency, Figs. 2(c) and (d) give the uncertainty maps of global motion and intensity fluctuation of residue, where the brighter regions correspond to larger uncertainty.

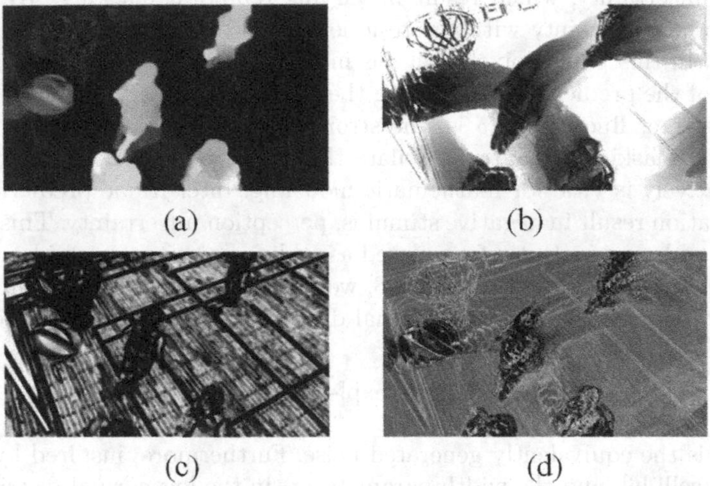

Fig. 2. (a) and (b): Stimulus saliency map caused by relative motion and duration, (c) and (d): Uncertainty map caused by global motion and intensity fluctuation of residue

3 Spatio-Temporal JND Model

We have computed the stimulus saliency driven by relative motion and duration as shown in Eqs. (5) and (10), and the uncertainty of the background motion and the intensity fluctuation of residue as shown in Eqs. (8) and (14), respectively. There is overlapping effect existing between these two groups of stimulus saliency and uncertainty. In order to remove the overlap, this paper adopts the nonlinear combination procedure of the NAMM model similar in [8], and the stimulus saliency and uncertainty are adjusted as follows:

$$I = I(v_r) + I(\tau) - C_1^{gr} \times min\{I(v_r), I(\tau)\}, \tag{15}$$

$$U = U(v_g) + U(\delta) - C_2^{gr} \times min\{U(v_g), U(\delta)\}. \tag{16}$$

where C_1^{gr} is the gain reduction parameter due to the overlapping between the stimulus saliency driven by relative motion and duration, C_2^{gr} is the gain reduction parameter due to the overlapping between the uncertainty of the background motion and the intensity fluctuation of residue, and $C_1^{gr} = C_2^{gr} = 0.3$ is used.

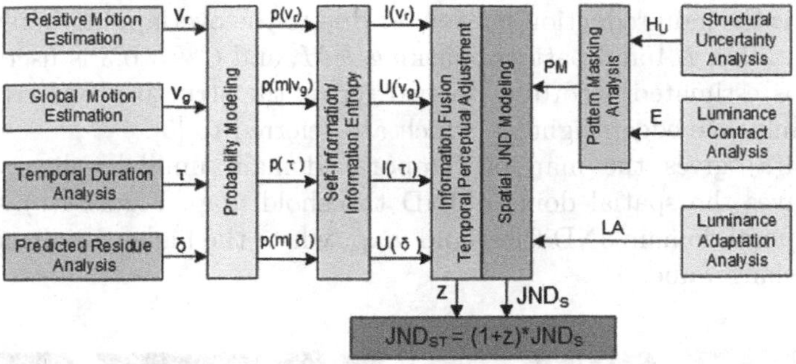

Fig. 3. The framework of the proposed spatiotemporal JND model

As analyzed above, there are several works on spatial JND model reported in the literature. This paper measures the temporal domain parameter including motion, duration and residue intensity fluctuation. They are further unified using information entropy and self information, $I(v_r)$, $I(\tau)$, $U(v_g)$, $U(\delta)$, and then fused to obtain the global saliency I and uncertainty U. These procedures are all illustrated in Fig. 3. Then, the following task it to elaborately adjust the prevailing spatial JND, remarked as JND_s, using U and I to derive the proposed spatio-temporally optimized JND model JND_{st}. Aiming at this goal, we employ an adjustment weight z centered about 0, and the final JND model is estimated adaptively as follows:

$$JND_{st} = (1 + z) \times JND_s. \tag{17}$$

Here, z is adjusted adaptively according to U and I, and dynamic range $[-\varpi, \varpi]$ of z is predefined for adjust strength control. For example $\varpi = 0.3$ can be used here.

Then, the final important task is to find an optimal mapping function between z and the pair (U, I). Following the intrinsic characteristics of HVS, there is intuitive relationship between z and (U, I). In general, the smaller I, the stronger noise masking effect appears, and the larger JND is. Similarly, the larger U, the stronger noise masking effect appears, and then the larger JND is. Thus, we define unified saliency $w = a_1 \times U - a_2 \times I$ to combine the stimulus saliency and uncertainty. Then, we find that the sigmoid function is relatively well-suited for modeling the relationship between w and z according to our experiments. As a result, we define the weight using the following function:

$$z = \varphi \times (\frac{1}{1 + e^{-\theta(w-b)}} - 0.5), \tag{18}$$

where a_1, a_2 are weighting control parameters, b is the central location which is calculated by w, and θ is the slop strength for curve shaping. a_1, a_2 and θ are all positive constants. $a_1 = 1$, $a_2 = 1$, $\varphi = 0.6$, and $\vartheta = 7$ are used.

Following the work in [5], luminance adaptation and pattern masking are taken into account for spatial JND modeling:

$$JND_S = LA + PM - C^{gr} \times min\{LA, PM\}, \tag{19}$$

where C^{gr} is the gain reduction parameter due to the overlapping between luminance adaptation LA and pattern masking PM, and $C^{gr} = 0.3$ is used. In addition, PM is estimated according to two terms the structural uncertainty H_U and the luminance edge height E, which are referred to [5].

Figure 4(a) gives the map of temporal domain unified saliency w, and Fig. 4(b) gives the spatial domain JND threshold map. Figure 4(c) shows the spatio-temporal domain JND threshold map, where the higher brightness means a large masking value.

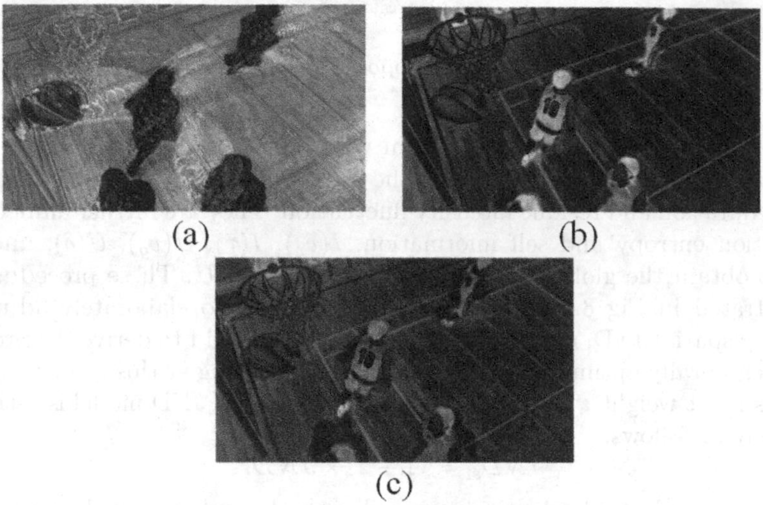

Fig. 4. (a) the map of temporal perception weight z, (b) the map of spatial JND threshold, (c) the map of spatiotemporal JND threshold

The framework of the proposed JND model is shown in Fig. 3. In this paper, we quantitatively measure the unified saliency I and uncertainty U in temporal domain, and then use U and I to adaptively adjust the spatial JND threshold to derive the final spatio-temporal JND threshold.

4 Experiment Results

An effective JND model should be able to add more noise into the insensitive regions and less into the sensitive regions. Under the same injected noise energy, a more accurate JND model would result in better perceptual quality. In order to demonstrate the effectiveness of the spatio-temporal JND model, the sensitive testing experiment is always adopted [8]. In this work, we compare the proposed model with three typical pixel-JND models, including Yang's model [8], Chen's model [4], and Wu's model [7]. For a testing video, the noise is injected with the guidance of its corresponding JND, which is formulated as follows:

$$F^{'}(x) = F(x) + \kappa \times rand(x) \times JND_{ST}(x), \tag{20}$$

where $F'(x)$ is the JND noise contaminated video, κ regulates the energy of JND noise, which makes the same energy for different JND models, and $rand(x)$ randomly takes +1 or −1.

Figure 5 gives the noise-contaminated images of four different JND models, including Yang et al.'s [8] model, Chen et al.'s [4] model, Wu et al.'s [7], and the proposed JND model. The "Backetball Drill" image is used for simulation and identical noise energy level (PSNR = 30 dB) is used. As shown in Fig. 5, (d) delivers better perceptual quality than other three noise contaminated images with identical noise energy levels. Therefore, the proposed JND model outperforms three typical pixel domain JND models (i.e., [4,7,8]).

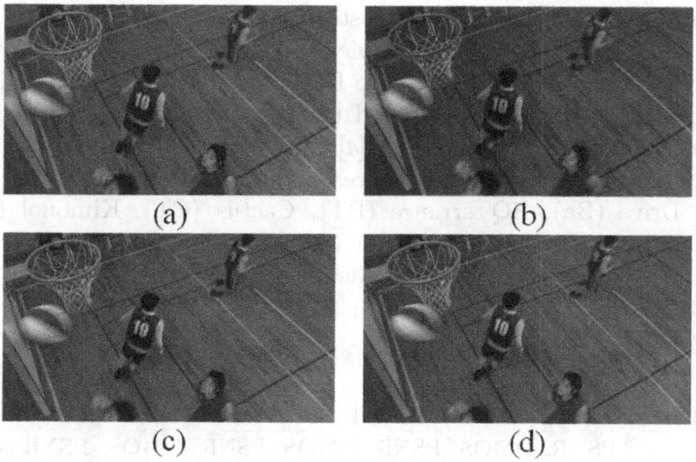

Fig. 5. Comparison of noise-contaminated images in the cases of four different JND models. (a) Yang et al.'s [8] model, (b) Chen et al.'s [4] model, (c) Wu et al.'s [7], (d) the proposed JND model.

In order to verify the effectiveness of our proposed spatio-temporal JND model, we performed subjective quality assessment experiments using several test video sequences. It aims to measure visibility of distortions in JND-distortion injected videos. In the experiments, the DSCQS (double stimulus continuous quality scale) method is used for subjective evaluations [3]. Figure 6 shows the presentation strategy of the DSCQS method, where A (a reference sequence) and B (a sequence to be compared) are pseudo-randomly ordered for each presentation. The subjects give visual quality scores for each A and B in a voting time. In order to measure perceptual qualities of the JND-imparied video (distorted video by a JND profile) compared to the original video, the DMOS (differential mean opinion score) value is calculated based on the subject's voting scores for A and B by

$$DMOS = MOS_{JND} - MOS_{ORI}. \quad (21)$$

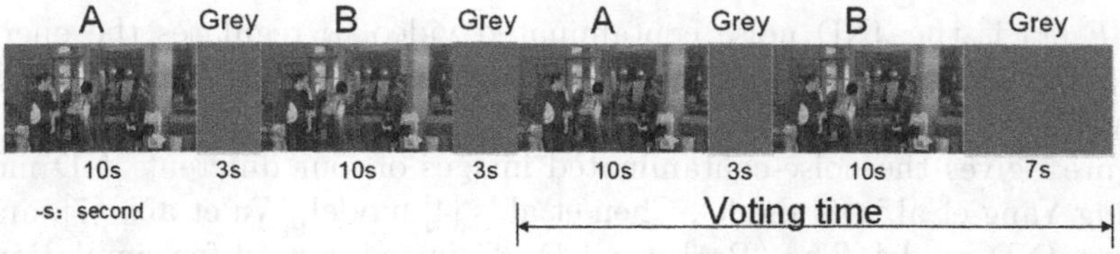

Fig. 6. The presentation strategy of the DSCQS method, where A (a reference sequence) and B (a sequence to be compared) are pseudo-randomly ordered for each presentation.

where MOS_{ORI} is the measured MOS value for the original video and MOS_{JND} is the measured MOS value from the distorted video by a JND profile.

Better JND model means that it yields distorted video with lower PSNR value (more distortion) with closer zero DMOS (perceptual quality difference). The proposed JND model is compared to three prevailing pixel-domain JND model, Yang's model [8], Chen's model [4], and Wu's model [7]. We use a test set including nine monochrome test sequences, including five full-HD test sequences, Basketball Drive (Ba), BQTerrance (BT), Cactus (CT), Kimonol (Ki), and ParkScene (Pa), and other four QVGA test sequences, Basketball Drill (BD), BQMall (BM), PartyScene (PS), and RaceHorse (RH).

Table 1. Subjective experimental results

TestSequence	Yang [8]		Chen [4]		Wu [7]		Proposed	
	PSNR	DMOS	PSNR	DMOS	PSNR	DMOS	PSNR	DMOS
Ba	36.52	−1.00	35.42	−0.87	34.10	−3.01	31.78	−1.34
BT	34.41	−1.00	33.51	−0.67	32.26	−5.78	31.01	−2.00
CT	33.35	−2.67	33.29	−0.47	32.54	−4.31	30.50	−0.68
Ki	31.61	−12.33	31.12	−3.47	32.01	−12.56	30.00	−8.37
Pa	32.05	−18.67	31.92	−2.67	31.45	−15.34	30.40	−11.35
BD	36.01	0.00	36.60	−7.47	34.17	−0.98	32.45	−0.83
BM	34.34	0.00	34.85	−8.20	32.97	−3.78	31.01	−3.45
PS	34.41	0.00	35.10	−0.60	32.01	−1.96	30.34	−1.33
RH	35.02	−3.67	35.30	−1.73	32.98	−10.98	31.13	−7.86
Avg	34.19	−4.37	34.12	−3.05	32.72	−6.52	30.96	−4.13

Table 1 shows the performance comparison results of four candidate JND models in terms of PSNR and DMOS. As shown in the table, the average PSNR results of Yang's, Chen's, Wu's and our proposed JND model are 34.19 dB, 34.12 dB, 32.72 dB, and 30.96 dB, respectively, and the corresponding average DMOS results are −4.37, −3.05, −6.52, and −4.13, respectively. Overall, performance improvement in terms of PSNR and DMOS are observed, and these results further confirm that the proposed JND model is superior to the existing pixel-domain model, with average 2.7 dB lower PSNR given that DMOS is close to zero.

5 Conclusions

In this paper, we propose an improved JND model via fully exploiting temporal HVS characteristics. This paper measures the stimulus saliency driven by relative motion and temporal duration along motion trajectory, and the uncertainty driven by global motion and intensity fluctuation of residue. Self-information and information entropy are used to quantitatively measure the stimulus saliency and uncertainty. With the homogenized parameters, we build the computational temporal JND weight model, and finally propose the spatiotemporal JND model by fusing the temporal weight and spatial JND threshold model. The experiment results verify that the proposed JND model yields significant performance improvement with much higher capability of distortion concealment (average 2.7 dB lower PSNR) compared to state-of-the-art JND profiles.

Acknowledgement. This work was supported by the Natural Science Foundation of China (NSFC) under Grants 61572449, 61931008, 61901150 and 61972123,Key R&D projects 2018YFC0830106, and by Natural Science Foundation of Zhejiang Province under Grants Q19F010030 and Y19F020124.

References

1. Bae, S.H., Kim, M.: A DCT-based total JND profile for spatio-temporal and foveated masking effects. IEEE Trans. Circ. Syst. Video Technol. **27**(6), 1196–1207 (2017)
2. Black, M.J., Anandan, P.: The robust estimation of multiple motions: parametric and piecewise-smooth flow fields. Comput. Vis. Image Underst. **63**(1), 75–104 (1996)
3. BT, R.I.R.: Methodology for the subjective assessment of the quality of television pictures (2002)
4. Chen, Z., Guillemot, C.: Perceptually-friendly H.264/AVC video coding based on foveated just-noticeable-distortion model. IEEE Trans. Circ. Syst. Video Technol. **20**(6), 806–819 (2010)
5. Wu, J., Lin, W., Shi, G., Wang, X., Li, F.: Pattern masking estimation in image with structural uncertainty. IEEE Trans. Image Process. **22**(12), 4892–4904 (2013)
6. Stocker, A.A., Simoncelli, E.P.: Noise characteristics and prior expectations in human visual speed perception. Nat. Neurosci. **9**(4), 578–585 (2006)
7. Wu, J., Li, L., Dong, W., Shi, G., Lin, W., Kuo, C.C.J.: Enhanced just noticeable difference model for images with pattern complexity. IEEE Trans. Image Process. **PP**(99), 1 (2017)
8. Yang, X., Ling, W., Lu, Z., Ong, E., Yao, S.: Just noticeable distortion model and its applications in video coding. Signal Process. Image Commun. **20**(7), 662–680 (2005)

9. Zhao, Y., Yu, L., Chen, Z., Zhu, C.: Video quality assessment based on measuring perceptual noise from spatial and temporal perspectives. IEEE Trans. Circ. Syst. Video Technol. **21**(12), 1890–1902 (2011)
10. Zhou, W., Qiang, L.: Video quality assessment using a statistical model of human visual speed perception. J. Opt. Soc. Am. A Opt. Image. Sci. Vis. **24**(12), 61–69 (2007)

Down-Sampling Based Video Coding with Degradation-Aware Restoration-Reconstruction Deep Neural Network

Minh-Man Ho[1], Gang He[2], Zheng Wang[2], and Jinjia Zhou[1,3](✉)

[1] Graduate School of Science and Engineering, Hosei University, Tokyo, Japan
jinjia.zhou.35@hosei.ac.jp
[2] Xi'dian University, Xi'an, China
[3] JST, PRESTO, Tokyo, Japan

Abstract. Recently deep learning techniques have shown remarkable progress in image/video super-resolution. These techniques can be employed in a video coding system for improving the quality of the decoded frames. However, different from the conventional super-resolution works, the compression artifacts in the decoded frames should be concerned with. The straightforward solution is to integrate the artifacts removing techniques before super-resolution. Nevertheless, some helpful features may be removed together with the artifacts, and remaining artifacts can be exaggerated. To address these problems, we design an end-to-end restoration-reconstruction deep neural network (RR-DnCNN) using the degradation-aware techniques. RR-DnCNN is applied to the down-sampling based video coding system. In the encoder side, the original video is down-sampled and compressed. In the decoder side, the decompressed down-sampled video is fed to the RR-DnCNN to get the original video by removing the compression artifacts and super-resolution. Moreover, in order to enhance the network learning capabilities, uncompressed low-resolution images/videos are utilized as a ground-truth. The experimental results show that our work can obtain over **8%** BD-rate reduction compared to the standard H.265/HEVC. Furthermore, our method also outperforms in reducing compression artifacts in subjective comparison. Our work is available at https://github.com/minhmanho/rrdncnn.

Keywords: Super-resolution · Video compression · Deep learning

1 Introduction

Video media has become one of the widest applications in the digital era, depending on the development and popularization of video coding technology. Video

Supported by JST, PRESTO Grant Number JPMJPR1757 Japan.

Y. M. Ro et al. (Eds.): MMM 2020, LNCS 11961, pp. 99–110, 2020.
https://doi.org/10.1007/978-3-030-37731-1_9

coding technology has been iteratively developed for nearly 30 years and has continued the hybrid coding architecture of transform coding and predictive coding. Nowadays, people's video playback devices are increasingly diversified; however, network bandwidth and storage restrictions are strict under many usage scenarios. Even with the popular advanced coding standard H.265/HEVC, the quality of the reconstructed video is still poor under extreme bandwidth conditions due to lossy coding, though many techniques (e,g. deblocking filter and sample adaptive offset) are applied reduce information loss as much as possible. Therefore, an efficient framework is required to reduce the bit-rate and keep high video quality. There are two significant problems: various distortions which brought from video compression, and the compression ratio of the encoder. As many achievements of deep learning techniques, de-noising, and super-resolution works thus are reasonable to address them respectively.

Down-Sampling Based Coding (DBC). Shen et al. [1] propose the seminal work of down-sampling based coding framework, where a super-resolution technique is employed to restore the down-sampled frames to their original resolutions. Recently, deep-learning-based super-resolution techniques outperform traditional methods and inspire researchers to improve the DBC framework. Li et al. [2] propose the CNN-based block up-Sampling for intraframe coding. Lin et al. [3] improve [2]'s work by leveraging information between frames as block-level down- and up-sampling into inter-frame coding. However, these block-based DBC methods ignore the useful information of the whole frame. Furthermore, compression artifacts are roughly learned and inferred. Feng et al. [12] apply a frame-based DBC system with an extra enhancement network to remove the compression artifacts before super-resolution. However, some useful features may be removed together with the artifacts, which will degrade the performance of super-resolution. We thus propose an end-to-end deep neural network to fully address compression degradation and learn super-resolution.

Deep-Learning Approach for Reducing the Compression Artifacts. Images/video resolution rapidly increases from 480p and 720p, to 1080p, 4K, and 8K. The frame rate also increases from 30 fps to 60fps and 120fps. Under limited bandwidth, videos are encoded with a high compression ratio by sacrificing quality. According to recent deep-learning super-resolution achievements, transferring the low-size bit-stream for high-resolution images/videos is possible. Similar to the related concept [12], we down-sample the source video before encoding, then up-sample, and reconstruct images/videos after decoding. The bit-stream capacity thus is much lower. Furthermore, the images/videos still meet quality requirements compared to the standard H.265/HEVC.

Single Image Super-Resolution (SISR) based on deep learning recently achieves outstanding performance on multiple scales. SISR aims to generate high-resolution (HR) images from a given low-resolution (LR) images. Like the promotion of deep-learning techniques, Dong et al. [8] proposed a CNN based SRCNN network structure to learn an end-to-end mapping from low-resolution to high-resolution. The network includes three layers: patch extraction, non-linear mapping, and reconstruction. This work opened the door to the application of deep learning to image super-resolution. Kim et al. [9] showed a VDSR network, which can effectively improve image performance by learning residuals and increasing network depth to 20 layers; furthermore, Adjustable Gradient Clipping is used to solve their convergence problem. Zhang et al. [10] propose DnCNN network for residual learning in super-resolution task. Zhang et al. [11] propose the very deep Residual Channel Attention Networks (RCAN) and channel attention mechanism to exploit the abundant low-frequency information. However, these works perform only on bicubic degradation, forgo or naively train their models on other distortions, which usually happens in daily multimedia such as noise, video compression artifact, JPEG compression; therefore, the existing super-resolution works have poor performance on the unseen distortion.

Recent Super-Resolution Works in Handling Degradation. To address the various degradation in super-resolution, Zhang et al. [4] synthesize bicubic degradation and Gaussian Noise maps and feed them to train together with LR. Zhao et al. [5] propose an unsupervised learning network to learn unseen degradation and reconstruct the output. Bulat et al. [6] use Generative Adversarial Network (GAN) to learn how to degrade and down-sample high-resolution images; from that point, they can achieve the degradation as their super-resolution network expectation. Chen et al. [7] directly train their models on JPEG degradation using an end-to-end deep convolution neural network. In the video coding field, we deal with various degradation such as blocking artifacts, ringing artifacts, which usually occurs in video compression techniques. The most similar work [12] uses a refinement network before super-resolution to reduce compression artifacts, the bicubic degradation of decoded images/videos thus are more precise. However, they still suffer from distortion due to imperfect refinement. To address the problem, we adopt DnCNN [10] and propose an end-to-end restoration-reconstruction deep neural network (RR-DnCNN) using the degradation-aware technique as two loss functions: restoration and reconstruction. Our network thus is capable of effectively dealing with video compression distortion and bicubic degradation.

The main contributions of this paper include the following aspects.

- Our down-sampling based video coding system achieve a high compression ratio while keeping the video quality at low bit-rates, compared to the standard H.265/HEVC.
- In our network architecture, we present the degradation-aware technique in our restoration-reconstruction deep neural network (RR-DnCNN) to deal with compression degradation, which is worse to be exaggerated.
- Since video compression degradation is various (e.g., blocking artifacts, ringing artifacts) due to varied video codec configurations, we have to find the most suitable degradation of compressed videos for our training data. Additionally, compressed videos for training are good if they show the learning capability and cover other types of degradation. We thus analysis related codec configurations for our training data.

2 Proposed Video Coding System

2.1 System Overview

In our study, we leverage the superior of deep-learning super-resolution techniques to reduce bit-rate and enhance the video quality for our down-sampling based video coding system. The video coding framework consists of down-sampling, HEVC codec, and a super-resolution network. We first perform bicubic down-sampling of High-Resolution (HR) as its Low-Resolution (LR) for HEVC codec. After decoding bit-stream, the super-resolution network removes compression artifacts and maps the Decoded Low-Resolution (DLR) to its HR at the decoding end, as shown in Fig. 1. Due to video compression degradation in lossy coding, we design an end-to-end restoration-reconstruction deep neural network (RR-DnCNN) using the proposed degradation-aware technique for our loss function.

The advantages of our degradation-aware technique are as follows: (1) Breaking minimizing error from DLR → HR to DLR → LR → HR defines the targets for each part inside the network. The LR is treated as transitional ground-truth. (2) Our up-sampled low-resolution inside the network is refined and adaptive for the reconstruction part. The super-resolution result is thus precise.

In super-resolution, the luminance component in YUV format is crucial for humans to see the objects in detail; therefore, our network takes Y component as $X \in \mathbb{R}^{H \times W \times 1}$ from the HEVC decoder as DLR. X is restored and exaggerated to have $\hat{Y}$ using our RR-DnCNN as h. Our target is to minimize the error between $\hat{Y}$ and the ground-truth HR. Instead of fully inference from X to $\hat{Y}$,

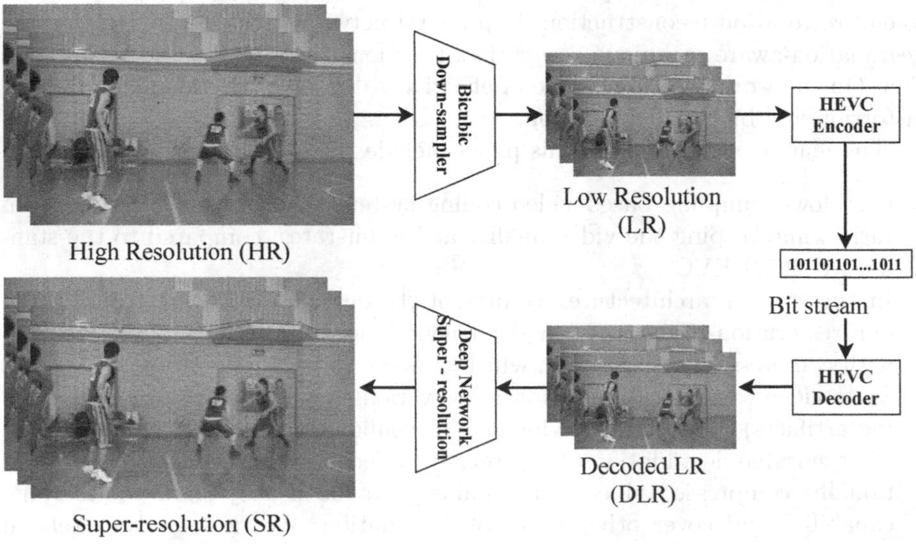

Fig. 1. The proposed super resolution based video coding system.

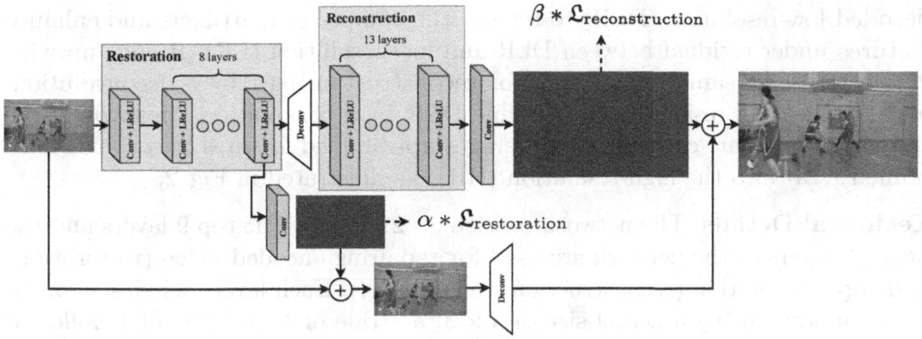

Fig. 2. Architecture of the proposed restoration-reconstruction deep neural network (RR-DnCNN)

we present the degradation-aware technique to treat the LR as our transitional ground-truth. Additionally, residual learning is applied to learn texture features of the image and speed up the network convergence, defined as:

$$\hat{X}, R_{res}, R_{rec} = h(X) \tag{1}$$

where R_{res} represents the inferred residual between LR and DLR for restoration; meanwhile, R_{rec} represents the inferred residual between refined X as $\hat{X}$ and HR. Inside our network, X is refined to have $\hat{X}$ as:

$$\hat{X} = X + R_{res} \tag{2}$$

then up-sampled by deconvolution, combined to reconstruction residual R_{rec} to have the final $\hat{Y}$ as:

$$\hat{Y} = Deconvolution(\hat{X}) + R_{rec} \tag{3}$$

2.2 Restoration-Reconstruction Deep Neural Network (RR-DnCNN)

The proposed restoration-reconstruction deep neural network (RR-DnCNN) restores and reconstructs the decoded low-resolution (DLR); however, DLR contains compression distortion such as deblocking artifacts, ringing artifacts, which become more distorted after exaggeration. Our network thus has two parts restoration and reconstruction. Each layer consists of a convolution module and a Leaky Rectified Linear Unit (Leaky ReLU) activation function. Reconstruction part includes a convolution with a high kernel size of 5, padding of 2 to take large-overall information (e.g., motions, edges), and 8 layers followed.

We ponder the existing conditions and the characteristics of video coding. The degradation-aware technique treats the uncompressed low-resolution video as a transitional ground-truth to enhance the learning capabilities. Our network thus has two parts: restoration and reconstruction. The restoration part takes the decoded low-resolution (DLR) to remove the compression artifacts and enhance features under residual between DLR and low-resolution (LR). It ends up with 2 directions: up-sampling features for reconstruction part by a deconvolution, and synthesizing residual map to refine DLR by a convolution. Meanwhile, the reconstruction part continuously leverages up-sampled features to converts from refined DLR into the high-resolution (HR), as illustrated in Fig. 2.

Technical Details. The network consists of 22 layers. The top 9 layers and the next 13 layers of the network are used for repairing encoded video (restoration) and super-resolution (reconstruction), respectively. Each layer includes a convolution module using a kernel size of 3 × 3, a stride of 1, padding of 1, followed by a Leaky Rectified Linear Units (Leaky ReLU) with negative slope of 0.01. Different from other layers, the convolution in the first layer uses 64 filters of size 5 × 5 × 1 to generate 64 feature maps and cover useful information. The depth channel of 64 is maintained in the network. At the end of each part, we use a convolution that uses one filter of size 3 × 3 × 64 to generate residual maps.

2.3 Loss Function

Our losses computed using Mean Square Error as:

$$MSE = \frac{1}{N} \sum_{i=1}^{N} \|R_i - R_i^*\|^2 \tag{4}$$

where N is number of elements in a batch, R_i represents the ground-truth residuals, while R_i^* can be the ith R_{res} or i^{th} R_{rec}. In baseline, Zhang et al. [10] use the loss of $0.5 * MSE$ for their residual learning. However, the true LR is treated as our transitional ground-truth in the middle of the overall network. We thus add loss weights of α and β to balance learning. Our total loss function is defined as:

$$\mathfrak{L} = \alpha * \mathfrak{L}_{\text{restoration}} + \beta * \mathfrak{L}_{\text{reconstruction}} \tag{5}$$

where $\mathfrak{L}_{\text{restoration}}$ minimizes loss of (LR - X) and R_{res}, while $\mathfrak{L}_{\text{reconstruction}}$ minimizes loss of (HR - *Deconvolution*$(\hat{X})$) and R_{rec}. Since various compression degradation of DLR is difficult to restore, we empirically set the loss weights in the Eq. 5 as $\alpha = 0.5, \beta = 0.005$.

2.4 Training Configuration

The standard HEVC leverages low-level information inside a frame or motion information between consecutive frames. Consequently, compressed videos contain various distortion. On the learning capability, we explore the characteristic of compression degradation, which is produced from three default configurations such as Random Access (RA), Low Delay P (LDP), and All Intra (AI) at QP = 37. Furthermore, we also observe and validate the models on the video

Table 1. Ablation studies in PSNR. We train our models using configuration Random Access (RA), Low Delay P (LDP), All Intra (AI) and test on decoded low-resolution video *BasketballDrive* 960 × 576, which is compressed in RA, LDP, AI, respectively. The ***bold*** values show the best PSNR for configuration comparison.

Configuration for training			PSNR on			Average
RA	LDP	AI	RA	LDP	AI	
✓			**31.99**	31.83	**33.21**	**32.34**
	✓		31.92	**31.84**	33.06	32.27
		✓	31.95	31.82	33.2	32.32

BaseketballDrive. As shown in Fig. 3, training on compressed videos in AI outperforms others in convergence, while the LDP is the most difficult to be converged. However, in the validation, the model trained on RA outperforms others in PSNR, as shown in Table 1. Also, RA has a promising convergence; we thus choose the RA to train our primary model.

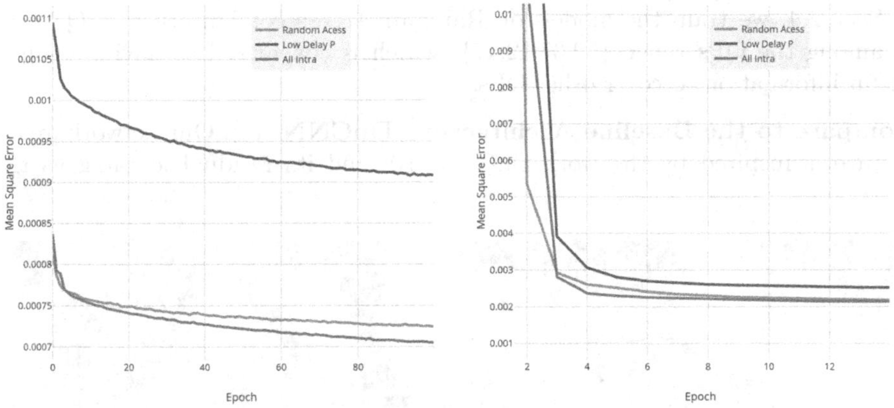

Fig. 3. Training processes of 3 domains Random Access, Low Delay P, and All Intra at QP = 37 in Mean Square Error. *Left*: restoration loss, *right*: reconstruction loss.

3 Experimental Results and Comparison

3.1 Experiments

Data Preparation. Uncompressed videos are significant to provide reliable analysis and understand video compression behavior for training and testing our models. We thus use 34 uncompressed videos as 18,487 frames from Xiph Video Test Media in CIF 352 × 288 for training, and standard test videos in 1080p, and 2K. Regarding video codec, HEVC version 16.20 is used to synthesize the decoded low-resolution. However, our scheme tends to encode the down-sampled videos at scale ×2. We thus resize 1080p to 1920 × 1152 to satisfy the coding unit (CU) requirement. Since our work is super-resolution, all experiments are conducted on only the Y component.

Data Augmentation. In training process, after down-sampling at scale ×2, the CIF decreases from 352 × 288 to 176 × 144. To vary our training data, we step-by-step apply random crop as 120 × 120, random flip in horizontal and vertical dimensions, and random rotation in 0, 90, 180, 270°. Finally, Y values are normalized in the range [0, 1].

Training Details. We training our models using Adam Optimizer [13] with initial learning rate of 0.0001, coefficients $\beta_1 = 0.9, \beta_2 = 0.999$, batch size of 16. Every 100 epochs cost approximately 24 h on Tesla V100.

3.2 Results and Comparison

We evaluate our work on the standard test videos and compare to DnCNN [10], the standard H.265/HEVC in compression proficiency using BD-rate, BD-psnr measurement as an objective comparison. Furthermore, we visualize results as a subjective comparison in the same bit-rate with H.265/HEVC. As conducted in Sect. 2.4, we train the models on Random Access configuration at QP = 37 in among the QPs range {32,37,42,47}, which is considered as having enough useful information to cover other QPs.

Compare to the Baseline Architecture DnCNN [10]**.** Our network architecture is inspired by the work DnCNN [10] and its residual learning as the

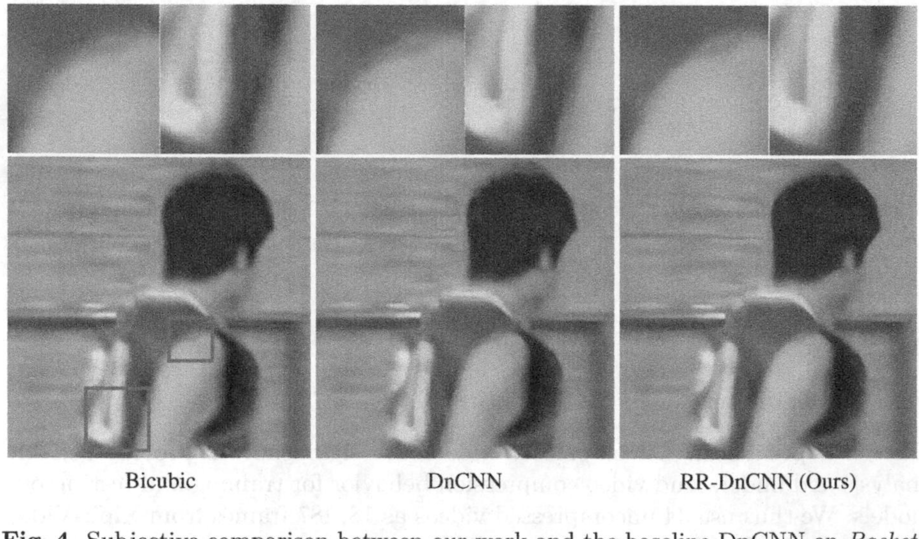

Fig. 4. Subjective comparison between our work and the baseline DnCNN on *BasketBallDrive* test sequence at QP = 37 compressed using Low Delay P configuration. Our method provides less distortion and more refined edges.

Table 2. Architecture comparison between bicubic, DnCNN, and our RR-DnCNN in PSNR on *BasketBallDrive* sequence compressed at QP = 37 using Random Access (RA), Low Delay P (LDP), and All Intra (AI). Our network outperforms others as ***bold*** values.

Method	PSNR on			
	RA	LDP	AI	Avg
Bicubic	31.48	31.37	32.63	31.83
DnCNN	31.6	31.46	32.64	31.9
RR-DnCNN (ours)	**31.99**	**31.83**	**33.21**	**32.34**

Table 3. Objective comparison between our proposed method and the standard HEVC in QPs = {32,37,42,47}. Ours outperform HEVC in the average BD-rate, BD-psnr.

Resolution	Sequence	Random Access		Low Delay P		All Intra	
		BD-rate	BD-psnr	BD-rate	BD-psnr	BD-rate	BD-psnr
2560×1600	People	−4.73	0.16	−3.65	0.15	−5.6	0.19
	Traffic	−8.23	0.28	−7.53	0.24	−9.72	0.42
1920×1080	Kimono	−12.36	0.4	−14.53	0.5	−8.75	0.36
	ParkScene	−7.88	0.19	−9.99	0.24	−6.85	0.19
	Cactus	−2.81	0.01	−2.58	0.02	−5.67	0.19
	BasketballDrive	−3.32	0.02	−8.09	0.25	−2.47	0.03
	Bluesky	−11.66	0.49	−9.43	0.31	−12.3	0.66
	Pedestrian	−11.89	0.43	−15.15	0.67	−11.51	0.52
	RushHour	−13.61	0.52	−15.3	0.64	−11.33	0.6
Average		−8.5	0.28	−9.58	0.33	−8.24	0.35

baseline; therefore, we train our RR-DnCNN and DnCNN in 100 epochs and compare them in both objective (PSNR) and subjective way. The baseline has its loss function $0.5 * MSE$ to learn the residual between input and output. However, compression distortion is various and hard to learn. We thus fairly adjust their loss weight to 0.005. Regarding objective comparison, we evaluate the models on the test sequence *BasketBallDrive* compressed in 3 configurations Random Access, Low Delay P, and All Intra. As described in Table 2, our RR-DnCNN outperforms others in three domains. Although DnCNN can reduce artifacts of compression from bicubic, it still contains significant distortion, especially regions around edges. In contrast, our method provides not only fewer artifacts but also more refined edges, as illustrated in Fig. 4.

Compare to the Standard HEVC. Overall, our scheme can reduce **58.88%** bit-rate by encoding ×2 down-sampled sequence, compared to HEVC at the same QP (estimated on the compared test sequences in Random Access compression). However, the quality in PSNR is also reduced. We thus propose the RR-DnCNN to compensate for the lossy information and enhance video quality. To prove our

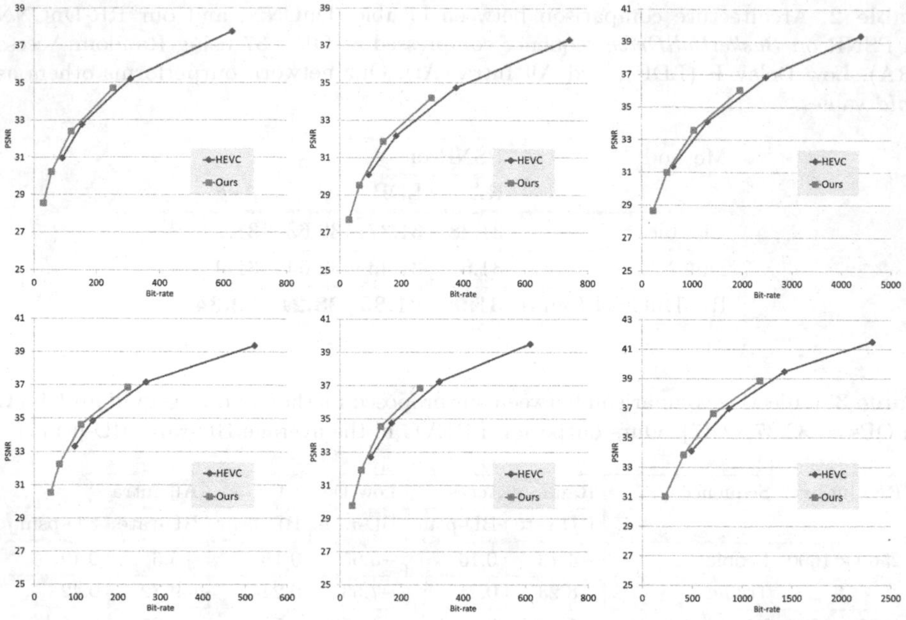

Fig. 5. Rate-distortion curves of our method compared to the standard HEVC on test sequences *Kimono* (*top-row*), *Rush Hour* (*bottom-row*) compressed by Random Access, Low Delay P, and All Intra (*left-to-right*) at QPs={32,37,42,47}. Our method apparently outperforms HEVC in three domain.

compression proficiency for transmission of ultra-high-definition video at low bit-rates, we compare our work to HEVC in two aspects: objective evaluation using BD-rate and BD-psnr measurement, and subjective evaluation at the same bit-rate. In an objective way, we evaluate compared methods on test sequences having the resolution of 2560 × 1600, 1920 × 1152. As shown in Table 3, our method outperforms the standard HEVC on all domains Random Access, Low Delay P, and All Intra in (**BD-rate, BD-psnr**) measurement as (**-8.5, 0.28**), (**-9.58, 0.33**), (**-8.24, 0.35**) correspondingly. Furthermore, our rate-distortion (RD) curves show the capability of compressing more efficient on the test videos *Kimono* and *Rush Hour*, as illustrated in Fig. 5. Subjectively, we visualize the results of ours and HEVC on *Kimono*, *Pedestrian*, and *Rush Hour* at the approximate bit-rate. As shown in Fig. 6, our method provides less distortion as higher PSNR; meanwhile, the standard HEVC results contain ringing distortion and artifacts. For further illustration, please check out our supplemental video of subjective comparison.

Fig. 6. Subjective comparison between our work and the standard HEVC in the approximate bit-rate condition. Our method outperforms in providing less video compression distortion as refined edges and surfaces in higher PSNR. We highlight and zoom out several places corresponding to red rectangles for easier comparison.

4 Conclusion

We propose an end-to-end restoration-reconstruction deep neural network (RR-DnCNN) using the degradation-aware technique to address various compression distortion from video coding for transmission of ultra-high-definition video at low bit-rates. To enhance learning capability and provide reliable experiments, we train and test our models on the uncompressed videos, and found that training on Random Access can recover compression degradation in overall configurations. As a result, our network outperforms the baseline DnCNN in providing refined edges and fewer artifacts as a higher **0.44** dB in PSNR. Compared to the standard HEVC, our work saves over **8%** in BD-rate, **0.28** dB in BD-psnr. Furthermore, our RR-DnCNN shows the superior in addressing video compression distortion more effective than HEVC in the same bit-rate condition.

References

1. Shen, M., Xue, P., Wang, C.: Down-sampling based video coding using super-resolution technique. IEEE Trans. Circ. Syst. Video Technol. **21**(6), 755–765 (2011)
2. Li, Y., et al.: Convolutional neural network-based block up-sampling for intraframe coding. IEEE Trans. Circ. Syst. Video Technol. **28**(9), 2316–2330 (2018)
3. Lin, J., Liu, D., Yang, H., Li, H., Feng, W.: Convolutional neural network-based block up-sampling for HEVC. IEEE Trans. Circ. Syst. Video Technol. (2018)
4. Feng, L., Zhang, X., Zhang, X., Wang, S., Wang, R., Ma, S.: A Dual-Network Based Super-Resolution for Compressed High Definition Video. In: Hong, R., Cheng, W.-H., Yamasaki, T., Wang, M., Ngo, C.-W. (eds.) PCM 2018. LNCS, vol. 11164, pp. 600–610. Springer, Cham (2018). https://doi.org/10.1007/978-3-030-00776-8_55
5. Zhao, T., Zhang, C., Ren, W., Ren, D., Hu, Q.: Unsupervised degradation learning for single image super-resolution. arXiv preprint: arXiv:1812.04240 (2018)
6. Bulat, A., Yang, J., Tzimiropoulos, G.: To learn image super-resolution, use a GAN to learn how to do image degradation first. In: Ferrari, V., Hebert, M., Sminchisescu, C., Weiss, Y. (eds.) ECCV 2018, Part VI. LNCS, vol. 11210, pp. 187–202. Springer, Cham (2018). https://doi.org/10.1007/978-3-030-01231-1_12
7. Chen, H., He, X., Ren, C., Qing, L., Teng, Q.: CISRDCNN: super-resolution of compressed images using deep convolutional neural networks. Neurocomputing **285**, 204–219 (2018)
8. Dong, C., Loy, C.C., He, K., Tang, X.: Image super-resolution using deep convolutional networks. IEEE Trans. Pattern Anal. Mach. Intell. **38**(2), 295–307 (2015)
9. Kim, J., Lee, J.K., Lee, K.M.: Accurate image super-resolution using very deep convolutional networks. In: Proceedings of the IEEE Conference on Computer Vision and Pattern Recognition (2016)
10. Zhang, K., Zuo, W., Chen, Y., Meng, D., Zhang, L.: Beyond a Gaussian denoiser: residual learning of deep cnn for image de-noising. IEEE Trans. Image Process. **26**(7), 3142–3155 (2017)
11. Zhang, Y., Li, K., Li, K., Wang, L., Zhong, B., Fu, Y.: Image super-resolution using very deep residual channel attention networks. In: Ferrari, V., Hebert, M., Sminchisescu, C., Weiss, Y. (eds.) ECCV 2018, Part VII. LNCS, vol. 11211, pp. 294–310. Springer, Cham (2018). https://doi.org/10.1007/978-3-030-01234-2_18
12. Zhang, K., Zuo, W., Zhang, L.: Learning a single convolutional super-resolution network for multiple degradations. In: Proceedings of the IEEE Conference on Computer Vision and Pattern Recognition (2018)
13. Kingma, D.P., Ba, J.: Adam: a method for stochastic optimization. arXiv preprint: arXiv:1412.6980 (2014)

Beyond Literal Visual Modeling: Understanding Image Metaphor Based on Literal-Implied Concept Mapping

Chengpeng Fu[1], Jinqiang Wang[1], Jitao Sang[1,3(✉)], Jian Yu[1], and Changsheng Xu[2,3]

[1] Beijing Jiaotong University, Beijing, China
{brainfu,markwang,jtsang,jianyu}@bjtu.edu.cn
[2] National Lab of Pattern Recognition, Institute of Automation, CAS, Beijing, China
csxu@nlpr.ia.ac.cn
[3] Peng Cheng Laboratory, Shenzhen, China

Abstract. Existing ultimedia content understanding tasks focus on modeling the literal semantics of multimedia documents. This study explores the possibility of understanding the implied meaning behind the literal semantics. Inspired by human's implied imagination process, we introduce a three-step solution framework based on the mapping from literal to implied concepts by integrating external knowledge. Experiments on self-collected metaphor image dataset validate the effectiveness in identifying accurate implied concepts for further metaphor understanding in controlled environment.

Keywords: Image metaphor understanding · Concept mapping · External knowledge

1 Introduction

"A picture is worth a thousand words". For most existing image content understanding algorithms, the "thousand words" mainly involve with the literal semantics explicitly demonstrated in images, e.g., image annotation [1] addresses what subjects physically appear, visual relation extraction [2] addresses the interaction between appeared subjects, image captioning [3] generates natural description based on the detected subjects and their interaction. However, it is recognized humans have advanced requirements of using image as carrier to express and deliver information beyond literal semantics [4]. Taking the political metaphor image in Fig. 1(a) for example, state-of-the-art image annotation algorithm can successfully recognize the appeared donkey/elephant and even their weared suits, while image captioning further derives description like "A donkey and an elephant with suits shake hands with each other". This yet obviously fails to capture the underlying information behind the image.

Chengpeng Fu and Jinqiang Wang contribute equally.

Y. M. Ro et al. (Eds.): MMM 2020, LNCS 11961, pp. 111–123, 2020.
https://doi.org/10.1007/978-3-030-37731-1_10

As illustrated in Fig. 1(b), humans typically understand metaphor image by exploiting their knowledge to map the detected literal concepts to the corresponding implied concepts and then decoding the underlying information in the implied domain. By imitating the above process, we attempt to address the problem of automatic image metaphor understanding by empowering algorithm with external knowledge and conduct image modeling with the mapped implied concepts. Realizing this can lead to a three-step framework as illustrated in Fig. 2: *literal concept detection* recognizes the concept explicitly appearing in the image, *literal-implied concept mapping* aims to identify the corresponding implied concept for each recognized literal concept, and *metaphor captioning* finally generates the metaphorical description based in the implied domain. Since the first and third steps can be respectively viewed as applications of the existing image annotation and captioning techniques, this study will focus on introducing a solution for the second step: *literal-implied concept mapping*.

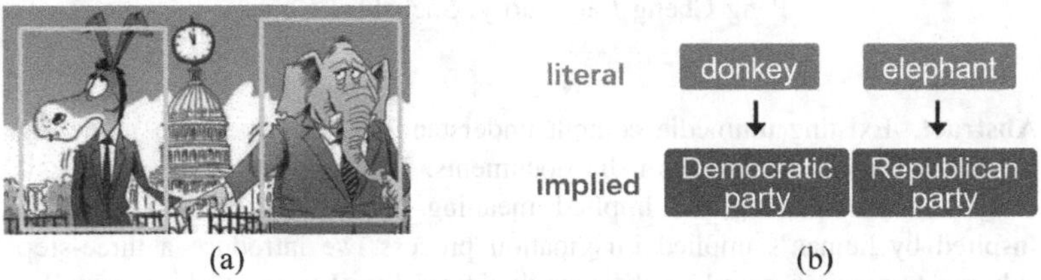

Fig. 1. Example metaphor image (a), and literal-implied concept mapping illustration (b).

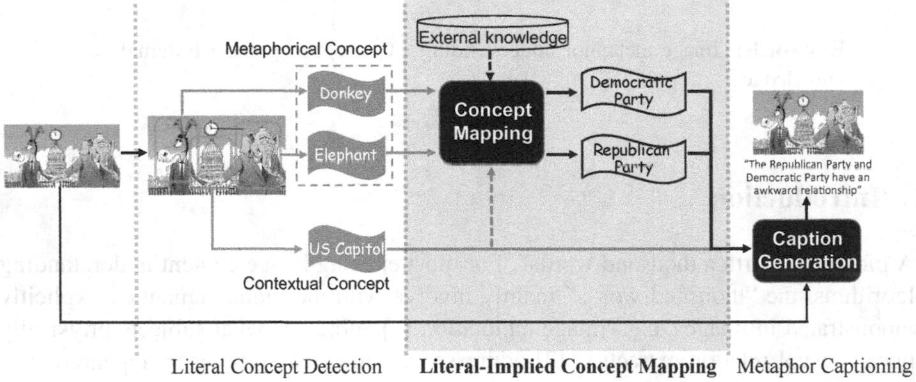

Fig. 2. The three steps in automatic image metaphor understanding.

The basic idea of *literal-implied concept mapping* is to activate implied concepts that are compatible with each other and collectively contribute to a coherent metaphor description. Specifically, a two-stage solution is proposed: (1) reference graph construction, to measure the compatibility between concepts by encoding external knowledge including both expert knowledge base and crowdsourcing co-occurrence; and (2) implied concept activation, to identify the most probable implied concepts by considering the coherence between, which is approximated by node centrality importance ranking in the derived reference graph.

The main contributions of this work can be summarized in two-fold:

– For the first time, we positioned the problem of image metaphor understanding, which extends visual modeling from literal semantics to implied domain.
– A two-stage solution is introduced for the task of *literal-implied concept mapping*. Experimental results on self-collected dataset validate its effectiveness in the controlled environment.

The rest of the paper is organized as follows: Sect. 2 elaborates the two-stage solution for literal-implied concept mapping, Sect. 3 reports preliminary experimental results and discussion, Sect. 4 reviews the related metaphor modeling studies in natural language modeling, and Sect. 5 concludes this work with future directions.

2 Literal-Implied Concept Mapping

2.1 Motivation and Problem Definition

The concepts directly recognized at the stage of *literal concept detection* can be further divided into two groups: (1) metaphorical concept, denoting the concept to be mapped to implied domain (e.g., "donkey" and "elephant" in Fig. 3(a)); and (2) contextual concept, denoting the concept stimulating imagination and indicative of the implied domain (e.g., "US Capitol" in Fig. 3(a)).

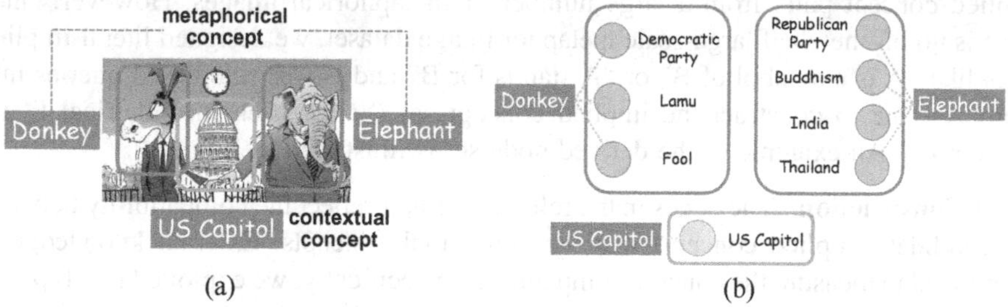

Fig. 3. (a) The metaphorical and contextual concepts. (b) Nodes in reference graph construction.

Each metaphorical concept can correspond to multiple implied concepts, e.g., "elephant" has implied concepts such as "Republican Party", "Thailand", "India" and "Buddhism". The core problem in *literal-implied concept mapping* is to select for each metaphorical concept which implied concept to activate. The basic idea behind is that: given a particular image, the activated implied concept should be compatible with other concepts (including both contextual concepts and the implied concepts of other metaphorical concepts) and collectively contributes to a coherent metaphor description. To achieve this goal, we propose a two-stage solution for *literal-implied concept mapping:* the measurement of compatibility between different candidate implied concepts leads to the first stage of *reference graph construction*, and exploiting the compatibility to activate most probable implied concept for each metaphorical literal concept is addressed in the second stage of *graph-based implied concept activation.* Before elaborating the details of the two stages, we first formally define the problem of *literal-implied concept mapping:*

Definition 1(Literal-implied concept mapping). Given detected contextual concept set $\mathcal{C} = \{c_1, \ldots, c_L\}$*, and metaphorical concept set* $\mathcal{M} = \{m_1, \ldots, m_D\}$*, for each metaphorical concept* $m_d \in \mathcal{M}$*, its corresponding implied concept set is denoted by* $I^{m_d} = \{i_1^{m_d}, \ldots, i_K^{m_d}\}$*, where K is the number of candidate implied concepts. The goal of literal-implied concept mapping is to identity the most probable implied concept* $i_*^{m_d}$ *for each metaphorical concept* $m_d \in \mathcal{M}$*.*

2.2 Reference Graph Construction

We define reference graph as an undirected graph $G = <V, E>$, where V is the set of vertexes and E is the set of edges. We construct reference graph based on the detected literal concepts and introduced external knowledge. The following details the construction of nodes and edges respectively.

Node Construction. The reference graph consists of two types of nodes: the first type directly corresponds to the contextual concept $c_l \in \mathcal{C}$ and is called contextual node; while the other type is the candidate implied concept i^{m_d} generated from each metaphorical concept m_d, which is called candidate implied node. An intuitive way to discover the candidate implied concepts is to extract the frequently co-occurrence literal-implied concept pairs from a large number of metaphorical images. However, since there is no off-the-shelf large-scale metaphor image dataset, we designed literal-implied rules like “A is a symbol of B” or “A stands for B” and issued rule-based queries into search engine to construct the implied concept set I^{m_d} for each metaphorical literal concept m_d. An example of the derived node set is illustrated in Fig. 3(b).

Edge Construction. The edges in the reference graph reflect the compatibility between the candidate implied concepts and the contextual concepts. External knowledge is introduced to measure the concept compatibility. Specifically, we exploited two types of external knowledge as expert knowledge base and crowdsourcing co-occurrence[1] in this study. The external knowledge is integrated to construct the edges in two ways: (1) KB-based edge extraction, to extract the direct edges and the intermediate nodes from the expert Knowledge Base (KB). This way derives an unweighted reference graph, as shown in Fig. 4(a). (2) Embedding-based edge weight estimation, to estimate the compatibility between the embedded representation of the concepts. Concept embeddings are obtained either by co-occurrence, knowledge base, or their combination. This way derives a weighted reference graph (as shown in Fig. 4(b)), where the weight is typically calculated by the cosine similarity between the embeddings[2].

---

1 To guarantee the quality of the derived concept compatibility, we use professional news corpus for co-occurrence calculation.

2 The edges with calculated weight below 0 are removed from the graph.

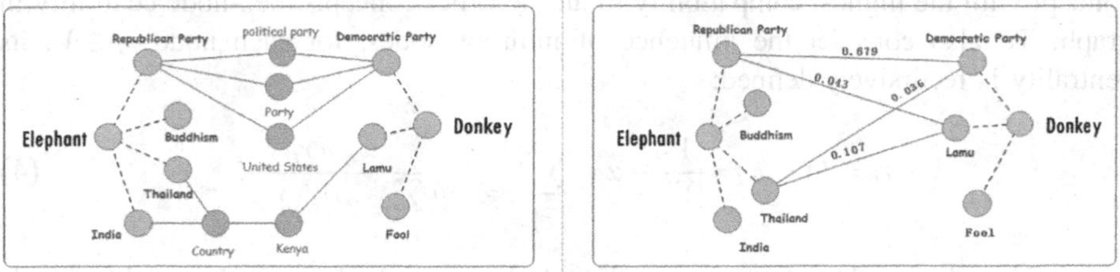

(a) (b)

Fig. 4. Examples of edge construction between metaphorical implied concepts in the reference graph: (a) KG-based edge extraction; (b) Embedding-based edge weight estimation. The dotted lines denote the correspondence between the metaphorical concept and its implied concepts, which are not included in the derived reference graph.

2.3 Graph-Based Implied Concept Activation

Given the constructed reference graph G, the goal is to activate one implied concept for each metaphorical literal concept based on their collective compatibility. Assuming $\bar{i}^{m_d} \in I^{m_d}$ is one candidate implied concept corresponding to metaphorical literal concept m_d, the implied concept set $\bar{I} = \{\bar{i}^{m_1}, \ldots, \bar{i}^{m_D}\}$ denotes one activation configuration. The problem can thus be formulated to find the configuration $\bar{I}^* = \{\bar{i}_*^{m_1}, \ldots, \bar{i}_*^{m_D}\}$, where the compatibility among the activated implied concepts and contextual concept set C is the highest among all possible configurations. The objective function can be written as follows:

$$\bar{I}^* = arg\max\nolimits_{\bar{I}} g(C, \bar{I}), \tag{1}$$

where $g(\cdot)$ denotes the group-wise compatibility function. An approximation can be made to transform the calculation of compatibility to pair-wise:

$$\bar{I}^* \approx arg\max\nolimits_{\bar{I}} \sum\nolimits_{l=1}^{L} \sum\nolimits_{d=1}^{D} p_c(c_l, \bar{i}^{m_d}) + \sum\nolimits_{d_1 \neq d_2} p_i(\bar{i}^{m_{d_1}}, \bar{i}^{m_{d_2}}), \tag{2}$$

where $p_c(\cdot), p_i(\cdot)$ respectively denote the pair-wise compatibility function between contextual concept and implied concept, and between the implied concepts. In this study, we do not distinguish between these two functions and instantiate them both with the edge weight w_{ab} from the derived reference graph[3]. With $O = C \cup \bar{I}$ denoting the new concept set, the above objective function can be then written as:

$$\bar{I}^* \approx arg\max\nolimits_{\bar{I}} \sum\nolimits_{a \neq b, o_a \notin C \, or \, o_b \notin C} w_{ab} \tag{3}$$

Solving this objective function is still a NP-hard problem. Moreover, this approximation focuses on the direct neighbor and ignores the influence of transitive nodes. Therefore, we further approximate this problem by selecting candidate implied

[3] Weight $w_{ab} \in \{0, 1\}$ in case of unweighted graph and $w_{ab} \in \mathbb{R}^+$ in case of weighted graph.

concept with the highest compatibility to all the other concepts, i.e., node centrality in graph. To also consider the influence of indirect nodes, for each node $v_i \in V$, its centrality is recursively defined:

$$r_i = (1-\alpha) * \frac{1}{|\mathcal{V}|} + \alpha * \sum\nolimits_{v_j \in \mathcal{N}(v_i)} \frac{w_{ij} * r_j}{\sum\nolimits_{v_k \in \mathcal{N}(v_j)} w_{jk}}, \quad (4)$$

where $|\mathcal{V}|$ is the number of vertexes in the reference graph, $\mathcal{N}(v_i)$ is the neighbor node set of v_i, α is a weight parameter belonging to $(0, 1)$. Solving the above objective function involves with a typical random walk process and is guaranteed to converge. The converged centrality scores are calculated as follows:

$$\boldsymbol{r} = \frac{(1-\alpha)(I - \alpha W^T D^{-1})^{-1} \cdot 1}{|\mathcal{V}|} \quad (5)$$

where $\boldsymbol{r} \in \mathbb{R}^{|\mathcal{V}| \times 1}$ is the centrality scores for each concept node, $W = (w_{ij})_{|\mathcal{V}| \times |\mathcal{V}|}$ is the weight matrix, $D = diag\left(\sum\nolimits_{v_j \in \mathcal{N}(v)} w_{1j}, \ldots, \sum\nolimits_{v_j \in \mathcal{N}(v_i)} w_{|\mathcal{V}|j}\right)$, $\mathbf{1}$ is a column vector of all ones.

For each metaphorical concept m_d, the implied concept with the highest centrality score is activated for further metaphor understanding:

$$\bar{i}_*^{m_d} = arg \max\nolimits_{i_k}^{m_d} r_{i_k}^{m_d} \quad (6)$$

3 Experiment

3.1 Experimental Setting

Metaphor Image Dataset. Since there is no off-the-shelf metaphor image dataset, we build a small-scale image metaphor dataset[4] for performance evaluation. The metaphor images are collected from stock image websites and 54 images are manually filtered with obvious metaphor meaning and easy-to-detect literal concepts. 10 graduate students help annotate the metaphorical literal concepts, contextual concepts and the ground-truth implied concepts included in each image. The concept with most endorsement is selected as the final annotation. Some example images are shown in Fig. 5. Among the resultant 54 metaphor images, 37 include contextual concepts. 28 unique metaphorical literal concepts are involved, with each image involving with 1–4 metaphorical literal concepts. The distribution of images with different number of metaphorical concepts is summarized in Table 1.

[4] Dataset is available on https://github.com/ADaM-BJTU/Metaphor-Image-Dataset.

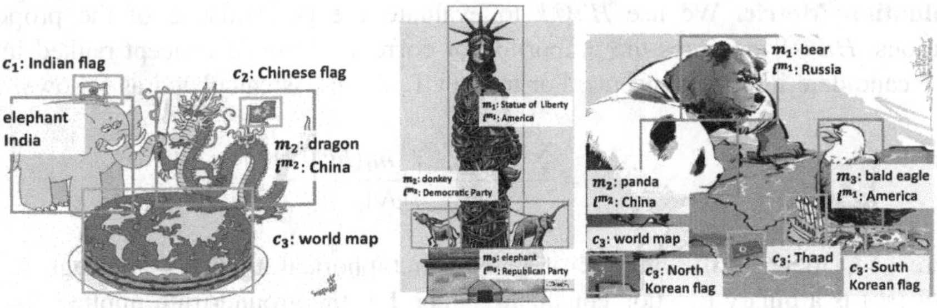

Fig. 5. Example metaphor images.

Table 1. The statistics of included metaphorical concepts in collected metaphor image dataset.

# metaphorical concept	1	2	3	4
# image	22	27	3	2

Table 2. The size distribution of implied concept set.

# implied concept	2	3	4	5	6	7	8	9
# metaphorical literal concept	4	2	5	5	2	4	2	4

Implementation Details. As claimed in Introduction, this study focuses on the second step of *literal-implied concept mapping* and assumes the metaphorical and contextual concepts are readily detected. In implementation, we directly use the annotated metaphorical and contextual concepts of each image as input.
Regarding the node construction in the reference graph, the implied concepts for each metaphorical literal concept are identified via rule-based search detailed in Sect. 2.2. Typically each metaphorical literal concept has 2–9 implied concepts, and the average number is 5.4. The detailed statistic is shown in Table 2.

Regarding the introduced external knowledge, *ConceptNet*5.5 [5] is utilized as the expert knowledge base, which contains over 8 million nodes and 21 million edges. Google News dataset is selected as the corpus to estimate crowdsourcing co-occurrence.

Regarding the two ways to exploit these external knowledge for edge construction, the 1-hop and 2-hop relations in *ConceptNet5.5* are extracted as the intermediate nodes to connect between implied and contextual concepts in the way of KB-based edge extraction. In the way of embedding-based edge weight estimation, concept embeddings are obtained considering three types of external knowledge: (1) *Word2Vec* [6] -based co-occurrence, where the concept embeddings are learned based on their co-occurrence patterns in Google News corpus; (2) *DeepWalk* [7] -based knowledge base, where random walk is conducted along the knowledge graph and derived concept embeddings can thus encode global knowledge structure; and (3) *NumberBatch* [5], which considers both the co-occurrence and knowledge base information.

Evaluation Metric. We use *Hit@k* to evaluate the performance of the proposed solutions. *Hit@k* measures the proportion of correctly implied concept ranked in the top *k* candidate implied concepts. For test set T, *Hit@k* is calculated as follows:

$$Hit@k = \frac{\sum_{\upsilon \in T} \sum_{t=1}^{|\mathcal{M}_\upsilon|} m_t(hit@k)}{\sum_{\upsilon \in T} |\mathcal{M}_\upsilon|} \quad (7)$$

where $|\mathcal{M}_\upsilon|$ denotes the number of unique metaphorical concepts in image υ, and $m_t(hit@k)$ is a binary function equalizing either 1 if the ground-truth implied concept appears in the top-k activated results for the metaphorical concept m_t, or 0 if otherwise.

3.2 Results and Analysis

Performance Comparison. As introduced in previous subsection, we implemented different ways for reference graph construction, including KB-based edge extraction (denoted by *EdgeExtraction*), and three strategies to exploit the external knowledge for concept embedding learning, i.e., *Word2Vec*-based co-occurrence, *DeepWalk*-based knowledge base, *NumberBatch* to integrate co-occurrence and knowledge base. To validate the motivation for modeling the compatibility between concepts and graph construction, we also implemented a baseline directly calculating the similarity between the *Word2Vec* embeddings of metaphorical concept and its implied concepts. The implied concept with the maximum similarity is activated. We denote this baseline as *Naive Similarity*. *Hit@1* and *Hit@2* of each method are summarized in Fig. 6(a).

A quick observation is that by modeling the compatibility between concepts, the four methods instantiating the proposed two-stage solution significantly outperform the *Naive Similarity* baseline. It is obvious that, without considering the influence of contextual concepts and other metaphorical concepts, *Naive Similarity* will activate the same implied concept for given literal concept in all cases. Figure 7 shows the activated implied concepts for the same literal concept "elephant" by *NumberBatch*. This validates the advantage of collectively considering the different contextual concepts as well as other metaphorical concepts.

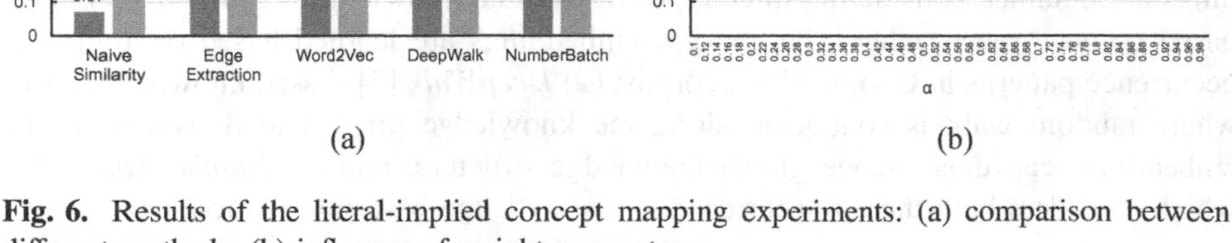

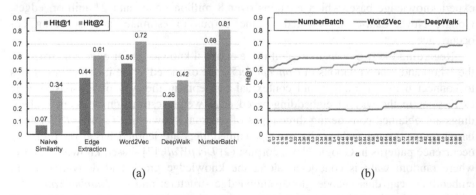

Fig. 6. Results of the literal-implied concept mapping experiments: (a) comparison between different methods; (b) influence of weight parameter α.

Fig. 7. The activated implied concept results on different images by *NumberBatch*.

Among the methods implementing the proposed solution, *DeepWalk* obtains inferior performance possibly due to the limited local neighborhood considered for node embedding. The additional consideration of intermediate concept nodes and flexible modeling of concurrence information contribute to the superior performance of *EdgeExtraction* and *Word2Vec* respectively. By combining the co-occurrence and knowledge base information, *NumberBatch* obtains the best activation accuracy, demonstrating the significance of integrating more external knowledge.

Parameter Analysis. Figure 6(b) shows the performance by varying the value of weight parameter α in *Eq.* (4). It is shown for all three examined methods, the activation accuracy basically improves as α increases. We recall that α controls the relative importance between walking with uniform probability and walking with the distribution decided by edge weight. The fact that larger α leading to superior performance is possible due to the reason that, the proposed method derives a compact reference graph with basically no isolated concept nodes, which reduces the importance to re-start with uniform distribution.

The Influence of Contextual Concept. The goal of introducing contextual concept is to exploit its indicative role to help activate suitable implied concept. In Fig. 8(a), we reported the concept activation accuracy with different numbers of contextual concepts. It is shown that more contextual concepts generally contribute to superior implied concept activation performance. To further demonstrate the influence of contextual concept, for the same image whose number of contextual concepts is greater than 0: (1) We removed the annotated contextual concepts and only retained the implied concepts in the reference graph (denoted as *w/o context*); (2) We added non-indicative concepts into the reference graph, e.g., "clock" in Fig. 3(a) (denoted as *w/n.i.context*). *NumberBatch* is used for reference graph construction. The results are showed in Fig. 8(b), where *w/context* denotes the proposed solution considering indicative contextual concepts. Two observations are derived: (1) Removing contextual concept significantly reduce the concept activation accuracy, which is consistent with the results from Fig. 8(a). (2) Adding non-indicative concepts tends to import noise to measure the collective compatibility, demonstrating the importance of automatically identifying highly-indicative contextual concepts. This is also one of the key directions in our future work.

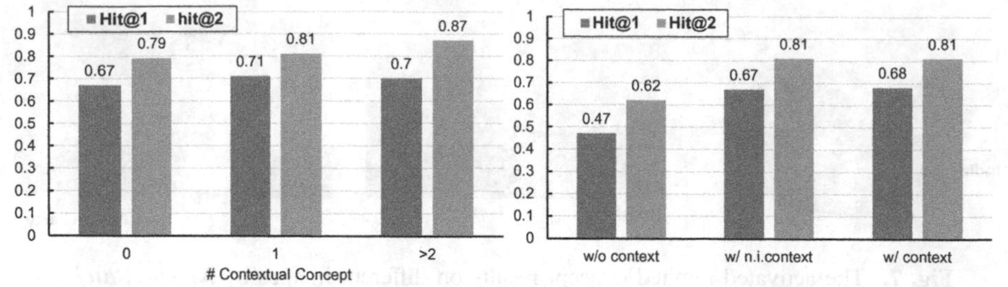

(a) (b)

Fig. 8. Concept activation accuracy: (a) with different number of contextual concepts; (b) w/and w/o contextual concepts.

3.3 Failure Cases and Limitation Discussion

The Coverage of Implied Concept Set. Figure 9(a) shows one failure case where the metaphorical concept "stone" is incorrectly activated as "firmness". By examining the implied concept set of "stone", we found that the ground-truth implied concept "stress" is not even included. After adding the missing ground-truth implied concept into the final implied concept set for reference graph construction, the *Hit@1* and *Hit@2* performance of *NumberBatch* increase from 0.68 and 0.81 to 0.72 and 0.84 respectively. This demonstrates the significance of acquiring a complete implied concept set.

The Quality of External Knowledge. Figure 9(b) shows another failure case. In this case, the incorrect implied concept activation is due to the poor measurement of the compatibility between the ground-truth implied concept of "Peace Party" and "War Party". A large knowledge base like *ConceptNet* still cannot cover all the necessary knowledge for metaphor understanding, especially some commonsense knowledge. When constructing reference graph using KB-based edge extraction, there exist no low-hop paths between the nodes of "Peace Party" and "War Party". Also, the method *NumberBatch* trained with *ConceptNet* gives a very low weight of 0.089 between these two implied concepts, which leads to the wrong activation result.

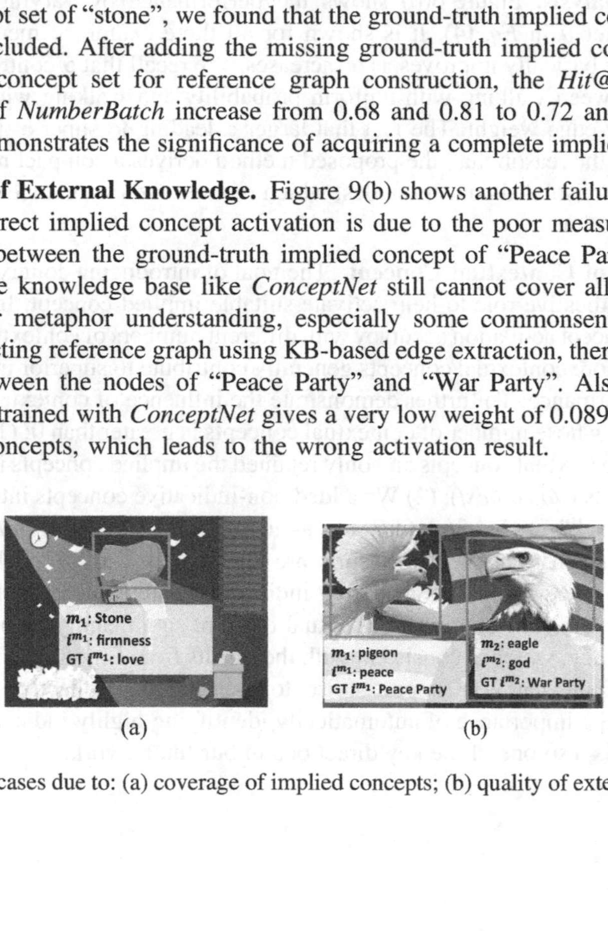

(a) (b)

Fig. 9. Failure cases due to: (a) coverage of implied concepts; (b) quality of external knowledge.

4 Related Work in Text Metaphor Modeling

Metaphor modeling has been initially introduced and studied in the field of Natural Language Processing (NLP) [8–12]. Metaphor in NLP also involves with two types of concepts as source and target concepts, which roughly correspond to the literal and implied concepts in image metaphor. According to the explicit appearance of source and target concepts, metaphor in NLP divides into three categories [13] (exampled on the left of Fig. 10): (1) Both source concept (e.g., "money") and target concept (e.g., "time") explicitly appear in the text; (2) Only source concept (e.g., "claws") is explicit, where the corresponding target concept can be "hands"; (3) Only target concept (e.g., "words") is explicit, where the corresponding source concept is something sharp like "arrow" or "knife".

Among the above three categories, the first two also exist in image metaphor modeling. The top right image in Fig. 10 shows one example of the first category, where the literal concept "cigarette" and implied concept "maze" both appear. The middle right image is one example of the second category, where only literal concepts "dragon" and "bear" appear. However, the third category almost does not exist in image metaphor. The metaphorical relationship in this category is typically indicated by the unusual verb in the text (e.g., "cut"). In metaphor image, these verbs are usually replaced by some concrete literal concepts (e.g., "arrow" in top bottom image), which makes the image transform to the second category. Considering that the first category of metaphor image explicitly embodies both literal and implied concepts, which poorly imitates the humans' typical process of metaphor understanding, this study actually addresses automatic image metaphor understanding for the second category.

It is noted that even within the same category, metaphor image and metaphor text differ much from each other in the following two aspects: (1) The quantity of literal concepts. Metaphor text usually involves with only one literal/source concept, while metaphor image involves with 1-4 implied concepts according to our collected dataset; (2) The dissimilarity between literal and implied concepts. In metaphor text, the source and target concepts typically belong to similar domains (e.g., "claws" and "hands") or share some obvious features (e.g., "money" and "time"). While in metaphor image, the literal and implied concept usually fall into concrete and abstract domains respectively, where their between relationship can only be recognized by importing additional information. The above two differences make the existing NLP solutions [8–12] to text metaphor modeling failed in addressing image metaphor understanding, which necessities the construction of reference graph to model the complex relationships among concepts, as well as the exploitation of external knowledge for literal-implied concept mapping.

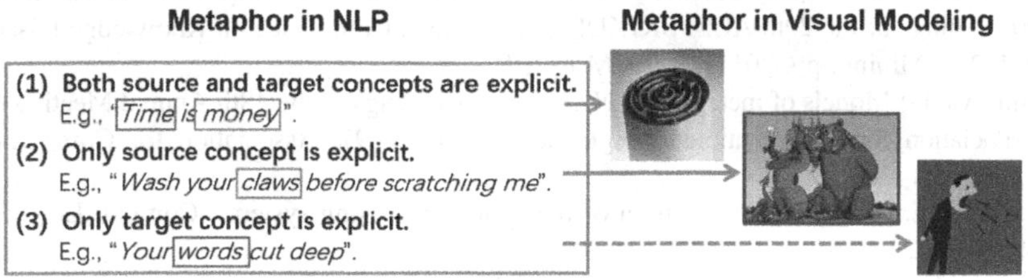

Fig. 10. Metaphor in NLP and visual modeling.

5 Conclusion and Future Work

This paper positioned the problem of image metaphor understanding and introduced a preliminary three-step solution framework. Preliminary experimental results validate the possibility of mapping from literal to implied concepts for metaphor understanding with the help of external knowledge. We hope this paper could serve to draw attention to the studies on multimedia modeling beyond literal semantics.

In addition to addressing the coverage/quality issues of implied concept and external knowledge as discussed in Sect. 3.3, this early work can also be extended at least along the following two directions: (1) automatizing the step of *literal concept detection* and integrating the step of *metaphor captioning* to give an overall realization to the problem of image metaphor understanding; (2) collecting more metaphor images to construct a large-scale dataset and exploring the end-to-end solution by considering metaphor style and other information.

Acknowledgement. This work is supported by the National Key R&D Program of China (Grant No. 2018AAA0100604), the National Natural Science Foundation of China (Grant No. 61632004, 61832002, 61672518, 61632115), and the Beijing Municipal Science & Technology Commission (No. Z181100008918012).

References

1. Deng, J., Dong, W., Socher, R., Li, L.J., Li, K., Fei-Fei, L.: Imagenet: a large-scale hierarchical image database. In: 2009 IEEE Conference on Computer Vision and Pattern Recognition, pp. 248–255. IEEE (2009)
2. Lu, C., Krishna, R., Bernstein, M., Fei-Fei, L.: Visual relationship detection with language priors. In: Leibe, B., Matas, J., Sebe, N., Welling, M. (eds.) ECCV 2016. LNCS, vol. 9905, pp. 852–869. Springer, Cham (2016). https://doi.org/10.1007/978-3-319-46448-0_51
3. Vinyals, O., Toshev, A., Bengio, S., Erhan, D.: Show and tell: a neural image caption generator. In: Proceedings of the IEEE Conference on Computer Vision and Pattern Recognition, pp. 3156–3164 (2015)
4. Drechsel, B.: The Berlin wall from a visual perspective: comments on the construction of a political media icon. Vis. Commun. **9**(1), 3–24 (2010)
5. Speer, R., Chin, J., Havasi, C.: Conceptnet 5.5: an open multilingual graph of general knowledge. In: Thirty-First AAAI Conference on Artificial Intelligence (2017)
6. Mikolov, T., Sutskever, I., Chen, K., Corrado, G.S., Dean, J.: Distributed representations of words and phrases and their compositionality. In: Advances in Neural Information Processing Systems, pp. 3111–3119 (2013)
7. Perozzi, B., Al-Rfou, R., Skiena, S.: Deepwalk: online learning of social representations. In: Proceedings of the 20th ACM SIGKDD International Conference on Knowledge Discovery and Data Mining, pp. 701–710. ACM (2014)
8. Shutova, E.: Models of metaphor in NLP. In: Proceedings of the 48th Annual Meeting of the Association for Computational Linguistics, pp. 688–697. Association for Computational Linguistics (2010)
9. Shutova, E.: Design and evaluation of metaphor processing systems. Comput. Linguist. **41** (4), 579–623 (2015)

10. Shutova, E., Kiela, D., Maillard, J.: Black holes and white rabbits: metaphor identification with visual features. In: Proceedings of the 2016 Conference of the North American Chapter of the Association for Computational Linguistics: Human Language Technologies, pp. 160–170 (2016)
11. Shutova, E., Sun, L., Gutiérrez, E.D., Lichtenstein, P., Narayanan, S.: Multilingual metaphor processing: experiments with semi-supervised and unsupervised learning. Comput.l Linguist. **43**(1), 71–123 (2017)
12. Veale, T., Shutova, E., Klebanov, B.B.: Metaphor: a computational perspective. Synthesis Lect. Hum. Lang. Technol. **9**(1), 1–160 (2016)
13. Li, H., Zhu, K.Q., Wang, H.: Data-driven metaphor recognition and explanation. Trans. Assoc. Comput. Linguist. **1**, 379–390 (2013)

Oral Session 3A: Color Processing and Art

Deep Palette-Based Color Decomposition for Image Recoloring with Aesthetic Suggestion

Zhengqing Li(✉), Zhengjun Zha(✉), and Yang Cao(✉)

Department of Automation, University of Science and Technology of China, Hefei 230027, China
lizq@mail.ustc.edu.cn, {zhazj,forrest}@ustc.edu.cn

Abstract. Color edition is an important issue in image processing and graphic design. This paper presents a deep color decomposition based framework for image recoloring, allowing users to achieve professional color edition through simple interactive operations. Different from existing methods that perform palette generation and color decomposition separately, our method directly generates the recolored images by a light-weight CNN. We first formulate the generation of color palette as an unsupervised clustering problem, and employ a fully point-wise CNN to extract the most representative colors from the input image. Particularly, a pixel scrambling strategy is adopted to map the continuous image color to a compact discrete palette space, facilitating the CNN focus on color-relevant features. Then, we devise a deep color decomposition network to obtain the projected weights of input image on the basis colors of the generated palette space, and leverage them for image recoloring in a user-interacted manner. In addition, a novel aesthetic constraint derived from color harmony theory is proposed to augment the color reconstruction from user-specified colors, resulting in an aesthetically pleasing visual effect. Qualitative comparisons with existing methods demonstrate the effectiveness of our proposed method.

Keywords: Palette extraction · Color decomosition · Image recoloring · Color harmony

1 Introduction

Image recoloring is one of the most common tasks in photo editing, which enables locally and globally color modifications of the original image to match the desirable color style. Typically, the recolored image should preserve the details of the original image, maintain perceptual uniformity and identity, as well as natural and harmonic. Thus, it is a challenging task to achieve an effective user-interacted image recoloring.

Image recoloring has been widely studied in the past years and a variety of methods have been proposed. Typically, the example based method is introduced by [1,2], which apply a statistical transformation to adjust the color from the reference image to the similar regions in the original image. Stroke based

Y. M. Ro et al. (Eds.): MMM 2020, LNCS 11961, pp. 127–138, 2020.
https://doi.org/10.1007/978-3-030-37731-1_11

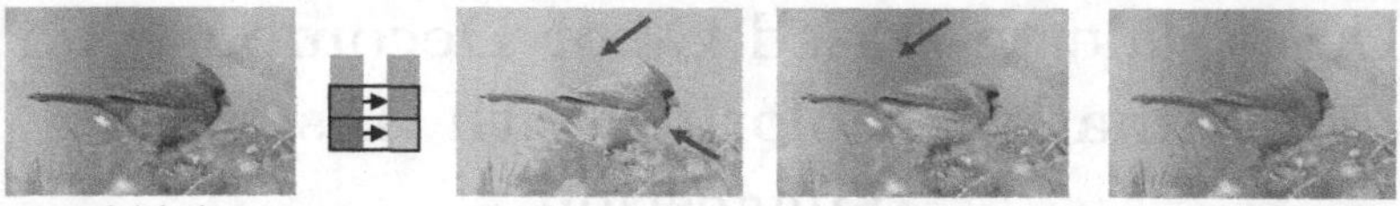

Fig. 1. A comparison of image recoloring among our proposed method and that of [9,13]. Artifacts are marked with arrow. CUB-200-2011 dataset. [15].

methods [3–8] propose to recolor images by propagating the desired color edits, e.g. scribles, on different regions to similar pixels.

Most current works focus on the palette-based image recoloring methods, which explores the intended color concept and pursue the ease of operation. For example, [9] provides a color transfer algorithm that recolors the input image to a target palette. [10–12] divide the task into two parts: palette extraction and image decomposition, and solve them separately. They decompose images into layers based on an addictive color mixing model, and project the colors of the image into a palette. [11] uses k-means algorithm to cluster the colors of the input image into a palette, and proposes a color decomposition optimization to generate layers. [12] computes the convex hull vertices of pixels in RGB-space as basis colors, and [13,14] extended it to 5D RGBXY-space to extract palettes and also solved an optimization problem to get decomposed layers. However, these non-data driven methods are time consuming and may cause some artifacts with unnatural or less vivid appearance as shown in Fig. 1.

Different from existing methods, we propose a deep learning based image recoloring framework in an end-to-end manner, which combines palette extraction and image decomposition to generate aesthetically pleasing recoloring results. Figure 2 demonstrates our proposed model architecture. Based on the powerful feature representation ability of CNN model, we have achieved real-time image recoloring with less artifacts and natural appearance. In our method, we assume that colors in the image can be represented as a linear combination of basic colors in the palette. Firstly, we pretrain a fully point-wise Palette Extraction Network (PE-Net) to summarize the colors of the input image. In view of the fact that the extracted palette is independent of the image content, we use a pixel scrambling strategy to make CNN pay more attention to the statistics of image colors. Then, Deep Color Decomposition Network (DCD-Net) is proposed to generate the weighted layers corresponding to the extracted palette by PE-Net. To exactly represent the mapping between the intended palett color and the corresponding layers, we leverage region prior knowledge as the guidance of DCD-Net for outputting sparse color decomposition. Then, we compute a multiplication of layers with the user-interacted palette to recolor original images. We optimize the parameters of the whole network by narrowing the gap between the original image and the reconstructed image in a self-supervised manner. Finally, we present a novel constraint derived from color harmony theory to generate an aesthetically pleasing recolored image.

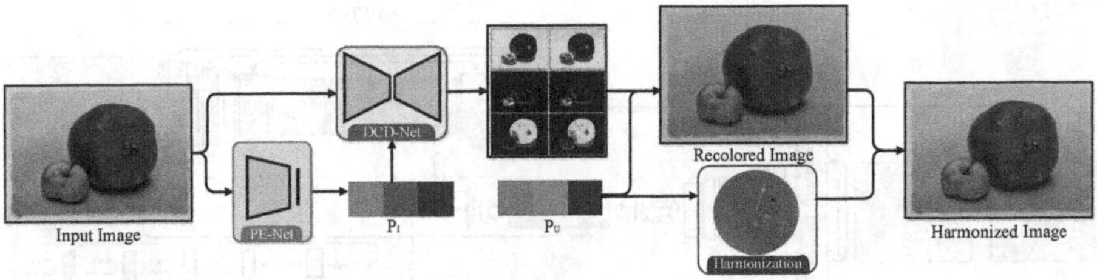

Fig. 2. Overview of our architecture. Given an input image, Palette Extraction Network(PE-Net) extractes the main colors of the image as palette P_I. Deep Color Decomposition Network(DCD-Net) decomposes the image into corresponding weighted maps based on P_I. Then our approach can help users achieve recoloring by applying matrix multiplication to a user modified P_U and the weighted maps. Finally, the recolored image is ajusted to be asethetically pleasing by a color harmonization process.

Our proposed framework has the following advantages:

1. We propose a light-weight CNN model for image recoloring in an end-to-end manner, which combines palette extraction and color decomposition together to generate weight maps with elaborate details. Furthermore, a novel constraint derived from color harmony theory is introduced to guide the generation of aesthetically pleasing recoloring results.
2. We present a fully point-wise network to map continuous color space to a compressed discrete palette space with a pixel scrambling strategy. Consequently, a DCD-Net constraint by a region prior loss is proposed to achieve image decomposition.
3. Extensive evaluations demonstrate the superiority of our proposed method over state-of-the-arts.

2 Proposed Method

In this section, we first introduce the problem of image recoloring. Then a palette extraction network (PE-Net) is proposed to generate a color palette comprising of a set of the most representative colors of the input image. Subsquently, we present our deep color decomposition network (DCD-Net) that learns to decompose an image into weighted layers according to the extracted palette colors. At last, we take color harmony into account, to assist and guide users in editing palette and recoloring. Figure 3 shows our network architecture.

2.1 Palette Extraction Network

We propose a Palette Extraction Network (PE-Net) to map any input colors to a representative discrete palette color space. Considering that the extraction of palette color does not require spatial information of the input image [9–14], we scramble all pixels and use the pixel-shuffled image as the input of the PE-Net. This pixel scrambling strategy makes the statistical properties of image colors more easily to be perceived by a CNN. Since the scrambled pixels are

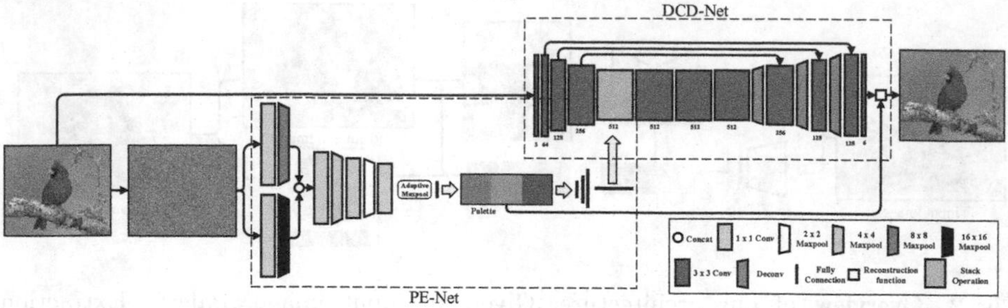

Fig. 3. Architectures of two networks used in our model: (a) PE-Net takes image with scrambled pixels as input, and outputs main colors as image palette. (b) DCD-Net. During training, DCD-Net learns to produce sparse weight maps that can reconstruct the input image with the palette which is the output of pretrained PE-Net. At test time, firstly the network decompose the input image into seperate weighted maps given palette extracted from itself, and then users can obtain a recolored image by recombining a new palette with weighted maps.

independent identically distributed, we use an extremely efficient fully pointwise CNN with multi-scale module [16] to extract representative palettes. The details of PE-Net are shown in Table 1.

A suitable palette P is expected to capture the most representative colors of the input image, and the difference between two basic colors in the palette should be as large as possible. We define a reconstruction error that measures the Euclidean distance between palette colors and image colors. The image color C_i is best matched with c^j in palette P.

$$\mathcal{L}_2 = \sum_{i=1}^{N} \left\| C_i - c^j \right\|^2, c^j \in P. \tag{1}$$

However, accurately estimating the luminosity of the palette color is of less importance than estimating its hue. Thus, we present a luminosity independent metric, which is widely used in color constancy problem [17]. The error metric is the angle between RGB triplet of the estimated palette color c^j and the pixel color C_i in the input image.

$$\mathcal{L}_{Ang} = arc\cos\left(\frac{C_i \cdot c^j}{\|C_i\| \, \|c^j\|}\right). \tag{2}$$

Equivalently, we use Euclidean distance of normalized color as loss function to optimize the parameters:

$$\mathcal{L}_{\cos} = \sum_{i=1}^{N} \left\| {C_i}^* - {c^j}^* \right\|^2, c^j \in P, \tag{3}$$

where ${C_i}^*$ and ${c^j}^*$ represent the normalized C_i and c^j, respectively. Mathematically, it is equivalent to optimize the vectorial angel between C_i and c^j.

Table 1. Details of Palette Extraction Network

layer	input	num	stride	layer	input	num	stride
Conv1-1, Conv1-2	256×256×3	128	0	Conv3	61×61×256	512	0
Maxpool1-1, 1-2*	256×256×128	1	2	Maxpool3	61×61×512	1	2
Conv2	125×125×128	256	0	Conv4	30×30×512	512	0
Maxpool2	125×125×256	1	2	AdapMaxpool	30×30×512	1	-

* The padding is 0 except that of MaxPool1-2 is 4.

Therefore, the loss function for palette extraction is given by

$$\mathcal{L} = \sum_{i=1}^{N} \left\| C_i - c^j \right\|^2 + \lambda \left\| C_i{}^* - c^{j*} \right\|^2. \tag{4}$$

We utilize the above algorithm to extract the palette and generate the corresponding mask. For example, the mask for palette color c^j is a binary map where the position of '1' indicates that the color of the pixel at that location is closest to c^j.

2.2 Deep Color Decomposition Network

According to [10,11], given a digital image, the color C_i of the i-th pixel can be represented as a combination of palette colors c^i:

$$C_i = \sum_{j=1}^{|P|} w_i^j c^j, \tag{5}$$

where weights w_i^j with $\sum_{j=1}^{|P|} w_i^j = 1$, P is the palette of the image, j is the j-th color in the palette P. Through this formula, we can decompose the image into separate weighted maps according to the given palette, which can be also named as decomposition layers.

However, there are infinitely many solutions to satisfy the above formula. This means that every pixel is generally affected by more than one color in the palette. Once we replace one color of the palette, the entire image but not the region of the modified color, will be recolored. Thus, the ambiguity during decomposition causes inconsistency between recolored image and the intention of users.

To address this issue, we map each pixel color to a basic color, so that we can convey users' intention conveniently by modifying palette. Specificaly, users can edit palette to change the color of certain image region. The total loss function $\mathcal{L}$ defined as follows:

$$\mathcal{L} = \lambda_{Re}\mathcal{L}_{Re} + \lambda_{RA}\mathcal{L}_{RA}, \tag{6}$$

where $\mathcal{L}_{Re}$ is to measure reconstruct error, $\mathcal{L}_{RA}$ is a region-aware loss to guarantee tue sparsity of weights, and λ_{Re} and λ_{RA} are both positive weights for balancing two loss functions. $\mathcal{L}_{Re}$ and $\mathcal{L}_{RA}$ are defined as:

$$\mathcal{L}_{Re} = \sum_{i=1}^{N} \|C_i - \sum_{j=1}^{\|P\|} w_i^j c^j\|^2, \mathcal{L}_{RA} = \sum_{i=1}^{N} \| \sum_{j=1}^{\|P\|} (1 - m_i^j) w_i^j \|^2. \quad (7)$$

where w_i^j denotes a weight measuring of the j-th basis color contributes to the formation of pixel i's color. When $m_i^j = 1$, it means that the color of pixel i is affected by the j-th basic color. When $m_i^j = 0$, it means that the j-th color is not involved with the generation of pixel i. Here, we define that there is only one case that m_i^j is 1 for each pixel i. For convenience, we mark $\{\{w_i^j\}_{j=1}^{|P|}\}_{i=1}^{N}$ as $M \in \mathbb{R}^{N \times |P|}$, which is a mask obtained by the method in Sect. 2.1. Note that we decompose *ab* channels of each pixel into weight maps respectively in the CIE *Lab* color space. The luminance channel L is not reconstructed to avoid artifacts and undesirable luminance changes in reconstructed image or recolored image.

By adding these constraints, we eliminate the ambiguities during image decomposition so that each pixel is primarily generated by the closest color in the palette. Then a recolored image is generated by computing a multiplication of weighted maps with a new palette.

To decompose a image into layers, we propose a Deep Color Decomposition Network (DCD-Net), which adopts U-Net architecture in [18] as backbone. In convolution block 1 to 4, the tensor sizes of input are halved spatially with the stride, or the tensor dimensions are doubled with the stride. The output of feature extraction module will be fused with the palette feature maps. For decoder part, convolution layers reduce tensor dimensions by half and upsampling layers double the wide and height of the tensor. The last convolution layer is with Sigmoid function to limit the range of the output. The output tensor are combined with palettes to reconstruct original images or obtain recolored images.

The input palette plays an important role in supervised learning, which allows the network to detect prominent edges and apply palette colors to suitable locations of the image. We utilize PE-Net to extract a palette consisting of three dominant colors of the ground truth image. During the training phase, we integrate the features of input images with three palette maps into the network. As shown in the 'Stack Operation' of Fig. 3 which is a similar operator in [19], the palette colors are processed through 3 fully connected layers, with size of 1×1 and 128, 256, 512 channels respectively, and the feature map is repeated spatially to match the feature of Conv4 in DCD-Net. In order to recover spatially detailed information, skip connections are adopted in the networks, guiding the input and output images to share the locations of prominent edges. The output of DCD-Net are 6 weighted maps, which are operated with the input palette of ab channels and the generated mask to calculate loss.

2.3 Color Harmonization

To provide a pleasant visual perception for users, we introduce color harmonization theory into image recoloring. Figure 4 shows eight harmonic templates proposed by Matsuda [20], which define the relationship of the hue distribution.

A group of colors that fall in the shadows of the templates are harmonious colors. While color harmony is mainly affected by the hue channel, we map image colors into LCh space (Lightness, Chroma, and hue)

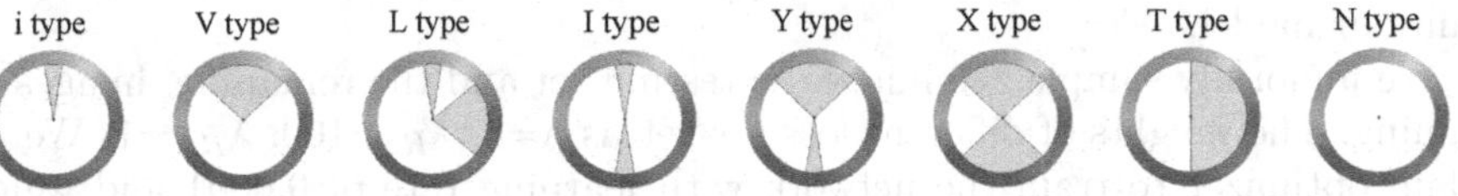

Fig. 4. Harmonic templates on the hue wheel.

Given an image, we seek to find a closest harmonic template to its extracted palette P. In the process of matching templates, we can generate several new harmonious palettes while remaining initial properties. A template is defined as $T_m(\alpha)$, where α is an associated angle varying in $[0, 2\pi]$ and m is the type. Then, we measure the distance between a template $T_m(\alpha)$ and a palette P as:

$$F(P, T_m(\alpha)) = \sum_{c^i \in P} W(c^i) \cdot L(c^i) \cdot C(c^i) \cdot D(c^i, T_m(\alpha)), \quad (8)$$

where $L(c^i)$ is the lightness and $C(c^i)$ is the chroma of palette color c^i. $W(c^i)$ is a normalized weight, which indicates how many pixels in the image are represented by c^i and normalized by the total number of pixels. $D(c^i, T_m(\alpha))$ refers to the arc-length difference on the Hue wheel. If users expect the color c^i to remain unchanged, $D(c^i, T_m(\alpha))$ is equal to infinity. More generally, $D(c^i, T_m(\alpha))$ is defined as:

$$D(c^i, T_m(\alpha)) = \begin{cases} 0 \;\; \textit{if } c^i \textit{ is in the shadows} \\ \left\| H(c^i) - E_{T_m(\alpha)}(c^i) \right\| \;\; \textit{else} \end{cases}, \quad (9)$$

where $H(c^i)$ is the hue of c^i , and $E_{T_m(\alpha)}$ is the border hue of the shadows in the template . Our goal is to find the closest harmonious palette under the template:

$$\alpha_m^* = \arg \min_{\alpha} F(P, T_m(\alpha)). \quad (10)$$

Apparently, the best template to fit the original palette and image is:

$$m^* = \arg \min_{m} F(P, T_m(\alpha_m^*)). \quad (11)$$

3 Experimental Results

In this section, we firstly compare the palette extraction results of our method with the state-of-the-arts. Then we evaluate the effectiveness of region-aware loss $\mathcal{L}_{RA}$, and illustrate the performance of our proposed color decomposition model. In the next, we compare the image recoloring results of our method with the state-of-the-arts. Finally, we present the image recoloring result in accordance with the theory of color harmony.

3.1 Datasets and Settings

Refer to the colorization methods in [21], we use CUB-200-2011 dataset [15] as the training dataset. This dataset contains 200 species of birds with a total of 11788 images. Due to its extensive color distribution, it is very appropriate to train our model.

We uniformly sample 240 images as testing set and the remaining images for training. The weights of different loss are set as λ=5, λ_{Re}=100, λ_{RA}=1. We use Adam optimizer to train the network with learning rate of 0.0001 and weight decay of 2e-6 for both two networks. Based on the parameters above, PE-Net is trained in 50 epochs with a batch-size of 50, and DCD-Net is trained in 30 epochs with a batch-size of 20. The model is trained and tested on a PC with NIVIDIA GTX1080 GPU×2 using Pytorch architecture.

3.2 Evaluation

Comparison of Palette Extraction Results Against SOTA. In Fig. 5, we compare our approach with the previous palette extraction methods [9,13]. As [13] assumes a palette size is at least 4, so we choose the palette size is 4 in (a). One can see that the base colors extracted by our method can represent the color distribution of the image, and the correlation between any two palette colors is lower than clustering based method proposed by [9].

Fig. 5. Comparison between our approach and other automatic palette extraction methods. (a)-(c) are results of [9,13], and our proposed method.

Evaluation on the $\mathcal{L}_{RA}$ Loss. To verify the effectiveness of our proposed region prior knowledge, we perform an experiment that compares the decomposition maps, reconstructed images and recoloring results by the models with and without region-aware loss. As shown in Fig. 6 (a), the weighted maps generated by the model with $\mathcal{L}_{RA}$ loss provide more sparse details, and there is little color distortion in the reconstructed image. The reason for this is that our proposed region-aware loss function promotes each pixel to be constrained by its closest color in the palette. Similarly, as show in Fig. 6 (b), the recovered and recolored image of the model with $\mathcal{L}_{RA}$ loss achieves better performance, where the editing region (i.e. the red bird) no longer affects the background color.

This is because our network enables to pay more attention to the details and generates high-quality image recoloring results.

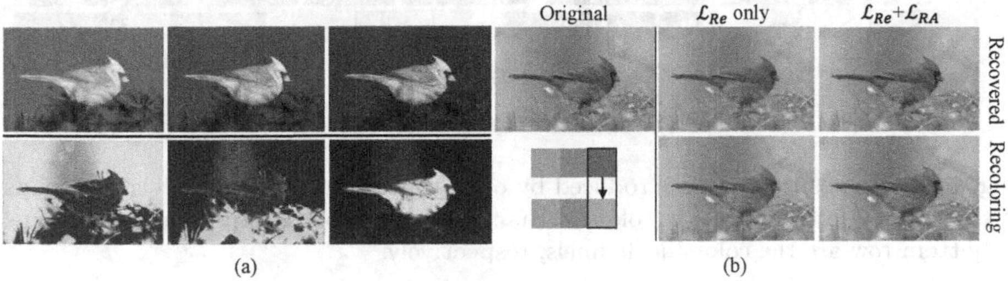

Fig. 6. Decomposition results (a), recovered images and recolored images (b) produced by our proposed method. The weighted maps in top row of (a) are for three palette colors' a channels in Lab space without using $\mathcal{L}_{RA}$ loss, The maps in bottom row of (a) are the same channels using $\mathcal{L}_{RA}$ loss.

Evaluation on Proposed Color Decomposition Model. To demonstrate the performance of our proposed DCD-Net, we perform an experiment to decompose images into separate layers, and then perform matrix multiplication with given palettes to reconstruct original images. Figure 7 shows that our decomposed layers reconstruct the original image without visually perceptible differences. It is because our proposed DCD-Net achieves a tradeoff between the sparsity and smoothness. On the one hand, it can generate sparse weight maps, which fit well with the corresponding color region in details. On the other hand, the decomposed layers preserve spatial smoothness in the region with high weights.

Comparison of Recoloring Results Against SOTA. To evaluate our approach comprehensively, we compare the recolored results of our proposed method to other palette-based recoloring approaches in the perspective of quality and speed. Firstly, to illustrate the effectiveness of our layer decompositions, we present the comparison results of our DCD-Net and the approach of [9] and [13] in Fig. 8 (a). As can be seen, the result of Chang et al.'s method introduces color artifacts, e.g., there exist undesirable color distortions in the background of the yellow bird, the girl's hair, and the meadow. Furthermore, it also exhibits blurred details and different illuminations from original images. The result of Tan et al.'s method has fewer artifacts, but it generates dividing lines in the color transition area, e.g. the cloud and sky. As a contrast, our results contain fewer unpleasant artifacts, such as noise, unrelated color changes, and undesirable illumination changes.

Since there is no public code for [22] to test arbitrary images, we cite its results directly from the CVPR workshop paper, and try to achieve similar recoloring results with our proposed method. As can be seen in Fig. 8 (b), our method generates visual pleasing recoloring results. As a contrast, there are

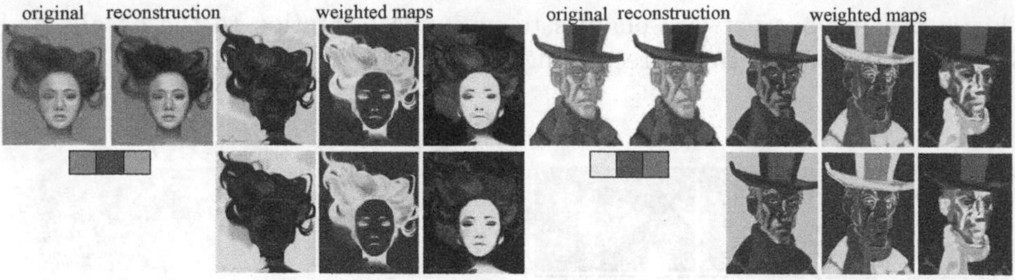

Fig. 7. Decomposition results produced by our proposed method. The weighted maps in top row are for three palette colors' a channels in Lab space, respectively. The maps in bottom row are the colors' b channels, respectively.

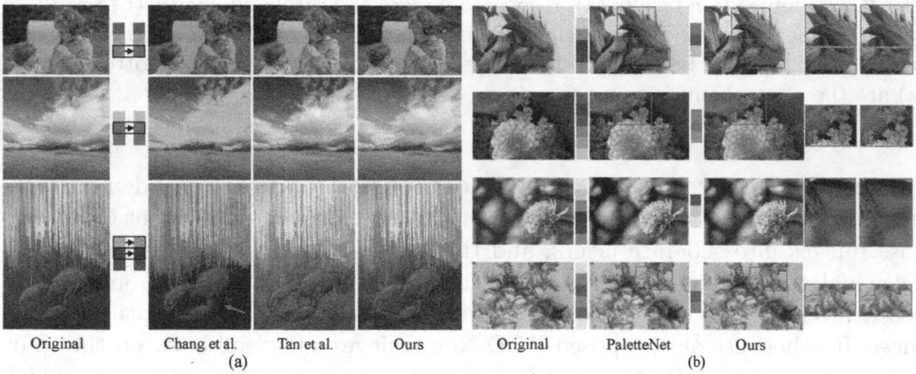

Fig. 8. A comparison of image recoloring between our proposed method and that of [9,13,22]. Artifacts are marked with arrows and red boxes. (Color figure online)

some artifacts residual, e.g. color distortion and color bleed, in the results of PaletteNet, as shown in the region marked by the red boxes.

Then we test the computation time of our proposed method on the NIVIDIA GTX 1080 GPU, using the input image with the size of 256×256. It takes an average of 100 epochs to get a reliable testing value. The average computation time is 0.0297 s, which shows that our method can achieve real-time image recoloring. To the best of our knowledge, most of the color decomposition methods [10–12,23] take a few seconds to hundreds of seconds to recolor an image.

Image Recoloring Accordance to Color Harmonization. Figure 9 shows some recoloring examples of our proposed method, which are in accordance with color harmonization theory. Several candidates for recoloring are provided based on user-modified palette, which provide aesthetically pleasing recoloring results. As can be seen, the color transfer of specific region improves the overall effect of the image, while also reflecting the user's intention. It demonstrates that our proposed method is useful and suitable for designers and amateurs to enhance their artistic work with a pleasant visual perception.

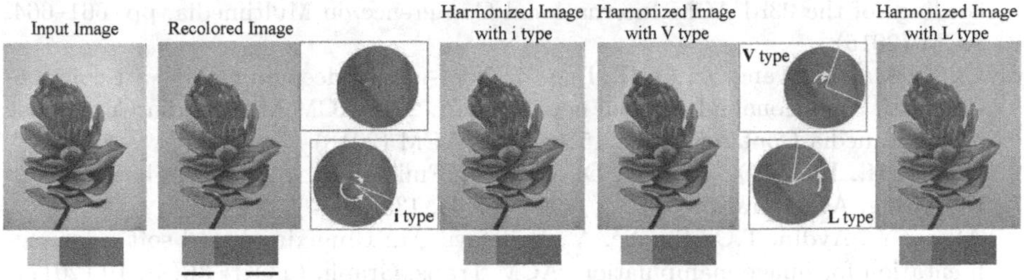

Fig. 9. Recolored images by changing palettes and the results of templates fitting to the palette edited by users. From left to right: original image, user recolorings, harmonized image of i type, harmonized image of V type and harmonized image of L type.

4 Conclusion

This paper has presented a light weight CNN to achieve palette-based image recoloring. We first extract a set of representative colors from the input image using a light fully point-wise CNN. Then we propose a deep color decomposition network to segment an image into palette-based weighted layers, and leverage them for a user-interacted image recoloring. In addition, we introduce color-harmonic constraint to augment the image recoloring process to generate visual pleasing results. Experimental results illustrate our method is user-friendly, sufficiently fast and visual meaningful to produce natural and harmonious recoloring results.

References

1. Reinhard, E., Adhikhmin, M., Gooch, B., Shirley, P.: Color transfer between images. IEEE Comput. Graph. Appl. **21**(5), 34–41 (2001)
2. Gupta, R.K., Chia, A.Y.S., Rajan, D., Ng, E.S., Zhiyong, H.: Image colorization using similar images. In: Proceedings of the 20th ACM International Conference on Multimedia, pp. 369–378. ACM (2012)
3. Levin, A., Lischinski, D., Weiss, Y.: Colorization using optimization. In: ACM Transactions on Graphics (tog), vol. 23, pp. 689–694. ACM (2004)
4. Li, Y., Ju, T., Hu, S.M.: Instant propagation of sparse edits on images and videos. In: Computer Graphics Forum. vol. 29, pp. 2049–2054. Wiley Online Library (2010)
5. Ding, X., Xu, Y., Deng, L., Yang, X.: Colorization using quaternion algebra with automatic scribble generation. In: Schoeffmann, K., Merialdo, B., Hauptmann, A.G., Ngo, C.-W., Andreopoulos, Y., Breiteneder, C. (eds.) MMM 2012. LNCS, vol. 7131, pp. 103–114. Springer, Heidelberg (2012). https://doi.org/10.1007/978-3-642-27355-1_12

6. Chen, X., Zou, D., Li, J., Cao, X., Zhao, Q., Zhang, H.: Sparse dictionary learning for edit propagation of high-resolution images. In: Proceedings of the IEEE Conference on Computer Vision and Pattern Recognition, pp. 2854–2861 (2014)
7. Matsui, Y.: Challenge for manga processing: sketch-based manga retrieval. In: Proceedings of the 23rd ACM International Conference on Multimedia, pp. 661–664. ACM (2015)
8. Ci, Y., Ma, X., Wang, Z., Li, H., Luo, Z.: User-guided deep anime line art colorization with conditional adversarial networks. In: 2018 ACM Multimedia Conference on Multimedia Conference, pp. 1536–1544. ACM (2018)
9. Chang, H., Fried, O., Liu, Y., DiVerdi, S., Finkelstein, A.: Palette-based photo recoloring. ACM Trans. Graph. (TOG) **34**(4), 139 (2015)
10. Aksoy, Y., Aydin, T.O., Smolić, A., Pollefeys, M.: Unmixing-based soft color segmentation for image manipulation. ACM Trans. Graph. (TOG) **36**(2), 19 (2017)
11. Zhang, Q., Xiao, C., Sun, H., Tang, F.: Palette-based image recoloring using color decomposition optimization. IEEE Trans. Image Process. **26**(4), 1952–1964 (2017)
12. Tan, J., Lien, J.M., Gingold, Y.: Decomposing images into layers via RGB-space geometry. ACM Trans. Graph. (TOG) **36**(1), 7 (2017)
13. Tan, J., Echevarria, J., Gingold, Y.: Efficient palette-based decomposition and recoloring of images via rgbxy-space geometry. In: SIGGRAPH Asia 2018 Technical Papers, p. 262. ACM (2018)
14. Tan, J., Echevarria, J., Gingold, Y.: Palette-based image decomposition, harmonization, and color transfer. arXiv preprint (2018). arXiv:1804.01225
15. Wah, C., Branson, S., Welinder, P., Perona, P., Belongie, S.: The caltech-ucsd birds-200-2011 dataset (2011)
16. Zhang, J., Cao, Y., Wang, Y., Wen, C., Chen, C.W.: Fully point-wise convolutional neural network for modeling statistical regularities in natural images. arXiv preprint (2018). arXiv:1801.06302
17. Hordley, S.D., Finlayson, G.D.: Re-evaluating colour constancy algorithms. In: Proceedings of the 17th International Conference on Pattern Recognition, 2004, ICPR 2004, vol. 1, pp. 76–79. IEEE (2004)
18. Ronneberger, O., Fischer, P., Brox, T.: U-Net: convolutional networks for biomedical image segmentation. In: Navab, N., Hornegger, J., Wells, W.M., Frangi, A.F. (eds.) MICCAI 2015. LNCS, vol. 9351, pp. 234–241. Springer, Cham (2015). https://doi.org/10.1007/978-3-319-24574-4_28
19. Tanno, R., Matsuo, S., Shimoda, W., Yanai, K.: DeepStyleCam: a real-time style transfer app on iOS. In: Amsaleg, L., Guðmundsson, G.Þ., Gurrin, C., Jónsson, B.Þ., Satoh, S. (eds.) MMM 2017. LNCS, vol. 10133, pp. 446–449. Springer, Cham (2017). https://doi.org/10.1007/978-3-319-51814-5_39
20. Tokumaru, M., Muranaka, N., Imanishi, S.: Color design support system considering color harmony. In: 2002 IEEE World Congress on Computational Intelligence, 2002 IEEE International Conference on Fuzzy Systems, FUZZ-IEEE 2002. Proceedings (Cat. No. 02CH37291). vol. 1, pp. 378–383. IEEE (2002)
21. Cho, W., et al.: Text2colors: guiding image colorization through text-driven palette generation. arXiv preprint (2018). arXiv:1804.04128
22. Cho, J., Yun, S., Mu Lee, K., Young Choi, J.: Palettenet: image recolorization with given color palette. In: Proceedings of the IEEE Conference on Computer Vision and Pattern Recognition Workshops, pp. 62–70 (2017)
23. Lin, S., Fisher, M., Dai, A., Hanrahan, P.: Layerbuilder: layer decomposition for interactive image and video color editing. arXiv preprint (2017). arXiv:1701.03754

On Creating Multimedia Interfaces for Hybrid Biological-Digital Art Installations

Carlos Castellanos[1(✉)], Bello Bello[2], Hyeryeong Lee[3], Mungyu Lee[3], Yoo Seok Lee[3], and In Seop Chang[3]

[1] School of Interactive Games and Media, Rochester Institute of Technology, Rochester, NY 14623, USA
carlos.castellanos@rit.edu

[2] Emerging Digital Practices Program, University of Denver, Denver, CO 80208, USA

[3] School of Earth Sciences and Environmental Engineering, Gwangju Institute of Science and Technology, Gwangju, KR, USA

Abstract. This paper discusses the application of real-time multimedia technologies to artworks that feature novel interfaces between human and non-human organisms (in this case plants and bacteria). Two projects are discussed: *Microbial Sonorities*, a real-time generative sound artwork based on bacterial voltages and machine learning, and *PlantConnect*, a real-time multimedia artwork that explores human-plant interaction via the human act of breathing, the bioelectrical and photosynthetic activity of plants and computational intelligence to bring the two together. Part of larger investigations into alternative models for the creation of shared experiences and understanding with the natural world, these projects explores complexity and emergent phenomena by harnessing the material agency of non-human organisms and the capacity of emerging multimedia technologies as mediums for information transmission, communication and interconnectedness between the human and non-human. While primarily focusing on technical descriptions of these projects, this paper also hopes to open up dialog about how the combination of emerging multimedia technologies and the often aleatoric unpredictability that living organisms can exhibit, can be beneficial to digital arts and entertainment applications.

Keywords: Electronic art · Interactive art · Plants · Microbial fuel cells · Clustering · Machine learning · Sound · Light · Breath · Computer vision · Bacteria · Photosynthesis · CO2

1 Introduction

In recent years, new media artists have increasingly utilized multimedia technologies to create interfaces with living organisms and the natural environment [1], in what is sometimes called "techno-ecological" practices [2]. Many of these artworks feature systems that might be referred to as biocybernetic interfaces: the bridging of the living world with the computational world. Artists marshal technologies such as robotics, bioenergy technologies, machine learning and computer vision to translate the often unseen processes of non-human organisms to human sensory ratios, in a speculative

Y. M. Ro et al. (Eds.): MMM 2020, LNCS 11961, pp. 139–150, 2020.
https://doi.org/10.1007/978-3-030-37731-1_12

attempt at creating some kind of meaningful and aesthetically potent connection between the two. The integration of biological systems has had an almost visceral appeal to artists, as systems may not only exhibit unexpected or unconceived patterns of behavior that purely digital or mechanical systems may not, but many artists are also attracted to the thematic blurring of boundaries between digital and biological worlds, as ways of experiencing the enigmatic "otherness" of non-human species [3].

The projects discussed in this paper feature plants, bacteria and microbial fuel cell technology (MFC). These are technologies and materials that are becoming of increasing interest to new media artists (see for example [2, 4]). More than just using digital technologies to bridge the living world with the computational world, what these kinds of works show us is that environmental and emerging bioenergy technologies and even the simple act of "speaking" to plants or "listening" to bacteria have cultural and aesthetic dimensions that should be further explored, with multimedia technologies having a role to play in that exploration. Indeed, all manner of digital arts and entertainment applications can benefit from the often aleatoric unpredictability that living organisms can exhibit.

In this paper, two projects by the author and his collaborators are discussed. The first is *Microbial Sonorities*, a real-time generative sound artwork based on bacterial voltages and machine learning. The second is *PlantConnect*, a real-time multimedia artwork that explores human-plant interaction via the human act of breathing, the bioelectrical and photosynthetic activity of plants and computational intelligence to bring the two together. The artistic motivations behind these projects center upon speculative investigations into alternative models for the creation of shared experiences and understanding with the natural world (in this case plants and bacteria). Thus the multimedia techniques employed (computer vision, machine learning, generative sound, etc.) are important in creating these experiences. We believe that by creating unconventional combinations, through various mediums and materials (in this case custom electronics, computational modeling, plants, bacteria, lights and generative sound), we are attempting to achieve new ways of looking at a particular aspect of human experience (in this case our relationship with plants and the microbial world)— recognizing how elements relate that maybe we didn't think related before. While mostly consisting of technical overviews, it is hoped that these works can facilitate a discussion about how multimedia systems can be modeled and constructed so as to better facilitate these experiences and be of use to artists, cultural mangers and cultural institutions.

2 A Primer on Microbial Fuel Cell Technology

Microbial fuel cells (MFCs) are an emerging bioenergy technology for generating electricity from biomass using microorganisms found in diverse environments such as wastewater, soil and lakes [5]. MFCs convert chemical energy to electrical energy via the action of anaerobic bacteria that metabolize organic matter. Generally, MFCs are used under the conditions of an aerobic cathode with air or oxygenated water and an anaerobic anode in wastewater or other organic matter (see Fig. 1). The organic matter is metabolized by the bacteria, generating electrons and protons. The electrons attach to the MFC's anode while at the cathode, oxygen together with electrons and protons are reduced to water. Positive hydrogen ions are also released and are directed through the membrane to the cathode side. In dual chamber designs, a proton exchange membrane is used as a separator between the cathode and anode, while single-chamber designs relay on the organic material (e.g. soil) as a natural separator, where the bottom is under anaerobic conditions and the top is aerobic (the cathode is exposed to air or oxygenated water). In addition to power generation, MFCs can also be used are part of or in conjunction with waste processing systems and remediation of contaminated lakes and rivers [6].

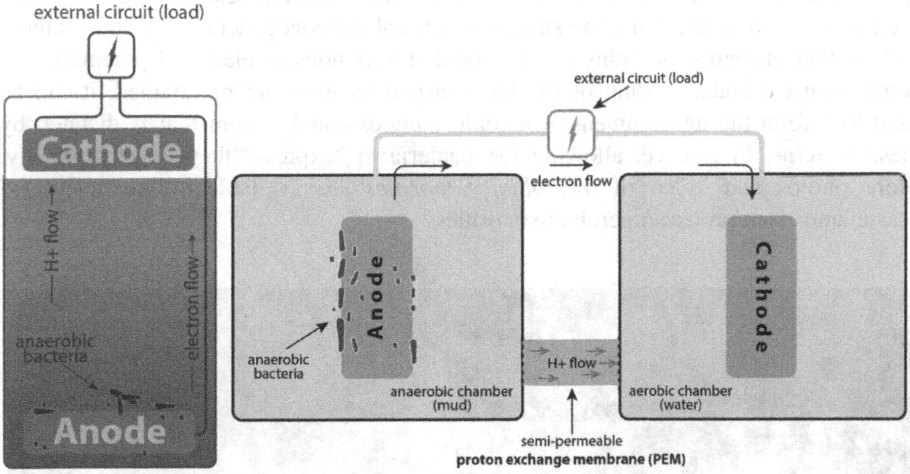

Fig. 1. Single-chamber (left) and dual chamber MFC designs.

Plant-based Microbial Fuel Cells. There are many types and implementations of MFC technology. *PlantConnect* uses an array of 16 plant microbial fuel cells (P-MFCs) as the core element of the system. P-MFCs use naturally occurring and known processes around the roots of plants (typically aquatic plants) to produce electricity [7]. The plant produces organic matter via photosynthesis under the influence of sunlight. Most of this organic matter ends up in the soil as root material or exudates where it is metabolized by anaerobic bacteria, resulting in the release of electrons as described above. P-MFCs have been placed on roofs as a sort of green roof electricity generation system [7].

3 Microbial Sonorities: A Hybrid Bio-Electronic Generative Sound System

Microbial Sonorities explores the use of sound to investigate the bioelectric and behavioral patterns of microorganisms (Fig. 2). Based upon inquiries into emerging bioenergy technologies and ecological practices as artifacts of cultural exploration, the piece features a hybrid biological-electronic system wherein variations in electrical potential from an array of microbial fuel cells are translated into rhythmic, amplitude and frequency modulations in modular electronic and software-based sound synthesizers. The research focuses on three primary areas: (1) Microbial Fuel Cells (MFCs), (2) Modular hardware and software synthesizers: The bioelectrical fluctuations of the MFCs are used as modulation and trigger sources for a Eurorack-based modular synthesizer and/or a custom-designed software synthesizer built in the Max/MSP/Jitter visual programming environment (http://cycling.com, hereafter referred to as "Max"). This entails building electronic circuits to amplify the electrical signals generated by the bacteria and software to translate the signals into control voltage (CV) sources appropriate for the synthesizer. (3) Machine Learning: Machine-learning algorithms are used as a way of interpreting the shifting electrical patterns generated by the bacteria, with statistical regression being used to predict variations in electrical potential. If a comprehensive understanding of the bioelectrical patterns can be attained, it can be used to inform the development of a sonic compositional system that is dictated by these patterns. In essence, allowing the bacteria to "express" themselves sonically. More photos and video of *Microbial Sonorities* are available online at https://ccastellanos.com/projects/microbial-sonorities/

Fig. 2. *Microbial Sonorities* installed at Washington state university, Pullman, Washington, USA in 2016. The modular synthesizers are shown in the center behind four microbial fuel cells.

3.1 System Overview

The current system set-up typically consists of four MFCs, a Eurorack modular synthesizer system, an Arduino microcontroller (arduino.cc) and the Max/MSP/Jitter visual programming environment (cycling74.com, hereafter referred to as "Max"). The biomatter used for the MFCs is usually fresh compost or if possible, benthic mud from a local lake or other aquatic body. Voltage from each MFC is amplified and connected to an analog input on the Arduino. In some cases it may also be plugged directly into the control voltage input on one of the Eurorack modules.

The piece operates on two temporal scales. The first, referred to as "immediate", consists of a simple linear mapping of voltage to pitch for each MFC. Transient voltage spikes are also detected and mapped to sound. The second time scale, "longitudinal" is a longer-term (from 48 h or greater) mixing of Eurorack synth patches. Each MFC is assigned a synthesizer patch according to its current "life stage". A life stage is simply a point in the overall voltage curve over which a typical MFC travels over the course of anywhere from 48 h to several weeks before it "dies" (i.e. when the bacteria run out of organic matter to metabolize. Four life stages have been identified and assigned a synthesizer patch. A regression curve, using a neural network, was then created to mix/transition between the four different sounds/patches. Training data for the network was created simply by drawing a curve in Max's **itable** object that matches a typical MFC voltage curve. The x coordinates of the **itable** represent discreet time steps (0-50 h), while the y coordinates represent voltages (0–1000 mV). While the piece is running, a running average of the voltage for each MFC is sent out to the neural network application once every 30 min as UDP messages. In essence then, the MFCs and the software together function as a sort of hybrid "smart mixer".

Machine Learning Model. The regression curve used for the mixing of synthesizer patches was created using a simple, three-layer neural network. It consisted of an input layer with two inputs for voltage and time, one hidden layer (with 3 nodes) and an output layer with two outputs representing the x/y coordinates of the quad mix. This model was copied four times (one for each MFC). The neural network was built using the Wekinator library (http://github.com/fiebrink1/wekinator).

4 PlantConnect: A Speculative Human-Plant Interface

An extension of *Microbial Sonorities*, *PlantConnect* (Fig. 3) measures the photosynthetic and bioelectrical activity from an array of P-MFCs and translates them into light and sound patterns using machine learning in real-time.

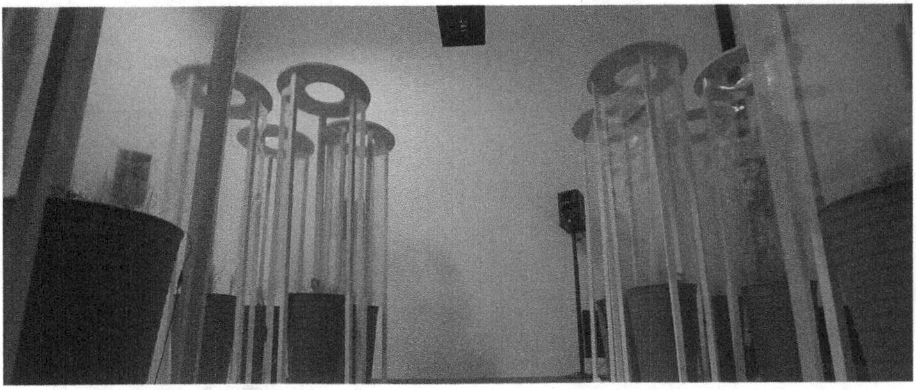

Fig. 3. The *PlantConnect* installation.

For this piece we began by asking: how might we utilize intelligent computational technologies to create systems that harness emerging bioenergy technologies and interface with the non-human world in such a way as to create novel aesthetic experiences? *PlantConnect* was exhibited in 2019 at the Asia Culture Center in Gwangju, Korea as part of the Arts & Creative Technology (ACT) Festival and the International

Symposium on Electronic Art (ISEA 2019). More photos and video of *PlantConnect* are available online at and https://ccastellanos.com/projects/plantconnect/.

4.1 System Overview

As seen in Fig. 4, when a participant blows or whistles into a CO2 sensor located within the array of plants, it causes the CO2 levels to surpass a baseline threshold. This in turn triggers an array of 16 grow lights and a set of software sound instruments. Participants thus receive an immediate visual and sonic response. The lights are directed at the plants (from 2 m above) and thus contribute to their photosynthesis. There is one light for each plant. The photosynthesis levels are obtained from housings containing a plant and a CO2 sensor placed near it (discussed below). When the light above the plant turns on, it causes the CO2 levels near the plant to decrease. These levels are translated into interpolation parameters for the software sound instruments and spatialization module of the system. Meanwhile the voltage signals from the P-MFCs are read by a standard microcontroller and analyzed to find the minimum & maximum voltage values. These thresholds determine the on/off patterns of the lights when they are triggered by human breath/CO2. Once the CO2 levels on the breath sensor fall below the baseline threshold, the lights turn off. This can take anywhere from 1 to 10 s.

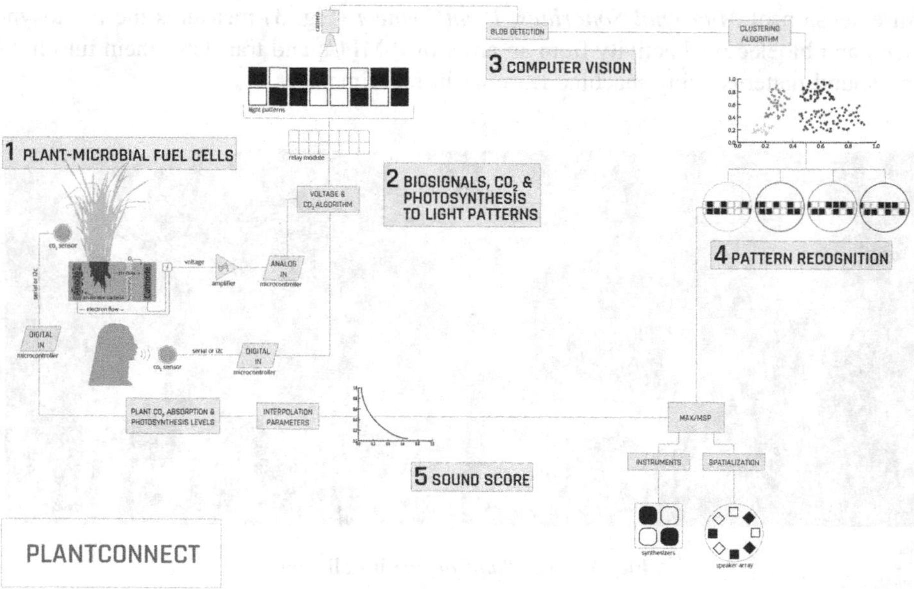

Fig. 4. *PlantConnect* system diagram.

Using two digital video cameras and a simple blob detection algorithm, the system then detects the on/off state of the lights in the light array, relative to the background.

This data is then sent to a clustering algorithm that performs rudimentary pattern recognition. This data is then sent to the sound instruments and spatialization module to create the generative sound environment. In this way, the machine learning algorithm —and by extension the plants—select instruments and alter their amplitude, duration, pitch, and other parameters. This is all discussed further in the succeeding sections below. A system diagram is shown in Fig. 4.

As mentioned above, when a participant blows or whistles into the CO2 sensor located in the center of the space, it triggers each grow light to turn on but only if the voltage of its associated P-MFC is above the requisite threshold. The result is an unpredictable and varied patterns of lights and sound that are experienced as a reaction by the plants to human breath and light. The entire sound, computer vision and machine learning portion of the system was built using Max (version 8.0.5). The project runs on two Apple Macintosh computers. One computer (the "CV/ML" computer) handles the computer vision and machine learning tasks, while the other (the "sound" computer) handles generative sound and communication with the microcontroller. Data is sent from the CV/ML computer as UDP messages from Max over a standard Ethernet connection to the sound computer that is also running Max, with the sound instruments loaded. The sensor readings, P-MFC voltage readings and light control system were built on the Arduino microcontroller platform. The following subsections detail each of the aforementioned elements of the system.

Plants and Plant Housings. The plants used in this project are Oryza Sativa (Asian rice, Fig. 5). The anodes are attached to insulated copper wire inside of a waterproof acrylic housing. They are then submerged about 5 cm below the surface so they are not exposed to oxygen. We have also built housings for the plants (Fig. 1). Though they also serve an aesthetic purpose in the piece, these housings are necessary for properly measuring changes in CO2 absorption from the plants themselves, irrespective of changes in the surrounding CO2 levels in the space. They also provide sufficient ventilation to allow for adequate air flow (and thus not risking the CO2 continually rising inside the housing) [8].

Fig. 5. P-MFCs for the *PlantConnect* project.

The P-MFCs were built using carbon fiber as the anode and cathode material (obtained from US Composites). Our design is taken mostly from [9]. Thus we refer the reader to that article for details of the design and construction of the P-MFCs for this project.

Biosignals, CO2, Light and Photosynthesis. All signal acquisition and light control is handled by a single Arduino Mega 2560 microcontroller. Acquiring voltages from the P-MFCs is a simple matter of connecting each cathode (which in this case is the positive lead) to an analog input of the Arduino. However, the voltages are not acquired from each individual P-MFC. Instead, groups of 4 P-MFCs are wired together in series to make a single voltage source that is then connected to an Arduino analog input. As there are 16 P-MFCs, this amounts to 4 groups of 4 P-MFCs (hereafter referred to as “P-MFC groups”) and thus a total of 4 voltage sources. The P-MFC groups are arranged in a reverse C arrangement.

While the system is running, the voltage signals in each MFC group are analyzed to continuously find the minimum & maximum values. These values are used to generate a set of dynamic thresholds. A total of four thresholds are generated, one for each light and P-MFC in the group. These thresholds determine which lights activate and thus determine the on/off patterns of the light array. The thresholds are spaced apart evenly from each other. For example if the minimum voltage value of a given P-MFC group is currently 10 mV and the maximum value is currently 100, then the two middle values will be 40 and 70. Each of these values will set each light in the group to an active state successively in a clockwise manner when it is surpassed. For example, light 1 is set to active when the voltage surpasses 10 mV, light 2 is set to active when the voltage surpasses 40 mV, light 6 set to active when 70 mV is surpassed and light 5 is set when 100 mV is surpassed. When a participant blows on the CO2 breath sensor (and the sensor value goes above the predetermined threshold) it will trigger the active lights to actually turn on. The lights themselves are 20 W led grow lights (obtained from ackegrowlight.com) that emit a warm white color. They are connected through two 8-channel relays, which are controlled by the Arduino. When plants are actively photosynthesizing, they absorb greater amounts of CO2 than when they are not photosynthesizing (e.g. at night). In our project, the P-MFCs' levels of photosynthesis are obtained by measuring CO2 near the plants. The sensor (a SenseAir K-30FR obtained from CO2Meter.com) returns the CO2 levels in parts per million and sends the data via a standard serial/RS232 connection to the Arduino. The breath CO2 sensor is also connected via serial/RS-232 to the Arduino. Here, we keep a running median of the nine most recent CO2 levels. This helps to establish a baseline level with respect to the surrounding environment. Thus the threshold for triggering lights and sound is a predetermined level above this baseline (20 ppm by default). Readings are taken at a rate of two per second.

Computer Vision. A simple blob detection algorithm is used to differentiate the lights from the background. This is a relatively simple task as the piece is installed in a rather dark space. In order to achieve blob detection easily and reliably within the Max environment, a third party library, **cv.jit** (https://jmpelletier.com/cvjit/) was used. The **cv.jit.blobs.centroids** object returns a list of blob centroid coordinates. Two USB digital video cameras (Mobius Maxi, www.mobius-actioncam.com) were mounted between the plants and the grow lights (just over 2 m from the floor) to provide the video feeds. They were pointed directly at the lights and connected to the CV/ML computer running Max. The two video feeds were combined and together produced a streaming image that captured all the lights in the space. The video feed was then virtually cut up into 4 rows and 8 columns, for a total 32 cells. In our default configuration, the video image is 640 × 360 pixels. Thus each grid is 80 × 90 pixels. This grid is the reason for using blob detection (as opposed to simply reading the on/off states from the microcontroller). The size of the lights and the fact that each light panel takes up to 500 ms to reach full brightness means that a single light may actually register as more than one blob as it may spill over to another row or column. Both of these factors serve to add an element of variety and aleatoric behavior to the system (for example the system may very quickly switch between several different cluster assignments for the same light pattern, resulting in an erratic "glitchy" sound).

Blobs are analyzed and the x/y coordinate of each blob's centroid (center of mass) is returned. A list of 32 binary numbers corresponding to the location of each centroid within the grid of 32 cells is then output, with 0 being "off" and 1 being "on"). This list determines which "voice" of the sound instrument (which essentially corresponds to pitch) gets played. For example, if the first light is turned on and the blob centroid is located at pixel location (40, 55), index 0 (the first item in the list) will be set to 1 and thus will trigger the sound instrument to play its lowest pitch. Depending on how the system is configured, the duration of each triggered voice is set to a fixed amount at runtime or is determined by whether the blob detection algorithm recognizes the light (essentially as long as the light is on, its corresponding voice stays on). Pitches (or which voice gets played) are arranged left-to-right and top-to-bottom in the 4 × 8 grid. Thus the first voice 1 would be the top left and voice 32, the bottom right of the grid.

Clustering/Pattern Recognition. The same list of 32 binary numbers that is sent to the sound instruments is also sent to the machine learning module. In this project we apply a fuzzy c-means clustering algorithm to the data. Fuzzy c-means clustering (FCM) [10] is a method of clustering (a type of unsupervised machine learning) that allows a given data point to belong to more than one cluster. A membership grade (in our case a floating point number between 0.0 and 1.0) is calculated for each data point which indicates the degree to which that point belongs to each cluster. Frequently used in pattern recognition tasks, FCM assigns membership in a cluster by calculating the distance between the cluster centroid and the data point. The closer the data point is to the cluster centroid the higher its membership grade for that cluster (i.e. the closer it is to 1.0).

In our project, we use the **ml.fcm** object from the **ml.*** package for Max [11]. We first initialize the object by assigning it a fuzz coefficient of 1.05, selecting the number of clusters to calculate (in our case four) and a termination threshold of 0.01 (the default). The fuzz factor effects how "crisp" or "fuzzy" the cluster memberships are (higher numbers return fuzzier membership grades), while the termination threshold effects the speed and accuracy of the cluster calculation (higher values produce quicker, more approximate clusters). We then generate one thousand random data points as a sort of training set. Each data point has 32 dimensions (corresponding to the possible location of each centroid within the grid of 32 cells) and consists of ones and zeros.

Once this is done and the live video feed is turned on, the system is ready to perform real-time clustering of incoming light patterns. When the system is running and new data on the light on/off patterns is received, a query is made to the **ml.fcm** object which then outputs a list of 4 membership grades (one for each cluster). These numbers are used to set the volume of each sound instrument (0.0 = minimum volume, 1.0 = maximum volume). In essence, the FCM algorithm is used as a sort of mixer for the sound instruments, generating a variety of sounds that would be unlikely or even impossible for a human-controlled mixer to achieve.

Generative Sound. The real-time data representing the shifting light patterns along with the output of the FCM algorithm are translated into a series of UDP messages that control the sound instruments and a spatialization module within the Max environment. These messages essentially function as note on/off messages to "play" the instruments. Five sound instruments have been constructed, each with its own distinct timbre. Four of these instruments correspond to the four cluster memberships generated by the FCM algorithm (and will henceforth be referred to as the "cluster instruments"). These instruments require human interaction (via breath/CO2) to be activated. A fifth instrument is the default instrument. It plays continuously, requiring no human action to be heard.

Instruments and Data Mappings. The default sound instrument simply maps the voltage levels from each P-MFC group to pitch (the higher the voltage, the higher the pitch). In addition, any transient spikes in the CO2 levels from any of the P-MFCs are also sonified by the default instrument (and are heard as transient spikes in the pitch). The cluster instruments receive CO2 levels as well. However in this case we add up the CO2 level of each plant of each P-MFC group and get an average of those readings. Then we take the five most recent averages and obtain the median value. These values are then used as interpolation parameters for the spatialization module (discussed below).

Finally, the CO2 readings are also collected and used to construct an envelope function (using the Max **function** object, essentially a breakpoint function editor) that is used as a modulation source for the cluster instruments. Each instrument uses this modulation data differently. For example, one instrument uses it to crossfade between different wavetables, while another uses it to alter the depth factor (the amount of deviation around a center frequency) of modulation oscillator and to crossfade between two control signals.

PlantConnect also features 8-speaker sound spatialization using circular panning. By default, sounds related to readings taken from each P-MFC group are sent to the two adjacent speakers closest to that group. In addition, whenever a light is triggered above a particular P-MFC in a group, the sound instrument will be heard on the two adjacent speakers closest to that group, in a manner similar to L-R panning. The idea being that the sound instrument is heard near the P-MFC whose lights are currently on (and thus triggering sound). Finally, CO2 levels of each P-MFC influence the amount spatialization spread between all the speakers. The median value of the five most recent averaged CO2 readings of each P-MFC group is used to determine the amount that the triggered sound instrument spreads from its "home" location (the two adjacent speakers closest to it) to the other speakers. When triggered, the sound spreads in both a clockwise and counter clockwise direction from this home location.

5 Evaluation

This work comes from an art and design tradition, rather than the science and engineering approaches underlying most research on computational media and human computer interaction. Scientific methods such as usability testing and statistical data analysis, which try to arrive at objective facts about a technology being evaluated, stand in contrast to the more subjective and interpretive approaches taken in interactive and new media art. Whereas the former is more utilitarian, an artistic approach to the design of a technological system is often centered upon meaning, experience and the systems' aesthetic and cultural implications rather than the technologies used to implement them. Furthermore, evaluations are often done informally in studio or gallery settings or via descriptions and scenarios [12]. This reflects a concern with the evocative potential of the work and its ability to offer new insights and spur the imagination [13]. It may even require a less technically rigid, "under-engineered" design approach in order to increase the range of possible (even if less reliable) outcomes [14], thus making traditional scientific and engineering measures less relevant (and even counterproductive). In recent years, there has been a move away from a singular focus on narrow functional and utility-oriented evaluation of interactive technologies towards broader concerns with understanding of activities that are less goal directed and more experience-based [15].

While to date, no formal user studies have been performed or data collected on the works discussed here, informal participant observation have been performed by Castellanos that may infer as to the participant experience. In *Microbial Sonorities* for example, two days of viewer observation revealed a consistent pattern of behavior. Almost everyone who observed the piece would bend down and lean in very closely to observe the MFCs from just inches away. In *PlantConnect* (also after two days of observation), after the initial surprise of the triggering of lights and sound, participants would again observe closely (in this case by often walking around and looking up as well as down and close to the plants). In all, most viewers stayed with the works considerably longer than is typical for most artworks [16], and did so in a manner (looking around, perhaps confused but curious or even delighted) that is suggests that they appreciated (if only partially "getting") what was going on the works (one observer referred to *Microbial Sonorities* as a "swamp music" system which is perhaps as good explanation as any the artist could give). Though the evaluations presented here are preliminary and provisional it suggests that these works—after the initial novelty and surprise—evoke a curiousness about the systems and perhaps an awareness that there are process and possibilities being revealed that were perhaps previously unknown or not considered.

6 Conclusions

The projects presented here are sort of hybrid art/science research projects exploring the cultural and aesthetic dimensions that arise from novel intersections of environmental data, emerging bioenergy technologies, machine learning and "primitive" living organisms. They showcase possible novel uses of multimedia techniques and technologies in arts and entertainment.

Special thanks to the Energy and Biotechnology Laboratory, School of Earth Sciences and Environmental Engineering, Gwangju Institute of Science and Technology (GIST) for their invaluable assistance.

References

1. Weintraub, L.: To Life!: Eco Art in Pursuit of a Sustainable Planet. University of California Press, Berkeley (2012)
2. Smite, R., Smits, R.: Emerging techno-ecological art practices - towards renewable futures. Acoust. Space **11**, 129–139 (2012)
3. van Eck, W., Lamers, M.H.: Hybrid biological-digital systems in artistic and entertainment computing. Leonardo **46**(2), 151–158 (2013)
4. Interspecifics. http://interspecifics.cc/work/. Accessed 17 Oct 2019/10/17
5. Logan, B.: Microbial Fuel Cells. Wiley-Interscience, Hoboken (2008)
6. An, J., et al.: Floating-type microbial fuel cell (FT-MFC) for treating organic-contaminated water. Environ. Sci. Technol. **43**(5), 1642–1647 (2009)
7. Helder, M., et al.: Electricity production with living plants on a green roof: environmental performance of the plant-microbial fuel cell. Biofuels, Bioprod. Biorefin. **7**(1), 52–64 (2013)
8. Murphy, J.Y., Ham, J.M., Owensby, C.E.: Design and testing of a novel gas exchange chamber. Acad. Res. J. Agric. Sci. Res. **2**(3), 34–46 (2014)
9. Moqsud, M.A., et al.: Compost in plant microbial fuel cell for bioelectricity generation. Waste Manage. **36**, 63–69 (2015)
10. Dunn, J.C.: A fuzzy relative of the ISODATA process and its use in detecting compact well-separated clusters. J. Cybernet. **3**, 32–57 (1973)
11. Smith, B.D., Garnett, G.E.: Unsupervised play: machine learning toolkit for max. In: Proceedings of NIME 2012 (2012)
12. Gaver, W., Martin, H.: Alternatives: exploring information appliances through conceptual design proposals. In: Proceedings of CHI 2000 (Den Haag, The Netherlands). ACM Press, New York (2000)
13. Gaver, B.: Provocative awareness. Comput. Support. Coop. Work (CSCW) **11**(3), 475–493 (2002)
14. Penny, S.: Embodied cultural agents: at the intersection of art, robotics and cognitive science. In: AAAI Socially Intelligent Agents Symposium, pp. 103–105. AAAI Press (1997)
15. Jeon, M., Fiebrink, R., Edmonds, E.A., Herath, D.: From rituals to magic: interactive art and HCI of the past, present, and future. Int. J. Hum.-Comput. Stud. **131**, 108–119 (2019)
16. Cascone, S.: The Average Person Spends 27 Seconds Looking at a Work of Art. Now, 166 Museums Are Joining Forces to Ask You to Slow Down. Artnet News, April 4, 2019. https://news.artnet.com/art-world/slow-art-day-2019-1508566. Accessed 17 Oct 2019

Image Captioning Based on Visual and Semantic Attention

Haiyang Wei, Zhixin Li(✉), and Canlong Zhang

Guangxi Key Lab of Multi-source Information Mining and Security,
Guangxi Normal University, Guilin 541004, China
lizx@gxnu.edu.cn

Abstract. Most of the existing image captioning methods only use the visual information of the image to guide the generation of the captions, lack the guidance of effective scene semantic information, and the current visual attention mechanism cannot adjust the focus intensity on the image. In this paper, we first propose an improved visual attention model. At each time step, we calculate the focus intensity coefficient of the attention mechanism through the context information of the model, and automatically adjust the focus intensity of the attention mechanism through the coefficient, so as to extract more accurate image visual information. In addition, we represent the scene semantic information of the image through some topic words related to the image scene, and add them to the language model. We use attention mechanism to determine the image visual information and scene semantic information that the model pays attention to at each time step, and combine them to guide the model to generate more accurate and scene-specific captions. Finally, we evaluate our model on MSCOCO dataset. The experimental results show that our approach can generate more accurate captions, and outperforms many recent advanced models on various evaluation metrics.

Keywords: Image captioning · Visual attention · Scene semantics · Encoder-decoder framework

1 Introduction

Image captioning is to generate a reasonable natural language description for a given image according to its content. It is an important research field of artificial intelligence. The image captioning contains the recognition of image content and the work of natural language generation. It is a cross-cutting task. The image usually contains a large amount of explicit and implicit visual semantic information, but there is a semantic gap between the information modes of images and texts. It is difficult to fully represent the visual information in an image by natural language. Recent studies of image captioning show that methods based on deep learning can handle this complex task. These approaches are usually based on an encoder-decoder framework from machine translation, and the main idea of which is to treat the image captioning task as translating an image into a

Y. M. Ro et al. (Eds.): MMM 2020, LNCS 11961, pp. 151–162, 2020.
https://doi.org/10.1007/978-3-030-37731-1_13

text description. A CNN is used as the encoder for image encoding and RNN as the decoder to generate text descriptions. This approach has achieved a breakthrough in image captioning, so the encoder-decoder framework has become the standard configuration of image captioning algorithms.

Although some progress has been made, image captioning is still a challenging task. How to make better use of image information? How to generate descriptive sentences more accurately? Still a question to consider. At present, visual attention mechanisms play an important role in image captioning. At each time step, the attention mechanism can focus on some salient regions of the image according to the current contextual information of the decoder, so as to provide accurate and effective visual information guidance for word generation. However, the current visual attention still has problems. Most of the visual attention is the 'soft' attention mechanism [20], and the attention distribution is generated on the image regions by softmax function. However, due to the calculation method of softmax function, if the numerical range of the incoming softmax function is large, the generated attention distribution will be relatively concentrated, and the model will be relatively 'hard'. If the numerical range is small, the model will be relatively 'soft'. In the process of captions generation, the model needs to pay attention with different focus intensity to the image for the generation of different types of words. For example, when generating nouns, the model may require 'hard' attention, focusing on some specific objects of the image. When generating conjunctions and prepositions, the model may require 'soft' attention, distracting attention on all regions of the image. In addition, most image captioning systems lack guidance of scene semantic information. Most image captioning systems use CNNs to extract image features directly, or use object detectors to extract the features of some salient regions on the image, to represent the information of the image. In fact, the potential scene semantic information in the image is rarely utilized. However, for the image captions generation, the scene semantic information is very important [4]. This is because there may be different scene meanings for the same visual region features. For example, the same grass, the scene can be the grass of the park or the football field.

To resolve the above-mentioned problems, we propose an image captioning approach based on visual and semantic attention. The overall structure of our model is shown in Fig. 1. First, we introduced a focus intensity coefficient to improve the traditional visual attention mechanism. The focus intensity coefficient is used to adjust the focus intensity of the attention mechanism on the image at each time step, so that the model can capture more accurate visual information. Furthermore, we added the scene semantic information of the image to the language model. Specifically, we used the LDA model to cluster all the caption texts in the dataset, and then used the topic category of the caption texts to represent the scene category of images. The topic category was represented by a series of topic words obtained by clustering. Because the scene topic information of the image was obtained by analyzing the caption texts, we obtained some global information of the generated text, which allowed us to predict which important words would be included in the sentence to be generated.

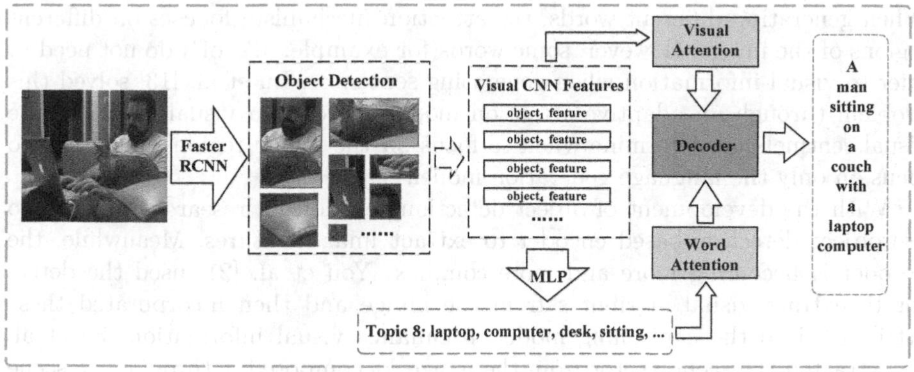

Fig. 1. The overall structure diagram of our model.

In each time step, we used the attention mechanism to determine which topic words the decoder would focuses on, and combined the visual information of the image to guide the decoder to generate more accurate captions.

The main contributions of this paper are as follows:

- We propose an improved visual attention model that extracts the visual information of the image more accurately by automatically adjusting the focus intensity of the attention mechanism.
- We propose a scene semantic extraction method that combines unsupervised and supervised methods, and incorporate the scene words into the decoder as a priori knowledge through the attention mechanism.
- We combine visual features and scene semantic features. Make full use of the visual and semantic information of the image to guide the decoder to generate more accurate captions.
- We perform a set of experiments on MSCOCO dataset, and the results prove the effectiveness of our method quantitatively and qualitatively.

2 Related Works

The early image captioning Encoder-Decoder framework [9,14,19] simply connects CNN and RNN. The vector output from the last fully connected layer of the CNN is used to represent the features of the image. However, this approach can only obtain the global features of the image, which means that not only will a part of the image features be lost, but also that the image in the decoding process will not be able to be analyzed. In order to better encode image information, Xu et al. [20] introduced the visual attention mechanism in the image captioning system. They remove the last fully connected layer of CNN and use the output feature vector of the convolutional layer as the spatial features of the image. At each time step, image attention features are connected with word embedding vectors and input into the LSTM to predict the generated word.

When generating different words, the attention mechanism focuses on different regions of the image. However, some words(for example: ‘a’, ‘of’) do not need to refer to visual information when generating sentences. Lu et al. [13] solved this problem through an adaptive attention model based on a visual sentinel. The visual sentinel can determine when to focus on the image regions and when to focus on only the language generation model.

With the development of object detection technology, researchers began to use object detection-based encoder to extract image features. Meanwhile, the decoder is becoming more and more complex. You et al. [21] used the detector to extract visual attributes from the image and then incorporated these attributes into the captioning model to enhance visual information. Fu et al. [5] extracted the scene vector from the image, decomposed it through the scene LSTM, and then added the scene context to the model. Anderson et al. [1] proposed a bottom-up and top-down attention model. They used the Faster R-CNN [3] object detector to select a set of candidate regions with high confidence, and used the average convolutional features of these regions as the visual features of the image. Gu et al. [6] proposed a coarse-to-fine multi-level prediction framework. They use multiple decoders to generate captions, and each decoder runs on the basis of the previous level, producing increasingly refined image captions. Jiang et al. [8] proposed a recurrent fusion network (RFNet). They use multiple encoders to extract image features, and use multiple LSTMs to fuse the information in a recurrent way.

3 Models

3.1 Overview

Encoder. We use the pre-trained Faster R-CNN [3] to extract features of a set of candidate regions from the input image as image encoding features. The encoded image features can be represented as $\boldsymbol{V} = (\boldsymbol{v}_1, \boldsymbol{v}_2, ..., \boldsymbol{v}_L)$, where L is the number of candidate regions in the image. For each selected region i, $\boldsymbol{v}_i \in \mathbb{R}^C$ represents the average convolutional feature of the region.

Decoder. In the classic Encoder-Decoder model, LSTM is typically used as the decoder to build a language generation model. At each time step $t \in [1, T]$, the attention feature $\boldsymbol{V}_t$ of the image and the word y_{t-1} generated by the previous time step are input into the LSTM. The LSTM outputs the hidden state $\boldsymbol{h}_t$ and then predicts the generated word by $\boldsymbol{h}_t$. In this way, the LSTM decodes step by step to generate the final word sequence $\boldsymbol{Y} = (y_1, y_2, ..., y_T)$.

$$\boldsymbol{V}_t = Att(\boldsymbol{V}, \boldsymbol{h}_{t-1}) \tag{1}$$

$$\boldsymbol{x}_t = \boldsymbol{W}_e y_{t-1} \tag{2}$$

$$\boldsymbol{h}_t = LSTM([\boldsymbol{V}_t; \boldsymbol{x}_t], \boldsymbol{h}_{t-1}) \tag{3}$$

$$y_t \sim \boldsymbol{p}_t = softmax(\boldsymbol{h}_t) \tag{4}$$

where $Att(\cdot)$ is the visual attention function, which is used to calculate the attention features of the image. $\boldsymbol{x}_t$ is the word embedding vector, $\boldsymbol{h}_t \in \mathbb{R}^H$ is the hidden state of the LSTM, and $\boldsymbol{p}_t \in \mathbb{R}^{|D|}$ is the probability vector to predict the generated word(D is the dictionary containing all the words).

Visual Attention Mechanism. The visual attention mechanism originates from the study of human vision, which is essentially the weighted integration of image regions features $\boldsymbol{V} = (\boldsymbol{v}_1, \boldsymbol{v}_2, ..., \boldsymbol{v}_L)$, $\boldsymbol{V}_t = \sum_{i=1}^{L} \alpha_{t,i}\boldsymbol{v}_i$. The weight distribution is calculated according to the hidden state $\boldsymbol{h}_{t-1}$ of the previous step and the visual features of the image.

$$e_{t,i} = \boldsymbol{W}_a^T \tanh(\boldsymbol{W}_v \boldsymbol{v}_i + \boldsymbol{W}_h \boldsymbol{h}_{t-1}) \tag{5}$$

$$\alpha_{t,i} = \frac{\exp(e_{t,i})}{\sum_{i=1}^{L} \exp(e_{t,i})} \tag{6}$$

where $\boldsymbol{W}_v \in \mathbb{R}^{K \times C}, \boldsymbol{W}_h \in \mathbb{R}^{K \times H}$ and $\boldsymbol{W}_a \in \mathbb{R}^{K}$. The $\alpha_{t,i}$ is the attention weight of the i-th image region at the t-time step.

3.2 Improved Visual Attention Model

In the process of captions generation, due to the different types of words, the model needs different focus intensity to integrate visual information for the generation of different words. As shown in Eq. (6), the traditional visual attention mechanism output the final attention distribution through the softmax function. If the numerical range of e is large, the exponentiation will further widen the gap between the numerical values, and the weight distribution of the final output will be relatively concentrated; otherwise, the weight distribution will be relatively dispersed. Therefore, we propose an adaptive focus intensity visual attention. The model can control the focus intensity of visual attention and integrate visual information better for different generated words.

We set a focus intensity coefficient η to control the focus intensity of the visual attention mechanism: $\eta_t = \lambda^{\beta_t}$, where λ is a hyperparameter, β is obtained by learning from the model itself.

$$\beta_t = \tanh(\boldsymbol{W}_b^T \bar{\boldsymbol{V}} + \boldsymbol{W}_d^T \boldsymbol{h}_{t-1}) \tag{7}$$

where $\boldsymbol{W}_b \in \mathbb{R}^C, \boldsymbol{W}_d \in \mathbb{R}^H$, $\bar{\boldsymbol{V}}$ represents the average features of all regions of the image. Add the focus intensity coefficient to Eq. (6) that becomes:

$$\alpha_{t,i} = \frac{\exp(\eta_t e_{t,i})}{\sum_{i=1}^{L} \exp(\eta_t e_{t,i})} \tag{8}$$

We apply the improved visual attention mechanism to the decoder structure proposed by Anderson et al. [1] to construct the language model. The structure is shown in Fig. 2, where IV-Att is our improved visual attention mechanism. The specific decoding operations are as follows:

$$\boldsymbol{h}_t^V = LSTM^V([\bar{\boldsymbol{V}}; \boldsymbol{x}_t; \boldsymbol{h}_{t-1}^L], \boldsymbol{h}_{t-1}^V) \tag{9}$$

$$\boldsymbol{V}_t = Att(\boldsymbol{V}, \boldsymbol{h}_t^V) \tag{10}$$

$$\boldsymbol{h}_t^L = LSTM^L([\boldsymbol{V}_t; \boldsymbol{h}_t^V], \boldsymbol{h}_{t-1}^L) \tag{11}$$

$$y_t \sim \boldsymbol{p}_t = softmax(\boldsymbol{h}_t^L) \tag{12}$$

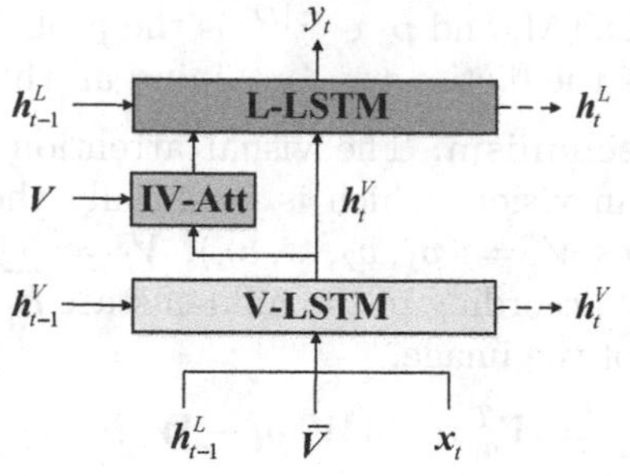

Fig. 2. The improved visual attention captioning model.

At each time step, V-LSTM is use to integrate current information and provide context information input for the attention mechanism. The L-LSTM is used to predict word generation.

3.3 Scene Semantic Information Extraction

At present, most image captioning systems lack the guidance of scene semantic information. However, for image captioning, the scene semantic information is very important for sentence generation. In this section, we introduce how to extract the scene semantic information from images.

We first use an unsupervised method to cluster all caption texts in the dataset. Specifically, we combine multiple descriptive sentences of each image in the dataset into one document, and then use LDA (Latent Dirichlet Allocation) model to cluster all the documents. All caption documents in the dataset are divided into N topic categories, each of which is represented by a series of topic words. We choose the M words with the highest probability to represent a topic category $U_i = \{w_{i,1}, w_{i,2}, w_{i,3}, ..., w_{i,M}\}$, $i \in [1, N]$. After classification, the topic category of caption document is taken as the scene category of the corresponding image.

Next, we use the classified image data to train a MLP (Multi-Layer Perception) by supervised learning method. Input the visual features of the image, and output the scene topic category corresponding to the image, so as to classify the images without captions.

3.4 Combine Image Vision and Scene Semantics

To enable the model to generate more accurate and scene-appropriate captions, we propose an image captioning approach that combines image vision and scene semantics. We use some topic words to represent the scene semantic information of the image and add them to the language model, so that the model can get some scene information of the image. Furthermore, combine the visual information of the image to guide the model to generate more accurate captions.

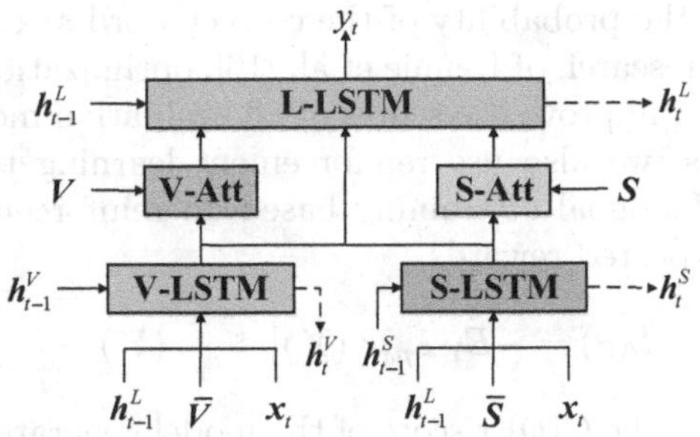

Fig. 3. The captioning model combining image vision and scene semantics.

We expand on the structure of Fig. 2, adding scene semantic information of the image to the model to guide the generation of captions. Figure 3 is our structure diagram, where S-LSTM represents the scene LSTM and S-Att represents the scene word attention mechanism. The specific operations are as follows:

$$\boldsymbol{S} = \boldsymbol{W}_e U_i \tag{13}$$

$$\boldsymbol{h}_t^S = LSTM^S([\bar{\boldsymbol{S}}; \boldsymbol{x}_t; \boldsymbol{h}_{t-1}^L], \boldsymbol{h}_{t-1}^S) \tag{14}$$

$$\boldsymbol{S}_t = Att(\boldsymbol{S}, \boldsymbol{h}_t^S) \tag{15}$$

where U_i represents the scene topic words of the image, and we transform them into the word embedding vector $\boldsymbol{S}$,$\boldsymbol{S} \in \mathbb{R}^{M \times H}$. $\bar{\boldsymbol{S}}$ represents the average feature of M words. Similar to V-LSTM, S-LSMT is used to integrate current information and provide context information input for the scene attention mechanism. In addition, we set up a control gate to control the importance of current visual information and scene information.

$$\boldsymbol{g}_t = \sigma(\boldsymbol{W}_g[\boldsymbol{h}_t^V; \boldsymbol{h}_t^S; \boldsymbol{V}_t; \boldsymbol{S}_t]) \tag{16}$$

$$\boldsymbol{V}_t = \boldsymbol{g}_t \odot \boldsymbol{V}_t; \boldsymbol{S}_t = (1 - \boldsymbol{g}_t) \odot \boldsymbol{S}_t; \tag{17}$$

$$\boldsymbol{h}_t^L = LSTM^L([\boldsymbol{h}_t^V; \boldsymbol{h}_t^S; \boldsymbol{V}_t; \boldsymbol{S}_t], \boldsymbol{h}_{t-1}^L) \tag{18}$$

where $\boldsymbol{g}_t \in \mathbb{R}^H$, $\odot$ denotes the vector dot product. Finally, the image attention information $\boldsymbol{V}_t$, the scene words attention information $\boldsymbol{S}_t$, the hidden state $\boldsymbol{h}_t^V$ and $\boldsymbol{h}_t^S$ are input into L-LSTM together, and the output $\boldsymbol{h}_t^L$ is used to predict the word output at the current time step.

3.5 Training Objective

In the training of the model, we first use the cross entropy loss to train. Minimize the cross entropy loss of the model by giving the reference sentence $\boldsymbol{Y} = (y_1, y_2, ..., y_T)$ of the image:

$$L(\theta) = -\sum_{t=1}^{T} \log p_t(y_t) \tag{19}$$

That is to maximize the probability of the correct word at each time step.

According to the research of Rennie et al. [16], optimization of the evaluation metric CIDEr [18] can improve the scores of all evaluation metrics of the model. To get better results, we also use reinforcement learning to further optimize the CIDEr metric. The goal of training based on reinforcement learning is to minimize negative expected rewards.

$$L(\theta) = -E_{\boldsymbol{Y} \sim p_\theta}[r(\boldsymbol{Y})] \approx -r(\boldsymbol{Y}) \tag{20}$$

where $r(\boldsymbol{Y})$ represents the CIDEr score of the model generated sentence $\boldsymbol{Y}$. The gradient $\nabla_\theta L(\theta)$ can be approximated by the Monte Carlo method as:

$$\begin{aligned} \nabla_\theta L(\theta) &= -E_{\boldsymbol{Y} \sim p_\theta}[r(\boldsymbol{Y}) \nabla_\theta \log p_\theta(\boldsymbol{Y})] \\ &\approx -r(\boldsymbol{Y}) \nabla_\theta \log p_\theta(\boldsymbol{Y}) \end{aligned} \tag{21}$$

We follow the SCST training method proposed by Rennie et al. [16], using sentence $\hat{\boldsymbol{Y}}$ generated by the model during testing as a baseline.

$$\nabla_\theta L(\theta) \approx -(r(\boldsymbol{Y}) - r(\hat{\boldsymbol{Y}})) \nabla_\theta \log p_\theta(\boldsymbol{Y}) \tag{22}$$

The training method based on reinforcement learning makes the model consistent in the training and testing process. It optimizes the sentence generation directly on the evaluation metric, which can greatly improve the overall performance of the model.

4 Experiments

4.1 Dataset and Metric

We conduct experiments in MSCOCO dataset. 5000 images for verification and 5000 images for testing. The training set contains 113,287 images, each image contains 5 manually annotated sentences. We preprocess the text by analyzing the captions text of the MSCOCO dataset. We replace low-frequency words that occur less than 5 times with 'UNK' to create a dictionary containing 9466 words. The maximum length of the captions is set to 16. Finally, we use the BLEU(1-4)(B) [15], METEOR(M) [2], ROUGE-L(R) [11], CIDEr(C) [18] and SPICE(S) [2] as evaluation metrics to evaluate the quality of the generated sentences.

4.2 Implementation Details

We encode the input image using the Faster R-CNN [3] pre-trained on the Visual Genome Dataset. Each image selects 36 candidate regions, and each region is represented by a 2048-dimensional vector output from ResNet [7]. The input image is encoded into a matrix of 36 × 2048. In the process of scene semantic extraction, we cluster all caption documents of the dataset into 60 topic categories, and each category selects the top 20 words with the highest probability to represent. In the model, the number of neurons in the LSTM is set to 1024. The size of the attention layer and the word embedding layer are also 1024. The focus intensity coefficient λ in the attention mechanism is set to 5.

In the training process, the model is trained with Adam optimizer [10] under the cross-entropy loss. The initial learning rate is 4×10^{-4}, and the batch size is 100. Then, we run the reinforcement learning-based training method to optimize the CIDEr evaluation metric. At this stage, the learning rate is 5×10^{-5}. At the end of each training epoch, we evaluate our model on the validation set. Finally, we choose the model with the highest CIDEr score on the verification set for testing. During the test, we use the beam search to generate sentences, and the beam size is set to 5.

4.3 Results and Analysis

Quantitative Analysis. Table 1 shows the performance comparison of our model with the baseline model on MSCOCO dataset, where IVAIC represents the improved visual attention model and VASS represents the model that combines image visual and scene semantics. It can be seen that our model shows significant improvement compared with the baseline model. For cross entropy loss training, although the BLEU-1 score of our model is slightly worse than the baseline model, it is significantly higher than the baseline model in other evaluation metrics. After CIDEr optimization, our model outperformed the baseline method in all evaluation metrics, especially the BLEU-4 score improved by 2.6 and the CIDEr score improved by 6.6. This is mainly because our visual model can adjust the focus intensity of the attention mechanism and extract more accurate visual information. Moreover, the scene semantic information is added to the model, so that the model can obtain more prior knowledge and generate better captions. Table 2 shows the performance comparison of our model with other advanced models. It can be seen that our model still has a strong competitive advantage. The final results fully demonstrate the effectiveness of our model.

Table 1. Performance comparison with baseline model.

Approach	Cross-Entropy Loss						CIDEr Optimization					
	B-1	B-4	M	R	C	S	B-1	B-4	M	R	C	S
Up-Down [1]	**77.2**	36.2	27.0	56.4	113.5	20.3	79.8	36.3	27.7	56.9	120.1	21.4
IVAIC	76.5	36.2	27.6	56.4	113.7	20.5	79.5	37.9	27.8	58.1	122.3	21.5
VASS	76.9	**36.4**	**27.9**	**56.5**	**114.0**	**20.8**	**80.5**	**38.9**	**28.3**	**58.8**	**126.7**	**21.7**

Qualitative Analysis. Because the images of the dataset have no real scene category label, it is impossible to show the quality of scene category classification from a quantitative perspective. Therefore, we instead show the effect of scene classification from a qualitative perspective. Figure 4 shows our scene classification effect. It can be seen that our method can classify images well and extract

Table 2. Performance comparison with other advanced models (XE is the result of cross entropy loss training and RL is the result of reinforcement learning optimization).

Approach	B-1	B-2	B-3	B-4	M	R	C	S
Google NIC [19]	66.6	46.1	32.9	24.6	-	-	-	
Stack-Cap [6]	78.6	62.5	47.9	36.1	27.4	56.9	120.4	20.9
RFNet [8]	79.1	63.1	48.4	36.5	27.7	57.3	121.9	21.2
CAVP [12]	80.1	64.7	50.0	38.6	28.3	58.5	126.3	21.6
EICP [17]	79.3	-	-	36.4	-	57.5	124.0	21.2
IVAIC(XE)	76.5	59.7	46.3	36.2	27.6	56.4	113.7	20.5
VASS(XE)	76.9	60.1	46.5	36.4	27.9	56.5	114.0	20.8
IVAIC(RL)	79.5	63.9	49.6	37.9	27.8	58.1	122.3	21.5
VASS(RL)	**80.5**	**65.3**	**51.0**	**38.9**	**28.3**	**58.8**	**126.7**	**21.7**

Fig. 4. Scene classification effect.

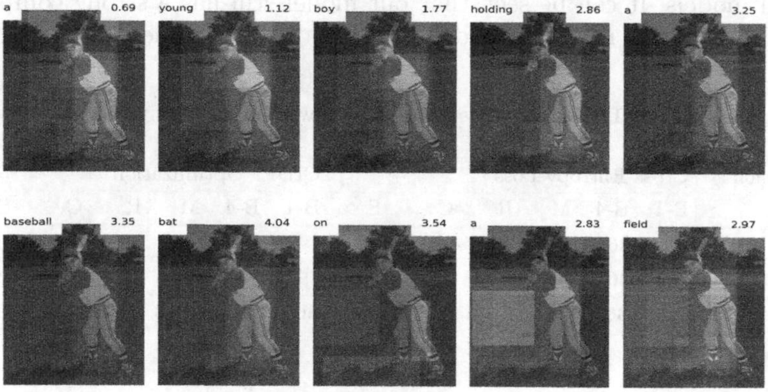

Fig. 5. Visual attention visualization

accurate scene topic words. Figure 5 show that visualization effect of the attention weights of the visual attention model, with the focus intensity coefficient in the upper right corner. We can see that the improved attention mechanism is more focused at most of the time step, especially on the small objects such as "bat". Figure 6 shows the visualization of the scene word attention during word generation. As we can see from the figure, when generating sentences, the model will focus on some important words related to the whole scene. For example, the "man", "wearing", "black" in the left image, and the "children", "game", "people", "team" in the right image.

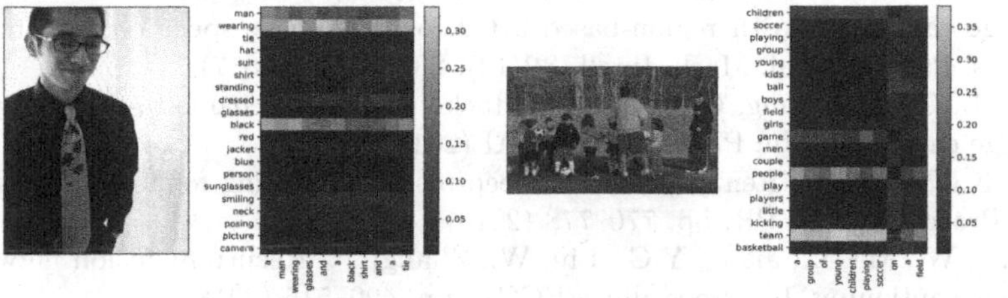

Fig. 6. Scene words attention visualization

5 Conclusions

In this paper, we propose an image captioning approach that combines image visual features and scene semantics. We introduce a focus intensity coefficient into the attention mechanism. It can automatically adjust the focus intensity of the attention mechanism to obtain more accurate visual information. Furthermore, we incorporate the scene semantic information of the image into the model, and combine the visual information of the image with the scene semantic information to guide the model to generate more accurate captions. Finally, the experimental results on the MSCOCO dataset show that our model has a significantly improvement on all evaluation metrics compared with the baseline model. Compared with other advanced approaches, our approach also has significant advantages.

Acknowledgments. This work is supported by the National Natural Science Foundation of China (Nos. 61966004, 61663004, 61762078, 61866004), the Guangxi Natural Science Foundation (Nos. 2016GXNSFAA380146, 2017GXNSFAA198365, 2018GXNSFDA281009), the Research Fund of Guangxi Key Lab of Multi-source Information Mining and Security (16-A-03-02, MIMS18-08), the Guangxi Special Project of Science and Technology Base and Talents (AD16380008), Innovation Project of Guangxi Graduate Education(XYCSZ2019068), the Guangxi "Bagui Scholar" Teams for Innovation and Research Project, Guangxi Collaborative Innovation Center of Multi-source Information Integration and Intelligent Processing.

References

1. Anderson, P., et al.: Bottom-up and top-down attention for image captioning and visual question answering. In: Proceedings CVPR, pp. 6077–6086 (2018)
2. Banerjee, S., Lavie, A.: Meteor: an automatic metric for MT evaluation with improved correlation with human judgments. In: Proceedings ACL, pp. 65–72 (2005)
3. Dai, J., Li, Y., He, K., Sun, J.: R-FCN: object detection via region-based fully convolutional networks. In: Proceedings NIPS, pp. 379–387 (2016)
4. Fang, H., et al.: From captions to visual concepts and back. In: Proceedings CVPR, pp. 1473–1482 (2015)
5. Fu, K., Jin, J., Cui, R., Sha, F., Zhang, C.: Aligning where to see and what to tell: Image captioning with region-based attention and scene-specific contexts. IEEE Trans. Pattern Anal. Mach. Intell. **39**(12), 2321–2334 (2017)
6. Gu, J., Cai, J., Wang, G., Chen, T.: Stack-captioning: coarse-to-fine learning for image captioning. In: Proceedings AAAI (2018)
7. He, K., Zhang, X., Ren, S., Sun, J.: Deep residual learning for image recognition. In: Proceedings CVPR, pp. 770–778 (2016)
8. Jiang, W., Ma, L., Jiang, Y.G., Liu, W., Zhang, T.: Recurrent fusion network for image captioning. In: Proceedings ECCV, pp. 499–515 (2018)
9. Karpathy, A., Fei-Fei, L.: Deep visual-semantic alignments for generating image descriptions. In: Proceedings CVPR, pp. 3128–3137 (2015)
10. Kingma, D.P., Ba, J.: Adam: A method for stochastic optimization. arXiv preprint (2014). arXiv:1412.6980
11. Lin, C.Y.: Rouge: a package for automatic evaluation of summaries. Text Summarization Branches Out, pp. 74–81 (2004)
12. Liu, D., Zha, Z.J., Zhang, H., Zhang, Y., Wu, F.: Context-aware visual policy network for sequence-level image captioning. arXiv preprint (2018). arXiv:1808.05864
13. Lu, J., Xiong, C., Parikh, D., Socher, R.: Knowing when to look: adaptive attention via a visual sentinel for image captioning. In: Proceedings CVPR, pp. 375–383 (2017)
14. Mao, J., Xu, W., Yang, Y., Wang, J., Huang, Z., Yuille, A.: Deep captioning with multimodal recurrent neural networks (m-rnn). arXiv preprint (2014). arXiv:1412.6632
15. Papineni, K., Roukos, S., Ward, T., Zhu, W.J.: Bleu: a method for automatic evaluation of machine translation. In: Proceedings of the 40th Annual Meeting on Association for Computational Linguistics, pp. 311–318. Association for Computational Linguistics (2002)
16. Rennie, S.J., Marcheret, E., Mroueh, Y., Ross, J., Goel, V.: Self-critical sequence training for image captioning. In: Proceedings CVPR, pp. 7008–7024 (2017)
17. Shuster, K., Humeau, S., Hu, H., Bordes, A., Weston, J.: Engaging image captioning via personality. In: Proceedings CVPR, pp. 12516–12526 (2019)
18. Vedantam, R., Lawrence Zitnick, C., Parikh, D.: Cider: consensus-based image description evaluation. In: Proceedings CVPR, pp. 4566–4575 (2015)
19. Vinyals, O., Toshev, A., Bengio, S., Erhan, D.: Show and tell: a neural image caption generator. In: Proceedings CVPR, pp. 3156–3164 (2015)
20. Xu, K., et al.: Show, attend and tell: neural image caption generation with visual attention. In: Proceedings ICML, pp. 2048–2057 (2015)
21. You, Q., Jin, H., Wang, Z., Fang, C., Luo, J.: Image captioning with semantic attention. In: Proceedings CVPR, pp. 4651–4659 (2016)

An Illumination Insensitive and Structure-Aware Image Color Layer Decomposition Method

Wengang Cheng[1,2(✉)], Pengli Dou[1], and Dengwen Zhou[1,2]

[1] North China Electric Power University, Beijing 102206, China
{wgcheng,1172227003,zdw}@ncepu.edu.cn

[2] Engineering Research Center of Intelligent Computing for Complex Energy Systems, Ministry of Education, Beijing, China

Abstract. To decompose of an image into a set of color layers can facilitate many image editing manipulations, but the high-quality layering remains challenging. We propose a novel illumination insensitive and structure-aware layer decomposition approach. To reduce the influence of non-uniform illumination on color appearance, we design a scheme of letting the decomposition work on the reflectance image output by intrinsic decomposition, rather than the original image commonly used in previous work. To obtain fine layers, we leverage image specific structure information and enforce it by encoding a structure-aware prior into a novel energy minimization formulation. The proposed optimization considers the fidelity, our structure-aware prior and permissible ranges simultaneously. We provide a solver to this optimization to get final layers. Experiments demonstrate that our method can obtain finer layers compared to several state-of-the-art methods.

Keywords: Color layer · Image editing · Illumination · Structure

1 Introduction

In digital image editing, layers organize and composite images. They are used to separate and represent different elements of an image, whether as a background or as a homogeneous color stroke [1]. These layers offer intuitive access to image manipulations, and thus image editing becomes easier. Given layers, artists can apply per-layer modifications, ranging from subtle details sharping to dramatic hue shifting, and in turn evaluate the effects interactively, as combining multiple layers can determine the final image straightforward. However, layers are usually not available except source files provided, e.g., .PSD file of Adobe Photoshop. In most cases, there is no approach to meaningful layers for those images acquired by commonly used devices such as digital cameras and scanners.

The goal of this research is to decompose an image into a set of layers for editing purpose. This problem has been addressed by several most recently published works. Without loss of generality, we follow their basic definitions [2–4]: a color layer is defined as a homogeneous color segment, while all the decomposed layers from a specific image

Y. M. Ro et al. (Eds.): MMM 2020, LNCS 11961, pp. 163–175, 2020.
https://doi.org/10.1007/978-3-030-37731-1_14

can mix together by a linear additive mode to reconstruct the given image. Actually, in high end programs like Adobe Photoshop, there are different kinds of layers, and two layers can blend using any one of several modes. The simplification for layers blending in those works is reasonable, although not complete, as the conversion between linear combination and normal blending option in Photoshop existed indeed [2, 5]. Although it seems that difficulties are alleviated somewhat under above blending simplification, the optimal decomposition is still challenging for its ill-posed nature. High-quality layers are not always accessible and this decomposition technique is far from mature.

We argue that a good decomposition should meet two criteria, i.e., a global appearance criterion and a local structure criterion. For the global concern, the extracted layers should respect an image's natural color composition to facilitate color-based management. As lighting condition affects color appearance, it would be better to remove the illumination effect for recovering the original appearance of scenes or objects, especially for images captured in non-ideal lighting conditions. For the local one, the layering results should coincide with the image's structure to ensure fine editing effects. On one side, spatial coherency should be maintained, and thus pixels within a homogenous color region share similar layering values. On the other side, layering should appear changes where there are intensive structure boundaries and texture variations. Simultaneously, for those regions with mixed colors, the pixels should belong to different layers with proper weights.

Based on the previous considerations, we address two challenges in layer decomposition: designing a decomposition scheme relatively free of illumination conditions, and pursuing fine decomposition regarding to image structure. We propose a novel illumination insensitive and structure-aware layer decomposition approach. For reliable color representation and palette extraction, the approach works on illumination independent reflectance image output by intrinsic image decomposition. To leverage the image specific structure information, we give a novel energy optimization that embeds our structure-aware prior for layering estimation. Experiments validate the proposed method.

1.1 Related Work

Previous work give the term layer different meanings in various areas, scenarios or contexts. In computational photography, an edge-persevering filter is often used to decompose an image into a piecewise smooth base layer and a detail layer [6, 7]. As a fundamental computer vision problem, intrinsic image decomposition separates an image into a reflectance layer and a shading layer to describe the underlying physical properties of the scene and illumination [8]. In computer graphics, image matting can also be considered as typical layer operations with alpha values. Unlike above definitions, this work regards the layer as a homogenous color segments of an image for editing purposes. To avoid ambiguity, the word "component" rather than "layer" is used to describe the output of intrinsic image decomposition, e.g., reflectance component, when we utilize this technique.

Recent years have witnessed increasing research efforts and encouraging achievements on layer decomposition for editing purposes. In some literatures, this technique was also named as soft color segmentation, such as in the pioneer work proposed by [9].

Typically, layer decomposition consists of two steps. First, a color palette is generated to represent an image's color composition and thus each layer can be attached to one dominant color. Second, designing a decomposition method to obtain layers under a color blending model. It can be carried out step by step [3, 4], simultaneously [2] or iteratively [9]. For palette extraction, clustering is an intuitive way, such as K-means or its variations used in [4, 10–12], Gaussian mixture models (GMMs) employed in [12]. A regression learning method was proposed in [13] to palette extraction based on human-extracted theme data. On the decomposition sub-problem, attempts were made to bind each layer to one representative color or one color distribution. [9] presented a global objective function modeled by image-level color statistics and pixel-level color mixture, and then designed an alternating optimization solution. [2] proposed a sparse color unmixing scheme with palette adjustment involved. A color decomposition optimization is explored in [4] to build the relationship between the pixels' and the basis colors.

Despite progresses, previous methods did not pay much attention to the input image's intrinsic color. They assumed that the input image were captured under uniform illumination [2–4]. It really holds true for some photos, but can't apply to most images. As color is directly affected by lighting, the real-world images often invalidate the underlying assumption and frustrate existing methods inevitably. Our method introduces intrinsic decomposition for illumination removal and takes the reflectance component rather than the original image for the subsequent layer estimation, which alleviates the influence of illumination on layers decomposition to some extent.

Meanwhile, revealing image structure in layer decomposition is necessary to fine image editing. A good layering result requires both smoothing color transitions and preserving fine structure details. Lin et al. [3] used manifold consistency to ensure the layer's smoothness successfully. Similarly, Zhang et al. [4] incorporated a smooth term considering the difference between layering values of current pixel and those of neighboring pixels. However, their layers could not agree well with texture details as they did not consider an image's structure. Aksoy et al. [2] used the guided filter as an additional step to refine the already generated layers. To respect the image's structure well, we propose a unified solution for structure-aware layer decomposition. A novel energy formulation that embeds our specific structure-aware smooth prior is proposed for layering map estimation.

1.2 Contributions

To summarize, our contributions in this research are list as follow.

- We present a strategy to reduce the influence of illumination variations on layer decomposition. Non-uniform illumination is pervasive for captured images, but it hampers delicate color analysis. We propose to use the reflectance component rather than the original image for color layer decomposition. Experiments verify it is effective.
- We propose a structure-aware layer decomposition method. To reveal fine structure in layering results, we model our problem with a novel energy optimization, considering the fidelity, our structure-aware prior and permissible ranges simultaneously. We

provide a solver to this optimization. Experiments demonstrate that our method can produce finer layers than several state-of-art methods.

The remainder of this paper is organized as follows. Section 2 describes the proposed approach, followed by the experiments and evaluations in Sect. 3. Finally, we close with a summary.

2 The Proposed Method

The framework of our proposed image layer decomposition system is illustrated in Fig. 1. Given an input image as shown in Fig. 1(a) and the number of expected layers *N*, we first get the reflectance component via intrinsic image decomposition to reduce the influence of illumination. Then, a palette with *N* dominant colors is extracted from this reflectance component via a clustering-based method. We encode our decomposition ideas with an elaborately designed energy minimization formulation and provide a solver to this optimization to get the final layers. The resulting layers can be used for many image manipulations. As an example, we demonstrate a recoloring application in Fig. 1(d) based on a user-modified color palette right side.

Fig. 1. The framework of the proposed image layer decomposition system. Given (a) an input image, the intrinsic decomposition is performed to remove illumination and get the reflectance component as in (b), and a palette is extracted from (b). The final layers (c) can obtained by our structure-aware layering optimization. The layering results can facilitate various image editing manipulations, and we demonstrate a recoloring application in (d).

2.1 Problem Formulation

The layer decomposition in this work is to slice a given image $\boldsymbol{I}$ into N homogeneous layers $\boldsymbol{L} = \{\boldsymbol{L}_1, \boldsymbol{L}_2, \cdots, \boldsymbol{L}_N\}$, where each layer is corresponding to a representative color. In other words, each pixel p in an image will be associated with N-dimensional vector $\mathbf{w}_p = \left(w_p^1, w_p^2, \ldots, w_p^N\right)^T$, where w_p^i is the weight of pixel p belonging to layer $\boldsymbol{L}_i$. Therefore, to solve the weight vector for each pixel becomes our task. Once this vector obtained, the final layers can be represented by a set of weight maps $\boldsymbol{W}$.

Above all, to ensure a faithful decomposition, the expected layers L from a specific image $\boldsymbol{I}$ should reconstruct the given image $\boldsymbol{I}$ well. That is, based on the additive color mixing model, the color $\boldsymbol{C}_p$ of each pixel p should be represented as a linear combination of the colors from the palette $\mathbf{C} = \{\boldsymbol{C}_1, \boldsymbol{C}_2, \cdots, \boldsymbol{C}_N\}$. There is:

$$\boldsymbol{C}_p = \sum\nolimits_{i=1}^{N} \boldsymbol{C}_i w_p^i \tag{1}$$

Meanwhile, the weights for each pixel should sum to unity, i.e., $\sum_{i=1}^{N} w_p^i = 1$ which can be treated as the *unity constraint*, and all the weight should lie in a meaningful range, $w_p^i \in [0, 1]$, which can be regarded as the *box constraint.*

So far, our problem can be formulated as: Given an image $\boldsymbol{I}$ and the number of layers N, we seek to infer a weight vector $\mathbf{w}_p = \left(w_p^1, w_p^2, \ldots, w_p^N\right)^T$ for each pixel under above constraints.

2.2 Illumination Removal and Palette Extraction

It is quite common in many images that illumination variations make some parts bright and others dark, which is not proper for the layer decomposition directly. However, the same task with an intrinsic decomposition is straightforward since the reflectance of an object is constant. The intrinsic decomposition provides a powerful means to reason about light and object colors that has proven to be useful to many image editing applications [14]. Therefore, we use this necessary tool to reduce illumination variations.

For the estimated reflectance, we want pixels that take similar chromaticity also have similar reflectance, and it is piecewise-constant and sparse, which will favor our layering method to obtain natural and controllable results. As the priors utilized in the [8] coincide well with our intension, we use this method for reflectance estimation.

Furthermore, our color palette $\mathbf{C} = \{\boldsymbol{C}_1, \boldsymbol{C}_2, \cdots, \boldsymbol{C}_N\}$ is also obtained from the reflectance component $\boldsymbol{R}$, which ensure a precise and robust color modal. In the experiments, we use a variant of k-means clustering for palette extraction as in [4].

2.3 Structure-Aware Layer Decomposition

We cast our structure-aware layer decomposition as an energy function as:

$$argmin_W \; E_r + \lambda_s E_s + \lambda_u E_u + \lambda_b E_b \tag{2}$$

where E_r, E_s, E_u and E_b are energy terms accounting for different constraints. The parameter λ_s, λ_u and λ_b are used to balance the importance of different terms.

Reconstruction Error Term. For a pixel p, the final weight vector w_p, together with the color palette C, should reconstruct its original color as close as possible. Derived from Eq. (1), the reconstruction error for each pixel p can be measured by $|C_p - \sum_{i=1}^{N} c_i w_p^i|$. Hence, the reconstruction error term for an image is defined as:

$$E_r = \sum\nolimits_p \left\| C_p - \sum\nolimits_{i=1}^{N} c_i w_p^i \right\|_F^2 \tag{3}$$

In matrix form, this term is expressed as:

$$E_r = \|\boldsymbol{CW} - \boldsymbol{R}\|_F^2 \tag{4}$$

where $\boldsymbol{W}$ is a PN-by-1 matrix, $\boldsymbol{W} = \langle w_1, w_2, \ldots, w_p \rangle^T$. P is the total number of pixels depending on the resolution of the reflectance component R. The reflectance R is a 3P-by-1 vector $\boldsymbol{R} = \langle R_r, R_g, R_b \rangle^T$. The matrix $\boldsymbol{C}$, with size $3P \times (PN)$, is expressed as:

$$\boldsymbol{C} = \begin{pmatrix} c_{r1}\boldsymbol{I}_p \ c_{r2}\boldsymbol{I}_p \ \ldots \ c_{rN}\boldsymbol{I}_p \\ c_{g1}\boldsymbol{I}_p \ c_{g2}\boldsymbol{I}_p \ \ldots \ c_{gN}\boldsymbol{I}_p \\ c_{b1}\boldsymbol{I}_p \ c_{b2}\boldsymbol{I}_p \ \ldots \ c_{bN}\boldsymbol{I}_p \end{pmatrix} \tag{5}$$

where c_{dj} is channel d of the j-th color element of a color palette with $d \in \{r, g, b\}$ and $j \in \{1, 2, \ldots, N\}$. $\boldsymbol{I}_p$ is the $P \times P$ identity matrix.

Structure-Aware Smooth Term. Smooth term is a commonly used prior for solution regularization, which takes many forms and implementations. In previous work, spatial smoothness prior is most frequently used one [3, 4, 8, 15]. To the layering problem, it says that for a pixel p, its layering value w_p^i should not be very different from layering values w_q^i within a local neighbor region, $q \in \mathcal{N}(p)$. Two state-of-the-art work, Lin et al.'s method [3] and Zhang et al.'s method [4] adopted and developed this basic assumption. Specially, Lin et al.'s [3] extended the neighbor region to the whole image to preserve the image's manifold. Basically, $\|\nabla \boldsymbol{W}\|_1$ can be one typical form of spatial smoothness. However, the spatial smoothness prior may easily lead to over smoothed results and some variations along image edge should take but cannot present well. High-quality layers should respect the input image's structure to ensure refined image manipulations. To this end, we give a structure-aware smooth term as:

$$E_s = \|\nabla \boldsymbol{W} - \boldsymbol{G}\|^2 \tag{6}$$

where $\boldsymbol{G}$ is the transformed gradient of the reflectance $\boldsymbol{R}$. The simplest one is $\boldsymbol{G} = \nabla \boldsymbol{R}$, which might manifest the input image's specific structure. Meanwhile, we observe the reflectance component $\boldsymbol{R}$ is much smoother than the original image $\boldsymbol{I}$, as spatial smoothness has been enforced during the intrinsic image decomposition processing. Consequently, the reflectance $\boldsymbol{R}$ keeps object boundaries and eliminates spurious variations caused by illumination, which is much proper for our task. For fine layering details, we adopt a nonlinear gradient amplification scheme:

$$\boldsymbol{G} = \left(1 + \lambda e^{-|\nabla \widehat{\boldsymbol{R}}|/\sigma}\right) \circ \nabla \widehat{\boldsymbol{R}} \tag{7}$$

where

$$\nabla \widehat{R} = \begin{cases} 0, & if\ |\nabla R| < \varepsilon \\ \nabla R, & \text{otherwise} \end{cases} \tag{8}$$

Thus, those details with lower gradient magnitude get stronger enlargement, while less adjustment occurs for higher gradient magnitude as these details are prominently distinct to be captured already. We suppress the noise by removing very small gradients before the amplification.

Unity Error Term. To normalize each layer's contribution w_p^i to a pixel color, we require the layering values over all layers w_p to add up to unity. We penalize the error of out of permissible range as:

$$E_u = \sum_p \left\| \sum_{j=1}^{N} w_p^j - 1 \right\|^2 = \left\| UW - \hat{I} \right\|^2 \tag{9}$$

where U is a $P \times PN$ indicator matrix with ones in the columns where they could contribute to the weights for a specific pixel. $\hat{I}$ is a $P \times 1$ vector of ones. The element of U is determined by:

$$u_{ij} = \begin{cases} 1 & if\, j - i \equiv 0 \ \ (mod\, P) \\ 0 & if\, j - i \not\equiv 0 \ \ (mod\, P) \end{cases} \tag{10}$$

Range Error Term. This term encourages layering values W to lie in the range [0, 1]. The out-of-bounds penalty is:

$$E_b = \| BW - T \|^2 \tag{11}$$

where B is indicator matrix with ones where the weights do not satisfy the box constraint. The size of matrix B is $M \times PN$ and M is the number of values violating the box constraint. B is a zero matrix initially. T is a vector of target bounds. Specially, we find the layering weights less than lower bound or greater than upper bound and set the corresponding target bounds as 0 or 1, respectively.

2.4 Solution

Substituting the energy terms into Eq. (2), we obtain the energy function as follows:

$$argmin_W \| CW - R \|^2 + \lambda_s \| \nabla W - G \|^2 + \lambda_u \left\| UW - \hat{I} \right\|^2 + \lambda_b \| BW - T \|^2 \tag{12}$$

As only quadratic terms available, the object function is convex and can find its minimum. Meanwhile, it is a classical least square problem. By differentiating Eq. (12) with respect to W and setting the derivative to 0, we get the following:

$$C^T CW - C^T R + \lambda_s D^T DW - \lambda_s D^T G + \lambda_u U^T UW - \lambda_u U^T \hat{I} + \lambda_b B^T BW - \lambda_b B^T T = 0 \tag{13}$$

$$\left(C^T C + \lambda_s D^T D + \lambda_u U^T U + \lambda_b B^T B \right) W = C^T R + \lambda_s D^T G + \lambda_u U^T \hat{I} + \lambda_b B^T T \tag{14}$$

where D is a PN $\times$ PN discrete gradient operator.

The solution can be obtained by solving a linear system. However, some resulting values may violate the box constraint as the initial B is a zero matrix, and this term does not work currently. A possible problem bring about by these out-of-bounds values, especially the values far away from the bounds, is that a slight change on color palette may lead to large impact on editing results. To relieve this problem, we adopt an iterative way. We first solve the energy minimization problem in Eq. (12) and pick out the values which have violated the box constraint. Accordingly, we update the matrix $\boldsymbol{B}$ of Eq. (11) for above unexpected values. Then, we go to next iterative until a satisfying result.

Our processing for layer composition can be summarized as the following algorithm.

Algorithm 1 The proposed layer decomposition algorithm

Input: Image $\boldsymbol{I}$, number of layers N, coefficient λ_s, λ_u, λ_b

Output: Resulting layer maps $\{w_p^j\}_{j=1}^N$

1: Perform palette extraction to get basis color $\boldsymbol{C}$.

2: Perform intrinsic decomposition to get reflectance image $\boldsymbol{R}$.

3: Initialize the W matrix to the solution of the unconstrained linear problem, $\lambda_s = 0.01, \lambda_u = 0.1, \lambda_e = 0.1, t = 0$

4: **repeat**

5: With λ_s, λ_u, and λ_b, solve Equation (2) for $\{w_p^j\}_{j=1}^N$.

6: With $\{w_p^j\}_{j=1}^N$, update matrix $\boldsymbol{B}$. $\boldsymbol{T}$ and M change w.r.t. $\boldsymbol{B}$ accordingly.

7: $t \leftarrow t + 1$

8: **until** $\mathrm{M} < 1 \times 10^4$ or $t > 5$

---

3 Experimental Evaluations

It is particularly challenging to evaluate layer decomposition methods. The most difficult issue might be the benchmark, as ground-truth layers for a given image are unavailable indeed. Even existed, the ground truth is undoubtedly controversial. Consequently, we conduct our evaluation qualitatively and quantitatively. For qualitative evaluations, we first present the layers generated by different method for comparison. As recoloring is a typical application benefitting from layers, we also demonstrate the recoloring result for visual inspection. For quantitative evaluations, we design several metrics for quality assessment. As no standard dataset available, we collect the images used in the related work [3, 4] and grab some other images from Flickr and Pixabay as our dataset, which covers a variety of scenes, lighting conditions and structures.

We compare the proposed method (Ours) with two most relevant state-of-the-art work, Lin et al.'s method (Lin's) [3] and Zhang et al.'s method (Zhang's) [4]. To testify the effect of illumination elimination, we also implement two additional methods. One is the letting our method work on the original image other than the reflectance component, and the other is making Lin's method work on the reflectance component. They are abbreviated as Ours_O and Lin's_R, respectively. For fair comparisons, the same color palette extraction scheme is used for all the methods. All the codes are in Matlab and execute at same setting to ensure the fairness of time comparison.

3.1 Qualitative Evaluations

As a qualitative evaluation, we get the layers obtained by different methods for visual inspection. A representative example is illustrated in Fig. 2, where we show the extracted color palette and the resulting layers by all competing methods.

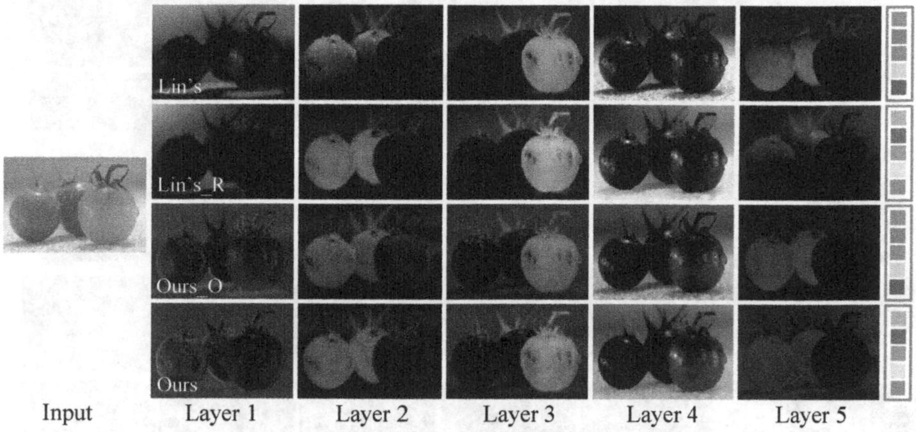

Fig. 2. Comparison of the generated layers.

In this example, the layers produced by all methods can get relatively homogenous color. However, the Lin's [3] and Ours_O are prone to misallocation of similar color into multiple layers, as illustrated in the 5th layers. The reason lies in the fact that uneven illumination drives red tomato show color variations. Nevertheless, our perception keeps unchanged as it's one of typical memory colors. As the reflectance component can indicate intrinsic color, Ours and Lin's_R get reliable color palette and robust decomposition to lighting conditions.

As another qualitative evaluation, we get and compare the corresponding recolored images by different methods on some sample images. Specially, we replace the extracted color palette with a user-modified one, and update the layers based on the new palette. Then, the transformed layers are mixed to produce the final recoloring. Several representative examples are illustrated in Fig. 3.

All methods work relatively well for ideal cases. However, for images with non-ideal lighting conditions, Lin's [3], Zhang's [4] and Ours_O easily result in unnatural recolored appearance, as shown in the results for Image #I. Due to the influence of illumination, the head of the old man shares similar color with the sofa. In this case, color distortion is introduced by non-uniform illumination. We only want to recolor the sofa, but these methods let the old man take superiors color finally, while Lin's_R performs somewhat better than the other three methods. Affected by some non-homogeneous layers, spurious color occurs for Image #III, where the ground is recolored undesirably by Zhang's [4] and Lin's_R. Our method can get natural recoloring for these images.

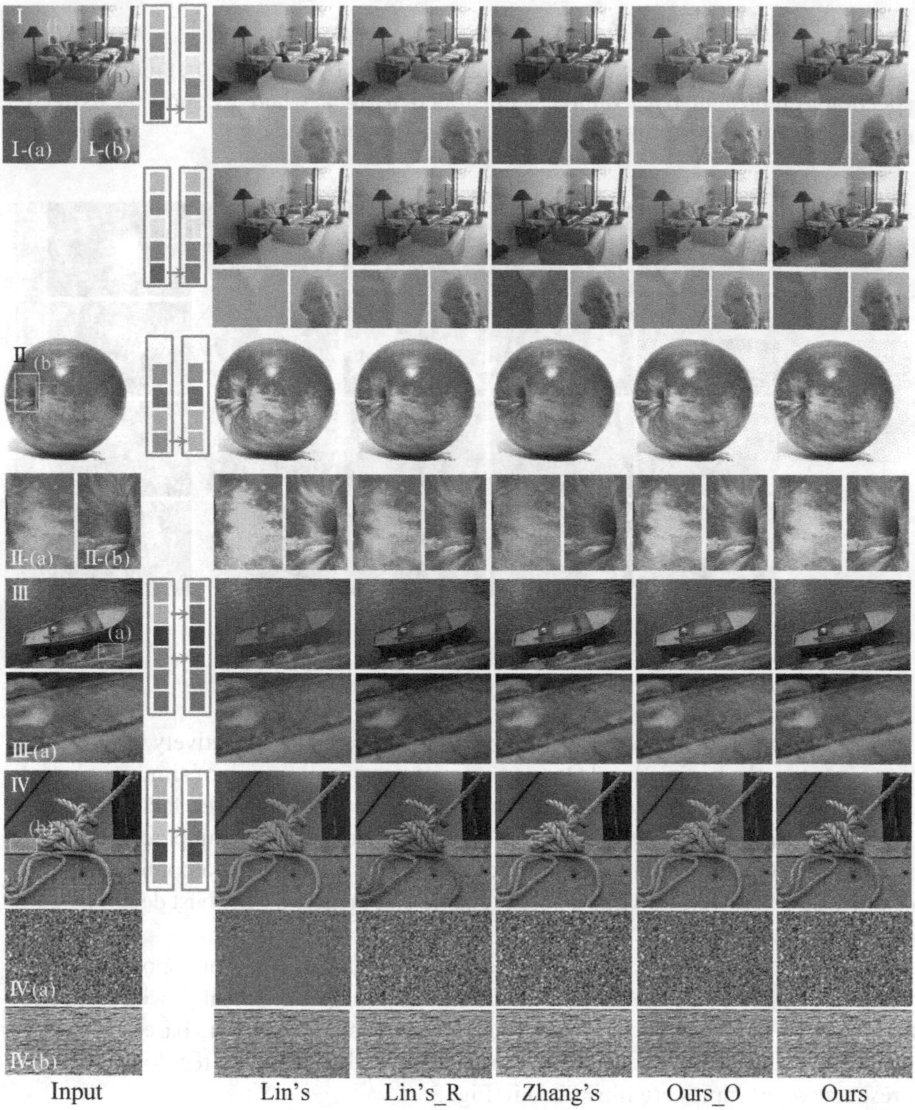

Fig. 3. Comparison of the recoloring results.

As for the structure-preserving, Lin's [3] and Lin's_R cannot not work very well, as illustrated by the results for Image #I and Image #IV. It is resulting from that the spatial distribution of layers cannot agree well with the input image's structure. Relatively, Ours_O is better than Lin's and Lin's_R. Meanwhile, we also observe that the structure information is also easily affected by the illumination conditions. As a result, Ours_O still cannot get good edge for sofa in Image #I. Among them, Zhang's [4] get relatively better structure preserving results as it adopts a smooth term considering color changes of pixels. However, Zhang's [4] sometimes cannot get smooth transitions, which makes the recoloring results less natural, e.g., the recoloring result of the apple in Image #II. For pixels located in smooth boundary regions, the layering weights distribution of Ours tends to be disperse rather than concentrated, which fits well with physical truth. Our method has good abilities of preserving structure and presenting vivid and natural color, e.g., the recoloring result of the apple in Image #II maintaining natural appearance and fine structure.

Overall, our method gets better performance than state-of-art methods in term of layer color quality, smooth transition and structure preserving, and we get much natural recolored appearance.

3.2 Quantitative Evaluations

There is no standard objective metrics for layering decomposition. To measure the different aspects of layer's quality, we use the following metrics for quality evaluation in terms of different aspects: (1) Root Mean Squared Error (RMSE) [16]: It is used to measure the fidelity which is the difference between the input image and the reconstructed image based on the weighted layers; (2) Average Color Variance (ACV): It is used to measure the color homogeneity of each final layer, calculated as the sum of three variances on RGB averaged over all layers; (3) Structural SIMilarity index (SSIM) [17]: It is used to measure the perceived change in structural information between the original image and the reconstructed image.

Table 1. The mean of several metrics on our dataset

Method	Lin's	Lin's_R	Zhang's	Ours_O	Ours
RMSE	0.017453	0.014345	0.049106	0.019882	**0.015829**
ACV	0.015565	0.020421	0.049928	**0.009026**	0.010853
SSIM	0.932851	0.988816	0.985156	0.986665	**0.995240**

Table 1 shows the average values of these metrics on our dataset. Ours has the smallest RMSE, which means it obtains faithful layering. Our_O and Ours can get homogenous intra-layer color, as demonstrated by the ACV metric. Meanwhile, we have the highest SSIM, which indicates the structure awareness of Ours is superior to other methods. Although incomplete, evaluations on these metrics can also verify our method partially.

In terms of time cost, our method (365.25 s) takes much more than Lin's [3] (119.71 s), Lin's_R(130.83 s), and it is slighter slower than Ours_R (309.04 s), while it is more efficient than Zhang's [4] (534.92 s). The values in brackets are average time for each method on our dataset with size of 500 * 375 under same computation environments.

4 Conclusions and Future Work

We proposed an illumination insensitive and structure-aware layer decomposition method. To reduce the influence of illumination variations, we first got the reflectance component via intrinsic decomposition. The palette extraction and layer decomposition optimization were performed on the reflectance component. To reveal fine structure in layering results, we proposed a structure-aware energy optimization function, considering the fidelity, our structure-aware smooth prior and permissible ranges simultaneously, and provided a solver to this optimization to get the final layers. Experiments demonstrate that our method can produce fine layers.

Our approach does have limitations. The fixed number of items in a color palette sometimes leads to uncontrollable layers, thus an adaptive scheme is preferred. Meanwhile, our layers are not associated with semantic concepts, which surely restricts its applications and is also list in our future work.

Acknowledgement. This work is partially supported by the National Key R&D Program of China (2018YFC0831404, 2018YFC0830605), the Fundamental Research Funds for the Central Universities(2016MS27), the NCEPU High-quality Graduate Course Construction Project and the NCEPU Education Reform Project (2019YB029).

References

1. En.wikipedia.org. (2019). Layers (digital image editing) https://en.wikipedia.org/wiki/Layers_(digital_image_editing). Accessed 31 July 2019
2. Aksoy, Y., Aydin, T.O., Smolić, A., et al.: Unmixing-based soft color segmentation for image manipulation. ACM Trans. Graph. **36**(2), 19 (2017)
3. Lin, S., Fisher, M., Dai, A., et al.: LayerBuilder: layer decomposition for interactive image and video color editing. arXiv preprint arXiv:1701.03754, 2017
4. Zhang, Q., Xiao, C., Sun, H., et al.: Palette-based image recoloring using color decomposition optimization. IEEE Trans. Image Process. **26**(4), 1952–1964 (2017)
5. Koyama, Y., Goto, M.: Decomposing images into layers with advanced color blending. Comput. Graph. Forum **37**(7), 397–407 (2018)
6. Farbman, Z., Fattal, R., Lischinski, D., et al.: Edge-preserving decompositions for multi-scale tone and detail manipulation. ACM Trans. Graph. **27**(3), 67 (2008)
7. Bae, S., Paris, S., Durand, F.: Two-scale tone management for photographic look. ACM Trans. Graph. **25**(3), 637–645 (2006)
8. Bell, S., Bala, K., Snavely, N.: Intrinsic images in the wild. ACM Trans. Graph. **33**(4), 159 (2014)
9. Tai, Y.W., Jia, J., Tang, C.K.: Soft color segmentation and its applications. IEEE Trans. Pattern Anal. Mach. Intell. **29**(9), 1520–1537 (2007)
10. Chang, H., Fried, O., Liu, Y., DiVerdi, S., Finkelstein, A.: Palette-based photo recoloring. ACM Trans. Graph. (TOG) **34**(4), 139 (2015)
11. Nguyen, R.M.H., Price, B., Cohen, S., et al.: Group-theme recoloring for multi-image color consistency. Comput. Graph. Forum **36**(7), 83–92 (2017)
12. Phan, H.Q., Fu, H., Chan, A.B.: Color orchestra: ordering color palettes for interpolation and prediction. IEEE Trans. Visual. Comput. Graph. **24**(6), 1942–1955 (2017)
13. Lin, S., Hanrahan, P.: Modeling how people extract color themes from images. In: Proceedings of the SIGCHI Conference on Human Factors in Computing Systems, pp. 3101–3110. ACM (2013)
14. Bonneel, N., Kovacs, B., Paris, S., et al.: Intrinsic decompositions for image editing. Comput. Graph. Forum **36**(2), 593–609 (2017)

15. Li, M., Liu, J., Yang, W., et al.: Structure-revealing low-light image enhancement via robust Retinex model. IEEE Trans. Image Process. **27**(6), 2828–2841 (2018)
16. Armstrong, J.S., Collopy, F.: Error measures for generalizing about forecasting methods: empirical comparisons. Int. J. Forecast. **8**(1), 69–80 (1992)
17. Wang, Z., Bovik, A.C., Sheikh, H.R., et al.: Image quality assessment: from error visibility to structural similarity. IEEE Trans. Image Process. **13**(4), 600–612 (2004)

CartoonRenderer: An Instance-Based Multi-style Cartoon Image Translator

Yugang Chen(✉), Muchun Chen, Chaoyue Song, and Bingbing Ni(✉)

Shanghai Jiao Tong University, Shanghai, China
{cygashjd,Brunestod,beyondsong,nibingbing}@sjtu.edu.cn

Abstract. Instance based photo cartoonization is one of the challenging image stylization tasks which aim at transforming realistic photos into cartoon style images while preserving the semantic contents of the photos. State-of-the-art Deep Neural Networks (DNNs) methods still fail to produce satisfactory results with input photos in the wild, especially for photos which have high contrast and full of rich textures. This is due to that: cartoon style images tend to have smooth color regions and emphasized edges which are contradict to realistic photos which require clear semantic contents, i.e., textures, shapes etc. Previous methods have difficulty in satisfying cartoon style textures and preserving semantic contents at the same time. In this work, we propose a novel "CartoonRenderer" framework which utilizing a single trained model to generate multiple cartoon styles. In a nutshell, our method maps photo into a *feature model* and renders the *feature model* back into image space. In particular, cartoonization is achieved by conducting some transformation manipulation in the feature space with our proposed *Soft-AdaIN*. Extensive experimental results show our method produces higher quality cartoon style images than prior arts, with accurate semantic content preservation. In addition, due to the decoupling of whole generating process into *"Modeling-Coordinating-Rendering"* parts, our method could easily process higher resolution photos, which is intractable for existing methods.

Keywords: Non-photorealistic rendering · Neural style transfer · Image generation

1 Introduction

Cartoon style is one of the most popular artistic styles in today's world, especially in online social media. To obtain high quality cartoon images, artists need to draw every line and paint every color block, which is labor intensive. Therefore, a well-designed approach for automatically rendering realistic photos in cartoon style is of a great value. Photo cartoonization is a challenging image stylization task which aims at transforming realistic photos into cartoon style images while preserving the semantic contents of the photos. Recently, image stylized rendering has been widely studied and several inspirational methods

Y. M. Ro et al. (Eds.): MMM 2020, LNCS 11961, pp. 176–187, 2020.
https://doi.org/10.1007/978-3-030-37731-1_15

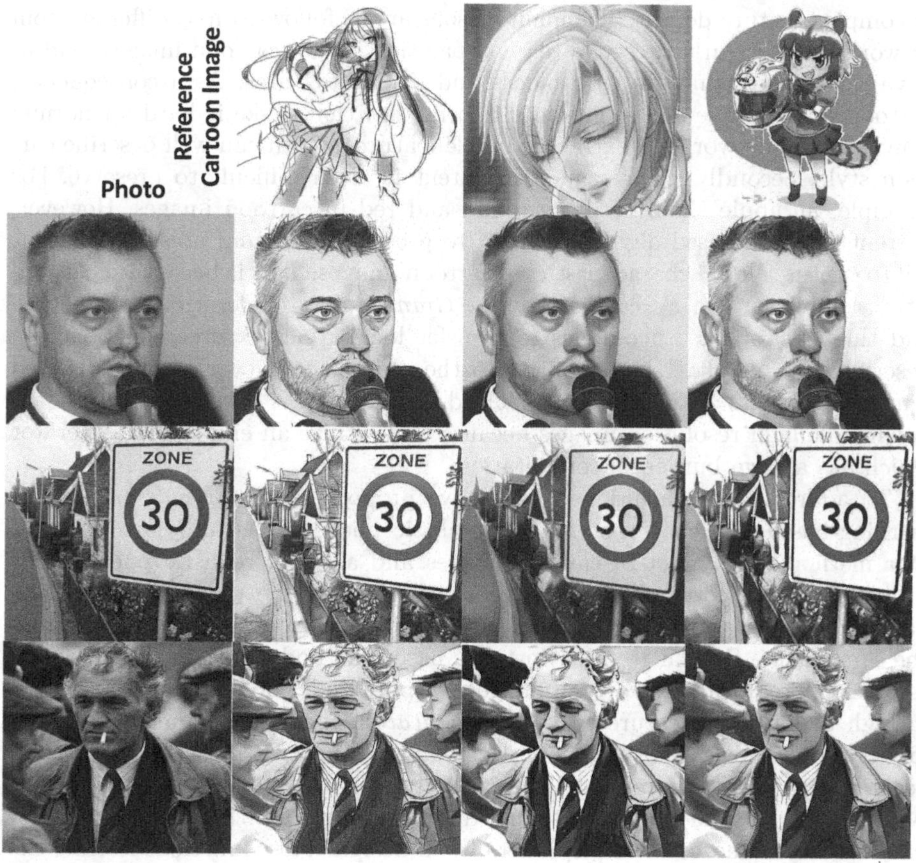

Fig. 1. Some cartoonization results of *CartoonRenderer* with different reference cartoon images.

have been proposed based on Convolutional Neural Network (CNN). Gatys [5] formulates image stylized rendering as an optimization problem that translating the style of an image while preserving its semantic content. This method produces promising results on transforming images in traditional oil painting styles, such as *Van Gogh*'s style and *Monet*'s style. However, it suffers from long running time caused by tremendous amount of computation. Based on Gatys's pioneering work, some researchers have devoted substantial efforts to accelerating training and inference process through feed-forward network, such as [2,6,8,12,16]. Some methods follow this line of idea that employs a feedforward network as generator to generate stylized results and achieve significant success. Since cartoon style is one of artist styles, many existing methods used for artistic style transfer can also be used to transform realistic photographs into cartoon style. However, even state-of-the-art methods fail to stably produce acceptable results with input content photos in the wild, especially for the high resolution photographs that full of complex texture details. The main reasons are as follows. First, different from artworks in other artistic styles (e.g. oil painting style), cartoon images tend to have clear edges, smooth color blocks and simple textures. As a consequence, cartoon images have sparse gradient information that make it hard for normal convolutional networks to extract valuable features which can well describe cartoon style. Secondly, clear semantic content is often difficult to preserve. For example, an apple should still be round and red in cartoon images. However, current instance-based algorithms tend to preserve local and noisy details but fail to capture global characteristics of cartoon images. This is because such algorithms purely utilize *Perceptual Loss* or *Gram-Matrix* to describe image style, and this type of loss encourages to transfer local style textures which can be described by "strokes" but conflicts to the objective that preserving detailed semantic contents at the same time. Third, current GAN- based algorithms cannot handle high resolution images because they utilize an end-to-end generator which has a large burden in computation.

To address issues mentioned above, we propose *CartoonRenderer*, a novel learning-based approach that renders realistic photographs into cartoon style. Our method takes a set of cartoon images and a set of realistic photographs for training. No correspondence is required between the two sets of training data. It is worth noting that we also do not require cartoon images coming from the same artist. Similar to other instance based methods, our *CartoonRenderer* receives photograph and cartoon image as inputs and models them respectively in high dimensional feature space to get *"feature model"s.* Inspired by AdaIN [6], we propose *Soft-AdaIN* for robustly align the *"feature-model"* of photograph according to the *"feature-model"* of cartoon image. Then, we use a *Rendering Network* to generate output cartoonized photograph from the aligned *"feature-model"*. Furthermore, we employ a set of well-designed loss functions to train the *CartoonRenderer*. Except for using pre-trained VGG19 [13] model to compute content loss and style loss, we add extra reconstruction loss and adversarial loss to further preserve detailed semantic content of photographs to be cartoonized. Our method is capable of producing high-quality cartoonized photographs, which are substantially better than state-of-the-art methods. Furthermore, due to the decoupling of whole generating process into *"Modeling-Coordinating-Rendering"* parts, our method is able to process high resolution photographs (up to 5000 * 5000 pixels) and maintain high quality of results, which is infeasible for state-of-the-art methods.

2 Related Works

Non-photorealistic Rendering (NPR). Non-photorealistic rendering is an alternative to conventional, photorealistic computer graphics, aiming to make visual communication more effective and automatically create aesthetic results resembling a variety existing art styles. The main venue of NPR is animation and rendering. Some methods have been developed to create images with flat shading, mimicking cartoon styles. Such methods use either image filtering or formulations in optimization problem. However, applying filtering or optimization uniformly to the entirely image does not give the high-level abstraction that an artist would normally do, such as making object boundaries clear. To improve the results, alternative methods rely on segmentation of images have been proposed, although at the cost of requiring some user interaction. Dedicated methods have also been developed for portraits, where semantic segmentation can be derived automatically by detecting facial components. Nevertheless, such methods cannot cope with general images. Turning photos of various categories into cartoons such as the problem studied in this paper is much more challenging.

3 Methodology

The task of instance based photo cartoonization is to generate cartoon style version of the given input image, according to some user specified style attributes. In our method, the style attributes are provided by the reference cartoon image. Our model learns from a quantity of unpaired realistic photographs and cartoon images to capture the common characteristics of cartoon styles and re-renders the photographs into cartoon styles. The photographs and cartoon images are not required to be paired and the cartoon images are also not required to be classified by artists. This brings significant feasibility in model training.

For the sake of discussion, let $\mathcal{P}$ and $\mathcal{C}$ be the photograph domain and cartoon domain respectively. Inspired by object modeling and rendering techniques with deep neural networks in the field of computer graphics [10], we formulate photograph cartoonization as a process of *Modeling-Coordinating-Rendering*:

`Modeling`: $\forall p \in \mathcal{P}, \forall c \in \mathcal{C}$, we construct the *feature model* of a photograph and a cartoon image as Ψ_p and Ψ_c respectively. The *feature model* consisting of multi-scale feature maps represent the style characteristics.

`Coordinating`: Align the *feature model* of photographs Ψ_p according to the *feature model* of cartoon image Ψ_c and gets the coordinated *feature model* Ψ_y, i.e, which possesses p's content representation with c's style representation.

`Rendering`: Generate the cartoonized photograph y ($y \in \mathcal{C}$) from the coordinated *feature model* Ψ_y which can be considered as reconstruction.

In a nutshell, we propose a novel instance based method *"CartoonRenderer"* to render the input photo p into cartoon style result y according to reference cartoon image c, which can be described as $y = G(p, c)$. G represents the non-linear mapping function of whole *"Modeling-Coordinating-Rendering"* process. It is worth noting that style attributes are provided by input cartoon image c, so single trained *"CartoonRenderer"* can be used to render different cartoon styles by feeding different reference images. Results with different reference cartoon images are demonstrated in Fig. 1. We present the detail of our model architecture in Sect. 3.1 and propose a series of loss functions for training G in Sect. 3.2.

3.1 Model Architecture

As demonstrated in Fig. 2, our *CartoonRenderer* is consist of three parts: Modeling, Coordinating and Rendering. In addition, a discriminator D is employed to produce adversarial loss. *CartoonRenderer* follows the auto-encoder architecture. The *Modeling network* is used to map input images into feature spaces. Different from traditional encoder used in Adain [6] and MUNIT [7], our *Modeling network* maps input image into multiple scales feature spaces instead of single fixed scale feature space. The *Coordinating* part of *CartoonRenderer* is consist of four *Soft-AdaIN* blocks, corresponding to the number of elements in *feature model*. Each *Soft-AdaIN* block is used to align the corresponding scale's element in feature models of photo Ψ_p according to the feature model of cartoon image Ψ_c. At last, we train a *Rendering network* to reconstruct back y from the coordinated *feature models* Ψ_y.

Modeling Network. The *Modeling network* is used to construct the *feature model* of input image. The great success of U-Net [11] based methods in high precision segmentation has proved that the coarse contextual information embedded in shallow features plays important role for preserving detailed semantic contents. The shallow features have relatively small receptive field that make it sensitive to local and detailed texture information, meanwhile, the deep features can better at describing global and abstract textures' characteristics. Both local and global texture information are important for generating high-quality images. So we utilize multiple scales of feature responses instead of fixed single scale to represent the images. The collection of multi-scale features can be recognized as a high dimensional *feature model*, which contains local and global semantic information and be able to well-represent the input image in terms of content and style. We employ the top few layers of a VGG19 [13] network (up to $31-th$ layer) as the modeling network. According to the definition of content loss and style loss used in [4,14,15], we choose the $4-th$, $11-th$, $18-th$ and $31-th$

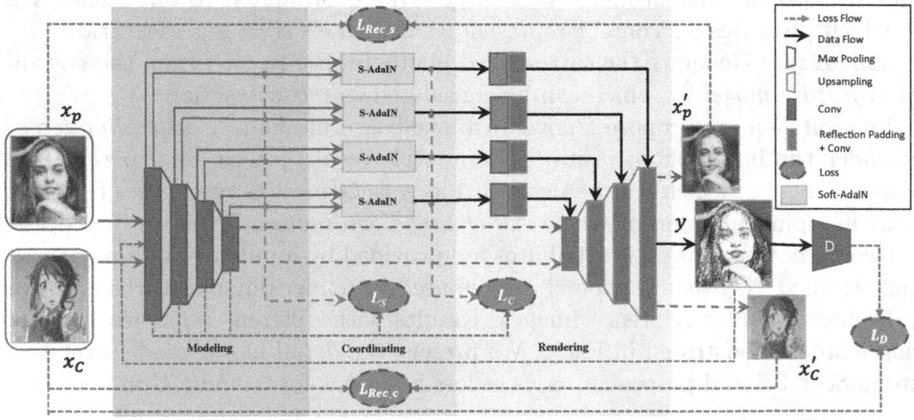

Fig. 2. The whole framework of our method. x_p represents the input photo and x_c represent the input cartoon image. x'_p and x'_c represent the reconstructed results and y represents the cartoonized target result.

layers' output to construct the *feature model.* We define the *feature model* of input image x as:

$$\Psi_x = \{f_4(x), f_{11}(x), f_{18}(x), f_{31}(x)\},$$

where $f_i(x)$ be the $i-th$ layer's feature response of input x. Ψ_x can be recognized as a "model" of input image x in the space spanned by multi-scale feature subspaces. The feature model Ψ_x represents image x on different scales.

***Soft-AdaIN* for Robust Feature Coordinating.** *AdaIN* proposed in [6] adaptively computes the affine parameters from the style input instead of learning affine parameters:

$$AdaIN(x_c, x_s) = \sigma(x_s)(\frac{x_c - \mu(x_c)}{\sigma(x_c)}) + \mu(x_s).$$

AdaIN [6] first scale the normalized content input with $\sigma(x_s)$ and then add $\mu(x_s)$ as a bias. $\sigma(x)$ and $\mu(x)$ are the channel-wise mean and variance of input x. As mentioned in Sect. 1, cartoon images tend to have quite unique characteristics which far away from realistic photos, which means that there is a huge gap between the distributions of photos and cartoon images. *AdaIN* [6] explicitly replace the feature statistics of photo with corresponding feature statistics of cartoon image, which will break the consistency and continuity of feature map. The non-consistency and non-continuity will cause obvious artifacts as shown in Fig. 3c.

To circumvent this problem, we designed *Soft-AdaIN*. The *Soft-AdaIN* is used to align the *feature model* of photographs for cartoon stylizing. As shown in Fig. 2, *Coordinating* part consists of four *Soft-AdaIN* blocks. *Soft-AdaIN* also receives a content input and a style input. In this paper, we denote content input (which comes from photographs) as x_p and style input (which comes from cartoon images) as x_c. Two mini convolutional networks θ_p and θ_c are used to further extract features of x_p and x_c. Since the shape of x_p and x_c maybe mismatch, we adopt global average pooling to pool $\theta_p(x_p)$ and $\theta_c(x_c)$ into $1*1*ch$ tensors, where ch is the channel number of x_p and x_c. The pooled $\theta_p(x_p)$ and $\theta_c(x_c)$ are concatenated in channel dimension as a $1*1*(2*ch)$ tensor. Then we employ 2 fully-connection layers to compute channel-wise weight $\omega(x_p, x_c)$ from the concatenated tensor. $\omega(x_p, x_c)$ is a $1*1*ch$ tensor. In fact, $\omega(x_p, x_c)$ can be recognized as channel-wise weights for adaptively blend feature statistics of photo input and cartoon input:

$$\sigma'(x_p, x_c) = \sigma(x_c) * \omega(x_p, x_c) + \sigma(x_p) * (1.0 - \omega(x_p, x_c)),$$
$$\mu'(x_p, x_c) = \mu(x_c) * \omega(x_p, x_c) + \mu(x_p) * (1.0 - \omega(x_p, x_c)).$$

Our proposed *Soft-AdaIN* scales the normalized content input with $\sigma'(x_p, x_c)$ and shift it with $\mu'(x_p, x_c)$:

$$Soft\text{-}AdaIN(x_p, x_c) = \sigma'(x_p, x_c)(\frac{x_p - \mu(x_p)}{\sigma(x_p)}) + \mu'(x_p, x_c).$$

We employ *Soft-AdaIN* to coordinate the *feature model* of realistic photo according to *feature model* of cartoon image. For $\forall p \in \mathcal{P}, \forall c \in \mathcal{C}$, we have

$$\Psi_p = \{f_4(p), f_{11}(p), f_{18}(p), f_{31}(p)\},$$
$$\Psi_c = \{f_4(c), f_{11}(c), f_{18}(c), f_{31}(c)\}.$$

To perform feature coordination, we conduct *Soft-AdaIN* on each element in Ψ_p and Ψ_c:

$$t^\lambda = Soft\text{-}AdaIN(f_\lambda(p), f_\lambda(c)),$$
$$\Psi_y = \{t^\lambda\}, \lambda = 4, 11, 18, 31,$$

where Ψ_y is the coordinated *feature model* for generating output cartoonized result y.

Rendering Network. The *Rendering Network* is used to render *feature model* Ψ_x into image space. Our *Rendering Network* has similar architecture as the expansive path of *U-Net* [11]. As shown in Fig. 2, *Rendering Network* is consist of 4 blocks. The first 3 blocks have two paths: a concatenation path and upsampling path, and the last block only has a upsampling path. The concatenation path receives corresponding scale's element in *feature-model* (t^{18}, t^{11} and t^4 for the first, second and third blocks' concatenation path respectively). The upsampling path receives proceeding block's output (the first block receives t^{31} as input) and is used to expansion the feature responses. We use *Reflection Padding* before each $3 * 3$ convolutional layer to avoid border artifacts. Obviously, the output of concatenation path and output of upsampling path have the same size, so we can concatenate them along the channel dimension. The concatenated feature map then be fed into another activation layer and become the final output of current block. The last block is a pure upsampling block without concatenation path, and its upsampling path have the same structure as preceding blocks do. All activation functions in *Rendering Network* are *ReLU*. By adopting such multi-scale architecture, the *Rendering Network* is able to make full use of both local and global texture information for generating the output images.

3.2 Loss Function

The loss function used to train the *CartoonRenderer* consists of three parts: (1) the style loss $\mathcal{L}_S(G)$ which guides the output to have the same cartoon style as the input cartoon image; (2) the content loss $\mathcal{L}_C(G)$ which preserves the photographs' semantic content during cartoon stylization; (3) the adversarial loss $\mathcal{L}_{adv}(G, D)$ which further drives the generator network to render input photographs into desired cartoon styles; and (4) the reconstruction loss $\mathcal{L}_{Recon}(G)$ which guides the rendering network to reconstruct origin input images from corresponding un-coordinated *feature models*. We formulate the loss function into a simple additive from:

$$\mathcal{L}_{adv}(R, D) = \omega_{style}\mathcal{L}_S(R) + \omega_{con}\mathcal{L}_C(R) + \omega_{recon}\mathcal{L}_{recon}(R) + \omega_{adv}\mathcal{L}_{adv}(R, D),$$

where ω_{style}, ω_{con}, ω_{recon} and ω_{adv} balance the four losses. In all our experiments. We set $\omega_{recon} = 0.0001$, $\omega_{adv} = 1$, $\omega_{style} = 20$ and $\omega_{con} = 1$ to achieve a good balance of style and content preservation.

Content Loss and Style Loss. Similar to AdaIN [6], we reuse the elements in the *feature model* (feature maps extracted by *modeling network*) to compute the style loss function and content loss function. The *modeling network* is initialized with a pre-trained VGG-19 [13]. The content loss is defined as:

$$\mathcal{L}_{con}(G) = \sum_{\lambda} \| Norm(f_\lambda(G(x,y))) - Norm(f_\lambda(x)) \|_1, \lambda = 4, 11, 18, 31,$$

where $Norm(x) = [x - mean(x)]/var(x)$ is used to normalize feature maps with channel-wise mean and variance.

Unlike other style transferring methods [3,6], we define the semantic content loss using the sum of $\mathscr{L}_1$ sparse regularization of normalized VGG feature maps instead of origin feature maps. This is due to the fact that statistics of feature maps affect the image's style. Directly using feature maps to compute content loss will introduce some restriction on style, which drives output image very similar to input photograph. The normalization operation eliminates representation of image style from feature maps, so the $\mathscr{L}_1$ sparse regularization of normalized feature maps better describes the differences between semantic contents of photograph and cartoon images. To preserve both local and global semantic contents, we compute $\mathscr{L}_1$ sparse regularization of every feature map in *feature model* and use the sum of them as final content loss.

For style loss $\mathcal{L}_{style}(G)$, we adopt the same method as used in AdaIN [6]. The style loss is defined as:

$$\mathcal{L}_{style}(G) = \sum_{\lambda} \| \sigma(f_\lambda(G(x,y))) - \sigma(f_\lambda(x)) \|_2 + \sum_{\lambda} \| \mu(f_\lambda(G(x,y))) - \mu(f_\lambda(x)) \|_2$$

Adversarial Loss $\mathcal{L}_{adv}$. Because the content loss and style loss mentioned before are both regularization in feature spaces. If there is not explicit restriction in image space, the generated images tend to be inconsistent among different parts and usually contain some small line segments. So we introduce the adversarial training strategy. We use the multi-scale discriminator proposed in [7] to distinguish between real cartoon images and generated cartoonized photographs. $\mathcal{L}_{adv}$ is defined as:

$$\mathcal{L}_{adv}(G, D) = E[logD(x_i)] + E[log(1 - D(G(x_i, y_j)))].$$

The adversarial loss explicitly add restriction to the generated images in image space, which drives the whole generated images more smooth and consistent among different parts. Some ablation study in Sect. 4.3 proves that the adversarial loss plays important role for producing high-quality cartoonized images.

Reconstruction Loss $\mathcal{L}_{Recon}$. The reconstruction loss is consist of two parts: the reconstruction loss for photo images $\mathcal{L}_{Recon\_p}$ and the reconstruction loss for cartoon images $\mathcal{L}_{Recon\_c}$. For input images x_p and x_c, we directly render the un-coordinated *feature model* Ψ_p and Ψ_c and get reconstructed images x'_p and x'_c. Reconstruction loss is defined as:

$$\begin{aligned}\mathcal{L}_{Recon}(G) &= \mathcal{L}_{Recon\_p}(G) + \mathcal{L}_{Recon\_c}(G),\\ &= \parallel x'_p - x_p \parallel_2 + \parallel x'_c - x_c \parallel_2 .\end{aligned}$$

The reconstruction loss is used to ensure the *Rendering network*'s generalization ability. *Rendering network* do not participate in cartoonization process and all cartoonization processes are limited in *Coordinating* part. By adopting reconstruction loss, we make *Rendering network* focus on reconstructing images from *feature models*, which prompts the *Rendering network* be able to render any type image, no matter it is photo in cartoon image.

4 Experiments

We implement our approach in PyTorch1.0 and Python language. All experiments were performed on an NVIDIA Titan X GPU.

CartoonRenderer can generate high-quality cartoonized images by using various cartoon images for training, which are easy to obtain since we do not require paired or classified images. Our model is able to efficiently learn different cartoon sub-styles. Some of results are shown in Fig. 1.

To compare *CartoonRenderer* with state of the art methods, we collected the training and test data as presented in Sect. 4.1. In Sect. 4.2, we present the comparison between *CartoonRenderer* and representative stylization methods.

4.1 Data

The training and test data contains realistic photos and cartoon images. All the training images are randomly cropped to 256 × 256.

Realistic Photos. We collect 220,000 photos in all, some of which come from MSCOCO [9] dataset and others come from the Internet. 200,000 photos are used for training and 20,000 for testing. The shortest width of each image is greater than 256 to ensure random cropping is feasible.

Cartoon Images. We collect 80,000 high-quality cartoon images from the Internet for training, another 10000 cartoon images sampled from Danbooru2018 [1] dataset are used for testing.

4.2 Comparison with State of the Art

In this subsection, we compare our results with CycleGAN [17], AdaIN [6] and CartoonGAN [3]. 200 epochs are trained for all the them.

Refer to Fig. 3, we show the qualitative results generated by different methods, and all of the test data are *never* observed during the training phase. It is clear that CycleGAN [17] and AdaIN [6] can not work well with the cartoon styles. In contrast, CartoonGAN and our *CartoonRenderer* produce high-quality results. To preserve the content of the input images well, we add the identity loss to CycleGAN [17], but the stylization results are still far from satisfactory. AdaIN [6] successfully generates images with smooth colors but suffers from serious artifacts. CartoonGAN [3] produces clear images without artifacts, but the generated results are too close to the input photos and the color distribution is very monotonous. In other words, the extent of cartoonization with CartoonGAN [3] is not enough. In contrast, our method apparently produces higher-quality cartoonized images, which have high contrast between colors and contains very clear edges.

Fig. 3. Cartoonization results of different methods

For more details, we show close-up views of one result in Fig. 4. Obviously, our method performs much better than others in detail. Even the details of eyelashes and pupils are well preserved and re-rendered in cartoon style.

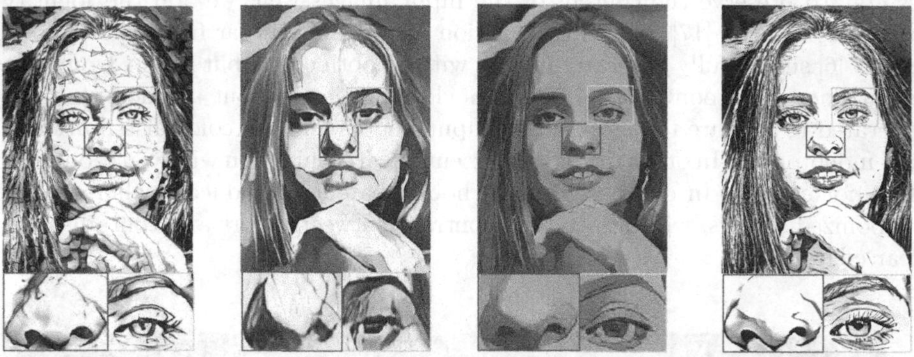

(a) AdaIN (b) CycleGAN (c) CartoonGAN (d) Ours

Fig. 4. The detailed performance of different methods

5 Conclusion

In this work, we propose a novel "CartoonRenderer" framework which utilizing a single trained model to generate multiple cartoon styles. In a nutshell, our method maps photo into a *feature model* and render the *feature model* back into image space. Our method is able to produce higher quality cartoon style images than prior art. In addition, due to the decoupling of whole generating process into *"Modeling-Coordinating-Rendering"* parts, our method could easily process higher resolution photos (up to 5000 × 5000 pixels).

Acknowledgment. This work was supported by National Natural Science Foundation of China (61976137, U1611461), 111 Project (B07022 and Sheitc No.150633) and the Shanghai Key Laboratory of Digital Media Processing and Transmissions. This work was also supported by SJTU-BIGO Joint Research Fund, and CCF-Tencent Open Fund.

References

1. Anonymous, the Danbooru community, Branwen, G., Gokaslan, A.: Danbooru 2018: a large-scale crowdsourced and tagged anime illustration dataset, January 2019
2. Chen, T.Q., Schmidt, M.: Fast patch-based style transfer of arbitrary style (2016)
3. Chen, Y., Lai, Y.K., Liu, Y.J.: CartoonGAN: generative adversarial networks for photo cartoonization, pp. 9465–9474, June 2018. https://doi.org/10.1109/CVPR.2018.00986

4. Dumoulin, V., Shlens, J., Kudlur, M.: A learned representation for artistic style (2016)
5. Gatys, L.A., Ecker, A.S., Bethge, M.: Image style transfer using convolutional neural networks. In: Computer Vision and Pattern Recognition (2016)
6. Huang, X., Belongie, S.: Arbitrary style transfer in real-time with adaptive instance normalization (2017)
7. Huang, X., Liu, M.Y., Belongie, S., Kautz, J.: Multimodal unsupervised image-to-image translation (2018)
8. Karras, T., Laine, S., Aila, T.: A style-based generator architecture for generative adversarial networks (2018)
9. Lin, T.-Y., et al.: Microsoft COCO: common objects in context. In: Fleet, D., Pajdla, T., Schiele, B., Tuytelaars, T. (eds.) ECCV 2014. LNCS, vol. 8693, pp. 740–755. Springer, Cham (2014). https://doi.org/10.1007/978-3-319-10602-1_48
10. Nguyen-Phuoc, T., Li, C., Balaban, S., Yang, Y.: RenderNet: a deep convolutional network for differentiable rendering from 3D shapes (2018)
11. Ronneberger, O., Fischer, P., Brox, T.: U-Net: convolutional networks for biomedical image segmentation (2017)
12. Sanakoyeu, A., Kotovenko, D., Lang, S., Ommer, B.: A style-aware content loss for real-time HD style transfer (2018)
13. Simonyan, K., Zisserman, A.: Very deep convolutional networks for large-scale image recognition. Computer Science (2014)
14. Ulyanov, D., Lebedev, V., Vedaldi, A., Lempitsky, V.: Texture networks: feed-forward synthesis of textures and stylized images (2016)
15. Ulyanov, D., Vedaldi, A., Lempitsky, V.: Improved texture networks: maximizing quality and diversity in feed-forward stylization and texture synthesis (2017)
16. Yao, Y., Ren, J., Xie, X., Liu, W., Liu, Y.J., Wang, J.: Attention-aware multi-stroke style transfer (2019)
17. Zhu, J.Y., Park, T., Isola, P., Efros, A.A.: Unpaired image-to-image translation using cycle-consistent adversarial networks. In: IEEE International Conference on Computer Vision (2017)

Oral Session 4A: Detection and Classification

Multi-condition Place Generator for Robust Place Recognition

Yiting Cheng[1], Yankai Wang[2], Lizhe Qi[2], and Wenqiang Zhang[1](✉)

[1] Shanghai Key Laboratory of Intelligent Information Processing, School of Computer Science, Fudan University, Shanghai, China
wqzhang@fudan.edu.cn

[2] Academy for Engineering and Technology, Fudan University, Shanghai, China

Abstract. As an image retrieval task, visual place recognition (VPR) encounters two technical challenges: appearance variations resulted from external environment changes and the lack of cross-domain paired training data. To overcome these challenges, multi-condition place generator (MPG) is introduced for data generation. The objective of MPG is two-fold, (1) synthesizing realistic place samples corresponding to multiple conditions; (2) preserving the place identity information during the generation procedure. While MPG smooths the appearance disparities under various conditions, it also suffers image distortion. For this reason, we propose the relative quality based triplet (RQT) loss by reshaping the standard triplet loss such that it down-weights the loss assigned to low-quality images. By taking advantage of the innovations mentioned above, a condition-invariant VPR model is trained without the labeled training data. Comprehensive experiments show that our method outperforms state-of-the-art algorithms by a large margin on several challenging benchmarks.

Keywords: Visual place recognition · Content-based image retrieval · Data augmentation · Image translation

1 Introduction

The visual place recognition has been traditionally viewed as an image retrieval task. Given a query image, a robust place recognition system is required to find the same location quickly and correctly from a large-scale database. It plays a vital role in Simultaneous Localization And Mapping (SLAM), and has been widely applied in applications such as mobile robotics [13] and autonomous driving [20]. VPR was traditionally settled with handcraft features [12,21,22], while with the development of deep learning [5,9], models based on CNNs have achieved impressive success in long-term and condition-robust place recognition [1,2,14,25,27] in the last few years. To remove the need for large data volume in supervised CNN based model [1,2], the unsupervised methods based on auto-encoder architecture

---

This work was supported by the National Natural Science Foundation of China (No. 81373555), Special Fund of the Ministry of Education of China (No. 2018A11005) and Jihua Lab under Grant No.Y80311W180.

Y. M. Ro et al. (Eds.): MMM 2020, LNCS 11961, pp. 191–202, 2020.
https://doi.org/10.1007/978-3-030-37731-1_16

are introduced by [14,25,27]. These methods are shown to be competitive on several datasets, but due to the limited cross-domain training samples, the performance significantly deteriorates when tested on other datasets.

To further improve the generalization ability of unsupervised VPR model, we propose MPG to synthesize places under different environmental conditions. The synthesized places are desired to keep their identities, meanwhile present different styles from the original one. Then abundant cross-domain correspondences can be obtained without data collection. MPG is constructed by extending StarGAN with a novel edge-preserving loss, which insists on preserving the edges of the original image, because the outlines of landmarks are crucial to make a place distinguishable. Although the proposed MPG promotes the synthesis process of our framework, distortion and noise are still incurred by generated images, and there is a gap of image quality among different target domains, the standard triplet loss [7] is reshaped to construct RQT loss to solve this problem. The relative quality is calculated by utilizing discriminative knowledge of discriminator; then it can be used as a coefficient of triplet loss for different samples.

The main contributions of this paper are as follows: (1) MPG with edge-preserving loss is proposed to preserve the identity information of place during the image-to-image translation. (2) RQT loss is proposed to tackle the issue of quality degradation brought by generated images. (3) With all the innovations, VPR model is trained to achieve the new state-of-the-art on three representative datasets.

2 Related Work

2.1 Unsupervised Deep Learning Based Visual Place Recognition

Unsupervised learning strategy has been introduced in deep learning based VPR due to the lack of training data. In [27], Xiang and Tao propose a method automatically learn features with the Stacked Denoising Auto-encoder (SDA) [23]. Inspired by [27], Merrill and Huang [14] propose an unsupervised architecture to construct training pairs with viewpoint variations. Windrim *et al.* [25] extend Spectral Angle-Stacked Autoencoder [24] to learn illumination-invariant features. These auto-encoder based networks have shown competitive performance; however, as training samples only belong to limited domains, the performance weakens when facing condition changes. Yin *et al.* [28] propose a feature separation method to extract condition-robust features with weakly supervision, this work combats appearance changes between multi-domain, but the specific training for each dataset is required in this approach, which leads to a limited generalization ability. With the above observation, as a data augmentation method, unsupervised GANs are utilized to generate multi-condition images for robust VPR model training in this paper.

2.2 Data Augmentation by Image Translation

Some works perform data augmentation by image-to-image translation for VPR. Based on CycleGAN, [11,19] preprocess the images by translating the images of two traverses to the same domain. Performance on the specific dataset is enhanced without the domain shift, however, considering the real-time requirement of VPR, the prepossessing procedure which runs at approximately 1–3 Hz on GPU is impractical before every query.

GAN-based image translation is also introduced for end-to-end training in other tasks. Synthesized images are utilized to learn a condition-invariant feature extractor for cross-domain tasks [8,30] or address the domain shift problem between different datasets [4,29]. Hu *et al.* propose CAPG-GAN [8] to synthesize faces with arbitrary views for face recognition, similar framework is introduced in [30] to adapt the camera style variation for person re-identification (ReID). In [30], L1 distance between the transferred image and the original image is added in CycleGAN loss to preserve the color consistency during image translation. [4] considers the problem of identity preserving in person transfer, the translated image is constrained to be semantically close with the corresponding original one. Inspired by these methods, MPG with edge-preserving loss is presented for the specific place generation task in this paper.

3 Proposed Method

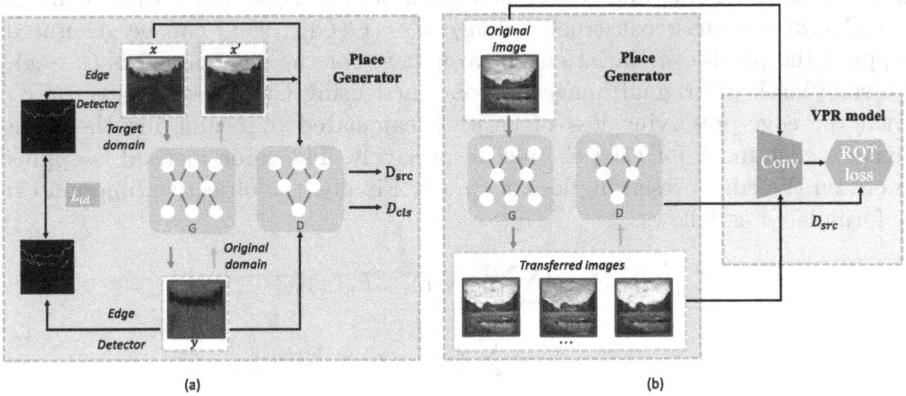

Fig. 1. The pipeline of our framework. (a) MPG training. (b) VPR model training.

Our prime goal is to generate cross-domain images for condition-invariant VPR model training. The pipeline of our framework is shown in Fig. 1, which consists of MPG model as an image translator and VPR model as a feature extractor. First, MPG is trained to generate samples under different conditions. Second, the samples for VPR training are constructed with original images and multi-condition images synthesized by MPG. Finally, the VPR model is trained with RQT loss for feature extraction. The details of the above steps are introduced in the rest of this section respectively.

3.1 MPG for Image Translation

StarGAN Review. StarGAN contains a generator G and a discriminator D. The generator is proposed to translate an input image x from the source domain into the target domain, the objective of the discriminator is two-fold: (1) identifying whether the input x is real or fake (generated); (2) distinguishing the source and target domain of an input x, $D : x \rightarrow (D_{src}(x), D_{cls}(x))$. The overall StarGAN loss function is expressed as:

$$L_{style}(G, D) = L_{GAN}(G, D) + \lambda_{cls} L_{cls} + \lambda_{rec} L_{rec}, \tag{1}$$

where $L_{GAN}(G, D)$ is the adversarial loss for the mapping function G and discriminator D, L_{cls} is the domain classification loss that forces G to generate images classified to the correct target domain, L_{rec} is the reconstruction loss to preserve the content after a cycle mapping. λ_{cls} and λ_{rec} penalize the importance between the above losses.

Edge-Preserving Loss. In VPR, the edges of scenes are not readily changed along with conditions, so we can describe the identity of place with edge information. Inspired by this characteristic, the edge-preserving loss builds a constraint that keeps the edge fixed during generation. Given the original image x, target domain label c, and source domain label c', the style-transferred image $y = G(x, c)$ and the reconstructed image $x' = G(G(x, c), c')$ can be generated. Suppose the pixel-level variation between (x, y) of the i_{th} channel is $(y - x)_i$, the edge mask of original image x is obtained using Canny edge detector E_d. Then the edge-preserving loss of (x, y) is calculated by evaluating the variations on edge mask for each channel respectively. The same method is applied to obtain the edge-preserving loss of (y, x'). Finally, the objective function can be formulated as follows,

$$\begin{aligned} L_{id}(G) = &\mathbb{E}_{x,y}[\sum_i \|(y - x)_i \circ E_d(x)\|_2] \\ &+ \mathbb{E}_{y,x'}[\sum_i \|(x' - y)_i \circ E_d(y)\|_2], \end{aligned} \tag{2}$$

where $\circ$ represents the Hadamard product, then the full loss function of MPG is formulated as,

$$L_{MPG}(G, D) = L_{Style} + \lambda L_{id}, \tag{3}$$

where L_{Style} imposes constraint on style transfer, L_{id} emphasizes on identity-preserving. λ is a parameter controls the relative importance of the above two constraints. Examples of images generated by MPG are shown in Fig. 2. It is apparent that images are translated to different styles conditioned on the target domain label, and the identity information of the original place is well preserved.

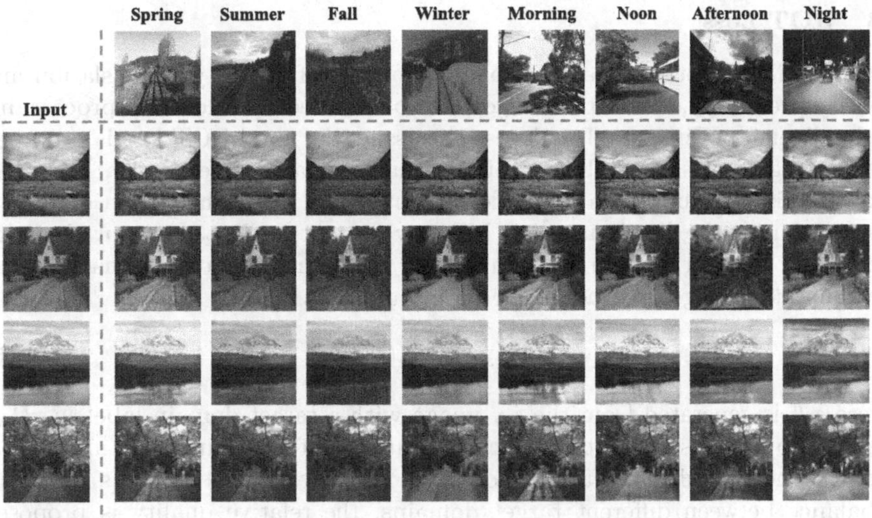

Fig. 2. Multi-condition image-to-image place generation results by MPG.

3.2 Training Samples Construction

Suppose that we have M different domains ($M = M_1 + M_2 + \cdots + M_n$) in all of N training datasets, the image-to-image mappings are learned between every domain pairs with MPG. The Places [31] dataset P is a large-scale dataset for scene recognition, it can be regarded as a source domain, which contains n_P images belonging to diverse locations. Followed [26], we train our VPR model with triplet network. For training triplets construction, MPG can be utilized to generate a set of images $B = \{x_i, x_{i*}^1, x_{i*}^2, \cdots, x_{i*}^M\}_{i=1}^b$, where b is the number of original samples in a training batch of P, x_i is the i_{th} original image of training batch, $x_{i*}^1, x_{i*}^2, \cdots, x_{i*}^M$ are corresponding synthesized images which are in the style of domain $1, 2, \cdots, M$ respectively. For every original image x_i, positive pair is generated by randomly choosing two images from $C = \{x_i, x_{i*}^1, x_{i*}^2, \cdots, x_{i*}^M\}$, the negative sample can be naturally found by randomly selecting from $B' = \{x_j, x_{j*}^1, x_{j*}^2, \cdots, x_{j*}^M | x_j \in B, i \neq j\}$. Once the triplets are constructed, the training of VPR model is the same as a supervised one. We adopt The triplet loss function $Wohlhart - Lepetit$ loss proposed by [26],

$$L_{Triplet} = max\left\{0, 1 - \frac{\|E(x_N) - E(x_A)\|_2}{margin + \|E(x_P) - E(x_A)\|_2}\right\}, \quad (4)$$

where x_A, x_P, x_N is the anchor, positive and negative of a triplet respectively, the $margin$ is a parameter which limits the separability of the negative pairs compared to positive ones. The value of $L_{Triplet}$ is limited in $[0, 1]$, which is demonstrated to counterbalance the output of the network. The $margin$ is set to 1 in all our experiments.

3.3 RQT Loss

Although MPG obtains the desirable capabilities of both style translation and identity-preserving, the distortions cannot be avoided in generation process due to the diversity of images. To address this issue, the novel RQT loss is proposed by lowering the loss contribution of low-quality images. Specifically, RQT loss takes the image quality as a coefficient for triplet loss. The image quality is measured using the discriminator of MPG, whose output $D_{src}(x)$ naturally judge the quality of input x while distinguishing x between real and fake image. Given the generated image x_{i*}^{m}, the image quality $q(x_{i*}^{m})$ is defined as:

$$q(x_{i*}^{m}) = D_{src}(x_{i*}^{m}), \tag{5}$$

where x_{i*}^{m} is generated from the i_{th} image with a target domain label m, D_{src} is the output of discriminator, which indicates whether an image is an original image or generated one. Furthermore, we can observe that there is a quality imbalance between different target domains, the relative quality is proposed by comparing the absolute quality with the average quality of corresponding domain:

$$q_r(x_{i*}^{m}) = \frac{q(x_{i*}^{m})}{\sum_{j=1}^{n_P} q(x_{j*}^{m})/n_P}, \tag{6}$$

where n_P is the number of images in dataset P, $q_r(x_{i*}^{m})$ indicates the relative quality by calculating a ratio as a normalization. Finally, the relative quality of a triplet Trq is evaluated by calculating the average relative quality among the anchor, positive and negative. Intuitively, coefficient Trq reduces the loss contribution from images with low quality, and a threshold t is set to filter the triplets with unacceptable low quality,

$$T_{rq} = avg(q_r(x_A), q_r(x_P), q_r(x_N)) \tag{7}$$

$$L_{RQT} = \begin{cases} T_{rq} * L_{Triplet}, & T_{rq} > t \\ 0, & otherwise, \end{cases} \tag{8}$$

4 Experiment

4.1 Datasets

Training Dataset. Nordland [18], St. Lucia [6], and Day-night Car Dataset [15] are used to train MPG. Note that the supervised image-to-image pair-wise information is not utilized in our MPG training. Traverses of Nordland are taken toward four seasons through Norway. St. Lucia is collected in 5 different times of day in a suburb, which contains illumination and shadow changes. Day-night Car is gathered on day/late afternoon/evening, therefore great illumination changes are supported in this dataset. Trained with the above three datasets, MPG is supposed to learn how scenes change under different seasons and illuminations.

Testing Dataset. The testing datasets are public benchmarks collected from geographically separated locations. The Gardens Point dataset consists of day-left and night-right traverses along the same route. The Campus Loop dataset [14] contains both indoor and outdoor images, two sequences were recorded on a cloudy day with snow and a sunny day following the same route respectively. The above two datasets show various changes in illumination, weather, and viewpoint. The FAS [17] dataset was collected through long journeys between different seasons with slightly viewpoint changes. We test on the first 450 images in each traverse to evaluate the long-term appearance robustness of the VPR model.

4.2 Experiment Settings

The official version of StarGAN is adopted as our MPG architecture, we empirically set $\lambda_{cls} = 1$, $\lambda_{rec} = 10$, $\lambda = 1$ in all of our experiments. After the MPG training completed, we randomly choose 200 images from each scene category of Places as original images. In this way, the environmental diversity is guaranteed when generate samples under different domains.

To extract the robust features for place recognition, the architecture of Calc [14] is adopted as our baseline, which only contains three convolutional layers and extracts a 1064-dim vector as feature descriptor. In this way, the efficiency of our VPR model could be ensured by the lightweight architecture and compact descriptor. Also, the random projective transformation algorithm in [14] is used to preprocess the training samples with a probability of 0.5, by which the samples are generated under different viewpoints. We fine-tune the Calc [14] with the original and generated images, use the Adam optimizer [10] with a batch size of 16, a learning rate of 0.0002 and set weight decay to 0.0005.

5 Results

5.1 Evaluation of Edge-Preserving Loss

Image Translation Results. Figures 3 and 4 show the synthesis results with StarGAN and MPG respectively, we can observe that MPG is demonstrated to yield sharper and cleaner images with substantially higher quality.

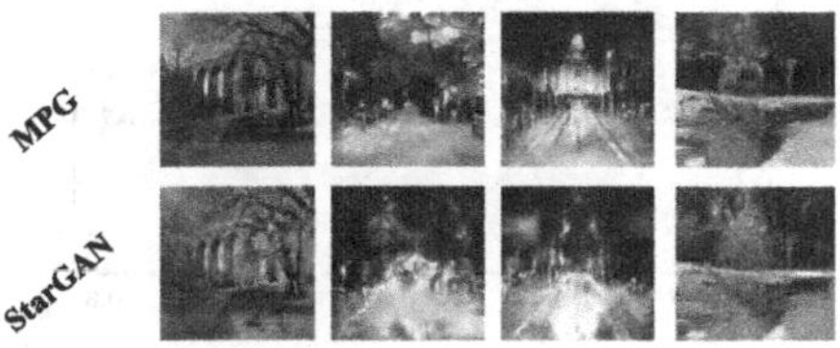

Fig. 3. The comparison of place synthesis results.

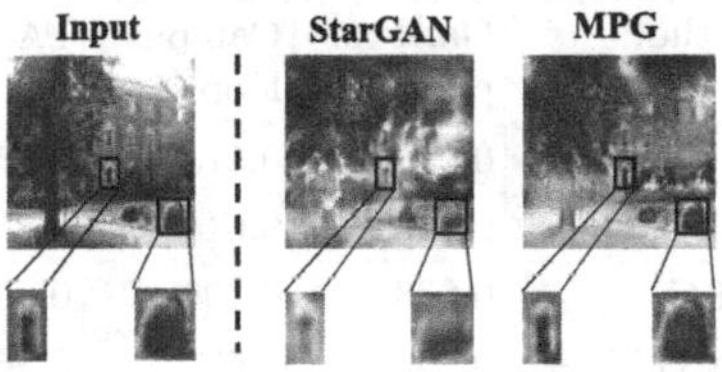

Fig. 4. The details of place synthesis results.

Table 1. The average distance between the original images and generated images under different target domains.

	Spring		Summer		Fall		Winter		Morning		Noon		Afternoon		Night	
	L1	L2	L1	L2	L1	L2	L1	L2	L1	L2	L1	L2	L1	L2	L1	L2
StarGAN	0.923	1.353	1.038	1.507	1.148	1.652	1.033	1.479	1.068	1.530	1.061	1.524	1.078	1.556	1.426	1.971
MPG	**0.818**	**1.252**	**0.892**	**1.337**	**0.987**	**1.447**	**0.950**	**1.382**	**0.900**	**1.338**	**0.960**	**1.413**	**0.959**	**1.425**	**1.302**	**1.816**

Furthermore, the identity-preserving capability of StarGAN and MPG is compared with quantitative analysis. We evaluate this capability by calculating the average distance between the original images and style-transferred images in the feature level. To extract features which are discriminative to the place information, our baseline VPR model Calc [14] is adopted as a feature extractor. As shown in Table 1, images generated by MPG are semantically closer to original images in both L1 and L2 distance. In this way, we demonstrate that MPG performs better in identity-preserving.

Results on VPR Datasets. MPG is constructed with edge-preserving loss based on StarGAN. As shown in Table 2, compared with StarGAN, MPG gains +8.75%, +14.7%, +1.29% increase in AUC when tested on Gardens Point, Campus Loop, FAS respectively. The improvement suggests that the novel edge-preserving loss is essential to preserve the place information through place generation. Greater improvement is shown tested on Gardens Point and Campus Loop dataset, which highlights the superiority of the edge-preserving loss when facing challenging environments with complex changes.

5.2 Evaluation of RQT Loss

Results on VPR Datasets. As shown in Table 2, the StarGAN+RQT model shows further improvement compared with StarGAN on three benchmarks. And compared with MPG, the full version model MPG+RQT also leads to +5.52%,

Table 2. AUC under different components of our framework.

Methods	Gardens point	Campus loop	FAS
Calc (basel.)	0.722	0.575	0.837
StarGAN	0.766	0.614	0.853
MPG	0.833	0.704	0.864
StarGAN + RQT	0.794	0.630	0.868
MPG+RQT (full version)	**0.879**	**0.742**	**0.873**

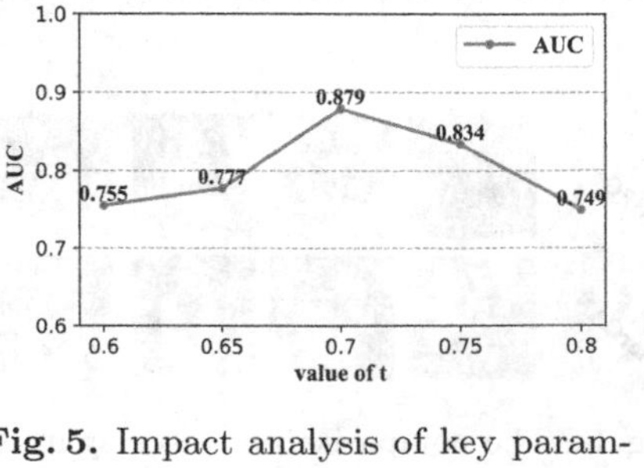

Fig. 5. Impact analysis of key parameter t in Eq. 8.

+5.40%, +1.04% increase on dataset Gardens Point, Campus Loop and FAS respectively, which achieves the best performance. The results indicate the necessity of considering the gap of quality among original and generated samples, by which the impact of image distortion is relieved.

Impact Analysis of Key Parameter t. In Fig. 5, the impact of t on the Gardens Point dataset is studied. t is a threshold controls the tolerance of low-quality triplets. When t is set to 0, the loss from all triples will be calculated with the coefficient Trq; a larger t means a stricter strategy of sample selection for VPR model training. We vary t from 0.6 to 0.8 to find a proper hyperparameter, the best AUC is obtained when the t is set to 0.7.

5.3 Comparison with State-of-the-Art Data Augmentation Methods

To further validate our full version model, we compare it with state-of-the-art data augmentation methods, StarGAN [3], Camstyle [30] and SPGAN [4]. The baseline VPR model Calc [14] is fine-tuned with the same settings described in Sect. 4.2 with original and generated images. As shown in Table 3, all the above data augmentation methods are demonstrated to be effective to promote VPR task, while AUC results show our proposed model achieves the best performance among these state-of-the-art methods.

As we mentioned before, the generated images are proposed to be style-transferred to different domains and to maintain its identity information. StarGAN and Camstyle make less improvement because the second objective is not considered during image translation. SPGAN train a feature learner to preserve the semantics of the original images, despite the competing results, Table 3 shows the superior of MPG to SPGAN. We speculate that the reason is that the semantic consistency constraint of SPGAN limits the essential changes in illumination and color to meet the style of target domain, while our edge-preserving loss relaxes the constraint as boundary consistency to achieve a balance between style translation and identity-preserving.

Table 3. Comparison with state-of-the-art data augmentation methods.

Methods	Gardens Point	Campus Loop	FAS
Calc (basel.)	0.722	0.575	0.837
StarGAN	0.766	0.614	0.853
CamStyle	0.777	0.709	0.859
SPGAN	0.805	0.648	0.864
Ours	**0.879**	**0.742**	**0.873**

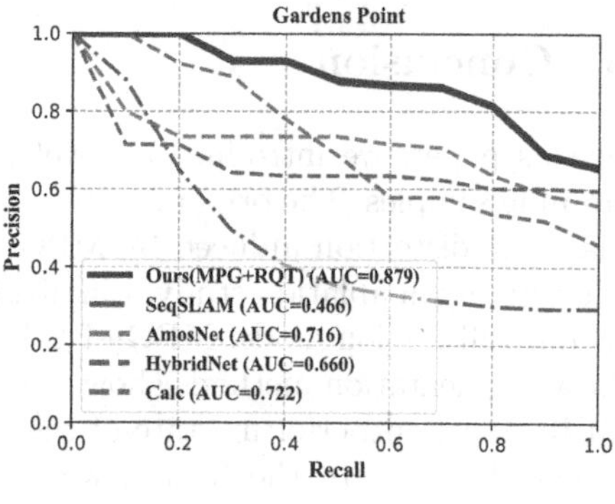

Fig. 6. Comparison results on the Gardens Point dataset.

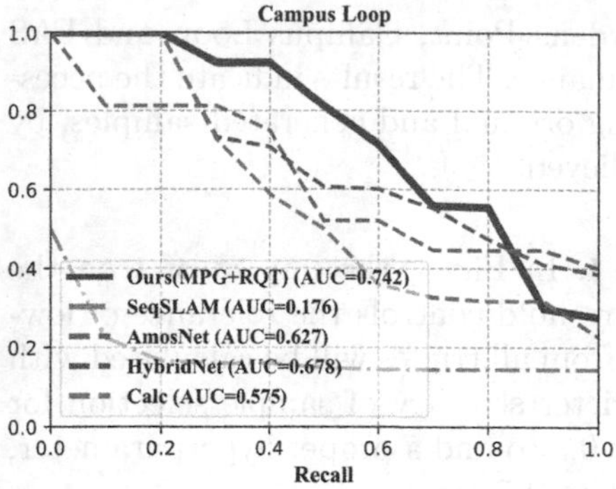

Fig. 7. Comparison results on the Campus Loop dataset.

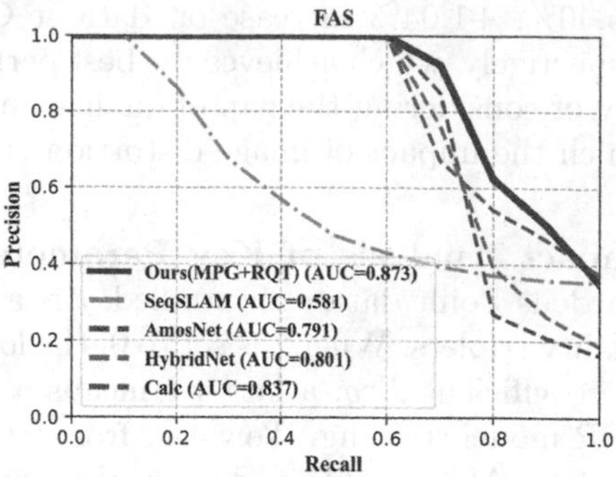

Fig. 8. Comparison results on the FAS dataset.

5.4 Comparison with State-of-the-Art VPR Methods

We compare our full version method MPG+RQT with the State-of-the-art methods Calc [14], SeqSLAM [16], HybridNet [2] and AmosNet [2]. For a fair comparison, while the descriptors of our method are 1064-dim vectors, we adopt the fc8 layer of HybridNet [2] and AmosNet [2], from which 2543-dim features can be produced. Note that the HybridNet [2] and AmosNet [2] are supervised methods and SeqSLAM [16] relies on additional sequence information, while our VPR model is trained without any labels, and sequence information is not utilized.

As shown in Figs. 6, 7, and 8, our full version method MPG+RQT achieves the new state-of-the-art on all the three benchmarks. The AUC on Gardens Point dataset is 0.879, which makes 21.7% increase compared with previous state-of-the-art method calc [14]. On the Campus Loop dataset, our method outperforms the second best method HybridNet [2] (0.678) with the AUC 0.742. Our method also achieves the best performance (0.873) on the FAS dataset. Therefore, the comparison results demonstrate the superiority and robustness of our VPR model.

6 Conclusion

In this paper, we introduce a novel place generator MPG to synthesize VPR training samples. The original triplet loss is replaced by a novel RQT loss to alleviate the distortion induced by MPG. The effectiveness of MPG and RQT loss is evaluated in ablation study. Finally, the VPR model is substantially promoted by our full version model MPG+RQT, and the comparison with state-of-the-art data augmentation methods shows its superiority. We also demonstrate that our VPR model outperforms state-of-the-art VPR methods on three representative public datasets. In the future, we will extend the environmental diversity by appending more weather condition in MPG training, by this means, the robustness of VPR model will be enhanced.

References

1. Arandjelovic, R., Gronat, P., Torii, A., Pajdla, T., Sivic, J.: NetVLAD: CNN architecture for weakly supervised place recognition. In: Proceedings of the IEEE Conference on Computer Vision and Pattern Recognition, pp. 5297–5307 (2016)
2. Chen, Z., et al.: Deep learning features at scale for visual place recognition. In: 2017 IEEE International Conference on Robotics and Automation (ICRA), pp. 3223–3230. IEEE (2017)
3. Choi, Y., Choi, M., Kim, M., Ha, J.W., Kim, S., Choo, J.: StarGAN: unified generative adversarial networks for multi-domain image-to-image translation. In: Proceedings of the IEEE Conference on Computer Vision and Pattern Recognition, pp. 8789–8797 (2018)
4. Deng, W., Zheng, L., Ye, Q., Kang, G., Yang, Y., Jiao, J.: Image-image domain adaptation with preserved self-similarity and domain-dissimilarity for person re-identification. In: Proceedings of the IEEE Conference on Computer Vision and Pattern Recognition, pp. 994–1003 (2018)
5. Girshick, R., Donahue, J., Darrell, T., Malik, J.: Rich feature hierarchies for accurate object detection and semantic segmentation. In: Proceedings of the IEEE Conference on Computer Vision and Pattern Recognition, pp. 580–587 (2014)
6. Glover, A.J., Maddern, W.P., Milford, M.J., Wyeth, G.F.: FAB-MAP+ RatSLAM: appearance-based SLAM for multiple times of day. In: 2010 IEEE International Conference on Robotics and Automation, pp. 3507–3512. IEEE (2010)
7. Gomez-Ojeda, R., Lopez-Antequera, M., Petkov, N., Jiménez, J.G.: Training a convolutional neural network for appearance-invariant place recognition. CoRR abs/1505.07428 (2015). http://arxiv.org/abs/1505.07428
8. Hu, Y., Wu, X., Yu, B., He, R., Sun, Z.: Pose-guided photorealistic face rotation. In: Proceedings of the IEEE Conference on Computer Vision and Pattern Recognition, pp. 8398–8406 (2018)
9. Jiang, S., Min, W., Mei, S.: Hierarchy-dependent cross-platform multi-view feature learning for venue category prediction. IEEE Trans. Multimedia **21**(6), 1609–1619 (2018)
10. Kingma, D.P., Ba, J.: Adam: a method for stochastic optimization. CoRR abs/1412.6980 (2015)
11. Latif, Y., Garg, R., Milford, M., Reid, I.: Addressing challenging place recognition tasks using generative adversarial networks. In: 2018 IEEE International Conference on Robotics and Automation (ICRA), pp. 2349–2355. IEEE (2018)
12. Liu, Y., Zhang, H.: Visual loop closure detection with a compact image descriptor. In: 2012 IEEE/RSJ International Conference on Intelligent Robots and Systems, pp. 1051–1056. IEEE (2012)
13. McManus, C., Churchill, W., Maddern, W., Stewart, A.D., Newman, P.: Shady dealings: robust, long-term visual localisation using illumination invariance. In: 2014 IEEE International Conference on Robotics and Automation (ICRA), pp. 901–906. IEEE (2014)
14. Merrill, N., Huang, G.: Lightweight unsupervised deep loop closure. In: Robotics: Science and Systems XIV, Carnegie Mellon University, Pittsburgh, Pennsylvania, USA, 26–30 June 2018 (2018). http://www.roboticsproceedings.org/rss14/p32.html
15. Milford, M., et al.: Sequence searching with deep-learnt depth for condition-and viewpoint-invariant route-based place recognition. In: Proceedings of the IEEE Conference on Computer Vision and Pattern Recognition Workshops, pp. 18–25 (2015)

16. Milford, M.J., Wyeth, G.F.: SeqSLAM: visual route-based navigation for sunny summer days and stormy winter nights. In: 2012 IEEE International Conference on Robotics and Automation, pp. 1643–1649. IEEE (2012)
17. Naseer, T., Burgard, W., Stachniss, C.: Robust visual localization across seasons. IEEE Trans. Rob. **34**(2), 289–302 (2018)
18. Olid, D., Fácil, J.M., Civera, J.: Single-view place recognition under seasonal changes. arXiv preprint arXiv:1808.06516 (2018)
19. Porav, H., Maddern, W., Newman, P.: Adversarial training for adverse conditions: robust metric localisation using appearance transfer. In: 2018 IEEE International Conference on Robotics and Automation (ICRA), pp. 1011–1018. IEEE (2018)
20. Sattler, T., et al.: Benchmarking 6DOF outdoor visual localization in changing conditions. In: Proceedings of the IEEE Conference on Computer Vision and Pattern Recognition, pp. 8601–8610 (2018)
21. Singh, G., Kosecka, J.: Visual loop closing using gist descriptors in manhattan world. In: ICRA Omnidirectional Vision Workshop (2010)
22. Sünderhauf, N., Protzel, P.: BRIEF-Gist-closing the loop by simple means. In: 2011 IEEE/RSJ International Conference on Intelligent Robots and Systems, pp. 1234–1241. IEEE (2011)
23. Vincent, P., Larochelle, H., Lajoie, I., Bengio, Y., Manzagol, P.A.: Stacked denoising autoencoders: Learning useful representations in a deep network with a local denoising criterion. J. Mach. Learn. Res. **11**(Dec), 3371–3408 (2010)
24. Windrim, L., Melkumyan, A., Murphy, R., Chlingaryan, A., Nieto, J.: Unsupervised feature learning for illumination robustness. In: 2016 IEEE International Conference on Image Processing (ICIP), pp. 4453–4457. IEEE (2016)
25. Windrim, L., Ramakrishnan, R., Melkumyan, A., Murphy, R.J.: A physics-based deep learning approach to shadow invariant representations of hyperspectral images. IEEE Trans. Image Process. **27**(2), 665–677 (2018)
26. Wohlhart, P., Lepetit, V.: Learning descriptors for object recognition and 3D pose estimation. In: Proceedings of the IEEE Conference on Computer Vision and Pattern Recognition, pp. 3109–3118 (2015)
27. Xiang, G., Tao, Z.: Unsupervised learning to detect loops using deep neural networks for visual SLAM system. Auton. Robots **41**(1), 1–18 (2017)
28. Yin, P., et al.: A multi-domain feature learning method for visual place recognition. In: 2019 IEEE International Conference on Robotics and Automation (ICRA) (2019)
29. Zhong, Z., Zheng, L., Luo, Z., Li, S., Yang, Y.: Invariance matters: exemplar memory for domain adaptive person re-identification. In: Proceedings of the IEEE Conference on Computer Vision and Pattern Recognition, pp. 598–607 (2019)
30. Zhong, Z., Zheng, L., Zheng, Z., Li, S., Yang, Y.: Camera style adaptation for person re-identification. In: Proceedings of the IEEE Conference on Computer Vision and Pattern Recognition, pp. 5157–5166 (2018)
31. Zhou, B., Lapedriza, A., Khosla, A., Oliva, A., Torralba, A.: Places: a 10 million image database for scene recognition. IEEE Trans. Pattern Anal. Mach. Intell. **40**(6), 1452–1464 (2017)

Guided Refine-Head for Object Detection

Lingyun Zeng[1], You Song[1(✉)], and Wenhai Wang[2]

[1] Beihang University, Beijing, China
{zenglingyun,songyou}@buaa.edu.cn
[2] Nanjing University, Nanjing, China
wangwenhai362@163.com

Abstract. In recent years, multi-stage detectors improve the accuracy of object detection to a new level. However, due to multiple stages, these methods typically fall short in the inference speed. To alleviate this problem, we propose a novel object detector—Guided Refine-Head, which is made up of a newly proposed detection network called Refine-Head and a knowledge-distillation-like loss function. Refine-Head is a two-stage detector, and thus Refine-Head has faster inference speed than multi-stage detectors. Nonetheless, Refine-Head is able to predict bounding boxes for incremental IoU thresholds like a multi-stage detector. In addition, we use knowledge-distillation-like loss function to guide the training process of Refine-Head. Therefore, besides fast inference speed, the proposed Guided Refine-Head also has competitive accuracy. Abundant ablation studies and comparative experiments on MS-COCO 2017 validate the superiority of the proposed Guided Refine-Head. It is worth noting that Guided Refine-Head achieves the AP of 38.0% at 10.4 FPS, surpassing Faster R-CNN by 1.8% at the similar speed.

Keywords: Object detection · Two-stage detector · Knowledge distillation

1 Introduction

Facilitated by the development of deep learning techniques [6,14,16–18,27], remarkable progress for object detection has been made in recent years. Currently, the popular object detection methods can be generally divided into two categories: two-stage detectors [7,10,11,13,24] and one-stage detectors [19,21,23]. In general, two-stage detectors typically have high accuracy due to two key processes: proposal generation (e.g. RPN [24]) and feature extraction (e.g. RoIPool [10]). However, these additional processes are often time-consuming and will be a bottleneck for efficiency optimization. In contrast one-stage detectors directly perform category and position prediction, making them more suitable for real-time applications. However, there is still room for improvement in the accuracy of one-stage detectors. So, "*How to achieve a better balance between accuracy and speed?*" is always a challenge for object detection.

Recently, multi-stage detectors (e.g. Cascade R-CNN [4]) push the accuracy of object detection to a new level. Unlike two-stage detectors, multi-stage

Y. M. Ro et al. (Eds.): MMM 2020, LNCS 11961, pp. 203–214, 2020.
https://doi.org/10.1007/978-3-030-37731-1_17

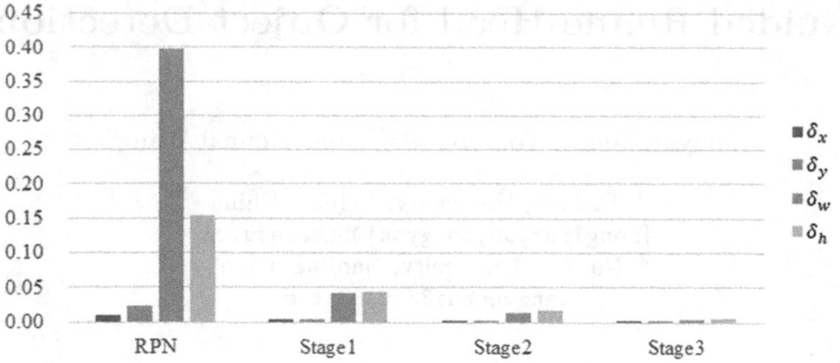

Fig. 1. The statistical histogram of δ_x, δ_y, δ_w and δ_h of RPN and the three stages of Cascade R-CNN [4].

detectors refine the bounding boxes by cascaded stages with incremental IoU thresholds, and this progressive optimal framework greatly improved the quality of the predicted bounding boxes. However, the shortcoming of the multi-stage detector is also obvious. It suffers from low speed because there are many stages in the pipeline. Therefore, a natural question emerges: *Can there be a faster way to refine the bounding boxes progressively?*

An intuitive solution is to reduce the multi-stage detector to the two-stage detector. First of all, we analyze the feasibility of this method from the perspective of Cascade R-CNN. As shown in Fig. 1, the δ_x, δ_y, δ_w and δ_h of the last three stages of Cascade R-CNN are very small, which indicates that the proposals given by the last three stages are similar. Furthermore, in Cascade R-CNN, the input feature of a stage is extracted based on the proposal predicted by the previous stage. Therefore, there are little differences among the input features of the last three stages, *which make it possible to merge these stages into a single one.* Motivated by the analysis, in this paper, we propose a novel two-stage detector, named Guided Refine-Head, which can progressively refine the bounding boxes like a multi-stage detector. Concretely, we firstly propose a Refine-Head to predict bounding boxes for different IoU thresholds. Note that, compared with the three separate networks in Cascade R-CNN, our proposed Refine-Head is a single network, and thus the speed of Refine-Head is faster. Inspired by knowledge distillation [15], we then use the soft labels and intermediate features of Cascade R-CNN to guide the training of Refine-Head. This process makes the result of Refine-Head more consistent with Cascade R-CNN, and let Refine-Head achieve close accuracy to Cascade R-CNN. The Refine-Head with the training guidance is Guided Refine-Head. Generally speaking, there are two benefits of our proposed Guided Refine-Head. Firstly, our method is actually a two-stage detector, which consumes shorter training and inference time compared with Cascade R-CNN. Secondly, our method keeps the setting of incremental IoU thresholds and uses knowledge distillation to guide the training process, which ensures the accuracy of our method.

To explore the effectiveness of our proposed Guided Refine-Head. We firstly conduct ablation studies on Guided Refine-Head. The ablation experiments mainly focus on the design of Refine-Head and loss function. We also compare Guided Refine-Head with other state-of-the-art methods, on the challenging COCO detection task [20]. Notably, with the similar backbone (e.g. ResNet50), Guided Refine-Head can achieve AP of 38.0% which is 1.8% better than Faster R-CNN [24], and the FPS of Guided Refine-Head is 50% faster than Cascade R-CNN [4]. These experiment results validate the superiority of the proposed Guided Refine-Head.

To summary, our contributions are listed as follows:

(1) We propose a novel Guided Refine-Head. Compared with Cascade R-CNN, the proposed Guided Refine-Head has close accuracy but faster speed;
(2) We propose a knowledge-distillation-like loss function to guide the training of Refine-Head, which can make the predicted bounding boxes more accurate;
(3) We conduct abundant ablation experiments to explore the efficiency of Guided Refine-Head and make comparisons with other state-of-the-art methods.

2 Related Work

2.1 Object Detection

Object detection has been extensively studied for decades. In the pre-deep learning era, object detectors [1,28] are based on sliding windows and use hand-crafted features to make object classification and location. With the remarkable success of Deep Convolutional Neural Networks (CNNs) [6,14,16–18,27], approaches based on CNNs have been actively explored for object detection. Currently, deep learning based detectors can be generally divided into two categories: two-stage detectors and one-stage detectors. For two-stage detectors, such as R-CNN [11], Fast R-CNN [10], SPP [13], Faster R-CNN [24], R-FCN [7], they first generate a sparse set of proposals, and then refine the proposals by region classifiers and location regressors. With proposal generator (e.g. selective search [26], RPN [24]), two-stage detector usually match the target objects well and have high accuracy. At the same time, due to the extra process, the speed of the two-stage detector is usually not fast. Different from two-stage methods, one-stage detectors such as SSD [21], YOLO [23], RetinaNet [19]), ignores the proposal generation step by directly making predictions with manually predefined anchors and thus reduce the inference time significantly. However, manually pre-defined anchors are usually sub-optimal and sometimes unreasonable, and few of them can match ground truths well. Therefore, one-stage detectors are difficult to precisely locate objects, which makes them less accurate than two-stage detectors.

2.2 Knowledge Distillation

CNNs are computationally expensive. Therefore, the trade-offs between speed and accuracy becomes a new challenge in deep learning technology. Knowledge distillation is one of the ways to solve this problem. Bucila et al. [3] compress large, complex ensembles into smaller, faster models by mimicking the output of the larger models. Subsequently, inspired by [3], [2] compress the deeper model to shallower but wider ones, in which the compressed model mimics the "logits". Hinton et al. [15] propose knowledge distillation as a more general case of [3], in which the prediction of the teacher model is viewed as a "soft label" and temperature cross-entropy loss is proposed to guide the training of student model. Specifically, for object detection, Shen et al. [25] consider the effect of distillation and hint frameworks in learning a compact object detection model. However, their methods are designed for pedestrian detection, which may not be well adapted to general object detection tasks. Different from [25], Chen et al. [5] apply knowledge distillation to multi-class detection models to find better accuracy-speed trade-off.

3 Proposed Method

In this section, we firstly propose Refine-Head and explain how it refines the bounding boxes progressively like a multi-stage detector. Next, we show the details of Guided Refine-Head, including how the Guided Refine-Head works during the training and testing phases. At last, we describe the design of the loss function in detail.

3.1 Refine-Head

As mentioned in Sect. 1, multi-stage detectors (e.g. Cascade R-CNN) often have high accuracy but suffer from low speed. To achieve a better trade-off between accuracy and speed, we propose a novel object detector—Refine-Head. Specifically, the proposed Refine-Head has two advantages. Firstly, it is a two-stage detector which is faster than Cascade R-CNN. Secondly, it can predict bounding boxes for different IoU thresholds like Cascade R-CNN, and thus it has high accuracy.

A high-level overview of the Refine-Head is illustrated in Fig. 2. Firstly, we get a sparse set of initial proposals P_0 from RPN [24] like most two-stage detectors. Then, we use RoIAlign [12] to extract the features F_0 of P_0 from the feature maps generated by the backbone, and the size of the extracted features F_0 are $7 \times 7 \times 256$. Finally, we use three groups of fully connected layers (FCs) to refine the extracted features F_0 and predict bounding boxes for different IoU thresholds ($\text{IoUs} = 0.5, 0.6, 0.7$). In more detail, for each group, there are two FCs with the output size of 1024, followed by a classifier and a regressor. We feed the features F_0 to the first group of FCs to get the refined features F_1 and refined proposals P_1. The same operation is applied between the second and third groups, and we get refined features $\{F_2, F_3\}$ and refined proposals $\{P_2, P_3\}$, in which the proposals P_3 are the final results of Refine-Head.

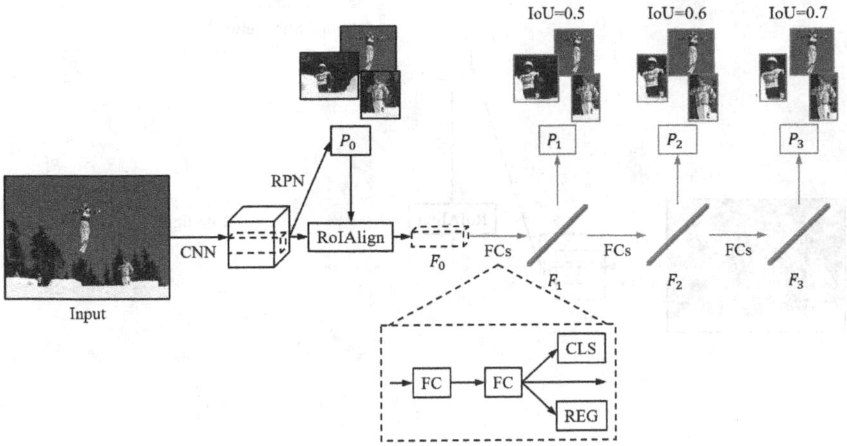

Fig. 2. The overall architecture of Refine-Head. P_0, P_1, P_2 and P_3 refer to proposals generated by RPN [24] and the three FCs groups respectively. FCs represents fully connection group which has several FC layers. F_1, F_2 and F_3 are features generated by the three FCs groups. "CLS" and "REG" represent classification and location regression respectively.

3.2 Guided Refine-Head

The refined-head replaces multiple stages with two stages, which improves the speed but also reduces the accuracy. To alleviate this problem, we propose Guided Refine-Head, in which we use the soft labels and intermediate features of Cascade R-CNN to guide the training of Refine-Head. As shown in Fig. 3, the proposed Guided Refine-Head is composed of two sub-networks: Guided Sub-Network (G-Net) and Mimic Sub-Network (M-Net). G-Net follows the same structure as Cascade R-CNN, and its high accuracy makes it a good guide for M-Net. M-Net follows the same structure as Refine-Head, whose details can be found in Fig. 2. Note that, G-Net is only used to guide the training of M-Net during the training phase. We drop G-Net and use only M-Net for inference during the testing phase. Therefore, Guided Refine-Head can achieve higher accuracy than Refine-Head at the same inference speed.

The overall framework of Guided Refine-Head is illustrated in Fig. 3. In the training phase, G-Net firstly produces intermediate features $\{F_1^G, F_2^G, F_3^G\}$ and results (i.e. categories and locations of bounding boxes) $\{P_1^G, P_2^G, P_3^G\}$. At the same time, M-Net also generates the corresponding features $\{F_1^M, F_2^M, F_3^M\}$ and results $\{P_1^M, P_2^M, P_3^M\}$. Note that, the size of F_i^G or F_i^M is 1024, and P_i^G or P_i^M consists of category vectors and location vectors, whose size is C and 4, respectively. Here, C is the category number of the dataset. After that, we typically use the ground truth labels to supervise the predicted results of G-Net and M-Net (see L_G and L_M in Fig. 4). In addition, we use soft label loss and feature loss to encourage the features and results of M-Net be similar to that of G-Net (see L_{soft} and L_{feat} in Fig. 4). In practice, this guiding process is only

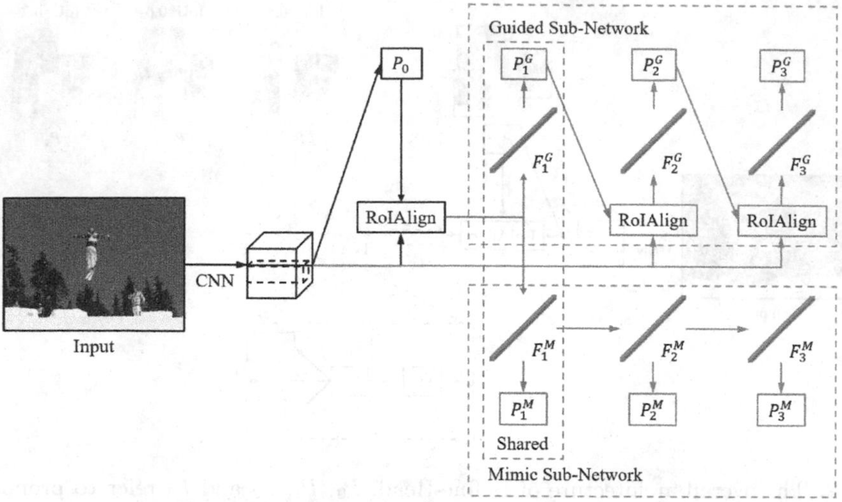

Fig. 3. The illustration of Guided Refine-Head. In Guided Sub-Network (G-Net), F_i^G refers to intermediate features generated by RoIAlign [12] and P_i^G represents the proposals (i.e. the categories and locations of bounding boxes). In Mimic Sub-Network (M-Net), F_i^M and P_i^M represent features and proposals which is corresponding to F_i^G and P_i^G. Note that G-Net and M-Net share the same network in the first part. (Color figure online)

performed on (F_i^G, F_i^M) and (P_i^G, P_i^M) when $i = 2, 3$, because G-Net and M-Net share a same network in the first part (see the blue dashed box in Fig. 3). In other words, F_1^G and P_1^G is the same as F_1^M and P_1^M, respectively. In the testing phase, only M-Net is used for inference, and we treat P_3^M produced by M-Net as the final result.

3.3 Loss Function

The overall loss function can be written as Eq. 1.

$$L = L_{RPN} + L_G + L_M + \alpha L_{feat} + \beta L_{soft} \tag{1}$$

Here, L_{RPN} is implemented from [24]. Both L_G and L_M are multi-stage loss which is the same as [4]. L_{feat} and L_{soft} are feature loss and soft label loss respectively. The α and β are used to balance the importance among L_{RPN}, L_G, L_M, L_{feat} and L_{soft}. We set α to 0.5 and β to 0.1 in our experiments. The details of L_{RPN}, L_G and L_M can be found in [24] and [4]. We emphatically presents the design of L_{feat} and L_{soft} as follows.

L_{feat} is used to make the features of M-Net be similar to that of G-Net. As discussed in Sect. 3.2, L_{feat} only calculates between F_i^G and F_i^M, when $i = 2, 3$. Thus, L_{feat} can be formulated as Eq. 2.

$$L_{feat} = \sum_{i=2}^{3} smooth_{L1}(F_i^G - F_i^M). \tag{2}$$

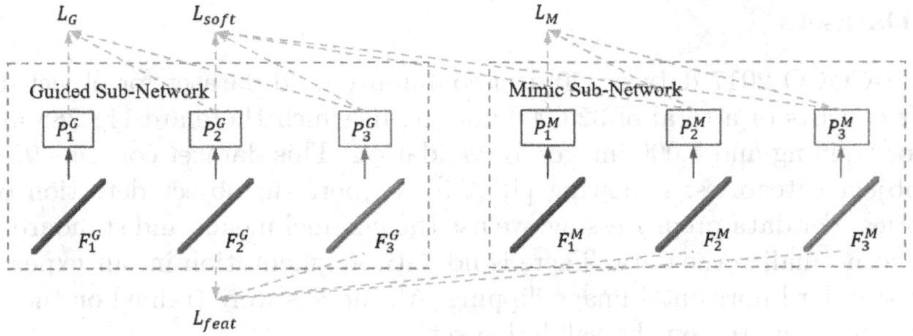

Fig. 4. The detail of loss functions in Guided Refine-Head. L_G and L_M represent multi-stage loss which is the same as [4]. L_{soft} and L_{feat} refer to soft label loss and feature loss respectively, which are calculated between each pair of (P_i^G, P_i^M) and (F_i^G, F_i^M) respectively when $i = 2, 3$.

Here, $smooth_{L1}$ [10] is used to measure the distance between F_i^G and F_i^M. Note that, F_i^G comes from G-Net, and is regarded as a "soft ground truth". So F_i^G do not require gradient.

L_{soft} consists of a soft category loss L_{soft}^C and a soft location loss L_{soft}^L, which are corresponding to category vectors and location vectors in P_i^G and P_i^M. L_{soft} only works on P_i^G and P_i^M, when $i = 2, 3$. So L_{soft} can be written as follows:

$$L_{soft} = \sum_{i=2}^{3} L_{soft}^C + L_{soft}^L, \tag{3}$$

where

$$L_{soft}^C = -\sum c_{P_i^G} \cdot log(c_{P_i^M}), \tag{4}$$

and

$$L_{soft}^L = smooth_{L1}(l_{P_i^G} - l_{P_i^M}). \tag{5}$$

Here, $c_{P_i^G}$ and $c_{P_i^M}$ refer to the category vectors in P_i^G and P_i^M respectively. $l_{P_i^G}$ and $l_{P_i^M}$ refer to the location vectors in P_i^G and P_i^M respectively. Note that, P_i^G is also a "soft ground truth" and do not require gradient.

4 Experiments

In this section, we first briefly introduce MS-COCO 2017 and present the details of the implement. Then, we conduct ablation studies for Guided Refine-Head. At last, we evaluate the proposed Guided Refine-Head on MS-COCO 2017 dataset and make comparisons with other state-of-the-art detectors.

4.1 Datasets

The MS-COCO 2017 dataset [20] is a commonly used dataset for object detection. It consists of a total of 328,000 images, in which there are 118,288 images used for training and 5,000 images for validation. This dataset contains 91 common object categories. Following [4,7,24], we perform object detection on 81 categories. For data preprocessing, we use the channel means and standard deviations to normalize the data. There is no data augmentation in our experiment except standard horizontal image flipping. All models were trained on the training set and evaluated on the validation set.

4.2 Implement Details

We use the ResNet [14] pre-trained on ImageNet [8] as our backbone. All the networks are optimized by using stochastic gradient descent (SGD). We use ~118K training images to train the model and report the result on validation set on MS-COCO 2017. We train all models with mini-batch size 16 on 8 GPUs (2 images per GPU) for 90K iterations. The initial learning rate is set to 0.002, and is divided by 10 at 60K and 80K iterations and finally terminates at 90K iterations.

During training, the α and β of loss balance is respectively set to 0.5 and 0.1. For simplicity, all regressors in our proposed model is class agnostic. The sampling of the RPN stage follows [24] and we use 256 RoIs per image. In the detection head, we apply three groups of fully connected layers (FCs) to refine the features extracted by ROIAlign and predict bounding boxes for different IoU thresholds (IoUs $= \{0.5, 0.6, 0.7\}$). In addition, we train G-Net and M-Net simultaneously in the experiment of Guided Refine-Head.

4.3 Ablation Study

The Influence of the FCs Group Structure. As is mentioned in Sect. 3.1, we use three groups of FCs and each FCs group has two FCs followed by a classifier and a regressor. To find a suitable structure for FCs group, we design two types

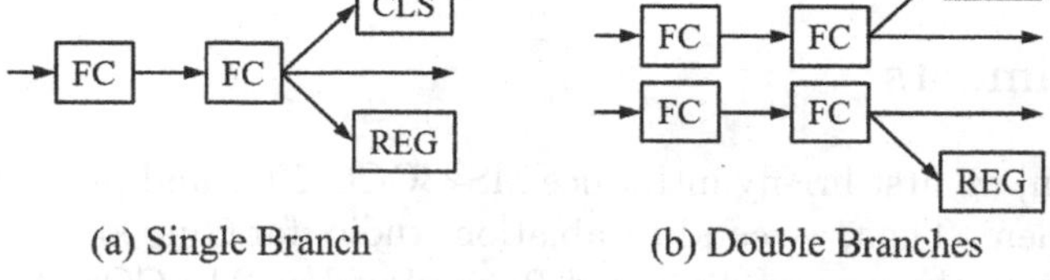

Fig. 5. The detail of FCs group structure. (a) is the single branch structure, in which the classifier and regressor share a single feature. (b) is double branches structure, in which the categories and locations are generated by separate branches. "CLS" and "REG" represent classification and location regression respectively.

Table 1. The results of models with different FCs group structures. All speeds are reported on a single Titan Xp GPU and the input size is 1333 × 800 × 3.

Model	FPS	AP	AP_{50}	AP_{75}	AP_S	AP_M	AP_L
Refine-Head (Single Branch)	**10.4**	37.3	58.2	40.7	20.9	41.2	47.7
Refine-Head (Double Branches)	9.5	**37.6**	**58.3**	**41.1**	**21.5**	**41.3**	**49.1**

Table 2. The results of models with different number of FCs in all FCs groups. All speeds are reported on a single Titan Xp GPU and the input size is 1333 × 800 × 3.

FC number	FPS	AP	AP_{50}	AP_{75}	AP_S	AP_M	AP_L
1	**10.8**	36.9	57.8	40.1	**21.6**	40.4	47.8
2	10.4	**37.3**	**58.2**	**40.7**	20.9	**41.2**	**47.7**
3	10.4	37.0	57.9	40.4	20.8	40.6	47.9
4	10.2	36.8	57.8	40.0	21.2	40.2	48.1
5	10.1	36.7	57.6	40.1	20.7	40.6	47.5

of structures: the single branch structure and the double branches structure. As shown in Fig. 5(a), the classifier and regressor in the single branch structure share a single feature generated by two FCs. In contrast, the classifier and regressor in the double branches structure are individual and have no shared feature (see Fig. 5(b)). From Table 1, we can find that compared with the double branches structure, the Refine-Head using the single branch structure has similar accuracy (AP: 37.3 vs. 37.6) but faster speed (FPS: 10.4 vs. 9.5). The results illustrate that the single branch structure shown in Fig. 5(a) is a suitable structure for FCs group. Therefore, we use the single branch structure as default in the following experiments.

The Influence of the Number of FCs. To investigate the effect of the number of FCs in FCs groups on the performance of Refine-Head, we use single branch structure as default and train Refine-Head with different numbers of FCs in FCs groups. Concretely, we vary the number of FCs in all FCs groups from 1 to 5 and compare their performance. Table 2 shows the experiment results, from which we can find that the AP on the validation set drops when the number of FCs is too large or too small and the AP reaches its peak value when the number of FCs is 2. To keep a good balance between accuracy and speed, we set the number of FCs to 2 by default in the following experiments.

The Effectiveness of the Loss Function. As mentioned in Sect. 3.3, the loss function can be divided into three parts: L_{gt} (i.e. $L_{RPN} + L_G + L_M$), L_{soft} and L_{feat}. To explore the effectiveness of these parts, we remove one of them from the pipeline respectively and compare their performance. Compared with the model only with L_{gt} (see Table 3 #1), the APs of models with L_{feat} (see Table 3 #2) and L_{soft} (see Table 3 #3) increases the AP by 0.2 and 0.6 respectively.

Furthermore, the model with both L_{feat} and L_{soft} can make about 0.7 improvement on AP (see Table 3 #4) , which indicates the both L_{soft} and L_{feat} are helpful for the accuracy of Guided Refine-Head.

Table 3. The results of models with different settings of loss. L_{gt} is $L_{RPN} + L_G + L_M$. L_{feat} and L_{soft} are feature loss and soft label loss respectively.

#	Loss			AP	AP_{50}	AP_{75}	AP_S	AP_M	AP_L
	L_{gt}	L_{feat}	L_{soft}						
1	✓			37.3	**58.2**	40.7	20.9	41.2	47.7
2	✓	✓		37.5	58.1	41.1	20.8	41.1	48.8
3	✓		✓	37.9	58.1	41.6	21.4	41.4	49.2
4	✓	✓	✓	**38.0**	58.1	**41.8**	**21.7**	**41.6**	**49.4**

Fig. 6. Qualitative results of Guided Refine-Head on MS-COCO 2017.

4.4 Comparisons with State-of-the-Art Results

To test the robustness of Guided Refine-Head in object detection, we evaluate it on MS-COCO 2017, which contains rich objects in various challenge scenes. Due to the large scale of the dataset, in order to fully exploit the potential of the Guided Refine-Head, we adopt ResNet50 and ResNet101 as the backbone. During testing, we scale the input image to (1333, 800). The comparisons with other state-of-the-art methods are shown in Table 4. The first group of detectors in Table 4 are one-stage detectors, and the second group multi-stage, and the last group two-stage. As is reported by the results, the proposed Guided Refine-Head achieve AP of 39.7% at 9.0 FPS and AP of 38.0% at 10.4 FPS, without any bells and whistles. Notably, with the similar backbone (e.g. ResNet50), Guided Refine-Head has higher accuracy (AP: 38.0% vs. 36.2%) than Faster R-CNN at the same speed (FPS: 10.4 vs. 10.5), and the FPS of Guided Refine-Head is 1.5 times of Cascade R-CNN. Some qualitative illustrations are shown in Fig. 6. The proposed Guided Refine-Head strike a good balance between accuracy and speed in object detection.

Table 4. The single-scale results on MS-COCO 2017. The FPS denoted by "*" is obtained by retesting the model on our machine and may be slightly different from the result reported in the corresponding original paper.

Method	Backbone	Input resolution	FPS	AP	AP_{50}	AP_{75}	AP_S	AP_M	AP_L
YOLOv2 [23]	DarkNet-19	608×608	40	21.6	44.0	19.2	5.0	22.4	35.5
SSD [22]	VGG-16	512×512	25.4	26.8	46.5	27.8	9.0	28.9	41.9
RetinaNet [19]	ResNet-50-FPN	800×800	12.1	35.7	55.0	38.5	18.9	38.9	46.3
AttractioNet [9]	VGG-16+Wide ResNet	600×600	-	32.0	51.4	33.4	14.1	35.6	48.5
Cascade R-CNN [4]	ResNet-50-FPN	1333×800	7.6*	40.5	59.0	44.0	22.3	44.1	53.3
Faster R-CNN [24]	ResNet-50-FPN	1333×800	10.5*	36.2	58.1	39.2	21.4	39.9	46.2
Faster R-CNN [24]	ResNet-101-FPN	1333×800	9.1*	38.4	60.0	41.6	21.9	42.7	49.9
Guided Refine-Head (ours)	ResNet-50-FPN	1333×800	10.4	38.0	58.1	41.8	21.7	41.6	49.4
Guided Refine-Head (ours)	ResNet-101-FPN	1333×800	9.0	39.7	59.6	43.8	22.5	43.4	52.5

5 Conclusion and Future Work

In this paper, we propose a novel Guided Refine-Head for object detection to successfully achieve a better trade-off between precision and speed. We firstly analyze the feasibility of the proposed Refine-Head, which can improve the detection accuracy compared with the Faster R-CNN, while maintaining the detection speed. Secondly, we introduce Guided Refine-Head, which achieve close accuracy to Cascade R-CNN with fast speed. The experiments on object detection benchmark demonstrate the superior performance of the proposed method.

There are multiple directions to explore in the future. Firstly, we will explore whether the parallel structure can achieve the same or even better results than the series structure of this paper. Then we will further optimize the network so that it has a faster speed and higher accuracy. We are cleaning our codes and will release them soon.

References

1. Alexe, B., Deselaers, T., Ferrari, V.: Measuring the objectness of image windows. IEEE Trans. Pattern Anal. Mach. Intell. **34**(11), 2189–2202 (2012)
2. Ba, J., Caruana, R.: Do deep nets really need to be deep? In: NeurIPS (2014)
3. Bucilă, C., Caruana, R., Niculescu-Mizil, A.: Model compression. In: SIGKDD (2006)
4. Cai, Z., Vasconcelos, N.: Cascade R-CNN: Delving into high quality object detection. In: CVPR (2018)
5. Chen, G., Choi, W., Yu, X., Han, T., Chandraker, M.: Learning efficient object detection models with knowledge distillation. In: NeurIPS (2017)
6. Chen, Y., Li, J., Xiao, H., Jin, X., Yan, S., Feng, J.: Dual path networks. In: NeurIPS (2017)
7. Dai, J., Li, Y., He, K., Sun, J.: R-FCN: object detection via region-based fully convolutional networks. In: NeurIPS (2016)
8. Deng, J., Dong, W., Socher, R., Li, L.J., Li, K., Fei-Fei, L.: Imagenet: a large-scale hierarchical image database. In: CVPR (2009)

9. Gidaris, S., Komodakis, N.: Attend refine repeat: active box proposal generation via in-out localization. arXiv preprint (2016). arXiv:1606.04446
10. Girshick, R.: Fast R-CNN. In: ICCV (2015)
11. Girshick, R., Donahue, J., Darrell, T., Malik, J.: Rich feature hierarchies for accurate object detection and semantic segmentation. In: CVPR (2014)
12. He, K., Gkioxari, G., Dollár, P., Girshick, R.: Mask R-CNN. In: Proceedings of the IEEE International Conference on Computer Vision, pp. 2961–2969 (2017)
13. He, K., Zhang, X., Ren, S., Sun, J.: Spatial pyramid pooling in deep convolutional networks for visual recognition. IEEE Trans. Pattern Anal. Mach. Intell. **37**(9), 1904–1916 (2015)
14. He, K., Zhang, X., Ren, S., Sun, J.: Deep residual learning for image recognition. In: CVPR (2016)
15. Hinton, G., Vinyals, O., Dean, J.: Distilling the knowledge in a neural network. arXiv preprint (2015). arXiv:1503.02531
16. Hu, J., Shen, L., Sun, G.: Squeeze-and-excitation networks. In: CVPR (2018)
17. Huang, G., Liu, Z., Weinberger, K.Q., van der Maaten, L.D.: Densely connected convolutional networks. In: CVPR (2017)
18. Li, X., Wang, W., Hu, X., Yang, J.: Selective kernel networks. In: CVPR (2019)
19. Lin, T.-Y., Goyal, P., Girshick, R., He, K., Dollár, P.: Focal loss for dense object detection. In: ICCV (2017)
20. Lin, T.-Y., et al.: Microsoft coco: common objects in context. In: ECCV (2014)
21. Liu, W., et al.: SSD: single shot multibox detector. In: ECCV (2016)
22. Masnadi-Shirazi, H., Vasconcelos, N.: Cost-sensitive boosting. IEEE Trans. Pattern Anal. Mach. Intell. **33**(2), 294–309 (2010)
23. Redmon, J., Divvala, S., Girshick, R., Farhadi, A.: You only look once: unified, real-time object detection. In: CVPR (2016)
24. Ren, S., He, K., Girshick, R., Sun, J.: Faster R-CNN: towards real-time object detection with region proposal networks. In: NeurIPS (2015)
25. Shen, J., Vesdapunt, N., Boddeti, V.N., Kitani, K.M.: In teacher we trust: learning compressed models for pedestrian detection. arXiv preprint (2016). arXiv:1612.00478
26. Uijlings, J.R.R., Van De Sande, K.E.A., Gevers, T., Smeulders, A.W.M.: Selective search for object recognition. Int. J. Comput. Vis. **104**(2), 154–171 (2013)
27. Wang, W., Li, X., Lu, T., Yang, J.: Mixed link networks. In: IJCAI (2018)
28. Zitnick, C.L., Dollár, P.: Edge boxes: locating object proposals from edges. In: ECCV (2014)

Towards Accurate Panel Detection in Manga: A Combined Effort of CNN and Heuristics

Yafeng Zhou[1], Yongtao Wang[1(✉)], Zheqi He[1], Zhi Tang[1], and Ching Y. Suen[2]

[1] Wangxuan Institute of Computer Technology, Peking University, 128 Zhongguancun North Street, Beijing, China
wyt@pku.edu.cn

[2] Concordia University, 1455 Boulevard de Maisonneuve Ouest, Montreal, Canada

Abstract. Panels are the fundamental elements of manga pages, and hence their detection serves as the basis of high-level manga content understanding. Existing panel detection methods could be categorized into heuristic-based methods and CNN-based (Convolutional Neural Network-based) ones. Although the former can accurately localize panels, they cannot handle well elaborate panels and require considerable effort to hand-craft rules for every new hard case. In contrast, detection results of CNN-based methods could be rough and inaccurate. We utilize CNN object detectors to propose coarse guide panels, then use heuristics to propose panel candidates and finally optimize an energy function to select the most plausible candidates. CNN assures roughly localized detection of almost all kinds of panels, while the follow-up procedure refines the detection results and minimizes the margin between detected panels and ground-truth with the help of heuristics and energy minimization. Experimental results show the proposed method surpasses previous methods regarding panel detection F1-score and page accuracy.

Keywords: Panel detection · Manga analysis · Region-based Convolutional Neural Networks · Energy minimization · Object detection

1 Introduction

In this paper, we focus on the accurate detection of manga panels. Based on our observation of manga image panels, almost every one of them could be compactly represented by a quadrilateral. Hence, to extract manga panels is to extract outer quadrilateral bounding boxes of panels. It serves as a fundamental process for assorted higher-level manga processing techniques.

Our main contribution is a new pipeline of accurate panel detection. We combine R-CNN (Region-based Convolutional Neural Networks), heuristics, and energy minimization into a two-phase procedure to solve the task of accurate panel localization. CNN assures that our method could handle vast cases of panels that previous rule-based methods cannot, because it does not explicitly depend on the borderlines or corners of panels, the gaps between panels or the

Y. M. Ro et al. (Eds.): MMM 2020, LNCS 11961, pp. 215–226, 2020.
https://doi.org/10.1007/978-3-030-37731-1_18

connectivity of drawings with a panel. Our algorithm could give fallback results even in extreme cases, such as concave polygons or arbitrary shapes. However, vanilla R-CNN methods could only produce up-right rectangles (bounding boxes) of panels. The detection results of R-CNN are referred to as **panel proposals** in this work. To refine and transform the extracted rectangles into quadrilaterals, we attach a post-processing procedure to the R-CNN network. In the post-processing stage, we first extract multiple quadrilateral panels (called **panel candidates**) from each panel proposal using heuristics. Then we choose the most convincing panel candidate(s), and this selection procedure is formulated as an optimal labeling problem with an energy function that consists of both unary and pairwise potentials. It forces spatial coherence on near-neighbor panels and elevates page-level accuracy as shown in the experiments section.

The rest of this paper is organized as follows. Section 2 introduces previous works closely related to our topic and analyzes possible application of our work on these methods. Section 3 describes in detail our pipeline, its parameter settings and why we design such a procedure. Experiments are included in Sect. 4. Lastly, we conclude in Sect. 5.

2 Previous Works on Panel Detection

We divide previous methods into heuristic-based methods and CNN-based ones and subdivide the former into division-line-based methods, connected-component-based methods, line-combination-based methods, and learning-assisted methods.

2.1 Division-Line-Based Methods

Tanaka et al. [20] proposed a division line based manga image segmentation algorithm. They implicitly assumed that all manga images have a pure white background and black foreground pixels. Also, their method required that a continuous white margin exists between neighboring panels. Hence by identifying division lines using density gradient accumulation in the gaps between foreground panels, the manga page could be segmented recursively. However, all these assumptions lead to poor generalization ability of the proposed method. [10] further improved Tanaka et al.'s method concerning detection accuracy. Tanaka et al.'s method roughly segmented manga pages into loose parts and made sure each part contains only one panel, while Ishii et al. brought in Harris corner point detection to accurately locate panels on the foundation of division line-based methods.

2.2 Connected-Component-Based Methods

Arai et al. [2] extended Yamada et al.'s architecture by adding data transcoding procedures. They used both connected components and division lines to extract panels, the former for simple panels and the latter for connected panels, but, they also assumed the white background. Even with thresholding to every input image, this assumption could lead to problems. Also, like most previous methods, their method could not generalize to panels without borderlines. Ho et al. [8] proposed to apply morphological operations to connected components to separate connected panels. They dilated the components N times and then eroded them N times to erase the parts between connected panels, while the variable N was derived from the foreground component size and the page size. This method could tackle some cases of panel adhesion at the cost of shape information loss, and could deal with panels with any shape as long as the corresponding connected component is integral. Pang et al. [17] further improved connected component based methods. Their method could deal with hard cases like connected panels, as well as partly borderless panels near page boundaries. For connected panels, they accumulated pixel values along the horizontal and vertical direction to compute the horizontal and vertical division lines respectively. Their method is more robust than the method mentioned in [2]. For partly borderless panels near page boundaries, they manually inserted missing borders. However, it is notable that this method could not handle entirely borderless panels, partly borderless panels that appear in the central page, panels with broken connected components, or panels that are partially or wholly contained within other panels.

2.3 Line-Combination-Based Methods

[9,13,14,21] proposed to extract line segments and then cluster or combine them to form panel candidates. Several strategies were introduced to deal with hard cases like connected panels and borderless panels in these works respectively. With further validation, the qualified candidates were treated as panels. Their methods all followed a similar pipeline but differed in the panel candidate-generating process. Li et al. [13] performed two-round clustering on the extracted line segments. In the first round, redundant line segments were filtered out, and collinear overlapped line segments were merged into one. In the second round, lines were clustered into panels via Finite-State Machines (FSM). Liu et al. [14] categorized line segments into four classes with respect to their relative position to the center point, and then manually chose one line segment from these four classes each and combine them to make panel candidates. For connected panels, they tried to separate them using division lines. Wang et al. [21] conducted connected component searching and then categorized components into different cases. For each case, different line segment combination and filtering strategies were used. All these three methods could handle connected panels and partly borderless panels near page boundaries, but for more complex cases such as entirely borderless panels, these methods would fail. Hung et al. [9] combine Harris corner point detection and LSD (Line Segment Detector) to extract candidate panel corners and candidate panel borders. Next, they do feature-matching and apply different strategies for different situations. Additionally, they deal with break-out panels by detecting uncovered image regions and using a single eroded non-overlapping convex hull under the assumption that no more than one borderless panel exists in a single manga page.

2.4 Learning-Assisted Methods

Previous works like [5,11] brought in machine learning and achieved good results on a relatively large dataset. Typically, various visual cues were used. Han et al. [5] first utilized Multi-Layer Perceptrons (MLP) to find horizontal and vertical cutting positions and then performed recursive XY-cut at these positions. Li et al. [11] introduced a novel panel detection method via tree-shaped Conditional Random Fields (CRF). They extracted three levels of visual patterns, connected components/edge segments/line segments, and obtained multiple features for each of these patterns. With proper training on a small dataset, CRF would be able to infer the labels of these patterns. After further post-processing of these labels, they achieved final panel results with convex polygon shapes. He et al. [7] applied neural network object detection methods (Fast R-CNN [3]) to panel detection and gained state-of-the-art performances on their large dataset. To deal with the lack of localization accuracy of R-CNN, they attached a shape regression network to the R-CNN regressor. The joined network was a VGG-16 network with a quadrilateral regressor. Despite the high overhead, the experimental results proved that their method outperformed previous methods both in panel-level and page-level metrics. Nguyen et al. [16] extend the existing Mask R-CNN head by adding a relation branch to associate different elements in manga. Their multi-task-learning method could detect panels, characters, and balloons, and infer the relationship between them.

3 Proposed Method

We propose a two-phase algorithm that could consistently detect elaborate panels with little margin between detected panel and its corresponding ground-truth. The first stage consists of R-CNN. It could handle various complicated panels and produce acceptable detection results, which we call **panel proposals**. The second stage is post-processing with heuristics and energy minimization. In this stage, we generate one or multiple tightly bounded **panel candidates** from each of the aforementioned rough panel proposals, then we construct a graphical model in which we treat every candidate as a node and the connections between them as edges, and last we inference the model to select the most plausible panel candidates.

Different from [21] that only relies on connected components to separate line segments into batches, we depend on R-CNN outputs that are more reliable than connected components. Also, we take into account the interaction between neighboring candidates. Moreover, there is no need for us to tune parameters for different situations as they finetune three dataset-dependent constants: α, β, and γ.

3.1 Panel Proposal Generation with R-CNN

We follow the two-stage pipeline as described in the R-CNN papers [3,18], only in our case objects are panels. Object proposals could be generated by selective

Fig. 1. Pipeline of our method (Nichijou, ©Keiichi Arawi/Kadokawa Shoten, Volume 7, Page 145)

search or RPN (Region Proposal Networks), and both methods prove effective to locate panels according to our experiments. The R-CNN pipeline judges a proposal by the IoU (Intersection over Union) between it and the ground-truth, and hence it does not directly solve our problem of accurately localizing quadrilateral manga panels. Although a higher AP (Average Precision) threshold requires R-CNN to yield more accurate bounding boxes of objects, the network still cannot produce quadrilateral enclosing boxes. After all, the criterion of positive detection in R-CNN is the IoU of a bounding box rather than the point distance required by the panel detection task (Fig. 1).

Consequently, we concatenate a following post-processing process to the R-CNN to extract tight-bounded panels from these loose panel proposals.

3.2 Panel Candidate Generation with Heuristics

In this stage, we generate multiple panel candidates from each panel proposal. The procedure consists of two steps: line segment selecting and combining. Considering that a CNN-detected panel may not fully contain the corresponding ground-truth panel, we increase the height and width of a detected rectangle by $0.05 \cdot imageHeight$ and $0.05 \cdot imageWidth$ respectively. Secondly, we deal with CNN-extracted panels one by one. Take an extracted panel as an example, we extract line segments using line segment detector (e.g. LSD, ELSD, EDLines, or other methods) from the image region corresponding to it, filter and combine these line segments to form possible panels.

Next, we discuss the line segment selection and combination process in detail. We deal with panel proposals output by R-CNN one by one in each image. After proposal extension, we try to match these proposals with convex hulls of every single chain segment extracted from that image page. Also, small chains inside some other bigger chain are removed beforehand. The matching threshold is set to 0.9 and 0 (>0 means they overlap), i.e.

$$intersection\left(convHull\left(chain\right), proposal\right)/convHull\left(chain\right) > 0.9$$

We denote the matched chain segments as $C_{0.9}$ and C_0 respectively. At the same time, we use the matching denominator, *proposal* with a lower threshold (0.7) and denote matching results as $C_{0.7}$. Depending on the matching result, different line selection strategies are used for further line segments combination.

1. If the $C_{0.9}$ matching result is one-to-one (one proposal to one chain) correspondence, we presume this proposal does contain only one panel. Then we extract line segments from the matching chain segment and use all of them for proposal formation.
2. If the $C_{0.9}$ result is one-to-many (one proposal to multiple chains), it is possible that this proposal contains more than one panel. It could be that those panels are connected with each other, or that the chain of a panel is broken into pieces due to projecting line drawings or speech text. The strategy is similar to the one-to-one situation. We use all line segments from all matched chain segments.
3. If the result, $C_{0.9}$, is one-to-nil, whether there is any chain segment that overlaps with a particular panel. For a panel proposal: if C_0 is empty, this proposal is considered a false positive and removed; if $C_{0.7}$ is empty while C_0 is not, we use all line segments that lie within the extended proposal; if $C_{0.7}$ is not empty, we use line segments that come from all matched chain segments and lie within the extended proposal. If the extended proposal does not fully contain a line segment, we crop and use the line part inside the proposal.

If the quantity of candidate line segments exceeds 20, it could be that the potential panel does not have a complete close boundary so that many line segments are extracted from the inner drawings. In this scenario, we directly use the CNN-output panel as a panel candidate, because the combination of these wrongly extracted line segments could be time-consuming and in practice only makes things worse. Other than that, for all cases, we add the borderlines of the original (unextended) R-CNN panel proposal into candidate line segments as auxiliary lines, but these supplementary line segments will not contribute to the compactness as mentioned in Sect. 3.3.

Next, we combine these selected line segments and calculate their intersection points to form panel candidates. Specifically, we classify line segments into vertical ones ver and horizontal ones hor, and then exhaust all $(hor_i, ver_j, hor_k, ver_l)$ combination and assume they are borderlines of a panel candidate. At last, we would get four intersection points pt_1, pt_2, pt_3 and pt_4 from (hor_i, ver_j), (ver_j, hor_k), (hor_k, ver_l) and (ver_l, hor_i) respectively. We propose several rules to restrict line segments combination:

1. T-junctions are not allowed unless one of the two line segments to be joined is close to the page border. T-junction happens when one line segment intersects with the other line segment in the middle of it, as Fig. 2 shows.
2. We roughly limit both the ratio of panel height to page height and the ratio of panel width to page width to the range of 1/20 to 20. The ratio of panel area to page area should be more than 0.0015.
3. We heuristically constrain the quantity of panel candidates under 20 to ensure the efficiency of the inference. In our experiments, we sort panel candidates in decreasing order of compactness and keep the top 20.

Fig. 2. Illustration of (a) T-junction, and (b) L-junction. Black solid lines are line segments, while black dashed lines are extended lines. Together they form a panel.

3.3 Panel Candidate Selection with Energy Minimization

Next, we select the most plausible panel candidates with reference to local and neighbor constraints. Local constraints describe the confidence of a panel candidate being a true panel, while neighbor constraints encode the relationship between associated candidates. Two types of neighbor interaction are used in this work: **supportive interaction** and **opposing interaction**. **Supportive interaction** exists between non-intersecting contiguous panel candidates when the adjacent sides of the two candidates are parallel and overlapping along the horizontal (for the up-and-down structure) or vertical (for the left-and-right structure) direction. Also, we consider two candidates supportive for each other if they satisfy the aforementioned conditions and their horizontal or vertical distance is below $0.1 \cdot imgWidth$ or $0.1 \cdot imgHeight$ depending on their structure. **Opposing interaction** occurs between intersecting neighbor panels if their IoU is above a preset threshold (set to 10% in our experiments to allow a margin for slight offsets). Our energy minimization process is implemented with the help of OpenGM [1].

We denote panel features as X, their labels as Y (1 for a true panel, -1 otherwise), the set of panels as S, and the energy as a function of three terms:

$$E(Y,X) = \overbrace{\sum_{i \in S} A_i(y_i, X)}^{\text{unary potential}} + \overbrace{\underbrace{\sum_{i \in S} \sum_{j \in SN_i} I_{ij}^{(1)}(y_i, y_j, X)}_{\text{supportive interaction}} + \underbrace{\sum_{i \in S} \sum_{j \in ON_i} I_{ij}^{(2)}(y_i, y_j, X)}_{\text{opposing interaction}}}^{\text{pairwise potentials}} \tag{1}$$

$$A_i(y_i, X) = y_i \cdot comp(x_i) \tag{2}$$

The first term of this energy function is association (or unary) potential. It measures the energy when panel i is given the label y_i. Currently, the feature of the panel is merely the panel's compactness, i.e. the ratio of the total length of candidate line segments lying along panel's borderlines to the panel's perimeter.

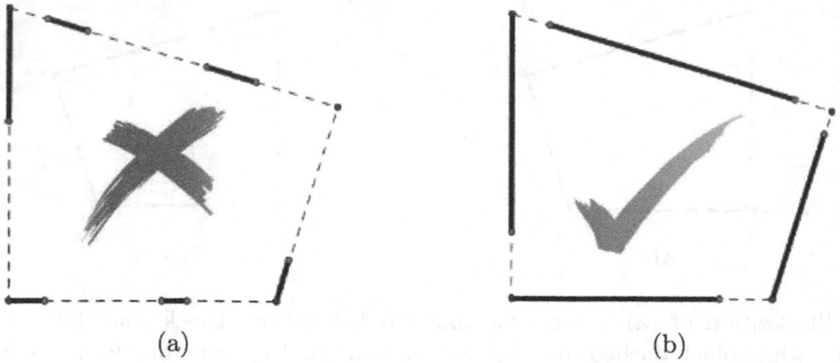

Fig. 3. Formed quadrilaterals are regarded as panels only if they are compact. (a) A loose panel candidate; (b) A compact panel candidate.

Auxiliary line segments coming from the original R-CNN panel proposal are not involved in the compactness calculation (Fig. 3).

The second and third terms are interaction (or pairwise) potentials. They assure that current labels of panels agree with explicit constraints between associated panel candidates.

$$I_{ij}^{(1)}(y_i, y_j, X) = \begin{cases} w_1 \cdot \phi^{(1)}(x_i, x_j) & \text{if } y_i \neq y_j \\ 0 & \text{if } y_i = y_j \end{cases} \tag{3}$$

$$I_{ij}^{(2)}(y_i, y_j, X) = \begin{cases} w_2 \cdot \phi^{(2)}(x_i, x_j) & \text{if } y_i = y_j = 1 \\ 0 & \text{if } y_i \neq y_j \text{ or } y_i = y_j = -1 \end{cases} \tag{4}$$

The second term encourages neighboring candidates with similar shapes to share the same label and penalizes the situation in which their labels differ. w_1 is fixed as 1 while $\phi^{(1)}(x_i, x_j)$ is dependent on the closeness of the two neighboring panels. In our experiments, all neighboring candidates with different labels are given a constant penalty, i.e. $\phi^{(1)}(x_i, x_j)$ is fixed as 1 for neighbor panels. To avoid the situation in which many neighbor panels overwhelm the model and it tends to give positive labels to all nodes with supportive interaction, we deliberately control the magnitude of supportive interaction potential to be significantly smaller than the other two potentials while still encouraging connected nodes to have the same label. As for the third term, it penalizes opposing candidates when they have the same label. In our experiments, we calculate $\phi^{(2)}(x_i, x_j)$ according to their extent of overlapping (IoU of the two overlapping panels), i.e. $\phi^{(2)}(x_i, x_j) = \text{IoU}(x_i, x_j)$, and w_2 is fixed to 400.

As for inference, we use ICM (Iterated Conditional Modes) instead in our experiments. Moreover, for better performance, we find all nodes with conflict and initialize the labels of these conflicting nodes according to the unary energy. Only the node with highest compactness among all conflicting nodes is given a positive label.

4 Experiments

4.1 Experimental Setup

Datasets. We use a dataset called Manga30K. It consists of 29 845 manga pages, 169 421 panels in total. We still follow the 2/1/1 split setting of train/val/test (2:1:1, 10571/5286/5285). The majority comes from the Manga109 dataset [15], which is a dataset first introduced in the arXiv-version paper disclosed in 2015 and is made up of 109 volumes portrayed by professional Japanese manga artists, and the rest comes from various manga titles published in Japan, Mainland China, Hong Kong S.A.R, United States. We labeled the corner points of all 169 421 panels, most of which are quadrilateral panels. For those panels without borderlines, their panels are labeled with reference to neighboring panels and should be compact regarding inner line drawings. Notice that only quadrilateral ones are used in our experiments.

Evaluation Metrics. Metrics used in previous papers are two-fold, panel-level metrics and page-level metric(s). Correct detection of a page relies on correct detection of all panels within that page. Meanwhile, the criterion for correct detection of a panel depends on the output shape of the method being evaluated. Methods that produce results with rough rectangle shapes adopt IoU-based criterion usually and set the threshold to either 0.7 or 0.9. Methods that output results with tightly bounded quadrilateral shapes often use endpoint distance-based criterion, and threshold the distance margin as 50 pixels even though a fixed pixel threshold could lead to problems when the resolution of manga images varies significantly.

To fully show the superiority of the proposed method, we adopt both the endpoint-distance-based and polygon(quadrangle)-IoU-based criteria but make the threshold resolution-sensitive ($0.02 \cdot imageHeight$ for endpoint distance, 0.9 for IoU). Also, we enforce a one-to-one matching between detection and ground-truth, i.e., repetitive detections of the same panel are treated as false detections. Also, both panel-level metrics (precision, recall, F1-score) and page-level metric (accuracy) are used in our experiments.

4.2 Experimental Results

To fully demonstrate the performance of our method, we compare it with (1) heuristic rules-based methods [12,14,17,21], (2) R-CNN baselines, both Fast R-CNN with VGG-16 [19] as the base net and Faster R-CNN with either VGG-16 [19] or ResNet-101 [6] as the base net.

Currently, our unary potentials depend solely on the compactnesss of panels. For a panel candidate with missing borderlines (low compactness), if it overlaps with other panel candidates, the conflict interaction between them would overwhelm the unary energy and force our method to give this panel candidate a negative label. Consequently, it results in the recall loss as shown in Table 1. But the post-processing stage brings a sharp increase in localization accuracy, and hence a gain in F1-score all in all.

Table 1. Performance comparison with previous methods on Manga109

Method		IoU criterion			
		Precision	Recall	F1 score	Page accuracy (#)
Liu [14]		0.7407	0.6298	0.6808	0.2969 (1569)
Li [12]		0.7094	0.5426	0.6149	0.232 (1226)
Pang [17]		0.6835	0.6093	0.6443	0.3082 (1629)
Wang [21]		0.7252	0.6165	0.6665	0.2744 (1450)
Fast VGG	Vanilla	0.781	0.7732	0.7771	0.4062 (2147)
	Our method	**0.867**	**0.802**	**0.8332**	**0.4553 (2406)**
Faster VGG	Vanilla	0.679	0.6974	0.6881	0.2903 (1534)
	Our method	0.8435	0.7735	0.807	0.4271 (2257)
Faster ResNet	Vanilla	0.7214	0.7417	0.7314	0.3504 (1852)
	Our method	0.8588	0.7915	0.8238	0.4496 (2681)
Method		Distance criterion			
		Precision	Recall	F1 score	Page accuracy (#)
Liu [14]		0.7315	0.622	0.6723	0.2914 (1540)
Li [12]		0.6882	0.5264	0.5965	0.2265 (1197)
Pang [17]		0.6805	0.6066	0.6414	0.2954 (1561)
Wang [21]		0.7107	0.6042	0.6531	0.2624 (1387)
Fast VGG	Vanilla	0.7706	0.7629	0.7667	0.4172 (2205)
	Our method	**0.8486**	**0.7847**	**0.8154**	0.4197 (2218)
Faster VGG	Vanilla	0.7077	0.7269	0.7172	0.3457 (1827)
	Our method	0.8258	0.7572	0.79	0.3796 (2006)
Faster ResNet	Vanilla	0.7497	0.7707	0.7601	**0.4278** (2261)
	Our method	0.8469	0.7803	0.8122	0.4193 (2216)

Contrast with Heuristic-Rule Based Methods. [12] performs the worst in both metrics. Methods of Liu et al. [14], Pang et al. [17], and Wang et al. [21] perform comparably. [12] and [14] use chain segment analysis while [21] exploits connected components. Both of them propose to combine line segments extracted from chain segments and outer component contours respectively, to form panel candidates and filter them with proper hand-crafted rules. Although the rules differ, they serve the same purpose and the involved line segment extracting algorithm is much the same. [17] utilizes merely connected components but explores thoroughly the relation between components and panels. It performs best among heuristic-based methods, but it is time-consuming and it takes ~3 s for one image on our i7-4930K machine. Moreover, all of them suffer from markedly lower recall than the proposed method, because they could not handle hard cases well and would miss more panels than the proposed method does. On panel-level metrics, R-CNN baselines have an edge over the best-performing rule-based method [21]. On page-level metrics, R-CNN baselines appear to enjoy considerable advantages over all rule-based methods, a huge ~10% increase in terms of page accuracy.

Contrast with R-CNN Baselines. Fast R-CNN with VGG-16 as the base net, Faster R-CNN with VGG-16, and Faster R-CNN with ResNet-101 are tested in our experiments. Results are tested on the dataset with the help of MX-RCNN [4], the distributed MXNet-version implementations of R-CNN. Hyper-parameters remain the same with original MX-RCNN, except that we change anchor ratios to (0.3, 0.7, 1.5) considering the typical aspect ratios of manga panels. Experimental results demonstrate that, even vanilla R-CNN methods can outperform previous heuristic-based methods. Under the distance and IoU criterion, with the combination of R-CNN and the proposed post-processing procedure, the F1 score of panel detection could increase obviously, and the page accuracy is comparable for VGG-16 and ResNet. At a low cost, the proposed method could be applied to all R-CNN based methods and beats all previous methods. Under the IoU metric, the loss in recall outweighs the gain in precision, which leads to a loss in F1 score and worse page accuracy.

5 Conclusion

In this paper, we manage to combine heuristics, loss minimization, and CNN for the task of fine-grained manga panel detection. Our two-phase method could generalize to various kinds of manga images, and deal with hard cases neither one of the three techniques could handle individually. For CNN panel detection methods, our method could be easily incorporated into them and improve detection results immediately. Experimental results show that our method achieves a higher page-level accuracy and a higher or equal panel-level performance over previous methods. Also, it is notable that the proposed method could give acceptable compromise results even when failing.

Acknowledgments. This work is supported by National Natural Science Foundation of China under Grant 61673029. This work is also a research achievement of Key Laboratory of Science, Technology and Standard in Press Industry (Key Laboratory of Intelligent Press Media Technology). The authors gratefully acknowledge financial support from China Scholarship Council.

References

1. Andres, B., Beier, T., Kappes, J.H.: OpenGM: A C++ library for discrete graphical models, Jun 2012. http://arxiv.org/abs/1206.0111
2. Arai, K., Tolle, H.: Automatic e-comic content adaptation. Int. J. Ubiquitous Comput. **1**(1), 1–11 (2010)
3. Girshick, R.: Fast R-CNN. In: ICCV, vol. 2015 Inter, pp. 1440–1448 (2015)
4. Guo, J.: MX-RCNN: faster R-CNN in MXNet with distributed implementation and data parallelization (2017). https://github.com/precedenceguo/mx-rcnn
5. Han, E.J., Wong, C.O., Jung, K.C., Lee, K.H., Kim, E.Y.: Efficient page layout analysis on small devices. J. Zhejiang Univ.-Sci. A **10**(6), 800–804 (2009)
6. He, K., Zhang, X., Ren, S., Sun, J.: Deep residual learning for image recognition. In: CVPR, pp. 770–778 (2016)

7. He, Z., Zhou, Y., Wang, Y., Tang, Z.: SReN: shape regression network for comic storyboard extraction. In: AAAI, pp. 4937–4938 (2017)
8. Ho, A.K.N., Burie, J.C., Ogier, J.M.: Panel and speech balloon extraction from comic books. In: Proceedings - 10th IAPR International Workshop on Document Analysis Systems, DAS 2012, pp. 424–428. IEEE (2012)
9. Hung, S.H., Lai, Y.C., Wong, S.C., Chiu, C.H., Yao, C.Y.: Arbitrary screen-aware manga reading framework with parameter-optimized panel extraction. IEEE MultiMedia **26**(2), 55–65 (2019)
10. Ishii, D., Watanabe, H.: A study on frame position detection of digitized comics images. In: Workshop on Picture Coding and Image Processing (PCSJ), Nagoya, vol. 2010, pp. 124–125 (2010)
11. Li, L., Wang, Y., Suen, C.Y., Tang, Z., Liu, D.: A tree conditional random field model for panel detection in comic images. Pattern Recogn. **48**(7), 2129–2140 (2015)
12. Li, L., Wang, Y., Tang, Z., Gao, L.: Automatic comic page segmentation based on polygon detection. Multimedia Tools Appl. **69**(1), 171–197 (2014)
13. Li, L., Wang, Y., Tang, Z., Liu, D.: Comic image understanding based on polygon detection. In: Zanibbi, R., Coüasnon, B. (eds.) Proceedings SPIE 8658, Document Recognition and Retrieval XX. vol. 8658, p. 86580B. International Society for Optics and Photonics, Feb 2013
14. Liu, D., Wang, Y., Tang, Z., Li, L., Gao, L.: Automatic comic page image understanding based on edge segment analysis. In: Coüasnon, B., Ringger, E.K. (eds.) Document Recognition and Retrieval XXI, vol. 9021, pp. 90210J–90210J-12. International Society for Optics and Photonics, Dec 2013
15. Matsui, Y., Ito, K., Aramaki, Y., Fujimoto, A., Ogawa, T., Yamasaki, T., Aizawa, K.: Sketch-based manga retrieval using manga109 dataset. Multimedia Tools Appl. **76**(20), 21811–21838 (2017)
16. Nguyen, N.V., Rigaud, C., Burie, J.C.: Comic MTL: optimized multi-task learning for comic book image analysis. Int. J. Doc. Anal. Recogn. (IJDAR), 1–20 (2019)
17. Pang, X., Cao, Y., Lau, R.W., Chan, A.B.: A robust panel extraction method for manga. In: Proceedings of the ACM International Conference on Multimedia - MM 2014, pp. 1125–1128. ACM Press, New York, New York, USA (2014)
18. Ren, S., He, K., Girshick, R., Sun, J.: Faster R-CNN: towards real-time object detection with region proposal networks. In: NIPS, pp. 91–99 (2015)
19. Simonyan, K., Zisserman, A.: Very deep convolutional networks for large-scale image recognition. In: International Conference on Learning Representations (ICLR), pp. 1–14, Sep 2015
20. Tanaka, T., Shoji, K., Toyama, F., Miyamichi, J.: Layout analysis of tree-structured scene frames in comic images. In: IJCAI International Joint Conference on Artificial Intelligence, pp. 2885–2890 (2007)
21. Wang, Y., Zhou, Y., Tang, Z.: Comic frame extraction via line segments combination. In: Proceedings of the International Conference on Document Analysis and Recognition, ICDAR, vol. 2015-Novem, pp. 856–860. IEEE (2015)

Subclass Deep Neural Networks: Re-enabling Neglected Classes in Deep Network Training for Multimedia Classification

Nikolaos Gkalelis and Vasileios Mezaris(✉)

CERTH-ITI, 6th Km Charilaou-Thermi Road, P.O. BOX 60361, Thessaloniki, Greece
{gkalelis,bmezaris}@iti.gr

Abstract. During minibatch gradient-based optimization, the contribution of observations to the updating of the deep neural network's (DNN's) weights for enhancing the discrimination of certain classes can be small, despite the fact that these classes may still have a large generalization error. This happens, for instance, due to overfitting, i.e. to classes whose error in the training set is negligible, or simply when the contributions of the misclassified observations to the updating of the weights associated with these classes cancel out. To alleviate this problem, a new criterion for identifying the so-called "neglected" classes during the training of DNNs, i.e. the classes which stop to optimize early in the training procedure, is proposed. Moreover, based on this criterion a novel cost function is proposed, that extends the cross-entropy loss using subclass partitions for boosting the generalization performance of the neglected classes. In this way, the network is guided to emphasize the extraction of features that are discriminant for the classes that are prone to being neglected during the optimization procedure. The proposed framework can be easily applied to improve the performance of various DNN architectures. Experiments on several publicly available benchmarks including, the large-scale YouTube-8M (YT8M) video dataset, show the efficacy of the proposed method (Source code is made publicly available at: https://github.com/bmezaris/subclass_deep_neural_networks).

Keywords: DNN · Neglected classes · Subclasses · Cross-entropy loss

1 Introduction and Related Work

Deep neural networks (DNNs) have shown a breakthrough performance in many machine learning problems and are currently witnessing a significant commercial deployment in several application domains such as multimedia understanding, self-driving cars, IoT and other. The state-of-the-art DNNs for classification tasks consist of a series of weight layers, nonlinear activation functions and downsampling operators and on top of them an output layer typically equipped with a

Y. M. Ro et al. (Eds.): MMM 2020, LNCS 11961, pp. 227–238, 2020.
https://doi.org/10.1007/978-3-030-37731-1_19

sigmoid or softmax activation function modeling c categorical probability distributions [16,21]. An important aspect on the design of a DNN is the choice of the cost function and the optimization algorithm. The cross-entropy (CE) loss and the stochastic gradient descent (SGD) combined with the back-propagation (BP) algorithm for updating the DNN parameters are almost always the sole choice in practice [12]. The great success of those DNNs is based on their extraordinary ability to extract nonlinear features at different layers guided by the SGD-BP algorithm in order to transform a set of c (possibly) nonlinear classification tasks in the input space of the DNN to c linear ones in the input space of the output layer. More specifically, for the ith output node a gradient update to the correct direction is generated, whose length is proportional to the training error of the ith class, guiding the overall network to extract the desired features and producing a linearly separable subspace for the ith classification task. In [19], it is shown that the application of the CE loss with gradient descent on separable data convergences to the max-margin solution with a logarithmic convergence rate. Moreover, it is shown that the above analysis is also valid in deep networks if after a certain number of iterations the weight vectors of the last weight layer are assumed fixed and the class distributions at its output are considered linearly separable (or piecewise linearly separable). However, as we show in this paper not all weight vectors in the last layer yield a linearly separable problem simultaneously and thus not all class separating hyperplanes converge to the max-margin solution with the same rate. Instead, there is an antagonism, where the extraction of discriminant features for certain classes is emphasized during the optimization of the DNN, while other classes are partially neglected yielding a "less" linearly separable problem in the input space of the output layer for these classes, and thus a separating margin that is suboptimal.

The limitation of DNNs to treat all classes fairly during the training procedure has been mostly studied in the context of class imbalanced learning [15]. Moreover, the identification of classes receiving little attention during training as described above is a relatively unexplored topic. To this end, a new criterion for identifying such neglected classes is proposed. This criterion computes the contribution of positive and negative observations in the gradient update of the weight vectors in the output layer and combines the computed quantities to form a stable measure for the likelihood that the underlying class is going to be neglected. Moreover, in order to turn the attention of the DNN on the identified neglected classes, we resort to a subclass partitioning strategy. Subclass-based classification techniques have been successfully used in the shallow learning paradigm. In [10], learning vector quantization (LVQ) is used to find a set of cluster centers for each class and classification is performed by finding the closest class center. In [7], mixture discriminant analysis (MDA) fits a Gaussian mixture density to each class, extending the linear discriminant analysis (LDA) to the non-normal setting. In [5], nonlinear classification problems are solved by splitting the original set of classes to subclasses and embedding the binary problems in a problem-dependent subclass error-correcting output codes (SECOC) design. In [6,20], a set of kernel subclass discriminant analysis techniques are proposed in order to deal with nonlinearly separable subclasses, and it is shown that the identification of the optimum kernel parameters can be performed more easily exploiting the subclass partitions.

Motivated by the above works, a subclass DNN (SDNN) framework is proposed, where the neglected classes are augmented and partitioned to subclasses, and subsequently a novel subclass CE (SCE) loss, which emphasizes the separation of subclasses belonging to different classes, is applied to train the network. In this way, the network is trained to derive a piecewise linear subspace for the neglected classes, imposing a less strict requirement for the extraction of nonlinear features for these classes. Thus, the DNN is trained more effectively with respect to the neglected classes, increasing its overall generalization performance. The novel SDNN framework is compared with state-of-the-art approaches in 3 popular benchmarks (CIFAR10, CIFAR100 [11] and SVHN [14]) and in the large-scale YT8M video dataset [1] for the task of multiclass and multilabel classification, respectively. The results show that in most cases the proposed SDNNs obtain significant performance improvements.

The rest of the paper is structured as follows: Sect. 2 presents the proposed method and Sect. 3 describes the experimental evaluation. Conclusions are drawn in Sect. 4.

2 Proposed Method

2.1 Identification of Neglected Classes

Suppose a DNN with a sigmoid output layer (SG)

$$\mathbf{h}_\kappa = \mathbf{W}^T \mathbf{x}_\kappa + \mathbf{b}, \tag{1}$$

$$q_{i,\kappa} = \frac{1}{1 + \exp(-h_{i,\kappa})}, \tag{2}$$

where $\mathbf{W} = [\mathbf{w}_1, \dots, \mathbf{w}_c] \in \mathbb{R}^{f \times c}$, $\mathbf{b} = [b_1, \dots, b_c]^T$ are the weight matrix and bias vector of the SG layer, and c is the number of classes. Moreover, assuming a batch of n training observations, the vectors $\mathbf{x}_\kappa = [x_{1,\kappa}, \dots, x_{f,\kappa}]^T$, $\mathbf{h}_\kappa = [h_{1,\kappa}, \dots, h_{c,\kappa}]^T$, $\mathbf{q}_\kappa = [q_{1,\kappa}, \dots, q_{c,\kappa}]^T$, $\mathbf{y}_\kappa = [y_{1,\kappa}, \dots, y_{c,\kappa}]^T$, are associated with the κth training observation in the batch, and are the input and output vector of the linear part of the SG layer, the output vector of the SG layer, and the class indicator vector, respectively. The ith component of $\mathbf{y}_\kappa$ is the label of the κth observation with respect to the ith class, i.e. $y_{i,\kappa}$ equals one if $\mathbf{x}_\kappa \in \omega_i$ and zero otherwise, and ω_i denotes the ith class. For training the DNN, the minibatch stochastic gradient descent (SGD) and the CE loss are used

$$L = -\frac{1}{n} \sum_{\kappa=1}^{n} \sum_{i=1}^{c} (y_{i,\kappa} \ln(q_{i,\kappa}) + (1 - y_{i,\kappa}) \ln(1 - q_{i,\kappa})). \tag{3}$$

Under this framework, the weight vector associated with the ith class is updated at each iteration as below

$$\mathbf{w}_i = \mathbf{w}_i - \eta \mathbf{g}_i, \tag{4}$$

where, $\mathbf{g}_i = \frac{1}{n}\sum_{\kappa=1}^{n} \zeta_{i,\kappa}\mathbf{x}_\kappa$ is the gradient of L with respect to $\mathbf{w}_i$, η is the learning rate and $\zeta_{i,\kappa} = q_{i,\kappa} - y_{i,\kappa}$. Noting that $q_{i,\kappa} \in [0,1]$ we observe that $\zeta_{i,\kappa} \in [-1,1]$, with $\zeta_{i,\kappa} \approx 0$ when the right answer for $\mathbf{x}_\kappa$'s label is provided by SG layer's unit i, and $\zeta_{i,\kappa}$ moving towards $|1|$ as the likelihood of unit i to provide a wrong answer increases

$$\zeta_{i,\kappa} = \begin{cases} 1 \text{ if } q_{i,\kappa} = 1, y_{i,\kappa} = 0, \\ -1 \text{ if } q_{i,\kappa} = 0, y_{i,\kappa} = 1, \\ 0 \text{ if } q_{i,\kappa} == y_{i,\kappa}. \end{cases} \tag{5}$$

These properties of $\zeta_{i,\kappa}$ can aid the correct operation of the gradient-based learning approach, i.e., shrinking the gradient in (4) when the right answer is obtained, and providing a strong gradient otherwise, forcing the overall network to act quickly in order to correct the mislabeled observations. However, this is not always the case. For instance, considering that the contribution to the summand in (4) of different observations may cancel out, the gradient may shrink despite the fact that many observations are misclassified. To see this, we rewrite the gradient as

$$\mathbf{g}_i = \frac{1}{n}(\tilde{\boldsymbol{\delta}}_i - \hat{\boldsymbol{\delta}}_i) = \frac{1}{n}\boldsymbol{\delta}_i, \tag{6}$$

$$\hat{\boldsymbol{\delta}}_i = \sum_{\mathbf{x}_\kappa \in \omega_i} -\zeta_{i,\kappa}\mathbf{x}_\kappa, \tag{7}$$

$$\tilde{\boldsymbol{\delta}}_i = \sum_{\mathbf{x}_\kappa \notin \omega_i} \zeta_{i,\kappa}\mathbf{x}_\kappa, \tag{8}$$

where $\hat{\boldsymbol{\delta}}_i$, $\tilde{\boldsymbol{\delta}}_i$ equal zero when the positive and negative observations, respectively, are classified correctly. Note that $-\zeta_{i,\kappa}, \mathbf{x}_\kappa \in \omega_i$ and $\zeta_{i,\kappa}, \mathbf{x}_\kappa \notin \omega_i$ are less than one and always positive, and thus $\hat{\boldsymbol{\delta}}_i$, $\tilde{\boldsymbol{\delta}}_i$ are the weighted means of the target and non-target class, respectively, weighted with the likelihood derived from the DNN that this observation belongs to the respective category or not. When $\hat{\boldsymbol{\delta}}_i$, $\tilde{\boldsymbol{\delta}}_i$ are close to each other, the overall gradient $\boldsymbol{\delta}_i$ approaches zero and $\mathbf{w}_i$ remains relatively unchanged, despite the fact that many observations are still not classified correctly by unit i. When this undesired effect appears, the network gradually stops to optimize the weights of the different layers below for extracting discriminant features associated with such "neglected" classes, paying more attention on improving the training classification rates of classes which still produce a strong gradient at each iteration. A unit i with large $\|\hat{\boldsymbol{\delta}}_i\|$, $\|\tilde{\boldsymbol{\delta}}_i\|$ and at the same time small difference between these two quantities reflects a high likelihood that the associated class is not getting the required attention and is going to be neglected in subsequent iterations. Based on the analysis above, every τ minibatch iterations we compute the following measure for estimating how likely a class is to be neglected

$$\theta_i = \frac{1}{n\tau}\sum_{l=p-\tau+1}^{\tau} \frac{\|\hat{\boldsymbol{\delta}}_{i,l}\| + \|\tilde{\boldsymbol{\delta}}_{i,l}\|}{\|\boldsymbol{\delta}_{i,l}\|}, \tag{9}$$

where $\hat{\boldsymbol{\delta}}_{i,l}$, $\tilde{\boldsymbol{\delta}}_{i,l}$ are the gradient terms (7), (8) at the lth minibatch iteration, $\|\|$ is the vector norm operator and p is the current iteration. The identification of the most neglected class $\imath$ is then performed by using a simple argmax rule

$$\imath = \underset{i}{\operatorname{argmax}}(\theta_i). \tag{10}$$

2.2 SDNNs

The major consequence of neglecting a class during the optimization procedure is that the trained DNN will fail to learn an appropriate feature mapping where the neglected classes are linearly separable. To alleviate this unwanted behavior we propose the use a clustering algorithm to derive a subclass partition for those classes that are prone to be neglected. By exploiting this partition it is expected that it will be generally easier for the DNN to learn a nonlinear mapping where the subclasses are linearly separable. Under this framework, the easiest way to extend the CE criterion would be to treat each subclass as a class. However, this loss will treat equivalently the costs associated with misclassifying an observation to the non-target subclasses without examining which non-target subclasses are associated with the target class of the observation and which not. To this end, we propose the following loss in order to favor the separability of those subclasses that correspond to different classes

$$L = -\frac{1}{n}\sum_{\kappa=1}^{n}\sum_{i=1}^{c}\sum_{j=1}^{H_i}(y_{i,j,\kappa}\ln(q_{i,j,\kappa}) + (1 - y_{i,\kappa})\ln(1 - q_{i,j,\kappa})), \tag{11}$$

where, $y_{i,j,\kappa}$ is the label of the κth training observation in the batch associated with jth subclass of class i, i.e., $y_{i,j,\kappa}$ equals one if $\mathbf{x}_\kappa \in \omega_{i,j}$ and zero otherwise, and $h_{i,j,\kappa}$, $q_{i,j,\kappa}$ are the input and output to the activation function of the (i,j) unit associated with $\mathbf{x}_\kappa$. Note, that in the second summand of (11) the class label $y_{i,\kappa}$ is utilized instead of the subclass label $y_{i,j,\kappa}$ in order to emphasize the separation of subclasses belonging to different classes, as explained above.

2.3 Subclass Partitioning and Augmentation

Any clustering algorithm and augmentation approach can be applied to derive a subclass division of the neglected classes. However, for large-scale datasets such as the YT8M [1], it may be infeasible to use computationally demanding clustering approaches such as k-means. To this end, the lightweight approach described in Algorithm 1 for partitioning the observations of the ith class into two subclasses is proposed. It is based on the computation of the distance of each class observation to $\mathbf{m}$, which is the mean along all observations in the training set and used as a representation of the rest-of-world class. Moreover, data augmentation can be performed to the neglected classes by applying extrapolation in the feature space for each observation as proposed in [3]

$$\acute{\mathbf{x}}_{i,j,\kappa} = \lambda(\mathbf{x}_{i,j,\kappa} - \check{\mathbf{x}}_{i,j}) + \mathbf{x}_{i,j,\kappa}, \tag{12}$$

Algorithm 1. Subclass partitioning algorithm

Input: $\{\mathbf{x}_{i,1}, \dots, \mathbf{x}_{i,n_i}\}$, $\mathbf{m}$

Output: $\mathbf{x}_{i,j,\kappa}$, $\check{\mathbf{x}}_{i,j}$, $\kappa = 1, \dots, n_{i,j}$, $j = 1, 2$

1: Compute $d_j = \|\mathbf{x}_{i,j} - \mathbf{m}\| \; \forall j$

2: Sort $\mathbf{x}_{i,j}$'s in descending order according to the d_j's: $\{\tilde{\mathbf{x}}_{i,1}, \dots, \tilde{\mathbf{x}}_{i,n_i}\}$

3: Compute $n_{i,1} = \lfloor n_i/2 \rfloor$, $n_{i,2} = n_i - n_{i,1}$

4: Set $\{\mathbf{x}_{i,1,1}, \dots, \mathbf{x}_{i,1,n_{i,1}}\} = \{\tilde{\mathbf{x}}_{i,1}, \dots, \tilde{\mathbf{x}}_{i,n_{i,1}}\}$ (i.e., we assign the observations with the highest d_j's to the 1st subclass; the remaining observations go to the 2nd subclass as shown in step 5)

5: Set $\{\mathbf{x}_{i,2,1}, \dots, \mathbf{x}_{i,2,n_{i,2}}\} = \{\tilde{\mathbf{x}}_{i,n_{i,1}+1}, \dots, \tilde{\mathbf{x}}_{i,n_i}\}$

6: Set $\check{\mathbf{x}}_{i,1} = \tilde{\mathbf{x}}_{i,1}$, $\check{\mathbf{x}}_{i,2} = \tilde{\mathbf{x}}_{i,n_i}$ (these quantities are used in (12) for the augmentation)

where, $\lambda \in [0, 1]$ and $\check{\mathbf{x}}_{i,1}$, $\check{\mathbf{x}}_{i,2}$ are the observations of class i with the largest and smallest distance from $\mathbf{m}$, respectively. Using the approach described in this section, both class partitioning and augmentation can be performed very efficiently on-line without the need to load the whole dataset or large parts of it in memory.

3 Experiments

3.1 Validation of the Neglection Criterion

In order to verify the validity of the proposed criterion we train and evaluate a VGG16 network for 420 epochs in the CIFAR10 dataset and record the testing CCR_i, the neglection measure θ_i, and the gradient vectors $\boldsymbol{\delta}_i$, $\hat{\boldsymbol{\delta}}_i$ and $\tilde{\boldsymbol{\delta}}_i$ for each epoch and class i, $i = 0, \dots, 9$. The exact details of the network architecture and the training procedure are provided in Sect. 3.2. The recorded values for θ_i and CCR_i are shown in Fig. 1, while the length of the three gradients plotted between the epochs 100 and 200 are depicted in Fig. 2. We observe the following: (i) There is a clear correlation between the generalization error rate and the neglection criterion. More specifically, as shown in Fig. 1 the neglection values can be used to rank the classes in terms of their expected generalization performance. (ii)

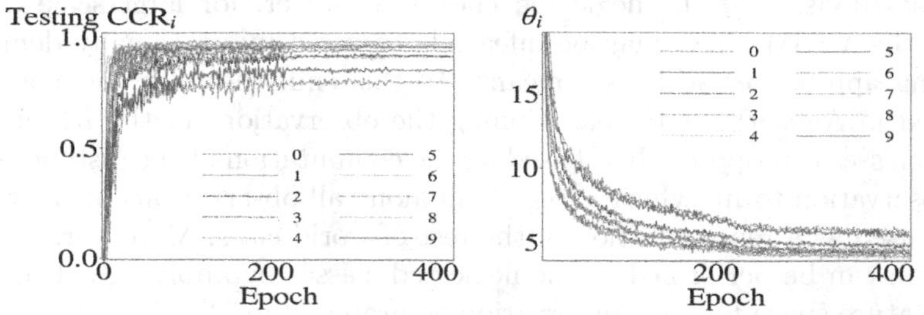

Fig. 1. Testing CCR_i and neglection measure θ_i for the CIFAR10 dataset.

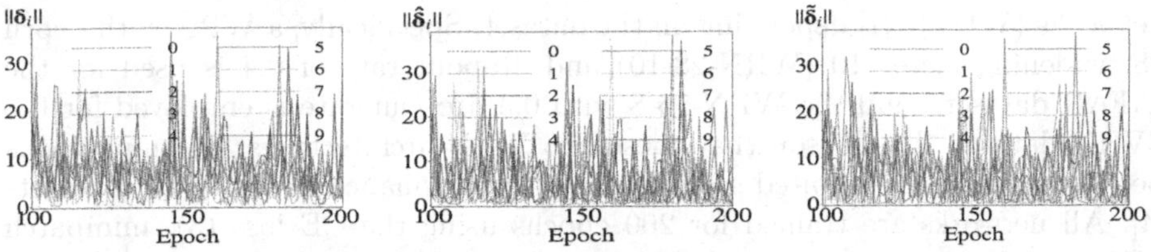

Fig. 2. Length of gradient vectors $\boldsymbol{\delta}_i$, $\hat{\boldsymbol{\delta}}_i$ and $\tilde{\boldsymbol{\delta}}_i$ for the CIFAR10 dataset.

From the CCR rates, the classes can be roughly categorized into two groups, i.e., one group with classes 3 and 5 that attain a rather low CCR and another group with the rest of the classes having better CCR rates. Looking at the 0 to 30 epoch temporal segment we observe that the classes of the first group clearly exhibit a smaller rate of CCR increase, while the majority of the ones in the second group almost attain their steady-state condition during this period. Moreover, after the 10th epoch a CCR gap between the first and second group of more than 10% in absolute values is observed, which stabilizes after the 230th epoch. Exactly the same conclusions can be drawn from the evolution of the θ_i values, where in this case a gap of 1 unit between the two groups is observed after the 30th epoch. (iii) The norm of the gradient update $\|\boldsymbol{\delta}_i\|$ alone, or its contributing parts $\|\hat{\boldsymbol{\delta}}_i\|$, $\|\tilde{\boldsymbol{\delta}}_i\|$, exhibit high fluctuations and a rather noisy behavior, and their direct observation does not provide any valuable information concerning the generalization performance of the classes during the training procedure.

From the above analysis we can see that a group of classes is neglected during the optimization procedure and that the proposed criterion can be used to identify these classes, verifying the theoretical analysis in Sect. 2.1.

3.2 Multiclass Classification Using SDNNs

Datasets. For the experimental evaluation of the proposed approach in the problem of multiclass classification the following 3 datasets are used: (i) The CIFAR-10 and CIFAR-100 datasets [11] consist of 60000 32 × 32 color images each, drawn from 10 and 100 classes, respectively. Both datasets are divided to a training and test partition with 50000 and 10000 images respectively. (ii) The street view house numbers (SVHN) dataset [14] contains 630420 color images of 32 × 32 pixel resolution, similar to the CIFAR datasets. They depict house numbers extracted from Google Street View images, i.e., each image belongs to one of ten classes. The dataset is split to a training, testing and an extra partition of 73257, 26032 and 531131 images, respectively. Following the standard procedure for this dataset, the training and extra partitions are combined in our experiments to form a new training partition.

Experimental Setup. Two modern DNN architectures are used for the evaluation of the proposed approach, namely, the VGG16 [16] with batch normalization after every convolutional layer, and two variants of the wide residual networks (WRN) [21] depending on the dataset. Specifically, a WRN with depth 28, widening factor 10 (WRN-28-10) and dropout rate of 0.4 is used for the CIFAR datasets, and the WRN-16-8 with 0.3 dropout rate is employed for the SVHN dataset. The reason that these two WRN architectures are employed is because they have exhibited state-of-the-art performance in the above datasets [4]. All networks are trained for 200 epochs using the CE loss (3), minibatch SGD with Nesterov momentum of 0.9, batch size of 128, weight decay of 0.0005, and an exponential learning rate schedule set to decrease at the 60th, 120th and 160th epoch. For the CIFAR datasets, the initial learning rate is set to 0.1 and reduced by a factor of 0.1 according to the learning rate schedule above, while for the SVHN dataset an initial learning rate and reduction factor of 0.01 and 0.2 are used, respectively. The images are normalized per-channel to zero mean and unit variance, and data augmentation is performed during training following [4], i.e., 4 pixels zero-padding and random cropping, horizontal mirroring with 50% probability, and cutout 16×16 and 8×8 for the CIFAR-10, CIFAR-100 datasets, respectively. The SVHN undergoes the same normalization, however, only 20×20 cutout is used to augment this dataset.

The subclass VGG16 (SVGG16) and WRN (SWRN) are created as explained in the following. The original VGG16 and WRN are executed for 30 epochs in order to compute a reliable neglection score θ_i for each class. In this way, 2 classes from the CIFAR10 and SVHN (20% of the total classes) and 10 classes from the CIFAR100 (10% of the total classes) with the highest θ_i's are selected, i.e., the classes with labels 3, 5 from CIFAR10, 1, 3 from SVHN and 0, 11, 18, 35, 53, 55, 62, 69, 72, 88 from CIFAR100. In order to alleviate any class imbalance problems resulting from the partitioning to subclasses, the selected classes are first doubled in size using the augmentation method described in [9], and then the k-means algorithm is applied to create two new subclasses from each class. The augmented datasets are then used to train SVGG and SWRN using the SCE loss (11) and the training procedure described above for the conventional networks. Learning is performed using the training partition of the datasets and the performance of each method is measured using the correct classification rate (CCR) along all classes achieved by the trained network in the test set.

All networks are implemented in PyTorch, extending the code provided in [4, 21], and the experimental evaluation is performed in an Intel i7 3770K@3.5 GHz PC with 32 GB RAM, Windows 10, and Nvidia GeForce GPU (GTX 1080 Ti).

Results. The evaluation results in terms of CCR and training times in hours are shown in Table 1. The testing times are only a few seconds in all cases (spanning the range of 5 s for VGG16 in CIFAR10 to 12 s for SWRN in SVHN). From the obtained results we can see that the proposed SVGG16 and SWRN outperform the conventional networks in all datasets, with differences in performance from 0.21% (SWRN over WRN in SVHN) to ≈2.5% (SVGG16 over VGG16 in CIFAR100). Considering that the CCR rates obtained with the WRN combined with cutout regularization [4] are currently among the state-of-the-art performances, even the small improvements obtained with the proposed approach are

Table 1. Accuracy rates and training times (hours) in 3 datasets

	VGG16 [16]	SVGG16	WRN [4]	SWRN
CIFAR10	93.5% (2.6 h)	94.8% (2.7 h)	96.92% (7.1 h)	**97.14%** (8.1 h)
CIFAR100	71.24% (2.6 h)	73.67% (2.6 h)	81.59% (7.1 h)	**82.17%** (7.5 h)
SVHN	98.16% (29.1 h)	98.35% (34.1 h)	98.70% (33.1 h)	**98.81%** (42.7 h)

considered significant. Moreover, we observe that the training time overhead caused by the application of the subclass approach is negligible for the medium size CIFAR datasets, and relatively small for the much larger SVHN dataset.

3.3 Multilabel Classification Using SDNNs

Dataset. The YT8M [1] is utilized to evaluate the proposed approach for the task of multilabel classification. This is the largest publicly available multilabel video dataset consisting of 6134598 videos annotated with one or more labels from 3862 classes (3.4 labels per video on average). For facilitating the comparison of different classification techniques the dataset is already divided to a training, evaluation and testing partition, consisting of 3888919, 1112356 and 1133323 videos, respectively. Visual and audio feature vectors in $\mathbb{R}^{1024}$ and $\mathbb{R}^{128}$, respectively, are already provided at video-level as well as at frame-level granularity. The data is stored in Tensorflow's tfrecord file format (3844 shards for each data partition and granularity level), which offers very efficient import and preprocessing functionalities for large-scale datasets.

Experimental Setup. For the evaluation, a rather simple convolutional neural network (CNN) is utilized with a convolutional, a max-pooling, a dropout and a SG layer of c outputs. The convolutional layer consists of 64 one-dimensional (1D) filters and is equipped with a rectification (ReLU) nonlinearity. Each filter has a receptive field of size 3 and stride 1, and zero padding is applied in order to preserve the spatial size of the input signals. The max-pooling layer employs a filter of size 2 and stride 2, while a keep-rate of 0.7 is used for the dropout layer. The CE loss (3) combined with the minibatch SGD-BP algorithm and weight decay of 0.0005 is used for training the CNN. The training is performed over 5 epochs with an exponential learning rate schedule, initial learning rate of 0.001, learning rate decay 0.95 in every epoch, and batch size of 512.

For the construction of the subclass CNN (SCNN), the CNN above is initially applied in the training set for $\frac{1}{3}$ of an epoch in order to obtain a neglection value θ_i (9) for each YT8M class and the 386 classes with the highest θ_i are selected, i.e., 10% of the total number of classes. The selected classes are then partitioned to $H_i = 2$ subclasses using the efficient on-line algorithm described in Algorithm 1, avoiding the loading of the whole dataset or large parts of it in memory, which would be infeasible for the YT8M dataset. Moreover, data augmentation is performed to the neglected classes using the extrapolation technique described in Sect. 2.3, setting $\lambda = 0.5$. In this way the number of observations in each subclass partition is doubled. The resulting SCNN is trained using the proposed SCE loss (11) and the training procedure described for the conventional CNN. For completeness, a standard logistic regression (LR) classifier is also evaluated using the same training procedure with initial learning rate of 0.001.

We performed experiments with the video-level visual features, as well as with audio-visual features produced by concatenating the video-level visual and audio feature vectors. In all cases L2-normalization was applied. The models are trained and evaluated using the YT8M training and validation set respectively. The labeling information for the testing set is not provided and for this reason it is excluded from the evaluation. Nevertheless, as reported in relevant works [8] the performance difference on the validation and test set is negligible. The evaluation metrics of the YT8M Video Understanding Challenge [1] are used to report our results, namely, Hit@1, precision at equal recall rate (PERR), mean average precision (mAP), and global average precision at 20 (GAP@20), with the latter being the official metric of the YT8M challenge for ranking the different participating teams. The models are implemented in Tensorflow and the evaluation is performed in the same PC used in Sect. 3.2.

Table 2. Evaluation results in YT8M

	Visual			Visual + Audio		
	LR	CNN	SCNN	LR	CNN	SCNN
Hit@1	82.4%	82.5%	**83.2%**	82.3%	85.2%	**85.7%**
PERR	71.9%	72.2%	**72.9%**	71.8%	75.4%	**75.9%**
mAP	41.2%	42.3%	**45.2%**	40.1%	45.6%	**47.9%**
GAP@20	77.1%	77.6%	**78.6%**	77%	80.7%	**82.2%**
T_{tr} *(min)*	**18.7**	59.2	66.2	**18.9**	60.3	67.1

Table 3. Comparison with the best single-model approaches in YT8M

	[8]	[13]	[2]	[18]	SCNN
GAP@20	82.15%	80.9%	**82.5%**	82.25%	82.2%

Results. The evaluation results in terms of Hit@1, PERR, mAP, GAP@20 and training time (T_{tr}) in minutes for each method are shown in Table 2. Moreover, in Table 3 we show state-of-the-art results achieved from single-model approaches in YT8M. From the analysis of the obtained results we observe the following: (i) The SCNN attains the best results, outperforming the conventional CNN by 1% and 1.5% GAP using the visual and audio-visual features, respectively. Both networks outperform the standard LR. (ii) By exploiting the audio information both CNN and SCNN attain a significant performance gain of more than 3%. On the other hand, a degradation in performance is observed for the LR model, which most likely does not have the capacity to exploit the additional discriminant information provided by the audio modality. (iii) As shown in Table 3, our SCNN method achieving a GAP of 82.2% performs in par with the best single-model approaches reported in [2,8,13,18]. This is an excellent performance considering that our SCNN exploits only the video-level feature vectors provided by the YT8M dataset in contrast to the top-performers in the competition, which additionally exploit the frame-level visual features and build upon stronger and much more computationally-demanding feature vector descriptors such as Fisher Vectors, VLAD, BoW, and other [2,18]. We should also note that the best performing approach [17] in the YT8M competition achieved a GAP score of 88.9%. However, this is achieved using an ensemble of classifiers and a variety of feature descriptors (e.g. NetVLAD, FVNet, DBoF), whose extraction and use would increase the computation requirements by at least an order of magnitude; thus this approach cannot be fairly compared with our proposed approach that creates a single model using the video-level descriptors already provided in the YT8M dataset.

4 Conclusions

In this paper, a novel SDNN framework was proposed and evaluated in two different multimedia classification tasks. Firstly, a new criterion is used for the identification of neglected classes during the initial stages of the DNN training. Subsequently, the identified classes are partitioned to subclasses and augmented in order to formulate an easier, piecewise linear classification problem for the DNN, and a new cross-entropy loss function emphasizing the discrimination of subclasses belonging to different classes is utilized. In this way, SDNNs are forced to pay more attention to the neglected classes, increasing effectively the overall classification performance. The experimental evaluation in two different problem domains, specifically, multiclass classification in three popular benchmarks (CIFAR10, CIFAR100 and SVHN) and multilabel classification using the YT8M dataset, which is the largest publicly available dataset for this task, demonstrated the efficacy of the proposed approach.

Acknowledgments. This work was supported by the EUs Horizon 2020 research and innovation programme under grant agreement H2020-780656 ReTV.

References

1. Abu-El-Haija, S., et al.: YouTube-8M: a large-scale video classification benchmark. arXiv:1609.08675 (2016)
2. Bober-Irizar, M., Husain, S., Ong, E.J., Bober, M.: Cultivating DNN diversity for large scale video labelling. In: CVPR Workshops (2017)
3. DeVries, T., Taylor, G.W.: Dataset augmentation in feature space. In: ICLR Workshops, Toulon, France, April 2017

4. Devries, T., Taylor, G.W.: Improved regularization of convolutional neural networks with cutout. arXiv:1708.04552 (2017)
5. Escalera, S., et al.: Subclass problem-dependent design for error-correcting output codes. IEEE Trans. Pattern Anal. Mach. Intell. **30**(6), 1041–1054 (2008)
6. Gkalelis, N., Mezaris, V., Kompatsiaris, I., Stathaki, T.: Mixture subclass discriminant analysis link to restricted Gaussian model and other generalizations. IEEE Trans. Neural Netw. Learn. Syst. **24**(1), 8–21 (2013)
7. Hastie, T., Tibshirani, R.: Discriminant analysis by Gaussian mixtures. J. Roy. Stat. Soc. Series B **58**(1), 155–176 (1996)
8. Huang, P., Yuan, Y., Lan, Z., Jiang, L., Hauptmann, A.G.: Video representation learning and latent concept mining for large-scale multi-label video classification. arXiv:1707.01408 (2017)
9. Inoue, H.: Data augmentation by pairing samples for images classification. arXiv:1801.02929 (2018)
10. Kohonen, T.: Learning vector quantization. In: Self-Organizing Maps, chap. 6. Springer Series in Information Sciences. Springer, Heidelberg (1995). https://doi.org/10.1007/978-3-642-97610-0_6
11. Krizhevsky, A.: Learning multiple layers of features from tiny images. Technical report, Department of Computer Science, University of Toronto (2009)
12. Le Cun, Y., Bottou, L., Bengio, Y., Haffner, P.: Gradient based learning applied to document recognition. Proc. IEEE **86**(11), 2278–2324 (1998)
13. Na, S., Yu, Y., Lee, S., Kim, J., Kim, G.: Encoding video and label priors for multi-label video classification on YouTube-8M dataset. In: CVPR Workshops (2017)
14. Netzer, Y., Wang, T., Coates, A., Bissacco, A., Wu, B., Ng, A.Y.: Reading digits in natural images with unsupervised feature learning. In: NIPS Workshops, Venice, Italy, pp. 2999–3007, October 2017
15. Sarafianos, N., Xu, X., Kakadiaris, I.A.: Deep imbalanced attribute classification using visual attention aggregation. In: Ferrari, V., Hebert, M., Sminchisescu, C., Weiss, Y. (eds.) ECCV 2018. LNCS, vol. 11215, pp. 708–725. Springer, Cham (2018). https://doi.org/10.1007/978-3-030-01252-6_42
16. Simonyan, K., Zisserman, A.: Very deep convolutional networks for large-scale image recognition. In: ICLR, San Diego, CA, USA, May 2015
17. Skalic, M., Austin, D.: Building a size constrained predictive model for video classification. In: CVPR Workshops (2017)
18. Skalic, M., Pekalski, M., Pan, X.E.: Deep learning methods for efficient large scale video labeling. In: CVPR Workshops (2017)
19. Soudry, D., Hoffer, E., Nacson, M.S., Gunasekar, S., Srebro, N.: The implicit bias of gradient descent on separable data. JMLR **19**(70), 1–57 (2018)
20. You, D., Hamsici, O.C., Martinez, A.M.: Kernel optimization in discriminant analysis. IEEE Trans. Pattern Anal. Mach. Intell. **33**(3), 631–638 (2011)
21. Zagoruyko, S., Komodakis, N.: Wide residual networks. In: BMVC, York, UK, September 2016

Automatic Material Classification Using Thermal Finger Impression

Jacob Gately[1], Ying Liang[2], Matthew Kolessar Wright[1], Natasha Kholgade Banerjee[1], Sean Banerjee[1], and Soumyabrata Dey[1](✉)

[1] Clarkson University, 8 Clarkson Avenue, Potsdam, NY 13699, USA
{gatelyjm,kolessmj,nbanerje,sbanerje,sdey}@clarkson.edu
[2] Cornell University, Ithaca, NY 14850, USA
yl2864@cornell.edu

Abstract. Natural surfaces offer the opportunity to provide augmented reality interactions in everyday environments without the use of cumbersome body-mounted equipment. One of the key techniques of detecting user interactions with natural surfaces is the use of thermal imaging that captures the transmitted body heat onto the surface. A major challenge of these systems is detecting user swipe pressure on different material surfaces with high accuracy. This is because the amount of transferred heat from the user body to a natural surface depends on the thermal property of the material. If the surface material type is known, these systems can use a material-specific pressure classifier to improve the detection accuracy. In this work, we address to solve this problem as we propose a novel approach that can detect material type from a user's thermal finger impression on a surface. Our technique requires the user to touch a surface with a finger for 2 s. The recorded heat dissipation time series of the thermal finger impression is then analyzed in a classification framework for material identification. We studied the interaction of 15 users on 7 different material types, and our algorithm is able to achieve 74.65% material classification accuracy on the test data in a user-independent manner.

Keywords: Multimaterial classification · Thermal imaging · Natural surface interface · Time series

1 Introduction

Sensor modalities outside the visible light domain such as depth, hyperspectral, and thermal cameras have begun to permeate the consumer space, and their ubiquity enables the spread of novel applications in the consumer domain. One such application is the use of any natural surface as a touchscreen interface to communicate with computing devices. While traditionally natural surface interaction has been performed in the color domain [1–3], a number of approaches [4–8] have demonstrated the effectiveness of using thermal sensors to perform natural surface interaction. Some of these works [6,8] attempted to detect swipe

Y. M. Ro et al. (Eds.): MMM 2020, LNCS 11961, pp. 239–250, 2020.
https://doi.org/10.1007/978-3-030-37731-1_20

pressure because this can add a new dimension to the vocabulary space of swipe and gesture actions. For example, the same swipe pattern with different pressure can carry different meanings for the interacting computing device. One of the main challenges of this task is the manifestation of swipe pressure as heat signature varies with different surface materials. This is because the amount of heat transferred from the user body to a surface depends on the thermal property of the surface material. For example, swipe actions with similar pressure on concrete and wood surfaces would appear differently while recorded using a thermal camera. On the other hand, a hard swipe on a concrete surface can look similar to a soft swipe on a wood surface. Figure 1 illustrate the problem with an example. As a result, pressure detection accuracy suffers a great deal while performed across different materials. Our work aims to solve this problem with automatic material detection which should precede the swipe pressure classification. Once the surface material is identified using our method, a material-specific classifier can be applied to detect the swipe pressure.

To perform automatic material classification using thermal images, we proposed a novel approach where a user needs to touch the surface of a material for 2 s with his finger. The thermal finger impression left on the surface is then tracked for 50 s. The time series of decaying heat signature of the thermal finger impression is used in a random forest based classification framework to detect the surface material. The algorithm is tested on data captured from 15 different users interacting with 7 different material types including blackboard, polyester fabric, cotton cloth, concrete, drywall, laminate, and wood. The classification accuracy achieved on the test data set is 52% compared to the random guess probability of 14.29%. Further investigation suggests that thermal signature decay patterns of blackboard and concrete are almost similar. Similar behavior observed for thermal patterns of drywall, laminate, and wood. See Fig. 3 for details. This suggests us to cluster 7 material types into 4 classes (Class 1 - blackboard and concrete, class 2 - polyester fabric, class 3 - cotton cloth, class 4 - drywall, laminate, and wood) based on their thermal impressions. Since the appearance of swipe pressure in the thermal domain depends on the amount of heat transferred onto the surface and its decay pattern, we concluded that swipes with similar pressure would display a similar thermal signature on materials of each of these four classes. The classification accuracy achieved for the detection of 4 material classes is 74.65%. Compared to the probability of random guess (25%) this is a significant improvement.

The main contribution of this paper is a novel user-independent material detection method. We selected 7 different material types that commonly found in indoor scenarios, and we demonstrated that they can be divided into 4 clusters based on their thermal behaviors. The method should assist in improving the accuracy of the systems which aim to perform user swipe pressure classification on different material surfaces. This can be achieved by first detecting the thermal class of a material, and then using a pressure classifier specific to the thermal property of the material.

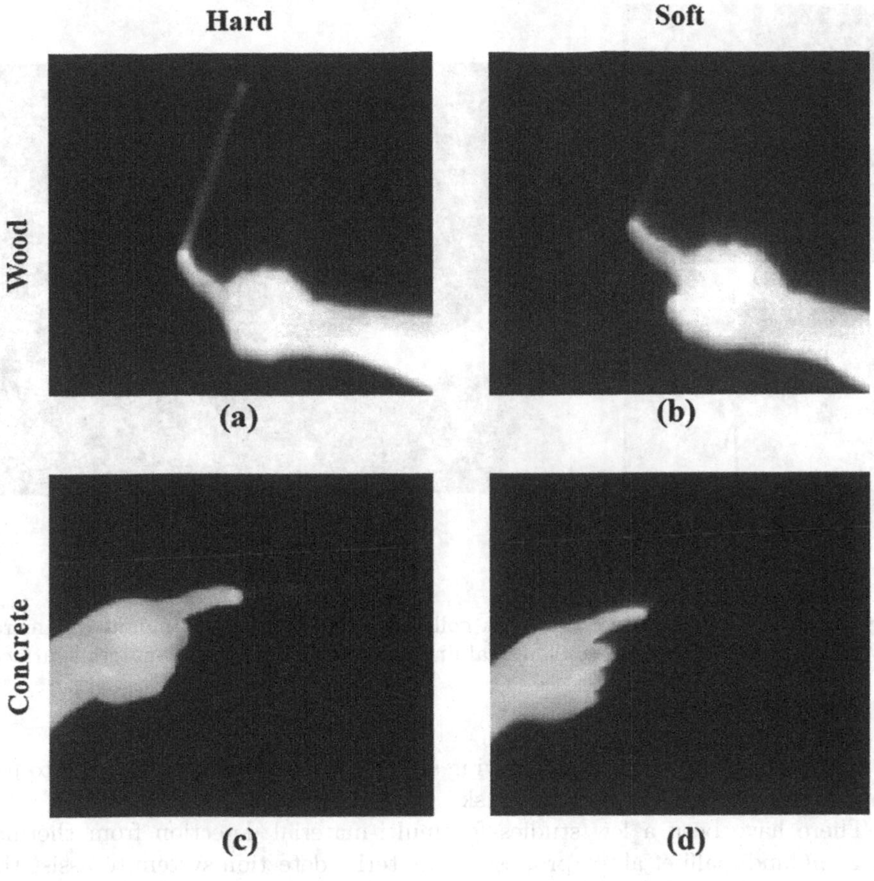

Fig. 1. This example illustrates how swipes with similar pressure can appear very different on different materials. (a) Hard swipe on wood, (b) soft swipe on wood, (c) hard swipe on concrete, (d) soft swipe on concrete.

2 Related Work

There have been several approaches that attempt to solve the problem of interaction with projected content on natural surfaces. While some of the work [1–3] used color cameras to detect user actions and gestures, others [4–8] leveraged on thermal domain data to address the problem. Few of the work [6–8] gone ahead to solve the problem of swipe pressure detection. While detection of swipe pressure can open a new dimension of user interaction with natural surfaces, accurate detection of swipe pressure across different materials type can be challenging. This is mainly because the amount of heat transferred to different material types is different even if the swipe pressure is similar. The problem is demonstrated in Fig. 1. Our work proposes to solve this problem by first detecting a

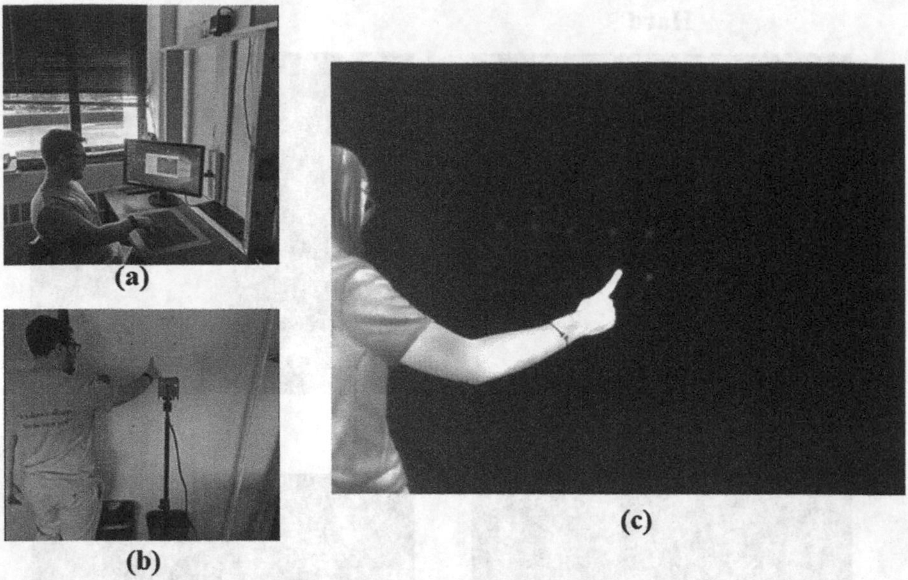

Fig. 2. Thermal finger impression data collection setup. (a) Table mounted camera. (b) Tripod mounted camera. (c) Thermal finger impression data on a material surface.

surface material type, and then allowing swipe pressure detection systems to use material-specific classifiers for the task.

There have been a few studies for multi-material detection from thermal images. Gundupalli et al. [9] proposed a material detection system to assist the segregation of recyclables items. However, they require to heat the materials in a dark hot chamber with controlled temperature. Cho et al. [10] use a thermal camera integrated into a mobile phone to capture thermal images of indoor and outdoor materials, and they utilize thermal texture information for material classification. Unlike this method, our material surfaces are smooth and do not display much texture information in the thermal domain. Aujeszky et al. [11] performed material classification using laser excitation step thermography. Bai et al. [12], use a heat lamp to heat up the local environment and capture the thermal signature of the materials. Our method, on the other hand, does not require any specific hardware system, and it can classify materials that otherwise are difficult to identify with texture features.

3 Data Collection

All the data is captured using a Sierra Olympic Viento-G thermal camera with a 9 mm lens. The data is recorded at 30 frames per second (fps) rate and stored as 16 bit TIFF images with 640 × 480 pixels resolution. We collected data from 15 users interacting with 7 different materials such as blackboard, polyester fabric, cotton cloth, concrete, drywall, laminate, and wood. Five different samples for each material, scattered across 8 different rooms of two buildings, are used in this process. The indoor temperature during data collection was between 65° to 70° Fahrenheit. Before the data collection, we made sure that the users' hand temperature is close to normal human body temperature in the range of 95° to 100° Fahrenheit. For each material sample, users are asked to provide 10 thermal finger impressions. As a result, we collected 5250 (7 materials × 5 samples × 15 users × 10 finger impressions) finger impression examples in total for all users on all material samples. For thermal finger impression data, users are asked to touch the material surface for approximately 2 s with their index finger. The transferred heat from the finger to the material surface (thermal finger impression) is recorded for 50 s to get the diminishing heat pattern. For the entire duration of data recording, the camera setup is arranged in such a way that the camera axis remains normal to the material surface. The data capturing procedure is illustrated in Fig. 2.

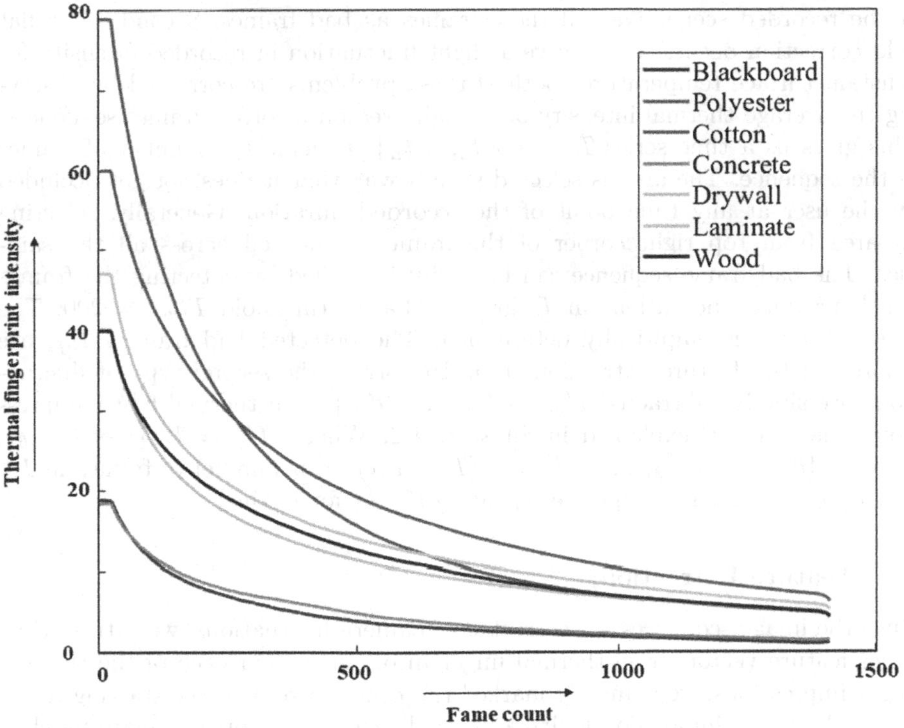

Fig. 3. A plot of average time series patterns for 7 different material types. The horizontal axis is corresponding to the frame number relative to the first recorded frame. The vertical axis represents the background-subtracted average pixel value for all thermal finger impression instances of a material type.

4 Method

Our method comprises of data pre-processing, feature extraction, and classification. The following sections explain the steps in detail.

4.1 Data Pre-processing

We performed mainly two tasks under data pre-processing. Data cleanup, and camera fluctuation correction. In the data cleanup step, we rejected some of the recorded data due to various reasons such as high frame drop rate, thermal finger impression being occluded by the user body part, and a user provides multiple finger impressions in very close proximity that cannot be segregated from each other. We rejected approximately 10% of the data in this process.

We observed different camera fluctuations while analyzing the data. One of the case being the camera automatically performs flat field corrections while recording the data. In this process, it records around 10 frames with high intensity fluctuations which is completely uncorrelated with the thermal signature of the recorded scene. We call these frames as bad frames. Second, after flat field correction occurs, we observe a slight fluctuation in recorded intensity for constant surface temperature. Both of these problems are corrected by observing the average thermal intensity of a small area on recorded frames sequences. This gives us a time series $T_c = \{t_1, t_2, ..., t_n\}$, n being the number of frames in the sequence. The area is selected such a way that it does not get occluded by the user at any time point of the recorded duration. Generally, selecting an area from top right corner of the frame works well across all the samples. The bad frame sequence can be easily identified by detecting the frames which produce fluctuations in T_c greater than a threshold $Th_{bf} = 200$. The value of Th_{bf} is empirically determined. The detected bad frames, T_{bf}, are ignored in the feature extraction step. To correct the second type of fluctuations, we simply subtracted $T'_c = \{t'_1, t'_2, ..., t'_{n'}\}$ from thermal finger impression time series F explained in Subsect. 4.2. Where, $T'_c = T_{c-bf} - T^1{}_{c-bf}$, $T_{c-bf} = \{t^{c-bf}{}_1, t^{c-bf}{}_2, ..., t^{c-bf}{}_{n'}\} = (T_c - T_{bf})$, n' is number of frames in T'_c and T_{c-bf}. $T^1{}_{c-bf}$ is a sequence repeating $t^{c-bf}{}_1$ for n' times.

4.2 Feature Extraction

Once the image sequences are corrected of camera fluctuations, we extract time series feature vectors from thermal finger impressions. For each of the thermal finger impressions, we manually marked the center pixel and the starting frame where the finger impression is first observed. An 11×11 pixels square patch is then selected around the center pixels as a Region of Interest (ROI). We used the background subtraction technique to compute the mean thermal intensity difference caused by the finger impression ROI. For this purpose, we computed the background model bg as the average of the first 10 frames of a recording sequence. Suppose the frame sequence starting from the first frame marked for the thermal finger impression is $S = \{s_1, s_2, ..., s_{1500}\}$. The length of the sequence is 1500 as we observed the finger impression for 50 s at 30 fps rate. The time series feature $F = \{f_1, f_2, f_{1500}\}$ is then computed as $f_i = mean(differ(s_{ROI,i}, bg_{ROI}))$, $i \in [1, 1500]$. Where $s_{ROI,i}$ is the ROI on frame s_i, bg_{ROI} is the ROI on the background model. The operation $differ(s_{ROI,i}, bg_{ROI})$ performs pixel-wise subtractions of bg_{ROI} from $s_{ROI,i}$. Finally, $mean(.)$ computes the average of all pixel-wise differences in $differ(s_{ROI,i}, bg_{ROI})$.

As expected, the extracted time series features mostly follow a non-increasing curve. Figure 3 displays the time series computed by averaging all finger impression time series for each of the 7 material types. As it can be seen, the time series patterns of blackboard and concrete are very similar. The same is applicable for drywall, laminate, and wood. This suggested us to club blackboard and concrete in one cluster and drywall, laminate, and wood in another cluster. Below are the features we considered for the classification framework. Before computing the features, a one-dimensional median filter with window size 51 is used for denoising the time series.

Raw Time Series: This is the 1500 dimensional time series F computed for each of the thermal finger impressions.

Relative Time Series: 1500 dimensional time series F' constructed by computing absolute differences of f_1 and each element of F. Sometimes, feature vectors of different samples of the same material can show some variance in absolute values. This feature can help to preserve the decay pattern of the time series ignoring the variance of absolute values. We used the 3000-dimensional concatenation of F and F' as the feature vector.

Polynomial Coefficients: We fitted a polynomial of degree 2 and a polynomial of degree 3 on each of the time series. The 7 polynomial coefficients (3 coefficients of the polynomial of degree 2 followed by 4 coefficients of the polynomial of degree 3) are used as a feature vector.

Median Samples: A time series F is divided into k equal parts. The median values of each part are computed constructing a k dimensional feature vector. This helps to ignore local distortion of features due to unexpected noise. Different value of k is used starting from 10 to 100 with a stride of 10.

Relative Median Samples: A k dimensional median samples vector is computed on F', and it is concatenated with the k dimensional median samples on F. Therefore, a k relative median samples feature vector is a $2 \times k$ dimensional vector.

4.3 Classification

We divided our data set into two parts. The first part consists of data from users 1 to 10 and we call it the training set. The second part consists of data from users 11 to 15 and this is called the test set. We used a random forest classifier implemented in Weka 3.8.3 release [13]. Random forest is a powerful classification model that can naturally handle multiclass classification, robust against nonlinear decision boundaries, and has a relatively low training cost. Therefore, we believe, it would be wise to validate our dataset with a random forest classifier. The training set is used for 10 fold cross validation using each of the features described in Subsect. 4.2. Finally, the best features, i.e. the 3000 dimensional relative times series, and 200 (100 + 100) dimensional relative median samples, are used for classification on the test set. All the experiments are repeated twice, first time for 7 material types and second time for 4 clusters formed by grouping the materials based on their thermal behavior. Cluster 1 is blackboard and concrete, cluster 2 is polyester fabric, cluster 3 is cotton cloth, and class 4 is drywall, laminate, and wood.

5 Results

We performed 10 fold cross validation on the training data set. The results of the experiments are reported in Figs. 4 and 5. Compared to the 7 class classification setup, the 4 class setup improved the best detection accuracy by 21.5%. This is mainly because we cluster together the materials with confusing thermal decay patterns into the same classes. As it can be seen, the raw relative time series feature received the best classification accuracy in both 7 class and 4 class classification setups. However, 200-dimensional relative median samples feature also received high detection rates which are very close to the highest accuracy. While it can be computationally expensive to train a classifier with the 3000-dimensional raw relative time series feature, training with the relative median sample feature is comparatively economical. Therefore, it can serve as a balance between classification accuracy and computational expense. Plots in Fig. 5 suggest that increasing k from 10 to 100 in median sample features and relative median samples features improve the detection rates around 3% for both 7 class and 4 class classification setups.

While the cross-validation on the training set is used only for the selection of the best performing features, the actual validation of our system is performed in a user-independent fashion by training the model using the complete training set and measuring the accuracy on the test set. Please note, our training set contains the data from user 1 to 10, and the test set contains the data from user 11 to 15. The best two performing features, raw relative time series, and 200-dimensional relative median samples are selected for the same. The confusion matrices in Fig. 6 shows the performance of both the features in two different classification scenarios. The confusion matrices in Fig. 6(a), and (b) support our earlier prediction that thermal signatures of materials within classes blackboard-concrete and drywall-laminate-wood are similar. That is the reason that the materials within the same classes are interchangeably getting falsely detected. Irrespective of that, we received around 52% and 75% accuracy in 7 class and 4 class scenarios. Compare to the random guess probability of 14.28% and 25%, this is a significant achievement. Moreover, user samples of the training set and the test

(a)

Material	Raw	Raw Rel.	Coeffs.	Med 100	Rel Med 200
Blackboard	65.5263	66.3158	52.6316	61.0526	65
Polyester	74.6512	80	69.3023	75.1163	81.1628
Cotton	87.7551	89.3878	87.551	88.5714	87.7551
Concrete	49.7561	48.5366	47.0732	50.2439	51.4634
Drywall	56.7442	56.9767	45.3488	58.3721	59.3023
Laminate	36.25	40.25	30.75	38.25	38.5
Wood	30.8333	36.9444	28.0556	31.6667	34.4444
Overall	58.76	61.1	53.07	59.07	61.03

(b)

Material Class	Raw	Raw Rel.	Coeffs.	Med 100	Rel Med 200
1	87.5949	88.481	82.7848	82.0253	87.9747
2	69.3023	72.093	60.6977	57.2093	72.093
3	85.9184	85.9184	85.9184	81.0204	85.5102
4	81.1765	81.7647	77.0588	72.2689	81.7647
Overall	81.97	82.86	77.69	81.83	82.66

Material Class: 1 = Blackboard-Concrete, 2 = Polyester, 3 = Cotton, 4 = Drywall-Laminate-Wood.

Fig. 4. Classification accuracy on the training set is reported (a) for 7 material classes and (b) 4 material classes. Columns 2 to 6 are accuracies for raw time series, relative time series, polynomial coefficients, median samples, and relative median samples features respectively. All numbers are in percentage.

set are completely separated. This strongly suggests that our algorithm is user-independent i.e. given it trained on enough training examples, it can produce good detection accuracy on unknown test data produced by users outside of the subjects in the training set.

6 Discussion

In this paper, we proposed a multi-material detection algorithm that can classify commonly available indoor materials into thermally equivalent clusters. To this process, we employ a novel approach where a user has to briefly touch a surface leaving its thermal finger impression on the material. The decaying heat pattern of the finger impression is then analyzed in a machine learning framework to identify the surface material. The work would be valuable especially for the systems that allow users to use the natural surfaces as touch screen interfaces. We demonstrated the capability of our method as we achieved 75% accuracy

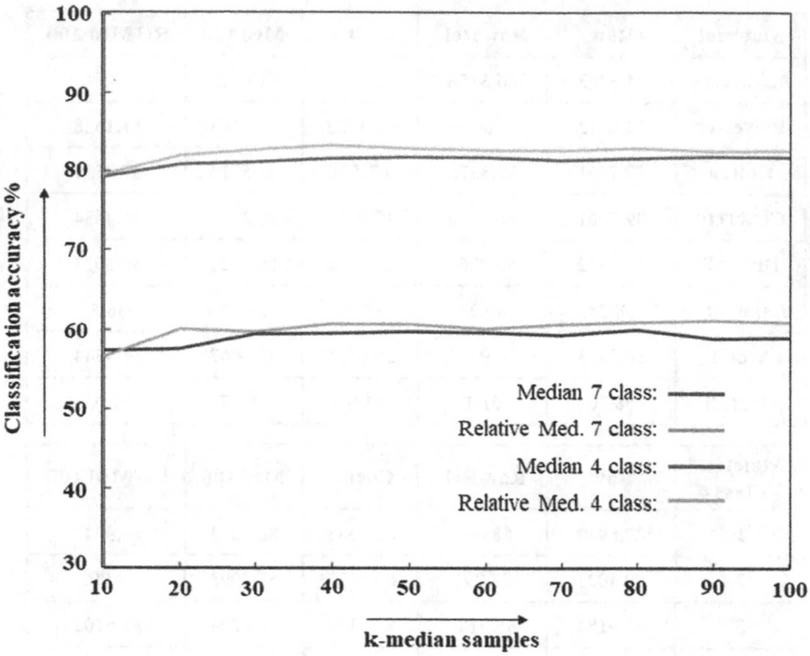

Fig. 5. Figure shows the accuracy of the training set on k-median samples and relative k-median samples features. k varies from 10 to 100 with a stride of 10.

in classifying 7 different materials into 4 classes based on the similarity of their thermal behavior. Moreover, we experimentally proved that our algorithm is user-independent. There can be two major reasons behind this. First, our defined task for the thermal finger impression is simple i.e. touching the surface material for two seconds with the index finger. Therefore, the between users' thermal finger impression variations for the same material are less compared to between material variations. Second, the heat decay patterns of a material surface are only dependent on the amount of heat transferred to the surface. Since there is not much variation in thermal finger impressions generated by different users, the decay patterns of the same material type are also not user dependent. This implies that our algorithm does not need to train on new user data to successfully able to predict a material type.

As part of the future work, we want to combine RGB color images with thermal finger impression to further improve our classification accuracy. We believe that the surface texture information in the color domain can assist our classifier with complementary information that would help to improve the prediction capability of our system. Furthermore, we have plans to benchmark our algorithm against different parameter changes such as room temperature and humidity differences, user hand temperature changes, within-class material variances such

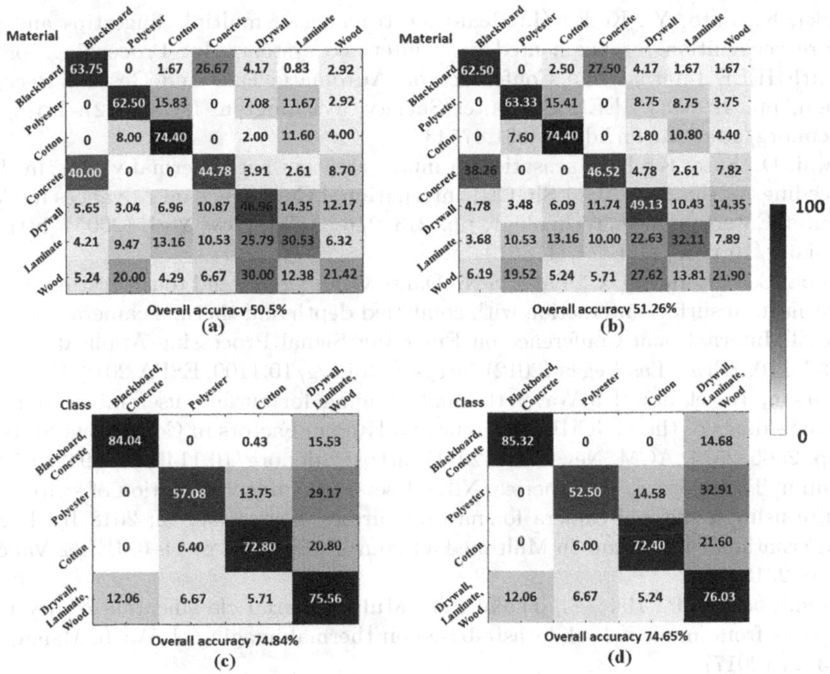

Fig. 6. Figure shows the confusion matrices computed on the test set. Accuracy is computed on (a) relative time series and 7 classes, (b) 200 dimensional relative median samples and 7 classes, (c) relative time series and 4 classes, and (d) 200 dimensional relative median samples, and 4 classes. All numbers are in percentage values.

as the same material with different textures. Finally, we would want to use different classification models such as the support vector machine, and deep neural network.

Acknowledgements. This work was partially supported by the National Science Foundation (NSF) grant #1730183.

References

1. Kurz, D.: Thermal touch: thermography-enabled everywhere touch interfaces for mobile augmented reality applications. In: 2014 IEEE International Symposium on Mixed and Augmented Reality, pp. 9–16. IEEE, Munich (2014). https://doi.org/10.1109/ISMAR.2014.6948403
2. Wilson, A.D.: Playanywhere: a compact interactive tabletop projection-vision system. In: Proceedings of the 18th Annual ACM Symposium on User Interface Software and Technology, pp. 83–92. ACM, New York (2005)
3. Mistry, P., Maes, P.: Sixthsense: a wearable gestural interface. In: ACM SIGGRAPH ASIA 2009 Sketches, pp. 11. ACM, New York (2009). https://doi.org/10.1145/1667146.1667160

4. Oka, K., Sato, Y., Koike, H.: Real-time tracking of multiple fingertips and gesture recognition for augmented desk interface systems. In: Proceedings of the Fifth IEEE International Conference on Automatic Face and Gesture Recognition, pp. 429–434. IEEE Computer Society, Washington, DC (2002). http://dl.acm.org/citation.cfm?id=874061.875437
5. Iwai, D., Sato, K.: Heat sensation in image creation with thermal vision. In: Proceedings of the 2005 ACM SIGCHI International Conference on Advances in Computer Entertainment Technology, pp. 213–216. ACM, New York (2005). https://doi.org/10.1145/1178477.1178510
6. Saba, E.N., Larson, E.C., Patel, S.N.: Dante vision: in-air and touch gesture sensing for natural surface interaction with combined depth and thermal cameras. In: 2012 IEEE International Conference on Emerging Signal Processing Applications. pp. 167–170, IEEE, Las Vegas (2012). https://doi.org/10.1109/ESPA.2012.6152472
7. Larson, E., et al.: HeatWave: thermal imaging for surface user interaction. In: Proceedings of the SIGCHI Conference on Human Factors in Computing Systems, pp. 2565–2574. ACM, New York (2011). https://doi.org/10.1145/1978942.1979317
8. Dunn, T., Banerjee, S., Banerjee, N.K.: User-independent detection of swipe pressure using a thermal camera for natural surface interaction. In: 2018 IEEE 20th International Workshop on Multimedia Signal Processing, pp. 1–6. IEEE, Vancouver (2018)
9. Gundupalli, S.P., Hait, S., Thakur, A.: Multi-material classification of dry recyclables from municipal solid waste based on thermal imaging. J. Waste Manag. **70**, 13–21 (2017)
10. Cho, Y., Bianchi-Berthouze, N., Marquardt, N., Julier, S.J.: Deep thermal imaging: proximate material type recognition in the wild through deep learning of spatial surface temperature patterns. In: Proceedings of the 2018 CHI Conference on Human Factors in Computing Systems, pp. 1–13. ACM, Montreal (2018). https://doi.org/10.1145/3173574.3173576
11. Aujeszky, T., Korres, G., Eid, M.: Thermography-based material classification using machine learning. In: 2017 IEEE International Symposium on Haptic, Audio and Visual Environments and Games, pp. 1–6. IEEE, Abu Dhabi (2017). https://doi.org/10.1109/HAVE.2017.8240344
12. Bai, H., Bhattacharjee, T., Chen, H., Kapusta, A., Kemp, C.: Towards Material Classification of Scenes Using Active Thermography. In: 2018 IEEE/RSJ International Conference on Intelligent Robots and Systems, pp. 4262–4269, IEEE, Madrid (2018). https://doi.org/10.1109/IROS.2018.8594469
13. Frank, E., Hall, M.A., Witten, I.H.: The WEKA Workbench. Online Appendix for "Data Mining: Practical Machine Learning Tools and Techniques". Morgan Kaufmann, Burlington (2016)

Oral Session 5A: Face

Face Attributes Recognition Based on One-Way Inferential Correlation Between Attributes

Hongkong Ge, Jiayuan Dong, and Liyan Zhang(✉)

Nanjing University of Aeronautics and Astronautics,
Nanjing, People's Republic of China
gehongkong@nuaa.edu.cn, dongjybaobao@gmail.com, zhangly84@126.com

Abstract. Attributes recognition of face in the wild is getting increasingly attention with the rapid development of computer vision. Most prior work tend to apply separate model for the single attribute or attributes in the same region, which easily lost the information of correlation between attributes. Correlation (*e.g.,* one-way inferential correlation) between face attributes, which is neglected by many researches, contributes to the better performance of face attributes recognition. In this paper, we propose a face attributes recognition model based on *one-way inferential correlation (OIR)* between face attributes (*e.g.,* the inferential correlation from goatee to gender). Toward that end, we propose a method to find such correlation based on data imbalance of each attribute, and design an *OIR-related attributes classifier* using such correlation. Furthermore, we cut face region into multiple region parts according to the category of attributes, and use a novel approach of face feature extraction for all regional parts via transfer learning focusing on multiple neural layers. Experimental evaluations on the benchmark with multiple face attributes show the effectiveness on recognition accuracy and computational cost of our proposed model.

Keywords: Face recognition · Attributes correlation · Deep learning

1 Introduction

Face attributes contain a series of biological characteristics of human face, providing a wide variety of identity information like gender, age, race, hair style, accessories, *etc.* The purpose of face attributes recognition is to detect the attributes of a human face. In recent years, many applications based on face attributes have emerged, and these applications include *face verification* [1], *video surveillance* [2] (*e.g.,* detecting the person with sunglasses automatically), *face retrieval* [3] (*e.g.,* finding the person with given attributes and filtering the face database automatically), *social media* [4] (*e.g.,* recommending makeups for the given face automatically), *etc.* The emergence of these applications embodies the great research value of the study of face (especially for face in the wild) attributes recognition.

Y. M. Ro et al. (Eds.): MMM 2020, LNCS 11961, pp. 253–265, 2020.
https://doi.org/10.1007/978-3-030-37731-1_21

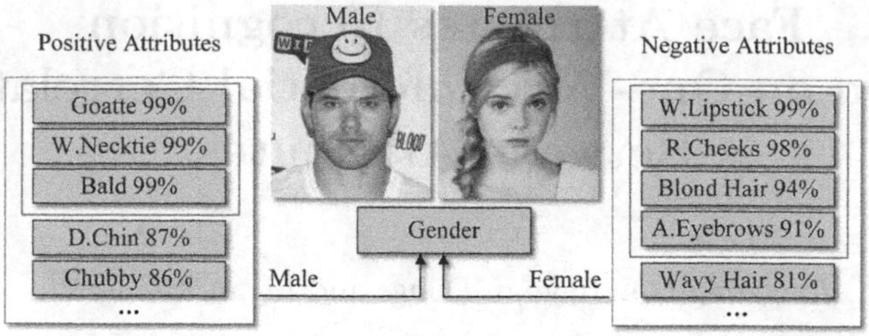

Fig. 1. An example of contribution of *OIR* between attributes to face attributes recognition, where gender is the attribute to be identified, and positive (negative) attributes with high probability contribute to the recognition of male (female).

Face in the wild is close to our daily life, but faced with the problem of illumination, occlusion, pose, expression, *etc.* Over the past several years, people attempt to use deep neural networks for face attributes recognition in order to solve these problems. However, most prior work tend to select the holistic face image as the input of their networks, which may neglect the capture of local information related to attributes. Meanwhile, the high complexity of networks could be reduced without the decreasing of recognition accuracy. Moreover, the relationship between attributes is not taken into account in the process of recognition, which contributes to better recognition performance. Figure 1 shows the contribution of *OIR* between attributes to face attributes recognition. For Gender, some positive attributes (*e.g.,* Goatee, Wearing Necktie, Bald, *etc.*) and negative attributes (*e.g.,* Wearing Lipstick, Rosy Cheeks, Blond Hair, *etc.*) contribute to Male and Female respectively.

Faced with these problems, we propose a face attributes recognition model based on *OIR* between attributes. Firstly, we find *OIR* between attributes according to the distribution of labelled data set, and filter them for each attribute. Then, we design a novel method of feature extraction via transfer learning from multiple neural layers. Besides, faces are cut into multiple region parts according to the categories of attributes, and we extract features for all region parts. Finally, we add *OIR* constraint in our *OIR-related attributes classifier*. Experimental evaluations on a large face in the wild database show the effectiveness on recognition accuracy and computational cost of our proposed model.

The rest of this paper is organized as follows. The related researches are listed in Sect. 2. The method to find all *OIR* between face attributes is presented in Sect. 3. Section 4 contains the architecture of our complete model. The performance of proposed model is shown in Sect. 5. Section 6 contains the conclusion of this paper.

2 Related Work

Attributes recognition of face in the wild is getting increasingly attention with the rapid development of computer vision, and a lot prior work contributes to the progress of face attributes recognition. There are three main steps: (i) face detection; (ii) face feature extraction; (iii) attributes recognition. The work of state-of-the-art face detection and alignment in [5–7] facilitates our research in face attributes recognition.

Researches can be divided into *holistic methods* [8] and *regional methods* [9] according to the input region of a face image. Liu et al. [8] proposed LNets to detect face region, and select the holistic region as the input of attributes recognition. Srinivas et al. [9] extracted features from six regions of a detected face. The regional methods outperform holistic ones, making full use of regional feature. However, the cutting methods in [9] is too rough to be attribute-related.

For feature extraction, Kumar et al. [10] extracted hand-crafted feature for attributes recognition. Recently, feature extraction methods in face recognition [11,12] achieved great progress, and many researchers have proposed feature extraction methods via deep learning. Cottrell et al. [11] used autoencoder for feature learning. Zhong et al. [12] captured face area through their proposed FaceNet, and then used VGG-16 [13] for feature learning. However, the complexity of networks in their work is high, and transferring feature from pre-trained CNNs can solve this problem. Transfer learning for feature extraction is used in [14], but most prior work is limited to last layer of CNNs.

Looking back on the prior work, approaches for face attributes recognition can be grouped into *single-task learning (STL)* and *multi-task learning (MTL)*. In *STL* [8,12], a separated SVM classifier was trained for each attributes. In *MTL* [15,16], the joint attributes classifier was trained for related attributes. The former focus on capturing the feature of attribute to be recognized without considering the relationship between attributes, while the latter is the opposite. Moreover, the relationship considered in the prior work is not much helpful for attributes recognition, and the relationship (*one-way inferential correlation* in this paper) that contributes to attributes recognition is not explored. Although *MTL* could capture some common features between attributes, it also decentralize the feature of the attribute that is recognized. The average face attributes recognition accuracy of 40 attributes in [8,16] were both 87%, and advantage of *STL* or *MTL* did not show up. In order to make full use of the advantage of *STL* and *MTL*, we find all *OIR* between attributes according to the distribution of labelled data set, and then add them into *OIR-related attributes classifier* for each attribute.

3 One-Way Inferential Correlation

Correlation between face attributes is important to face attributes recognition, however, such correlation is not mutual. Taking correlation between Beard and Male as an example, we can easily see the unidirectionality of correlation. When beard is identified for a face, there is a high inferential probability that this face belongs to a male. On the contrary, when a face is recognized as a male, the existence of beard is still uncertain. This is easy to explain: females generally do not have beard, but it is uncertain whether males have beard or not. We call such correlation *one-way inferential correlation (OIR)*, and the direction of *OIR* between Beard and Male is from the former to the latter.

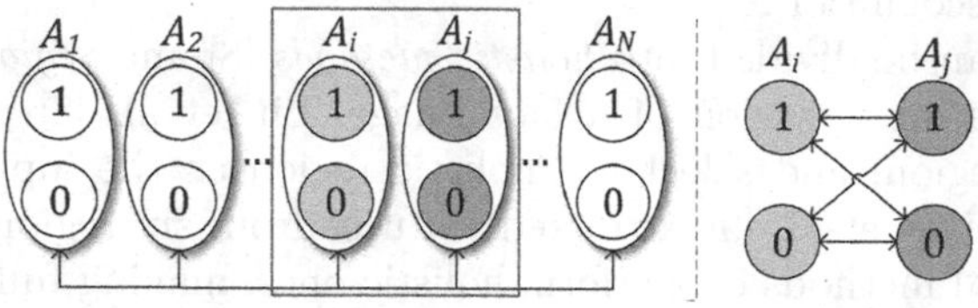

Fig. 2. *OIR* between face attributes. (Color figure online)

In the process of recognizing face attributes, it will be helpful to consider all attributes that have *OIR* with the attribute to be recognized. As shown in Fig. 1, Gender is the attribute to be recognized; Positive and negative attributes are attributes that have *OIR* with Male and Female; Probability after each attribute is the inferential probability of the corresponding *OIR*. Obviously, there will be positive effect on recognition if attributes with high probability (attributes in red box) are considered.

Firstly, the dataset labelled with multiple face attributes is required in this section. In Fig. 2, $\{A_1, A_2, ..., A_N\}$ are N face attributes; $\{1, 0\}$ are binary values of each attribute. *OIR* may exist between any two attributes, and all possible correlation between A_i and A_j (in red box) are shown on the right. In order to find *OIR* between A_i and A_j, the prior and posterior attribute should be determined first, and the direction of *OIR* is from prior one to posterior one. Supposing that we set A_i (A_j) as prior (posterior) attribute, and the inferential probability $P(A_j|A_i)$ is calculated as:

$$P(A_j = n|A_i = m) = (N_m^n)/N_m; \ m, n \in \{1, 0\} \tag{1}$$

In (1), N_m^n and N_m are total numbers of face images, and we define them as: N_1 (the number of faces with attribute $A_i = 1$); N_1^0, N_1^1 ($A_j = 0$, 1 and $A_i = 1$); N_0 ($A_i = 0$); N_0^0, N_0^1 ($A_j = 0$, 1 and $A_i = 0$).

After that initial *OIR* (Oir_1, Oir_2) is determined, which contains three information (*i.e.*, prior attribute, posterior attribute, and inferential probability). The *OIR* with larger probability in $P(A_j = 0, 1|A_i = 1)$ and $P(A_j = 0, 1|A_i = 0)$ are selected as candidates for Oir_1 and Oir_2 respectively, and if inferential probability is greater than *pass-rate*, the corresponding $Oir_{\{1,2\}}$ can be determined as initial *OIR*. The value of *pass-rate* equals to *PI* plus *Pivot*, and if it's greater than 1, we change the value to 0.99. *PI* is the data imbalance rate of posterior attribute here, and *Pivot* is a manual valve we set. The reason for above is that data imbalance will disturb the judgment of reasonable *OIR*. For example, if face images with A_j=0 account for the majority of dataset (*e.g.*, 90%), and $P(A_j = 0|A_i = 1)$ is calculated to be 91%. It is unreasonable to say: there is a high inferential probability that $A_j = 0$ when $A_i = 1$ is already identified, though inferential probability is as high as 91%, and the reason is that such probability may be the result of data imbalance instead of attributes correlation. Finally, only the legal initial *OIR* will be retained, and the illegal *OIR* is defined as: the posterior attributes of Oir_1 and Oir_2 are same, but the prior attributes are different.

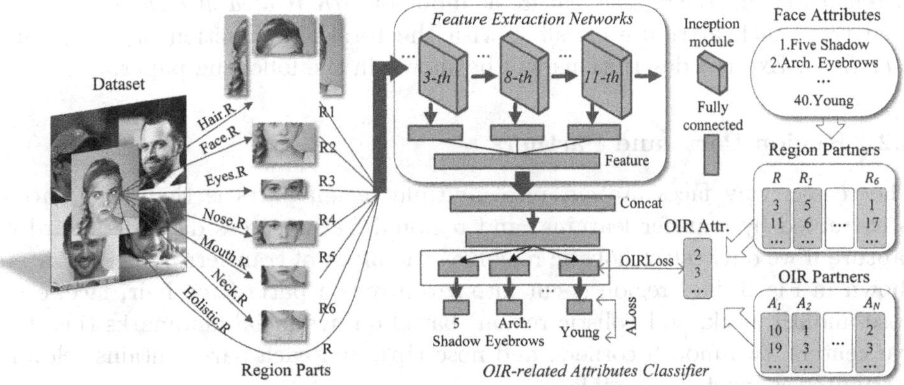

Fig. 3. Framework of the proposed face attributes recognition model. Region parts are regional and holistic regions selected from human faces, and features are extracted from all of these regions via designed feature extraction networks. *OIR* constraint is applied to *OIR-related attributes classifier* for face attribute.

The *OIR* from A_i to A_j is found by above method, and if we set A_i as posterior attribute, all *OIR* between A_i and A_j will be found. Hence, the method to find *OIR* between all attributes is described as: set $\{A_1, A_2, ..., A_N\}$ as posterior attribute in turn, and $\{A_1, A_2, ..., A_N\}$ as prior attribute for each posterior attribute, then search for legal *OIR* for all prior-posterior attribute pairs.

4 Face Attributes Recognition Model

The correlation found in last section will be applied to *OIR-related attributes classifier* of the proposed face attributes recognition model. Moreover, regional feature together with holistic one, and the face feature extraction transferring from multiple neural layers are applied to enhance our model.

4.1 Framework

Figure 3 shows the framework of the proposed face attributes recognition model. All face attributes in dataset are divided into seven categories (*i.e.*, one holistic, and six regional categories). Attributes belonging to the same category are put into the same region partner, and faces are cut into multiple region parts according to these categories. *OIR* partners contain attributes which have *OIR* with the attribute to be recognized, and we select those in partners belonging to the same region as the attribute recognized. Thus, *OIR attr.* is the final correlation applied to *OIR-related attributes classifier*.

The process of face attributes recognition contains three steps: (i) select a face image from dataset and perform facial landmark detection, then cut the face region into multiple region parts; (ii) extract feature via multiple layers of inception networks from each region, then concatenate these features into final face feature; (iii) select face feature as input of *OIR-related attributes classifier*, then train each attribute classifier with the total loss function of $ALoss$ and $OIRLoss$. Explicit descriptions will be shown in the following paper.

4.2 Region Parts and Partners

The reason why faces are cut into multiple region parts is that face feature is extracted by transfer learning, and regional feature cross dataset is hard to capture if we only select holistic region as the input of transferring networks. As shown in Fig. 3, face region is cut into seven region parts (*i.e.*, hair, face, eyes, nose, mouth, neck, and holistic region) based on five facial landmarks (i.e., two eye centers, two mouth corners, and nose tip), and each part contains relevant attributes as much as possible.

In region partners, attributes in gray box belong to the same region. R and $R_{\{1,\ldots,6\}}$ correspond to holistic, hair,..., neck region in turn. In *OIR* partners, $A_{\{1,\ldots,N\}}$ are face attributes to be recognized, and those in gray box are attributes which have *OIR* with corresponding face attributes. The size of partners may be large, thus we focus on those belonging to the same region as the attribute to be recognized.

4.3 Feature Extraction Networks

Face attributes recognition is a multi-instance multi-label task, and CNNs have shown great advantages in dealing with such task. Further, the semantics of layers at different levels is explored in [17]. The semantics of labels is not that abstract for layers near input of networks, and these neural layers focus on the feature of input. On the contrary, layers near output are like semantic detectors, which are close to semantic description space of labels. Hence, different abstract level of feature will be utilized in this paper.

In order to speed up the process of face feature extraction, we transfer the pre-trained CNNs (*i.e.*, Inception networks [19]) to our work. Inception networks is exquisitely designed and contains hundreds of neural layers, which performs well on ImageNet. There are five convolutional layers and two pooling layers, followed by eleven inception modules which contain lots of convolutional, pooling and concatenate layers. Inception V3 is selected as the basic face *feature extraction networks* because of the cross-dataset advantage it shows. A novel method of face feature extraction focusing on multiple neural layers (*i.e.*, *3-th*, *8-th*, and *11-th* module in Fig. 3) is designed as: $Module_{\{3,8,11\}} \rightarrow Pool_{\{3,8,11\}}(18, 17, 8) \rightarrow FC_{\{3,8,11\}}(288, 768, 2048) \rightarrow Feature$, where $Module_{\{3,8,11\}}$ are the outputs of *3-th*, *8-th*, and *11-th* inception module; $Pool_{\{3,8,11\}}$ are average pooling layers, and the values of kernel size and strides are in parentheses behind; $FC_{\{3,8,11\}}$ are fully connected layers, and sizes are in parentheses; $Feature$ in *feature extraction networks* is concatenated by $FC_{\{3,8,11\}}$.

The reasons for the selection of above modules include: (i) feature will be too large if all modules of Inception networks are considered, which boosts computational cost of feature extraction and attributes classifier; (ii) features extracted by close neural layers in deep networks tend to capture similar semantic description, which provide homologous effect on attributes recognition; (iii) 11 modules in Inception V3 are grouped into three modules groups (*i.e.*, {*1,2,3-th* module}, {*4,5,6,7,8-th* module}, {*9,10,11-th* module}), and modules in the same group have similar network structure.

4.4 OIR-related Attributes Classifier

Exploring correlation between labels is helpful in multi-instance multi-label classification, especially the *OIR* in face attributes recognition as showed in Sect. 3. In Fig. 3, the *OIR Attr.* of each attribute to be recognized is utilized in the corresponding binary *OIR-related attributes classifier*. Those fully connected layers (in red box) are designed to capture information of *OIR Attr.*, and the complete face attributes recognition model is designed as: $Face_i \rightarrow Feature_{r=\{R,R1,...,R6\}}(3104) \rightarrow Concat(3104 \times 7) \rightarrow FC_1(2048) \rightarrow FC_2(?) \rightarrow FC_3(2)$, where $Face_i$ is the face region of *i-th* image; $Feature_r$ is the feature extracted from *r-th* region, and $Concat$ concatenate all these features; $FC_{\{1,2,3\}}$ are fully connected layers; The size of each layer is showed behind, and notice that the size of FC_2 is determined by the number of corresponding *OIR Attr.*

Loss function of *OIR-related attributes classifier* contains $ALoss$ and $OIRLoss$. $OIRLoss$ captures information of *OIR Attr.*, which is formulated as:

$$OIRLoss = -\frac{1}{N}\sum_{i=1}^{N}\sum_{j=1}^{Q} y_{i,j}\log\left(p_{i,j}\right) \tag{2}$$

$$p_{i,j} = \frac{\exp\left(FC_2^{i,j}\right)}{\sum \exp\left(FC_2^{i,j}\right)} \tag{3}$$

$ALoss$ is a binary loss for final attributes classifier, which is formulated as:

$$ALoss = -\frac{1}{N}\sum_{i=1}^{N}\left(y_{i,k}\log\left(q_{i,k}\right) + \left(1 - y_{i,k}\right)\log\left(1 - q_{i,k}\right)\right) \tag{4}$$

$$q_{i,k} = \frac{\exp\left(FC_3^{i,k}\right)}{\sum \exp\left(FC_3^{i,k}\right)} \tag{5}$$

In (2)–(5), N is the number of face images; k is the index of attribute to be recognized; Q is the number of *OIR Attr.*; $y_{(i,j)} \in \{1, 0\}$ is the ground-truth of *j-th* attribute belonging to *i-th* face; $p_{(i,j)}$ and $q_{(i,k)}$ are probabilities that the value of *j-th* and *k-th* attribute belonging to *i-th* face is 1; $FC_2^{i,j}$ is the *j-th* neural value of FC_2, and $FC_3^{i,k}$ is the first neural value of FC_3.

Fig. 4. Face images with 40 binary attributes from the CelebA, faced with the problems of illumination, occlusion, pose, expression, *etc.*

Table 1. The indexes and definitions of 40 attributes, and all attributes are listed in the corresponding region (hair, face, eyes, nose, mouth, neck, and holistic region).

Idx	Attr. Def	29	R. Hairline	23	Mustache	13	B. Eyebrows	7	Big Lips	*Holistic Region*	
Hair Region		33	Straight Hair	25	No Beard	16	Eyeglasses	22	Mouth S. O	3	Attractive
5	Bald	34	Wavy Hair	26	Oval Face	24	Narrow Eyes	32	Smiling	11	Blurry
6	Bangs	36	Wearing Hat	30	Rosy Cheeks	*Nose Region*		37	W. Lipstick	14	Chubby
9	Black Hair	*Face Region*		31	Sideburns	8	Big Nose	*Neck Region*		19	H. Makeup
10	Blond Hair	1	5 O Shadow	*Eyes Region*		28	Pointy Nose	15	Double Chin	21	Male
12	Brown Hair	17	Goatee	2	A. Eyebrows	35	W. Earrings	38	W. Necklace	27	Pale Skin
18	Gray Hair	20	H. C. bones	4	B U. Eyes	*Mouth Region*		39	W. Necktie	40	Young

5 Experiments

5.1 Dataset and Settings

CelebA is a large-scale face attribute database with more than *200K* celebrity faces in the wild, each with 40 attribute annotations. The face images (showed in Fig. 4) in CelebA contain variations in illumination, occlusion, pose, expression, *etc.* All face attributes in this dataset are divided into seven categories, and attributes belonging to the same category are put into the same region. In Table 1, the index and definition of each attribute is shown in corresponding region, and these are region partners defined.

10-fold cross-validation is applied to evaluate the performance of the proposed method. For all face images in dataset, an open source *SeetaFace Engine* [7] is applied to detect the face and five landmarks. The training and testing are performed on a Nvidia Titan X GPU.

5.2 OIR for OIR-related Attributes Classifier

Firstly, the data imbalance rate *PI* is needed. The positive and negative sample proportions of each attribute are calculated, and the larger are selected as *PI*. The index and *PI* rate of each attribute are showed in Table 2.

Table 2. Data imbalance rate *PI* of 40 attributes.

Idx.	1	2	3	4	5	6	7	8	9	10	11	12	13	14	15	16	17	1	19	20
PI (%)	89	73	51	80	98	85	76	77	76	85	95	79	86	94	95	93	94	96	61	54
Idx.	21	22	23	24	25	26	27	28	29	30	31	32	33	34	35	36	37	38	39	40
PI (%)	58	52	96	88	83	72	96	72	92	93	94	52	79	68	81	95	53	88	93	77

Parameter *Pivot* is set to 0.1 for most attributes (except for 0.3 for attribute #3, #9, #21), and the *OIR* of 40 attributes on CelebA is found by the method in Sect. 3. The *OIR* (inferential probabilities) is showed in Fig. 5, where indexes of 40 prior attributes are on the vertical axis; posterior attributes are on the horizontal axis; the black block of each attribute represents the value of 1, and the white block is the opposite; the colorful blocks are inferential probabilities from prior to posterior attributes, which are higher in red color. For each posterior attribute, *OIR partners* are the corresponding prior attributes in colorful blocks.

Table 3. *OIR* Attributes of 40 face attributes.

Id	*OIR* Attr				
1	19, 21, 35, 37	14	3, 10, 19, 37	28	8
2	5, 18, 21, 25, 31, 39	15	3, 10, 19, 21, 37	29	6, 36
3	5, 11, 14, 15, 16, 18, 23, 40	16	19, 30	30	1, 17, 20, 23, 25, 31
4	N	17	10, 19, 21, 37	31	10, 19, 21, 35, 37, 38
5	6, 9, 10, 12, 33, 34, 36	18	2, 3, 19, 37, 40	32	20, 30
6	5, 18, 29, 36	19	1, 5, 17, 21, 23, 25, 31, 39	33	5, 34, 36
7	18, 39	20	1, 17, 23, 25, 30, 31	34	5, 18, 29, 33, 36
8	28	21	1, 5, 19, 23, 25, 31, 37, 39	35	1, 31, 39
9	5, 10, 12, 18, 36	22	32	36	5, 6, 9, 10, 12, 29, 33
10	5, 9, 12, 36	23	6, 10, 19, 21, 27, 35, 37	37	1, 5, 17, 21, 23, 25, 31, 39
11	30	24	N	38	39
12	5, 9, 10, 18, 29, 36	25	17, 23, 30, 31	39	10, 19, 21, 30, 35, 37
13	N	26	1, 23	40	2, 3, 18, 19, 21, 37
		27	17, 23, 30		

OIR partners of each posterior attribute can be divided into two categories (C0 and C1) according to their location. Partners belonging to C1 are in same region as the corresponding prior attributes, which is the opposite for C0. Moreover, *pass-rate* of prior attribute is different for C0 ($Pivot = 0.1$) and C1 ($Pivot = 0.2$).

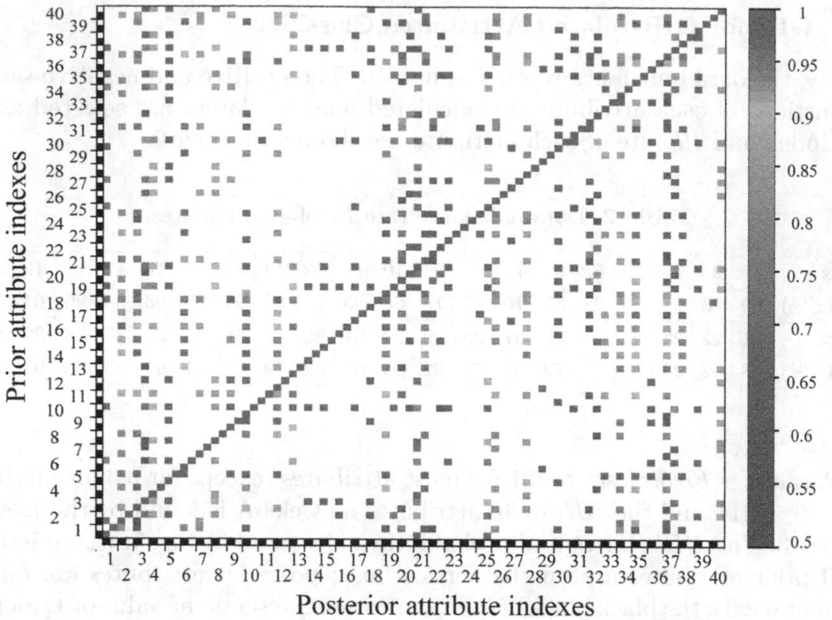

Fig. 5. *OIR* matrix of the 40 face attributes provided with CelebA, and the direction of *OIR* is from the prior to the posterior attributes. Posterior attributes need to be recognized, and those prior attributes having high inferential probabilities (blocks in red) with posterior attributes are applied to the corresponding attribute classifier. (Color figure online)

Attributes in the same region share some common local features, thus partners in C1 are preferred. Meanwhile, attributes with high inferential probabilities in different regions should also be considered. Only one of C0 and C1 is selected for each posterior attribute. C1 is selected if the attributs in C1 are more than 3; Otherwise, the larger between C1 and C0 is selected. The size of partners may be large and we focus on the attributes (no more than 8) with higher inferential probabilities, and the final *OIR* Attributes of each attribute are showed in Table 3.

5.3 Methods for Comparisons

The proposed method is compared with four competitive and one designed approaches, *i.e.,* FaceTracer [19], PANDA-1, LNets+ANet [8], CTS-CNN [12], and Proposed-p. FaceTracer extracts HOG and color histograms as features, and then trains SVM for face attributes recognition. PANDA-1 is based on PANDA [20], which ensemble multiple CNNs extracting features from the corresponding human part and then trains SVM classifier. LNets+ANet detects face region by LNets and then extracts features by ANet, then a separate Linear SVM is trained for each attribute. CTS-CNN contains the similar idea, applying FaceNet and VGG-16 features for recognizing face attributes. Proposed-p is similar to proposed method except for: (i) only the holistic region is selected as input; (ii) only the last layer of Inception networks is extracted as features; (iii) no *OIR* considered in attributes recognition.

5.4 Performance

The results on CelebA by the proposed method and several state-of-the-art approaches are reported in Table 4. The proposed method outperforms all these approaches for the most the 40 attributes, and the average accuracy (90.7%) is the highest among them. The proposed method achieve excellent performance both on holistic and regional attributes. Compared with the data imbalance rate, the recognition accuracy of each attribute is higher at different degree, which shows that the face attributes feature rather than data imbalance information is captured in our model. Comparing the results of proposed-p and proposed, we find that *OIR* is more helpful to the recognition of attributes which are subtle to recognize (*e.g.*, attribute #30 "Rosy Cheeks"). Instead of extracting feature from holistic face region, extracting features from multiple attribute-related regions captures more regional information. At the same time, extracting from multiple neural layers ultilizes features at different level.

Table 4. Recognition accuracy (in %) for 40 face attributes on CelebA by the proposed method and several state-of-the-art approaches. The proposed method outperforms all these approaches for the most the 40 attributes, and the average accuracy (90.7%) is the highest among them.

Approach	Attribute indexes																				
	1	2	3	4	5	6	7	8	9	10	11	12	13	14	15	16	17	18	19	20	21
FaceTracer	85	76	78	76	89	88	64	74	70	80	81	60	80	86	88	98	93	90	85	84	91
PANDA-1	88	78	81	79	96	92	67	75	85	93	86	77	86	86	88	98	93	94	90	86	97
LNets+ANets	91	79	81	79	98	**95**	68	78	88	**95**	84	80	**90**	91	92	**99**	95	97	90	87	98
CTS-CNN	89	**83**	**82**	79	96	94	70	79	87	93	87	79	87	88	89	**99**	94	95	**91**	87	**99**
Proposed-p	90	79	76	81	97	92	75	80	86	93	93	81	89	92	94	98	95	96	86	84	96
Proposed	**92**	82	80	**82**	**99**	**95**	**85**	**83**	**90**	**95**	**96**	**86**	**90**	**95**	**96**	**99**	**97**	**98**	89	**90**	98
	22	23	24	25	26	27	28	29	30	31	32	33	34	35	36	37	38	39	40	Ave.	
FaceTracer	87	91	82	90	64	83	68	76	84	94	89	63	73	73	89	89	68	86	80	81.1	
PANDA-1	**93**	93	84	93	65	91	71	85	87	93	**92**	69	77	78	96	**93**	67	91	84	85.4	
LNets+ANets	92	95	81	**95**	66	91	72	89	90	96	**92**	73	80	82	**99**	**93**	71	93	87	87.3	
CTS-CNN	92	93	78	94	67	85	73	87	88	95	**92**	73	79	82	96	**93**	73	91	86	86.6	
Proposed-p	88	94	85	90	68	90	72	90	87	95	89	74	80	86	97	88	80	90	86	87.1	
Proposed	89	**96**	**93**	93	**74**	**97**	**75**	**93**	**94**	**97**	90	**83**	**85**	**87**	**99**	**93**	**87**	**97**	**88**	**90.7**	

Further, some attributes tend to be recognized at lower recognition accuracy. We correct the mis-labelled labels and filter the images in low quality, and slight improvement shows up. However, the recognition of some attributes (e.g.

attribute #28 "Pointy Nose") still need to be improved, and we will explore the better recognition performance on these subtle attributes in the future work.

The computational cost of the proposed method is competitively. For face feature extraction and attributes recognition, the proposed methods takes 7 ms on a Titan X GPU. This is faster than the cost of feature learning reported in LNets+ANet (14 ms). Moreover, the face detection only takes 5 ms, compared with 35 ms reported in [8]. Results above show the effectiveness of the proposed model on recognition accuracy and computational cost.

6 Conclusion

In order to integrate the correlation between of attributes into face attributes recognition, this paper proposed a face attributes recognition model based on *one-way inferential correlation (OIR)* between face attributes. A method to find all *OIR* between attributes is designed according to the distribution of labelled database, and we applied *OIR* constraint to the designed *OIR-related attributes classifier*. Moreover, we cut faces into multiple *region parts* according to the category of attributes, and used a novel method of face feature extraction for all parts via transfer learning focusing on multiple neural layers. Experimental evaluations on the benchmark (CelebA) with 40 face attributes show the effectiveness on recognition accuracy and computational cost of the proposed methods. Recognition on subtle attributes which have low recognition accuracy will be explored in the future work.

Acknowledgment. This work was supported in part by the National Natura Science Foundation of China under Grant 61572252, Grant 61772268 and Grant 61720106006, and in part by the Natural Science Foundation of Jiangsu Province under Grant BK20190065.

References

1. Song, F., Tan, X., Chen, S.: Exploiting relationship between attributes for improved face verification. Comput. Vis. Image Underst. **122**(4), 143–154 (2014)
2. Kim, J., Pavlovic, V.: Attribute rating for classification of visual objects. In: Proceedings of the ICPR, pp. 1611–1614. IEEE, Tsukuba (2012)
3. Xia, S., Shao, M., Fu, Y.: Toward kinship verification using visual attributes. In: Proceedings ICPR, pp. 549–552. IEEE, Tsukuba (2012)
4. Qi, G., Aggarwal, C., Tian, Q., et al.: Exploring context and content links in social media: a latent space method. IEEE Trans. Pattern Anal. Mach. Intell. **34**(5), 850–862 (2012)
5. Sun, Y., Wang, X., Tang, X.: Deep convolutional network cascade for facial point detection. In: Proceedings of the IEEE Conference on CVPR, pp. 3476–3483. IEEE, Portland (2013) https://doi.org/10.1109/CVPR.2013.446
6. Li, J., Zhang, Y.: Learning SURF cascade for fast and accurate object detection. In: Proceedings of the IEEE Conference on CVPR, pp. 3468–3475. IEEE, Portland (2013)

7. SeetaFace Engine. https://github.com/seetaface/SeetaFaceEngine
8. Liu, Z., Luo, P., Wang, X., et al.: Deep learning face attributes in the wild. In: Proceedings of the IEEE ICCV, pp. 3730–3738. IEEE, Santiago (2015) https://doi.org/10.1109/ICCV.2015.425
9. Srinivas, N., Atwal, H., Rose, D.C., et al.: Age, Ggender, and fine-grained ethnicity prediction Uusing convolutional neural networks for the east Asian face dataset. In: Proceeding of the IEEE Conference on FG, pp. 953–960. IEEE, Washington (2017)
10. Kumar, N., Berg, A.C., Belhumeur, P.N., et al.: Attribute and simile classifiers for face verification. In: Proceedings of the IEEE ICCV, pp. 365–372. IEEE, Kyoto (2009) https://doi.org/10.1109/ICCV.2009.5459250
11. Cottrell, G.W., Metcalfe, J.: EMPATH: face, emotion, and gender recognition using holons. In: Proceedings of the NIPS, pp. 564–571. DBLP, Denver (1990)
12. Zhong, Y., Sullivan, J., Li, H.: Face attribute prediction using off-the-shelf CNN features. In: Proceedings of the ICB, pp. 1–7. IEEE, Halmstad (2016)
13. Simonyan, K., Zisserman, A.: Very deep convolutional networks for large-scale image recognition. ArXiv e-prints, September 2014
14. Zeng, T., Ji, S.: Deep convolutional neural networks for multi-instance multi-task learning. In: Proceedings IEEE ICDM, pp. 579–588. IEEE, Atlantic City (2016)
15. Hand, E.M., Chellappa, R.: Attributes for improved attributes: a multi-task network for attribute classification. ArXiv e-prints, April 2016
16. Ehrlich, M., Shields, T.J., Almaev, T., et al.: Facial attributes classification using multi-task representation learning. In: Proceedings of the IEEE CVPRW, pp. 752–760. IEEE, Las Vegas (2016)
17. Dong, M., Pang, K., Wu, Y., et al.: Transferring CNNS to multi-instance multi-label classification on small datasets. In: Proceedings of the IEEE ICIP, pp. 1332–1336. IEEE, Beijing (2017)
18. Szegedy, C., Vanhoucke, V., Ioffe, S., et al.: Rethinking the inception architecture for computer vision. In: Proceedings of the IEEE CVPR, pp. 2818–2826. IEEE, Las Vegas (2016) https://doi.org/10.1109/CVPR.2016.308
19. Kumar, N., Belhumeur, P., Nayar, S.: FaceTracer: a search engine for large collections of images with faces. In: Forsyth, D., Torr, P., Zisserman, A. (eds.) ECCV 2008. LNCS, vol. 5305, pp. 340–353. Springer, Heidelberg (2008). https://doi.org/10.1007/978-3-540-88693-8_25
20. Zhang, N., Paluri, M., Ranzato, M., et al.: PANDA: Pose aligned networks for deep attribute modeling. In: Proceedings of the IEEE CVPR, pp. 1637–1644. IEEE, Columbus (2014). https://doi.org/10.1109/CVPR.2014.212

Eulerian Motion Based 3DCNN Architecture for Facial Micro-Expression Recognition

Yahui Wang[1], Huimin Ma[1(✉)], Xinpeng Xing[2], and Zeyu Pan[1]

[1] Department of Electronic Engineering, Tsinghua University, Beijing, China
{wangyh17,mhmpub,pzy17}@mails.tsinghua.edu.cn
[2] Shenzhen Key Laboratory of Information Science and Technology, Graduate School at Shenzhen, Tsinghua University, Shenzhen, China
xing.xinpeng@sz.tsinghua.edu.cn

Abstract. Facial micro-expressions are fast and subtle muscular movements, which typically reveal the underlying mental state of an individual. Due to low intensity and short duration of micro-expressions, the task of micro-expressions recognition is a huge challenge. Our method adopts a new pre-processing technique on the basis of the Eulerian video magnification (EVM) for micro-expressions recognition. Further, we propose a micro-expressions recognition framework based on the simple yet effective Eulerian motion-based 3D convolution network (EM-C3D). Firstly, Eulerian motion feature maps are extracted by employing multiple spatial scales temporal filtering approach, then the multi-frame Eulerian motion feature maps are directly fed into the 3D convolution network with a global attention module (GAM) to encode rich spatiotemporal information instead of being added to the raw images. Our algorithm achieves state-of-the-art result 69.76% accuracy and 65.75% recall rate on the CASME II dataset, which surpasses all baselines. Cross-domain experiments are also performed to verify the robustness of the algorithm.

Keywords: Facial micro-expression · Eulerian motion magnification · 3D ConvNets · Emotion recognition

1 Introduction

Facial expression conveys almost all subtle emotional nuances in face-to-face meetings, furthermore, facial micro-expression (FME) especially reflects the authentic psychological state of an individual [5]. FMEs are brief and involuntary muscle movements to hide genuine emotion, which typically last between 40 and 200 ms [6] and usually difficult to detect. For each sample, the frame for a facial video sequence for which the intensity of the action unit (AU) starts to rise is called Onset frame, and when the amplitude reaches a peak, it is named Apex frame, and the disappearing frame is dubbed Offset frame [19]. As shown in the Fig. 1, the combination of local motion in the face area constitutes a

Y. M. Ro et al. (Eds.): MMM 2020, LNCS 11961, pp. 266–277, 2020.
https://doi.org/10.1007/978-3-030-37731-1_22

micro-expression. Automatic FME recognition faces two significant challenges [13], the first challenge is spotting that aims to identify micro-expression from continuous long facial video clips, and another challenge is the recognition that is classified micro-expression to specific emotional states or objective classes, objective classification is labeled based on several activated facial AU combinations. This paper focuses on the second challenge.

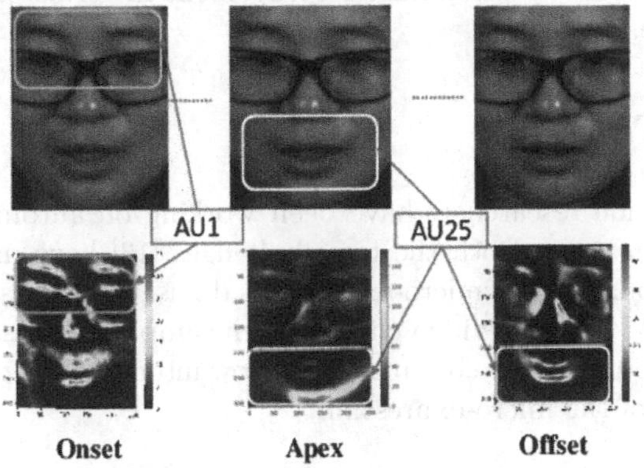

Fig. 1. An example utilizing Eulerian motion feature maps for visualizing AUs movement from the CASME II dataset (sub15/EP04/02 raw image sequence), Onset, Apex and Offset cropped raw images (top row), motion visualization of the top row images (bottom row), the blue and red values represent the low and high intensity (Color figure online)

In micro-expression recognition domains, the analysis procedures consist of two steps: feature extraction and classification, precisely capturing the long-range distance texture and temporal context feature for each sample is the key challenge. The feature extraction method based on texture discriminator has limited effect in the temporal dimension, while the optical flow characteristics of the Lagrangian view need to calculate the temporal variation in the pixel level repeated iteratively, leading to wasted computing resources. This paper proposes a Eulerian motion-based 3D convolutional architecture (EM-C3D) for FME recognition. Although inspired by previous Eulerian Video Magnification (EVM) [18] was used as a pre-process tool in several works about FME recognition [10,17], achieve limited performance improvement. Due to the low intensity of the FME, even after the superposition of motion magnification, the dynamic motion information still be reduced in the subsequent processing of feature extraction. Considering this point, we only extract the Eulerian motion as the feature map and leverage a relatively shallow 3D convolutional neural network (3D ConvNet) [14] trained on Chinese Academy of Sciences Micro-Expression dataset II (CASME II) [19] and Spontaneous Micro-Facial Movement Dataset (SAMM) [4] and reach impressive results in the recognition task.

In summary, our contributions in this paper are as follows:

1. An Eulerian motion-based feature map is proposed for extracting efficient spatiotemporal representation, which leads to improved results and even easier to calculate than optical flow.
2. We design a useful and straightforward sequential 3D convolutional network with a global attention module to automatically generate discriminative high-level semantic vectors.
3. We verify the effectiveness of the structure on the CASME II and SAMM datasets and achieve performance improvement in terms of recognition rate and recall rate.

2 Related Work

The computer vision researchers have been working on automatic FME recognition for over ten years. Both the two challenges [13] have made considerable progress. Most spontaneous micro-expression datasets such as CASME II [19], SMIC [11], SAMM [4] are a video clip for each sample. It is essential to extract robust spatiotemporal feature because of the low intensity and complex temporal dynamic texture of the micro-expression.

2.1 Hand-Crafted Features

In general, micro-expression feature descriptors can be categorized into either texture based approaches or dense optical flow approaches. Before extracting the hand-designed features, the face area is usually divided into well-designed regions of interest (ROI). To characterize the local appearance and dynamic texture, for example, the Local Binary Pattern (LBP) operator with Three Orthogonal Planes is called LBP-TOP [21] has been extended to deal with this problem [19] and achieves impressive performance. Subsequently, improved methods based on LBP-TOP [7,8] were proposed to boost the capabilities of FME recognition algorithms. Motion representation based on optical flow is also applied to FME problems. Such as optical flow orientations and optical strain information be extracted as the spatiotemporal descriptor. Liu et al. [12] proposed an effective Main Directional Mean Optical-flow (MDMO) that considers both local statistic motion information and spatial location to recognize FME. Zhang et al. [20] extracted optical flow orientation histogram and LBP-TOP feature in each facial region respectively, and the two kind of features are concatenated region-by-region to generate local statistical descriptor.

2.2 Deep Learning Methods

Deep learning methods are also developed for recognizing micro-expression in recent years, Khor et al. [9] utilized the enriched version of the Long-term Recurrent Convolutional Network (ELRCN) to identify micro-expressions, while Peng et al. [3] adopted a two-dimensional landmark feature and CNN-LSTM architecture for effectively capturing temporal information to recognize facial

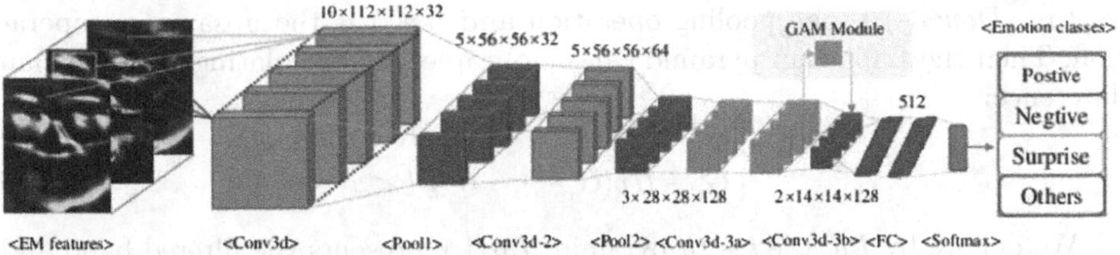

Fig. 2. Overall structure of our approach

micro-expressions. Monu et al. [15] proposed a Lateral Accretive Hybrid Network (LEARNet) to capture micro-level motion by the cross decoupled relationship between convolution layers.

3 The Proposed Method

The proposed Eulerian motion-based FME recognition algorithm consists of two steps: extracting Eulerian motion feature map and employing the 3D convolution network with a global attention module to identify the emotional classes. The overall structure of our approach is given in Fig. 2.

3.1 Eulerian Motion Feature Map Extraction

From the Eulerian perspective, the motion of an object is not explicitly estimated, pixel values variation through multiple spatial scales to appraise [18]. The architecture proposed in this work utilities both spatial and temporal processing method to extract and amplify the motion of each frame in FME video sequences. The extraction process follows the pipeline illustrated in Fig. 3. Firstly, we decompose the cropped raw images to multiple scales spatial components by building standard Laplacian pyramid [2], and the purpose of this procedure is to improve the spatial signal-to-noise ratio in the multiple spatial scales. In general cases, the temporal processing is performed by extracting frequency interested on multiple scale spatial bands, and the conventionally used filter methods are the ideal filter, Butterworth filter, and IIR filter.

We adopt Butterworth band-pass filter keeping frequencies between 0.4–4 Hz, corresponding 24–240 heart rates per minute to make image signals smooth in the experiment. Next, the filtered multiple scale bands used to reconstruct Eulerian motion feature map. Specifically, for the $i-th$ frame of an FME video sequence, $N-level$ Gaussian pyramid G_i^N, is calculated by:

$$G_i^k = \begin{cases} I_i, & k = 0 \\ Down(G^{k-1} \otimes g_{m\times m}), & k > 0 \end{cases} \tag{1}$$

Where G_i^k is the $k-th$ Gaussian pyramid of the $i-th$ frame, I_i is the image intensity of the $i-th$ frame, $g_{m\times m}$ means that Gaussian filter kernel with sizes

$m \times m$. $Down(\cdot)$ is the pooling operation and $Up(\cdot)$ is the upsampling operation. Then the Laplacian pyramid can be obtained by calculating the Gaussian difference:

$$Lp_i^l = \begin{cases} G_i^N, & l = N \\ G_i^l - Up(G_i^{l+1}), & 0 \le l < N-1 \end{cases} \tag{2}$$

We denote by Lp_i^l the $l-th$ pyramid, Lpf_i^l represents the filtered band and $f(\cdot)$ is the Butterworth filter, the reason for choosing the Butterworth filter for temporal filtering is because it is spatially and temporally smoother than the video sequence reconstructed by the ideal filter.

$$Lpf_i^l = f(Lp_i^l), l = 0, 1...N \tag{3}$$

To reconstruct the image from Lpf_i^l, we follow the below procedure:

$$EM_i = \sigma \cdot rec(Lpf_i^1, Lpf_i^2, ..., Lpf_i^N) \tag{4}$$

We define σ as the magnification factor and $rec(\cdot)$ as the Laplacian pyramid Lpf_i^j $j = 1, 2, ..., N$ reconstructed function to rebuild the new image. The principle of Eulerian motion magnification is specifically inferred in [18]. The EM feature maps of each sample are extracted to represent the dynamic motion information of the face and to eliminate redundant information. To reduce the shift in color space, we convert the image to the YIQ channels before extracting the EM feature and attenuate the IQ channels variation when reconstructing the RGB image.

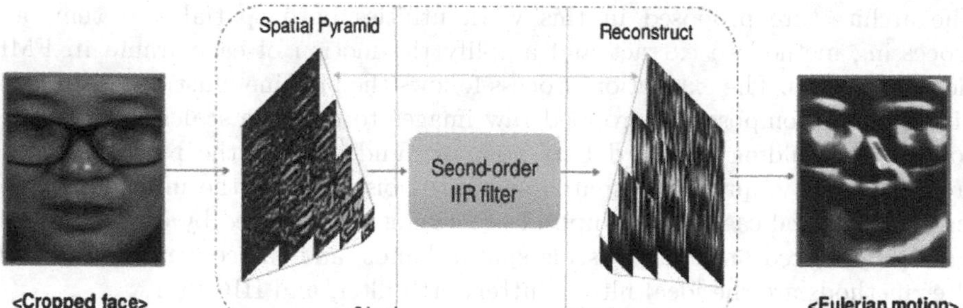

Fig. 3. The flowchart of the proposed Eulerian motion feature map extraction

3.2 Learning Features with 3D ConvNets

The Eulerian motion feature maps characterize the dynamic motion information of the micro-expression. For encoding the global texture and temporal context information to local feature, we utilize the 3D Convnet to learn a model which can be used to extract discriminant features automatically. Deep learning methods aim at modeling the local motion and global texture in higher dimensions. 3D Convent and 3D pooling operations can characterize temporal information better [14] and obtain scale-invariant features. Global attention module encodes a wider range of spatial and temporal context information to local feature. EM-C3D receives the Eulerian motion frames as the input of neural networks.

EM-C3D Architecture. The shape of the input tensor for the proposed architecture is $\langle d \times h \times w \times c \rangle$, where d is the temporal depth of the EM frames, h and w is the height and width of a single frame, c is the channels of the frame, general case the value is 3. In our settings, we resize the EM frames to a standard size of $\langle 112 \times 112 \times 3 \rangle$ based on the rule that the cropped face appears in the center of the image. We design the temporal depth as 10 for each sample in order to reduce redundant information between frames in a dataset acquired at high frame rates.

The C3D network is widely used in action recognition and scene and object recognition in [14]. To transfer the C3D architecture to our micro-expression recognition task, we adjust the structure of the network and reduce the numbers of the layers of the network. Our EM-C3D network have four convolution layers and two pooling layers, Fig. 2 illustrates the pipeline, in the first four layers of the network, convolution operations and pooling operations is performed two times, followed by two convolution layers. The function of the pooling layer is to maintain feature invariant and reduce the number of parameters to prevent over-fitting. After Conv3d-3b layer we feed the feature map into our global attention module. Next, we expand the tensor of this layer output into a 1-dimensional vector, then feed it into two fully-connected layers and a Softmax layer to predict the emotion class.

Basic 3D Convolution Layer. The output feature map of a standard 3D convolution assuming with stride one and padding one is computed as:

$$Q_{N,t,s,s} = \sum_{h,i,j,M} K_{h,i,j,M,N} \cdot P_{t+h-1,s+i-1,s+j-1,M} \tag{5}$$

A standard 3D convolutional layer takes as input a feature map $P \in \mathbb{R}^{M \times t \times s \times s}$ and produces a feature map $Q \in \mathbb{R}^{N \times t \times s \times s}$, $\langle h \times i \times j \rangle$represents the size of the three-dimensional convolution kernel K, where s is the spatial width and height of a volume input feature map, t represents the time dimension, and M is the input channels, N is the output channels.

Global Attention Module. We explore a global attention module based on the Non-local block [16] method to encode wider spatial and temporal information to local high-level semantic vectors, which has been proved to be highly effective in capturing long-range dependencies. The structure of our global attention module is illustrated in Fig. 4.

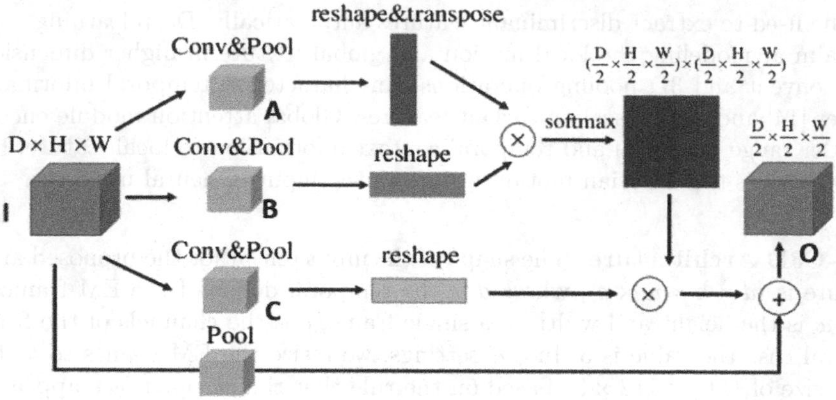

Fig. 4. The details of global attention module

Given a single channel feature map $I \in \mathbb{R}^{D\times H\times W}$, we first feed it into a 3D convolution layer and a 3D pooling layer to generate two new feature maps $A \in \mathbb{R}^{\frac{D}{2}\times\frac{H}{2}\times\frac{W}{2}}$ and $B \in \mathbb{R}^{\frac{D}{2}\times\frac{H}{2}\times\frac{W}{2}}$, respectively. The features A and B are reshaped to a vector, then we perform a matrix multiplication between the transpose of A and B, attention weights are determined by a softmax layer. Meanwhile, we feed feature into a convolution layer and a pooling layer to generate a new feature $C \in \mathbb{R}^{\frac{D}{2}\times\frac{H}{2}\times\frac{W}{2}}$. Next, we perform a multiplication between the reshape vector of C and the attention map. Finally, we reshape the result of multiplication to $\mathbb{R}^{\frac{D}{2}\times\frac{H}{2}\times\frac{W}{2}}$ and perform a element-wise sum operation to generate the output $O \in \mathbb{R}^{\frac{D}{2}\times\frac{H}{2}\times\frac{W}{2}}$.

Loss Function. Cross entropy loss was chosen to reduce the fitting error. A multiple classes categorical probability distribution can be defined by the softmax function. The softmax function φ takes as input a C-dimensional vector Z and outputs a C-dimensional vector Y of real values between 0 and 1.

$$Y_c = \varphi(Z)_c = \frac{e^{Z_c}}{\sum_{d=1}^{N} e^{Z_d}} \tag{6}$$

where $\sum_{d=1}^{N} e^{Z_d}$ acts as a regularizer to make sure that $\sum_{c=1}^{C} Y_c = 1$. Cross-entropy loss with softmax function is used as the output layer extensively. y_r is the ground truth, and p_r is the predictive value. The process of minimizing the fitting error is the process of finding the minimum value of the loss function L.

$$L = -\sum_{r} y_r log(p_r) \tag{7}$$

Considering that the existing micro-expression datasets are small-scale, we use the Leaky RELU activation functions and drop out opreation after the last two convolution layers to avoid over-fitting. The number of channels for the four convolutional layers and the two fully connected layers is $\langle 32, 64, 128, 128, 512, 512 \rangle$, the size of the convolution kernel and the pooling kernel are similar to those in C3D [14].

4 Experiments

In this section, we compare the proposed method with other state-of-the-art algorithms in FME recognition task. Such as Main Directional Mean Optical-flow (MDMO) [12], LBP-TOP [19]. For evaluating the performance of our approach, we use two datasets: the CASME II [19] and SAMM [4] datasets. Two set of experiments were carried out: single domain experiments were performed only on the CASME II dataset, cross domain experiments were conducted on the CASME II and SAMM datasets together.

4.1 Experimental Details

Evaluation Datasets. CASME II [19] is currently the most widely used spontaneous micro-expression dataset to evaluate FME algorithm performance, and it contains 255 samples from 26 participants with an average of 22 years old. All FME video clips are labeled with action units and emotional labels. Emotion labels are divided into five categories: Happiness, Disgust, Repression, Surprise, Others. SAMM [4] is a new dataset with 159 micro-expression samples from 32 subjects developed by Manchester Metropolitan University in 2018, and seven emotional labels are marked. To efficiently evaluate performance when conducting cross-domain experiment, we unify the emotional labels of the two datasets into four classes: Positive, Negative, Surprise, and Others.

Implementation Details. Both datasets provide pre-cropped video clips and can be directly used. Eulerian feature maps have been extracted for all samples according to the method in 2.1. All Eulerian motion frames are resized to $112 * 112$ pixel resolution to match the spatial size of the EM-C3D networks. We train our model with 2 NVIDIA TITAN X GPU under Tensorflow [1] and Keras. The whole training procedures for EM-C3D takes 255 iterations with the learning rate initialized at 0.01 and decreased by iteration steps. Leave-One-Subject-One (LOSO) cross-validation was adopted to evaluate performance.

4.2 Single Domain Experiment

In this experiment, we evaluate the proposed method on CASME II dataset. Unweighted Average Recall (UAR) and Accuracy were selected as indicators for evaluating performance. The experiment results for UAR and accuracy for different FME algorithms are summarized in Table 1. The proposed algorithm achieves an excellent performance of 69.76% accuracy on the CASME II dataset

Table 1. Performance of proposed methods vs. other methods for micro-expression recognition, by Leave-One-Subject-One (LOSO) Cross-Validation on CASMEII dataset

Methods	UAR	Accuracy/WAR
LBP-TOP [19]	0.3523	0.6483
MDMO [12]	0.6175	0.6737
VGG16+LSTM (reproduced) [9]	0.5386	0.6523
2-dimensional landmark feature (reproduced) [3]	0.5225	0.6129
C3D (raw images) [14]	0.2975	0.4975
2-stream C3D	0.3008	0.5122
EM-C3D (Ours)	0.6525	0.6784
EM-C3D+GAM (Ours)	**0.6575**	**0.6976**

Table 2. Micro-expression recognition rates (%) of EM-C3D in CASMEII under different parameter settings

Parameter settings		Recognition rate
Spatial levels (l)	Amplification factor (σ)	
l = 3	$\sigma = 5$	0.5385
	$\sigma = 10$	0.5677
	$\sigma = 15$	0.5217
l = 5	$\sigma = 5$	0.6539
	$\sigma = 10$	**0.6976**
	$\sigma = 15$	0.6721

and increased by 4.93% compared to LBP-TOP in the recognition rate, which is equivalent to MDMO method. Also, our algorithm's UAR is 4.0% points higher than MDMO, reaching 65.75%. Our global attention module improves performance significantly, where EM-C3D with global attention module exceeds EM-C3D without global attention module by 1.92% in terms of accuracy. We further compare our method with existing methods [3,9] on the CASME II dataset. We show the confusion matrices of the proposed method and the state-of-the-art algorithm MDMO in Fig. 4. The proposed algorithm has a recall rate of 0.09 lower than the MDMO in the category of Postive, and the performance in the other three types is better than MDMO, especially in the category of Surprise, the proposed method has a recall rate 13% higher than MDMO. The comparison experiments under different parameter settings are shown in Table 2. Employing multi-frame Eulerian motion feature map, EM-C3D achieves the best LOSO recognition rate (0.6976) at $l = 5, \sigma = 10$. The relatively shallow pyramid layer has a weaker ability to extract motion information, and a more appropriate magnification factor will improve the accuracy of recognition (Fig. 5).

For verifying the effort of the EM feature maps, we conduct two sets of comparative experiments. The first set of experiment replaces the EM feature

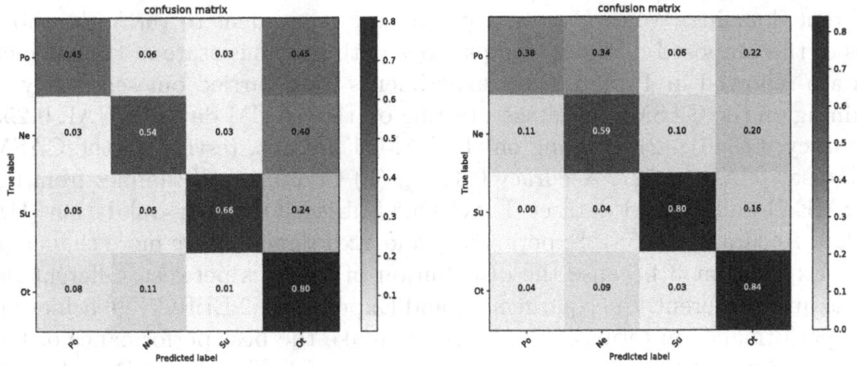

Fig. 5. The confusion matrix of MDMO (left) VS. the proposed EM-C3D algorithms (right) on CASMEII

maps feed into the convolutional networks with cropped FME images, and the recognition rate of the model was reduced by 18.09% since the raw frames contain large amounts of redundant information, and a relatively shallow network can not well characterize high-dimensional semantics. Another experiment is designed as a two-stream network, the input of one branch of the network is the raw images, and the input of the other branch is the EM features. After the pooling3 layer, the two feature vectors of the high-level semantics are concatenated together. This set of experiments is 18.54% lower than the single-stream C3D that only inputs the EM features in recognition rate. From the two sets of comparison experiments, we conclude that the dynamic motion information of EM clips significantly improves the recognition accuracy of the model.

4.3 Cross Domain Experiment

Table 3. Experimental results for cross-domain evaluation

Train/Test	Performance	LBP-TOP [19]	ELRCN [9]	Ours
CASMEII/SAMM	UAR	0.2766	**0.3927**	0.2933
	Accuracy	0.4532	0.4765	**0.5346**
SAMM/CASMEII	UAR	0.2937	**0.2983**	0.2727
	Accuracy	0.3927	0.3657	**0.4235**
CASMEII+SAMM	UAR	0.3706	0.4207	**0.5490**
	Accuracy	0.5365	0.6248	**0.6658**

Cross-domain FME recognition is more challenging than the single-domain FME recognition because of the inconsistency of the feature distribution from different domains. We conduct a cross-domain experiment to verify the robustness of the proposed method. Comparisons with previous state-of-the-art methods are reported in Table 3, three experiments were carried out separately: (1) Training on the CASME II dataset, testing on the SAMM dataset (UAR 0.2933, Accuracy 0.5346). (2) Training on the SAMM dataset, testing on the CASME II dataset (UAR 0.2727, Accuracy 0.4235). (3) Combines all samples from both CASME II and SAMM dataset, Leave-One-Subject-One cross-validation (UAR 0.5490, Accuracy 0.6658). Experiment 1 and Experiment 2 are more challenging than Experiment 3 because the distribution of features between different data sets is quite different. In Experiment 1 and Experiment 2 ELRCN [9] achieve the best performance in terms of the UAR, we make the best performance of UAR and accuracy in Experiment 3 compared the two other methods. Our algorithm shows strong robustness on the cross-domain experiment.

5 Conclusion

This paper proposes an Eulerian motion-based 3D convolutional neural network, the Eulerian Motion (EM) feature map of the facial image is extracted by Laplacian pyramid and temporal processing, then high-dimensional spatiotemporal features are extracted by a 3D convolutional neural network with a global attention module for emotion classification. The proposed method achieves a competitive recognition rate of 69.76% and recall rate of 65.75% on the CASME II dataset, which surpasses the handcrafted feature Main Directional Mean Optical-flow (MDMO) and other baselines. Besides, we demonstrate that EM clips can provide more discriminative high-level semantic information than raw images on the existing data scale through similar comparison experiments.

Acknowledgments. This work is supported by National Key Basic Research Program of China (No. 2016YFB0100900) and National Natural Science Foundation of China (No. 61773231).

References

1. Abadi, M.: TensorFlow: learning functions at scale. ACM SIGPLAN Not. **51**(9), 1 (2016). https://doi.org/10.1145/3022670.2976746
2. Burt, P.J., Adelson, E.H.: The Laplacian pyramid as a compact image code. Fundam. Pap. Wavelet Theory **31**(4), 28 (2006)
3. Choi, D.Y., Kim, D.H., Song, B.C.: Recognizing fine facial micro-expressions using two-dimensional landmark feature. In: 2018 25th IEEE International Conference on Image Processing (ICIP). IEEE (2018)
4. Davison, A.K., Lansley, C., Costen, N., Tan, K., Yap, M.H.: SAMM: a spontaneous micro-facial movement dataset. IEEE Trans. Affect. Comput. **9**(1), 116–129 (2018). https://doi.org/10.1109/taffc.2016.2573832
5. Ekman, P., Friesen, W.V.: Nonverbal leakage and clues to deception (1969)
6. Ekman, P., Friesen, W.V.: Constants across cultures in the face and emotion. J. Pers. Soc. Psychol. **17**(2), 124–129 (1971)

7. Huang, X., Wang, S.J., Zhao, G., Piteikainen, M.: Facial micro-expression recognition using spatiotemporal local binary pattern with integral projection. In: 2015 IEEE International Conference on Computer Vision Workshop (ICCVW). IEEE (2015). https://doi.org/10.1109/iccvw.2015.10
8. Huang, X., Zhao, G., Hong, X., Zheng, W., Pietikäinen, M.: Spontaneous facial micro-expression analysis using spatiotemporal completed local quantized patterns. Neurocomputing **175**, 564–578 (2016)
9. Khor, H.Q., See, J., Phan, R.C.W., Lin, W.: Enriched long-term recurrent convolutional network for facial micro-expression recognition. In: 2018 13th IEEE International Conference on Automatic Face & Gesture Recognition (FG 2018). IEEE (2018). https://doi.org/10.1109/fg.2018.00105
10. Li, X., et al.: Towards reading hidden emotions: a comparative study of spontaneous micro-expression spotting and recognition methods. IEEE Trans. Affect. Comput. **9**(4), 563–577 (2018). https://doi.org/10.1109/taffc.2017.2667642
11. Li, X., Pfister, T., Huang, X., Zhao, G., Pietikainen, M.: A spontaneous micro-expression database: inducement, collection and baseline. In: 2013 10th IEEE International Conference and Workshops on Automatic Face and Gesture Recognition (FG). IEEE (2013). https://doi.org/10.1109/fg.2013.6553717
12. Liu, Y.J., Zhang, J.K., Yan, W.J., Wang, S.J., Zhao, G., Fu, X.: A main directional mean optical flow feature for spontaneous micro-expression recognition. IEEE Trans. Affect. Comput. **7**(4), 299–310 (2016)
13. Merghani, W., Davison, A., Yap, M.: Facial micro-expressions grand challenge 2018: evaluating spatio-temporal features for classification of objective classes. In: 2018 13th IEEE International Conference on Automatic Face & Gesture Recognition (FG 2018). IEEE (2018)
14. Tran, D., Bourdev, L., Fergus, R., Torresani, L., Paluri, M.: Learning Spatiotemporal Features with 3D Convolutional Networks. In: 2015 IEEE International Conference on Computer Vision (ICCV). IEEE (2015)
15. Verma, M., Vipparthi, S.K., Singh, G., Murala, S.: Learnet dynamic imaging network for micro expression recognition. arXiv preprint arXiv:1904.09410 (2019)
16. Wang, X., Girshick, R., Gupta, A., He, K.: Non-local neural networks. In: Proceedings of the IEEE Conference on Computer Vision and Pattern Recognition (CVPR), pp. 7794–7803 (2018)
17. Wang, Y., et al.: Effective recognition of facial micro-expressions with video motion magnification. Multimedia Tools Appl. **76**(20), 21665–21690 (2016). https://doi.org/10.1007/s11042-016-4079-6
18. Wu, H.Y., Rubinstein, M., Shih, E., Guttag, J., Durand, F., Freeman, W.: Eulerian video magnification for revealing subtle changes in the world. ACM Trans. Graph. **31**(4), 1–8 (2012). https://doi.org/10.1145/2185520.2185561
19. Yan, W.J., et al.: CASME II: an improved spontaneous micro-expression database and the baseline evaluation. PLoS ONE **9**(1), e86041 (2014)
20. Zhang, S., Feng, B., Chen, Z., Huang, X.: Micro-expression recognition by aggregating local spatio-temporal patterns. In: Amsaleg, L., Guðmundsson, G., Gurrin, C., Jónsson, B., Satoh, S. (eds.) MMM 2017. LNCS, vol. 10132, pp. 638–648. Springer, Cham (2017). https://doi.org/10.1007/978-3-319-51811-4_52
21. Zhao, G., Pietikainen, M.: Dynamic texture recognition using local binary patterns with an application to facial expressions. IEEE Trans. Pattern Anal. Mach. Intell. **29**(6), 915–928 (2007)

Emotion Recognition with Facial Landmark Heatmaps

Siyi Mo[1], Wenming Yang[1(✉)], Guijin Wang[2], and Qingmin Liao[2]

[1] Graduate School at Shenzhen/Department of Electronic Engineering, Tsinghua University, Shenzhen, China
msy17@mails.tsinghua.edu.cn, yang.wenming@sz.tsinghua.edu.cn

[2] Graduate School at Shenzhen/Department of Electronic Engineering, Tsinghua University, Beijing, China
{wangguijin,liaoqm}@tsinghua.edu.cn

Abstract. Facial expression recognition is a very challenging problem and has attracted more and more researchers' attention. In this paper, considering that facial expression recognition is closely related to the features of key facial regions, we propose a facial expression recognition network that explicitly utilizes the landmark heatmap information to precisely capture the most discriminative features. In addition to directly adding the information of facial fiducial points in the form of landmark heatmaps, we also propose an end-to-end network structure--heatmap aiding emotion network (HAE-Net) by embedding the landmark detection module based on stack-based hourglass network into the facial expression recognition network. Experiments on CK+, RAF and AffectNet databases show that our method achieves better results compared with the state-of-the-art methods, which demonstrates that adding additional landmark information, as well as joint training of landmark detection and expression recognition, are beneficial to improve recognition performance.

Keywords: Facial expression recognition · Facial landmark detection · Facial landmark heatmaps

1 Introduction

Emotion recognition aims to identify the expression from an input facial image, and the classic problem is to classify it as one of the seven basic expressions–angry, disgust, fear, happy, sad, surprise and neutral [12]. Recently, it has attracted more and more attention from both academic and industrial communities due to its wide range of applications in many fields such as human-computer interaction and facial animations.

With the development of deep learning algorithms, a series of networks such as VGG [23], Resnet et al. [3], have been proposed and widely used in image classification [7], face recognition [21] and many other tasks. Since the convolutional neural network (CNN) can learn the high-level feature representation of

Y. M. Ro et al. (Eds.): MMM 2020, LNCS 11961, pp. 278–289, 2020.
https://doi.org/10.1007/978-3-030-37731-1_23

the image, many researchers built up facial expression recognition systems based on it and achieve great performance. For example, Ali et al. [15] proposed a deep neural network architecture based on Inception layer [20] for facial expression recognition problem. These methods mainly extract spatial information, but do not consider the characteristics associated with expressions.

As a special classification task related to facial analysis, facial expression specific prior knowledge in facial images can be used to boost the recognition performance. For example, according to the fact that facial expression is mainly caused by changes of fiducial points location, [5] designed a temporal geometry network that used normalized coordinates of facial landmarks from consecutive frames to learn temporal geometric features. However, using sequences of facial landmarks requires to collect more data and it is not suitable for static image recognition.

In this paper, we mainly focus on the task of static facial expression recognition. Since the expression process of the expression is closely associated with the movements of the facial key parts such as eye, nose and mouth, et al., it is possible to improve the recognition accuracy by capturing the features of these parts through the facial fiducial point positions. Based on this, we design an expression recognition system that can simultaneously utilize appearance information and geometry information. Figure 1 illustrates the proposed framework. We fed the facial landmark heatmaps to the network as extra aiding information while using the CNN network to extract texture features from facial images.

Different from using sequences of facial landmark points [5,24,28,30], we only pay attention to facial fiducial points of a single image expressing peak emotion. Besides, instead of directly using the coordinates of facial landmark points like [13], we add the geometry information in the form of landmark heatmaps to the appropriate layer of the network. Here the heatmaps are generated by the Gaussian kernels centered on the locations of facial landmarks, indicating the probability of occurrence of each component. Thus adding a heatmap map is equivalent to increasing facial structure information, including the location information of the facial organs, visibility and the relationship between them.

In summary, the main contributions of this paper are:

(1) We propose to exploits facial landmark heatmaps as geometry prior knowledge in a convolutional neural network for the facial expression recognition task. Through these heatmaps, we can focus on the most discriminative part of the extracted features;
(2) We design an end-to-end network that uses predicted heatmaps estimated by a facial landmark heatmap detection network to refine the expression features, and we call it Heatmap Aiding Emotion Network;
(3) Experiments on three databases achieve better accuracy than other state-of-art methods.

2 Related Work

The method we propose is mainly related to the knowledge of the expression recognition using geometry information and facial landmark detection network. We first introduce the relevant work and then illustrate the motivation of our work.

2.1 Expression Recognition Using Facial Landmarks

To improve the accuracy of expression recognition, most approaches tend to add prior knowledge. Among them, facial landmark points prior knowledge is added most as the facial key parts surrounded by them contain the most descriptive information related to expression.

Many methods use facial landmark prior knowledge to get better recognition results. One common practice is to use coordinates of fiducial points as input and apply a neural network to extract features, which is called geometry features. For example, Zhang et al. [30] proposed a part-based hierarchical bidirectional recurrent neural network (PHRNN) to simulate facial morphological variation and dynamic changes of expression by gradually adding landmark information of a single face organ in each BRNN layer. Some also design relevant new feature representations using coordinates of facial landmark points. Tang et al. [24] design a 39-dimensional feature based on the coordinates of facial landmark points to represent the facial geometry information of a single frame. Another approach is to develop multi-task learning methods to simultaneously perform expression recognition and facial landmark detection. For example, Hu et al. [4] proposed an end-to-end soft sharing strategy that automatically learned which layers to share and improved the recognition accuracy by using an auxiliary task: facial landmark detection; Tautkute et al. [25] expanded the latest facial landmark detection network–Deep alignment network [6] to a multi-task network by adding a classification loss function. Then the facial image can be classified into the corresponding expression category while performing facial landmark detection.

In recent years, the landmark information has been added to the network in the form of a heatmap, which has made great progress in face super-resolution reconstruction [1]. Inspired by these work, we believe that if landmark heatmap information is added in the process of extracting image texture features, it can provide auxiliary information to enhance the expression recognition performance. Different from the above methods that directly use coordinates of facial landmark points, we first exploit facial landmark points to generate the ground-truth heatmaps and then concatenate the convolutional feature maps extracted from the original image with the landmark heatmaps to emphasize the features at the locations of facial key parts.

2.2 Landmark Heatmap Regression

Heatmap regression models, which aim to predict landmark heatmaps, have achieved excellent performance in tasks such as pose estimation [17] and face alignment [27]. Motivated by this, to enable end-to-end training, we incorporate the heatmap estimate network module to our network, as shown in Fig. 3.

Since one of our goals is to generate the likelihood heatmaps for facial fiducial points, we employ the network in [17], which consists of stacked hourglass modules. As shown in [17], the stacked-hourglass network achieved a compelling result as it is built by a repeated bottom-top and top-bottom mechanism which enables the network to fuse multi-scale features.

One of our contributions is to show that when integrating a facial landmark heatmap estimation network to an expression-recognition network and training them jointly, we can get higher recognition accuracy.

3 Proposed Method

We first introduce the framework of the proposed method that exploits extra facial landmark prior information, and then describe the end-to-end network structure, which we call Heatmap Aiding Emotion Network (HAE-Net).

3.1 Framework

The overall framework of our proposed method is shown in Fig. 1. We first use the feature extraction part to get the feature maps from the original images. Then we generate the facial landmark heatmaps with facial detection module. Finally, both convolutional feature maps and landmark heatmaps are concatenated and fed into the identification net to get the final predicted expressions.

To better illustrate the effectiveness of the jointly training of facial expression and landmark heatmap prediction, we also first design a basic network—Conv_heatmap that uses the ground-truth heatmaps directly. It contains two inputs, one is the facial image and the other is the ground-truth heatmap. Comparative experiments can be seen in the fourth part of the paper.

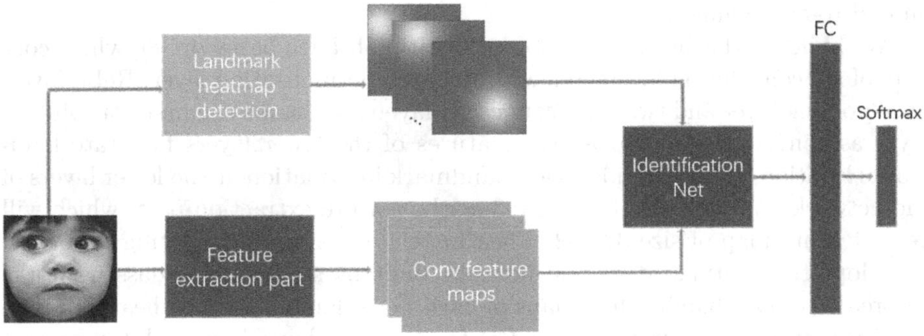

Fig. 1. The framework of our method.

We choose to leverage the heatmap information for two reasons. First, using a convolutional neural network only extracts the texture features from original images, but using extra landmark heatmaps as prior knowledge adds facial shape information [2]. Second, the landmark heatmap not only provides the locations of facial fiducial points but also indicates the visibility of each point around facial components and the relationships between them [29], which is beneficial to extract the features of the facial parts closely related to the expression. As shown in Fig. 2, the landmark heatmap of 37 channels and the original image are shown together in a single image.

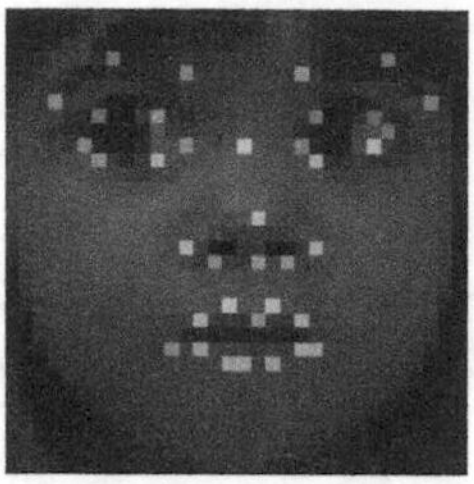

Fig. 2. The generated heatmap using 37 facial landmarks. We visualize it in a single image by adding up the 37 channels of the generated heatmaps.

3.2 Heatmap Aiding Emotion Network

Figure 3 illustrates the structure of our proposed Heatmap Aiding Emotion Network (HAE-Net). HAE-Net consists of two parts: a landmark heatmap prediction branch and a facial expression recognition branch. Each orange block represents one or more residual blocks in the top landmark heatmap prediction branch. The blue block represents the convolutional layer, while the yellow block indicates the fully connected layer. Particularly, the batch normalization layer, ReLu layer and max-pooling layer are not drawn here. The entire network can be trained in an end-to-end manner.

We build up the facial expression recognition branch based on [8], which consists of six convolution layers followed by batch normalization layer, ReLu layer, max-pooling layer and two fully connected layers. We name the first convolution layer as conv_1, and so on. As the features of the lower layers facilitate landmarks location [18], we decide to add landmark information at the lower layers of the network. We use conv_1 to conv_3 as the feature extraction part, which will get a feature map of size $32 * 32$. Then instead of directly predicting locations, we adopt the heatmap detection network built by stacked hourglass networks to predict the probability heatmaps of each facial landmark. The heatmap estimation network is mainly composed of four stacked hourglass modules, each of which outputs a predicted landmark heatmap for supervising the training of the network. Specifically, the hourglass network is based on an encoding-decoding structure, in which the features are first downsampled to a low resolution using convolutional and max-pooling layers and then upsampled to the original resolution. Meanwhile, features extracted in the downsampling layers are combined with the features at the upsampling layers. In this way, the network can capture effective information from features of multiple scales. At last, the heatmaps obtained through the landmark detection network are combined with the lower

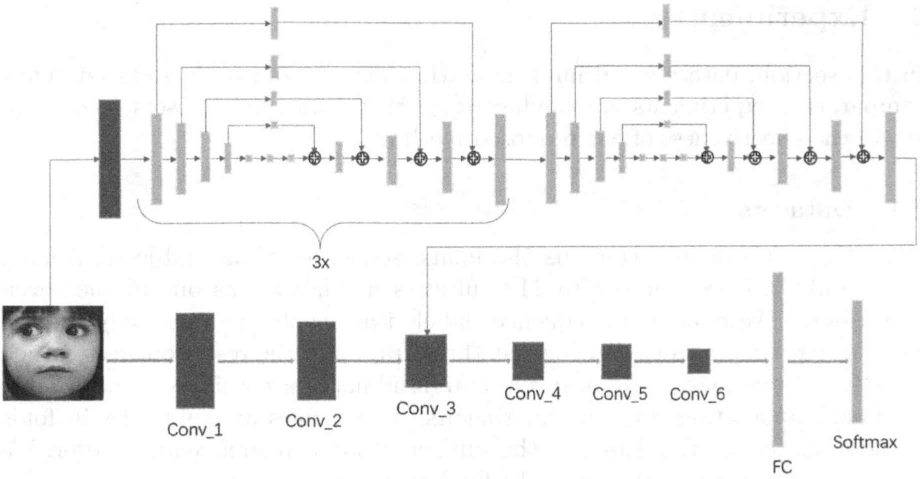

Fig. 3. The structure of Heatmap Aiding Emotion Network. HAE-Net consists of two parts: a landmark heatmap prediction branch (top) and a facial expression recognition branch (bottom).

layer features extracted by the feature extraction part to further extract the high-level features to improve the recognition performance.

By adding intermediate supervision in the stacked hourglass networks, the heatmap loss is as follows:

$$L_{Heatmap\_loss} = \sum_{i=1}^{n} \|H_i - H^*\|_2 \tag{1}$$

where H_i is the i-th output of hourglass modules, and H* is the ground-truth generated heatmap.

Cross-entropy is used to supervise the learning of expression classification, namely:

$$L_{Softmax\_loss} = -\frac{1}{N}\left(\sum_{i=1}^{N} y_i \cdot \log(f(x_i))\right) \tag{2}$$

where N is the total number of samples, x_i represents the i-th sample, y_i is the true label, and f(x_i) is the predicted output. Thus, the final loss function of the network is:

$$L_{Total\_loss} = L_{Softmax\_loss} + \lambda \cdot L_{Heatmap\_loss} \tag{3}$$

where λ is used to balance the influences of heatmap loss and softmax loss.

With this method, we can not only locate the landmarks but also exploit the landmark information to improve facial expression recognition performance.

4 Experiments

In this section, datasets and implementation details are first introduced. Then comparative experiments are conducted on three different datasets to demonstrate the effectiveness of our proposed method.

4.1 Datasets

CK+ [12]: This dataset contains 593 image sequences of 327 subjects. Among them, only 327 sequences with 118 subjects are labeled as one of the seven expressions. We remove the sequences labeled as "contempt" and only use the first (neutral expression) and the last three frames of the rest sequences, which results in 1308 images. We also select 37 landmarks accordingly from original landmark annotations for our experiments. The images are split into 10 folds without subject overlap based on the subject identity in an ascending order. We use the average of the 10 runs as the final accuracy.

RAF [8]: This dataset contains around 30k facial images under natural conditions downloaded from the Internet. It provides two types of images: basic expressions and composite expressions, as well as their corresponding 5 landmark locations labeled manually and 37 landmark locations automatically annotated with the face++ API [14]. In this paper, only images labeled with seven basic expressions categories and 37 landmark annotations are used, which contain 12271 training samples and 3068 testing samples.

AffectNet [16]: This dataset is the largest database for emotion recognition that contains more than 1,000,000 images, about half of which are manually annotated for the presence of seven discrete facial expressions, 68 facial landmark locations and the intensity of valence and arousal. Here we only select images with seven basic expressions and pick out 37 landmarks from original landmark annotations for our experiments.

4.2 Implement Details

For CK+ and RAF dataset, we crop the face region based on the ratio of inter-pupil distance. For Affect dataset, we crop the face region according to the bounding box coordinates. Then the cropped faces are aligned according to the center coordinates of the left and right eyes and resized to the same size 128 * 128. We also use 37 landmarks to generate the heatmaps as extra input or ground truths for training. We implement data augmentation by random cropping, rotating and flipping. The model is trained using RMSprop optimizer with an initial learning rate of 2.5e−4. To train the HAE-Net, we set the coefficient λ empirically as 50 for all of the datasets.

4.3 Results and Analysis

We measured the performance of the proposed network architecture on three datasets: CK+, RAF and AffectNet. To measure the results more comprehensively, we choose two metrics: accuracy which is defined as the proportion of the correct results to all predictions and average accuracy which can be obtained by calculating the average diagonal value of the confusion matrix.

Result of CK+ Dataset. As shown in the Table 1, the accuracy of Conv_Heatmap is about 1% higher than Baseline, which indices that adding the landmark heatmaps helps refine the features. HEA-Net gets about 1% higher accuracy compared with Conv_Heatmap. We owe this to the jointly training of facial landmark detection and facial expression recognition.

The results of our comparison with other methods are listed in Table 1. HEA-Net surpasses most methods by a large margin. However, we do not outperform the method Lopes et al. [11] and Hu et al. [4]. The explanations are as follows. Lopes et al. [11] use extra synthetic samples to train the network, whereas we only train our network on the original database. Although the accuracy of our method is lower than Lopes et al. [11], the average accuracy of HAE-Net is comparable to it, which demonstrates that our proposed method is useful for all seven expressions. Hu et al. [4] pretrained the network on the large dataset–LSEMSW and then used the augmented CK+ database to finetune the network, while we train our network all from scratch.

Table 1. Accuracy and average accuracy on CK+ dataset.

Methods	Validation settings	Accuracy	Average accuracy
Rivera et al. [22]	8-fold	0.8930	0.8594
LBP+SVM [19]	10-fold	0.9140	0.8914
AUDN [10]	10-fold	0.9370	-
Lopes et al. [11]	8-fold	0.9880	0.9575
Hu et al. [4]	5-fold	0.9640	-
Baseline	10-fold	0.9436	0.9427
Conv_Heatmap	10-fold	0.9583	0.9484
HEA-Net	10-fold	0.9624	0.9557

The confusion matrix of HAE-Net on the CK+ Dataset is displayed in Fig. 4. The expression angry gets relatively low accuracy compared with other emotions and it is easily classified into the neutral expression. The reason may be that the angry expression is closely related to the action unit frowning, but there is no facial landmarks representing the position between the eyebrows. The features most related to the angry may not be captured well, thus it will be easily classified into the neutral expression with most training samples.

Result of RAF Dataset. The results of the different methods on the RAF database are shown in Table 2. We train all of our networks from scratch using training samples and evaluate the performance on testing samples. Comparing

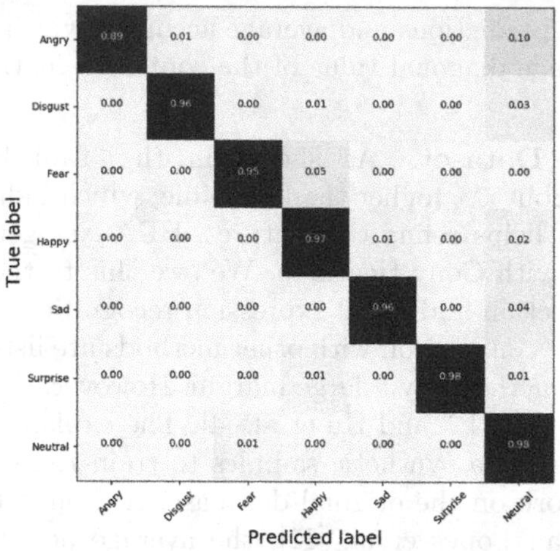

Fig. 4. Confusion matrix of HAE-Net on the CK+ dataset.

the results of the Baseline with Conv_Heatmap, it can be seen that adding the landmark heatmap information can bring about performance improvement. Further, the result of HAE-Net surpasses that of Conv_Heatmap, which shows that jointly training landmark heatmap detection and expression recognition is beneficial to improve the accuracy of expression recognition. FSN [31] proposed a feature selection mechanism to filter unrelated features, while gACNN [9] learned adaptive weights for different key facial patches extracted by facial landmarks and the whole image and then integrates the local representations with global representations. As is shown in Table 2, the results of our method are better than any of them.

Table 2. Accuracy and average accuracy on RAF dataset.

Methods	Accuracy	Average accuracy
FSN [31]	-	0.7246
gACNN [9]	0.8507	-
Baseline	0.8478	0.7377
Conv_Heatmap	0.8550	0.7564
HEA-Net	0.8664	0.7671

Table 3. Accuracy and average accuracy on AffectNet dataset.

Methods	Accuracy	Average accuracy
RAN-ResNet18 [26]	0.5297	-
gACNN [9]	0.5878	-
Baseline	0.5620	0.5628
Conv_Heatmap	0.5769	0.5757
HEA-Net	0.5886	0.5871

From the confusion matrix shown in Fig. 5, we can observe that the accuracy for happy is the highest, but the accuracy of fear is the lowest. We can also find that disgust expression is difficult to distinguish from angry and the fear expression is confused most with sad and neutral.

Result of AffectNet Dataset. The results of AffectNet dataset are presented in Table 3. Similar to the case of RAF dataset, our proposed HAE-Net achieves the best accuracy of all the methods, which verifies the superiority of our method.

The confusion matrix of HAE-Net is shown in Fig. 6. We note that in the case of happy and neutral, our network performs well, but the performance of disgust and surprise is relatively poor. Particularly, neutral and surprise, angry and neutral, disgust and angry, sad and neutral are easily confused with each other in this dataset.

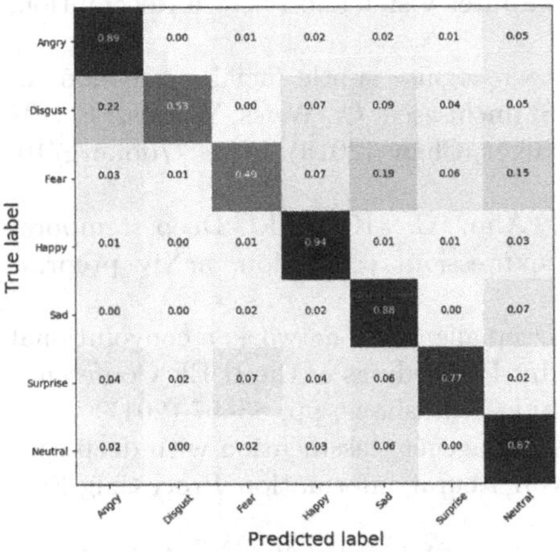

Fig. 5. Confusion matrix of HAE-Net on the RAF dataset.

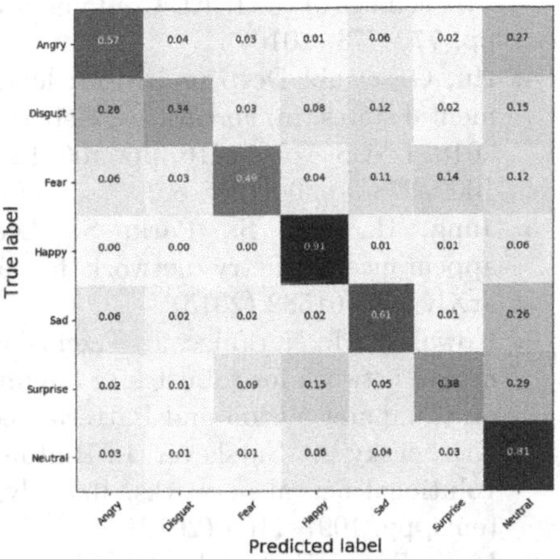

Fig. 6. Confusion matrix of HAE-Net on the AffectNet dataset.

5 Conclusion

In this work, we propose an expression recognition method that exploits landmark heatmap information explicitly and further present an end-to-end expression recognition network structure -- HAE-Net which is embedded with a facial landmark detection module. We conduct comparative experiments on three databases and get compelling results, which show that (1) directly adding additional landmark information helps to capture the discriminate features related to emotions; (2) HAE-Net can further improve the recognition accuracy by jointly training the facial landmark detection and expression recognition.

Acknowledgement. This work was partially supported by the National Natural Science Foundation of China (No. 61471216 and No. 61771276) and the Special Foundation for the Development of Strategic Emerging Industries of Shenzhen (No. JCYJ20170307153940960 and No. JCYJ20170817161845824).

References

1. Bulat, A., Tzimiropoulos, G.: Super-fan: integrated facial landmark localization and super-resolution of real-world low resolution faces in arbitrary poses with GANs. In: Proceedings of the IEEE Conference on Computer Vision and Pattern Recognition, pp. 109–117 (2018)
2. Chen, Y., Tai, Y., Liu, X., Shen, C., Yang, J.: Fsrnet: End-to-end learning face super-resolution with facial priors. In: Proceedings of the IEEE Conference on Computer Vision and Pattern Recognition, pp. 2492–2501 (2018)
3. He, K., Zhang, X., Ren, S., Sun, J.: Deep residual learning for image recognition. In: Proceedings of the IEEE Conference on Computer Vision and Pattern Recognition, pp. 770–778 (2016)
4. Hu, G., et al.: Deep multi-task learning to recognise subtle facial expressions of mental states. In: Ferrari, V., Hebert, M., Sminchisescu, C., Weiss, Y. (eds.) ECCV 2018. LNCS, vol. 11216, pp. 106–123. Springer, Cham (2018). https://doi.org/10.1007/978-3-030-01258-8_7
5. Jung, H., Lee, S., Park, S., Lee, I., Ahn, C., Kim, J.: Deep temporal appearance-geometry network for facial expression recognition. arXiv preprint arXiv:1503.01532 (2015)
6. Kowalski, M., Naruniec, J., Trzcinski, T.: Deep alignment network: a convolutional neural network for robust face alignment. In: Proceedings of the IEEE Conference on Computer Vision and Pattern Recognition Workshops, pp. 88–97 (2017)
7. Krizhevsky, A., Sutskever, I., Hinton, G.E.: Imagenet classification with deep convolutional neural networks. In: Advances in Neural Information Processing Systems, pp. 1097–1105 (2012)
8. Li, S., Deng, W., Du, J.: Reliable crowdsourcing and deep locality-preserving learning for expression recognition in the wild. In: Proceedings of the IEEE Conference on Computer Vision and Pattern Recognition, pp. 2852–2861 (2017)
9. Li, Y., Zeng, J., Shan, S., Chen, X.: Occlusion aware facial expression recognition using CNN with attention mechanism. IEEE Trans. Image Process. **28**(5), 2439–2450 (2018)
10. Liu, M., Li, S., Shan, S., Chen, X.: Au-inspired deep networks for facial expression feature learning. Neurocomputing **159**, 126–136 (2015)
11. Lopes, A.T., de Aguiar, E., De Souza, A.F., Oliveira-Santos, T.: Facial expression recognition with convolutional neural networks: coping with few data and the training sample order. Pattern Recogn. **61**, 610–628 (2017)
12. Lucey, P., Cohn, J.F., Kanade, T., Saragih, J., Ambadar, Z., Matthews, I.: The extended cohn-kanade dataset (ck+): a complete dataset for action unit and emotion-specified expression. In: 2010 IEEE Computer Society Conference on Computer Vision and Pattern Recognition-Workshops, pp. 94–101. IEEE (2010)
13. Majumder, A., Behera, L., Subramanian, V.K.: Automatic facial expression recognition system using deep network-based data fusion. IEEE Trans. Cybern. **48**(1), 103–114 (2016)
14. Megvii, I.: Face++ research toolkit (2013). http://www.faceplusplus.com
15. Mollahosseini, A., Chan, D., Mahoor, M.H.: Going deeper in facial expression recognition using deep neural networks. In: 2016 IEEE Winter Conference on Applications of Computer Vision (WACV), pp. 1–10. IEEE (2016)
16. Mollahosseini, A., Hasani, B., Mahoor, M.H.: Affectnet: a database for facial expression, valence, and arousal computing in the wild. IEEE Trans. Affect. Comput. **10**(1), 18–31 (2017)

17. Newell, A., Yang, K., Deng, J.: Stacked hourglass networks for human pose estimation. In: Leibe, B., Matas, J., Sebe, N., Welling, M. (eds.) ECCV 2016. LNCS, vol. 9912, pp. 483–499. Springer, Cham (2016). https://doi.org/10.1007/978-3-319-46484-8_29
18. Ranjan, R., Patel, V.M., Chellappa, R.: Hyperface: a deep multi-task learning framework for face detection, landmark localization, pose estimation, and gender recognition. IEEE Trans. Pattern Anal. Mach. Intell. **41**(1), 121–135 (2017)
19. Rivera, A.R., Castillo, J.R., Chae, O.O.: Local directional number pattern for face analysis: face and expression recognition. IEEE Trans. Image Process. **22**(5), 1740–1752 (2012)
20. Russakovsky, O., et al.: Imagenet large scale visual recognition challenge. Int. J. Comput. Vision **115**(3), 211–252 (2015)
21. Schroff, F., Kalenichenko, D., Philbin, J.: Facenet: a unified embedding for face recognition and clustering. In: Proceedings of the IEEE Conference on Computer Vision and Pattern Recognition, pp. 815–823 (2015)
22. Shan, C., Gong, S., McOwan, P.W.: Facial expression recognition based on local binary patterns: a comprehensive study. Image Vis. Comput. **27**(6), 803–816 (2009)
23. Simonyan, K., Zisserman, A.: Very deep convolutional networks for large-scale image recognition. arXiv preprint arXiv:1409.1556 (2014)
24. Tang, Y., Zhang, X.M., Wang, H.: Geometric-convolutional feature fusion based on learning propagation for facial expression recognition. IEEE Access **6**, 42532–42540 (2018)
25. Tautkute, I., Trzcinski, T., Bielski, A.: I know how you feel: Emotion recognition with facial landmarks. In: Proceedings of the IEEE Conference on Computer Vision and Pattern Recognition Workshops, pp. 1878–1880 (2018)
26. Wang, K., Peng, X., Yang, J., Meng, D., Qiao, Y.: Region attention networks for pose and occlusion robust facial expression recognition. arXiv preprint arXiv:1905.04075 (2019)
27. Wu, W., Qian, C., Yang, S., Wang, Q., Cai, Y., Zhou, Q.: Look at boundary: a boundary-aware face alignment algorithm. In: Proceedings of the IEEE Conference on Computer Vision and Pattern Recognition, pp. 2129–2138 (2018)
28. Yan, J., Zheng, W., Cui, Z., Tang, C., Zhang, T., Zong, Y.: Multi-cue fusion for emotion recognition in the wild. Neurocomputing **309**, 27–35 (2018)
29. Yu, X., Fernando, B., Ghanem, B., Porikli, F., Hartley, R.: Face super-resolution guided by facial component heatmaps. In: Ferrari, V., Hebert, M., Sminchisescu, C., Weiss, Y. (eds.) ECCV 2018. LNCS, vol. 11213, pp. 219–235. Springer, Cham (2018). https://doi.org/10.1007/978-3-030-01240-3_14
30. Zhang, K., Huang, Y., Du, Y., Wang, L.: Facial expression recognition based on deep evolutional spatial-temporal networks. IEEE Trans. Image Process. **26**(9), 4193–4203 (2017)
31. Zhao, S., Cai, H., Liu, H., Zhang, J., Chen, S.: Feature selection mechanism in CNNs for facial expression recognition. In: BMVC, p. 317 (2018)

One-Shot Face Recognition with Feature Rectification via Adversarial Learning

Jianli Zhou[1,2], Jun Chen[1,2(✉)], Chao Liang[1,2], and Jin Chen[1,2]

[1] National Engineering Research Center for Multimedia Software, School of Computer Science, Wuhan University, Wuhan, China
chenj.whu@gmail.com

[2] Key Laboratory of Multimedia and Network Communication Engineering, Wuhan, Hubei, China

Abstract. One-shot face recognition has attracted extensive attention with the ability to recognize persons at just one glance. With only one training sample which cannot represent intra-class variance adequately, one-shot classes have poor generalization ability, and it is difficult to obtain appropriate classification weights. In this paper, we explore an inherent relationship between features and classification weights. In detail, we propose *feature rectification generative adversarial network* (FR-GAN) which is able to rectify features closer to corresponding classification weights considering existing classification weights information. With one model, we achieve two purposes: without fine-tuning via back propagation as previous CNN approaches which are time consuming and computationally expensive, FR-GAN can not only (1) generate classification weights for new classes using training data, but also (2) achieve more discriminative test feature representation. The experimental results demonstrate the remarkable performance of our proposed method, as in MS-Celeb-1M one-shot benchmark, our method achieves 93.12% coverage at 99% precision with the introduction of novel classes and remains a high accuracy at 99.80% for base classes, surpassing most of the previous approaches based on fine-tuning.

Keywords: Face recognition · One-shot learning · Adversarial rectification

1 Introduction

In recent years, face recognition based on deep learning techniques such as Convolutional Neural Networks (CNN) has shown powerful performance [16–18],

This research was supported partially by National Key R&D Program of China (2017YFC0803700), National Nature Science Foundation of China (U1611461, U1736206, 61876135, 61872362, 61671336, 61801335), Technology Research Program of Ministry of Public Security (2016JSYJA12), Hubei Province Technological Innovation Major Project (2016AAA015, 2017AAA123, 2018AAA062), Nature Science Foundation of Hubei Province (2018CFA024) and Nature Science Foundation of Jiangsu Province (BK20160386).

Y. M. Ro et al. (Eds.): MMM 2020, LNCS 11961, pp. 290–302, 2020.
https://doi.org/10.1007/978-3-030-37731-1_24

and it is related to a wide range of applications, such as multimedia analysis and surveillance [13,21]. Some models have even exceeded humans given sufficient training data [9,14]. Thanks to large-scale training datasets, CNN can learn essential features by powerful learning ability. However, it is hard to collect a large amount of training data for each identity (i.e. *base classes*), some identities only have few samples or even one (i.e. *novel classes*), which lack sufficient discrimination information. In this condition, mining the ability of intelligent algorithms to effectively learn new category from a single sample is a very challenging problem, which known as *one-shot learning*. To explore this problem, Guo *et al.* [4] designed MS-Celeb-1M one-shot face dataset composed of Base Set and Novel Set, Base Set consists of 20,000 identities, each with 50–100 training images and Novel Set contains 1,000 identities, each with only one training image.

To study this task, many researchers have proposed various valuable solutions. Existing methods on one-shot face recognition generally fall into three categories: loss-based methods, training data hallucination methods and classifier-based methods.

Loss-Based Methods. Intuitively, some methods focus on constructing novel loss function to alleviate data imbalance. Guo *et al.* [4] proposed CCS loss to gain a better face feature representation and UP loss to promote the norm of classification weights. In [20], shifting center loss was introduced to adjust the clustering center to handle scarce data. Zhao *et al.* [7] proposed an enforced softmax loss to learn discriminative compact feature representation by narrowing the decision boundaries of each class. These methods can improve the accuracy performance through training by directly using unbalanced datasets. However, the long-tail phenomenon of training datasets still exists, which drops generalization ability of the feature representation model. Furthermore, when novel classes emerge, the network needs to be fine-tuned on all prior training data with samples from novel classes, which is inefficient and time-consuming.

Training Data Hallucination Methods. Since one sample cannot fully reflect the intra-class variance, a general strategy is training data hallucination. Along this line, Choe *et al.* [1] implemented GAN to generate faces under various poses and attributes. Similarly, method in [2] introduced a generative framework to synthesize more effective novel data by referring to the data variation of Base Set. However, the quality of the samples produced by GAN is unstable. For classes with limited samples, e.g. novel classes, the generated samples can bring positive effect by enlarging the data space. For classes with sufficient samples, e.g. base classes, the generated samples may lead to negative effect due to their noisy interference to existing real data distribution.

Classifier-Based Methods. Besides, since the classifier which based on plain softmax performs poor performance in one-shot recognition problem, Wu *et al.* [23] proposed a hybrid classifier model with two classifiers of CNN and Nearest Neighbor (NN) model to handle different kinds of sets. Although the method does not require back propagation when new identities appear, it heavily relies

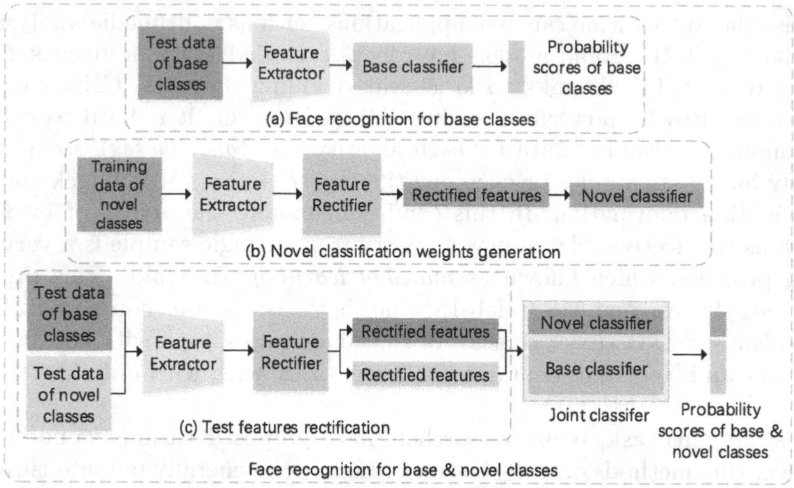

Fig. 1. Overview of our method. To recognize both base and novel classes, first, (a) a feature extractor and a base classifier are learned which can only recognize base classes. Then, (b) the rectifier generates rectified training features of novel classes as novel classifier, and (c) it rectifies the test features of both base and novel classes in the same way. Finally, the novel classifier is concatenated to the base classifier, and the joint classifier takes as input the rectified test features and outputs the probability scores of both base and novel classes.

on threshold adjustment. In a separate way, Qi *et al.* [12] extracted features from samples of new classes as classification weights of new classes. Nonetheless, it is merely for the sake of a better initialization parameter for fine-tuning, and the method cannot balance the performance of both base and novel classes well simultaneously. Obviously, it is easy to find that features and classifiers are two decisive factors to the recognition performance, but their internal connection is neglected.

In this paper, we empirically show that fine-tuning on imbalanced dataset is likely to cause degradation of model, and we propose an one-shot face recognition method that can adapt rapidly to new identities without back propagation, while remaining or even improving the original performance on base classes at the same time. Specifically, we discuss the difference between feature space and classification weight space, and impose a feature rectifier to alleviate their gap. Moreover, considering the sensitivity of GAN to slight disturbance in parameters and structure choice, we employ GAN to generate features instead of images of real scenario. Thereafter, the low dimension output enables the network to generate more reliable results.

The main contributions of our paper are three folds. (1) To the best of our knowledge, we employ GAN to learn the internal relationship between classification weights and features for the first time. (2) We propose a feature rectifier to generate features which adapted to the manifold of pre-existing classification

Table 1. Top-1 accuracy on MS-Celeb-1M one-shot face Development Set [4]. "Pre-Trained" denotes the pre-trained classifier on Base Set, and "Direct Embedding" denotes the new classifier by directly embedding features from Novel Set as classification weights.

	Base classes	Novel classes
Pre-Trained	99.64%	/
Direct Embedding	80.32%	92.16%

weights, and the novel classes weights can be generated directly by the rectifier simultaneously. (3) Extensive experiments on MS-Celeb-1M one-shot face dataset demonstrate the superiority of our proposed method.

2 Proposed Method

In this section, we first explain the motivation of our proposed method, then design FR-GAN and present the details as well as the training process. An overview of our method is provided in Fig. 1.

2.1 Motivation

Face recognition involves two important parts, feature extraction and feature classification. In the case of one-shot learning, in order to recognize novel classes one must be able to get classification weight vectors appropriately, which is a challenging problem due to scarce training samples. In [12], novel classification weights were initialized by class center

$$c_i = \frac{1}{N}\sum_{n=1}^{N}\phi(I_i^n), \tag{1}$$

where $\phi(\cdot)$ denotes the feature extractor and I_i^n is the n-th training example of the novel class i, the class center c_i represents the average of features from the ith class. For one-shot classes, the class center equals the only training feature.

However, under the supervision of cross entropy loss, not only does the classification weight W_i contain information about i^{th} class, but it's also influenced by neighboring samples from other classes. Formally, according to the standard version of cross entropy loss

$$L_s = -\,log\,p(x_i), \tag{2}$$

where $p(x_i)$ is the estimated probability that feature x_i from class i which defined as

$$p(x_i) = \frac{e^{W_i^T x_i}}{e^{W_i^T x_i} + \sum_{j\neq i} e^{W_j^T x_i}}, \tag{3}$$

the gradient of W_i is calculated as

$$\frac{\partial L_s}{\partial W_i} = (p(x_i) - 1)x_i, \tag{4}$$

and the gradient of W_k belonging to other classes is calculated as

$$\frac{\partial L_s}{\partial W_k} = \frac{e^{W_k^T x_i}}{\sum_j e^{W_j^T x_i}} x_i. \tag{5}$$

Equations 4 and 5 demonstrate, for training samples x_i, the direction of W_i move closer to it, while the direction of other classification weights will tend to stay away from it. So, there is an essential difference between features and classification weights, and directly embedding features into the network as classification weights is not optimal. To make this statement more convincing, we use a simple experiment to illustrate. On MS-Celeb-1M one-shot training dataset, after training a 20,000-way classifiers using Base Set, we directly set classification weights for novel classes using features from Novel Set to obtain a 21,000-way classifiers. The performance is evaluated on MS-Celeb-1M one-shot face Development Set [4]. The result shows when 1,000 new classes are added, the recognition accuracy of base classes severely degrades. Top-1 accuracy is shown in Table 1. The explanation is that, under the setup of our experiment, the distances between features and corresponding classification weight are prone to farther than other features in some cases. More specifically, we assume that the classification weights and features are not lie on the same manifold.

2.2 FR-GAN

Based on the previous analysis, in view of the average impact of all features of the same classes, the generation of new classification weights has two kinds of learning directions: (1) closer to the class center of related class, and (2) farther from the others. As an average of all features in the same class, when the number of samples are sufficient, the class center represents an ideal face, removing non-identity factors such as posture and expression [24]. However, for novel classes, the class center is equivalent to the only training sample, and it is possibly placed on the edge of intra-class variance illustrated in Fig. 2(a) and (b), thus losing the guiding significance. To this end, we introduce a novel FR-GAN that shifts the features to adapts the distribution of existing classification weights shown in Fig. 2(c).

Before we train FR-GAN, we pre-train a classifier on base classes, which includes a feature extractor $\phi(\cdot)$ and a set of classification weights $W_{base} = \{W_i\}_{i=1}^{K}$, where K is the number of base classes, and W_i is the classification weight of ith base class. For training set of FR-GAN, in our paper, we just use the features $X_{base} = \bigcup_{i=1}^{K} \{x_i^n\}_{n=1}^{N}$, where N is the number of training examples of ith base class, and take the set of classification weights W_{base} as labels. We assume that the features are generic enough and the classification weights

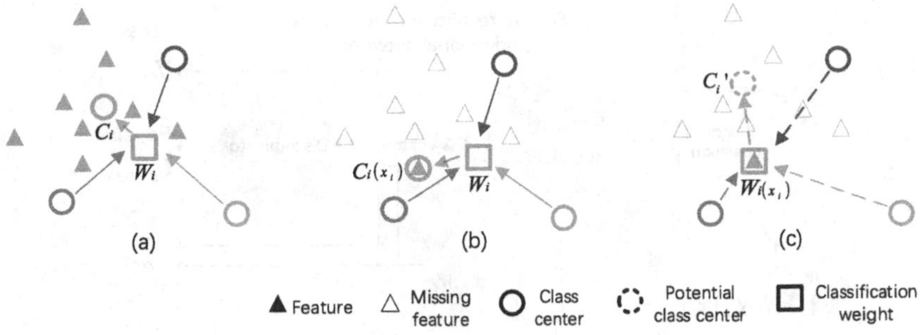

Fig. 2. The full line denotes the component of updating direction of classification weights in backward propagation process, and the dotted line indicates the potential rectification direction as directed by FR-GAN. To learn a classification weights W_i for the red class, it will be closer to the related class center C_i and move away from other class centers. (a) When training samples are adequate, the class center C_i is representative enough to guide the update of the classification weights W_i. (b) If the red class has only one available training sample x_i, just like the novel classes, the class center C_i is determined by the single sample x_i which may lie on the margin of intra-class variance. In this case, the class center is actually biased and cannot provide useful information. (c) By learning the potential class centers C_i' and referring to the existing classification weights, FR-GAN rectifies training sample x_i to generate discriminative classification weights W_i.

are appropriate, so FR-GAN can learn valuable inherent mapping from these features to their corresponding classification weights. This approach allows the rectifier to fundamentally grasp the holistic distribution of classification weights of base classes, so it is the most suitable training set, and it also reflects the effective utilization of data. To make the process of training and testing as consistent as possible, each training sample is treated as the only sample of corresponding class, just like samples from the novel classes. Training process of FR-GAN is shown in Fig. 3.

Attention Mechanism. Considering the adjacent classification weights have the greatest influence on feature x_i, we model its effect using an attention mechanism. Inspired from [10], we employ temporal convolutions and soft attention to design a rectifier, its architecture is shown in Fig. 4. Attention mechanism allows model to aggregate contextual information and focus on some useful pieces, finding similarities or distinctions. Given x_i with corresponding weights W_i, we filter out the 10 weight vectors $NN_{10}(x_i)$ nearest to x_i except W_i, then concatenate $NN_{10}(x_i)$ with x_i as W_c. The new feature x_i' is represented as a sum of the original feature x_i with a residual part produced by rectifier $R(W_c)$, which can be written as:

$$x_i' = x_i + R(W_c). \tag{6}$$

In the training process of feature extractor, similar to [19], we normalize features and weights to optimize the angle between classes better. On the contrary,

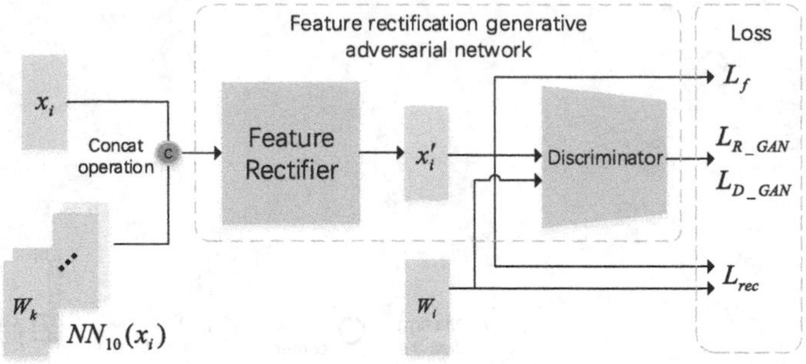

Fig. 3. Illustration of the training process of FR-GAN. W_i is the classification weight corresponding to x_i. $NN_{10}(x_i)$ denotes the 10 nearest classification weight to x_i except W_i, the concatenation of them are fed into the feature rectifier to obtain discriminative feature x_i'. The adversarial loss L_{R_GAN}/L_{D_GAN}, the reconstruction loss L_{rec} and the focal loss L_f are employed to supervise the training process of FR-GAN jointly.

in the training process of FR-GAN, we do not normalize feature x_i. The reason is that we consider the L_2 norm can reflect the quality of examples, if the value is small, there may be interference of pose, illumination or resolution. We hope the rectifier can learn this implied information in features and control the rectification strength based on it.

Adversarial Reconstruction. To enhance the ability of learning distribution, We employ the GAN framework [3]. It contains the rectifier R shown in Fig. 4 and a discriminator D. The discriminator is a sequential network with two fully connected layers in which the first one maps from 2048 dimensions to 2048 dimensions and the second one maps from 2048 dimensions to 1 dimension, the activation function between them is Leakey ReLU. The GAN loss function for the rectifier and the discriminator of FR-GAN is formally expressed as:

$$L_{R\_GAN} = E[1 - log(D(x_i'))], \tag{7}$$

$$L_{D\_GAN} = -E[log(D(W_i))] - E[1 - logD(x_i')]. \tag{8}$$

In contrast to image generation, we consider feature generation to be a more credible approach. In our case, generating a color image of 224 × 224 pixels requires an output of 150,528 dimensions, while generating features requires only 2,048 dimensions. Furthermore, image generation is mainly to provide better visual quality for human perspective, and feature generation is more straightforward for machine recognition.

Cosine Reconstruction. To make the rectifier more constrained, a reconstruction loss function is defined to ensure identity-preserving. In our case, we only concentrate on the angle, so the reconstruction loss is formulated as:

$$L_{rec} = cos(\theta_i), \tag{9}$$

where θ_i is the angle between generated x_i' and W_i.

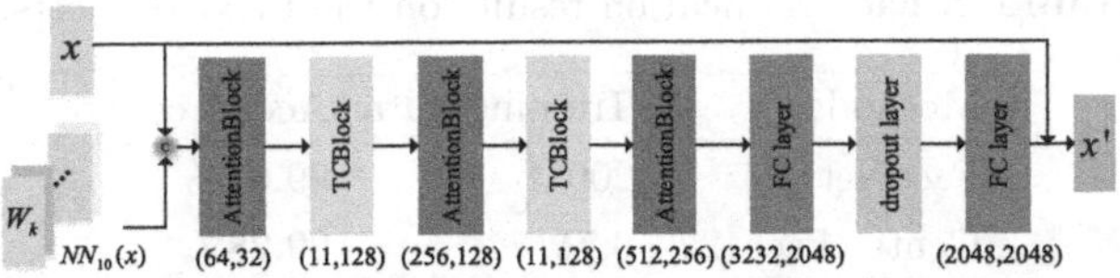

Fig. 4. Architecture of rectifier. See details about AttentionBlock and TCBlock in [10].

Global Constraints. In addition to using corresponding weight vector for local constraints, we apply cross entropy loss for global supervision. In particular, we notice there are always some hard samples in face datasets, such as very similar faces or faces with poor illumination and posture. These hard samples often account for a small number, resulting in an imbalance of sample quality. Peculiarly, this is fatal for one-shot classes, because it's likely that the unique training sample is a hard sample so a good clustering center is difficult to optimize. We use focal loss [8] by reshaping standard cross entropy loss to focus on hard examples. The focal loss is formulated as:

$$L_f = -(1 - p(x_i'))^\gamma log(p(x_i')), \tag{10}$$

where γ is a focusing parameter, $p(x_i')$ is cosine softmax function defined as,

$$p(x_i) = \frac{e^{s\cos(\theta_i)}}{e^{s\cos(\theta_i)} + \sum_{j\neq i} e^{s\cos(\theta_j)}}, \tag{11}$$

subject to

$$W^* = \frac{W}{\|W\|}, x^* = \frac{x}{\|x\|}, \cos(\theta_j) = W_j^{*T} x_i^*, \tag{12}$$

where s is a scaling term that makes convergence more sufficient, the W_j is the classification weight of the j-th class, and θ_j is the angle between W_j and x_i.

In view of GAN's instability and the problem of over-fitting, we consider L_2 regularization term. Regularization limits the information that the rectifier can encode, forcing it to learn valuable optimal direction in a limited space. At the same time, it may be able to reduce the probability of producing irregular output. Finally, considering all of above, the system training optimization goal can be written as:

$$L_R = \lambda_g L_{R\_GAN} + \lambda_{rec} L_{rec} + \lambda_f L_f + \lambda_r \|x'\|^2, \tag{13}$$

$$L_D = L_{D\_GAN}, \tag{14}$$

where $\lambda_g, \lambda_{rec}, \lambda_f, \lambda_r$ are hyperparameters to control the weighting of each loss.

It is worth noting that the rectifier can be used not only to generate classification weights using training data, but also to enhance test features at test time. Because its constraint function determines that for different samples belonging to the same identity, after the rectification, they should all be clustered to same angle as possible. In experiments, this approach proved to greatly improve the performance of the model.

Table 2. Face verification results on the LFW datasets.

Methods	Training data	Accuracy
FaceNet [14]	200M	99.63%
Center Face [22]	0.7M	99.28%
DeepFR [11]	2.6M	98.95%
Deep Face [18]	4M	97.35%
Ours	1.1M	98.96%

3 Experiments

In this section, we will verify both components of our solution on MS-Celeb-1M one-shot benchmark and LFW.

3.1 Experimental Setup

MS-Celeb-1M one-shot face recognition task mainly focus on the performance in Novel Set by using coverage rate at precision 99% and 99.9% as evaluation metrics while the Top-1 accuracy rate in Base Set is also supervised. Coverage and precision are defined as m/n, c/m respectively, where n is the total number of images and c the number of images that are correct in the recognized m images.

We train the feature extractor with ResNet-50 architecture [6]. In the training phase, we rescale images to 240×240 pixels and then randomly cropped to 224×224 pixels, subtracting mean value from each color channel. We employ random horizontal mirroring and random grayscaling. The optimizer of both networks is SGD with weight decay of $5e^{-4}$ and momentum of 0.9. Focusing parameter is set to $\gamma = 2$ as same as [8]. We find $\lambda_g = 0.1, \lambda_{rec} = 1, \lambda_f = 0.5, \lambda_r = 0.001$ work well. Notice only Base Set is used for training our both networks.

3.2 Representation Learning

We investigate the feature representation performance of our feature extractor in LFW, which is a standard face verification testing dataset. The accuracy with other methods are shown in Table 2. It can be seen that our method achieves comparable performance with a part of MS-Celeb-1M one-shot dataset on LFW verification task, giving discriminative feature representation.

3.3 One-Shot Face Recognition

In this subsection, we check the performance of our solutions on MS-celeb-1M Development Set, and compare it with previous one-shot learning methods. The results are shown in Table 3. For the pre-trained model, the Top-1 accuracy on

Table 3. Comparison on Development Set. As shown in the table, our method achieves the state-of-the-art performance without fine-tuning.

Method	base classes, Top-1 Accuracy	novel classes, C@P=0.99
SGM [5]	99.80%	27.23%
DM [15]	99.88%	88.32%
Shifting [20]	98.00%	88.87%
Hybrid [23]	99.58%	92.78%
Pre-trained	99.64%	/
Direct Embedding	80.32%	92.16%
Fine-Tuning	99.40%	80.60%
FR_1	91.78%	92.14%
FR_2(w/o L_{GAN})	97.78%	91.12%
FR_2(w/o L_f)	97.89%	91.98%
FR_2(ours)	99.80%	**93.12%**

Base Set is 99.64%. Combining the above test, they demonstrate that we have proper features and classification weights, which provide valuable training data for FR-GAN.

Similar to the method in [12], "Fine-Tuning" denotes that, after embedding the features of Novel Set into the classifiers directly just like "Direct Embedding", we freeze the parameters of the feature extractor and fine-tune the new classifiers in entire training datasets, where the samples from Novel Set are duplicated by 60 times. The drawback of this approach is that, the novel classification weights merely reconcile the distance to other classes, rather than learn their underlying class center. Intuitively, this means that fine-tuning can help the novel classes cause less interference to other classes, but its own performance will suffer as the experimental results show. As we can see from the results, for performance of base classes and novel classes, neither of these two methods can improve one without reducing the another.

For our method, FR_1 in Table 3 means that we only employ feature rectifier to generate new classification weights, while FR_2 means we also rectify the testing features from both base and novel classes, and the effect of this on base classes is shown to be very notable. Since the base classes are those rectifier have seen during training phase, we conjecture that the rectifier has better rectification ability for features of base classes and makes features of the same classes converge more closely. Besides, we illustrate the cases of training without L_f and training without L_{GAN}, both of them will degrade the recognition performance of our model. Figure 5 shows Precision-Recall curves. With the help of GAN, our method has better generalization capability. Similarly, training with focal loss brings performance gains, showing that focusing on poor quality samples is beneficial to generating ideal novel classification weights.

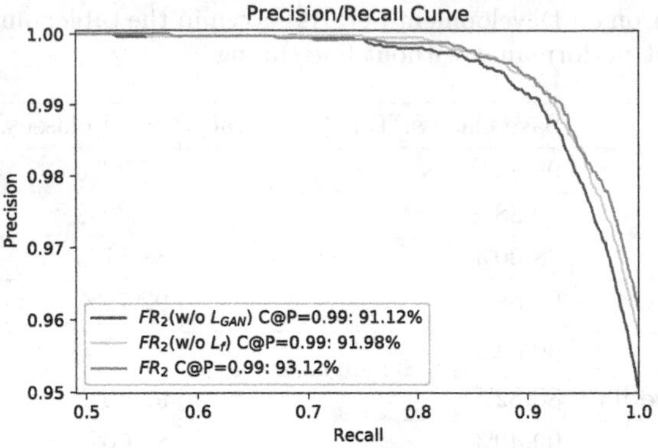

Fig. 5. Precision-recall curves on MS-celeb-1M development novel set.

In addition, it's remarkable that our method is able to add novel classes without any degradation of the performance in base classes, even with a slight improvement, which is essentially different from other algorithms. The evaluation results in Table 3 show that our method brings a significant performance gain in MS-Celeb-1M one-shot face recognition task.

4 Conclusion

In this paper, we explore the relationship between features and classification weights and propose a novel model called FR-GAN for one-shot face recognition. The core idea of our method is to learn a latent mapping from feature space to classification weight space. By referring to the distribution of existing classification weights, FR-GAN realizes two goals: it (1) generates classification weights of novel classes using training novel data, and also (2) outputs more discriminative features at test time. The evaluation results show the superiority of our method in one-shot face recognition task.

References

1. Choe, J., Park, S., Kim, K., Park, J.H., Kim, D., Shim, H.: Face generation for low-shot learning using generative adversarial networks. In: 2017 IEEE International Conference on Computer Vision Workshop (ICCVW), pp. 1940–1948. IEEE (2017)
2. Ding, Z., Guo, Y., Zhang, L., Fu, Y.: One-shot face recognition via generative learning. In: 2018 13th IEEE International Conference on Automatic Face & Gesture Recognition (FG 2018), pp. 1–7. IEEE (2018)
3. Goodfellow, I.J., et al.: Generative adversarial nets. In: International Conference on Neural Information Processing Systems (2014)
4. Guo, Y., Zhang, L.: One-shot face recognition by promoting underrepresented classes. arXiv preprint arXiv:1707.05574 (2017)

5. Hariharan, B., Girshick, R.: Low-shot visual recognition by shrinking and hallucinating features. In: Proceedings of IEEE International Conference on Computer Vision (ICCV), Venice, Italy (2017)
6. He, K., Zhang, X., Ren, S., Sun, J.: Deep residual learning for image recognition. In: Proceedings of the IEEE Conference on Computer Vision and Pattern Recognition, pp. 770–778 (2016)
7. Jian, Z., Yu, C., Wang, Z., Yan, X., Feng, J.: Know you at one glance: a compact vector representation for low-shot learning. In: IEEE International Conference on Computer Vision Workshop (2017)
8. Lin, T.Y., Goyal, P., Girshick, R., He, K., Dollár, P.: Focal loss for dense object detection. IEEE Trans. Pattern Anal. Mach. Intell. (2018)
9. Liu, J., Deng, Y., Bai, T., Wei, Z., Huang, C.: Targeting ultimate accuracy: face recognition via deep embedding. arXiv preprint arXiv:1506.07310 (2015)
10. Mishra, N., Rohaninejad, M., Chen, X., Abbeel, P.: A simple neural attentive meta-learner (2018)
11. Parkhi, O.M., Vedaldi, A., Zisserman, A., et al.: Deep face recognition. In: BMVC, vol. 1, p. 6 (2015)
12. Qi, H., Brown, M., Lowe, D.G.: Low-shot learning with imprinted weights. In: Proceedings of the IEEE Conference on Computer Vision and Pattern Recognition, pp. 5822–5830 (2018)
13. Ruan, W., et al.: Multi-correlation filters with triangle-structure constraints for object tracking. IEEE Trans. Multimedia **21**(5), 1122–1134 (2018)
14. Schroff, F., Kalenichenko, D., Philbin, J.: Facenet: a unified embedding for face recognition and clustering. In: Proceedings of the IEEE Conference on Computer Vision and Pattern Recognition, pp. 815–823 (2015)
15. Smirnov, E., Melnikov, A., Novoselov, S., Luckyanets, E., Lavrentyeva, G.: Doppelganger mining for face representation learning. In: 2017 IEEE International Conference on Computer Vision Workshop (ICCVW), pp. 1916–1923. IEEE (2017)
16. Sun, Y., Chen, Y., Wang, X., Tang, X.: Deep learning face representation by joint identification-verification. In: Advances in Neural Information Processing Systems, pp. 1988–1996 (2014)
17. Sun, Y., Liang, D., Wang, X., Tang, X.: Deepid3: face recognition with very deep neural networks. arXiv preprint arXiv:1502.00873 (2015)
18. Taigman, Y., Yang, M., Ranzato, M., Wolf, L.: Deepface: closing the gap to human-level performance in face verification. In: Proceedings of the IEEE Conference on Computer Vision and Pattern Recognition, pp. 1701–1708 (2014)
19. Wang, H., et al.: Cosface: large margin cosine loss for deep face recognition. In: Proceedings of the IEEE Conference on Computer Vision and Pattern Recognition, pp. 5265–5274 (2018)
20. Wang, L., Li, Y., Wang, S.: Feature learning for one-shot face recognition. In: 2018 25th IEEE International Conference on Image Processing (ICIP), pp. 2386–2390. IEEE (2018)
21. Weijian, R., Wu, L., Qian, B., Jun, C., Yuhao, C., Tao, M.: Poinet: pose-guided ovonic insight network for multi-person pose tracking. In: ACM International Conference on Multimedia (2019)
22. Wen, Y., Zhang, K., Li, Z., Qiao, Y.: A discriminative feature learning approach for deep face recognition. In: Leibe, B., Matas, J., Sebe, N., Welling, M. (eds.) ECCV 2016. LNCS, vol. 9911, pp. 499–515. Springer, Cham (2016). https://doi.org/10.1007/978-3-319-46478-7_31

23. Wu, Y., Liu, H., Fu, Y.: Low-shot face recognition with hybrid classifiers. In: 2017 IEEE International Conference on Computer Vision Workshop (ICCVW), pp. 1933–1939. IEEE (2017)
24. Yin, X., Yu, X., Sohn, K., Liu, X., Chandraker, M.: Feature transfer learning for face recognition with under-represented data. In: Proceedings of the IEEE Conference on Computer Vision and Pattern Recognition, pp. 5704–5713 (2019)

Visual Sentiment Analysis by Leveraging Local Regions and Human Faces

Ruolin Zheng, Weixin Li(✉), and Yunhong Wang

Beijing Advanced Innovation Center for Big Data and Brain Computing,
Beihang University, Beijing 100191, China
{zhengruolin,weixinli,yhwang}@buaa.edu.cn

Abstract. Visual sentiment analysis (VSA) is a challenging task which attracts wide attention from researchers for its great application potentials. Existing works for VSA mostly extract global representations of images for sentiment prediction, ignoring the different contributions of local regions. Some recent studies analyze local regions separately and achieve improvements on the sentiment prediction performance. However, most of them treat regions equally in the feature fusion process which ignores their distinct contributions or use a global attention map whose performance is easily influenced by noises from non-emotional regions. In this paper, to solve these problems, we propose an end-to-end deep framework to effectively exploit the contributions of local regions to VSA. Specifically, a Sentiment Region Attention (SRA) module is proposed to estimate contributions of local regions with respect to the global image sentiment. Features of these regions are then reweighed and further fused according to their estimated contributions. Moreover, since the image sentiment is usually closely related to humans appearing in the image, we also propose to model the contribution of human faces as a special local region for sentiment prediction. Experimental results on publicly available and widely used datasets for VSA demonstrate our method outperforms state-of-the-art algorithms.

Keywords: Visual sentiment analysis · Attention mechanism · Local regions

1 Introduction

Visual sentiment analysis (VSA) aims to predict the emotional reactions of humans towards visual stimuli e.g. images. Psychological studies have proved that visual contents can stimulate various human emotions [6,7]. Thus, researchers started to design algorithms to analyze visual sentiments automatically, which have great application potentials in various domains e.g. business, politics, sociology, etc. However, VSA is a challenging task compared to other general computer vision and multimedia tasks, e.g. object recognition and detection, since emotional reactions of humans are subjective and the analysis needs a much higher-level understanding of image contents.

Y. M. Ro et al. (Eds.): MMM 2020, LNCS 11961, pp. 303–314, 2020.
https://doi.org/10.1007/978-3-030-37731-1_25

In the literature, hand-crafted features are commonly used during the past decades to predict image sentiment, e.g. color, texture and shape [9,20–22]. Recently, due to the successful applications of convolutional neural network (CNN) in the fields of multimedia, computer vision, etc., many researchers use CNNs to extract deep features for visual sentiment analysis [1,18], which can be learnt automatically from data and achieve satisfactory performance compared with hand-crafted ones. However, most of these studies extract high-level sentiment features only globally from the whole image. Some recent studies find that analyzing local regions can help improve the image sentiment prediction performance [11,13,15–17]. These methods generally follow two ways to use local information for sentiment prediction. One is to generate a global attention map by a branch of CNN architecture to focus on regions that are more related to image sentiment [13,15,17]. The other is to first generate region proposals and then rank them by both region features and sentiment scores, and regions ranked higher are treated as more related to the image sentiment and thus their sentiment features will be highlighted in the final prediction [11,16]. However, for methods using global attention maps, they directly compute the sentiment map of the whole image, without fully considering each region, and their performance is easily affected by noises from non-emotional regions. For the latter one, they only deal with regions independently in the ranking stage, not relating them to the global sentiment. And the highlighted regions are treated equally in the image sentiment prediction process, ignoring their distinct contributions and thus limiting the final performance. Hence, how to effectively model the contributions of different local regions to visual sentiment analysis still remains a problem.

Moreover, humans are usually the important parts in the image undoubtedly, and they can evoke more emotional reactions of people seeing the image, since people are more likely to feel empathy with humans in images. So, we believe that the image sentiment is closely related to humans in the image if they appear, especially their faces, which, however, has not been considered in previous work for VSA to our best knowledge.

To solve the aforementioned issues, in this paper, we propose an end-to-end deep framework for visual sentiment analysis by leveraging local regions and human faces. Specifically, we estimate the contribution of each local region with respect to the global image sentiment, and reweigh and further fuse these region features according to their different contributions. For estimating the region contributions, we propose a Sentiment Region Attention (SRA) module, which computes the weights based on the global sentiment features and region features. The SRA module is effectively embedded in the whole framework, so our network can predict the image sentiment in an end-to-end way. Also, to consider the contribution of humans in images to VSA, we extract facial sentiment features from human faces in images and fuse them to the final sentiment features. We evaluate the proposed method on three commonly used datasets for visual sentiment analysis, including Flickr and Instagram (FI) [19], ArtPhoto [9] and EmotionROI [10], and the experimental results show the superiority of our method compared with state-of-the-art approaches.

2 Related Work

Existing methods for image sentiment analysis can roughly be divided into two categories, one based on manually designed features, and the other using deep learning frameworks. Early hand-crafted features are designed primarily according to psychological principles. Machajdik et al. [9] defined a set of basic features to represent emotional contents, including color, texture, image components, etc. Based on these basic features, Zhao et al. [20] proposed a more robust algorithm based on the artistic rules of images. Zhao et al. [21,22] proposed multi-task hypergraph learning to predict people's emotional responses and studied the subjective emotions of images.

In recent years, with the successful applications of deep networks, many researchers began to use deep models to learn the image sentiment representations, and achieved better performance compared to the hand-crafted features. DeepSentiBank [1] constructed the concept of visual sentiment based on classification of adjective nouns pairs (ANPs), and used ANPs for predicting the sentiment of images. You et al. [18] trained a CNN model on large-scale sentiment datasets and employed a progressive strategy to make use of noisy machine labeled data. However, most of these previous methods try to extract a global representation from the whole image, without considering the different contributions of local regions to VSA.

Some recent studies used local region information in visual sentiment prediction, since it is obvious that different local areas can contribute differently to human emotional responses of the whole image. Some of them learn a global attention map to model which region contributes more to the sentiment stimulation. You et al. [17] used CNN to extract emotional features, and then used an attention model with a visual attribute detector to calculate the emotional consistency of local regions and full images. Yang et al. [15] used the fully convolutional network to calculate a sentiment map as the global attention map, and combined it with the global sentiment feature map extracted from the whole image to classify the image sentiments. Song et al. [13] supervised the sentiment attention map generation with a saliency map acquired from the saliency detection method. However, these methods generally fail to fully consider the contribution of each local region only with a global attention map, and more importantly, their performance is easily influenced by noises from non-emotional regions.

Other methods try to detect and rank the affective regions based on region appearance and sentiment features. Yang et al. [16] ranked the regions by their object scores and sentiment scores calculated by EdgeBox and fine-tuned VGG, and then fused the global sentiment features and the sentiment features of top ranked regions. However, the sentiment score of each region proposal is computed approximately through the CNN fine-tuned using the dataset containing whole images, which makes the framework not possible to be trained in an end-to-end way. Rao et al. [11] fine-tuned Faster R-CNN with EmotionROI [10] to acquire the object scores and sentiment scores, and combined them to calculate the final scores of the ROIs. Sentiment features extracted from the top ROIs are concatenated with the global sentiment features extracted from the Faster R-CNN backbone. However, all the region features are treated equally in the concatenation process.

In this paper, we propose to estimate the contribution of each local region to the prediction of image sentiment. Region features are then reweighed based on their contributions, and further fused with the global sentiment features in the final prediction. We also add facial sentiment features to the final classification to improve prediction results.

3 Method

The overall structure of our end-to-end network is illustrated in Fig. 1. Specifically, we use two backbone convolutional neural networks to extract global sentiment features from the whole image and the facial sentiment features from the human faces, and utilize object detection methods to get region proposals as another input. In our Sentiment Region Attention (SRA) module, we compute the contribution of each local region with respect to the global sentiment feature and reweigh the region features based on their corresponding estimated contributions. The final features used in the classifier are obtained by concatenating the global sentiment features, the weighted region object features and the facial sentiment features.

3.1 Sentiment Region Attention Module

Local regions are helpful to the prediction of image sentiment. As shown in Fig. 2, the sentiment of images is concentrated in some local regions. Existing works studying the representation and extraction of local region information have not well modeled the contribution of each region to global sentiment. Therefore, inspired by the wide and successful use of attention mechanism in various tasks e.g. machine translation [14], object detection [5], etc., we propose a Sentiment Region Attention (SRA) module to estimate contributions of different regions with respect to the global image sentiment.

For a general attention module, the inputs are a query and keys of dimension d_k, and values of dimension d_v. Dot product is used to calculate the similarity of the query and all keys. A softmax function is applied to the dot product result to obtain the weights on the values. Given a query q, all keys K and values V, the output value is obtained by weighted average over input values:

$$output = softmax(\frac{qK^T}{\sqrt{d_k}})V. \qquad (1)$$

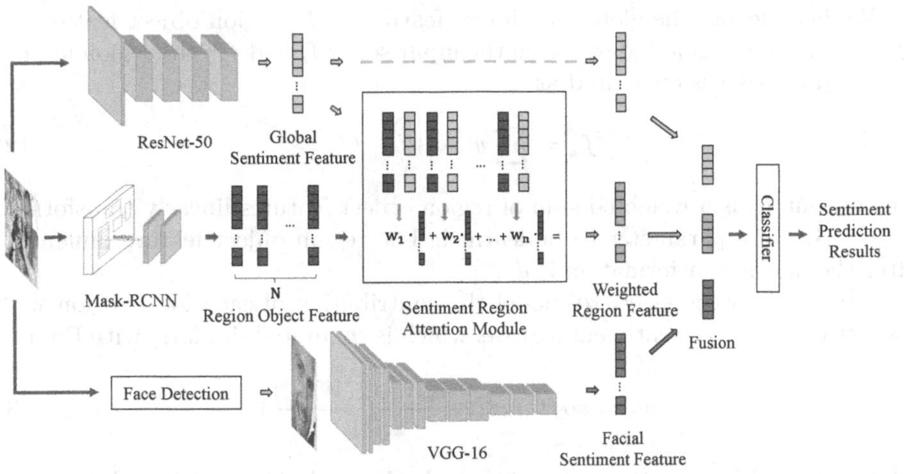

Fig. 1. The overall structure of our model for visual sentiment analysis. Give an input image, we first extract the global sentiment features of the whole image, the facial sentiment features of the human face located by a face detector, and the local region proposals along with their corresponding object features. Then, we compute the contribution of each region based on our Sentiment Region Attention (SRA) module. Finally, the region features are reweighed and further fused with the global sentiment features and the facial sentiment features to predict sentiment of the input image.

For our visual sentiment analysis task, in the SRA module we consider the contribution of each region with respect to the global image sentiment. The global sentiment feature is regarded as the query q. All the region object features are the keys K and the values V are also the region object features.

Fig. 2. Images from EmotionROI dataset [10]. The bounding boxes indicate the regions which evoke emotion reactions mostly, annotated by 15 users.

We here denote the global sentiment feature as f_s, region object features as f_o^n, and n is the region index. Given the input set of f_s and f_o^n, the region feature weighted by SRA is computed as

$$f_w = \sum w_n \cdot (W_v \cdot f_o^n). \tag{2}$$

The output f_w is a weighted sum of region object features linearly transformed by W_v. W_v is a parameter to be learned. The region object feature dimension after the linear transformation is d_v.

We use the weights w_n to model the contribution of each local region with respect to the global sentiment feature, which is computed similarly with Eq. 1 as

$$w_n = softmax(\frac{dot(W_k f_o^n, W_q f_s)}{\sqrt{d_k}}) \tag{3}$$

where W_k and W_q are the parameters to be learned. They project the original features f_s and f_o^n into subspaces to measure the sentiment contribution of each region. d_k is the feature dimension after projection.

Now we obtain one weighted region feature f_w based on the global sentiment feature and region object features. The SRA module aggregates in total N_w weighted region features by concatenation:

$$f_W = concat(f_w^1, f_w^2, ..., f_w^{N_w}) \tag{4}$$

where f_W denotes the output of our SRA module. The dimension of the output f_W is $d_v \times N_w$. We set $d_v \times N_w$ equal to the dimension of global sentiment feature d_s, which means that d_v is set as $\frac{d_s}{N_w}$.

3.2 Facial Sentiment Feature Extraction

Humans in images can evoke more emotional reactions of the viewers, since they are more likely to feel empathy with humans in images. We believe that the image sentiment is strongly associated with humans, especially their faces, in the image if they appear. Some examples are shown in Fig. 3. So we propose to extract facial sentiment features and fuse them with the global sentiment features and weighted region features to the final prediction.

We first locate the human faces appearing in the image by a face detector. Given an image as input, from the face detector, we get the bounding boxes of faces and use the largest one to extract facial sentiment features based on a CNN network. If there are no faces in the image, we pad the features with zeros.

3.3 Sentiment Prediction

Our network contains five parts: global sentiment feature extraction, facial sentiment features extraction, region object feature extraction, SRA module and sentiment classifier. The structure of our network is shown in Fig. 1.

Fig. 3. Images with different sentiment from FI dataset [19]. As we can see, human faces are usually closely associated with the image sentiment.

First, we extract region object features, global sentiment features and facial sentiment features. Given an input image, we extract N region proposals and their object features using Mask R-CNN [3]. We use outputs of the fully connected layer after ROIAlign as object features for each region. In another two branches, ResNet-50 [4] is used to extract the global sentiment features from the whole image, and VGG-16 [12] is used to extract the facial sentiment features from the human face which is located by a face detector.

We then use the proposed SRA module to calculate the weighted region features, which are further concatenated with the global sentiment features and the facial sentiment features. The obtained sentiment features F_S are finally used to predict the image sentiment. The C-categories classifier is built using fully connected layers. The sentiment score is computed as

$$score(y_i = c|F_S, W) = softmax(W^T F_S) \tag{5}$$

where y_i is the predicted sentiment. W is the set of model parameters to be learned. We employ the negative log likelihood to compute the loss:

$$loss = -p(y_i = c)log(score(y_i = c|F_S, W)). \tag{6}$$

4 Experiments

4.1 Datasets

Our experiments are conducted on public datasets including Flickr and Instagram (FI) [19], ArtPhoto [9] and EmotionROI [10]. FI dataset is currently the largest well-labeled dataset, collected by querying with eight sentiment categories (i.e. amusement, awe, anger, disgust, fear, sadness, excitement and contentment) as keywords from social website. A group of 225 Amazon Mechanical

Turk (AMT) participants were asked to label the images. FI dataset contains 23,308 images which receive at least three agreements in the labeling stage. ArtPhoto dataset contains 806 artistic photographs from a photo sharing site and the ground truth labels for eight categories provided by the owner of each image. EmotionROI dataset is collected from Flickr and contains 1980 images with six categories (i.e. joy, surprise, fear, sad, disgust, anger).

In our experiment, similar to previous works [13,16], we focus on the binary sentiment prediction, and thus we convert the eight sentiment categories in FI and ArtPhoto dataset and the six sentiment categories in EmotionROI dataset into positive and negative categories according to their sentiment semantics. In detail, we set amusement, awe, contentment and excitement, joy, surprise as positive sentiments, and anger, fear, sadness (sad) and disgust as negative sentiments.

4.2 Implementation Details

We use Mask R-CNN [3] which is pre-trained on MS COCO dataset [8] to extract local regions and their object features. The number of proposal regions N is set as 50. Outputs of the fully connected layer after ROIAlign are used as the region object features, whose dimension is 1024. We also add the normalized coordinates of the upper left corner and the normalized area (divided by length and width of the image) into the region object feature. We use Dlib[1] to locate human faces in images and use the largest face to extract facial sentiment features. So, the inputs of our network include an image, its corresponding region object features, and the bounding box of the largest human face in it. The backbone networks used for extracting the global sentiment features and facial sentiment features are ResNet-50 [4] and VGG-16 [12], respectively. We first initialize the networks with weights pre-trained on ImageNet [2]. We also remove the fully connected layer of them for classification, which is used to extract sentiment features. The dimension of the global sentiment feature d_s is 2048 and the dimension of the facial sentiment feature d_f is 512. In the Sentiment Region Attention (SRA) module, we set $d_k = 64$, $N_w = 16$, and $d_v = 2048/16 = 128$. The classifier contains 2 fully connected layers for predicting the sentiment. The class weights of positive samples and negative ones are inversely proportional to the corresponding sample ratio in the training set (e.g., in FI the weights are set as 1:2.43). We fine-tune all layers with Stochastic Gradient Descent (SGD). The learning rate is set as 1e-4. We use a weight decay of 2e-5 and momentum of 0.9. The total number of iterations for optimization is 30. The FI datasets are split randomly into 80% training, 5% validation and 15% testing. The ArtPhoto datasets and the EmotionROI datasets are randomly split into 80% training and 20% testing. All of our experiments are carried out on one NVIDIA GTX 1080 Ti GPU.

[1] http://dlib.net/.

4.3 Results

We compare the proposed method with several state-of-the-art algorithms for visual sentiment task, including DeepSentiBank, PCNN, Affective region discovery.

Table 1. Comparison with the state-of-art methods on visual sentiment datasets.

Method	FI	ArtPhoto	EmotionROI
DeepSentiBank [1]	61.54	68.73	70.11
PCNN [18]	75.34	70.96	73.58
Affective region discovery [16]	86.35	74.80	81.26
Ours	87.01	78.13	82.58

Fig. 4. Example results of our SRA module. We show the top weighted three regions in each image, where the colors red, blue, and green mark the sentiment related regions in the descending order. (Color figure online)

PCNN proposed by You et al. [18] is a progressive CNN architecture. DeepSentiBank [1] is a visual sentiment concept classification based on CNNs for discovering Adjective Noun Pairs (ANPs). Affective region discovery [16] ranks the affective region by its region object score and sentiment score for sentiment classification.

Table 1 shows the comparison results. Our network performs favorably against the other methods for sentiment classification since the local region information has been better used in our SRA module. We also show some qualitative results of the top weighted regions from SRA in Fig. 4. As we can see, the top weighted regions our method detect are associated with image sentiment closely.

We also conduct an ablation study in the experiment using the FI dataset, in which a number of variants of our model are compared to justify our design choices. In detail, we first use fine-tuned ResNet-50 as our baseline. And we do several experiments: (1) treating all region object features equally which are then concatenated with the global sentiment features (so the SRA Module is not used), (2) training the backbone CNN for the whole image first and then fixing its layers and training the SRA and the classifier (so the whole network is not trained in an end-to-end way), (3) only using SRA with global sentiment features and (4) only using facial sentiment features with global sentiment features. The results are shown in Table 2 (the baseline result is shown in the first row, and results for the variants (1) to (4) are shown in the second to the fifth rows of the table). These results indicate that global sentiment features, facial sentiment features and region object features all contain sentiment related cues. Our SRA module and facial sentiment features are effective for visual sentiment analysis, and the end-to-end training also brings performance improvement.

Table 2. Ablation study on FI dataset.

Method	ResNet-50	Region	End-to-End	Face	SRA	Accuracy
Baseline	w/	w/o	w/	w/o	w/o	84.95
(1) Region (equally average)	w/	w/	w/	w/o	w/o	85.26
(2) SRA (not end-to-end)	w/	w/	w/o	w/o	w/	85.68
(3) SRA (end-to-end)	w/	w/	w/	w/o	w/	86.16
(4) Face	w/	w/o	w/	w/	w/o	86.01
(5) SRA and face	w/	w/	w/	w/	w/	87.01

5 Conclusion

Visual sentiment analysis is an interesting yet challenging task, which attracts wide attention of researchers. Existing methods can not make full use of local regions for visual sentiment analysis, and in this paper, we propose a Sentiment Region Attention (SRA) module to estimate the contribution of each local region to the prediction of image sentiment with respect to the whole image and also use facial sentiment features to help the prediction. The SRA module is embedded into the framework effectively and thus our model can predict the image sentiment in an end-to-end way. Experimental results demonstrate the effectiveness of the proposed method.

Acknowledgement. This work is funded by the National Key Research and Development Plan (No. 2016YFC0801002) and National Natural Science Foundation of China (No. 61806016).

References

1. Chen, T., Borth, D., Darrell, T., Chang, S.F.: DeepSentiBank: visual sentiment concept classification with deep convolutional neural networks. arXiv preprint arXiv:1410.8586 (2014)
2. Deng, J., Dong, W., Socher, R., Li, L.J., Li, K., Li, F.F.: ImageNet: a large-scale hierarchical image database. In: IEEE Conference on Computer Vision and Pattern Recognition, pp. 248–255 (2009)
3. He, K., Gkioxari, G., Dollár, P., Girshick, R.: Mask R-CNN. In: IEEE International Conference on Computer Vision, pp. 2961–2969 (2017)
4. He, K., Zhang, X., Ren, S., Sun, J.: Deep residual learning for image recognition. In: IEEE Conference on Computer Vision and Pattern Recognition, pp. 770–778 (2016)
5. Hu, H., Gu, J., Zhang, Z., Dai, J., Wei, Y.: Relation networks for object detection. In: IEEE Conference on Computer Vision and Pattern Recognition, pp. 3588–3597 (2018)
6. Lang, P.J.: A bio-informational theory of emotional imagery. Psychophysiology **16**(6), 495–512 (1979)
7. Lang, P.J., Bradley, M.M., Cuthbert, B.N.: Emotion, motivation, and anxiety: brain mechanisms and psychophysiology. Biol. Psychiatry **44**(12), 1248–1263 (1998)
8. Lin, T.-Y., et al.: Microsoft COCO: common objects in context. In: Fleet, D., Pajdla, T., Schiele, B., Tuytelaars, T. (eds.) ECCV 2014. LNCS, vol. 8693, pp. 740–755. Springer, Cham (2014). https://doi.org/10.1007/978-3-319-10602-1_48
9. Machajdik, J., Hanbury, A.: Affective image classification using features inspired by psychology and art theory. In: Proceedings of the 18th ACM International Conference on Multimedia, pp. 83–92 (2010)
10. Peng, K.C., Sadovnik, A., Gallagher, A., Chen, T.: Where do emotions come from? Predicting the emotion stimuli map. In: 2016 IEEE International Conference on Image Processing (ICIP), pp. 614–618 (2016)
11. Rao, T., Li, X., Zhang, H., Xu, M.: Multi-level region-based convolutional neural network for image emotion classification. Neurocomputing **333**, 429–439 (2019)
12. Simonyan, K., Zisserman, A.: Very deep convolutional networks for large-scale image recognition. arXiv preprint arXiv:1409.1556 (2014)
13. Song, K., Yao, T., Ling, Q., Mei, T.: Boosting image sentiment analysis with visual attention. Neurocomputing **312**, 218–228 (2018)
14. Vaswani, A., et al.: Attention is all you need. In: Advances in Neural Information Processing Systems, pp. 5998–6008 (2017)
15. Yang, J., She, D., Lai, Y.K., Rosin, P.L., Yang, M.H.: Weakly supervised coupled networks for visual sentiment analysis. In: IEEE Conference on Computer Vision and Pattern Recognition, pp. 7584–7592 (2018)
16. Yang, J., She, D., Sun, M., Cheng, M.M., Rosin, P.L., Wang, L.: Visual sentiment prediction based on automatic discovery of affective regions. IEEE Trans. Multimedia **20**(9), 2513–2525 (2018)
17. You, Q., Jin, H., Luo, J.: Visual sentiment analysis by attending on local image regions. In: Thirty-First AAAI Conference on Artificial Intelligence, pp. 231–237 (2017)
18. You, Q., Luo, J., Jin, H., Yang, J.: Robust image sentiment analysis using progressively trained and domain transferred deep networks. In: Twenty-Ninth AAAI Conference on Artificial Intelligence, pp. 381–388 (2015)

19. You, Q., Luo, J., Jin, H., Yang, J.: Building a large scale dataset for image emotion recognition: the fine print and the benchmark. In: Thirtieth AAAI Conference on Artificial Intelligence, pp. 308–314 (2016)
20. Zhao, S., Gao, Y., Jiang, X., Yao, H., Chua, T.S., Sun, X.: Exploring principles-of-art features for image emotion recognition. In: Proceedings of the 22nd ACM International Conference on Multimedia, pp. 47–56 (2014)
21. Zhao, S., Yao, H., Gao, Y., Ding, G., Chua, T.S.: Predicting personalized image emotion perceptions in social networks. IEEE Trans. Affect. Comput. **9**(4), 526–540 (2016)
22. Zhao, S., et al.: Predicting personalized emotion perceptions of social images. In: Proceedings of the 24th ACM International Conference on Multimedia, pp. 1385–1394 (2016)

Oral Session 6A: Image Processing

Prediction-Error Value Ordering for High-Fidelity Reversible Data Hiding

Tong Zhang[1], Xiaolong Li[2], Wenfa Qi[1], and Zongming Guo[1](✉)

[1] Wangxuan Institue of Compuer Technology, Peking University, Beijing 100871, China
{zhangtong1204,qiwenfa,guozongming}@pku.edu.cn

[2] Institute of Information Science, Beijing Jiaotong University, Beijing 100044, China
lixl@bjtu.edu.cn

Abstract. Prediction-error expansion (PEE) is the most widely utilized reversible data hiding (RDH) technique. However, the performance of PEE is far from optimal since the correlations among prediction-errors are not fully exploited. Then, to enhance the embedding performance of PEE, a new RDH method named prediction-error value ordering (PEVO) is proposed in this paper. The main idea of PEVO is to exploit the inter-correlations of prediction-errors by combining PEE with the recent RDH technique of pixel value ordering. Specifically, the prediction-errors within an image block are first sorted, and then the maximum and minimum prediction-errors of the block are predicted and modified for data embedding. By the proposed approach, the image redundancy is better exploited and promising embedding performance is achieved. Experimental results demonstrate that the proposed PEVO embedding method is better than the PEE-based ones and some other state-of-the-art works.

Keywords: Reversible data hiding · Prediction-error expansion · Prediction-error value ordering

1 Introduction

As the rapid development of the Internet and multimedia technique, the security of the transmitted information becomes a major concern in the digital age. Data hiding is the technique that can embed secret message into the multimedia data for copyright protection, secret communication, and so on. Reversible data hiding (RDH) is an important branch of this literature [1]. By RDH, the cover medium can be restored without any distortion after data extraction. Due to its special characteristic, RDH has been widely applied in sensitive scenes including medical, military image processing and remote sensing, etc.

This work was supported by the National R&D project of China under contract No. 2018YFB0803702 and the National Natural Science Foundation of China (Nos. 61972031 and U1636206).

Y. M. Ro et al. (Eds.): MMM 2020, LNCS 11961, pp. 317–328, 2020.
https://doi.org/10.1007/978-3-030-37731-1_26

Many RDH methods have been proposed in recent years, and they are mainly based on lossless compression, difference expansion (DE), histogram shifting (HS), and prediction-error expansion (PEE). The lossless compression based method is proposed at the early stage, and its main idea is to losslessly compress a feature set of the cover image to produce vacant space for data embedding. The DE technique is proposed in [2], in which every two neighboring pixels are paired and then the difference between them is expanded to embed data. The HS method is firstly proposed by Ni *et al.* in [3]. In this method, the pixel intensity histogram of the cover image is first generated and then the data embedding is realized by modifying the generated histogram. To further improve the embedding performance, PEE is proposed in [4] by replacing the pixel intensity histogram with the prediction-error histogram (PEH). The PEH is generated by counting the frequency of prediction-errors and its shape of the distribution is like a Laplace distribution which is suitable for reversible embedding. The local correlation of neighboring pixels is exploited in PEE, and thus better embedding performance is achieved compared with DE and HS.

Following PEE, many subsequent works have been proposed so far. Some of them focus on the investigation of advanced predictors that aims to generate more sharply distributed PEH [5–8]. Other approaches are also proposed including double-layered embedding [9], adaptive expansion-bin-selection [10–12], high dimensional histogram modification [13,14], and multiple histograms modification [15], etc.

Although efficient, the performance of PEE-based methods is far from optimal. For the conventional PEE such as [9,11], the prediction-errors are processed independently, so that the correlations among them are not fully utilized. On the other hand, for the two-dimensional (2D) histogram modification based methods such as pairwise PEE [13,14], only the correlations between two adjacent prediction-errors are considered, and the histogram modification manner is heuristically designed without considering the specific image content.

In this paper, to enhance the embedding performance of PEE, inspired by the recent RDH technique of pixel value ordering (PVO) [5], a new method named prediction-error value ordering (PEVO) is proposed. Instead of processing the prediction-errors independently in the conventional PEE, the inter-correlations of prediction-errors are considered and utilized in the proposed method. First, the cover image is divided into non-overlapping equal-sized blocks, and the prediction-errors within each block are sorted according to their values. After that, for each selected block, the largest (smallest) prediction-error is predicted by the second largest (smallest) prediction-error and then modified for data embedding. Here, the complexity of each block is first computed and only the smooth ones (i.e., the ones with a complexity less than a given threshold) are utilized for data embedding. The experimental results show that the proposed PEVO embedding method has better marked image quality than the PEE-based ones including the conventional PEE [11] and pairwise PEE [13], and it also outperforms some other state-of-the-art works [16,17].

The remainder of this paper is organized as follows. The related works are introduced in Sect. 2. The details of the proposed method are given in Sect. 3. The experimental results and comparisons with other methods are shown in Sect. 4. Finally, the paper is concluded in Sect. 5.

2 Related Works

The proposed method combines PEE with PVO. In this section, the PEE-based embedding methods are first introduced and then the PVO-based methods are presented briefly.

2.1 PEE

We first review the main steps of the conventional PEE. The first step is to predict the cover pixels to obtain the prediction-error sequence. Under the raster-scan order, the cover pixels are collected as a sequence consisting of N pixels: $(x_1, ..., x_N)$. A predictor is then employed to predict each pixel x_i based on the local content to get the predicted value $\widehat{x}_i$, and the prediction-error is defined as $e_i = x_i - \widehat{x}_i$. By counting the frequency of prediction-errors, the PEH is generated. Next, the reversible data embedding is realized by modifying the generated PEH. In Sachnev *et al.*'s method [9], the highest two histogram bins are selected as the expansion bins to maximum the embedding capacity. In Wang *et al.*'s method [11], the expansion bins are adaptively determined to improve the embedding performance. Specifically, a pair of bins (a, b) with $a < b$ are selected for expansion embedding, and the bins between a and b remain unchanged, while the other bins are shifted to create vacancy to ensure the reversibility. That is, for a prediction-error e_i, it is modified to $\widetilde{e}_i$ by

$$\widetilde{e}_i = \begin{cases} e_i - 1, & \text{if } e_i < a \\ e_i - m, & \text{if } e_i = a \\ e_i, & \text{if } a < e_i < b \\ e_i + m, & \text{if } e_i = b \\ e_i + 1, & \text{if } e_i > b \end{cases} \tag{1}$$

where $m \in \{0, 1\}$ is the to-be-embedded binary bit. Finally, x_i is changed to $\widehat{x}_i + \widetilde{e}_i$ to derive the marked pixel.

By pairing every two adjacent prediction-errors, the so-called pairwise PEE is proposed in [13]. The 2D histogram of the prediction-error pair is first generated, and then the secret data is embedded into the cover image by modifying the generated 2D histogram based on a specifically designed 2D mapping.

2.2 PVO

In PVO [5], the cover image is first divided into non-overlapping equal-sized blocks. For each block with n pixels, sort the pixel values $(x_1, ..., x_n)$ to get

$x_{\sigma(1)} \leq ... \leq x_{\sigma(n)}$, where $\sigma : \{1, ..., n\} \rightarrow \{1, ..., n\}$ is the unique one-to-one mapping such that $\sigma(i) < \sigma(j)$ if $x_{\sigma(i)} = x_{\sigma(j)}$ and $i < j$. Then, the second largest value $x_{\sigma(n-1)}$ is used to predict the maximum $x_{\sigma(n)}$, and the corresponding prediction-error is $e_{\max} = x_{\sigma(n)} - x_{\sigma(n-1)}$. Notice that, $e_{\max}$ is always non-negative, and thus the PEH of $e_{\max}$ is defined within the interval $[0, \infty)$. Since the highest bin for this PEH is typically 1, the bin 1 is expanded to embed data, the bin 0 is unmodified, while the other bins are simply shifted for reversibility. The minimum of each block is also utilized for data embedding in PVO, and the similar embedding process is omitted here.

As an extension of PVO, the improved PVO (IPVO) proposed in [18] redefines the prediction-error by considering the spatial order between the top two largest pixels. Specifically, the new prediction-error is defined as $e_{\max} = x_u - x_v$, where $u = \min(\sigma(n-1), \sigma(n))$ and $v = \max(\sigma(n-1), \sigma(n))$. Here, the new defined prediction-error $e_{\max}$ takes value in $(-\infty, \infty)$, which is similar to the histogram of the conventional PEE. Then, the bins 0 and 1 are expanded for reversible embedding. Different from PVO, more smooth pixel blocks can be utilized by IPVO to embed data. Also, the minimum of each block is taken for data embedding in IPVO.

Pairwise PVO [17] extends PVO into 2D form by considering a prediction-error pair within a block. Using the third largest value $x_{\sigma(n-2)}$, the two prediction-errors $e^1_{\max}$ and $e^2_{\max}$ are defined as $e^1_{\max} = x_u - x_{\sigma(n-2)}$ and $e^2_{\max} = x_v - x_{\sigma(n-2)}$, where (u, v) is defined above in IPVO. Then, based on the 2D PEH of $(e^1_{\max}, e^2_{\max})$, a histogram modification rule (i.e., a 2D mapping) is designed to embed data. This method is experimentally verified better than PVO and IPVO.

Besides, many improved PVO-based methods are recently proposed based on involving more embedding pixels per block [18], dynamic block partition [21], pixel-wise embedding [20], multistage blocking strategy [22], and so on.

3 Proposed Method

3.1 PEVO

The main idea of PEVO is to exploit the inter-correlations of prediction-errors by combining PEE with PVO. For this purpose, various PVO-based methods can be applied in the proposed method. For clarity, we now just describe in detail the combination with the original PVO [5] as an example here.

First, the cover image is divided into non-overlapping blocks with size $n_1 \times n_2$. Here, to ensure the prediction is consistent at the decoder end, double-layered embedding manner is adopted to partition the cover pixels into two sets, i.e., the blank set and the shadow set (see Fig. 1 for an illustration). We first predict and modify the pixels in the blank set (i.e., first-layer embedding), and then implement the same operation on the shadow set (i.e., second-layer embedding). Each of the embedding layer is embedded with half of the given payload, where the payload consists of the secret data and the auxiliary information for blind extraction. Specifically, for each blank pixel $x_{i,j}$ within a block, based on its four

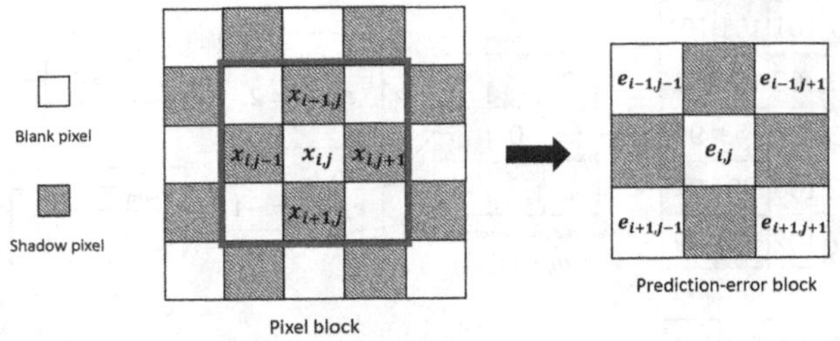

Fig. 1. A 3×3 sized pixel block. Within this block, five blank prediction-errors $\{e_{i-1,j-1}, e_{i-1,j+1}, e_{i,j}, e_{i+1,j-1}, e_{i+1,j+1}\}$ are generated.

neighboring pixels, the rhombus prediction is performed to derive its prediction denoted $\widehat{x}_{i,j}$ (see Fig. 1 for an illustration). The corresponding prediction-error is $e_{i,j} = x_{i,j} - \widehat{x}_{i,j}$.

Then, the derived blank prediction-errors within the block are sorted. The second largest prediction-error denoted e_{i_1,j_1} is used to predict the largest prediction-error denoted $e_{i',j'}$. The corresponding re-computed prediction-error is defined as $e_{\max} = e_{i',j'} - e_{i_1,j_1}$. Similarly, the re-computed prediction-error for the minimum is obtained by $e_{\min} = e_{i'',j''} - e_{i_2,j_2}$, where e_{i_2,j_2} is the second smallest prediction-error and $e_{i'',j''}$ is the smallest prediction-error.

The next steps are the same as PVO, for the histogram of $e_{\max}$ ($e_{\min}$), the bin 1 (-1) is expanded for embedding data, the bin 0 is unchanged, while the other bins are shifted to create vacant space. That is to say, the above defined $e_{\max}$ ($e_{\min}$) will be modified according to the embedding rule of PVO to derive $\widetilde{e}_{\max}$ ($\widetilde{e}_{\min}$). After that, the largest prediction-error $e_{i',j'}$ is modified as $\widetilde{e}_{i',j'} = e_{i_1,j_1} + \widetilde{e}_{\max}$, and the smallest prediction-error $e_{i'',j''}$ is modified as $\widetilde{e}_{i'',j''} = e_{i_2,j_2} + \widetilde{e}_{\min}$. Finally, the marked values for $x_{i',j'}$ and $x_{i'',j''}$ are determined as $\widehat{x}_{i',j'} + \widetilde{e}_{i',j'}$ and $\widehat{x}_{i'',j''} + \widetilde{e}_{i'',j''}$, respectively. Here, the other blank pixels $x_{i,j}$ in the block with $(i,j) \notin \{(i',j'),(i'',j'')\}$ are just unchanged.

For better illustration, an example of the proposed PEVO in the first-layer embedding is shown in Fig. 2. For the 3×3 sized block with highlighted border, by performing rhombus prediction on the blank pixels in the block, five prediction-errors scanned with the raster-scan order are obtained as $(0, 3, 0, 2, -1)$. Then, these prediction-errors are sorted to get the maximum $e_{i',j'} = 3$ and the second largest value $e_{i_1,j_1} = 2$, the minimum $e_{i'',j''} = -1$ and the second smallest value $e_{i_2,j_2} = 0$, and thus $e_{\max} = 1$ and $e_{\min} = -1$. Next, take the maximum for example, $e_{\max}$ is expanded to $\widetilde{e}_{\max} = 2$ when embedding data bit "1", and the largest prediction-error $e_{i',j'}$ is modified to $\widetilde{e}_{i',j'} = e_{i_1,j_1} + \widetilde{e}_{\max} = 4$. Finally, the marked value of $x_{i',j'}$ is obtained as $\widehat{x}_{i',j'} + \widetilde{e}_{i',j'} = 104$.

Moreover, to further improve the embedding performance, the noise level for each block is computed to distinguish the smooth blocks and the textured ones. For PEVO, the noise level for first-layer embedding is computed by considering a context as shown in Fig. 3, and it is defined as the sum of three parts:

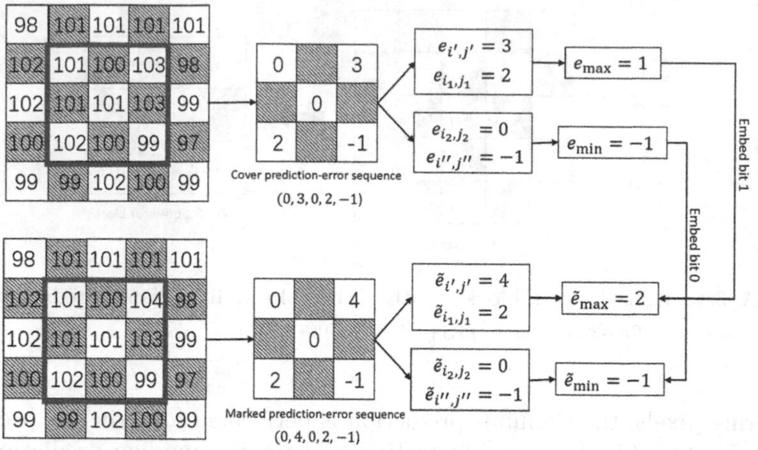

Fig. 2. Example of the proposed PEVO for a 3 × 3 sized block, where the largest and smallest prediction-errors are marked in red and blue, respectively. Here, only the first-layer embedding for blank pixels is shown for illustration. (Color figure online)

the diagonal absolute difference between the shadow values, the vertical and horizontal absolute difference between every consecutive pixels in the context. Then, for a given threshold T, only the blocks with noise level less than T are utilized for data embedding, and the other blocks are just skipped and unchanged. Besides, the parameters of block size n_1 and n_2 are also adaptively determined according to the embedding payload. In this way, the optimal parameters are obtained by traversing all the combinations of T ($0 \leq T \leq 1024$), n_1 and n_2 ($n_1, n_2 \in \{2, 3, 4, 5\}$ with $n_1 \times n_2 \geq 6$) to minimize the embedding distortion.

After the first-layer embedding, the second-layer embedding is implemented in a similar way. Therefore, for an image block, the proposed PEVO embedding method can embed at most four bits into each block by modifying four pixels.

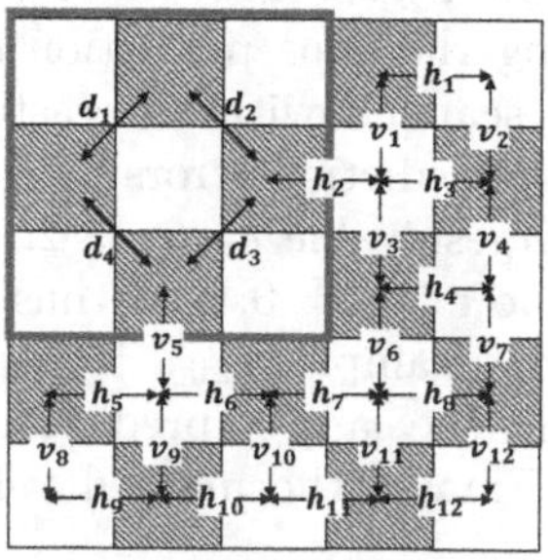

Fig. 3. A 3 × 3 sized block (i.e., the block with highlighted border) with its context (i.e., the other 16 pixels) to compute its noise level for first-layer embedding, where its noise level is defined as $\sum_{i=1}^{4} d_i + \sum_{j=1}^{12} v_j + \sum_{k=1}^{12} h_k$.

3.2 Data Embedding and Extraction Procedures

To restore the cover image blindly, some auxiliary information needs to be embedded along with the secret message. To address the overflow and underflow problem, the cover pixels whose values are 0 and 255 are modified to 1 and 254 in advance, and a location map (LM) is constructed to record those modifications. Specifically, if the pixel value is 0 or 255, then add a bit 1 in LM, and if the pixels value is 1 or 254, then add a bit 0 in LM. Finally, LM is compressed losslessly using arithmetic coding to get the compressed LM (CLM), and its length is denoted as S_{CLM}. In this way, for example, for a 512×512 sized cover image, the auxiliary information includes

- block size parameters n_1 and n_2 (4 bits),
- noise level threshold T (10 bits),
- the index of the last modified block (16 bits),
- location map (S_{CLM} bits),
- the value of S_{CLM} (18 bits).

The data embedding process is briefly described as follows. First, perform the rhombus predictor on the blank pixels to get the prediction-errors. Then, for each block, calculate its noise level. Next, for the block with noise level less than T, implement the data embedding process for blank pixels as introduced above. Finally, repeat the above steps for shadow pixels in the second-layer embedding. The extraction process is in the inverse order of the embedding process. We first implement the data extraction and cover pixels restoration for shadow pixels. Then, repeat the same process for blank pixels to derive the embedded secret message and the cover image.

Notice that, the proposed PEVO embedding method can be combined with various PVO-based methods. That is to say, after generating the prediction-errors, the corresponding PVO-based method can be implemented in a double-layered way. Here, we just introduce the PEVO combined with the original PVO [5]. We also implement the PEVO combined with IPVO [18] and pairwise PVO [17], respectively. The detailed implementation process is omitted here for simplicity, and we just show the embedding results comparison for PEVO combined with these three PVO-based methods in Fig. 4. The experiment result proves that, the embedding performance is better if a better PVO-based method is applied with the proposed PEVO. It can be seen that, according to this figure, for images Lena and Airplane, the PEVO with pairwise PVO outperforms the PEVO combined with the other two methods whatever the embedding capacity is. Then, in the next section, pairwise PVO is applied to the proposed PEVO for performance comparison.

4 Experimental Results

In this section, we evaluate the performance of the proposed method with the prior arts of pairwise PVO [17], pairwise PEE [13], multiple HS [11] and

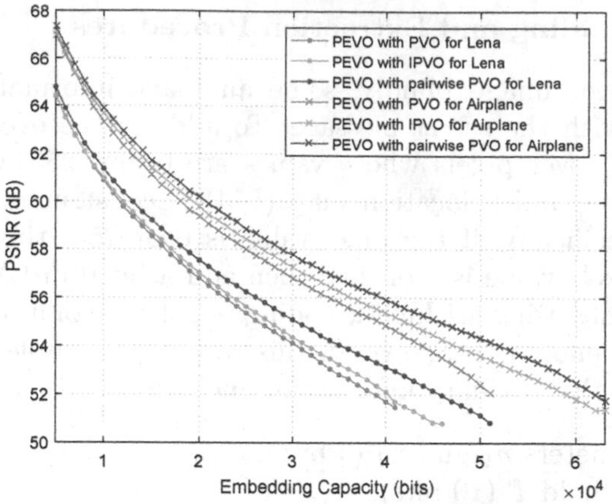

Fig. 4. Performance comparison between the PEVO with PVO [5], the PEVO with IPVO [18] and the PEVO with pairwise PVO [17], for the images Lena and Airplane.

skewed HS [16]. Eight standard 512 × 512 sized gray-scale images including Lena, Baboon, Airplane, Barbara, Lake, Boat, Elaine and Peppers are used in the experiment. The distortion-capacity curve is plotted in Fig. 5, in which the embedding capacity is ranged from 5,000 bits to the maximum embedding capacity that PEVO can provides, and the step size is set as 1,000 bits. One can see that the proposed method can yield the best performance among these methods for most cases. For better illustration, the performance comparisons when the embedding capacity is 10,000 and 20,000 bits are shown in Table 1.

Pairwise PVO is the state-of-the-art technique among PVO-based methods, in which the PVO embedding is represented in a high-dimensional form. In pairwise PVO, the spatial and value information of the top two largest pixels of each block are considered, and a reversible 2D mapping is designed for data embedding. Referring to Fig. 5, the proposed method has better marked image quality for all the embedding capacities and images. The average PSNR value of the proposed method is 0.91 dB higher that of pairwise PVO when the embedding capacity is 10,000 bits, and 0.73 dB higher when the embedding capacity is 20,000 bits.

Pairwise PEE is the PEE technique that implements on the 2D PEH. A sequence of prediction-error pairs is generated by considering every adjacent prediction-errors as a unit. Then the pairwise modification mechanism is employed for data embedding. According to Fig. 5, the proposed method can yield a higher PSNR for most cases. However, for some test images with high embedding capacity, pairwise PEE outperforms the proposed one, e.g., for the image Airplane with an embedding capacity larger than 25,000 bits. Actually, the advantage of the proposed method is mainly in the cases of moderate capacity. In general, the proposed one is better than pairwise PEE, and the average

PSNR gain is 1.31 and 1.11 dB for an embedding capacity of 10,000 and 20,000 bits, respectively.

Multiple HS is a state-of-the-art PEE-based method. In this method, multiple peak and zero bins of the generated PEH are selected for expansion embedding. Moreover, the genetic algorithm is utilized to determine the nearly optimal expansion bins for performance optimization. According to Fig. 5, the proposed method has better embedding performance for most cases, but for some images such as Baboon and Airplane, the PSNR of our method is lower than that of multiple HS when the embedding capacity is high. Generally, according to Table 1, it can be seen that, compared with multiple HS, our improvement is 1.51 and 0.99 dB for the embedding capacity of 10,000 and 20,00 bits, respectively.

Skewed HS is the most recent PEE-based method. The PEH of the past PEE-based methods is typically symmetrically distributed, but in skewed HS, a pair of extreme predictors are employed to generate two skewed histograms where the distribution shape is asymmetrical and the bins are concentrated on one side. The benefit of the skewed histogram is that it can reduce the number of shifted pixels to decrease the embedding distortion. Referring to Fig. 5, the proposed method is better than skewed HS for most test images. However, for example, for the image Baboon, skewed HS outperforms the proposed PEVO when the embedding capacity is larger than 10,000 bits. The reason is that, the image Baboon is very textured, while the utilization of skewed histograms has the advantage of reducing the distortion caused by shifted bins. Generally, for an embedding capacity of 10,000 and 20,00 bits, the average PSNR gains of the proposed PEVO compared with skewed HS are 1.08 and 0.85 dB, respectively.

Table 1. Comparison of PSNR (in dB) between the proposed method and pairwise PVO [17], pairwise PEE [13], multiple HS [11] and skewed HS [16] for the embedding capacity of 10,000 bits and 20,000 bits

Image	EC = 10,000 bits					EC = 20,000 bits				
	[17]	[13]	[11]	[16]	Proposed	[17]	[13]	[11]	[16]	Proposed
Lena	60.41	59.77	60.11	59.92	61.34	56.69	56.29	56.60	56.67	57.54
Baboon	54.41	55.23	55.09	55.99	56.03	–	–	–	–	–
Airplane	62.85	63.78	61.96	63.66	63.89	59.11	60.16	59.49	60.12	60.18
Barbara	60.40	59.49	60.67	59.95	61.42	56.35	56.25	57.10	56.52	57.55
Lake	59.28	58.67	57.37	58.24	59.81	54.37	53.76	53.14	53.67	54.40
Boat	58.06	57.56	57.43	57.67	58.67	53.70	53.37	53.61	53.74	54.52
Elaine	57.63	58.10	56.63	58.33	58.70	53.02	52.92	52.21	53.11	53.60
Peppers	59.07	56.25	58.03	56.93	59.52	55.02	52.86	54.32	53.59	55.60
Average	**59.01**	**58.61**	**58.41**	**58.84**	**59.92**	**55.47**	**55.09**	**55.21**	**55.35**	**56.20**

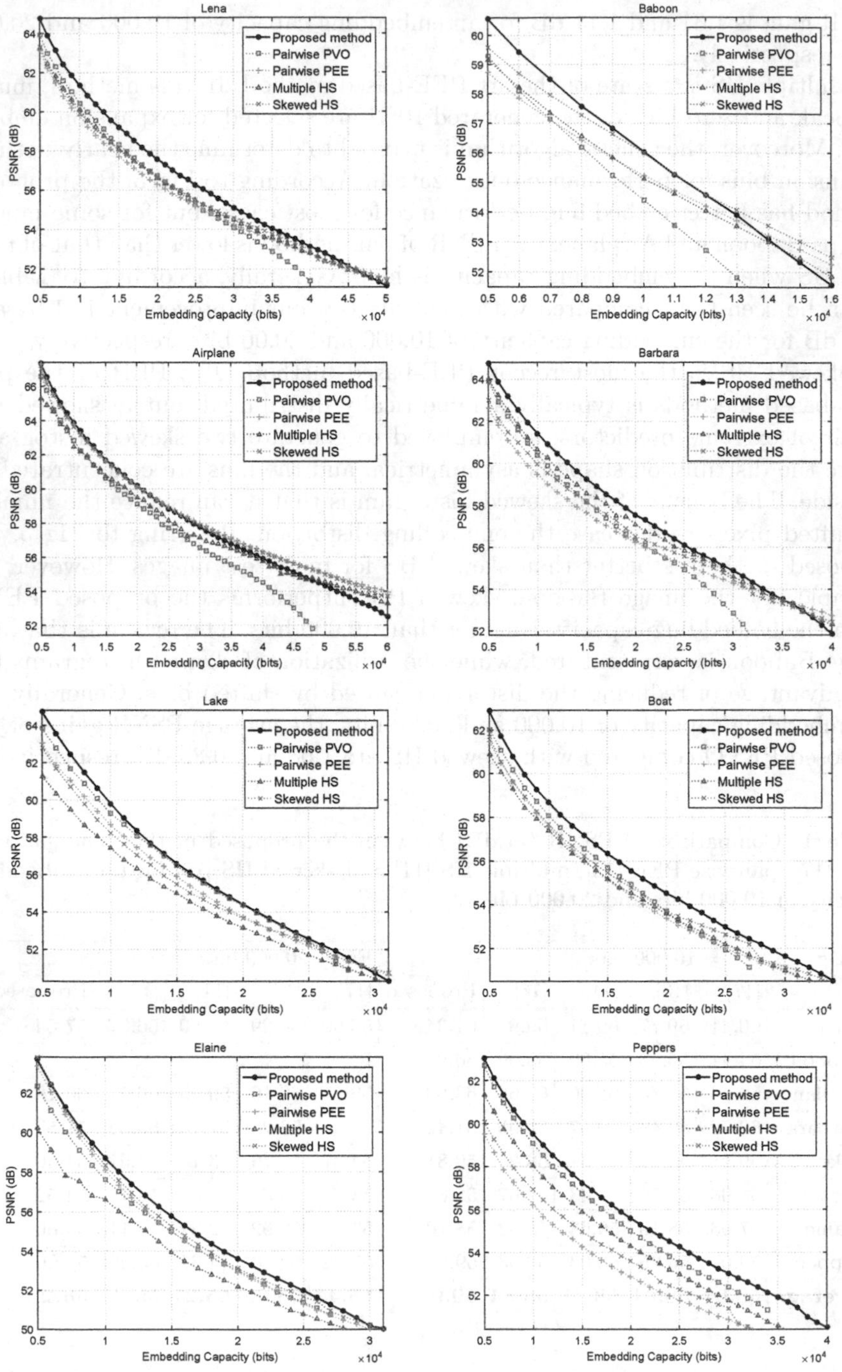

Fig. 5. Performance comparison between the proposed method and pairwise PVO [17], pairwise PEE [13], multiple HS [11] and skewed HS [16].

5 Conclusions

In this paper, a high-fidelity RDH method named PEVO is proposed. The proposed method is the first attempt to combine the traditional PEE with the PVO technique. The cover image is divided into blocks and the correlations among the local prediction-errors are considered. For each block, the prediction-errors are sorted, and then the maximum and minimum are predicted and modified to embed data. The experiment results show that the proposed method outperforms the PVO-based method like pairwise PVO [17] in terms of embedding capacity and marked image quality. It is also demonstrated that PEVO outperforms the PEE-based methods [11,13,16] for moderate embedding capacity. In the further, we plan to optimize the parameters selection mechanism and improve the embedding performance for the cases of high embedding capacity.

References

1. Shi, Y.Q., Li, X., Zhang, X., Wu, H.T., Ma, B.: Reversible data hiding: advances in the past two decades. IEEE Access **4**, 3210–3237 (2016)
2. Tian, J.: Reversible data embedding using a difference expansion. IEEE Trans. Circuits Syst. Video Technol. **13**(8), 890–896 (2003)
3. Ni, Z., Shi, Y.Q., Ansari, N., Su, W.: Reversible data hiding. IEEE Trans. Circuits Syst. Video Technol. **16**(3), 354–362 (2006)
4. Thodi, D.M., Rodríguez, J.J.: Expansion embedding techniques for reversible watermarking. IEEE Trans. Image Process. **16**(3), 721–730 (2007)
5. Li, X., Li, J., Li, B., Yang, B.: High-fidelity reversible data hiding scheme based on pixel-value-ordering and prediction-error expansion. Sig. Process. **93**(1), 198–205 (2013)
6. Dragoi, I.C., Coltuc, D.: Local-prediction-based difference expansion reversible watermarking. IEEE Trans. Image Process. **23**(4), 1779–1790 (2014)
7. Ma, B., Shi, Y.Q.: A reversible data hiding scheme based on code division multiplexing. IEEE Trans. Inf. Forensics Secur. **11**(9), 1914–1927 (2016)
8. Chen, H., Ni, J., Hong, W., Chen, T.S.: High-fidelity reversible data hiding using directionally enclosed prediction. IEEE Signal Process. Lett. **24**(5), 574–578 (2017)
9. Sachnev, V., Kim, H.J., Nam, J., Suresh, S., Shi, Y.Q.: Reversible watermarking algorithm using sorting and prediction. IEEE Trans. Circuits Syst. Video Technol. **19**(7), 989–999 (2009)
10. Hwang, H.J., Kim, H.J., Sachnev, V., Joo, S.H.: Reversible watermarking method using optimal histogram pair shifting based on prediction and sorting. TIIS **4**(4), 655–670 (2010)
11. Wang, J., Ni, J., Zhang, X., Shi, Y.Q.: Rate and distortion optimization for reversible data hiding using multiple histogram shifting. IEEE Trans. Cybern. **47**(2), 315–326 (2017)
12. Coatrieux, G., Pan, W., Cuppens-Boulahia, N., Cuppens, F., Roux, C.: Reversible watermarking based on invariant image classification and dynamic histogram shifting. IEEE Trans. Inf. Forensics Secur. **8**(1), 111–120 (2013)
13. Ou, B., Li, X., Zhao, Y., Ni, R., Shi, Y.Q.: Pairwise prediction-error expansion for efficient reversible data hiding. IEEE Trans. Image Process. **22**(12), 5010–5021 (2013)

14. Dragoi, I.C., Coltuc, D.: Adaptive pairing reversible watermarking. IEEE Trans. Image Process. **25**(5), 2420–2422 (2016)
15. Li, X., Zhang, W., Gui, X., Yang, B.: Efficient reversible data hiding based on multiple histograms modification. IEEE Trans. Inf. Forensics Secur. **10**(9), 2016–2027 (2015)
16. Kim, S., Qu, X., Sachnev, V., Kim, H.J.: Skewed histogram shifting for reversible data hiding using a pair of extreme predictions. IEEE Trans. Circuits Syst. Video Technol. (2018)
17. Ou, B., Li, X., Wang, J.: High-fidelity reversible data hiding based on pixel-value-ordering and pairwise prediction-error expansion. J. Vis. Commun. Image Represent. **39**, 12–23 (2016)
18. Peng, F., Li, X., Yang, B.: Improved PVO-based reversible data hiding. Digit. Signal Proc. **25**, 255–265 (2014)
19. Ou, B., Li, X., Zhao, Y., Ni, R.: Reversible data hiding using invariant pixel-value-ordering and prediction-error expansion. Sig. Process. Image Commun. **29**(7), 760–772 (2014)
20. Qu, X., Kim, H.J.: Pixel-based pixel value ordering predictor for high-fidelity reversible data hiding. Sig. Process. **111**, 249–260 (2015)
21. Wang, X., Ding, J., Pei, Q.: A novel reversible image data hiding scheme based on pixel value ordering and dynamic pixel block partition. Inf. Sci. **310**, 16–35 (2015)
22. He, W., Cai, J., Zhou, K., Xiong, G.: Efficient PVO-based reversible data hiding using multistage blocking and prediction accuracy matrix. J. Vis. Commun. Image Represent. **46**, 58–69 (2017)
23. Weng, S., Shi, Y., Hong, W., Yao, Y.: Dynamic improved pixel value ordering reversible data hiding. Inf. Sci. **489**, 136–154 (2019)

Classroom Attention Analysis Based on Multiple Euler Angles Constraint and Head Pose Estimation

Xin Xu[1,2](✉) and Xin Teng[1]

[1] School of Computer Science and Technology, Wuhan University of Science and Technology, Wuhan 430065, China
xuxin0336@163.com
[2] Hubei Province Key Laboratory of Intelligent Information Processing and Real-Time Industrial System, Wuhan University of Science and Technology, Wuhan 430065, China

Abstract. Classroom attention analysis aims to capture rich semantic information to analyze how the students are reacting to the lecture. However, there are some challenges for constructing a uniform attention model of students in the classroom. Each student is an individual and it is hard to make a unified judgment. The orientation of the head reflects the direction of attention, but changes in posture and space can interfere with the direction of attention. Aiming to solve these, this paper proposes a scoring module for converting the head Euler angle and attention in the classroom. This module takes the head Euler angle in three directions as input, and introduces spatial information to correct the angle. The key idea of the proposed method lies in introducing the mutual constraint of multiple Euler angles with the head spatial information, aiming to make attention model less susceptible to the difference of head information. The mutual constraint of multiple Euler angles can provide more accurate head information, while the head spatial information can be utilized to correct the angle. Extensive experiments using classroom video data demonstrate that the proposed method can achieve more accurate results.

Keywords: Classroom attention analysis · Euler Angle · Head pose estimation · Scoring module

1 Introduction

With the development of informationalized classrooms, there are many classroom videos that can be used to analyze the quality of teaching in traditional education and the enthusiasm of students in the classroom. Through the assessment of the quality of these teachings, which help to support constructive concept development, allowing the teacher to be more focus to teaching the subject while working to help the students to understand the topic individually. Raca et al. [15] analyzed the student's body language, and linked the characteristics of the student and different attention instead of analyzing the individual behavior in the classroom. In order to research the attention of the classroom, Dillenbourg et al. [13] designed a classroom detection system, which

Y. M. Ro et al. (Eds.): MMM 2020, LNCS 11961, pp. 329–340, 2020.
https://doi.org/10.1007/978-3-030-37731-1_27

quantifies the estimation of body movement and the gaze direction by means of questionnaires, and then the obtained information was statistically processed. However, it is also mentioned that each student has a set of independent customary movements and postures, which cannot be easily handled uniformly. Raca et al. [14] developed a multi-camera system to observe the actions of teacher and the reactions of students in the whole classroom, which analyzes the interaction between students and teachers by getting teachers to use mobile eye trackers and students to get information through questionnaire. Qin et al. [12] analyzed the behavior of students through classroom video, including several behaviors of individual student or a group of students, and explored the relationship between these behaviors and grade. It indicated that the research will be directed toward the expression recognition and head posture. Shao et al. [20] mainly focused on teaching-related behaviors in the classroom, including standing and raising hands of the students, as well as the actions of the teachers.

However, most studies mainly analyze the behavior of students in the classroom, but the gestures and movements of the students in the classroom usually occluded resulting in incomplete information, making it difficult to judge them accurately. Relatively, the head information about students is reserved in the classroom. In order to make better use of head information, a classroom attention analysis system is proposed in our paper. Unlike static single-head pose analysis, it is a challenging problem to analyze attention through head postures in classroom scenarios due to different head information obtained by unconstrained scene, angle and position changes. In order to solve this problem, the paper proposed a scoring module to unify conversion of different students' head information. The scoring module is utilized to convert head Euler angle to score for attention analysis. Head Euler angles include pitch angle, yaw angle and rotation angle. In order to accurately analyze the head information in the classroom, the Euler angles are constrained in three directions, for the purpose of responding the change of the head angle caused by the position, the head spatial information is utilized to correct the heads information of different students. The experiments are conducted on the collected classroom video data and demonstrate that the proposed method can accurately analyze attention.

2 Related Work

Attention analysis of the classroom is based on the head pose estimation, which mainly includes three steps.

(1) Detecting the face in the classroom. Some face detection algorithms have achieved good results on public datasets, such as *single shot multibox detector* (SSD) [8], *Multi-task Cascaded Convolutional Networks* (MTCNN) [26], Faster R-CNN [17], *Single Stage Headless Face Detector* (SSH) [10]. SSD is an object detection algorithm that directly predicts the coordinates and categories of bounding boxes with no proposal. MTCNN uses a 3-layer convolutional network cascaded to obtain candidate frames and bounding box regression of these candidate frames. Faster R-CNN introduces a region recommendation network (RPN), which shares the image convolution feature with the target detection network, thus realizing the region recommendation process with almost no cost. SSH adapts multi-scales feature map detection modules for convolution layers with different network depth to improve

speed and accuracy. Since face detection is only a pre-processing stage and SSH [10] method has a good effect in our classroom scene, we directly choose this method as our first step.

(2) Estimating the head posture of the face. Recently, numerous works have developed on head pose estimation. Patacchiola et al. [11] used the AFLW dataset and trained a relatively shallow network through regression loss for in-depth research. Kumar et al. [7] proposed an improved GoogLeNet [23] structure, using the AFLW dataset to roughly train the pose estimation while working together through the key points of the face. Ranjan et al. [16] proposed a multi-task convolutional neural network for simultaneous detection of face, gender, key points and head pose. It is implemented by improving AlexNet [6] based on the R-CNN [4] method. Chang et al. [3] used a simple CNN to regress the 3D head pose and applied the head pose for face alignment. Ruiz et al. [18] introduced the method of RGB combined classification and regression constraints to predict Euler angles, which can improve the accuracy of pose estimation. Above methods are not aimed at low resolution scene, and our classroom scenarios exist a lot of the low resolution of small face, in order to solve this problem, when we input images, we will compress the images with different qualities. Images with different qualities will enable the model to learn the features under different resolutions, which can effectively overcome the problems caused by low resolution and improve the robustness of the model.

(3) Performing attention analysis on the obtained head information. Matsumoto et al. [9] described a real-time stereo face tracking and gaze detection system, which is based on the close relationship between head posture and gaze direction movement to human interfaces. Ba et al. [1] focused on attention of natural meeting, and used a geometric model which is based on results from cognitive science on saccadic eye motion to recognize visual attention in natural meetings. Voit et al. [24] presented work on recognizing the visual focus of attention during dynamic meeting scenarios, and collected a dataset of meeting using the proposed new approach to deduce visual focus by means of head orientation as first clue and show. At present, many methods can only estimate attention in a specific direction. Meanwhile, changes in head posture in complex situations will seriously affect the stability of the model. In order to accurately judge all directions of attention, our system improves the accuracy by constraining Euler angles in three directions, and meanwhile introduces spatial information to overcome the head Euler Angle changes caused by unconstrained conditions, so as to improve the robustness of the model.

3 The Proposed Method

This paper mainly detects and estimates the head posture and then analyze student's attention. We obtain the classroom scene video through the camera, and then detect the face and head posture of student from the video to analyze their attention. In this section, the face detection and head pose estimation method are described first, then the module from head posture to attention analysis is introduced. The flowchart of the proposed method is illustrated in Fig. 1.

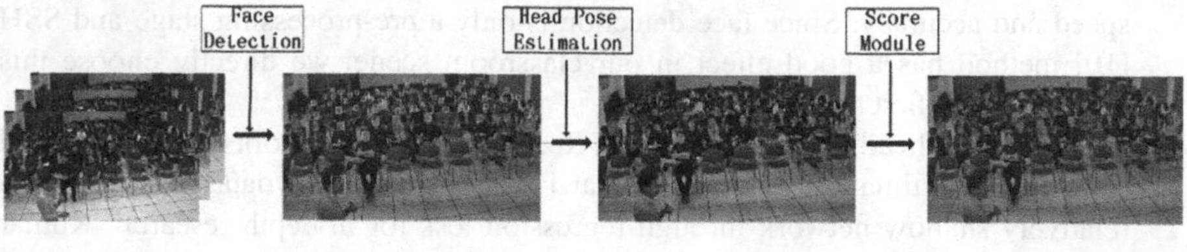

Fig. 1. Flowchart of the attention analysis system.

3.1 Face Detection

In order to obtain a good face detection model, the proposed model for face detection is based on SSH [10]. The detection module (Fig. 2) includes classification and regression. The first path is the ordinary 3 × 3 convolution, and the second path is the information module. Aiming to obtain more context information and larger receptive field, multiple 3 × 3 convolution is used instead of 7 × 7 convolution, at the same time, it can improve the depth of the network and improve the effect of neural network under certain conditions. Then the feature graphs of the two paths are fused for classification and regression tasks. Finally, this module is connected to three different convolution layers of VGG16 [22] to correspond to the feature diagrams of different sizes, so as to improve the model effect.

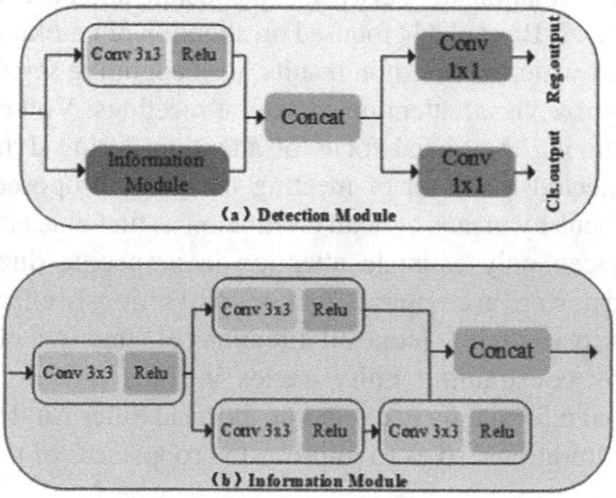

Fig. 2. Detection module and information module

3.2 Head Pose Estimation

The traditional head posture is to obtain the Euler Angle through the mapping relationship between 2D key points and 3D world coordinate system. However, this method requires highly accurate facial key points and is not suitable for classroom scenes.

Inspired by [18], the head pose estimation model is proposed. The model structure is shown in Fig. 3. The model mainly sets 2 loss functions for each Angle. First, Euler angles are classified according to the Angle interval. Then the regression loss can be calculated by comparing the classification results with the actual Angle. Finally, regression loss and classification loss are combined to calculate the final loss for each Euler angle, which is computed by:

$$L = C(y, \widehat{y}) + \alpha_1 \bullet MSE(y, \widehat{y}) \tag{1}$$

where C and MSE represent the Cross Entropy Loss and MSE Loss respectively, α_1 denote the weight coefficient. Meanwhile, in order to better adapt to the head pose estimation in the classroom, we filtered the data. When we use 300W-LP [19] as the data set for training, we will select pictures with the maximum Angle of −90–+90 as the training pictures, which will help us learn more effective features to improve the model performance. Influenced by Shao [21], in addition to random cropping and mirroring the image, we compressed the selected image quality, and then put it into the network for training, so as to increase the robustness of the model for low-quality image and suitable for the estimation of small face pose in the classroom.

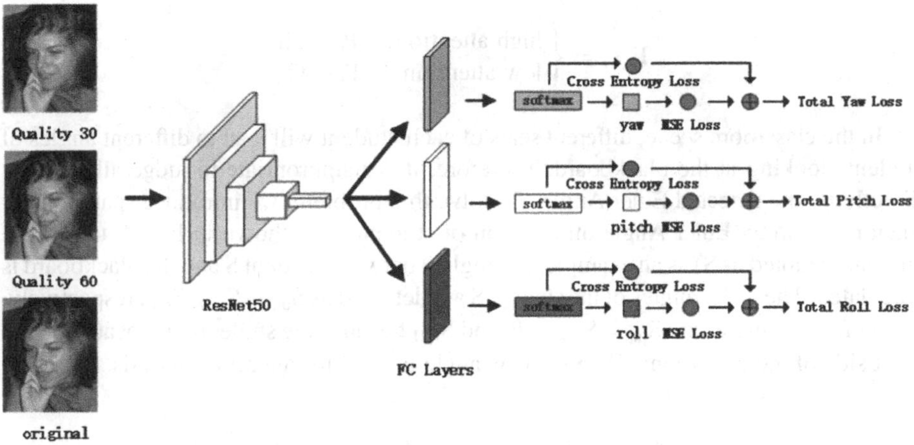

Fig. 3. Head pose estimation model structure. The images are compressed with the JPEG qualities of 30 and 60 respectively.

3.3 Attention Analysis Based on Head Pose Estimation

Attention analysis based on the head pose estimation is to put the Euler angles in three directions into the scoring module, and judge the attention by comparing the obtained score on the threshold. When students concentrate on class, they may look up at the blackboard and the teacher, and their heads will not shake frequently. Inattention is manifested in low head angle, looking left and right. First of all, we divided the collected data into two categories by voting combined with the above description.

Then we use the head pose estimation method mentioned in Sect. 3.2 for angle estimation. Let FK = $\{x_k, y_k, z_k\}$ represents the set of Euler angles of the head pose of the Kth student in a frame. Where x_k represents the pitch angle of the student, y_k represents the yaw angle of the student, z_k represents the rotation angle of the student.

Finally, we conducted multiple regression fitting for the three angles after feature scaling, and the calculation formula is as follows:

$$P_s = \alpha\, xk + \beta\, yk + \gamma\, z_k + b \tag{2}$$

Where α, β and γ represent Weight after training, b represents bias. And then we mapped Ps to be between 0 and 1 through sigmoid function, so as to carry out probability comparison later. Sigmoid formula is as follows:

$$P_t = \frac{1}{1 + e^{-P_s}} \tag{3}$$

During the training, we labeled high attention as 1 and low attention as 0. The final score is judged by (4), and the module larger than the threshold (denoted as Th and set as 0.5) judges to high attention, and the module below the threshold Th is judged to low attention.

$$F(x) = \begin{cases} \text{high attention}, & P_t \geq Th \\ \text{low attention}, & P_t < Th \end{cases} \tag{4}$$

In the classroom scene, different seats of each student will lead to different angles of students looking at the blackboard. Therefore, it is inappropriate to judge all students directly by the detected Euler Angle. To solve this problem, we introduce spatial information to correct Euler Angle information of students. As shown in Fig. 4, taking the student (denoted as S) as an example, the angle θ between student S and the blackboard is calculated. The Euler angles of the student S are detected as S_{pitch}, S_{raw}, S_{roll}, respectively. The corrected angles are S_{pitch}, $S_{raw} - \theta$, and S_{roll} because the students are located on the right side of the classroom. Then the new angle is used for attention analysis.

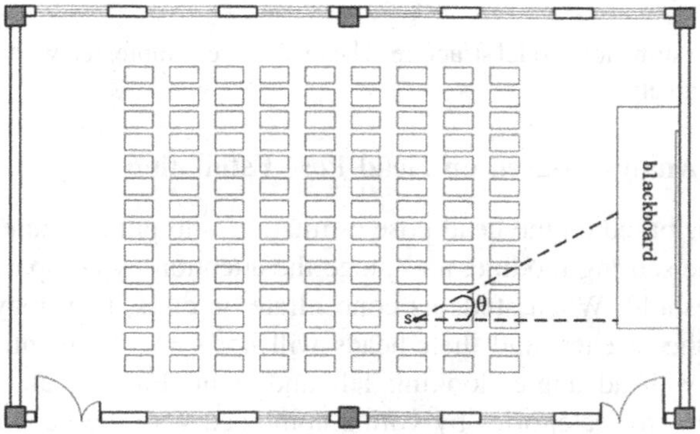

Fig. 4. Classroom setting plan

The above method is to judge the image of a single frame, but the state of a single frame cannot clearly represent the state of students in a period of time. In order to reflect the state of students for a period of time, so we adopt the method of equal interval sampling to judge. As shown in the Fig. 5, the sampling interval t_w is defined to be 20 s and interval time $t = t_p^i - t_{p-1}^i$ is defined to be 2 s. Then we judge the 10 segments by a single frame image, and finally use the result calculated by formula (5) to represent a state of students within 20 s.

$$S_{state} = \frac{\sum_{i=1}^{p} \{F(x)\}}{p} \tag{5}$$

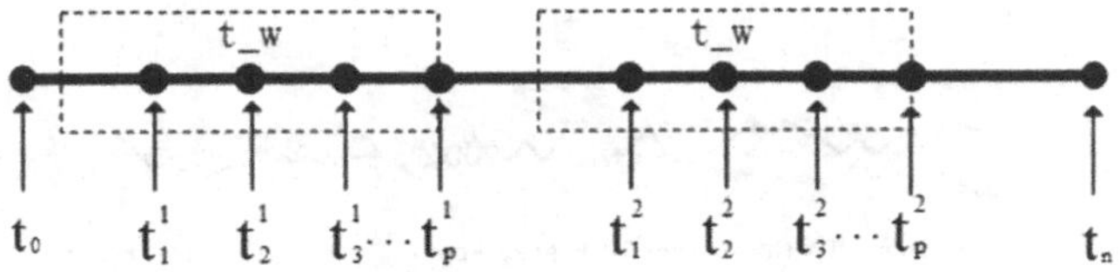

Fig. 5. Equidistant sampling

4 Experiment

We conducted experiments in actual classroom scenarios to evaluate the performance of the proposed method. First, the face detection model and the head pose estimation model are trained, and then the classroom video in the real scene is collected, and finally the experiments results based on accuracy show the advantages of the proposed algorithm.

4.1 Dataset

We use the WIDER dataset [25] on the face to train our face detector. The data consists of 32,203 images and 393,703 face images, 40% of which are training sets, 10% are cross-validated set, and 50% are used as test sets. The datasets of head pose we use are the AFLW2000 [27] and 300W-LP [19]. The AFLW2000 contains 2000 identity information and each face is annotated with 68 3d key points. The 300W-LP dataset includes more than 122450 head pose images. The classroom test video was collected by the camera directly above the classroom blackboard and when we do the recording, we tell the students that everything is done voluntarily. A total of several videos of different periods were recorded, and contains 5376 attention of the students in videos are marked. We label each frame of the video by 3 people. When the same student in the same frame is marked as high attention by more than 2 people, it is defined as high attention, and less than 2 people are marked as low attention.

4.2 Experimental Results

Face Detection. We compare the three methods SSD, Faster-RCNN, and our method. Then we use *true positive* (TP), which estimates the number of correct detections, and *false positive* (FP), which estimates the number of false alarms, as metrics. The details are shown in the Fig. 6. Our model has added detection module, which can detect faces of different scales, so the effect is better than the other two methods. There are more false detection and missed detection in the other two methods, and our method has better effect in the classroom scene.

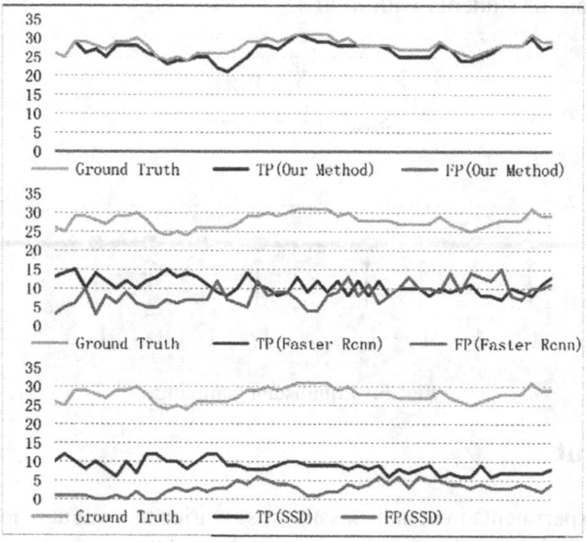

Fig. 6. Compare the results of different methods on 50 frames. Hand-labeled ground truth is illustrated by green line. Blue line is the TP result. Red line is the FP result. Our method is more stable than the other two methods, with no false detection and high accuracy. (Color figure online)

Head Pose Estimation. The proposed head pose model is tested on the AFLW2000, and the absolute value of the difference among the pitch, yaw, and roll. The labeled value is the estimated value error. For all test pictures, the error is averaged to get the average error. We use the current mainstream methods for comparison. Results can be seen in Table 1.

Table 1. Mean average error of Euler angles across different methods on the AFLW2000 dataset [27], Our method has the least error.

	Yaw	Pitch	Roll	MAE
3DDFA [27]	5.400	8.530	8.250	7.393
FAN [2]	6.358	12.277	8.714	9.116
Dlib [5]	23.153	13.633	10.545	15.777
DeepGaze [11]	11.04	7.150	4.400	7.53
HopeNet [18]	6.470	6.559	5.436	6.155
Ours	6.323	6.560	5.330	**6.071**

Attention Analysis Test. We compared our method with several other common methods. One classroom video was randomly selected from the dataset, and two-thirds of video was used as the training set and one-third as the test which is called dataset1. In order to verify the robustness of the method, we will randomly select 3 different classrooms video as the test which is called dataset2, and then take the average accuracy as our evaluation standard. The detailed information is shown in the Table 2. Since our method has been improved for low-resolution face in the classroom scene during training, the accuracy has been improved. Meanwhile, we can see that the accuracy has been improved after the correction of Euler Angle through spatial information, which proves the effectiveness of our method. Our method is also the best in dataset2, which proves the robustness of our method.

Table 2. Accuracy on different datasets. Dataset1 and training set students are the same, but the time period is different. Dataset2 consists of three different courses, with different time and different students.

	Dataset1 accuracy	Dataset2 accuracy
3DDFA [27]	76.49%	76.83%
FAN [2]	60.22%	57.93%
Dlib [5]	71.08%	67.72%
DeepGaze [11]	68.67%	64.19%
HopeNet [18]	81.9%	84.45%
Ours	86.57%	85.42%
Ours + spatial information	**87.87%**	**86.30%**

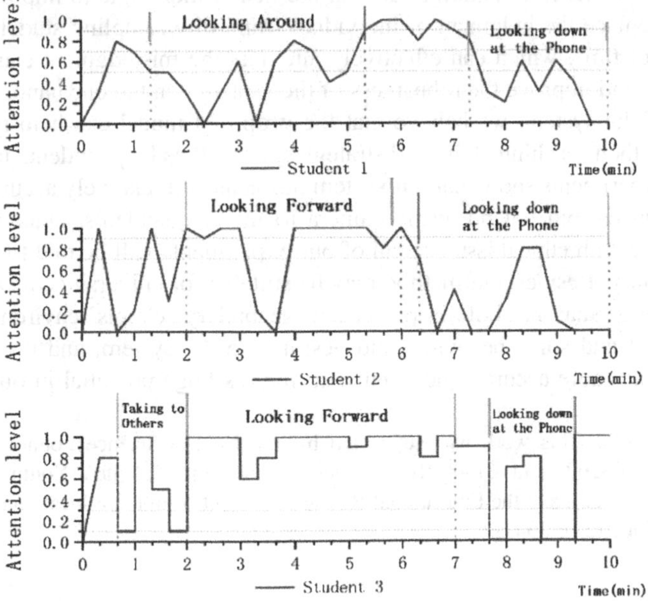

Fig. 7. Line chart for three student's attention analysis on 10-min period. Time is on the horizontal axis and the attention level on the vertical one. The blue line represents the results of students' attention obtained by our method and the red interval represents the results marked by students in real scenes. (Color figure online)

As mentioned in Sect. 3.3, in order to give a more accurate description of students, we adopted the method of equidistant sampling, and took 20 s as an interval to represent the status of students. Figure 7 shows the results of attention analysis of students within 10 min of class.

The blue line represents the results of students' attention obtained by our method, while the red interval represents the results marked by students in real scenes. We find that our method can accurately reflect the level of students' attention. Student 1 looks around between 1 min and 20 s to 5 min and 20 s, with relatively low concentration. It is not a good performance to lower the head to play with the phone between 7 min and 20 s to 10 min. Student 2 looked up at the blackboard for 2 to 6 min, and his attention was relatively high, while his attention was low when he looked down at the phone for 6 min and 20 s to 10 min. Students 3 chatted with others within 40 s to 2 min, and then played with the phone between 7 min and 9 min, resulting in low attention. However, he looked at the blackboard between 2 min to 7 min, resulting in increased attention.

5 Conclusion

This paper proposed an attention analysis system, which analyzes the attention of students in the classroom through multiple Euler angles constraint and head pose estimation. At the same time, in order to solve the problem raised by different head information, we designed a scoring module to process header information uniformly and introduce spatial information to correct the head Euler angle to improve accuracy. Finally, we replace the judgment of individual frames by sampling students' attention for a period of time, which can effectively alleviate the misjudgment caused by individual frames and improve the robustness of the system. On the one hand, according to the results of the system, we believe that the proposed model can help teachers constantly adjust their teaching skills and strategies, as well as help students improve their efficiency. Experiments show that our system has achieved relatively accurate results in classroom. On the other hand, using camera to monitor students' behavior is a controversial topic with ethical issue, so all of our experiments will be told to students and will be voluntary. Besides, our method may be suitable for university education and the same assumption may not hold in primary or secondary schools' environment. In the future, we will add some behaviors and gestures to the system, and use more information to make more accurate judgments, so there's huge potential in our work.

Acknowledgments. This work was supported by the Natural Science Foundation of China (61602349, U1803262, and 61440016), Hubei Chengguang Talented Youth Development Foundation (2015B22), and the Educational Research Project from the Educational Commission of Hubei Province (2016234).

References

1. Ba, S.O., Odobez, J.M.: Recognizing visual focus of attention from head pose in natural meetings. IEEE Trans. Syst. Man Cybern. Part B (Cybern.) **39**(1), 16–33 (2008)
2. Bulat, A., Tzimiropoulos, G.: How far are we from solving the 2D & 3D face alignment problem? (And a dataset of 230,000 3D facial landmarks). In: Proceedings of the IEEE International Conference on Computer Vision, pp. 1021–1030 (2017)
3. Chang, F.J., Tuan Tran, A., Hassner, T., Masi, I., Nevatia, R., Medioni, G.: FacePoseNet: making a case for landmark-free face alignment. In: Proceedings of the IEEE International Conference on Computer Vision, pp. 1599–1608 (2017)
4. Girshick, R., Donahue, J., Darrell, T., Malik, J.: Rich feature hierarchies for accurate object detection and semantic segmentation. In: Proceedings of the IEEE Conference on Computer Vision and Pattern Recognition, pp. 580–587 (2014)
5. Kazemi, V., Sullivan, J.: One millisecond face alignment with an ensemble of regression trees. In: Proceedings of the IEEE Conference on Computer Vision and Pattern Recognition, pp. 1867–1874 (2014)
6. Krizhevsky, A., Sutskever, I., Hinton, G.E.: ImageNet classification with deep convolutional neural networks. In: Advances in Neural Information Processing Systems, pp. 1097–1105 (2012)
7. Kumar, A., Alavi, A., Chellappa, R.: KEPLER: keypoint and pose estimation of unconstrained faces by learning efficient H-CNN regressors. In: 2017 12th IEEE International Conference on Automatic Face & Gesture Recognition (FG 2017), pp. 258–265. IEEE (2017)
8. Liu, W., et al.: SSD: single shot multibox detector. In: Leibe, B., Matas, J., Sebe, N., Welling, M. (eds.) ECCV 2016. LNCS, vol. 9905, pp. 21–37. Springer, Cham (2016). https://doi.org/10.1007/978-3-319-46448-0_2
9. Matsumoto, Y., Zelinsky, A.: An algorithm for real-time stereo vision implementation of head pose and gaze direction measurement. In: Proceedings Fourth IEEE International Conference on Automatic Face and Gesture Recognition (Cat. No. PR00580), pp. 499–504. IEEE (2000)
10. Najibi, M., Samangouei, P., Chellappa, R., Davis, L.S.: SSH: single stage headless face detector. In: Proceedings of the IEEE International Conference on Computer Vision, pp. 4875–4884 (2017)
11. Patacchiola, M., Cangelosi, A.: Head pose estimation in the wild using convolutional neural networks and adaptive gradient methods. Pattern Recogn. **71**, 132–143 (2017)
12. Qin, J., Zhou, Y., Lu, H., Ya, H.: Teaching video analytics based on student spatial and temporal behavior mining. In: Proceedings of the 5th ACM on International Conference on Multimedia Retrieval, pp. 635–642. ACM (2015)
13. Raca, M., Dillenbourg, P.: System for assessing classroom attention. In: Proceedings of 3rd International Learning Analytics & Knowledge Conference. No. CONF (2013)
14. Raca, M., Dillenbourg, P.: Holistic analysis of the classroom. In: Proceedings of the 2014 ACM Workshop on Multimodal Learning Analytics Workshop and Grand Challenge, pp. 13–20. ACM (2014)
15. Raca, M., Tormey, R., Dillenbourg, P.: Sleepers' lag-study on motion and attention. In: Proceedings of the Fourth International Conference on Learning Analytics and Knowledge, pp. 36–43. ACM (2014)
16. Ranjan, R., Patel, V.M., Chellappa, R.: HyperFace: a deep multi-task learning framework for face detection, landmark localization, pose estimation, and gender recognition. IEEE Trans. Pattern Anal. Mach. Intell. **41**(1), 121–135 (2017)

17. Ren, S., He, K., Girshick, R., Sun, J.: Faster R-CNN: towards real-time object detection with region proposal networks. In: Advances in Neural Information Processing Systems, pp. 91–99 (2015)
18. Ruiz, N., Chong, E., Rehg, J.M.: Fine-grained head pose estimation without keypoints. In: Proceedings of the IEEE Conference on Computer Vision and Pattern Recognition Workshops, pp. 2074–2083 (2018)
19. Sagonas, C., Tzimiropoulos, G., Zafeiriou, S., Pantic, M.: 300 faces in-the-wild challenge: the first facial landmark localization challenge. In: Proceedings of the IEEE International Conference on Computer Vision Workshops, pp. 397–403 (2013)
20. Shao, B., Jiang, F., Shen, R.: Multi-object detection based on deep learning in real classrooms. In: Geng, X., Kang, B.-H. (eds.) PRICAI 2018. LNCS (LNAI), vol. 11013, pp. 352–359. Springer, Cham (2018). https://doi.org/10.1007/978-3-319-97310-4_40
21. Shao, Z., Ding, S., Zhu, H., Wang, C., Ma, L.: Face alignment by deep convolutional network with adaptive learning rate. In: 2016 IEEE International Conference on Acoustics, Speech and Signal Processing (ICASSP), pp. 1283–1287. IEEE (2016)
22. Simonyan, K., Zisserman, A.: Very deep convolutional networks for large-scale image recognition. arXiv preprint arXiv:1409.1556 (2014)
23. Szegedy, C., et al.: Going deeper with convolutions. In: Proceedings of the IEEE Conference on Computer Vision and Pattern Recognition, pp. 1–9 (2015)
24. Voit, M., Stiefelhagen, R.: Deducing the visual focus of attention from head pose estimation in dynamic multi-view meeting scenarios. In: Proceedings of the 10th International Conference on Multimodal Interfaces, pp. 173–180. ACM (2008)
25. Yang, S., Luo, P., Loy, C.C., Tang, X.: Wider face: a face detection benchmark. In: Proceedings of the IEEE Conference on Computer Vision and Pattern Recognition, pp. 5525–5533 (2016)
26. Zhang, K., Zhang, Z., Li, Z., Qiao, Y.: Joint face detection and alignment using multitask cascaded convolutional networks. IEEE Signal Process. Lett. **23**(10), 1499–1503 (2016)
27. Zhu, X., Lei, Z., Liu, X., Shi, H., Li, S.Z.: Face alignment across large poses: a 3D solution. In: Proceedings of the IEEE Conference on Computer Vision and Pattern Recognition, pp. 146–155 (2016)

Multi-branch Body Region Alignment Network for Person Re-identification

Han Fang[1,2], Jun Chen[1,2(✉)], and Qi Tian[3]

[1] National Engineering Research Center for Multimedia Software, School of Computer Science, Wuhan University, Wuhan, China
{fanghan,chenj}@whu.edu.cn

[2] Hubei Key Laboratory of Multimedia and Network Communication Engineering, Wuhan University, Wuhan, China

[3] Department of Computer Science, University of Texas at San Antonio, San Antonio, TX 78249-1604, USA
qitian@cs.utsa.edu

Abstract. Person re-identification (Re-ID) aims to identify the same person images from a gallery set across different cameras. Human pose variations, background clutter and misalignment of detected human images pose challenges for Re-ID tasks. To deal with these issues, we propose a Multi-branch Body Region Alignment Network (MBRAN), to learn discriminative representations for person Re-ID. It consists of two modules, i.e., body region extraction and feature learning. Body region extraction module utilizes a single-person pose estimation method to estimate human keypoints and obtain three body regions. In the feature learning module, four global or local branch-networks share base layers and are designed to learn feature representation on three overlapping body regions and the global image. Extensive experiments have indicated that our method outperforms several state-of-the-art methods on two mainstream person Re-ID datasets.

Keywords: Person re-identification · Keypoints detection · Feature fusion

1 Introduction

Given a particular probe image, person re-identification (Re-ID) [17] aims to identify the same person images from a gallery set across different cameras. Due to its extensive applications in video surveillance and security system, person Re-ID has attracted more and more attention in recent years.

Most of the person Re-ID methods concentrate on two phases, i.e., feature representation learning and distance metric learning.

Feature representation learning aims to learn a discriminative feature to represent the appearances of different persons. With increasing popularity of deep neural networks, more and more researchers tend to employ deep learning based feature representations rather than hand-crafted features. Plenty of

Y. M. Ro et al. (Eds.): MMM 2020, LNCS 11961, pp. 341–352, 2020.
https://doi.org/10.1007/978-3-030-37731-1_28

existing methods learn the discriminative feature from the whole human images, which depict the global cues but may lose local information. This issue has been valued in recent work [5,6,8]. [8] puts forward a Part-based Convolutional Baseline (PCB) which carries out unified partition on the convolution layer and learns the characteristics of division classification. In addition, some studies [1,7,9–12,36] make full use of the latest human pose estimation and attention models for locating human body parts to alleviate the problems of pose misalignment and background interference.

Distance metric learning targets to reduce the distance among features of images containing the same person. Inspired by the great success of Convolutional Neural Networks (CNN) in large-scale image classification competition such as Alexnet [13], subsequent methods [14–16] begin to design algorithms based on deep learning and have achieved remarkable improvements. This paper mainly takes the feature learning phase into consideration and adopts cosine distance as distance metric method.

Large variations on persons such as human pose, background clutter and misalignment of detected human images make identifying a person from a large-scale gallery a challenging task. As we can see from Fig. 1(a), in the several images of the same boy with the red T-shirt and blue plants, there has been a very marked change in his posture. Since the human body regions are detected by existing object detection methods such as DPM [3] or Faster-RCNN [4], the detected bounding boxes may be inaccurate. For example, as showed in Fig. 1(b), human body part cannot be sufficiently aligned across the three images such as the head region in the blue bounding box. The dislocation on the space is able to make the CNN feature maps of the same area completely different so they can not be compared directly. If the background of images is quite complex and varied, pedestrians as the foreground are difficult to spot even for humans. As showed in Fig. 1(c), it becomes difficult for the naked eye to identify the pedestrian due to the background occlusion. As Fig. 1(d) shows, all three men dressed in white tops and black trousers look very similar in appearance, but in reality they have completely different identities.

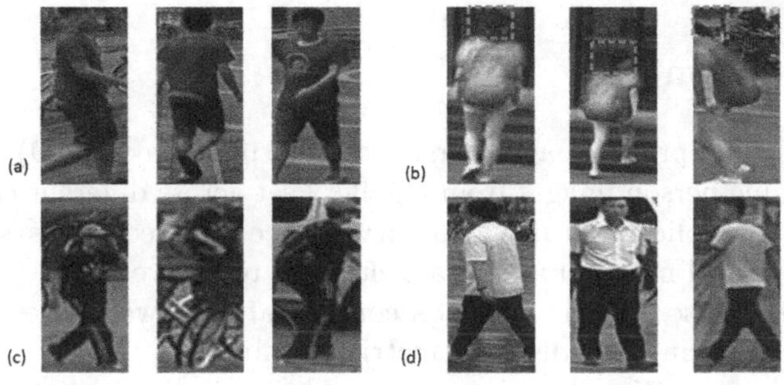

Fig. 1. Challenges of person Re-ID. (a) Human pose variations. (b) Misalignment of detected human images. (c) Background clutter. (d) Similar appearance with different IDs. (Color figure online)

To deal with above issues, [7] proposes a 4-stream network to obtain global features and head, upper body and lower body part-based features at the same time, and then conduct multiple features fusion to get GLAD descriptor. However, GLAD lacks the characteristics of strong robustness to variations on the human pose and camera viewpoint. Compared with GLAD [7], which also adopts pose estimation, we do not consider the head region because many detected pedestrian images are incomplete without the head region, or they are on the back. As a result, the head region is not sufficiently discriminative but will introduce noise to model training.

In this paper, we propose a feature learning strategy combining global and local information based on human pose estimation. Since deep learning mechanism can capture approximate attention on the whole body from the image, it is also probable to capture more concentrated saliency preferences for local features extracted from different body regions. Based on this idea, we put forward a simple yet effective Multi-branch Body Region Alignment Network (MBRAN) with two modules, i.e., body region extraction and feature learning. Body region extraction module utilizes a single-person pose estimation method to estimate human keypoints. Three coarse part regions, i.e., upper-body, lower-body and middle-body are hence generated based on these keypoints. To mine the global and local information of pedestrian images simultaneously, four global or local branch-networks share several convolutional layers and are designed to learn feature representation on three overlapping body regions and the global image, respectively. They are combined on the loss level and their complementary aspects are leveraged to enhance the final Re-ID accuracy.

The main contributions of this paper are: **(I)** By combining four branch-networks, a simple yet effective Multi-branch Body Region Alignment Network (MBRAN) is proposed to learn discriminative global and local feature representation simultaneously. **(II)** We use multiple cross entropy loss and triplet loss with different weights to train the CNN model and further improve the obtained fused feature. **(III)** Extensive experiments have indicated that our method outperforms several state-of-the-art methods on two mainstream Re-ID datasets.

2 Related Work

This work is related with deep learning based person Re-ID and human pose estimation for person Re-ID. The following parts simply review previous work on these two categories, respectively.

2.1 Deep Learning Based Person Re-ID

Deep learning shows sufficient performance in multimedia and computer vision areas and has become the mainstream method for person Re-ID. [18] first introduces deep siamese network architecture into Re-ID and combines the body part features. [20] merges slices of part features with LSTM network and combines with global features learned from classification metric learning. [19] rearranges human part patches to generate a new pose-aligned human image. The above methods all lack the characteristics of robustness to variations on the human pose and camera viewpoint.

2.2 Human Pose Estimation

Human pose estimation is a fundamental task in computer vision, aiming to estimate joint locations of human body. Human body parts, generated by pose estimation, can provide useful contextual cues to help localize body joints in some challenging scenarios. Recently, research efforts have been devoted to both single- and multi-person pose estimation problems, via exploring network architecture engineering [21], enhancing training supervision [22], and improving inference strategy [23]. [24] puts forward a novel Parsing Induced Learner (PIL) to assist human pose estimation by effectively exploiting parsing information. PIL learns to predict certain pose model parameters from parsing features and adapts the pose model to extracting complementary useful features. In this paper, we use PIL for person Re-ID tasks.

3 Multi-branch Body Region Alignment Network

In this section, the proposed MBRAN is introduced in detail. As showed in Fig. 2, we first detect several body regions from an input person image, and then learn feature representation from both the global and local body regions. In the following, we introduce the body region extraction module and feature learning module, respectively.

3.1 Body Region Extraction

The detected images are taken in unconstrained environment, and are easily affected by human pose, background clutter and camera viewpoint in person Re-ID. It motivates us to consider body regions that could be easily and reliably detected under various viewpoint and pose changes. Human pose estimation has been studied for many years and has achieved remarkable improvements. Human body parts, generated by pose estimation, can provide useful contextual cues to help localize body joints in person re-identification.

More concretely, we utilize PIL [24], a single-person pose estimation method, to estimate only six keypoints, i.e., head, neck, left-hip, right-hip, left-knee, right-knee, respectively on respectively on the human image. As depicted in Fig. 3, according to these keypoints, we can coarsely divide a human image into three overlapping part regions: upper-body, middle-body and lower-body, respectively. Specifically, the upper-body is from the top of the head to the waist. The lower-body is from the waist to the feet, and the middle-body is from the neck to the knees. Since the keypoints of the pedestrian foot is not adequately stable, we chose the lower edge of the image to replace the foot in the lower-body.

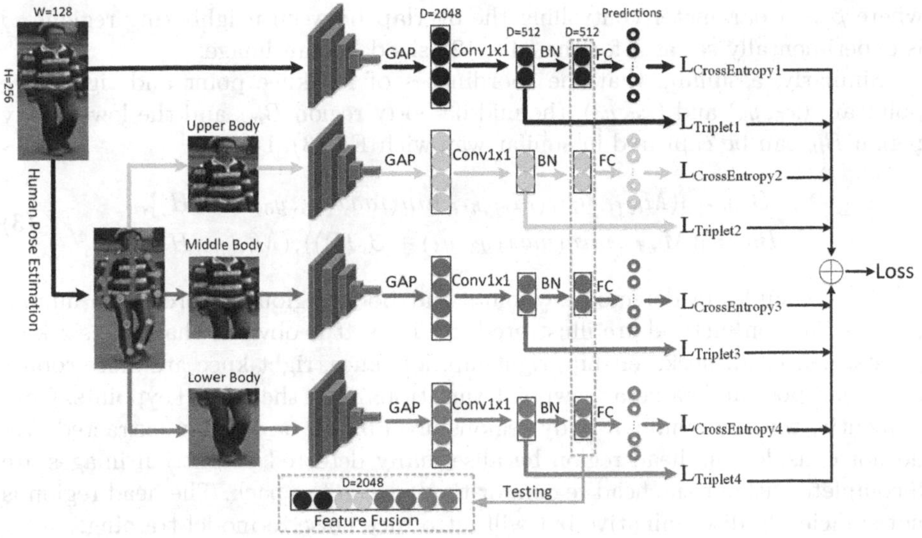

Fig. 2. Overview of the proposed Multi-branch Body Region Alignment Network with two modules, i.e., body region extraction and feature learning. Body region extraction module utilizes a single-person pose estimation method to estimate human keypoints. A CNN composed of four branch-networks is proposed in feature learning module. These branch-networks share base layers and are designed to learn feature representation on three overlapping body regions and the global image.

Assuming that the size of pedestrian image is $W \times H$ and x and y represent the horizontal and vertical coordinates of the keypoints, respectively. To make full use of the 16 keypoints obtained from pose estimation, we use them to reposition the left and right margins of pedestrian images to reduce the influence of inaccurate bounding boxes and background clutter with Eq. (1), i.e.,

$$\begin{aligned} M_{left} &= \max(\min(x_1, x_2, ..., x_{16}) - \theta, 0), \\ M_{right} &= \min(\max(x_1, x_2, ..., x_{16}) + \theta, W), \end{aligned} \tag{1}$$

where θ is a parameter controlling the left and right boundaries of pedestrian images. θ is experimentally set as 8 for the 64×128 sized human image.

We only need head, neck, left-hip and right-hip keypoints to locate the upper-body of the pedestrian. Suppose the coordinates of head, neck, left-hip and right-hip keypoints are (x_1, y_1), (x_2, y_2), (x_3, y_3) and (x_4, y_4). According to the experimental results, a few keypoints are still wrong when tested directly on the Re-ID dataset. To handle the keypoints of these exceptions, we need to make some constraints on the boundary of the bounding boxes so we crop the upper-body region B_{ub} with Eq. (2), i.e.,

$$B_{ub} = [(M_{left}, max(y_1 - \beta, 0)), (M_{right}, min(max(y_3, y_4) + \beta, H)], \tag{2}$$

where β is a parameter controlling the overlap between neighboring regions. β is experimentally set as 4 for the 64×128 sized human image.

Similarly, assuming that the coordinates of left-knee point and right-knee point are (x_5, y_5) and (x_6, y_6), the middle-body region B_{mb} and the lower-body region B_{lb} can be captured in similar way with Eq. (3), i.e.,

$$\begin{aligned} B_{mb} &= [(M_{left}, y_2), (M_{right}, min(max(y_5, y_6) + \beta, H)], \\ B_{lb} &= [(M_{left}, min(max(y_3, y_4) + \beta, H))), (M_{right}, H)], \end{aligned} \tag{3}$$

Some samples of detected keypoints and body regions according to human pose estimation method are illustrated in Fig. 3. It is obvious that, the six keypoints, i.e., head, neck, left-hip, right-hip, left-knee, right-knee are more robust to human pose and camera viewpoint variations than the other keypoints. Consequently, the three human body regions are able to be reliably extracted. We do not consider the head region because many detected pedestrian images are incomplete without the head region, or they are on the back. The head region is not sufficiently discriminative but will introduce noise to model training.

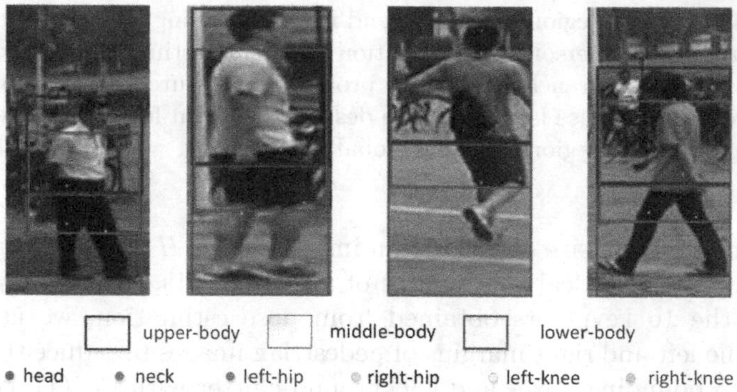

Fig. 3. Some samples of detected keypoints and generated three body regions. The six keypoints used in our method are emphasized with different colors. (Color figure online)

3.2 Feature Learning

Existing deep neural networks such as GoogLeNet [25], VGGNet [26], and ResNet have been exploited to learn global feature on the whole person image for person Re-ID. To adequately leverage global and local information for feature learning, we propose the MBRAN. As showed in Fig. 2, the proposed network includes one branch-network for global feature learning and three branch-networks for body region feature learning, respectively. These branch-networks share the base layers of CNN and can be initialized by exiting network structures and parameters.

More concretely, we use the ResNet-50 as the backbone network with some modifications and initialize it with pre-trained parameters on ImageNet. At first, the average pooling layer has been replaced by Global Average Pooling (GAP). Next, the stride of the conv4-1 is set to 1 so the size of extracted feature maps will be $\frac{1}{16}$ of the input image size. After that, each 2048-dim feature vector is fed into a 1×1 convolutional layer to reduce the dimensions from 2048 to 512. For each global or local branch, we adds a batch normalization (BN) layer and a classifier FC layer after 1×1 convolutional layer, which followed by a softmax function to predict the ID of each input image.

For the global feature learning, the input image is the original image which resized to 128×256. The upper-body region is resized to 128×128 as the network input. For middle-body and lower-body branch-networks, the input size is 128×128, too. These branch-networks are trained in different classification tasks to classify the global or local body regions into correct person classes. As depicted in Fig. 2, we train them together with sharing weights in base layers of ResNet-50 to avoid overfitting.

At the testing stage, assuming that K channels of feature maps are generated, we ultimately generate an K-dimension feature vector by GAP on each branch-network. The feature vectors extracted on global and three local body regions are concatenated as the final feature representation, i.e.,

$$\mathbf{f} = [\mathbf{f}_g, \lambda_1 \mathbf{f}_{ub}, \lambda_2 \mathbf{f}_{mb}, \lambda_3 \mathbf{f}_{lb}], \tag{4}$$

where $\mathbf{f}_g$ represents the learned feature on the global image, $\mathbf{f}_{ub}$, $\mathbf{f}_{mb}$ and $\mathbf{f}_{lb}$ are features generated from the three branch-networks, respectively. λ_1, λ_2 and λ_3 represents the weights of local features, respectively. Consequently, $\mathbf{f}$ is an $4K$ dimensional vector, which adequately leverages global and local information. We experimentally set K as 512 to generate an 2048-dim feature vector.

3.3 Loss Function

To further strengthen the discrimination ability of the learned feature representation of our MBRAN, we use cross entropy loss for classification, and triplet loss for metric learning in the training stage, which are both widely used in existing person Re-ID methods based deep learning.

Given an image, we denote t as truth person ID label and p_j as ID prediction value of class j. The cross entropy loss is computed as:

$$L_{CrossEntropy} = -\sum_{j=1}^{J} q_j log(p_j) \begin{cases} q_j = 0, t \neq j \\ q_j = 1, t = j \end{cases} \tag{5}$$

Since person IDs of the testing set have not appeared in the training set, it is extremely important to prevent the person Re-ID model from overfitting training IDs and label smoothing [27] is a widely used method which changes the construction of q_j to:

$$q_j = \begin{cases} \frac{\epsilon}{C}, t \neq j \\ 1 - \frac{C-1}{C}\epsilon, t = j \end{cases} \tag{6}$$

where ϵ is a small constant to encourage the model to be less confident on the training set. We experimentally set ϵ as 0.1. C represents numbers of person IDs in the training set.

In addition, We adopt the triplet loss with batch hard mining [28] to enhance ranking performances. This loss function is formulated as follows:

$$L_{Triplet} = \sum_{p=1}^{P}\sum_{k=1}^{K}(max \, \|I - I_{+}\|_2^2 - min \, \|I - I_{-}\|_2^2 + \alpha) \tag{7}$$

where I is the anchor image, I_{+} is the positive example with I, and I_{-} is the negative example. The distance between positive pair $\langle I, I_{+}\rangle$ or negative pair $\langle I, I_{-}\rangle$ is obtained by computing L2 distance of output features. α is the margin of triplet loss. In this paper, We set α as 0.3.

As showed in Fig. 2, after gaining the cross entropy loss and triplet loss of each branch, the final loss function of the proposed MBRAN is defined as:

$$L_{final} = \sum_{i=1}^{4} \omega_i (L_{CrossEntropy_i} + L_{Triplet_i}) \tag{8}$$

where $L_{CrossEntropy_1}$, $L_{Triplet_1}$ represent the obtained loss of global branch and the other are the loss of local branch. ω_i is the balanced weight of global or local branch network. We experimentally set four weights as 0.52, 0.16, 0.16, 0.16.

4 Experiment

4.1 Implementation

We use Pytorch framework to implement the proposed method. To estimate keypoints for body region extraction, we use PIL [24], a single-person pose estimation method, pre-trained on the Look into Person dataset [29]. During the feature learning stage, an initial learning rate is set as 0.00035, and is divided by 10 after every 40 epochs. Fine-tuning is applied on the target training set to avoid overfitting. On Market-1501 [2] and DukeMTMC-reID [30], we train our network with 120 epochs. All experiments are conducted on a server equipped with GeForce Titan X GPU, Intel i7 CPU, and 128 GB memory.

4.2 Datasets and Protocols

The experiments to evaluate our method are made on two mainstream Re-ID datasets: Market-1501 [2] and DukeMTMC-reID [30]. It is essential to recommend these datasets and their evaluation protocols before we display our results.

Market-1501. This dataset includes images of 1,501 persons captured from 6 different cameras. The whole dataset is divided into training set with 12,936 images of 751 persons and testing set with 3,368 query images and 19,732 gallery images of 750 persons. It also contains 500,000 images as some distractors.

DukeMTMC-reID. This dataset contains 1,812 identities captured by 8 cameras. A number of 1,404 identities appear in more than two cameras, and the rest 408 IDs are distractor images. Using the evaluation protocol specified in [31], the training and testing sets both have 702 IDs. In general, there are 2,228 query images, 16,522 training images and 17,661 gallery images.

Evaluation Protocols. For the person re-ID task, we use the Cumulative Matching Characteristic (CMC) curve at Rank1 and the mean average precision (mAP). For each query, its average precision (AP) is computed from its precision-recall curve. Then mAP is the mean value of average precisions across all queries. The presumption is that CMC reflects retrieval precision, while mAP reflects the recall. In this paper, we conduct experiments in single-query mode only.

4.3 Evaluation on Feature Learning

Our feature is learned by a MBRAN on the global and local body regions. The four branch networks are trained with shared parameters in base layers. Here, we compare different feature fusion strategies to test the validity of our feature learning method. The experimental results on Market-1501 are depicted in Table 1. It is obvious that the global feature performs better than features on local regions. This may be because the global image contains more visual information thus reasonably owns better discriminative power. The performance of the middle region is the best among three body regions. This also corresponds to our identification of a person primarily based on his middle torso.

By combining all the global and local feature, "global+upper-body+middle-body+lower-body" outperforms all of the global and fused local features. What's more, it dramatically outperforms "baseline" by 1.5% on Rank1 and 3.4% on mAP. Above experiments show the effectiveness of our feature fusion strategy.

Table 1. Comparison of different feature fusion strategies on Market-1501.

Fusion strategy	Rank1	mAP
baseline	93.8	83.7
global	94.1	85.0
upper-body	82.9	61.4
middle-body	87.1	71.3
lower-body	83.2	66.0
upper-body+middle-body+lower-body	94.6	83.8
global+upper-body	94.8	85.5
global+middle-body	94.9	85.9
global+lower-body	94.8	85.6
global+upper-body+lower-body	95.0	86.2
global+upper-body+middle-body+lower-body	**95.3**	**87.1**

4.4 Comparison with State-of-the-Art Methods

We compare our proposed MBRAN with recent state-of-the-art methods on two mainstream datasets to show our significant performance advantage over several existing methods.

Results on Market-1501. As showed in Table 2, our MBRAN achieves the mAP of 87.1% and Rank1 accuracy 95.3%, which both surpass several existing methods. Our MBRAN outperforms PCB by 1.5% and 5.5% on Rank1 and mAP, respectively. For GLAD, which also adopts pose estimation method, our MBRAN dramatically outperforms it by 5.4% and 13.2% on Rank1 and mAP, respectively. Unlike GLAD, we choose the stronger discriminative body region rather than the head region because lots of detected images are incomplete without the head region, or they are on the back.

Results on DukeMTMC-ReID. As depicted in Table 2, our MBRAN obtains the mAP of 76.9% and Rank1 accuracy 87.1%, which both surpass several existing methods. Mancs is closest competitor, which leverages attention-based learning for person Re-ID. Our MBRAN outperforms it by 2.2% and 5.1% on Rank1 and mAP, respectively.

Table 2. Comparison of some state-of-the-art methods.

Type	Method	Market1501		DukeMTMC-ReID	
		Rank1	mAP	Rank1	mAP
Stripe-based	AlignedReID [5]	92.6	82.3	81.2	67.4
	PCB+RPP [8]	93.8	81.6	83.3	76.9
Attention-based	HA-CNN [32]	91.2	75.7	80.5	63.8
	Mancs [33]	93.1	82.3	84.9	71.8
Pose-guided	SVDNet [35]	82.3	62.1	76.7	56.8
	PAR [9]	81.0	63.4	–	–
	PDC [34]	84.1	63.4	–	–
	AACN [1]	85.9	66.9	76.8	59.3
	GLAD [7]	89.9	73.9	–	–
	MBRAN (Ours)	**95.3**	**87.1**	**87.1**	**76.9**

5 Conclusion

In this paper, we propose a Multi-branch Body Region Alignment Network (MBRAN) to learning discriminative representations for person Re-ID tasks. It consists of two modules, i.e., body region extraction and feature learning. Body region extraction module utilizes a single-person pose estimation method to estimate human keypoints and obtain three body regions. In the feature learning module, four global or local branch-networks share base layers and are designed to learn feature representation on three overlapping body regions and the global image. Extensive experiments have indicated that our method outperforms several state-of-the-art methods on two mainstream person Re-ID datasets.

Acknowledgement. This research was partially supported by National Key R&D Program of China (2017YFC0803700), National Nature Science Foundation of China (U1611461, 61876135), Hubei Province Technological Innovation Major Project (2017AAA123, 2018AAA062), and Nature Science Foundation of Jiangsu Province (BK20160386).

References

1. Xu, J., Zhao, R., Zhu, F., et al.: Attention-aware compositional network for person re-identification. In: CVPR (2018)
2. Zheng, L., Shen, L., Tian, L., Wang, S., Wang, J., Tian, Q.: Scalable person re-identification: a benchmark. In: ICCV (2015)
3. Felzenszwalb, P.F., Girshick, R.B., McAllester, D., Ramanan, D.: Object detection with discriminatively trained partbased models. TPAMI **32**(9), 1627–1645 (2010)
4. Ren, S., He, K., Girshick, R., Sun, J.: Faster R-CNN: towards real-time object detection with region proposal networks. In: NIPS (2015)
5. Zhang, X., et al.: AlignedReID: surpassing human-level performance in person re-identification. arXiv (2017)
6. Yao, H., et al.: Large-scale person re-identication as retrieval. In: ICME (2017)
7. Wei, L., Zhang, S., Yao, H., Gao, W., Tian, Q.: GLAD: global-local-alignment descriptor for pedestrian retrieval. In: ACM MM (2017)
8. Sun, Y., Zheng, L., Yang, Y., Tian, Q., Wang, S.: Beyond part models: person retrieval with refined part pooling (and a strong convolutional baseline). In: Ferrari, V., Hebert, M., Sminchisescu, C., Weiss, Y. (eds.) ECCV 2018. LNCS, vol. 11208, pp. 501–518. Springer, Cham (2018). https://doi.org/10.1007/978-3-030-01225-0_30
9. Su, C., Li, J., Zhang, S., Xing, J., Gao, W., Tian, Q.: Pose driven deep convolutional model for person re-identification. In: ICCV (2017)
10. Zhao, L., Li, X., Wang, J., Zhuang, Y.: Deeply-learned part-aligned representations for person re-identification. In: ICCV (2017)
11. Zheng, L., Huang, Y., Lu, H., Yang, Y.: Pose invariant embedding for deep person re-identification. arXiv (2017)
12. Saquib Sarfraz, M., Schumann, A., Eberle, A., Stiefelhagen, R.: A pose-sensitive embedding for person reidentification with expanded cross neighborhood re-ranking. In: CVPR (2018)
13. Krizhevsky, A., Sutskever, I., Hinton, G.E.: ImageNet classification with deep convolutional neural networks. In: NIPS (2012)
14. Liao, S., Hu, Y., Zhu, X., Li, S.Z.: Person reidentification by local maximal occurrence representation and metric learning. In: CVPR (2015)
15. Yi, D., Lei, Z., Liao, S., Li, S.Z.: Deep metric learning for person re-identification. In: ICPR (2014)
16. Zhang, L., Xiang, T., Gong, S.: Learning a discriminative null space for person re-identification. In: CVPR (2016)

17. Zheng, L., Yang, Y., Hauptmann, A.G.: Person reidentification: past, present and future. arXiv (2016)
18. Li, W., Zhao, R., Xiao, T., Wang, X.: DeepReID: deep filter pairing neural network for person re-identification. In: CVPR (2014)
19. Su, C., Li, J., Zhang, S., Xing, J., Gao, W., Tian, Q.: Posedriven deep convolutional model for person re-identification. In: ICCV (2017)
20. Bai, X., Yang, M., Huang, T., Dou, Z., Yu, R., Xu, Y.: DeepPerson: learning discriminative deep features for person re-identification. arXiv (2017)
21. Newell, A., Yang, K., Deng, J.: Stacked hourglass networks for human pose estimation. In: Leibe, B., Matas, J., Sebe, N., Welling, M. (eds.) ECCV 2016. LNCS, vol. 9912, pp. 483–499. Springer, Cham (2016). https://doi.org/10.1007/978-3-319-46484-8_29
22. Chen, Y., Shen, C., Wei, X.-S., Liu, L., Yang, J.: Adversarial PoseNet: a structure-aware convolutional network for human pose estimation. In: ICCV (2017)
23. Cao, Z., Simon, T., Wei, S.-E., Sheikh, Y.: Realtime multiperson 2D pose estimation using part affinity fields. In: CVPR (2017)
24. Nie, X.: Human pose estimation with parsing induced learner. In: CVPR (2018)
25. Szegedy, C., et al.: Going deeper with convolutions. In: CVPR (2015)
26. Simonyan, K., Zisserman, A.: Very deep convolutional networks for large-scale image recognition. arXiv (2014)
27. Szegedy, C., Vanhoucke, V., Ioffe, S., Shlens, J., Wojna, Z.: Rethinking the inception architecture for computer vision. In: CVPR (2016)
28. Hermans, A., Beyer, L., Leibe, B.: In defense of the triplet loss for person re-identification. arXiv (2017)
29. Gong, K., Liang, X., Shen, X., Lin, L.: Look into person: self-supervised structure-sensitive learning and a new benchmark for human parsing. In: CVPR (2017)
30. Ristani, E., Solera, F., Zou, R., Cucchiara, R., Tomasi, C.: Performance measures and a data set for multi-target, multi-camera tracking. In: Hua, G., Jégou, H. (eds.) ECCV 2016. LNCS, vol. 9914, pp. 17–35. Springer, Cham (2016). https://doi.org/10.1007/978-3-319-48881-3_2
31. Zheng, Z., Zheng, L., Yang, Y.: Unlabeled samples generated by GAN improve the person re-identification baseline in vitro. arXiv (2017)
32. Li, W., Zhu, X., Gong, S.: Harmonious attention network for person re-identification. In: CVPR (2018)
33. Wang, C., Zhang, Q., Huang, C., Liu, W., Wang, X.: Mancs: a multi-task attentional network with curriculum sampling for person re-identification. In: Ferrari, V., Hebert, M., Sminchisescu, C., Weiss, Y. (eds.) ECCV 2018. LNCS, vol. 11208, pp. 384–400. Springer, Cham (2018). https://doi.org/10.1007/978-3-030-01225-0_23
34. Zhao, L., Li, X., Zhuang, Y., Wang, J.: Deeply-learned part-aligned representations for person re-identification. In: ICCV (2017)
35. Sun, Y., Zheng, L., Deng, W., Wang, S.: SVDNet for pedestrian retrieval. In: ICCV (2017)
36. Ruan, W., Liu, W., Bao, Q., Chen, J., Cheng, Y., Mei, T.: POINet: pose-guided ovonic insight network for multi-person pose tracking. In: ACM MM (2019)

DeepStroke: Understanding Glyph Structure with Semantic Segmentation and Tabu Search

Wenguang Wang[1,2], Zhouhui Lian[1,2(✉)], Yingmin Tang[1,2], and Jianguo Xiao[1,2]

[1] Wangxuan Institute of Computer Technology, Peking University, Beijing, China
{wangwenguang,lianzhouhui,tangyingmin,xiaojianguo}@pku.edu.cn
[2] Center For Chinese Font Design and Research, Peking University, Beijing, China

Abstract. Glyphs in many writing systems (e.g., Chinese) are composed of a sequence of strokes written in a specific order. Glyph structure interpreting (i.e., stroke extraction) is one of the most important processing steps in many tasks including aesthetic quality evaluation, handwriting synthesis, character recognition, etc. However, existing methods that rely heavily on accurate shape matching are not only time-consuming but also unsatisfactory in stroke extraction performance. In this paper, we propose a novel method based on semantic segmentation and tabu search to interpret the structure of Chinese glyphs. Specifically, we first employ an improved Fully Convolutional Network (FCN), DeepStroke, to extract strokes, and then use the tabu search to obtain the order how these strokes are drawn. We also build the Chinese Character Stroke Segmentation Dataset (CCSSD) consisting of 67630 character images that can be equally classified into 10 different font styles. This dataset provides a benchmark for both stroke extraction and semantic segmentation tasks. Experimental results demonstrate the effectiveness and efficiency of our method and validate its superiority against the state of the art.

Keywords: Stroke extration · Semantic segmentation · Data sets

1 Introduction

Stroke is the basic component of glyphs in many writing systems (e.g., Chinese). Stroke extraction plays an important role in applications such as offline character recognition, writing style analysis, aesthetic visual quality evaluation, handwriting synthesis, etc. Up to now, a number of stroke extraction approaches for Chinese characters have been proposed, which can be roughly classified into two categories: unsupervised methods and data-driven methods. However, those existing methods are typically time-consuming and poor in performance due to costly but inaccurate correspondence estimation between target and reference glyphs. Consequently, we exploit the state-of-the-art sematic segmentation technique to handle the stroke extraction task.

Y. M. Ro et al. (Eds.): MMM 2020, LNCS 11961, pp. 353–364, 2020.
https://doi.org/10.1007/978-3-030-37731-1_29

Sorting out the correct order of segmented strokes is also critical in order to understand the structure of a Chinese glyph. Stroke order refers to the order how the strokes of a glyph are written, which has been clearly defined in the official standard.

Figure 1 illustrates an overview of the proposed model which takes the binary image and character encoding (CE) of a Chinese character as input. Then, the proposed DeepStroke is utilized to predict the stroke category to which each pixel belongs. We employ popular FCNs models as the backbone of the proposed DeepStroke. In order to fully understand the glyph structure, we also need to get the correct stroke order. Thereby, we further process the segmentation results and generate all independent stroke images. Then, the tabu search algorithm is employed to match the segmented independent strokes with the reference data in a standard KAITI style to get the correct stroke order. In this manner, a given Chinese glyph image (in the resolution of about 300 × 300) can be precisely decomposed into ordered strokes in less than 120 ms.

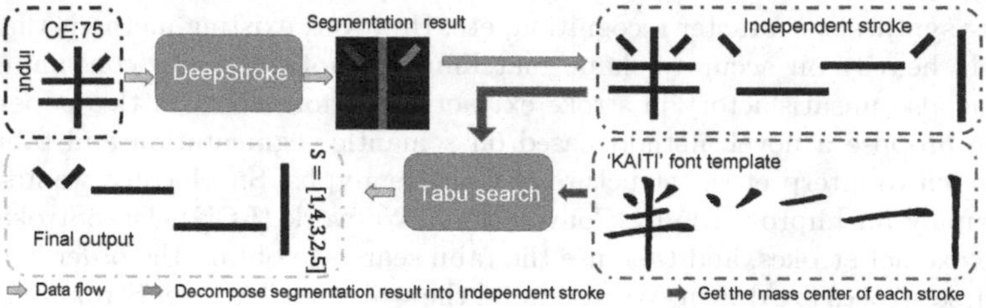

Fig. 1. An overview of our method.

As we know, building large-scale annotated databases is critical in the community of machine learning. In this paper, we construct the Chinese Character Stroke Segmentation Dataset (CCSSD) using 10 different font libraries including LTH font, HLJ font, SS font and so on. There are 6763 images of frequently-used Chinese characters in each font style and every pixel in these images is labeled with the corresponding stroke category. Previous stroke extraction methods usually test their own data and use different metrics, which makes it difficult to fairly compare the effectiveness of the methods. CCSSD can be used as a benchmark to solve this problem.

To sum up, major contributions of this paper are threefold. (1) To the best of our knowledge, this is the first work to apply the semantic segmentation technique to extract strokes from Chinese character images. The proposed method takes much less time but results in better stroke extraction performance compared to other traditional approaches. (2) We are the first to convert the stroke ordering problem into a Traveling Salesman Problem (TSP) to effectively solve it through tabu search with specially designed fitness function. (3) We build a large-scale database (CCSSD) for stroke extraction and sematic segmentation of

Chinese characters, which can serve as a benchmark for fair comparison and is expected to further promote investigations in this field.

2 Related Work

Stroke Extraction. Currently, there exist two categories of methods for glyph stroke extraction: unsupervised methods and data-driven methods. Most unsupervised methods [9,11] do not need template characters by using feature point and contour information. However, those unsupervised methods can only extract basic strokes (e.g., Heng, Shu), which means that composed strokes would be incorrectly segmented into several basic strokes. Data-driven methods [4,10] typically require a standard font library as reference data, in which all characters have been decomposed into independent strokes. Strokes of the target glyph can be obtained according to the shape matching results since the stroke information of the reference glyph is available. However, data-driven methods perform well only when the target glyph is similar to the corresponding reference data, making them less versatile.

Semantic Segmentation. Traditionally, semantic segmentation systems rely heavily on the hand-crafted features combined with classifiers. Thanks to the success of Deep Learning, large numbers of deep neural network models have been proposed for the semantic segmentation problem. [6] is the first to use fully convolutional networks (FCNs) to solve this problem. FCN is not only effective but also elegant because of its capability of conducting end-to-end training. After that, several variants based on FCNs have been presented, such as DeepLab [1,2], PSPNet [14].

3 Chinese Character Stroke Segmentation Dataset

3.1 Data Set

There is no benchmark publicly available for the fair comparison of stroke extraction methods until 2016 [4], which means that most of these kinds of papers test on their own data and use different metrics. What is worse, the benchmark proposed in [4] only has 4 types of font style and 639 characters for each type, which is too small to be used for performance evaluation of different methods. To overcome these difficulties, we propose the Chinese Character Stroke Segmentation Dataset (CCSSD).

Classes and Annotations. We use unique attributes of Chinese character images to create a tool for semi-automatic extraction of strokes. We only need to manually mark the skeleton of each stroke in each Chinese character in stroke order. Marking the skeleton of one stroke takes about 3 s. On average, there are 10.6 strokes per Chinese character, which means that annotating a Chinese character takes about 31.8 s. CCSSD consists of ten different fonts including

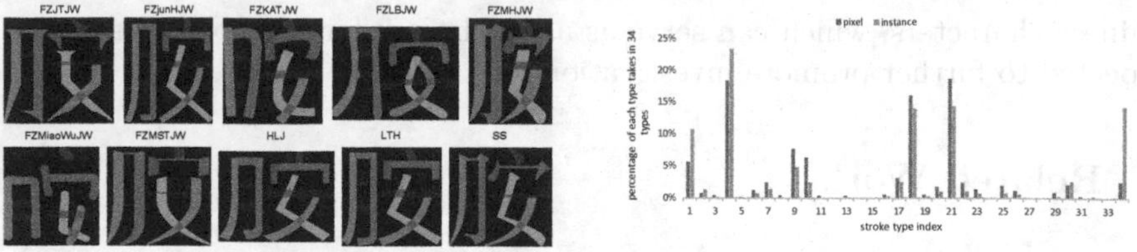

(a) Examples of a character with different styles in CCSSD.

(b) Instance and pixel proportion of other 34 types.

Fig. 2. Information of CCSSD

LTH, HLJ, SS, FZLBJW and so on. Each font has 6763 binary images of Chinese characters, and each pixel on the images is marked with the stroke type to which it belongs. We divide the strokes into 33 categories.

Ambiguous Cases. Strokes might overlap with each other in a character image, many semantic segmentation datasets, such as PASCAL Context [7], classify the overlapping area as the category which is in forefront. However, it is unsuitable for our task since the overlapping areas belong to all crossed strokes. Therefore, we add a new category named "cross" denoting the overlapping region. Dealing with overlapping areas in this way provides great convenience for subsequent processing.

Dataset Splits. We split our CCSSD in two ways: inside font and outside font. For inside font, we randomly divide those 6763 characters in each font into a training set with 3415 Chinese characters and a test set of 3349 Chinese characters. For outside font, we divide 10 fonts into a test set of 3 font including HLJ, SS, FZLBJW and a training set of other 7 fonts.

Statistical Analysis. We find that the proportion of background in all images of 10 fonts is 63.7%, which means that the background takes the largest proportion in all categories. We next calculated the proportion of instances and pixels that exclude the background in Fig. 2(b), we can find that CCSSD is extremely unbalance in the categories.

3.2 Metrics

Let us first review the frequently-used evaluation metrics for common-purpose semantic segmentation and scene parsing that are defined as:

mean IOU (M-IOU):

$$(1/n_{cl}) \sum_i n_{ii}/(t_i + \sum_j n_{ji} - n_{ii}), \tag{1}$$

We propose the following two new metrics base on M-IOU and our task, background IOU (B-IOU):

$$n_{00}/(t_0 + \sum_j n_{j0} - n_{00}), \tag{2}$$

foreground frequency weighted IOU (FFW-IOU):

$$(\sum_{k,k\neq 0} t_k)^{-1} \sum_{i,i\neq 0} t_i n_{ii}/(t_i + \sum_j n_{ji} - n_{ii}). \tag{3}$$

Where n_{ij} is the number of pixels in class i predicted to belong to class j, n_{cl} denotes the number of different stroke classes, and $t_i = \sum_j n_{ij}$ is the total number of pixels in class i.

For the background that occupies the largest proportion in the image, we use B-IOU to evaluate the performance on background type. For the extremely unbalance existing in our dataset, we use FFW-IOU to respect the foreground accuracy. And M-IOU is used to evaluate if the test model can get balance performance in the unbalance categories.

4 Method Description

Figure 1 depicts the pipeline of our method. We first employ the proposed DeepStroke to get stroke segmentation results. Then, we decompose those stroke segmentation results into independent strokes by analysing the connected region. Finally, we utilize the tabu search algorithm to match the segmented independent strokes with the reference data in a standard KAITI style to get the correct stroke order.

4.1 DeepStroke

As shown in Fig. 3, the proposed DeepStroke consists of the following three parts: the FCN backbone, the Stroke List module, and the Inference module. All FCN models which are designed for semantic segmentation task can be used as the backbone of our model. Here, we mainly introduce the version of DeepStroke using DeepLabV3+ [3] which is comparable to the state of the art. There is still much room for improvement when using DeeplabV3+ for stroke extraction due to the special characteristic of Chinese glyphs. As shown in Fig. 3, two new modules which are annotated as Stroke List and Inference in the diagram are integrated into the backbone to build our model.

Stroke List Module. When segmenting strokes in different categories, our network can only judge from the distribution of black and white pixels in the input image. On the contrary, typical semantic segmentation tasks use three-channel color images as input, that means segmentation can be made based on the pixel's color value. What is worse, some stroke categories are so similar in shapes (i.e., the pixel distribution) that even human beings can not correctly distinguish them, such as HengZhe and HengZG. Moreover, complex strokes can be disassembled into simple strokes, which also increases the discrimination difficulty of the network. For example, HengZZZ can be disassembled into two Heng strokes and two Shu strokes. So it is quite difficult for the network to determine whether the stroke is HengZZZ or the combination of Heng and Shu strokes by using only pixel distribution information. In order to solve the problem that some stroke categories are indistinguishable (we call these categories hard classes), we design a new module called Stroke List. This branch requires an additional input named character encoding (CE) which ranges from 1 to 6763. In addition, we establish a 6763×35 table in advance to store the quantity information of each stroke category owned by each Chinese character. Specially, the value of the first column in the table is always 1, representing existence of the background class. Character encoding is to tell the network which Chinese character is entered and select the corresponding $1 \times 1 \times 35$ stroke list from the above-mentioned table. Then, we up-sample the $1 \times 1 \times 35$ stroke list and concatenate it with the ASPP output. The Stroke List branch gives the network strong guidance with character information, allowing the network to generate only the stroke categories owned by the input Chinese characters. Our experiments show that the additional cost of adding this module is small but the resulting effect is significant.

Inference Module. Using binary images as input increases the difficulty of distinguishing between each stroke category but reduces the difficulty of distinguishing between the background and the stroke (foreground) categories. Since the background and foreground pixels are easily distinguishable in the origin input image, we propose the Inference module to reuse the information of input image and make the accuracy of classifying the foreground category and the background category 100%. As shown in Fig. 3, we have a probability map (got by a softmax layer) of 35 channels in the Inference module. For common purpose FCN models, it will take a argmax operation in the probability map when inference. We do a simple modification by replacing the channel 0 (representing the background probability) with the input binary image. Our experiments demonstrate that this simple modification can make the foreground and background be correctly distinguished.

4.2 Stroke Ordering via Tabu Search

After processing a given character image via DeepStroke, we get the category of each pixel in the image. However, the ultimate aim of our task is to extract independent strokes with correct order from the images. As shown in the right part of Fig. 1, we solve this problem in the following two steps. First, we extract independent strokes without correct order labels directly from the output of DeepStroke. Second, we compare the result of first step with the correponding reference data in the KAITI font style and use the tabu search algorithm to get the correct order for each stroke. Details of these two steps are presented as follows.

Step 1: getting independent strokes. Thanks to the convenience brought by adding a new categories named cross category (introduced in Sect. 3), we

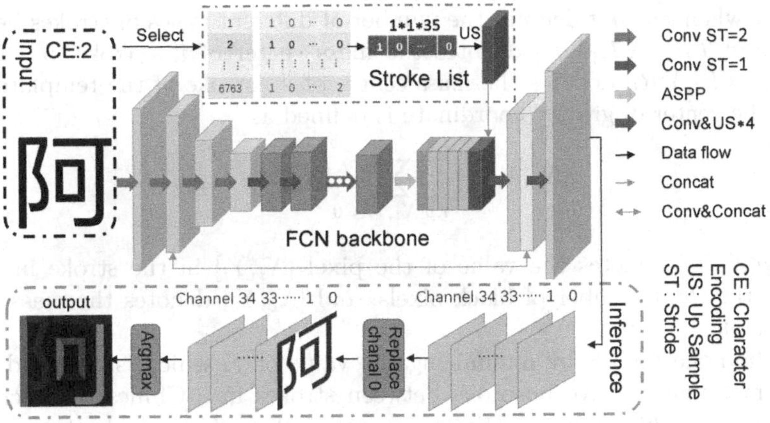

Fig. 3. The architecture of our DeepStroke

can extract independent strokes easily. Our stroke extraction method is base on the processing of connected regions. To be Specific, we repeatedly combine the connected region of the cross category with that of each stroke category, and finally obtain the independent strokes in various stroke categories.

Step 2: getting stroke order via the tabu search. The aim of this step is to obtain a digital sequence S by comparing the sequence of stroke barycentric coordinates of "independent stroke" and "KAITI template". The digital sequence S represents the rank each stroke belongs to. For example, in Fig. 1, the digital sequence should be $[1,4,3,2,5]$. This digital sequence represents that the first stroke in the independent strokes is the first stroke for the Chinese character input, the second stroke in the independent strokes is the fourth stroke for the character and so on. Finding such a digital sequence is a variant of the traveling salesman problem (TSP). TSP is an NP-hard problem in combinatorial optimization, and it can be effectively addressed via many intelligent optimization methods including the tabu search algorithm used in this paper. Our definition of the fitness function is different from the classical TSP. We define our fitness function f as

$$f = \lambda t + \sum_{i=1}^{N} \sqrt{(XT_{S_i} - XR_i)^2 + (YT_{S_i} - YR_i)^2} \tag{4}$$

$$t = \sum_{i=1}^{N} I(TT_{S_i} \neq TR_i), \tag{5}$$

where S is the digital sequence that we want to calculate, N is the number of strokes the input Chinese character has, λ is a hyper-parameter which will be set later, TT_i denotes the stroke categories of ith stroke of unsorted strokes ("independent stroke" in Fig. 1), TR_i denotes the stroke categories of ith stroke of template strokes ("KAITI font template" in Fig. 1), $I(x) = 0$ when $x = 0$,

$I(x) = 1$ when $x \neq 0$, t denotes the number of different types of strokes between $TT[S]$ and TR, $[XT_i, YT_i]$ denotes the mass center of ith stroke in unsorted strokes, $[XR_i, YR_i]$ denotes the mass center of ith stroke of the template character. The center of gravity coordinate is defined as

$$[X_c, Y_c] = \sum_{i, p[X_i, Y_i]=0} [X_i, Y_i]/T, \tag{6}$$

where $p[X_i, Y_i]$ denotes the value of the pixel $[X_i, Y_i]$ in the stroke image, T denotes the total number of black pixels, and $[X_c, Y_c]$ denotes the mass center of the stroke image.

We find the best S by minimizing the value of f, which is designed based on the fact that relative positions between strokes in a Chinese character are considerably stable. We use the mass center of a given stroke to represent the stroke's position. Minimizing the second term of the fitness function is to get a S which could make $[XT[S], YT[S]]$ be more similar with $[XR, YR]$. However, optimizing only the second term of f is not enough because mass centers can not explicitly represent the related position of strokes. The mass centers of some strokes can be quite close to each others. Thereby, we add a penalty term to the fitness function, in which λ should be a large value to enforce $TT[S]$ and TR having the same category sequence. For example, given a Chinese character input (i.e., TT = [DianZuo, Heng, Heng, DianYou, Shu], TR = [DianZuo, DianYou, Heng, Heng, Shu]) shown in Fig. 1, if $S = [1, 4, 3, 2, 5]$, then $TT[S]$ and TR have the same category sequence. Experiments show that our method is able to find the correct stroke order for Chinese characters with high accuracy.

5 Experiments

In this section, we first evaluate the performance of existing semantic segmentation methods and the proposed DeepStroke. Then, we employ the output of DeepStroke to get independent strokes in correct order via the tabu search.

5.1 Performance of Baseline and DeepStroke

We first evaluate the performance of different baseline methods on our dataset. Most settings of the baseline are the same as the provided code but the iteration time chosen as 50000. The performance of each baseline is shown in Table 2. We can see that there is still much room for improvement in the original semantic segmentation methods for our benchmark.

Just like DeepLabV3, we perform bootstrapping (**BS**) on hard classes. As shown in Table 1, we employ DeepLab-lfov as the backbone of our DeepStroke and examine the impact of the proposed two modules (i.e., Stroke List module (SL) and Inference module (Inf)) and the bootstrapping (BS) on accuracy when added to the selected backbone. We can observe that bootstrapping brings about

Table 1. The ablation study conducted on the test set of LTH when employing DeepLab-lfov as the backbone: **BS**: bootstrapping. **SL**: Stroke List module. **Inf**: Inference module.

BS	SL	Inf	Metric		
			M-IOU	FFW-IOU	B-IOU
			68.996%	71.179%	85.128%
✓			71.726%	71.569%	85.191%
✓	✓		81.095%	80.560%	90.264%
✓	✓	✓	93.056%	94.414%	100%

Table 2. Comparison of different models evaluated on the test set of LTH font. **DLab**: DeepLab. **DStroke**: DeepStroke.

Model	M-IOU	FFW-IOU	B-IOU	Model	M-IOU	FFW-IOU	B-IOU
fcn-32s [8]	44.572%	47.591%	64.154%	DLab-lfov [1]	68.996%	71.179%	85.128%
fcn-16s [8]	57.838%	70.056%	87.789%	DLab-resnet [2]	74.472%	80.167%	92.548%
fcn-8s [8]	73.442%	84.290%	96.919%	DLabV3+ [3]	87.337%	94.056%	99.622%
PSPNet [14]	67.766%	83.610%	99.694%	DStroke-lfov	93.056%	94.414%	100%
DASPP [12]	78.695%	89.586%	98.390%	DStroke-resnet	89.875%	92.373%	100%
BiSeNet [13]	78.975%	90.818%	98.277%	DStroke-V3+	95.848%	96.783%	100%

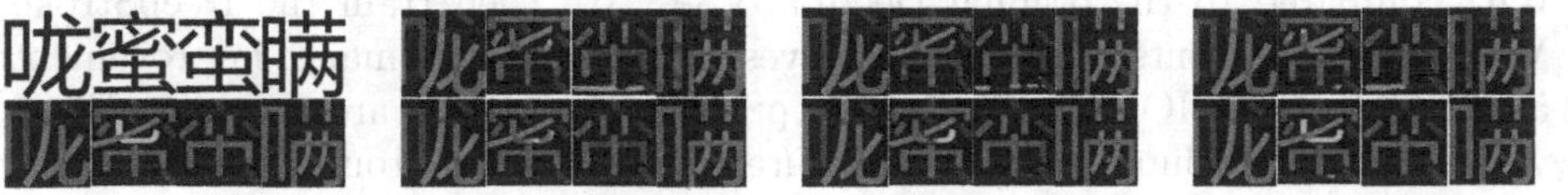

(a) input&GT (b) lfov (c) resnet (d) V3+

Fig. 4. Segmentation results of different models.

3% improvement in M-IOU. With the Stroke List module, all three types of metrics by more than 5%. The Inference module increases the values of all three types of metrics by more than 9.7%. Through above analyses, a conclude can be made that the proposed modules can significantly improve the performance of the original segmentation networks.

In Table 2, we compare the performance of different models, including 8 existing segmentation networks and three DeepStroke models whose backbones are the baseline in Table 2, respectively. In Table 2, the model DStroke-lfov means a DeepStroke model that employs DeepLab-lfov as its backbone. We can see that the proposed modules help to achieve significant performance improvements on models with different backbones. Figure 4(b), (c), (d) show the results of different models, where the name of each subgraph indicates different backbones used. The first row of each subgraph shows results of the original network and the second row represents the results of the DeepStroke model using this network as

(a) HLJ (b) SS (c) FZLBJW

Fig. 5. Ground truth (first row of each subfigure) and segmentation results (second row of each subfigure) of our method for different fonts when employing DeepStroke-V3+(MF) model.

its backbone. Specially, in the 2nd–4th column of Fig. 4, we depict images that contain hard classes to show the superiority of our models.

In the aforementioned experiments, models are all trained on the training set of LTH font and tested on the test set of LTH font. However, the more important thing we want to know is whether the model is able to accurately segment character images in unseen font styles. Thus, we also train the models on all the images in one or several fonts and use the trained models to process all 6763 character images in the three test fonts (HLJ, SS, FZLBJW), which are not involved in the training procedure. From Table 3, we can see that the performance of DeepLabV3+ which is only trained on LTH font is poor while our modified DeepStroke-V3+ model achieves a 11%–26% performance improvement in FFW-IOU compared to the original DeepLabV3+. We then train the DeepStroke-V3+ model on 7 fonts, which also achieves significant performance improvement: 5%–24% in FFW-IOU. Results of DeepStroke-V3+ (MF) are shown in Fig. 5, where the first column of each subfigure represents the ground truth and the second column represents segmentation results.

In the bottom part of Table 3, we show the performance of the Lian's method [5] and Chen's method [4]. Compared to these methods, our model is more effective (sets the new state of the art) and much more efficient (20 s–30 s per image for the Lian's and Chen's method and 34 ms per image for ours (GTX1070 GPU, 50k iterations, 10.5 h of training time)).

Our method can also handle handwritten Chinese characters. The only thing that needs to be added is to binarize the original image first. To better evaluate

Table 3. Performance (FFW-IOU) on three unseen test fonts and handwritten data: **LTH**: The model is only trained on LTH font. **MF**: The model is trained on other 7 fonts of CCSSD. DeepStroke: DeepStroke-V3+.

Method	HLJ	SS	FZLBJW	Handwritten data
DeepLabV3+(LTH)	78.693%	62.235%	39.678%	–
DeepStroke(LTH)	89.816%	80.828%	65.444%	–
DeepStroke(MF)	95.124%	96.632%	89.476%	73.347%
Lian's method [5]	88.660%	91.798%	88.285%	71.976%
Chen's method [4]	71.958%	72.197%	67.749%	46.907%

Fig. 6. Segmentation results of some handwritten characters.

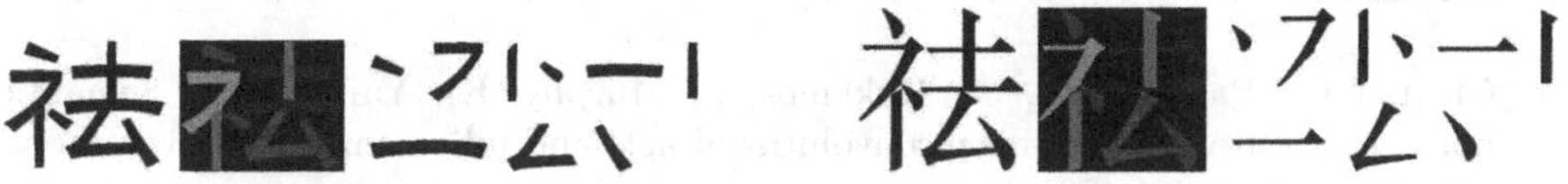

(a) HLJ (b) SS

Fig. 7. Getting independent stroke in correct order.

segmentation performance on handwritten data, we built a small dataset containing 70 character images written by different persons. Table 3 compares the performance of different methods and some segmentation examples are shown in Fig. 6. Although our method clearly outperforms other two approaches, for segmentation of handwritten Chinese characters, there is much room to improve.

5.2 Obtaining Stroke Order via Tabu Search

To evaluate the performance of stroke ordering, we propose a new metric called ordering accuracy (o.acc), which is obtained by computing the percentage of the correctly ordered characters in the font library. With λ set to 100, iteration times of the tabu search set to 30, segmentation results of DeepStroke-V3+ (MF) employed as input, we get o.acc values of 88.0%, 91.4% and 76.0% on HLJ, SS and FZLBJW, respectively. Some results are shown in Fig. 7. These operations take an average of 84 ms for each character image on an i7-6700k machine. It can be concluded that the accuracy of stroke ordering is positively correlated to the segmentation performance.

6 Conclusion

This paper proposed a novel method to understand the structure of Chinese glyph effectively and efficiently. Specifically, DeepStroke makes full use of the characteristics of Chinese characters, which greatly improves the segmentation performance. The tabu search algorithm is delicately used for getting correct stroke order. These operations take less than 120 ms per image. We also established a dataset called CCSSD to fill the gaps in the segmentation data of Chinese strokes. CCSSD also provides a benchmark for both stroke extraction and semantic segmentation tasks. We believe that both the dataset and our proposed method will further promote the investigation in this direction.

Acknowledgments. This work was supported by National Natural Science Foundation of China (Grant No.: 61672056 and 61672043) and Key Laboratory of Science, Technology and Standard in Press Industry (Key Laboratory of Intelligent Press Media Technology).

References

1. Chen, L.C., Papandreou, G., Kokkinos, I., Murphy, K., Yuille, A.L.: Semantic image segmentation with deep convolutional nets and fully connected CRFs. Comput. Sci. **4**, 357–361 (2014)
2. Chen, L.C., Papandreou, G., Kokkinos, I., Murphy, K., Yuille, A.L.: DeepLab: semantic image segmentation with deep convolutional nets, atrous convolution, and fully connected CRFs. arXiv preprint arXiv:1606.00915 (2016)
3. Chen, L.C., Zhu, Y., Papandreou, G., Schroff, F., Adam, H.: Encoder-decoder with atrous separable convolution for semantic image segmentation (2018)
4. Chen, X., Lian, Z., Tang, Y., Xiao, J.: A benchmark for stroke extraction of Chinese characters. Acta Scientiarum Naturalium Universitatis Pekinensis **2**, 4 (2016)
5. Lian, Z., Xiao, J.: Automatic shape morphing for Chinese characters. In: SIGGRAPH Asia 2012 Technical Briefs, p. 2. ACM (2012)
6. Long, J., Shelhamer, E., Darrell, T.: Fully convolutional networks for semantic segmentation. In: Proceedings of the IEEE Conference on Computer Vision and Pattern Recognition, pp. 3431–3440 (2015)
7. Mottaghi, R., et al.: The role of context for object detection and semantic segmentation in the wild. In: IEEE Conference on Computer Vision and Pattern Recognition, pp. 891–898 (2014)
8. Shelhamer, E., Long, J., Darrell, T.: Fully convolutional models for semantic segmentation. TPAMI (2016)
9. Sun, Y., Qian, H., Xu, Y.: A geometric approach to stroke extraction for the Chinese calligraphy robot. In: 2014 IEEE International Conference on Robotics and Automation (ICRA), pp. 3207–3212. IEEE (2014)
10. Wang, C., Lian, Z., Tang, Y., Xiao, J.: Automatic correspondence finding for Chinese characters using graph matching. In: Seventh International Conference on Image and Graphics, pp. 545–550 (2013)
11. Wang, X., Liang, X., Sun, L., Liu, M.: Triangular mesh based stroke segmentation for Chinese calligraphy. In: 2013 12th International Conference on Document Analysis and Recognition (ICDAR), pp. 1155–1159. IEEE (2013)
12. Yang, M., Yu, K., Zhang, C., Li, Z., Yang, K.: DenseASPP for semantic segmentation in street scenes. In: Proceedings of the IEEE Conference on Computer Vision and Pattern Recognition, pp. 3684–3692 (2018)
13. Yu, C., Wang, J., Peng, C., Gao, C., Yu, G., Sang, N.: BiSeNet: bilateral segmentation network for real-time semantic segmentation. arXiv preprint arXiv:1808.00897 (2018)
14. Zhao, H., Shi, J., Qi, X., Wang, X., Jia, J.: Pyramid scene parsing network (2016)

3D Spatial Coverage Measurement of Aerial Images

Abdullah Alfarrarjeh[1(✉)], Zeyu Ma[2], Seon Ho Kim[1], and Cyrus Shahabi[1]

[1] Integrated Media Systems Center, University of Southern California, Los Angeles, USA
{alfarrar,seonkim,shahabi}@usc.edu

[2] Electronic Engineering Department, Tsinghua University, Beijing, China
mzy16@mails.tsinghua.edu.cn

Abstract. Unmanned aerial vehicles (UAVs) such as drones are becoming significantly prevalent in both daily life (e.g., event coverage, tourism) and critical situations (e.g., disaster management, military operations), generating an unprecedented number of aerial images and videos. UAVs are usually equipped with various sensors (e.g., GPS, accelerometers and gyroscopes) so provide sufficient spatial metadata that describe the spatial extent (referred to as aerial field-of-view) of recorded imagery. Such spatial metadata can be used efficiently to answer a fundamental question about how well a collection of aerial imagery covers a certain area spatially by evaluating the adequacy of the collected aerial imagery and estimating their sufficiency. This paper provides an answer to such questions by introducing 3D spatial coverage measurement models to collectively quantify the spatial and directional coverage of a geo-tagged aerial image dataset. Through experimental evaluation using real datasets, the paper demonstrates that our proposed models can be implemented with highly efficient computation of 3D space geometry.

Keywords: Geo-tagged aerial image · 3D spatial coverage · Aerial field of view

1 Introduction

As various drone applications begin to use more images for monitoring tasks (e.g., disaster management, event coverage)[1], such applications are looking for a more systematic way to collect and manage aerial images. These needs are highlighted by current trends in the use of drones. Excel (the utility provider for the Denver area) just received Federal Aviation Administration (FAA) permission to use

[1] In the near future, aerial images can be potentially used for smart city applications, e.g., street cleanliness classification [1] and material recognition [3].

A. Alfarrarjeh and Z. Ma—These authors contributed equally to this work.
Z. Ma—This author contributed to the work during his research visit at USC.

Y. M. Ro et al. (Eds.): MMM 2020, LNCS 11961, pp. 365–377, 2020.
https://doi.org/10.1007/978-3-030-37731-1_30

drones out of visual site of the operator for inspecting transmission lines [14]. The use of drones for offshore facilities is growing both in the US Gulf of Mexico as well as the North Sea.

When we deal with a large amount of geo-tagged visual data, especially including drone imagery data, there exist well-known challenges. Most data are being collected and stored in an independent and decentralized way, so there are few systematic methods to know the availability of data, to measure the coverage of visual information, or to efficiently access needed data with regarding a specific region of interest. For example, when we have thousands of geo-tagged images in Los Angeles, how do we intuitively measure how much they visually cover the city? How do we identify unrecorded street blocks in the dataset? Collaboratively collecting visual data in a centralized system to answer the questions is challenging due to the size of data, which requires a huge cost to move around the data over the network, especially in a situation when data bandwidth is constrained such as in disasters. Furthermore, even in the presence of a comprehensive shared visual dataset, deciding what visual data is relevant to an application is challenging, especially because it is task-dependent and computationally intensive if we rely solely on traditional computer vision techniques [9,18]. Lastly, timely data collection becomes critical in some applications such as situation awareness in disasters. While crowdsourcing using autonomous sensors (i.e., drones) over a wide area is technically feasible and many approaches to coordinate such a collection have been studied with traditional data, spatial crowdsourcing techniques [5,12] for visual data remain ineffective or impractical. We argue that this is due primarily to the lack of a good measure of visual coverage, which is essential in defining the degree to which a data collection task is completed.

To overcome the challenges, especially with aerial images, we devise 3D spatial coverage measurement models to quantify the visual coverage and completeness of the aerial images relevant to a region of interest. UAVs are usually equipped with various sensors (e.g., GPS, accelerometers, and gyroscopes) so provide spatial metadata that describes the recorded imagery. However, spatial metadata of images by themselves do not provide a full visual understanding of their recorded regions. Hence, there is a need to define appropriate models for measuring the spatial coverage of a geo-tagged image dataset collectively based on human visual perception (e.g., Fig. 1). In this paper, we extend the spatial coverage models for ground-level 2D images proposed by Alfarrarjeh *et al.* [2] to 3D aerial images. One baseline model (referred to as *Volume Coverage Measurement Model*) calculates the percentage of the overlapping volume between a certain 3D space and the collectively covered volume of a set of images (Fig. 2). The other model calculates the coverage percentage with respect to various Euler-angle directions to assure the visibility of the region from all viewable angles (*Euler-based Directional Coverage Measurement Model*). The third model further extends the spatial coverage to comprise the measurement at fine-granular sub-regions (e.g., 3D cells) of the interested region (especially, when it is large) and then aggregate the local measurements by weighting the coverage of each sub-region (*Weighted Cell Coverage Measurement Model*).

Estimating 3D space coverage, in reality, is associated with two main issues. One is the computational complexity of the models that inevitably include time-consuming geometric operations on complex 3D objects. Therefore, we propose an efficient approximate measurement solution using the Monte Carlo algorithm. Another issue is the scalability of the models when a dataset grows large while the region of interest remains relatively small compared with the geographical region of the whole dataset. To address this issue, we propose a filtering approach to quickly calculate the coverage using only a subset of selected images.

Through experimental evaluation on two real drone imagery datasets [16,17], we validated the proposed models. The results demonstrate that our approaches efficiently provided the 3D spatial coverage measurement of drone images intuitively complying with human visual perception [2]. Also, our filtering and approximate geometrical approaches enabled the models to properly address both scalability and efficiency challenges while preserving the validity of the models.

Fig. 1. A set of aerial field of views

Fig. 2. A range query in 3D space

2 Related Work

To the extent of our knowledge, there is no existing work in the measurement of the 3D spatial coverage of aerial images for a geographical 3D space. However, there are several works [9,18] relevant to our problem. Papatheodorou *et al.* [18] examined the problem of maximizing the area coverage when controlling autonomous robots to record videos. Del Bue *et al.* [9] utilized 3D reconstruction algorithms (e.g., [19]) to control robot movement in order to obtain full visual coverage of a given area. But such content-based methods are time-consuming and requires many similar images to cover all features for each specific place. Different from these works, the methods proposed in [2] quantify the spatial coverage based only on the geospatial metadata carried with images. This relevant work only considers the spatial coverage problem in 2D space while this paper is extending the problem to the 3D case.

Regarding 3D geometric calculation, which is relative to the approaches we are to use, there are also some work. For example, Bringmann and Friedrich [8] investigated the approximation approach of several geometry problems, including the volume calculation problem. But they did not pose the problem in a real-world scenario.

3 Preliminaries and Problem Description

3.1 3D Field of View Model

A UAV is typically equipped with a camera as well as various sensors (e.g., GPS, 3-axis accelerometer and gyroscope). Hence, the collected visual data (i.e., an aerial image or an aerial video frame) can be conveniently tagged with spatial metadata which is referred to as *Aerial Field of View (f)*. An f is defined in Definition 1 and illustrated in Fig. 3. The Aerial field-of-view dataset $\mathcal{F}$ is a set of n fs (i.e., $\mathcal{F} = \{f_1, f_2, \cdots f_n\}$).

Definition 1 (Aerial Field of View [15]**).** *Given an aerial image I_j, the aerial field of view f_j is represented by the eight parameters acquired at the image capturing time, $f_j \equiv \langle lat, lng, hgt, \theta_y, \theta_p, \theta_r, \alpha, R\rangle$, where lat and lng are the GPS coordinates (i.e., latitude and longitude) of the camera location, hgt is the camera height with respect to the ground, θ_y, θ_p, and θ_r are three rotation angles of the camera pose (θ_y is the yaw angle rotating around the vertical axis, θ_p is the pitch angle arotating around the lateral axis, θ_r is the roll angle rotating around the longitudinal axis), α is the camera visible angle, and R is the maximum visible distance.*

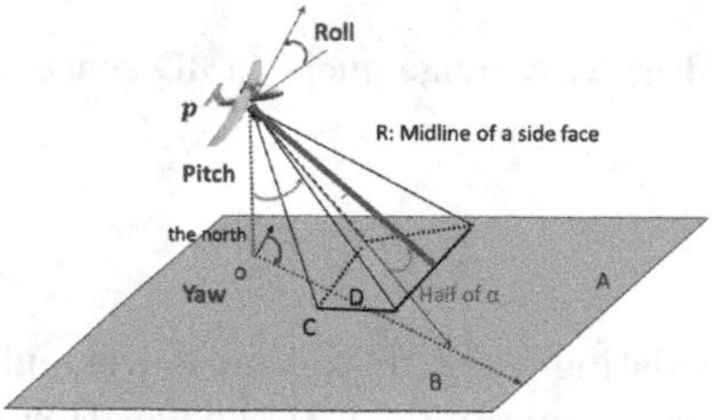

Fig. 3. Aerial field of view (f)

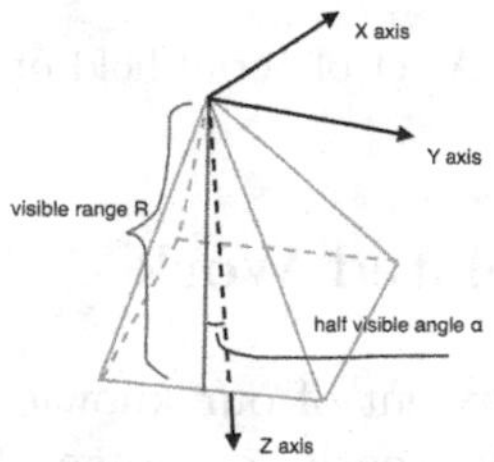

Fig. 4. A pyramid corresponding to an f in the local coordinate system

3.2 Problem Description

Given a dataset $\mathcal{F}$ and a query region in 3D space R_q (e.g., a cubic region), the 3D spatial coverage measurement problem is formulated as calculating the geo-awareness percentage of $\mathcal{F}$ to the visual space located in R_q.

3.3 Converting Spatial Metadata into the 3D World System

Each f is a set of raw sensor readings. Therefore, the first step is to convert these readings into a geometric object in the 3D world system, i.e., each f is represented as a pyramid. Then, the parameters composing an f is converted into the five 3D points constituting a pyramid (i.e., $\forall f_i \in \mathcal{F} : f_i := \langle p_{i0}, p_{i1}, p_{i2}, p_{i3}, p_{i4}\rangle$).

This conversion is performed using a transformation between two coordinate systems: local and world. The local coordinate system is defined by placing the camera location at the origin (i.e., the camera location is at (0, 0, 0)) with the x-axis pointing forward, the y-axis pointing to the right, and the z-axis pointing downward. The world coordinate system is defined with the x, y, and z axes pointing to the East, the North, and upward, respectively.

In the local coordinate system, without loss of generality, we assume that the camera is attached at the bottom of a UAV, so the generated pyramid of an f_i is positioned to point downwards. Also, for simplicity, we assume that R represents the length of the mid-line of a side face of the pyramid (red line in Fig. 4) and α is twice the angle between the z-axis and the mid-line (see Fig. 4). Next, the pyramid is oriented and translated according to Eq. 1–3[2], where A is the rotation transform matrix between the two systems according to θ_y, θ_p and θ_r, and x_i, y_i, and z_i are the world position converted from lat, lng, and hgt. We will not dive into the details here.

$$p_{i,0}^{local} = (0, 0, 0) \tag{1}$$

$$p_{i,j}^{local} = (\pm R\sin(\alpha), \pm R\sin(\alpha), R\cos(\alpha)), j = \{1, 2, 3, 4\} \tag{2}$$

$$p_{i,j}^{world} = A \cdot p_{i,j}^{local} + (x_i, y_i, z_i), j = \{0, 1, 2, 3, 4\} \tag{3}$$

4 Coverage Measurement Models in the 3D Space

4.1 Overview of 2D Spatial Coverage Measurement Models

Alfarrarjeh *et al.* [2] presented three space coverage measurement models using the 2D field-of-view descriptor [6] of ground-level images. The first model only considers estimating the percentage of the overlapped area covered by $\mathcal{F}$ within a query range (referred to as *Area Coverage Measurement Model* (ACM)). However, the second model measures the percentage of the covered area with respect to various viewable directions to ensure the visibility of the region from all viewable angles (referred to as *Directional Coverage Measurement Model* (DCM)). The third model adds a further level of measurement by estimating the visibility at a finer granularity by dividing the area of a large query range into smaller cells and evaluating the visibility per cell; then it aggregates the weighted results into one (referred to as *Cell Coverage Measurement Model* (CCM)).

4.2 Proposed 3D Spatial Coverage Measurement Models

Estimating the 3D spatial coverage of aerial images is an analogous problem to that in the 2D area. Therefore, we adapt the previously discussed models to fit in the 3D space. In particular, ACM is extended to consider calculating the volume coverage of $\mathcal{F}$ with respect to R_q as shown in Eq. 4 (referred to as *Volume Coverage Measurement Model* (VCM)). This model requires calculating the union

[2] Regarding Eq. 2, each combination of signs corresponds to the four different points.

and intersection operations of 3D objects. Performing such operations on $\mathcal{F}$ in 3D space is very time-consuming because each of these operations generates a complex polyhedral structure (see Fig. 5). DCM is extended to measure the coverage considering viewing directions in the three Euler angles (i.e., yaw, pitch, and roll) (see Fig. 6), referred to as *Euler-based Directional Coverage Measurement Model* (ECM). The third model (*Weighted Cell Coverage Measurement Model* (WCM)) divides R_q into 3D cells (see Fig. 7). Thereafter, it measures the coverage per 3D cell, and then performs a weighted aggregation of the coverage of all cells. The weighted aggregation can be done in various ways. One way is to consider the relative volume of each cell with respect to that of R_q. However, this approach might weigh all cells equally if they have the same volume. Alternatively, each cell is weighted with respect to its distance from the subset of $\mathcal{F}$ covering that cell as shown in Eqs. 5–6.

$$VCM(R_q, \mathcal{F}) = \frac{Volume(Overlap(R_q, Union(\mathcal{F})))}{Volume(R_q)} \tag{4}$$

$$Weight(c_j) = (1 - \frac{Avg.(Distance(f_i, c_j) | f_i \in \mathcal{F}, f_i \cap c_j)}{MaxDist}), \forall c_j \in Cells \tag{5}$$

$$MaxDist = \max(Distance(f_i, c_j) | \forall f_i \in \mathcal{F}, \forall c_j \in Cells, f_i \cap c_j) \tag{6}$$

Fig. 5. Union and overlap in 3D

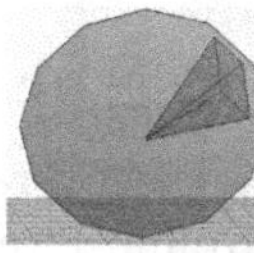

Fig. 6. Direction division in 3D

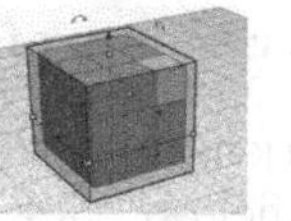

Fig. 7. R_q division in 3D cells

4.3 Practical Challenges and Solutions

There exist significant issues that arise when one uses the 3D coverage models in practice. One issue is efficiency, i.e., whether the coverage models can compute many geometric operations with complex 3D objects in a reasonable amount of time. Another issue is scalability, when the coverage models have to be capable of measuring the coverage for a large-scale dataset as $\mathcal{F}$ grows. We address these challenges by the proposed solutions as follows:

Subsetting $\mathcal{F}$. One way to calculate the coverage of $\mathcal{F}$ with respect to R_q is to use a brute-force approach (i.e., iterating the whole set and considering all objects in $\mathcal{F}$ in the geometrical operations). $\mathcal{F}$ can be potentially large, while R_q might be small compared to the region covered by $\mathcal{F}$. Therefore, a preprocessing step by filtering $\mathcal{F}$ to select only a subset of $\mathcal{F}$ can speed up the calculation of the spatial coverage; hence addressing the scalability issue. Towards this purpose, we propose a filtering approach based on organizing $\mathcal{F}$ in an auxiliary structure (i.e., spatial index structure) which enables retrieving a subset of $\mathcal{F}$ with respect to R_q. One of the state-of-the-art index structures[3] to organize such types of 3D objects is Kd-tree [7]. Storing each 3D object representing an $f \in \mathcal{F}$ can be performed in two ways. One way is to use a bounding box (e.g., cube or sphere) which simplifies storing such complex objects (i.e., pyramids); however using these bounding boxes produces dead space in the storage, while still complicates the organization because of storing high-dimensional objects; hence degrading the performance of the querying operation. Alternatively, our proposed approach simplifies the storage by storing only one point for each f in a Kd-tree. Querying the kd-tree is done in two steps: First, R_q is enlarged by the maximum value of R in $\mathcal{F}$ to consider the spatial extent of each f rather than a single point representing an f (examples are f_1 and f_3 in Fig. 8). Thereafter, the second step prunes any falsely retrieved f (e.g., f_2 in Fig. 8) resulted from the enlargement of R_q. The pseudocode of the approach is provided in Algorithm 1. The cost of building the Kd-tree is $\mathcal{O}(n)$ while the cost of searching it is $\mathcal{O}(\log n)$. Since building a Kd-tree is performed once, filtering based on the Kd-tree is more efficient than the brute-force approach.

Algorithm 1. Subsetting $\mathcal{F}(\mathcal{F}; R_q)$

$\forall f_i \in \mathcal{F}$ is represented by five points $(p_{i0}, p_{i1}, p_{i2}, p_{i3}, p_{i4})$
$\delta = max(f_i.R, \forall f_i \in \mathcal{F})$
Build a KD-tree $(\mathcal{T})$ using p_{i0} $\forall f_i \in \mathcal{F}$
R'_q = Enlarge R_q by δ
$\mathcal{F}' = RangeQuery(\mathcal{T}, R'_q)$
$\mathcal{F}'' = \{\}$
for $f_j \in \mathcal{F}'$ **do**
    if f_j *intersects* R_q **then**
        $\mathcal{F}'' = \mathcal{F}'' \cup f_j$
    end if
end for
return $\mathcal{F}''$

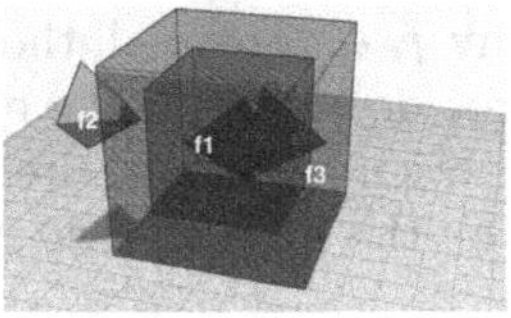

Fig. 8. Subsetting $\mathcal{F}$ using Algorithm 1 (f_1 and f_3 are true-positive, and f_3 is false positive)

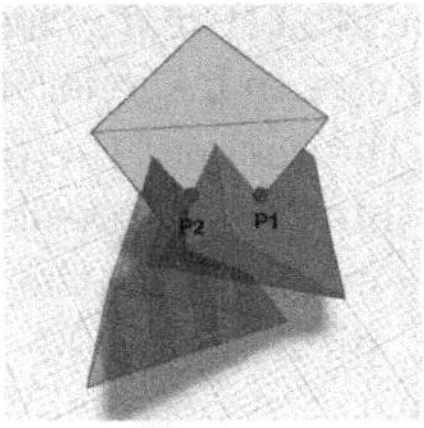

Fig. 9. Union or intersection between polyhedrons

[3] Other index structures include R-tree [11], Quad-tree [10], and Grid.

Approximating Geometric Operations. The proposed coverage models comprise executing multiple union and intersection operations. To analyze the efficiency of our models, we analyze asymptotically the time complexity of these operations. Given that the cost of the union and intersection operations is a function of the number of vertices, the complexity analysis of these two operations can be made by estimating the number of vertices. Our analysis is fundamentally based on the Euler's Polyhedral Formula (see Eq. 7) which specifies the characteristics of a polyhedron where V is the number of vertices, F is the number of faces, and E is the number of edges. Moreover, the faces of a polyhedron can be represented by triangles for simplicity. If a face is not a triangle, lines can be drawn to divide the face into triangles (this process is known as *triangulation*). Subsequently, since every face is a triangle and in a polyhedron every edge joins 2 triangular faces, the number of edges in a triangulated polyhedron is defined in Eq. 8. Based on Eqs. 7–8, the numbers of F and E are all linear in V.

$$V + F - E = 2 \tag{7}$$

$$3 \cdot F = 2 \cdot E \tag{8}$$

When a union operation is performed on n polyhedrons (referred to as $Poly_i, i \in \{1, 2, ..., n\}$ with V_i vertices, F_i faces, and E_i edges), the vertices in the new structure comprise the "original" vertices of each $Poly_i$ and a "new" set of vertices where each one is produced from either an intersection of a face of $Poly_i$ with an edge of $Poly_j$ ($i \neq j$, see point p_1 in Fig. 9) or an intersection of three faces of $Poly_i$, $Poly_j$ and $Poly_k (i \neq j \wedge j \neq k \wedge k \neq i)$ (see point p_2 in Fig. 9). As a result, the total number of the vertices ($V_{\mathbf{total}}$) of the new structure resulting from this operation is bounded by Eq. 9. By further computation, the total time complexity is bounded by $\mathcal{O}(N^4)$[4].

$$V_{\mathbf{total}} \leq \sum_{i \neq j} E_i \cdot F_j + \sum_{i \neq j, j \neq k, k \neq i} F_i \cdot F_j \cdot F_k + \sum V_i = \mathcal{O}(N^3) \tag{9}$$

Because of the high cost of the union and intersection operations on $\mathcal{F}$, especially when it is large, an approximate solution is needed in practice. To address this issue, we utilize a randomized method, particularly the Monte-Carlo method [8]. In particular, to estimate the coverage of $\mathcal{F}$ w.r.t. R_q using Monte-Carlo, a set of random points can be generated within R_q, and then the coverage is estimated by calculating the ratio of the points that are within any $f_i \in \mathcal{F}$ over all the points (see Algorithm 2). Theoretically, the estimation error decreases in the order of $\mathcal{O}(m^{-0.5})$[5], where m is the number of iterations. When choosing a relatively large value[6] of m (e.g., 1000), the error introduced by the Monte-Carlo method is negligible.

[4] The proof is omitted due to space limitation. In practice, it can be lower, but still prohibitive.
[5] The proof is omitted due to limited space.
[6] m can be further reduced in ECM and WCM, which we will not discuss here.

Algorithm 2. Coverage Calculation Using Monte-Carlo Algorithm ($\mathcal{F}$; R_q)

```
count = 0
m = number of iterations, n =| F |
for i = {1, ..., m} do
    Generate a random point p_i within R_q
    for f_j ∈ F do
        if p_i intersects f_j then
            count = count + 1
            break
        end if
    end for
end for
return r = count / n
```

Table 1. Parameter values for the 3D spatial coverage models

Parameter	Value
# sectors for angle division	2, 4, $\underline{8}$, 16
# cells for cube division	4^3, $\underline{8^3}$, 16^3, 32^3

5 Evaluation

Datasets and Experimental Setup. To evaluate the efficiency and effectiveness of our coverage measurement models, we conducted several experiments using two real datasets recorded by Autonomous System Lab at the Swiss Federal Institute of Technology Zurich. The first dataset (referred to as $DS1$) [16] consists of a 1-h flight trajectory while the second one (referred to as $DS2$) [17] is an 81-h flight trajectory. Both datasets are collected at different places of open fields in Switzerland. $DS1$ contains 17k fs which cover a geographical region of size $1,009 \times 1,077\,\text{m}^2$ with a maximum height of 1,082 m, while $DS2$ contains 645k fs covering a region of size $1,228 \times 1,304\,\text{m}^2$ with a maximum height of 911 m. In these two datasets, the yaw angle varies widely while both pitch and roll angles are almost constant. Hence, ECM considers the division using only the yaw angle. Both datasets provide metadata for all parameters of each f except for R (i.e., maximum visible distance) and α (i.e., visibility width). Given that the value of R depends on the properties of the camera lens, in our evaluation, R is either 50 m (default), 100 m, or 150 m (assuming the recording mission is to monitor other close flying objects) and the value of α is 45°. To conduct our evaluation, we consider a query region (R_q) as one geographical MBR per dataset which bounds all fs in each dataset. Alternatively, R_q can be a small region (i.e., with a volume of 100 m^3) within the maximum geographical bound. Therefore, we conducted experiments using both the maximum and small regions. To evaluate the spatial coverage for each R_q using our models, we varied the values of the model parameters, as shown in Table 1 (the default value of each parameter is underlined). For implementing the models, we used the

PyCSG library (https://github.com/timknip/pycsg) for geometric operations. The source code of the proposed approaches is available at https://github.com/mazeyu/3D_Spatial_Coverage_Model, and these approaches are demonstrated by a web-based visualization tool presented in [4].

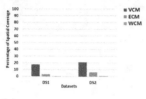

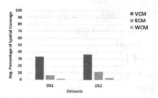

(a) w.r.t. the whole region (b) w.r.t. 100 small regions

Fig. 10. Spatial coverage using VCM, ECM, and WCM for two datasets

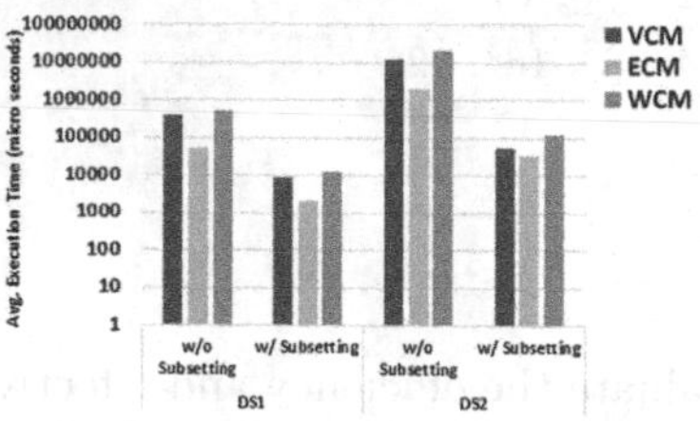

Fig. 11. Impact of subsetting on execution time (base-10 logarithmic scale)

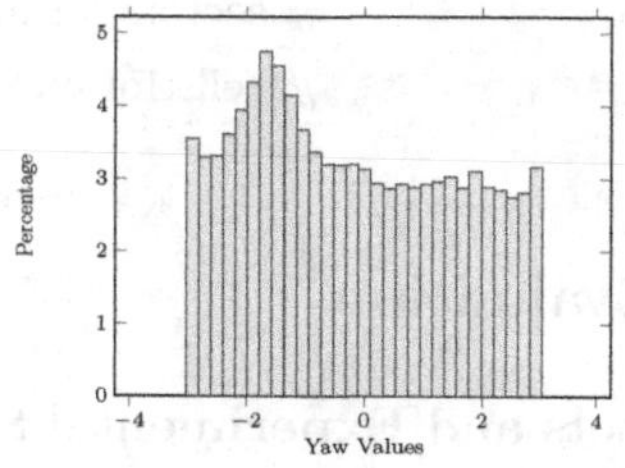

Fig. 12. $\mathcal{F}$ distribution among values of yaw for $DS2$

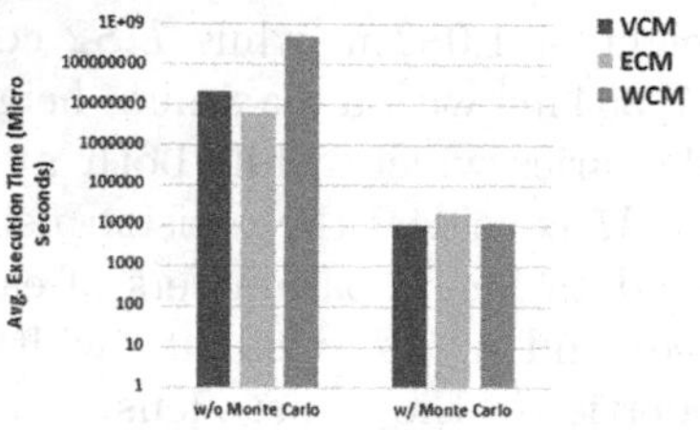

Fig. 13. Execution time of coverage measurements using all models w/ and w/o Monte Carlo using $DS1$ (base-10 logarithmic scale)

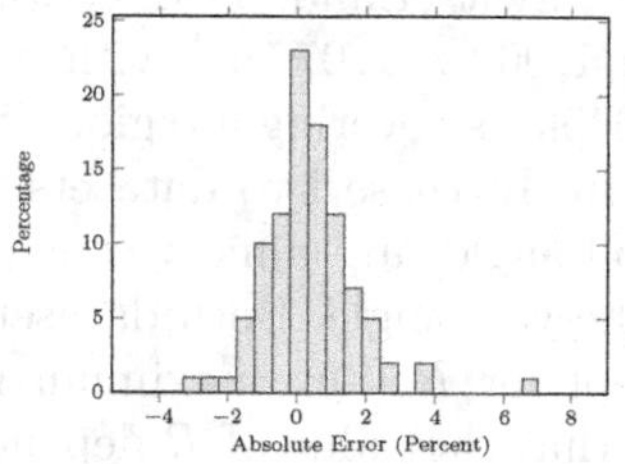

Fig. 14. Absolute error distribution of VCM w/ Monte Carlo using $DS1$

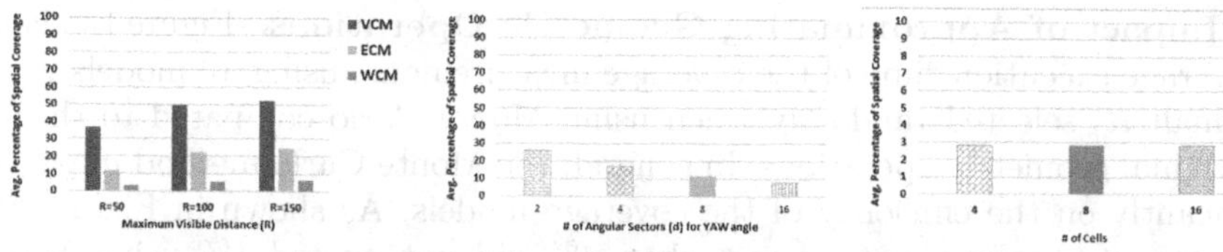

(a) All Coverage models w/ varying R (b) using ECM and varying # of angular sectors (c) using WCM w/ varying # of cells

Fig. 15. Spatial coverage w.r.t. 100 small regions within the region of $DS2$

Spatial Coverage Measurement. Figure 10 shows the 3D spatial coverage measurements using VCM, ECM, and WCM w.r.t. two cases of R_q. In Fig. 10a, R_q is the region containing $\mathcal{F}$ for each of $DS1$ and $DS2$. In general, the measured coverage using the three models varies significantly where VCM reports the highest coverage percentage while WCM reports the lowest one. The coverage by VCM is always the highest because it considers neither directional coverage nor fine-granular coverage. Conversely, WCM is the most conservative method because the coverage is calculated per various small cells in different directions. This observation complies with the user study reported in [2] from which our models are derived. Moreover, because of the high density of $DS2$ compared to $DS1$, $DS1$ has lower coverage than that of $DS2$ using the three models. To validate our observation, we measured the coverage using 100 small R_qs (each of volume 100 m^3) selected randomly within the region of each dataset, as shown in Fig. 10b. The same observations hold; however, the coverage for the small R_qs is higher than that of the large R_q because each small R_q is potentially covered by many fs where $f.R$ is larger than the diameter of a small R_q.

The Impact of Subsetting $\mathcal{F}$. Figure 11 compares the efficiency of the coverage models when using the subsetting approach and without using it by reporting the average execution time of the spatial coverage measurements using all models w.r.t. 100 small R_q selected randomly. In general, the subsetting approach enables significantly expediting the execution of the coverage measurements using all models across the two datasets[7]. Noticeably, the execution time of the coverage measurement using ECM is less than that of VCM in these particular datasets because the distribution of $\mathcal{F}$ on various yaw angles is almost uniform (see Fig. 12). Such a distribution potentially splits $\mathcal{F}$ equally into various yaw sectors; hence decreases the execution time of geometric operations required by ECM for each sector. Meanwhile, since each $f \in \mathcal{F}$ potentially spans across multiple small 3D cells of R_q; the coverage measurement of each f is replicated across multiple cells which eventually increases the execution time of coverage measurement using WCM compared to both VCM and ECM.

[7] Subsetting does not affect the accuracy of the coverage models.

The Impact of Approximating Geometric Operations. Figure 13 shows the average execution time of the coverage measurements using all models w.r.t. 100 small R_q selected randomly when using Monte Carlo compared to that of the original geometric operations. In general, the Monte Carlo method impacted significantly on the efficiency of the coverage models. As shown in Fig. 14, the frequency of absolute errors larger than 4% did not exceed 1% using Monte Carlo, and the average of the absolute value of error was around 1%.

The Impact of Varying Model Parameters. As shown in Fig. 15b, the coverage reported by ECM decreases by increasing the number of angular sectors. By considering more sectors, ECM becomes more conservative because the subset of $\mathcal{F}$ overlapping with R_q should cover it from various viewing angles. On the other hand, the coverage of WCM has not decreased significantly when varying the number of cells, as shown in Fig. 15c. The reported coverage has not changed because of the large volume of each object of $\mathcal{F}$ which enables them to cover R_q at fine granularity (i.e., small cells of R_q).

The Impact of Varying R. Figure 15a shows the evaluation of the coverage models by varying R. In general, when increasing R, the reported coverage by all models increases. Increasing R enlarges the volume of each object in $\mathcal{F}$; hence increases the chances of covering a larger region in R_q which potentially affects the coverage measured by the three models. Note that the value of R is application dependent and will be determined by the properties of aerial images.

6 Conclusion

This paper proposes three coverage measurement models of aerial images utilizing their spatial metadata. Geo-parameters tagged with each image describes the aerial field-of-view that can be interpreted as a 3D object. The proposed models calculate the coverage by considering three main characteristics: volume, 3D-Euler directions, and locality at fine-granular viewpoints. To overcome the challenges of efficiency and scalability in a large dataset, we also devised supportive approaches: filtering and approximate geometric approaches. In the experimental evaluation using large-scale real geo-tagged UAV datasets, our approaches significantly expedited the performance of the coverage models without scarifying their accuracy. As part of our future work, we plan to implement the models on a data management platform for geo-tagged aerial images and integrate these coverage models into our visionary framework (Translational Visual Data Platform, TVDP [13]) for smart cities.

Acknowledgment. This work was supported in part by NSF grants IIS-1320149 and CNS-1461963, the USC Integrated Media Systems Center, and unrestricted cash gifts from Oracle and Google.

References

1. Alfarrarjeh, A., et al.: Image classification to determine the level of street cleanliness: a case study. In: BigMM, pp. 1–5. IEEE (2018)
2. Alfarrarjeh, A., et al.: Spatial coverage measurement of geo-tagged visual data: a database approach. In: BigMM, pp. 1–8. IEEE (2018)
3. Alfarrarjeh, A., et al.: Recognizing material of a covered object: a case study with graffiti. In: ICIP, pp. 2491–2495. IEEE (2019)
4. Alfarrarjeh, A., et al.: A web-based visualization tool for 3D spatial coverage measurement of aerial images. In: Cheng, W.-H., et al. (eds.) MMM 2020. LNCS, vol. 11962, pp. 715–721. Springer, Cham (2020)
5. Alfarrarjeh, A., et al.: Scalable spatial crowdsourcing: a study of distributed algorithms. In: MDM, vol. 1, pp. 134–144. IEEE (2015)
6. Ay, S.A., et al.: Viewable scene modeling for geospatial video search. In: MM, pp. 309–318. ACM (2008)
7. Bentley, J.L.: Multidimensional binary search trees used for associative searching. Commun. ACM **18**(9), 509–517 (1975)
8. Bringmann, K., Friedrich, T.: Approximating the volume of unions and intersections of high-dimensional geometric objects. CG **43**(6), 601–610 (2010)
9. Del B., A., et al.: Visual coverage using autonomous mobile robots for search and rescue applications. In: SSRR, pp. 1–8. IEEE (2013)
10. Finkel, R.A., Bentley, J.L.: Acta informatica **4**(1), 1–9 (1974)
11. Guttman, A.: R-trees: A dynamic Index Structure for Spatial Searching. In: SIGMOD, pp. 47–57. ACM Press (1984)
12. Kazemi, L., Shahabi, C.: GeoCrowd: enabling query answering with spatial crowdsourcing. In: SIGSPATIAL GIS, pp. 189–198. ACM (2012)
13. Kim, S.H., et al.: TVDP: translational visual data platform for smart cities. In: ICDEW, pp. 45–52. IEEE (2019)
14. Lillian, B.: Xcel energy kicks off drone inspections beyond line of sight (2018). https://unmanned-aerial.com/xcel-energy-kicks-off-drone-inspections-beyond-line-of-sight
15. Lu, Y., Shahabi, C.: Efficient indexing and querying of geo-tagged aerial videos. In: SIGSPATIAL GIS, pp. 1–10. ACM (2017)
16. Oettershagen, P., Stastny, T., Mantel, T., Melzer, A., Rudin, K., Gohl, P., Agamennoni, G., Alexis, K., Siegwart, R.: Long-endurance sensing and mapping using a hand-launchable solar-powered UAV. In: Wettergreen, D.S., Barfoot, T.D. (eds.) Field and Service Robotics. STAR, vol. 113, pp. 441–454. Springer, Cham (2016). https://doi.org/10.1007/978-3-319-27702-8_29
17. Oettershagen, P., et al.: Design of small hand-launched solar-powered UAVs: from concept study to a multi-day world endurance record flight. J. Field Robot. **34**(7), 1352–1377 (2017)
18. Papatheodorou, S., et al.: Collaborative visual area coverage. Robot. Auton. Syst. **92**, 126–138 (2017)
19. Sameer, A., et al.: Building Rome in a day. In: ICCV, pp. 72–79. IEEE Computer Society (2009)

Oral Session 7A: Learning and Knowledge Representation

Instance Image Retrieval with Generative Adversarial Training

Hongkai Li[1], Cong Bai[1(✉)], Ling Huang[1], Yugang Jiang[2], and Shengyong Chen[3]

[1] College of Computer Science and Technology, Zhejiang University of Technology, Hangzhou, China
congbai@zjut.edu.cn

[2] College of Computer Science, Fudan University, Shanghai, China

[3] College of Computer Science and Engineering, Tianjin University of Technology, Tianjin, China

Abstract. While generative adversarial training becomes promising technology for many computer vision tasks especially in image processing domain, it has few works so far on instance level image retrieval domain. In this paper, we propose an instance level image retrieval method with generative adversarial training (ILRGAN). In this proposal, adversarial training is adopted in the retrieval procedure. Both generator and discriminator are redesigned for retrieval task: the generator tries to retrieve similar images and passes them to the discriminator. And the discriminator tries to discriminate the dissimilar images from the images retrieved and then passes the decision to the generator. Generator and discriminator play min-max game until the generator retrieves images that the discriminator can not discriminate the dissimilar images. Experiments on four widely used databases show that adversarial training really works for instance level image retrieval and the proposed ILRGAN can get promising retrieval performances.

Keywords: Instance image retrieval · Generative adversarial training · 1 × 1 convolution kernel

1 Introduction

The method of retrieving similar images by analyzing image visual content is called content-based image retrieval (CBIR), which starts to be investigated from 1970s [27]. In CBIR community, instance level image retrieval is a more challenging problem as the relevancy is defined at the instance level, in which given a query image of an object or scene, the images that containing the same object or scene are retrieved in the database that may be captured under different angles or with different illumination [32]. Before 2010s, local feature based methods have dominated the instance image retrieval, as two of pioneering works have been introduced into the retrieval community: SIFT [18,20] and

Y. M. Ro et al. (Eds.): MMM 2020, LNCS 11961, pp. 381–392, 2020.
https://doi.org/10.1007/978-3-030-37731-1_31

BoVW [17,28]. In 2012, AlexNet achieved impressive accuracy in ILSRVC challenge. After this, retrieval community starts to investigate deep learning based methods [3,4,10,30]. Most of deep learning based retrieval methods use deep convolutional neural network (CNN) [6,9,22,26] to extract compact feature vectors and employ approximate nearest neighbor (ANN) search method for retrieval. In 2014, generative adversarial network (GAN) [8] is proposed as a kind of adversarial training framework to generate images that are similar to the input images. GAN is composed of two models. A generative model G captures data distribution to generate unreal samples. A discriminative model D estimates the probability of the sample coming from natural data rather than G. These two models play a mini-max game via adversarial training. Since GAN shows promising potential on deep learning based tasks, more and more GAN-based applications have been developed in recent years, including image retrieval. These GAN-based image retrieval can be divided three categories: class level image retrieval based on compact features [7,13,29], cross-modal retrieval [14,31] and sketch based image retrieval [1,11]. These researches on GAN-based retrieval tend to take advantage of image generating from GAN to offer more training samples or to perform data augmentation for image retrieval. However, the objective of GAN is to synthesize images that are similar with the input images, while the objective of instance image retrieval is retrieving similar images with the query image. The final objective of GAN and that of instance level image retrieval are both to get similar images. But the inputs of them are totally different. So is it possible to incorporates adversarial training directly with retrieval procedure by redesigning the generative adversarial process?

For addressing the above problems, this paper proposes a new instance level image retrieval method: instance level retrieval with generative adversarial training (ILRGAN). ILRGAN adopts adversarial training in the retrieval process by redesigning the generative adversarial networks. Given a query image describing a particular object or scene, the generator tries to retrieve similar images containing the same object or scene in image database by continually optimizing its parameters to minimize the difference between the retrieved images output and the query image input. In contrast, the discriminator tries to discriminate the dissimilar images from the retrieval results by maximizing the discrimination of the retrieved images and the query image. An adversarial reward function is designed to make generator and discriminator to play min-max game until the discriminator can not discriminate the dissimilar images from the images retrieved by the generator. Finally the well-trained generator is used to retrieve images. In summary, the contributions of this paper can be summarized as follows:

(1) A novel end-to-end instance image retrieval framework, ILRGAN, is proposed. To our best of knowledge, this is the first try to adopt adversarial training in the retrieval process for instance image retrieval. Furthermore, no additional annotated data is needed for training this framework.
(2) Novel generator and discriminator are designed. They are composed of 1×1 one-layer convolutional network with new designed objective function.

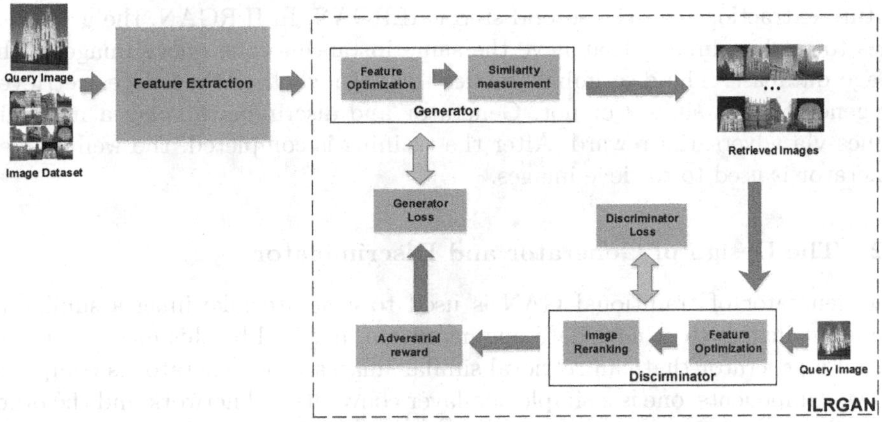

Fig. 1. Overview of ILRGAN framework. The input of ILRGAN is the feature vectors of the query image and that of gallery images. The generator retrieves similar images by optimizing the input feature, followed by the similarity measurement. The generator loss is composed by image sequences retrieved, parameters of generator network and adversarial reward. The discriminator discriminates images retrieved from generator whether they are similar or not and re-ranks the retrieved images for eliminating the dissimilar images. The discriminator loss is composed by image ranking, parameters of the discriminator network. The judgement of similarity from discriminator is output as adversarial reward impacting on the generator loss to adjust the parameters of generator.

A new adversarial reward function is also designed for connecting discriminator and generator for adversarial training.

(3) Extensive experiments have been conducted on four widely used benchmark databases. The experimental results shows the that the adversarial training could improve the retrieval performance without significantly increasing the retrieval time.

The rest of the paper is organized as follows: Sect. 2 presents the details of ILRGAN. Section 3 shows the experimental results in different aspects followed by the conclusions in Sect. 4.

2 The Proposal

In this section, we detail an end-to-end instance level retrieval framework, named ILRGAN. This framework is composed of a generator and a discriminator for adopting adversarial training in the retrieval procedure. Details of the proposal are shown in follows.

2.1 Overview

The overview of ILRGAN is shown in Fig. 1. As shown in this figure, the entire instance image retrieval process is divided into two stages. The first step is feature extraction, and the second step is ILRGAN. In ILRGAN, the generator tries to retrieve images that have the same instance as the query image in the image database. The discriminator tries to judge whether the images retrieved by generator are similar or not. Generator and discriminator play a max-min games via adversarial reward. After the training is completed, the well trained generator is used to retrieve images.

2.2 The Design of Generator and Discriminator

The generator of traditional GAN is used to generate fake images similar to the input images to achieve data augmentation. Inspired by this mechanism, we design a generator that can retrieval similar images. The generator is composed of two components, one is a simple one-layer convolutional network and the other is similarity measurement. Generator optimizes the features of query image and that of images in database by 1×1 convolution kernel firstly. Then the cosine distance is calculated between optimized feature of input image and that of images in the database in order to sort the images according to the similarity. As a result, the output of generator is the feature of top k retrieved images. With this new-designed generator, it could retrieve similar images from the input gallery images. So the generator model can be written as follow:

$$G_\theta(s'|q, I) \tag{1}$$

where q is the input query image, I is the image database, and s' is the state obtained by iterative optimization of the parameter θ. The input of the generator model is the feature vectors of the query image and that of gallery images. All these features are optimized by convolutional network, followed by the calculation of cosine distance between the query and the gallery images. Then the top k images ranked by the distances are output.

The discriminator of traditional GAN is used to discriminate whether the input images are the fake images generated by generator or not. In our framework, we redesign the discriminator to determine whether the images retrieved by generator are similar to the query image or not. The discriminator is composed of two components: convolutional network for optimizing the features and image re-ranking for adjusting the dissimilar images. So the discriminator model can be written as:

$$D_\phi(s|q, R) \tag{2}$$

where q is the input query image, R are the images retrieved by generator, and s is the ideal state of the discriminator model by iterative optimization of the parameter ϕ. The input of the discriminator model is the feature vectors of the query image and the feature vectors of top k similar images retrieved by generator. The k sequence is re-ranked according to the cosine distance of the feature vectors, thus the discriminator outputs a new sequence.

1×1 convolution kernel [19] is used in the convolutional network of generator and discriminator. There are three reasons of this choice. First, 1×1 convolution kernel possesses better feature extraction ability of local patches, which is needed in instance level retrieval. Second, it is easy to decrease or increase the channel number of the network with less network parameters. Third, it can integrate the information across channels.

2.3 Adversarial Training in ILRGAN

The discriminator will establish an adversarial reward to the generator according to the adjusted ranking of image sequence. This reward impacts on the generator's loss function, which acts as the adversarial training to update the parameters of generator. The reward function is defined as:

$$reward = \delta(d_\phi(q, R)) \tag{3}$$

The adversarial training mentioned above will repeat until the output image sequence of discriminator is the same with the output of image sequence of generator. The generator and the discriminator play a min-max game, so the whole optimization function of ILRGAN is defined as:

$$\begin{aligned} f^{G,D} = \underset{\theta}{\min}\underset{\phi}{\max} \sum_{n=1}^{N} \mathbb{E}_{D \sim G_{true(s'|q_n,I)}}[logD_\phi(s|q_n, R)] \\ + \mathbb{E}_{D \sim G_{\theta(s'|q_n,I)}}[1 - logD_\phi(s'|q_n, I)] \end{aligned} \tag{4}$$

In this equation, the state of the generator is s' and the state of the discriminator is s. $D \sim G_{true(s'|q_n,I))}$ represents the ideal state of the discriminator, while $D \sim G_{\theta(s'|q_n,I)}$ represents the state of the current generator selection. In the optimization, ϕ needs to be maximized, and θ needs to be minimized, which means the generator continues to reduce the distances between input and output, and the discriminator is constantly expanding. Here we set the ideal state that the generator select images with the cosine distance as zero. Thus no annotated information is needed in the adversarial training.

D_ϕ estimates the probability of query image q relevant to image database I or retrieved images R, which is given by the sigmoid function of the discriminator score:

$$D_\phi(s|q_n, I) = \delta(d_\phi(q, I)) = \frac{exp(d_\phi(q, I))}{1 + exp(d_\phi(q, I))} \tag{5}$$

d_ϕ is the distance calculation function in which the cosine distance is used. The cosine distance function is defined as:

$$d_\phi(q|I) = \frac{\sum_{i=1}^{n} q_i I_i}{\sqrt{\sum_{i=1}^{n} q_i^2}\sqrt{\sum_{i=1}^{n} I_i^2}} \tag{6}$$

q and R are both feature vectors after passing through the discriminator network. q is the feature vectors of the input query image, and R is the feature vectors of the K image sequence retrieved by the generator.

2.4 The Optimization of Generator and Discriminator

In the optimization of the discriminator for ϕ, Eq. 5 is substituted to Eq. 4, so the objective function of discriminator is converted into:

$$
\begin{aligned}
f^D = \underset{\phi}{argmax} \sum_{n=1}^{N} \mathbb{E}_{D \sim G_{true(s'|q_n,I)}} [log\delta(d_\phi(q|R))] \\
+ \mathbb{E}_{D \sim G_{\theta(s'|q_n,I)}} [1 - log\delta(d_\phi(q|I))]
\end{aligned} \tag{7}
$$

This objective function is a continuous function, so the stochastic gradient descent is used to optimize it.

The generator needs adversarial reward from the discriminator for the optimization of θ, that means, only the parameters of the discriminator model $D_\phi(s)$ are stable in advance, the generator can be optimized. When $D_\phi(s)$ is stable, only the last part of Eq. 4 remains to be optimized and after Eq. 5 is substituted to Eq. 4, we can get the objective function of generator as follows:

$$
\begin{aligned}
f^G &= \underset{\phi}{argmin} \sum_{n=1}^{N} \mathbb{E}_{D \sim G_{\theta(s'|q_n,I)}} [1 - logD_\phi(s'|q_n, I)] \\
&= \underset{\phi}{argmin} \sum_{n=1}^{N} \mathbb{E}_{D \sim G_{\theta(s'|q_n,I)}} [log(1 + \delta(d_\phi(q|I))]
\end{aligned} \tag{8}
$$

The above objective function is a discrete function, so the advanced gradient algorithm (Adam) is used for parameter optimization.

2.5 The Overall Algorithm

Finally, we conclude the adversarial training in the retrieval process written in the algorithm shown as follows:

3 Experiments

In this section, we conduct experiments to evaluate ILRGAN from two aspects on four widely used instance retrieval benchmark databases. Firstly, the effect of adversarial training is investigated. And then, ILRGAN is compared with state-of-the-art methods. The experimental details are described in the following.

3.1 Databases

Oxford5k [24]. The Oxford5K dataset uses Oxford's 11 landmark names to crawl a total of 5063 images from the Flickr to build the image database. The dataset defines five queries for each landmark through hand-drawn bounding boxes, resulting in a total of 55 Regions of Interest (ROI). Each image is assigned

Algorithm 1. Adversarial training for instance image retrieval

Input: The feature vectors of the image database and that of the query image;
Initialize the weights of generator $G(s')$ and discriminator $D(s)$;
repeat
    for *epoch* **do**
        The generator $G(s')$ retrieves the similar images from the database to train the discriminator $D(s)$;
        for *d-epochs* **do**
            Calculate the distance between the query image and the sequence of images retrieved by the generator and obtain the reward;
            Optimize the parameters of $D(s)$ by the stochastic gradient descent;
        end
        for *g-epochs* **do**
            Calculate the distance between the query image and the gallery images;
            Optimize the parameters of $G(s')$ by Adam algorithm;
        end
    end
until *convergence*;

one of four labels, good, ok, junk, or bad. The 'good' and 'ok' label indicate that the ROIs of the query are well-matched, while the bad means non-match.

Paris6k [23]**.** The Paris6K dataset uses 11 landmark names of the Parisian landmark to crawl total 6412 images from the Flickr to build the database. This database has five queries per landmark also, so this database has 55 queries with bounding boxes. Moreover, the dataset also has the same four types of labels as Oxford5K.

Flickr100k [23]**.** The Flickr100K dataset includes 99,782 high-definition images of the 145 most popular labels from the Flickr. This dataset is usually added to the Oxford5k dataset or Paris6k dataset to form Oxford 105K or Paris106K to test the scalability of the retrieval framework.

3.2 Evaluation Criteria

Mean Average Precision (mAP) is used to measure the performance that shows an overall evaluation. Given a query image, all the images in the database will be ranked based on their similarity scores. The average precision at K is defined as follows:

$$precision@K = \frac{\sum_{i=1}^{k} R_e(i)}{K} \tag{9}$$

Table 1. With or without ILRGAN

Methods	mAP(%)		Time(s)	
	Oxford5k	Paris6k	Oxford5k	Paris6K
R-MAC	70.01	85.4	0.091	0.109
R-MAC + ILRGAN	**74.06**	**86.86**	0.109	0.127
R-MAC + RA	76.8	**87.5**	0.091	0.109
R-MAC + RA + ILRGAN	**79.36**	87.38	0.109	0.145

where $R_e(i)$ is expressed as the ground truth relevance between the query image and the i-th ranked image. $R_e(i) \in [0, 1]$, where 0 is irrelevant, and 1 is related. Mean average precision (mAP) is defined as follows:

$$mAP(Q) = \frac{1}{|Q|} \sum_{i=0}^{Q} \frac{1}{m} \sum_{k=1}^{m} precision \tag{10}$$

where Q is the set of query images and m is the number of relevant images in the database.

3.3 Experimental Details

Network Settings: One layer 1×1 convolution network is used both in generator and discriminator as its simplicity and can not add too much computing burdens in the retrieval. We initialize the network parameters by random normal initialization.

Framework Input: The framework input could be any kind of feature vectors, either the traditional SIFT or the CNN-based deep features or the local features weighted by each region score. We finally use the local deep features [16] for evaluating the performance of ILRGAN in the comparison with start-of-the arts. We should emphasize that only the feature vectors are input into ILRGAN and no label information of the images is needed. Thus we claim that we train the ILRGAN in an unsupervised way.

Framework Output: After the adversarial training, we use the well trained generator model to retrieve instance images. The output of the framework is the images in the database that have the similar instance level content as the query image.

Database Preparation: Due to the task specificity of the instance retrieval, the images of the retrieval results of each category are divided into four labels [25]: good, ok, junk, and bad. So we can choose good and ok as training

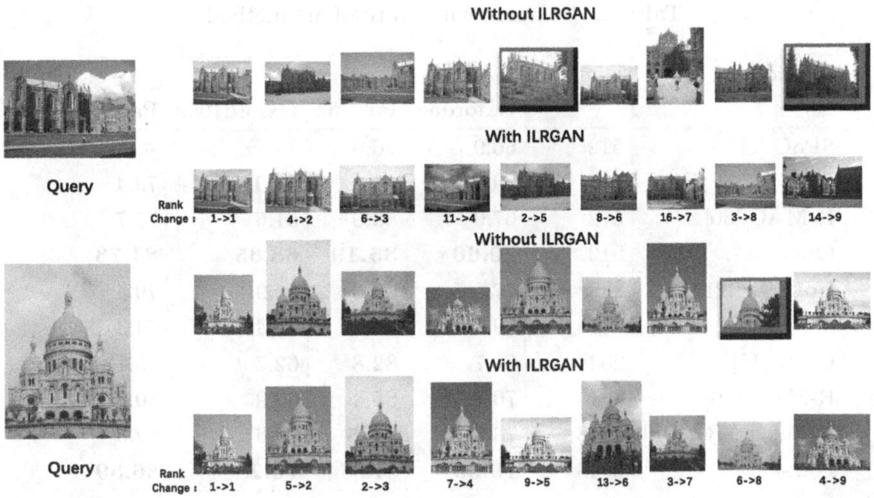

Fig. 2. Retrieval results with and without ILRGAN for the same query image. Ranking changes are shown as "A -> B". A means the image rank without ILRGAN and B means the image rank with ILRGAN. The retrieved images that do not have same label with query are marked in red box. (Color figure online)

set. For objective evaluation of the performance, we use cross validation evaluation. That is to say, we train ILRGAN with Paris6k for testing on Oxford5k and Oxford105k, and use Oxford5k for testing on Paris6k and Paris106k. This is the same as R-MAC [30], CroW [15] and SDCF [12].

3.4 Experiment Results

With or Without ILRGAN. One of our main contribution is adopting adversarial training in the retrieval process. So we conduct contrast experiments to see whether the adversarial training improve the retrieval performance or not. To do this, R-MAC [30]is used as the baseline method. Furthermore, the method improving R-MAC with regional attention [16] (R-MAC + RA) is also used as the baseline method. To do the comparison, we obtain the feature vectors of R-MAC and that of (R-MAC + RA) from their proposed network, and use them as the input of the ILRGAN. Furthermore, the online retrieval is also compared. Table 1 shows the contrast results: the time cost increased by the adversarial training is about 0.02–0.03 s. From this table, we could conclude that the adversarial training do improve the retrieval performance with slightly time increase.

Furthermore, we visualize the changes of sequence of retrieved images after ILRGAN using under the same query image in Fig. 2. We can see that the ranks of the same image have changed. However, the images with the same instance target are still in the top position. But some retrieved images that do not have the same label are disappeared in the top position when ILRGAN is adopted.

Table 2. Compare with state-of-art methods

Methods	Dim.	mAP(%)			
		Oxford5k	Paris6k	Oxford105k	Paris106K
SPoC [2]	512	66.9	76.5	–	–
GatedSQU [5]	512	69.4	81.3	63.9	73.4
R-MAC [30]	512	67.0	83.0	61.6	75.7
Ours	512	**70.66**	**85.19**	**68.65**	**84.73**
BoDVW [21]	Bow-10k	77.6	85.0	74.9	79.4
SDCF [12]	2048	69.1	81.7	65.4	74.3
Crow [15]	2048	68.7	82.8	62.7	75.1
R-MAC [30]	2048	70.1	85.4	66.9	80.8
R-MAC + RA [16]	2048	76.8	**87.5**	73.6	82.5
Ours	2048	**79.36**	87.38	**79.25**	**86.59**

Comparison with State-of-Art Methods. Finally, we compare ILRGAN with several state-of-the-art retrieval methods focusing on instance retrieval, including SPoC [2], GatedSQU [5], BoDVW [21], SDCF [12], Crow [15], R-MAC [30] and R-MAC + RA [16].

For fair comparison, the dimension of feature vector used in the adversarial training is either 512D or 2048D, depending on the feature vectors used by the competitors. Table 2 shows the performance comparisons with competitors on four databases. From this table, we could see that the proposed ILRGAN gets the best performance with a 3%–6% improvement comparing the second best method on Oxford5k, Oxford105k and Pairs106k. The performance of ILRGAN on Paris6k gets the second place with slight gap and outperforms other methods obviously. We thus argue that adding adversarial training after feature extraction could improve retrieval performance on instance image retrieval.

4 Conclusions

In this paper, we propose a novel instance image retrieval method named ILRGAN, which adopts adversarial training in the retrieval process rather than using adversarial training for data augmentation or feature representation. To do this, new generator and new discriminator are proposed. With the new objective functions, no additional label information is need for training ILRGAN. Comprehensive experiments have been done on two aspects, including the effect of adversarial training and the comparison with state-of-the art methods. Experimental results show that adversarial training do improve the retrieval performance and ILRGAN could get better performance comparing with state-of-the-art methods.

Acknowledgement. This work is funded by Zhejiang Provincial Natural Science Foundation of China under Grant No. LY18F020032, Natural Science Foundation of China under Grant No. 61976192, 61502424 and U1509207. The source code of this work will be released on http://www.escience.cn/people/congbai/index.html.

References

1. Yelamarthi, S.K., Reddy, S.K., Mishra, A., Mittal, A.: A zero-shot framework for sketch based image retrieval. In: Ferrari, V., Hebert, M., Sminchisescu, C., Weiss, Y. (eds.) ECCV 2018. LNCS, vol. 11208, pp. 316–333. Springer, Cham (2018). https://doi.org/10.1007/978-3-030-01225-0_19
2. Babenko, A., Lempitsky, V.: Aggregating local deep features for image retrieval. In: Proceedings of the IEEE International Conference on Computer Vision, pp. 1269–1277 (2015)
3. Babenko, A., Slesarev, A., Chigorin, A., Lempitsky, V.: Neural codes for image retrieval. In: Fleet, D., Pajdla, T., Schiele, B., Tuytelaars, T. (eds.) ECCV 2014. LNCS, vol. 8689, pp. 584–599. Springer, Cham (2014). https://doi.org/10.1007/978-3-319-10590-1_38
4. Bell, S., Bala, K.: Learning visual similarity for product design with convolutional neural networks. ACM Trans. Graph. **34**(4), 98:1–98:10 (2015)
5. Chen, Z., Lin, J., Chandrasekhar, V., Duan, L.Y.: Gated square-root pooling for image instance retrieval. In: 2018 25th IEEE International Conference on Image Processing (ICIP), pp. 1982–1986. IEEE (2018)
6. Cong, B., Ling, H., Xiang, P., Zheng, J., Chen, S.: Optimization of deep convolutional neural network for large scale image retrieval. Neurocomputing **303**, 60–67 (2018)
7. Dizaji, K.G., Zheng, F., Nourabadi, N.S., Yang, Y., Deng, C., Huang, H.: Unsupervised deep generative adversarial hashing network. In: 2018 IEEE/CVF Conference on Computer Vision and Pattern Recognition, pp. 3664–3673 (2018)
8. Goodfellow, I., et al.: Generative adversarial nets. In: Advances in Neural Information Processing Systems, pp. 2672–2680 (2014)
9. Gordo, A., Almazán, J., Revaud, J., Larlus, D.: Deep image retrieval: learning global representations for image search. In: Leibe, B., Matas, J., Sebe, N., Welling, M. (eds.) ECCV 2016. LNCS, vol. 9910, pp. 241–257. Springer, Cham (2016). https://doi.org/10.1007/978-3-319-46466-4_15
10. Gordo, A., Almazán, J., Revaud, J., Larlus, D.: End-to-end learning of deep visual representations for image retrieval. Int. J. Comput. Vis. **124**(2), 237–254 (2017)
11. Guo, L., Liu, J., Wang, Y., Luo, Z., Wen, W., Lu, H.: Sketch-based image retrieval using generative adversarial networks. In: Proceedings of the ACM on Multimedia Conference, pp. 1267–1268 (2017)
12. Hoang, T., Do, T.T., Le Tan, D.K., Cheung, N.M.: Selective deep convolutional features for image retrieval. In: Proceedings of the 25th ACM International Conference on Multimedia, pp. 1600–1608. ACM (2017)
13. Huang, L., Bai, C., Lu, Y., Chen, S., Tian, Q.: Adversarial learning for content-based image retrieval. In: 2019 IEEE Conference on Multimedia Information Processing and Retrieval (MIPR), pp. 97–102 (2019)
14. Huang, X., Peng, Y., Yuan, M.: MHTN: modal-adversarial hybrid transfer network for cross-modal retrieval. IEEE Trans. Cybern. 1–13 (2018). https://doi.org/10.1109/TCYB.2018.2879846

15. Kalantidis, Y., Mellina, C., Osindero, S.: Cross-dimensional weighting for aggregated deep convolutional features. In: Hua, G., Jégou, H. (eds.) ECCV 2016. LNCS, vol. 9913, pp. 685–701. Springer, Cham (2016). https://doi.org/10.1007/978-3-319-46604-0_48
16. Kim, J., Yoon, S.E.: Regional attention based deep feature for image retrieval. In: British Machine Vision Conference (BMVC). BMVA (2018)
17. Li, H., Sun, F., Liu, L., Ling, W.: A novel traffic sign detection method via color segmentation and robust shape matching. Neurocomputing **169**, 77–88 (2015)
18. Li, H., Wang, X., Tang, J., Zhao, C.: Combining global and local matching of multiple features for precise item image retrieval. Multimedia Syst. **19**(1), 37–49 (2013)
19. Lin, M., Chen, Q., Yan, S.: Network in network. arXiv preprint arXiv:1312.4400 (2013)
20. Lowe, D.G.: Distinctive image features from scale-invariant keypoints. Int. J. Comput. Vis. **60**(2), 91–110 (2004)
21. Lv, Y., Zhou, W., Tian, Q., Li, H.: Scalable bag of selected deep features for visual instance retrieval. In: Schoeffmann, K., et al. (eds.) MMM 2018. LNCS, vol. 10705, pp. 239–251. Springer, Cham (2018). https://doi.org/10.1007/978-3-319-73600-6_21
22. Mei, S., Min, W., Duan, H., Jiang, S.: Instance-level object retrieval via deep region CNN. Multimedia Tools Appl. **78**(10), 13247–13261 (2018)
23. Philbin, J., Chum, O., Isard, M., Sivic, J., Zisserman, A.: Lost in quantization: improving particular object retrieval in large scale image databases. In: 2008 IEEE Conference on Computer Vision and Pattern Recognition, pp. 1–8, June 2008
24. Philbin, J., Chum, O., Isard, M., Sivic, J., Zisserman, A.: Object retrieval with large vocabularies and fast spatial matching. In: 2007 IEEE Conference on Computer Vision and Pattern Recognition, pp. 1–8. IEEE (2007)
25. Radenović, F., Iscen, A., Tolias, G., Avrithis, Y., Chum, O.: Revisiting Oxford and Paris: large-scale image retrieval benchmarking. In: Proceedings of the IEEE Conference on Computer Vision and Pattern Recognition, pp. 5706–5715 (2018)
26. Radenović, F., Tolias, G., Chum, O.: CNN image retrieval learns from bow: unsupervised fine-tuning with hard examples. In: Leibe, B., Matas, J., Sebe, N., Welling, M. (eds.) ECCV 2016. LNCS, vol. 9905, pp. 3–20. Springer, Cham (2016). https://doi.org/10.1007/978-3-319-46448-0_1
27. Rui, Y., Huang, T.S., Chang, S.F.: Image retrieval: current techniques, promising directions, and open issues. J. Vis. Commun. Image Represent. **10**(1), 39–62 (1999)
28. Sivic, Z.: Video Google: a text retrieval approach to object matching in videos. In: Proceedings Ninth IEEE International Conference on Computer Vision, vol. 2, pp. 1470–1477. IEEE (2003)
29. Song, J., He, T., Gao, L., Xu, X., Hanjalic, A., Shen, H.T.: Binary generative adversarial networks for image retrieval. In: AAAI Conference on Artificial Intelligence, pp. 394–401 (2018)
30. Tolias, G., Sicre, R., Jégou, H.: Particular object retrieval with integral max-pooling of CNN activations. In: International Conference on Learning Representations (ICRL), San Juan, Puerto Rico, pp. 1–12 (2016)
31. Xu, X., He, L., Lu, H., Gao, L., Ji, Y.: Deep adversarial metric learning for cross-modal retrieval. World Wide Web **22**(2), 657–672 (2019)
32. Zheng, L., Yang, Y., Tian, Q.: SIFT meets CNN: a decade survey of instance retrieval. IEEE Trans. Pattern Anal. Mach. Intell. **40**(5), 1224–1244 (2017)

An Effective Way to Boost Black-Box Adversarial Attack

Xinjie Feng[1(✉)], Hongxun Yao[1(✉)], Wenbin Che[1], and Shengping Zhang[2]

[1] Harbin Institute of Technology, Harbin Shi, China
[2] Harbin Institute of Technology, Weihai Shi, China
{fengxinjie,h.yao,chewenbin,s.zhang}@hit.edu.cn

Abstract. Deep neural networks (DNNs) are vulnerable to adversarial examples. Generally speaking adversarial examples are defined by adding input samples a small-magnitude perturbation, which is hardly misleading human observers' decision but would lead to misclassifications for a well trained models. Most of existing iterative adversarial attack methods suffer from low success rates in fooling model in a black-box manner. And we find that it is because perturbation neutralize each other in iterative process. To address this issue, we propose a novel boosted iterative method to effectively promote success rates. We conduct the experiments on ImageNet dataset, with five models normally trained for classification. The experimental results show that our proposed strategy can significantly improve success rates of fooling models in a black-box manner. Furthermore, it also outperforms the momentum iterative method (MI-FSGM), which won the first places in NeurIPS Non-targeted Adversarial Attack and Targeted Adversarial Attack competitions.

Keywords: Neural network · Deep learning · Adversarial attack

1 Introduction

Deep Neural Networks (DNNs) have achieved great successes in a variety of computer vision applications ranging from image recognition [6–8], object detection [5,13,14] to semantic segmentation [2,11,15]. However, DNNs are also limited by their vulnerability to adversarial examples [4,19], which are crafted by adding small noises to accurate classified images. Such examples would make a well-trained model output inaccurate predictions. For this reason, it is very important to evaluate DNNs with adversarial attacks before they are deployed.

In general, adversarial examples can be generated in two manners: white-box and black-box. The main difference is that the former knows the knowledge of the structure and parameters of the given model while the latter does not. Many methods can easily generate successful white-box examples. The transferability [10,12,19] property of deep neural network models makes black-box attacks practical in real-world applications, i.e., adversarial examples crafted by one model will make other models output wrong predictions. For white-box attack, one-step

Y. M. Ro et al. (Eds.): MMM 2020, LNCS 11961, pp. 393–404, 2020.
https://doi.org/10.1007/978-3-030-37731-1_32

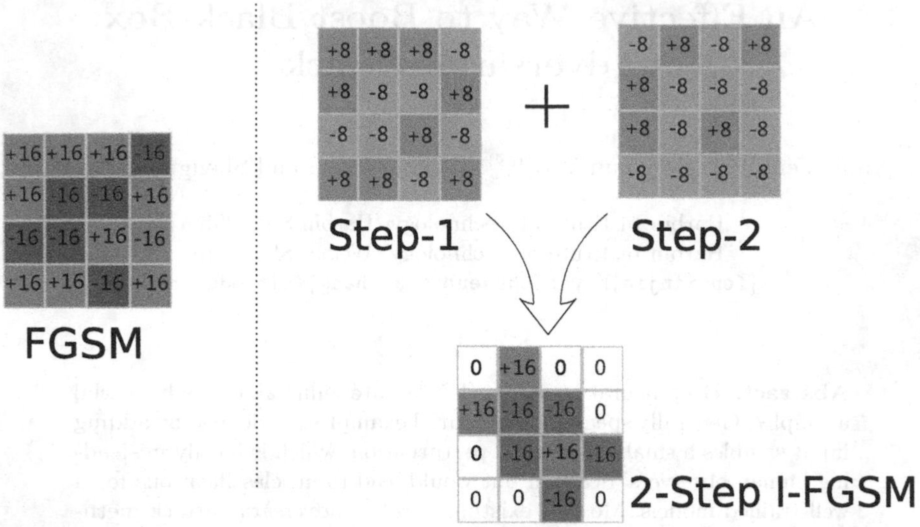

Fig. 1. Illustration of the difference between perturbations generated by I-FGSM and FGSM respectively, where the noise bound $\epsilon = 16$.

gradient-based methods such as fast gradient sign [4] (FGSM) are basic methods to generate adversarial examples, and iterative variants of gradient-based methods [9] (I-FGSM) performs better than one-step gradient-based methods. Whereas the situation is quite opposite in a black-box manner [3]. In our opinion, iterative methods learn more knowledge of the given model, thus degenerate the generative abilities to attack other kind of models.

To study the degeneration of black-box attack for iterative methods, we compare the variance of perturbations generated by fast gradient sign method (FGSM) [4] and a two-step iterative gradient-based methods (I-FGSM) [9] for inception_v3 [18] model. We find that almost all the pixel are changed by perturbation for FGSM, while just half pixels are completely unchanged for the two-step iterative gradient-based I-FGSM. We illustrate this phenomenon in Fig. 1, in which we can see that perturbation generated in different step get opposite direction which sumed to zero finally, thus make the attack strength weak. In detail, generated perturbation is either -8 or $+8$ for each pixel each step(we ignore zero as the probability of gradient to be exactly zero is nearly zero). Therefore, for a two-step I-FGSM method, there is 50% to generate a zero perturbation for each pixel.

Based on the above findings, we propose a simple but very effective way to boost iterative methods for black-box attack. Concretely, the perturbations generated at different iterations can be avoided being suppressed, resulting in a comparable magnitude after the final iteration. We refer to our boosting iterative attack method as BI-FGSM in the following.

Figure 2 illustrates adversarial examples crafted by I-FGSM and our proposed method BI-FGSM respectively, using Resnet50 model. In the upper row are original images which are labeled as banana and Monastery. In the middle row are samples generated by I-FGSM, and they are predicted as banana and mosque for inception_v3 (black-box manner attack), which means the attack failed for banana and success for Monastery. Adversarial examples generated by our proposed method BI-FGSM are listed in the bottom row. They all successfully fool inception_v3 model in black-box manner. We must point out that, monastery being classified as mosque is acceptable even for human eyes, but it is seriously being classified as a hog. In this way, we can say that our attack method is more successful.

Experiments show that our methods outperforms the benchmark work Momentum iterative fast gradient sign method (MI-FGSM) which won the first places in NeurIPS Non-targeted Adversarial Attack and Targeted Adversarial Attack competitions. And we also study the underlying reasons for such promotions in the extensive experiments.

2 Preliminary and Related Works

This section introduces the preliminary knowledge and related works of adversarial attack. Given an image, a pretrained model G can output the ground truth label y, such that $G(x) = y$. The goal of adversarial attack is to find an example $\hat{x}$ in the vicinity of x that makes model G output a wrong prediction, such that $G(\hat{x})! = y$. In most cases, we define the vicinity of input x measured by L_p norm. The adversarial perturbation is required to be less than an allowed value ϵ such that $\|x - \hat{x}\|_p \leq \epsilon$, where p could be 0, 1, 2, ∞.

2.1 Attack Methods

In this paper, we only take non-target attack methods into consideration, because target methods are almost the same. There are four main kinds of methods for non-targeted attack:

One-step gradient-base methods generate adversarial examples through maximizing the cross-entropy loss $L(G(x), y)$ via one step. Measured by L_∞ norm bound, one-step gradient-base methods generate adversarial examples as:

$$\begin{aligned} \hat{x} &= x + \epsilon * sign(\nabla x L(G(x), y)) \\ \hat{x} &= Clip(\hat{x}, 0, 255) \end{aligned} \tag{1}$$

where $\nabla x L(G(x), y)$ is the gradient of loss $L(G(x), y)$ w.r.t x. And the function $Clip(.)$ means clip the $\hat{x}$ between 0 and 255 to make a valid image. Fast gradient sign method (FGSM) [4] is the most popular one-step gradient-base method.

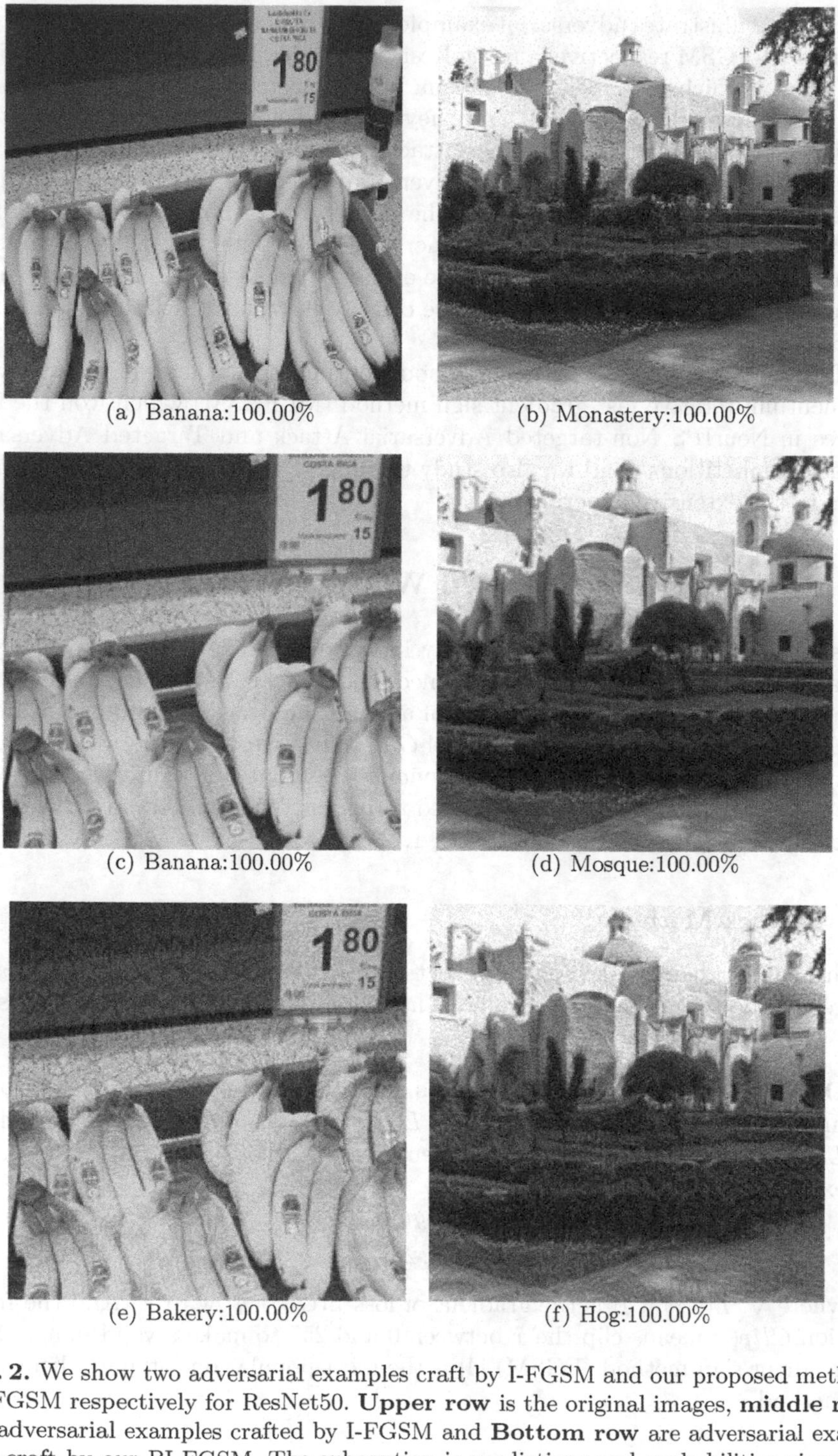

(a) Banana:100.00% (b) Monastery:100.00%

(c) Banana:100.00% (d) Mosque:100.00%

(e) Bakery:100.00% (f) Hog:100.00%

Fig. 2. We show two adversarial examples craft by I-FGSM and our proposed method BI-FGSM respectively for ResNet50. **Upper row** is the original images, **middle row** are adversarial examples crafted by I-FGSM and **Bottom row** are adversarial examples craft by our BI-FGSM. The subcaption is predictions and probabilities given by inception_v3 in black-box attack manner.

Iterative methods iteratively perform fast gradient with a small norm bound $\alpha = \epsilon/N$, generating more powerful examples than one-step gradient-base methods. It can be written as follows:

$$\begin{aligned} \hat{x}_0 &= x \\ \hat{x}_t &= \hat{x}_{t-1} + \alpha * sign(\nabla x L(G(\hat{x}_{t-1}), y)) \\ \hat{x}_N &= Clip(\hat{x}_N, 0, 255) \end{aligned} \tag{2}$$

where N is the number of iteration steps. Some previous literatures [9,20] show that iterative methods are more powerful for white-box attack, but perform worse in black-box manner. In our opinion, this is mainly because perturbations generated in different phases may suppress each other, as shown in Fig. 1. It proofs our hypothesis about statistics of perturbation variance for iterative methods and one-step gradient-base method. Our statistics show that with more iterations, variance will be decreasingly smaller.
Momentum iterative gradient-based methods [3] boosts iterative methods by integrating momentum into iterative FGSM, and exhibits the state of the art transferability for black-box attack. It can be summarized as follows:

$$\begin{aligned} g_0 &= 0 \\ \hat{x}_0 &= x \\ g_t &= \mu * g_{t-1} + \frac{\nabla x L(G(\hat{x}_{t-1}), y)}{\|\nabla x L(G(\hat{x}_{t-1}), y)\|_1} \\ \hat{x}_t &= \hat{x}_{t-1} + \alpha * sign(g_t) \\ \hat{x}_N &= Clip(\hat{x}_N, 0, 255) \end{aligned} \tag{3}$$

where μ is the decay factor of momentum and g is the momentum who accumulates all the gradient directions in an iterative manner. The direction of perturbation is no longer decided by gradient, but by momentum.
Optimization-based methods obtain adversarial examples by solving a constrained problem as:

$$\arg\min_{\hat{x}} \lambda \|x - \hat{x}\|_p - L(G(\hat{x}), y) \tag{4}$$

We note that $\hat{x}$ is required to be close to x so that it can become an adversarial example. However, as there is no guarantee that the condition $\|x - \hat{x}\|_p \leq \epsilon$ can be satisfied, optimization-based methods also lack the efficacy in black-box attacks just like iterative methods [1].

3 Methodology

In this section, we give more details about how we utilize our boosting strategy in iterative methods. Specifically, we would incorporate it in two existing popular attacks: I-FGSM and MI-FGSM, and explain why our boosting method can make them work well for both white-box and black-box attacks.

3.1 Boosting Iterative Methods

As discussed above, attacking noise generated in different steps may suppress each other for iterative fast gradient sign methods. The main reason is that gradient sign has only two likely directions. The noise would either be weaken or reinforced after two iterations. To overcome this limitation, we modify the iterative method in a simple but effective way as:

$$\hat{x} = x + \epsilon * sign(\hat{x}_N - x) \tag{5}$$

where $\hat{x}_N$ is the output of iterative methods. We adopt $sign(\hat{x}_N - x)$ as the main directions for each pixel. In this way we not only keep the valid direction of iterative perturbations, but also maintain the magnitude of fast gradient sign methods. In another regard, we can think of the iterative process as a gradient voting. The result gives rise to the main direction of our desired perturbations. We illustrate the entire process of generating our adversarial examples in Algorithm 1. The input is the same as iterative methods, which contains a model G, a real example x and the ground-truth label y of x, the bound of perturbation ϵ and iteration steps N. We acquire main directions of perturbations by the iterative process, and use this directions to perturb input example x. The generated examples can fool the given model G. We refer to this boosted attack method as B(boosting)I-FGSM.

Algorithm 1. BI-FGSM

Input: a model G; a real example x; ground-truth label y;the bound of perturbations ϵ; and the number of iterations N

Output: An adversarial example $\hat{x}$ with $\|x - \hat{x}\|_p \leq \epsilon$

1: $\alpha = \epsilon/N$
2: $\hat{x}_0 = x$
3: **for** $i = 0; i < N; i++$ **do**
4: $\quad \hat{x}_{t+1} = \hat{x}_t + \alpha * sign(\nabla x L(G(\hat{x}_t), y))$;
5: **end for**
6: $\hat{x} = x + \epsilon * sign(\hat{x}_N - x)$;
7: $\hat{x} = Clip(\hat{x}, 0, 255)$;
8: **return** $\hat{x}$;

3.2 Boosting Momentum Iterative Methods

Similar to BI-FGSM, we also design a boosting version of momentum iterative methods. Algorithm 2 illustrates details of Boosting Momentum iterative methods B(boosting)MI-FGSM. Different from I-FGSM, gradient directions are accumulated in the iterative process by momentum g. We adopt the final direction of momentum g as the main direction of perturbation.

Based on the above description, it is obvious that our methods satisfy the L_∞ norm bounding constraint $\|x - \hat{x}\|_\infty \leq \epsilon$, ensuring our attack methods is valid. Generally speaking, our proposed boosting way can be deemed as combining the strength of FGSM and the gradient directions of I-FGFSM.

Algorithm 2. BMI-FGSM

Input: a model G; an example x; a real example x and ground-truth label y; The size of perturbation ϵ; iterations N ;and decay factor μ.

Output: An adversarial example $\hat{x}$ with $\|x - \hat{x}\|_p \leq \epsilon$

1: $\alpha = \epsilon/N$
2: $g_0 = 0$
3: $\hat{x}_0 = x$
4: **for** $i = 0$; $i < N$; $i++$ **do**
5: $\quad g_{t+1} = \mu * g_t + \frac{\nabla x L(G(\hat{x}_t), y)}{\|\nabla x L(G(\hat{x}_t), y)\|_1}$;
6: $\quad \hat{x}_{t+1} = \hat{x}_t + \alpha * sign(g_{t+1})$;
7: **end for**
8: $\hat{x} = x + \epsilon * sign(\hat{x}_N - x)$;
9: $\hat{x} = Clip(\hat{x}, 0, 255)$;
10: **return** $\hat{x}$;

4 Experiments

4.1 Models and Dataset

We conduct experiments on the ImageNet dataset [16] to validate the effectiveness of our proposed methods. We adopt five mainstream models from Pytorch model zoo: vgg16 [17], inception_v3 [18], resnet50, renset101, and resnet152 [6]. These five models have different structures and magnitudes, representing the most popular deep learning frameworks at present.

It is meaningless to study images which are not correctly classified. Therefore, we randomly select 1,000 images from ImageNet validation dataset which are correctly classified by all above five models.

We compare our proposed methods BI-FGSM and BMI-FGSM to one-step gradient method FSGM, iterative methods I-FGSM and momentum iterative methods MI-FGSM. Here we report the results based on L_∞ norm bounding constraint for non-targeted attacks. We set the perturbation bound ϵ as 16, the number of iterations as 10, the decay factor of momentum as 1.0. This setup is reported as the best choice in [3].

4.2 Attacking Results

We summarize the attacking results in Table 1. We provide both the top-1 and top-5 prediction accuracy of adversarial images crafted by the above five models using five attack methods. The success attack rate is defined exactly as $1 - accuracy(top_x)$. So the lower prediction accuracy becomes, the higher success attack rate will be. The diagonal of table shows the white-box attack results, highlighted in bold. We can observe that for all iterative methods, the white-box attack almost achieved the same success rate. But the situation is different for black-box attack.

We highlight the best black-box attack success rate (i.e., the lowest top-1 accuracy) in red. It is obvious that our proposed method BI-FGSM outperforms the other four methods in all black-box tests. Specifically, our BI-FGSM outperforms the benchmark method MI-FGSM by an average of 4.6%. In particular, the promotion for inception_v3 is 9.1% on average. Furthermore, our proposed method BMI-FGSM also outperforms MI-FGSM, even though the promotion is not so remarkable.

We also find that our proposed BMI-FGSM is weaker than our BI-FGSM. The difference between them lies in the gradient directions. Therefore, we believe our boosting way, say "gradient voting", works better than "gradient accumulation".

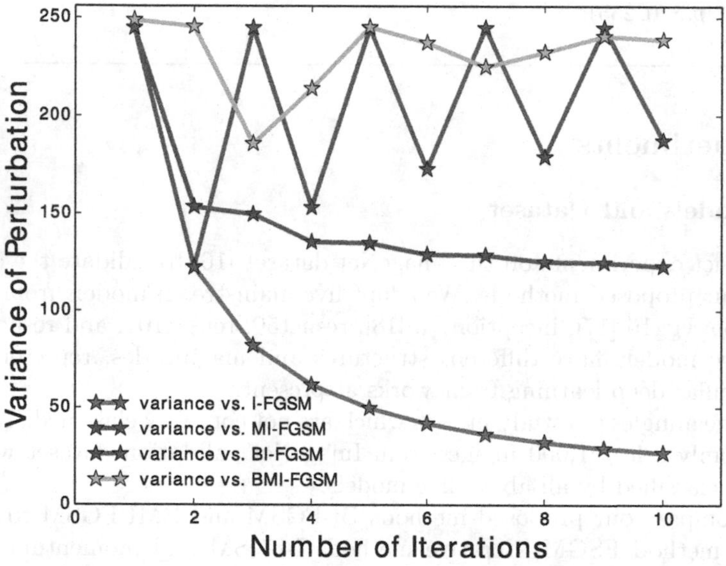

Fig. 3. Variance of perturbations crafted by four iterative methods which are I-FGSM, MI-FGSM, BI-FGSM and BMI-FGSM.

4.3 Variance of Perturbations

In this part, we analyze the underlying reason of the above four iterative methods by counting the average variance of perturbations. All methods are performed on the 1,000 validation images. We visualize the results in Fig. 3. Intuitively, lower variance means the weaker strength of perturbation. We find that the variance of perturbation crafted by I-FGSM keeps at a very low value after 3 steps, and gradually decreases afterwards. In our opinion, this is the main reason of why the success rate of I-FGSM drops for black-box attack.

Although the variance of perturbation crafted by MI-FGSM gradually drops with the growth of iteration, the variance keeps at a higher value which is almost 5 times than I-FGSM after 4 steps. Therefore, MI-FGSM achieved more powerful perturbations than I-FGSM and manifest high success rate.

Table 1. The top-1 and top-5 accuracy of five models we study after non-targeted adversarial attacks respectively using FGSM, I-FGSM BI-FGSM MI-FGSM and BMI-FGSM, the lower accuracy the better successful attack. Each row mean the adversarial examples is crafted by the first column model to attack the rest column models. Black bold indicates the white-box attack and red indicates the best attack methods.

	Attack	vgg16	Inception_v3	Resnet50	Resnet101	Resnet152
vgg16	FGSM	**8.10/20.60**	60.70/84.00	51.40/78.90	61.70/85.70	65.90/87.40
	I-FGSM	**0.80/2.50**	70.50/92.00	57.90/88.40	69.10/93.00	72.10/94.10
	BI-FGSM	**0.80/2.00**	50.60/76.80	36.00/67.40	46.70/77.10	53.20/79.90
	MI-FGSM	**1.00/2.90**	54.00/80.70	38.50/71.80	49.90/81.20	53.80/84.20
	BMI-FGSM	**1.10/3.60**	54.10/81.50	37.50/72.70	50.20/80.90	53.50/83.70
inception_v3	FGSM	45.60/71.80	**23.10/51.40**	62.10/88.20	69.00/89.70	74.30/92.40
	I-FGSM	76.90/95.10	**3.10/6.20**	83.10/97.80	86.40/98.40	88.00/98.50
	BI-FGSM	42.00/68.10	**3.00/7.60**	60.20/85.40	67.50/91.10	71.70/89.80
	MI-FGSM	56.40/82.90	**3.00/5.20**	69.20/90.90	73.90/94.40	78.30/94.60
	BMI-FGSM	48.30/75.10	**3.10/8.30**	67.00/88.90	71.90/92.60	75.40/93.10
resnet 50	FGSM	34.30/60.80	58.80/83.10	**17.20/45.20**	53.00/81.10	60.90/84.60
	I-FGSM	57.60/87.40	70.70/94.50	**0.00/2.20**	58.10/90.50	62.90/93.50
	BI-FGSM	29.30/58.50	51.70/79.60	**0.00/2.20**	35.50/71.70	41.70/78.10
	MI-FGSM	35.70/68.20	55.70/82.80	**0.10/2.00**	35.80/74.60	42.70/78.70
	BMI-FGSM	30.00/62.40	54.90/82.50	**0.10/2.90**	35.60.73.30	42.50/78.40
resnet 101	FGSM	36.50/61.10	60.90/86.00	50.30/78.40	**20.20/48.90**	59.20/84.00
	I-FGSM	63.50/89.80	72.40/94.10	56.50/89.30	**0.00/3.40**	61.70/90.30
	BI-FGSM	33.10/62.50	52.40/81.00	31.90/69.80	**0.00/3.90**	38.00/76.30
	MI-FGSM	40.50/72.70	57.60/85.00	35.10/74.70	**0.00/2.20**	41.00/80.20
	BMI-FGSM	34.90/65.60	56.30/83.70	34.90/74.40	**0.00/3.30**	40.40/80.10
resnet 152	FGSM	36.30/64.60	58.80/84.90	51.30/79.60	36.30/64.60	**23.20/56.90**
	I-FGSM	60.70/89.40	69.70/93.30	53.60/89.10	52.20/89.40	**0.20/3.70**
	BI-FGSM	31.60/64.10	48.70/79.80	31.10/68.50	30.50/68.50	**0.20/3.70**
	MI-FGSM	39.20/72.20	52.50/82.30	33.40/74.20	33.60/73.20	**0.30/2.80**
	BMI-FGSM	34.90/65.30	52.40/81.90	32.50/73.20	33.00/73.50	**0.30/3.00**

We also observe that the variance of BI-FGSM fluctuates with iteration. For odd number of iterations, it is scarcely possible to generate zero noise, because it will remain at least one perturbation for each pixel. So the variance keeps the highest all the time. But for even number of iterations, some pixels remain unchanged. And we also find that the "left" pixels gradually become less with the growth of iteration.

For BMI-FGSM, the variance keeps a high value, and becomes stable after 5 iterations, and higher than MI-FGSM all the time. The only difference between BMI-FGSM and MI-FGSM is the strength of perturbations, bringing higher attack success rate for BMI-FGSM. But we can see that the promotion of BMI-FGSM is not so remarkable, as the MI-FGSM already has a high variance.

Overall, we must say that the success attack rate is influenced by both strength and directions of generated perturbations.

4.4 Number of Iterations N

We finally explore the influence of iteration numbers on the attack success rate for I-FGSM and BI-FGSM. We use adversarial images crafted by ResNet50 model to attack all the five models. We plot the top-1 and top-5 accuracy in Fig. 4.

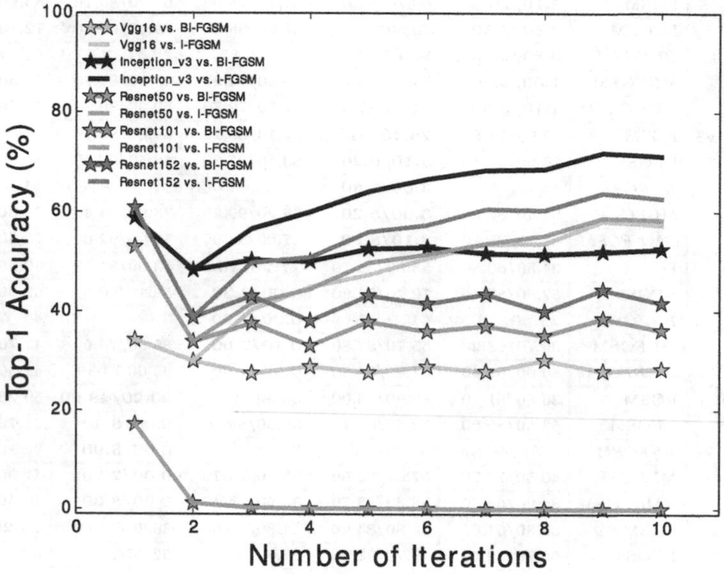

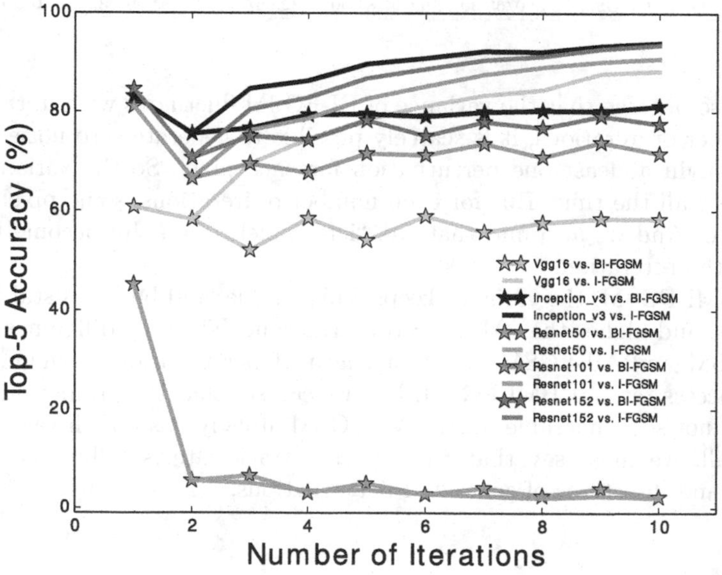

Fig. 4. Illustration of influence of the number of iterations on the accuracy for I-FGSM and BI-FGSM, left is top-1 accuracy and right is top-5. (Color figure online)

For white-box attack (orange curve in Fig. 4) top-1 accuracy almost equal to zero in just two steps. For our BI-FGSM, it becomes steady after three steps, and keeps a lower top-1 and top-5 accuracy. But for I-FGSM, attack success rate decreases gradually for all of the four black-box attacks.

Therefore, our proposed BI-FGSM is more robust to the number of iterations, whereas I-FGSM method become weaker as increase the number of iterations for black-box attacks.

5 Conclusion

In this paper, we propose a simple but effective way to boost iterative methods for black-box attack. Experiments show that our methods outperform the benchmark method MI-FGSM. We conduct extensive experiments to explain why our methods work in practice. We also study the influence of perturbation strength and gradient directions of attack success rate, and the influence of the number of iterations for all four iterative method in both white-box attack and black-box attack.

References

1. Carlini, N., Wagner, D.: Towards evaluating the robustness of neural networks. In: 2017 IEEE Symposium on Security and Privacy (SP), pp. 39–57. IEEE (2017)
2. Chen, L.C., Papandreou, G., Kokkinos, I., Murphy, K., Yuille, A.L.: DeepLab: semantic image segmentation with deep convolutional nets, atrous convolution, and fully connected CRFs. IEEE Trans. Pattern Anal. Mach. Intell. **40**(4), 834–848 (2018)
3. Dong, Y., et al.: Boosting adversarial attacks with momentum. In: Proceedings of the IEEE Conference on Computer Vision and Pattern Recognition, pp. 9185–9193 (2018)
4. Goodfellow, I.J., Shlens, J., Szegedy, C.: Explaining and harnessing adversarial examples (2014). arXiv preprint arXiv:1412.6572
5. He, K., Gkioxari, G., Dollár, P., Girshick, R.: Mask R-CNN. In: Proceedings of the IEEE International Conference on Computer Vision, pp. 2961–2969 (2017)
6. He, K., Zhang, X., Ren, S., Sun, J.: Deep residual learning for image recognition. In: Proceedings of the IEEE Conference on Computer Vision and Pattern Recognition, pp. 770–778 (2016)
7. Huang, G., Liu, Z., Van Der Maaten, L., Weinberger, K.Q.: Densely connected convolutional networks. In: Proceedings of the IEEE Conference on Computer Vision and Pattern Recognition, pp. 4700–4708 (2017)
8. Krizhevsky, A., Sutskever, I., Hinton, G.E.: ImageNet classification with deep convolutional neural networks. In: Advances in Neural Information Processing Systems, pp. 1097–1105 (2012)
9. Kurakin, A., Goodfellow, I., Bengio, S.: Adversarial examples in the physical world (2016). arXiv preprint arXiv:1607.02533
10. Liu, Y., Chen, X., Liu, C., Song, D.: Delving into transferable adversarial examples and black-box attacks (2016). arXiv preprint arXiv:1611.02770

11. Long, J., Shelhamer, E., Darrell, T.: Fully convolutional networks for semantic segmentation. In: Proceedings of the IEEE Conference on Computer Vision and Pattern Recognition, pp. 3431–3440 (2015)
12. Metzen, J.H., Genewein, T., Fischer, V., Bischoff, B.: On detecting adversarial perturbations (2017). arXiv preprint arXiv:1702.04267
13. Redmon, J., Farhadi, A.: YOLOv3: an incremental improvement (2018). arXiv preprint arXiv:1804.02767
14. Ren, S., He, K., Girshick, R., Sun, J.: Faster R-CNN: towards real-time object detection with region proposal networks. In: Advances in Neural Information Processing Systems, pp. 91–99 (2015)
15. Ronneberger, O., Fischer, P., Brox, T.: U-Net: convolutional networks for biomedical image segmentation. In: Navab, N., Hornegger, J., Wells, W.M., Frangi, A.F. (eds.) MICCAI 2015. LNCS, vol. 9351, pp. 234–241. Springer, Cham (2015). https://doi.org/10.1007/978-3-319-24574-4_28
16. Russakovsky, O., et al.: Imagenet large scale visual recognition challenge. Int. J. Comput. Vis. **115**(3), 211–252 (2015)
17. Simonyan, K., Zisserman, A.: Very deep convolutional networks for large-scale image recognition (2014). arXiv preprint arXiv:1409.1556
18. Szegedy, C., Vanhoucke, V., Ioffe, S., Shlens, J., Wojna, Z.: Rethinking the inception architecture for computer vision. In: Proceedings of the IEEE Conference on Computer Vision and Pattern Recognition, pp. 2818–2826 (2016)
19. Szegedy, C., et al.: Intriguing properties of neural networks (2013). arXiv preprint arXiv:1312.6199
20. Tramèr, F., Kurakin, A., Papernot, N., Goodfellow, I., Boneh, D., McDaniel, P.: Ensemble adversarial training: attacks and defenses (2017). arXiv preprint arXiv:1705.07204

Crowd Knowledge Enhanced Multimodal Conversational Assistant in Travel Domain

Lizi Liao[1(✉)], Lyndon Kennedy[2], Lynn Wilcox[2], and Tat-Seng Chua[1]

[1] NGS, National University of Singapore, Singapore, Singapore
liaolizi.llz@gmail.com, chuats@comp.nus.edu.sg
[2] FXPAL, Palo Alto, USA
{kennedy,wilcox}@fxpal.com

Abstract. We present a new solution towards building a crowd knowledge enhanced multimodal conversational system for travel. It aims to assist users in completing various travel-related tasks, such as searching for restaurants or things to do, in a multimodal conversation manner involving both text and images. In order to achieve this goal, we ground this research on the combination of multimodal understanding and recommendation techniques which explores the possibility of a more convenient information seeking paradigm. Specifically, we build the system in a modular manner where each modular construction is enriched with crowd knowledge from social sites. To the best of our knowledge, this is the first work that attempts to build intelligent multimodal conversational systems for travel, and moves an important step towards developing human-like assistants for completion of daily life tasks. Several current challenges are also pointed out as our future directions.

Keywords: Multimodal assistant · Conversational systems · Travel

1 Introduction

Conversational agents and travel go hand in hand. In fact, artificial intelligence is set to be a game-changer for this industry, through helping travelers and companies simplifying their travel arrangements and streamlining business procedures. Although conversational agents in travel offer big commercial potential, it is non-trivial to build such an intelligent system to meet user needs. As illustrated in the example in Fig. 1, the most critical problems lie in how to correctly understand user's intention and find out which venue meets user's requirements. The system needs to extract useful information such as "center of the city" and "moderate price" while also figure out Sushi restaurant from the user offered image. After obtaining such information, it should also be able to present some venue candidates for user to select by considering constraints as well as the matching between user intention and venue features.

Y. M. Ro et al. (Eds.): MMM 2020, LNCS 11961, pp. 405–418, 2020.
https://doi.org/10.1007/978-3-030-37731-1_33

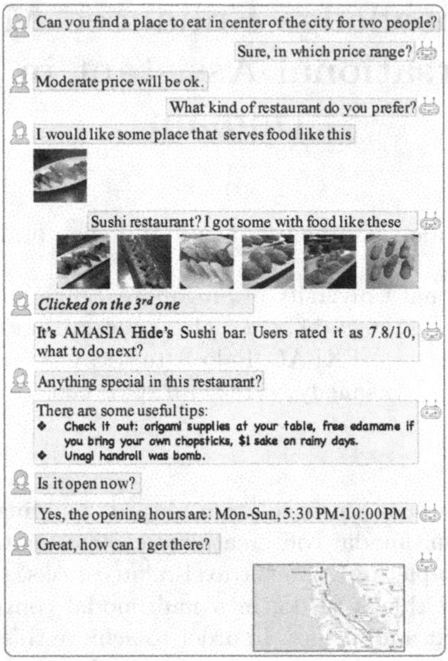

Fig. 1. An example of crowd knowledge enhanced multimodal conversational assistant.

For the first utterance understanding problem, a number of recent works in both industry and academia have developed natural language understanding (NLU) techniques for parsing user utterances into predefined semantic slots [13,18]. However, developing a structured ontology for NLU can be very difficult in cold-start stage where domain experts have to define the slot and possible values such as food type and price range. This is especially so in travel domain where the slot value structure is much more complicated. Typically, it involves several sub-topics such as restaurant, hotel and sightseeing *etc.* We observe enormous differences between the semantic slots of these sub-topics. For example, users might talk about "omakase" for Japanese restaurant while "rooftop garden" for hotel. Previous data-driven works for slot induction are mostly based upon human-human dialogue corpus [5,16]. However, it is hard to collect a large scale human-human dialogue data in travel scenario. Moreover, to enable the ability of communicating with images, moving beyond natural language understanding to multimodal understanding is another essential requirement.

Regarding the second problem of venue recommendation, there have been some existing efforts aiming to find appropriate venues in conversational systems. Many task-oriented dialogue systems try to form queries and feed them to database systems to retrieve the desired venues [2,3,17]. However, such methods heavily rely on the exact match of constraints which is rather sensitive to even slight language variations. It also has other limitations such as the weakness on modeling relationships between venues. Another line of works leverage memory networks to 'softly' incorporate venue entries in external Knowledge Bases

(KBs) [12,14]. However, there exist various relationships between venues, even the simplest 'nearby' relation, that still are hard to capture. The most recent studies such as [8,10,15] start to integrate conversational system with recommendation components, but the recommendation part only focus on learning the interplay between users and items, and the information slots about items are rather simple.

To deal with the aforementioned problems, we propose to leverage rich crowd sourced knowledge in social sites to build multimodal conversational assistant in travel domain. Generally speaking, we make use of user generated reviews, posted photos and meta data such as ratings *etc.* First of all, by analyzing user reviews and guided with salient terms, we are able to construct more fine-grained and user-friendly slot ontology for language understanding. Further with the help of images via taxonomy based learning, the system can largely narrow down the possible user intentions. Second, we leverage recommendation techniques to rank venues for user. Certain constraints such as location, ratings are used to filter venue candidates first, then we construct venue matching neural network where user intention and venue features are mapped for similarity computation to obtain the recommendation scores for the remaining venue candidates. Last but not the least, the reviews and meta data also provide good source for answering related user queries.

2 Crowd Sourced Knowledge

With user contributed services flourishing, social media sites become popular venues for users to express judgments of things and share their daily life experiences. The abundant user generated contents provide an useful source for conversational assistants to generate intelligent responses. For instance, Foursquare City Guide provides abundant user ratings, reviews, posted photos and meta information about each venue such as location, opening hours *etc.* The ratings are accumulated by many different users, thus provide a general sense of the restaurant for potential customers. The reviews are often commented based on existing user experiences, hence would offer detailed information such as popular dishes or dining environment. The posted photos largely come from smart phone camera shooting in location, which gives direct feeling of the venue and serves as a convenient way to pinpoint user intention. Finally, the meta data associated such as location and opening hours would work as answers for certain user queries.

Moreover, Foursquare also provides venue taxonomy which is termed as Foursquare Venue Category Hierarchy. There is a total of 937 nodes in the original taxonomy in Foursquare website, and ten major branches ranging from Food, Event, to Residence. In our work, we focus on five main branches which are heavily queried by travelers: Food, Nightlife Spot, Outdoors & Recreation, Shop & Service, and Arts & Entertainment. Organizing venues from general to specific, the taxonomy provides powerful support for narrowing down user's search intention.

3 Conversational Multimodal Assistant

In order to enable the interactive search scenario and make good use of crowd sourced knowledge at hand, we design the conversational multimodal assistant in modular-based fashion to fulfill the complicated task. The general workflow is shown in Fig. 2. Our framework has four modules: a multimodal understanding module, a venue recommender, a dialogue management component and a response generator. The multimodal understanding module parses text and image input to semantic representations. The dialogue management module maintains the dialogue context and determines what content to express next. The recommendation module finds the most appropriate venues for users. The response generation module converts actions to text and image responses. In what follows, we elaborate on these modules one by one.

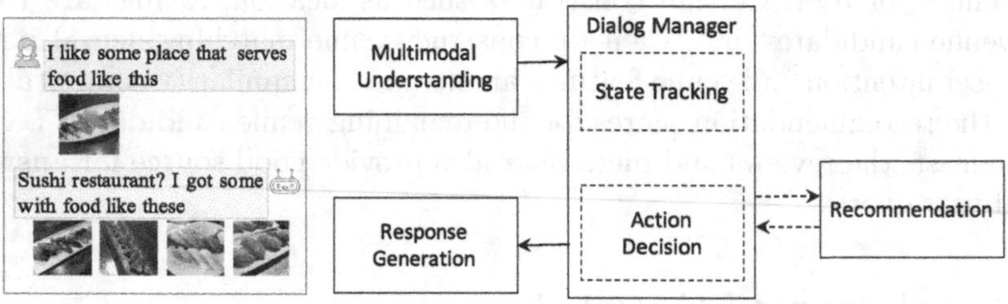

Fig. 2. The modular-based multimodal conversational system overview.

3.1 Multimodal Understanding

Given an utterance u which might contain text, image, or both, the multimodal understanding module generates its corresponding internal representation $\mathcal{U}$:

$$\mathcal{U} = <\mathcal{D}, \mathcal{C}, \mathcal{M}, \mathcal{A}, \mathcal{I}>. \tag{1}$$

$\mathcal{D}$ denotes the domain that u is talking about (we consider the five major branches in Foursquare taxonomy as domain candidates), which determines the possible slots and narrows down the possible venues. $\mathcal{C}$ contains a set of constraints that are popular to filter venues such as location and time. $\mathcal{M}$ denotes user's intent expressed by the utterance u (The most frequent query intents are like *Inform value, Request info, Recommend, Ask opinion, Negation, Chitchat*). $\mathcal{A}$ denotes a set of attributes or slot values extracted from u. $\mathcal{I}$ indicates the image(s) provided or picked by user.

Slot Ontology Construction. To facilitate utterance understanding, we first build a domain specific and relative comprehensive slot ontology. We not only include traditional slot values such as $\{num\_of\_people$ $=$

two, $price\_range = moderate\}$ adopted from existing works, but also enclose salient terms harvested from crowd sourced knowledge in social site reviews like $\{romantic, wagyu\ beef\}$. To obtain the salient terms, given the user reviews $\{r_1, \cdots, r_N\}$, we first extract term candidates $\{a_1, \cdots, a_M\}$ which are usually expressed by users in the form of adjective, noun or noun phrases. Since each review r_i can be associated with an upvote number l_i, we define the impact of review as $\tau_i = (\frac{1+l_i}{1+l_{max}})^\eta$, which also implicitly shows the importance of term candidates contained in the review. Intuitively, aside from frequency counting, representative term candidates in each domain usually appear in representative reviews, as these reviews often are carefully written and attract higher impact. Therefore, similar to [9], we formalize the extraction of salient terms as the co-selection of representative reviews and representative terms contained. We denote the representativeness score of a review set $\mathcal{X}$ as weighted sum of the scores regarding each term candidate,

$$\mathcal{R}(\mathcal{X}) = \sum_{a_i \in \{a_1, \cdots, a_M\}} w_i \mathcal{R}_i(\mathcal{X}), \tag{2}$$

where the weight w_i can be manually defined or otherwise set as 1. To avoid redundancy of candidate terms during selection, we define the score for a specific term candidate using the diminishing return property which is also known as submodularity in discrete optimization:

$$\mathcal{R}_i(\mathcal{X}) = 1 - \prod_{r_j \in \mathcal{X}} (1 - \mathcal{R}_i(r_j)), \quad \mathcal{R}_i(r_j) = \tau_j \frac{\sum_{a_k \in A_j} fsim(a_s, a_i)}{|A_j|}.$$

where A_j denotes the candidates contained in r_j and $fsim(\cdot, \cdot) \in [0, 1]$ denotes the similarity score between two term candidates, which is calculated from fuzzy matching [4]. We solve the maximization of Eq. 2 via greedy algorithm.

Intention Understanding. With the constructed slot ontology, the extraction of attributes can be cast as a sequence labeling problem. Since the domain, intent are closely related to slot values, we adopt an attention-based neural network model for joint domain determination, intent detection and attribute extraction in multitask setting as in [11]. As shown in Fig. 3, an attention mechanism is introduced to enable the encoder-decoder architecture to align and decode simultaneously. Specifically, at each decoding step i, the decoder state $\mathbf{s}_i$ is calculated as a function of the previous decoder state $\mathbf{s}_{i-1}$, the previous emitted label and the aligned encoder hidden state $\mathbf{h}_i$. The context vector $\mathbf{c}_i$ is calculated as a weighted average of the RNN hidden states $\mathbf{h}_1, \mathbf{h}_2, \cdots, \mathbf{h}_n$ [1]:

$$\mathbf{c}_i = \sum_{j=1}^{N} \alpha_{ij} \mathbf{h}_j, \tag{3}$$

$$\alpha_{ij} = \frac{exp(\mathbf{e}_{ij})}{\sum_{k=1}^{N} exp(\mathbf{e}_{ik})}, \tag{4}$$

$$\mathbf{e}_{ik} = g(\mathbf{s}_{i-1}, \mathbf{h}_k), \tag{5}$$

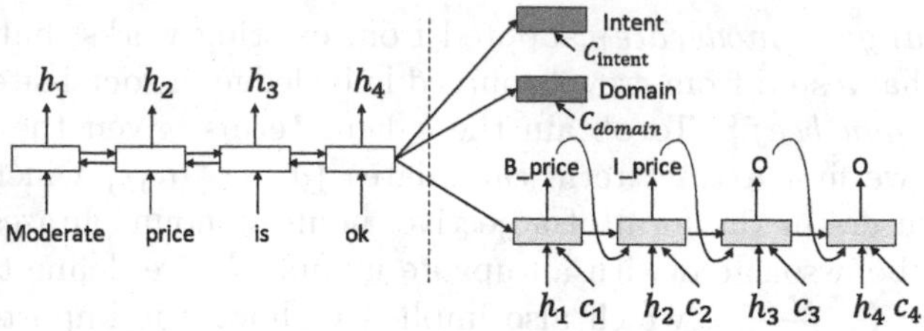

Fig. 3. Encoder-decoder model for joint intent detection, domain determination and attribute extraction.

where g is a feed forward neural network. At each decoding step, the explicit aligned input is the encoder state $\mathbf{h}_i$. The context vector $\mathbf{c}_i$ provides additional information to the decoder and can be seen as a continuous bag of weighted features $(\mathbf{h}_1, \mathbf{h}_2, \cdots, \mathbf{h}_n)$.

Regarding constraints $\mathcal{C}$, we currently consider location, time and ratings. Such constraints are important to consider separately. For example, user might indicate that the restaurant should be with rating score of over four and located nearby. In such case, we directly filter out restaurants based on rating and location, which is more straightforward and effective. Another observation on constraint extraction is that the typical linguistic constructs of such constraints are relatively fixed, hence we can directly apply simple regular expressions and patterns to extract them.

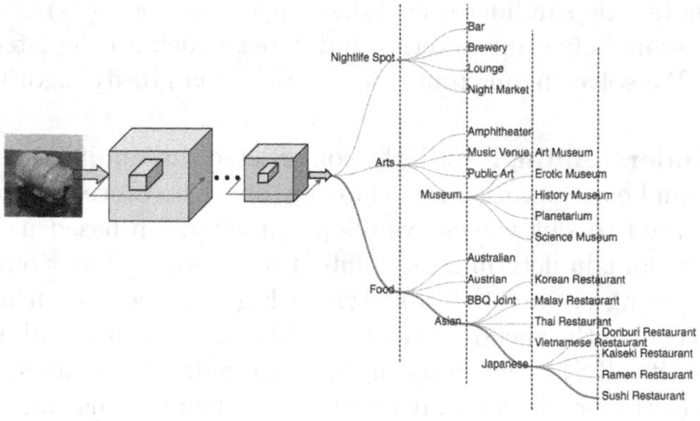

Fig. 4. Layer by layer image classification guided by venue taxonomy. Due to space limitation, only part of the taxonomy is illustrated.

The images provided by user are processed by ResNet [7] with the help of venue taxonomy in a layer-by-layer style. The learning model is shown in Fig. 4. The image goes through ResNet to obtain pool5 vector features which are then feed to the first layer of classifier. If the largest resulting score exceeds a certain threshold which we view as the credibility threshold, the vector features will be feed to the next layer classifier. We continue this procedure until no score of a layer exceeds the threshold. Then a credible venue category in certain granularity is obtained. In our experiment, we set the threshold of each layer to 0.8 for convenience. It can be empirically set for each classifier differently. At the same time, the vector feature can be used during venue recommendation which we will elaborate soon.

3.2 Venue Recommendation

Different from traditional task-oriented dialogue systems that use database query to find venues and suffer from limitation of exact match, we leverage recommendation techniques to find a match between user intention and venues. Generally speaking, to obtain user intention representation $\mathbf{v}_{int}$, the user intention $\{\mathcal{D}, \mathcal{A}, \mathcal{I}\}$ in Eq. 1 is fed into a two layer fully connected neural nets. $\mathcal{D}$ and $\mathcal{A}$ are represented as one-hot representation while $\mathcal{I}$ uses the pool5 vector feature obtained via ResNet. Such representations are concatenated together. Note that the $\mathcal{C}$ in user intention is directly used to filter venues, instead of being packed into the network. For obtaining the venue representation $\mathbf{v}_{ven}$, information about venue is also fed into a Multi-Layer Perceptron (MLP) network. Then, the representations are used to calculate a matching score for ranking. We leverage the triplet loss to train the network where for each ground truth venue, we pair a sampled negative venue with it. The representation obtained for the sampled venue is denoted as $\mathbf{v}'_{ven}$. Suppose we have N training samples, the training loss is calculated as below:

$$\mathcal{L} = \frac{1}{N}\sum_{i=1}^{N} max\{0, m - (cos(\mathbf{v}_{int_i}, \mathbf{v}_{ven_i}) - cos(\mathbf{v}_{int_i}, \mathbf{v}'_{ven_i}))\}$$

where m is a predefined margin.

The recommendation module is triggered by the dialogue management module when certain conditions are satisfied. The results returned by recommendation is a list of venues obtained via ranking the matching scores.

3.3 Dialogue Management

Most of previous dialogue system works rely on labeled data as supervision to train statistical models for dialogue state tracking and policy learning. However, annotated data is scarce for many practical scenarios especially for complex ones like travel, we thus manually define a set of rules for dialogue management to enable the completion of a full-fledged system. Generally speaking, the update of dialogue state mainly depends on domain $\mathcal{D}$ and intention $\mathcal{M}_t$. For dialogue policy, we pre-define a set of actions such as *Proactive Questioning, Candidate Listing, Venue Recommendation, Question Answering, Review Summary, API call* and *Chitchat.* We then set a list of activation conditions for triggering these actions. More details will be provided in Appendix.

3.4 Response Generation

For text response part, we apply both IR-based, template-based and summarization-based response generation.

- For the *Chitchat* action, we apply IR-based method to generate response $\hat{o}$ for a given user utterance u. The general idea is that given a collection of query-response pairs $\{q_i, o_i\}$, the method finds an existing query q that is most similar to u and return q's response o as the response $\hat{o}$ for u.
- Regarding the *Review Summary* action, the venue usually has already been fixed. Given the reviews about the venue, we apply extractive summarization technique as in [9] to select representative sentences and organize them as response.
- For other actions, we define a set of rules to map semantic representation into natural language. For example, if the next detailed action is *require(food=$V)* in *Proactive Questioning* type, the possible language templates can be "Do you like a $V restaurant?" or "How about $V food?".

To generate image responses, we purely rely on retrieval-based method. It usually corresponds to the *Candidate Listing* action, and user often have offered an image or provided enough attribute value to find a venue. Based on these information, the recommendation module returns a list of venue candidates, and the corresponding photos make up the image response list.

4 Evaluations

4.1 Data

To harvest crowd sourced knowledge from Foursquare City Guide, we use python selenium webdriver to simulate user scroll, click actions *etc.* The crawler is applied to San Francisco and the detailed information is shown in Table 1. Initially, we crawled 456,060 user posted venue photos. After brief inspection, we observe that the photos are too noisy to be used directly. We thus apply ResNet-50 to extract image features and use DBSCAN [6] to cluster these images in each venue subcategory. By manually tuning the clustering density, we filter out images by clusters. For example, we continuously observe user Selfie clusters in almost every venue subcategory. After the filtering procedure, we obtain about 80K high quality images. The detailed results for each domain are shown as in Fig. 5.

Table 1. Foursquare data crawled for San Francisco.

# Venues	# Reviews	# Photos (raw)	# Photos (filtered)
13,942	386,053	456,060	80,641

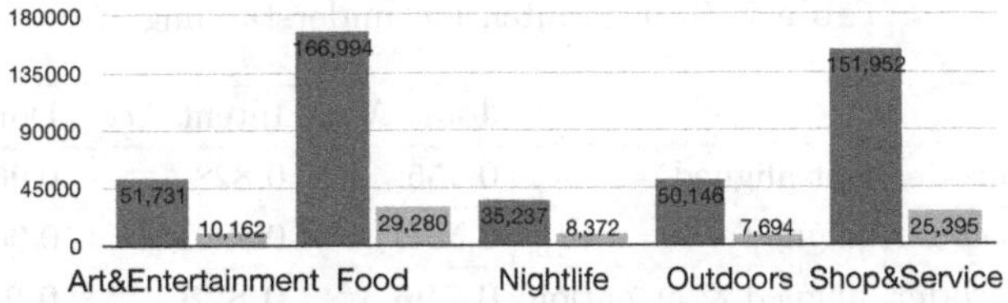

Fig. 5. The difference of photo numbers between the original data (blue) and the data after filtering process (green). (Color figure online)

Aside from the crawled data from social sites, the multimodal dialogue data in travel is still not available. We thus have to make use of whatever available to mitigate the problem. Therefore, to train our Chitchat response generation, we leverage the Microsoft Research Social Media Conversation Corpus which contains 4,232 three-step conversational snippets extracted from Twitter logs. To get more comprehensive slot ontology, we adopt the MultiWOZ dataset [3] to get the traditional slot values. Together with the crawled social site data, we use it to help training our language understanding model.

4.2 Evaluation on Multimodal Understanding

The training setting of the joint intent detection model is as follows: we use LSTM cell as the basic RNN unit and word embedding size is set to 128; the word embeddings are randomly initialized and fine-tuned during mini-batch training; dropout rate of 0.5 is applied to the non-recurrent connections and the maximum norm for gradient clipping is set to 5; and we use Adam optimization method with initial learning rate 0.01. The evaluation metric for domain classification and intent classification is accuracy, while the metric for attribute extraction (or slot filling in other works) is joint accuracy. We compare the performance of joint detection model with several baselines as in Table 2.

To train the image-based venue classification model, we leverage the filtered user posted photo data. We use the pre-trained ResNet50 model to extract pool5 image features and train classifiers layer by layer guided by the venue taxonomy. We set the threshold of going deeper layer to 0.8. The evaluation metric used here is top-5 accuracy where we view an output as correct if the ground truth class is among the top-5 guesses. We compare the performance of our layered method with that of multi-label and multi-class version of ResNet where multi-label assumes mutual independence relation among the class labels and multi-class assumes exclusive relation among class labels.

Joint Intent Detection. Table 2 shows the joint training model performance on intent classification, domain classification and attribute extraction as compared to previous methods. As shown in this table, we observe that the encoder-decoder network with aligned inputs and attention mechanism performs the best. Not to our surprise, the pure attention-based encoder-decoder model (in the first

Table 2. Test on intention understanding.

Model	Joint Acc.	Intent Acc.	Domain Acc.
Encoder-decoder, not aligned	0.455	0.828	0.963
Encoder-decoder, aligned	0.524	0.826	0.962
Encoder-decoder, aligned & attention	**0.596**	**0.828**	**0.963**

line) that does not utilize explicit alignment information performs poorly. It indicates that letting the model to learn the alignment from training data itself does not seem to be appropriate for the attribute extraction task. Line 2 and line 3 show the joint accuracy scores of the non-attention and attention-based encode-decoder models that utilize the aligned inputs. The attention-based model gives a slightly better score than the non-attention-based one. By investigating the attention learned by the model, we find that the attention weights are more likely to be evenly distributed across words while there are a few cases where we observe insightful attention that the decoder pays to the input sequence. It might partly explain the observed performance gain when attention is enabled. For intent accuracy and domain accuracy scores, the performance difference among the joint model and its variations is marginal. This might be due to the fact that the classifiers only directly connect to the last hidden vector of the utterance, and thus the input alignment mechanism does not affect them much.

Image-Based Venue Category Classification. The results for image-based venue category classification are shown in Table 3. We observe that classifying images in the layer-by-layer style with the help of venue taxonomy achieves the best performance. It manages to obtain 0.93% relative gain compared to the Multi-class model and 1.88% relative gain compared to the Multi-label model with regard to Top-5 accuracy score. Although such improvement might not be obviously observed when inspecting the final classification result, the layer-by-layer classification paradigm is essential for improving the conversation experience. This is because the venue taxonomy organizes venues from general to specific and the higher level nodes are usually more general thus easier to separate than the lower ones. In addition, adding threshold constraints for going deeper layers ensures that the class label obtained is of high reliability. During conversation, a piece of general but reliable information is much safer than specific but unreliable information. It facilitates users in specifying or navigating to more specific venues. On the other hand, a classification error appeared in specific venue in utterance understanding might lead to serious problem in later conversation thus affect the completion of task and user satisfaction.

Table 3. Layered image classification results comparison.

	Multi-label	Multi-class	Layered model
Top-5 accuracy	0.744	0.751	**0.758**

4.3 Evaluation on Venue Recommendation

Our recommender works on well-organized dialogue states $\mathcal{S}$, we can thus make use of the crawled social site data to simulate our recommendation scenario. Specifically, to construct a training instance, we sample information from review and venue meta data as the user intention, and use the remaining information to obtain venue representation. The recommendation module is trained via mini-batch and the Adam optimization method with an initial learning rate of 0.01 is applied. The word embedding setting and dropout are the same to that of the multimodal understanding experiments. We compare with database query and memory network [14] methods. The *matching net (w/o)* denotes our method without using salient terms in user intention.

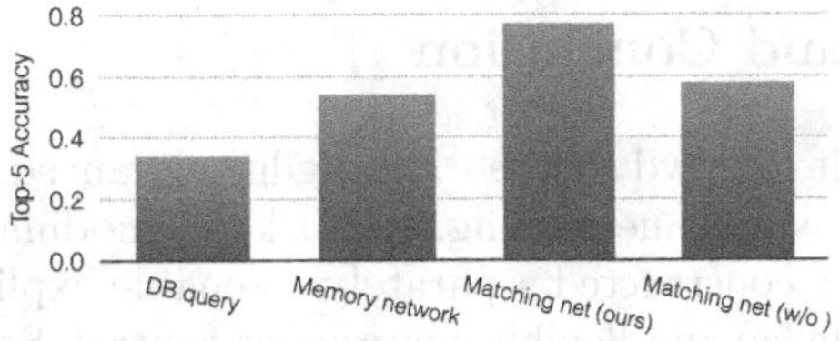

Fig. 6. Test on venue recommendation.

The performance comparison are shown in Fig. 6. It is obvious that the triplet loss enhanced matching network achieves the best performance. Not to our surprise, the DB query method performs the worst which is largely due to the exact matching mechanism. It will be affected by even slight language variations. The memory network actually resembles our matching net in the sense that it also learns representations for user intention and venues, and calculates similarity scores between them for matching. However, the triplet loss training in our matching net enhances the model's capability in finding the correct answer. When salient terms are ignored as *matching net (w/o)*, we also observe a performance drop which further validates the usefulness of crowd sourced knowledge.

4.4 System Evaluation

To further evaluate the usefulness of incorporating crowd sourced knowledge, we build a demo system to carry out human evaluation. The one enriched with crowd sourced knowledge is termed as *with CSK* while the one without is termed as *w/o CSK*. We recruit ten participants and set up ten goals for them to chat with the demo. Each goal consists of complete slot values, a user posted photo and meta data of the venue except those that are unique such as address and phone number. After each dialogue, the participants are asked to give scores regarding how fluent and how informative the responses are (from zero to five and the larger the better). We also report the success rate of these goals. The compiled results are shown in Table 4. It shows that when the crowed sourced knowledge is incorporated, the informativeness of responses increases a lot. It is as expected since the user reviews and information from API better helps the user. Also, with the help of detailed salient terms and photos, the system can pinpoint the venue easier as shown by the increased success rate.

Table 4. Human evaluation on system performance.

Method	Fluency	Informativeness	Success rate
w/o CSK	**3.51**	1.67	0.16
with CSK	3.39	**3.34**	**0.45**

5 Discussion and Conclusion

In this work, we built a crowd sourced knowledge enhanced multimodal conversational agent for travel venue seeking. It works in modular-based style where four core modules are constructed separately to enable explicit incorporation of crowd sourced knowledge and flexible component control. Specifically, the introduction of multimodal understanding and venue recommendation techniques into the system encourages a more convenient information seeking paradigm that is more natural, prompt as well as intelligent.

However, in order to build human-like multimodal agents, there are still many challenges. One of the most prominent challenges at this "cold-start" stage is the lack of large scale dialogue data. Without such training data, we cannot use statistical models to train dialogue management module as well as the response generation module, which is critical for increasing the intelligence level of agents. To construct a full-fledged system, we can only resort to rule-based methods for such modules at this stage. Nevertheless, such system provides us with an option to start constructing a large scale dataset with further help of crowdsourcing services such as Amazon Mechanical Turk, which we view as our future work. Another challenge lies in the design of internal representation of dialogue. Although semantic frame styled representation is rather straightforward, its flexibility and efficiency is relatively limited.

Appendix A: State Tracking

State tracking refers to the maintenance of the dialogue state $\mathcal{S}_t$ which is the representation of the conversation session until time t. Based on the state $\mathcal{S}_{t-1}$ in former time step and the multimodal understanding result $\mathcal{U}_t$ for utterance in time step t, the dialogue state is obtained as follows:

$$\mathcal{S}_t = \mathcal{G}(\mathcal{S}_{t-1}, <\mathcal{M}_t, \mathcal{D}_t, \mathcal{C}_t, \mathcal{A}_t, \mathcal{I}_t>), \tag{6}$$

where $\mathcal{G}$ refers to a set of rules. We generally summarize the rules as below:

(1) if $\mathcal{M}_t = Chitchat$, then $\mathcal{S}_t = \mathcal{S}_{t-1}$;
(2) if domain $\mathcal{D}_t$ is changed: $\mathcal{S}_t$ will be updated totally based on $\mathcal{U}_t$;
(3) if domain $\mathcal{D}_t$ is not changed: if $\mathcal{M}_t \neq Negation$, $\mathcal{S}_t$ will inherit information stored in $\mathcal{S}_{t-1}$;
(4) if domain $\mathcal{D}_t$ is not changed: if $\mathcal{M}_t = Negation$, $\mathcal{S}_t$ will inherit information stored in $\mathcal{S}_{t-1}$ while update the parts according $\mathcal{U}_t$;
(5) if the time interval between two consecutive utterances exceeds a pre-defined length at time t, then $\mathcal{S}_t$ will be cleaned.

Tracking dialogue states is the key to elevate user experience on multi-turn conversation. The main reason that we do not follow the previous works to learn models is because of the lack of dialogue data to train statistical tracking models. We leave leveraging session-level labeled dialogue data to improve the state tracking task as our future work.

Appendix B: Action Decision

At each turn of conversation between user and agent, the dialogue management module takes the current state tracking results as input, and outputs the corresponding actions. Due to the lack of large-scale dialogue training data, we also resort to a set of rules. Intuitively, the main action types considered and the conditions for triggering it are as below:

- *Proactive Questioning.* This action will be triggered when (a) a recommendation intent is detected, (b) a domain is detected, and (c) no enough constraints or attributes is detected in $\mathcal{S}_t$. This action is often used to obtain more constraints or attributes to narrow down the search space.
- *Candidate Listing.* This action is often triggered when recommendation results are obtained or the *Show more* intent is detected. As each venue in our dataset is associated with Foursquare photos, we implement candidate listing via a list of images where each image corresponds to a venue. In the interface, user can conveniently choose a venue by simply clicking its corresponding image.
- *Venue Recommendation.* This action is triggered when the intent $\mathcal{I}_t$ in $\mathcal{S}_t$ is *Recommendation*, and it will retrieve results from the recommendation module.
- *Question Answering.* It will be triggered when a venue is selected and one of its slot names are detected in $\mathcal{U}_t$ without value around. It returns the missing attribute value by looking up the venue database.
- *Review Summary.* This action will be triggered when a venue is selected and the intent $\mathcal{I}_t$ in $\mathcal{S}_t$ is *Ask opinion*. It will summarize the reviews of the target venue and present in organized form.
- *API call.* It will be triggered when a venue is selected and the *Map direction* intent is present in $\mathcal{I}_t$. The Google Map API will be called with the start position and destination. Currently, only the Map API is integrated. However, other APIs such as weather report can also be integrated with proper modifications.

– *Chitchat.* This action will be triggered when none travel venue seeking related intent is detected. As pointed out by [18], nearly 80% of utterances are chitchat queries for e-commerce bots. If the system cannot reply to them, then the conversation may not be able to continue. Thus, it will activate the chitchat response generation to obtain a reply.

References

1. Bahdanau, D., Cho, K., Bengio, Y.: Neural machine translation by jointly learning to align and translate. arXiv preprint arXiv:1409.0473 (2014)
2. Bordes, A., Weston, J.: Learning end-to-end goal-oriented dialog. In: The 3rd International Conference on Learning Representations, pp. 1–14 (2016)
3. Budzianowski, P., et al.: MultiWOZ - a large-scale multi-domain wizard-of-oz dataset for task-oriented dialogue modelling. In: EMNLP, pp. 5016–5026 (2018)
4. Chaudhuri, S., Ganjam, K., Ganti, V., Motwani, R.: Robust and efficient fuzzy match for online data cleaning. In: SIGMOD, pp. 313–324. ACM (2003)
5. Chen, Y.N., Wang, W.Y., Rudnicky, A.I.: Leveraging frame semantics and distributional semantics for unsupervised semantic slot induction in spoken dialogue systems. In: 2014 IEEE Spoken Language Technology Workshop, pp. 584–589 (2014)
6. Ester, M., et al.: A density-based algorithm for discovering clusters in large spatial databases with noise. In: KDD, vol. 96, pp. 226–231 (1996)
7. He, K., Zhang, X., Ren, S., Sun, J.: Deep residual learning for image recognition. In: CVPR, pp. 770–778 (2016)
8. Li, R., Kahou, S.E., Schulz, H., Michalski, V., Charlin, L., Pal, C.: Towards deep conversational recommendations. In: NIPS, pp. 9748–9758 (2018)
9. Liao, L., He, X., Ren, Z., Nie, L., Xu, H., Chua, T.S.: Representativeness-aware aspect analysis for brand monitoring in social media. In: IJCAI, pp. 310–316 (2017)
10. Liao, L., Takanobu, R., Ma, Y., Yang, X., Huang, M., Chua, T.: Deep conversational recommender in travel. arxiv:1907.00710 (2019)
11. Liu, B., Lane, I.: Attention-based recurrent neural network models for joint intent detection and slot filling. arXiv preprint arXiv:1609.01454 (2016)
12. Madotto, A., Wu, C.S., Fung, P.: Mem2seq: effectively incorporating knowledge bases into end-to-end task-oriented dialog systems. In: ACL, pp. 1468–1478 (2018)
13. Rieser, V., Lemon, O.: Natural language generation as planning under uncertainty for spoken dialogue systems. In: Krahmer, E., Theune, M. (eds.) EACL/ENLG - 2009. LNCS (LNAI), vol. 5790, pp. 105–120. Springer, Heidelberg (2010). https://doi.org/10.1007/978-3-642-15573-4_6
14. Sukhbaatar, S., et al.: End-to-end memory networks. In: NIPS, pp. 2440–2448 (2015)
15. Sun, Y., Zhang, Y.: Conversational recommender system. In: SIGIR, pp. 235–244 (2018)
16. Tur, G., Jeong, M., Wang, Y.Y., Hakkani-Tür, D., Heck, L.: Exploiting the semantic web for unsupervised natural language semantic parsing. In: Thirteenth Annual Conference of the International Speech Communication Association (2012)
17. Wen, T.H., et al.: A network-based end-to-end trainable task-oriented dialogue system. In: EACL, pp. 438–449 (2017)
18. Yan, Z., Duan, N., Chen, P., Zhou, M., Zhou, J., Li, Z.: Building task-oriented dialogue systems for online shopping. In: AAAI, pp. 4618–4625 (2017)

Improved Model Structure with Cosine Margin OIM Loss for End-to-End Person Search

Haoran Chen[1], Minghua Zhu[1(✉)], Xuesong Cai[1(✉)], Jufeng Luo[2], and Yunzhou Qiu[2]

[1] MOE Engineering Research Center for Software/Hardware Co-Design Technology and Application, East China Normal University, Shanghai, China
mhzhu@sei.ecnu.edu.cn, sh_cxs@163.com
[2] Shanghai Internet of Things Co., Ltd., Shanghai, China

Abstract. End-to-end person search is a novel task that integrates pedestrian detection and person re-identification (re-ID) into a joint optimization framework. However, the pedestrian features learned by most existing methods are not discriminative enough due to the potential adverse interaction between detection and re-ID tasks and the lack of discriminative power of re-ID loss. To this end, we propose an Improved Model Structure (IMS) with a novel re-ID loss function called Cosine Margin Online Instance Matching (CM-OIM) loss. Firstly, we design a model structure more suitable for person search, which alleviates the adverse interaction between the detection and re-ID parts by reasonably decreasing the network layers shared by them. Then, we conduct a full investigation of the weight of re-ID loss, which we argue plays an important role in end-to-end person search models. Finally, we improve the Online Instance Matching (OIM) loss by adopting a more robust online update strategy, and importing a cosine margin into it to increase the intra-class compactness of the features learned. Extensive experiments on two challenging datasets CUHK-SYSU and PRW demonstrate our approach outperforms the state-of-the-arts.

Keywords: End-to-end person search · Re-ID loss weight · Improved model structure · Cosine margin OIM loss

1 Introduction

Person re-identification (re-ID), referring to the task of identifying a target person across multi-camera surveillance systems [11,16,23], is an important and fast-growing research topic in computer vision. However, a typical re-ID system cannot be used directly in practical applications, since most advanced re-ID algorithms are based on manually cropped pedestrians, which are hard to get in real-world scenarios. Under such circumstance, the task of person search, which considers pedestrian detection and person re-ID jointly, has gradually become a hot research topic in the area of intelligent surveillance and analysis.

Y. M. Ro et al. (Eds.): MMM 2020, LNCS 11961, pp. 419–430, 2020.
https://doi.org/10.1007/978-3-030-37731-1_34

There are currently two types of methods for person search: two-stage methods [1,7,22,26] and end-to-end methods [8,14,20,21]. Two-stage methods handle this problem by utilizing separate supervised models respectively for pedestrian detection and person re-ID, tackling each task sequentially, while end-to-end methods leverage joint optimization deep neural networks to unify the two tasks. In general, end-to-end methods have more advantages than two-stage methods, for example, the detection and re-ID parts can better adapt with each other through joint optimization to reduce the influence of false alarms and detection misalignments [21], and the shared representations between the two parts can make person search more time-efficient.

However, end-to-end methods always face three important issues. The first is that sharing representations between detection and re-ID parts would adversely affect the model performance, which is firstly analyzed in [1]. The second is that the performance of end-to-end models is highly dependent on an appropriate choice of the weighting between the losses of the two parts, when adopting a multi-task deep learning manner [2,4,13]. And the last one is that the widely adopted Online Instance Matching (OIM) loss function [21] for the supervision of re-ID part lacks the power of discrimination, since it only considers the inter-class variance of pedestrian features while ignores the intra-class compactness.

In this paper, we aim to resolve the aforementioned issues. Firstly, we propose an Improved Model Structure (IMS) to alleviate the adverse interaction between the detection and re-ID parts while maintaining sufficient helpful shallow contextual information shared by them. Different from these methods [8,14,20,21], our IMS reduces the network layers shared by the two parts, making them concentrate more on their respective tasks while achieving the end-to-end advantages at the same time. Secondly, we find that it is not an effective way to easily set uniform weights on the detection loss and the re-ID loss, which is adopted by all recent end-to-end works [8,14,21]. We observe that the scale values of the Faster R-CNN [12] loss (detection loss) and the OIM loss (re-ID loss) are quite different, which would cause the model to converge to an unfavorable parameter space. Therefore, we conduct a full study of the re-ID loss weight, aiming to explore its impact on the performance of model. Finally, we improve the OIM loss by designing a more effective update strategy for the online lookup table and importing a cosine margin into the OIM loss. Different from [1,8,14,21], our update manner utilizes the weighted average information of the features with the same label in a batch, which is more robust. Moreover, as a variant of the conventional Softmax loss [18], the OIM loss only considers the inter-class variance of features while ignores the intra-class compactness. To this end, our proposed Cosine Margin OIM loss (CM-OIM) formulates a cosine margin via $\cos\theta - m$ for the OIM loss, minimizing the intra-class variance by forming margins between the feature clusters of different classes. Compared with these methods [8,19] which introduce center loss [17] to their models, our approach requires less memory space since we do not need to maintain an additional buffer to store the numerous category center vectors. Furthermore, the CM-OIM loss is conceptually simpler and more geometrically interpretable, which can be easily embedded into any person search model for better performance without making any changes to it. Extensive experiments on two benchmarks CUHK-SYSU [21] and PRW [26] show that our approach is more efficient than the state-of-the-art end-to-end person search methods.

2 Related Work

In this section we first review the recent works of person search, then we review the prior works aiming at improving the discriminative power of the Softmax loss, which is related to our proposed method.

2.1 Person Search

Person search has attracted much research attention over the past few years, especially since the publication of [21]. As the best of our knowledge, [22] is the first work to introduce a unified framework for person search by using hand-crafted features to model pedestrian commonness and uniqueness. After that, [26] releases a large-scale benchmark dataset for person search called PRW, and uses a variety of separated models to fully investigate the combination of pedestrian detection and person re-ID. [20] proposes the first successful end-to-end deep framework to address the person search problem by modifying the Faster R-CNN detector, and [21] proposes a non-parametric loss function called Online Instance Matching (OIM) loss for the supervision of re-ID part, which is widely used in recent works. In [8,19], center loss is introduced into the model to increase the intra-class compactness of features. [14] leverages the similarities between the labeled identities and unlabeled identities to extend the labeled samples, which can be treated as a semi-supervised learning method. [7] achieves more precise location of the target person by recursively shrinking the search area, which can get better search efficiency. [1] states that solving the detection and re-ID tasks separately would achieve better performance than jointly, and they use a two-stage method to solve person search rather than an end-to-end model.

2.2 Improvements of the Softmax Loss

The Softmax loss is a classical loss function for the classification tasks. In order to acquire better feature embeddings, [10] proposes a large margin softmax (L-Softmax), which adds angular constraints to each identity. To further improve the L-Softmax, angular Softmax (A-Softmax) [9] is proposed by normalizing the weights, and it achieves better performance on many face recognition benchmarks. After that, [15] proposes additive margin Softmax (AM-Softmax) by introducing an additive angular margin for the Softmax loss, which is intuitively appealing and more interpretable.

3 Proposed Method

We propose an Improved Model Structure (IMS) for end-to-end person search, which is an improvement of the Original Model Structure (OMS) in [21], as shown in Fig. 1.

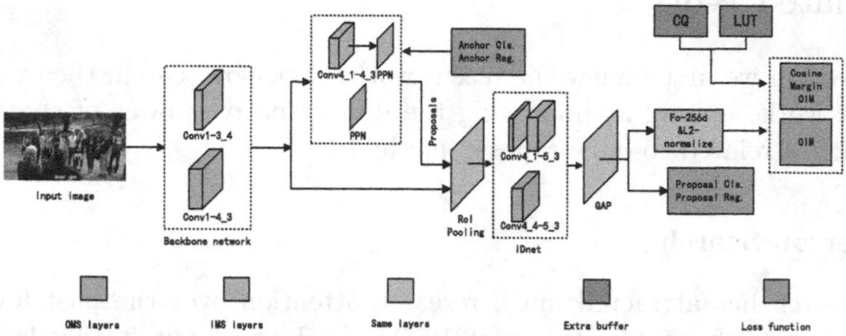

Fig. 1. Comparison of the IMS and the OMS (**Best viewed in color**). Within the dotted line is the difference between the IMS (upper) and the OMS (lower). (Color figure online)

3.1 Improved Model Structure

Specifically, we adopt the ResNet-50 [3] as our base CNN model, which consists of a 7×7 convolutional layer named conv1 and four blocks named conv2_x to conv5_x each containing 3, 4, 6, 3 residual units respectively. We exploit the conv1 to conv3_4 as the backbone network shared by the Pedestrian Proposal Network (PPN) and the IDentification net (IDnet).

The shallow feature maps generated by the stem will be divided into two routes. One of the routes sends these feature maps to feature extraction layers composed of the duplicated conv4_1 to conv4_3 (does not share parameters with the corresponding layers in the IDnet), followed by the PPN to produce some pedestrian candidates. The other sends them to the RoI-Pooling layer to pool a $512 \times 40 \times 20$ region feature for each candidate produced by the PPN. The PPN structure is consistent with the RPN [12]. The IDnet is composed of the conv4_1 to conv5_3, followed by a Global Average Pooling (GAP) layer to get a 2048 dimensional feature vector for each proposal. Strictly speaking, the IDnet should only focus on identifying pedestrians and the losses for detection should be removed. However, through experiments we find that it is necessary to add a Softmax classifier and a linear regression after the GAP, which can further reduce the false alarms and misalignments by using the advanced semantics. Finally, to get more discriminative features for the re-ID task, a fully-connected (Fc) layer followed by a L2-normalized block is leveraged to project these features into a L2-normalized 256 dimensional subspace. The overall objective is given by:

$$\mathcal{L}_{all} = \mathcal{L}_{a\_Cls} + \mathcal{L}_{a\_Reg} + \mathcal{L}_{p\_Cls} + \mathcal{L}_{p\_Reg} + \lambda \mathcal{L}_{re\text{-}ID}, \quad (1)$$

where the first four losses make up the Fast R-CNN loss, and the whole network is jointly trained in a multi-task learning manner.

Different from the OMS, the detection part (the PPN) and the re-ID part (the IDnet) in the IMS share network layers from the conv1 to the conv3_4, while in the OMS, they share the conv1 to the conv4_3, at the same time, both the two parts get more layers to focus more on their respective tasks. Moreover, the IMS sets the aspect ratio of pooling features to 2:1, which is more suitable for pedestrian proposals. By using such a compromise approach, the adverse effects between the detection part and the re-ID part caused by the shared representations can be mitigated, meanwhile, the useful shallow contextual information can be preserved partly.

3.2 Cosine Margin OIM Loss

After obtaining the L2-normalized 256 dimensional pedestrian features, [21] proposes an Online Instance Matching (OIM) loss for the supervision, which maintains an online lookup table (LUT) $\boldsymbol{V} \in \mathbb{R}^{D \times L}$ to store the features of all labeled identities, where D is the feature dimension and L is the number of classes in the train set, together with a circular queue (CQ) $\boldsymbol{U} \in \mathbb{R}^{D \times Q}$ to store the unlabeled, where Q is a fixed value close to L. The OIM loss is defined as:

$$\mathcal{L}_{\mathbf{OIM}} = \frac{1}{N}\sum_{i=1}^{N} -\log \frac{e^{\boldsymbol{v}_t^T \boldsymbol{x}_i/\tau}}{\sum_{j=1}^{L} e^{\boldsymbol{v}_j^T \boldsymbol{x}_i/\tau} + \sum_{k=1}^{Q} e^{\boldsymbol{u}_k^T \boldsymbol{x}_i/\tau}}, \tag{2}$$

where N is the number of labeled identity features in a batch, and $\boldsymbol{x}_i$ denotes the i-th normalized 256 dimensional feature whose label is t ($t \in [1, C]$, C is the number of classes for labeled identities). After each iteration, the LUT and CQ are updated. Different from [1,8,14,21] which adopt the following update strategy:

$$\boldsymbol{v}_t = \gamma \boldsymbol{v}_t + (1-\gamma)\boldsymbol{x}, \tag{3}$$

which is done sequentially for each sample with class t in a batch, we update the t-th column of the LUT in the $(l+1)$th iteration by:

$$\boldsymbol{v}_t^{l+1} = \mu \boldsymbol{v}_t^{l} + (1-\mu)\frac{1}{N_t}\sum_{i=1}^{N_t} C_i \boldsymbol{x}_i, \tag{4}$$

where N_t is the number of the features whose label is t in a batch and $\boldsymbol{x}_i$ denotes the feature with the label t. The C_i is the confidence that $\boldsymbol{x}_i$ is recognized as a pedestrian, which is obtained by the Softmax classifier of IDnet. Unlike the γ which is fixed to a constant value, the μ increases linearly with epochs increasing.

Our approach is based on two considerations: (1) since the sample features generated in a batch do not have a priority relationship, leveraging their weighted average information is a more robust way; (2) in the early stage of training, since the $\boldsymbol{v}$ is not reliable enough, the μ is required to be smaller to update the $\boldsymbol{v}$

rapidly; after a period of training, the $\boldsymbol{v}$ becomes stable, thus the μ needs to be larger to resist the interference noise.

Since all the pedestrian features are L2-normalized, we can rewrite the OIM loss as:

$$\mathcal{L}_{\mathbf{OIM}} = \frac{1}{N}\sum_{i=1}^{N} -\log \frac{e^{s\cdot\cos(\theta_t, i)}}{e^{s\cdot\cos(\theta_t, i)} + \sum_{j=1, j\neq t}^{L} e^{s\cdot\cos(\theta_j, i)} + \sum_{k=1}^{Q} e^{s\cdot\cos(\psi_k, i)}}, \quad (5)$$

where θ_j, i denotes the angle between $\boldsymbol{x}_i$ and $\boldsymbol{v}_j$ while ψ_k, i denotes the angle between $\boldsymbol{x}_i$ and $\boldsymbol{u}_k$. The s is a scaling factor with the value equal to $1/\tau$.

Equation (5) shows that the OIM loss aims at maximizing the probability of $\boldsymbol{x}$ being recognized as its label. However, it dose not optimize the feature embeddings explicitly to minimize the intra-class difference, which causes the features learned not sufficiently discriminative. To this end, we import a cosine margin into the OIM loss, which is naturally incorporated into the cosine formulation of the OIM loss.

Formally, the Cosine Margin OIM (CM-OIM) loss is defined as:

$$\mathcal{L}_{\mathbf{CM\text{-}OIM}} = \frac{1}{N}\sum_{i=1}^{N} -\log \frac{e^{s\cdot(\cos(\theta_t, i)-m)}}{e^{s\cdot(\cos(\theta_t, i)-m)} + \sum_{j=1, j\neq t}^{L} e^{s\cdot\cos(\theta_j, i)} + \sum_{k=1}^{Q} e^{s\cdot\cos(\psi_k, i)}}, \quad (6)$$

where the m is a hyper-parameter indicating the cosine margin. Our CM-OIM loss has a clear geometric interpretation, as shown in Fig. 2. As illustrated in Fig. 2, we compare the decision boundary of the CM-OIM to the OIM. For simplicity of analysis, we consider the binary-classes cases. Let $\boldsymbol{x}$ denote the feature vector labeled C_1. $\boldsymbol{f}_1$ denotes the feature vector with class C_1 stored in the LUT, and $\boldsymbol{f}_2$ denotes the feature vector with class C_2 in the LUT or CQ. All these vectors are of 2 dimensions and L2-normalized, which means that their end points are on a circle with radius 1. The OIM loss aims to force $\boldsymbol{f}_1^T\boldsymbol{x} > \boldsymbol{f}_2^T\boldsymbol{x}$ (i.e., $\cos(\theta_1) > \cos(\theta_2)$) in order to classify $\boldsymbol{x}$ correctly, therefore, the decision boundary is given by: $\cos(\theta_1) = \cos(\theta_2)$, as depicted in Fig. 2(a), which is the

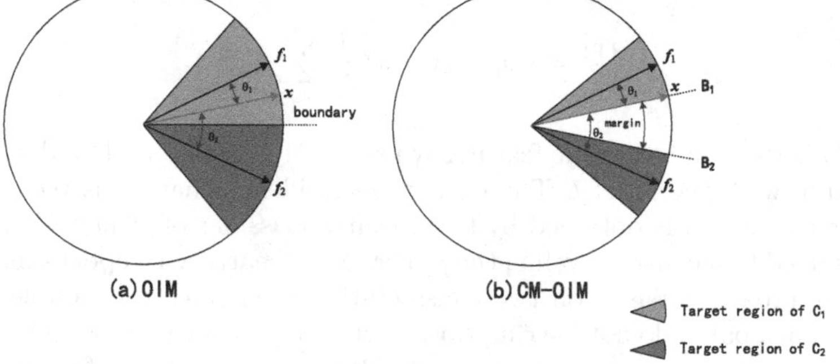

Fig. 2. Geometrical interpretation of OIM loss (a) and CM-OIM loss (b).

angular bisector of $\boldsymbol{f}_1$ and $\boldsymbol{f}_2$. From Fig. 2(a) we can see that the two target regions are bordered, which makes the features near the boundary difficult to classify.

In contrast, our CM-OIM loss makes the boundary a marginal region instead of a single vector. As shown in Fig. 2(b), we get a new boundary B_1 for class C_1, in which $\cos(\theta_1) - m = \cos(\theta_2)$. In this way, the new classification criteria will be more strongly required to classify $\boldsymbol{x}$ correctly, eventually forming certain cosine margins between categories on the hypersphere manifold. Consequently, both inter-class separability and intra-class compactness are encouraged by the CM-OIM loss, with the features learned more discriminative.

4 Experiments and Analysis

In this section, we first introduce two benchmark datasets and evaluation setups, followed by the discussion of the re-ID loss weight. After that, we give our experimental results and analysis.

4.1 Datasets and Metrics

CUHK-SYSU. CUHK-SYSU [21] contains 18,184 scene images, 8,432 labeled identities, and 96,143 annotated pedestrian bounding boxes in total (23,430 boxes are labeled specific ID). The standard train/test split [21] is adopted in this paper, where 11,206 images and 5,532 identities are used for training, while the remaining overall 6,978 gallery images and 2,900 query persons for testing. The gallery size is set to 100 if not specified.

PRW. PRW [26] consists of 11,816 scene images, 932 labeled identities, and 43,110 pedestrian bounding boxes (34,304 boxes are ID labeled). Following [1], we use 5,134 images and 482 identities for training, while 6,112 gallery images and 2,057 query persons for testing. The gallery size is set to 6,112.

Evaluation Metrics. We adopt the same evaluation metrics as in [1,8,21]: mean Average Precision (mAP) which is derived from the object detection tasks, and Common Matching Characteristic (CMC top-K) which is inherited from the person re-ID problem.

4.2 Implementation Details

We implement our model based on Pytorch. ImageNet-pretrained ResNet-50 is exploited for parameters initialization. We use SGD with a batch size of 1 to train the model on a NVIDIA GTX1080Ti GPU, and initialize the learning rate as 0.001, which is decayed by a factor of 0.1 at 60 k and 100 k iterations respectively and kept unchanged until the model converges at 140 K iterations. The μ is linearly increased from 0 to 0.5 with epoch increasing in Eq. (4). Following [15], the scaling factor s is set to 30 and the cosine margin m is set to 0.35 in Eq. (6).

4.3 Experiments on Hyper-parameter λ

The hyper-parameter λ controls the re-ID loss weight over the whole network loss function, which is set to 1 in all recent end-to-end person search works [8,14,21]. However, we observe that when λ is set to 1, the scale values of the OIM loss and the Faster R-CNN loss are quite different in the process of training, and the mAP result at convergence is not good enough, as illustrated in Fig. 3. Note that the Faster R-CNN loss is the sum of four losses, and the model structure used and parameter settings are consistent with [21].

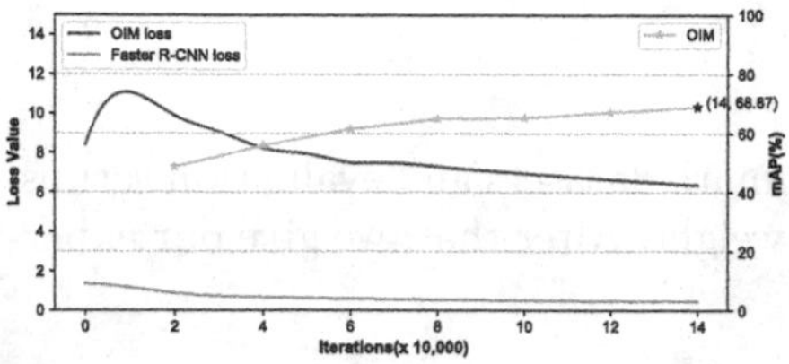

Fig. 3. The smoothing loss and mAP curve.

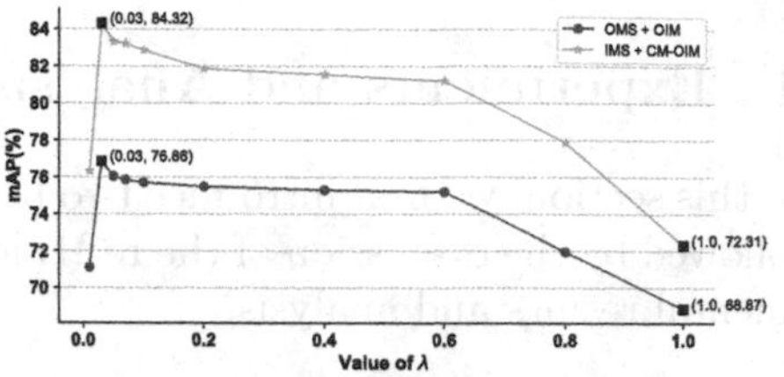

Fig. 4. The mAP accuracy of person search on CUHK-SYSU using various re-ID loss weights.

Figure 3 shows that the loss values of the OIM are much larger than that of the Faster R-CNN when setting equivalent weights for them, which would lead to a considerable imbalance between their contribution to the gradient during training. As a result, the final trained model would not converge to a good parameter space. Therefore, we conduct targeted experiments to investigate the sensitiveness of the value of λ.

For fairness, we first use the Original Model Structure (OMS) with the OIM loss and parameter settings in [21], varying λ from 0.01 to 1.0 to learn different models under CUHK-SYSU dataset (using the standard split). The person search accuracies of these models are shown in Fig. 4.

It can be clearly seen that setting λ to 1 does not achieve good mAP performance, while proper choice of it, e.g., $\lambda = 0.03$, can achieve a better result. It is noteworthy that when λ is set to 1, the mAP of the model we reproduce (68.87%) is lower than that reported in [21] (75.5%), but when setting a reasonable value to λ (0.03), it can obtain a better result (76.86%). Based on the mAP versus λ curve depicted in Fig. 4, it can be observed that the weight of re-ID loss plays an important role in the end-to-end person search performance.

We then test the mAP performance of IMS + CM-OIM (our method) with the change of λ, as shown in Fig. 4. Unlike the standard split, we divide the CUHK-SYSU train set into 5 equal folds, using 4 of them for training, and 1 for validation. Based on the experimental results, we set the re-ID loss weight to 0.03 in the next following experiments.

4.4 Comparison with State-of-the-Art Methods

In this subsection, we report the experimental results of our method on CUHK-SYSU and PRW datasets, and compare them with several state-of-the-art methods, including the end-to-end methods OIM [21], IAN (ResNet-50 as backbone networks) [19], JDI + IEL [14], IPSN + Center-loss [8], and the two-stage methods NPSM [7] and MGTS [1]. At the same time, several methods using hand-crafted re-ID features reported in [21] are also compared.

Results on CUHK-SYSU. The comparative results are shown in Table 1, where the Faster R-CNN detector based on ResNet-50 is denoted as "CNN", and the VGG-based detector is marked as "CNN_v". It can be seen that the pedestrian features extracted by deep learning based methods have much better discriminability than the hand-crafted features. Compared with the best end-to-end person search methods (IPSN + Center-loss and IAN), our approach achieves about 4% increase on mAP and 4.7% on top-1 matching rate, and compared with the best two-stage method (MGTS), our proposed method still makes a slight increase in both mAP and top-1 accuracy, which can demonstrate the effectiveness of our method. For a more comprehensive comparison, we also set different gallery sizes of {50, 100, 500, 1000, 2000, 4000} to evaluate our model and compare with other end-to-end methods, as visualized in Fig. 5. It can be observed that our method outperforms all the counterparts by a notable margin under all gallery sizes, which can prove the robustness of our proposed method.

Table 1. Comparisons between our method and state-of-the-arts

Method	CUHK-SYSU		PRW	
	mAP (%)	top-1 (%)	mAP (%)	top-1 (%)
CNN + DSIFT + Euclidean [24]	34.5	39.4	–	–
CNN + DSIFT + KISSME [5,24]	47.8	53.6	–	–
CNN + BoW + Cosine [25]	56.9	62.3	–	–
CNN + LOMO + XQDA [6]	68.9	74.1	–	–
NPSM [7]	77.9	81.2	24.2	53.1
CNN_v + MGTS [1]	83.0	83.7	32.6	72.1
OIM [21]	75.5	78.7	21.3	49.9
IAN [19]	76.3	80.1	22.1	60.2
JDI + IEL [14]	79.4	79.7	24.3	69.5
IPSN + Center-loss [8]	79.8	79.9	21.0	63.1
IMS + CM-OIM (Ours)	**83.5**	**84.8**	**32.8**	**72.2**

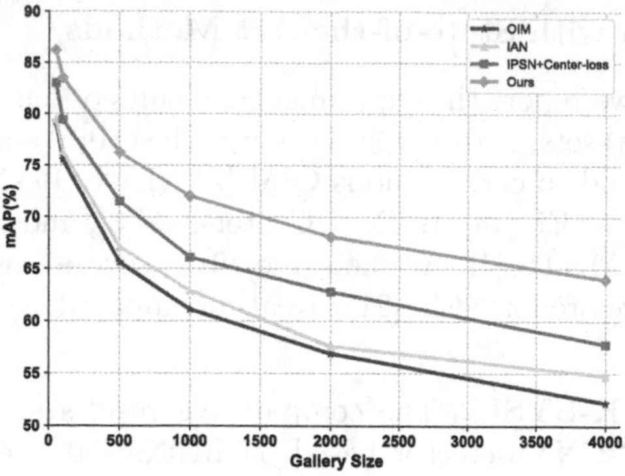

Fig. 5. The mAP accuracy on CUHK-SYSU with different gallery sizes.

Results on PRW. The results on the PRW dataset are shown in Table 1. Compared with CUHK-SYSU, all the models get worse results, but our method still shows a better performance.

4.5 Analysis of the Component Study

Table 2 shows the results of the component study on CUHK-SYSU. The U means the proposed update strategy. It can be observed that the IMS has a certain degree of improvement over the OMS, proving that the IMS effectively reduces the adverse interaction between detection and re-ID parts from the structural point of view. Furthermore, the CM-OIM loss can notably improve person search performance, since the introduced cosine margin makes the pedestrian features learned have smaller intra-class distance, and the problem of unbalanced contribution of multiple losses is solved by setting an appropriate re-ID loss weight. Meanwhile, our proposed update strategy makes the features stored in the LUT more reliable, which also improves the model performance to some extent.

Table 2. Visual component study on CUHK-SYSU

OMS	IMS	OIM	CM-OIM	U	mAP(%)	top-1(%)
✓		✓			75.5	78.7
✓			✓		81.1	82.6
	✓	✓			77.8	80.2
	✓		✓		82.6	83.9
✓		✓		✓	77.6	80.3
	✓		✓	✓	**83.5**	**84.8**

5 Conclusion

In this paper, we propose an Improved Model Structure (IMS) with a powerful re-ID loss (CM-OIM) for end-to-end person search. Specifically, the IMS reduces the shared layers of the detection and re-ID parts to effectively alleviate the adverse effects between them, making them focus more on their own tasks. Then, we conduct a full investigation of the weight of re-ID loss, optimizing the whole model to a better parametric state by adopting a multi-task leaning manner with a proper re-ID loss weight. Furthermore, the CM-OIM loss introduces a cosine margin to the OIM loss to increase the intra-class compactness, making the learned features much more discriminative. Meanwhile, we design a novel update strategy for the re-ID loss, which is proved to be more robust. Experimental results on two standard benchmarks demonstrate that our proposed method achieves better mAP and top-1 accuracy than existing state-of-the-art methods.

Acknowledgments. This work has been supported by Science and Technology Commission of Shanghai Municipality (No. 17511106902), Shanghai Youth Science and Technology Development Funds (No. 18QB1403900), Shanghai Artificial intelligence development project (No. 2018-RGZN-02009).

References

1. Chen, D., Zhang, S., Ouyang, W., Yang, J., Tai, Y.: Person search via a mask-guided two-stream CNN model. In: Ferrari, V., Hebert, M., Sminchisescu, C., Weiss, Y. (eds.) ECCV 2018. LNCS, vol. 11211, pp. 764–781. Springer, Cham (2018). https://doi.org/10.1007/978-3-030-01234-2_45
2. Eigen, D., Fergus, R.: Predicting depth, surface normals and semantic labels with a common multi-scale convolutional architecture. In: Proceedings of the IEEE International Conference on Computer Vision, pp. 2650–2658 (2015)
3. He, K., Zhang, X., Ren, S., Sun, J.: Deep residual learning for image recognition. In: Proceedings of the IEEE Conference on Computer Vision and Pattern Recognition, pp. 770–778 (2016)
4. Kendall, A., Gal, Y., Cipolla, R.: Multi-task learning using uncertainty to weigh losses for scene geometry and semantics. In: Proceedings of the IEEE Conference on Computer Vision and Pattern Recognition, pp. 7482–7491 (2018)
5. Koestinger, M., Hirzer, M., Wohlhart, P., Roth, P.M., Bischof, H.: Large scale metric learning from equivalence constraints. In: 2012 IEEE Conference on Computer Vision and Pattern Recognition, pp. 2288–2295. IEEE (2012)
6. Liao, S., Hu, Y., Zhu, X., Li, S.Z.: Person re-identification by local maximal occurrence representation and metric learning. In: Proceedings of the IEEE Conference on Computer Vision and Pattern Recognition, pp. 2197–2206 (2015)
7. Liu, H., et al.: Neural person search machines. In: Proceedings of the IEEE International Conference on Computer Vision, pp. 493–501 (2017)
8. Liu, H., Shi, W., Huang, W., Guan, Q.: A discriminatively learned feature embedding based on multi-loss fusion for person search. In: 2018 IEEE International Conference on Acoustics, Speech and Signal Processing (ICASSP), pp. 1668–1672. IEEE (2018)

9. Liu, W., Wen, Y., Yu, Z., Li, M., Raj, B., Song, L.: Sphereface: deep hypersphere embedding for face recognition. In: Proceedings of the IEEE Conference on Computer Vision and Pattern Recognition, pp. 212–220 (2017)
10. Liu, W., Wen, Y., Yu, Z., Yang, M.: Large-margin softmax loss for convolutional neural networks. In: ICML, vol. 2, p. 7 (2016)
11. Loy, C.C., Xiang, T., Gong, S.: Multi-camera activity correlation analysis. In: 2009 IEEE Conference on Computer Vision and Pattern Recognition, pp. 1988–1995. IEEE (2009)
12. Ren, S., He, K., Girshick, R., Sun, J.: Faster R-CNN: towards real-time object detection with region proposal networks. In: Advances in Neural Information Processing Systems, pp. 91–99 (2015)
13. Sermanet, P., Eigen, D., Zhang, X., Mathieu, M., Fergus, R., LeCun, Y.: Overfeat: integrated recognition, localization and detection using convolutional networks. arXiv preprint arXiv:1312.6229 (2013)
14. Shi, W., Liu, H., Meng, F., Huang, W.: Instance enhancing loss: deep identity-sensitive feature embedding for person search. In: 2018 25th IEEE International Conference on Image Processing (ICIP), pp. 4108–4112. IEEE (2018)
15. Wang, F., Cheng, J., Liu, W., Liu, H.: Additive margin softmax for face verification. IEEE Signal Process. Lett. **25**(7), 926–930 (2018)
16. Wang, X.: Intelligent multi-camera video surveillance: a review. Pattern Recogn. Lett. **34**(1), 3–19 (2013)
17. Wen, Y., Zhang, K., Li, Z., Qiao, Y.: A discriminative feature learning approach for deep face recognition. In: Leibe, B., Matas, J., Sebe, N., Welling, M. (eds.) ECCV 2016. LNCS, vol. 9911, pp. 499–515. Springer, Cham (2016). https://doi.org/10.1007/978-3-319-46478-7_31
18. Wu, S., Chen, Y.C., Li, X., Wu, A.C., You, J.J., Zheng, W.S.: An enhanced deep feature representation for person re-identification. In: 2016 IEEE Winter Conference on Applications of Computer Vision (WACV), pp. 1–8. IEEE (2016)
19. Xiao, J., Xie, Y., Tillo, T., Huang, K., Wei, Y., Feng, J.: IAN: the individual aggregation network for person search. Pattern Recogn. **87**, 332–340 (2019)
20. Xiao, T., Li, S., Wang, B., Lin, L., Wang, X.: End-to-end deep learning for person search **1**(2). arXiv preprint arXiv:1604.01850 (2016)
21. Xiao, T., Li, S., Wang, B., Lin, L., Wang, X.: Joint detection and identification feature learning for person search. In: Proceedings of the IEEE Conference on Computer Vision and Pattern Recognition, pp. 3415–3424 (2017)
22. Xu, Y., Ma, B., Huang, R., Lin, L.: Person search in a scene by jointly modeling people commonness and person uniqueness. In: Proceedings of the 22nd ACM International Conference on Multimedia, pp. 937–940. ACM (2014)
23. Yu, S.I., Yang, Y., Hauptmann, A.: Harry Potter's Marauder's Map: localizing and tracking multiple persons-of-interest by nonnegative discretization. In: Proceedings of the IEEE Conference on Computer Vision and Pattern Recognition, pp. 3714–3720 (2013)
24. Zhao, R., Ouyang, W., Wang, X.: Unsupervised salience learning for person re-identification. In: Proceedings of the IEEE Conference on Computer Vision and Pattern Recognition, pp. 3586–3593 (2013)
25. Zheng, L., Shen, L., Tian, L., Wang, S., Wang, J., Tian, Q.: Scalable person re-identification: a benchmark. In: Proceedings of the IEEE International Conference on Computer Vision, pp. 1116–1124 (2015)
26. Zheng, L., Zhang, H., Sun, S., Chandraker, M., Yang, Y., Tian, Q.: Person re-identification in the wild. In: Proceedings of the IEEE Conference on Computer Vision and Pattern Recognition, pp. 1367–1376 (2017)

Effective Barcode Hunter via Semantic Segmentation in the Wild

Feng Ni(✉) and Xixin Cao(✉)

School of Software and Microelectronics, Peking University, Beijing, China
nifeng@pku.edu.cn, cxx@ss.pku.edu.cn

Abstract. Barcodes are popularly used for product identification in many scenarios. However, locating them on product images is challenging. Half-occlusion, distortion, darkness or targets being too small to recognize can often add to the difficulties using conventional methods. In this paper, we introduce a large-scale diverse barcode dataset and adopt a deep learning-based semantic segmentation approach to address these problems. Specifically, we use an efficient method to synthesize 30000 well-annotated images containing diverse barcode labels, and get Barcode-30 k, a large-scale dataset with accurate pixel-level annotated barcode in the wild. Moreover, to locate barcode more precisely, we further propose an Effective Barcode Hunter - BarcodeNet. It is a semantic segmentation model based on CNN (Convolutional Neural Network) and is mainly formed with two novel modules, Prior Pyramid Pooling Module (P3M) and Pyramid Refine Module (PRM). Additional ablation studies further demonstrate the effectiveness of BarcodeNet, and it yields a high mIoU result of 95.36% on the proposed synthetic Barcode-30 k validation-set. To prove the practical value of the whole system, we test the BarcodeNet trained on train-set of Barcode-30 k on a manually annotated testing set that only collected from cameras, it achieves mIoU of 90.3%, which is a very accurate result for practical applications.

Keywords: Synthesize image · Semantic segmentation · CNN

1 Introduction

Digital sign is able to represent rich information of the attached product, such as its identification number and the production date. It usually has a relative regular shape in 2D images. Barcode and QR code, the most widely appeared digital signs in common life, are employed in factories and supermarkets massively. Using computer vision algorithms to help accurately detect, segment and recognize these digital signs will greatly promote the development of automation in these industries. With the powerful deep Convolutional Neural Networks, the performance of most visual tasks has been greatly improved. For instance, deep learning methods [2–5, 8, 21, 24, 26, 30] have achieved a breakthrough in the field of semantic segmentation.

Y. M. Ro et al. (Eds.): MMM 2020, LNCS 11961, pp. 431–442, 2020.
https://doi.org/10.1007/978-3-030-37731-1_35

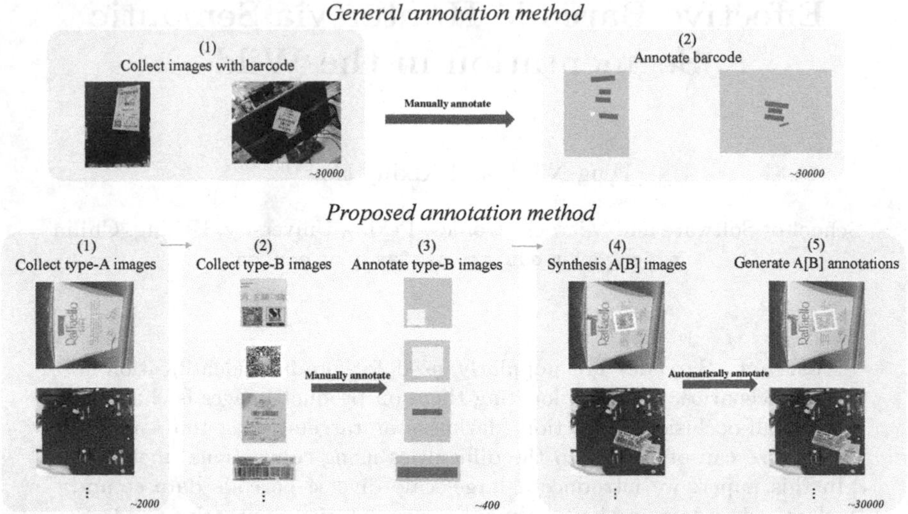

Fig. 1. Comparison of the annotation steps between general method and the method driven by our proposed synthesis strategy. The upper subfigure is general annotation method, the bottom subfigure is our proposed annotation steps. Synthesizing operation saves a lot of annotation time. **In this paper, the sensitive information on images is pixelated into the mosaic.** (Color figure online)

Images with barcode and QR code, we call them barcode images in this paper for simplicity. It's not easy to directly apply existing semantic segmentation methods (such as FCN [21], PSPNet [30], SegNet [1], Deeplab [3], DeepLabv3 [5] and so on) to segment QR code and barcode pixels from barcode images due to the following two problems:

1. **No well-annotated dataset:** Barcode images of existing barcode dataset such as [23,27,28] are taken closer than 30 cm and under clear lighting, while no annotated barcode images are taken at more common conditions, e.g., around 0.5 m to 2 m to the targets. Moreover, annotating pixel-level labels as supervised segmentation tasks need is very time-consuming, especially when the target barcode is even too small to be noticed by human eyes.
2. **No off-the-shelf deep models:**: State-of-the-art networks, including PSP-Net and DeepLabv3 [5], are mainly designed for irregular object segmentation, such as car and pedestrian, which mostly have soft borders. Digital signs, like barcodes, always appear with regular shapes. Unlike objects with high-level semantics, digital signs contain plenty of structural texture information. However, no models take use of very shallow features for segmentation recently.

To solve the above two problems, we first propose a method for synthesizing dataset as shown in Fig. 1. Specifically, we use around 2000 type-A images and around 400 type-B images to create a large dataset with ~30000 barcode images (namely Barcode-30 k). The synthetic barcode dataset Barcode-30 k includes cases of one or more barcodes on images, as well as different scales, different rotation angles and different cropping ratios, which will help models improve the generalization abilities.

Considering the nature of digital signs, we designed a semantic segmentation network - BarcodeNet, based on PSPNet but more accurate than it for segmenting regular barcode and QR code. Our BarcodeNet introduces a pyramid structure to help learn both the rich semantic information and structural information from the feature maps. Specifically, the Prior Pyramid Pooling module (P3M) uses global prior information to guide local location distribution, which considers more details for large targets. And the other Pyramid Refine module (PRM) helps learn the shallow features of the images, aiming at refining more regularized boundaries for the segmented pixels. Also, shallow features can help recognize barcode images.

In the following content, we will introduce the related work of recent segmentation researches and existing barcode dataset in Sect. 2. And in Sect. 3, we describe the strategy to synthesize a barcode dataset. In Sect. 4, we introduce the proposed BarcodeNet. Then, experiments are shown in Sect. 5, discussing problems about barcodes in Sect. 6. The inference model and code of BarcodeNet will be publicly available soon.

2 Related Work

2.1 Traditional Segmentation Methods

Mostly based on the low-level visual cues of the pixel itself, traditional semantic segmentation approaches usually rely on domain knowledge to extract features and then apply them with post processing methods such as Texton Forests [12], SVM [7] and Conditional Random Fields (CRFs) [13]. However, for more challenging segmentation tasks, these methods will meet a significant limitation and were quickly replaced by effective deep learning algorithms.

2.2 Deep-Learning Segmentation Methods

In the past few years, CNN-based networks [9,22] have been proposed and make a breakthrough in the field of segmentation. Fully convolutional network (FCN) [21] includes the implementation of deconvolution layer, upsampling and skip architecture to fuse the high-level and low-level features. Dilated convolution [26] and DeepLab (v1,v2,v3,v3+) [3–5] use subsequent convolution layers to expand the receptive field and maintain resolution. Other segmentation networks such as encoder-decoders [1], region-based representations [2,8], and cascaded networks [17] also contribute to the trend of research. In order to achieve higher accuracy, several supporting techniques are merged, including ensembling features [3], multi-stage training [21], additional training data from other datasets [3], object proposals [20], CRF-based post processing [24] and pyramid-based feature re-sampling [30].

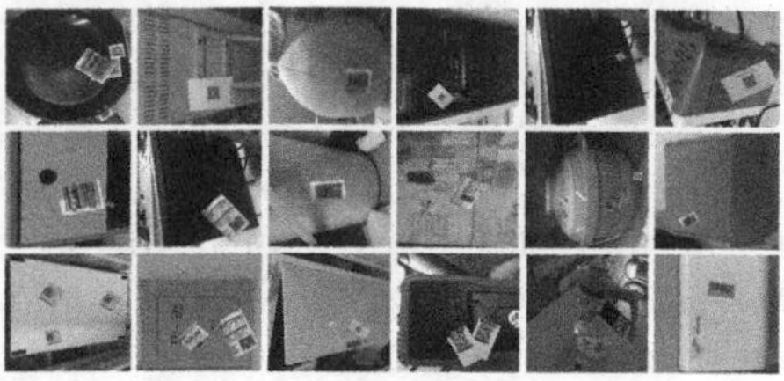

Fig. 2. Examples of Barcode-30 k.

Scene		Percentage	
Indoor	Supermarket	25	60
	Factory	10	
	Office	10	
	Laboratory	10	
	Other	5	
Outdoor	Billboard	10	40
	Poster	10	
	Street sign	10	
	Railing	5	
	Other	5	

Fig. 3. Distribution of type-A images.

2.3 Barcode Segmentation

Research on segmentation algorithm of barcode in the past were mainly focusing on images taken within 30 cm and in each image there was only one no-overlapped complete barcode. [15] proposed an adaptive segmentation method based on Mathematic Morphological, [19] presents a segmentation algorithm for 2D color barcode image based on gradient features. Xu et al. [25] developed an approach for detecting blur 2D barcodes based on coded exposure algorithms. Li et al. [14] propose two 2-D barcode image segmentation algorithms under complex background. Li and Zhao et al. [16] proposeda a cascaded strategy for accurate detection of 1D barcode with deep convolutional neural network.

3 Synthesize Barcode Images

In this section, we mainly introduce the synthesizing strategy for barcode images. Specifically, we describe how to collect and annotate images, and the detailed synthesizing steps in Sect. 3.1. Then in Sect. 3.2, we introduce the Barcode-30 k dataset, which is gained by above synthesis strategy. Note that, we overallly annotate these digital signs into 2 categories: *Barcode* and *QR code*, indicated as green and yellow mask as shown in Fig. 1.

3.1 Synthesis Strategy

Digital signs need rare context information to localize because they are always pasted randomly on various backgrounds, which is available for us to generate similar images. To build a large-scale barcode dataset, we synthesize barcode images by affixing smaller images with barcode (name type-B images in Fig. 1) to relative larger background images (name type-A images in Fig. 1) following a series of transformation rules. What we should annotate manually is the type-B images, their pixels are easy to label due to the regular target areas.

In order to simulate, we set some basic rules to synthesize: Each synthesized image (denote as A[B]) contains at least one sampled type-B image; A[B] should contain less than 10 type-B imagest, half contain same type-B images and half contain different type-B images, the number of type-B images in one type-A image obedience to a poisson-distribution. Most importantly, type-B images should randomly be transformed by multiple operations, including half-cut, distorting, lighting-darken and made into low-resolution.

A more detailed description of the strategy is listed as follows:

(1) For each background image of type-A, we randomly (50%) select one type-B image or randomly (50%) select T type-B images as Selected type-B images (STB1). Then get a number K that from Poisson-distribution ($\lambda = 2$) and sample K times type-B images from $STB1$ randomly with repeated samples, denote the K type-B images as $STB2$.
(2) For each barcode image in $STB2$, apply a series of transformation steps: Resizing by the ratio from 0.2 to 5; Rotating by the ratio from $-45°$ to $45°$; Cropping a corner randomly (10%) with a ratio from 0.5 to 1; lighting-darkening with a ratio from 1 to 0.5; Resizing twice (zoom in and zoom out) to make into low-resolution. After these, $STB2$ images are prepared.
(3) These $STB2$ images are randomly pasted on type-A image. Only one post processing step, any pixels that beyond the size range of the type-A image, directly crop off. By the way, the pixel-level labels of A[B] images are automatically generated within the pasting processing.

3.2 Barcode-30 K Dataset

We generate Barcode-30 k following 2 steps: collecting original type-A and type-B images, synthesizing the simulated data using the above synthetic strategy.

For type-A images, we have selected some representative places from indoor and outdoor situations, containing a diverse number of different scenes. As shown in Fig. 3, in our daily life, supermarkets, laboratories, and offices that contain most of the indoor scenes, in which there are plenty of goods, devices, express delivery boxes, etc. Meanwhile streets, parking lots and parks cover most outdoor scenes, in which the most common things are billboards, cars, etc. The distance between camera and targets are mostly from half meters to 2 m. As for type-B images, we mainly take images that have barcodes and QR codes with a close distance, so that bring convenience for annotation step.

Finally, we selected 2000 type-A images, and 400 type-B images which we have accurate annotated. Based on these images, with the above synthesis strategy, we synthesize a dataset that contains 30,000 Barcode images, called Barcode-30 k. Some sampled images from Barcode-30 k are shown in Fig. 2, the barcodes are just similar to those posted by people who posted small advertisements. Barcode-30 k not only contains large number of well-annotated images, but also is with enough diversity. It includes two kinds of label information: QR code and bar code. The synthesis process of Barcode-30 k provides guidance for many segmentation tasks and detection tasks for regular targets.

4 BarcodeNet

Refer to the overall network architecture shown in Fig. 4. Similar to PSPNet [30], BarcodeNet obtains global and local pixel classification features by pooling multi-scale features based on Res5. In addition, the features of Res1 are

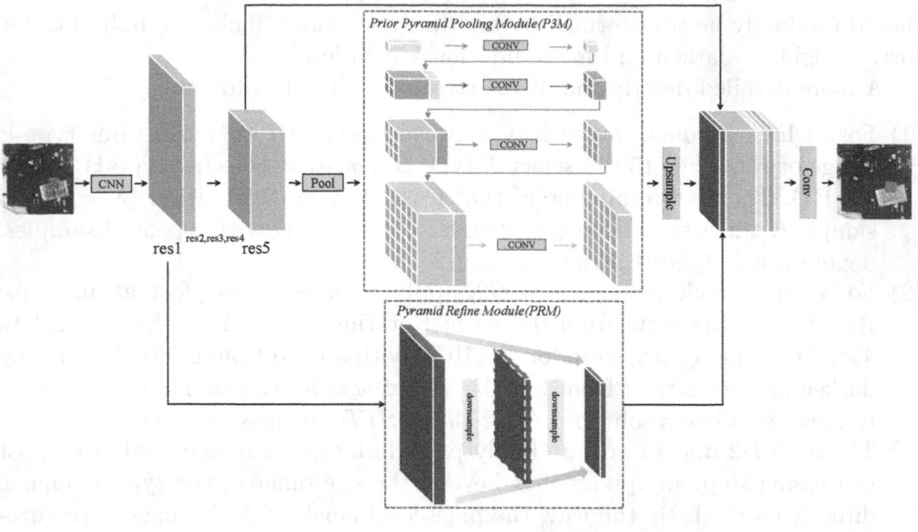

Fig. 4. Illustration of our framework - BarcodeNet.

extended to be utilized, because shallow features have stronger structural information, which is effective for apperceiving regular objects [29]. The backbone of BarcodeNet is ResNet101 [11], more powerful to extract representative features compared with shallow networks, e.g. VGG16. BarcodeNet is mainly formed by two pyramid pooling modules, the top Prior Pyramid Pooling Module (P3M) and the bottom Pyramid Refine Module (PRM) shown in Fig. 4. The P3M is designed for aggregating contextual information, the global average pooling operations based on multi-scale global features could learn global representative features for objects ranges among different scales. And the PRM is adept at using shallow features to learn regular geometrical boundaries. The two modules are described in detail in the following, and moreover, we also expound the effective optimization method for ResNet-FCN like network [30].

Prior Pyramid Pooling Module (P3M): Pyramid Pooling module (P2M) is introduced to learn global knowledge by pooling with multi-scale kernels [10, 18, 30]. However, no methods ever considered their relations, i.e., global guidance between each other. Considering the fact that feature maps in original pyramid pooling module (P2M) lack semantic information and all layers directly make predictions without guidance, resulting worse segmentations. Besides P2M, to further strengthen semantic information relationship between feature maps with different scales, we propose a hierarchical global prior, containing information with different scales and varying among different sub-regions. Specifically, we added another branch from the output feature map of upper pooling module to the input of next pooling module. As illustrated in Fig. 4, the blue lines connecting adjacent two-layer features indicate the priority information we introduced. Then we directly upsample the feature maps of prior pyramid pooling module to generate the same size feature as the original feature map via bilinear interpolation.

Pyramid Refine Module (PRM): Different from the general segmentation task, the barcode always have regular outlines, and therefore, the structural information of shallow feature maps is of great significance. This inspired us to utilize another pyramid module from the output of shallow features, as illustrated in Fig. 4. To keep the structural features of shallow positions, we try to make PRM as simplistic as possible. In detail, two groups of Conv(3×3)+BN+ReLU are used continuously to construct PRM part, note that both Conv strides are set as 2 to match the size of Res5 feature. The Pyramid Refine Module (PRM) learns shallow features like edges, textures and streaks from feature Res1, which leads to refine out more regularized boundaries for the targets.

Finally, multiple kinds of features generated by P3M and PRM, and the raw Res5 feature are concatenated as the final representative feature. This powerful feature fusion system makes good use of global image-level priors, multi-scale features and structural information.

5 Experiments

In this section, we evaluate our approach BarcodeNet on the proposed dataset. To measure the performance, we focused our experiments on mIoU (mean of Intersection over Union) percentage, which becomes a standard for semantic segmentation. To compare different modules and different settings of our method, we conduct experiments on a mini subset of Barcode-30 k - Barcode-3 k, which is evenly sampled by the ratio of 1:10. Finally, to evaluate ultimate performance of BarcodeNet, we change to full Barcode-30 k. Note that the training and validation ratio is split by 4:1 for both.

Table 1. Segmentation results of different structures.

Method	Backbone	Input size	Mean Acc	FPS	mIoU
FCN-8s [21]	VGG-16	480 × 480	85.38	9.17	82.00
PSPNet [30]	ResNet-101	473 × 473	92.15	5.88	89.23
PSPNet-P3M	ResNet-101	473 × 473	93.26	5.63	90.36
BarcodeNet	ResNet-101	473 × 473	**94.24**	5.23	**91.63**

5.1 Configurations of BarcodeNet

We train models with end-to-end manners on 2 NVIDIA GTX1080Ti GPUs, optimized by synchronized SGD with a weight decay of 0.001 and momentum of 0.9. Giving a batch size of 8 and an initial learning rate of 0.001, we then reduce the learning rate down to 0.0001 when it comes to 50 epochs, and 0.00001 when 80 epochs, it can reach optimum performance at 90 epochs. We have adopted FCN-8s as our baseline, and selected PSPNet as the main comparison. To enhance performance, we pretrained all models using Cityscapes [6].

5.2 Validate P3M and PRM

The segmentation results of our methods are shown in Table 1. With our proposed BarcodeNet, the best mIoU results reaches 91.63%. And compared to the baseline FCN-8s, BarcodeNet outperforming it by nearly 10%. Specifically, by using Pyramid Pooling module that PSPNet introduced, the mIoU then improved by 7.23% compared with FCN-8s baseline. As for P3M, we validate their contribution by evaluate PSPNet-P3M, which replace Pyramid Pooling module with Prior Pyramid Pooling Module. Notably, P3M improves by 1.1%, with very little added modelweights. Since shallower layer feature contains more structural information in deep networks, PRM is specially designed for refining structural information. Using both P3M and PRM in PSPNet, it becomes our BarcodeNet. It improved the mIoU by 2.4% compared with the original PSPNet, and 1.3% compared with the PSPNet using P3M, which shows the importance of fusing refined structural information by PRM. More clearly visual comparisons can be seen in Fig. 5. In addition, Barcode that trained on full Barcode-30 k training set can achieve mIoU of 0.9536.

Table 2. PRM from different shallow features.

PRM feature	Layers	Mean Acc	barcode IoU	QR code IoU	mIoU
Res5	Encoder-Decoder	93.09	83.25	89.32	90.65
Res4	Encoder-Decoder	93.30	83.53	89.65	90.76
Res3	Encoder-Decoder	93.63	83.76	89.93	90.94
Res2	Two Convs	93.96	84.05	90.18	91.13
Res1	**Two Convs**	**94.24**	**84.72**	**90.73**	**91.63**

5.3 Evaluate the Structure of PRM

Fix the P3M, we conduct experiments to verify different PRM modules. The role of PRM module in BarcodeNet is to aggregate more shallow features to the final fusion features as refinement of the regular position at boundaries. The PRM module obviously has different structural settings, and it can also learn shallow information from features from different depths. Shown in Table 2, we compare the guidance knowledge from different depths as shallow feature (Res1, 2, 3, 4, 5). For Res1 and Res2, we connect the two conv layers directly and set the stride parameter to 2 to get the same scale with final features. For Res3, 4 and 5, we use Encode-Decode structure to connect the features into the Conv layer and the Deconv layer. Experiments show that the guidance of Res1 feature can bring more improvement, and from a unified perspective, the shallower layer gets better results.

In addition, we also validate how to use shallow information, whether by directly pooling or through the convolutional layers to learn the features we need. Table 3 compares these different operations. The experimental results show

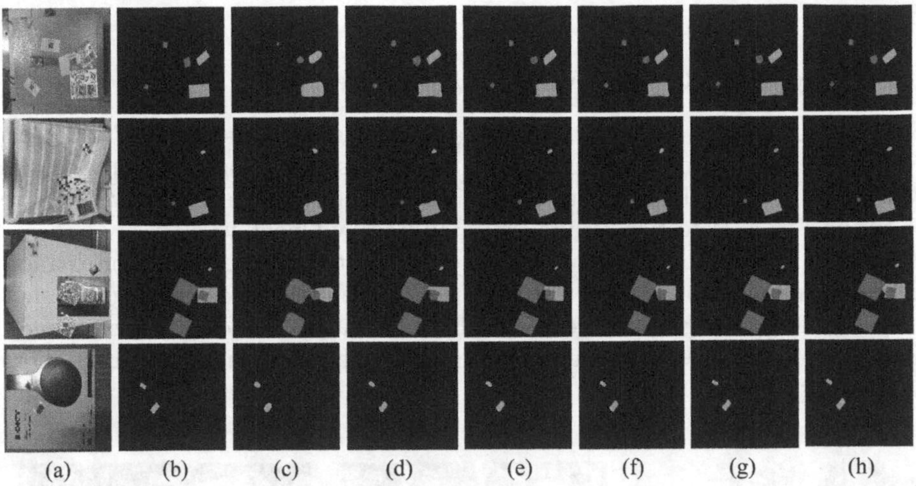

Fig. 5. Visual comparison on Barcode-30 k data. (a) Image. (b) Ground truth. (c) FCN-8s [26]. (d) PSPNet[24]. (e) PSPNet-P3M. (f) PSPNet-P3M-PRM (Res5). (g) PSPNet-P3M-PRM (Res1-Avgpooling). (h) BarcodeNet (Res1-2Convs).

Table 3. PRM of different operations.

PRM feature	Layers	Mean Acc	Barcode IoU	QR code IoU	mIoU
Res1	Maxpooling (s = 4)	93.55	83.75	90.00	91.06
	Avgpooling (s = 4)	93.94	84.12	90.31	91.28
	Two Convs (s = 2)	**94.24**	**84.72**	**90.73**	**91.63**

that the two-layer convolution PRM structure works better, allowing the final BarcodeNet to reach mIoU of 0.9163.

5.4 More Visual Comparisons

More visualization comparisons between BarcodeNet and other methods are shown in Fig. 5. Our baseline model FCN-8s has two main problems. One is that it missed a lot of tiny barcodes. Another is the blurred boundaries, both leading to poor segmentation results.

Then PSPNet gets a large improvement, shown in the third column of Fig. 5. However, the boundaries and corners are still not good enough. When further replacing P2M with P3M module, connecting PRM from Res5, change to connecting PRM from Res1 by average pooling, and change to connecting PRM from Res1 by two Convs, the results are gradually more accurate, and the problem that PSPNet suffers from has been greatly relieved.

In addition, segmentation results of real images are shown in Fig. 5. We select challenging cases for visualization of our powerful BarcodeNet. Note that we use the BarcodeNet pre-trained on full Barcode-30 k training set.

6 Discussion

6.1 Why Barcode Segmentation, Not Detection?

Segmentation task and the detection task for digital signs are very different. For one thing, on the conditional that they are small, dense, overlapped, and randomly cut, it will be hard to detect. Some sampled false positive results are shown in Fig. 6. Detection results are computed by OpenCV.

For another, segmentation results support post-processing steps for extracting more useful information, e.g., using the maximum outside rectangle to shot the barcodes, getting target areas with different shapes, not only limited to rectangle targets. However, detection results of specific bounding boxes have more limitations.

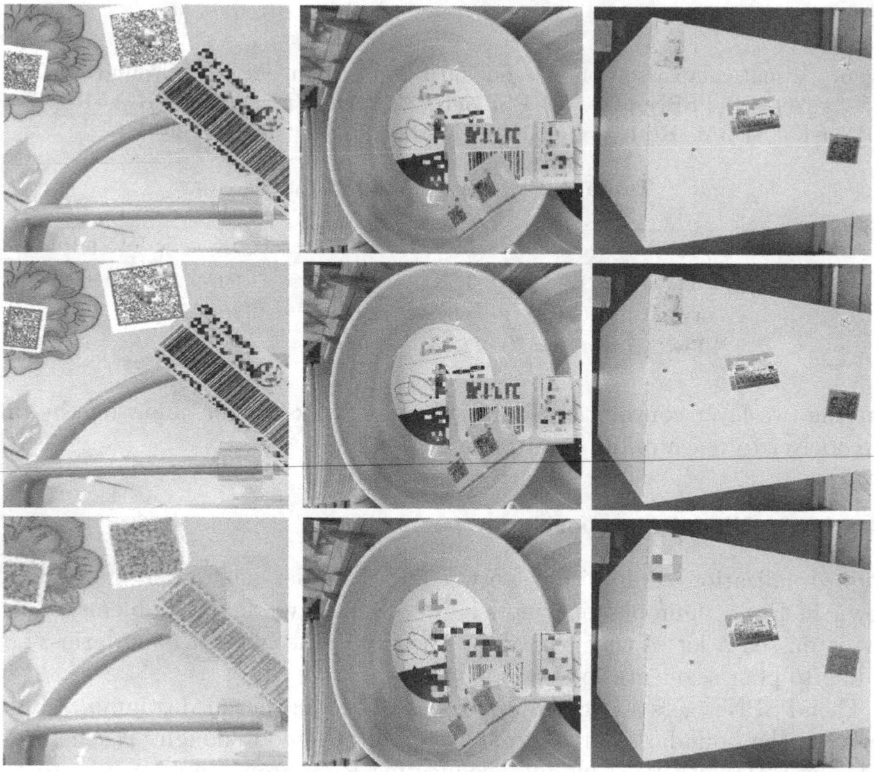

(a) Truncated (b) Overlapped (c) Small

Fig. 6. Compare qualitative results between barcode detection and segmentations in situations of (a) truncated, (b) overlapped and (c) small objects.

6.2 Generalization of Our Method

Though we mainly focus on barcode images in this paper, note that the synthesis strategy and the network BarcodeNet can be well extended for other targets with similar properties, such as LOGOs, traffic sighs, billboards segmentation, etc. Our synthesis strategy requires little annotations cost, and it provides guidance for time-critical segmentation tasks.

7 Conclusion

In this paper, we firstly propose a method for barcode image synthesis, by which we introduce a large-scale barcode image dataset, Barcode-30 k. Furthermore, according to the appearance characteristics of digital signs, we introduce Effective Barcode Hunter, a pyramid semantic segmentation network called BarcodeNet. It reached a high mIoU of 0.9536 on the Barcode-30 k validation set. Also, when applied to segment real images, the BarcodeNet pre-trained on Barcode-30 k can get great segmentation results. What's more, this method and model can be extended to the semantic segmentation of other objects with regular shapes.

References

1. Badrinarayanan, V., Kendall, A., Cipolla, R.: SegNet: a deep convolutional encoder-decoder architecture for scene segmentation. TPAMI **39**(12), 2481–2495 (2017)
2. Caesar, H., Uijlings, J., Ferrari, V.: Region-based semantic segmentation with end-to-end training. In: Leibe, B., Matas, J., Sebe, N., Welling, M. (eds.) ECCV 2016. LNCS, vol. 9905, pp. 381–397. Springer, Cham (2016). https://doi.org/10.1007/978-3-319-46448-0_23
3. Chen, L.C., Papandreou, G., Kokkinos, I., Murphy, K., Yuille, A.L.: DeepLab: semantic image segmentation with deep convolutional nets, atrous convolution, and fully connected CRFs. TPAMI **40**(4), 834–848 (2018)
4. Chen, L.C., Papandreou, G., Kokkinos, I., Murphy, K., Yuille, A.L.: Semantic image segmentation with deep convolutional nets and fully connected CRFs. In: ICLR (2015)
5. Chen, L., Papandreou, G., Schroff, F., Adam, H.: Rethinking atrous convolution for semantic image segmentation. CoRR. arXiv:1706.05587 (2017)
6. Cordts, M., et al.: The cityscapes dataset for semantic urban scene understanding. In: CVPR, pp. 3213–3223 (2016)
7. Cortes, C., Vapnik, V.: Support-vector networks. Mach. Learn. **20**(3), 273–297 (1995)
8. Dai, J., He, K., Sun, J.: Convolutional feature masking for joint object and stuff segmentation, pp. 3992–4000 (2014)
9. Garcia-Garcia, A., Orts-Escolano, S., Oprea, S., Villena-Martinez, V., Garcia-Rodriguez, J.: A review on deep learning techniques applied to semantic segmentation (2017)

10. He, K., Zhang, X., Ren, S., Sun, J.: Spatial pyramid pooling in deep convolutional networks for visual recognition. TPAMI **37**(9), 1904–16 (2015)
11. He, K., Zhang, X., Ren, S., Sun, J.: Deep residual learning for image recognition. In: CVPR, pp. 770–778 (2016)
12. Johnson, M., Shotton, J., Cipolla, R.: Semantic texton forests for image categorization and segmentation **5**(7), 1–8 (2008)
13. Lafferty, J.D., Mccallum, A., Pereira, F.C.N.: Conditional random fields: Probabilistic models for segmenting and labeling sequence data. In: ICML, pp. 282–289 (2001)
14. Li, J.H., Wang, W.H., Rao, T.T., Zhu, W.B., Liu, C.J.: Morphological segmentation of 2-D barcode gray scale image. In: ICISAI, pp. 62–68 (2017)
15. Li, J., Wang, Y.W., Chen, Y., Wang, G.: Adaptive segmentation method for 2-D barcode image base on mathematic morphological. Res. J. Appl. Sci. Eng. Technol. **6**(18), 3335–3342 (2013)
16. Li, J., Zhao, Q., Tan, X., Luo, Z., Tang, Z.: Using deep convnet for robust 1D barcode detection. In: ICIISA, pp. 261–267 (2017)
17. Lin, G., Milan, A., Shen, C., Reid, I.: RefineNet: multi-path refinement networks for high-resolution semantic segmentation (2016)
18. Liu, W., Rabinovich, A., Berg, A.C.: ParseNet: looking wider to see better. Computer Science (2015)
19. Liu, Z., He, L., Liang, R.: Research on segmentation algorithm of 2D color barcode based on mobile phone. In: ICCEE (2012)
20. Noh, H., Hong, S., Han, B.: Learning deconvolution network for semantic segmentation, pp. 1520–1528 (2015)
21. Shelhamer, E., Long, J., Darrell, T.: Fully convolutional networks for semantic segmentation. TPAMI **39**(4), 640–651 (2017)
22. Thoma, M.: A survey of semantic segmentation (2016)
23. Wachenfeld, S., Terlunen, S., Jiang, X.: Robust 1-D barcode recognition on camera phones and mobile product information display (2010)
24. Xie, S., Girshick, R., Dollar, P., Tu, Z., He, K.: Aggregated residual transformations for deep neural networks, pp. 5987–5995 (2016)
25. Xu, W., Mccloskey, S.: 2D barcode localization and motion deblurring using a flutter shutter camera. In: Applications of Computer Vision, pp. 159–165 (2011)
26. Yu, F., Koltun, V.: Multi-scale context aggregation by dilated convolutions (2015)
27. Zamberletti, A., Gallo, I., Carullo, M., Binaghi, E.: Neural image restoration for decoding 1-D barcodes using common camera phones. In: VISAPP 2010 - ICCV, pp. 5–11 (2010)
28. Zamberletti, A., Gallo, I., Albertini, S.: Robust angle invariant 1D barcode detection. In: ACPR, pp. 160–164 (2013)
29. Zeiler, M.D., Fergus, R.: Visualizing and understanding convolutional networks. In: Fleet, D., Pajdla, T., Schiele, B., Tuytelaars, T. (eds.) ECCV 2014. LNCS, vol. 8689, pp. 818–833. Springer, Cham (2014). https://doi.org/10.1007/978-3-319-10590-1_53
30. Zhao, H., Shi, J., Qi, X., Wang, X., Jia, J.: Pyramid scene parsing network. In: CVPR, pp. 6230–6239 (2017)

Oral Session 7B: Video Processing

Wonderful Clips of Playing Basketball: A Database for Localizing Wonderful Actions

Qinyu Li[1,3], Lijun Chen[1], Hanli Wang[1,2(✉)], and Xianhui Liu[1]

[1] Department of Computer Science and Technology, Tongji University, Shanghai, China
hanliwang@tongji.edu.cn
[2] Shanghai Institute of Intelligent Science and Technology, Tongji University, Shanghai, China
[3] Department of Computer Science, Lanzhou City University, Lanzhou, China

Abstract. Video highlight detection, or wonderful clip localization, aims at automatically discovering interesting clips in untrimmed videos, which can be applied to a variety of scenarios in real world. With reference to its study, a video dataset of Wonderful Clips of Playing Basketball (WCPB) is developed in this work. The Segment-Convolutional Neural Network (S-CNN), a start-of-the-art model for temporal action localization, is adopted to localize wonderful clips and a two-stream S-CNN is designed which outperforms its former on WCPB. The WCPB dataset presents the specific meaning of wonderful clips and annotations in playing basketball and enables the measurement of performance and progress in other realistic scenarios.

Keywords: Video highlight detection · Wonderful clip localization · Temporal action localization · Two-stream segment-convolutional neural network

1 Introduction

The huge amount of unstructured videos make it more and more time-consuming and expensive to generate high quality video clips. As we know, people are not always keeping their minds on the entire video during watching. As the integral video is usually unstructured and it is really a tedious job to browse it manually, video highlight detection is becoming increasingly important, which aims at finding the clips that mainly draw people's attention. Namely, the clips, named wonderful clips in this paper, refer to the video clips which people are more interested in than others.

This work was supported in part by National Natural Science Foundation of China under Grant 61622115 and Shanghai Engineering Research Center of Industrial Vision Perception & Intelligent Computing (17DZ2251600).

Y. M. Ro et al. (Eds.): MMM 2020, LNCS 11961, pp. 445–454, 2020.
https://doi.org/10.1007/978-3-030-37731-1_36

Recognition (or classification) of human actions in videos is significant for video understanding and has drawn considerable interests in the research community. It is usual to classify trimmed videos for this task. Various datasets and methods have been developed for action recognition [2,4,6,8,13]. For temporal action localization, the input videos are often untrimmed. Besides action categories, the corresponding temporal location shall be computed as well. In fact, action recognition is a particular case of temporal action localization with default temporal locations, and action recognition models can be extended to temporal action localization [1,7,11,12,19].

As compared to general temporal action localization, video highlight detection, or wonderful clip localization, concentrates on a relatively small part of a composite action, *i.e.*, wonderful clip localization produces interesting video fragments rather than fragments of ordinary actions that are likely to contain a quite long period of mundane frames. The methods for temporal action localization can be extended to wonderful clip localization feasibly. Specifically designed features are used in highlight detection in broadcast sport videos due to the well-defined structure and rules in early literature [10,14,16,18]. Highlight detection is highly dependent on the domain of interest and data-driven methods, especially deep learning techniques which require large-scale training data. Yao *et al.* [17] introduce a highlight detection dataset of 100 h videos for 15 unique sport categories and propose a two-stream network structure with AlexNet [5] and Convolutional 3D (C3D) [3,15] networks.

In general, it is subjective to judge whether a video clip is interesting or not, hence it is formidable to measure the degree of interest for a video clip. With regard to localizing wonderful clips, a dataset about Wonderful Clips of Playing Basketball (WCPB) is designed as the benchmark to evaluate wonderful clip localization approaches quantitatively and uniformly. Inspired by the Segment-Convolutional Neural Network (S-CNN) [12] model and chained multi-stream networks [20], a new network architecture is proposed to evaluate the proposed WCPB dataset. The main contributions of this work include the following two folds. First, the WCPB dataset is developed to evaluate wonderful clip localization approaches. This dataset is emphasized on playing basketball to acquire a distinct and unambiguous explanation of wonderful clips. To the best of our knowledge, it is the video highlight detection dataset with the largest number of hours and instances for basketball. Second, the temporal action localization model S-CNN [12] is evaluated on WCPB to localize wonderful clips, and a two-stream S-CNN is further designed to improve the performances, which can be considered as a primary baseline for future study.

2 Proposed WCPB Dataset

The proposed WCPB dataset consists of 13886 wonderful clips annotated from 788 videos. While other datasets contain several actions, WCPB concentrates on playing basketball and collects a large number of labels per action. Before annotation, the specific meaning of wonderful clips about playing basketball is defined to collect appropriate videos and distinguish wonderful clips from mundane clips.

2.1 Data Collection

Fig. 1. Illustration of wonderful clips about playing basketball. (a) Jump Shot. (b) Layup or Dunk. (c) Turn and Shot.

For wonderful clip localization, several wonderful clips (referred to as instances) of an input video are expected to be predicted. Each instance includes a label which stands for the description of the clip content, the start and the end time showing the temporal locations. As shown in Fig. 1, three kinds of actions about playing basketball are selected, including **Jump Shot**, **Layup or Dunk**, and **Turn and Shot**. Since the annotators may not have professional knowledge about playing basketball, it is sometimes difficult for them to distinguish the clips. In order to address this issue, these three wonderful clip labels are defined as follows.

- Jump Shot. A player is attempting to make a shot and there is an obvious action of jumping. The start time is required to be annotated at the time when the player is on the point of jumping. The clip is finished when the falling of the player is completed. Briefly speaking, the time when the body of the player departs from and reaches the playground are selected as the start and the end time respectively.
- Layup or Dunk. The significant difference of this one from Jump Shot is that the player does not simply jump on the spot before shooting. There can be a running up with the basketball in hands. If the player does not jump at all, it is universally acknowledged that it is not interesting enough. In other words, the wonderful clip begins when the player is moving and there is no dribbling before throwing the ball. The end time is the same as that of Jump Shot.

- Turn and Shot. In this situation, for the reason that the existence of turning around makes the clip attractive, turning is involved as part of the clip. The clip comprises a turning around and one of the two clips introduced above, without a long standstill. Dribbling is excluded and the player turns by more than 180°.

To get untrimmed videos with wonderful clips meeting the aforementioned standards, an offline collection of videos is taken in the first place. Videos are taken at basketball courts of different places in the daytime and nighttime. For the same event of playing basketball, several video-recorders work simultaneously to capture the sport from different directions. The whole proceeding of playing basketball is set between two players of half-court. Among collected videos, wonderful clip labels are generated by crowd-sourcing annotators online. Afterwards, a group of people, who are told about the criteria and then pass the corresponding test, will check the annotations offline. As a consequence, 788 videos with 13886 instances are generated, and all the videos are converted to the MP4 format.

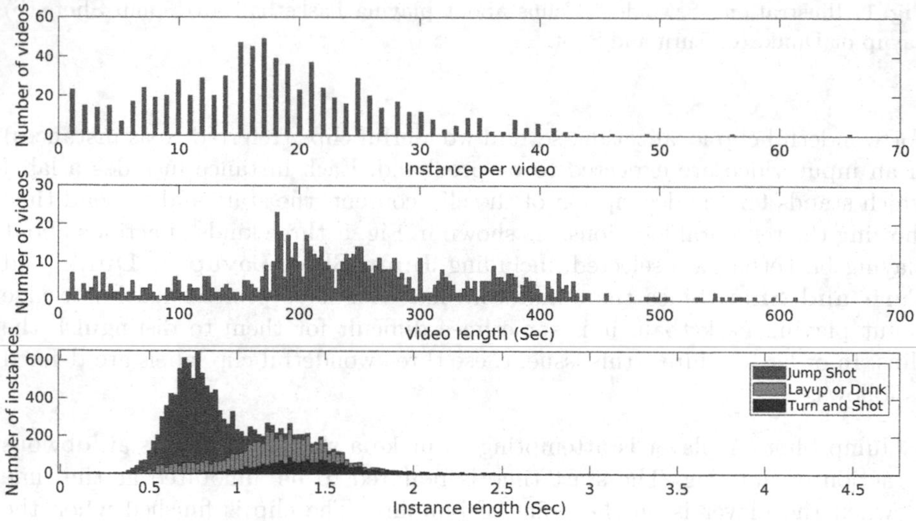

Fig. 2. Statistics in WCPB. The top plot shows the distribution of instances per video, the middle plot is the histogram of video length, and the bottom plot shows the histogram of instance length.

2.2 WCPB Characteristics

The total time of all these 788 videos is 52.71 h. The distribution of video length and instance length for each category are illustrated in Fig. 2. In addition, the statistics of temporal annotations for each category are shown in Table 1, where "Avg Len", "Max Len" and "Min Len" stand for the average, the maximum and the minimum time length of the instance for each category, and "Ratio" represents the time percentage of all instances against the entire videos for each category.

Table 1. Annotation statistics about each WCPB category.

Category	Instances	Avg Len	Max Len	Min Len	Ratio
All	13886	0.99	4.54	0.14	7.24
Jump Shot	8088	0.80	2.59	0.14	3.39
Layup or Dunk	3915	1.17	2.96	0.14	2.41
Turn and Shot	1883	1.45	4.54	0.22	1.44

Moreover, three distinct splits of video subsets are generated for evaluation purpose. For each split, the ratio of number of instances for training, validation and testing is about 3:1:1, with the statistics of these three splits summarized in Table 2.

Table 2. Statistics of three splits.

Subset	Train		Validation		Test	
	Video	Instance	Video	Instance	Video	Instance
Split1	478	8333	154	2820	156	2733
Split2	473	8341	155	2787	160	2758
Split3	472	8339	169	2778	147	2769

The performance on the proposed WCPB dataset can be evaluated by two ways. One is the mean Average Precision (mAP), and the other is to regard all the three kinds as positive and compute the Average Precision (AP). Moreover, similar to temporal action localization, the Intersection over Union (IoU) similarity measure [2] is considered to judge the validity of the prediction. In this work, the evaluation is reported for the values of IoU threshold from 10% to 90% with an interval of 10%.

3 Baseline Model on WCPB

To evaluate the proposed WCPB dataset, the S-CNN [12] model is employed first as the baseline model, and then a two-stream S-CNN model is designed with an extra pose stream.

3.1 S-CNN Model

In [12], three segment-based C3D networks, the proposal, classification and localization networks, are adopted to address the task of temporal action localization. The proposal network is set as a binary classifier to detect potential positive segments, while the classification and localization networks deal with multi-class problems to distinguish different categories. Moreover, the localization network is added with a new loss function (called overlap) about IoU to softmax for considering temporal overlap and is initialized with the classification network. In this work, the overlap loss is similarly employed for the proposal network.

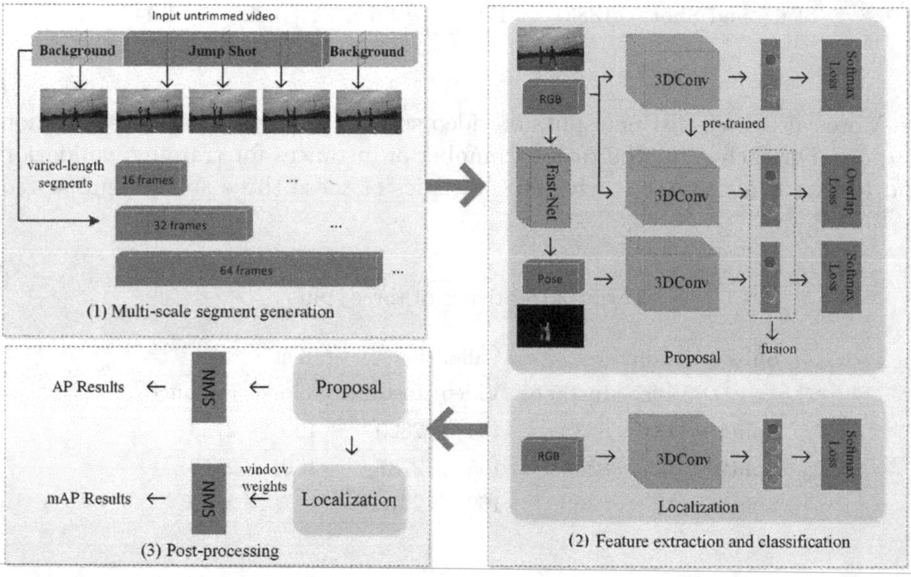

Fig. 3. Overview of the proposed two-stream S-CNN architecture.

3.2 Two-Stream S-CNN Model

Besides raw images, another visual cue, pose feature, is taken into consideration in this work. The pose feature is extracted from the raw images by Fast-Net [9] for human body part segmentation trained on the action recognition datasets [20]. Figure 3 illustrates the architecture of the proposed two-stream S-CNN model. Multi-scale segment generation is conducted to produce segments with varied lengths by temporal sliding window. For the RGB stream, a fixed number of raw images (*e.g.*, 16) uniformly sampled from a segment are fed into a C3D network with binary classification for proposal and another with multiple classification for localization. During training, the proposal network with softmax loss is first learned and then used as initialization for the one with overlap loss. For the pose stream, pose frames are generated from RGB frames related to the same segment via a trained network and fed into the proposal network with softmax loss. During prediction, the prediction scores from the two proposal networks are combined by weighted average and only positive segments (exceeding the threshold) are input to the localization network. The prediction scores of the localization network are refined by multiplying with the class-specific frequency for the distribution of segment length (window weight) in the training set to obtain the segments with more common lengths.

4 Experimental Evaluation

The input videos are decomposed into frames by 25 frames per second. The length of temporal sliding window is set as 16, 32, 64 or 128 frames and there is a 75% overlap of frames between two adjacent sliding windows. The threshold for positive segments is 0.7, and Non-Maximum Suppression (NMS) is applied to remove redundant results. The configuration of the C3D networks and hyper-parameters for overlap function are set according to the traditional S-CNN [12].

Five configurations of proposal network are evaluated in this work, including (1) **RGB_P1** and **Pose_P1**: the softmax loss is applied for the proposal network, (2) **RGB_P2**: the overlap loss is used by the proposal network, (3) **RGB_P3**: the proposal network with the overlap loss fine-tuned based on RGB_P1, and (4) **Fusion_P1**: late fusion of RGB_P3 and Pose_P1. The input frames for RGB_P1, RGB_P2 and RGB_P3 are raw images, while pose features are used for Pose_P1. If not mentioned, the network is pre-trained on the Sports-1M dataset [15]. The overlap IoU threshold is stated as θ in the following result tables.

Table 3. The AP results of the proposal networks with different settings on split1.

θ	0.1	0.2	0.3	0.4	0.5	0.6	0.7	0.8	0.9
RGB_P1	88.77	87.60	77.76	63.17	44.46	28.29	15.21	5.04	0.26
RGB_P2	88.11	86.13	76.72	60.66	42.13	26.87	14.29	4.43	0.20
RGB_P3	88.70	86.95	77.76	66.76	49.03	30.84	16.51	5.64	0.27
Pose_P1	82.74	81.19	73.53	64.47	48.49	28.44	15.54	5.06	0.25
Fusion_P1	**90.76**	**89.51**	**81.68**	**71.17**	**53.18**	**32.20**	**17.59**	**5.88**	**0.28**

First, the comparative results of the aforementioned five proposal network settings on the split1 dataset are shown in Table 3, where the network weights are learned using mini-batch Stochastic Gradient Descent (SGD) with a batch size of 6, momentum of 0.9, weight decay of $5e^{-4}$ and initial learning rate of $1e^{-4}$ with the exception of $1e^{-3}$ for the last fully connected layer. For RGB_P1, RGB_P2 and RGB_P3, the learning rate is decreased by a factor of 10 every $10k$ iterations and the maximum iteration is $30k$. For Pose_P1, the learning rate is decreased by a factor of 10 every $30k$ iterations and the maximum iteration is $60k$.

For RGB_P3, the pre-trained RGB_P1 is with a learning rate decreased by a factor of 10 every $60k$ iterations and the maximum iteration is $90k$. For Fusion_P1, the weights of the two streams are both 0.5. It can be seen that the overlap loss function can generally improve the proposal network with pre-training just like classification for localization in THUMOS'14 and the proposed two-stream architecture is better than others. Therefore, the setting of Fusion_P1 is chosen in our model.

Table 4. The mAP results of the localization networks with different settings on split1.

θ	0.1	0.2	0.3	0.4	0.5	0.6	0.7	0.8	0.9
Pose_L1	34.73	33.39	30.11	25.32	18.18	12.04	6.07	1.97	0.10
RGB_L1	36.47	35.22	31.41	27.78	19.00	12.52	6.63	2.36	0.13
RGB_L2	35.42	33.81	29.16	23.20	16.08	10.35	5.41	1.78	0.08
RGB_L3	44.62	43.77	41.07	36.28	25.04	16.67	9.13	3.22	0.18
RGB_L4	45.92	45.52	42.92	38.30	26.24	17.45	9.61	3.46	0.17
RGB_L5	43.38	43.46	40.96	36.65	25.80	16.67	9.33	3.27	0.18
RGB_L6	**46.00**	**46.39**	**44.82**	39.57	27.83	18.03	10.05	3.58	0.18
RGB_L7	40.29	40.98	41.75	39.23	30.59	22.71	13.07	5.05	0.28
RGB_L8	40.63	41.42	43.93	**41.52**	**32.55**	**23.91**	**13.64**	**5.27**	**0.29**

In order to investigate the characteristics of WCPB further, the results of localization are reported along with different proposals. Nine model configurations are evaluated, including (1) **RGB_L1** and **Pose_L1**: the softmax loss is applied with multi-scale segment generation, (2) **RGB_L2**: the overlap loss is used with multi-scale segment generation, (3) **RGB_L3**: the softmax loss is applied with RGB_P1, (4) **RGB_L4**: the softmax loss is applied with RGB_P3, (5) **RGB_L5**: the softmax loss is applied with Pose_P1, (6) **RGB_L6**: the softmax loss is applied with Fusion_P1, and (7) **RGB_L7** and **RGB_L8** are respectively RGB_L4 and RGB_L6 with window weight. The mAP results are shown in Table 4 on the split1 dataset, where it can be observed that the proposal network plays an important role to generate good localization performances. Moreover, the classification network generally outperforms the localization network because of the unbalanced number of training samples for each class. In addition, the window weight is beneficial for relatively high IoU results. Finally, the settings of RGB_L6 and RGB_L8 are chosen for θ from 0.1 to 0.3 and from 0.4 to 0.9, respectively. The AP and mAP performances on the entire WCPB dataset are shown in Tables 5 and 6.

Table 5. AP performance on WCPB.

θ	0.1	0.2	0.3	0.4	0.5	0.6	0.7	0.8	0.9
Split1	90.76	89.51	81.68	71.17	53.18	32.20	17.59	5.88	0.28
Split2	89.06	87.56	79.88	68.81	50.46	31.07	17.34	5.38	0.26
Split3	87.61	85.84	77.09	67.49	50.88	34.32	18.67	5.71	0.27
Average	89.14	87.64	79.55	69.16	51.51	32.53	17.87	5.66	0.27

Table 6. mAP performances over the three classes on WCPB.

θ	0.1	0.2	0.3	0.4	0.5	0.6	0.7	0.8	0.9
Split1	46.00	46.39	44.82	41.52	32.55	23.91	13.64	5.27	0.29
Split2	44.01	44.07	42.19	38.42	29.58	21.70	12.59	4.20	0.22
Split3	45.45	45.10	43.10	38.87	30.75	23.19	13.34	4.99	0.25
Average	45.15	45.19	43.37	39.60	30.96	22.93	13.19	4.82	0.25

5 Conclusion

In this paper, a video dataset is established as the benchmark for wonderful clip localization in basketball. The specific meaning of wonderful clip about playing basketball is detailed on the dataset. Then, the S-CNN model is conducted to predict the temporal locations of wonderful clips on the proposed WCPB dataset. Furthermore, together with S-CNN, a two-stream S-CNN is proposed by adding the pose cue. In the future, it is desired to extend wonderful clips to other realistic scenarios, for which a lot of efforts are needed to make precise definitions.

References

1. Escorcia, V., Caba Heilbron, F., Niebles, J.C., Ghanem, B.: DAPs: deep action proposals for action understanding. In: Leibe, B., Matas, J., Sebe, N., Welling, M. (eds.) ECCV 2016. LNCS, vol. 9907, pp. 768–784. Springer, Cham (2016). https://doi.org/10.1007/978-3-319-46487-9_47
2. Idrees, H., et al.: The THUMOS challenge on action recognition for videos "in the wild". Comput. Vis. Image Underst. **155**, 1–23 (2017)
3. Ji, S., Xu, W., Yang, M., Yu, K.: 3D convolutional neural networks for human action recognition. IEEE Trans. Pattern Anal. Mach. Intell. **35**(1), 221–231 (2013)
4. Karpathy, A., Toderici, G., Shetty, S., Leung, T., Sukthankar, R., Fei-Fei, L.: Large-scale video classification with convolutional neural networks. In: Proceedings of CVPR 2014, pp. 1725–1732, June 2014
5. Krizhevsky, A., Sutskever, I., Hinton, G.E.: ImageNet classification with deep convolutional neural networks. In: Proceedings of NIPS 2012, pp. 1097–1105, December 2012

6. Kuehne, H., Jhuang, H., Garrote, E., Poggio, T., Serre, T.: HMDB: a large video database for human motion recognition. In: Proceedings of ICCV 2011, pp. 2556–2563, November 2011
7. Lin, T., Zhao, X., Shou, Z.: Single shot temporal action detection. In: Proceedings of ACM MM 2017, pp. 988–996, October 2017
8. Niebles, J.C., Chen, C.-W., Fei-Fei, L.: Modeling temporal structure of decomposable motion segments for activity classification. In: Daniilidis, K., Maragos, P., Paragios, N. (eds.) ECCV 2010. LNCS, vol. 6312, pp. 392–405. Springer, Heidelberg (2010). https://doi.org/10.1007/978-3-642-15552-9_29
9. Oliveira, G.L., Burgard, W., Brox, T.: Efficient deep models for monocular road segmentation. In: Proceedings of IROS 2016, pp. 4885–4891, October 2016
10. Rui, Y., Gupta, A., Acero, A.: Automatically extracting highlights for TV baseball programs. In: Proceedings of ACM MM 2000, pp. 105–115, October 2000
11. Shou, Z., Chan, J., Zareian, A., Miyazawa, K., Chang, S.F.: CDC: convolutional-de-convolutional networks for precise temporal action localization in untrimmed videos. In: Proceedings of CVPR 2017, pp. 1417–1426, July 2017
12. Shou, Z., Wang, D., Chang, S.F.: Temporal action localization in untrimmed videos via multi-stage CNNs. In: Proceedings of CVPR 2016, pp. 1049–1058, June 2016
13. Soomro, K., Roshan Zamir, A., Shah, M.: UCF101: a dataset of 101 human actions classes from videos in the wild, December 2012. CoRR abs/1212.0402
14. Tang, H., Kwatra, V., Sargin, M.E., Gargi, U.: Detecting highlights in sports videos: cricket as a test case. In: Proceedings of ICME 2011, pp. 1–6, July 2011
15. Tran, D., Bourdev, L., Fergus, R., Torresani, L., Paluri, M.: Learning spatiotemporal features with 3D convolutional networks. In: Proceedings of ICCV 2015, pp. 4489–4497, December 2015
16. Wang, J., Xu, C., Chng, E., Tian, Q.: Sports highlight detection from keyword sequences using HMM. In: Proceedings of ICME 2004, pp. 599–602, June 2004
17. Yao, T., Mei, T., Rui, Y.: Highlight detection with pairwise deep ranking for first-person video summarization. In: Proceedings of CVPR 2016. pp. 982–990, June 2016
18. Yow, D., Yeo, B., Yeung, M., Liu, B.: Analysis and presentation of soccer highlights from digital video. In: Proceedings of ACCV 1995, pp. 499–503, December 1995
19. Zhao, Y., Xiong, Y., Wang, L., Wu, Z., Tang, X., Lin, D.: Temporal action detection with structured segment networks. In: Proceedings of ICCV 2017, pp. 2933–2942, October 2017
20. Zolfaghari, M., Oliveira, G.L., Sedaghat, N., Brox, T.: Chained multi-stream networks exploiting pose, motion, and appearance for action classification and detection. In: Proceedings of ICCV 2017, pp. 2923–2932, October 2017

Structural Pyramid Network for Cascaded Optical Flow Estimation

Zefeng Sun[1], Hanli Wang[1,2](✉), Yun Yi[1,3], and Qinyu Li[1,4]

[1] Department of Computer Science and Technology, Tongji University, Shanghai, China
hanliwang@tongji.edu.cn
[2] Shanghai Institute of Intelligent Science and Technology, Tongji University, Shanghai, China
[3] Department of Mathematics and Computer Science, Gannan Normal University, Ganzhou, China
[4] Department of Computer Science, Lanzhou City University, Lanzhou, China

Abstract. To achieve a better balance of accuracy and computational complexity for optical flow estimation, a Structural Pyramid Network (StruPyNet) is designed to combine structural pyramid processing and feature pyramid processing. In order to efficiently distribute parameters and computations among all structural pyramid levels, the proposed StruPyNet flexibly cascades more small flow estimators at lower structural pyramid levels and less small flow estimators at higher structural pyramid levels. The more focus on low-resolution feature matching facilitates large-motion flow estimation and background flow estimation. In addition, residual flow learning, feature warping and cost volume construction are repeatedly performed by the cascaded small flow estimators, which benefits training and estimation. As compared with state-of-the-art convolutional neural network-based methods, StruPyNet achieves better performances in most cases. The model size of StruPyNet is 95.9% smaller than FlowNet2, and StruPyNet runs at 3 more frames per second than FlowNet2. Moreover, the experimental results on several benchmark datasets demonstrate the effectiveness of StruPyNet, especially StruPyNet performs quite well for large-motion estimation.

Keywords: Optical flow estimation · Convolutional neural network · Structural pyramid

1 Introduction

Optical flow estimation is a time-honoured research field dating back to several decades ago. Before deep learning is applied to optical flow estimation,

This work was supported in part by National Natural Science Foundation of China under Grants 61622115 and 61962003, and Shanghai Engineering Research Center of Industrial Vision Perception & Intelligent Computing (17DZ2251600).

Y. M. Ro et al. (Eds.): MMM 2020, LNCS 11961, pp. 455–467, 2020.
https://doi.org/10.1007/978-3-030-37731-1_37

most variational methods [2,12,16,21] follow [7] to constrain themselves with the assumption of brightness constancy, spatial smoothness and so on. Therefore, these methods formulate complex energy functions at the cost of expensive computational overhead, limiting their scope for real-time applications.

In recent years, to deal with the weaknesses of variational methods, deep learning is booming on this research field. Many effective convolutional neural network (CNN)-based methods [4,8,9,15,19,20] are proposed and achieve competitive performances on the challenging benchmarks [3,5,14]. Most methods try to achieve a balance of accuracy and computational complexity. Considering memory limitation during training, PWC-Net [19] doesn't predict full-resolution flow directly. Instead, it predicts flow with 1/16 of full resolution and finally up-samples the predicted flow to full resolution by the bilinear method. But the final up-sampling from 1/16 of full resolution to full resolution makes many flow details lost and reduces the accuracy. In LiteFlowNet [8], the siamese feature pyramid has one less feature down-sampled than PWC-Net. So the resolution of feature pairs is 4 times that of PWC-Net, which causes the GPU memory footprint almost 4 times that of PWC-Net. Meanwhile, the large GPU memory footprint in LiteFlowNet constrains the number of parameters and the refinement of network architectures. Although feature pyramid processing is a critical component in PWC-Net and LiteFlowNet, it requires intensive computations and memory usage.

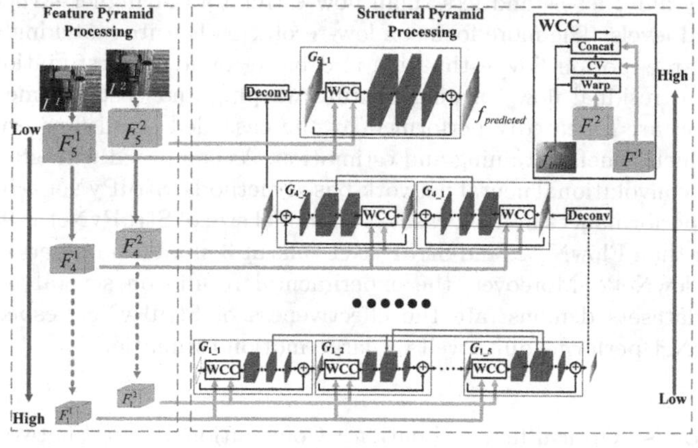

Fig. 1. An overview of the proposed StruPyNet.

To achieve a better balance of accuracy and computational complexity, a Structural Pyramid Network (StruPyNet) is designed, which consists of feature pyramid processing and structural pyramid processing as shown in Fig. 1. The feature pyramid is an inverted pyramid which has 5 levels to extract multi-scale feature pairs in a bottom-up manner, and the structural pyramid also has 5 levels to estimate multi-resolution flows. For an efficient distribution of parameters and computations among all the structural pyramid levels, the numbers of cascaded small flow estimators are respectively 5, 4, 3, 2 and 1 from the bottom level to the top level in the structural pyramid. Each structural pyramid level is connected to its adjacent structural pyramid level with a de-convolutional layer for up-sampling and transporting flow fields. Benefiting from the structural pyramid, StruPyNet pays more efforts on extracting correlation from low-resolution feature pairs that contain rich global structure information, which enhances the capability for large-motion flow estimation and background flow estimation. Moreover, residual flow learning, feature warping and cost volume construction are performed for 15 times by 15 cascaded small flow estimators to better extract correlation and refine sub-pixels. The proposed StruPyNet outperforms other state-of-the-art CNN-based methods such as FlowNet2 [9], LiteFlowNet [8] and PWC-Net [19] on the KITTI datasets [5,14], and achieves competitive results on the Sintel dataset [3]. Moreover, the model size of StruPyNet is less than that of FlowNet2 and PWC-Net. To sum up, the main contributions of this work are as follows:

- StruPyNet is designed by combining feature pyramid processing and structural pyramid processing to achieve the balance of accuracy and computational complexity, which enhances the capability for large-motion flow estimation and background flow estimation.
- To flexibly distribute parameters at all levels of the structural pyramid, the small flow estimator is designed. By cascading small flow estimators, StruPyNet executes residual flow learning, feature warping and cost volume construction repeatedly to strengthen feature matching and sub-pixel refinement.
- To enhance feature propagation and supplement the missing feature matching information, intra-pyramid-level and inter-flow-estimator dense connections are constructed at each structural pyramid level, except the highest one.

The rest of this paper is organized as follows. Section 2 discusses the related works. The proposed StruPyNet is detailed in Sect. 3. The experimental results are presented in Sect. 4. Finally, Sect. 5 concludes this work.

2 Related Work

Variational Methods. Based on the work of Horn and Schunck [7], many variational methods have been proposed. In DeepFlow [21], a descriptor matching algorithm is blended with the variational method to handle large motions in flow estimation. In PatchMatch Filter [12], a PatchMatch-based randomized search, an efficient edge-aware image filtering and a novel super pixel-based search strategy are integrated to establish dense correspondence. To cope with the detailed flow estimation problem, rich descriptors are integrated into the typical energy formulation [2]. In EpicFlow [16], a sparse-to-dense matching is done by edge-preserving interpolation and the dense matches are further optimized finely by a variational method.

Traditional Machine Learning Methods. Black *et al.* apply Principal Component Analysis (PCA) to make the model self-learn computing flow fields [1]. Sun *et al.* construct a statistical model that learns both the brightness constancy variation and the spatial properties of optical flow [18]. In PCA-Flow [22], Wulff *et al.* propose a model that learns the principal components of natural flow fields and adopt a sparse-to-dense method to estimate optical flow.

CNN-Based Methods. FlowNet [4] is a pioneer CNN-based method for optical flow estimation but its performance is limited due to its large model size. The successive work of FlowNet is FlowNet2 [9] which consists of several FlowNets cascaded together. Although FlowNet2 achieves excellent results, its model size is several times that of FlowNet, which may cause proneness of over-fitting. SPyNet [15], which combines deep learning with a classical spatial image pyramid structure, performs on a par with FlowNet but with a much smaller model size as compared with FlowNet. But the performance of SPyNet is limited by its simple CNN architecture. As a solution, DSPyNet is proposed in [20], which employs an efficient CNN architecture. DSPyNet exceeds FlowNet and SPyNet on most benchmarks but is still inferior to FlowNet2. Sun *et al.* propose PWC-Net [19] where spatial pyramid structure, feature warping and cost volume are fused. In LiteFlowNet [8], Hui *et al.* cascade three lightweight networks executing descriptor matching, sub-pixel refinement and flow regularization respectively at each pyramid level. PWC-Net and LiteFlowNet obtain similar performances and both outperform FlowNet2 on some benchmarks. But there is still room to improve the balance of accuracy and computational complexity.

Unlike the baseline methods, the proposed StruPyNet has a novel structural pyramid processing to achieve a better balance between accuracy and computations. Different from PWC-Net [19] and LiteFlowNet [8] that have the same flow estimators at each pyramid level, StruPyNet has different numbers of cascaded small flow estimators at different structural pyramid levels. More cascaded small flow estimators at the lower structural pyramid level receive lower-resolution feature pairs from higher feature pyramid levels, and less cascaded small flow estimators at the higher structural pyramid level receive higher-resolution feature pairs from lower feature pyramid levels. This leads to a more efficient distribution of parameters and computations among all the structural pyramid levels.

3 Proposed Structural Pyramid Network

3.1 Feature Pyramid Processing

Feature pyramid processing, which has been widely employed in various fields, such as object detection [6,17], semantic segmentation [11] and flow estimation [8,19], is critical for performance improvement. A siamese feature pyramid network is designed based on the feature pyramid extractor in PWC-Net [19] to extract multi-scale feature pairs (F_L^1, F_L^2) from the input image pairs (I^1, I^2), as shown in the left part of Fig. 1. It has 5 levels (excluding the input level) and down-samples feature maps for 5 times, which requires one less down-sampling operation than PWC-Net [19] and quadruples the resolution of feature maps input into small flow estimators. Therefore, the resolution of the predicted flow is quadrupled to 1/4 of full resolution and more flow details are saved when up-sampled to full resolution. The channel numbers of the feature maps from the lowest level to the highest level are separately 16, 32, 64, 96 and 128. More useful information is contained through feature extraction during down-sampling, and the feature space is more discriminative for matching. Moreover, global structure information is captured by convolution operations at high feature pyramid levels, which leads to more accurate estimation of large-motion flow and background flow.

3.2 Structural Pyramid Processing

Small Flow Estimator. The small flow estimator is a small-scale CNN with three techniques: residual flow learning, feature warping and cost volume construction. It has been verified that residual flow learning, feature warping and cost volume construction improve the performance of flow estimation in [8,9,15,20]. The residual flow learning rather than complete flow learning reduces the range of predicted numbers and makes the small flow estimator G easier to infer flow vectors. In each small flow estimator, the shortcut connections for the addition of the initial flow and the predicted residual flow lead to an easy training process. As a replacement of image warping, feature warping has many advantages compared with image warping, as it focuses on only the feature space instead of the RGB space and further reduces the distance of feature matching. To briefly represent the architecture of G, the warping layer, the cost volume layer and the concatenation layer are combined into one block, called WCC block, as shown in the top-right part of Fig. 1. Let the feature warping in the WCC block be denoted as:

$$\widetilde{F^2}(x,y) = F^2(x+u(x,y), y+v(x,y)), \tag{1}$$

where $F^2(x,y)$ is the feature vector at the (x,y) position in F^2, $u(x,y)$ and $v(x,y)$ are the horizontal and vertical components of the flow vector in the initial flow $f_{initial}$. The cost volume, as a higher-level representation of flow, is constructed to measure how well the feature patches in the feature map F^1 match the same feature patches in the feature map F^2. In the WCC block, the cost volume is defined as:

$$CV(x,y) = (F^1(x,y) \cdot \widetilde{F^2}(x+r_1, y+r_2))/N, \tag{2}$$

where $r_1, r_2 \in [-d, d]$, and N is the length of feature vector $F^1(x,y)$. In order to reduce the computational complexity, a short range of d pixels is set for a partial cost volume construction instead of a global one. Then, the flow inference formulation in the small flow estimator G is

$$f_{predicted} = \underbrace{G(concat(CV, f_{initial}, F^1))}_{f_{residual}} + f_{initial}, \tag{3}$$

where the *concat* function concatenates feature maps along the channel dimension, and CV is calculated by Eq. (2).

The detailed CNN architecture of the small flow estimator is shown in Table 1. We integrate the inception sub-module and the 1×1 convolutional layer to improve the representation efficiency. The last layer is set with a 7×7 kernel size for a wider capture of context information. And intra-pyramid-level and inter-flow-estimator dense connections increase the input channel number of Conv2, which will be detailed in Sect. 3.2.

Table 1. The detailed architecture of the X-th small flow estimator G_{L_X} at the L-th structural pyramid level. Ch_Num is $(L-1)*32+81+2$ when $L \geq 2$ and $16+81+2$ when $L = 1$. 81 and 2 are the channel numbers of the cost volume and the initial flow respectively.

Layer name	Kernel size	#Ch. In/Out	Input	Layer name	Kernel size	#Ch. In/Out	Input
WCC	–	-/Ch_Num	F_L^1, F_L^2, $f_{initial}^{L\text{-}X}$	Conv4	3×3	64/64	Conv3
Inception	–	Ch_Num/160	WCC	Conv5	3×3	64/32	Conv4
Conv1	1×1	160/64	Inception	Conv6	3×3	32/16	Conv5
Conv2	3×3	(X*64)/64	Conv1, Dense connections	Conv7	3×3	16/8	Conv6
Conv3	3×3	64/64	Conv2	Conv8	7×7	8/2	Conv7

Structural Pyramid. As shown in the middle part of Fig. 1, structural pyramid processing is proposed to achieve a better balance of accuracy and computational complexity. The structural pyramid has the same number of levels as the feature pyramid. Each structural pyramid level is connected to its adjacent structural pyramid level with a de-convolutional layer for up-sampling and transporting flow fields. Different structural pyramid levels have different numbers of cascaded small flow estimators, which are respectively 5, 4, 3, 2 and 1 from the bottom level to the top level. At each structural pyramid level, all the small flow estimators are fed with the same feature pairs from the corresponding feature pyramid level in the inverted feature pyramid. Consequently, small flow estimators at the lower structural pyramid level receive lower-resolution feature pairs from the higher feature pyramid level and the ones at the higher structural pyramid level receive higher-resolution feature pairs from the lower feature pyramid level. The more cascaded small flow estimators at a structural pyramid level means a more powerful capability for flow refinement. Therefore, lower structural pyramid levels, which have more cascaded small flow estimators, provide higher-quality flow to higher structural pyramid levels through the de-convolutional layer. This helps reduce the burden of flow refinement for small flow estimators at higher structural pyramid levels.

The structural pyramid allows more feature warping and cost volume construction operations with a marginal extra cost. The proposed StruPyNet executes the feature warping and the cost volume construction 15 times, while PWC-Net [19] and LiteFlowNet [8] execute these operations only 5 times.

More operations of feature warping and cost volume construction help feature matching and sub-pixel refinement, which further improve performances.

Intra-Pyramid-Level and Inter-Flow-Estimator Dense Connections. The small flow estimator inevitably loses some feature matching information due to its limited representation power during flow estimation. To address this issue, intra-pyramid-level and inter-flow-estimator dense connections are proposed in the structural pyramid processing to strengthen feature propagation and supplement the feature matching information that has been lost in previous flow estimators. Each cascaded small flow estimator G shares its feature map output from the 1×1 convolutional layer to all subsequent estimators at the same structural pyramid level. Then these shared feature maps are concatenated together as the input of next convolutional layers in subsequent estimators, as shown in Fig. 1 and Table 1. This implementation also makes training more effective.

3.3 Network Training

Let P denote the set of the learnable parameters in StruPyNet. The training loss $\mathcal{L}_{G_{L\_X}}$ of the X-th small flow estimator G_{L_X} at the L-th structural pyramid level is defined as Eq. (4), therefore the total training loss $\mathcal{L}(P)$ is calculated as Eq. (5).

$$\mathcal{L}_{G_{L\_X}} = \sum_{(x,y)} (|f_{predicted}^{L\_X}(x,y) - f_{gt}^{L\_X}(x,y)|_k + \epsilon)^q, \tag{4}$$

$$\mathcal{L}(P) = \sum_{L=1}^{5} \alpha_L \sum_{X=1}^{6-L} \mathcal{L}_{G_{L\_X}} + \gamma |P|_2^2, \tag{5}$$

where $f_{predicted}^{L\_X}(x,y)$ and $f_{gt}^{L\_X}(x,y)$ respectively represent the predicted flow vectors and ground-truth flow vectors at the (x,y) position, $|\cdot|_k$ computes the l_k norm, $k \in [1,2]$, ϵ is a parameter for fine-tuning, and $q \leq 1$ determines how much penalty should be given to outliers.

At different structural pyramid levels, the ground-truth flow is down-scaled by 20 and down-sampled to different sizes to match the predicted flow sizes for the Average End Point Error (AEPE) computation over all pixels. The weights of AEPE losses from the lowest structural pyramid level to the highest structural pyramid level are separately set as: $\alpha_1 = 0.32$, $\alpha_2 = 0.08$, $\alpha_3 = 0.02$, $\alpha_4 = 0.01$ and $\alpha_5 = 0.005$. The trade-off weight γ is set to be 0.0004.

To achieve optimal generalization performances, there are three training stages. At Stage 1, the models are trained on the FlyingChairs dataset [4] and then fine-tuned on the Things3D dataset [13] at Stage 2. At Stage 3, the models are further fine-tuned on the corresponding Sintel and KITTI datasets. At Stages 1 and 2, Eq. (4) is employed as the loss function with $k = 2$, $\epsilon = 0$ and $q = 1$, while $k = 1$, $\epsilon = 0.01$ and $q = 0.4$ at Stage 3.

The initial flow is up-scaled for the warping layer in each cascaded small flow estimator following the protocol in [19], and the pixel range d for the partial cost volume construction is set to 4 in each small flow estimator. At Stages 1

Table 2. Comparison of AEPEs and Fl-all indexes tested by models at Stage 1. A postfix "-pre" is added behind model names. The best 2 results in each column are highlighted in bold.

Method	FlyingChairs	Sintel clean	Sintel final	KITTI2012	KITTI2015	
	Validation	Train	Train	Train	Train	Train (Fl-all)
FlowNetS [4]	2.71	4.50	5.45	8.26	–	–
FlowNetC [4]	2.19	4.31	5.87	9.35	–	–
SPyNet [15]	2.63	4.12	5.57	9.12	–	–
DSPyNet [20]	2.05	3.51	5.22	9.20	–	–
LiteFlowNet-pre [8]	**1.57**	**2.78**	**4.17**	**4.56**	**11.58**	**32.59%**
PWC-Net-pre [19]	2.00	3.33	4.59	5.14	13.20	41.79%
StruPyNet-pre	**1.63**	**2.72**	**4.09**	**4.22**	**11.10**	**31.90%**

and 3, the same training schedule as FlowNet2 [9] is applied. At Stage 2, we explore a new fine-tuning schedule on the Things3D dataset. Instead of S_{fine} in FlowNet2 [9], a new learning rate schedule S_{new_fine} is explored where only 60K iterations are needed for fine-tuning on the Things3D dataset, *i.e.*, starting from $1e^{-5}$ and reducing the learning rate by half at the 5K, 12K and 35K iterations. Furthermore, the related ablation experiments will be shown in Sect. 4.2, which verifies that StruPyNet is easier to train and fine-tune.

Table 3. Comparison of AEPEs and Fl-all indexes tested by models fine-tuned at Stage 2. The best 2 results in each column are highlighted in bold.

Method	Sintel clean	Sintel final	KITTI2012	KITTI2015	
	Train	Train	Train	Train	Train (Fl-all)
FlowNet2 [9]	**2.02**	**3.54**	4.01	**10.08**	29.99%
LiteFlowNet [8]	2.48	4.04	**4.00**	10.39	**28.50%**
PWC-Net [19]	2.55	3.93	4.14	10.35	33.67%
StruPyNet	**2.40**	**3.84**	**3.79**	**9.95**	**28.52%**

4 Experimental Results

4.1 Main Results

The proposed StruPyNet is evaluated on several public benchmarks at the aforementioned stages, and the results at each stage are compared with baseline methods. The Caffe framework [10] is employed to implement the proposed model, and all experiments are run on 4 Titan-X GPUs in an Ubuntu16.04 server with Intel(R) Xeon(R) CPU E5-2683 v3. In experiments, besides AEPE, two other popular employed metrics are also presented, including Fl-all (the percentage of flow outliers averaged over all regions) and Fl-bg (the percentage of flow outliers averaged over background regions).

Evaluation of Stage 1. As shown in Table 2, the proposed StruPyNet-pre obtains the best result on all datasets except on the validation set of FlyingChairs. StruPyNet-pre is on par with LiteFlowNet-pre [8] on the validation set of FlyingChairs, and obtains better results than PWC-Net-pre [19] on all datasets. For example, the AEPE of StruPyNet-pre is 2.1 smaller than that of PWC-Net-pre on the KITTI2015 training set [14]. The Sintel dataset [3] and KITTI datasets [5,14] contain many large motions. Therefore, we attribute the advantages of StruPyNet-pre to the novel structural pyramid processing, which enhances the capability for large-motion flow estimation.

Table 4. Comparison of AEPEs and Fl-all indexes tested by models at Stage 3. A postfix "-ft" is added behind model names. The best 2 results in each column are highlighted in bold. "Noc" and "All" stand for Non-occluded pixels and all regions, respectively.

Method	Sintel clean	Sintel final	KITTI2012	KITTI2015			
	Test	Test	Test	Noc Fl-bg	Noc Fl-all	All Fl-bg	All Fl-all
FlowNetS-ft [4]	6.96	7.76	9.1	–	–	–	–
FlowNetC-ft [4]	6.85	8.51	–	–	–	–	–
SPyNet-ft [15]	6.64	8.36	4.7	–	–	–	–
DSPyNet-ft [20]	6.22	7.45	5.5	–	–	–	–
FlowNet2-ft [9]	**4.16**	5.74	1.8	7.24%	6.94%	10.75%	11.48%
LiteFlowNet-ft [8]	4.54	**5.38**	**1.6**	**5.58%**	**5.49%**	**9.66%**	**9.38%**
PWC-Net-ft [19]	**3.86**	**5.13**	**1.7**	6.14%	6.12%	**9.66%**	9.60%
StruPyNet-ft	4.40	5.51	**1.7**	**5.42%**	**5.53%**	**9.00%**	**9.15%**

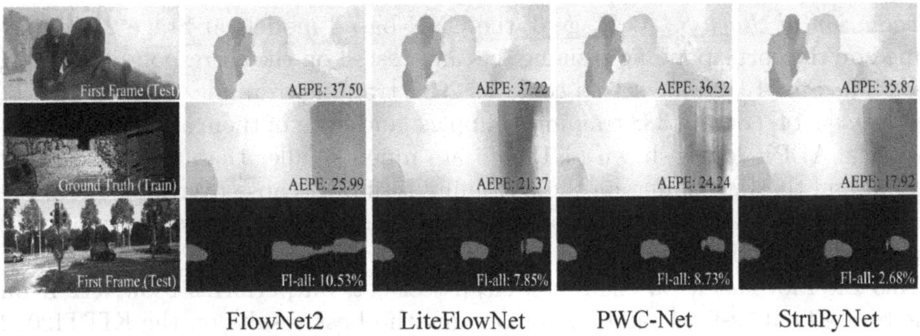

Fig. 2. Visual results of optical flow estimated by four CNN-based methods on the datasets of Sintel (Row 1), KITTI2012 (Row 2) and KITTI2015 (Row 3).

Evaluation of Stage 2. In Table 3, the results are better than that in Table 2, which shows that fine-tuning on more flow datasets at Stage 2 can reinforce the generalization ability of CNN-based models. Thank to the structural pyramid,

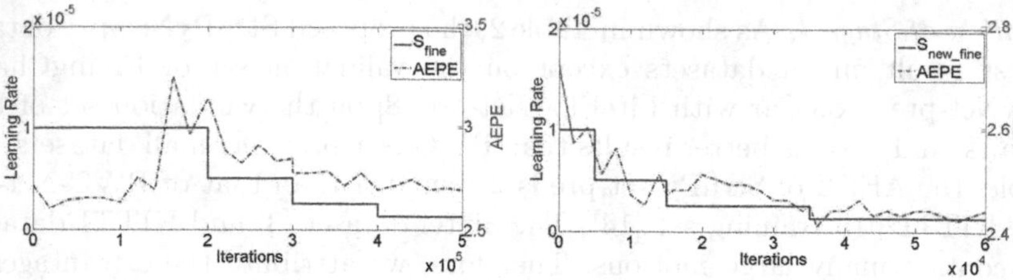

Fig. 3. Comparison between S_{fine} and S_{new_fine} during fine-tuning on Things3D. AEPEs are tested every 20K iterations when S_{fine} is used and every 2K iterations when S_{new_fine} is used on the Sintel Clean dataset.

Table 5. Comparison of AEPEs and Fl-all indexes between S_{fine} and S_{new_fine}. The results are all tested on the training sets. The percentages in the parentheses indicate Fl-all index.

	Sintel clean	Sintel final	KITTI2012	KITTI2015
S_{fine}	2.69	3.98	4.03	10.57 (28.98%)
S_{new_fine}	2.40	3.84	3.79	9.95 (28.52%)

the proposed StruPyNet outperforms baseline methods on the KITTI training sets [5,14]. On the Sintel dataset [3], StruPyNet is a little inferior to FlowNet2 [9], but is superior to PWC-Net [19] and LiteFlowNet [8]. The Sintel dataset contains some small and blur motions, so StruPyNet may do a little worse in coping with small and blur motions. Although FlowNet2 [9] performs better in coping with small and blur motions than StruPyNet, it has almost 24 times larger model size than StruPyNet.

Evaluation of Stage 3. At Stage 3, the CNN-based models at Stage 2 are fine-tuned on the corresponding training sets and tested on the corresponding testing sets. The Sintel training set [3] contains 2082 training examples and the KITTI datasets [5,14] contain 388 training examples, and both of them are small. Therefore, the AEPE losses shown in Table 4 are much smaller than that in Tables 2 and 3, and the fine-tuning on these training sets may cause over-fitting and the models have weaker generalization abilities. Thus, the results are less important than that in Tables 2 and 3 for performance evaluation. StruPyNet-ft outperforms LiteFlowNet-ft on the Sintel clean test set, outperforms FlowNet2-ft on the Sintel final test set, and almost obtains the best results on the KITTI2012 and KITTI 2015 testing sets. These results indicate the powerful capability of StruPyNet for large-motion flow estimation and background flow estimation. Moreover, a visualization of several optical flow estimated by four competing CNN-based methods on the datasets of Sintel, KITTI2012 and KITTI2015 is shown in Fig. 2.

Table 6. Comparison of AEPEs and Fl-all indexes between StruPyNet-pre with DC and w/o DC. The results are all tested on the training sets. The percentages in the parentheses indicate Fl-all index.

	FlyingChairs	Sintel clean	Sintel final	KITTI2012	KITTI2015
With DC	1.63	2.72	4.09	4.22	11.10 (31.90%)
W/o DC	1.69	2.81	4.13	4.54	11.94 (32.83%)

4.2 Ablation Experiments

Learning Rate Schedule on the Things3D Dataset. A new learning rate schedule S_{new_fine} is explored for fine-tuning on the Things3D dataset [13]. The comparison between S_{fine} and S_{new_fine} is shown in Fig. 3. The use of S_{fine} can't get the AEPE loss reduced, and unexpected over-fitting even appears after 150K iterations. However, the proposed S_{new_fine} makes the AEPE loss decrease to a low level with only 60K iterations. Table 5 shows the comparison of results tested on all the training sets using models fine-tuned on the Things3D dataset with S_{fine} and S_{new_fine} respectively. In conclusion, this experiment demonstrates that the structural pyramid is easier to train and fine-tune, and has a good generalization ability.

Evaluation of Dense Connections. Intra-pyramid-level and inter-flow-estimator Dense Connections (DC) improve flow estimation accuracy and the representation power of the proposed StruPyNet. To verify the effectiveness, StruPyNet is trained with intra-pyramid-level and inter-flow-estimator dense connections (*i.e.*, with DC) and without intra-pyramid-level and inter-flow-estimator dense connections (*i.e.*, w/o DC) separately on the FlyingChairs dataset [4]. The results are summarized and compared in Table 6, where it can be observed that StruPyNet with DC gains lower AEPEs on all the training sets than that without DC.

4.3 Analysis of Computational Cost

It is well known that a fully convolutional network can be fed with feature maps of variable resolutions but the output channel numbers of every convolutional layer are fixed during forward propagation. So its computational complexity is proportional to the resolution of input. Actually, the proposed small flow estimator is a fully convolutional network without feature down-sampling and up-sampling. In StruPyNet, the feature pairs which are input into small flow estimators at lower structural pyramid levels have a lower resolution than that at higher structural pyramid levels. Therefore, although lower structural pyramid levels have more cascaded flow estimators than higher structural pyramid levels, the computational complexity of lower structural pyramid levels is less than that of higher structural pyramid levels. This leads to a more efficient distribution of parameters and computations among all the structural pyramid levels and reduces memory footprint during training.

The comparison of model size is shown in Fig. 4, where it can be observed that the proposed StruPyNet is 23.2% smaller than PWC-Net [19] and has around 24 times fewer parameters than FlowNet2 [9]. Furthermore, the run time of the competing models is tested with the same testing configuration: 1024×448 image pairs as input on a Titan-X GPU. The comparison of run time shows that although StruPyNet is 34% larger than LiteFlowNet [8], it runs at about 13 frames per second (fps), which is almost the same as that of LiteFlowNet. This verifies the efficiency of structural pyramid processing. Moreover, the proposed StruPyNet is faster than FlowNet2 [9] which runs at 10 fps.

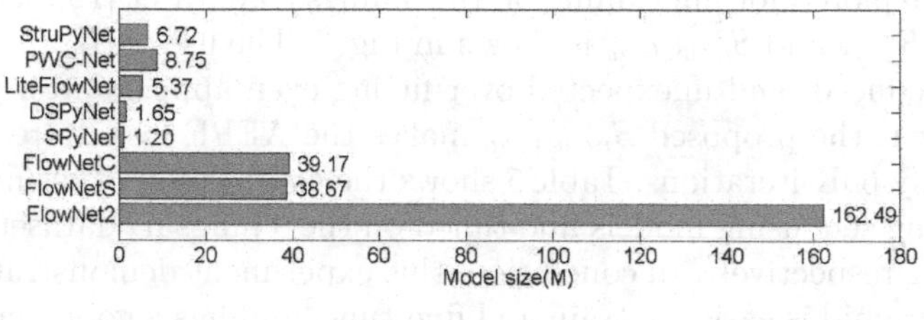

Fig. 4. Comparison of model size.

5 Conclusion

To achieve a better balance of accuracy and computational complexity, StruPyNet is proposed to combine structural pyramid processing with feature pyramid processing. The structural pyramid processing consists of 15 small flow estimators that are cascaded and flexibly deployed at different structural pyramid levels to form the pyramid shape, and achieves an efficient distribution of parameters and computational complexity among all structural pyramid levels. By focusing more on low-resolution feature matching, StruPyNet learns well-performing capability to cope with very large motions and background motions. Additionally, StruPyNet allows more operations of feature warping and cost volume construction by cascading small flow estimators, which eases the difficulty of flow estimation to some extent. The experimental results demonstrate that StruPyNet, whose model size is 95.9% smaller than that of FlowNet2 and 23.2% smaller than that of PWC-Net, achieves better performances than baseline methods in most cases, and StruPyNet runs at 3 more fps than FlowNet2. As a future research perspective, structural pyramid processing is expected to be employed in other dense prediction applications, *e.g.*, semantic segmentation. The code of StruPyNet will be made available to the public.

References

1. Black, M.J., Yacoob, Y., Jepson, A.D., Fleet, D.J.: Learning parameterized models of image motion. In: CVPR, pp. 561–567, June 1997

2. Brox, T., Malik, J.: Large displacement optical flow: descriptor matching in variational motion estimation. IEEE Trans. Pattern Anal. Mach. Intell. **33**(3), 500–513 (2011)
3. Butler, D.J., Wulff, J., Stanley, G.B., Black, M.J.: A naturalistic open source movie for optical flow evaluation. In: Fitzgibbon, A., Lazebnik, S., Perona, P., Sato, Y., Schmid, C. (eds.) ECCV 2012. LNCS, vol. 7577, pp. 611–625. Springer, Heidelberg (2012). https://doi.org/10.1007/978-3-642-33783-3_44
4. Dosovitskiy, A., Fischery, P., Ilg, E., Hausser, P.: FlowNet: learning optical flow with convolutional networks. In: ICCV, pp. 2758–2766, December 2015
5. Geiger, A., Lenz, P., Urtasun, R.: Are we ready for autonomous driving? The KITTI vision benchmark suite. In: CVPR, pp. 3354–3361, June 2012
6. Girshick, R.: Fast R-CNN. In: ICCV, pp. 1440–1448, December 2015
7. Horn, B.K., Schunck, B.G.: Determining optical flow. J. Artif. Intell. **17**(1), 185–203 (1980)
8. Hui, T.W., Tang, X., Chen, C.L.: LiteFlowNet: a lightweight convolutional neural network for optical flow estimation. In: CVPR, pp. 8981–8989, June 2018
9. Ilg, E., Mayer, N., Saikia, T., Keuper, M., Dosovitskiy, A., Brox, T.: FlowNet 2.0: evolution of optical flow estimation with deep networks. In: CVPR, pp. 2462–2470, December 2017
10. Jia, Y., et al.: CAFFE: convolutional architecture for fast feature embedding. In: ACM MM, pp. 675–678, November 2014
11. Lin, G., Milan, A., Shen, C., Reid, I.D.: RefineNet: multi-path refinement networks for high-resolution semantic segmentation. In: CVPR, pp. 5168–5177, June 2017
12. Lu, J., Yang, H., Min, D., Do, M.N.: Patch match filter: efficient edge-aware filtering meets randomized search for fast correspondence field estimation. In: CVPR, pp. 1854–1861, June 2013
13. Mayer, N., et al.: A large dataset to train convolutional networks for disparity, optical flow, and scene flow estimation. In: CVPR, pp. 4040–4048, June 2016
14. Menze, M., Geiger, A.: Object scene flow for autonomous vehicles. In: CVPR, pp. 3061–3070, June 2015
15. Ranjan, A., Black, M.J.: Optical flow estimation using a spatial pyramid network. In: CVPR, pp. 2720–2729, June 2017
16. Revaud, J., Weinzaepfel, P., Harchaoui, Z., Schmid, C.: EpicFlow: edge-preserving interpolation of correspondences for optical flow. In: CVPR, pp. 1164–1172, June 2015
17. Shrivastava, A., Gupta, A., Girshick, R.B.: Training region-based object detectors with online hard example mining. In: CVPR, pp. 761–769, June 2016
18. Sun, D., Roth, S., Lewis, J.P., Black, M.J.: Learning optical flow. In: Forsyth, D., Torr, P., Zisserman, A. (eds.) ECCV 2008. LNCS, vol. 5304, pp. 83–97. Springer, Heidelberg (2008). https://doi.org/10.1007/978-3-540-88690-7_7
19. Sun, D., Yang, X., Liu, M., Kautz, J.: PWC-Net: CNNs for optical flow using pyramid, warping, and cost volume. In: CVPR, pp. 8934–8943, June 2018
20. Sun, Z., Wang, H.: Deeper spatial pyramid network with refined up-sampling for optical flow estimation. In: Hong, R., Cheng, W.-H., Yamasaki, T., Wang, M., Ngo, C.-W. (eds.) PCM 2018. LNCS, vol. 11164, pp. 492–501. Springer, Cham (2018). https://doi.org/10.1007/978-3-030-00776-8_45
21. Weinzaepfel, P., Revaud, J., Harchaoui, Z., Schmid, C.: DeepFlow: large displacement optical flow with deep matching. In: CVPR, pp. 1385–1392, June 2013
22. Wulff, J., Black, M.J.: Efficient sparse-to-dense optical flow estimation using a learned basis and layers. In: CVPR, pp. 120–130, June 2015

Real-Time Multiple Pedestrians Tracking in Multi-camera System

Muchun Chen[1(✉)], Yugang Chen[1], Truong Tan Loc[2], and Bingbing Ni[1]

[1] Shanghai Jiao Tong University, Shanghai, China
{Brunestod,cygashjd,nibingbing}@sjtu.edu.cn
[2] Minivision, Tan Uyen, Vietnam
ttanloc@gmail.com

Abstract. This paper proposes a novel 3D realtime multi-view multi-target tracking framework featured by a global-to-local tracking by detection model and a 3D tracklet-to-tracklet data association scheme. In order to enable the realtime performance, the former maximizes the utilization of temporal differences between consecutive frames, resulting in a great reduction of the average frame-wise detection time. Meanwhile, the latter accurately performs multi-target data association across multiple views to calculate the 3D trajectories of tracked objects. Comprehensive experiments on PETS-09 dataset well demonstrate the outstanding performance of the proposed method in terms of efficiency and accuracy in multi-target 3d trajectory tracking tasks, compared to the state-of-the art methods.

Keywords: Multi-view multi-object tracking · Tracking by detection · Computer vision · Deep learning

1 Introduction

Object tracking is an important topic in the field of computer vision and has various applications such as sport analysis and security. In recent decades, despite the fact that fruitful progresses have been achieved in object tracking, most of them mainly focus on solving tracking tasks in single view settings. In addition, the previous works on multi-view object tracking based on deep learning usually suffer from the heavy computation, which makes it difficult to meet the realtime requirement. In this paper, we present a deep-learning-based multi-view multi-target object tracking framework in combination with a proposed global-to-local tracking by detection approach, which is capable of accelerating the object tracking process, making it possible to track multiple objects across multiple cameras at a realtime performance.

According to [21], there are commonly three main paradigms of multi-view object tracking tasks including track-first, fuse-first and manifold-based. Firstly, manifold-based paradigm performs multi-view object tracking by projecting features on a manifold using Locally Linear Embedding [17] in combination with

Y. M. Ro et al. (Eds.): MMM 2020, LNCS 11961, pp. 468–479, 2020.
https://doi.org/10.1007/978-3-030-37731-1_38

Caratheodory-Fejer (CF) interpolation theory, making it robust against model uncertainty and occlusion. However, this method heavily depends on the foreground segmentation and assumption of a large overlapping field of view across cameras. Moreover, this paradigm does not calibrate the relative spatial positions between cameras, resulting in the impossibility of calculating the accurate 3D positions of tracked targets. Secondly, the fuse-first approach projects detection results from each individual view to a common one, then applies tracking [1–3,6,7,11,12]. Those multi-view tracking methods [2,3,7,11,12] rely on the background subtraction, sparsity and geometric constraints and occlusion reasoning, whose performance degrades in complex environment. Lastly, the track-first methods perform detection and tracking in each individual camera view, then project and associate the results in the common view [13,16,22,23]. Since deep learning based methods [15,20,24] are well-known for outperforming traditional pedestrian detection methods in single image, they are also implemented in multi-view tracking tasks [1,6]. Moreover, the success of deep-learning-based pedestrian detection makes the track-first paradigm popular in multi-view people tracking. Thanks to the advances on deep-learning-based detection networks, detectors have been able to detect people with high precision in the wild. As a result, those accurate single-view detection results greatly boost the effectiveness of multi-view tracking systems. Although deep detection networks have achieved great progress in multi-view tracking system, their inevitably heavy computation makes it impossible for realtime applications.

In a nutshell, this paper makes the followings contributions:

1. Firstly, we propose a global-to-local tracking-by-detection strategy to fully utilize the efficiency of CNNs and reduce the computation consumption, which makes it possible to track people in multi cameras in real time.
2. Secondly, we propose a tracklet-to-tracklet data association pipeline to predict accurate 3D trajectories efficiently.
3. Lastly, we combine all those elements into a realtime multi-view multi-targets detection and tracking system.

Comprehensive experiments well demonstrate the effectiveness and efficiency of the proposed new multi-view tracking system.

2 Related Works

2.1 Deep Learning Based Detection

The trade-off between precision and speed leads to two major categories of Object Detection frameworks including Two-staged network and One-staged one:

1. Two-staged network: R-CNN [8] first proposes CNN-based Object detection method, it sifts thousands promising regions with selective search, then classifies those regions by CNN. Fast R-CNN [9] alleviates the time-consuming shortcoming of R-CNN by classifying the high-dimensional representation of

the region of interest (ROI) in the feature space. Faster R-CNN [20] further proposes the Region Proposal Network (RPN) to reduce the computational burden of selective search.
2. One-staged network: YOLO [19] directly obtains the bounding box from feature space regression, which realizes one-step prediction and significantly speed up the detection pipeline. SSD [15] utilizes multi-scale features to improve prediction accuracy of YOLO. RetinaNet [14] further introduces focal loss, which mitigates the accuracy degradation caused by sample imbalance of one-staged detection.

However, these frameworks must sacrifice speed or detection accuracy, which is contrary to the application scenario of multi-view tracking. Our framework leverages the advantages of both pipelines, using a two-staged model in non-trivial frames to achieve highly accurate results to ensure tracking effectiveness, and a one-stage model for trivial frames to ensure real-time tracking.

2.2 Tracking by Detection

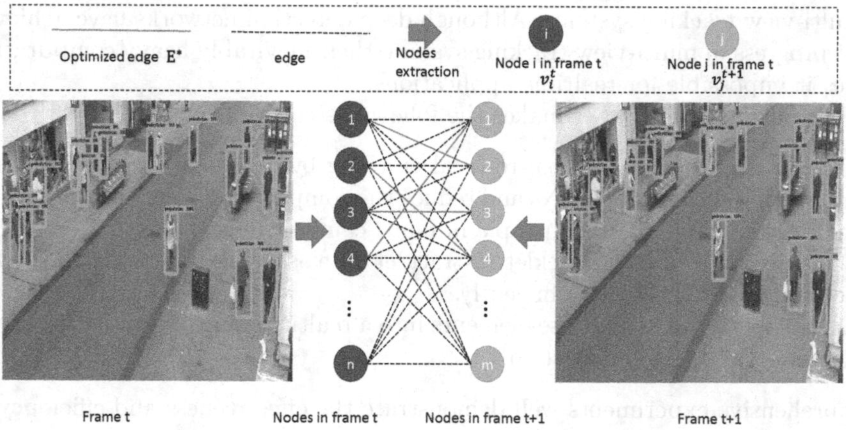

Fig. 1. Tracking by detection can be modeled as a graph maximum matching problem. The optimized edges indicate the tracking result.

Tracking-by-detection is a common approach to track multiple objects. With the ideal assumption of the availability of a high speed and precise detector, tracking is a much simpler problem, which can even be done without using image information [5].

Consequently, tracking by detection can be modeled as a graph maximum matching problem. As shown in Fig. 1, the undirected graph is denoted by $G = (V, E)$. The vertex set V consists of two disjoint sets $V^t = \{v_i^t | i = 1, 2, ..., n\}$ and $V^{t+1} = \{v_i^t | i = 1, 2, ..., m\}$, which represent the detection results in frame t and frame $t+1$ respectively. Each node in the graph represents a detection result, and two nodes connected by an edge represent the same person. The edges between

V^t and V^{t+1} are described by a $n \times m$ adjacency matrix $A_{t,t+1}$, which has the following form

$$A_{t,t+1}(i,j) = \begin{cases} 1 & (v_i^t, v_j^{t+1}) \in E \\ 0 & else. \end{cases} \tag{1}$$

In addition, a $n \times m$ distance matrix $D_{t,t+1}$ is defined to represent the dissimilarity between nodes in V^t and V^{t+1}. The dissimilarity can be measured by Euclidean distance, bounding box IOU and distance in image feature space.

Then a global optimization objective L is denoted by the following form

$$L = \underset{E}{\arg\min} \quad A^{\mathrm{T}} D. \tag{2}$$

The optimized edges E^* indicate the tracking result.

3 Methodology

3.1 Overall Pipeline

Our pipeline is shown in Figs. 2 and 3. Given synchronized video streams as the input to our system, we split each stream into chunks, each of which has equal time intervals containing N frames. The first frame of each chunk is the non-trivial keyframe on which we perform the global detection, while the rest are trivial frames on which we perform the motion prediction and local detection. Next, the tracklets, which are the tracking results of chunks on each individual view, are stored in the Tracking Pool. Each view has an individual Tracking Pool. Then, each tracklet is mapped to a common global view via a Homography Transformation, on which the data association between tracklets is performed. Finally, the associated results are back-projected back to each view in order to refine the corresponding Tracking Pool.

3.2 Global-to-Local Tracking by Detection

Let C_i be the i-th camera in the multiple camera system. Given a video stream from the camera C_i, we denote frames as $[f_0, f_1, f_2, \cdots f_n, \cdots]$. The video stream is split into equal-time-interval chunks, each of which contains N frame. Next, the detection is conducted on every first frame, so-called keyframe, of each chunk, resulting in global detecting results of $[f_0, f_N, f_{2*N} \cdots]$. Each detected person is associated with a unique tracklet, which is a collection of tracking results in a chunk. All tracklets are stored and managed in a "Tracklet Pool" denoted as TP_i corresponding to i-th camera. In addition, it is worth to mention that the detecting results are not perfectly accurate. Saying that, there might be some false positives, false negatives and occlusions happening in each particular view. However, by combining 2D and 3D information, our proposed algorithm is capable of addressing these issues. In each chunk, our tracking pipeline in 2D views can be summarized as follows:

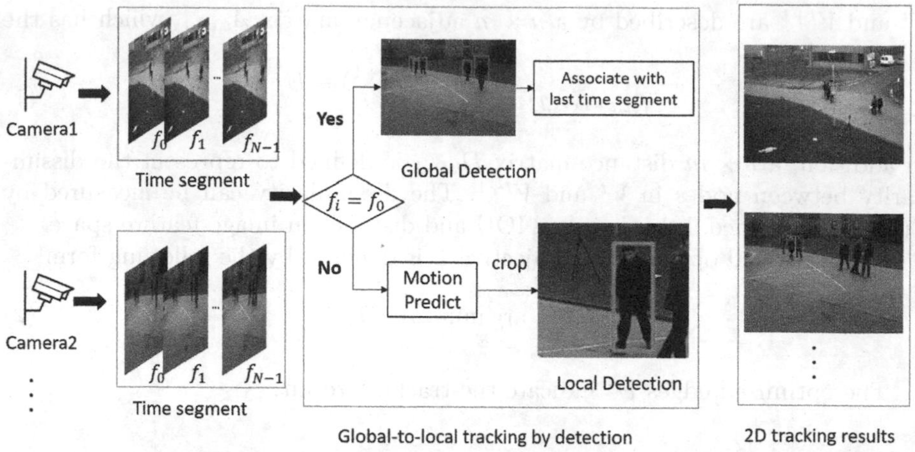

Fig. 2. The pipeline of global-to-local tracking by detection. We split each video stream into chunks. The first frame of each chunk is the non-trivial keyframe on which we perform the global detection, while the rest are trivial frames on which we perform the motion prediction and local detection.

1. We firstly apply a global pedestrian detector to the keyframe f_0 to get the detection results $\{p_0, p_1, \ldots, p_i, \ldots\}$, where p_i is the i-th detected people. Denoting the tracking results in Tracking Pool TP of the previous chunk as $\{t_0, t_1, \ldots, t_i, \ldots\}$, we associate $\{p_0, p_1, \ldots, p_i, \ldots\}$ and $\{t_0, t_1, \ldots, t_i, \ldots\}$ by the simple Hungarian Algorithm [18]. Next, we create a tracklet tp_i for each p_i and assign it a track ID according to the associated results. If a p_i has no association result, we assign "new" to it. Noted that the associated tracklets contain the history information of trajectories of all previous chunks.
2. As for the rest of other frames in the chunk, we employ a Kalman filter and a LSTM model to predict the next position of each tp_i in current frame based on its history stored in TP. Then, we take the mean of the two predictions as the final predicted position. According to the predicted position, we crop a region of interest (ROI) from the current frame. The size of the ROI is determined by the size of last tracked bounding box. Next, we apply a local detector on the cropped ROI to retrieve the refined postion of the object. Since the size of ROI is much smaller than the whole frame and the scale of p_i relatively remains the same as the previous result, the detecting speed is extremely fast. We set the local detection threshold to 0.8. If the local detector fails to detect people in the ROI, the tracking result will be the predicting center and the size of the last bounding box. If there are more than 1 results whose score higher than the threshold, we choose the one whose center is closest to the predicting one.
3. Finally, we map all TP to the global 3D view, and we use tracklet-to-tracklet association to link all mapped tracklets. Then, a back-projection will be performed to map 3D trackets back to each 2D view in order to update the Tracking Pool of each view.

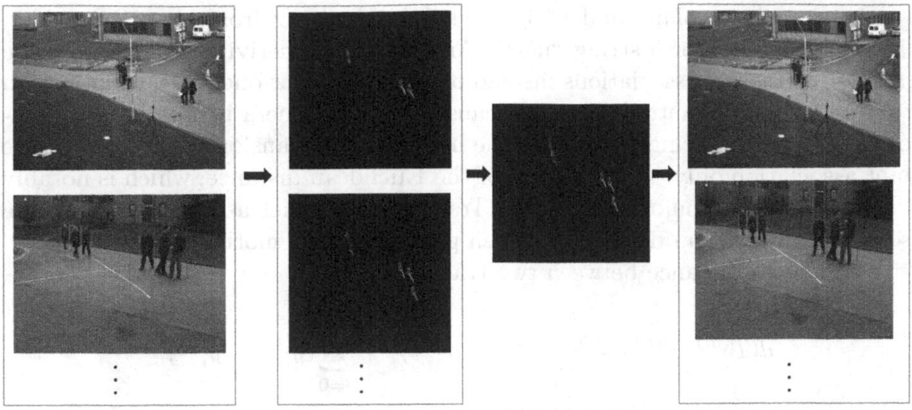

Fig. 3. Each Tracklet is mapped to a common global view, on which the data association between tracklets is performed via a Homography Transformation. Finally, the associated results are back-projected back to each view in order to refine the corresponding Tracking Pool.

3.3 Data Association in Common View

Homography Transformation. In order to associate the data from multiple views, the calibration information must be available. Intrinsic and extrinsic parameters of each camera are estimated using a pattern plane. Those parameters will be used to map information from one view to another.

Our system exploits homography transformation to implement data association in the common view. Considering c synchronized cameras, we denote the image taken by each camera in frame t by $I_1^t, I_2^t, ..., I_c^t$. Let π^h represent the plane in the common view which is parallel to the image floor at height h. Homographies of camera i at height h is denoted as H_i^h, which projects points in the camera views to their corresponding locations in the top view of the ground plane at height h by following form

$$q = H_i^h p \;\; \forall p \in I_i, \tag{3}$$

where p is a pixel in camera frame and q is its projected location.

Tracklets Distance. Inheriting from global-to-local tracking by detection single view tracking results, the data from each camera is constructed as tracklets. Our data association in the common view makes use of independent 2D tracking results in each view, and constructs trajectories in the common view through tracklet-to-tracklet associations. We denote tracklets transformed into the common view as Eq. 3 from ith camera by $\mathcal{T}^i = \{T_1^i, T_2^i, ..., T_{N_i}^i\}$ and currently maintained 3D trajectories by $\mathcal{T}^0 = \{T_1^0, T_2^0, ..., T_{N_0}^0\}$. Every tracklet $T = (x, y, h, id)$.

h is height of the plane and id is track ID inheriting from the 2D tracklet, which is an integer or a string "new". An addition underlying benefit from the tracklet-to-tracklet associations instead of point-to-point ones is the elimination of redundant 3D phantom points. Because the real camera is not a perfect pin-hole model, which brings noise into the homography transformation. The single point association only takes advance of the Euclidean distance, which is notably influenced by the homography noise. Tracklet-to-tracklet association can make use of both Euclidean distance between points and the motion information.

We define a distance between two tracklets

$$\begin{aligned} d(T^{(m)}, T^{(n)}) = &\sum_{i=0}^{K} (x_i^{(m)} - x_i^{(n)})^2 + \sum_{i=0}^{K} (y_i^{(m)} - y_i^{(n)})^2 \\ &+ \sum_{i=0}^{K-1} (x_{i+1}^{(m)} - x_i^{(m)} - x_{i+1}^{(n)} + x_i^{(n)})^2 \\ &+ \sum_{i=0}^{K-1} (y_{i+1}^{(m)} - y_i^{(m)} - y_{i+1}^{(n)} + y_i^{(n)})^2, \end{aligned} \tag{4}$$

which consists of the Euclidean distance and the first derivative of Euclidean distance. Because using homography transformation all points have the same height in the common view, the z axis is not taken into consideration.

Multi-view Tracklets Association. After defining a distance, we then use an approximate global method to link the tracklets in each view. In this paper, we do not focus on finding the optimal method. In contrast, we use a sub-optimal but fast and straightforward to be implemented association method which is sufficient in this task. The optimal association needs to find a global optimized path to link tracklets in each view, while the approximate method chooses a key view by uniformly random sampling in every time step, and we link other views to this key view. The detail of this approximate method is described in Algorithm 1.

Refinement via Back-Projection. Occlusion cases occur frequently in single view detection and tracking. Once the target is obscured by a obstruction, detector usually fail to recall this target. In addition, a single camera can not capture the whole view of the scene. Some objects may go out of the image boundary, although those objects are still in the scene. In order to solve this problem, we propose a back-projection process to map the associated 3D information back to each 2D image. Similar to the Eq. 3, back-projection process uses the inverse homography transformation in the form

$$p = (H_i^h)^{-1} q \quad \forall q \in \pi^h. \tag{5}$$

Algorithm 1. Tracklets association across views

input :
Currently maintained 3D trajectories $\mathcal{T}^0 = \{T_1^0, T_2^0, ..., T_{N_0}^0\}$;
Tracklets $\mathcal{T}^i = \{T_1^i, T_2^i, ..., T_{N_i}^i\}$ in multiple views;
Output:
Updated 3D trajectories $\mathcal{T}^* = \{T_1^*, T_2^*, ..., T_{N_*}^*\}$;

initialize the key tracklet set $\mathcal{T}^k$ using uniform random sampling;
for *each view* $i = 1, 2, ..., C$ *and* $i \neq k$ **do**
    calculate the optimal assignment from $\mathcal{T}^k$ to $\mathcal{T}^i$ using Hungary Algorithm
    updat each (x, y) position for assigned tracklets in $\mathcal{T}^k$ using moving average
    add unassigned tracklets in $\mathcal{T}^i$ into $\mathcal{T}^k$
end
for *each tracklet* T_i^k $i = 1, 2, ..., N_k$ *in* $\mathcal{T}^k$ **do**
    assign the *id* of T_i^k by voting from linked tracklets
end
for *each trajectory* T_i^0 $i = 1, 2, ..., N_0$ *in* $\mathcal{T}^0$ **do**
    find the tracking ID *id* in $\mathcal{T}^k$
    if *found* T_j^k **then**
        update T_i^0 using T_j^k
    end
    else
        kill T_i^0
    end
end
add tracklets whose id is "new" in $\mathcal{T}^k$ into $\mathcal{T}^0$ and assign a new integer as tracking ID for each of them
$\mathcal{T}^* \leftarrow \mathcal{T}^0$

After conducting the tracklet-totracklet association, we get the associated 3D trajectories $\mathcal{T}^*$. We only back-project the tracklets denoted by $\mathcal{T} = \{T_i \;\; i = 1, 2, ..., N\}$ back to the Tracking Pool of each view in last time step. The detail is described in Algorithm 2.

4 Experiments

4.1 Dataset

There are not many suitable multi-view multi-target pedestrian tracking datasets publicly available. To demonstrate the effectiveness of our proposed method, we performed a comprehensive experiment on the famous PETS-S2L2 dataset. Our training set includes three video sequences PETS09-S2L1, TUD-Stadtmitte and AVG-TownCentre, with a total of 1424 frames and 12780 annotated bounding boxes. Those training data are used to train our global and local detectors. Our test set is the more complex PETS09-S2L2, which has 436 frames and a total of 9641 annotated bounding boxes. In particular, the PETS09 has 8 cameras,

Algorithm 2. Tracklets back-projection

input :
  Associated 3D trajectories $\mathcal{T}^* = \{T_1^*, T_2^*, ..., T_{N_*}^*\}$;
  Tracking Pool of each view $\{\mathcal{TP}^1, \mathcal{TP}^2, ..., \mathcal{TP}^C\}$

Output:
  Updated Tracking Pool of each view $\{\mathcal{TP}^1, \mathcal{TP}^2, ..., \mathcal{TP}^C\}$;

initialize the updated tracklets $\mathcal{T} = \{T_i \;\; i = 1, 2, ..., N\}$ from $\mathcal{T}^*$;
for *each view* $i = 1, 2, ..., C$ **do**
  for *tracklet* T *in* $\mathcal{T}$ **do**
    back-project T into t^i
    if T *in view* i **then**
      update corresponding position and track ID of 2D tracklet t in view i
    end
    else
      add t^i into $\mathcal{TP}^i$
    end
  end
end

and the PETS09-S2L2 uses 1, 2, 3 and 4 cameras. Only annotations of the first frame are available. Calibration parameters are available for all cameras.

We use the CLEAR MOT metrics [4] to evaluate the performance of our methods. This benchmark evaluates trackers comprehensively by several metrics, such as multiple object tracking precision (MOTA), multiple object tracking precision (MOTP), false positives (FP), false negatives(FN), identity switches (ID Sw.), mostly tracked targets (MT), mostly lost targets (ML), fragments (Frag.) and the FPS indicator Hz.

4.2 Implementation Detail

The entire system is implemented in C++. The global detector is faster-RCNN whose backbone is Resnet-50. The local detector is Single Shot Detector (SSD) whose backbone is Mobilenet-V1. The global and local detectors are implemented in tensorflow C++ API. As for the global detector, the training data is frames in the training set. It uses 5 scales $(0.25, 0.5, 1.0, 2.0)$ and 3 aspect ratios $(0.5, 1.0, 2.0)$. The height stride and width stride are set to 16. It is finetuned from a pre-trained model which is trained on COCO dataset. The number of class is set to 1, because we only want to detect pedestrians. Since the model is not trained from scratch, the initial learning rate is set to 0.0003. The number of steps in the whole training process is 100000, and the learning rate decrease to 0.00003 in 50000 steps. For the local detector, the training data is cropped from frames in the training set. If the size of target's bounding box is denoted as (w, h), we crop the frame with size $A \times A$ which is defined as $(w + p) \times (h + p) = A^2$, where $p = \frac{w+h}{2}$. In addition, in order to eliminate the center bias, we auggment the training data by performing a random translation within 30 pixels and a random resize which varies from 0.85 to 1.15. Then the cropped image is resized to 128×128. The aspect ratios is set to $(0.33, 0.5, 1, 2, 3)$. The model is also fine-tuned from a pre-trained model which is trained on COCO dataset. The learning rate decays from 0.005 to 0.000005 during 500000 steps.

4.3 Performance

Table 1. Performance on PETS-09. It can be seen that our system has the best speed performance and can almost meet the real-time requirement.

Tracker	Tracking mode	MOTA (%)	MOTP (%)	MT (%)	ML (%)	FP	FN	ID.SW	Frag	Hz1	Hz2
Ours	Online	45.1	55.3	17.2	8.1	913	4112	267	266	-	19,0
DBN	Online	57.6	63.6	28.6	4.8	805	3,049	231	245	0.1	<0.1
MOANA	Online	57.6	57.0	40.5	7.1	1,453	2,531	107	386	19.6	6.2
GPDBN	Online	55.5	65.5	21.4	4.8	638	3,480	174	202	0.1	<0.1
MCFPHD	Offline	50.3	55.8	19.0	9.5	869	3,761	158	258	17.7	6.0
SVT	Offline	47.2	56.6	11.9	4.8	1,140	3,710	245	292	1.9	1.6
LP3D	Offline	45.4	54.1	16.7	7.1	1,407	3,593	268	296	83.5	8.2
GustavHX	Online	42.6	58.2	14.3	4.8	1,399	3,980	155	202	0.0	0.0
LPSFM	Offline	41.3	55.7	7.1	16.7	640	4,776	243	271	8.4	4.4
AMIR3D	Online	32.2	56.2	2.4	4.8	913	4,729	891	1,018	1.2	1.1
KalmanSFM	Online	32.2	55.1	4.8	2.4	1,549	4,091	893	889	30.6	7.0

The performance is shown in Table 1. It is worth noting that the time-performance test of other trackers excludes the time consumption of the detectors, and it is denoted by Hz1. We measure the time consumption of all modules for our method including detectors, and it is denoted by Hz2. We add the mean time consumption of faster-RCNN with Resnet-50 [10] backbone to estimate the Hz2 of other trackers. It can be seen that our system can almost meet the real-time requirement. To achieve this performance, we set the interval of time segment $N = 10$ and we use a platform equipped by 4 GTX1080Ti. The global detector runs at about 110ms per frame. For the local one, we reduce the depth of the backbone to 75% and process the input images, which are resized into 128×128, in batch. Because of those the processes, we reduce the time consumption of the local detector to about 2ms per frame.

Because of the limited power of local detectors, the false negative (FN) is much higher than the most powerful multi-view multi-object trackers. We get a comparable false positive (FP) due to using a powerful global detector. In addition, it is proven that the suboptimal association method in 3D view does not cause an increasement of ID switch. In another word, we almost meet the realtime requirement and the accuracy does not decay too much. Our method gets a balance between efficiency and accuracy.

5 Conclusion

In this paper, we balance the efficiency and accuracy of multi-view multi-object 3d tracking and propose a novel real-time multi-view multi-object 3d tracking framework. Two novel modules are designed to enable realtime as well as accurate performance, which are global-to-local tracking detection module and tracklet-to-tracklet 3D tracking association. Our method gets appealing results on PETS-09 dataset.

Acknowledgment. This work was supported by National Natural Science Foundation of China (61976137, U1611461), 111 Project (B07022 and Sheitc No. 150633) and the Shanghai Key Laboratory of Digital Media Processing and Transmissions. This work was also supported by SJTU-BIGO Joint Research Fund, and CCF-Tencent Open Fund.

References

1. Baqué, P., Fleuret, F., Fua, P.: Deep occlusion reasoning for multi-camera multi-target detection. CoRR abs/1704.05775 (2017). http://arxiv.org/abs/1704.05775
2. Berclaz, J., Fleuret, F., Fua, P.: Multiple object tracking using flow linear programming. In: 2009 Twelfth IEEE International Workshop on Performance Evaluation of Tracking and Surveillance, pp. 1–8, December 2009. https://doi.org/10.1109/PETS-WINTER.2009.5399488
3. Berclaz, J., Fleuret, F., Turetken, E., Fua, P.: Multiple object tracking using k-shortest paths optimization. IEEE Trans. Pattern Anal. Mach. Intell. **33**(9), 1806–1819 (2011)
4. Bernardin, K., Stiefelhagen, R.: Evaluating multiple object tracking performance: the clear mot metrics. Eurasip J. Image Video Process. **2008**(1), 246309 (2008)
5. Bochinski, E., Eiselein, V., Sikora, T.: High-speed tracking-by-detection without using image information. In: 2017 14th IEEE International Conference on Advanced Video and Signal Based Surveillance (AVSS), pp. 1–6, August 2017. https://doi.org/10.1109/AVSS.2017.8078516
6. Chavdarova, T., Fleuret, F.: Deep multi-camera people detection. CoRR abs/1702.04593 (2017). http://arxiv.org/abs/1702.04593
7. Fleuret, F., Berclaz, J., Lengagne, R., Fua, P.: Multicamera people tracking with a probabilistic occupancy map. IEEE Trans. Pattern Anal. Mach. Intell. **30**(2), 267–282 (2008). https://doi.org/10.1109/TPAMI.2007.1174
8. Girshick, R., Donahue, J., Darrell, T., Malik, J.: Rich feature hierarchies for accurate object detection and semantic segmentation. In: IEEE Conference on Computer Vision and Pattern Recognition (2014)
9. Girshick, R.B.: Fast R-CNN. CoRR abs/1504.08083 (2015). http://arxiv.org/abs/1504.08083
10. He, K., Zhang, X., Ren, S., Sun, J.: Deep residual learning for image recognition. CoRR abs/1512.03385 (2015). http://arxiv.org/abs/1512.03385
11. Khan, S., Shah, M.: Tracking multiple occluding people by localizing on multiple scene planes. IEEE Trans. Pattern Anal. Mach. Intell. **31**, 505–19 (2009). https://doi.org/10.1109/TPAMI.2008.102

12. Kim, K., Davis, L.S.: Multi-camera tracking and segmentation of occluded people on ground plane using search-guided particle filtering. In: Leonardis, A., Bischof, H., Pinz, A. (eds.) ECCV 2006. LNCS, vol. 3953, pp. 98–109. Springer, Heidelberg (2006). https://doi.org/10.1007/11744078_8
13. Leal-Taixe, L.: Branch-and-price global optimization for multi-view multi-target tracking. In: IEEE Conference on Computer Vision and Pattern Recognition (2012)
14. Lin, T.Y., Goyal, P., Girshick, R., He, K., Dollar, P.: Focal loss for dense object detection. In: The IEEE International Conference on Computer Vision (ICCV), October 2017
15. Liu, W., et al.: SSD: single shot multibox detector. CoRR abs/1512.02325 (2015). http://arxiv.org/abs/1512.02325
16. Liu, W., Camps, O.I., Sznaier, M.: Multi-camera multi-object tracking. CoRR abs/1709.07065 (2017). http://arxiv.org/abs/1709.07065
17. Morariu, V.I., Camps, O.I.: Modeling correspondences for multi-camera tracking using nonlinear manifold learning and target dynamics. In: Proceedings of the 2006 IEEE Computer Society Conference on Computer Vision and Pattern Recognition, CVPR 2006, vol. 1, pp. 545–552. IEEE Computer Society, Washington (2006). https://doi.org/10.1109/CVPR.2006.189
18. Munkres, J.: Algorithms for the assignment and transportation problems. J. Soc. Ind. Appl. Math. **5**(1), 32–38 (1957)
19. Redmon, J., Divvala, S., Girshick, R., Farhadi, A.: You only look once: unified, real-time object detection. In: The IEEE Conference on Computer Vision and Pattern Recognition (CVPR), June 2016
20. Ren, S., He, K., Girshick, R.B., Sun, J.: Faster R-CNN: towards real-time object detection with region proposal networks. CoRR abs/1506.01497 (2015). http://arxiv.org/abs/1506.01497
21. Taj, M., Cavallaro, A.: Multi-view multi-object detection and tracking. In: Cipolla, R., Battiato, S., Farinella, G.M. (eds.) Computer Vision. SCI, vol. 285, pp. 263–280. Springer, Heidelberg (2010). https://doi.org/10.1007/978-3-642-12848-6_10
22. Wen, L., Lei, Z., Chang, M.C., Qi, H., Lyu, S.: Multi-camera multi-target tracking with space-time-view hyper-graph. Int. J. Comput. Vis. **122**(2), 313–333 (2017)
23. Xu, Y., Liu, X., Yang, L., Zhu, S.C.: Multi-view people tracking via hierarchical trajectory composition. In: Computer Vision and Pattern Recognition (2016)
24. Zhang, S., Benenson, R., Omran, M., Hosang, J., Schiele, B.: How far are we from solving pedestrian detection? (2016)

Learning Multi-feature Based Spatially Regularized and Scale Adaptive Correlation Filters for Visual Tracking

Ying She[1(✉)] and Yang Yi[1,2,3]

[1] School of Data and Computer Science, Sun Yat-sen University, Guangzhou, China
shey@mail2.sysu.edu.cn,issyy@mail.sysu.edu.cn
[2] School of Information Science, Xinhua College of Sun Yat-sen University, Guangzhou, China
[3] Guangdong Province Key Laboratory of Big Data Analysis and Processing, Guangzhou, China

Abstract. Visual object tracking is a challenging problem in computer vision. Although the correlation filter-based trackers have achieved competitive results both on accuracy and robustness in recent years, there is still a need to improve the overall tracking performance. In this paper, to tackle the problems caused by Spatially Regularized Discriminative Correlation Filter (SRDCF), we suggest a single-sample-integrated training scheme which utilizes information of the previous frames and the current frame to improve the robustness of training samples. Moreover, manually designed features and deep convolutional features are integrated together to further boost the overall tracking capacity. To optimize the translation filter, we develop an alternating direction method of multipliers (ADMM) algorithm. Besides, we introduce a scale adaptively filter to directly learn the appearance changes induced by variations in the target scale. Extensive empirical evaluations on the TB-50, TB-100 and OTB-2013 datasets demonstrate that the proposed tracker is very promising for various challenging scenarios.

Keywords: Visual object tracking · Single-sample-integrated training · Multi-feature fusion · Scale adaptive · Calculation optimization

1 Introduction

Visual object tracking is a fundamental problem in computer vision with various practical applications in areas such as video surveillance, human-machine interaction, biomedical image analysis and modern military. In generic visual tracking, the task is to predict the motion trajectory of the target according to

Supported by National Natural Science Foundation of China (No. 61672546 and No. 61573385), and Guangzhou Science and Technology Project (No. 201707010127).

Y. M. Ro et al. (Eds.): MMM 2020, LNCS 11961, pp. 480–491, 2020.
https://doi.org/10.1007/978-3-030-37731-1_39

the given initial location of it. This problem is challenging because of several factors, such as motion blur, fast motion, low resolution, out of view, in-plane rotation, illumination variation, scale variation and out-of-plane rotation.

Recently, Discriminative Correlation Filters (DCFs) have received considerable attention in visual tracking. Benefited from that the DCFs can be trained efficiently in the frequency domain via Fast Fourier Transform (FFT), the tracking speed of the DCFs are competitive. However, SRDCF [6] formulates its model on multiple images which breaks the structure of the circulant matrix, thus leading to a computational burden. What's more, SRDCF only exploits manually designed features such as grayscale intensity, Histogram of Oriented Gradients (HOG) [5,16] and Color Name (CN) [17] for target model construction. When encountered with a more challenging scene, the tracker drifts easily. Moreover, SRDCF applies the iterative Gauss-Seidel method to solve the model, which still remains high computational complexity. Besides, SRDCF adopts an exhaustive scale search, which is time-consuming and struggles when encountered with large scale variations.

In this paper, our model Multi-feature based Spatially Regularized and Scale Adaptive Correlation Filters (MSRSA-DCF) copes with the above problems in four aspects. Firstly, we propose a single-sample-integrated training scheme to learn the translation filter. Secondly, we exploit both manually designed features and deep features to train a more discriminative filter. Thirdly, an ADMM method is developed for solving the translation filter. Finally, a scale adaptive filter [7] is introduced for accurate scale estimation.

The rest of this paper is organized as follows. Section 2 briefly outlines some relevant prior work in visual object tracking. Section 3 describes our model MSRSA-DCF in detailed. Section 4 evaluates it on three benchmarks and shows that MSRSA-DCF achieves favorable performance. Section 5 concludes the paper.

2 Related Work

In this section, our recent work on visual object tracking are firstly introduced. Besides, we also describe the motivation to propose our MSRSA-DCF.

In 2018, a hierarchical framework [20] which consists of three appearance models including local-histogram-based model, weighted alignment pooling model and sparsity-based discriminative model was proposed. In 2019 [21], we proposed an appearance model based on a correlation filter with deep CNN features and a dynamic model using improved pyramid optical flow method. In the detection phase, a cascade classifier and P-N learning scheme are employed to tackle the challenge of model drift.

Recently, Correlation filter-based trackers have achieved excellent performance, showing great robustness to challenging situations and operating at real-time. Bolme et al. [2] proposed the Minimum Output Sum of Squared Error (MOSSE) filter, which runs in hundreds of frames per second. Henriques et al. [9] introduced kernel methods and employed ridge regression to train filters. Subsequently, Henriques et al. [10] formulated the Kernelized Correlation Filer (KCF) via kernel trick and incorporated multi-channel features in a Fourier domain. To suppress unwanted boundary effects, Danelljan et al. [6] introduced a spatial regularization term in the learning to penalize the filter coefficients depending on their spatial location. However, SRDCF brings about a heavy computational burden in the following two parts. Firstly, several historical samples incorporated breaks the circulant matrix structure. Secondly, Gauss-Seidel method still needs to solve a large amount of system of linear equations although using the property of sparse matrix. Therefore, in this paper, we train the translation filter with an integrated sample and introduce an ADMM algorithm to solve it efficiently.

What's more, all trackers described above employ an exhaustive scale search to estimate the target size, which is computational expensive. Danelljan et al. [8] proposed to learn correlation filters based on a scale pyramid representation, which can be incorporated into any tracking method. Based on the above work, Danelljan et al [7] extended the Discriminative Scale Space Tracker (DSST) [8] by investigating strategies to achieve a light computation. Therefore, in this paper, we introduce the scale adaptive filter fDSST [7] to directly learn the appearance changes induced by variations in the target scale.

Traditional correlation filters are usually trained with manually designed features which have higher resolution. Recently using convolutional neural networks has gained popularity in visual tracking, due to its robust feature representation of images. Recent results [4,13] show that features extracted from convolutional layer activations encode more semantic information, thus learning a more discriminative model. Therefore, in this paper, we integrate deep convolutional features for target model construction.

3 Our Approach (MSRSA-DCF)

In this section, the architecture of our MSRSA-DCF is firstly described. Then we illustrate our contributions based on SRDCF in four aspects. Section 3.2 presents our multi-feature fusion scheme. Section 3.3 presents the single-sample-integrated training scheme. Section 3.4 describes how we optimize the translation filter and Sect. 3.5 displays the introduced scale filter.

3.1 Overview

As Fig. 1 shown, an overview of the MSRSA-DCF architecture is given to describe the proposed tracking algorithm. During visual tracking, we firstly extract features of the first frame to initialize a translation filter and a scale adaptive filter. In the subsequent frames, based on the single-sample-integrated training scheme, the specific region is cropped in the current frame according to the target location and scale predicted by the previous frame. Then we integrate features from previous frames with the current one to improve the robustness of training samples. Both manually designed features and deep convolutional features are extracted to train a more discriminative filter. Thirdly, we apply the translation filter for location estimation, which is achieved by minimizing

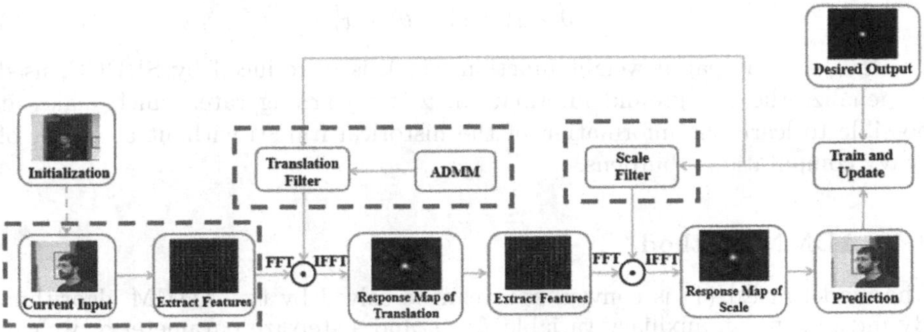

Fig. 1. Overview of the MSRSA-DCF architecture. The leftmost red box indicates that we extract both manually designed features and deep features to train the filter with a single-sample-integrated scheme. The middle one shows that we employ the ADMM method to solve the translation filter. The rightmost one demonstrates that we introduce a scale adaptively filter. (Color figure online)

the $L^2-error$ of the correlation response compared to the desired output. Especially, an ADMM method is used to solve the filter efficiently. After that, we perform the similar procedure for scale estimation. Finally, we update filters iteratively with predicted target states.

3.2 Multi-feature Fusion Scheme

In the training phase, with the given target location in frame number t, our aim is to learn a multi-channel convolution filter f from a sample which integrates current frame information with the previous one. When extracting features, we employ manually designed features including grayscale intensity, HOG and CN. Besides, we take the activation of the third convolutional layer from imagenet-vgg-2048 network [3] as the convolutional feature. The network is trained on the ImageNet dataset to cope with image classification. When extracting deep features, the sample should be resized to 224 × 224 to fit the input size of the network. Then we exploit both manually designed features and deep convolutional features for target model construction.

3.3 Single-Sample-Integrated Training Scheme

We assume that the sample of the $(t) - th$ frame is x_t and the sample of the previous frame is x_{t-1}. All samples have the same spatial size $M \times N$ and consist of a d dimension feature map extracted from an image region. We denote the feature layer $l \in \{1, ..., d\}$ of x_t by x_t^l and the desired output y is a scalar valued function. The filter can be obtained by minimizing the $L^2-error$ between the convolution response of the filter on the sample x_t and the label y,

$$\varepsilon(f) = \arg\min_f \frac{1}{2}\|\sum_{l=1}^{d} x_t^l * f^l - y\|^2 + \frac{1}{2}\sum_{l=1}^{d} \|\omega \cdot f^l\|^2. \quad (1)$$

$$x_t^l = \theta \times x_t^l + (1-\theta) \times x_{t-1}^l. \tag{2}$$

Here, ω is a spatial weight function which is introduced by SRDCF, used to penalize the background information. θ is a learning rate, which makes it possible to learn the information of the historical frames without at a cost of heavy computational burdens.

3.4 ADMM Method

The model in Eq. (1) is convex, so it can be solved by the ADMM algorithm. By introducing an auxiliary variable $f = g$ and a stepsize parameter γ, we can formulate the Eq. (1)'s Augmented Lagrangian form as

$$L(\omega, g, s) = \frac{1}{2}\|\sum_{l=1}^{d} x_t^l * f^l - y\|^2 + \frac{1}{2}\sum_{l=1}^{d}\|\omega \cdot f^l\|^2 + \sum_{l=1}^{d}(f^l - g^l)^T s^l + \frac{\gamma}{2}\sum_{l=1}^{d}\|f^l - g^l\|^2. \tag{3}$$

Here, s is the Lagrange multiplier. We assume that $h = \frac{1}{\gamma}s$, so Eq. (3)'s Augmented Lagrangian form can be transformed as

$$L(\omega, g, h) = \frac{1}{2}\|\sum_{l=1}^{d} x_t^l * f^l - y\|^2 + \frac{1}{2}\sum_{l=1}^{d}\|\omega \cdot f^l\|^2 + \frac{\gamma}{2}\sum_{l=1}^{d}\|f^l - g^l + h^l\|^2. \tag{4}$$

According to the ADMM formulation, the globally optimal solution (Eq. (4)) can be decomposed into the following smaller and easier local sub-problems for solving (Eq. (5)).

$$\begin{cases} f^{i+1} = \arg\min_f \|\sum_{l=1}^{d} x_t^l * f^l - y\|^2 + \gamma\|f - g + h\|^2. \\ g^{i+1} = \arg\min_g \|\sum_{l=1}^{d} \omega \cdot g^l\|^2 + \gamma\|f - g + h\|^2. \\ h^{i+1} = h^i + f^{i+1} - g^{i+1} \end{cases} \tag{5}$$

Specially, by applying Parseval's formula to the first row of Eq. (5), the filter f can be further obtained by minimizing Eq. (6) over the Discrete Fourier Transform (DFT) coefficients $\hat{f}$,

$$\arg\min_{\hat{f}} \|\sum_{l=1}^{d} \hat{x}_t^l \cdot \hat{f}^l - \hat{y}\|^2 + \gamma\|\hat{f} - \hat{g} + \hat{h}\|^2. \tag{6}$$

Then we introduce a vectorization of Eq. (6), where $V_k(f) \in \mathrm{R}^d$ represents the vector whose all d channels have the k-th elements of f. $V_k(\hat{f})$ can be further solved by taking the derivative of Eq. (7), as Eq. (8) shown.

$$\arg\min_{V_k(\hat{f})} \|V_k(\hat{x}_t)^{\mathrm{T}} V_k(\hat{f}) - \hat{y}_k\|^2 + \gamma\|V_k(\hat{f}) - V_k(\hat{g}) + V_k(\hat{h})\|^2. \tag{7}$$

$$V_k(\hat{f}) = \frac{1}{\gamma}(I - \frac{V_k(\hat{x}_t)V_k(\hat{x}_t)^{\mathrm{T}}}{\gamma + V_k(\hat{x}_t)^{\mathrm{T}}V_k(\hat{x}_t)})(V_k(\hat{x}_t)\hat{y_k} + \gamma V_k(\hat{g}) - \gamma V_k(\hat{h})) \quad (8)$$

We can get the filter f by the inverse DFT of $\hat{f}$. In the detection phase, the correlation score corresponding to the test sample $z \in \mathrm{R}^d$ and the filter is computed, as Eq. (9) shown. The estimate of the current target location can be obtained by finding the maximum corresponding score.

$$S_f(z) = \sum_{l=1}^{d} z^l * f^l \quad (9)$$

3.5 Scale Adaptive Filter

Considering that position changes of the target between adjacent frames are more obvious than scale changes, it's difficult to ensure both accurate position prediction and scale estimation by only one filter. We therefore first apply the translation filter at the previous target location and scale. By maximizing the translation correlation scores, we obtain the relative change in location compared to the previous frame.

The scale filter then adopts a nonlinear exponential scaling form to perform scale adaptive changes, that is, the scale filter collects samples using variable patch sizes centered around the new target location. Specially, We assume that all samples have the same spatial size $M \times N$ and the size of the scale filter is s. For each $n \in \{\lfloor -\frac{s-1}{2} \rfloor, \ldots, \lfloor \frac{s-1}{2} \rfloor\}$, we extract sample features of size $a^n M \times a^n N$, where a denotes the scale factor. After that, the scale filter is trained in a similar way as translation filter. By maximizing the scale correlation scores, we finally obtain the relative change in scale compared to the previous frame.

4 Experiments

In this section, we first discuss the implementation details and the related evaluation protocols. Then we verify the effectiveness of our tracking algorithm through extensive experiments on three challenging benchmarks: TB-50 [19], TB-100 [19] and OTB-2013 [18]. The results display that our MSRSA-DCF is competitive with several state-of-the-art trackers: CSK [9], KCF [10], SAMF [12], LCT [14], Staple [1], DCF_CA [15], SAMF_CA [15], STAPLE_CA [15] and SRDCF [6].

4.1 Implementation Details

Our MSRSA-DCF is implemented with MATLAB 2018b and all the experiments are run on a PC equipped with Intel i7-4790 CPU. Following some settings of SRDCF [6], STRCF [11] and fDSST [7], we employ grayscale intensity, HOG and CN with a cell size of 4×4 pixels, while the deep feature with a cell size of 16×16 pixels. We employ the imagnet-vgg-2048 network to extract the deep feature, which is trained on the ImageNet dataset for image classification. The sample learning rate θ is set to 0.012. The extracted features are processed by a Hann window, as described in [2]. As for the scale filter, the standard deviations for the desired correlation output of the translation filter is set to $\frac{1}{16}$ while 1.5 is set to the scale filter. We set the size of the scale filter s to 33 with the scale factor a of 1.02.

4.2 Evaluation Protocols

To test our model effectively, we use one-pass evaluation (OPE), temporal robustness evaluation (TRE) and spatial robustness evaluation (SRE) on TB-50 and TB-100. Experimental results are displayed via success plots and precision plots [18]. The precision plots show the percentage of frames whose predicted location is within a given threshold of the ground truth location. The success plots illustrate the percentage of frames where the overlap ratio between the predicted bounding box and the ground truth is higher than a threshold.

Then we display the attributed-based evaluation on OTB-2013 dataset to demonstrate that our proposed MSRSA-DCF outperforms state-of-the-art methods in various challenging situations. In addition, an ablation study on TB-50, TB-100 and OTB-2013 datasets is performed to further certify our contributions to the overall performance.

4.3 The TB-50 Benchmark

As shown in Fig. 2, we compare the proposed MSRSA-DCF with other state-of-the-art trackers on TB-50 benchmark, which consists of 50 video sequences. We can conclude from Fig. 2 that MSRSA-DCF achieves favorable performance in terms of accuracy and robustness.

4.4 The TB-100 Benchmark

As shown in Fig. 3, we compare the proposed MSRSA-DCF with other state-of-the-art trackers on TB-100 benchmark, which consists of 100 video sequences. We can conclude from Fig. 3 that MSRSA-DCF achieves favorable performance in terms of accuracy and robustness.

4.5 The OTB-2013 Benchmark

On OTB-2013 benchmark, we perform qualitative evaluation and quantitative evaluation based on 8 different challenging factors on 50 video sequences.

Qualitative Evaluation. For presentation clarity, we display tracking results on 5 challenging sequences. As shown as Fig. 4, our MSRSA-DCF can localize the target more precisely through the overall tracking process.

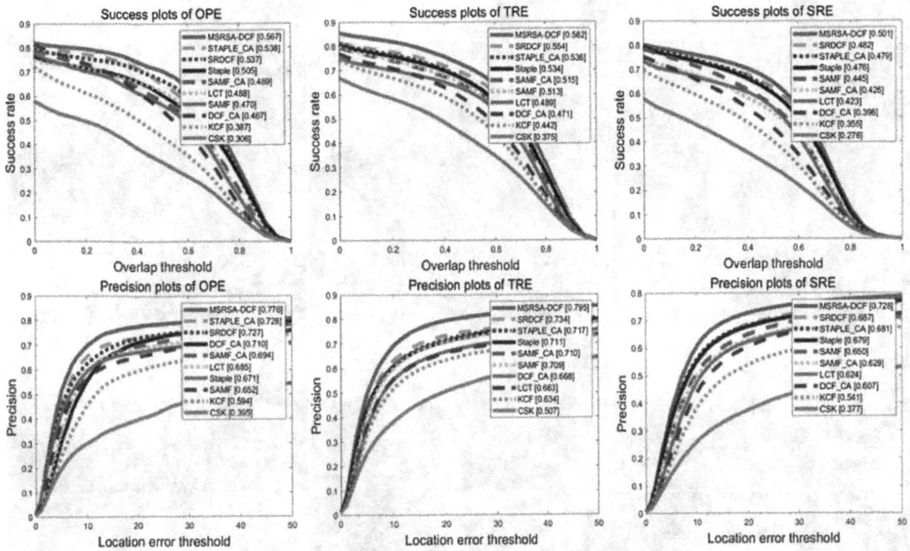

Fig. 2. A comparison of success plots and precision plots with the state-of-the-art trackers on TB-50 benchmark.

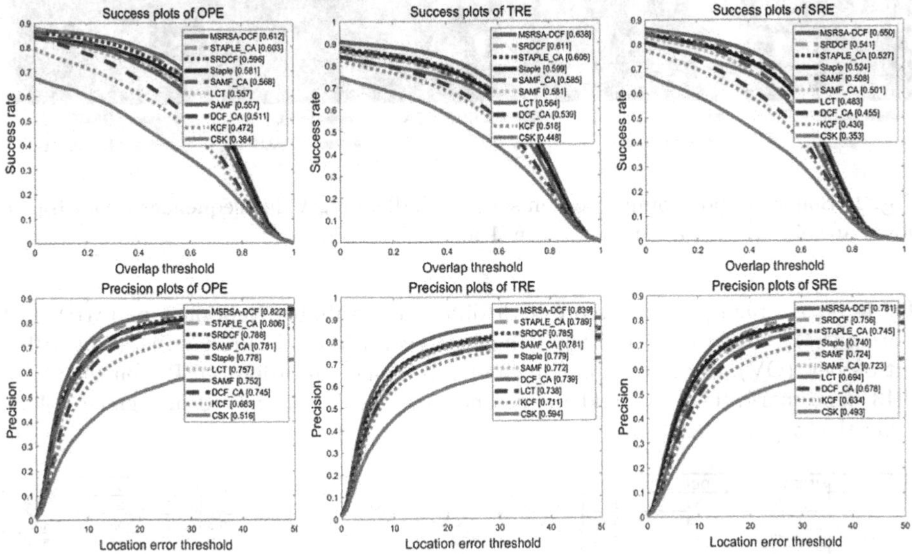

Fig. 3. A comparison of success plots and precision plots with the state-of-the-art trackers on TB-100 benchmark.

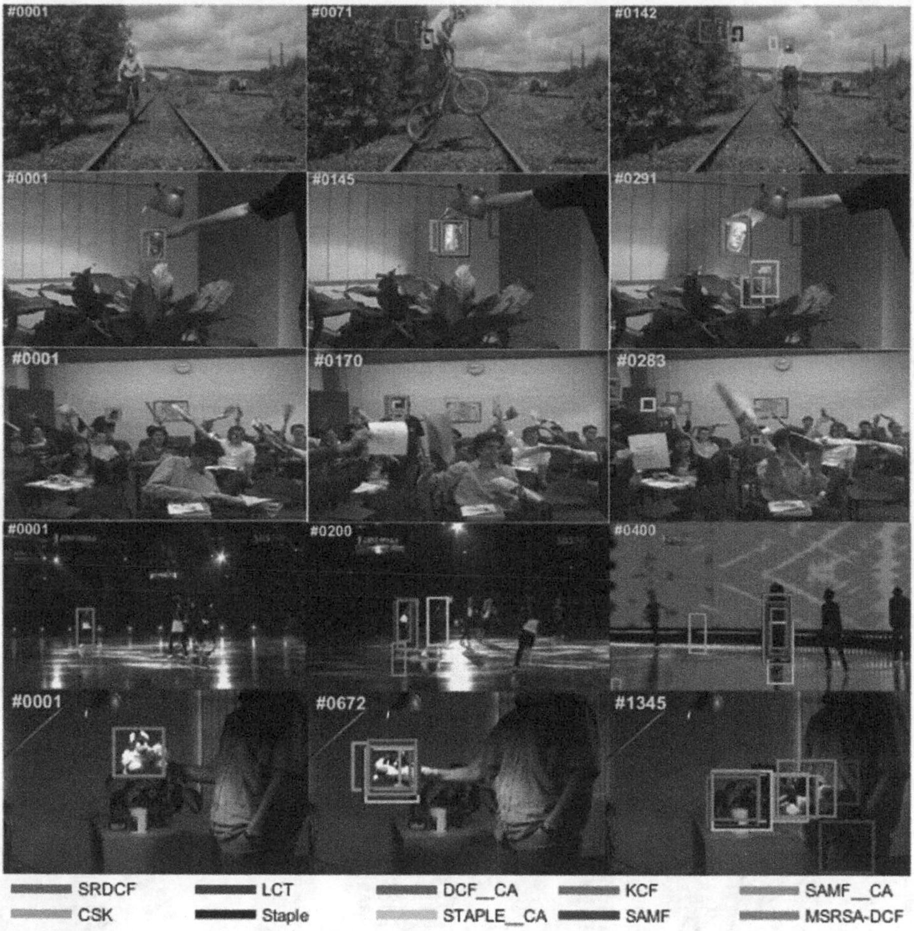

Fig. 4. Bounding box comparison on several challenging video sequences (from top to down are biker, coke, freeman4, skating1 and sylvester).

Table 1. Average precision score with different attributes (motion blur (MB), fast motion (FM), scale variation (SV), illumination variation (IV), in-plane rotation (IPR), out-of-view (OV), low resolution (LR) and out-of-plane rotation (OPR)) on the OTB-2013 benchmark. The best and the second best results are in red and green colors, respectively.

	MSRSA-DCF	SRDCF	STAPLE_CA	SAMF_CA	LCT	DCF_CA	SAMF	Staple	KCF	CSK
MB	0.779	0.750	0.686	0.666	0.624	0.667	0.554	0.628	0.588	0.364
FM	0.725	0.708	0.703	0.646	0.638	0.628	0.607	0.597	0.555	0.400
SV	0.848	0.753	0.761	0.711	0.741	0.701	0.721	0.703	0.645	0.521
IV	0.822	0.717	0.747	0.734	0.766	0.739	0.659	0.699	0.685	0.475
IPR	0.816	0.759	0.816	0.731	0.796	0.779	0.704	0.766	0.717	0.546
OV	0.834	0.620	0.655	0.719	0.716	0.617	0.706	0.618	0.585	0.411
LR	0.663	0.518	0.542	0.547	0.352	0.400	0.525	0.550	0.381	0.411
OPR	0.821	0.798	0.793	0.760	0.841	0.759	0.763	0.752	0.704	0.543

Table 2. Averge success score with different attibutes (motion blur (MB), fast motion (FM), scale variation (SV), illumination variation (IV), in-plane rotation (IPR), out-of-view (OV), low resolution (LR) and out-of-plane rotation (OPR)) on the OTB-2013 benchmark. The best and the second best results are in red and green colors, respectively.

	MSRSA-DCF	SRDCF	STAPLE_CA	SAMF_CA	LCT	DCF_CA	SAMF	Staple	KCF	CSK
MB	0.593	0.570	0.535	0.532	0.500	0.498	0.460	0.505	0.443	0.322
FM	0.565	0.544	0.543	0.509	0.520	0.469	0.485	0.479	0.419	0.329
SV	0.631	0.563	0.551	0.515	0.537	0.444	0.506	0.527	0.395	0.362
IV	0.610	0.549	0.567	0.552	0.565	0.502	0.503	0.535	0.457	0.370
IPR	0.600	0.556	0.594	0.546	0.586	0.547	0.521	0.572	0.496	0.402
OV	0.673	0.497	0.531	0.611	0.599	0.510	0.613	0.512	0.493	0.369
LR	0.523	0.426	0.425	0.421	0.286	0.326	0.388	0.438	0.312	0.286
OPR	0.604	0.585	0.577	0.561	0.615	0.520	0.557	0.556	0.474	0.388

Quantitative Evaluation. To facilitate better analysis on the tracking performance, we further evaluate all the trackers on OTB-2013 benchmark with 8 attributes. Tables 1 and 2 demonstrate that our proposed MSRSA-DCF can well handle a variety of challenging factors and outperform state-of-the-art methods in almost all the challengings.

4.6 Ablation Study on Three Benchmarks

To further investigate the effectiveness of each component we proposed, we report the performation of different variants of MSRSA-DCF in Table 3 on OTB-2013, TB50 and TB100 benchmarks, where MSRSA-DCF(-CNN) represents the tracker trained without deep convolutional features; MSRSA-DCF(-scale_filter) represents the tracker adopting exhaustive scale search rather than a scale adaptive filter; MSRSA-DCF(-sample_integrated) represents the tracker trained without adopting the single-sample-integrated scheme; MSRSA-DCF(-ADMM) represents the tracker solved without ADMM. We can conclude from Table 3 that four components of our proposed MSRSA-DCF contribute to the improvement of the overall performance.

Table 3. Ablation study of the proposed tracker on OTB-2013, TB50 and TB100 benchmarks. Mean_Pre represents the mean precision score and Mean_Suc represents the mean success score. FPS denotes frame per second. The best results are in red color.

	OTB-2013		TB-50		TB-100		Mean
	Mean_Pre	Mean_Suc	Mean_Pre	Mean_Suc	Mean_Pre	Mean_Suc	FPS
MSRSA-DCF	0.818	0.62	0.776	0.567	0.822	0.612	5.5
MSRSA-DCF(-CNN)	0.793	0.604	0.714	0.532	0.774	0.588	--
MSRSA-DCF(-scale_filter)	0.811	0.615	0.759	0.549	0.808	0.597	1.3
MSRSA-DCF(-sample_integrated)	0.401	0.288	0.342	0.243	0.401	0.275	--
MSRSA-DCF(-ADMM)	--	--	--	--	--	--	0.7

5 Conclusions

In this paper, we propose MSRSA-DCF to address the problems of SRDCF. We employ a single-sample-integrated training scheme to learn the previous frame's feature information. Moreover, both manually designed features and deep convolutional features are extracted to train a more discriminative translation filter. Besides, an ADMM algorithm is used to solve the filter. To adapt to the appearance changes of the object, we introduce a scale adaptive filter. At last, through evaluation of TB-50, TB-100 and OTB-2013 benchmarks, the proposed tracker is validated to achieve a competitive performance.

References

1. Bertinetto, L., Valmadre, J., Golodetz, S., Miksik, O., Torr, P.H.S.: Staple: complementary learners for real-time tracking. In: 2016 IEEE Conference on Computer Vision and Pattern Recognition (CVPR). IEEE, June 2016. https://doi.org/10.1109/cvpr.2016.156
2. Bolme, D., Beveridge, J.R., Draper, B.A., Lui, Y.M.: Visual object tracking using adaptive correlation filters. In: 2010 IEEE Computer Society Conference on Computer Vision and Pattern Recognition. IEEE, June 2010. https://doi.org/10.1109/cvpr.2010.5539960
3. Chatfield, K., Simonyan, K., Vedaldi, A., Zisserman, A.: Return of the devil in the details: delving deep into convolutional nets. In: Proceedings of the British Machine Vision Conference 2014. British Machine Vision Association (2014). https://doi.org/10.5244/c.28.6
4. Cimpoi, M., Maji, S., Vedaldi, A.: Deep filter banks for texture recognition and segmentation. In: 2015 IEEE Conference on Computer Vision and Pattern Recognition (CVPR). IEEE, June 2015. https://doi.org/10.1109/cvpr.2015.7299007
5. Dalal, N., Triggs, B.: Histograms of oriented gradients for human detection. In: 2005 IEEE Computer Society Conference on Computer Vision and Pattern Recognition (CVPR). IEEE (2005). https://doi.org/10.1109/cvpr.2005.177
6. Danelljan, M., Hager, G., Khan, F.S., Felsberg, M.: Learning spatially regularized correlation filters for visual tracking. In: 2015 IEEE International Conference on Computer Vision (ICCV). IEEE, December 2015. https://doi.org/10.1109/iccv.2015.490
7. Danelljan, M., Hager, G., Khan, F.S., Felsberg, M.: Discriminative scale space tracking. IEEE Trans. Pattern Anal. Mach. Intell. **39**(8), 1561–1575 (2017). https://doi.org/10.1109/tpami.2016.2609928
8. Danelljan, M., Häger, G., Khan, F.S., Felsberg, M.: Accurate scale estimation for robust visual tracking. In: Proceedings of the British Machine Vision Conference 2014. British Machine Vision Association (2014). https://doi.org/10.5244/c.28.65
9. Henriques, J.F., Caseiro, R., Martins, P., Batista, J.: Exploiting the circulant structure of tracking-by-detection with kernels. In: Fitzgibbon, A., Lazebnik, S., Perona, P., Sato, Y., Schmid, C. (eds.) ECCV 2012. LNCS, vol. 7575, pp. 702–715. Springer, Heidelberg (2012). https://doi.org/10.1007/978-3-642-33765-9_50
10. Henriques, J.F., Caseiro, R., Martins, P., Batista, J.: High-speed tracking with kernelized correlation filters. IEEE Trans. Pattern Anal. Mach. Intell. **37**(3), 583–596 (2015). https://doi.org/10.1109/tpami.2014.2345390

11. Li, F., Tian, C., Zuo, W., Zhang, L., Yang, M.H.: Learning spatial-temporal regularized correlation filters for visual tracking. In: 2018 IEEE/CVF Conference on Computer Vision and Pattern Recognition. IEEE, June 2018. https://doi.org/10.1109/cvpr.2018.00515
12. Li, Y., Zhu, J.: A scale adaptive kernel correlation filter tracker with feature integration. In: Agapito, L., Bronstein, M.M., Rother, C. (eds.) ECCV 2014. LNCS, vol. 8926, pp. 254–265. Springer, Cham (2015). https://doi.org/10.1007/978-3-319-16181-5_18
13. Liu, L., Shen, C., van den Hengel, A.: The treasure beneath convolutional layers: cross-convolutional-layer pooling for image classification. In: 2015 IEEE Conference on Computer Vision and Pattern Recognition (CVPR). IEEE, June 2015. https://doi.org/10.1109/cvpr.2015.7299107
14. Ma, C., Yang, X., Zhang, C., Yang, M.H.: Long-term correlation tracking. In: 2015 IEEE Conference on Computer Vision and Pattern Recognition (CVPR). IEEE, June 2015. https://doi.org/10.1109/cvpr.2015.7299177
15. Mueller, M., Smith, N., Ghanem, B.: Context-aware correlation filter tracking. In: 2017 IEEE Conference on Computer Vision and Pattern Recognition (CVPR). IEEE, July 2017. https://doi.org/10.1109/cvpr.2017.152
16. Sun, S., Guo, Q., Dong, F., Lei, B.: On-line boosting based real-time tracking with efficient HOG. In: 2013 IEEE International Conference on Acoustics, Speech and Signal Processing. IEEE, May 2013. https://doi.org/10.1109/icassp.2013.6638064
17. van de Weijer, J., Schmid, C., Verbeek, J., Larlus, D.: Learning color names for real-world applications. IEEE Trans. Image Process. **18**(7), 1512–1523 (2009). https://doi.org/10.1109/tip.2009.2019809
18. Wu, Y., Lim, J., Yang, M.H.: Online object tracking: a benchmark. In: 2013 IEEE Conference on Computer Vision and Pattern Recognition. IEEE, June 2013. https://doi.org/10.1109/cvpr.2013.312
19. Wu, Y., Lim, J., Yang, M.H.: Object tracking benchmark. IEEE Trans. Pattern Anal. Mach. Intell. **37**(9), 1834–1848 (2015)
20. Yi, Y., Cheng, Y., Xu, C.: Visual tracking based on hierarchical framework and sparse representation. Multimed. Tools Appl. **77**(13), 16267–16289 (2018). https://doi.org/10.1007/s11042-017-5198-4
21. Yi, Y., Luo, L., Zheng, Z.: Single online visual object tracking with enhanced tracking and detection learning. Multimed. Tools Appl. **78**(9), 12333–12351 (2019). https://doi.org/10.1007/s11042-018-6787-6

Unsupervised Video Summarization via Attention-Driven Adversarial Learning

Evlampios Apostolidis[1,2], Eleni Adamantidou[1], Alexandros I. Metsai[1], Vasileios Mezaris[1](✉), and Ioannis Patras[2]

[1] Information Technologies Institute, Centre for Research and Technology Hellas, Thermi-Thessaloniki, Greece
{apostolid,adamelen,alexmetsai,bmezaris}@iti.gr

[2] School of Electronic Engineering and Computer Science, Queen Mary University of London, London, UK
i.patras@qmul.ac.uk

Abstract. This paper presents a new video summarization approach that integrates an attention mechanism to identify the significant parts of the video, and is trained unsupervisingly via generative adversarial learning. Starting from the SUM-GAN model, we first develop an improved version of it (called SUM-GAN-sl) that has a significantly reduced number of learned parameters, performs incremental training of the model's components, and applies a stepwise label-based strategy for updating the adversarial part. Subsequently, we introduce an attention mechanism to SUM-GAN-sl in two ways: (i) by integrating an attention layer within the variational auto-encoder (VAE) of the architecture (SUM-GAN-VAAE), and (ii) by replacing the VAE with a deterministic attention auto-encoder (SUM-GAN-AAE). Experimental evaluation on two datasets (SumMe and TVSum) documents the contribution of the attention auto-encoder to faster and more stable training of the model, resulting in a significant performance improvement with respect to the original model and demonstrating the competitiveness of the proposed SUM-GAN-AAE against the state of the art (Software publicly available at: https://github.com/e-apostolidis/SUM-GAN-AAE).

Keywords: Video summarization · Unsupervised learning · Attention mechanism · Adversarial learning

1 Introduction

Recent advances in video capturing and storage technology, combined with the widespread use of social networks (e.g. Facebook) and video hosting platforms (e.g. YouTube), facilitate the recording and sharing of huge volumes of video content. Thousands of hours of video are uploaded every day on the Web, aiming to attract the viewers' attention. However, in several cases, browsing through long videos to find the content that a viewer prefers is a highly time-consuming and tedious process. Hence, the provision of a concise summary that conveys the

Y. M. Ro et al. (Eds.): MMM 2020, LNCS 11961, pp. 492–504, 2020.
https://doi.org/10.1007/978-3-030-37731-1_40

main concept of the video enables the viewer to quickly grasp an idea without having to watch the entire content, thus allowing time-efficient browsing of large video collections and increasing the potential of a video to be consumed.

Several methods have been proposed to automate video summarization, and the researchers' focus was recently attracted by deep learning architectures. In this direction, annotated datasets were built to facilitate training and evaluation. However, since video summarization is a highly-subjective task we argue that supervised learning approaches, which rely on the use of a single ground-truth summary, cannot fully explore the learning potential of such architectures. Hence, we focused on developing an unsupervised method for video summarization. Starting from [16] and building on a variation of this model [5], we scrutinized features of the architecture and the training process that could be fine-tuned to improve the model's performance. The resulting architecture SUM-GAN-sl (Sect. 3.1) has a reduced number of parameters, updates the model's components in an incremental manner, and follows a stepwise label-based approach for training the adversarial part. Then, inspired by the efficiency of attention mechanisms in spotting the attractive parts of a data sequence, we extended SUM-GAN-sl by: (a) directly introducing an attention layer within the variational auto-encoder of the model (SUM-GAN-VAAE; Sect. 3.2), and (b) replacing this component with a deterministic attention auto-encoder (SUM-GAN-AAE; Sect. 3.3). Experiments on the SumMe and TVSum datasets (Sect. 4), document the improvements that are attained in comparison to the original SUM-GAN model, show the inability of variational attention to enhance the training capacity of the architecture, highlight the contribution of the attention auto-encoder to faster and more stable training of the model, and show the competitiveness of the proposed SUM-GAN-AAE architecture against the state of the art.

2 Related Work

Various approaches to video summarization were introduced over the last couple of decades, with the majority being trained supervisingly using ground-truth data. For the sake of space, we report here only on methods exploiting the learning efficiency of neural networks, which represent the current state of the art; while, special focus is put on approaches utilizing attention mechanisms. A number of supervised algorithms (e.g. [17]) use Convolutional Neural Networks (CNN) to extract information about the video semantics and use it to learn to identify the most suitable parts of the video. [21] tackles video summarization as a sequence labeling problem and performs keyframe selection using fully convolutional sequence models. [7] combines a soft, self-attention network with a 2-layer fully connected network to process the CNN features of the video frames and compute frame-level importance scores that are used for key-fragment selection.

Other supervised techniques utilize Recurrent Neural Networks (RNN) (e.g. Long Short-Term Memory (LSTM) units [12]) to capture temporal dependencies over sequential data. This idea was first introduced in [27], and further expanded in [30] and [31], with hierarchies of LSTMs that extract and encode data about the video structure, and identify the key-fragments of the video. [28]

combines LSTMs with Dilated Temporal Relational units to capture long-range dependencies at different temporal windows, while training relies on the generative adversarial framework. Other approaches introduce attention mechanisms to identify the most attractive parts of the video. [13] formulates video summarization as a sequence-to-sequence learning problem and proposes an LSTM-based encoder-decoder network with an intermediate attention layer. In [9], the typical encoder-decoder seq2seq model is replaced by a special attention-based seq2seq model that defines and ranks the different fragments of the video, and is combined with a 3D-CNN classifier which judges whether a fragment is from a ground-truth or a generated summary. [8] introduces an architecture with memory augmented networks for global attention modeling, and tackles video summarization by estimating the temporal dependency across the entire video.

Contrary to the above supervised approaches, a few unsupervised methods were proposed too. [16] selects a sparse subset of representative keyframes by training a summarizer to minimize the distance between videos and a distribution of their summaries using a Generative Adversarial Network (GAN). Similarly, [25] aims to maximize the mutual information between summary and video using an information-preserving metric, two trainable discriminators and a cycle-consistent adversarial learning objective. [32] formulates video summarization as a sequential decision-making process and trains a deep summarization network to produce diverse and representative video summaries via reinforcement learning. [29] extracts key motions of appearing objects and learns to produce an object-level video summarization in an unsupervised manner. Finally, [20] proposes an adversarial process that learns a mapping function from raw videos to human-like summaries, based on professional summary videos available online.

The contributions of our work are: (i) the introduction of an attention mechanism in an unsupervised learning framework, whereas all previous attention-based summarization methods [7–9,13] were supervised; (ii) the investigation of integrating attention into a variational auto-encoder for video summarization purposes; and (iii) the use of attention to guide the generative adversarial training of the model, rather than using it to rank the video fragments as in [9].

3 Proposed Approach

3.1 Building on Adversarial Learning

The starting point of our work is the unsupervised method of [16]. This algorithm selects the video keyframes by minimizing the distance between the deep feature representations of the original video and a reconstructed version of it based on the selected keyframes. The difficulty in defining a suitable similarity threshold was tackled by using adversarial learning and introducing a trainable discriminator network. So, the goal was to train the summarizer (that contains the generator) in order to maximally confuse the discriminator when trying to distinguish the original from the reconstructed video; a condition that indicates a highly representative keyframe summary. Based on an implemented variation of this model [5] (used to evaluate SUM-GAN when summarizing 360° videos [15]), we scrutinized features of the architecture and the training process that could be

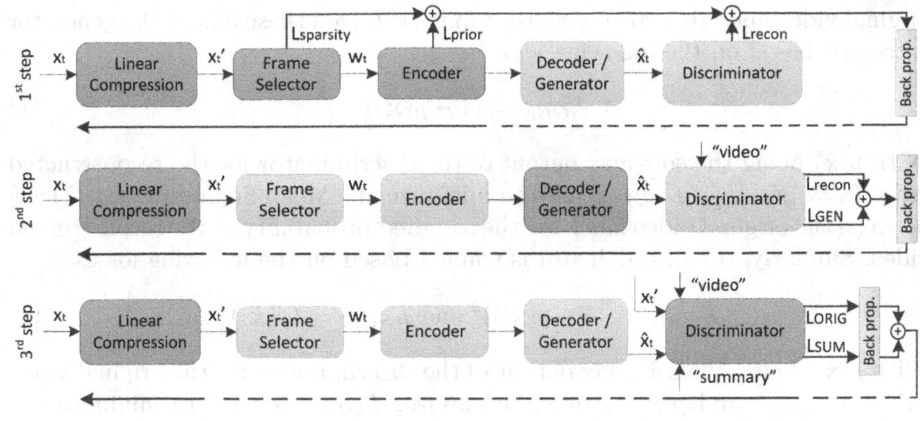

Fig. 1. Incremental training of SUM-GAN-sl. Adversarial learning follows a stepwise label-based approach. Dark-coloured boxes show updated parts in each backward pass.

fine-tuned to improve the model's performance. As depicted in the block-diagram of Fig. 1, we developed a new model (called SUM-GAN-sl and presented in [1]) that: (i) contains a linear compression layer which reduces the size of the input feature vectors and the number of learned parameters, (ii) follows an incremental approach for training the model's components, and (iii) applies a stepwise label-based learning strategy for the adversarial part of the architecture.

Given a video of T frames, x_t, x'_t, and $\hat{x}_t$ represent the original, compressed and reconstructed feature vectors respectively, with $t \in [1, T]$. In the first step of the training process the algorithm performs a forward pass of the model, computes the L_{recon}, L_{prior} and $L_{sparsity}$ losses, and updates the frame selector, the encoder and the linear compression layer. In the second step it performs a forward pass of the partially updated model, computes the L_{recon} and L_{GEN} losses, and updates the decoder and the linear compression layer. The third step is implemented in a fine-grained, stepwise manner based on a strategy used in [19] for unsupervised representation learning that targets the task of image generation. In particular, the compressed feature vectors of the original video (x'_t, $t \in [1, T]$) pass through the discriminator, the L_{ORIG} loss is calculated using a label-based approach and the gradients for this loss are computed via a backward pass. Subsequently, the same feature vectors pass through the updated summarizer, the reconstructed features ($\hat{x}_t$, $t \in [1, T]$) are forwarded to the discriminator, the L_{SUM} loss is calculated and the gradients from both the original video and the summary-based reconstructed version of it are accumulated with another backward pass. With the gradients accumulated, the algorithm updates the discriminator and the linear compression layer. This fine-grained computation of gradients helps the discriminator to develop higher discrimination efficiency.

With respect to the utilized losses for training the model, L_{recon}, L_{prior} and $L_{sparsity}$ are computed as in [16]. However, instead of using the L_{GAN} loss of the SUM-GAN model, we adopt a label-based approach where label "1" denotes the original video and label "0" the video summary. Given these labels, the generator is trained based on the following loss:

$$L_{GEN} = (1 - p(\hat{\mathbf{x}}))^2 \quad (1)$$

With $p(\hat{\mathbf{x}})$ being the soft-max output of the discriminator for the reconstructed video ($\hat{\mathbf{x}} = \{\hat{x}_t\}_{t=1}^{T}$), L_{GEN} is used to minimize the Mean Squared Error (MSE) between the original video label and the assigned probability to the reconstructed video. Similarly, the discriminator is trained based on the following losses:

$$L_{ORIG} = (1 - p(\mathbf{x'}))^2 \text{ and } L_{SUM} = (p(\hat{\mathbf{x}}))^2 \quad (2)$$

With $p(\mathbf{x'})$ being the soft-max output of the discriminator for the original video ($\mathbf{x'} = \{x'_t\}_{t=1}^{T}$) and $p(\hat{\mathbf{x}})$ as described above, L_{ORIG} is used to minimize the MSE between the original video label and the assigned probability to the original video, while L_{SUM} is used to minimize the MSE between the summary label and the assigned probability to the summary-based reconstruction of the video. This stepwise, label-based learning approach allows better training of the adversarial part of the model, via a more fine-grained update of the discriminator's gradients and the use of a more strictly defined learning task for the generator.

Given a trained model, the key-fragment summary for an unseen video is created based on the following process. The CNN feature vectors of the video frames pass through the linear compression layer and the frame selector, which computes frame-level importance scores. Then, after having the video segmented using the KTS algorithm [18] (other methods (e.g. [2,3]) could be used too), fragment-level importance scores are calculated by averaging the scores of each fragment's frames. Finally, following the approach of several summarization algorithms (e.g. [13,22,27,32]), the summary is created by selecting the fragments that maximize the total importance score, provided that the summary does not exceed 15% of video duration, by solving the 0/1 Knapsack problem.

3.2 Introducing an Attention Mechanism

The idea behind the use of an attention mechanism for video summarization is to implement a gradual decision-making approach that bases the selection of a piece of data from a data sequence on the previously seen ones. Inspired by [13], we extended the SUM-GAN-sl model (Sect. 3.1) by integrating an attention layer within the variational auto-encoder of the architecture. A recent work (see [4]) that aimed to build a method for natural language modeling, examined different settings for this integration and described the bypassing effect that the traditional (deterministic) attention mechanism has on the VAE's functionality, since the latter has no impact in the process. To avoid this effect, the authors of [4] proposed a variational attention mechanism where the attention vector is also modeled as Gaussian distributed random variables. Hence, the original VAE is extended as shown in Fig. 2, in order to compute a latent variable also for the attention vector and use it when generating the decoded representation of the input sequence. Based on the above, we extended the SUM-GAN-sl model with variational attention, forming the SUM-GAN-VAAE architecture. In particular,

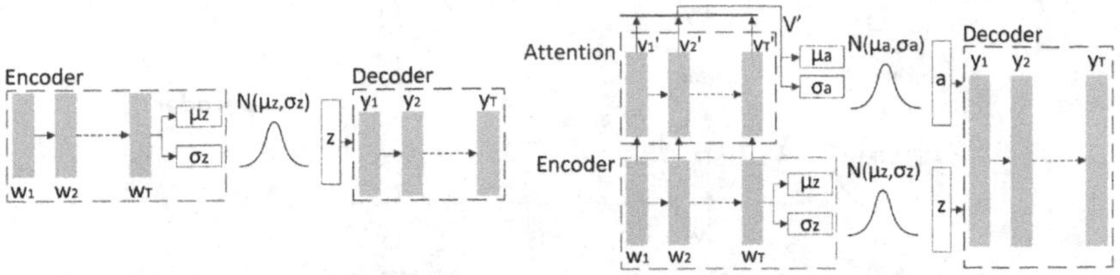

Fig. 2. Going from variational (left) to variational attention auto-encoder (right).

the attention weights of each frame were considered as random variables and a latent space was computed by the VAE for these values, too. Finally, the decoding part of this component was modified in order to update its hidden states based on both latent spaces (computed for the encoder's output and the attention values) during the reconstruction of the video.

3.3 Introducing an Attention Auto-encoder

The second alternative examined for integrating an attention mechanism to the SUM-GAN-sl model is based on the supervised attention-based encoder-decoder network of [13]. Since deterministic attention bypasses the functionality of VAE, the latter is entirely replaced by an attention auto-encoder (AAE) network. The architecture of the new model (called SUM-GAN-AAE) is shown in Fig. 3. Given the t_{th} frame of a video of T frames and using the notations from Sect. 3.1, $s_t,\ t \in [1, T]$ refers to the computed importance score by the frame selector, $w_t,\ t \in [1, T]$ corresponds to its weighted feature vector ($s_t \otimes x'_t$, where $\otimes$ denotes element-wise matrix multiplication) that is passed to the attention auto-encoder, and $\hat{x}_t,\ t \in [1, T]$ represents the reconstructed feature vector.

Focusing on the introduced AAE module of the architecture (see Fig. 4), after feeding the weighted feature vectors to the encoder, for any time-step t in $[2, T]$, the attention component receives the encoder output $\mathbf{V} = \{\nu_t,\ t \in [1, T]\}$ and the previous hidden state of the decoder h_{t-1}, then computes the attention energy vector e_t, with elements that represent the correlation between the t_{th} frame of the video and the entire set of video frames, using a score function (see below), and finally applies a soft-max function to normalize the attention

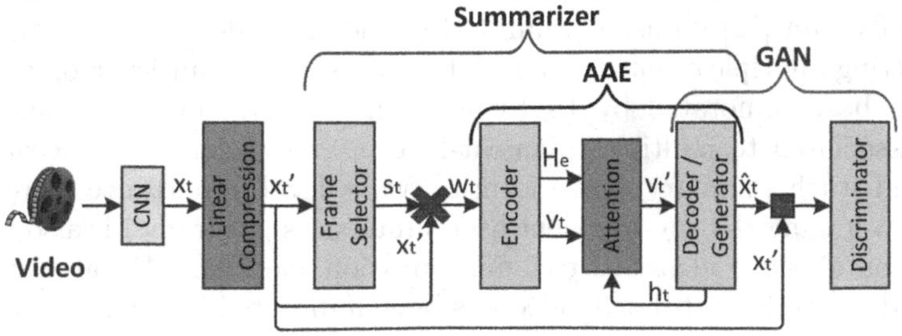

Fig. 3. The proposed SUM-GAN-AAE architecture.

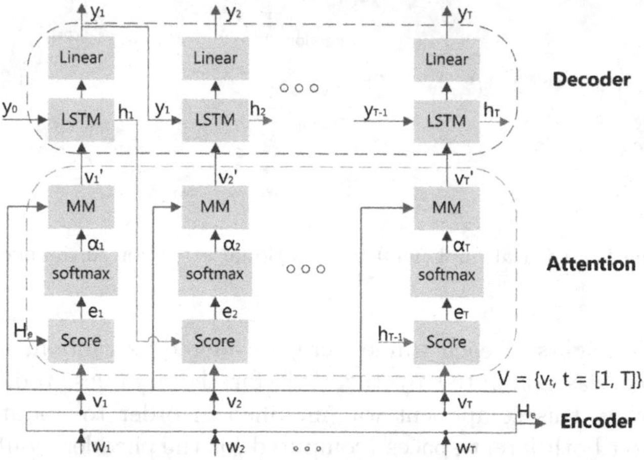

Fig. 4. The attention auto-encoder. Decoding is performed in a stepwise manner which involves the corresponding step of the attention component.

energies producing the attention weight vector a_t. For $t = 1$, as illustrated in Fig. 4, the attention component uses the hidden state of the last encoder's step ($\mathbf{H_e}$), since there is no previous hidden state of the decoder. Afterwards, the attention weight vector a_t is multiplied (an operation denoted by "MM" in Fig. 4) with the encoder's output, producing the context vector ν'_t, $t \in [1, T]$. The latter is fed to the decoder, which combines it with its output from the previous frame y_{t-1}, so as to incrementally reconstruct the video. The score function used in our implementation is a multiplicative one, i.e. $e^i_t = \nu^*_i W_a h_{t-1}$ where ν^*_i is the transposed encoder output for the i_{th} video frame, h_{t-1} is the hidden state of the decoder for $t - 1$, W_a is a learnable parameter and e^i_t is the relevance score (scalar value) before the normalization. The final attention weights a^i_t are computed based on the following normalization: $a^i_t = \exp(e^i_t)/\sum_{j=1}^{n} \exp(e^j_t)$.

4 Experiments

4.1 Experimental Settings

Datasets. The performance of the developed models is evaluated on the SumMe [10] and TVSum [22] datasets. SumMe includes 25 videos of 1 to 6 min. duration, covering multiple events from both first-person and third-person view. Each video has been annotated by 15–18 users in the form of key-fragments, and thus is associated to multiple fragment-level user summaries. Moreover, a single ground-truth summary in the form of frame-level importance scores (calculated by averaging the key-fragment user summaries per frame) is also provided. TVSum contains 50 videos of 1 to 5 min duration, capturing 10 categories of the TRECVid MED dataset. Each video has been annotated by 20 users in the form of frame-level importance scores, and a single ground-truth summary (computed by averaging all users' scores) is available.

Evaluation Approach. For fair comparison with the majority of SoA approaches, we adopt the key-fragment-based evaluation protocol from [27]. Similarity between an automatically created (A) and a user summary (U) is computed by the F-Score (as percentage), where (P)recision and (R)ecall measure the temporal overlap ($\cap$) between the summaries ($|| * ||$ denotes duration):

$$F = 2 \times \frac{P \times R}{P + R} \times 100, \text{ with } P = \frac{A \cap U}{||A||} \text{ and } R = \frac{A \cap U}{||U||} \quad (3)$$

So, given a video, we compare the generated summary with the user summaries for this video, and compute an F-Score for each pair of compared summaries. Then, we average the computed F-Scores (for TVSum) or keep the maximum of them (for SumMe, following [11]) and end up with the final F-Score for this video. The computed F-Scores for the entire set of testing videos are finally averaged to capture the algorithm's performance. This protocol is directly applicable on SumMe, as user annotations are already available in the form of key-fragments. For TVSum, frame-level annotations are converted to key-fragment annotations following [22,27]. The videos are segmented using the KTS method [18], and fragment-level importance scores are computed by averaging the scores of each fragment's frames. Video fragments are ranked based on the computed scores and the Knapsack algorithm is used to select the key-fragments and form the summary, such that it does not exceed 15% of the video's duration (an assumption made by most works in the literature). Finally, for fair comparison with a group of methods [9,13,16,24,25,28] that evaluate the generated summary for a given video by matching it with the single ground-truth summary for that video, we report our model's performance based on this approach too.

Implementation Details. Videos were downsampled to 2 fps. Feature extraction was based on the pool5 layer of GoogleNet [23] trained on ImageNet. The linear compression layer reduces the size of these vectors from 1024 to 500. Each component of the architecture is comprised of a 2-layer LSTM, with 500 hidden units, while the frame selector is a bi-directional LSTM. Training is based on the Adam optimizer and the learning rate for all components but the discriminator is 10^{-4}; for the latter one is 10^{-5}. Moreover, we followed the typical learning setting (see [16,27]) where the used dataset is split into two non-overlapping sets; one training set having 80% of data, and one testing set including the remaining 20% of data. Finally, we ran our experiments for 5 different random splits and we report the average performance over these runs.

4.2 Performance Evaluation

The developed models were initially evaluated for several values of the regularization factor σ, ranging between 0.05 and 0.5. Greater values were not examined as the models' performance was significantly reduced in (at least) one of the datasets for the highest tested value. In Table 1 we report our findings focusing on the proposed SUM-GAN-AAE model. As can be seen, this factor affects the model's efficiency (as reported in [16]) and thus, it needs fine-tuning. Moreover, the latter seems to be dataset-dependent, as the highest performance is achieved

Table 1. Performance (F-Score (%)) of SUM-GAN-AAE for different values of the regularization factor. Best performance is shown in bold.

	SumMe	TVSum
$\sigma = 0.05$	47.1	58.3
$\sigma = 0.1$	48.2	58.2
$\sigma = 0.15$	**48.9**	58.3
$\sigma = 0.3$	47.6	57.3
$\sigma = 0.5$	46.8	**59.6**

Table 2. Comparison (F-Score (%)) with different unsupervised video summarization approaches, on SumMe and TVSum. +/− indicate better/worse performance than SUM-GAN-AAE.

	SumMe	TVSum
Random summary	39.9 (−)	53.9 (−)
Tessellation [14]	41.4 (−)	**64.1** (+)
DR-DSN [32]	41.4 (−)	57.6 (−)
Online Motion-AE [29]	37.7 (−)	51.5 (−)
UnpairedVSN [20]	47.5 (−)	55.6 (−)
SUM-GAN-sl [1]	47.3 (−)	58.0 (−)
SUM-GAN-VAAE	45.7 (−)	57.6 (−)
SUM-GAN-AAE	**48.9**	58.3

for different values of σ in each dataset. For fair comparison with other methods that use a strictly defined set of parameters, in the following we refer to the SUM-GAN-AAE model with $\sigma = 0.15$, while the best performing SUM-GAN-sl and SUM-GAN-VAAE models were observed for $\sigma = 0.1$ and $\sigma = 0.3$ respectively.

The results of the comparative evaluation of these models against the performance of a randomly generated summary[1] and of other SoA unsupervised approaches on SumMe and TVSum are reported in Table 2. As a note, each method's score is from the corresponding paper, while the original SUM-GAN method is not listed in this table as it follows a different evaluation protocol; the comparison with it is reported in the sequel (see Tables 4 and 5). These results show that: (i) the performance of a few SoA methods is comparable (or even worse) to that of a random summary generator; (ii) the best approach on TVSum achieves random-level performance on SumMe, a fact that indicates it is a dataset-tailored technique, since it efficiently summarizes the TVSum videos but clearly fails to define good summaries for the SumMe videos; (iii) the introduction of variational attention reduces the efficiency of the SUM-GAN-sl model, possibly due to the difficulty in efficiently defining two latent spaces in parallel to the continuous updating of the model's components during the training; (iv) the replacement of the VAE with the AAE results in a noticeable performance improvement over the SUM-GAN-sl model. The latter indicates the contribution of the introduced attention mechanism in enhancing the decoder's ability to identify the most important frames to pay attention to, and in effectively guiding the learning of the adversarial component of the architecture. The applied training strategy efficiently backpropagates this knowledge to the frame selection component, resulting in a significantly improved performance compared to the SUM-GAN-sl model. Moreover, a study of the training curves of the adversarial part of these models (see Fig. 5) points out

[1] Importance scores were defined based on a uniform distribution of probabilities and the experiment was repeated 100 times.

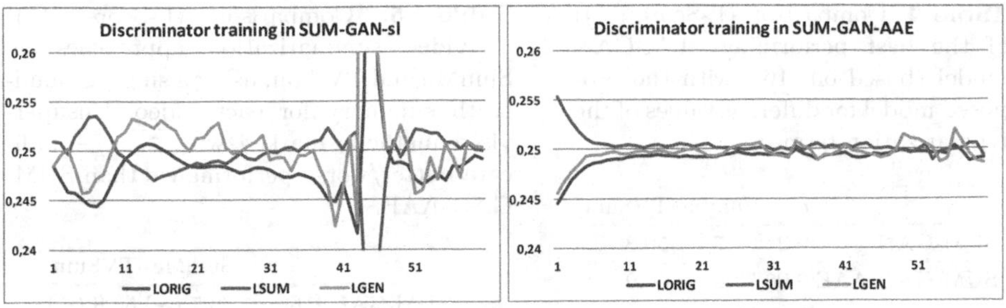

Fig. 5. Loss curves of the discriminator (L_{ORIG}, L_{SUM}) and generator (L_{GEN}) of SUM-GAN-sl and SUM-GAN-AAE models. Horizontal axis denotes training epochs.

Table 3. Comparison (F-Score (%)) of our *unsupervised* method with *supervised* video summarization approaches on SumMe and TVSum. +/− indicate better/worse performance than SUM-GAN-AAE.

	SumMe	TVSum		SumMe	TVSum
Random summary	39.9 (−)	53.9 (−)	MAVS [8]	40.3 (−)	**66.8** (+)
vsLSTM [27]	37.6 (−)	54.2 (−)	SUM-FCN [21]	47.5 (−)	56.8 (−)
dppLSTM [27]	38.6 (−)	54.7 (−)	SUM-DeepLab [21]	48.8 (−)	58.4 (+)
H-RNN [30]	41.1 (−)	57.7 (−)	DR-DSNsup [32]	42.1 (−)	58.1 (−)
Tessellationsup [14]	37.2 (−)	63.4 (+)	ActionRanking [6]	40.1 (−)	56.3 (−)
HSA-RNN [31]	44.1 (−)	59.8 (+)	UnpairedVSNpsup [20]	48.0 (−)	56.1 (−)
DQSN [33]	–	58.6 (+)	VASNet [7]	**49.7** (+)	61.4 (+)
DSSE [26]	–	57.0 (−)	SUM-GAN-AAE	48.9	58.3

that the AAE contributes to much faster and more stable training. On top of these findings, the SUM-GAN-AAE model performs consistently well in both datasets (being the best one on SumMe), and thus is the most competitive one among the compared approaches.

Our unsupervised SUM-GAN-AAE model was compared also against supervised methods for video summarization (which is a rather unfair comparison). Table 3 shows that: (i) the best methods on TVSum are highly-adapted to this dataset as they exhibit random-level performance on SumMe; (ii) only a few supervised methods surpass the performance of a random summary generator on both datasets. The performance of these methods ranges in 44.1–49.7 on SumMe, and in 56.1–61.4 on TVSum. Hence, the results of our unsupervised method make SUM-GAN-AAE comparable with SoA supervised algorithms.

For fair comparison with approaches evaluated using the single ground-truth summaries of each video of SumMe and TVSum (i.e. the different evaluation protocol adopted in [9,13,16,24,25,28]), we assessed our model also via this approach. Once again we considered different values for the regularization factor σ, to examine its impact on the model's efficiency according to this evaluation protocol and make our findings comparable with the ones in [16]. Table 4 indicates that the model's performance is, indeed, affected by the value of σ, while

Table 4. Comparison (F-Score (%)) of the best performing SUM-GAN model (based on [16]) with the proposed model for different values of the regularization term σ.

	σ	SumMe	TVSum
SUM-GAN	0.3	38.7	50.8
SUM-GAN-AAE	0.05	53.6	60.9
	0.1	55.4	59.9
	0.15	56.4	60.2
	0.3	56.0	59.8
	0.5	**56.9**	**63.9**

Table 5. Comparison (F-Score (%)) of video summarization approaches on SumMe and TVSum, using a single ground-truth summary for each video. Unsupervised methods marked with *. +/− indicate better/worse performance than SUM-GAN-AAE.

	SumMe	TVSum
* SUM-GAN [16]	38.7 (−)	50.8 (−)
* SUM-GANdpp [16]	39.1 (−)	51.7 (−)
SUM-GANsup [16]	41.7 (−)	56.3 (−)
SASUM [24]	45.3 (−)	58.2 (−)
DTR-GAN [28]	44.6 (−)	59.1 (−)
A-AVS [13]	43.9 (−)	59.4 (−)
M-AVS [13]	44.4 (−)	61.0 (−)
AALVS [9]	46.2 (−)	63.6 (−)
* Cycle-SUM [25]	41.9 (−)	57.6 (−)
* SUM-GAN-AAE	**56.9**	**63.9**

the effect of this hyper-parameter depends on the evaluation approach (best performance when using multiple human summaries was observed for $\sigma = 0.15$). Moreover, our method clearly outperforms the original SUM-GAN model on both datasets, even for the same value of σ. Finally, the comparison of the best performing instance of our model (for $\sigma = 0.5$) with other techniques that follow this evaluation protocol, indicates the superiority of the proposed approach in both datasets (see Table 5; methods' scores are from the corresponding papers).

5 Conclusions

We presented a video summarization method that combines the effectiveness of attention mechanisms in spotting the most attractive parts of the video and the learning efficiency of the generative adversarial networks for unsupervised training. Based on the SUM-GAN model, we built an improved variation that performs incremental training of the model's components, applies a stepwise label-based learning approach for the adversarial part and has a reduced number of network parameters. Two further extensions of the developed model were studied; one using a variational attention mechanism and another one using a deterministic attention auto-encoder. Experimental evaluations on the SumMe and TVSum datasets documented the positive contribution of the introduced attention auto-encoder component in the model's training and summarization performance, and highlighted the competitiveness of the proposed unsupervised SUM-GAN-AAE approach against SoA video summarization techniques.

Acknowledgments. This work was supported by the EUs Horizon 2020 research and innovation programme under grant agreement H2020-780656 ReTV. The work of Ioannis Patras has been supported by EPSRC under grant No. EP/R026424/1.

References

1. Apostolidis, E., et al.: A stepwise, label-based approach for improving the adversarial training in unsupervised video summarization. In: AI4TV, ACM MM 2019 (2019)
2. Apostolidis, E., et al.: Fast shot segmentation combining global and local visual descriptors. In: IEEE ICASSP 2014, pp. 6583–6587 (2014)
3. Apostolidis, K., Apostolidis, E., Mezaris, V.: A motion-driven approach for fine-grained temporal segmentation of user-generated videos. In: Schoeffmann, K., et al. (eds.) MMM 2018. LNCS, vol. 10704, pp. 29–41. Springer, Cham (2018). https://doi.org/10.1007/978-3-319-73603-7_3
4. Bahuleyan, H., et al.: Variational attention for sequence-to-sequence models. In: 27th COLING, pp. 1672–1682 (2018)
5. Cho, J.: PyTorch implementation of SUM-GAN (2017). https://github.com/j-min/Adversarial_Video_Summary. Accessed 18 Oct 2019
6. Elfeki, M., et al.: Video summarization via actionness ranking. In: IEEE WACV 2019, pp. 754–763 (2019)
7. Fajtl, J., Sokeh, H.S., Argyriou, V., Monekosso, D., Remagnino, P.: Summarizing videos with attention. In: Carneiro, G., You, S. (eds.) ACCV 2018. LNCS, vol. 11367, pp. 39–54. Springer, Cham (2019). https://doi.org/10.1007/978-3-030-21074-8_4
8. Feng, L., et al.: Extractive video summarizer with memory augmented neural networks. In: ACM MM 2018, pp. 976–983 (2018)
9. Fu, T., et al.: Attentive and adversarial learning for video summarization. In: IEEE WACV 2019, pp. 1579–1587 (2019)
10. Gygli, M., Grabner, H., Riemenschneider, H., Van Gool, L.: Creating summaries from user videos. In: Fleet, D., Pajdla, T., Schiele, B., Tuytelaars, T. (eds.) ECCV 2014. LNCS, vol. 8695, pp. 505–520. Springer, Cham (2014). https://doi.org/10.1007/978-3-319-10584-0_33
11. Gygli, M., et al.: Video summarization by learning submodular mixtures of objectives. In: IEEE CVPR 2015, pp. 3090–3098 (2015)
12. Hochreiter, S., et al.: Long short-term memory. Neural Comput. **9**(8), 1735–1780 (1997)
13. Ji, Z., et al.: Video summarization with attention-based encoder-decoder networks. IEEE Trans. Circ. Syst. Video Technol. 1 (2019)
14. Kaufman, D., et al.: Temporal tessellation: a unified approach for video analysis. In: IEEE ICCV 2017, pp. 94–104 (2017)
15. Lee, S., et al.: A memory network approach for story-based temporal summarization of 360 videos. In: IEEE CVPR 2018, pp. 1410–1419 (2018)
16. Mahasseni, B., et al.: Unsupervised video summarization with adversarial LSTM networks. In: IEEE CVPR 2017, pp. 2982–2991 (2017)
17. Otani, M., Nakashima, Y., Rahtu, E., Heikkilä, J., Yokoya, N.: Video summarization using deep semantic features. In: Lai, S.-H., Lepetit, V., Nishino, K., Sato, Y. (eds.) ACCV 2016. LNCS, vol. 10115, pp. 361–377. Springer, Cham (2017). https://doi.org/10.1007/978-3-319-54193-8_23

18. Potapov, D., Douze, M., Harchaoui, Z., Schmid, C.: Category-specific video summarization. In: Fleet, D., Pajdla, T., Schiele, B., Tuytelaars, T. (eds.) ECCV 2014. LNCS, vol. 8694, pp. 540–555. Springer, Cham (2014). https://doi.org/10.1007/978-3-319-10599-4_35
19. Radford, A., et al.: Unsupervised representation learning with deep convolutional generative adversarial networks. In: ICLR 2016 (2016)
20. Rochan, M., et al.: Video summarization by learning from unpaired data. In: IEEE CVPR 2019 (2019)
21. Rochan, M., Ye, L., Wang, Y.: Video summarization using fully convolutional sequence networks. In: Ferrari, V., Hebert, M., Sminchisescu, C., Weiss, Y. (eds.) ECCV 2018. LNCS, vol. 11216, pp. 358–374. Springer, Cham (2018). https://doi.org/10.1007/978-3-030-01258-8_22
22. Song, Y., et al.: TVSum: summarizing web videos using titles. In: IEEE CVPR 2015, pp. 5179–5187 (2015)
23. Szegedy, C., et al.: Going deeper with convolutions. In: IEEE CVPR 2015, pp. 1–9 (2015)
24. Wei, H., et al.: Video summarization via semantic attended networks. In: AAAI 2018, pp. 216–223 (2018)
25. Yuan, L., et al.: Cycle-SUM: cycle-consistent adversarial LSTM networks for unsupervised video summarization. In: AAAI 2019, pp. 9143–9150 (2019)
26. Yuan, Y., et al.: Video summarization by learning deep side semantic embedding. IEEE Trans. Circ. Syst. Video Technol. **29**(1), 226–237 (2019)
27. Zhang, K., Chao, W.-L., Sha, F., Grauman, K.: Video summarization with long short-term memory. In: Leibe, B., Matas, J., Sebe, N., Welling, M. (eds.) ECCV 2016. LNCS, vol. 9911, pp. 766–782. Springer, Cham (2016). https://doi.org/10.1007/978-3-319-46478-7_47
28. Zhang, Y., et al.: DTR-GAN: dilated temporal relational adversarial network for video summarization. In: ACM TURC 2019, pp. 89:1–89:6 (2019)
29. Zhang, Y., et al.: Unsupervised object-level video summarization with online motion auto-encoder. Pattern Recogn. Lett. (2018)
30. Zhao, B., et al.: Hierarchical recurrent neural network for video summarization. In: ACM MM 2017, pp. 863–871 (2017)
31. Zhao, B., et al.: HSA-RNN: hierarchical structure-adaptive RNN for video summarization. In: IEEE/CVF CVPR 2018, pp. 7405–7414 (2018)
32. Zhou, K., et al.: Deep reinforcement learning for unsupervised video summarization with diversity-representativeness reward. In: AAAI 2018, pp. 7582–7589 (2018)
33. Zhou, K., et al.: Video summarisation by classification with deep reinforcement learning. In: BMVC 2018 (2018)

Poster Papers

Efficient HEVC Downscale Transcoding Based on Coding Unit Information Mapping

Zhijie Huang, Yunchang Li, and Jun Sun(✉)

Wangxuan Institute of Computer Technology, Peking University, Beijing, China
{zhijiehuang,liyunchang,sunjun}@pku.edu.cn

Abstract. In this paper, a novel method that utilizes the information of coding unit (CU) from source video to accelerate the downscale transcoding process for High Efficiency Video Coding (HEVC) is proposed. Specifically, the CU depth and prediction mode information are first extracted into matrices in block level according to the decoded source video. Then we use the matrices to predict CU depth and prediction mode at CU level in the target video. Finally, some effective rules are introduced to determine CU partition and prediction mode based on the prediction. Our approach supports the spatial downscale transcoding with any spatial resolution downscaling ratio. Experiments show that the proposed method can achieve an average time reduction of 59.3% compared to the reference HEVC encoder, with a relatively small Bjøntegaard Delta Bit rate (BDBR) increment on average. Moreover, our approach is also competitive compared to the state-of-the-art spatial resolution downscale transcoding methods for HEVC.

Keywords: High Efficiency Video Coding · Downscale transcoding · Information mapping · CU partition · Prediction mode

1 Introduction

More and more people are beginning to transmit and share videos on mobile phones due to the increasing popularity of mobile devices. But owing to heterogeneous device capabilities and various networks, mobile services have faced many challenging issues in efficient video content sharing and delivery. To address such inefficiency, video transcoding is a common technique to provide videos in multiple resolutions and formats. And spatial downscale transcoding [1,15], one of the most effective transcoding approaches, can share and deliver videos efficiently when end-users have limited display capabilities or the bandwidth is constrained. Meanwhile, the standard High Efficiency Video Coding (HEVC) [16] can save approximately 50% bit-rate at similar video quality compared to the traditional video compression standards, H.264/Advanced Video Coding (AVC) [19] by adopting some advanced video coding techniques, e.g., the quad-tree structure of the coding unit (CU) partition. However, these techniques also lead

Y. M. Ro et al. (Eds.): MMM 2020, LNCS 11961, pp. 507–518, 2020.
https://doi.org/10.1007/978-3-030-37731-1_41

to extremely high computational complexity, as show in [5], the encoding time of HEVC is higher than H.264/AVC by 253% on average. Therefore, in order to make downscale transcoding for HEVC more efficient, it's critical to reduce the heavy computation.

In the reference software HM [3], the recursive process of the quad-tree CU partition occupies the largest proportion of the total encoding time on average, which is the major cause of HEVC heavy computation. Thus, instead of the brute-force recursive rate-distortion optimization (RDO) search, some researches such as [10,14,20] predict the CU depth in advance to simplify the process of CU partition, and some researches such as [7,11] make prediction mode decision in advance to accelerate CU partition. But these methods can only gain a limited speedup in the phase of encoding target video for arbitrary ratio downscale transcoding. In fact, since the contents of the videos do not change during the spatial resolution downscale transcoding, more efficient methods for downscale transcoding usually utilize the information obtained from the stage of decoding source bitstream to accelerate the encoding process. Nguyen et al. [13] utilizes the temporal correlation of depth levels among CUs and the continuity of the motion vector field in the precoded video to avoid the unnecessary exhaustive CU size search at certain depth levels. [9] and [17] analyse the CU structure during the decoding process and exploit it to accelerate CU partition in the encoding process. But their time saving are all less than 50%. And [13] and [17] are only evaluated in the case where the spatial resolution downscaling ratio is 2. In [6], a method applying feature selection based on a decision tree is proposed in a fast HEVC transcoding model for misaligned content. However, its performance varies depending on the shift and average transform size in the original sequence. Lin et al. [12] propose a method based on predicting CU depth in pixel level according to decoded partitioning of source videos to make early CU splitting or pruning decision without complex recursive search. Although it can achieve about 74% time reduction on average, the increase of Bjøntegaard Delta Bit rate (BDBR) [2] is about 6%. As can be seen, the above methods get either a high BDBR increase or a limited acceleration. In view of this, it's necessary to significantly reduce the encoding time of target videos with smaller increase of BDBR.

To this end, this paper proposes a novel downscale transcoding method that utilizes the information about CU partition depth and prediction mode to accelerate the downscale transcoding process for HEVC. First, during the decoding process, the CU depth and prediction mode information are extracted into matrices in block level. Then we use the matrices to predict CU partition depth and prediction mode at CU level. Based on the prediction, some efficient rules are proposed to determine CU partition and prediction mode of target videos, so that many unnecessary calculation can be skipped. Our approach supports the spatial downscale transcoding with any spatial resolution downscaling ratio. Experiments show that the proposed method can achieve 59.3% time reduction on average compared to the reference HEVC encoder, with 3.4% of BDBR increment on average. A comparsion with the state-of-the-art spatial resolution downscale transcoding methods for HEVC also shows the effectiveness of our method.

The rest of this paper is organized as follows. Section 2 reviews the CU encoding process of HEVC. Section 3 describes the proposed method to accelerate the spatial resolution downscale transcoder for HEVC. In Sect. 4, the experimental results and evaluations of the proposed method are presented. Section 5 concludes the paper.

2 Overview of CU Encoding Process

2.1 CU Partition

HEVC introduces a relatively flexible CU structure [8] by adopting a multi-level quadtree structure. As is presented in Fig. 1, CU partition process is a recursive search. Starting from the most basic coding tree unit (CTU), whose size is 64×64 pixels by default, a CTU can contain a single CU or can be further divided into four sub-CUs. Each sub-CU can choose whether to be divided into four smaller sub-CUs until the CU arrives the minimum size of 8×8. Each CU has a depth value which represents its level as well as the partition. The depth value is an integer ranging from 0 to 3, which correspond to the sizes of 64×64, 32×32, 16×16, and 8×8 respectively. It can be seen that a variety of possible CU sizes provide a very flexible CU partition for HEVC, where the encoder selects a CU partition scheme with the lowest rate distortion cost. Compared with H.264, as the number of alternative partitioning schemes increases, it is more likely to find the scheme with the lowest rate distortion cost. This is an important reason for the high efficiency of HEVC coding. However, more CU partitioning schemes also mean that the encoder need to take more time to check the rate distortion cost of each scheme. In the hierarchical recursive CU partition process, the encoder needs to check a total of 85 CUs (including 64 8×8 CUs, 16 16×16 CUs, 4 32×32 CUs, and 1 64×64 CU). But only certain CUs are selected, if we can utilize the CU depth information of decoded source videos to predict CU depth in advance, many unnecessary checks can be skipped with ignorable loss in rate-distortion (RD) performance.

2.2 Prediciton Mode

The prediction mode of HEVC can be classified into two categories, Intra mode and Inter mode. Furthermore, the Intra mode has 35 kinds of luma prediction modes and 5 kinds of chroma prediction modes. For Inter mode, it can be categorized as Skip mode, Merge mode and normal Inter mode. For Skip mode and Merge mode, the motion vector difference (MVD) is 0, so the motion parameters are directly obtained from the adjacent coded blocks. The difference between two modes is that Skip mode does not need encode MVD or prediction residuals, Merge mode does not need encode MVD but need encode prediction residuals. As for Inter mode, it need encode both MVD and prediction residuals. Moreover, for CUs in an inter-frame, both Intra mode and Inter mode can be adopted. During the process of HEVC prediction mode determination, even if we don't

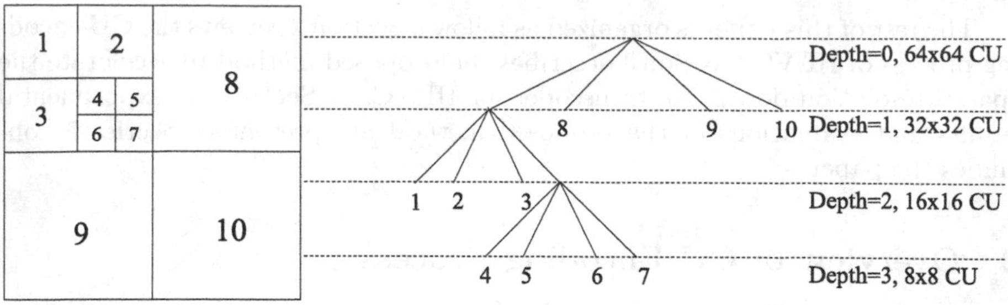

Fig. 1. CU partition process and CU structure

consider non-symmetric mode, the RD-cost of total 8 modes, one Skip mode, one Merge mode, one $2N \times 2N$ Inter mode, two $2N \times N$ Inter mode, two $N \times 2N$ Inter mode and one $2N \times 2N$ Intra mode need to be calculated for CU of each depth. And for the CU with maximum coding depth as well as the size of 8×8, another four RD-cost of $N \times N$ Intra mode need to be calculated. This also increases the CU partition computational complexity greatly. Thus, if we can utilize the prediction mode information of decoded source videos to predict prediction mode at CU level in advance, many mode analysis parts can be skipped.

3 CU Information Mapping Transcoder

In this section, we present our downscale transcoding method, which contains two parts, depth mapping and partition determination, prediction mode mapping and determination.

3.1 Depth Mapping and Partition Determination

In order to utilize the CU depth information of source videos to skip unnecessary checks in CU coding process, we need to predict the CU depth of target videos firstly. As mentioned in Sect. 2, the CU size can be 64×64, 32×32, 16×16, and 8×8. That is, any CU can be formed as some 8×8 blocks. Since the pixels in one CU have the same depth, all of the pixels in one 8×8 block have the same depth. So we define 8×8 block as the Basic Unit (BU). As shown in Fig. 2(a), when decoding the source video, the CU depth information is extracted into a matrix in BU level. Since the contents of the videos do not change during the spatial resolution downscale transcoding, the general tendency of CU depth is also unchanged. Therefore, in the encoding phase, we can apply the depth matrix to predict the specified block depth in the corresponding position. Specifically, the location of the block in the target video is mapped to the original video according to the downscale ratio. As only when the downscaling ratio is a power of 2, which means the size of every mapped CU is still a power of 2, the current CU block can be mapped to the corresponding location in the reference image without grid misalignment. Otherwise, as shown in Fig. 2(a), the boundary of

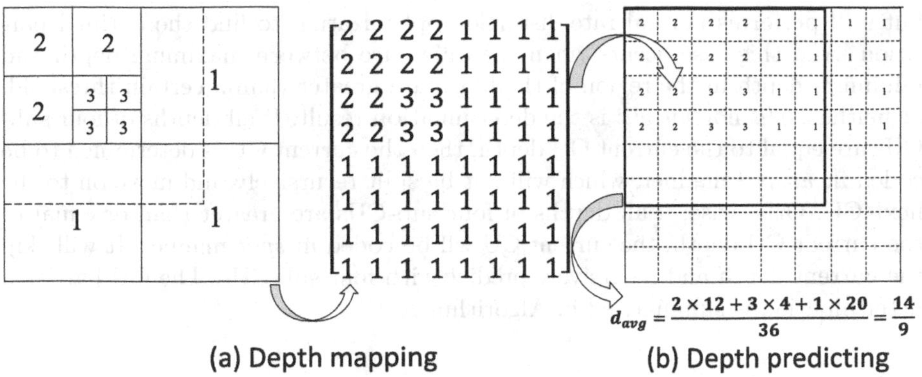

Fig. 2. CU depth mapping and prediction

mapped CUs can't be aligned with that in the reference image. To solve this problem, we define a set of BUs as X whose region has an intersection with the target block and the intersecting area is greater than 32, then the average depth is calculated by:

$$d_{avg} = \frac{\sum_{x \in X} d_x}{N} \tag{1}$$

where X is defined as above, d_x is the depth of BU x, N is the number of elements in the set X. As illustrated in Fig. 2(b), the average depth of the block (thick line) can be computed as above. Besides, since the spatial resolution downscaling makes the size of CU smaller, the depth of block will become larger. Thus, we need add a bias to correct the average value of depth. Here, we predict the depth of the target block as follows:

$$D_{pred} = d_{avg} + 0.5 \cdot log_2(r_w \cdot r_h) \tag{2}$$

where r_w and r_h are downscale ratios in width and height respectively. As can be seen, the calculation of Formula (2) may result in noninteger depth value. However, the depth of a CU is a integer value and can only be in {0, 1, 2, 3}. As a result, the final predicted depth can be denoted as:

$$D = \min(3, \lceil D_{pred} \rceil) \tag{3}$$

where $\lceil x \rceil$ is the smallest integer greater than or equal to x.

After computing the predicted depth, we can use it to avoid unnecessary rate-distortion calculations to accelerate the CU partition. In encoding process, we first assume that the current CU is split into four sub-CUs. Then we use the depth mapping method to predict the depths of four sub-CUs. At last, the CU partition decision will be one of the following three options: *split*, *unsplit* or *unsure* according to the predicted depth. When the result of partition decision is *unsure*, the current CU is not directly determined whether to split or not, but still performs normal rate-distortion optimization to find the optimal partition. And this case occurs when the difference between maximum depth and minimum depth in the region of the block are greater than a certain threshold, or neither *split* nor *unsplit* is the determination result. If all depths of four sub-CUs are equal to the current CU depth, then the current CU is determined to be coded in *unsplit* manner, which will not be split recursively and move on to the next CU. Otherwise, if all depths of four sub-CUs are greater than or equal to the current CU depth, the current CU wll be coded in *split* manner. It will skip the current depth and recursively predict with four sub-CUs. The CU partition determination is summarized in Algorithm 1.

Algorithm 1. CU partition determination Algorithm

Input: the mapping depth matrix, M; the depth of current CU, cur_depth;
Output: the predicted partition result of the current CU, $pred\_split$;

initial $max\_depth = 0$ and $min\_depth = 4$;
for $k = 1$ to 4 **do**
  compute the predicted depth of kth sub-CU $depth_k$ by Formula (1), (2), (3);
  update max_depth and min_depth;
end for
if $max\_depth - min\_depth > th_{unsure}$ **then**
  $pred\_split \leftarrow unsure$;
end if
if $cur\_depth = depth_k$ **then**
  $pred\_split \leftarrow unsplit$;
else if $cur\_depth \leq depth_k$ **then**
  $pred\_split \leftarrow split$;
else
  $pred\_split \leftarrow unsure$;
end if

3.2 Prediction Mode Mapping and Determination

In this paper, we propose a method based on prediction mode mapping at CU level. As mentioned above, although Skip mode and Merge mode belongs to Inter mode, the processes of Skip mode and Merge mode are different from normal Inter modes. Thus, the prediction mode is divided into three class, Intra mode, Inter mode and Skip/Merge mode. Then we need to determine which class mode to be selected as the final prediction mode. Different from depth, prediction mode is a categorical variable, which is completely discrete and incalculable. Consequently, the method of calculating the average value similar to CU depth prediction is not feasible here. The solution in this paper is as follows. First, we employ the same way as depth mapping to convert the prediction mode information into a matrix. Then similarly, the location of the block in the target video is mapped to the original video according to the downscale ratio. Afterwards, we calculate the respective proportion of the three class modes separately and utilize the weights to determine the prediction mode. The method of computing the proportion of each class mode is as follows:

$$W_i = \frac{\sum_{y \in Y_i} 1}{\sum_{x \in X} 1}, i = 1, 2, 3 \tag{4}$$

where Intra mode, Inter mode and Skip/Merge mode correspond to 1, 2, 3, W_i is the weight of class mode i, X a set of BUs whose region has an intersection with the target block and the intersecting area is greater than 32, Y_i is a subset of X and the prediction modes of all elements are i.

In the reference software HM, the CU coding is sequentially performed by four processes, the Skip/Merge mode check, the Inter mode check, the Intra mode check and recursive partition. In this paper, we computes the weights of three modes before CU coding, and uses the following rules to determine whether to skip some modes calculation:

(a) Unconditionally perform the Skip/Merge mode analysis part;
(b) If W_3 is greater than Th_{skip} and the RD-Cost of Skip mode is less than the Merge mode, then skip the Inter and Intra mode analysis part directly;
(c) If the sum of W_3 and W_2 are less than or equal to W_1, the Inter mode analysis part is skipped;
(d) If W_1 is less than or equal to Th_{intra}, the Intra mode analysis part is skipped.

For rule (a), the Skip/Merge mode exploits the continuity of the moving object in spatial and temporal domain, which associates the moving object covered by the current block with the moving object in the adjacent block in spatial and temporal domain. However, for one image at different resolutions, objects covered by the same size block in the corresponding position may be different. It's possible that a 64×64 CTU on the image at a larger resolution cannot cover a moving object, so it can be merged with surrounding blocks that cover the same moving object by using one motion vector. But on the image at a smaller resolution, the CTU can completely cover an independent moving object and cannot be merged with adjacent blocks. On the other hand, the Skip/Merge mode has a low computational complexity. Hence, skipping the Skip/Merge mode incorrectly will not achieve a significant promotion in coding speed, and it will result in a reduction in compression efficiency.

Rule (b) is a strategy for early jump out of mode calculation, in which the relation between RD-Cost of Skip mode and Merge mode are an important condition to ensure the accuracy of prediction. Since the Skip mode does not require coding residuals, if the RD-Cost of the Skip mode is smaller, which means the difference generated by motion compensation is small, the prediction accuracy is already high enough. And exceeding the threshold Th_{skip} also shows that the motion between the current block and the surrounding blocks is consistent, thus other modes can be skipped directly.

Rule (c) and rule (d) directly use the weights of each mode to determine the prediction mode. Note that the Skip/Merge mode is a special Inter mode, of which the motion vector difference is 0, so the actual weight of the Inter mode in rule (c) includes the weight of the Skip/Merge mode.

Finally, considering CU partition information and mode information reuse, the total CU coding process is shown in Fig. 3.

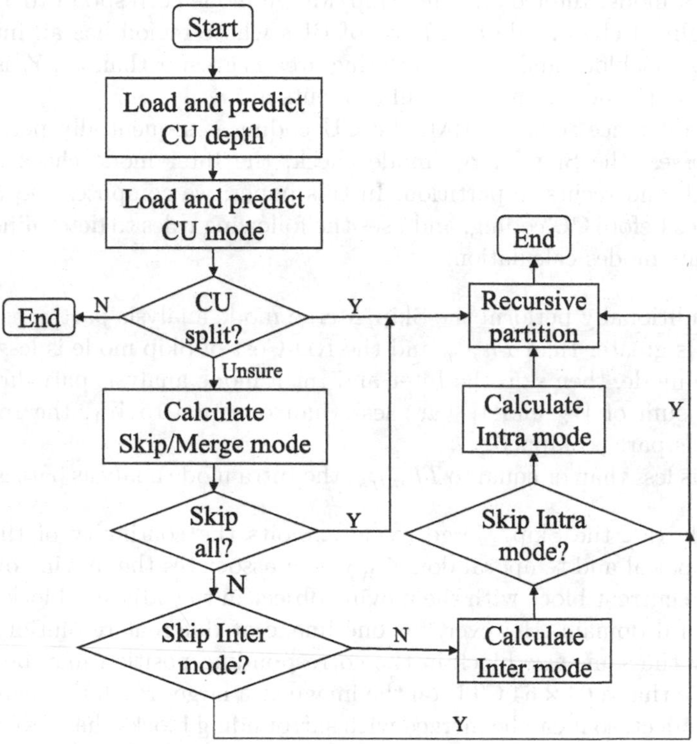

Fig. 3. Flowchart of CU coding process

4 Experimental Results

In this section, we implement the proposed method based on HEVC test model (HM) software 16.20 and perform a comparison of the reference HEVC transcoder and the proposed transcoding method for the evaluation. All experiments are performed on an Ubuntu server with a Xeon(R) E5-1680 CPU at 3.40 GHz. The 8-bit HEVC standard test sequences [16] from 1080p (1920 × 1080) and 720p (1280 × 720) are selected. The videos are encoded with four quantization parameters (QP) values 22, 27, 32, and 37 in random access (RA) setting, which is common used for downscale transcoding. Then the bitstream is decoded and downscaled to smaller resolution using bi-cubic interpolation. And 1080p video is downscaled to 720p and 480p, and 720p video is downscaled to 480p and 360p. Afterwards, the downscaled sequence is encoded by the original encoder and the proposed encoder with the same QP in RA setting. The performance of the proposed transcoding algorithm is evaluated in terms of the difference in computational time and Bjontegaard Delta bit rate (BDBR). The time savings are calculated as:

$$TS = \frac{T_{org} - T_{prop}}{T_{org}} \times 100\% \tag{5}$$

where T_{prop} denotes the overall encoding time of the proposed encoder and T_{org} are encoding time of the original encoder.

Table 1. Performance evalution of proposed downscale transcoder

Sequence	Source resolution	Target resolution	BDBR (%)	TS (%)
BasketBallDrive	1920 × 1080	1280 × 720	5.04	52.6
BQTerrace			3.23	57.4
Cactus			4.26	53.0
Kimono			3.57	52.0
ParkScene			3.86	50.0
BasketBallDrive		832 × 480	3.98	37.7
BQTerrace			3.27	46.2
Cactus			2.29	42.1
Kimono			2.72	48.2
ParkScene			3.30	48.0
FourPeople	1280 × 720	832 × 480	5.51	64.1
Johnny			1.03	71.0
KristenAndsara			1.98	63.6
SlideEdit			1.52	78.1
FourPeople		640 × 360	6.15	71.4
Johnny			2.35	77.5
KristenAndsara			3.14	72.4
SlideEdit			2.12	83.4
Average			3.29	59.4

Table 1 demonstrates the performance comparison between the proposed encoder and the original encoder. As can be seen, our proposed method can downscale transcoding with various scaling factors. And it can save 59.4% encoding time with about 3.40% BDBR inscrease on average, which shows the effectiveness of our method.

Considering both coding efficiency and speedup, we use the ratio of the BDBR and time saving (TS) as a performance metric [4]. Since the decrement of

Table 2. Comparsion with the state-of-the-art downscale transcoder

Method	Scaling factor	BDBR (%)	TS (%)	BDBR/TS
Temporal neighboring CU prediction [13]	2	0.88	40.50	2.17
Efficient downscale transcoder by Lin [12]	1.4	7.65	70.90	10.79
	1.5	5.00	66.87	7.48
	2	6.22	87.60	7.10
Machine learning based transcoder [18]	1.33	5.33	71.06	7.50
	1.5	5.32	71.21	7.47
	2	5.22	70.28	7.43
	4	6.15	68.03	9.04
Ours	1.5	3.33	60.21	5.53
	2	3.44	76.18	4.51
	2.28	3.11	44.44	7.00

BDBR and the increment of TS is inversely proportional, lower BDBR/TS value represents a better HEVC transcoding efficiency. Table 2 shows the comparing results of the proposed algorithm and the previous transcoding algorithms: the temporal neighboring CU prediction method proposed by Nguyen et al. [13], the HEVC transcoding method based on machine learning by Van et al. [18], the efficient arbitrary ratio downscale transcoding proposed by Lin [12]. Although algorithm [13] achieve a good performance at the scaling factor 2, it is limited with the scaling factor 2. Compared with other two arbitrary downscaling transcoder, our methods achieves the lowest BDBR/TS in case of scaling factor 1.5 and 2. Besides, the proposed method achieves the lowest average BDBR/TS 5.54 which is, 2.57 smaller than the BDBR/TS average of Efficient downscale transcoder by Lin and 2.17 smaller than the BDBR/TS average of the machine learning based transcoder.

5 Conclusions

In this paper, a fast downscale transcoding method based on CU information reuse is proposed. A CU information mapping approach is presented to predict CU depth and prediction mode. And some efficient CU splitting and CU prediction mode determination rules are proposed. The efficiency of the method is evaluated with respect to the time savings and the coding quality. The experimental results show that the proposed algorithm reduces the re-encoding time significantly and also has a relatively low quality loss.

Acknowledgment. This work was supported by National Natural Foundation of China under contract No. 61671025

References

1. Ahmad, I., Wei, X., Sun, Y., Zhang, Y.-Q.: Video transcoding: an overview of various techniques and research issues. IEEE Trans. Multimedia **7**(5), 793–804 (2005). https://doi.org/10.1109/TMM.2005.854472
2. Bjontegaard, G.: Calculation of average PSNR differences between RD-curves. In: Proceedings of the ITU-T Video Coding Experts Group (VCEG) Thirteenth Meeting, January 2001
3. Bossen, F.: Common HM test conditions and software reference configurations. In: Proceedings of the 11th Meeting, October 2012
4. Correa, G., Assuncao, P.A., Agostini, L.V., Cruz, L.A.D.S.: Fast HEVC encoding decisions using data mining. IEEE Trans. Circuits Syst. Video Technol. **25**(4), 660–673 (2015)
5. Correa, G., Assunção, P., Agostini, L., da Silva Cruz, L.: Performance and computational complexity assessment of high efficiency video encoders. IEEE Trans. Circuits Syst. Video Technol. **22**, 1899–1909 (2012). https://doi.org/10.1109/TCSVT.2012.2223411
6. De Praeter, J., De Cock, J., Van Wallendael, G., Van Leuven, S., Lambert, P., Van de Walle, R.: Efficient transcoding for spatially misaligned compositions for HEVC. In: 2014 IEEE International Conference on Image Processing (ICIP), pp. 2487–2491, October 2014. https://doi.org/10.1109/ICIP.2014.7025503
7. He, J., He, X., Li, X., Qing, L.: Fast inter-mode decision algorithm for high-efficiency video coding based on textural features. J. Commun. **9**, 441–447 (2014). https://doi.org/10.12720/jcm.9.5.441-447
8. Kim, I.K., Min, J., Lee, T., Han, W., Park, J.: Block partitioning structure in the HEVC standard. IEEE Trans. Circuits Syst. Video Technol. **22**, 1697–1706 (2012)
9. Kim, M., Sung, M., Kim, M., Ro, W.W.: Exploiting pseudo-quadtree structure for accelerating HEVC spatial resolution downscaling transcoder. IEEE Trans. Multimedia **20**(9), 2262–2275 (2018). https://doi.org/10.1109/TMM.2018.2804765
10. Leng, J., Sun, L., Ikenaga, T., Sakaida, S.: Content based hierarchical fast coding unit decision algorithm for HEVC. In: 2011 International Conference on Multimedia and Signal Processing, vol. 1, pp. 56–59, May 2011. https://doi.org/10.1109/CMSP.2011.167
11. Lin, K.M., Lin, J.R., Chen, M.J., Yeh, C.H., Lee, C.A.: Fast inter-prediction algorithm based on motion vector information for high efficiency video coding. EURASIP J. Image Video Process. **2018**(1), 99 (2018). https://doi.org/10.1186/s13640-018-0340-4
12. Lin, Z., Zhang, Q., Chen, K., Sun, J., Guo, Z.: Efficient arbitrary ratio downscale transcoding for HEVC. In: 2016 Visual Communications and Image Processing (VCIP), pp. 1–4, November 2016. https://doi.org/10.1109/VCIP.2016.7805465
13. Nguyen, V.A., Do, M.N.: Efficient coding unit size selection for HEVC downsizing transcoding. In: 2015 IEEE International Symposium on Circuits and Systems (ISCAS), pp. 1286–1289, May 2015. https://doi.org/10.1109/ISCAS.2015.7168876
14. Shen, X., Yu, L., Chen, J.: Fast coding unit size selection for HEVC based on Bayesian decision rule. In: 2012 Picture Coding Symposium, pp. 453–456, May 2012. https://doi.org/10.1109/PCS.2012.6213252
15. Shu, H., Chau, L.-P.: The realization of arbitrary downsizing video transcoding. IEEE Trans. Circuits Syst. Video Technol. **16**(4), 540–546 (2006). https://doi.org/10.1109/TCSVT.2006.871324

16. Sullivan, G.J., Ohm, J., Han, W., Wiegand, T.: Overview of the high efficiency video coding (HEVC) standard. IEEE Trans. Circuits Syst. Video Technol. **22**(12), 1649–1668 (2012). https://doi.org/10.1109/TCSVT.2012.2221191
17. Sung, M., Kim, M., Kim, M., Ro, W.W.: Accelerating HEVC transcoder by exploiting decoded quadtree. In: The 18th IEEE International Symposium on Consumer Electronics (ISCE 2014), pp. 1–2, June 2014. https://doi.org/10.1109/ISCE.2014.6884329
18. Van, L.P., De Praeter, J., Van Wallendael, G., De Cock, J., Van de Walle, R.: Performance analysis of machine learning for arbitrary downsizing of pre-encoded HEVC video. IEEE Trans. Consum. Electron. **61**(4), 507–515 (2015). https://doi.org/10.1109/TCE.2015.7389806
19. Wiegand, T., Sullivan, G.J., Bjontegaard, G., Luthra, A.: Overview of the H.264/AVC video coding standard. IEEE Trans. Circuits Syst. Video Technol. **13**(7), 560–576 (2003). https://doi.org/10.1109/TCSVT.2003.815165
20. Xiong, J., Li, H., Wu, Q., Meng, F.: A fast HEVC inter CU selection method based on pyramid motion divergence. IEEE Trans. Multimedia **16**(2), 559–564 (2014). https://doi.org/10.1109/TMM.2013.2291958

Fine-Grain Level Sports Video Search Engine

Zikai Song[1], Junqing Yu[1(✉)], Hengyou Cai[1], Yangliu Hu[1], and Yi-Ping Phoebe Chen[2]

[1] School of Computer Science and Technology, Center of Network and Computation, Huazhong University of Science and Technology, Wuhan, China
{skyesong, yjqing, caihengyou, huyangliu}@hust.edu.cn

[2] La Trobe University, Melbourne, VIC 3086, Australia
phoebe.chen@latrobe.edu.au

Abstract. It becomes an urgent demand how to make people find relevant video content of interest from massive sports videos. We have designed and developed a sports video search engine based on distributed architecture, which aims to provide users with content-based video analysis and retrieval services. In sports video search engine, we focus on event detection, highlights analysis and image retrieval. Our work has several advantages: (I) CNN and RNN are used to extract features and integrate dynamic information and a new sliding window model are used for multi-length event detection. (II) For highlights analysis. An improved method based on self-adapting dual threshold and dominant color percentage are used to detect the shot boundary. Affect arousal method are used for highlights extraction. (III) For image's indexing and retrieval. Hyper-spherical soft assignment method is proposed to generate image descriptor. Enhanced residual vector quantization is presented to construct multi-inverted index. Two adaptive retrieval methods based on hype-spherical filtration are used to improve the time efficient. (IV) All of previous algorithms are implemented in the distributed platform which we develop for massive video data processing.

Keywords: Video search engine · Event detection · Highlights analysis · Image retrieval

1 Introduction

Sports video, as one of the important video types, has long been a concern worldwide. In contrast to the rapid growth of sports video data, people with busy lifestyle often have little time to watch videos. It becomes an urgent demand that how to access and obtain video content which people are interested in. To date, the content-based video retrieval (CBVR) [1] offers a promising approach to meet this demand. It involves three main research topics: video analysis, video indexing and video retrieval. Video analysis aims at analyzing the content of video based on low-level features. Due to the existence of semantic gap, the semantic description of video content is hard to obtain, making it difficult for current semantic-based video retrieval. Although CBVR has achieved some good research results, a good commercial system has not yet appeared.

Y. M. Ro et al. (Eds.): MMM 2020, LNCS 11961, pp. 519–531, 2020.
https://doi.org/10.1007/978-3-030-37731-1_42

We designed and developed a fine-grain level sports video search engine on distributed architecture (Hereinafter referred to as sports video search engine), aiming at providing users with content-based sports video analysis and retrieval services.

The sports video search engine draws on the idea of platform-as-a-service (PaaS) and uses a distributed cluster as hardware support to distributed computing and storage of video. The front browser can search the video based on text and video content. Non-linear browsing of the searched video by means of video shots or video highlight curves can enhance user experience. Sports video event detection uses deep learning method to construct a event detection model. Highlights analysis consists of shot segmentation and highlights extraction based on affect arousal. Key frames extracted through event detection and highlights analysis will be used for image retrieval which uses content-based indexing and retrieval methods. The architecture of the sports video search engine is shown in Fig. 1.

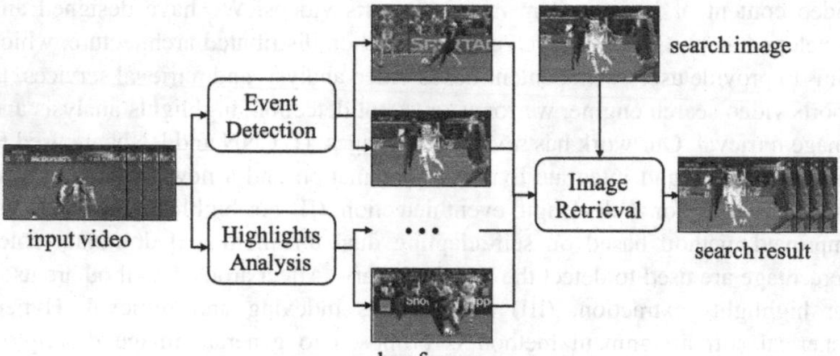

Fig. 1. Architecture of the sports video search engine.

The innovations of the sports video search engine are as follows.

- CNN and RNN are used to extract features and integrate dynamic information. A new sliding window model are also used for multi-length event detection.
- An improved method based on self-adapting dual threshold and dominant color percentage are used to detect the shot boundary. Affect arousal method are used for highlights extraction.
- Hyper-spherical soft assignment method is proposed to generate image descriptor. Enhanced residual vector quantization is presented to construct multi-inverted index. Two adaptive retrieval methods based on hype-spherical filtration are used to improve the time efficient.
- The upper application can regard the sports video search engine as a reliable cloud computing service, and the distributed processing of the video application can be realized by simply calling the API. The sports video search engine is reusable and can handle the various technical needs of multiple video applications.

2 Related Work

We will provide an overview of event detection, highlights analysis, image retrieval and video data processing platform.

Event detection. Currently, video event detection widely uses deep learning method [2, 3]. Ramanathan [4] uses the position information of player to identify key players with Attention Model and increase his role in basketball event detection. Ibrahim [5] comprehensively consider individual information and group activity information, further integrate the appearance and movement features of each player to form a group activity description in volleyball game. New CNN structures were proposed in [6] for the action detection problem, using CNN and sliding window to identify the action type and determine the boundary respectively. The combination of C3D and longer RNN is the basic model of the action detection network [7], and the temporal boundary is directly predicted according to the output hidden state of the RNN.

Highlights analysis. Based on the principle that video content changes will cause mood fluctuations of audience, Hanjalic [8] first proposed the idea of extracting highlights from the perspective of the audience's emotions. An emotional model is constructed by extracting features of the sports video that can cause emotional agitation of the audience, and then detecting the highlights in sports video based on the emotional agitation curve. This method overcomes the versatility of the previous methods, and has great application potential in the exciting shot extraction of sports video. However, there are also some problems, one is that it is time consuming to extract the video intensity features of the avi format, and another is that it is impossible to determine the start point and end point of the event specifically.

Image retrieval. Common image visual features include color histograms, GIST and SIFT. However, in recent years, researchers have paid more attention to the study of image descriptor based on visual words. Image descriptor based on the Bag-of-Feature (BOF) [9] calculates the BOF descriptor of the image according to the SIFT local features extracted from the image. Based on the BOF image description, a new algorithm called VLAD, which combines BOF and Fisher kernel, was proposed in [10]. Wengert [11] proposed the bag-of-color image descriptor based on CIE-Lab space. The inverted index structure based on visual words was originally proposed by [9]. After that, Inverted File with Asymmetric Distance Computation was proposed by [12] for the nearest neighbor search of feature descriptors. According to whether the number of nodes in each inverted list in the index structure is balanced, Jegou [13] proposed a balanced clustering mechanism to make the size of cluster more uniform. A penalty term is introduced and set the distance between the feature descriptor and the cluster center to the sum of Euclidean distance and penalty term.

3 Event Detection on Sports Video

Sports video event detection (SVED) uses deep learning method to construct a sports video event detection model. CNN and RNN are used to extract features and integrate dynamic information of video. Feature information is expanded by feature reorganization of multi-frame images. Then feature sequence is expanded by sliding window. And we use a new sliding window model for multi-length event detection.

3.1 Event Type Recognition

In video clip type recognition. CNN is used to extract features from video images while RNN is used to extract dynamic information from multiple feature sequences. And attention model is used to reconstruct adjacent features to enlarge the range of feature sequences. Event data set are used to train the network and predict the types of sports events that input video belong to. VGGNet [14], BN-Inception [15] and ResNet [16] are selected as feature extraction networks. After extracting the features of a single video frame, the next is to integrate the corresponding feature sequences of video frames. LSTM [17] network is used to extract the information contained in the feature sequences. Network structure is shown as Fig. 2(a).

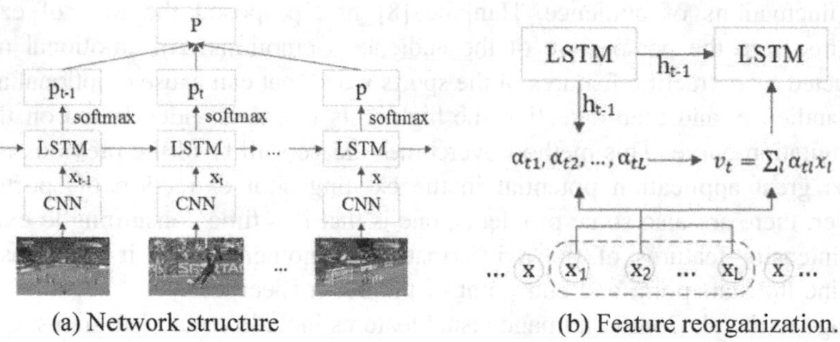

Fig. 2. Video type recognition.

In order to enhance the flow of feature information in LSTM network, the input feature sequence is reconstituted so that the network can obtain the input feature directly and reduce the loss. As shown in Fig. 2(b). For any point of time t, the input of LSTM is no longer a single feature but a combination of many features. The combination of multiple features further utilizes the Attention Model mentioned in [18] for weighted reorganization. Then we train the network and predict the types of sports events.

3.2 Event Boundary Detection

In long video event detection. An event time boundary determination module is added to RNN to detect events of various lengths of videos. Siding windows of different lengths are predicted by LSTM network to determine the event boundaries. And the event detection results are further screened by using the relationship between events and playback shots. For a complete video, detect playback fragments, and event boundary identified is performed outside of playback while event type recognition is performed inside of playback. A complete story is composed of related events and playback segments.

4 Highlights Analysis

Highlights analysis consists of both shot segmentation and highlights extraction. Shot segmentation uses an improved algorithm to detect shot boundary as well as motion vector method to extract playback scenes. Highlights extraction for sports video based on affect arousal method.

4.1 Shot Segmentation

Shot Boundary Detection. There are two types of shot boundaries: cut and gradual transition. The shot segmentation algorithm first detects candidate cut and gradual transition according to the self-adapting dual threshold and dominant color percentage, then determines whether the candidate transition is cut or gradual transition according to statistical confirmation method. The detail of boundary detection is shown in Fig. 3.

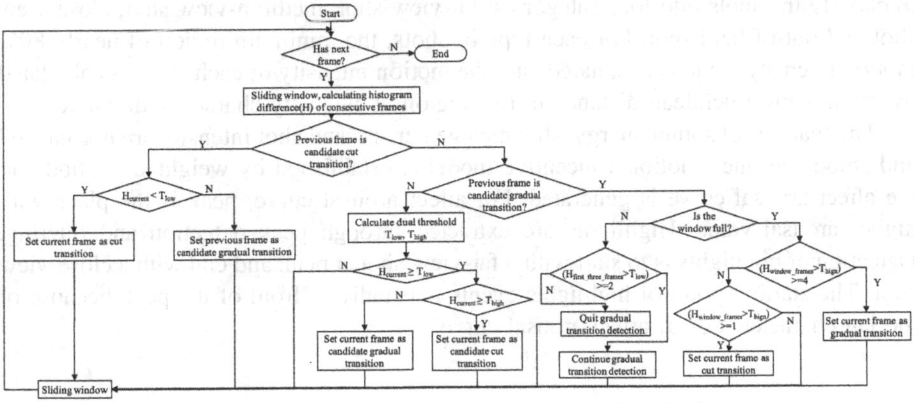

Fig. 3. Flow chart of boundary detection algorithm

Playback Extraction. Playback scenarios play a important role in detecting highlights. The algorithm detects the Logo region using motion vectors method. The playback detection is divided into two parts: learning and detection.

In learning, gradual transition is obtained by shot boundary detection algorithm, and the gradient length within a certain range is regarded as a candidate Logo transform set. Optical flow and motion vectors in each candidate Logo transform set are calculated. The sequence matching value which calculated by matching the gradient with the dynamic programming sequence determines whether the gradual transition is a logo gradual transition sequence. A gradual transition sequence with larger matching values is regarded as a logo sequence.

In detection, the color difference between the frame and L-pixels is compared. Some frames with higher similarity are chosen as candidate Logo and are constituted with adjacent frames. The sequence of Logo template is compared with learned template to determine whether it is a real Logo transform. Playback scenes are obtained by matching the adjacent Logo sequences.

4.2 Highlights Extraction

In sports videos, wonderful events are always accompanied by the increase of motion intensity, sound energy, shot change density and shot intensity.

The feature of sound energy is the short-term energy of sound, as shown in (1).

$$e(k) = \sum_{i=1}^{N} x(i)^2 \tag{1}$$

Where *e(k)* is sound energy of k_{th} frame and *x(i)* is the value of i_{th} sampling points in audio frame. Shot change density first detects the shot of the video, gets the length of each shot and then calculates the switching rate according to (2).

$$c(k) = e^{((1-n(k))/r)} \tag{2}$$

Where *n(k)* is the number of frames contained in k_{th} frame and *r* is a scaling constant.

In the aspect of shot intensity feature extraction, firstly, the method in [19] is used to classify the shots into four categories: far-view shot, medium-view shot, close-view shot and out-of-field shot. For each type of shots, the minimum region of nearly 80% motion intensity value is calculated, and the motion intensity of each shots is calculated by minimizing Euclidean distance in this region as intensity characteristic value.

The features of sound energy, shot change density and shot intensity are normalized and smoothed, the emotional incentive model is established by weighted method and the affect arousal curve is generated. For affect arousal curve, peak is the place with higher arousal value. Highlights are extracted through peak detection and filtering. Detection of highlights is to start with a far-view shot at peak and end with a close-view shot. The starting point of highlights events is usually in front of the peak because of the lag characteristics of affect arousal curve.

5 Indexing and Retrieval for Images

We can get key frames as retrieve images from event detection and highlights extraction. In the image retrieval algorithm. Hyper-spherical soft assignment method is proposed to generate image descriptor. And an enhanced residual vector quantization (ERVQ) is presented and used to construct multi-inverted index. To improve the time efficient, two adaptive retrieval methods based on hype-spherical filtration are proposed, which includes exhaustive filtration-based adaptive retrieval (EFAR) and non-exhaustive filtration-based adaptive retrieval (NEFAR).

5.1 Image Descriptor

Image descriptor is used to represent the visual content of the image, which is the fundamental factor that affects the performance of image retrieval. Image descriptors are generated by hyper-spherical soft assignment method. The algorithm is to construct a hypersphere for each cluster center in the feature space and assign the feature points to the corresponding cluster centers of hyperspheres containing the feature points in the spatial position.

K-means algorithm is used to train *k* clustering centers $C = \{c_1, \ldots, c_2, \ldots c_k\}$ and feature points $x_{ci} = \{x_{i1}, \ldots, x_{in}\}$ of each clustering center c_i. The maximum Euclidean distance of all feature points from c_i to Xc_i is defined as the $radius_i$ of the clustering center:

$$\text{radius}_i = max_{j=1,\ldots,n_i} d(c_i, x_{ij}) \tag{3}$$

Therefore, in the feature space, a hypersphere is constructed with each cluster center c_i as sphere center and $radius_i$ as the radius. The characteristic allocation mechanism of hyper-spherical soft assignment is as (4):

$$\text{b}_{ji} = \begin{cases} 0 & when\ d(x_j, c_i) > radius_i \\ 1 & when\ d(x_j, c_i) \le radius_i \end{cases} \tag{4}$$

Where $b_{ji} = 1$ indicates that x_j is allocated to ci, $b_{ji} = 0$ means that it is not allocated to c_i.

5.2 Multi-inverted Index

ERVQ method is used to quantify and encode the image features. Aiming at the problem of finding the nearest neighbor clustering centers accurately in feature quantization, a search method based on lower bound filtering is proposed. This method uses the distance lower bound to filter the non-neighboring clustering centers in low dimensional space. And a multi-dimensional inverted index structure is designed on the base of enhanced residual vector quantization. Each inverted index corresponds to a clustering, and its clustering center is used as index key to represent inverted table.

Figure 4 is a schematic diagram of the process of inserting image feature vector x into inverted index. After the quantized by ERVQ, the image feature vector is encoded and inserted into the inverted table according to the first M layer identification in the corresponding vector ID.

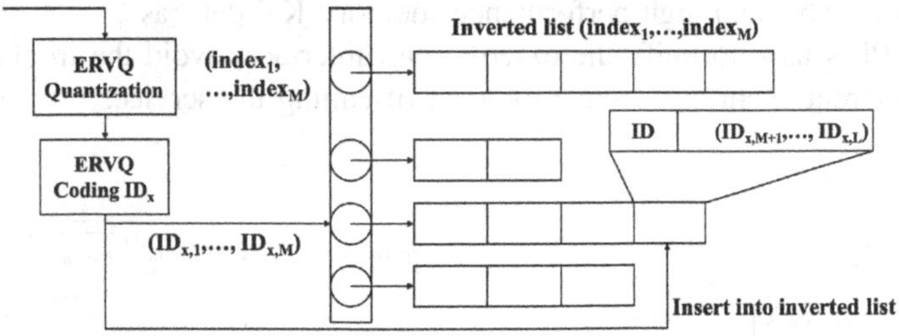

Fig. 4. Multi-inverted index based on ERVQ.

5.3 Adaptive Retrieval Method

On the basis of inverted index structure, adaptive retrieval methods including exhaustive filtration-based adaptive retrieval and non-exhaustive filtration-based adaptive retrieval are adopted to reduce the number of sorted feature points and improve the query speed under the same query precision as original retrieval method.

The key of exhaustive filtration-based adaptive retrieval is to determine a radius based on the position of query feature points. A hypersphere in feature space is constructed with the query feature points as center of sphere. The feature points locate outside the hypersphere are filtered out, and only sort feature points locate inside the hypersphere. Based on the standard inverted index structure, non-exhaustive filtration-based adaptive retrieval reduce the number of distance calculations and times of comparisons between distance and radius of hypersphere by adding inverted index layer to each inverted table.

6 Overall Structure of Platform

Using big data technology and PaaS design to realize sports video analysis platform based on distributed architecture. Taking sports video as research object, design a video processing platform with big data technology. Distributed technology is used to achieve fast and effective processing and simplify the development of upper-level applications.

6.1 Storage Layer

The storage layer is mainly composed of multiple storage modules, such as video storage, video metadata storage and small file storage. The overall architecture of the storage layer is shown in Fig. 5(a).

- HDFS storage for big data can guarantee high throughput, HBase component is introduced to store data with high real-time requirements.
- Elasticsearch is a distributed search and analysis engine can be used for full-text search, structured search and analysis.
- Redis is introduced for the needs of upper application cache to speed up data access, which is a stable and high-performance memory KV database.
- REST API is used to unify the external call interface, avoid the trouble of developing different client and reduce the cost of calling the service.

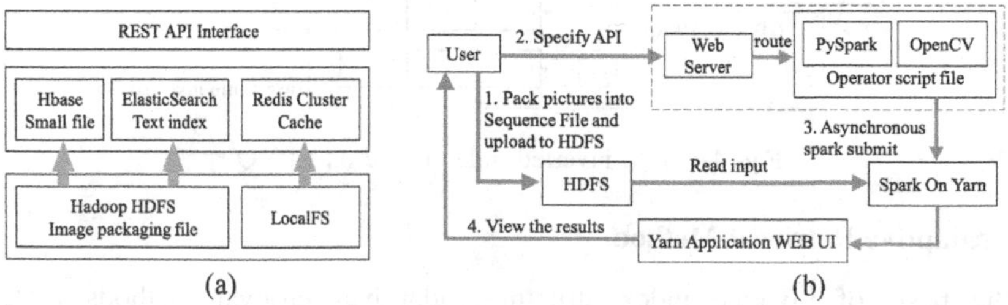

Fig. 5. (a) Schematic diagram of storage layer architecture. (b) Schematic diagram of computing layer architecture.

6.2 Computing Layer

There will be many computationally intensive operations in massive sports video processing. On the basis of storage layer, we encapsulate computing libraries by using distributed computing framework Spark to accelerate operation of common video images. The overall architecture is shown in Fig. 5(b). And steps in architecture are:

1. Video preprocessing. Call API of video storage module in the storage layer to decode native video into pictures and package them as a Sequence File to storage.
2. Launch a request. Specify the path and parameters of HTTP request. Route to the specified operation according to path.
3. Asynchronous submit task. SparkCV opens a Web Server, accepts request and routes to the corresponding operator. Task is asynchronously submitted to Spark for execution, returning detail URL in YARN Application WEB UI.
4. Observation results. User receives return URL and opens it to listen for the submission of application.

6.3 Application Scenarios

The soccer.findball.net is an application of sports video search engine. Figure 6(a) is football part. Home page mainly displays the latest videos, most comments, and most clicks. Click the corresponding link to enter video playback details page. Figure 6(b) is play details page, in the upper right corner of page is preview part of video, below it is highlight curve, the value on curve is brightness of video corresponding time. The soccer.findball.net can use the image and text to search for related videos. As shown in Fig. 6(c), video with high relevance to the search image is displayed. User can click link to start playing from the time point of the image.

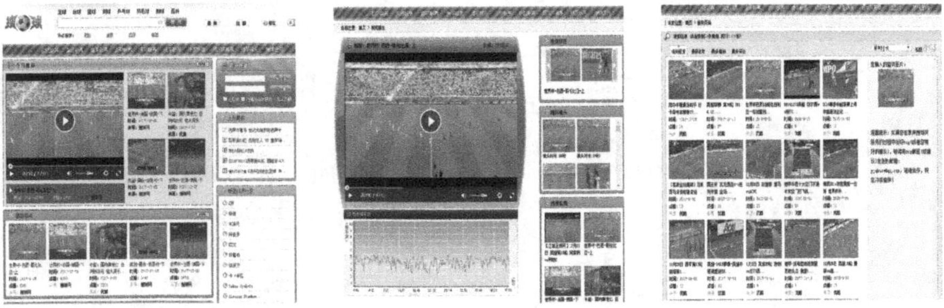

(a) Homepage (b) Play details (c) Search page

Fig. 6. Soccer.findball.net.

7 Experiment

7.1 Event Detection

In event detection, we have compared four methods (Devnet [20], LRCN [21], SST [22] and our methods SVED) on Soccer DataSet [23], evaluation indicators P and R represent for Precision and Recall. Results are shown in Table 1. As we can see, it is hard to get good performance in soccer event detection because of too many negative samples in a soccer video, and proportion of events is too small. However, no matter which method, the best result we got is the corner, since it always happens at the corners of the soccer field. Due to the scenes of shot and goal are basically the same, training sample of shot is much more than the goal, it is easy to misjudge the goal as shot. Above all, experimental results verify that our detection method has best performance when comparing with other detection algorithms.

Table 1. Detection results of four models.

Method	Devnet [20]		LRCN [21]		SST [22]		SVED	
	P	R	P	R	P	R	P	R
Goal	0.013	0.243	0.0	0.0	0.032	0.023	0.340	0.409
Shot	0.070	0.377	0.261	0.244	0.371	0.472	0.335	0.756
Corner	0.086	0.460	0.104	0.709	0.739	0.883	0.710	0.854
Freekick	0.028	0.153	0.063	0.659	0.561	0.376	0.054	0.729
Yellow	0.025	0.508	0.138	0.618	–	–	0.179	0.830
Foul	0.049	0.211	0.076	0.724	–	–	0.211	0.392
Mean	0.039	0.306	0.092	0.422	–	–	0.272	0.621

7.2 Highlights Analysis

The affect arousal curve generating by features of sound energy, shot change density and shot intensity is show in Fig. 7(a). Which is a 20 min' clip from American VS Czech video in 2006 World Cup. Detection result of highlight shots represented by red line box is shown in Fig. 7(b).

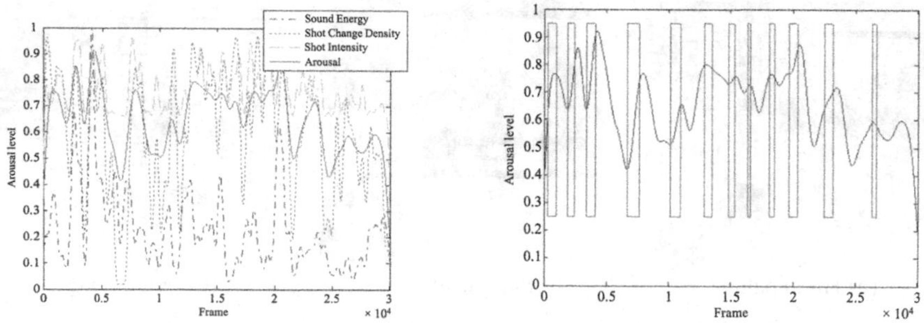

(a) Affect arousal curve (b) Highlights detection

Fig. 7. Highlights analysis in soccer video

7.3 Image Retrieval

For image descriptor experiment, we use the Holidays Dataset [24]. By applying hyperspherical soft assignment to the generation of image VLAD [25] descriptors, the accuracy of VLAD can be evaluated by the accuracy of image retrieval. We compare VLAD based on soft assignment of feature space with the methods proposed in this paper and VLAD. Table 2 shows retrieval performance of these three descriptors.

Table 2. Performance of different descriptors on Holidays dataset.

Descriptor	k	D	Holidays dataset			
			D	D' = 128	D' = 64	D' = 32
VLAD	64	8192	0.526	0.510	0.478	0.420
RNN_VLAD	64	8192	0.497	0.510	0.491	0.463
SSA-VLAD	64	8192	0.553	0.558	0.493	0.499

RNN-VLAD descriptor generation requires two parameters r and $\sigma2$, where r denotes the number of visual words assigned to each local feature and $\sigma2$ is the parameter needed to calculate weight vector. We set r = 3, $\sigma2 = 6250$. k denotes the number of data word, D denotes the original dimension of SSA-VLAD vector, D' denotes the dimension of SSA-VLAD after PCA. As can be seen from Table 3, in Holidays datasets, query results of SSA-VLAD are significantly better than VLAD and RNN-VALD.

For multi-inverted index experiment. Mean Average Precision (mAP) is used to measure the retrieval performance on SSA-VLAD image descriptor set. mAP is area under the recall-precision curve. Table 3 shows the performance comparison of ERVQ, RVQ, PQ and spectral hashing (SH) on SSA-VLAD imazhidaoge descriptor set. Coding length of PQ and SH is {32, 64}, coding length of ERVQ and RVQ is {32, 40}, initial clustering center number of codebook in ERVQ is k = 256, clustering center number of codebook in RVQ is k = 256, and corresponding number of codebook layers is $L \in \{4, 5\}$.

Table 3. Performance comparison of compete retrieval on SSA-VLAD image descriptors.

Methods	Parameters	mAP
RVQ	nbits = 32, k = 256, L = 4	0.448
RVQ	nbits = 40, k = 256, L = 5	0.489
ERVQ	nbits = 32, k = 256, L = 4	0.496
ERVQ	nbits = 40, k = 256, L = 5	0.505
PQ	nbits = 32	0.382
PQ	nbits = 64	0.445
SH	nbits = 32	0.302
SH	nbits = 64	0.383

As can be seen from Table 3, when using the same length of encoding, mean average precision of ERVQ retrieval is significantly higher than that of RVQ, PQ and SH. When the same accuracy is achieved, ERVQ requires less coding length.

8 Conclusions

We introduce a fine-grain level sports video search engine. The core algorithm in search engine including event detection, highlights analysis and image retrieval. The analysis results show that these algorithms achieve better results in processing sports videos. And we introduce the video processing platform focusing on storage layer and computing layer. In future, the algorithm in video search engine would achieve higher accuracy and faster speed to support the increased demand of video data processing. At same time, we should focus on optimizing the storage and computing layers of distributed architecture to further improve the stability and usability of the search engine.

Acknowledgments. We gratefully acknowledge the granted financial support from the National Natural Science Foundation of China (No. 61572211, 61173114, 61202300).

References

1. Geetha, P., Narayanan, V.: A survey of content-based video retrieval. J. Comput. Sci. **4**(6), 734 (2008)
2. Chao, Y.W., Vijayanarasimhan, S., Seybold, B., et al.: Rethinking the faster R-CNN architecture for temporal action localization. In: IEEE Conference on Computer Vision and Pattern Recognition (CVPR), pp. 1130–1139 (2018)
3. Lin, T., Zhao, X., Su, H., et al.: BSN: boundary sensitive network for temporal action proposal generation. In: European Conference on Computer Vision (ECCV), pp. 3–19 (2018)
4. Ramanathan, V., Huang, J., Abu-El-Haija, S., et al.: Detecting events and key actors in multi-person videos. In: IEEE Conference on Computer Vision and Pattern Recognition (CVPR), pp. 3043–3053 (2016)
5. Ibrahim, M.S., Muralidharan, S., Deng, Z., et al.: A hierarchical deep temporal model for group activity recognition. In: IEEE Conference on Computer Vision and Pattern Recognition (CVPR), pp. 1971–1980 (2016)
6. Lea, C., Flynn, M.D., Vidal, R., et al.: Temporal convolutional networks for action segmentation and detection. In: IEEE Conference on Computer Vision and Pattern Recognition (CVPR), pp. 1003–1012 (2017)
7. Krishna, R., Hata, K., Ren, F., et al.: Dense-captioning events in videos. In: IEEE International Conference on Computer Vision (ICCV), pp. 706–715 (2017)
8. Hanjalic, A.: Adaptive extraction of highlights from a sport video based on excitement modeling. IEEE Trans. Multimedia **7**(6), 1114–1122 (2005)
9. Sivic, J., Zisserman, A.: Video Google: a text retrieval approach to object matching in video. In: IEEE International Conference on Computer Vision (ICCV), pp. 1470–1477 (2003)
10. Jegou, H., Douze, M., Schmid, C., et al.: Aggregating local descriptors into a compact image representation. In: IEEE Conference on Computer Vision and Pattern Recognition (CVPR), pp. 3304–3311 (2010)
11. Wengert, C., Douze, M., Jegou, H.: Bag-of-colors for improved image search. In: 19th ACM International Conference on Multimedia, pp. 1437–1440 (2011)
12. Jegou, H., Douze, M., Schmid, C.: Product quantization for nearest neighbor search. IEEE Trans. Pattern Anal. Mach. Intell. **33**(1), 117–128 (2011)

13. Tavenard, R., Jegou, H., Amsaleg, L.: Balancing clusters to reduce response time variability in large scale image search. In: 9th International Workshop on Content-Based Multimedia Indexing (CBMI), pp. 19–24 (2011)
14. Simonyan, K., Zisserman, A.: Very deep convolutional networks for large-scale image recognition. arXiv preprint arXiv:1409.1556 (2014)
15. Ioffe, S., Szegedy, C.: Batch normalization: accelerating deep network training by reducing internal covariate shift. arXiv preprint arXiv:1502.03167 (2015)
16. He, K., Zhang, X., Ren, S., et al.: Deep Residual Learning for Image Recognition. arXiv preprint arXiv:1512.03385 (2015)
17. Hochreiter, S., Schmidhuber, J.: Long short-term memory. Neural Comput. **9**(8), 1735–1780 (1997)
18. Xu, K., Ba, J., Kiros, R., et al.: Show, attend and tell: neural image caption generation with visual attention. arXiv preprint arXiv:1502.03044 (2015)
19. Yu, J., Wang, N.: Shot classification for soccer video based on sub-window region. J. Image Graph. 1006–8961 (2008). 07-1347-06
20. Gan, C., et al.: DevNet: a deep event network for multimedia event detection and evidence recounting. In: IEEE Conference on Computer Vision and Pattern Recognition (2015)
21. Donahue, J., et al.: Long-term recurrent convolutional networks for visual recognition and description. In: IEEE Conference on Computer Vision and Pattern Recognition (2015)
22. Buch, S., et al.: SST: single-stream temporal action proposals. In: IEEE Conference on Computer Vision and Pattern Recognition (CVPR) (2017)
23. Yu, J.Q., Lei, A.P., Song, Z.K., et al.: Comprehensive dataset of broadcast soccer videos. In: IEEE International Conference on Multimedia Information Processing and Retrieval (2018)
24. Jegou, H., Douze, M., Schmid, C.: Hamming embedding and weak geometric consistency for large scale image search. In: Forsyth, D., Torr, P., Zisserman, A. (eds.) ECCV 2008. LNCS, vol. 5302, pp. 304–317. Springer, Heidelberg (2008). https://doi.org/10.1007/978-3-540-88682-2_24
25. Herve, J., Matthijs, D., Cordelia, S., et al.: Aggregating local descriptors into a compact image representation. In: IEEE Conference on Computer Vision and Pattern Recognition (CVPR), pp. 3304–3311 (2010)

The Korean Sign Language Dataset for Action Recognition

Seunghan Yang[1], Seungjun Jung[1], Heekwang Kang[2], and Changick Kim[1](✉)

[1] Korea Advanced Institute of Science and Technology (KAIST), Daejeon, Korea
{seunghan,seungjun45,changick}@kaist.ac.kr
[2] Samsung Electornics, Suwon, Korea
s2473k@kaist.ac.kr

Abstract. Recently, the development of computer vision technologies has shown excellent performance in complex tasks such as behavioral recognition. Therefore, several studies propose datasets for behavior recognition, including sign language recognition. In many countries, researchers are carrying out studies to automatically recognize and interpret sign language to facilitate communication with deaf people. However, there is no dataset aiming at sign language recognition that is used in Korea yet, and research on this is insufficient. Since sign language varies from country to country, it is valuable to build a dataset for Korean sign language. Therefore, this paper aims to propose a dataset of videos of isolated signs from Korean sign language that can also be used for behavior recognition using deep learning. We present the Korean Sign Language (KSL) dataset. The dataset is composed of 77 words of Korean sign language video clips conducted by 20 deaf people. We train and evaluate this dataset in deep learning networks that have recently achieved excellent performance in the behavior recognition task. Also, we have confirmed through the deconvolution-based visualization method that the deep learning network fully understands the characteristics of the dataset.

Keywords: Korean sign language (KSL) · Sign language recognition and analysis · Deep learning · Video recognition · Action recognition

1 Introduction

1.1 Sign Language Datasets

Many deaf people in the world are talking with each other using a sign language. A sign language, like a speech, has various expressions that reflect individual characteristics. For this reason, it is difficult for ordinary people to communicate with deaf people. Therefore, it is meaningful to design a system that automatically translates the sign language.

Y. M. Ro et al. (Eds.): MMM 2020, LNCS 11961, pp. 532–542, 2020.
https://doi.org/10.1007/978-3-030-37731-1_43

Fig. 1. A video sample (Bibimbap).

Previously, various sign language datasets are released and applied to behavior recognition models. In Germany, Forster *et al.* [7] present the RWTH-PHOENIX-Weather dataset for meteorological analysis, and Von Agris *et al.* [19] present SIGNUM containing essential words and sentences. In the United States, AM Martinez *et al.* [13] propose PurDue ASL, which is well suited to learning. Neidle *et al.* [14] release the Boston ASLLVD with more than 3300 words, and the CUNY ASL [12] which makes American sign language (ASL) animated. In Poland, PSL Kinect 30 [15] and PSL ToF 84 [10], which record the essential words of Polish sign language with Kinect camera and Time-of-flight camera, are released. In China, Chai *et al.* [3] have released a DEVISIGN-G/-D/-L dataset that contains RGB, depth, and skeleton information easy to learn for machine learning algorithms.

In Korea, however, there is no sign language dataset for network learning. Since sign languages are different from country to country, it is essential to build a suitable dataset for Korean sign language recognition. Therefore, we present the Korean Sign Language dataset (https://github.com/Yangseung/KSL) and contribute to the research and technological development of networks suitable for Korean sign language in the future.

1.2 Video Action Recognition

Recently, the number of studies in video-based behavior detection and recognition has significantly increased. Mainly, it is widely used for sports analysis, fire, and area monitoring through video analysis. Simonyan and Zisserman [16] design two-stream Convolutional Networks for action recognition using RGB and optical flow images. Tran *et al.* [18] use 3D ConvNets to obtain both spatial and temporal information. Wang *et al.* [20] propose Temporal Segment Networks (TSN), which win the first place in the CVPR 2016 ActivityNet Challenge. They cut videos into a fixed number of sequences and then sample the snippets in each sequence to represent the entire videos with fewer images. Carreira and Zisserman [2] propose Two-Stream Inflated 3D ConvNet (I3D), which combines two-stream networks with 3D ConvNets. This network also win the first place in the CVPR 2017 Charades Challenge. Long-term Recurrent Convolutional Networks (LRCN) proposed by

Donahue *et al.* [6], which combine CNN and LSTM to recognize behavior for the first time.

Table 1. Class names of the KSL dataset.

Hi	Name	Again	Cell phone	Introduction
Special	Sweat	Food	What	Read
How many	Where	Receive	Yesterday	Yet
Want	Meet	Thank	Day	Number
Please	Education	Finally	Visit	Bibimbap
Equal	Good	Location	Walk	Test
Born	One hour	Glad	Sorry	When
Guide	Parents	End	Success	Far
Hobby	Eat	We	Responsibility	10 min
You	Favor	Good	Meat	Fine
Subway	Who	Sister	Worry about	Seoul
Care	Movie	Do effort	Be friendly	Arrive
Study	Marry	Dinner	Face	Next
Bus	Family	Human	Effort	Experience
See	Age	Ride	Time	Now
No	Invite			

The development of action recognition networks has led to the development of sign language recognition networks. Yang and Zhu [21] propose CNN-based networks for Chinese sign language recognition. Their model shows high performance by extracting only the area corresponding to hand and then learning CNN-based networks. Also, Huang *et al.* [8] combine the 3D convolution modules [9] and Two Stream Networks [16] to extract the features of RGB and depth images and then improve the accuracy of Chinese sign language recognition using LS-HAN. Based on these studies, We expect that the existing action recognition networks will achieve excellent performance in Korean sign language recognition as well.

In summary, we release the Korean Sign Language (KSL) dataset. This dataset differs from previous sign language datasets in other countries in that it is taken in the background where real sign language could be used and included the most commonly used words for deaf people. We train and evaluate the KSL dataset with TSN, I3D, and LRCN. Finally, we visualize LRCN trained by the KSL dataset and analyze features different from previous behavior recognition datasets.

The main contribution of this paper is as follows.

1. To the best of our knowledge, we first present the Korean Sign Language (KSL) dataset suitable for deep neural network learning.

2. We train and evaluate the KSL dataset with representative networks in the field of behavior recognition, and analyze the results through a visualization technique.

2 The KSL Dataset Analysis

In this section, we explain how the KSL dataset is organized. We then analyze the KSL video clips and show how the experimental dataset is constructed.

The KSL dataset for Korean sign language recognition consists of sign language for 77 words of 20 people who use Korean sign language in real life (in Table 1). While existing datasets for other countries' sign language recognition are taken to target a specific situation, we aim to a real-life situation. Therefore, the 77 words are constructed by asking the participants of the data composition, which are frequently used in real life. Each sign language of the deaf people is recorded in one place, and the total background consists of 17 locations. In our dataset, facial expressions and hand movements can be identified clearly. Furthermore, the dataset consists of shooting angles and distances that can be applied to the actual video, and the background in which real-life sign language can be used. The total number of images is 1,229, and the total number of frames is 112,564. We take all images with a fixed camera with a resolution of 1280 * 720 and 30 fps. The KSL dataset consists of the original videos, RGB images, and optical flow images. The optical flow images are generated by the method proposed by Brox *et al.* [1]

2.1 The KSL Video Clips

The KSL video clips consist of fifteen women and five men, shown in different colors in Fig. 2. Among them, there are four girls aged 8–19, three women aged 20–39, and eight women aged 40–59. Also, there are two men aged 20–39, three men aged 40–59. The dataset is composed of various people, because the size of the hand varies according to age and gender, and the characteristics of sign language are different. For example, in the case of "face," the deaf people commonly turn their hands round in front of their face, but the number of times

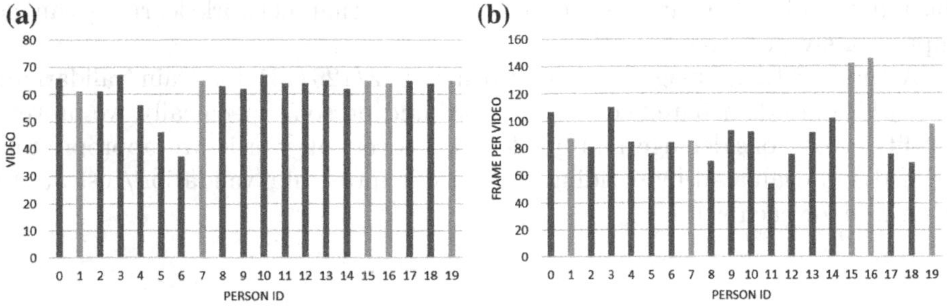

Fig. 2. (a) The number of videos per person, (b) The number of average frames per person (red: male, blue: female). (Color figure online)

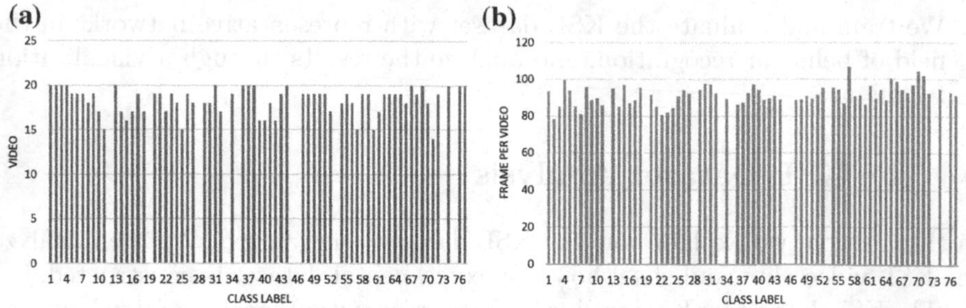

Fig. 3. (a) The number of videos per class, (b) The number of average frames per class.

is different for each person. In the case of "bibimbap,", which is the compound word in Korea, some people signify "bibimbap" in the order of "bibimbap," while others say it "bapbibim" (see Fig. 1). We construct the dataset considering these diversities. In addition, we consider right-handed, left-handed people, whose sign language behavior is symmetrical.

2.2 The KSL Dataset for Sign Language Recognition Experiments

In the sign language experiments using the deep learning network, the words are excluded from the experiments when the sign language motions are too different for each word. Moreover, if the sign of a small number of people is very different for one word, the images are excluded from the experiments. In detail, Korean sign language varies depending on the situation, such as speaking to friends or speaking to high people like the difference between "sorry" and "apologize" in English. In this case, the sign language of the word is different from each other and we exclude it on experiments. As a result, 67 words are used in the experiments (see Fig. 3).

The speed of sign language is different for each participant in the experiments, and we denote this as the average number of frames per video taken for each person in Fig. 2. Although the average number of frames per person and the number of videos are different, the average number of frames per video and the number of videos are distributed evenly so that network learning can be appropriately performed (see Fig. 3).

A total of 1,229 images are divided into 972/126/131 for train/validation/test, which are distributed equally by word and person. Specifically, we prevent overfitting to consider age and gender. Moreover, all words are appropriately learned and evaluated by dividing the dataset into train/validation/test at the same rate for each word.

3 Networks for Video Action Recognition and a Visualization Method

This section introduces the best-performing networks in existing behavior-aware tasks and describes methods for visualizing the network. Next section, we train and evaluate the KSL dataset on the introduced network and analyze them through a visualization technique, explained in this section.

3.1 Video Action Recognition

Temporal Segment Networks (TSN). In the video-based classification, it is essential to see the sequences of a video. Due to the limited capacity, it is difficult to learn to use all the frames of the video at once, and if the video is divided into fixed lengths, the network will only judge the action by seeing a limited length of a scene. In order to solve these problems mentioned above, TSN cuts the video V into K segments, and then randomly extracts one frame per segment to learn a total of K frames.

$$TSN(T_1, T_2, ..., T_K) = H(G(F(T_1; W), F(T_2; W), ..., F(T_K; W))). \quad (1)$$

Equation (1) shows a process in which TSN finally makes an inference through input frames. F is a CNN-based deep neural network, G is a segmental consensus function that combines the results of each of the K frames, and H is a softmax function for computing the probability of each class.

Two-Stream Inflated 3D ConvNet (I3D). RGB model and optical flow model are learned through 3D ConvNet using 3D convolution. With 3D convolution, the network is able to consider the data temporally and spatially, which is effective for video behavior recognition. After training each model, the outputs of the models are combined before Softmax to improve performance. However, using 3D ConvNet for both RGB and optical flow models makes it difficult to learn because the number of parameters is too large. So, in I3D, they use a pre-trained model with ImageNet [5] dataset and Kinetics [11] dataset to better make feature maps for video action recognition and improve performance by learning only the last layer.

Long-Term Recurrent Convolutional Networks (LRCN). LRCN improves performance by considering video in space and time with CNN + LSTM structures. The CNN-based networks generate the feature maps reflecting the spatial characteristics, and the LSTM networks classify the feature maps generated by the CNN-based networks. This result reflects the temporal characteristics. Inputs are continuous RGB images and optical flow images, and outputs are probabilities per class from LSTM. RGB model and optical flow model are trained and coupled together to increase performance before final inference. Moreover, they put a sequence of the video snippets several times and average the results from the LSTM to final classification.

3.2 A Visualization Method

We use the Deconvnet layer [22] to visualize which parts of the image the classifier looks at. The feature maps from the last convolution layer is reconstructed to the image pixel level through the Deconvnet layer, and reconstructed images are visualized. By solving the optimization problem of Eq. (2) using the result of the feature maps and the convolution kernels, the feature maps can be reconstructed to the pixel level. We denote that y_c^i is the feature map of the i-th coordinate of the c-th channel, $f_{k,c}$ is the k-th kernel of the c-th channel, we can find the result of the previous layer by finding z_k^i that minimizes Eq. (2). The result is put into y_c^i and it is repeated to restore the feature map to the image pixel level.

$$C_1(y^i) = \frac{\lambda}{2} \sum_{c=1}^{K_0} \| \sum_{k=1}^{K_1} z_k^i \oplus f_{k,c} - y_c^i \| + \sum_{k=1}^{K_1} |z_k^i|^p . \quad (2)$$

In Sect. 4.2, we visualize the behavior recognition network using the Deconvnet layer to verify the characteristic of the KSL dataset that is different from the existing dataset.

4 Experiments

We evaluate and visualize the KSL dataset with the best performing networks in existing behavior recognition tasks. We train the networks in two ways. The first is learning the model with ImageNet [5], which is made for image classification task of networks, then learning with the KSL dataset. Second, the network is

Table 2. Test accuracy on the KSL dataset.

Model	Pretrained		Accuracy	
	ImageNet	UCF-101	RGB (%)	Flow (%)
TSN	O	X	X	70.71
TSN	O	O	X	**79.80**
I3D	O	X	X	X
I3D	O	O	X	X
LRCN	O	O	27.06	54.14

Table 3. Test accuracy on the UCF-101 dataset.

Model	Pretrained	Accuracy		
	ImageNet	RGB (%)	Flow (%)	Fusion (%)
TSN	O	85.4	89.4	**94.9**
I3D	O	84.5	90.6	93.4
LRCN	O	71.12	76.95	82.92

first learned by the UCF-101 [17] dataset, which is for video behavior recognition tasks, then fine-tuned by the KSL dataset.

4.1 Results of the KSL Dataset

Table 2 shows the action classification results on the KSL dataset using TSN, I3D, and LRCN. When training with RGB video, CNN based TSN and I3D do not converge (accuracy below 5%), and only LRCN based on CNN + LSTM is learned. The CNN-based network cannot converge because it uses the spatial information in the image rather than the temporal information between images. On the other hand, since LRCN uses the feature maps extracted by CNN as an input to the LSTM, LRCN can consider time information. Therefore, LRCN using the RGB image achieve 27.06% on the KSL dataset.

TSN and LRCN show good results when learning with optical flow images, but I3D is not. Since the optical flow images already contain temporal information, it can be learned well in TSN. TSN learned by optical flow images show the highest accuracy among the three networks. I3D consist of 3D convolutions, which need a huge dataset because of the large number of parameters. For this reason, I3D should be pre-trained with behavior-aware datasets that have plenty of data, such as the UCF-101 dataset or Kinetics dataset. However, the existing behavior recognition datasets and the KSL dataset do not have common features, and therefore do not apply well.

In case of learning the KSL dataset with TSN pre-trained by ImageNet dataset used in image classification, the accuracy is 70.71%. Performance is lower than learning and evaluating additional behavior awareness dataset UCF-101 (79.80%). Because the KSL dataset is also a behavior-aware dataset, additional learning of the UCF-101 dataset characterizes its features better than otherwise.

Table 3 shows the accuracy of evaluating networks for the UCF-101 dataset. It is much more accurate than learning and evaluating with the KSL dataset. This is because the UCF-101 dataset behavior recognition task is easier than the sign language recognition task, which is discussed in detail in the next section.

4.2 A Visualization of Network

Figures 4 and 5 show the result of visualizing the feature maps of LRCN learned by the UCF-101 and the KSL dataset. LRCN is based on Vgg-M [4], and the feature maps are obtained from the fc6 layer and visualized using the Deconvet layer described in the previous section. Since the UCF-101 dataset has a different background for each class, and the background is the same within the same class, then the LRCN learned by UCF-101 classifies the actions by the backgrounds, not the human actions themselves. For example, in Fig. 4, LRCN classifies the action by looking at a person's face, not a hand gesture. On the other hand, it can be seen that LRCN learned by the KSL dataset classifies the action based on human hand movements (see Fig. 5). Through the visualization process, the KSL dataset can be confirmed to be a more difficult task to distinguish behaviors

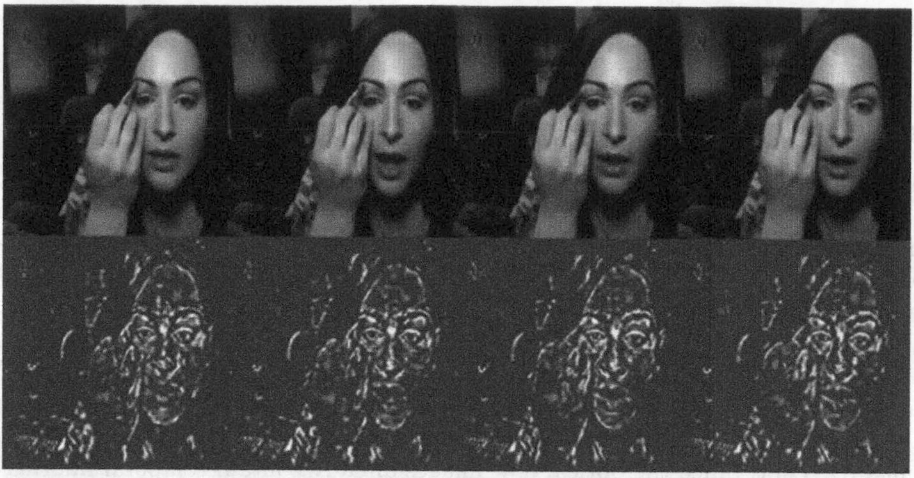

Fig. 4. Visualization of LRCN (the UCF-101 dataset).

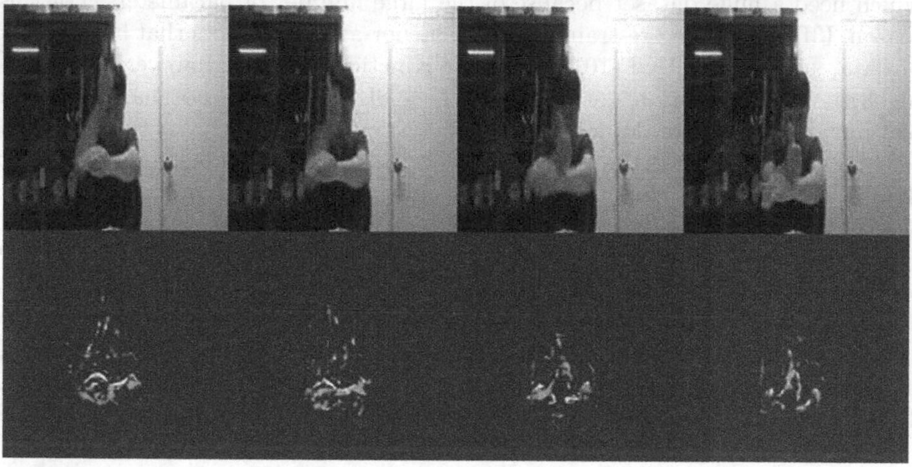

Fig. 5. Visualization of LRCN (the KSL dataset).

from hand movements compared to existing behavior recognition techniques that can use background information.

5 Conclusion

In this paper, we first present the Korean Sign Language (KSL) dataset suitable for deep learning network. We release original videos, RGB images, and optical flow images of the KSL dataset, contributing research and technology development for network suitable for Korean sign language in the future. Also, we evaluate the KSL dataset for the networks that achieve the highest performance in the field of behavior recognition. We visualize the network and confirm that sign language recognition is a difficult task to classify the action based on only hand movements, unlike existing ones.

References

1. Brox, T., Bruhn, A., Papenberg, N., Weickert, J.: High accuracy optical flow estimation based on a theory for warping. In: Pajdla, T., Matas, J. (eds.) ECCV 2004. LNCS, vol. 3024, pp. 25–36. Springer, Heidelberg (2004). https://doi.org/10.1007/978-3-540-24673-2_3
2. Carreira, J., Zisserman, A.: Quo vadis, action recognition? a new model and the kinetics dataset. In: proceedings of the IEEE Conference on Computer Vision and Pattern Recognition, pp. 6299–6308 (2017)
3. Chai, X., Wanga, H., Zhoub, M., Wub, G., Lic, H., Chena, X.: DEVISIGN: dataset and evaluation for 3D sign language recognition, Technical report, Beijing (2015)
4. Chatfield, K., Simonyan, K., Vedaldi, A., Zisserman, A.: Return of the devil in the details: delving deep into convolutional nets. arXiv preprint arXiv:1405.3531 (2014)
5. Deng, J., Dong, W., Socher, R., Li, L.J., Li, K., Fei-Fei, L.: ImageNet: a large-scale hierarchical image database. In: 2009 IEEE Conference on Computer Vision and Pattern Recognition, pp. 248–255. IEEE (2009)
6. Donahue, J., et al.: Long-term recurrent convolutional networks for visual recognition and description. In: Proceedings of the IEEE Conference on Computer Vision and Pattern Recognition, pp. 2625–2634 (2015)
7. Forster, J., et al.: RWTH-PHOENIX-Weather: a large vocabulary sign language recognition and translation corpus. In: LREC, pp. 3785–3789 (2012)
8. Huang, J., Zhou, W., Zhang, Q., Li, H., Li, W.: Video-based sign language recognition without temporal segmentation. In: Thirty-Second AAAI Conference on Artificial Intelligence (2018)
9. Ji, S., Xu, W., Yang, M., Yu, K.: 3D convolutional neural networks for human action recognition. IEEE Trans. Pattern Anal. Mach. Intell. **35**(1), 221–231 (2012)
10. Kapuscinski, T., Oszust, M., Wysocki, M., Warchol, D.: Recognition of hand gestures observed by depth cameras. Int. J. Adv. Rob. Syst. **12**(4), 36 (2015)
11. Kay, W., et al.: The kinetics human action video dataset. arXiv preprint arXiv:1705.06950 (2017)
12. Lu, P., Huenerfauth, M.: Collecting and evaluating the CUNY ASL corpus for research on American Sign Language animation. Comput. Speech Lang. **28**(3), 812–831 (2014)
13. Martínez, A.M., Wilbur, R.B., Shay, R., Kak, A.C.: Purdue RVL-SLLL ASL database for automatic recognition of American sign language. In: Proceedings of the Fourth IEEE International Conference on Multimodal Interfaces, pp. 167–172. IEEE (2002)
14. Neidle, C., Thangali, A., Sclaroff, S.: Challenges in development of the American Sign Language Lexicon Video Dataset (ASLLVD) corpus. In: Proceedings of the 5th Workshop on the Representation and Processing of Sign Languages: Interactions between Corpus and Lexicon, Language Resources and Evaluation Conference (LREC) 2012, CiteSeer (2012)

15. Oszust, M., Wysocki, M.: Polish sign language words recognition with Kinect. In: 2013 6th International Conference on Human System Interactions (HSI), pp. 219–226. IEEE (2013)
16. Simonyan, K., Zisserman, A.: Two-stream convolutional networks for action recognition in videos. In: Advances in Neural Information Processing Systems, pp. 568–576 (2014)
17. Soomro, K., Zamir, A.R., Shah, M.: Ucf101: a dataset of 101 human actions classes from videos in the wild. arXiv preprint arXiv:1212.0402 (2012)
18. Tran, D., Bourdev, L., Fergus, R., Torresani, L., Paluri, M.: Learning spatiotemporal features with 3D convolutional networks. In: Proceedings of the IEEE International Conference on Computer Vision, pp. 4489–4497 (2015)
19. Von Agris, U., Zieren, J., Canzler, U., Bauer, B., Kraiss, K.F.: Recent developments in visual sign language recognition. Univ. Access Inf. Soc. **6**(4), 323–362 (2008)
20. Wang, L., et al.: Temporal segment networks: towards good practices for deep action recognition. In: Leibe, B., Matas, J., Sebe, N., Welling, M. (eds.) ECCV 2016. LNCS, vol. 9912, pp. 20–36. Springer, Cham (2016). https://doi.org/10.1007/978-3-319-46484-8_2
21. Yang, S., Zhu, Q.: Video-based Chinese sign language recognition using convolutional neural network. In: 2017 IEEE 9th International Conference on Communication Software and Networks (ICCSN), pp. 929–934. IEEE (2017)
22. Zeiler, M.D., Fergus, R.: Visualizing and understanding convolutional networks. In: Fleet, D., Pajdla, T., Schiele, B., Tuytelaars, T. (eds.) ECCV 2014. LNCS, vol. 8689, pp. 818–833. Springer, Cham (2014). https://doi.org/10.1007/978-3-319-10590-1_53

SEE-LPR: A Semantic Segmentation Based End-to-End System for Unconstrained License Plate Detection and Recognition

Dongqi Tang, Hao Kong, Xi Meng, Ruo-Ze Liu, and Tong Lu(✉)

National Key Lab for Novel Software Technology, Nanjing University, Nanjing, China
{coura,hkong,AMew}@smail.nju.edu.cn, liuruoze@163.com, lutong@nju.edu.cn

Abstract. Most previous works regard License Plate detection and Recognition (LPR) as two or more separate tasks, which often leads to error accumulation and low efficiency. Recently, several new studies use end-to-end training to overcome these problems and achieve better results. However, challenges like misalignment and variable-length or multi-language LPs still exist. In this paper, we propose a novel Semantic segmentation based End-to-End multilingual LPR system SEE-LPR to solve these challenges. Our system has four components which are convolution backbone, LP capture, LP alignment, and LP recognition. Specifically, LP alignment is used to connect LP capture and LP recognition, allowing the gradient back-propagate through the whole network and can handle oblique LPs. Connectionist Temporal Classification (CTC) module used in LP recognition makes our system able to handle LPs with variable-length or multi-language. Comparative studies on several challenging benchmark datasets show that the proposed SEE-LPR system significantly outperforms the state-of-the-art systems in both accuracy and efficiency.

Keywords: License Plates · License Plate detection and Recognition · Deep learning

1 Introduction

Transportation, which is closely related to our daily travels, plays an essential role in our life. Today, License Plate detection and Recognition (LPR) systems have achieved great progress in various applications such as electronic toll, parking management, and unattended vehicle weighing. New deep networks [1,7,9,15,16] for LPR have also been explored recently.

Electronic supplementary material The online version of this chapter (https://doi.org/10.1007/978-3-030-37731-1_44) contains supplementary material, which is available to authorized users.

Y. M. Ro et al. (Eds.): MMM 2020, LNCS 11961, pp. 543–554, 2020.
https://doi.org/10.1007/978-3-030-37731-1_44

Despite tremendous progress and wide applications in this field, LPR still faces a lot of real-life challenges including multi-languages, multi-views, different illuminations, and real-time processing. For example, LPR systems used in parking only take the front view of car images without on-plane rotations, which is not always true in real life environments. Therefore, LRP in realistic unconstrained scenarios is still a very challenging problem.

Most existing research applies separated steps to develop an LPR system by ignoring the relations between detection and recognition. Error accumulation and computation cost may be brought, leading to poor accuracy and low efficiency. Recently, studies [10,17] used end-to-end training to handle these problems. But they didn't consider challenges like oblique LPs, variable-length and multi-language, making their performance still unsatisfactory.

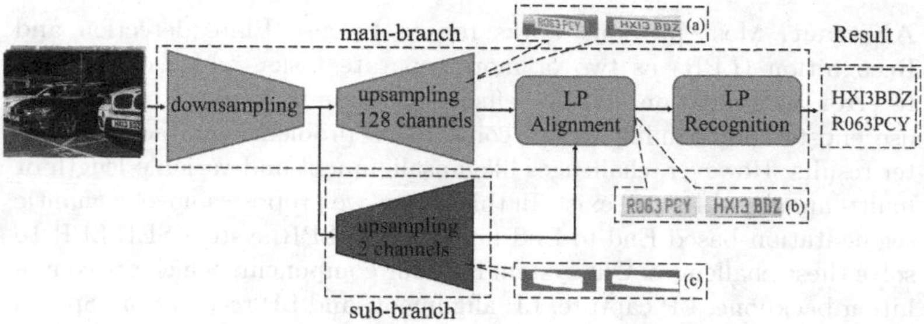

Fig. 1. Overall architecture for SEE-LPR. We apply the main-branch for LP recognition and the sub-branch for LP capture. And we adopt a novel LP alignment module to connect the two branches organically. We use input image in (a) and (b) to illustrate the alignment and recognition for LPs, actually all the operations are based on feature maps.

Considering the mentioned problems, in this paper, we propose a novel Semantic segmentation based End-to-End LPR system SEE-LPR as shown in Fig. 1. To overcome the multi-view situations of license plate (LP) images, we adopt Fully Convolutional Networks (FCN) [12] to apply semantic segmentation for accurately capturing the shape of LP regions. As for recognizing multilingual and variable-length cases, we use Bidirectional LSTM for encoding and Connectionist Temporal Classification (CTC) [4] for decoding to obtain the final results. In order to combine the detection and recognition steps to achieve end-to-end training, we proposed a novel LP alignment method transforming the LP region into a rectangular feature map and making the gradient propagate throughout the whole network. Last but not least, to get over the complexities in real scenes, we build an artificial dataset to simulate cases of different illuminations, defocus blur, motion blur, partial occlusion, etc.

Due to that the two branches in our end-to-end system can work together to perform detection and recognition simultaneously with the shared convolution, we shorten the computation time considerably. Also, the two branches can promote each other to achieve higher accuracy. Comparative results on challenging benchmark datasets, namely, OpenALPR, SSIG, AOLP(RP), OpenData-SYSU and EasyPR, show that the average accuracy of the proposed system (93.50%) is about 10% higher than recent state-of-the-art systems, that is, 13.43% higher than Li et al.'s (2017) [10] on AOLP(RP), 3.85% higher than Laroca et al.'s (2018) [9] on SSIG, and 18.40% higher than Xu et al.'s (2018) [17] on OpenData-SYSU.

Our main contributions can be summarized as follows.

- We propose a novel end-to-end LPR system SEE-LPR with a unified neural network for capturing and recognizing LPs simultaneously through one forward propagation, which is applicable to unconstrained scenarios.
- We introduce a novel alignment method for license plates, transforming the captured LP regions via semantic segmentation into rectangular feature maps, allowing our system to better adapt to oblique LPs.
- Comparative studies show that the proposed system achieving faster speed and higher accuracy than existing multi-stage systems and other end-to-end systems.

2 Related Works

Most previous approaches on LPR are divided into two or more subtasks to be settled one by one. Recently, researchers proposed several end-to-end systems to achieve higher accuracy and faster speed. We briefly introduce these two categories in this section.

2.1 Detection-Recognition Systems

Most existing systems implemented LPR with separated steps, such as car detection, LP detection from cars, character segmentation, and character recognition. In the early stages of LPR research, template matching [2], wavelet transform [19] and sliding windows [1] have been proposed. However, they face difficulties due to the powerlessness when meeting other objects similar to LPs in images. Benefited by deep learning based object detection methods [11,14], several recent LPR systems were proposed. However, most of them still have problems like complex pre-processing in [15] and tedious steps in [16]. Additionally, most works predict LPs in the form of rectangles, which may lead to a deviation with real LP shapes with perspective distortions.

2.2 End-to-End Systems

Although most existing methods are implemented with multi-stages, there are still a small number of end-to-end systems. Li et al. [10] and Xu et al. [17] made efforts on developing end-to-end LPR systems; however, both the two systems ignored perspective distortions caused by various views. The system in [17] utilized rectangles fitting LP regions and applied seven classifiers to predict each character in LPs, but it was only suitable for license plates with fixed-length labels, and required an additional training module for detection before end-to-end training.

In addition to end-to-end license plate detection and recognition, there are several end-to-end scene text detection and recognition methods (text spotting). Lyu et al. [13] proposed a unified network using a branch for finding text bounding boxes and another branch for segmenting characters as well as giving character recognition results. However, since each channel of the network stands for a specific character category, the computational overhead will be very heavy if the target alphabet set is too large.

3 Proposed System

As shown in Fig. 1, we propose a novel end-to-end system SEE-LPR with a unified network. Given an input image, the proposed system captures LP regions and output predictions for each region after LP alignment in one forward propagation. To clearly introduce the proposed SEE-LPR system, we describe the details from four aspects, that is, backbone network, LP capture, LP alignment, and LP recognition. More details on the proposed system will be introduced as follows.

3.1 Backbone Network

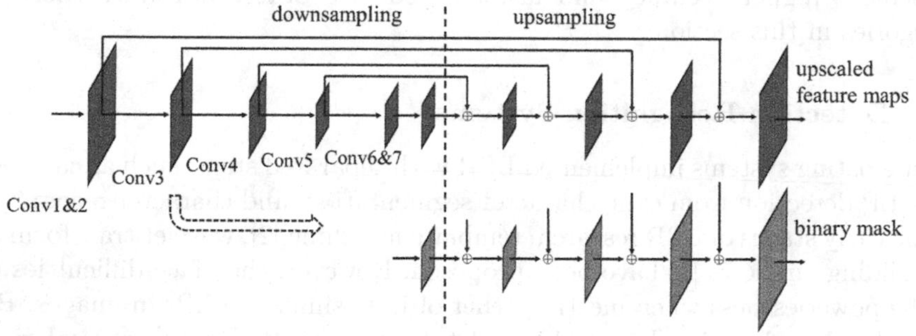

Fig. 2. Backbone Network (Conv1-Conv5 are operations from ResNet-50, Conv6 and Conv7 are convolutional layers with 3×3 kernel, fusion of feature maps from different convolutional stages during upsampling is applied with a cascade of bilinear interpolation and add operations).

Inspired by FCN, the backbone network of the proposed system consists of a downsampling path and an upsampling path with skip connections as shown in Fig. 2. Conv1-Conv5 in downsampling path are operations from ResNet-50 [6], and fully connected layers in ResNet-50 are replaced by convolutional layers Conv6 and Conv7 to achieve pixel-wise prediction. The upsampling path contains a 128-channel main-branch and a 2-channel sub-branch, in which we upscale the feature maps and apply feature fusion through a cascade of bilinear interpolation and add operations. And the scale of feature maps are firstly reduced to 1/32 and then enlarged to 1/2.

Note that the 2-channel sub-branch is used to capture LPs, and the 128-channel main-branch is for obtaining the final recognition results.

3.2 LP Capture

Inspired by the idea of semantic segmentation, we adopt FCN for capturing LPs in the input image. In detail, we apply binary classification for each pixel in the feature maps from the 2-channel sub-branch mentioned in Fig. 2. Given the predictions on pixels, we select positive pixels after Softmax and then group positive adjacent pixels together.

During training, the Cross-Entropy loss function H is utilized on LP/non-LP region prediction:

$$L_{ce} = H(y, \hat{y}) \tag{1}$$

in which y stands for prediction results for pixel-wise binary classification after Softmax, while $\hat{y}$ denotes the ground truth.

As the size of LPs may vary even in a single input image and too small ones may be ignored. Therefore, we give small sizes bigger weights. For the ith LP in an image, the weight for which is denoted by $w_i = S_{all}/(S_i N)$, where S_i is the area of the ith LP, S_{all} is the sum of all the areas, and N is the number of LPs in the input image.

Since lots of scene text regions in images can be regarded as LPs, we adopt Online Hard Example Mining (OHEM) to select negative pixels to reduce false detection. In detail, we select $r \times S_{all}$ negative pixels (r stands for the ratio of negative and positive pixels) with the highest losses and set their weights to ones, meanwhile set other weights to zeros. In this way, we obtain a weight matrix W and calculate the final sub-branch loss as follows:

$$L_s = \frac{1}{(1+r)S_{all}} rsum(W L_{ce}) \tag{2}$$

where $rsum$ stands for reduce sum.

3.3 LP Alignment

LP alignment aims to extract captured LP regions from the upscaled feature maps in the main-branch for further recognition. The alignment process can be divided into two steps, using quadrangles to fit the shape of LP regions and sampling points in main-branch to form rectangular feature maps.

Firstly, when given an LP region R captured by sub-branch, we select a quadrangle Q to fit the region through maximizing Intersection-over-Union (IoU) between Q and R. The determination for Q can be formulated as follows:

$$Q^* = \arg\max_{Q} IoU(Q, R) \tag{3}$$

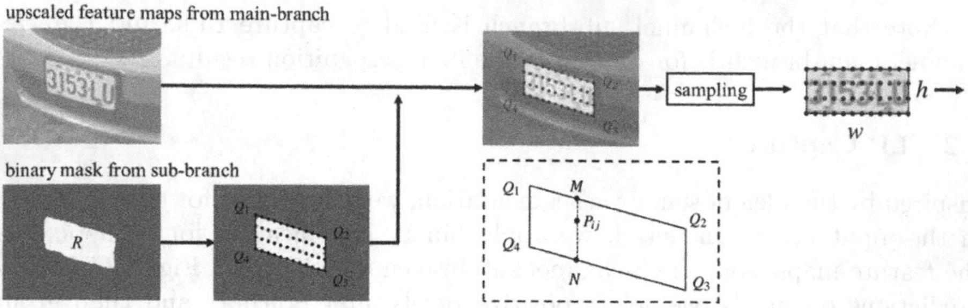

Fig. 3. LP alignment. Firstly, we use a quadrangle box to fit the LP region. Then sample $h \times w$ points in the box from upscaled feature map to form a rectangular feature map. The dashed box shows how to obtain the position of each sampling point.

Then, inspired by RoIAlign in [5], we sample $w \times h$ points from region Q in the main-branch as shown in Fig. 3. The position for each point P_{ij} $(1 \leq i \leq w, 1 \leq j \leq h)$ can be calculated as follows:

$$\overrightarrow{Q_1M} = \frac{i-1}{w-1}\overrightarrow{Q_1Q_2} \tag{4}$$

$$\overrightarrow{Q_1N} = \overrightarrow{Q_1Q_4} + \frac{i-1}{w-1}\overrightarrow{Q_4Q_3} \tag{5}$$

$$\overrightarrow{MP_{ij}} = \frac{j-1}{h-1}\overrightarrow{MN} = \frac{j-1}{h-1}(\overrightarrow{Q_1N} - \overrightarrow{Q_1M}) \tag{6}$$

$$\overrightarrow{Q_1P_{ij}} = \overrightarrow{Q_1M} + \overrightarrow{MP_{ij}} \tag{7}$$

Note that as text recognition is sensitive to the positions of the sampling points, we use float numbers while calculating quadrangle bounding box Q and sampling points. And the value at each position P_{ij} is obtained via bilinear interpolation.

Since license plates usually have a fixed shape, we keep the aspect ratio of h and w fixed. And the selection for values of h and w may affect the accuracy of the recognition results and the efficiency of the model forward propagation. In general, the larger the value of h, the higher the accuracy, as the larger of h, the more features are preserved for the LP region. On the other hand, smaller h will bring faster speed, for that the height of the extracted tensor h must be reduced to 1 through convolution and pooling operations before LSTM encoding. Therefore, the smaller h is, the fewer convolutions and poolings are required. And we need to strike a balance between accuracy and efficiency.

Particularly, when $h = 1$, we directly sample w points on the center line of the quadrangle box to form a $1 \times w$ feature map for LSTM encoding without extra convolution and pooling operation, we find that the recognition accuracy still stays at a relatively high level. This is for that through down sampling and up sampling, each point has a large receptive field, and the receptive field of the center line can cover the whole LP region in most cases.

3.4 LP Recognition

Table 1. Detailed structure for the CNN and LSTM based encoder (k and s represent for kernel size and stride, respectively, and N is the size of the alphabet $L' = L \cup \{blank\}$ used in our datasets.

Layer type	Parameters	Output channels	Feature shape
input		128	8×24
conv-bn-relu	k:$(3,3)$ s:$(1,1)$ p:$(1,1)$	256	8×24
conv-bn-relu	k:$(3,3)$ s:$(1,1)$ p:$(1,1)$	256	8×24
max-pool	k:$(2,2)$ s:$(2,2)$ p:$(0,0)$	256	4×12
conv-bn-relu	k:$(3,3)$ s:$(1,1)$ p:$(1,1)$	512	4×12
conv-bn-relu	k:$(3,3)$ s:$(1,1)$ p:$(1,1)$	512	4×12
max-pool	k:$(2,2)$ s:$(2,1)$ p:$(0,1)$	512	2×12
conv-bn-relu	k:$(2,2)$ s:$(1,1)$ p:$(0,0)$	512	1×12
BiLSTM		512	12
BiLSTM		N	12

After carrying out the LP alignment, the $h \times w$ feature maps are encoded by a CNN and LSTM based encoder, and the final results are decoded by a CTC decoder.

As shown in Table 1, take $h = 8$ and $w = 24$ as an instance, feature maps after alignment are firstly fed into a series of convolution and pooling layers for higher-level feature extraction, after which the heights of the feature maps are reduced to 1. Then the feature maps are permuted to sequence major form $\mathbb{R}^{W \times C}$ from channel major form $\mathbb{R}^{C \times 1 \times W}$ in order to apply sequential feature extraction through recurrent layers. We use two Bidirectional LSTMs for encoding, where the number of the final output channels N is the size of the alphabet $L' = L \cup \{blank\}$ used in our datasets.

The final results are obtained via a CTC decoder, which transforms the N-dimensional encoded sequence $h_1, h_2, ..., h_W \in \mathbb{R}^N$ into a text label with indefinite length. During training, CTC loss is used as the loss function of the main-branch, which is calculated as follows. Firstly, we obtain the probability distribution x_t over alphabet L' of each h_t. Then suppose the ground truth text label sequence $l = \{y_1, ..., y_T\}, T \leqslant W$, we define the conditional probability of the given ground truth label sequence l as the sum of the probabilities of all the paths π corresponding to it:

$$p(l|x) = \sum_{\pi \in \mathcal{B}^{-1}(l)} p(\pi|x) \tag{8}$$

where $\mathcal{B}$ defines a many-to-one map from the set of possible labels to the ground truth l after removing blanks and repeated labels. And $p(\pi|x)$ is the probability of obtaining path π when given x. Finally, we calculate our loss function for the main-branch as follows:

$$L_m = -\frac{1}{n}\sum_{i=1}^{n}\log p(l_i|x) \tag{9}$$

where n denotes the number of LPs in the input image.

3.5 End-to-End Training

For training the whole end-to-end neural network, since the sub-branch cannot provide accurate bounding boxes at the very beginning and some false detection may affect training the main-branch, we utilize the bounding boxes from ground truth during training and use the captured bounding boxes for testing.

The total loss for the network consists of two parts, namely, the sub-branch loss L_s and the main-branch loss L_m. As values of these two items may vary heavily, we adopt dynamically adjusted weights for each item to make the loss converge rapidly:

$$L = \lambda_s L_s + \lambda_m L_m \tag{10}$$

We update the two weights λ_s and λ_m every 100 iterations by the moving average values of each loss L_{sh} and L_{mh}.

$$\lambda_s = 1/L_{sh}, \lambda_m = 1/L_{mh} \tag{11}$$

4 Experimental Results

To evaluate the proposed SEE-LPR, we select several state-of-the-art academic LPR systems and competitive commercial LPR systems for comparison on popular benchmark datasets.

4.1 Benchmark Datasets

We choose several benchmark datasets, namely, OpenALPR (EU and BR), SSIG [3], AOLP [8], OpenData-SYSU [18] and EasyPR, due to the fact that they cover a lot of different types like varying situations and regions.

Table 2. Benchmark datasets for evaluation (D, E, C represent for digital numbers, English characters and Chinese characters, respectively).

Dataset	Size	Alphabet	Difficulty	Dataset	Size	Alphabet	Difficulty
OpenALPR (BR)	114	D/E	Low	AOLP (RP)	511	D/E	Medium
OpenALPR (EU)	108	D/E	Medium	SSIG (test-set)	804	D/E	High
OpenData-SYSU	1060	D/E/C	Medium	EasyPR	258	D/E/C	High

Table 2 shows a brief description for the datasets mentioned above. In these datasets, the AOLP dataset includes AC, LE and RP 3 subsets, in which RP is the hardest as it contains a lot of samples with oblique LPs. OpenData-SYSU contains 3383 images covering LPs of different regions as well as a lot of special ones such as plates from Consulate and Police Station, which are extremely diverse from common plates. From these data, we picked out all the single-line plate images and randomly choose one third as test data and else for training. Note that EasyPR is the most challenging dataset among the six datasets. It covers low resolution, low illumination, blur, raining, rotation, tilt and almost all kinds of situations.

4.2 Pretrain with Artificial Data

Since end-to-end systems usually require a large amount of training data, to overcome the scarcity of the existing training data, we established an artificial dataset LP2P (License-Plate-to-Pretrain). Firstly, we collected some fonts similar to the texts in our target LPs, and generated fake LP images based these fonts by computer rendering. Then we apply noising, blurring and shading processes to these artificial images. Finally, we insert the fake ones into LP regions in real image data (samples are attached in the supplemental material). To achieve better results, we use these artificial data to pretrain with 30 epochs and a few real data to fine-tune.

4.3 Experimental Results

Table 3. End-to-end accuracy on benchmark datasets.

System	OpenALPR		SSIG test-set	AOLP (RP)	OpenData SYSU	EasyPR
	(EU)	(BR)				
Sighthound	83.33%	**94.73%**	81.46%	83.47%	–	–
Amazon Rekog.	69.44%	83.33%	31.21%	68.25%	–	–
Baidu	–	–	–	–	84.81%	85.71%
HyperLPR	–	–	–	–	78.40%	72.43%
Silva and Rosito [16]	**93.52%**	91.23%	88.56%	**98.36%**	–	–
Laroca et al. [9]	–	–	85.45%	–	–	–
Li et al. [10]	–	–	–	83.63%	–	–
Hsu et al. [8]	–	–	–	85.70%	–	–
Xu et al. [17]	–	–	–	–	80.75%	74.81%
Ours (two-stage)	90.74%	92.10%	80.85%	91.19%	87.17%	76.36%
Ours (end-to-end)	**93.52%**	**94.73%**	**89.30%**	97.06%	**99.15%**	**87.26%**

Table 4. Speed (fps) comparison on benchmark datasets.

System	OpenALPR		SSIG test-set	AOLP (RP)	OpenData SYSU	EasyPR
	(EU)	(BR)				
Xu et al. [17]	–	–	–	—	13.7	10.6
Silva and Rosito [16]	2.3	2.1	3.1	4.2	–	–
Ours (two-stage)	8.3	7.1	9.1	10.9	9.4	7.8
Ours (end-to-end)	**16.5**	**13.7**	**16.6**	**22.8**	**17.2**	**15.4**

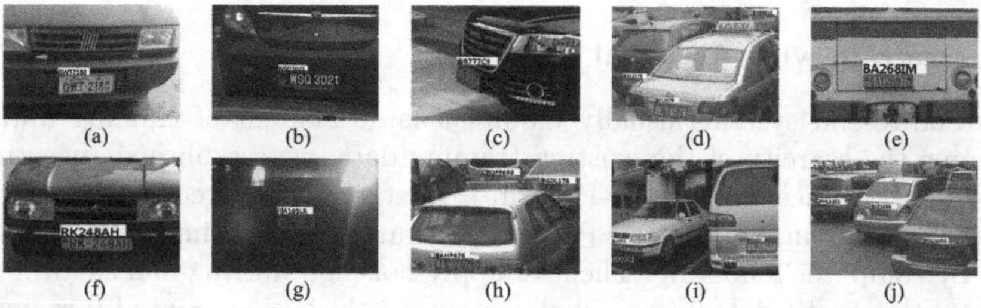

Fig. 4. Results for several samples covering weak illumination, low resolution, tilt angle, different regions, etc.

In our experiments, r is set to 3, both the initial weights λ_s and λ_m are set to 1. And h and w are set to 8 and 24 to achieve relatively high accuracy and fast speed. And we find that if we set h to 1, the accuracy would reduce to around 80% of the value when $h = 8$, while the speed would improve about 10% on OpenData-SYSU dataset.

And during training, data augmentations similar to the way in SSD [11] are applied during training. Firstly, input images are randomly rotated by 0°, 90°, 180°, or 270°. Then random clipping is performed with areas ranging from 0.1 to 1 and ratios of width and height ranging from 0.5 to 2. Next, color jittering, random noise and random blur are applied to the images. Finally, the images are resized to 512×512. And during testing, for images with a short side larger than 512, we rescale the image to let the short side be 512. And for the recognition results with length less than 5, we regard them as false detection and drop these results.

To show the performance of the proposed SEE-LPR, we compared it with some commercial systems, other competitive academic multi-stage systems [8–10,16] and another end-to-end system [17]. On OpenALPR, SSIG and AOLP datasets, we choose commercial systems Sighthound and Amazon Rekognition for comparisons. As for the two LP datasets OpenData-SYSU and EasyPR, since commercial systems mentioned above do not support Chinese characters, we use Baidu and HyperLPR instead. For ablation analysis, we also separate our end-to-end system into a detection and recognition based two-stage system, in which we adopt semantic segmentation for license plate detection and apply CNN, LSTM and CTC for license plate recognition on the original input images, respectively.

Table 3 shows the results on the benchmark datasets, from which we can find the proposed SEE-LPR has a significant improvement in accuracy compared others and outperforms state-of-the-art systems. Table 4 shows our end-to-end system is much faster than others. We choose systems [16,17] for comparison as they provide source code and we test the speed ourselves. Figure 4 shows results for some samples covering weak illumination, low resolution, tilt angle, different regions, etc. More detailed comparative results are attached in the supplemental material.

5 Conclusion

In this paper, we propose an end-to-end trainable license plate detection and recognition system SEE-LPR, in which we introduce semantic segmentation into the field of LPR to process LPs with different perspectives and come up with a novel alignment method for LPs. We also establish an artificial dataset LP2P for pretraining to overcome the scarcity problem of training data. Through experiments and empirical studies, we find the proposed SEE-LPR system shows advantages both in performance and efficiency. For future work, we plan to extend our system to deal with other cases of license plate such as double-line data.

Acknowledgment. This work is supported by the Natural Science Foundation of China under Grant 61672273 and Grant 61832008, and Scientific Foundation of State Grid Corporation of China (Research on Ice-wind Disaster Feature Recognition and Prediction by Few-shot Machine Learning in Transmission Lines).

References

1. Anagnostopoulos, C.N.E., Anagnostopoulos, I.E., Loumos, V., Kayafas, E.: A license plate-recognition algorithm for intelligent transportation system applications. IEEE Trans. Intell. Transp. Syst. **7**(3), 377–392 (2006)
2. Ashtari, A.H., Nordin, M.J., Fathy, M.: An iranian license plate recognition system based on color features. IEEE Trans. Intell. Transp. Syst. **15**(4), 1690–1705 (2014)
3. Gonçalves, G.R., da Silva, S.P.G., Menotti, D., Schwartz, W.R.: Benchmark for license plate character segmentation. J. Electron. Imaging **25**(5), 053034 (2016)
4. Graves, A., Fernández, S., Gomez, F., Schmidhuber, J.: Connectionist temporal classification: labelling unsegmented sequence data with recurrent neural networks. In: Proceedings of the 23rd International Conference on Machine Learning, pp. 369–376. ACM (2006)
5. He, K., Gkioxari, G., Dollár, P., Girshick, R.: Mask R-CNN. In: Proceedings of the IEEE international Conference on Computer Vision, pp. 2961–2969 (2017)
6. He, K., Zhang, X., Ren, S., Sun, J.: Deep residual learning for image recognition. In: Proceedings of the IEEE Conference on Computer Vision and Pattern Recognition, pp. 770–778 (2016)

7. Hsu, G.S., Ambikapathi, A.M., Chung, S.L., Su, C.P.: Robust license plate detection in the wild. In: IEEE International Conference on Advanced Video and Signal Based Surveillance, pp. 1–6 (2017)
8. Hsu, G.S., Chen, J.C., Chung, Y.Z.: Application-oriented license plate recognition. IEEE Trans. Veh. Technol. **62**(2), 552–561 (2013)
9. Laroca, R., et al.: A robust real-time automatic license plate recognition based on the YOLO detector, pp. 1–10 (2018)
10. Li, H., Wang, P., Shen, C.: Toward end-to-end car license plate detection and recognition with deep neural networks. IEEE Trans. Intell. Transp. Syst. **20**(3), 1126–1136 (2018)
11. Liu, W., et al.: SSD: single shot multibox detector. In: Leibe, B., Matas, J., Sebe, N., Welling, M. (eds.) ECCV 2016. LNCS, vol. 9905, pp. 21–37. Springer, Cham (2016). https://doi.org/10.1007/978-3-319-46448-0_2
12. Long, J., Shelhamer, E., Darrell, T.: Fully convolutional networks for semantic segmentation. In: Proceedings of the IEEE Conference on Computer Vision and Pattern Recognition, pp. 3431–3440 (2015)
13. Lyu, P., Liao, M., Yao, C., Wu, W., Bai, X.: Mask TextSpotter: an end-to-end trainable neural network for spotting text with arbitrary shapes. In: Proceedings of the European Conference on Computer Vision, pp. 67–83 (2018)
14. Redmon, J., Divvala, S., Girshick, R., Farhadi, A.: You only look once: unified, real-time object detection. In: Proceedings of the IEEE Conference on Computer Vision and Pattern Recognition, pp. 779–788 (2016)
15. Selmi, Z., Halima, M.B., Alimi, A.M.: Deep learning system for automatic license plate detection and recognition. In: 2017 14th IAPR International Conference on Document Analysis and Recognition (ICDAR), vol. 1, pp. 1132–1138. IEEE (2017)
16. Silva, S.M., Jung, C.R.: License plate detection and recognition in unconstrained scenarios. In: Ferrari, V., Hebert, M., Sminchisescu, C., Weiss, Y. (eds.) ECCV 2018. LNCS, vol. 11216, pp. 593–609. Springer, Cham (2018). https://doi.org/10.1007/978-3-030-01258-8_36
17. Xu, Z., et al.: Towards end-to-end license plate detection and recognition: a large dataset and baseline. In: Ferrari, V., Hebert, M., Sminchisescu, C., Weiss, Y. (eds.) ECCV 2018. LNCS, vol. 11217, pp. 261–277. Springer, Cham (2018). https://doi.org/10.1007/978-3-030-01261-8_16
18. Youting, Z., Zhi, Y., Xiying, L.: Evaluation methodology for license plate recognition systems and experimental results. IET Intell. Transp. Syst. **12**(5), 375–385 (2018)
19. Yu, S., Li, B., Zhang, Q., Liu, C., Meng, Q.H.: A novel license plate location method based on wavelet transform and emd analysis. Pattern Recogn. **48**(1), 114–125 (2015)

Action Co-localization in an Untrimmed Video by Graph Neural Networks

Changbo Zhai[1], Le Wang[1(✉)], Qilin Zhang[2], Zhanning Gao[3], Zhenxing Niu[3], Nanning Zheng[1], and Gang Hua[4]

[1] Xi'an Jiaotong University, Xi'an 710049, Shaanxi, People's Republic of China
lewang@xjtu.edu.cn
[2] HERE Technologies, Chicago, IL 60606, USA
[3] Alibaba Group, Hangzhou 311121, Zhejiang, People's Republic of China
[4] Wormpex AI Research, Bellevue, WA 98004, USA

Abstract. We present an efficient approach for action co-localization in an untrimmed video by exploiting contextual and temporal feature from multiple action proposals. Most existing action localization methods focus on each individual action instances without accounting for the correlations among them. To exploit such correlations, we propose the Graph-based Temporal Action Co-Localization (G-TACL) method, which aggregates contextual features from multiple action proposals to assist temporal localization. This aggregation procedure is achieved with Graph Neural Networks with nodes initialized by the action proposal representations. In addition, a multi-level consistency evaluator is proposed to measure the similarity, which summarizes low-level temporal coincidences, features vector dot products and high-level contextual features similarities between any two proposals. Subsequently, these nodes are iteratively updated with Gated Recurrent Unit (GRU) and the obtained node features are used to regress the temporal boundaries of the action proposals, and finally to localize the action instances. Experiments on the THUMOS'14 and MEXaction2 datasets have demonstrated the efficacy of our proposed method.

Keywords: Temporal action co-localization · Multi-level consistency evaluator

1 Introduction

The temporal action co-localization task aims to jointly locate the action instances of the same category within an untrimmed video, which includes simultaneous action recognition (identify the category of each action instance) and temporal localization (identify the temporal boundaries of each action instance).

Considerable progress has been made to address the temporal action localization problem in untrimmed videos [4–8,20,26,32,38,39]. Techniques including hand-crafted features (iDT) [32,37], Convolution Neural Networks (CNNs) [20,39] and 3-dimensional Convolution Networks (3D ConvNets) [4,24] have been

Y. M. Ro et al. (Eds.): MMM 2020, LNCS 11961, pp. 555–567, 2020.
https://doi.org/10.1007/978-3-030-37731-1_45

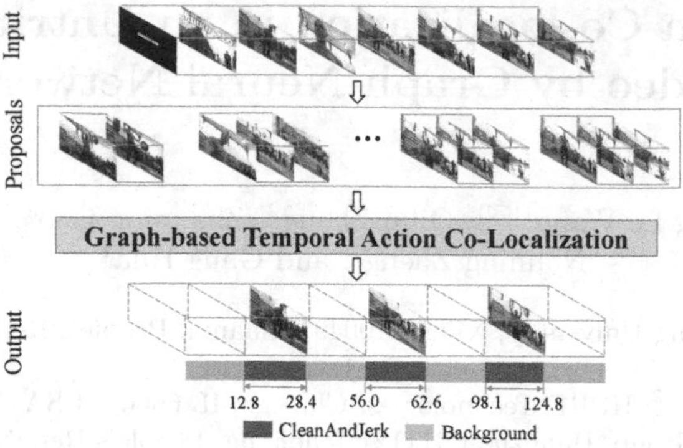

Fig. 1. Flowchart of the proposed G-TACL method. The input is an untrimmed video, which contains multiple action instances of the same category (*e.g.*, CleanAndJerk, marked with the red chunks at the bottom). There are a large number of background frames (marked with the gray chunks) not containing such action instances. The outputs are the predicted categories and the temporal boundaries of action instances. (Color figure online)

proposed and empirically demonstrated to be beneficial. However, the correlation between multiple action proposals of the video in the same category are usually neglected, which could otherwise be potentially beneficial due to the appearance and structure consistency between proposals. Similar strategy of exploiting the appearance and structural consistency of instances has been demonstrated in image/video object co-segmentation [16,18,31]. Actually, it is common that many videos contain multiple action instances of the same category, such as triple jump videos or clean and jerk videos about the Olympic Games. Therefore, a temporal action co-localization algorithm exploiting such correlations could be reasonably desirable.

Graph Neural Networks (GNNs) have been widely adopted in many areas including human-object interaction detection [21] and scene understanding [35]. The GNNs inherit the advantages of both CNNs and graphical models and have strong capabilities of representing and learning the correlation among targets [21]. Inspired by the success of GNNs, we devise the Graph-based Temporal Action Co-Localization (G-TACL) algorithm which represents the correlations using GNNs for co-localizing action instances.

Figure 1 illustrates the flowchart of our proposed action co-localization method. We first employ the Two-Stream network [26] to extract snippet-level features. And then a binary classifier is applied to compute the confidence score of whether each video snippet belongs to the action or not. To generate high-quality action proposals, a two-step thresholding strategy is utilized to group snippets according to confidence scores. Finally, we leverage the G-TACL to model the correlations among multiple action proposals and then iteratively update the action proposal features. The nodes of the graph are initialized by the representations of action proposals, and we propose a multi-level consistency evaluator which exploits high-level contextual similarity and low-level temporal coincidence between action proposals to construct the adjacency matrix. The node features are updated by GRU [3] and the updated features are employed to regress the temporal boundaries of action proposals and to obtain the final action co-localization result.

The primary contributions of this paper are summarized as follows. (1) We propose G-TCAL for video action co-localization, which takes advantage of the correlation among multiple action proposals of the same category in an untrimmed video. (2) We propose a multi-level consistency evaluator for G-TACL, which accounts for low-level temporal coincidences, features vector dot products and high-level contextual features similarities.

2 Related Work

Action Recognition. Action recognition involves the classification of actions in videos. Methods based on hand-crafted features [13,30] and deep neural networks [11,26,29] have been studied extensively. Karpathy *et al.* [11] propose to use CNNs for video classification. Simonyan *et al.* [26] propose the Two-stream architecture where two structurally identical 2D ConvNets are used respectively to process spatial and temporal information in videos. Tran *et al.* [29] propose to extract temporal and spatial features from multiple frames simultaneously by using 3D ConvNets.

Action Localization. Action localization mainly focuses on untrimmed videos that containing at least one action instance and numerous background scenes [17,25,32,34,37,39]. Wang *et al.* [32] combine manually crafted features representing motion and CNN features representing appearance for classification. To overcome the drawbacks of hand-crafted features and capture motion characteristics, Shou *et al.* [25] use multi-scale sliding windows and 3D ConvNet to determine the action category and a localization network for the temporal boundaries of action instances. Motivated by the original faster R-CNN [22], Xu *et al.* [34] propose R-C3D where they switch from classical exhaustive sliding windows to the 3D RoI Pooling that proposes temporal regions from a convolutional feature map. Zhao *et al.* [39] propose the Structured Segment Networks (SSN) where they introduce the structured temporal pyramid pooling to describe three major stages of an action proposal, and apply a decomposed discriminative model to jointly determine its category and completeness. Still, in the aforementioned literatures, the correlation among action proposals of the same category are not explicitly addressed as we speculate earlier.

Graph-Based Network. Graph is a natural data structure to represent relationships among entities. GNNs extend the powerful learning potential of neural networks to process graph data, and have recently become increasingly popular in various domains [9,14,21,28]. Li *et al.* [14] propose a situation recognition method based on GNNs, which can capture joint dependencies between roles in an image. Qi *et al.* [21] propose the Graph Parsing Neural Network (GPNN) to

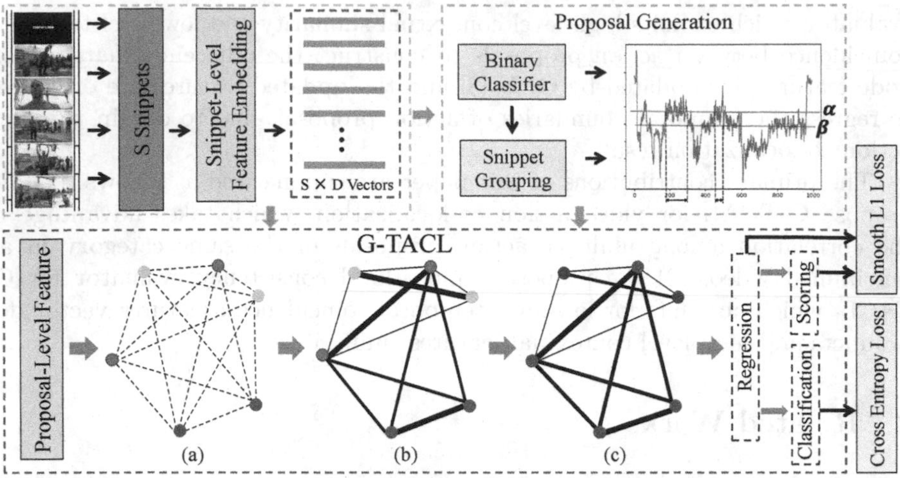

Fig. 2. Pipeline of the proposed temporal action co-localization method. It consists of three parts: feature extraction (upper-left), action proposal generation (upper-right) and G-TACL (bottom).

infer human-object interactions in images and videos. Since action instances of the same category are similar in context and appearance, we try to correlate and update the representations of the action proposals using GNNs.

3 Method

Let V denote an untrimmed video with T frames, $V = \{t_m\}_{m=1}^{M}$, where t_m is the m-th frame. V contains a set of action instances $G = \{g_n = (t_{s,n}, t_{e,n}, k_n)\}_{n=1}^{N_g}$, where N_g is the number of action instances, $t_{s,n}, t_{e,n}$, and k_n are the starting, ending frame and the action category of the n-th instance g_n, respectively. Our goal is to identify the action in video V and to predict the temporal boundaries and the category of each action instance. We adopt a two-stage framework, proposal-and-classification, *i.e.*, we first generate action proposals, and then process them using G-TACL to obtain the final action co-localization result. Figure 2 presents the pipeline of our proposed temporal action co-localization method.

3.1 Snippet-Level Feature Embedding

The goal of this step is to obtain the video representation. The original video is first split into multiple non-overlapping, fixed-length snippets. A pre-trained Two-stream networks [26] is applied to embed each snippet into a fixed-length feature vector[1].

[1] Note that our method is not restricted to any specific feature extractor.

For each snippet, we randomly sample one RGB frame and five consecutive optical flow images and feed them to the spatial stream and the temporal stream respectively, each producing in a 1024-dimensional feature vector. The snippet-level feature is obtained by concating the spatial and the temporal features. Specifically, given a video $V = \{s_i\}_{i=1}^{S}$ with S snippets, where s_i denotes the i-th snippet, the snippet-level feature embedding can be formulated as

$$F_i = [\mathcal{F}_{\text{rgb}}(s_i), \mathcal{F}_{\text{flow}}(s_i)], \tag{1}$$

where $\mathcal{F}_{\text{rgb}}$ and $\mathcal{F}_{\text{flow}}$ denote temporal and spatial stream, respectively. To sum up, the output of this step is the feature map $F \in \mathbb{R}^{S\times 2048}$.

3.2 Action Proposals Generation

Unlike conventional sliding windows-based proposal generation, we exploit the output scores of an "actionness" [33] binary classifier and design a dual threshold scheme. As illustrated in the upper right part of Fig. 2, this class-agnostic binary classifier estimates the actionness scores of input snippets. As noted in [39], there are many noisy frames in the untrimmed videos. Empirically, we design a dual threshold scheme, with separate action-starts threshold α and action-ends threshold β (typically $\beta < \alpha$). A new action proposal is obtained once its the actionness score spikes above α and until its actionness score falls below β. With different choices of α and β, a set of L proposals $\mathbb{P} = \{P_l\}_{l=1}^{L}$ can be obtained. In our experimental settings, $\alpha \in \{0.5, 0.6, 0.7, 0.8\}$ and $\beta \in \{\alpha - 0.2, \alpha - 0.1\}$ accordingly, therefore a total of 8 threshold combinations are explored.

3.3 G-TACL

With action proposals of the same action category, we can theoretically expect higher contextual correlations among them than those across different action categories. In addition, we expect that the quality of these action proposals also affect the contextual correlations. Specifically, we speculate that the correlations among high-quality action proposals of the same category should be higher than those among their low-quality counterparts. To leverage such information, we formulate such contextual correlations and information transfer/interaction with the GNNs and the iterative GRU [3] updates, respectively.

Defining Graph Nodes. In the training phase, only the proposals that satisfy one of the following two conditions are used as nodes: (1) Its IoU with ground-truth is greater than 0.5; (2) It has the largest IoU of all proposals with ground-truth. We denote the set of nodes as $\mathbb{X} = \{X_j\}_{j=1}^{N}$, where X_j is the j-th node. $X_j = (t_{s,j},\ t_{e,j},\ k_j,\ F_{X_j})$, where $t_{s,j}$, $t_{e,j}$, k_j, and F_{X_j} denote the starting, ending frame, action category and the feature representation of the corresponding proposal, respectively. F_{X_j} is obtained by concating the features of three parts:

$$F_{X_j} = [F_{X_j}^{s}, F_{X_j}^{c}, F_{X_j}^{e}], \tag{2}$$

where $F^s_{X_j}$, $F^c_{X_j}$, and $F^e_{X_j}$ denote the average of three snippets features before the proposal, the average of all snippets features covered by the proposal and the average of three snippets features after the proposal (*i.e.* the starting, course, and ending stage of a proposal), respectively.

Computing Adjacency Matrix. We use three kinds of relations to construct the consistency evaluator, noted as $\boldsymbol{A_1}$, $\boldsymbol{A_2}$, and $\boldsymbol{A_3}$ below, which represent low-level temporal coincidences, features vector dot products and high-level contextual similarities, respectively. First, if two nodes, X_p and X_q, have a high overlap in the time domain, then the proximity between them should be high. We calculate the overlap of temporal region between proposals (noted as $\mathcal{O}(X_p, X_q)$) to obtain $\boldsymbol{A_1}(p,q)$. Second, the similarity between vectors can be represented by their dot product. We calculate the dot product between F_{X_p} and F_{X_q} to obtain $\boldsymbol{A_2}(p,q)$. Third, we adopt a simple multi-layer perception model with one hidden layer to capture the contextual correlation between nodes. Specifically, we concat the features of two nodes and use two 1-dimensional convolution layer with kernel size of 3 to obtain the degree of contextual correlation $\boldsymbol{A_3}(p,q)$ of these two nodes. The final adjacency matrix is the weighted sum of $\boldsymbol{A_1}$, $\boldsymbol{A_2}$, and $\boldsymbol{A_3}$. It can be formulated as

$$\begin{cases} \boldsymbol{A_1}(p,q) = \mathcal{O}(X_p, X_q) = \dfrac{(t_{s,p}, t_{e,p}) \cap (t_{s,q}, t_{e,q})}{(t_{s,p}, t_{e,p}) \cup (t_{s,q}, t_{e,q})} \\ \boldsymbol{A_2}(p,q) = F_{X_p} \cdot F_{X_q} \\ \boldsymbol{A_3}(p,q) = \mathcal{F}_s([F_{X_p}, F_{X_q}]) \\ \boldsymbol{A}(p,q) = w_1 \cdot \boldsymbol{A_1} + w_2 \cdot \boldsymbol{A_2} + w_3 \cdot \boldsymbol{A_3} \end{cases}, \tag{3}$$

where $\mathcal{F}_s$ denotes the two 1-dimensional convolution layer and w_1, w_2, w_3 are constants to control the trade-off of those three terms (detailed in Sect. 4.3). The value in the adjacency matrix is the similarity between action proposals.

Updating Node Features. Our goal is to update the node features based on all other nodes in the graph and its own state during message propagation. We first aggregate features of all similar nodes with the message function, and then use the update function to update the node features. The message function is defined as

$$\boldsymbol{m_p} = \sum_q \boldsymbol{A}(p,q) \cdot F_{X_q}. \tag{4}$$

We use GRU [3] as the update function to update the node features. At each iteration η ($\eta = 1, \ldots, H$), the update function is formulated as

$$\begin{cases} \boldsymbol{o^\eta_p},\ \boldsymbol{h^\eta_p} = \mathrm{GRU}(\boldsymbol{h^{\eta-1}_p},\ \boldsymbol{m^\eta_p}) \\ F^\eta_{X_p} = \boldsymbol{o^\eta_p} \end{cases}, \tag{5}$$

where $\boldsymbol{m^\eta_p}$ denotes the aggregated features of node p at η-th iteration. We update F_{X_p} with the hidden state of the GRU.

Regression, Classification and Scoring. We use the updated node features to classify the actions of the nodes and regress the temporal boundaries t_s and

t_e, so that the regressed temporal region is better aligned with the target action instance. Since each action instance will generate multiple proposals, we need to compute the confidence score of each node to retrieve the results.

Specifically, for a node X_p, its temporal boundaries is $t_{s,p}$ and $t_{e,p}$, and the corresponding temporal center location and duration are $l = (t_{s,p} + t_{e,p})/2$ and $d = t_{e,p} - t_{s,p}$, respectively. We obtain the regression results by feeding the updated features into a stacked 1-dimensional convolution network with a hidden layer. The output consists of two elements Δl and Δd, which representing the predicted center location and length offset, respectively. The regressed center location, duration and new boundaries (localization result) can be calculated by

$$\begin{aligned} l' &= l + d \cdot \Delta l, \quad & d' &= d \cdot e^{\Delta d}, \\ t'_{s,p} &= l' - d'/2, \quad & t'_{e,p} &= l' + d'/2. \end{aligned} \tag{6}$$

The regressed proposals are then classified and scored based on the features of the regressed temporal location. We use a fully connected layer for classification and a stacked two 1-dimensional convolution layer for scoring. During the training phase, we fix the parameters of the feature embedding module and only learn the parameters of G-TACL. We calculate the regression loss and the scoring loss (Smooth L_1) based on the temporal boundaries after the regression, and use the classification result to calculate the classification loss (Cross Entropy).

4 Experiments

4.1 Datasets and Evaluation Metrics

We conduct extensive experiments on two benchmark datasets to evaluate the proposed method, including THUMOS'14 [10] and MEXaction2 [1].

THUMOS'14 dataset is challenging and widely used in temporal action localization task, which includes 20 action categories with temporal annotations. The validation set and test set contain 1, 010 and 1, 574 untrimmed videos, respectively. Each video contains multiple action instances. We only use 200 videos in validation set and 212 videos in test set in which temporal annotations are provided. We use the validation set for training and the test set for evaluation.

MEXaction2 dataset contains two action categories, *i.e.*, "Bull Charge Cape" and "Horse Riding". It is consisted of YouTube clips, UCF101 Horse Riding clips (these clips are trimmed videos), and untrimmed INA videos. We just use the INA subset of untrimmed videos in our experiments, which contains 38 training and 32 test videos of 2 categories. The average duration of INA videos is 39 minutes, of which less than 3% are action instances. We train the G-TACL with the training set and test it with the test set.

The mean average precision (mAP) with respect to different IoUs is used as evaluation metric, which is the conventional metric used in temporal action localization task. A prediction is considered correct if and only if the category label is correct and the temporal IoU with ground-truth exceeds the IoU threshold. Multiple mAP values under different IoU thresholds are reported.

4.2 Implementation Details

We implement the model and the evaluation pipeline using PyTorch. We refer the feature embedding module as SSN [39], and use the Inception-V3 [27] network pre-trained on Kinetics dataset [12] as the network backbone, with the last classification layer removed. We optimise the parameters of G-TACL in an end-to-end manner in 35 epochs using stochastic gradient descent (SGD), with an initial learning rate of 0.0001 annealed by 0.1 after epoch 15 and again at epoch 25, and a momentum fixed at 0.9. Empirically, the number of node features updates as little effect on the experimental results, therefore it is fixed at 1 ($H = 1$) for computational efficiency in our experiments.

4.3 Ablation Study

Evaluation of the G-TACL. To validate the efficacy of the proposed G-TACL, we compare it with a baseline aggregation strategy, specifically, G-TACL without node feature update, on THUMOS'14 dataset. The result is summarised in Table 1, where "Baseline" denotes no feature update and "G-TACL" denotes our proposed method. The results showed that our proposed G-TACL can significantly improve the performance of temporal action co-localization at all the IoU thresholds.

Comparison with Different Consistency Evaluators. We speculate that the three components of the consistency evaluator might not contribute equally on node feature update, and assess each of them by setting the weights of the others to 0. The results in Table 2 showed that every single component can boost the performance, and thus verified our speculation. We empirically tune the weights and find a ratio of $w_1 : w_2 : w_3 = 2 : 1 : 2$ yields reasonable performance.

The Effect of the Number of Iterations. Our proposed G-TCAL can iteratively update node features as detailed in Sect. 3.3. Table 3 presents the effect of

Table 1. Ablation study on node feature update. G-TACL outperforms G-TACL without 'node' feature update at multiple IoU thresholds on THUMOS'14 dataset.

IoU	0.3	0.4	0.5	0.6	0.7
Baseline	38.7	32.1	27.5	19.6	11.9
G-TACL	**49.4**	**39.5**	**31.1**	**22.0**	**14.7**

Table 2. Ablation study on consistency evaluator (IoU = 0.5). All the three parts in consistency evaluator are compatible and each single part can boost the performance.

$w_1 : w_2 : w_3$	mAP
0 : 0 : 0	27.5
1 : 0 : 0	29.7
0 : 1 : 0	29.1
0 : 0 : 1	30.1
2 : 1 : 2	**31.1**

Table 3. Exploration of the G-TACL with different number of iterations at multiple IoU thresholds on THUMOS'14 dataset.

IoU threshold	0.3	0.4	0.5	0.6	0.7
H = 1	49.4	39.5	**31.1**	**22.0**	**14.7**
H = 2	**49.8**	39.6	30.6	21.5	13.8
H = 3	49.4	**39.7**	30.8	21.7	13.9

the number of iterations. It can be seen that the number of iterations has little effect on performance. As more iterations will affect the computation efficiency, we set $H = 1$ in our experiments.

4.4 Comparison with State-of-the-Art Methods

We compare our method with a variety of recently proposed temporal action localization methods on THUMOS'14 dataset. As shown in Table 4, our method is comparable to other recent methods when IoU threshold <0.5 and outperforms them when IoU ≥ 0.5. This validated that our proposed G-TCAL can generate more accurate temporal boundaries and have better performance. Figure 3 visualizes the localization results of two action categories from the THUMOS'14.

Table 4. Comparison with the state-of-the-art temporal action localization methods on the THUMOS'14 test set. G-TACL yields comparable results when IoU threshold <0.5, and significantly outperforms other methods when IoU threshold ≥ 0.5.

IoU threshold	0.3	0.4	0.5	0.6	0.7
Oneata *et al.* [19]	28.8	21.8	15.0	8.5	3.2
Richard *et al.* [23]	30.0	23.2	15.2	–	–
Yuan *et al.* [38]	36.5	27.8	17.8	–	–
Shou *et al.* [25]	36.3	28.7	19.0	–	–
Duan *et al.* [4]	39.8	27.2	20.7	–	–
Shou *et al.* [24]	40.1	29.4	23.3	13.1	7.9
Xu *et al.* [34]	44.7	35.6	28.9	–	–
Lin *et al.* [15]	43.0	35.0	24.6	–	–
Buch *et al.* [2]	45.7	–	29.2	–	9.6
Zhao *et al.* [39]	**51.9**	**41.0**	29.8	19.6	10.7
Yang *et al.* [36]	44.1	37.1	28.2	20.6	12.7
G-TACL	49.4	39.5	**31.1**	**22.0**	**14.7**

Also, we compare our method with three existing methods on MEXaction2 dataset. As same as the compared methods, we summarise the mAP@IoU = 0.5 of each category in Table 5, our proposed method achieves the best performance.

Table 5. Comparisons with three existing methods on the MEXaction2 test set (IoU = 0.5).

Category	BullCHargeCape	HorseRiding	mAP
MEXaction2 [1]	0.3	3.1	1.7
Shou *et al.* [25]	11.6	3.1	7.4
Lin *et al.* [15]	**16.5**	5.5	11.0
G-TACL	10.0	**13.8**	**11.9**

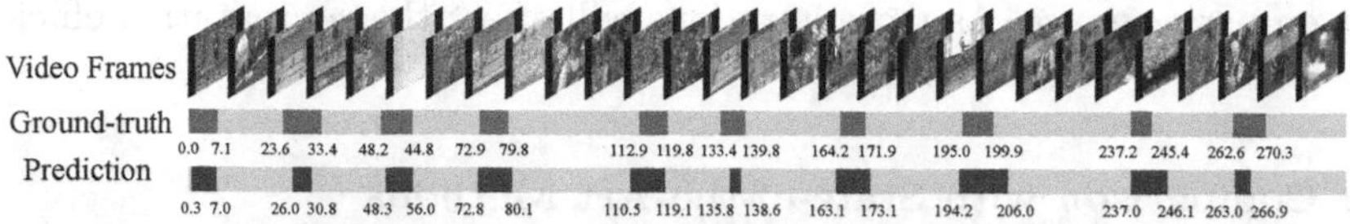

(a) An example of *HummerThrow*

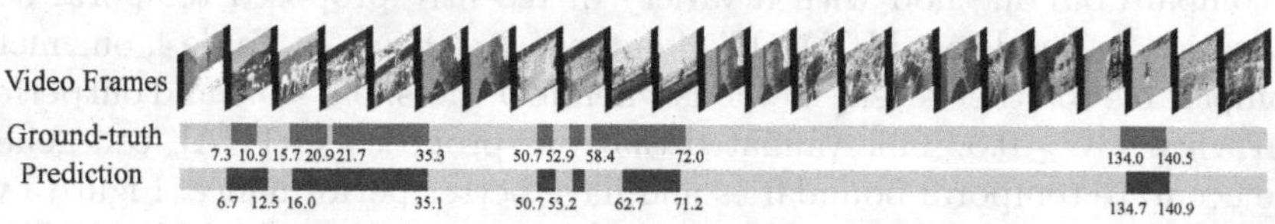

(b) An example of *HighJump*

Fig. 3. Qualitative examples of the proposed G-TACL on THUMOS'14 test set. The ground-truth temporal locations, predictions and backgrounds are illustrated by red, green and blue bars, respectively. (Color figure online)

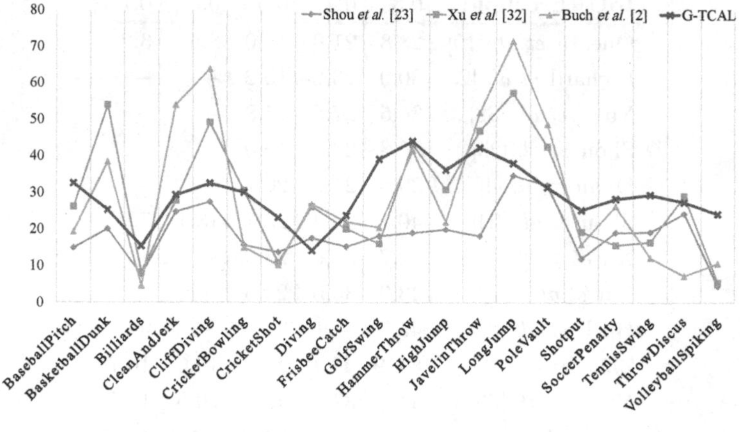

Fig. 4. The AP of each action category on THUMOS'14 test set (IoU = 0.5).

In this paper, we propose the G-TACL to model the contextual correlation between action proposals and update the features of nodes. We compute the AP of each category on the THUMOS'14 dataset and compare them with three existing method in Fig. 4. The results showed that our method obviously outperforms the others in more than half of the categories. In the process of information transfer, not only will the feature be enhanced, but also the feature may be weakened, so that our results on all categories are relatively average, unlike other results are particularly good or particularly poor.

5 Conclusion

In this paper, we propose a graph-based network (G-TACL) for temporal action co-localization in an untrimmed video. In contrast to previous methods, G-TACL can update node by aggregating similar contextual features, which is beneficial for precise temporal boundaries regression. In addition, we propose the multi-level consistency evaluator as an indicator of the similarity between proposals to calculate the adjacency matrix. Experiments on two datasets have verified the efficacy of our proposed method.

Acknowledgements. This work was supported partly by National Key R&D Program of China Grant 2018AAA0101400, NSFC Grants 61629301, 61773312, and 61976171, China Postdoctoral Science Foundation Grant 2019M653642, and Young Elite Scientists Sponsorship Program by CAST Grant 2018QNRC001.

References

1. Mexaction2. http://mexculture.cnam.fr/xwiki/bin/view/Datasets/Mex+ac-tion+dataset
2. Buch, S., Escorcia, V., Ghanem, B., Fei-Fei, L., Niebles, J.C.: End-to-end, single-stream temporal action detection in untrimmed videos. In: BMVC (2017)
3. Cho, K., Van Merriënboer, B., Bahdanau, D., Bengio, Y.: On the properties of neural machine translation: Encoder-decoder approaches. arXiv preprint arXiv:1409.1259 (2014)
4. Duan, X., et al.: Joint spatio-temporal action localization in untrimmed videos with per-frame segmentation. In: ICIP (2018)
5. Gao, Z., et al.: ER3: a unified framework for event retrieval, recognition and recounting. In: CVPR (2017)
6. Gao, Z., Wang, L., Jojic, N., Niu, Z., Zheng, N., Hua, G.: Video imprint. IEEE Trans. Pattern Anal. Mach. Intell. (2018)
7. Gao, Z., Wang, L., Zhang, Q., Niu, Z., Zheng, N., Hua, G.: Video imprint segmentation for temporal action detection in untrimmed videos. In: AAAI (2019)
8. Heilbron, F.C., Niebles, J.C., Ghanem, B.: Fast temporal activity proposals for efficient detection of human actions in untrimmed videos. In: CVPR (2016)
9. Jain, A., Zamir, A.R., Savarese, S., Saxena, A.: Structural-RNN: Deep learning on spatio-temporal graphs. In: CVPR (2016)
10. Jiang, Y., et al.: Thumos challenge: action recognition with a large number of classes (2014)

11. Karpathy, A., Toderici, G., Shetty, S., Leung, T., Sukthankar, R., Fei-Fei, L.: Large-scale video classification with convolutional neural networks. In: CVPR (2014)
12. Kay, W., et al.: The kinetics human action video dataset. arXiv preprint arXiv:1705.06950 (2017)
13. Laptev, I.: On space-time interest points. Int. J. Comput. Vis. **64**(2–3), 107–123 (2005)
14. Li, R., Tapaswi, M., Liao, R., Jia, J., Urtasun, R., Fidler, S.: Situation recognition with graph neural networks. In: ICCV (2017)
15. Lin, T., Zhao, X., Shou, Z.: Single shot temporal action detection. In: ACM MM (2017)
16. Liu, Z., et al.: Joint video object discovery and segmentation by coupled dynamic Markov networks. IEEE Trans. Image Process. **27**(12), 5840–5853 (2018)
17. Liu, Z., et al.: Weakly supervised temporal action localization through contrast based evaluation networks. In: ICCV (2019)
18. Lv, X., Wang, L., Zhang, Q., Zheng, N., Hua, G.: Video object co-segmentation from noisy videos by a multi-level hypergraph model. In: ICIP (2018)
19. Oneata, D., Verbeek, J., Schmid, C.: The LEAR submission at Thumos 2014. In: ECCV THUMOS Workshop (2014)
20. Paul, S., Roy, S., Roy-Chowdhury, A.K.: W-TALC: weakly-supervised temporal activity localization and classification. In: ECCV (2018)
21. Qi, S., Wang, W., Jia, B., Shen, J., Zhu, S.C.: Learning human-object interactions by graph parsing neural networks. In: ECCV (2018)
22. Ren, S., He, K., Girshick, R., Sun, J.: Faster R-CNN: towards real-time object detection with region proposal networks. In: NeurIPS (2015)
23. Richard, A., Gall, J.: Temporal action detection using a statistical language model. In: CVPR (2016)
24. Shou, Z., Chan, J., Zareian, A., Miyazawa, K., Chang, S.F.: CDC: convolutional-de-convolutional networks for precise temporal action localization in untrimmed videos. In: CVPR (2017)
25. Shou, Z., Wang, D., Chang, S.F.: Temporal action localization in untrimmed videos via multi-stage CNNs. In: CVPR (2016)
26. Simonyan, K., Zisserman, A.: Two-stream convolutional networks for action recognition in videos. In: NeurPIS (2014)
27. Szegedy, C., Vanhoucke, V., Ioffe, S., Shlens, J., Wojna, Z.: Rethinking the inception architecture for computer vision. In: CVPR (2016)
28. Tan, H., Wang, L., Zhang, Q., Gao, Z., Zheng, N., Hua, G.: Object affordances graph network for action recognition. In: BMVC (2019)
29. Tran, D., Bourdev, L., Fergus, R., Torresani, L., Paluri, M.: Learning spatiotemporal features with 3D convolutional networks. In: ICCV (2015)
30. Wang, H., Schmid, C.: Action recognition with improved trajectories. In: ICCV (2013)
31. Wang, L., Hua, G., Sukthankar, R., Xue, J., Niu, Z., Zheng, N.: Video object discovery and co-segmentation with extremely weak supervision. IEEE Trans. Pattern Anal. Mach. Intell. **39**(10), 2074–2088 (2017)
32. Wang, L., Qiao, Y., Tang, X.: Action recognition and detection by combining motion and appearance features. In: ECCV THUMOS Workshop (2014)
33. Wang, L., Qiao, Y., Tang, X., Van Gool, L.: Actionness estimation using hybrid fully convolutional networks. In: CVPR (2016)
34. Xu, H., Das, A., Saenko, K.: R-C3D: region convolutional 3d network for temporal activity detection. In: ICCV (2017)

35. Yang, J., Lu, J., Lee, S., Batra, D., Parikh, D.: Graph R-CNN for scene graph generation. In: ECCV (2018)
36. Yang, K., Qiao, P., Li, D., Lv, S., Dou, Y.: Exploring temporal preservation networks for precise temporal action localization. In: AAAI (2018)
37. Yuan, J., Ni, B., Yang, X., Kassim, A.A.: Temporal action localization with pyramid of score distribution features. In: CVPR (2016)
38. Yuan, Z.H., Stroud, J.C., Lu, T., Deng, J.: Temporal action localization by structured maximal sums. In: CVPR (2017)
39. Zhao, Y., Xiong, Y., Wang, L., Wu, Z., Tang, X., Lin, D.: Temporal action detection with structured segment networks. In: ICCV (2017)

A Novel Attention Enhanced Dense Network for Image Super-Resolution

Zhong-Han Niu[1(✉)], Yang-Hao Zhou[1], Yu-Bin Yang[1(✉)], and Jian-Cong Fan[2]

[1] State Key Laboratory for Novel Software Technology, Nanjing University, Nanjing 210023, China
niuzh@smail.nju.edu.cn, yangyubin@nju.edu.cn

[2] Provincial Key Laboratory for Information Technology of Wisdom Mining of Shandong Province, Shandong University of Science and Technology, Qingdao 266590, China

Abstract. Deep convolutional neural networks (CNNs) have recently achieved impressive performance in image super-resolution (SR). However, they usually treat the spatial features and channel-wise features indiscriminatingly and fail to take full advantage of hierarchical features, restricting adaptive ability. To address these issues, we propose a novel attention enhanced dense network (AEDN) to adaptively recalibrate each kernel and feature for different inputs, by integrating both spatial attention (SA) and channel attention (CA) modules in the proposed network. In experiments, we explore the effect of attention mechanism and present quantitative and qualitative evaluations, where the results show that the proposed AEDN outperforms state-of-the-art methods by effectively suppressing the artifacts and faithfully recovering more high-frequency image details.

Keywords: Image super-resolution · Spatial attention · Channel attention · Convolutional neural networks

1 Introduction

Single image super-resolution (SISR) refers to generate a high-resolution (HR) image from its low-resolution (LR) image accurately. As a fundamental low-level vision task, it has been widely used in computer vision applications, ranging from security [35], satellite [21], and medical imaging [18]. Single image SR is a highly ill-posed problem, since it may have many different plausible HR images consistent with the original LR image.

Recently, SISR has been attracted increasing attention in research community. Numerous methods based on deep convolutional neural network (CNN) have been proposed, which achieved significant improvements on conventional SR methods [27,28,32]. The pioneering work was done by Dong et al. [3], who proposed SRCNN to learn an end-to-end mapping between the interpolation image of LR and their HR image. Then, FSRCNN [4] was presented to accelerate the training and testing of SRCNN, which extracted features in LR images

Y. M. Ro et al. (Eds.): MMM 2020, LNCS 11961, pp. 568–580, 2020.
https://doi.org/10.1007/978-3-030-37731-1_46

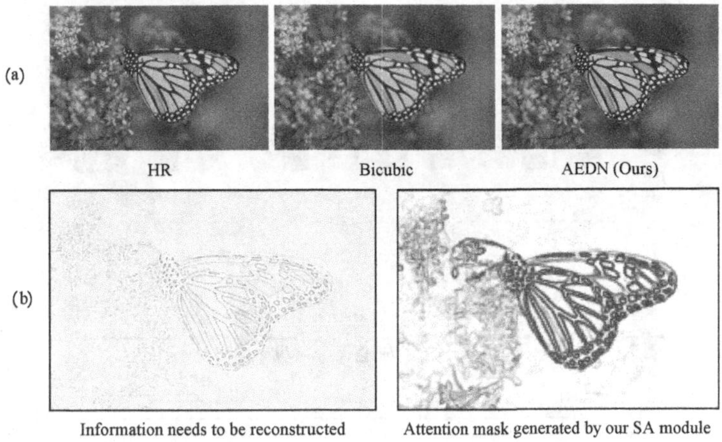

Fig. 1. (a) Monarch form Set14 [30] (left). Super-resolution result of Bicubic (middle) compared with our AEDN (right). [×4 upsampling]. (b) Information lost during down-sampling procedure (left), attention mask generated by our attention module (right).

upsampled at the end of the SR network. By stacking more convolutional layers with identity skip connections, VDSR [8], RED-Net [13] and IRCNN [31] were all proposed to achieve notable improvements. Currently, residual-based learning methods such as SRResnet [11] and EDSR [12] have been proposed to achieve better performance by taking advantage of deeper/wider networks. Furthermore, inspired by the DenseNet [6], SRDenseNet [23], MemNet [20] and RDN [34] were successfully designed by directly connecting each layer to all subsequent layers, providing an effective way to reuse feature maps.

However, previous works treat the spatial features and channel-wise features equally, restricting the adaptive ability of CNN. The difference between the HR and its corresponding SR via bicubic interpolation on RGB channels is shown in Fig. 1(b left), and the darker the area, the greater the difference. As the result demonstrates, the information discarding during the down-sampling procedure usually lies in the area, such as edges, texture, and other details. But none of the above CNN models have such a mechanism to pay more attention to the regions that may contain high-frequency information, and lacking flexible modulation ability in dealing with different types of complex textures. Although attention mechanism widely adopted in many high-level vision tasks, such as image classification [5,24], image caption [2,26] and visual question answering [25,29], little work has been down in SR task, because simply apply attention can decrease the reconstruction quality. Therefore, it is very significant to develop an attention mechanism that works effectively for SR tasks.

To resolve these problems, we exploit interdependencies among feature spaces and channels, proposing a novel attention-based architecture, called Attention Enhanced Dense Network (AEDN) as illustrated in Fig. 2. The attention

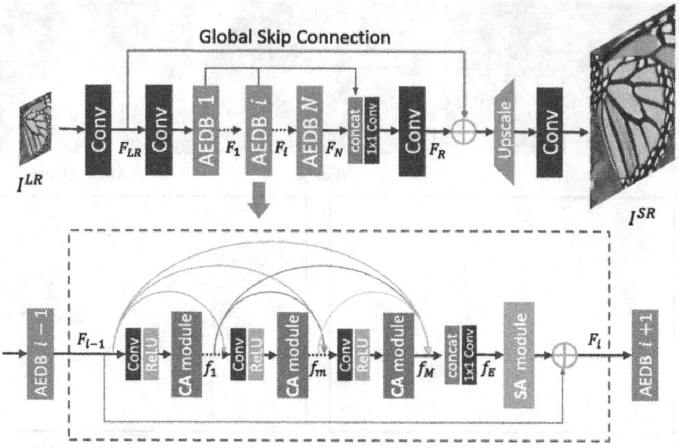

Fig. 2. The architecture of the attention enhanced dense network (AEDN).

modules in the proposed network work as feature selectors, which make use of all the hierarchical features and adaptively rescale each kernel and feature for different input. As it can be observed in Fig. 1(b, right), with the attention enhanced, the AEDN identifies the important areas and boundaries in need of reconstruction. Quantitative evaluations in Sect. 3.3 show that by exploiting both attention modules the proposed method achieves greatly improves. Our contributions are summarized as follows:

(1) We propose a novel spatial attention (SA) module to recalibrate the feature, forcing the network to pay more attention to the boundaries and areas where may contain more high-frequency information.
(2) We construct the channel attention (CA) module, which rescales the feature across channels. Moreover, for different types of images, the CA module could assign attention weights adaptively, which enhances the representational ability and learning capacity of networks.
(3) We apply both spatial attention and channel-wise attention in our network. The combination of SA and CA module helps the network concentrate on more useful channels and adaptively modulate feature representations, help the network achieved significant improvement over the state-of-the-art works in SISR.

2 Attention Enhanced Dense Network

2.1 Network Architecture

In this work, we use the densely connected framework as the basis of our model. This framework directly connecting each layer to all subsequent layers, which fully exploring the advantage of skip connections and providing an effective way to reuse feature maps. As shown in Fig. 2, our AEDN is composed of three parts:

low-frequency feature extraction, attention enhanced dense blocks (AEDBs), and upscale module in the end. Let I^{LR} and I^{SR} denote the input and output of our AEDN. The first convolution layer extracts low-frequency features F_{LR} from the LR image.

$$F_{LR} = \Phi_{conv}(I^{LR}) \tag{1}$$

As CNNs going deeper, it was difficult to train networks. Global skip connection was introduced to ease this problem, F_{LR} is directly delivered to the final reconstruction layer.

As an important component of the network, the proposed attention enhanced dense block (AEDB) integrates the CA module after each convolution and the SA module at the end of the block. With multiple attention modules, AEDB can generate adaptively attention-aware features for different images. The output of the m-th CA module f_m and feature f_E before SA module in AEDB can be obtained by

$$f_m = \Phi_{CA}[\Phi_{conv}(F_{i-1}, f_1, \cdots, f_{m-1})] \tag{2}$$
$$f_E = \Phi_{1\times 1conv}(F_{i-1}, f_1, \cdots, f_M) \tag{3}$$

Let F_{i-1} and F_i denote the input and output of the i-th AEDB respectively. The F_i can be formulated as

$$\begin{aligned} F_i &= \Phi_{AEDB}(F_{i-1}) \\ &= \Phi_{SA}(f_E) + F_{i-1} \end{aligned} \tag{4}$$

where $\Phi_{SA}(\cdot)$ and $\Phi_{CA}(\cdot)$ denote the spatial attention module and the channel-wise attention module, and more details will be presented in Sects. 2.2 and 2.3, respectively.

We utilize the sub-pixel convolution layer [17] in the upscale procedure. The output of AEDN can be obtained by

$$I^{SR} = \Phi_{Upscale}(F_{LR} + F_R) \tag{5}$$

where $\Phi_{Upscale}(\cdot)$ and F_R are the upscale net and reconstruction feature, respectively.

2.2 Spatial Attention Module

Details lying in the high-frequency region usually need to be recovered more accurately. However, previous works consider each feature map region equally, hindering the networks' expressiveness on the details of a given image. Hence, we introduce a novel spatial attention mechanism into the network, for paying more attention to the latent high-frequency regions.

The computation procedure of our SA module is depicted in Fig. 3. In contrast to the SA mechanism used in other high-level vision tasks, we do not apply any pooling layer in our SA module. Stacking convolutions (unpadded convolutions) enable our SA module with a large receptive field to exploit contextual

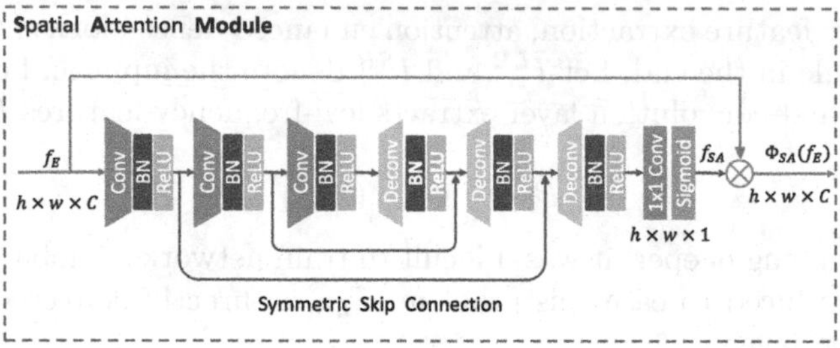

Fig. 3. The structure of spatial attention (SA) module. ⊗ denotes element-wise product.

information. This strategy helps the module to finally generate an elaborate attention mask. The SA module consists of several convolution, deconvolution operators and symmetric skip connection. Benefiting from symmetric skip connection, gradient could be directly passed from the bottom layers to top layers. Batch normalization (BN) is adopted after each convolution and before activation (ReLU). In the last layer, we use the sigmoid activation to control the output ranging from 0 to 1, predicting the probability that each pixel belongs to the high-frequency region.

Given the input feature $f_E \in \mathbb{R}^{h \times w \times C}$, a 2D spatial attention mask $f_{SA} \in \mathbb{R}^{h \times w \times 1}$ is generated by $\Phi_{SA}(\cdot)$, the final output SA module can be expressed as

$$\Phi_{SA}(f_E) = f_E * f_{SA} \tag{6}$$

By applying the element-wise product between feature and soft mask, the SA module generates a refined attention mask. As illustrated in Fig. 1 (b, right), the generated attention mask with high value is in accordance with the high-frequency region.

2.3 Channel Attention Module

Feature channels in CNN are response activations of corresponding convolutional filters. Previous studies treat channel features equally, hindering networks focusing on more informative features. To address this issue, channel attention is introduced to force the network to pay attention to different channels of image features adaptively.

In the structure of AEDB, every Conv layer is followed with a CA module, and the output of every CA module is connected to all the subsequent Conv layers. The structure of CA module is illustrated in Fig. 4. The operations of channel-wise attention including global average pooling and two fully connected (FC) layers followed by activations, by which the channel-wise attention weights f_{CA} are calculated

$$f_{CA} = \delta(W_1 \sigma(W_0 f_{avg})) \tag{7}$$

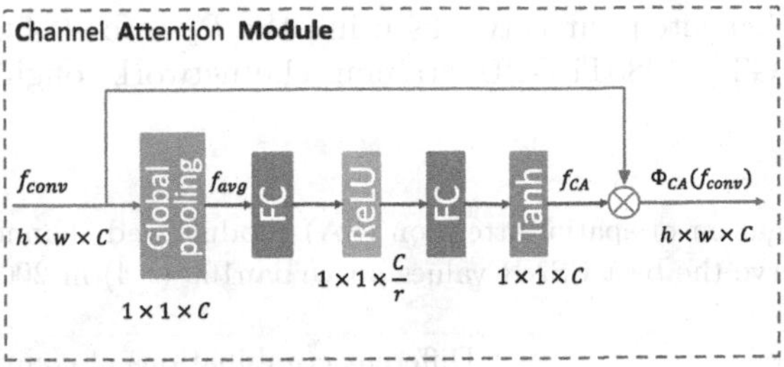

Fig. 4. The structure of channel attention (CA) module. ⊗ denotes element-wise product.

where δ and σ denote the Tanh and ReLU functions respectively. $f_{avg} \in \mathbb{R}^{1\times1\times C}$ denote C elements obtained by global average pooling operation. The first FC layer W_0 reduces the channels of f_{avg} with ratio r, then the second FC layer W_1 increases the number of channels back with ratio r. The CA module decides which channel should be emphasize emphasized or suppressed. The output can be formulated as

$$\Phi_{CA}(f_{conv}) = f_{CA} * f_{conv} \tag{8}$$

3 Experimental Results

3.1 Datasets and Metrics

In training progress, we train our network on the DIV2K dataset with 800 training images and validate on 10 images. For testing, we use five well-known benchmark datasets: Set5 [1], Set14 [30], B100 [14], Urban100 [7] and Manga109 [15]. To compare our model with other methods, we evaluate our reconstruction results on Y channel with two standard automated quantitative metrics: peak signal to noise ratio (PSNR) and structural similarity (SSIM) [12].

3.2 Training Details and Parameters

In this work, we set kernel size to be 3×3 for all Conv layers using about 64 filters (except the 1×1 Conv layer). We pad zero boundaries of each input feature map to keep size fixed except Conv operation in the SA module. Attention enhanced dense block (AEDB) includes 8 CA modules and we use 16 blocks in all. The reduction ratio r in the CA module is set to 16. Same as previous works, our AEDN is optimized with L_1 loss function.

Following settings of [12], LR color patches with a size of 32×32 are randomly cropped from LR images as inputs, and the mini-batch size is set to 16. We augment the training data via random horizontal flipping and 90° rotating. The network is optimized with ADAM [10] by setting $\beta_1 = 0.9$, $\beta_2 = 0.999$, $\xi = 10^{-8}$, and the initial learning rate is set to 10^{-4}, which is reduced to half for every 200 epochs. We implemented our networks using the PyTorch 0.4.0 framework [16] on an NVIDIA GTX 1080Ti GPU, training the network roughly takes one day for 200 epochs.

Table 1. Investigation of spatial attention (SA) module and channel attention (CA) module. We observe the best PSNR values on Urban100 (×4) in 200 epochs.

Module	Different combinations of components			
Spatial Attension (SA)	×	✓	×	✓
Channel Attension (CA)	×	×	✓	✓
PSNR on Urban100 (×4)	26.27	26.37	26.40	**26.50**

3.3 Attention Module Analysis

To demonstrate the effects of proposed SA and CA modules, we conduct an ablation experiment by removing each of the modules from AEDN respectively. Table 1 shows the quantitative evaluations of each attention module. It can be observed that the baseline without SA and CA modules performs very poorly (PSNR = 26.27). Each module can effectively improve the performance of the baseline, when adding both SA and CA to the baseline, the model achieves the best performance (PSRN = 26.50 dB).

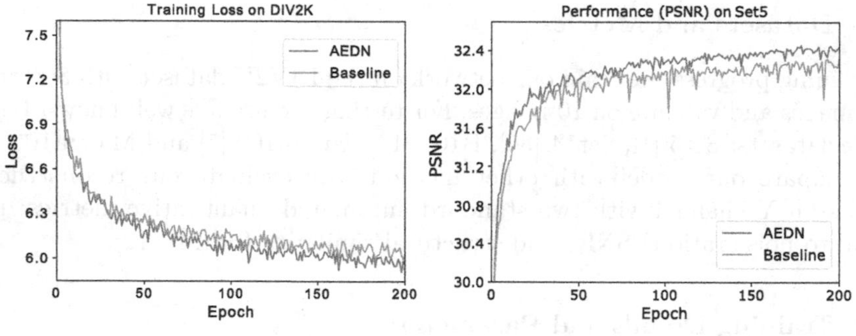

Fig. 5. Convergence analysis of AEDN (blue curves) and Baseline (brown curves). Left: training loss on the DIV2K dataset. Right: model performance (PSNR) on Set5. Both with scaling factor ×2 in 200 epochs. (Color figure online)

Furthermore, we visualize the convergence process of AEDN and Baseline. In Fig. 5, training curves of AEDN and Baseline are depicted in the left panel, model performance (PSNR) curves on Set5 are depicted in the right panel. It can be seen that the AEDN with attention mechanism yields lower training loss. The combination of SA and CA attention modules has a great ability to improve the generalization performance of the baseline. Results in Table 1 and Fig. 5 both exhibiting considerably generalization ability of our attention mechanism.

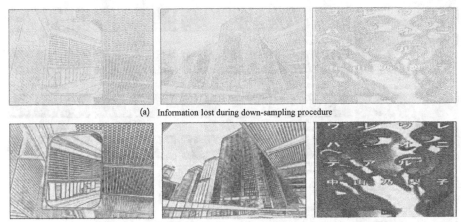

(a) Information lost during down-sampling procedure

(b) Spatial attention masks generated by our SA module

Fig. 6. (a) Information lost during down-sampling procedure. (b) Attention mask generated by our spatial attention (SA) module in the last AEDB.

To show the role of our attention mechanism, we visualize a typical example of the spatial attention masks f_{SA} in Fig. 6, which are generated by SA module in the last AEDB. Figure 6(a) shows the information lost $HR - BI(LR)$ during the down-sampling procedure such as edge or texture, where BI denotes the bicubic interpolation upsampling operation. We visualize the generated spatial attention masks in Fig. 6(b). It can be observed that the SA mask is almost identical to the $HR - BI(LR)$. This observation indicates that the SA module has the ability to forcing the network to pay more attention to the information loss and to recover more details correctly.

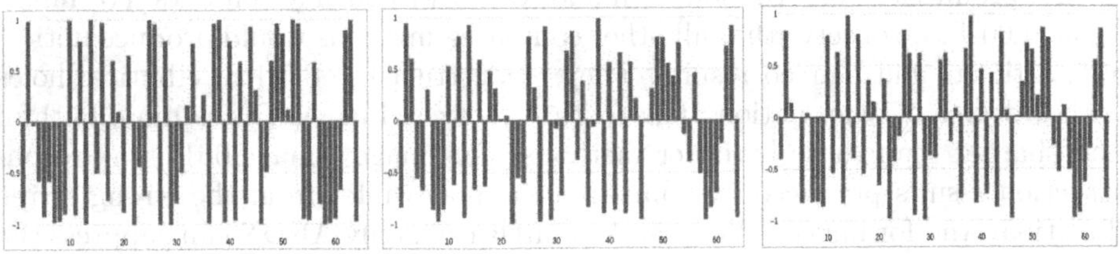

Fig. 7. The channel attention weights of 64 channels generated by the first channel attention (CA) module in the seventh AEDB (the same images with Fig. 6).

In Fig. 7, the channel attention weights f_{CA} across channels generated by the seventh AEDB. From Fig. 7 we can see that channel-wise attention weights of 64 channels are distinct. Some channels of the input feature maps are repressed while some other channels are relatively enlarged, which indicates that our CA modules work as feature selectors. Moreover, for different types of images, the

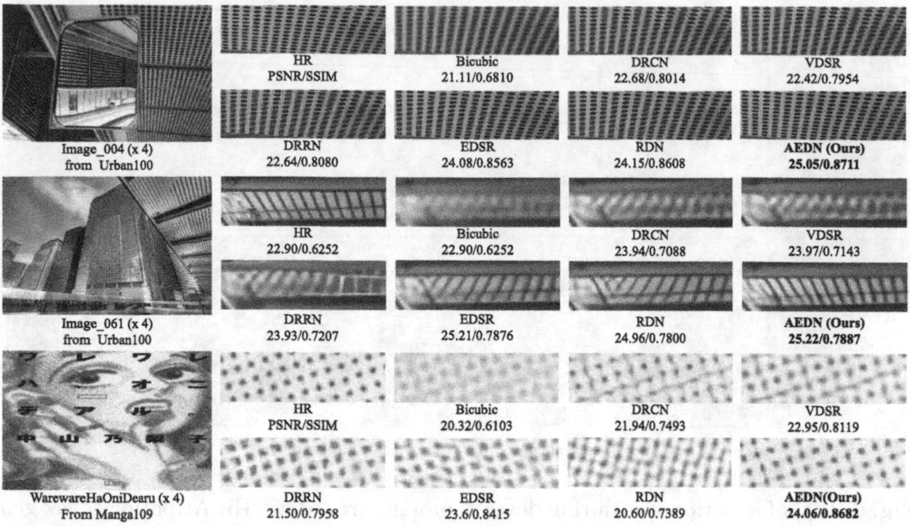

Fig. 8. Visual comparison for ×4 super-resolution. Red indicates the best. (Color figure online)

CA module could assign attention weights adaptively, capturing more important information. These results demonstrate that the SA and CA modules help the network concentrate on more important regions and adaptively modulate feature representations.

3.4 Comparison with State-of-the-Art Models

Visual comparisons of different methods are shown in Fig. 8. The proposed AEDN produces reconstruction with a lot of high-frequency contents. For image "image_004", we observe that all other compared methods would produce noticeable artifacts and blurred results. They reconstruct the original elliptical holes with a degree of deformation. The texture recovered by AEDN is more faithful and sharper than those by other methods. For image "image_061", the reconstruction results produced by compared methods suffer from the wrong stripe direction. And for image "WarewareHaOniDearu", only AEDN can suppress the blurring artifacts and generate the SR image with correct dots.

The quantitative evaluations for scale factor ×2, ×3, and ×4 are summarized in Table 2. Since the RCAN [33] which has about 400 convolutional layers is much deeper than our AEDN. For fair comparisons, we do not compare our model with it. We compare the proposed AEDN with 7 state-of-the-art SR algorithms: A+ [22], SRCNN [3], VDSR [8], DRCN [9], DRRN [19], EDSR [12], and RDN [34]. As the results show, our method outperforms other methods for all scale factors (×2, ×3, and ×4). Similar to [12,34], we introduce self-ensemble strategy to further improve the performance of AEDN, which is denoted as

Table 2. Quantitative results. Average PSNR/SSIM for scale factor ×2, ×3 and ×4 on datasets Set5, Set14, B100, Urban100, and Manga109. Red color indicates the best performance and blue indicates the second best.

Dataset	Scale	Bicubic	A+[22]	SRCNN [3]	VDSR [8]	DRCN [9]	DRRN [19]	EDSR [12]	RDN [34]	**AEDN** (ours)	**AEDN**+(ours)
Set5	×2	33.66/0.9299	36.54/0.9544	36.66/0.9542	37.53/0.9587	37.63/0.9588	37.74/0.9591	38.11/0.9601	38.24/0.9614	38.25/0.9615	38.30/0.9617
	×3	30.39/0.8682	32.58/0.9088	32.75/0.9090	33.66/0.9213	33.82/0.9226	34.03/0.9244	34.65/0.9282	34.71/0.9296	34.72/0.9297	34.80/0.9303
	×4	28.42/0.8104	30.28/0.8603	30.48/0.8628	31.35/0.8838	31.53/0.8854	31.68/0.8888	32.46/0.8968	32.47/0.8990	32.55/0.8996	32.67/0.9007
Set14	×2	30.24/0.8688	32.28/0.9056	32.42/0.9063	33.03/0.9124	33.04/0.9118	33.23/0.9136	33.92/0.9195	34.01/0.9212	34.05/0.9227	34.20/0.9232
	×3	27.55/0.7742	29.13/0.8188	29.28/0.8209	29.77/0.8314	29.76/0.8311	29.96/0.8349	30.52/0.8462	30.57/0.8468	30.61/0.8475	30.71/0.8487
	×4	26.00/0.7027	27.32/0.7491	27.49/0.7503	28.01/0.7674	28.02/0.7670	28.21/0.7720	28.80/0.7876	28.81/0.7871	28.89/0.7882	28.98/0.7895
BSD100	×2	29.56/0.8431	31.21/0.8863	31.36/0.8879	31.90/0.8960	31.85/0.8942	32.05/0.8973	32.32/0.9013	32.34/0.9017	32.37/0.9020	32.41/0.9232
	×3	27.21/0.7385	28.29/0.7835	28.41/0.7863	28.82/0.7976	28.80/0.7963	28.95/0.8004	29.25/0.8093	29.26/0.8093	29.30/0.8100	29.35/0.8109
	×4	25.96/0.6675	26.82/0.7087	26.90/0.7101	27.29/0.7251	27.23/0.7233	27.38/0.7284	27.71/0.7420	27.72/0.7419	27.77/0.7428	27.82/0.7439
Urban100	×2	26.88/0.8403	29.20/0.8938	29.50/0.8946	30.76/0.9140	30.75/0.9133	31.23/0.9188	32.93/0.9351	32.89/0.9353	33.17/0.9371	33.34/0.9383
	×3	24.46/0.7349	26.03/0.7973	26.24/0.7989	27.14/0.8279	27.15/0.8276	27.53/0.8378	28.80/0.8653	28.80/0.8653	29.00/0.8683	29.18/0.8707
	×4	23.14/0.6577	24.32/0.7183	24.52/0.7221	25.18/0.7524	25.14/0.7510	25.44/0.7638	26.64/0.8033	26.61/0.8028	26.77/0.8055	26.93/0.8090
Manga109	×2	30.80/0.9339	35.37/0.9663	35.60/0.9663	37.22/0.9729	37.60/0.9736	37.60/0.9736	39.10/0.9773	39.18/0.9780	39.36/0.9778	39.51/0.9782
	×3	26.95/0.8556	29.93/0.9089	30.48/0.9117	32.01/0.9310	32.42/0.9359	32.42/0.9359	34.17/0.9773	34.13/0.9484	34.39/0.9494	34.65/0.9506
	×4	24.89/0.7866	27.03/0.8439	27.58/0.8555	28.83/0.8809	29.18/0.8914	29.18/0.8914	31.02/0.9148	31.00/0.9151	31.25/0.9176	31.55/0.9200

AEDN+. Specially, for Urban100 and Manga109 datasets, which contain more complex patterns, our ADEN achieves great improvements.

Both quantitative and qualitative results demonstrate that with our attention mechanism, the proposed AEDN is easier to extract the high-frequency features for these complex details finally recover more plausible details.

4 Conclusion

In this paper, we proposed a novel attention enhanced dense network (AEDN), integrating both spatial attention (SA) and channel attention (CA) modules into the network. The attention modules, working as feature selectors, force the network to pay more attention to the high-frequency regions, and adaptively rescaling each spatial and channel-wise feature for different types of information. Based on the novel attention modules, the proposed AEDN reconstruct high-quality image with different upsampling factors, achieving better performance than the state-of-art methods.

Acknowledgements. This work is funded by the National Natural Science Foundation of China (No. 61673204), and the Fundamental Research Funds for the Central Universities (No. 14380046).

References

1. Bevilacqua, M., Roumy, A., Guillemot, C., Morel, M.L.A.: Low-complexity single-image super-resolution based on nonnegative neighbor embedding. In: Proceedings of the British Machine Vision Conference (BMVC) (2012)
2. Chen, L., et al.: SCA-CNN: spatial and channel-wise attention in convolutional networks for image captioning. In: Proceedings of the IEEE Conference on Computer Vision and Pattern Recognition (CVPR), pp. 5659–5667. IEEE (2017)
3. Dong, C., Loy, C.C., He, K., Tang, X.: Learning a deep convolutional network for image super-resolution. In: Fleet, D., Pajdla, T., Schiele, B., Tuytelaars, T. (eds.) ECCV 2014. LNCS, vol. 8692, pp. 184–199. Springer, Cham (2014). https://doi.org/10.1007/978-3-319-10593-2_13
4. Dong, C., Loy, C.C., Tang, X.: Accelerating the super-resolution convolutional neural networkD. In: Leibe, B., Matas, J., Sebe, N., Welling, M. (eds.) ECCV 2016. LNCS, vol. 9906, pp. 391–407. Springer, Cham (2016). https://doi.org/10.1007/978-3-319-46475-6_25
5. Hu, J., Shen, L., Sun, G.: Squeeze-and-excitation networks. In: Proceedings of IEEE Conference on Computer Vision and Pattern Recognition (CVPR), pp. 7132–7141. IEEE (2018)
6. Huang, G., Liu, Z., Van Der Maaten, L., Weinberger, K.Q.: Densely connected convolutional networks. In: Proceedings of the IEEE Conference on Computer Vision and Pattern Recognition (CVPR), pp. 4700–4708. IEEE (2017)
7. Huang, J.B., Singh, A., Ahuja, N.: Single image super-resolution from transformed self-exemplars. In: Proceedings of the IEEE Conference on Computer Vision and Pattern Recognition (CVPR), pp. 5197–5206. IEEE (2015)

8. Kim, J., Kwon Lee, J., Mu Lee, K.: Accurate image super-resolution using very deep convolutional networks. In: Proceedings of the IEEE Conference on Computer Vision and Pattern Recognition (CVPR), pp. 1646–1654. IEEE (2016)
9. Kim, J., Kwon Lee, J., Mu Lee, K.: Deeply-recursive convolutional network for image super-resolution. In: Proceedings of the IEEE Conference on Computer Vision and Pattern Recognition (CVPR), pp. 1637–1645. IEEE (2016)
10. Kingma, D., Ba., J.: Adam: a method for stochastic optimization. In: International Conference on Learning Representations (ICLR) (2015)
11. Ledig, C., Theis, L., Huszár, et al.: Photo-realistic single image super-resolution using a generative adversarial network. In: Proceedings of the IEEE Conference on Computer Vision and Pattern Recognition (CVPR), pp. 4681–4690. IEEE (2017)
12. Lim, B., Son, S., Kim, H., Nah, S., Lee, K.M.: Enhanced deep residual networks for single image super-resolution. In: Proceedings of the IEEE Conference on Computer Vision and Pattern Recognition (CVPR) Workshops, pp. 136–144. IEEE (2017)
13. Mao, X., Shen, C., Yang, Y.B.: Image restoration using very deep convolutional encoder-decoder networks with symmetric skip connections. In: Neural Information Processing Systems (NIPS), pp. 2802–2810 (2016)
14. Martin, D., Fowlkes, C., Tal, D., Malik, J.: A database of human segmented natural images and its application to evaluating segmentation algorithms and measuring ecological statistics. In: Proceedings of the IEEE International Conference on Computer Vision (ICCV). IEEE (2001)
15. Matsui, Y., Ito, K., Aramaki, Y., Fujimoto, A., Ogawa, T., Yamasaki, T., Aizawa, K.: Sketch-based manga retrieval using Manga109 dataset. Multimedia Tools Appl. (MTA) **76**(20), 21811–21838 (2017)
16. Paszke, A., Gross, S., Chintala, S., et al.: Automatic differentiation in PyTorch (2017)
17. Shi, W., Caballero, J., Huszár, F., et al.: Real-time single image and video super-resolution using an efficient sub-pixel convolutional neural network. In: Proceedings of the IEEE Conference on Computer Vision and Pattern Recognition (CVPR), pp. 1874–1883. IEEE (2016)
18. Shi, W., et al.: Cardiac image super-resolution with global correspondence using multi-atlas PatchMatch. In: Mori, K., Sakuma, I., Sato, Y., Barillot, C., Navab, N. (eds.) MICCAI 2013. LNCS, vol. 8151, pp. 9–16. Springer, Heidelberg (2013). https://doi.org/10.1007/978-3-642-40760-4_2
19. Tai, Y., Yang, J., Liu, X.: Image super-resolution via deep recursive residual network. In: Proceedings of the IEEE Conference on Computer Vision and Pattern Recognition (CVPR), pp. 3147–3155. IEEE (2017)
20. Tai, Y., Yang, J., Liu, X., Xu, C.: MemNet: a persistent memory network for image restoration. In: Proceedings of the IEEE Conference on Computer Vision and Pattern Recognition (CVPR), pp. 4539–4547. IEEE (2017)
21. Thornton, M.W., Atkinson, P.M., Holland, D.: Sub-pixel mapping of rural land cover objects from fine spatial resolution satellite sensor imagery using super-resolution pixel-swapping. IJRS **27**(3), 473–491 (2006)
22. Timofte, R., De Smet, V., Van Gool, L.: A+: adjusted anchored neighborhood regression for fast super-resolution. In: Cremers, D., Reid, I., Saito, H., Yang, M.-H. (eds.) ACCV 2014. LNCS, vol. 9006, pp. 111–126. Springer, Cham (2015). https://doi.org/10.1007/978-3-319-16817-3_8
23. Tong, T., Li, G., Liu, X., Gao, Q.: Image super-resolution using dense skip connections. In: Proceedings of the IEEE International Conference on Computer Vision (ICCV), pp. 4809–4817. IEEE (2017)

24. Wang, F., et al.: Residual attention network for image classification. In: Proceedings of the IEEE Conference on Computer Vision and Pattern Recognition (CVPR) (2017)
25. Xu, H., Saenko, K.: Ask, Attend and Answer: Exploring Question-Guided Spatial Attention for Visual Question Answering. In: Leibe, B., Matas, J., Sebe, N., Welling, M. (eds.) ECCV 2016. LNCS, vol. 9911, pp. 451–466. Springer, Cham (2016). https://doi.org/10.1007/978-3-319-46478-7_28
26. Xu, K., Ba, J., Kiros, et al.: Show, attend and tell: neural image caption generation with visual attention. In: Proceedings of the 32nd International Conference on Machine Learning (ICML), pp. 2048–2057 (2015)
27. Yang, C.Y., Yang, M.H.: Fast direct super-resolution by simple functions. In: Proceedings of the IEEE International Conference on Computer Vision (ICCV), pp. 561–568. IEEE (2013)
28. Yang, J., Wright, J., Huang, T.S., Ma, Y.: Image super-resolution via sparse representation. TIP **19**(11), 2861–2873 (2010)
29. Yang, Z., He, X., Gao, J., Deng, L., Smola, A.: Stacked attention networks for image question answering. In: Proceedings of the IEEE Conference on Computer Vision and Pattern Recognition (CVPR), pp. 21–29. IEEE (2016)
30. Zeyde, R., Elad, M., Protter, M.: On single image scale-up using sparse-representations. In: Boissonnat, J.-D., Chenin, P., Cohen, A., Gout, C., Lyche, T., Mazure, M.-L., Schumaker, L. (eds.) Curves and Surfaces 2010. LNCS, vol. 6920, pp. 711–730. Springer, Heidelberg (2012). https://doi.org/10.1007/978-3-642-27413-8_47
31. Zhang, K., Zuo, W., Gu, S., Zhang, L.: Learning deep CNN denoiser prior for image restoration. In: Proceedings of the IEEE Conference on Computer Vision and Pattern Recognition (CVPR), pp. 3929–3938. IEEE (2017)
32. Zhang, K., Gao, X., Tao, D., Li, X., et al.: Single image super-resolution with non-local means and steering kernel regression. TIP **11**, 12 (2012)
33. Zhang, Y., Li, K., Li, K., Wang, L., Zhong, B., Fu, Y.: Image super-resolution using very deep residual channel attention networks. In: Ferrari, V., Hebert, M., Sminchisescu, C., Weiss, Y. (eds.) ECCV 2018. LNCS, vol. 11211, pp. 294–310. Springer, Cham (2018). https://doi.org/10.1007/978-3-030-01234-2_18
34. Zhang, Y., Tian, Y., Kong, Y., Zhong, B., Fu, Y.: Residual dense network for image super-resolution. In: Proceedings of the IEEE Conference on Computer Vision and Pattern Recognition (CVPR), pp. 2472–2481. IEEE (2018)
35. Zou, W.W., Yuen, P.C.: Very low resolution face recognition problem. TIP **21**(1), 327–340 (2012)

Marine Biometric Recognition Algorithm Based on YOLOv3-GAN Network

Ping Liu, Hongbo Yang(✉), and Jingnan Fu

Beijing Information Science and Technology University, Beijing, China
anonbo@bistu.edu.cn

Abstract. With the rise of the marine ranching field, the object recognition applications on underwater catching robots have become more and more popular. However, due to the influence of uneven underwater light, the underwater images are easily encountered with problems such as color distortion and underexposure, which seriously affects the accuracy of underwater object recognition. In this work, we propose a marine biometric recognition algorithm based on YOLOv3-GAN network, which jointly optimizes the training of image enhancement loss (*LossGAN*) and classification and location loss (*LossYOLO*) in the network, and it is different from the traditional underwater object recognition approaches which usually consider image enhancement and object detection separately. Consequently, our proposed algorithm is more powerful in marine biological identification. Moreover, the anchor box is further modified by k-means method to cluster the object box size in the network detection part, which makes the anchor box more in line with the object size. The experimental results demonstrate that the mean Average Precision (mAP) and the Recall of the YOLOv3-GAN network are above 6.4% and 4.8% higher than that of the YOLOv3 network. In addition, the image enhancement part in the YOLOv3-GAN network can provide high quality images which benefit for other applications in the marine surveillance field.

Keywords: YOLOv3-GAN network · YOLOv3 network · GAN network · Image enhancement · Object recognition and detection

1 Introduction

In recent years, object recognition based on underwater robots has been widely used in the intelligent field of marine ranching. However, as light travels underwater, the degree of distortion varies with the wavelength, which results in low resolution of the underwater image. The distorted image makes it difficult to improve the accuracy of object detection algorithm. The detection accuracy and speed of marine biological target recognition and detection algorithms are often difficult to meet the requirements at the same time. To solve the above problems, the traditional marine biometric recognition algorithm adopts the "two-step" approach to improve the detection accuracy: firstly, the image quality is improved by enhancing the underwater image using an image enhancement method, and then the enhanced images are trained by the detection network. The underwater image enhancement methods and object recognition detection algorithms currently used are introduced below.

Y. M. Ro et al. (Eds.): MMM 2020, LNCS 11961, pp. 581–592, 2020.
https://doi.org/10.1007/978-3-030-37731-1_47

Currently, underwater image enhancement methods are mainly divided into two categories: the first is a physical model-based approach [1]. This method draws on the image imaging mechanism, and studies the scattering and absorption of incident light by suspended particles in water to establish a reasonable underwater imaging model. On this basis, the undegraded image is reversed. However, due to the complexity and variety of the underwater imaging process, the existing models generally have the disadvantages of too simple parameters and poor passability, which restricts the use of such methods. The second category is based on a non-physical model approach. It is also divided into two categories: image enhancement based on traditional method and image enhancement based on deep learning. The traditional underwater image enhancement method is aimed at the degradation of underwater image quality, such as contrast reduction, color cast, image blur, etc., and the corresponding image enhancement technology is selected to flexibly construct the processing scheme. The image enhancement method based on deep learning mainly uses unsupervised or semi-supervised feature learning and hierarchical feature extraction to learn tasks from examples, such as UGAN-P [2] underwater image enhancement network.

At present, the object detection and recognition algorithms based on deep learning are mainly divided into two categories: (1) Two stage object detection algorithm. The detection problem is divided into two phases. Firstly, candidate regions are generated, and then classifying and refining the candidate regions.. Typical examples of such algorithms are R-CNN [3], Fast R-CNN [4], Faster R-CNN [5], etc. (2) One stage object detection algorithm. It realizes simultaneous detection and classification, and directly output the class probability and position coordinate value of the object. Typical algorithms such as YOLOv1 [6], YOLOv2 [7], YOLOv3 [8], SSD [9] and Corner Net [10] and so on.

At present, most of the research on underwater image enhancement is based on the improvement of visual effect in image quality, thus ignoring its practical use in life, that is, improving the accuracy of detection and recognition. This research, which divides underwater image enhancement and object detection into two tasks, limits the current development of marine biometrics. Inspired by the above, we proposed a YOLOv3-GAN network. The principle of the network is to add the underwater image enhancement GAN network into the YOLOv3 detection and recognition network. The intention of this approach is to enhance and detect the underwater image at the same time, so that the purpose of underwater image enhancement is clearer.

The main research content of this paper is divided into two parts: dataset preparation and model training. Its contribution mainly includes the following four aspects: (1) Design a multi-task YOLOv3-GAN network. This network can achieve both image enhancement and object detection simultaneously. Due to its strong expansibility, it is applicable not only to the ocean field studied in this paper, but also to other existing underwater scenes. (2) An underwater image enhancement network model is provided. It can generate real images and provide more high-definition images for the surveillance field. (3) The purpose of underwater image enhancement is clearer. Combined training and optimization of underwater image enhancement loss (*LossGAN*) and classification and regression loss (*LossYOLO*) make the marine biological recognition algorithm more systematic. (4) Anchor box is modified by k-means clustering size of dataset object box, which improves detection accuracy.

2 YOLOv3-GAN Marine Biological Recognition Algorithm

At present, marine biometric recognition technology is one of the important links for underwater capture robots to capture seafood. Its recognition accuracy and detection speed are affected by two aspects: (1) underwater image quality. (2) object detection algorithm. At present, the "two-step" method is used for recognition of marine biometrics. The underwater image is enhanced first, and then the enhanced image dataset is trained by using a suitable detection algorithm, and the trained model is evaluated on the test set. This paper proposes a "one-step" YOLOv3-GAN marine biometric recognition algorithm based on task. The core idea of this algorithm is to add underwater image enhancement network to the object detection network. It can implement a multi-tasking network that performs underwater image enhancement and object detection simultaneously. The proposed algorithm provides a new idea for the field of marine biological identification.

2.1 YOLOv3-GAN Network Structure

Figure 1 shows the structure diagram of YOLOv3-GAN network. The network is mainly divided into two parts: GAN image enhancement network and YOLOv3 object detection network.

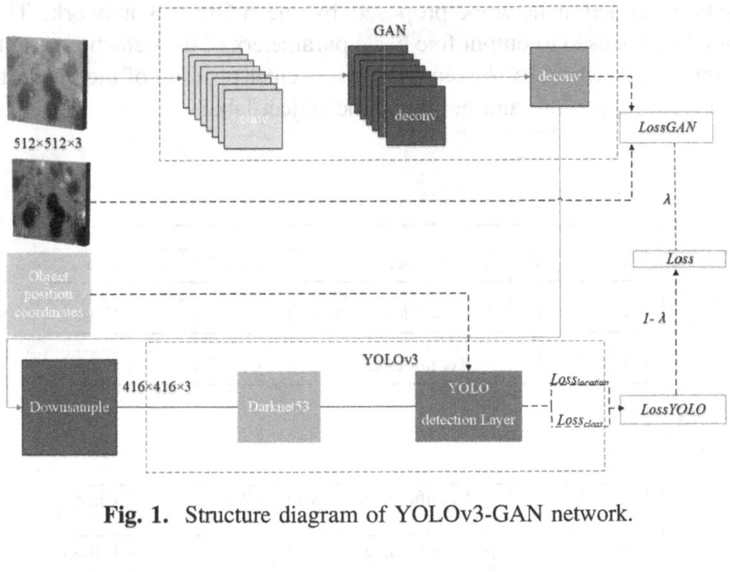

Fig. 1. Structure diagram of YOLOv3-GAN network.

The underwater image enhancement network part of the YOLOv3-GAN is a kind of generative adversarial net, similar to [2]. It can be found from Fig. 1 that the GAN network is designed in a completely symmetrical form consisting of 8 layers of convolution and 8 layers of deconvolution. Due to the structural similarity between input and output, it is also designed as "U-Net" [11].

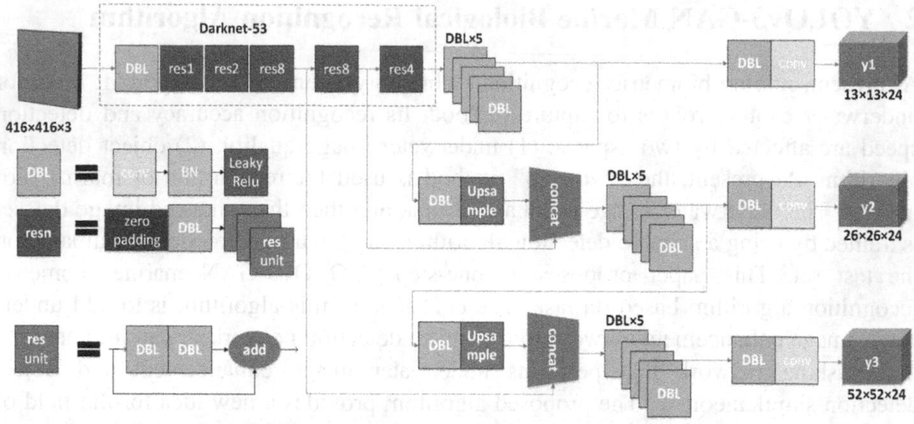

Fig. 2. Structure diagram of YOLOv3 network.

The detection network part of the YOLOv3-GAN network is the YOLOv3 network. Figure 2 shows the network structure diagram of YOLOv3. It is mainly composed of feature extraction layer Darknet53 and YOLO detection layer. The feature extraction layer is mainly composed of convolution layer, BN (Batch Normalization) layer and concatenate layer. LeakyRelu is used as the activation function. Darknet53 is a new feature extraction network proposed by the YOLOV3 network. The YOLO convolution layer is used to output five basic parameters of the detection result: (*bx*, *by*, *bw*, *bh*, confidence), where *bx*, *by* represents the center position of the object label, and *bw*, *bh* represents the width and height of the object label.

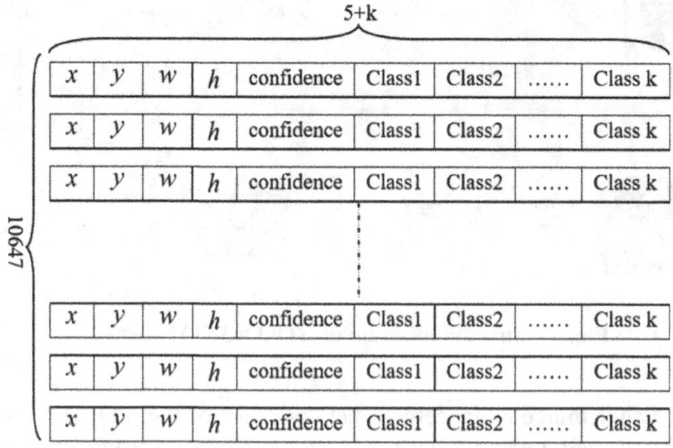

Fig. 3. YOLOv3 network output format.

As shown in Fig. 2, the size of the input image is 416 × 416 × 3, then the three scales of the network detection part are 13 × 13 × 3, 26 × 26 × 3, 52 × 52 × 3. Each box is responsible for the regression of three anchor boxes and takes one of them as the final detection result. As shown in Fig. 3, for an input image, the size of output [12] is 1 × (3 × (13 × 13 + 26 × 26 + 52 × 52) × (5 + k) = 1 × 10647 × (5 + k), k represents the number of classes. The underwater image dataset used in this paper has three classes.

Since the input and output of the two networks are inconsistent, we add a layer of down-sampling layer to connect the image enhancement GAN network with the YOLOv3 network. As shown in Fig. 1, the input of the GAN network selected in this paper is 512 × 512 × 3. Each time it passes through a layer of convolution, the size is reduced by 2 times. Each time a layer of deconvolution is passed, the size is doubled. This symmetrical network structure is caused by the concatenate connection during deconvolution. Therefore, the input size after the 8-layer convolution and 8-layer deconvolution is still 512 × 512 × 3. For detection network, the input image needs to be extracted through the Darknet53 network, and the maximum stride of the network is 32, which causes the input to be a specific size. In this paper, the input size of the detection network part is set to 416 × 416 × 3. Therefore, the down-sampling layer is used to interpolate the output of the image enhancement network with the input of the detection and recognition network.

2.2 YOLOv3-GAN Network Loss Function

In this paper, a new GAN loss function (*LossGAN*) is added to the detection algorithm for underwater image enhancement. Network input mainly includes three parts: original distorted image, real image generated by the trained UGAN-P image enhancement model and image position coordinate information. The purpose of adding real images in this paper is to reduce the deviation from the original distortion image after passing through the GAN enhanced network, that is, to optimize *LossGAN*. Therefore, the total loss function of this paper consists of two parts: underwater image enhancement loss (*LossGAN*) and classification location loss (*LossYOLO*).

The GAN enhanced network is mainly composed of a generator G and a discriminator D. From [13], it is found that with the improvement of the discriminator, the generator gradient disappears, which makes training difficult. At present, many different loss functions [14–17] have been proposed for the discriminator. The GAN enhanced network part of this paper uses the Wasserstein GAN (WGAN-GP) [15] loss function with gradient penalty:

$$L_{WGAN}(G,D) = E[D(X)] - E[D(G(Y))] + \lambda_{GP} E_{\hat{x}\sim P_{\hat{x}}}[(\|\nabla_{\hat{x}} D(\hat{x})\|_2 - 1)^2], \quad (2)$$

Where X is the true data distribution and Y is the distribution of the generator approximating learning X. $P_{\hat{x}}$ defined as a straight line sample between the paired points from the real data distribution and the generator distribution. λ_{GP} represents a weighting factor. E stands for the expected value.

In order to make G authentic and capture low frequencies in the image, UGAN-P also considers L1 loss:

$$L_{L_1} = E\left[\|X - G(Y)\|_1\right] \tag{3}$$

Often, the generated model produces a blurry image. A strategy to enhance the prediction of image gradients in the direct punishment generator is explored here. As proposed in [18], given the real image I^X, the predicted image $I^P = G(I^Y)$, the gradient difference loss (GDL) is given by:

$$L_{GDL}\left(I^X, I^P\right) = \sum_{i,j}\left\| \left|I^X_{i,j} - I^X_{i-1,j}\right| - \left|I^P_{i,j} - I^P_{i-1,j}\right| \right\|^{\alpha} + \left\| \left|I^X_{i,j-1} - I^X_{i,j}\right| - \left|I^P_{i,j-1} - I^P_{i,j}\right| \right\|^{\alpha}, \tag{4}$$

Where α is an integer greater than or equal to 1.

When considering GDL, the loss function of GAN enhanced network can be expressed as:

$$LossGAN = \min_G \max_D L_{WGAN}(G, D) + \lambda_1 L_{L_1}(G) + \lambda_2 L_{GDL} \tag{5}$$

The loss function of YOLOv3 uses the sum of the squared errors to integrate the location error of prediction box, IOU errors with or without objects and classification errors. The formula of total loss function [12] is as follows:

$$\begin{aligned} L_1 &= (2 - truth_w \times truth_h) \times \sum\nolimits_{r \in (x,y,w,h)} (truth_r - predict_r)^2 \\ L_2 &= \sum\nolimits_{r=0}^{k-1} ((r == truth_{class})?1 : 0 - predict_{class_r})^2 \\ L_3 &= (truth_{conf} - predict_{conf})^2 \\ LossYOLO &= \frac{1}{2}\sum\nolimits_{i=1}^{10647} \lambda_{obj} * (L_1 + L_2) + L_3, \end{aligned} \tag{6}$$

where λobj is set to 1 if the cell currently has an object, otherwise 0.

Finally, the formula of the total loss function of YOLOV3-GAN network is shown as follows:

$$Loss = \lambda LossGAN + (1 - \lambda) LossYOLO \tag{7}$$

3 Experiment

3.1 Dataset

Derwater Image and Label Dataset. The underwater image and label dataset provided by the Underwater Robot Picking Contest (URPC) official website. Images of seacucumbers, seaurchins, and scallops and their coordinates in the image are provided in the dataset. We processed 18,982 images into a usable dataset. The training set is set to 14,236 and the testing set is set to 4,746. The dataset has two purposes: one is to train the YOLOv3 network. The other is as the dataset of YOLOv3-GAN detection network part.

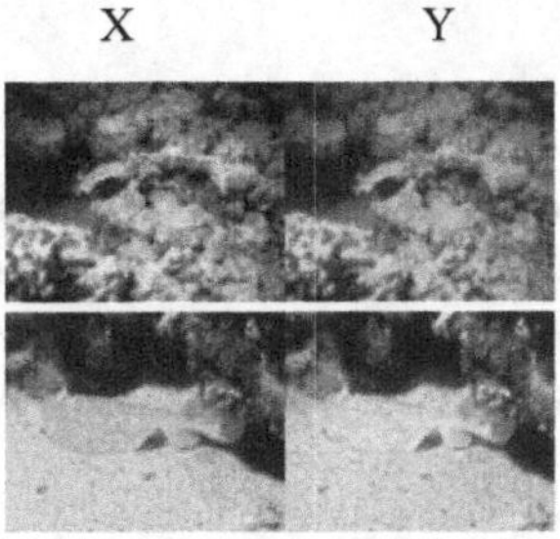

Fig. 4. UGAN-P network dataset format, pairwise distortion and real image.

UGAN-P Model Training Dataset. Since the network dataset format is a pair of real and distorted images, and it is difficult to obtain real underwater image dataset. We introduced the CycleGAN network [19] to produce datasets of paired images. The network contains two mapping functions G: X → Y and F: Y → X, as well as the related dual discriminators D_Y and D_X. D_Y encourages G to convert X to an output that is indistinguishable from domain Y, while D_X encourages F to convert Y to an output that is indistinguishable from domain X. It's consistent for the cycle of forward and backward, which is:

$$\begin{aligned} x \rightarrow G(x) \rightarrow F(G(x)) \approx x \\ y \rightarrow G(y) \rightarrow F(G(y)) \approx y \end{aligned} \tag{8}$$

According to the above principle, as shown in Fig. 4, given the undistorted image X, the CycleGAN model can generate a distorted image Y. The X and Y are connected in the form of Fig. 4, that is, the dataset of the UGAN-P network is obtained. There are 6128 available image datasets for UGAN-P network generated by CycleGAN network model.

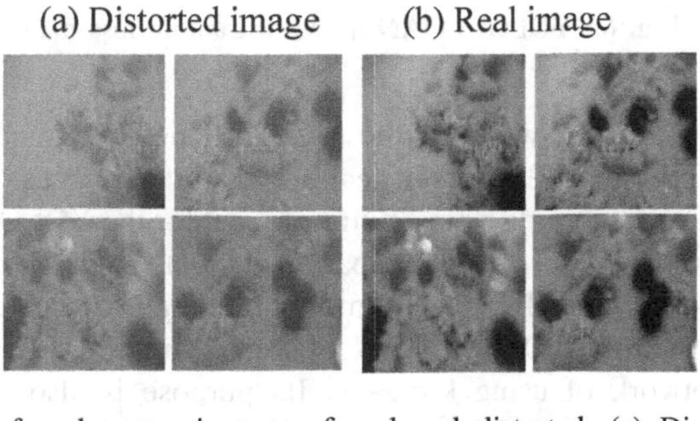

Fig. 5. Four pairs of underwater images of real and distorted. (a) Distorted images taken underwater, (b) Real images generated using the UGAN-P model.

YOLOv3-GAN Network Joint Training Dataset. A dataset used to jointly train the YOLOv3-GAN network. As shown in Fig. 5(a), there is a distortion image dataset with a total of 18,982 pictures. Figure 5(b) shows the 18,982 real images generated, which is the dataset of YOLOv3-GAN enhanced network part.

3.2 Model Training

Determination of the Value of the Anchor Box Parameter. We used k-means clustering on the detection network to determine the priori values of bounding box. We correct the anchor box size by k-means clustering the size of object box in the dataset. The values of the nine anchor boxes corresponding to our dataset are: (16 × 30), (40 × 15), (25 × 38), (15 × 71), (52 × 25), (36 × 51), (65 × 53), (47 × 80), (74 × 109).

Setting and Tuning of Super Parameters. The number of YOLOv3-GAN network training iterations is set to 30,000 times, and the initial learning rate is set to 0.01. It is found through tuning parameters that when the iteration is 20,000 and 23,000 times respectively, the corresponding learning rate is 0.007 and 0.005, and the network has certain convergence. Figure 6 shows the training loss graph of the whole network. From the graph we can see that the network basically converges when the number of iterations is 25,000.

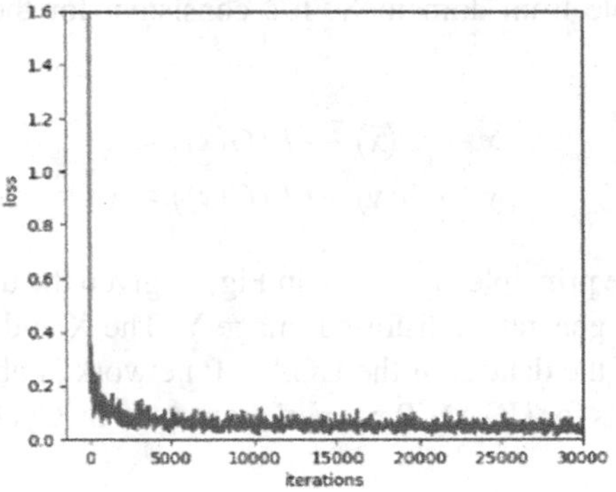

Fig. 6. YOLOv3-GAN network training loss map.

Network Training. Firstly, we train the UGAN-P network model. The dataset is shown in Fig. 6. There are 6128 pairs of real and distorted images. The model has two main purposes. One is to provide a pre-training model for the YOLOv3-GAN enhanced network part. The other is to generate a partial dataset of the YOLOv3-GAN image enhancement network. Secondly, network model training is carried out for YOLOv3 of using k-means clustering, YOLOv3-GAN network without k-means clustering and YOLOv3-GAN network of using k-means. Its purpose is also twofold: One is to compare the network system performance of YOLOv3 and YOLOv3-GAN proposed in this paper. The other is to evaluate whether the revised anchor box has an impact on the detection indicators in this paper.

3.3 Experimental Setup

The test evaluation indicators in this paper mainly use recall rate (Recall), mean Average Precision (mAP) and speed (Fps). The experimental environment includes Ubuntu 14.04, Pytorch 1.0, python 3.7. The server configuration used for training is: Intel Core i7-6700K CPU 4 000 GHz * 8, two Geforce GTX 2080Ti, two Nvidia TiTAN X, one Geforce GTX 1080Ti.

3.4 Experimental Results and Analysis

Two sets of experiments are carried out in this paper. The first set of experiments train the UGAN-P network model. Underwater distorted images can generate clear images through the trained UGAN-P model. It can be observed from Fig. 5(a) and (b) that the model has a great improvement in background definition of underwater images. In the second set of experiments, we use the YOLOv3-A (using k-mean clustering), YOLOv3-GAN-A (using k-mean clustering), and YOLOv3-GAN-B (without using k-mean clustering) three detection algorithms for model training and results testing. The recall rate (Recall), mean Average Precision (mAP) and speed (Fps) were used to evaluate the accuracy of the model. The results are summarized in Table 1.

Table 1. Recall, mAP and speed results of the three algorithm tests.

Methods	Recall	mAP	Fps
YOLOv3-A	88.5	76.1	20
YOLOv3-GAN-B	92.3	81.0	15
YOLOv3-GAN-A	**93.3**	**82.5**	14

The experimental results show that the mAP of YOLOv3-GAN network model test without k-means clustering increased by 4.9% compared with that of YOLOv3 network model test of using k-means clustering, and the Recall is increased by 3.8%. It shows that the detection accuracy of the YOLOv3-GAN network for underwater distortion images has great advantages compared with the YOLOv3 network. The YOLOv3-GAN network model using k-means improved mAP by 1.5% and Recall by 1% compared to the that without k-means. It is indicated that correcting the anchor box by k-means clustering the size of label box can improve the accuracy of object detection. It can also be seen from Table 1 that although the detection speed of the YOLOv3-GAN network proposed by us is 6Fps lower than that of YOLOv3, it can still meet the application requirements.

Table 2. The results comparison of YOLOv3-A, YOLOv3-GAN-B and YOLOv3-GAN-A

Methods	Threshold	Seacucumber	Seaurchin	Scallop
Ground truth		7	32	29
YOLOv3-A	0.5	4	27	18
YOLOv3-GAN-B	0.5	5	30	27
YOLOv3-GAN-A	0.5	7	32	29

Figure 7(a), (b) shows the test results of the two groups of network training. The green boxes marked in the first image of the two sets of pictures are real label boxes. The second, third, and fourth images are the test results of YOLOv3 using k-means, YOLOv3-GAN without k-means, and YOLOv3-GAN using k-means. The blue box in the image represents the tested object, and the red box represents the missed object. The results of the two groups of object detection are summarized as shown in Table 2.

Analysis of Table 2 shows that the number of objects missed detection using the YOLOv3 network is 13 compared to the YOLOv3-GAN network model without k-means. It missed 19 compared to the YOLOV3-GAN network model using k-means. YOLOV3-GAN, which did not use k-means, missed six objects than using k-means. In summary, two conclusions can be drawn through quantitative analysis: YOLOv3-GAN network is more accurate than YOLOv3 network in detecting underwater objects. Secondly, k-means clustering for object labels can improve detection accuracy.

(a) (b)

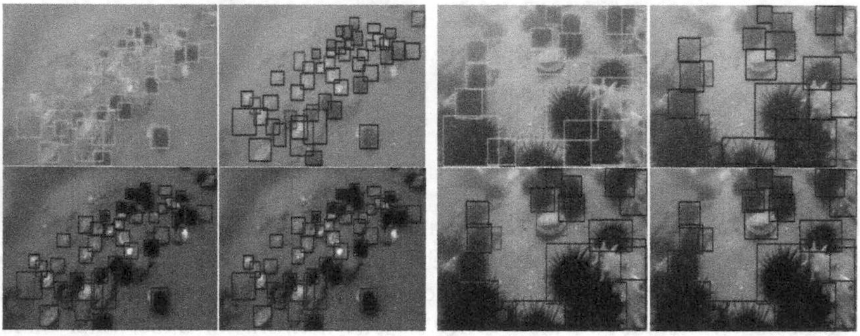

Fig. 7. (a) (b) is the result of two sets of network training test results.

4 Conclusion

This paper proposes a multi-task YOLOv3-GAN marine biometric recognition algorithm, which adds a new loss function *LossGAN* for underwater image enhancement. It breaks the limitations of traditional underwater image object detection and underwater image enhancement step by step, making the whole underwater object detection network more systematic. The purpose of image enhancement network in YOLOv3-GAN network is clearer than other underwater image enhancement networks. The images generated by our enhanced network model are also more conducive to the underwater object detection and recognition algorithm to learn the object features, thus improving the detection accuracy. The experimental results show that the YOLOv3-GAN network has improved detection accuracy and recall rate compared to YOLOv3. The YOLOv3-GAN network proposed by us has strong expansibility in application. It is suitable for other fields of underwater object detection and recognition, and has high scientific use and research value. It also has high scientific use and research value. At the same time, the GAN image enhancement model trained in this paper can generate more realistic images. This can provide a lot of clear images for the field of underwater surveillance.

References

1. Schettini, R., Corchs, S.: Underwater image processing: state of the art of restoration and image enhancement methods. EURASIP J. Adv. Signal Process. **2010**, 1–15 (2010)
2. Fabbri, C., Islam, M.J., Sattar, J.: Enhancing underwater imagery using generative adversarial networks (2018)
3. Girshick, R., Donahue, J., Darrell, T., Malik, J.: Rich feature hierarchies for accurate object detection and semantic segmentation. In: IEEE Conference on Computer Vision and Pattern Recognition (CVPR) (2014)
4. Girshick, R.: Fast R-CNN. Comput. Sci. (2015)
5. Ren, S., He, K., Girshick, R., et al.: Faster R-CNN: towards real-time object detection with region proposal networks. IEEE Trans. Pattern Anal. Mach. Intell. **39**(6), 1137–1149 (2017)
6. Redmon, J., Divvala, S., Girshick, R., et al.: You only look once: unified, real-time object detection. In: IEEE Conference on Computer Vision and Pattern Recognition, pp. 779–788. IEEE Computer Society (2016)
7. Redmon, J., Farhadi, A.: Yolo9000: better, faster, stronger. In: 2017 IEEE Conference on Computer Vision and Pattern Recognition (CVPR), pp. 6517–6525. IEEE (2017)
8. Redmon, J., Farhadi, A.: YOLOv3: an incremental improvement (2018)
9. Liu, W., et al.: SSD: single shot multibox detector. In: Leibe, B., Matas, J., Sebe, N., Welling, M. (eds.) ECCV 2016. LNCS, vol. 9905, pp. 21–37. Springer, Cham (2016). https://doi.org/10.1007/978-3-319-46448-0_2
10. Law, H., Deng, J.: CornerNet: detecting objects as paired keypoints (2018)
11. Ronneberger, O., Fischer, P., Brox, T.: U-Net: convolutional networks for biomedical image segmentation. In: Navab, N., Hornegger, J., Wells, W.M., Frangi, A.F. (eds.) MICCAI 2015. LNCS, vol. 9351, pp. 234–241. Springer, Cham (2015). https://doi.org/10.1007/978-3-319-24574-4_28
12. Shuo, L., Xuan, C., Rui, F.: YOLOv3 network based on improved loss function. Comput. Syst. Appl. (2019)
13. Arjovsky, M., Bottou, L: Towards principled methods for training generative adversarial networks. arXiv preprint arXiv:1701.04862 (2017)
14. Arjovsky, M., Chintala, S., Bottou, L.: Wasserstein GAN. arXiv preprint arXiv:1701.07875 (2017)
15. Gulrajani, I., Ahmed, F., Arjovsky, M., Dumoulin, V., Courville, A.: Improved training of wasserstein GANS. arXiv preprint arXiv:1704.00028 (2017)

16. Mao, X., Li, Q., Xie, H., Lau, R.Y.K., Wang, Z., Smolley, S.P.: Least squares generative adversarial networks. arXiv preprint arXiv:1611.04076 (2016)
17. Zhao, J., Mathieu, M., LeCun, Y.: Energy-based generative adversarial network. arXiv preprint arXiv:1609.03126 (2016)
18. Mathieu, M., Couprie, C., LeCun, Y.: Deep multi-scale video prediction beyond mean square error. arXiv preprint arXiv:1511.05440 (2015)
19. Zhu, J.-Y., Park, T., Isola, P., Efros, A.A.: Unpaired image-to-image translation using cycle-consistent adversarial networks. arXiv preprint arXiv:1703.10593 (2017)

Multi-scale Spatial Location Preference for Semantic Segmentation

Qiuyuan Han[1] and Jin Zheng[1,2](✉)

[1] School of Computer Science and Engineering, Beihang University, Beijing 100191, China
{qiuyuanhan,JinZheng}@buaa.edu.cn

[2] State Key Laboratory of Virtual Reality Technology and Systems, Beihang University, Beijing 100191, China

Abstract. This paper proposes a semantic segmentation network which can address the problem of adaptive segmentation for objects with different sizes. In this work, ResNetV2-50 is firstly exploited to extract features of objects, and then these features are fed into the reconstructed feature pyramid network (FPN), which includes multi-scale preference (MSP) module and multi-location preference (MLP) module. Aiming at objects with different sizes, the receptive fields of kernels need to be adjusted. MSP module concatenates feature maps of different receptive fields, and then combines them with the SE block in SE-Net to obtain scale-wise dependencies. In this way, not only multi-scale information can be encoded in feature maps with different degree levels of preference adaptively, but also multi-scale spatial information can be provided to MLP module. The MLP module combines the channels containing more accurate spatial location information with preference to replace traditional nearest interpolation upsampling in FPN. At last, the weighted channels equip with scale-wise information as well as more accurate spatial location information and yield precise semantic prediction for objects with different sizes. We demonstrate the effectiveness of the proposed solutions on the Cityscapes and PASCAL VOC 2012 semantic image segmentation datasets and our methods achieve comparable or higher performance.

Keywords: Semantic segmentation · Multi-scale · Multi-location · FPN · Receptive field

1 Introduction

Semantic segmentation has proven highly effective at automatic driving, image editing and other reality applications, whose objective is to label each pixel in the image with one of the object categories. With the rapid development of deep convolutional neural networks (CNNs) [10, 16, 17], it is no need to use hand-designed features and adjust them during experiments. Even though high-level segmentation representations can be acquired through CNNs, they may produce inaccurate locating information in practical application.

This work is supported by the NSFC (No. 61876014, No.61632001, No.61772054).

Y. M. Ro et al. (Eds.): MMM 2020, LNCS 11961, pp. 593–604, 2020.
https://doi.org/10.1007/978-3-030-37731-1_48

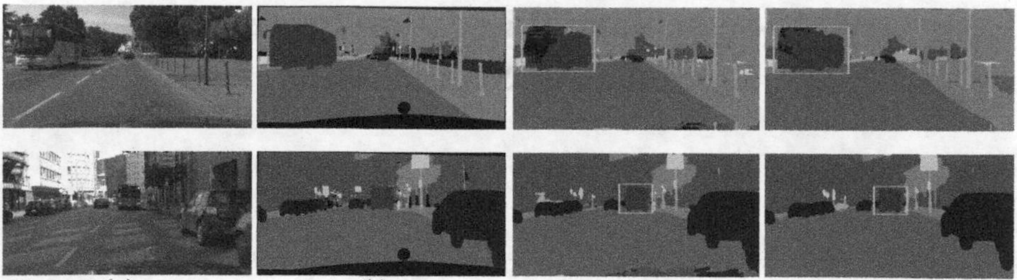
(a) (b) (c) (d)

Fig. 1. Visualization results produced by ResNetV2-50 combined with different modules on Cityscapes validation set. (a) Input image, (b) Ground truth, (c) ResNetV2-50 with traditional FPN, (d) ResNetV2-50 with our reconstructed FPN (including MSP and MLP modules).

To resolve the problem of segmenting objects with different sizes through enlarging the receptive fields, dilated convolution is proposed in [19]. The dilated convolution is employed in atrous spatial pyramid pooling (ASPP) module, which has been proposed in DeepLabv2 [3], and the module is put on feature maps performed multiple pooling operations. Even though rich semantic information can be obtained through a deep convolutional network, detailed information related to pixel location is missing due to the multiple pooling operations within the network backbone. In addition, cross-scale information is not combined as well.

To take advantage of low-level information with accurate location, the idea of feature pyramid network (FPN) [13] is proposed, which utilizes a top-down pathway to fuse low-level features containing more accurate locating information, and high-level features containing more semantic information. Though FPN is capable of merging cross-scale feature maps, the scale information of different receptive fields is not reflected in each feature map. Hence, in each feature map, the multiple scale information for the same class of objects with different sizes is not effectively utilized. It is difficult for FPN to obtain good segmentation results for objects with different sizes simultaneously. Just as shown in Fig. 1(c), the segmentation result of the smaller size 'bus' in the image below is perfect, while the larger size 'bus' in the image above is worse. The network fails to integrate the information of 'bus' with different sizes.

In order to acquire more accurate semantic segmentation for objects with different sizes, the appropriate receptive fields with scale and accurate pixel locating information need to be seized automatically. This paper reconstructs FPN, and integrates multi-scale preference (MSP) module and multi-location preference (MLP) module in FPN. MSP module captures multi-scale information, and endows them with different degrees of preference adaptively. In MSP, four kinds of dilated convolutions are applied on feature maps to capture various receptive fields and the SE block in [9] is employed to emphasize scale-wise information and suppress useless scale information. Furthermore, the proposed multi-location preference (MLP) module can combine the multiple scale-wise spatial location information provided by MSP module with preference for each segmentation class and upsample the feature maps simultaneously. As shown in Fig. 1(d), not only the segmentation result of the smaller size 'bus' in the image below is good, but

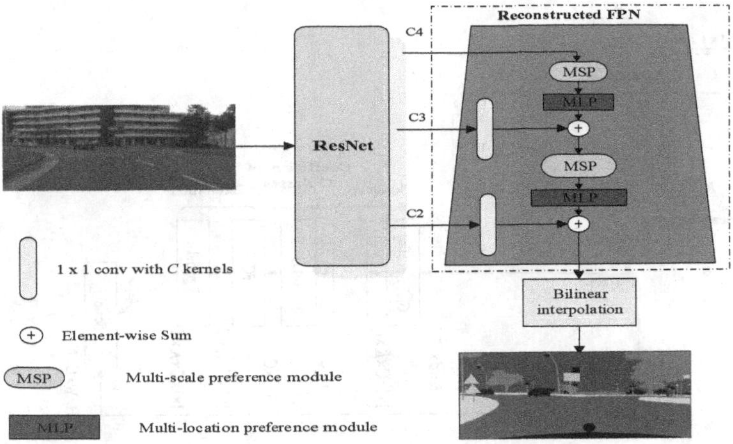

Fig. 2. An overview of the proposed network structure.

also the result of the larger one in image above is better than that of Fig. 1(c) apparently. That means, employing the combination of MSP and MLP modules enables the network to pay attention to the feature maps containing required cross-scale information and combine multi-scale spatial location information.

2 Related Work

Deep convolutional neural network based methods have made significant progress in image semantic segmentation. Several model variants are proposed to exploit multi-scale contextual information and combine low-level features for segmentation.

In order to enlarge receptive fields, dilated convolution [19] is adopted with enlarged convolution kernels applied on sparse locations with original weights, instead of max-pooling [18–21]. Compared with max-pooling, dilated convolution can get wider receptive fields without losing spatial location information. In DeepLabV2 [3], ASPP is introduced using the pyramid structure of dilated convolution to obtain multi-scale information. However, the module is placed after the fifth pooling operation, which does not take a series of feature maps of different scales into account. As shown in [11], the receptive fields of a network affect the performance on objects with different sizes. Dilated convolution with large dilation rate behaves well for large objects detection and segmentation, dilated convolution with small dilation rate behaves well for small objects detection and segmentation.

FPN [13] enables a model to acquire cross-scale features. It combines high-level feature maps, and semantically strong features with low-level feature maps, whose spatial location information are more accurate, via a top-down pathway and skip connections with high-level feature maps. In [14], it employs a structure called fully convolutional network (FCN) to produce semantic segmentation predictions. It performs nearest interpolation upsampling on high-level feature maps and then fuses with the 'score layer' consisting of 1×1 convolution. However, upsampling high-level class scores

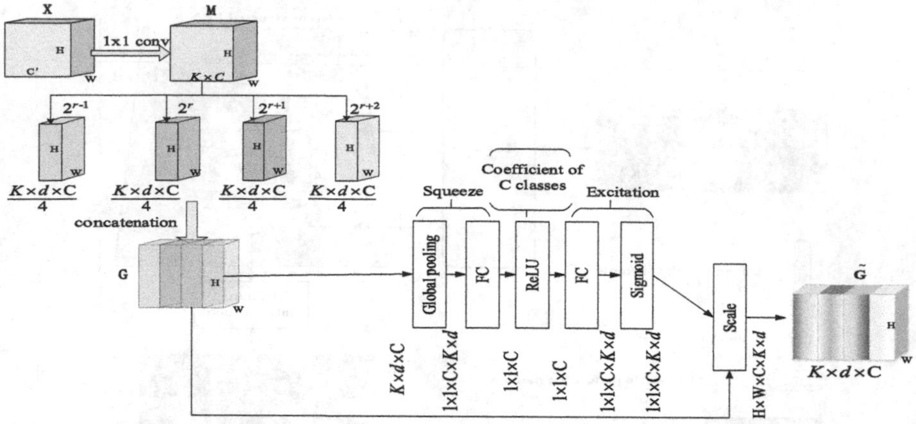

Fig. 3. MSP module. It extracts informative features of different scales selectively and adaptively by using four 3×3 dilated convolution with $2^{r-1}, 2^r, 2^{r+1}, 2^{r+2}$ dilate ratios and SE block in SE-Net. The variable r, descripted as dilate ratio index, is adjusted according to the feature map of different sizes, K is a multiple of C, d is a multiple of the input channels of feature maps.

directly reduces the details of segmentation result and bilinear upsampling for class prediction would yield same results unless adding non-linear filtering on the feature map as illustrated in [6].

Our approach is motivated by the success of the methods above. Dilated convolution can cover a wide range of receptive fields, and FPN can incorporate the low-level features with more accurate position information. Our method utilizes their outstanding features and improves on their deficiencies.

3 Methods

In this section, we first introduce the overall network structure, and then describe the proposed MSP module and MLP module in detail.

The network architecture is shown in Fig. 2. We adopt ResNetV2-50 [8] as backbone of our network. According to [13], we use the feature activations output of each stage's last residual block of ResNetV2-50 as the feature maps of bottom-up pathway, which are denoted as {C2, C3, C4} for block2, block3, block4 outputs. Firstly, feeding the high-level feature map C4 into MSP module which is explained in Sect. 3.1, and then doing upsampling in MLP, explained in Sect. 3.2, to upsample the result of MSP. Low-level maps undergo a 1×1 convolutional layer with C kernels and then merged with the corresponding upsampled maps by element-wise addition. Finally, we implement bilinear interpolation on the output of reconstructed FPN to turn it into the original size of image entered into the network. Throughout the paper, C means the number of classes for segmentation.

3.1 MSP Module

In order to obtain cross-context features and realize scale-wise dependencies efficiently and adaptively, we propose a multi-scale preference (MSP) module.

The structure of MSP module is illustrated in Fig. 3. In the first stage, the input feature maps $\mathbf{X} \in \mathbb{R}^{H\times W\times C'}$ are transformed to the feature maps $\mathbf{M} \in \mathbb{R}^{H\times W\times K\times C}$ by a 1×1 convolution, aiming to compress the number of channels.

In the second stage, the feature maps $\mathbf{M}$ are passed into four 3×3 dilated convolutions, each of which has a dilate ratio 2^{r-1}, $r \in \mathbb{Z}^+$. The dilate ratio index r needs to be set according to the sizes of $\mathbf{M}$. We set the number of output channels of each dilated convolution is:

$$q(d) = \left\lfloor \frac{K \times d \times C}{4} \right\rfloor, \tag{1}$$

where K is the amplification factor, and d is the influence factor. We assume $K \in 4\mathbb{Z}^+$ and $d \in \mathbb{Z}^+$. This step embeds the global distribution of C classes in specific receptive field. Then, the results of the four dilated convolution are concatenated into $\mathbf{G} \in \mathbb{R}^{H\times W\times (K\times d\times C)}$ which contains four different receptive fields.

After the first two stages, each segmentation class has $\frac{K\times d}{4}$ features for each receptive field, because $K \in 4\mathbb{Z}^+$ and $d \in \mathbb{Z}^+$, therefore, $\frac{K\times d}{4} \in \mathbb{Z}^+$. In the third stage, the feature maps $\mathbf{G}$ are fed into the SE block to selectively emphasise and suppress the role of each class in each receptive field. In the step of squeeze, the global spatial information is squeezed into a channel descriptor by using a global average pooling. The descriptor $\mathbf{d} \in \mathbb{R}^{C\times K\times d}$ is calculated by:

$$d_t = F_{sq}(\mathbf{g}_t) = \frac{1}{H \times W}\sum_{i=1}^{H}\sum_{j=1}^{W} g_t(i,j), \tag{2}$$

where $\mathbf{g}_t \in \mathbb{R}^{H\times W}$ is the t-th feature map in $\mathbf{G} \in \mathbb{R}^{H\times W\times (K\times d\times C)}$. The descriptor now is the coarse coefficients corresponding to $\frac{K\times d}{4}$ features of C classes in each receptive field. After the squeeze step, the global scale-wise dependencies are embedded in the descriptor, enabling the descriptor equipped with information of global receptive field. In the step of excitation, the descriptor is projected to the original size of it. Now, the channel descriptor represents precise coefficients representing the preference weights for each feature map.

At last, the final weighted feature maps $\widetilde{\mathbf{G}} \in \mathbb{R}^{H\times W\times (K\times d\times C)}$ are obtained by rescaling the features $\mathbf{G}$ with the scaling functions:

$$\widetilde{\mathbf{G}} = F_{scale}(\mathbf{g}_t, s_t) = s_t \cdot \mathbf{g}_t, \tag{3}$$

where $\widetilde{\mathbf{G}} = [\widetilde{\mathbf{g}}_1, \widetilde{\mathbf{g}}_2, ..., \widetilde{\mathbf{g}}_{C\times K\times d}]$, and $F_{scale}(\mathbf{g}_t, s_t)$ represents channel-wise multiplication between feature map $\mathbf{g}_t \in \mathbb{R}^{H\times W}$ and scalar s_t.

As a result, the information of C classes in different scales is strengthened or weakened in feature maps $\widetilde{\mathbf{G}}$. In Fig. 3, we use relatively dark and light color to represent the strengthened or weakened feature map of each class in different receptive fields. For clarity, we provide the detailed description of $\widetilde{\mathbf{G}}$ in Fig. 4. If K is set to 4 and d is set to 1, each class has one feature map in each receptive field so that each class has four

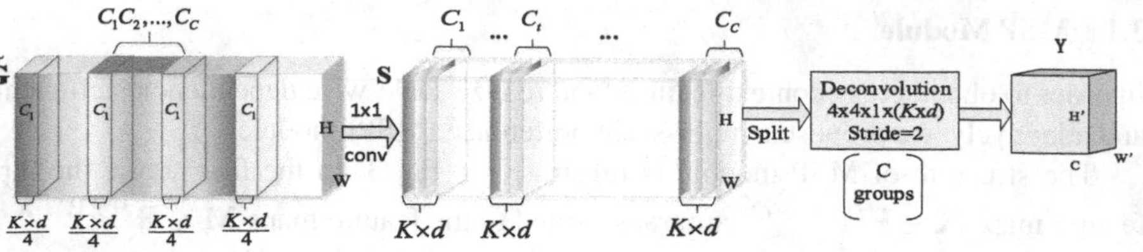

Fig. 4. MLP module. It fuses and upsamples informative features which are embedded with more accurate locating information of different scales.

different receptive fields locating information. Meanwhile, the information of the four feature maps may be strengthened or weakened as well after MSP module.

As a result, feature maps of one class have different preferences for different scales. Through MSP module, the attention to each class between multiple scales is recalibrated adaptively.

3.2 MLP Module

Direct upsampling, such as nearest interpolation upsampling in FCN may cause positional offset and inaccuracy, so we conduct a reconstructed upsampling incorporated in MLP module to replace nearest interpolation upsampling, and utilize the idea of 'score layer' in [13]. The comparison result between FCN-4s and FCN-32s tells us that the higher the sampling rate is, the more it decreases the performance of the model. Therefore, we upsample the spatial resolution of high-level feature maps by a factor of 2, as employed in FPN. In order to combine multi-scale locating information effectively, we produce a MLP module, which can dock with the MSP module perfectly.

As illustrated in Fig. 4, the input $\widetilde{\mathbf{G}}$ is the output of the MSP module in Fig. 3, in which each class carries locating information of different scales. As exhibited by $\widetilde{\mathbf{G}}$, each class possesses $\frac{K \times d}{4}$ spatial location information for each receptive field, $K \times d$ in total. The first step is to combine multi-scale information with preference. We append a 1×1 convolution on the feature maps $\widetilde{\mathbf{G}}$ to bind $K \times d$ feature maps together. This process facilitates class specialization with respect to the scale that it is needed as well. As a result, each class has $K \times d$ different specialized scale information covering four receptive fields, and each class of $K \times d$ feature maps contains the locating features of its scale.

Therefore, the next step is to fuse $K \times d$ feature maps into one feature map, which is the score map for one class. In other words, the purpose of this step is to combine spatial location information covering different scales. Then we tile the high-resolution score map with C groups overlapping deconvolution functions.

Firstly, the feature maps $\mathbf{S}$ are splitted into C groups. Each group $\mathbf{S}_{C_i}$ is generated by a slice function $F_{slice} : \mathbf{S} \rightarrow \mathbf{S}_{C_i}$, $\mathbf{S} \in \mathbb{R}^{H \times \mathbb{W} \times (K \times d \times C)}$, $\mathbf{S}_{C_i} \in \mathbb{R}^{K \times d}$.

$$\mathbf{S}_{C_i} = F_{slice}(\mathbf{S}, i) = \mathbf{S}_{K \times d \times i}^{K \times d \times (i+1)} \quad (4)$$

where i = 1, . . . , C.

The $K \times d$ feature maps with low resolution can be considered as $K \times d$ coefficients for each of C classes. Each group of $K \times d$ coefficients for each class is then multiplied by a set of deconvolution kernels and summed using a deconvolution layer. For the purpose of conducting 2× upsampled reconstruction, we use deconvolution kernels with a 4×4 pixel support and a stride of 2. The class score maps $\mathbf{Y} \in \mathbb{R}^{2H \times 2W \times C}$ are mapped from the $K \times d$ coefficients $\mathbf{S}_{c_i} \in \mathbb{R}^{k \times d}$ using deconvolution kernel $\mathbf{D} \in \mathbb{R}^{4 \times 4 \times K \times d \times C}$ through:

$$\mathbf{Y}_{C_i} = \mathbf{D}_{C_i} \otimes \mathbf{S}_{C_i} = \sum_{t=0}^{K \times d-1} \mathbf{D}_{C_i}^{t} \cdot \mathbf{S}_{C_i}^{t} \tag{5}$$

Here $\otimes$ denotes deconvolution convolution, $\mathbf{D}_{C_i} = \left[\mathbf{D}_{C,}^{0}, \mathbf{D}_{C,}^{1}, \ldots, \mathbf{D}_{C_i}^{K \times d-1}\right]$ and $\mathbf{S}_{C_i} = [\mathbf{S}_{C_1}^{0}, \mathbf{S}_{C_1}^{1}, \ldots, \mathbf{S}_{C_i}^{K \times d-1}]$, $i = 1, \ldots, C$ (for simplicity, biais terms are omitted). Since the score map of one class is produced by a summation through $K \times d$ channels covering four receptive fields, the spatial location information of the class in four scales is considered synthetically. Eventually, the feature map of class C_i is equivalent to be embedded with multi-scale locating information.

4 Experiments

We perform experiments on Cityscapes dataset [4] and PASCAL VOC 2012 dataset [5]. Experimental results demonstrate that MSP and MLP modules can exactly improve the performance of network. In the sections, we introduce the datasets, implementation details and series of ablation experiments. In the end, we report out results on Cityscapes and PASCAL VOC 2012 datasets.

4.1 Datasets and Implementation Details

Cityscapes. The dataset has 5,000 images in total captured from 50 different cities with high quality pixel-level notations of 19 semantic classes. There are 2,979 images in training set, 500 images in validation set and 1,525 images in test set of 2048 × 1024 pixels.

PASCAL VOC 2012. The PASCAL VOC 2012 semantic segmentation benchmark [5] contains 1,464 (*train*), 1,449 (*val*), and 1,456 (*test*) pixel-level annotated images for training, validation, and testing, respectively. The dataset contains 20 foreground object classes and one background class.

Implementation Details. We use multiple-scaled training images to augment training data and crop an image with the size of 512 × 512 for each batch randomly. We use momentum gradient descent with batch size of 20, momentum of 0.9 and weight decay of 0.0004. We train 60000 steps in total, using poly learning rate decay with learning rate starting from 0.01 on Cityscapes dataset and 0.007 on PASCAL VOC 2012 dataset. The performance is measured in terms of pixel intersection-over-union averaged across the 21 classes (mIoU) on PASCAL VOC 2012 segmentation benchmark and 19 classes on Cityscapes dataset, respectively. Our implementation is built on TensorFlow [1].

Table 1. Performance comparison for different strategies on Cityscapes validation set.

Methods	mIoU
ResNetV2-50	63.52
ResNetV2-50-FCN-2s	65.90
ResNetV2-50-MSP (r = 1)	67.58
ResNetV2-50-MSP (r = 2)	68.46
ResNetV2-50-MSP (r = 1, 2)	69.18
ResNetV2-50-MLP	68.04
ResNetV2-50-MSP-MLP (r = 1)	69.85
ResNetV2-50-MSP-MLP (r = 2)	73.27
ResNetV2-50-MSP-MLP (r = 1, 2)	74.67

4.2 Evaluation on Cityscapes

In this section, we show the results of the ablation studies on MSP and MLP modules. In the experiment, K is set to 4 and d is set to 1.

Ablation Study for MSP. Table 1 shows the evaluation results of the strategies, with switching the directly upsampled ResNetV2-50 to the proposed MSP and MLP modules. To verify the validity of the proposed modules, we train the upsampled ResNetV2-50 and others under the same condition. In the case of upsampling with nearest interpolation, employing MSP module outperforms the baseline FCN (ResNetV2-50) by 1.68% gain and 2.56% gain with r equaling to 1 and 2. Results show that MSP module is beneficial to semantic segmentation and using larger scale receptive fields is greater than using smaller ones in MSP. Due to the feature maps have different scales in the top-down pathway, the receptive fields are different in feature maps of each scale. Capturing different receptive fields of different scale feature maps is also implemented in our experiments. Therefore, we set $r = 1$ in the MSP module above and $r = 2$ in the MSP module below in Fig. 2, respectively. The result shows that ResNetV2-50-MSP with larger dilation rate for larger feature maps outperforms the baseline with 3.28% gain and better than the network with same dilate ratio index for different scale feature maps. Thus, setting different dilate ratio index for different scale feature maps is beneficial for semantic segmentation.

Ablation Study for MLP. As shown in Table 1, directly employing the MLP module on the top of ResNetV2-50 to replace the nearest interpolation upsampling in FCN ourperforms the baseline module by 2.14% gain. The result means that the MLP module is exactly good for determining multi-location preference for semantic segmentation.

Ablation Study for MSP and MLP Modules. Experimental results presented at the bottom of Table 1 illustrate that the combination of MSP and MLP modules improves the segmentation performance remarkably. Compared with the baseline, integrating the

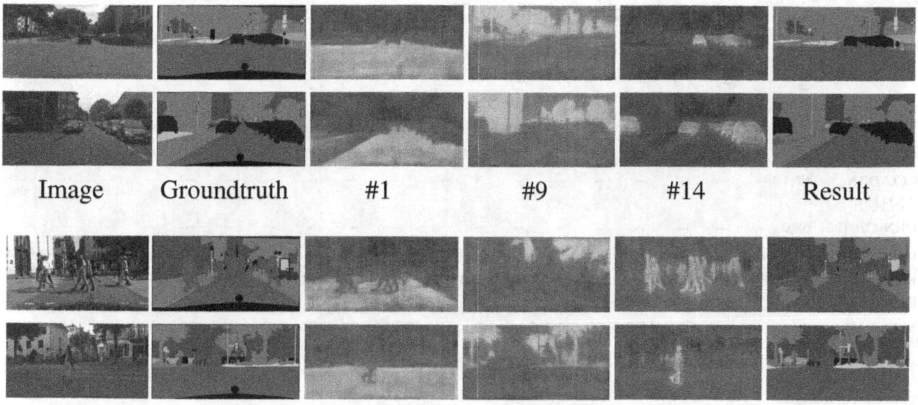

Fig. 5. Visualization results of our proposed MSP and MLP modules on Cityscapes validation set. For the first two columns, we show the input image, corresponding groundtruth. Meanwhile, we provide three channel maps from the intermediate outputs of the network after MLP module and the corresponding segmentation result. The channel maps of the two rows above are from 1th, 9th and 14th channels. The channel maps of the two rows below are from 1th, 9th and 12th channels.

two modules together, the performance improves to 69.85% in Mean IoU with r set to be 1, and further improves to 73.27% with r set to be 2. This means 3.95% and 7.37% performance enhancement respectively. Compared with using same dilate ratio index, employing different dilate ratio indexes for different scale feature maps yields a result of 74.67% in Mean IoU. Once again, it is advantageous to adopt different dilate ratio indexes for obtaining multi-scale receptive fields.

The results show that multi-scale spatial location information is utilized sufficiently.

Visualization Results. In order to verify the validity of our method, we extract the channels of the intermediate layer after MLP instead of the final output of the network. Through fusing the cross-scale information provided by MSP module, the t-th group of feature maps provides multi-scale spatial information for the t-th segmentation class. After combining the multi-scale spatial information of each group, the output of the group should belong to t-th class.

For each image in the first column of Fig. 5, we select three channel maps of the layer after MLP to display. The 1th, 9th and 14th channels in column 3, 4 and 5 of the two rows above corresponds to 'road', 'vegetation' and 'car' classes respectively. We find that the response of each specific semantic is prominent and consistent with the class to which it belongs. For example, the 14th channel map responds to the 'car' class and the 9th channel map responds to the 'vegetation' class exactly. We further select the image containing people for visualization shown in the next two rows of Fig. 5. The 12th channel map of the MLP output belongs to 'human' class. It is obvious that the 12th channel map responds to the 'human' class exactly and the response of other two

Table 2. Per-class results on Cityscapes benchmark test set.

Methods	Mean IoU	Road	Sidewalk	Building	Wall	Fence	Pole	Traffic light	Traffic sign	Vegetation	Terrian	Sky	Person	Rider	Car	Truck	Bus	Train	Motocycle	Bicycle
FCN-8s [13]	65.3	97.4	78.4	89.2	34.9	44.2	47.4	60.0	65.0	91.4	69.3	93.9	77.1	51.4	92.6	35.3	48.6	46.5	51.6	66.8
CCC-DRN-A50 [15]	67.1	–	–	–	–	–	–	–	–	–	–	–	–	–	–	–	–	–	–	–
DRN-C26 [20]	68.0	–	–	–	–	–	–	–	–	–	–	–	–	–	–	–	–	–	–	–
DeepLab-v2 [3]	70.4	97.9	81.3	90.3	48.8	47.4	49.6	57.9	67.3	91.9	69.4	94.2	79.8	59.8	93.7	56.5	67.5	57.5	57.7	68.8
RefineNet-Res101 [12]	**73.6**	**98.2**	83.3	91.3	47.8	50.4	56.1	**66.9**	71.3	92.3	**70.3**	94.8	80.9	**63.3**	**94.5**	**64.6**	**76.1**	**64.3**	**62.2**	**70**
MSP & MLP	70.6	98.0	**81.6**	**91.4**	**50.8**	**52.7**	**59.6**	**66.9**	**72.8**	**92.5**	70.1	**95.0**	**81.2**	60.1	94.2	51.3	68.1	54.5	55.7	69.7

Table 3. Comparison of our model with state-of-the-art methods on Cityscapes benchmark test set.

Methods	IoU Class	iIoU Class	IoU Cat	iIoU Cat
FCN-8s [14]	65.3	41.7	85.7	70.1
SegNet [2]	57.0	32.0	79.1	61.9
Dilation 10 [19]	67.1	42.0	86.5	71.1
DeepLab-v2 [3]	70.4	42.6	86.4	67.7
LRR-4x [6]	69.7	48.0	88.2	74.7
ResNetV2-50-MSP-MLP	**71.9**	47.8	**88.5**	74.1

channel maps are also consistent with the class they belong to. The result demonstrates that the semantic label distributed after MLP is consistent with the group.

Comparing with State-of-the-Art. We compare our method with others on per-class, shown in Table 2. DeepLab-v2 and RefineNet employ ResNet-101 [7] as their backbone of the network. The parameters of DRN-C26 [20] and CCC-DRN-A50 [15] are 20.62M and 16.79M respectively, and they are much larger than ours, which is 7.78M. Moreover, our model outperforms DRN-C26 by 2.6% gain and CCC-DRN-A50 by 3.5% gain respectively, and our model achieves comparable or higher performance.

We further compare our model with the existing methods related to the design of our model on the Cityscapes test set. As shown in Table 3, our model equipped with MSP and MLP modules achieves better performance in comparison to them. Besides, the backbone of our model is more lighter than others.

4.3 Evaluation on PASCAL VOC 2012 Dataset

To verify the effectiveness of the MSP and MLP modules and whether the combination of them is good for the performance exactly, we develop the experiments on PASCAL VOC 2012 segmentation benchmark. The results of mIoU with different strategies are shown in Table 4. In the case of using nearest interpolation upsampling, employing

Table 4. Comparison of segmentation results on PASCAL VOC 2012 dataset with different strategies.

Methods	mIoU
ResNetV2-50-FPN	66.41
ResNetV2-50-MSP ($r = 1$)	67.33
ResNetV2-50-MSP ($r = 1, 2$)	68.19
ResNetV2-50-MLP	68.25
ResNetV2-50-MSP-MLP ($r = 1$)	70.29
ResNetV2-50-MSP-MLP ($r = 1, 2$)	72.41

MSP module outperforms the baseline by 0.29% gain and 1.78% gain with dilate ratio index equals to 1 and 2, respectively. While using MLP module to replace the nearest interpolation upsampling in FCN brings 1.84% improvement. Compared with the baseline, the performance of integrating the two modules together outperforms baseline by 3.88% and 6.0% respectively, with r set to be 1 and 2 in different scale feature maps. ResNetV2-50-MSP-MLP shows more than 3% performance enhancement compared with the baseline ResNetV2-50-FPN. The results confirm that the MSP and MLP modules are beneficial for the semantic segmentation task and the combination of them can improve the performance further. Furthermore, the proposed MSP and MLP module are not restricted to a specific model.

5 Conclusion

In this paper, we present a MSP module and a MLP module for semantic segmentation. The proposed MSP module adaptively captures multi-scale information and obtains the scale-wise dependencies of classes, and the MLP module dock with MSP module perfectly by organizing the multi-scale spatial information. Specifically, the former module obtains a weighted scale-wise feature maps by using four different dilated convolutions and the latter one combines the multi-scale spatial information by using multiple slicing operations and deconvolutions to generate the feature map for each segmentation class. The ablation experiments illustrate that the combination of MSP and MLP module gives more precise locating information for objects with different sizes, and setting different dilation rates of dilated convolution for different scale feature maps can produce more precise semantic segmentation results.

References

1. Abadi, M., TensorFlow, A.A.B.P.: Large-scale machine learning on heterogeneous distributed systems. In: Proceedings of the 12th USENIX Symposium on Operating Systems Design and Implementation (OSDI 2016), Savannah, GA, USA, pp. 265–283 (2016)
2. Badrinarayanan, V., Kendall, A., Cipolla, R.: SegNet: a deep convolutional encoder-decoder architecture for image segmentation. IEEE Trans. Pattern Anal. Mach. Intell. **39**(12), 2481–2495 (2017)

3. Chen, L.C., Papandreou, G., Kokkinos, I., Murphy, K., Yuille, A.L.: DeepLAB: semantic image segmentation with deep convolutional nets, atrous convolution, and fully connected CRFs. IEEE Trans. Pattern Anal. Mach. Intell. **40**(4), 834–848 (2018)
4. Cordts, M., et al.: The cityscapes dataset for semantic urban scene understanding. In: Proceedings of the IEEE Conference on Computer Vision and Pattern Recognition, pp. 3213–3223 (2016)
5. Everingham, M., Eslami, S.A., Van Gool, L., Williams, C.K., Winn, J., Zisserman, A.: The Pascal visual object classes challenge: a retrospective. Int. J. Comput. Vis. **111**(1), 98–136 (2015)
6. Ghiasi, G., Fowlkes, C.C.: Laplacian pyramid reconstruction and refinement for semantic segmentation. In: Leibe, B., Matas, J., Sebe, N., Welling, M. (eds.) ECCV 2016. LNCS, vol. 9907, pp. 519–534. Springer, Cham (2016). https://doi.org/10.1007/978-3-319-46487-9_32
7. He, K., Zhang, X., Ren, S., Sun, J.: Deep residual learning for image recognition. In: Proceedings of the IEEE Conference on Computer Vision and Pattern Recognition, pp. 770–778 (2016)
8. He, K., Zhang, X., Ren, S., Sun, J.: Identity mappings in deep residual networks. In: Leibe, B., Matas, J., Sebe, N., Welling, M. (eds.) ECCV 2016. LNCS, vol. 9908, pp. 630–645. Springer, Cham (2016). https://doi.org/10.1007/978-3-319-46493-0_38
9. Hu, J., Shen, L., Sun, G.: Squeeze-and-excitation networks. In: Proceedings of the IEEE Conference on Computer Vision and Pattern Recognition, pp. 7132–7141 (2018)
10. Krizhevsky, A., Sutskever, I., Hinton, G.E.: ImageNet classification with deep convolutional neural networks. In: Advances in Neural Information Processing Systems, pp. 1097–1105 (2012)
11. Li, Y., Chen, Y., Wang, N., Zhang, Z.: Scale-aware trident networks for object detection. arXiv preprint arXiv:1901.01892 (2019)
12. Lin, G., Milan, A., Shen, C., Reid, I.: RefineNet: multi-path refinement networks for high-resolution semantic segmentation. In: Proceedings of the IEEE Conference on Computer Vision and Pattern Recognition, pp. 1925–1934 (2017)
13. Lin, T.Y., Dollár, P., Girshick, R., He, K., Hariharan, B., Belongie, S.: Feature pyramid networks for object detection. In: Proceedings of the IEEE Conference on Computer Vision and Pattern Recognition, pp. 2117–2125 (2017)
14. Long, J., Shelhamer, E., Darrell, T.: Fully convolutional networks for semantic segmentation. In: Proceedings of the IEEE Conference on Computer Vision and Pattern Recognition, pp. 3431–3440 (2015)
15. Park, H., Yoo, Y., Seo, G., Han, D., Yun, S., Kwak, N.: Concentrated-comprehensive convolutions for lightweight semantic segmentation. arXiv preprint arXiv:1812.04920 (2018)
16. Simonyan, K., Zisserman, A.: Very deep convolutional networks for large-scale image recognition. arXiv preprint arXiv:1409.1556 (2014)
17. Szegedy, C., et al.: Going deeper with convolutions. In: Proceedings of the IEEE Conference on Computer Vision and Pattern Recognition, pp. 1–9 (2015)
18. Wolterink, J.M., Leiner, T., Viergever, M.A., Išgum, I.: Dilated convolutional neural networks for cardiovascular MR segmentation in congenital heart disease. In: Zuluaga, M.A., Bhatia, K., Kainz, B., Moghari, M.H., Pace, D.F. (eds.) RAMBO/HVSMR -2016. LNCS, vol. 10129, pp. 95–102. Springer, Cham (2017). https://doi.org/10.1007/978-3-319-52280-7_9
19. Yu, F., Koltun, V.: Multi-scale context aggregation by dilated convolutions. arXiv preprint arXiv:1511.07122 (2015)
20. Yu, F., Koltun, V., Funkhouser, T.: Dilated residual networks. In: Proceedings of the IEEE Conference on Computer Vision and Pattern Recognition, pp. 472–480 (2017)
21. Zhao, H., Shi, J., Qi, X., Wang, X., Jia, J.: Pyramid scene parsing network. In: Proceedings of the IEEE Conference on Computer Vision and Pattern Recognition, pp. 2881–2890 (2017)

HRTF Representation with Convolutional Auto-encoder

Wei Chen[1], Ruimin Hu[1,2(✉)], Xiaochen Wang[1,3], and Dengshi Li[4]

[1] National Engineering Research Center for Multimedia Software, School of Computer Science, Wuhan University, Wuhan 430072, China
hrm@whu.edu.cn

[2] Hubei Key Laboratory of Multimedia and Network Communication Engineering, Wuhan University, Wuhan 430072, China

[3] Collaborative Innovation Center of Geospatial Technology, Wuhan 430079, China

[4] School of Mathematics and Computer Science, Jianghan University, Wuhan, China

Abstract. The head-related transfer function (HRTF) can be considered as some kind of filter that describes how a sound from an arbitrary spatial direction transfers to the listener's eardrums. HRTF can be used to synthesize vivid virtual 3D sound that seems to come from any spatial location, which makes it play an important role in the 3D audio technology. However, the complexity and variation of auditory cues inherent in HRTF make it difficult to set up an accurate mathematical model with the conventional methods. In this paper, we put forward an HRTF representation modeling based on convolutional auto-encoder (CAE), which is some type of auto-encoder that contains convolutional layers in the encoder part and deconvolution layers in the decoder part. The experimental evaluation on the ARI HRTF database shows that the proposed model provides very good results on dimensionality reduction of HRTF.

Keywords: HRTF · Representation · Convolutional auto-encoder · Deep auto-encoder · Denoising auto-encoder

1 Introduction

When a sound traveling from a spatial point to the listener's eardrums it may be modified by the diffraction and reflection properties of the pinna, head, and torso, etc. These modifications encode the cues that related to human auditory localization mechanism and usually be expressed as the head-related transfer function (HRTF). So, in theory, the HRTF can be used to generate virtual 3D audio that seems to come from an arbitrary spatial direction.

In practice, the methods to synthesize a virtual 3D sound can be divided into two types: The first method is to rebuild a virtual 3D sound field of a particular spatial zone by a certain number of loudspeakers. This kind of method usually needs stricter conditions for use, for example, a special configuration for the speakers, limited area of the "sweet spot", etc. The other kind of method

Y. M. Ro et al. (Eds.): MMM 2020, LNCS 11961, pp. 605–616, 2020.
https://doi.org/10.1007/978-3-030-37731-1_49

synthesis a 3D sound by using the HRTF, which can provide the virtual 3D sound experience through stereo headphones. The advantages of the second method are simple equipment and easy operating, which make it especially suitable for mobile devices.

However, the HRTF varies from person to person due to the difference in listener's anatomy. The ideal HRTF can be obtained by measurements, but unfortunately, measurements require precision instruments and special measurement environment (anechoic chamber) which let it difficult to apply in practice. Nevertheless, there are some public HRTF databases that contain high-spatial-resolution HRTF measurements. Therefore, exploit existing HRTF data and research the inherent features of HRTF measurements and set up the representation model is an important part of HRTF-based technology.

In this paper, we put forward an HRTF representation modeling based on convolutional auto-encoder (CAE). An auto-encoder is a type of neural network that is efficient in dimensionality reduction. The basic idea of auto-encoder is trying to compress data from a corrupted input into a low-dimensional code and try to decompress that code as well as reconstruct an output that as similar to the original data (the not-corrupted version of input) as possible. This process forces the auto-encoder to engage in capturing inherent features of the input in its hidden representation. Convolutional auto-encoder is some type of auto-encoder that contains convolutional layers in the encoder part and deconvolution layers in the decoder part. CAE can utilize the properties of convolutional neural network (CNN), which have been proven to have efficient expression ability of features.

In our approach, the HRTF is represented as a spectrum image and fed into a convolutional auto-encoder with pooling/un-pooling layers to represent the HRTF into a lower-dimensional representation. The experimental evaluation on the ARI HRTF database shows that the proposed model provides very good results on dimensionality reduction of HRTF.

2 Related Works

Several methods for HRTF representation have been proposed at the expense of minimum reconstruction error.

One of the typical representation methods is modeling HRTF with the pole/zero model [14,16], which can be constructed with an infinite impulse response (IIR) filter. However, low order pole/zero model can only fit the relatively coarse spectral patterns in HRTFs, and the order of pole/zero should increase to more than (40, 40) for sufficiently approximate the HRTF [3]. To overcome this problem, common-acoustical-pole and zero (CAPZ) model was put forward [4,10,12,15]. The CAPZ model expresses HRTF with two parts, which modeling direction-independent components of HRTF with the common acoustical poles, and the direction-dependent parts with zeros. Compared with the pole/zero model, CAPZ model requires fewer parameters, and the zero variations can be used to analyze the directional dependence of the HRTF.

However, research of CAPZ model is based on independent-samples, which may not be used to establish the HRTF representation model for multi-users.

Another conventional HRTF representation method is mapping the HRTF into some low-dimensional expressions, such as principal components analysis (PCA) [5,11,13], Locally Linear Embedding (LLE) [8,21], Isometric Feature Mapping (Isomap) [7,9]. Among these models, the PCA-based model is the most classical one that was first reported in [18]. The basic idea of PCA-based model is to represent the HRTF as linear combinations of basis functions. However, there are complex nonlinear correlations between the features of HRTF that may be difficult to describe using PCA. To this end, some nonlinear mapping methods using manifold learning had been proposed, such as LLE and Isomap. But different from the PCA-based model, the LLE and the Isomap do not offer explicit methods of reconstructing data from the low-dimensional version, which is required for some HRTF-based application such as HRTF interpolation and HRTF individualization [19], etc. Therefore, PCA is still an important method in HRTF representation.

In recent years, CAE has been proven to be effective in extracting high-level features in image processing task [22]. However, there was no report about representing HRTF with CAE model. In this paper, we put forward an HRTF representation model based on CAE and investigate the accuracy performance of reconstructing and the compression ratio of the proposed model.

3 Proposed Approach

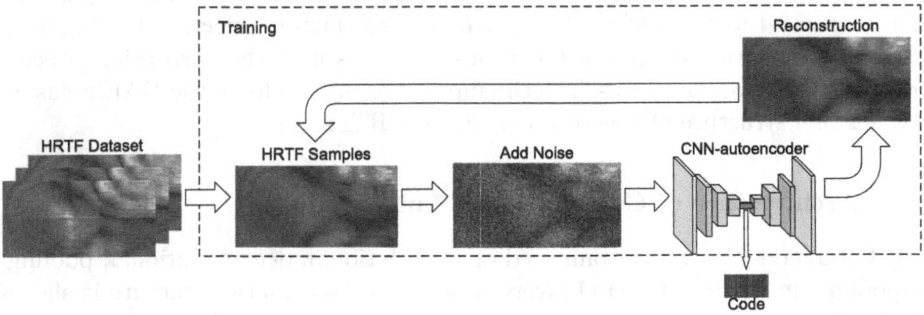

Fig. 1. The pipeline of the HRTF representation approach.

The pipeline of the proposed HRTF representation approach is summarized in Fig. 1.

First of all, we cluster neighboring spatial HRTFs and take the spectrum image of these HRTFs as input data, which will be handled by a corruption process before fed into the auto-encoder. The encode part consists of two levels of convolutional and pooling layers followed by a two-layer fully-connected network. And there is, inversely, one two-layer fully-connected network, two levels of un-pooling and deconvolution layers in the decoder part. And finally, the model is trained with minimizing the mean-absolute-error between input and output as the objective function.

The rest of this section will present the detail of our model, which includes HRTF preprocessing and the architecture of the CAE model.

3.1 HRTF Preprocessing

In this paper, the experimental samples are extracted from the ARI database which contains high-resolution HRTFs of more than 170 subjects (178 subjects at present) [1]. And only listener-specific directional transfer functions (DTFs) are considered, which are HRTFs with the direction-independent characteristics been removed [2].

The main processes are as follows:

1. Firstly, the HRTFs of each subject is grouped together and express as the spectrum image of these HRTFs.
2. Secondly, then the spectrum image will be converted to 16-bit gray-scale image.
3. Finally, a corrupted version of the spectrum image will be generated by adding artificial Gaussian noise.

The stochastic corruption process in the last step can be explained by the theory of denoising auto-encoder (DAE). The purpose of adding noise into the input is to add randomness in the learning process from input to reconstruction, which will force the hidden layers to capture more inherent features from the input. Some psychoacoustic studies have reported that the macroscopic patterns of the spectral features of HRTF are the critical factors affecting the human's auditory perception of spatial directions. In our study, the corruption process adds artificial Gaussian noise into the input, which may force the DAE focus on the internal structure of spectral features of HRTFs.

3.2 Architecture of Convolutional Auto-encoder

Our CAE model is mainly composed of convolutional, deconvolutional, pooling, unpooling and fully-connected layers, whose brief schematic structure is shown in Fig. 2.

There are two levels of convolutional and pooling layers in the encoder part. Each convolutional layer followed by a ReLU activation layer, and then a max-pooling layer with kernel shape of $(2, 2)$ that will reduce the previous convolutional layer's output by half. Then the output of the last pooling layer is reshaped into single dimension data by a flatten layer and feed into a two-layer full-connected forward network.

The architecture of the decoder part is the reverse schema of the encoder part. In which, the reshape layer transforms the single-dimension data into two dimensions. The deconvolutional layer reconstructs an input spectrum image from the feature map, which is actually can be considered as some kinds of the

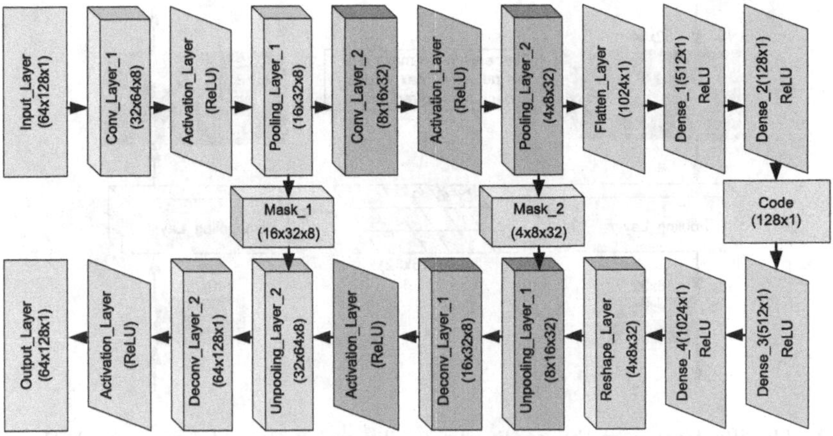

Fig. 2. The schematic structure of the CAE model.

Table 1. Detailed parameters of proposed CAE model.

Layers	Input shape	Output shape	Filter	Kernel/ Pool size	Stride	Layers	Input shape	Output shape	Filter	Kernel/ Pool size	Stride
Conv_1	$64 \times 128 \times 1$	$32 \times 64 \times 8$	8	(7, 7)	(2, 2)	Dense_3	128	512	–	–	–
Pool_1	$32 \times 64 \times 8$	$16 \times 32 \times 8$	–	(2, 2)	–	Dense_4	512	1024	–	–	–
Conv_2	$16 \times 32 \times 8$	$8 \times 16 \times 32$	32	(5, 5)	(2, 2)	Reshape	1024	$4 \times 8 \times 32$	–	–	–
Pool_2	$8 \times 16 \times 32$	$4 \times 8 \times 32$	–	(2, 2)	–	Unpool_1	$4 \times 8 \times 32$	$8 \times 16 \times 32$	–	(2, 2)	–
Flatten	$4 \times 8 \times 32$	1024	–	–	–	Deconv_1	$8 \times 16 \times 32$	$16 \times 32 \times 8$	8	(5, 5)	(2, 2)
Dense_1	1024	512	–	–	–	Unpool_2	$16 \times 32 \times 8$	$32 \times 64 \times 8$	–	(2, 2)	–
Dense_2	512	128	–	–	–	Deconv_2	$32 \times 64 \times 8$	$64 \times 128 \times 1$	1	(7, 7)	(2, 2)

convolutional layer. And the unpooling layer restores the pooled feature into the corresponding place of the output feature map.

The input shape and the parameters of the convolutional/deconvolutional, pooling/unpooling and dense layers are listed in Table 1.

It should be noted that the pooling operation is an irreversible process. In order to address this problem, the locations of maximum value are stored into a mask during the pooling operation which is used to reconstruct the approximate inverse operation during the unpooling process. The procedure of pooling and unpooling is illustrated in Fig. 3.

4 Experimental Evaluation

4.1 HRTF Database

The performance of proposed CAE model is evaluated using the ARI HRTF database [1], which contains in-the-ear HRTFs of 178 listeners. Each HRTF is 256-point length (5.33-ms duration) with 48 kHz sampling frequency and the relevant frequency ranged from 50 Hz to18 kHz.

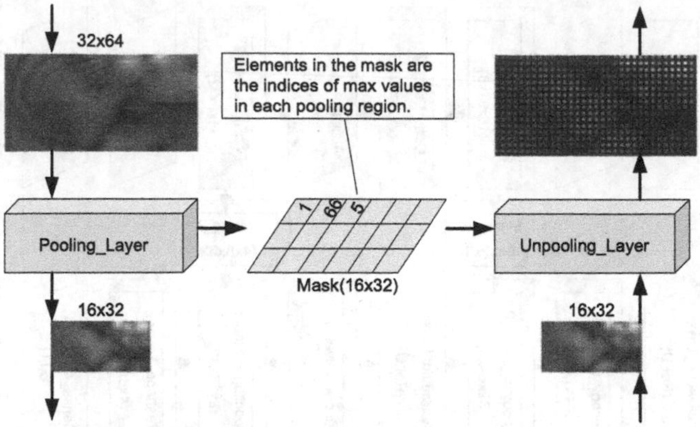

Fig. 3. The illustration of the pooling/unpooling procedure. In our model, the mask record the locations of the maxima of each pooling region. In the present case, the values in the mask range from 0 to 2047.

In this paper, the DTFs on the median plane (elevations ranged from −30° to 80°) are extracted to generate the dataset, and 178 listeners' DTFs are divided into two distinct sets. We take first 128 listeners' DTFs (with id from 'NH2' to 'NH252') as the training set, and take the latter 50 listeners' DTFs (with id from 'NH253' to 'NH834') as the testing set. And both the left and right DTFs are utilized to generate the dataset, thus we can obtain a training set of 256 samples and a testing set of 100 samples. Then all the HRTFs are transformed into directional transfer functions (DTFs) followed the methods from [17,20], and finally, each DTF is the 95-point length with a valid frequency range from 200 Hz to 18 kHz.

4.2 Deep CAE Model Training

All samples in the training set and the testing set will be considered as a spectrum image and transformed into a 16-bit grayscale image with the size of 64 × 128 pixels. And it should be noted that during the training process, before was fed into the CAE model, the training data will be pre-handled by a corruption process by which a certain amount (10%) of Gaussian noise will be added into the input. This process may help for the hidden layers in catching more inherent features, which can be explained by the theory of denoising autoencoder [6,23,24].

In the training phase, we use mean-absolute-error (MAE) as the loss function. And the samples from the training set will be passed into the corruption process firstly, and then the corrupted version of samples will be fed into the CAE model. Then the MAE between the input (original spectrum image before corrupted) and the output (a reconstructed spectrum image) will be calculated.

While in the testing phase, the samples will be fed directly into the CAE model, then the average spectral distortion of the reconstructed will be calculated as the performance metric of the model. The detailed initialization parameters used in this work are listed in Table 2.

Table 2. Parameters of the proposed CAE model.

Parameter	Value
Optimizer	Adam optimizer
Learning rate	0.001
Activation function	ReLU[a] (alpha = 0.2)
Loss function	Mean absolute error
Bath size	16
Epochs	50

[a]Rectified Linear Unitactivation function.

4.3 HRTF Representation Performance

We take the average spectral distortion (SD) of the reconstructed HRTFs as the performance evaluation metrics. The SD is calculated as

$$SD = \sqrt{\frac{1}{N}\sum_{n=1}^{N}\left(20\log 10\frac{|H(f_n)|}{\left|\hat{H}(f_n)\right|}\right)^2} \tag{1}$$

where $H(f_n)$ is the magnitude of the input HRTF at frequency f_n, and $\hat{H}(f_n)$ is the corresponding magnitude of reconstructed HRTF.

The average SD (ASD) is calculated as

$$ASD = \frac{1}{N}\sum_{n=1}^{N}\frac{1}{D}\sum_{d=1}^{D} SD_{n,d} \tag{2}$$

where N is the number of testing samples and D is the number of spatial directions, $SD_{n,d}$ represents the spectral distortion of n-th sample at d-th spatial direction.

We compared the proposed model with the PCA-based representation model, which is usually considered as the baseline method. Figure 4 shows the comparison of the CAE model and PCA-based model, in which the ASD result of PCA-based model is calculated with 48 principal components that explain about 99.9% variance of the training set. The mean ASD of 100 samples with our model is 2.26 dB, much better than the 3.63 dB achieved by PCA-based model. What's more, the variance of ASD with our model is also smaller than the PCA-based model (0.058 versus 1.536), which may indicate the stable and reliable performance of our model.

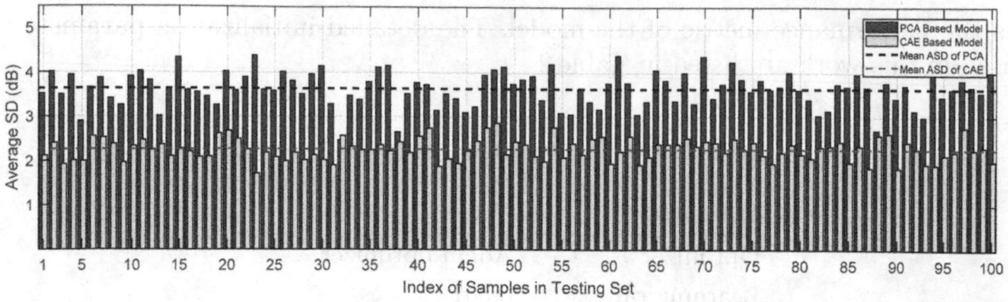

Fig. 4. Performance comparison of PCA-based model and proposed CAE model. The mean ASD of all 100 samples is 2.26 dB with the CAE model versus 3.63 dB with the PCA-based model. The PCA-based model is calculated with 48 principal components that capture about 99.9% variance of the training set.

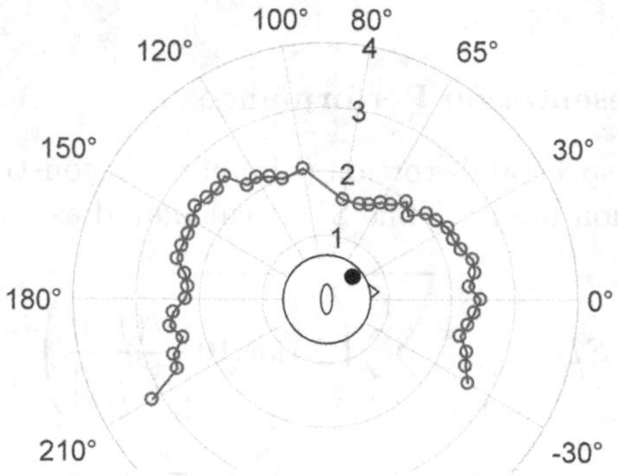

Fig. 5. ASD results of CAE model at different elevations. The values shown in the figure are the mean ASD result of 100 samples in the testing set, and the unit is the decibel (dB).

In order to further evaluate the performance of the CAE model, we investigated the ASD results of different elevations. The results are shown in Fig. 5, from which it can be seen that the ASD results are below 3 dB for most elevations, and the variance of ASD with different elevations is 0.09. And Fig. 6 shows three typical HRTF reconstruction results for an intuitive display.

We also compared the storage requirement of the CAE model with PCA-based models. It should be pointed out that, in our CAE model there are mask matrices that used to restore the locations of the maxima within the pooling region, these masks should also be considered as the storage requirement. Fortunately, however, the elements in the masks are only non-negative integers which can be compressed.

The storage requirement V of the PCA-based model is calculated as

$$V = (C + 100 \times 44 \times P) \times 8 \tag{3}$$

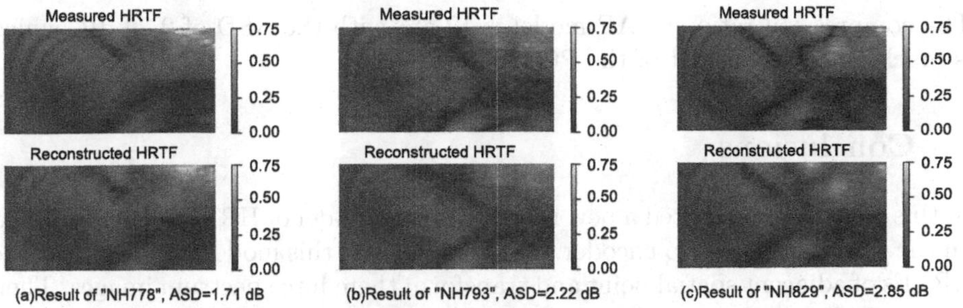

Fig. 6. HRTF reconstruction results of 3 typical testing samples. (a) shows the reconstruction result of sample "NH778" (left HRTF), who's ASD performance is the best of all the testing samples. (b) displays the result of "NH793" (left HRTF), and the corresponding ASD is 2.22 dB which is close to the average performance. (c) show the result of "NH829" (left HRTF), the corresponding ASD is 2.85 dB which is the worst of all the testing samples.

where C represents the number of elements in eigenvectors and P represents the number of principal components (PCs). 100 × 44 indicates that there are 100 samples, each of which contains 44 HRTFs of different elevations. And the 8 means each element takes up 8 bytes (64-bit float) of space. For example, the storage requirement of PCA-based model with 12 PCs is $(95 \times 12 + 100 \times 44 \times 12) \times 8 = 431520$ bytes.

The storage requirement $\hat{V}$ of the CAE model is calculated as

$$\hat{V} = ((M_1 + M_2) \times 2 + N \times 8) \times 100 \quad (4)$$

where N represents the length of encoding result, M_1 and M_2 represent the number of elements that needed for 2 mask matrices of the CAE model, respectively. Since the elements of the mask matrices are the indices of max values, they can be stored as 16-bit unsigned integers.

Table 3. Comparison of storage requirement between the CAE model and PCA-based models.

Method	Number of principal components	Storage requirement	Compression ratio[a]	ASD
PCA	42 (explain 99.03% of variance)	1510320 bytes	16.8%	10.13 dB
PCA	60 (explain 99.49% of variance)	2157600 bytes	23.9%	9.94 dB
PCA	85 (explain 99.90% of variance)	3056600 bytes	33.9%	3.63 dB
CAE	–	**1126400 bytes**	**12.5%**	**2.26 dB**

[a]The compression ratio is the ratio of storage requirement compared with the total bytes of original HRTFs (9011200 bytes).

Table 3 lists the comparison of storage requirement of proposed CAE model and the PCA-based model with different number of principal components.

The compression ratio of CAE model is 12.5% with the ASD of 2.26 dB, which is much better than that of the PCA-based model.

5 Conclusions

In this paper, we presented a new representation model of HRTF, which is based on the convolutional auto-encoder. The basic idea of this model is to compose the HRTFs of adjacent spatial point and transform them into spectrum images. Then a convolutional auto-encoder model is set up to extract the inherent features of HRTFs. The proposed CAE model is trained and evaluated with the ARI database which is a public HRTF database contains high-resolution HRTFs of 178 listeners.

The results of the experimental evaluation indicate that the average SD our CAE model is 2.26 dB, which may reduce 37% spectrum distortion compared with the PCA-based method (with 85 PCs). We also investigated the storage requirement of the proposed method, the compression ratio is 12.5% which is also better than the PCA-based model. These results indicate that our CAE model has an effective performance in HRTF representation task due to the advantages of expressing nonlinear relations of inherent features of HRTFs.

Acknowledgment. This work is supported by the National Key R&D Program of China (No. 2017YFB1002803), National Nature Science Foundation of China (No. 61701194, No. U1736206).

References

1. Ari hrtf database homepage. http://www.kfs.oeaw.ac.at/hrtf. Accessed 4 July 2019
2. Baumgartner, R., Majdak, P., Laback, B.: Modeling sound-source localization in sagittal planes for human listeners. J. Acoust. Soc. Am. **140**(4), 2456 (2016). https://doi.org/10.1121/1.4964753
3. Blommer, M., Wakefield, G.: Pole-zero approximations for head-related transfer functions using a logarithmic error criterion. IEEE Trans. Speech Audio Process. **5**(3), 278–287 (1997)
4. Chen, M.C., Hsieh, S.F.: Common acoustical-poles/zeros modeling for 3D sound processing. In: Proceedings of the 2000 IEEE International Conference on Acoustics, Speech, and Signal Processing (ICASSP), pp. 785–788. IEEE Signal Processing Society (2000)
5. Fink, K.J., Ray, L.: Individualization of head related transfer functions using principal component analysis. Appl. Acoust. **87**, 162–173 (2015)
6. Grais, E.M., Plumbley, M.D.: Single channel audio source separation using convolutional denoising autoencoders. In: 2017 IEEE Global Conference on Signal and Information Processing (GLOBALSIP 2017), pp. 1265–1269. IEEE (2017). https://doi.org/10.1109/GlobalSIP.2017.8309164

7. Grijalva, F., Martini, L., Florencio, D., Goldenstein, S.: A manifold learning approach for personalizing HRTFs from anthropometric features. IEEE/ACM Trans. Audio Speech Lang. Process. **24**(3), 559–570 (2016)
8. Grijalva, F., Martini, L.C., Florencio, D., Goldenstein, S.: Interpolation of head-related transfer functions using manifold learning. IEEE Signal Process. Lett. **24**(2), 221–225 (2017)
9. Grijalva, F., Martini, L.C., Masiero, B., Goldenstein, S.: A recommender system for improving median plane sound localization performance based on a nonlinear representation of HRTFs. IEEE Access **6**, 24829–24836 (2018)
10. Haneda, Y., Makino, S., Kaneda, Y., Kitawaki, N.: Common-acoustical-pole and zero modeling of head-related transfer functions. IEEE Trans. Speech Audio Process. **7**(2), 188–196 (1999)
11. Hugeng, Gunawan, D., Wahab, W.: Effective preprocessing in modeling head-related impulse responses based on principal components analysis. Sig. Process. Int. J. **4**(4), 201–212 (2010)
12. Iwaya, Y., Sato, W., Okamoto, T., Otani, M., Suzuki, Y.: Interpolation method of head-related transfer functions in the z-plane domain using a common-pole and zero model. In: 20th International Congress on Acoustics 2010, ICA 2010, Sydney, NSW, Australia, vol. 4, pp. 2936–2940 (2010)
13. Kistler, D.J., Wightman, F.L.: A model of head-related transfer-functions based on principal components-analysis and minimum-phase reconstruction. J. Acoust. Soc. Am. **91**(3), 1637–1647 (1992)
14. Kulkarni, A., Colburn, H.S.: Infinite-impulse-response models of the head-related transfer function. J. Acoust. Soc. Am. **115**, 1714–1728 (2004)
15. Liu, C.J., Hsieh, S.F.: Common-acoustic-poles/zeros approximation of head-related transfer functions. In: 2001 IEEE International Conference on Acoustics, Speech, and Signal Processing (ICASSP), pp. 3341–3344. IEEE Signal Processing Society (2001)
16. Mackenzie, J., Huopaniemi, J., Valimaki, V., Kale, I.: Low-order modeling of head-related transfer functions using balanced model truncation. IEEE Signal Process. Lett. **4**(2), 39–41 (1997)
17. Majdak, P., Goupell, M.J., Laback, B.: 3-D localization of virtual sound sources: effects of visual environment, pointing method, and training. Atten. Percept. Psychophys. **72**(2), 454–469 (2010)
18. Martens, W.L.: Principal components analysis and resynthesis of spectral cues to perceived direction. In: Proceedings of the International Computer Music Conference, Champaine-Urbana, IL (1987)
19. Meng, L., Wang, X., Chen, W., Ai, C., Hu, R.: Individualization of head related transfer functions based on radial basis function neural network. In: 2018 IEEE International Conference on Multimedia and Expo (ICME), pp. 1–6 (2018). https://doi.org/10.1109/ICME.2018.8486494
20. Middlebrooks, J.C.: Individual differences in external-ear transfer functions reduced by scaling in frequency. J. Acoust. Soc. Am. **106**(3), 1480–1492 (1999)
21. Ming, X., Binzhou, Y., Shuxia, G., Ying, G.: Head-related transfer function individualization based on locally linear embedding. In: Qiao, F., Patnaik, S., Wang, J. (eds.) ICMIR 2017. AISC, vol. 690, pp. 104–111. Springer, Cham (2018). https://doi.org/10.1007/978-3-319-65978-7_16

22. Turchenko, V., Chalmers, E., Luczak, A.: A deep convolutional auto-encoder with pooling – unpooling layers in caffe. Int. J. Comput. **18**(1), 8–31 (2019). http://www.computingonline.net/computing/article/view/1270
23. Vincent, P., Larochelle, H., Lajoie, I., Bengio, Y., Manzagol, P.A.: Stacked denoising autoencoders: learning useful representations in a deep network with a local denoising criterion. J. Mach. Learn. Res. **11**, 3371–3408 (2010)
24. Zeiler, M.D., Krishnan, D., Taylor, G.W., Fergus, R.: Deconvolutional networks. In: 2010 IEEE Conference on Computer Vision and Pattern Recognition (CVPR), pp. 2528–2535. IEEE Computer Society (2010). https://doi.org/10.1109/CVPR.2010.5539957

Unsupervised Feature Propagation for Fast Video Object Detection Using Generative Adversarial Networks

Xuan Zhang(✉), Guangxing Han, and Wenduo He

Institute for Network Sciences and Cyberspace, Tsinghua University, Beijing, China
{zhangx, hewd}@cernet.edu.cn,
hgxl4@mails.tsinghua.edu.cn

Abstract. We propose unsupervised Feature Propagation Generative Adversarial Network (denoted as FPGAN) for fast video object detection in this paper. In our video object detector, we detect objects on spare key frames using pre-trained state-of-the-art object detector R-FCN, and propagate CNN features to adjacent frames for fast detection via a light-weight transformation network. To learn the feature propagation network, we make full use of unlabeled video data and employ generative adversarial networks in model training. Specifically, in FPGAN, the generator is the feature propagation network, and the discriminator employs second-order temporal coherence and 3D ConvNets to distinguish between predicted and "ground truth" CNN features. In addition, Euclidean distance loss provided by the pre-trained image object detector is also adopted to jointly supervise the learning. Our method doesn't need any human labelling in videos. Experiments on the large-scale ImageNet VID dataset demonstrate the effectiveness of our method.

Keywords: Video object detection · Generative adversarial networks · Feature flow

1 Introduction

Currently, object detection [1–8] has achieved significant success owing to the rapid development of deep convolutional neural networks (DCNNs [13, 14]). In this paper, we consider object detection in video domain [9–12]. Fast and accurate video analysis is critical in many real-time applications, e.g., video surveillance and autonomous driving. Different from object detection in static images, videos provide additional temporal information [21] beyond static appearance features. Adjacent frames in a video usually have similar appearance. Naive frame-by-frame independent detection ignores this similarity in a video. Efficiently exploiting temporal coherence can largely accelerate detection in adjacent frames. In addition, dense labelling in videos is usually laborious and difficult to acquire, and we should pay more attention to unsupervised and semi-supervised learning with video data.

In this work, we aim to estimate feature flow for high-level CNN features in adjacent frames to build efficient video object detectors. In DFF [11], a light-weight

Y. M. Ro et al. (Eds.): MMM 2020, LNCS 11961, pp. 617–627, 2020.
https://doi.org/10.1007/978-3-030-37731-1_50

CNN network is employed to propagate CNN features along the temporal dimension for fast feature extraction in adjacent frames, and then the key problem can be described as feature flow estimation for adjacent frames, illustrated in Fig. 1. Once we can estimate feature flow in videos, we can obtain CNN features for adjacent frames fast and accurately. Previous method DFF needs labelled videos for model learning, and cannot fully exploit large scale of unlabeled video data. To deal with this problem, semi-DFF [12] decouples the learning of static object detection module and temporal feature propagation module, and proposes feature semantic loss for temporal module learning using unlabeled videos. Different to semi-DFF, we propose to exploit the temporal coherence in video data to learn the feature flow network by Feature Propagation Generative Adversarial Network (FPGAN) in this paper.

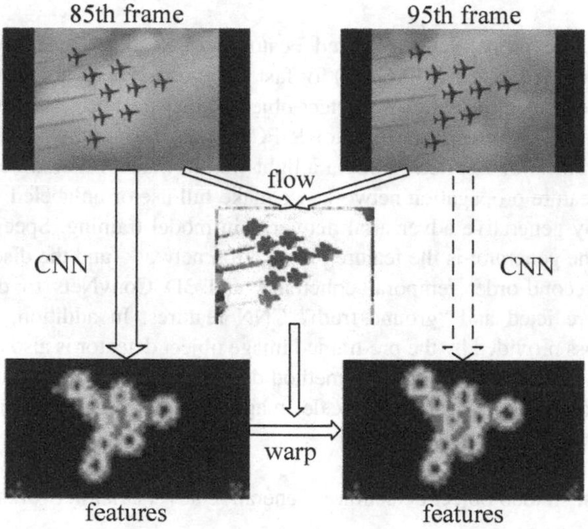

Fig. 1. The above two frames (ten frames apart) are selected from a video in ImageNet VID dataset. Independently extracting features for these two frames using modern CNN networks (e.g., ResNet-101 [14]) are time-consuming. Considering temporal coherence in videos, we propagate CNN features from one frame to another using a light-weight feature flow network and can detect objects in adjacent frames much faster.

Concretely, in FPGAN, we make full use of the pre-trained state-of-the-art image object detector and second-order temporal coherence in videos for model learning. For the feature propagation network, we adopt fully convolutional FlowNet in [25]. For the loss function, we employ feature regression loss as well as feature adversarial loss. For the feature regression loss, we first use pre-trained images object detectors to get "ground truth" CNN features, and then supervise the feature flow network predicting accurate CNN features within two adjacent frames using "ground truth" CNN features. However, as demonstrated in [17], simply minimizing the Euclidean distance between the predicted and "ground truth" CNN features will tend to produce blurry predicted features. In order to predict accurate CNN features for adjacent frames, we propose conditional adversarial loss to make the predicted features indistinguishable from "ground truth" features. Specifically, we introduce several reference frames which have equal interval with the aforementioned paired frames to make full use of the higher-order temporal coherence in videos [22]. Then instead of classifying CNN feature alone as in original GANs [18], the discriminator employs 3D convolutional networks [26] to classify the CNN features by examining the feature evolutions between equally spaced frames. Finally, our FPGAN is trained by the joint feature regression loss and adversarial loss to generate realistic CNN features for adjacent frames.

The proposed method attempts to address the drawbacks of previous works in DFF [11] and can learn high-level CNN feature evolution in video by unsupervised learning. To evaluate our method, we conduct several experiments on video object detection. Experimental results demonstrate that our FPGAN can learn non-trivial knowledge about motion and achieves improved accuracy compared to the unsupervised baseline methods, and also achieves significant speedup due to the light-weight feature flow network.

2 Related Work

Object Detection in Image. Currently, modern object detectors mainly consist of two-stage detectors [1–5] and one-stage detectors [6–8]. Two-stage detectors can achieve higher detection accuracy due to the cascade design. One-stage detectors can achieve higher running speed due to single shot fully convolutional design. R-FCN [4] belongs to two-stage detectors, and introduces position-sensitive RoI pooling layer to share the calculation in the 2nd stage, which greatly reduces the computation time and also enjoys high accuracy. In this paper, we employ R-FCN [4] as our default image object detector considering the balance of speed and accuracy.

Object Detection in Video. Video object detection is a rather new topic. Early methods work on box level. Kang et al. [9] propose to associate independent detections of adjacent frames to obtain stable and accurate detection results. Recent methods focus on the feature level and the model can be trained end-to-end. Shelhamer et al. [10] propose clockwork ConvNets to schedule different layers at different update rates. However, it ignores the evolution of high-level features and gets worse recognition accuracy. Our work is closely related to DFF proposed by Zhu et al. [11]. DFF proposes to propagate CNN features to adjacent frames via a flow field. Han et al. [12] propose semi-DFF to decouple the learning of the spatial and temporal module and propose feature semantic loss to learn the temporal module using unlabeled videos. Different to semi-DFF, we propose FPGAN to exploit the second-order temporal coherence in videos to learn the feature flow network, and FPGAN can further benefit from the feature semantic loss in semi-DFF and the box-level methods as well.

Image-to-Image Translation. A wide variety of applications in computer vision can be broadly described as image-to-image translation [15], which converts one image into another similar image, e.g., image super-resolution [16], style transfer [16], future frame prediction [17]. Naive per-pixel regression or classification loss would neglect the structural configuration of images [15]. Recently, GANs [18] are proposed to learn structure loss. The key to the success of GANs is the design of adversarial loss which forces the generated images to be indistinguishable from real images. Motivated by this idea, [15] employ paired training examples for image translation. Recent methods leverage large scale of unpaired training data for training using self-regularization [19] or cycle consistency [20]. Our problem can be treated as feature-to-feature translation problem, and we design FPGAN to efficiently propagate features along the temporal dimension.

Unsupervised Feature Learning with Unlabeled Videos. A new unsupervised learning method has been proposed as self-supervised learning. The key idea is to leverage the inherent structure of raw images or videos to formulate a strong supervision signal to train the network. We pay more attention to self-supervised learning with videos in this paper. [21] employs temporal smoothness of CNN features through time in videos for unsupervised learning. [22] further exploits second-order temporal coherence as a stronger supervision. Our method follows this idea and employs higher-order temporal coherence to classify CNN features. [23] employs tracking in videos to provide appearance variation of the same object. [24] proposes to leverage the temporal order of frames as supervision signal. [17] focuses on future frame prediction and uses adversarial loss for training.

3 Our Method

In this section, we introduce our method in detail, starting with our default object detector R-FCN for static images in Sect. 3.1. Based on the state-of-the-art image object detector R-FCN, we propose our video object detector with the feature flow network and describe the detailed architecture of our FPGAN and the unsupervised learning method in Sect. 3.2.

3.1 Object Detector R-FCN for Static Images

Given an input frame $I \in \mathbb{R}^{H_0 \times W_0 \times 3}$, a backbone feature extraction network (e.g., ResNet-101 [14]) is used to extract CNN features $f \in \mathbb{R}^{C_l \times H_l \times W_l}$, where C_l, H_l and W_l are the channel, height, width of CNN features at layer l. In the detection specific networks, object proposals are generated using RPN, and $k^2(C+1)$ position-sensitive score maps and $4k^2$ position-sensitive regression maps are produced simultaneously for proposal classification and (class-agnostic) bounding box regression respectively. Finally, position-sensitive RoI pooling layers are adopted to aggregate position-sensitive maps for final predictions.

3.2 Unsupervised Feature Propagation Using FPGAN

Considering the slow [21] and steady [22] feature evolutions in adjacent frames, we attempt to cheaply propagate CNN features from key frames to the adjacent frames via a light-weight transformation network. Then the key problem can be treated as feature-to-feature translation problem. Adversarial learning provides a good framework to approach this problem. In our case, the generative network G is our transformation network T_θ, where θ is the parameters. We aim to predict high-level CNN features $\hat{f}_a \in \mathbb{R}^{C_l \times H_l \times W_l}$ of the adjacent frame I_a, given the RGB input of the key frame I_k and the adjacent frame I_a as well as high-level CNN features f_k of the key frame I_k. In order to make the predicted features more realistic, conditional adversarial loss $\mathcal{L}_{adv}$ and Euclidean distance loss $\mathcal{L}_{l_2}$ are introduced to jointly train our transformation network. The architecture of our method is illustrated in Fig. 2.

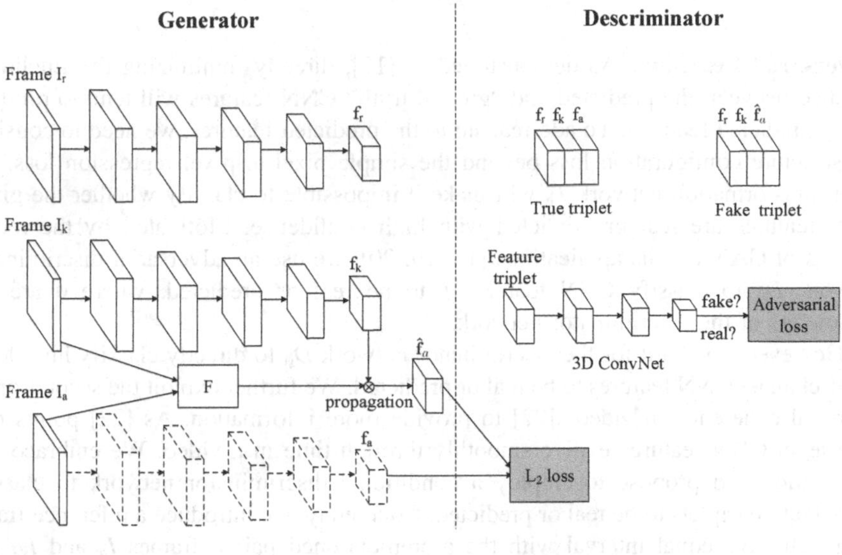

Fig. 2. Illustration of our FPGAN. The generative network is used to propagate CNN features from key frames to the adjacent frames. For the discriminator network, we introduce a reference frame I_r to construct real feature triple and fake triplet (similar to multiple reference frames). Our discriminator network employs 3D convolutional network to classify the triplets. In addition, we also employ Euclidean distance loss for training in our FPGAN.

Feature Propagation Sub-network. To propagate CNN features from key frames to adjacent frames, we adopt the CNN based state-of-the-art FlowNet [25] architecture (the "Simple" version) to compute the feature flow $\mathcal{F}(I_k, I_a)$ between the key frame I_k and its adjacent frame I_a. To better accommodate the amplitudes of CNN features, we multiply the predicted features with a learned scale field $\mathcal{S}(I_k, I_a)$ in an element-wise way [11]. The feature flow and scale field further adjust its size using bilinear interpolation to match the resolution of CNN features. The predicted feature $\hat{f}_a$ is

$$\hat{f}_a = T_{\text{è}}(I_k, I_a, f_k) = \mathcal{W}(f_k, \mathcal{F}(I_k, I_a)) * \mathcal{S}(I_k, I_a)$$

where $\mathcal{W}$ is bilinear interpolation operator which spatially warps the CNN features in key frames with the estimated feature flow. This bilinear interpolation is parameter-free and can be differentiated during training. The key frame interval is set to 10 frames by default for the balance of speed and accuracy.

Euclidean Distance Loss. It is laborious and difficult to acquire dense labelling in videos. We use the state-of-the-art R-FCN models to get "ground truth" CNN features f_a for frame I_a. Then, the "ground truth" CNN features can be directly employed to supervise our feature flow network by Euclidean distance loss

$$\mathcal{L}_{l_2}(f_a, \hat{f}_a) = \left\| f_a - \hat{f}_a \right\|_2 = \frac{1}{C_l H_l W_l} \sum_{c=1}^{C_l} \sum_{h=1}^{H_l} \sum_{w=1}^{W_l} \left(f_a(c,h,w) - \hat{f}_a(c,h,w) \right)^2$$

Adversarial Learning. As demonstrated in [17], directly minimizing the Euclidean distance between the predicted and "ground truth" CNN features will tend to produce blurry predicted features. To add realism to the predicted features. we need to consider the structure configuration loss beyond the simple pixel-to-pixel regression loss. An ideal transformation network $T_{\grave{e}}$ will make it impossible to classify whether the given CNN features are real or predicted with high confidence. Motivated by the recent success of GAN and its applications [15, 19, 20], we use an adversarial discriminator network $D_{\emptyset}$ to classify CNN features f to be real or predicted, where $\emptyset$ are the parameters of the discriminator network.

However, it is hard for the discriminator network $D_{\emptyset}$ to directly classify high-level multi-channel CNN features to be real or predicted. We further exploit the second-order temporal coherence in videos [22] to provide more information. As [22] points out, high level CNN features evolve smoothly through time in a video. We embrace this observation and propose to employ a conditional discriminator network to classify CNN feature triplets to be real or predicted. Concretely, we introduce a reference frame I_r, which have equal interval with the aforementioned paired frames I_a and I_k. For simplicity, we only introduce one reference frame here and it can be easily expanded to multiple reference frames. The number of reference frames is a hyper-parameter of our model. Suppose the temporal order of the frames is $r < k < a$, and their interval is $\Delta T = a - k = k - r$. Using the pretrained R-FCN, we can get "ground truth" features for all the frames. According to the second-order temporal coherence in [22], we can get

$$f_a - f_k \approx f_k - f_r$$

However, if our transformation network is not good enough, the predicted features cannot satisfy the aforementioned second-order temporal coherence

$$\hat{f}_a - f_k \neq f_k - f_r$$

Then we propose to employ 3D convolutional neural network for our discriminator $D_{\emptyset}$. 3D ConvNets [26] are good feature learning architectures which model appearance and motion information simultaneously. We use 3D convolutions to capture feature evolutions between equally spaced frames, which can classify the CNN feature triplets to be real or fake. Following the GAN approach [18], we model the learning as a two-player minimax game. The discriminator $D_{\emptyset}$ attempts to recognize the fake feature triplet $(f_r, f_k, \hat{f}_a)$ and real feature triplet (f_r, f_k, f_a). The generator $T_{\grave{e}}$ is responsible for 'fooling' the network $D_{\emptyset}$ into classifying the predicted feature triplet $(f_r, f_k, \hat{f}_a)$ to be real.

Original GANs [18] suffer from mode collapse and instable convergence. Our formulation of the adversarial loss follows Wasserstein GAN [27] to avoid these problems by minimizing an approximated Wasserstein distance

$$\begin{aligned}\min_{T}\max_{D} V(T,D) = & \mathbb{E}_{f_r, f_k, f_a \sim p(f)}[D_{\emptyset}(f_r, f_k, f_a)] \\ & - \mathbb{E}_{I_k, I_a \sim p(I), f_r, f_k \sim p(f)}[D_{\emptyset}(f_r, f_k, T_{\grave{e}}(I_k, I_a, f_k))] \\ & + \ddot{e}\mathcal{L}_{l_2}(f_a, T_{\grave{e}}(I_k, I_a, f_k))\end{aligned}$$

where $p(I)$ and $p(f)$ denote the true data distributions of video frames and CNN features, and $\ddot{e}$ is a hyper-parameter balancing the two losses, which is set to 10 by default. The discriminator network updates its parameters by maximizing the absolute difference between the output of real feature triplets and fake triplets predicted by our transformation network. The generator network updates its parameters by minimizing the joint losses of Euclidean distance loss and adversarial loss. We optimize the generator $T_{\grave{e}}$ and discriminator $D_{\emptyset}$ alternately according to WGAN [27].

4 Experiments and Analysis

4.1 Datasets

We comprehensively evaluate our method on ImageNet VID dataset. The VID dataset has 3862, 555, and 937 fully-annotated video snippets for the training, validation, and test sets respectively. The frame rate is 25 or 30 FPS for most snippets. There are 30 object categories, and they are a subset of the categories in the ImageNet DET dataset. To train R-FCN in static images, we also utilize ImageNet DET training dataset (only the same 30 category labels are used), as a common practice in [9, 11]. Following the protocols in [9, 11], evaluations are performed on the ImageNet validation set, and we report our results using the standard mean average precision (mAP) metric over all classes and also running speed (FPS).

4.2 R-FCN Trained on the ImageNet DET Dataset

In this experiment, we train R-FCN only using the ImageNet DET training set (totally 53639 training images for the same category in VID). Synchronized SGD is used to train R-FCN on 4 GPUs. Each mini-batch involves 1 image per GPU and thus the effective batch size is 4 images. We train R-FCN with learning rate 2.5×10^{-4} on the first 40K iterations and reduce it to 2.5×10^{-5} on the next 20 k iterations. After training R-FCN, we keep the parameters fixed and train the feature flow network with ImageNet VID training dataset as in Sect. 3.2.

We compare our FPGAN with a variety of baseline methods as below:

- **R-FCN frame**. We simply evaluate each frame independently using the trained R-FCN model. This is a strong baseline without any feature propagation module.
- **R-FCN copy**. In this case, only key frames are evaluated with R-FCN model, and the detection results of the adjacent frames are just copies of the key frames.
- **R-FCN flow**. We evaluate the key frames using R-FCN model, and propagate CNN features to adjacent frames using pre-trained FlowNet models in Flying Chairs [25].
- **FPGAN w/o l_2**. This is the method we propose in this paper. We first train R-FCN, and then fix the parameters in R-FCN and train the feature flow network only using the adversarial loss in our FPGAN.
- **FPGAN w/o GAN**. In this case, we train the feature flow network only using the Euclidean distance loss in our FPGAN.
- **FPGAN**. We train the feature flow network using both Euclidean distance loss and adversarial loss in our FPGAN, and this is the default model we refer to if not specified otherwise.

The evaluation results of all these methods are shown in Table 1. The R-FCN frame is a strong baseline and achieves the best result (59.3% mAP) among these methods. Simple methods, such as R-FCN copy and R-FCN flow, can largely improve the inference speed, but bring in large accuracy decrease (5.2% and 4.3% decrease in mAP). Our proposed FPGAN can learn accurate feature flow network and propagates CNN features from key frames to adjacent frames, and largely improves the detection accuracy compared to these simple methods (only 1.7% decrease in mAP) without any human labelling in the video or pre-trained optical flow network, and also enjoys high running speed (4 × speedup compared to the R-FCN frame, tested in TITAN X GPU).

Table 1. Performance comparison on the ImageNet VID validation set. The mean average precision over all classes and running speed are shown for a variety of methods. All methods use the same R-FCN model which is trained using ImageNet DET training set (only the same 30 category labels are used). We compare our FPGAN with other methods and also conduct ablation experiments in this table.

Approach	mAP (%)	Runtime (FPS)
R-FCN frame	59.31	7.5
R-FCN copy	54.12	60
R-FCN flow	55.05	30
FPGAN w/o l_2	54.36	30
FPGAN w/o GAN	57.51	30
FPGAN	57.65	30

We also explore deep into FPGAN. If we only use the adversarial loss in FPGAN, we can get better detection mAP compared to R-FCN copy. This indicates that our model starts to learn non-trivial motions with adversarial learning. Using the Euclidean distance loss, we can observe a large improvement compared to R-FCN copy and R-FCN flow. We then further combine these two losses in our FPGAN to jointly train the feature flow network, and can obtain slightly better model than using either of the two losses alone, which demonstrates the importance of the two losses.

4.3 R-FCN Trained on the ImageNet DET+VID Dataset

In this experiment, we first train R-FCN using the ImageNet DET training set (53639 training images) as well as ImageNet VID training set (57834 selected frames from the 3862 raw video snippets, as in [11, 12]), totally 111473 training images. We train R-FCN with roughly 120 k iterations following [4]. After this, we fix the parameter of R-FCN as in [12] and train the feature flow network using FPGAN as in Sect. 3.2. Note that the labels for the sampled frames in VID are only used to expand the training set of R-FCN, and we do not employ these labels anymore in our FPGAN by default.

Different to the training set in DET, there are more variant of objects in VID dataset, e.g., rare pose, partial occlusion and motion blur [9]. Given labelled training examples in VID dataset, we can learn better R-FCN model suitable to the video scene. The evaluation results of all these methods are shown in Table 2. We can observe a 10%–15% accuracy improvement in all methods due to better R-FCN model using labelled frames in VID dataset. In this case, the strong R-FCN frame baseline achieves 74.1% mAP which is slightly better than the result 73.9% in [11]. Simple methods like R-FCN copy and R-FCN flow bring in large accuracy decrease (8.5% and 6.8% decrease in mAP). We also observe similar improvement by using the proposed FPGAN to train the feature flow network in Sect. 4.2, which is 5.6% and 3.9% higher in mAP than the simple baselines R-FCN copy and R-FCN flow, and also is only 2.85% lower than R-FCN frame in mAP. Our FPGAN only needs unlabelled videos for training, and achieves real-time running speed. The experimental results demonstrate the effectiveness of our FPGAN.

Table 2. Performance comparison on the ImageNet VID validation set. The mean average precision over all classes and running speed are shown for a variety of methods. All methods use the same R-FCN model which is trained using both ImageNet DET training set (only the same 30 category labels are used) and ImageNet VID training set (use sampled frames as in [11]). We compare our FPGAN with other methods in this table.

Approach	mAP (%)	Runtime (FPS)
R-FCN frame	74.10	7.5
R-FCN copy	65.61	60
R-FCN flow	67.32	30
FPGAN w/o l_2	66.53	30
FPGAN w/o GAN	71.14	30
FPGAN	71.25	30

In DFF [11], R-FCN and the feature flow network are jointly trained using the combination of ImageNet DET and VID dataset, and achieves 72.9% mAP accuracy which is 1.7% higher than our method. However, our method attempts to learn the feature flow network using unsupervised learning by fully exploiting the temporal coherence in video data and the pre-trained R-FCN model, which is different to the supervised learning method DFF. Our method can still learn efficient video object detectors even if ground truth labels are unavailable in videos.

5 Conclusion

We aim to learn fast and accurate video object detectors given pre-trained image object detectors in this paper. The key problem we try to address is to propagate CNN features from key frame to adjacent frames fast and accurately using unlabelled videos. To achieve this goal, we propose Feature Propagation GAN (FPGAN) to fully exploit large scale unlabelled video data and pre-trained image object detectors. Adversarial loss and Euclidean distance loss are adopted to jointly supervise the learning of feature flow network. The discriminator in FPGAN employs 3D ConvNets to explicitly learn the feature evolutions between equally spaced frames, thus classifying feature triplets to be real or predicted. Comprehensive experiments are conducted on the ImageNet VID dataset and the results demonstrate the effectiveness of our method.

References

1. Girshick, R., Donahue, J., Darrell, T., Malik, J.: Region-based convolutional networks for accurate object detection and segmentation. In: CVPR, pp. 580–587 (2014)
2. Girshick, R.: Fast r-cnn. In: ICCV, pp. 1440–1448 (2015)
3. Ren, S., He, K., Girshick, R., Sun, J.: Faster r-cnn: towards real-time object detection with region proposal networks. In: NIPS, pp. 91–99 (2015)
4. Dai, J., Li, Y., He, K., Sun, J.: R-FCN: object detection via region-based fully convolutional networks. In: NIPS, pp. 379–387 (2016)
5. Han, G., Zhang, X., Li, C.: Revisiting faster R-CNN: a deeper look at region proposal network. In: ICONIP, pp. 14–24 (2017)
6. Redmon, J., Farhadi, A.: YOLO9000: better, faster, stronger. In: CVPR, pp. 7263–7271 (2017)
7. Liu, W., et al.: SSD: single shot MultiBox detector. In: Leibe, B., Matas, J., Sebe, N., Welling, M. (eds.) ECCV 2016. LNCS, vol. 9905, pp. 21–37. Springer, Cham (2016). https://doi.org/10.1007/978-3-319-46448-0_2
8. Han, G., Zhang, X., Li, C.: Single shot object detection with top-down refinement. In: ICIP, pp. 3360–3364 (2017)
9. Kang, K., et al.: Object detection in videos with tubelet proposal networks. In: CVPR, pp. 727–735 (2017)
10. Shelhamer, E., Rakelly, K., Hoffman, J., Darrell, T.: Clockwork convnets for video semantic segmentation. In: Hua, G., Jégou, H. (eds.) ECCV 2016. LNCS, vol. 9915, pp. 852–868. Springer, Cham (2016). https://doi.org/10.1007/978-3-319-49409-8_69
11. Zhu, X., Xiong, Y., Dai, J., Yuan, L., Wei, Y.: Deep feature flow for video recognition. In: CVPR, pp. 2349–2358 (2017)
12. Han, G., Zhang, X., Li, C.: Semi-supervised DFF: decoupling detection and feature flow for video object detectors. In: ACM Multimedia 2018. New York, NY, USA, pp. 1811–1819 (2018). https://doi.org/10.1145/3240508.3240693

13. Krizhevsky, A., Sutskever, I., Hinton, G.E.: ImageNet classification with deep convolutional neural networks. In: NIPS, pp. 1097–1105 (2012)
14. He, K., Zhang, X., Ren, S., Sun, J.: Deep residual learning for image recognition. In: CVPR, pp. 770–778 (2016)
15. Isola, P., Zhu, J.-Y., Zhou, T., Efros, A.A.: Image-to-image translation with conditional adversarial networks. In: CVPR (2017)
16. Johnson, J., Alahi, A., Fei-Fei, L.: Perceptual losses for real-time style transfer and super-resolution. In: Leibe, B., Matas, J., Sebe, N., Welling, M. (eds.) ECCV 2016. LNCS, vol. 9906, pp. 694–711. Springer, Cham (2016). https://doi.org/10.1007/978-3-319-46475-6_43
17. Mathieu, M., Couprie, C., LeCun, Y.: Deep multi-scale video prediction beyond mean square error. In: ICLR (2016)
18. Goodfellow, I., et al.: Generative adversarial nets. In: NIPS (2014)
19. Shrivastava, A., Pfister, T., Tuzel, O., Susskind, J., Wang, W., Webb, R.: Learning from simulated and unsupervised images through adversarial training. In: CVPR (2017)
20. Zhu, J.-Y., Park, T., Isola, P., Efros, A.A.: Unpaired image-to-image translation using cycle-consistent adversarial networks. In: ICCV (2017)
21. Wiskott, L., Sejnowski, T.J.: Slow feature analysis: unsupervised learning of invariances. Neural Comput. **14**(4), 715–770 (2002)
22. Jayaraman, D., Grauman, K.: Slow and steady feature analysis: higher order temporal coherence in video. In: CVPR (2016)
23. Wang, X., Gupta, A.: Unsupervised learning of visual representations using videos. In: ICCV 2015 (2015)
24. Lee, H.-Y., Huang, J.-B., Singh, M., Yang, M.-H.: Unsupervised representation learning by sorting sequences. In: ICCV (2017)
25. Dosovitskiy, A., et al.. Flownet: learning optical flow with convolutional networks. In: ICCV (2015)
26. Tran, D., Bourdev, L., Fergus, R., Torresani, L., Paluri, M.: Learning spatiotemporal features with 3D convolutional networks. In: ICCV (2015)
27. Arjovsky, M., Chintala, S., Bottou, L.: Wasserstein generative adversarial networks. In: ICML (2017)

OmniEyes: Analysis and Synthesis of Artistically Painted Eyes

Gjorgji Strezoski(✉), Rogier Knoester, Nanne van Noord, and Marcel Worring

Intelligent Sensory Information Systems, University of Amsterdam, Amsterdam, The Netherlands
rogier@knoester.com
{g.strezoski,n.j.e.vannoord,m.worring}@uva.nl

Abstract. Faces in artistic paintings most often contain the same elements (eyes, nose, mouth...) as faces in the real world, however they are not a photo-realistic transfer of physical visual content. These creative nuances the artists introduce in their work act as interference when facial detection models are used in the artistic domain. In this work we introduce models that can accurately detect, classify and conditionally generate artistically painted eyes in portrait paintings. In addition, we introduce the OmniEyes Dataset that captures the essence of painted eyes with annotated patches from 250 K artistic paintings and their metadata. We evaluate our approach in inpainting, out of context eye generation and classification on portrait paintings from the OmniArt dataset. We conduct a user case study to further study the quality of our generated samples, asses their aesthetic aspects and provide quantitative and qualitative results for our model's performance.

1 Introduction

Portrait painting is one of the most common painting genres in the art world, where the intent is to depict a human subject. Portraits are expected to show a good balance between photographic realism and an artistic accent of the characteristics that define the depicted individual. A direct indication of the quality of a painted portrait are facial features, as Gordon C. Aymar states: *"The eyes are the place one looks for the most complete, reliable, and pertinent information about the subject."*. However, artists have been know to modify the original appearance of the subjects eyes, to benefit the overall artwork appearance. For example, it is known that Jeanne in 'Portrait of Jeanne Hébuterne' painted by the Italian artist Amedeo Modigliani had blue eyes, but most of her portraits depict her with dark brown irises. This raises the question of the distribution of eye colors in portrait paintings, how does the presence of blue eyes compare to brown eyes? Do artists opt for brown eyes to enhance contrast even when the subject has blue irises? The recent increase in visual art collection availability [2,6,15,17,26] has made large scale research on topics like this possible.

Y. M. Ro et al. (Eds.): MMM 2020, LNCS 11961, pp. 628–641, 2020.
https://doi.org/10.1007/978-3-030-37731-1_51

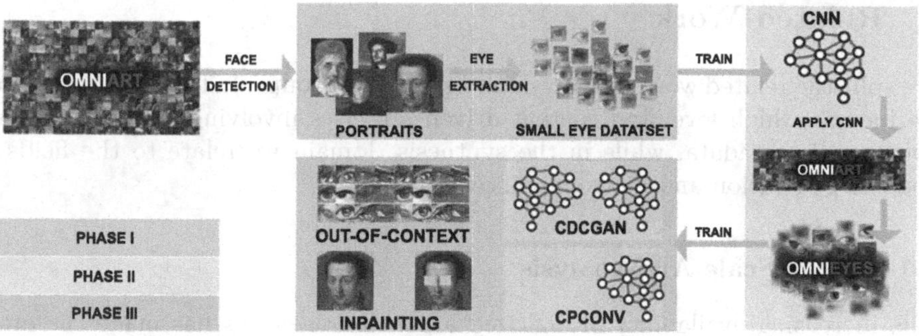

Fig. 1. The complete pipeline of the process for in and out of context painted eye generation. The process takes place in three phases with the arrows showing in the chronological order of the arrows from left to right.

Over the years there has been a fruitful collaboration between the fields of multimedia and art on both the analysis [2,3,5–7,17,20,25,26,30] and synthesis fronts [9,13,18,24,27,29,31]. High and low level annotations, natural language descriptions and curated metadata have improved our understanding of the visual content in art and the potential of applying multimedia and vision techniques in this domain. Applications in the artistic domain have also been helpful in artwork restoration scenarios [27]. In this work, we continue this trend by focusing on the study of art color in portrait paintings in the OmniArt dataset through generative and discriminative models.

Our approach takes place in three phases as depicted in Fig. 1. In the first phase we develop a pipeline to localize and extract eyes in paintings with their orientation and color of the iris using traditional image processing and computer vision methods. In the second phase we train a discriminative model that is able to disentangle the representations of eyes and the color of their irises. We use this model to create the OmniArt Eyes dataset containing more than 118 K painted eye samples, with their location within the painting, eye color, orientation and expanded artwork related metadata. Finally, in the third phase we use the OmniEyes dataset to train a conditional image inpainting model that generates painted eyes with respect to their context, and an out-of-context generative adversarial network that generates painted eyes that satisfy a conditional statement on color.

In this paper we note the following contributions:

- The OmniArt Eyes dataset containing 118 K eye samples with visual descriptions such as eye color, orientation and artwork specific metadata from the originating collection.
- An accurate detection, localization and color classification model for eyes in artistic painting.
- An in and out-of-context generative model able to generate painted eyes that satisfy a color conditional.

2 Related Work

We split the related work in analysis and synthesis groups. In the analysis domain we focus on high level and content driven analyses involving images and their contextual metadata, while in the synthesis domain we relate to the fields of content generation and image inpainting.

2.1 Large Scale Art Analysis

The increasing availability of digitized artwork collections has made the artistic domain attractive for performing large scale content based analyses. There have been multiple efforts to identify, characterize, and define styles as well as other high level metadata based on the visual content of the artwork reproduction. For example, Strezoski and Worring [26] introduced the OmniArt large scale artistic benchmark, where they define high level classification and detection tasks such as artist attribution, artwork type, genre, school, style and creation period estimation. In this effort, they link the artwork's metadata to cues in it's visual content. Garcia et al. [6] developed context aware embeddings for artwork analysis, accenting the textual modality by taking into account the social and historical context of the artwork's description.

On a lower, content based level, Cetinic et al. [2] perform analyses on how content and image lighting affect the projected sentiment. An even more fine-grained analysis is performed by Xi Shen et al. [22], who introduce a method for discovering locally repeating visual patterns in art collections. This leads to better understanding of the link between a study (usually a sketch) and the painting it was made for. Noticeable in [5,22] and supported by [32], depicting human figures and faces involves many small details that give the artwork it's character or appeal. As portrait painting is one of the most humanly relatable genres [11] in artistic painting and the facial features it contains haven't been studied on a large scale, in this work we focus on the large scale analysis of painted eyes and their context as facial features in artistic painting.

2.2 Art Generation and Artwork Inpainting

Regardless of the recent influx of GAN generated artworks, GANs by definition have no motivation to generate anything creative [4]. Since the generator is trained to generate images mimicking the training distribution, ultimately the generator just generates images that look like already existing art [21]. While not creative by itself, his behavior has benefits in terms of learning the building blocks of artworks in their own space. Guided by conditional statements these approaches can be of help for art conservators, curators, and historians. In this work we exploit this behavior of GANs to learn the structure of an artistically painted eye, disentangle it from the color of the iris and seamlessly merge the generated content with it's context.

Generative models have been proven useful in artwork restoration scenarios [27]. Specifically a model can estimate on how a restoration procedure of a damaged section would affect the appearance of an artwork. For example, in Eastern Europe icons in Orthodox Christian churches often suffer from damaged eyes. It was believed that removing the eyes from depictions of saints in churches would bring good health to whomever does it. In most of these cases no indication of the original state of these damaged icons is available. A generative models can help in estimating the appearance of the repaired image. These models that *fill in the gaps* are dubbed inpainting models. Typical deep learning based inpainting methods initialize the holes with some constant placeholder values e.g. the mean pixel value of ImageNet [19], which is then passed through a convolutional network. Due to the resulting artifacts, post-processing is often used to ameliorate the effects of conditioning on the placeholder values. In this work, we develop a iris color conditioned deep inpainting model that generates eyes that fit into the context of an artistically painted face.

3 Approach

Our approach is organized in three functional phases. The first phase is dedicated to constructing a small and accurate dataset containing eyes and eye colors. As in artistic painting the eyes do not follow the strict rules of nature and can significantly differ in appearance, conventional eye detection methods do not perform well in all cases. For this reason, in the first phase we built a *mini* dataset that has the purpose of being both accurate and large enough to train a deep model.

This model initiates phase two of our approach in which we detect, localize and classify eyes and their color from OmniArt. Phase two results in the OmniEyes dataset containing 118 K painted eyes from any style of artistic painting reproductions (drawings, sketches and prints included) present in OmniArt.

The third phase of our approach is generative. We train inpainting and out-of-context generative models. The inpainting model is tasked with conditionally inpainting eyes in portrait paintings. As the OmniEyes dataset follows the OmniArt resource identification convention, the eyes in the OmniEyes dataset are directly linked to their full size portraits where the context can be acquired. On the other hand, our out-of-context generative model is tasked with disentangling the structure of an eye from the color of it's iris.

3.1 Eye Detection and Eye Color Classification

Phase one begins with extracting and classifying eyes using traditional handcrafted features for maximal control over the outcome. For face detection we encode the image using HOG features and match the part of the encoded image that most resembles a generic HOG encoding of a face and align it to the center of the image [10]. On the aligned and centered facial images we extract 68 facial landmarks with OpenFace [1] out of which 6 denote the left eye and 6 denote the right eye in the image. The area encapsulated by these landmark, we consider eye proposals.

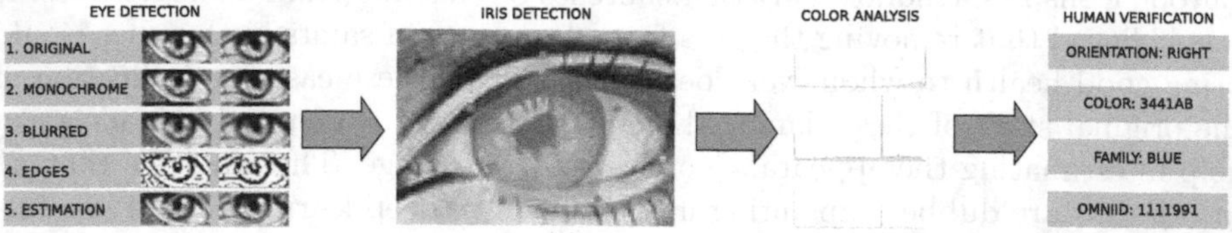

Fig. 2. Creating the *mini* curated dataset for training the convolutional neural network used for the entire dataset. This approach yielded 15000 detected eyes out of which 3000 were manually curated by human observers for maximum precision and clarity.

As eyes in artistic painting do not follow an exact building structure, these proposals are quite noisy and have to be filtered further. The next filtering step includes detecting an iris which in humans always has roughly the same shape (circle) and approximately in the same location within the eye. Using this assumption we apply the Circle Hough Transform to detect circles and partial arcs (in case the eyes are gazing on the side). This algorithm takes a single channel image and returns the location of the iris. We further reduce noise and artifacts in this step by applying a 3×3 Gaussian blur on the mono-channel images fed into the algorithm illustrated in Fig. 2.

The eye landmarks and the circle surrounding the iris are helpful in extracting the iris color. The intersection of the two areas marks the iris and the pixels within hold the color information. This intersection is used as circles can be detected in skin patterns outside of the eye in the larger skin area. We extract eye color in the HSV space by a center-wise weighted sum of color values. We designed the weights to counter the near complete black values of the pupil. The further away the pixel is from the centroid of the intersection polygon the higher the weight assigned to it is. This weight grows linearly in increments of one towards the edge where the weight is ten. We then create three clusters of these weighted pixels out of which we assume the color of the largest one to be the color of the iris. As the HSV color value is not usable in a classification setting, we map this value to one of the color families defined by the X11 standard (Table 1).

Table 1. The initial *mini* dataset for training the CNN model.

	Amber	Blue	Brown	Gray	Grayscale	Green	Hazel	Irisless	Red	Negative
Train	304	347	286	251	287	296	213	149	264	215
Val	51	62	57	49	49	56	41	20	45	31
Test	20	20	20	20	20	20	20	20	20	20

The resulting dataset is filtered manually as well. Non expert human observers (information studies master students) distilled 3000 (out of 15000 detected samples) completely accurate eyes and accompanying metadata. Our human observers additionally defined the Amber, Hazel, Irisless and Gray-scale categories as new categories we did not account for in the original X11 color mapping. As Amber and Hazel are variations of brown they can be considered part of that family, however there is a significant amount of consistent samples which demands a separate category. In grayscale images eye color is not obtainable from the image itself and irisless eyes cannot have an iris color. The Negative class is assigned to any region proposals that were proposed, but not accepted as valid eyes by our human observer. We attempted to cover as many of the possible variations of the Negative class. With defining these classes our categorization becomes more accurate and fine-grained.

This phase of our approach provides us with a small, but accurate, dataset of eyes and their color categories. In the next step we train a Convolutional Neural Network, which provides a large enough set of training examples, and can learn the artistic variations of painted eyes in it's parameter space with an abstraction to color.

3.2 The OmniEyes Dataset

We use the curated dataset from the previous phase to fine-tune already established architectures for CNNs such as [8,12,23] pretrained on the ImageNet dataset. For the fine-tuning process, we define a ten-way classification task over a subset of 250 K images in the OmniArt dataset and the ten color classes defined in the previous step.

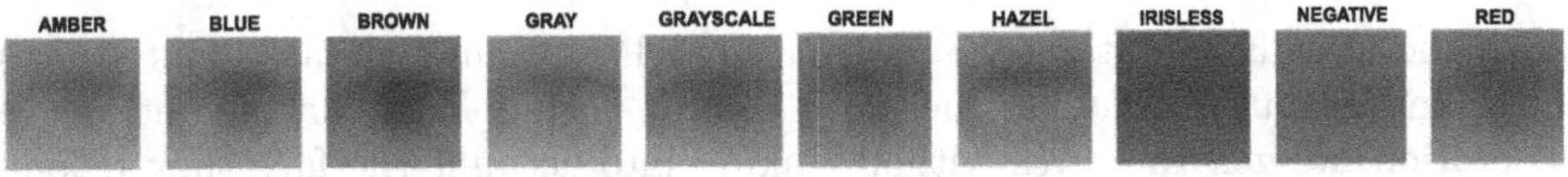

Fig. 3. Average eyes per class in the OmniEyes dataset. A clear color distinction between the classes is noticeable and a blurry eye structure is present in all of the classes including the Negative class. This indicates that even though out model performs well on the eye detection and color classification tasks, there are still eyes in the Negative pool to be discovered. (Color figure online)

With our best performing model we extracted and stored 118.576 samples of eyes (the distribution across classes is visible in Table 2). Our model discovered 214.618 proposals for faces within the 250 K images from the dataset, however a substantial amount of region proposals did not pass the threshold to be classified as eyes and were dropped in the Negative class. The average eye per class is visible in Fig. 3, where the centered colored iris indicates a clean selection.

The OmniEyes dataset shares the same structure of metadata and annotations as the OmniArt dataset, which allows for access to artwork s specific

Table 2. Number of samples per class in the OmniEyes dataset.

	Amber	Blue	Brown	Gray	Grayscale	Green	Hazel	Irisless	Red	Negative
Samples	3.114	18.926	42.094	7.637	16.234	5.220	1.578	18.282	5.491	96.042

metadata. For every eye sample we can access the artist, genre, creation period, type of artwork, collection, color palette, and concepts through the OmniId [26] (Fig. 4).

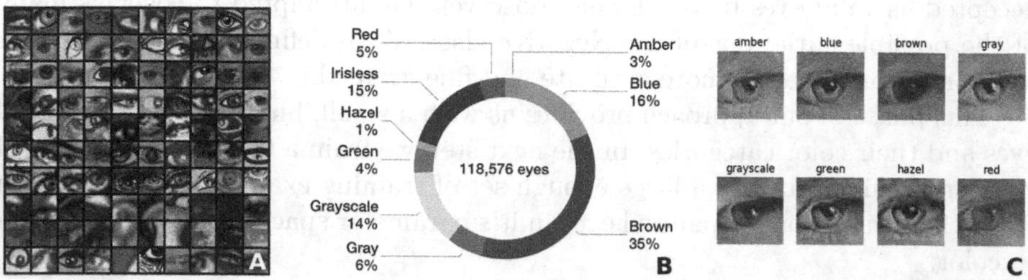

Fig. 4. A. For every class ten random samples are shown. The classes from top to bottom are amber, blue, brown, gray, gray-scale, green, hazel, iris-less, negative, and red. **B.** The distribution of colors of eyes in the OmniArt dataset. **C.** For each class an eye is generated with the same noise vector. The only difference in each eye is the eye color, meaning that the generator has learned to separate the eye color from other content. (Color figure online)

3.3 Painted Eye Generation and Eye Inpainting

With the OmniEyes dataset we create a model that can generate painted eyes in two modes, out of context generation and inpainting. With out-of-context eye generation, we generate eyes without taking into account the face they belong to, while for inpainting we train the model to fill a gap where the eyes in an artwork should be.

Our out-of-context generation relies on the Conditional Deep Convolutional Generative Adversarial Network (cDCGAN) from [16]. This architecture allows us to turn a random noise vector sampled from a normal distribution and a conditional statement into an image of an eye. We condition the generator network on the iris color. The generated feature vector is passed through a series of transposed convolutions which result in a 128×128 pixel image being forwarded to the discriminator network. The discriminator outputs two values, one regarding the color of the eye and the other indicating whether the newly generated sample belongs to the training set distribution. The complete architecture of the model is shown in Fig. 5.

The out-of-context GAN was trained for 200 epochs with a batch size of 64 and categorical cross-entropy for both the iris color and set attribution tasks on the OmniEyes training set (Fig. 6).

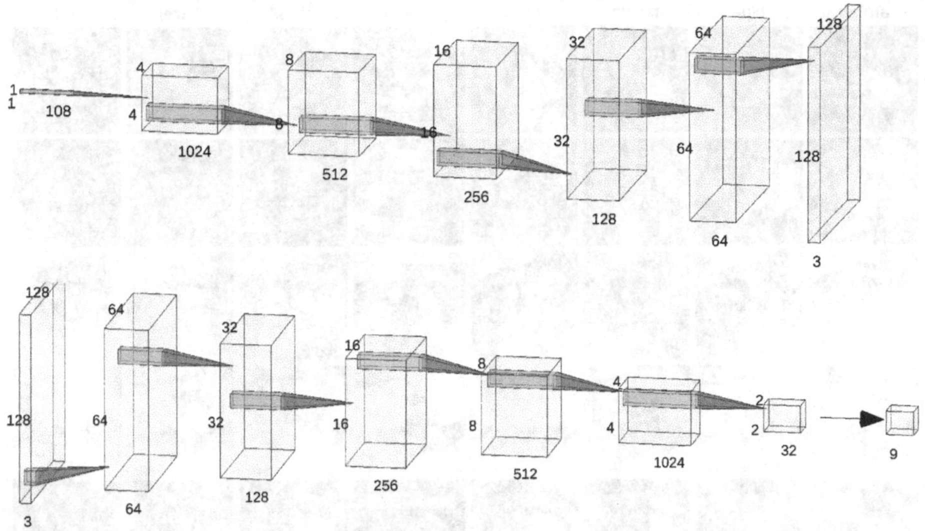

Fig. 5. The architectures of the generator (top) and discriminator network (bottom). The generator has noise and a one-hot vector denoting the eye color as input and through transposed convolutions transforms it into an image. The discriminator takes an image as input and uses convolutions to classify the realness and the eye color.

The inpainting model is based on an adapted version of the approach proposed by Liu et al. [14]. Our adaptation consists of conditioning the model to produce an output that satisfies the condition. Similar to the out-of-context generation, we condition the inpainting model on eye color based on the 10 classes present in the OmniEyes dataset. As the OmniEyes dataset follows the same naming convention as the OmniArt dataset, we can directly pull the complete portraits for which we have eye color information. For training we randomly pulled a selection of 80 K portrait paintings from the OmniArt dataset and their respective OmniEyes information. We tested on 20 K randomly pulled portraits of the remaining 170 K.

4 Results

We report quantitative, qualitative and human valuation results as part of our work. The quantitative results provide insight into the discriminative performance of our model. They also justify the choices in model architectures, as well as indicate the quality of the OmniEyes dataset and it's ability to train models. The qualitative results show the conditionally generated image quality. As an additional metric we conducted a human study where we evaluate how humans perceive the output from our model and how realistic the generated results are.

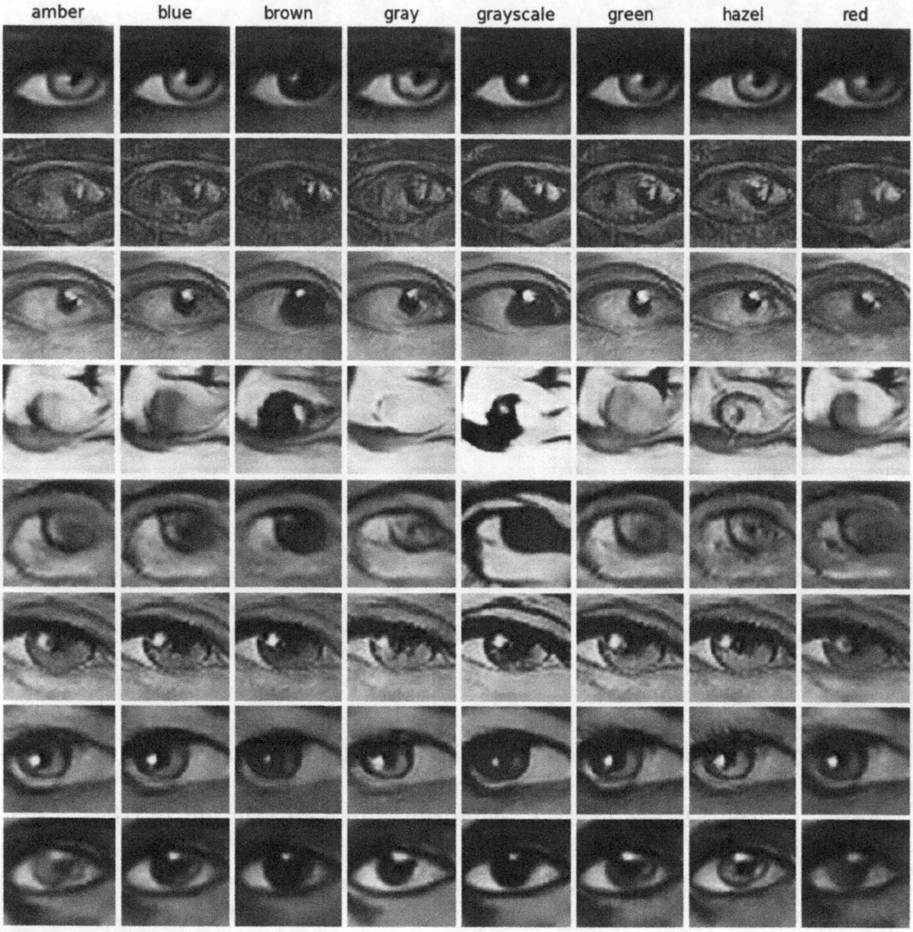

Fig. 6. Generated eyes from eight random vectors with our out-of-context generation module. Each column indicates the generated image in it's respective class indicated in the topmost row. Regardless of the eye structure, our models are able to disentangle the structure of an eye from the color of the iris and generate relevant samples to the conditioning class. A repeating phenomenon from the original training distribution is the tint in the skin tone of the generated image which reflects the color of the iris.

4.1 Quantitative Results

Our approach is quantitatively evaluated in both the classification and the generation tasks. For evaluating the classification performance on the OmniEyes dataset we report the accuracy over the ten iris color classes. However, for the out of context generation and inpainting tasks there is not a definitive good metric to evaluate our results. For this reason we follow the metrics used in previous inpainting and generation works [14, 24, 29] and report the l_1, PSNR, SSIM [28] and Inception scores (Table 3).

Table 3. Classification accuracy on the handpicked *mini* set for training the initial eye detection and classification net in the first row. We trained the same models with OmniEyes and compare their predictive performance.

Dataset	AlexNet	VGG-11	ResNet-18
MiniSet	60.0%	75.0%	84.0%
OmniEyes	69.2%	83.1%	94.3%

On the inpainting task the score of our model is always best if it is not conditioned on the color of the iris. Upon visual inspection of the generated patches, we can observe that a conditioning on the eye color introduces a slight color tint in the entire in-painted region. In Fig. 7 we can see how the white eye sections and skin of Mona Lisa's eye region adopts the tone of the generated iris. As these metrics are pixel based, it is expected that any changes to the original look will negatively impact performance (Table 4).

Table 4. Average inpainting scores on the frontal portraits subset in the OmniArt dataset. The original reconstruction score indicates the performance on returning the painting to it's original state, while the rest of the columns quantify the difference to the original when conditional generation is introduced.

Metric	Original	Amber	Blue	Brown	Gray	Grayscale	Green	Hazel	Irisless
l_1	1.02	1.58	1.76	1.05	4.11	3.16	1.62	1.22	1.99
PSNR	29.14	30.20	31.03	29.77	33.62	33.41	31.12	30.95	31.28
SSIM	0.89	0.82	0.79	0.86	0.78	0.71	0.80	0.80	0.69
Inception	0.22	0.46	0.51	0.46	0.92	1.29	0.72	0.55	1.01

4.2 Qualitative Study

Quantitative metrics usually provide a variation of content based measurable similarity to the ground-truth result. While a relevant indicator of generative model performance, the more difficult test is satisfying the attention to detail of the human eye.

Figure 7 displays the results of our inpainting approach to eyes in portraits. We picked three well known artworks for showcasing the performance of the model. The first column of Fig. 7 contains the masked image, the second the ground-truth and the subsequent columns contain the inpainted masked regions. We notice that the change in appearance is most subtle in the Mona Lisa as the iris color does not tint the complete eye region. The iris color tint is very prominent in the third sample, where also the white part of the eye is significantly larger than in the previous two.

For the human study of our generated content we created a simple web application. On entering the application the observer is presented with a short description of the task at hand, and a sample of generated painted eyes. As 16 image grid presents a light cognitive load and is ideal for the average screen size, the user is presented with two batches of 16 images where each image of an eye is 128 by 128 pixel large. Both batches contain samples from the training dataset and samples from our generator. Upon selecting the eyes the observer considers artificially generated, the next batch is displayed. after completing two batches of the study the observer's feedback is stored for further analysis. We assume the subjects of this study do not have experience with evaluating outputs from generative models and have the art connoisseurship of an average human.

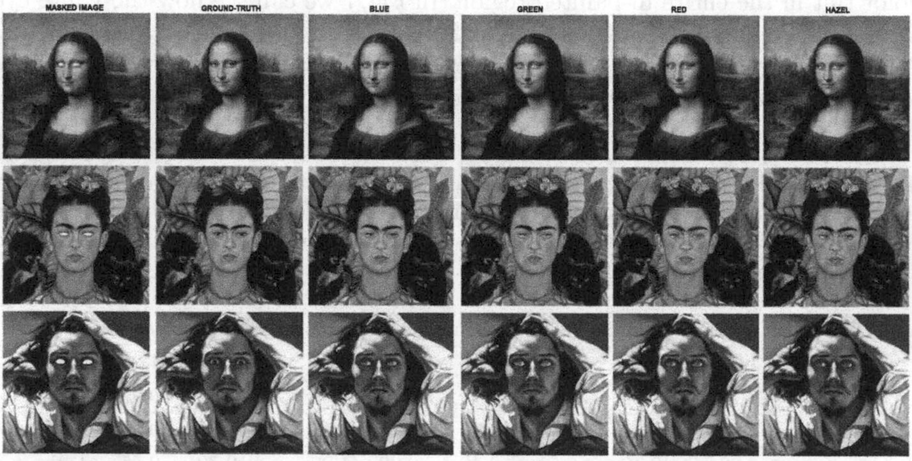

Fig. 7. Conditional inpainting results on selected portraits from the OmniArt dataset. For aligning the pixels where information is missing and needs to be filled in we use a standard layer mask that drops the missing pixels (marked in white) from the receptive field. The masks for the test images are manually generated.

In this study a total of 612 generated randomly generated eyes and 612 real painted eyes were shown to 53 users. Of the 612 generated eyes only 191 in total were marked to be fake by different observers. This means that in more than 2/3 of the cases our generator is able to fool a human observer as shown in Fig. 8. As this study is in the artistic domain it is not unusual for humans to misinterpret model generated artifacts as an artistic touch, or consider actual artist introduced elements as model generated content. However, even with taking into account the ambiguity of the discrimination task for the average user, our model manages to fool the human observer.

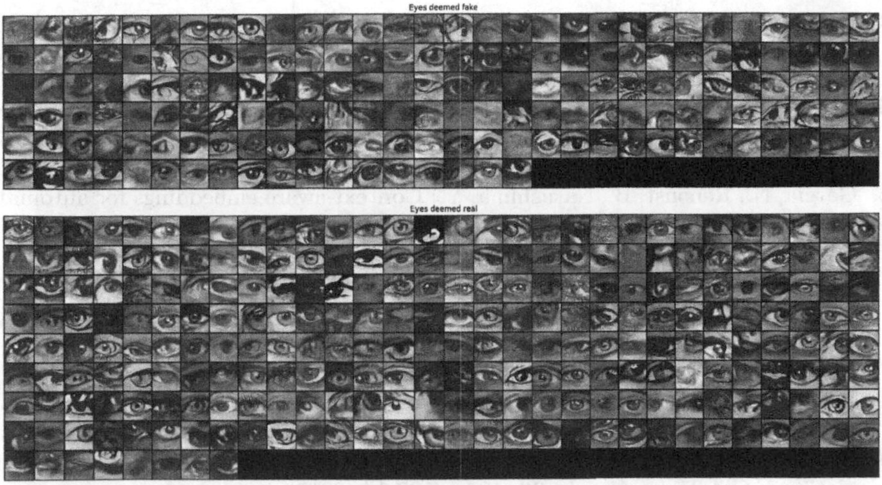

Fig. 8. All of the eyes above have been generated for the human study and none of them are real. The top row are the generated painted eyes that were marked by humans as fake, they correctly recognized them. The bottom row shows the generated painted eyes that humans thought were real, the generator was able to fool humans with these painted eyes.

5 Conclusion

In this work we develop and evaluate generative and analytical models for eye color in artistic portrait painting. Answering the questions posed in the introduction, portraits with faces containing blue colored irises are the second most common portraits after portraits with brown irises. In addition to analyzing the distribution of eye colors in 250 K paintings from the OmniArt dataset, we present inpainting and out-of-context generative models evaluated by non-expert humans. Finally, we introduce the OmniEyes dataset containing more than 118 K artistically painted eyes with descriptive and high level metadata. We hope our models, dataset and approach prove to be helpful for professionals in the field and offer them as pip packages as well as open source code.

References

1. Baltrušaitis, T., Robinson, P., Morency, L.P.: Openface: an open source facial behavior analysis toolkit. In: 2016 IEEE Winter Conference on Applications of Computer Vision (WACV), pp. 1–10. IEEE (2016)
2. Cetinic, E., Lipic, T., Grgic, S.: A deep learning perspective on beauty, sentiment, and remembrance of art. IEEE Access **7**, 73694–73710 (2019)
3. Ci, Y., Ma, X., Wang, Z., Li, H., Luo, Z.: User-guided deep anime line art colorization with conditional adversarial networks. In: 2018 ACM Multimedia Conference on Multimedia Conference, MM 2018, Seoul, Republic of Korea, October 22–26, 2018, pp. 1536–1544 (2018). https://doi.org/10.1145/3240508.3240661

4. Elgammal, A., Liu, B., Elhoseiny, M., Mazzone, M.: Can: creative adversarial networks, generating "art" by learning about styles and deviating from style norms. arXiv preprint (2017). arXiv:1706.07068
5. Elgammal, A., Liu, B., Kim, D., Elhoseiny, M., Mazzone, M.: The shape of art history in the eyes of the machine. In: Thirty-Second AAAI Conference on Artificial Intelligence (2018)
6. Garcia, N., Renoust, B., Nakashima, Y.: Context-aware embeddings for automatic art analysis. In: Proceedings of the 2019 on International Conference on Multimedia Retrieval, pp. 25–33. ACM (2019)
7. Goldfarb, D., Merkl, D.: Visualizing art historical developments using the getty ulan, wikipedia and wikidata. In: 2018 22nd International Conference Information Visualisation (IV), pp. 459–466. IEEE (2018)
8. He, K., Zhang, X., Ren, S., Sun, J.: Deep residual learning for image recognition. In: Proceedings of the IEEE Conference on Computer Vision and Pattern Recognition, pp. 770–778 (2016)
9. Iizuka, S., Simo-Serra, E., Ishikawa, H.: Globally and locally consistent image completion. ACM Trans. Graph. **36**, 107:1–107:14 (2017)
10. Kazemi, V., Sullivan, J.: One millisecond face alignment with an ensemble of regression trees. In: Proceedings of the IEEE Conference on Computer Vision and Pattern Recognition, pp. 1867–1874 (2014)
11. Kozbelt, A., Seeley, W.P.: Integrating art historical, psychological, and neuroscientific explanations of artists' advantages in drawing and perception. Psychology of Aesthetics, Creativity, and the Arts **1**(2), 80 (2007)
12. Krizhevsky, A., Sutskever, I., Hinton, G.E.: Imagenet classification with deep convolutional neural networks. In: Advances in Neural Information Processing Systems, pp. 1097–1105 (2012)
13. Li, Y., Liu, S., Yang, J., Yang, M.H.: Generative face completion. In: Proceedings of the IEEE Conference on Computer Vision and Pattern Recognition, pp. 3911–3919 (2017)
14. Liu, G., Reda, F.A., Shih, K.J., Wang, T.C., Tao, A., Catanzaro, B.: Image inpainting for irregular holes using partial convolutions. In: Proceedings of the European Conference on Computer Vision (ECCV), pp. 85–100 (2018)
15. Mao, H., Cheung, M., She, J.: Deepart: learning joint representations of visual arts. In: Proceedings of the 2017 ACM on Multimedia Conference, MM 2017, Mountain View, CA, USA, October 23–27, 2017, pp. 1183–1191 (2017). https://doi.org/10.1145/3123266.3123405
16. Mirza, M., Osindero, S.: Conditional generative adversarial nets. arXiv preprint (2014). arXiv:1411.1784
17. Oh, C.: Automatically classifying art images using computer vision (2018)
18. Pathak, D., Krahenbuhl, P., Donahue, J., Darrell, T., Efros, A.A.: Context encoders: feature learning by inpainting. In: Proceedings of the IEEE Conference on Computer Vision and Pattern Recognition, pp. 2536–2544 (2016)
19. Ren, S., He, K., Girshick, R., Sun, J.: Faster R-CNN: towards real-time object detection with region proposal networks. In: Advances in Neural Information Processing Systems, pp. 91–99 (2015)
20. Rodriguez, C.S., Lech, M., Pirogova, E.: Classification of style in fine-art paintings using transfer learning and weighted image patches. In: 2018 12th International Conference on Signal Processing and Communication Systems (ICSPCS), pp. 1–7. IEEE (2018)

21. Sbai, O., Elhoseiny, M., Bordes, A., LeCun, Y., Couprie, C.: Design: design inspiration from generative networks. In: Proceedings of the European Conference on Computer Vision (ECCV) (2018)
22. Shen, X., Efros, A.A., Aubry, M.: Discovering visual patterns in art collections with spatially-consistent feature learning. In: Proceedings IEEE Conference on Computer Vision and Pattern Recognition (CVPR) (2019)
23. Simonyan, K., Zisserman, A.: Very deep convolutional networks for large-scale image recognition. arXiv preprint (2014). arXiv:1409.1556
24. Song, Y., et al.: Contextual-based image inpainting: infer, match, and translate. In: Proceedings of the European Conference on Computer Vision (ECCV), pp. 3–19 (2018)
25. Strezoski, G., Groenen, I., Besenbruch, J., Worring, M.: Artsight: an artistic data exploration engine. In: 2018 ACM Multimedia Conference on Multimedia Conference, MM 2018, Seoul, Republic of Korea, October 22–26, 2018, pp. 1240–1241 (2018). https://doi.org/10.1145/3240508.3241389
26. Strezoski, G., Worring, M.: Omniart: a large-scale artistic benchmark. ACM Trans. Multimedia Comput. Commun. Appl. (TOMM) **14**(4), 88 (2018)
27. Van Noord, N., Postma, E.: Light-weight pixel context encoders for image inpainting. arXiv preprint (2018). arXiv:1801.05585
28. Wang, Z., Bovik, A.C., Sheikh, H.R., Simoncelli, E.P., et al.: Image quality assessment: from error visibility to structural similarity. IEEE Trans. Image Process. **13**(4), 600–612 (2004)
29. Yang, C., Lu, X., Lin, Z., Shechtman, E., Wang, O., Li, H.: High-resolution image inpainting using multi-scale neural patch synthesis. In: Proceedings of the IEEE Conference on Computer Vision and Pattern Recognition, pp. 6721–6729 (2017)
30. Yoshimura, Y., Cai, B., Wang, Z., Ratti, C.: Deep learning architect: classification for architectural design through the eye of artificial intelligence. In: Geertman, S., Zhan, Q., Allan, A., Pettit, C. (eds.) CUPUM 2019. LNGC, pp. 249–265. Springer, Cham (2019). https://doi.org/10.1007/978-3-030-19424-6_14
31. Yu, J., Lin, Z., Yang, J., Shen, X., Lu, X., Huang, T.S.: Generative image inpainting with contextual attention. In: Proceedings of the IEEE Conference on Computer Vision and Pattern Recognition, pp. 5505–5514 (2018)
32. Zaidel, D.W.: Neuropsychology of art: Neurological, Cognitive, and Evolutionary Perspectives. Psychology Press (2015)

LDSNE: Learning Structural Network Embeddings by Encoding Local Distances

Xiyue Gao[1,2,3], Jun Chen[1,2,3](✉), Jing Yao[1], and Wenqian Zhu[1]

[1] National Engineering Research Center for Multimedia Software, School of Computer Science, Wuhan University, Wuhan 430072, China
chenj.nercms@gmail.com

[2] Hubei Key Laboratory of Multimedia and Network Communication Engineering, Wuhan University, Wuhan 430072, China

[3] Collaborative Innovation Center of Geospatial Technology, Wuhan 430079, China

Abstract. Network embedding algorithms learn low-dimensional features from the relationships and attributes of networks. The basic principle of these algorithms is to preserve the similarities in the original networks as much as possible. However, existing algorithms are not expressive enough for structural identity similarities. Therefore, we propose *LDSNE*, a novel algorithm for learning structural representations in both directed and undirected networks. Networks are first mapped into a proximity-based low-dimension space. Then, structural embeddings are extracted by encoding local space distances. Empirical results demonstrate that our algorithm can obtain multiple types of representations and outperforms other state-of-the-art methods.

Keywords: Representation learning · Structural network embedding · Social multimedia

1 Introduction

A wide variety of social networks has become the hottest web application in recent years, and massive multimedia information has attracted widespread attention of researchers. When performing typical network mining tasks, such as node classification [10,11], link prediction [6] and clustering [5,17], classifiers require accurate features about nodes, edges, communities and other elements. Therefore, a large number of network embedding algorithms are proposed to represent a network as low dimensional vectors while the network similarities are preserved [1,3,7].

The evolution history of network embedding algorithms is the history of how to define similar node pairs in a network. In the early 2000s, Locally Linear Embedding (LLE) assumes that every node embedding is a linear combination of its neighbors embeddings. This method considers that nodes and their direct connected neighbours are similar, so called first-order proximity fusion method [16]. Since 2010, researchers found that not only neighbors, but also the neighbors

Y. M. Ro et al. (Eds.): MMM 2020, LNCS 11961, pp. 642–652, 2020.
https://doi.org/10.1007/978-3-030-37731-1_52

of neighbors may be similar to the node. GraRep considers k-order neighbors to learn embeddings [2]. HOPE uses the Katz Index, Rooted PageRank, Common Neighbors, and Adamic-Adar score to find those similar node pairs [13]. Recently, many methods perform random walks and a variable-length sliding window to obtain flexible order similar node pairs, and then use skip-gram models to shorten the distance of similar pairs in the embedding space [8,14]. Besides, Struc2vec considers that nodes with same structural identity are similar. Structural similarity does not depend on hop distance, which means neighbor nodes can be different, far away nodes can be similar [15].

However, these increasingly complex network embedding methods neglect the relationship between proximate and structural features. Consequently, these methods may lose the original network structure and not suitable for storage. For example, given a network, we generally choose to store its adjacency list instead of 2-hop relational adjacency list. Because it cannot reconstruct the original network, which is equivalent to partial data loss. In the same way, network embedding is also a network representation method, so the original network information should also be retained. Considering similarities of multi-hop and structure in the representation learning phase means that embeddings will be affected by a specific data analysis tasks. And each data analysis task will have a set of embeddings. Therefore, these methods are not beneficial to the understanding, the separation of representation and analysis and the data retention. Moreover, the resulting latent representations give poor performance on various prediction tasks over networks.

In this paper, we proposed *LDSNE*, which aims to learn structural network embeddings for both directed and undirected networks. This model completely separates representation learning process and data analysis process. Figure 1 shows the goal of representation learning of *LDSNE*, which ensures that networks embeddings learned from adjacency lists or matrices can reconstruct the original adjacency lists or matrices as little as possible loss of information. The representation learning process is like an auto-encoder. Next, in the data analysis process, we proposed an unsupervised model to extract structural identities by encoding local distances. Empirical results demonstrate that *LDSNE* achieved structural embeddings and significantly better performance than state-of-the-art methods.

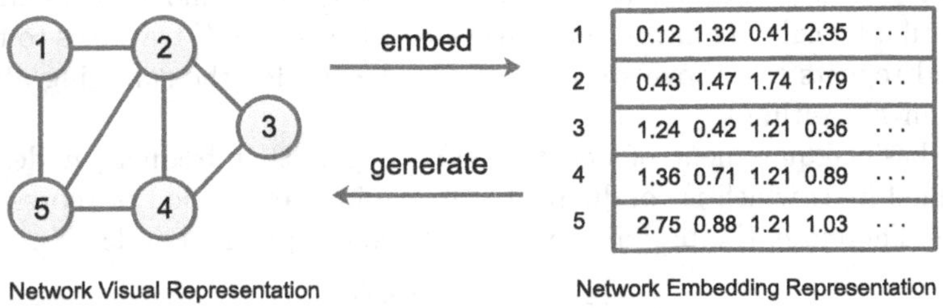

Fig. 1. Illustration of embedding and generating process of representation learning.

This paper is outlined as follows: we describe the preliminary concepts and define the representation learning problem in Sect. 2. We present details for representation learning using *LDSNE* in Sect. 3. In Sect. 4, we evaluate our algorithm using real-world networks. In Sect. 5, we present our conclusions.

2 Preliminary Information

In this section, we first introduce the definition of the network concept, and then provide formal definitions of the network embedding problem.

Definition 1 (Network). *A network is* $\mathbb{N} = (V, E)$ *in which* V *is the set of nodes and* E *is the set of edges between nodes, representing a relationship between two objects. Each edge* $e \in E$ *is an ordered pair* $e = (u, v)$*. If* $\mathbb{N}$ *is weighted, each edge* $e \in E$ *is a triple* $e = (u, v, w_{u,v})$*, in which* $w_{u,v}$ *indicates the strength of the relation. If* $\mathbb{N}$ *is undirected, we have* $(u, v) \equiv (v, u)$ *and* $w_{u,v} \equiv w_{v,u}$*. If* $\mathbb{N}$ *is directed, we have* $(u, v) \not\equiv (v, u)$ *and* $w_{u,v} \not\equiv w_{v,u}$*.*

Problem 1 ***(Network Embedding).*** Given an input network $\mathbb{N} = (V, E)$, the task of network embedding is to convert $\mathbb{N}$ into a d-dimensional space R^d. Learning embeddings of nodes in networks is to obtain a vector set $X^{|V|*d} \in R^d, d \ll |V|$, where $|V|$ is the number of nodes in $\mathbb{N}$, which requires $X^{|V|*d}$ can be used to reconstruct $\mathbb{N}$ with as little as possible loss of information.

3 Learning Structural Network Embeddings

3.1 Sampling Strategy

To train embeddings, the first step is to extract training samples from networks. *LDSNE* regards every edge in the original network as similar node pairs and samples disconnected nodes as dissimilar node pairs. We believe that 1-hop neighbors are sufficient to reconstruct the original network. And a node embedding can fully fuse its higher-hop neighbor embeddings after several iterations. Therefore, we adopt the following sampling strategy.

LDSNE traverses all nodes multiple times. When traversing to a node u, the algorithm first extracts a neighbor v_1^p of node u, and then extract k negative nodes $\{v_1^n, \cdots, v_k^n\}$ from the network by a negative sampling method. (u, v_1^p) is a similar node pair and $\{(u, v_1^n), \cdots, (u, v_k^n)\}$ are dissimilar node pairs. Then the algorithm starts looking for a next neighbor of node u, and repeats the above steps until all neighbors have been traversed. Then *LDSNE* traverses to the next node and repeats the above steps. The pseudocode for the sampling algorithm is given in Algorithm 1.

The basic requirement of negative sampling is that frequent nodes should be sampled first, which is conducive to the rapid stabilization of representation learning. Therefore, the probability of negative sampling to node v is:

$$p(v|V) = \frac{degree(v)}{\sum_{u \in V} degree(u)} \tag{1}$$

in which $degree()$ represents the degree of a node in the network.

Algorithm 1. Sampling algorithm of *LDSNE*

Input: Network $N = (V, E)$; Negative sampling times k
Output: Similar node pairs S; Dissimilar node pairs D

```
Initialize S, D
for u in V do
    ngb ← Get neighbors of u in N
    for v_1^p in ngb do
        {v_1^n, ···, v_k^n} ← Random sample k nodes in N
        Append (u, v_1^p) to S
        Append {(u, v_1^n), ···, (u, v_k^n)} to D
    end for
end for
return S, D
```

3.2 Simple Embedding Optimization

In the previous subsection, we have proposed a sampling method that can continuously output similar and dissimilar node pairs from networks. Next, *LDSNE* performs a simple optimization model for learning embeddings, which can shorten the distance between similar nodes and increase the distance between dissimilar nodes. Formally, given similar node pairs S and dissimilar node pairs D, we intend to optimize the following objective function, which maximizes weighted probability of similar node pairs and minimize probability of dissimilar node pairs.

$$L = min \prod_{(u^p,v^p)\in S} [1 - p(v^p|u^p)] \prod_{(u^n,v^n)\in D} p(v^n|u^n) \tag{2}$$

in which $p(v|u)$ represents the similarity probability of observing node v conditioned on node u. Here, we use a *sigmoid* unit parametrized by a dot product of embeddings as $p(v|u)$. But we have different embedding matrices in undirected and directed networks.

$$p(u|v) = \begin{cases} \sigma(X(u)X^T(v)) & \text{if } \textit{undirected network} \\ \sigma(X(u)Y^T(v)) & \text{if } \textit{directed network} \end{cases} \tag{3}$$

in which X and Y are embedding matrices that holds raw node representations and σ is the *sigmoid* function. Only one matrix is needed in undirected networks, but two matrices X and Y are needed to represent outgoing and incoming features in directed networks. And these two matrices need to be concatenated at the output stage. The pseudocode for embedding optimization is given in Algorithm 2.

3.3 Encoding Local Distances

Many node classification tasks are not determined by proximity similarities. For example, if we want to predict the social roles or social positions of individuals

Algorithm 2. Embedding optimization of *LDSNE*

Input: Similar node pairs S; Dissimilar node pairs D; Internal hidden weights θ; Embedding dimension d; Learning rate η

Output: Network embeddings $X^{|V|*d}$

Initialize embeddings $X^{|V|*d}$
for (u, v^p) **in** S **do**
  $e \leftarrow 0$
  $g \leftarrow \eta(1 - \sigma(X(u)\theta^T(v))$
  $e := e + g * \theta(u)$
  $\theta(v^p) := \theta(v^p) + g * X(u)$
  for (u, v^n) **in** N **do**
    $g \leftarrow \eta(\sigma(x(u)^T\theta(v))$
    $e := e + g * \theta(u)$
    $\theta(v^n) := \theta(v^n) + g * X(u)$
  end for
  $X(u) := X(u) + e$
end for
return X

in a social network [15], nodes need to be partitioned into equivalent classes with respect to their function in the network. Figure 2 shows that the proximal similarity between node u and node v are small because of the multiple-hop distance. But they are structurally similar because of their similar degrees and connected triangle numbers. However, simple network embeddings extract no structural information. Therefore, we propose the following method for extracting structural embeddings based on simple network embeddings.

Given simple network embeddings $X^{|V|*d}$, we extract the p-neighborhood embeddings for each node embedding. The algorithm considers more structural information as p becomes larger, but it also largely increase the complexity of computation. L2-norm is used to measure the neighborhood distance between node embeddings, and $l_2(u, v)$ is used to represent the L2-norm between node u and node v for short.

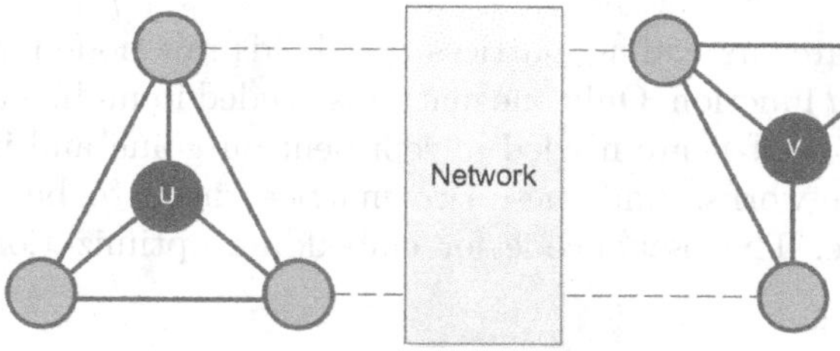

Fig. 2. An example of two nodes (u and v) that are structurally similar.

$$l_2(u, v) = \|X(u) - X(v)\|_2 = \sqrt{\sum_{i=1}^{d}(X(u)_i - X(v)_i)^2} \quad (4)$$

Figure 3 shows the node embedding $X(u_0)$ and its three neighboring embeddings. $X(u_1)$, $X(u_2)$ and $X(u_3)$ are used to represent neighbor nodes from near to far. Then, we sequentially send L2-norms between these embedding to node u_0 structural embedding $T(u_0)$, whose dimension is $F(p)$.

$$T(u_0)_i = l_2(u_x, u_y) \quad (5)$$

$$F(p) = p * (p + 1)/2 \quad (6)$$

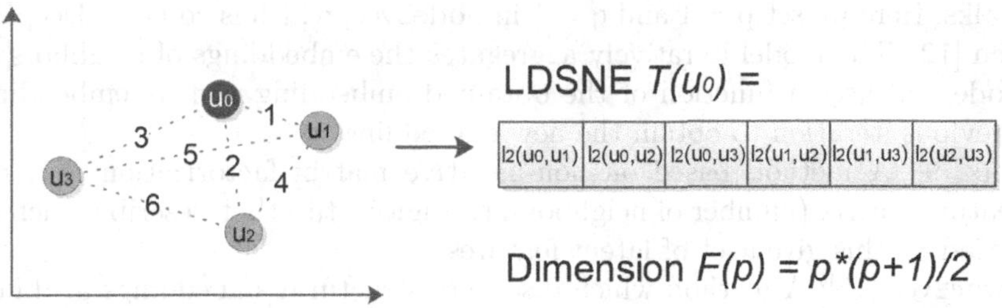

Fig. 3. Illustration of extracting structural embeddings based on simple node embeddings.

After traversing all the nodes, the whole structural embeddings $T^{|V|*F(p)}$ can be obtained. The structural embeddings can greatly preserve the structural features, and the operation such as rotating subgraphs in the embedding space will not change its structural embedding. Additionally, the structural embeddings usually have different dimension with the original simple network embeddings. Then back to node classification tasks, we solve it by inputting the learned structural embeddings to neural networks. The pseudocode for extracting structural embeddings is given in Algorithm 3.

4 Experiments

4.1 Baseline Methods

In this paper, we have the following representation learning methods for comparison.

- grarep [2]: This method integrates global structural information of the graph into embeddings.

Algorithm 3. Encoding Local Distances of *LDSNE*

Input: Network embeddings $X^{|V|*d}$; Neighbor size p
Output: Structural embeddings $T^{|V|*F(p)}$
Initialize T
for X_u to X **do**
$X_1, ..., X_p \leftarrow$ get p neighbor embeddings
$T(u) \leftarrow$ extract structure from $X_u, X_1, ..., X_p$ according to (4) (5) (??) (??) (6)
Append $T(u)$ to T
end for
return $T^{|V|*F(p)}$

- node2vec [8]: This approach learns feature representations by biased random walks. Here we set p = 1 and q = 1 in node2vec, which is equal to DeepWalk.
- gcn [12]: The model iteratively aggregates the embeddings of neighbors for a node and uses a function of the obtained embedding and its embedding at previous iteration to obtain the new embedding.
- roix [9]: A method based on non-negative matrix factorization of a node-feature matrix (number of neighbors, triangles, etc.) that describes each node based on this given set of latent features.
- struc2vec [15]: A method which discovers structural embeddings at different scales through a sequence of walks on a multilayered graph.
- GraphWave [4]: A method that represents each node's network neighborhood via a low-dimensional embedding by leveraging heat wavelet diffusion patterns.

4.2 Case Study: Barbell Network

Barbell network [4] is a synthetic network consisting of two dense cliques connected by a long chain as illustrated in Fig. 4(a). This network has 30 nodes and 101 edges. Because its significant number of nodes with the same structural identities, barbell network is always used to view the effects of structural network embeddings [4,15]. We believe that nodes with same colors in Fig. 4(a) have same structural identities.

Figure 4(b–e) show 2-dimensional PCA representations learned by grarep, node2vec, gcn and sne. We observed that all these methods can extract proximate features from the original network and grarep performs best. Figure 4(f–j) shows 2-dimensional PCA representations learned by struc2vec, graphWave and LDSNE. We observed that nodes with all these methods can extract structural features and LDSNE with higher p achieve best performance.

Next, we tested the need for embedding matrices for both directed and undirected networks. Figure 5 shows the loss curves on one embedding matrix and two embedding matrix respectively. We observed that one embedding matrix has a faster fitting speed in the undirected barbell network. But one

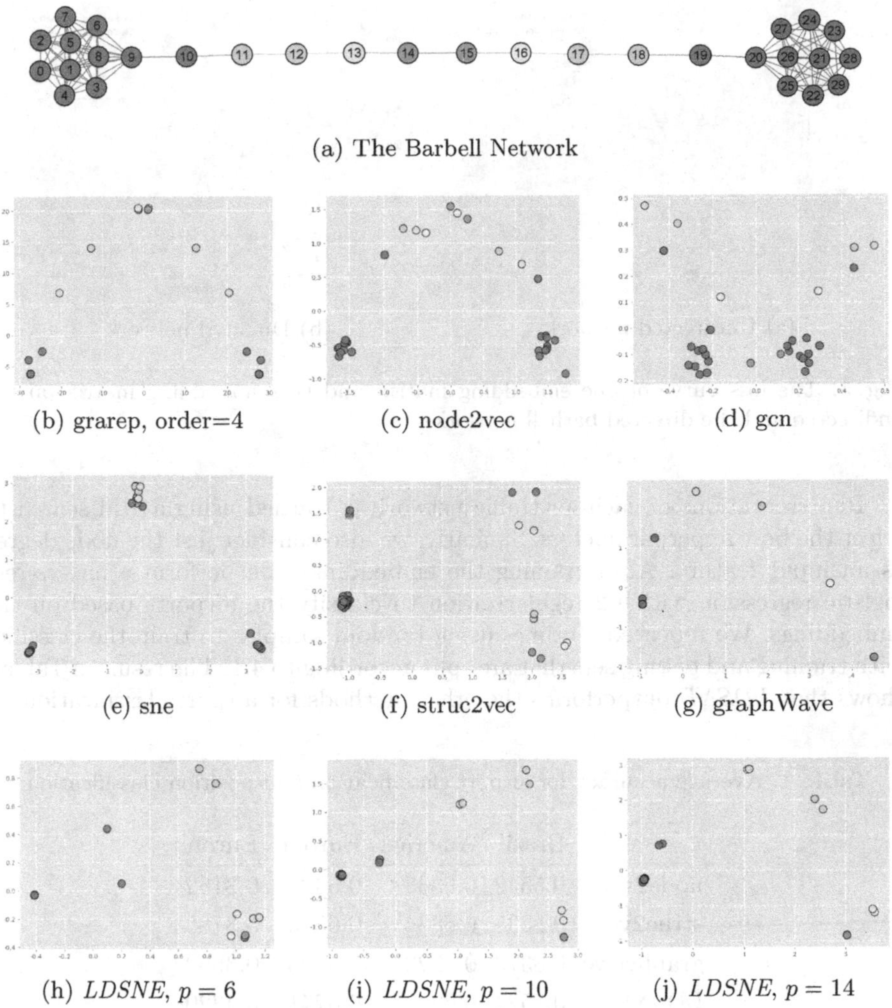

(a) The Barbell Network

(b) grarep, order=4 (c) node2vec (d) gcn

(e) sne (f) struc2vec (g) graphWave

(h) *LDSNE*, $p = 6$ (i) *LDSNE*, $p = 10$ (j) *LDSNE*, $p = 14$

Fig. 4. 2-dimensional network embeddings of the barbell network

embedding matrix cannot fit on the directed network, which indicated that directed networks need two matrices to represent the outgoing and incoming features.

4.3 Airport Classification in Air-Traffic Networks

To test the node classification performance of LDSNE, we perform it on airport classification tasks. Air-traffic networks [15] are Brazilian, American and European networks that nodes correspond to airports and edges indicate the existence of commercial flights. The label of each airport is assigned corresponding to their level of activity, therefore, classes are related more to the role played by the airport.

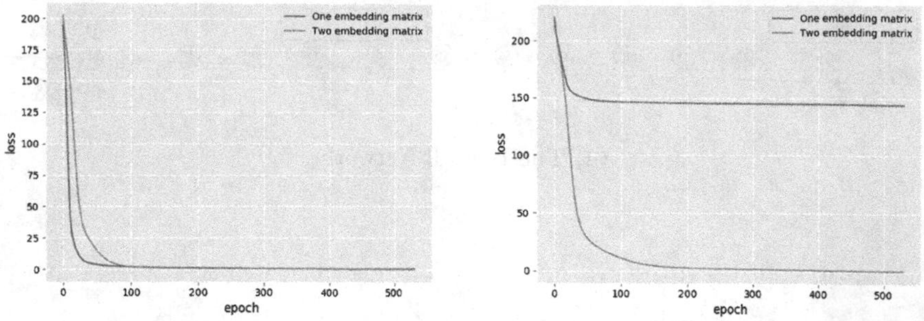

(a) Undirected network (b) Directed network

Fig. 5. The loss curve of one embedding matrix and two embedding matrix on the undirected and the directed barbell network.

Representations of each air-traffic network is learned using a grid search to select the best hyperparameters. Similarly, we also consider just the node degree as an input feature. After training the embeddings, we perform a one-vs-rest logistic regression with L2 regularization to classify the airports based on the embeddings. We repeated 10 times using random samples to train the classifier with training and testing sets that are split according to 4:1. The result in Table 1 shows that *LDSNE* outperforms the other methods for airport classification.

Table 1. Average accuracy for airport classification and position classification.

	Brazil	America	Europe	Enron
node2vec	0.5542	0.6335	0.5424	0.3152
struc2vec	0.8235	0.6834	0.6533	0.3785
graphwave	0.8319	0.6823	0.6623	0.3952
LDSNE	0.8524	0.6947	0.6741	0.4320

4.4 Position Classification in an Email Communication Network

Next we test our algorithm on a ground-truth label dataset - Enron email communication network, which consists of all the email communication in Enron company. Nodes in the network represent Enron employees and edges correspond to email communication between the employees. The node classification task is to predict the positions in Enron including CEO, president, vice president, director, manager, trader and employee.

After removing some people without jobs, there are 130 people left in training and testing set. However, some "top" job titles have very few people, such as CEO, it is necessary to manually assign these people to the training and testing set. Similarly, we choose the same classifier and testing method for airport classification. We show the classification accuracy performance in Table 1. *LDSNE* achieves average improvements of 9.3% to the best baseline method.

5 Conclusion

In this paper, we proposed *LDSNE*, a novel network embedding method of learning structural representations in networks. The structural representation is a concept of symmetry in networks which nodes are identified based on the network structure. We first proposed simple network embedding method to ensures that networks embeddings learned from adjacency lists or matrices can reconstruct the original adjacency lists or matrices with as little as possible loss of information. Next, we proposed a structural feature extraction model to encode local distances. Empirical results demonstrate that *LDSNE* achieved structural embeddings and significantly better performance than state-of-the-art methods.

References

1. Cai, H., Zheng, V.W., Chang, K.C.C.: A comprehensive survey of graph embedding: problems, techniques, and applications. IEEE Trans. Knowl. Data Eng. **30**(9), 1616–1637 (2018). https://doi.org/10.1109/tkde.2018.2807452
2. Cao, S., Lu, W., Xu, Q.: GraRep: learning graph representations with global structural information. In: Proceedings of the 24th ACM International on Conference on Information and Knowledge Management - CIKM 2015. ACM Press (2015). https://doi.org/10.1145/2806416.2806512
3. Cui, P., Wang, X., Pei, J., Zhu, W.: A survey on network embedding. IEEE Trans. Knowl. Data Eng. **31**(5), 833–852 (2018)
4. Donnat, C., Zitnik, M., Hallac, D., Leskovec, J.: Learning structural node embeddings via diffusion wavelets. In: Proceedings of the 24th ACM SIGKDD International Conference on Knowledge Discovery and Data Mining - KDD 2018, pp. 1320–1329. ACM Press, July 2018. https://doi.org/10.1145/3219819.3220025
5. Emmons, S., Kobourov, S., Gallant, M., Börner, K.: Analysis of network clustering algorithms and cluster quality metrics at scale. PLoS One **11**(7), e0159161 (2016). https://doi.org/10.1371/journal.pone.0159161
6. Gao, X., Chen, J., Huai, N.: Meta-circuit machine: inferencing human collaborative relationships in heterogeneous information networks. Inf. Process. Manage. **56**(3), 844–857 (2019). https://doi.org/10.1016/j.ipm.2019.01.002
7. Goyal, P., Ferrara, E.: Graph embedding techniques, applications, and performance: a survey. Knowl.-Based Syst. **151**, 78–94 (2018). https://doi.org/10.1016/j.knosys.2018.03.022
8. Grover, A., Leskovec, J.: node2vec: Scalable feature learning for networks. In: Proceedings of the 22nd ACM SIGKDD International Conference on Knowledge Discovery and Data Mining, KDD 2016, pp. 855–864. ACM (2016). https://doi.org/10.1145/2939672.2939754
9. Henderson, K., et al.: RolX structural role extraction and mining in large graphs. In: Proceedings of the 18th ACM SIGKDD International Conference on Knowledge Discovery and Data Mining - KDD 2012. ACM Press (2012). https://doi.org/10.1145/2339530.2339723

10. Ji, M., Han, J., Danilevsky, M.: Ranking-based classification of heterogeneous information networks. In: Proceedings of the 17th ACM SIGKDD International Conference on Knowledge Discovery and Data Mining, KDD 2011, pp. 1298–1306. ACM, New York (2011). https://doi.org/10.1145/2020408.2020603
11. Jian, L., Li, J., Liu, H.: Toward online node classification on streaming networks. Data Min. Knowl. Disc. **32**(1), 231–257 (2017). https://doi.org/10.1007/s10618-017-0533-y
12. Kipf, T.N., Welling, M.: Semi-supervised classification with graph convolutional networks. arXiv preprint arXiv:1609.02907 (2016)
13. Ou, M., Cui, P., Pei, J., Zhang, Z., Zhu, W.: Asymmetric transitivity preserving graph embedding. In: Proceedings of the 22nd ACM SIGKDD International Conference on Knowledge Discovery and Data Mining - KDD 2016. ACM Press (2016). https://doi.org/10.1145/2939672.2939751
14. Perozzi, B., Al-Rfou, R., Skiena, S.: DeepWalk: online learning of social representations. In: Proceedings of the 20th ACM SIGKDD International Conference on Knowledge Discovery and Data Mining - KDD 2014, pp. 701–710. ACM Press (2014). https://doi.org/10.1145/2623330.2623732
15. Ribeiro, L.F.R., Saverese, P.H.P., Figueiredo, D.R.: struc2vec: Learning node representations from structural identity. In: Proceedings of the 23rd ACM SIGKDD International Conference on Knowledge Discovery and Data Mining - KDD 2017 (2017)
16. Roweis, S.T.: Nonlinear dimensionality reduction by locally linear embedding. Science **290**(5500), 2323–2326 (2000). https://doi.org/10.1126/science.290.5500.2323
17. Zhou, Y., Liu, L.: Social influence based clustering and optimization over heterogeneous information networks. ACM Trans. Knowl. Discov. Data **10**(1), 1–53 (2015). https://doi.org/10.1145/2717314

FurcaNeXt: End-to-End Monaural Speech Separation with Dynamic Gated Dilated Temporal Convolutional Networks

Liwen Zhang[1(✉)], Ziqiang Shi[2], Jiqing Han[1], Anyan Shi[3], and Ding Ma[1]

[1] School of Computer Science and Technology, Harbin Institute of Technology, Harbin 150001, China
{15B903062,jqhan,madingcs}@hit.edu.cn

[2] Fujitsu Research and Development Center, Beijing 100027, China
shiziqiang@cn.fujitsu.com

[3] Shuangfeng First, Beijing, China
shi.anyan@protonmail.com

Abstract. Deep dilated temporal convolutional networks (TCN) have been proved to be very effective in sequence modeling. In this paper we propose several improvements of TCN for end-to-end approach to monaural speech separation, which consists of (1) multi-scale dynamic weighted gated TCN with a pyramidal structure (FurcaPy), (2) gated TCN with intra-parallel convolutional components (FurcaPa), (3) weight-shared multi-scale gated TCN (FurcaSh) and (4) dilated TCN with gated subtractive-convolutional component (FurcaSu). All these networks take the mixed utterance of two speakers and maps it to two separated utterances, where each utterance contains only one speaker's voice. For the objective, we propose to train the networks by directly optimizing utterance-level signal-to-distortion ratio (SDR) in a permutation invariant training (PIT) style. Our experiments on the public WSJ0-2mix data corpus result in 18.4 dB SDR improvement, which shows our proposed networks can lead to performance improvement on the speaker separation task.

Keywords: Speech separation · Cocktail party problem · Sequence modeling · Temporal convolutional networks · Permutation invariant training

1 Introduction

Multi-talker monaural speech separation has a vast range of applications in speech or speaker recognition tasks. However, there are two difficulties in this speech separation problem, the first is that the prior information of the target speaker is unknown, and a truly practical system must be speaker-independent; the second is that the beamforming algorithm cannot be used for a single microphone signal. Many traditional methods, such as computational auditory scene

Y. M. Ro et al. (Eds.): MMM 2020, LNCS 11961, pp. 653–665, 2020.
https://doi.org/10.1007/978-3-030-37731-1_53

analysis (CASA) [10,20,30], non-negative matrix factorization (NMF) [13,23], and probabilistic models [29], do not solve these two difficulties well.

Recently, lots of deep learning based methods have been proposed for this task. These methods can be roughly divided into three categories. The first category is based on deep clustering (DPCL) [8,11], which maps the time-frequency (TF) features into embedding vectors, then these vectors are clustered into several classes corresponding to different speakers, and finally the cluster centroids of these classes are used as masks to inversely transform the TF features to the separated clean voices; the second category is the permutation invariant training (PIT) [12,35], which solves the label permutation problem by minimizing the lowest error output among all possible permutations for N mixing sources assignment; the third category is the end-to-end speech separation in time-domain [17,18,27], which is a natural way to surpass the upper bound of source-to-distortion ratio improvement (SDRi) in short-time Fourier transform (STFT) mask estimation based methods, such that real-time processing requirements can be satisfied.

This paper is based on the end-to-end method [17,18,27], which has achieved better results than DPCL or PIT based approaches. For most DPCL and PIT based methods, the STFT is used as the front-end, the mixed speech signal is first transformed from one-dimensional signal in time-domain to two-dimensional spectrum signal in TF-domain, and then the mixed spectrum is separated to result in spectrums corresponding to different source speeches by a deep clustering or mask estimation method, and finally the cleaned source speech signal can be restored by an inverse STFT on each spectrum. However, such framework has several limitations. Firstly, it is unclear whether the STFT is the optimal (even assume the parameters the STFT depends on are optimal, such as frame size, window type, etc.) transformation of the signal for speech separation. Secondly, most STFT based methods usually assume that the phase of the separated signal is equal to the mixture phase, which is generally incorrect and can impose an obvious upper bound on separation performance by using the ideal masks. To solve these problems, several speech separation models that operate directly on time-domain speech signals [17,18,27] were proposed.

Inspired by these first results, we propose FurcaNeXt, which is a general name for a series of fully end-to-end time-domain separation methods that includes: (1) multi-scale dynamic weighted gated temporal convolutional networks (TCN) with a pyramidal structure (FurcaPy): due to the influence of different word lengths and speech speeds, multiple TCN branches with different temporal receptive field scales are introduced, and the weights of these branches are automatically determined by a "weightor" network; (2) deep gated dilated temporal convolutional networks (TCN) with intra-parallel convolutional components (FurcaPa): to reduce the variance of this model, two convolutional related modules in each dilated convolutional module are replaced by two intra-parallel convolutional modules which replicate the weight matrices; (3) weight-shared multi-scale gated TCN (FurcaSh): a simple design is proposed to achieve the functions of FurcaPy but without increasing the number of network parameters; (4) dilated

TCN with gated subtractive-convolutional component (FurcaSu): inspired by the work of highway network [24], in which two additional non-linear transformations act as gates that can dynamically pay attention to some part of the input and suppress the other part, in addition, based on the work in [34], two identical transformation function branches were proposed to simplify the highway network module.

2 Speech Separation with TCN

Monaural speech separation aims to estimate the individual target signals from a linearly mixed single-microphone signal, in which the target signals overlap in the TF-domain. Let $x_i(t), i = 1, .., S$ and $y(t)$ denote the S target speech signals and the mixed speech signal, respectively. The mixed signal can be defined as

$$y(t) = \sum_{i=1}^{S} x_i(t), \tag{1}$$

then, the goal of monaural speech separation is estimating each individual target speech signal, $x_i(t)$, from the given mixed speech signal, $y(t)$. In this work it is assumed that the number of target signals is known.

To deal with this ill-posed problem, Luo et al. [18] introduced TCN [2,14] which was proposed as an alternative to recurrent neural networks (RNN) for speech separation task. As shown in Fig. 1, each layer in the TCN contains a 1-D convolution block with an increasing dilation factor, d, which is increased exponentially. Dilated convolution has made a huge success in WaveNet [26] for audio generation, and when the dilation factor grows exponentially, a very large temporal receptive field can be provided for the network by stacking only a few dilated convolutional layers. The large temporal receptive field allows the network to capture the long range temporal dependence of different resolutions within the input sequences. The stacked structure introduces a time hierarchy: the upper layer can access longer input subsequences and learn representations on larger time scales. In addition, with the adoption of residuals and skip connections, local information from the lower layers can be spreaded through the hierarchy.

There are two important elements in the original TCN [2], one is the dilated convolutions, and the other is residual connections. Dilated convolutions follow the work of [26], it is defined as

$$(x *_d k)(p) = \sum_{s+dt=p} x(s)k(t), \tag{2}$$

where x is the 1-D input signal, k is the filter(aka kernel), and d is the dilation factor. Therefore, dilation is equivalent to introducing a fixed step size between every two adjacent filter taps, and the receptive field of the TCN can be increased by increasing the dilation factor, d. In this work, we increase d exponentially (the exponent value is 2) with the depth of the network. As shown in Fig. 1, the TCN has four layers of 1-D Conv modules with dilation factors of 1, 2, 4, 8, respectively. Each 1-D Conv module is a residual block [7], which contains one layer of dilated convolution (Depth-wise conv [9]), two layers of 1×1 convolutions (1×1 Conv), two non-linearity activation layers (Parametric Rectified Linear Unit, PReLU [6]), and two global normalization layers [18] (Normalization).

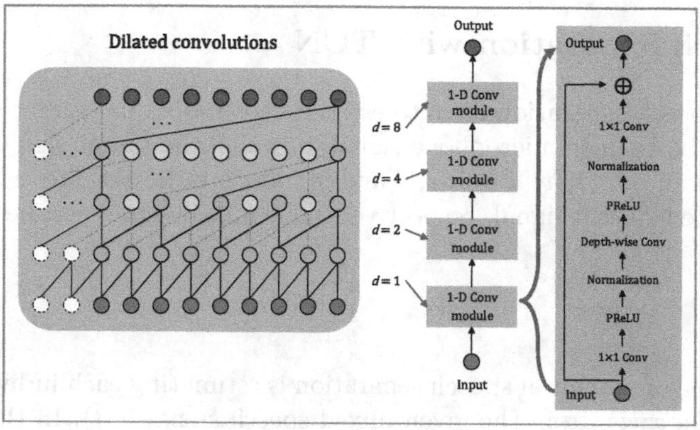

Fig. 1. The structure of TCN.

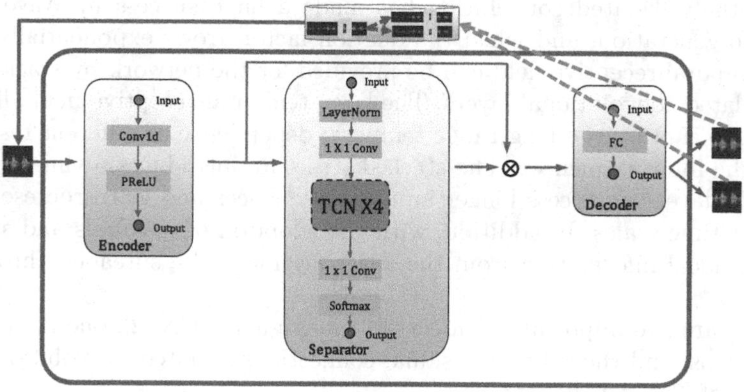

Fig. 2. The pipeline of TCN based speech separation in [18].

The TCN-based speech separation method in [18] consists of three processing stages, as shown in Fig. 2: encoder (Conv1d is followed by a PReLU activation), separator (consisted in the order by a LayerNorm, a 1×1 conv, 4 TCN layers, 1×1 conv, and a softmax operation) and decoder (a FC layer). First, the encoder module is used to convert short segments of the mixed waveform into their corresponding representations. Then, each representation is presented to the separator module to estimate the multiplication function (mask) of the corresponding source and encoder output for each time step. Finally, a linear decoder module is used to reconstruct the source waveform by transforming the masked encoder features.

3 Speech Separation with FurcaNeXt

Nonlinear gated activation had been successfully used on sequence modeling [4,26], it can control the flow of information and may help the network to model more complex interactions. In this regard, we introduce the gating operations into the original TCN. As illustrated in Fig. 3, two gates are added to each 1-D convolutional module in the plain TCN, one is corresponding to the first 1×1 convolutional layer in the 1-D convolutional module, the other is corresponding to all the layers from the depth-wise convolutional layer to the output 1×1 convolutional layer. Based on this gated TCN, a speech separation pipeline called FurcaPorta is presented in this work. Additionally, we also make several improvements to our gated TCN and speech separation framework: FurcaPorta.

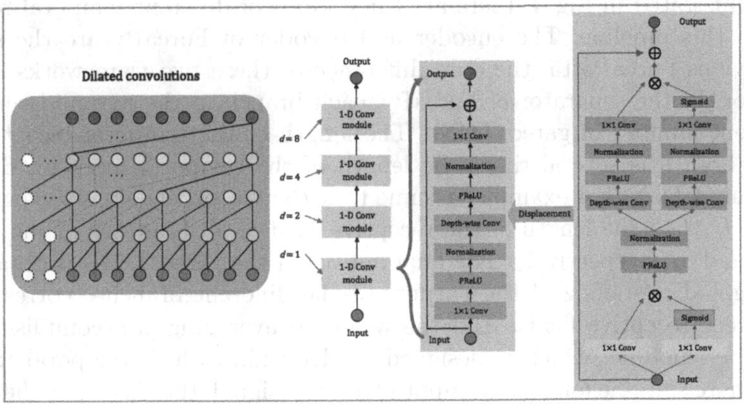

Fig. 3. The structure of gated TCN.

3.1 FurcaPy: Multi-scale Dynamic Weighted Gated TCN with a Pyramidal structure

Since the word lengths and pronunciation characteristics (e.g. speed) of various speakers are different, the utterances always have the feature of temporal scale variation. Speech separation may be benefit from considering multiple temporal receptive fields. As shown in Fig. 1, the temporal receptive field of the TCN is fixed. In order to handle the temporal scale variation problem, a multi-scale dynamic weighted gated TCN with a pyramidal structure is proposed for the speech separation pipeline, which is called FurcaPy.

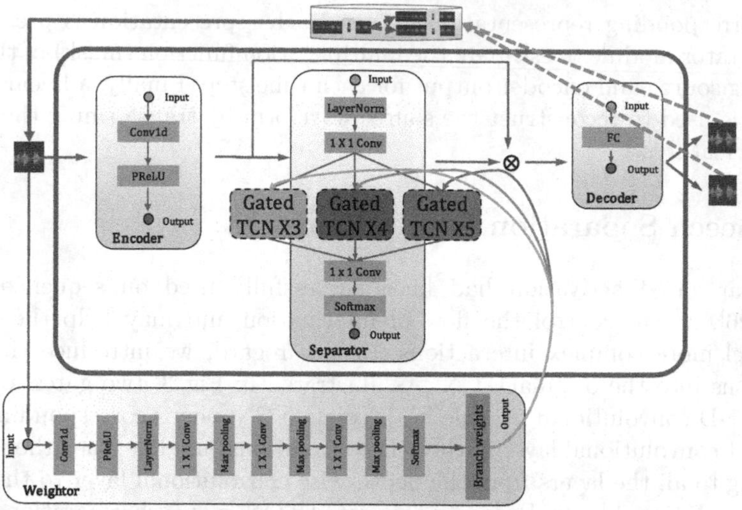

Fig. 4. The pipeline of FurcaPy speech separation.

As illustrated in Fig. 4, there are three kinds of different temporal receptive fields in this pipeline. The encoder and decoder of FurcaPy are the same as the previous FurcaPorta, the only difference of these two frameworks is in the separator. In the separator of FurcaPy, each branch in the pyramid consists of a different number of gated TCNs. The length of the temporal receptive field of each branch is several times the length of the temporal receptive field of a single gated TCN. For example, assume that the receptive field of a single gated TCN is L, then the length of the receptive field of all branches in the Fig. 4 is $3L$,$4L$, and $5L$, respectively. The final output of the gated TCNs is obtained by the weighted averaging of the outputs of the different branches corresponding to different receptive fields. And the weighted averaging is accomplished by a "weightor" module, which is designed to determine which temporal receptive field is more suitable for current input utterance signal, that is to say, the weights of different gated TCNs are determined dynamically by a "weightor" network for each utterance. The "weightor" is composed of a common multi-layer 1-D convolutional neural network as shown in Fig. 4 and it mainly consists of one layer of Conv1d, PReLU and LayerNormal, 3 layers of 1×1 Conv and max pooling, and a final Softmax layer.

3.2 FurcaSh: Weight-Shared Multi-scale Gated TCN

Since multiple branches of gated TCNs and a "weightor" module are adopted, FurcaPy will increase the number of parameters of the network several times, and the processing speed of the network will decrease a lot. Compared with FurcaPorta, FurcaPy is much more time consuming, and in many cases, there is no way to meet the requirements of real-time processing for such network. To deal with these problems, we propose a new network structure that can achieve multi-scale receptive fields of two levels without increasing the number of network parameters. As shown in Fig. 5, the first level of multi-scale temporal receptive fields is the dilated 1-D conv module level, where the outputs corresponding to different dilated factors are summed and averaged to result in the final output of this gated TCN; the second level is in the stacked gated TCNs, where the outputs of four gated TCNs are summed and averaged to result in the separator. In each level, the weights of different temporal receptive fields are <u>sh</u>ared, we call this new structure FurcaSh.

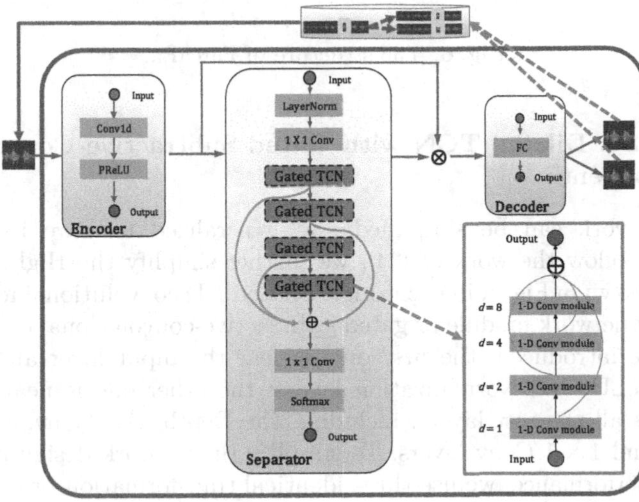

Fig. 5. The pipeline of FurcaSh speech separation.

3.3 FurcaPa: Gated TCN with Intra-parallel Convolutional Components

The performance of a single predictive model can always be improved by ensemble, that is to combine a set of independently trained networks. The most commonly used method is to do the average of the outputs of the trained models, which can at least help to reduce the variance of the performance. As shown in Fig. 6, in the different layers of each 1-D convolutional module of the gated TCN in FurcaPorta, two identical <u>pa</u>rallel branches are added. We call this structure FurcaPa. In each single dilated 1-D convolutional module layer, two intra-parallel convolutional components are introduced, the first one is near the input layer and covers the Conv1d, PReLU, and Normalization layers; the other one is near the output and it covers all the rest layers, including the Depthwise conv, PReLu, Normalization and 1×1 Conv layers. The reason why we do this ensemble in two places is to reduce the sub-variances of each block. Then, the final output of each intra-parallel convolutional components is obtained by averaging the outputs of all the parallel branches.

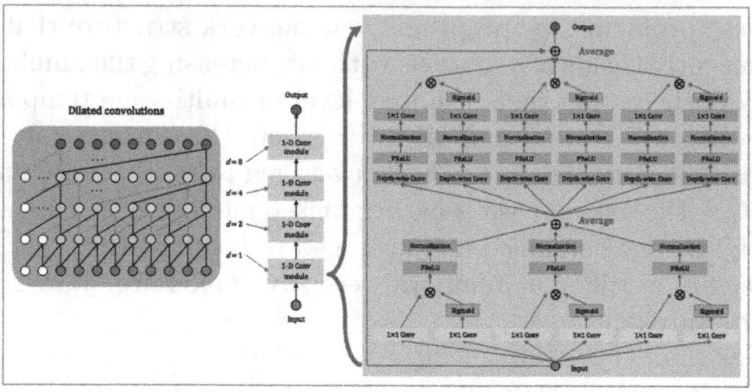

Fig. 6. The structure of FurcaPa.

3.4 FurcaSu: Dilated TCN with Gated Subtractive-Convolutional Component

Highway network can be simplified and generalized to have better performance [34]. Follow the work of [34], we further simplify the Highway network module, as shown in Fig. 7, in each single dilated 1-D convolutional module layer, two Highway network module or gated subtractive-convolutional components as we called are introduced, the first one is near the input layer and covers the Conv1d, PReLU, and Normalization layers; the other one is near the output and it covers all the rest layers, including the Depth-wise Conv, PReLu, Normalization and 1 × 1 Conv layers. To simplify the network design and improve the system performance, we use three identical transformation branches instead of three different transformation functions from the original Highway network module. As illustrated in Fig. 7, the transformation branch in the right side is regarded as the attention gate, and the other two branches are signal transformations, and their outputs are subtracted and then gated.

3.5 Perceptual Metric: Utterance-Level SDR Objective

Since the loss function of many STFT-based methods is not directly applicable to waveform-based end-to-end speech separation, perceptual metric based loss function is tried in this work. The perception of speech is greatly affected by distortion [1,33]. Generally in order to evaluate the performance of speech separation, the BSS_Eval metrics that includes signal-to-distortion ratio (SDR), signal-to-Interference ratio (SIR), signal-to-artifact ratio (SAR) [5,28], and short-time objective intelligibility (STOI) [25] have been often employed. In this work we directly use SDR, which is one of the most commonly used metrics to evaluate the performance of source separation, as the training objective. SDR measures the amount of distortion introduced by the output signal and is defined as the ratio between the energy of the clean signal and the energy of the distortion.

SDR captures the overall separation quality of the algorithm. There is a subtle problem here. In this work, our main concern is the quality of the whole

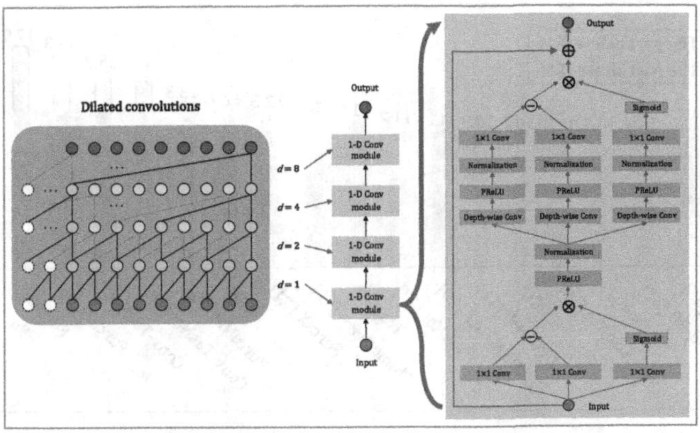

Fig. 7. The structure of FurcaSu.

separated utterance. Therefore, we first concatenate the outputs of FurcaNeXt into a complete utterance and then compare it with the input full utterance to calculate the SDR in the utterance-level instead of calculating the SDR for one frame at a time. In specific, if the output of the network is denoted as s, which should ideally be equal to the target source, x, then SDR can be given as [5,28]

$$\tilde{x} = \frac{\langle x, s \rangle}{\langle x, x \rangle} x, \tag{3}$$

$$e = \tilde{x} - s, \tag{4}$$

$$\mathrm{SDR} = 10 * \log_{10} \frac{\langle \tilde{x}, \tilde{x} \rangle}{\langle e, e \rangle}, \tag{5}$$

where the distortion, e, is defined as the difference between the normalized target source, $\tilde{x}$, and the network output, s. Then our target is to maximize SDR or minimize the negative SDR as loss function respect to the s.

In order to solve tracing and permutation problem, the PIT training criteria [12,35] is employed in this work. We calculate the SDRs for all the permutations of the target sources and network output, pick the maximum one, and take the negative as the loss. It is called the uSDR loss in this work.

4 Experiments

4.1 Dataset and Neural Network

We evaluated our system on two-speaker speech separation problem using WSJ0-2mix dataset [8,11], which contains 30 h of training and 10 h of validation data. The mixtures are generated by randomly selecting 49 male and 51 female speakers and utterances in Wall Street Journal (WSJ0) training set si_tr_s, and mixing them at various signal-to-noise ratios (SNR) uniformly between 0 dB and 5 dB.

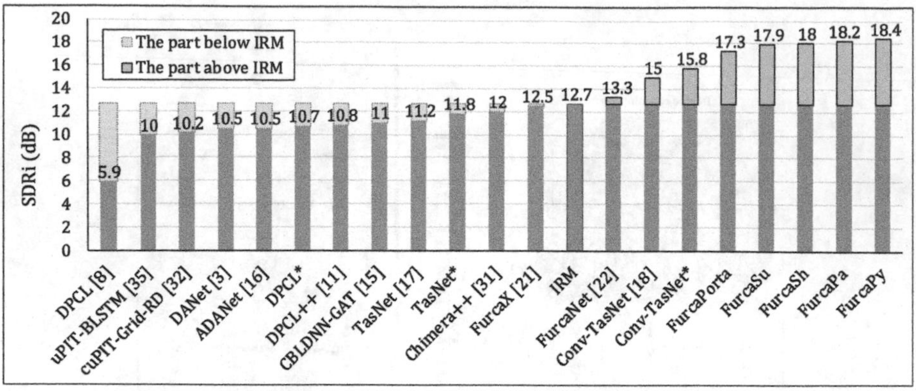

Fig. 8. SDRi (dB) in a comparative study of different separation methods on the WSJ0-2mix dataset. * indicates our reimplementation of the corresponding method.

5 h of evaluation set is generated in the same way, using utterances from 16 unseen speakers from si_dt_05 and si_et_05 in the WSJ0 dataset.

We evaluate the systems with the SDR improvement (SDRi) [5,28] metric, which was used in [3,11,12,16,32]. The original SDR is defined as the average SDR of mixed speech, $y(t)$, for the original target speech, $x_1(t)$ and $x_2(t)$, is 0.15. Figure 8 demonstrates the average SDRi obtained by the different structures in FurcaNeXt and almost all the results in the past two years, where IRM denotes the ideal ratio mask that is applied to the STFT, $Y(t, f)$, of the mixed speech signal, $y(t)$, to obtain the separated speech. IRM is evaluated to show the upper bound of STFT-based methods, which is given as

$$M_s = \frac{|X_s(t,f)|}{\sum_{s=1}^{S} |X_s(t,f)|}, \tag{6}$$

where $X_s(t, f)$ is the STFT of $x_s(t)$.

Furthermore, as baselines, we reimplemented several classical approaches, such as DPCL [8], TasNet [17] and Conv-TasNet [18]. Compared with these baselines an average increase of nearly 2.6 dB SDRi is obtained. Among those different structures in FurcaNeXt, FurcaPy has achieved the most significant performance improvement compared with baseline systems, and it break through the upper bound of STFT based methods a lot (nearly 6 dB).

5 Conclusion

In this paper we investigated the effectiveness of deep dilated temporal convolutional networks for multi-talker monaural speech separation. We propose a series structures under the name of FurcaNeXt to speech separation. Benefits from the strength of end-to-end processing, the novel gating mechanism and dynamic weighted module, the best performance of structure in FurcaNeXt achieve 18.4 dB SDRi on the public WSJ0-2mix data corpus, results in 16% relative improvement. Although SDR is widely used and can be regarded as an effective metric for speech separation, it still has some limitations [19]. Hence, in our future work, maybe SNR can be used to evaluate our models. It would be interesting to see how consistent the SDR and SNR are.

Acknowledgment. We would like to thank Jian Wu, Yi Luo, and Zhong-Qiu Wang at for valuable discussions on WSJ0-2mix database, DPCL, and end-to-end speech separation.

References

1. Assmann, P., Summerfield, Q.: The perception of speech under adverse conditions. In: Speech Processing in the Auditory System, pp. 231–308. Springer, New York (2004). https://doi.org/10.1007/0-387-21575-1_5
2. Bai, S., Kolter, J.Z., Koltun, V.: An empirical evaluation of generic convolutional and recurrent networks for sequence modeling. arXiv preprint arXiv:1803.01271 (2018)
3. Chen, Z., Luo, Y., Mesgarani, N.: Deep attractor network for single-microphone speaker separation. In: 2017 IEEE International Conference on Acoustics, Speech and Signal Processing (ICASSP), pp. 246–250. IEEE (2017)
4. Dauphin, Y.N., Fan, A., Auli, M., Grangier, D.: Language modeling with gated convolutional networks. In: International Conference on Machine Learning, pp. 933–941 (2016)
5. Févotte, C., Gribonval, R., Vincent, E.: Bss_eval toolbox user guide-revision 2.0 (2005)
6. He, K., Zhang, X., Ren, S., Sun, J.: Delving deep into rectifiers: surpassing human-level performance on imagenet classification. In: Proceedings of the IEEE International Conference on Computer Vision, pp. 1026–1034 (2015)
7. He, K., Zhang, X., Ren, S., Sun, J.: Deep residual learning for image recognition. In: Proceedings of the IEEE Conference on Computer Vision and Pattern Recognition, pp. 770–778 (2016)
8. Hershey, J.R., Chen, Z., Le Roux, J., Watanabe, S.: Deep clustering: discriminative embeddings for segmentation and separation. In: 2016 IEEE International Conference on Acoustics, Speech and Signal Processing (ICASSP), pp. 31–35. IEEE (2016)
9. Howard, A.G., et al.: Mobilenets: Efficient convolutional neural networks for mobile vision applications. arXiv preprint arXiv:1704.04861 (2017)
10. Hu, K., Wang, D.: An unsupervised approach to cochannel speech separation. IEEE Trans. Audio, Speech, Language Processing **21**(1), 122–131 (2013)
11. Isik, Y., Roux, J.L., Chen, Z., Watanabe, S., Hershey, J.R.: Single-channel multi-speaker separation using deep clustering. arXiv preprint arXiv:1607.02173 (2016)
12. Kolbæk, M., et al.: Multitalker speech separation with utterance-level permutation invariant training of deep recurrent neural networks. IEEE/ACM Trans. Audio Speech Lang. Process. (TASLP) **25**(10), 1901–1913 (2017)
13. Le Roux, J., Weninger, F.J., Hershey, J.R.: Sparse nmf half-baked or well done? Mitsubishi Electric Research Labs (MERL), Cambridge, MA, USA, Technical Report, no. TR2015-023 (2015)

14. Lea, C., Vidal, R., Reiter, A., Hager, G.D.: Temporal convolutional networks: a unified approach to action segmentation. In: Hua, G., Jégou, H. (eds.) ECCV 2016. LNCS, vol. 9915, pp. 47–54. Springer, Cham (2016). https://doi.org/10.1007/978-3-319-49409-8_7
15. Li, C., Zhu, L., Xu, S., Gao, P., Xu, B.: CBLDNN-based speaker-independent speech separation via generative adversarial training (2018)
16. Luo, Y., Chen, Z., Mesgarani, N.: Speaker-independent speech separation with deep attractor network. IEEE/ACM Trans. Audio Speech Lang. Process. **26**(4), 787–796 (2018)
17. Luo, Y., Mesgarani, N.: Tasnet: time-domain audio separation network for real-time, single-channel speech separation. arXiv preprint arXiv:1711.00541 (2017)
18. Luo, Y., Mesgarani, N.: Tasnet: Surpassing ideal time-frequency masking for speech separation. arXiv preprint arXiv:1809.07454 (2018)
19. Roux, J.L., Wisdom, S., Erdogan, H., Hershey, J.R.: SDR-half-baked or well done? arXiv preprint arXiv:1811.02508 (2018)
20. Shao, Y., Wang, D.: Model-based sequential organization in cochannel speech. IEEE Trans. Audio Speech Lang. Process. **14**(1), 289–298 (2006)
21. Shi, Z., Lin, H., Liu, L., Liu, R., Hayakawa, S., Han, J.: Furcax: end-to-end monaural speech separation based on deep gated (de)convolutional neural networks with adversarial example training. In: Proceedings of the ICASSP (2019)
22. Shi, Z., et al.: Furcanet: An end-to-end deep gated convolutional, long short-term memory, deep neural networks for single channel speech separation. arXiv preprint arXiv:1902.00651 (2019)
23. Smaragdis, P., et al.: Convolutive speech bases and their application to supervised speech separation. IEEE Trans. Audio Speech Lang. Process. **15**(1), 1 (2007)
24. Srivastava, R.K., Greff, K., Schmidhuber, J.: Highway networks. arXiv preprint arXiv:1505.00387 (2015)
25. Taal, C.H., Hendriks, R.C., Heusdens, R., Jensen, J.: A short-time objective intelligibility measure for time-frequency weighted noisy speech. In: 2010 IEEE International Conference on Acoustics Speech and Signal Processing (ICASSP), pp. 4214–4217. IEEE (2010)
26. Van Den Oord, A., et al.: Wavenet: a generative model for raw audio. CoRR abs/1609.03499 (2016)
27. Venkataramani, S., Casebeer, J., Smaragdis, P.: Adaptive front-ends for end-to-end source separation. In: Proceedings of the NIPS (2017)
28. Vincent, E., Gribonval, R., Févotte, C.: Performance measurement in blind audio source separation. IEEE Trans. Audio Speech Lang. Process. **14**(4), 1462–1469 (2006)
29. Virtanen, T.: Speech recognition using factorial hidden markov models for separation in the feature space. In: Ninth International Conference on Spoken Language Processing (2006)
30. Wang, D., Brown, G.J.: Computational Auditory Scene Analysis: Principles, Algorithms, and Applications. Wiley-IEEE Press, New York (2006)
31. Wang, Z.Q., Le Roux, J., Hershey, J.R.: Alternative objective functions for deep clustering. In: Proceedings of the IEEE International Conference on Acoustics, Speech and Signal Processing (ICASSP) (2018)
32. Xu, C., et al.: Single channel speech separation with constrained utterance level permutation invariant training using grid LSTM (2018)

33. Yang, W., Benbouchta, M., Yantorno, R.: Performance of the modified bark spectral distortion as an objective speech quality measure. In: Proceedings of the 1998 IEEE International Conference on Acoustics, Speech and Signal Processing, vol. 1, pp. 541–544. IEEE (1998)
34. Yousef, M., Hussain, K.F., Mohammed, U.S.: Accurate, data-efficient, unconstrained text recognition with convolutional neural networks. arXiv preprint arXiv:1812.11894 (2018)
35. Yu, D., Kolbæk, M., Tan, Z.H., Jensen, J.: Permutation invariant training of deep models for speaker-independent multi-talker speech separation. In: 2017 IEEE International Conference on Acoustics, Speech and Signal Processing (ICASSP), pp. 241–245. IEEE (2017)

Multi-step Coding Structure of Spatial Audio Object Coding

Chenhao Hu[1,2], Ruimin Hu[1,2(✉)], Xiaochen Wang[1,2], Tingzhao Wu[1,2], and Dengshi Li[1,3]

[1] National Engineering Research Center for Multimedia Software, School of Computer Science, Wuhan University, Wuhan, China
Tingzhao_Wu@126.com
{huchenhao,hrm,clowang}@whu.edu.cn

[2] Hubei Key Laboratory of Multimedia and Network Communication Engineering, Wuhan University, Wuhan, China

[3] School of Mathematics and Computer, Jianghan University, Wuhan, China
reallds@126.com

Abstract. The spatial audio object coding (SAOC) is an effective method which compresses multiple audio objects and provides flexibility for personalized rendering in interactive services. It divides each frame signal into 28 sub-bands and extracts one set object spatial parameters for each sub-band. Objects can be coded into a downmix signal and a few parameters by this way. However, using same parameters in one sub-band will cause frequency aliasing distortion, which seriously impacts listening experience. Existing studies to improve SAOC cannot guarantee that all audio objects can be decoded well. This paper describes a new multi-step object coding structure to efficient calculate residual of each object as additional side information to compensate the aliasing distortion of each object. In this multi-step structure, a sorting strategy based on sub-band energy of each object is proposed to determine which audio object should be encoded in each step, because the object encoding order will affect the final decoded quality. The singular value decomposition (SVD) is used to reduce the increasing bit-rate due to the added side information. From the experiment results, the performance of proposed method is better than SAOC and SAOC-TSC, and each object can be decoded well with respect to the bit-rate and the sound quality.

Keywords: Audio object coding · Residual coding · Spatial audio

1 Introduction

The spatial audio system based on channel coding has become popular as it provides more immersive listening experience than mono or stereo audio coding techniques, but it still has limitations [1,2]. On the one hand, this method cannot adapt to non-standard playback environment. When the number and position of

Y. M. Ro et al. (Eds.): MMM 2020, LNCS 11961, pp. 666–678, 2020.
https://doi.org/10.1007/978-3-030-37731-1_54

loudspeakers is not match standard requirements, the spatial orientation information of audio will be obviously distorted. On the other hand, it is difficult for audio channel coding to support the interactive audio services. The personalized adjustment of the channel based method will lead to the change of all the object signals contained in the channel.

Therefore, Fraunhofer and other international well-known research institutions, research on the new spatial audio system based on object (see Fig. 1), and the spatial audio object coding (SAOC) scheme [3] is proposed to directly compress and transmit multiple independent audio objects in recorded scenes. The original audio scenes are reconstructed by using the transmitted down-mixed signals and metadata (also known as side information), and personalized rendering is allowed according to the needs of users. These both ensure the users can get the best experience afforded by diverse device configurations, and give new opportunities for personalized interactive content [4].

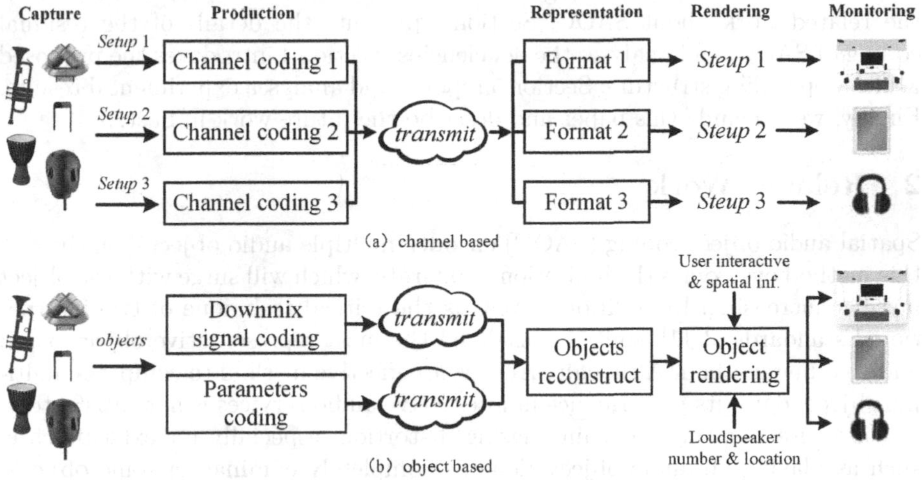

Fig. 1. The spatial audio pipeline for (a) channel-based and (b) object-based audio. In this paper, we only focus on the coding and decoding part of spatial audio system.

Due to its characteristics of loose coupling with playback devices and independent processing of object, spatial audio systems adopting this technology became the trend of future audio systems to meet the key requirements of immersive personalized audio-visual experience. For instance, hearing-impaired users could improve speech intelligibility by adjusting the balance between dialog and background sounds [5], or football fan might choose to hear the match as if they are seated with their own team's fans in the stadium [6]. Furthermore, the SAOC scheme could be used in teleconference and VR games [1,7].

In the SAOC scheme, the same parameters are used in one sub-band in order to get lower coding bit-rate. This leads to aliasing distortion in frequency domain

[8], which seriously reducing listening experience, such as one audio object signal will mix with other object signal components. Even worse, this problem will affect subsequent rendering and interactive services of spatial audio. Some studies used residual signal to improve the decoding sound quality [9,10]. However, these methods only can improve the listening experience of one target object, others still have aliasing distortion problem. This paper presents a new multi-step coding structure to efficient calculate residual of each object as added information to compensate the loss of aliasing distortion. In this multi-step structure, a sorting strategy based on sub-band energy of each object is proposed to determine which audio object should be encoded in each step, because the objects' encoding order will affect the final decoded quality. The singular value decomposition (SVD) is used to reduce the bit rate increased by the added side information. From experiment results, the residual information can be compressed to a normal level by SVD. And every audio object can be successfully decoded with respect to the sound quality by using the proposed Multi-step coding structure.

The rest of this paper is organized as follows. In Sect. 2, we briefly review the related work about SAOC. Section 3 presents the details of the residual coding of SAOC, and analyses the deficiencies. Section 4 introduces the proposed Multi-step coding structure. Section 5 reports and analyses experimental results. Finally, we conclude this paper and describe the future work in Sect. 6.

2 Related Work

Spatial audio object coding (SAOC) encodes multiple audio objects jointly, and this method overcomes the limitation of bit-rate, which will surge with the object number increasing. In addition, SAOC is the critical technique of two international standards [3,11], so it is considered the most representative object-based audio coding method. Although SAOC is an effective method to compress multiple objects data, its performance in interactive audio services is not satisfactory. It will cause frequency domain aliasing distortion, especially for extreme case, such as playing an audio object alone or completely eliminating some objects. Therefore, a number of improved methods (use SAOC as the baseline) have been proposed to enhance the decoding sound quality.

Koo K et al. proposed variable sub-band analysis to improve the decoding quality of SAOC [12], because frequency domain aliasing decreases as the sub-band number increases. Kim K et al. proposed efficient residual coding to improve the target object quality for interactive audio services [9,10], but the listening quality of other objects is difficult to guarantee. Zheng X et al. proposed a Psychoacoustic-based Analysis-By-Synthesis (PABS) approach for encoding multiple audio objects [13]. This compression framework exploits sparsity in the perceptual time-frequency domain to ensure the decoding quality. Jia M et al. encoded multiple simultaneously active audio objects based on intra-object sparsity [14]. This method assumes that the energy of an audio object primarily concentrates in only a few time-frequency instants of each frame. Jia M et al. also proposed psychoacoustic coding method to preserve the important time-frequency bins [15]. Villemoes L et al. from Dolby proposed an approach to improve the performance by adding one or more decorrelators to the decoding process [16]. Ting W et al. proposed a sub-band partition method of higher resolution frequency, and applied the non-negative matrix factorization (NMF) method to reduce the increasing bit-rate caused by sub-band division [17]. Furthermore, Ting W's team first analyze how the object distortion varies with sub-band frequency resolution, and find a way to determine the optimal resolution to reduce aliasing distortion [8]. Zhang S et al. proposed a sparse auto-encoder method to get a sparser signal representation, and extracted ideal binary mask for each object as side information [18].

The essence of these studies is try to reduce the frequency aliasing distortion. These studies can be divided into two categories, one is to modify sub-band division [8,12,16,17], another is to utilize sparsity of objects [13–15,18]. Whereas, sub-band has upper division limitation and bit-rate will surge with frequency resolution; the sparsity will decrease as audio object number increases, the sound quality is not ideal. SAOC with residual coding can compensate aliasing distortion satisfactorily. But existing studies [9,10] only eliminate aliasing distortion of one target object, others still have poor listening experience. This paper try to solve this problem and control the bit-rate at a normal level.

3 Framework of SAOC Residual Coding Method

3.1 Overview

Kim K et al. proposed using residual to compensate object signal decoding error of SAOC [9,10]. This method is called SAOC of Two step coding (SAOC-TSC). And the basic conceptual structure of SAOC residual coding is shown in Fig. 2.

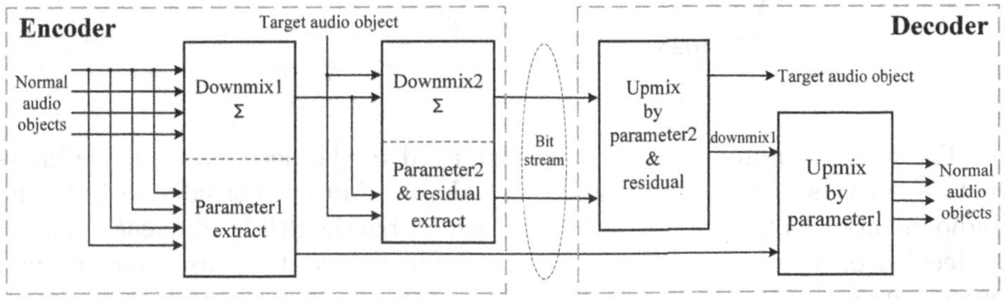

Fig. 2. Basic conceptual structure of SAOC residual coding, composed of two parts, encoder and decoder.

In the encoding part, the first step is to dispose normal audio objects, it generates normal-objects downmix signal (D1) and object level difference (OLD); the second step is to handle target audio object with D1, it generates all-objects downmix signal (D2), channel level difference (CLD) and the residual of target object. Before the parameter extraction, object signals are transformed into time-frequency (TF) domain. The spatial parameters OLD and CLD are the power ratio between the input TF data. The parameters are calculated as follows:

$$OLD_i(j,k) = \frac{P_i(j,k)}{P_M(j,k)}, CLD(j,k) = 10\log_{10}\frac{P_t(j,k)}{P_{dm}(j,k)} \begin{cases} 1 \le i \le N \\ 1 \le j \le L \\ 1 \le k \le M \end{cases} \quad (1)$$

where $P_i(j,k) = \sum_{b=A_{k-1}}^{A_k-1}[S_i(j,b)]^2$ is the power of the ith normal object and P_M is the maximum power of the normal object at the kth sub-band of jth frame. Calculate like $P_i(j,k)$, P_t is the power of target object and P_{dm} is the power of D1. In the calculation of sub-band power, $S_i(j,b)$ is the frequency signal of the ith object, b is the frequency point index. Furthermore, A_{k-1} and $A_k - 1$ are the beginning and ending points of the kth sub-band, respectively. The sub-band frequency signals are obtained by applying human auditory characteristic according to Table 1. N, L, and M are the number of normal object, frame, and sub-band. The derivation of residual can be seen in [9,10].

Table 1. Partition boundaries of sub-band (DCT size of 2048, sampling rate of 44.1 kHz).

A_0	A_1	A_2	A_3	A_4	A_5	A_6	A_7	A_8
0	3	7	11	15	19	23	27	31
A_9	A_{10}	A_{11}	A_{12}	A_{13}	A_{14}	A_{15}	A_{16}	A_{17}
39	47	55	63	79	95	111	127	159
A_{18}	A_{19}	A_{20}	A_{21}	A_{22}	A_{23}	A_{24}	A_{25}	A_{26}
191	223	255	287	319	367	415	479	559
A_{27}	A_{28}							
655	1025							

The final downmix signal D2 is transmitted to the decoder with side information consists of parameters and residual. In addition, considering both the audio quality and the bit-rate, effective residual bandwidth in frequency domain is decided on 0–5.5 kHz. Then, in the decoding part, the target and normal objects are separately reconstructed by two steps. First, using residual and gain factors calculated by OLD, target object and downmix signal D1 can be reconstructed from D2. Second, using gain factors calculated by CLD, normal objects can be reconstructed from D1. The gain factors of audio objects can be calculated as

$$G_i(j,k) = \sqrt{\frac{OLD_i(j,k)}{\sum_{p=1}^{N} OLD_p(j,k)}}, G_t(j,k) = \sqrt{\frac{1}{1+10^{-\frac{CLD(j,k)}{10}}}} \quad (2)$$

where $G_i(j,k)$ is used to reconstruct normal objects and $G_t(j,k)$ is used to reconstruct target object. Objects can be separated after gain factors multiply by downmix signal transformed into frequency domain. Besides, target object has residual information to reduce its aliasing distortion.

3.2 Discussion of SAOC-TSC

The residual framework contributes to the enhancement of sound quality, but only one target object can be decoded perfectly. The residual coding method SAOC-TSC is suit for the application of Karaoke and Solo greatly by only eliminate the aliasing distortion of one target audio object. It is not appropriate yet when support other main application scenarios of spatial object audio, like teleconference, VR games and music remix, where the users will base on their own need to amplification and attenuation of the level and adjust the spatial information of any audio object.

Figure 3 is an example to show the decoding quality by comparing spectrogram difference of original and reconstructed signals. It is obvious that the original and reconstructed signal of target object almost have similar spectrogram. However, in the spectrogram of normal object, the reconstructed signal is quite different from the original signal. The reconstructed normal object has undesired harmonic components that came from other objects and it also has many spectral nulls, some differences are presented with a red wireframe outline in Fig. 3.

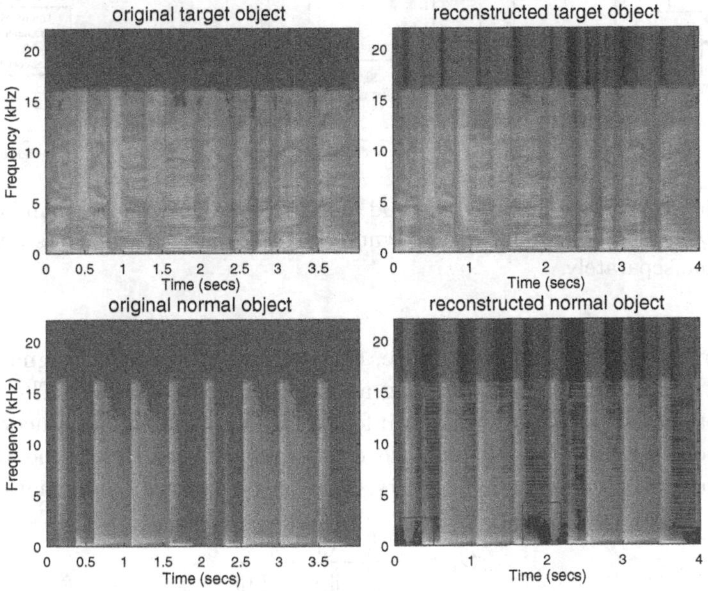

Fig. 3. Spectrogram comparison of original and the reconstructed signals. The first line is the target object comparison, the second line is the normal object comparison.

4 Our Proposed Method

4.1 The Structure of Multi-step SAOC

In order to decoding every audio object to a satisfactory level of perception, we need to encode each object gradually and obtain the residual matrix in each step. In addition, the encoding order of audio objects will affect the final decoding sound quality. We proposed a frequency energy sorting strategy and a cyclic choose module to settle this issue properly. Figure 4 is the overview of multi-step SAOC (MS-SAOC). It should be noted that the number N, D, Q and E in this figure will satisfy the following condition:

$$N = E + 1 = D + 1 = Q + 1 \tag{3}$$

the first object decoded in last step can be estimated by downmix signal and penultimate object, so the number of residual and spatial parameter will be less.

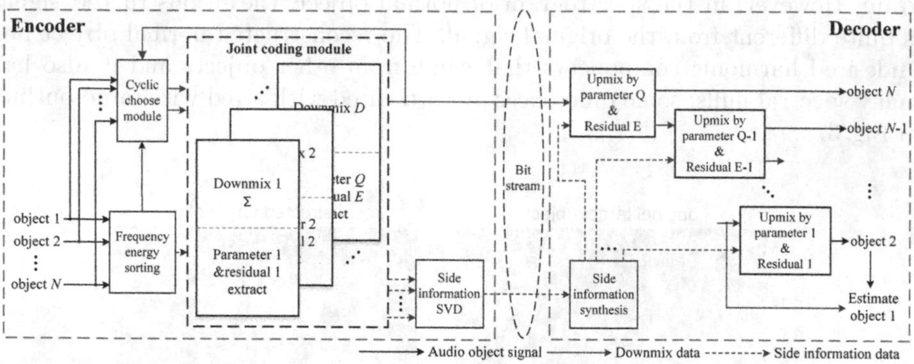

Fig. 4. The structure of proposed method multi-step SAOC. N is the number of audio objects. D, Q, E is the number of downmix signal, spatial parameters and residual information, separately.

In our multi-step SAOC structure, the original audio object signals serve as the input to frequency energy sorting and cyclic choose module. The frequency energy sorting outputs contain order information and TF signals. Encoding order information will be utilized in cyclic choose module to determine which two signals should be the encoded targets. The encoding order information can be calculated as follows:

$$O_i = \frac{\|S_i(j,b)\|}{\sum_{i=1}^{N} \|S_i(j,b)\|} \tag{4}$$

where O_i is used for objects sorting, and $S_i(j,b)$ is the frequency domain signal of the ith input object, j is the frame number, b is the frequency bins. In this paper, we sort O_i from largest to smallest. For example, cyclic choose module will first pick up two largest objects as coding target couple into joint coding module. Like SAOC and SAOC-TSC, joint coding calculates downmix signal and extracts side information. Then, downmix signal is fed back to cyclic choose module as new coding target in the next step. In the next loop, cyclic choose module just pick up one object to form a new coding target couple with the downmix signal in previous step. In this way, N audio objects can be coded in $N-1$ steps. After N-1 steps, residual information will be compressed by SVD and transmitted to decoder with spatial parameters and final downmix signal. The decoder part is the reverse of the encoder part. The coding target couples will be recovered by side information gradually.

4.2 Extraction of Side Information

Our side information consists of spatial parameters and residual matrix, which is extracted after Discrete Cosine Transform (DCT). Different from SAOC-TSC and SAOC, we directly calculate gain factors as spatial parameters. Notice the difference in formulas between step 1 and other steps. These parameters can be calculated in each sub-band as follows:

$$G_o(i,j,k) = \begin{cases} \sqrt{\frac{[P_o(i+1,j,k)]}{[P_o(i,j,k)+P_o(i+1,j,k)]}} & ,i=1 \\ \sqrt{\frac{[P_o(i+1,j,k)]}{[P_o(i+1,j,k)+P_d(i-1,j,k)]}} & ,2 \le i \le N-1 \end{cases} \tag{5}$$

$$P_o(i,j,k) = \sum_{b=A_{k-1}}^{A_k-1} [S_i(j,b)]^2, 1 \le i \le N \tag{6}$$

$$P_d(i,j,k) = \sum_{b=A_{k-1}}^{A_k-1} \left[X_{i-1}(j,b)^2 + S_{i+1}(j,b)^2\right], 1 \le i \le N-1. \tag{7}$$

where $j,k,b \in N^+$ is same as Eq. (1). $G_o(i,:,:)$ is the gain factor matrix of $i+1$ object in i^{th} step. $P_o(i,:,:)$ and $P_d(i,:,:)$ is the sub-band frequency power of ith object and downmix signal in i^{th} step, respectively. The sub-band division is shown in Table 1. $S_i(j,b)^2$ is the frequency signal of the ith object, $X_i(j,b)^2$ is the downmix TF signal in i^{th} step. Especially, $X_0(j,b) = S_1(j,b)$ when $i=1$. $[A]/[B]$ is the Hadamard division, divided element by element.

The residual information $R(i,j,b)$ can be represented by using the gain factors and two target coding objects output from cyclic choose module as follows:

$$\begin{cases} R(i,j,b) = \frac{G_d(i,j,k) \cdot S_{i+1}(j,b) - G_o(i,j,k) \cdot X_{i-1}(j,b)}{G_d(i,j,k)+G_o(i,j,k)} \\ G_d(i,j,k) = \sqrt{1-G_o(i,j,k)^2} \end{cases} ,1 \le i \le N-1 \tag{8}$$

where $R(i,:,:)$ is the residual matrix of $i+1$ object in i^{th} step. $G_d(i,:,:)$ is the gain factor matrix of ith downmix signal. Especially, $X_0(j,b) = S_1(j,b)$ when $i=1$. Audio object signal can be reconstructed in frequency domain as follows:

$$\begin{cases} S_i(j,b)' = G_o(i-1,j,k) \cdot X_{i-1}(j,b)' + R(i-1,j,b) & ,2 \le i \le N \\ S_1(j,b)' = X_1(j,b)' - S_2(j,b)' & ,i=1 \\ X_i(j,b)' = G_d(i,j,k) \cdot X_{i+1}(j,b)' - R(i+1,j,b) & ,1 \le i \le N-2 \end{cases} \tag{9}$$

where S_i' and X_i' is the reconstructed object and downmix signal respectively. $X_{N-1}' \approx X_{N-1}$, because the final downmix is transmitted directly to the decoder as input. Otherwise, in Eqs. (8) and (9), frequency bins in one sub-band will use the same gain factor. In this way, G_d and G_o will be filled to the same length as S and X. The dot-product in these equations is viable.

4.3 Residual Compressing Based on SVD

We encode audio objects step by step to relieve the aliasing distortion of every audio object, but the increased number of residual information also leads to a significant increase in coding bit-rate. Therefore, we apply SVD to achieve dimensional reduction to reduce the bit-rate of side information coding. SVD can decompose a large size matrix into three matrices [19]. That is to say, the residual matrix R can be decomposed into matrices U, Λ and V. We can approximate it with a small number of top r singular values and corresponding singular vectors. Because of the limitation of space, the calculation of SVD is not derived here.

5 Experiments and Data Analysis

5.1 Experiments Conditions

In the experiments, we evaluate the performance of three object-based spatial audio coding methods (SAOC, SAOC-TSC and MS-SAOC). The downmix signal is coded with MPEG AAC at 128 kbps. And spatial parameters is coded by lossless coding method. The time-frequency transform is achieved by DCT, with hanning window, 2048 sample points per frame and 50% overlapping.

The audio object signals used in the experiments are selected from QUASI database [20]. This database is suit for evaluating object-based spatial audio coding methods. The sample rate of audio is 44.1 KHz, and residual bandwidth is 0–5.5 kHz. We choose five actual recording segments each consists of six objects for experiments, and continues about 60 s, as shown in Table 2.

Table 2. Performance evaluation items.

Index	Name	List of audio objects
A	one we love	bass, drums, gtr-acoustik, gtr-arpeg, gtr-solo, lead-vocal
B	good soldier	guitar, keyboards, vibes, prophet, tamb, lead-vocal
C	sunrise	acoustik-gtr, ele-gtrs, lead-vocal, bass, drums, piano
D	Ana	acoustik-gtr, alto, drm-kit, chop-gtr, kick, organ
E	remember the name	bang, bass, chorus beeps, hihat, kick, snare

In objective experiments, we use signal-to-distortion ratio (SDR) and signal-to-interference ratio (SIR) as the performance metrics, and the calculation of them is implemented in BSS-EVAL toolbox [21]. The larger value of SDR and SIR represents the better coding performance. To further evaluate the sound quality, we select 20 listeners to do multiple stimuli with hidden reference and anchor (MUSHRA) test [22] as subjective experiments.

5.2 Bit-Rate of Compressed Residual Information

As r value of SVD reduce, the bit-rate of residual will be decline, but sound quality will be worse. On the contrary, the bit-rate of residual will rise when r value increase. Considering the bit-rate and sound quality, r singular values is better to choose 35. This will maintain bit-rate at a normal level without obvious sound quality loss. The average residual bit-rate of the selected items before and after SVD is shown in Table 3. As a result, the residual information bit-rate can be reduced by SVD. The total residual information for six objects is 30.15 kbps, not much different from SAOC-TSC.

Table 3. Residual information bit-rate of per object.

SAOC-TSC(FRC)	MS-SAOC before SVD	MS-SAOC after SVD
15 kbps	14.11 kbps	6.03 kbps

5.3 Objective and Subjective Tests

We evaluate the performance of different methods on five item segments. First, the SDR and SIR [21] are estimated with the original audio objects and their reconstructed results. Table 4 shows its results. It can be seen that MS-SAOC with *down* sorting strategy has the best SDR and SIR, so we will choose this method to do subjective tests. In terms of SDR value, our method has minimum numerical error between reconstructed object and original object. In terms of SIR value, the degree of frequency aliasing distortion of MS-SAOC is the least.

The MUSHRA scores of five item segments with 95% confidence interval are shown in Fig. 5. Figure 5(a) confirms that the MS-SAOC audio quality is the best. Because of the multi-step residual calculation, the deviation from mean to maximum of our proposed MS-SAOC is smaller than that of SAOC-TSC. In Fig. 5(b), SAOC-TSC only has one high score object, and most object scores of our method are better than SAOC and SAOC-TSC. This illustrates we have reconstructed most objects well. But the object scores of our method show a decreasing trend, the object 1 reconstructed in first step has the best sound quality, the object 6 reconstructed in last step has the worst sound quality. Because we use the reconstructed downmix signal to recover couple objects in the next step, this lead to the error propagation and cause the bad quality in last step. Overall, our approach improved the sound quality of most objects.

Table 4. Objective results. (*down* means the encoding sort is descending order, and the object has lower energy will be decoded first. *up* is the reverse of *down*)

SDR	SAOC	SAOC-TSC	MS-SAOC(*up*)	MS-SAOC(*down*)
item A	3.35	4.31	9.43	15.63
item B	3.82	4.63	10.45	13.79
item C	2.36	4.30	13.64	14.87
item D	8.68	11.65	16.71	18.21
item E	6.76	9.06	13.62	16.28
average	**4.99**	**6.05**	**12.77**	**15.76**
SIR	SAOC	SAOC-TSC	MS-SAOC(*up*)	MS-SAOC(*down*)
item A	6.89	11.92	19.85	21.47
item B	8.14	9.45	19.01	21.79
item C	5.75	8.13	17.77	21.19
item D	15.73	19.65	23.87	27.46
item E	13.14	17.57	21.69	26.90
average	**9.93**	**13.34**	**20.43**	**23.76**

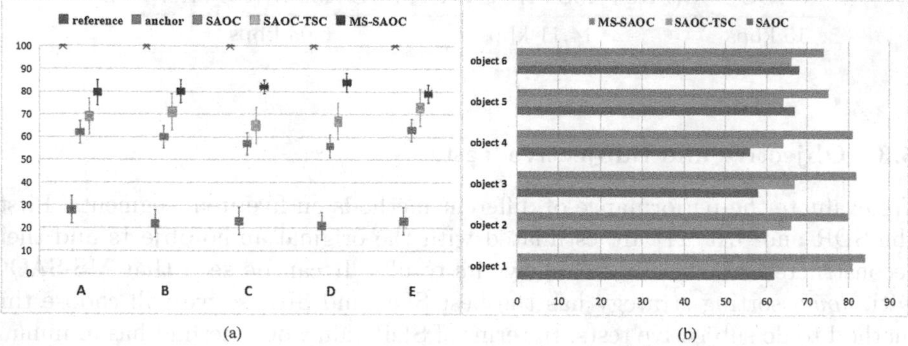

Fig. 5. Subjective experiment results. (*a*) is the average MUSHRA scores of five item segments. (*b*) is the MUSHRA scores of the six audio objects in item E.

6 Conclusions

We propose an object coding method MS-SAOC to reconstruct all objects well. We extract residual and spatial information of all objects by cyclic choose module and use SVD to compress the residual information. To decide which object will be coded in every step, we propose a frequency energy sorting strategy. The bit-rate experiments show that the residual bit-rate will reduce to a normal level after SVD. The objective and subjective experiments show that our method has better sound quality for most objects in all items. The results also show that our method has the problem of error propagation, which means there is still room for improvement in our approach. In future studies, we aim to adjust the sorting strategy to find the optimum coding sequence, also we will eliminate error propagation to further improve sound quality and reduce residual bit-rate.

Acknowledgement. This work was supported by National Key R&D Program of China (No. 2017YFB1002803) and National Nature Science Foundation of China (No. 61701194, No. U1736206).

References

1. Breebaart, J., Engdegård, J., Falch, C., et al.: Spatial audio object coding (saoc)-the upcoming MPEG standard on parametric object based audio coding. Audio Eng. Soc. Convention Audio Eng. Soc. **124**, 613–627 (2008)
2. Füg, S., Hoelzer, A., Borss, C., Ertel, C., Kratschmer, M., Plogsties, J.: Design, coding and processing of metadata for object-based interactive audio. In: Audio Engineering Society Convention 137. Audio Engineering Society (2014)
3. Herre, J., Hilpert, J., Kuntz, A., Plogsties, J.: Mpeg-h 3D audio–the new standard for coding of immersive spatial audio. IEEE J. Sel. Top. Signal Process. **9**(5), 770–779 (2015)
4. Coleman, P., Franck, A., Francombe, J., et al.: An audio-visual system for object-based audio: from recording to listening. IEEE Trans. Multimedia **20**(8), 1919–1931 (2018)
5. Shirley, B., Oldfield, R., et al.: Clean audio for tv broadcast: an object-based approach for hearing impaired viewers. J. Audio Eng. Soc. **63**(4), 245–256 (2015)
6. Oldfield, R., Shirley, B., Spille, J.: Object-based audio for interactive football broadcast. Multimedia Tools Appl. **74**(8), 2717–2741 (2015)
7. Kasuya, T., et al.: Livration: remote VR live platform with interactive 3D audio-visual service (2019)
8. Wu, T., Hu, R., Wang, X., Ke, S.: Audio object coding based on optimal parameter frequency resolution. Multimedia Tools and Appl. **78**(15), 20723–20738 (2019)
9. Kim, K., Seo, J., Beack, S., Kang, K., Hahn, M.: Spatial audio object coding with two-step coding structure for interactive audio service. IEEE Trans. Multimedia **13**(6), 1208–1216 (2011)
10. Lee, B., Kim, K., Hahn, M.: Efficient residual coding method of spatial audio object coding with two-step coding structure for interactive audio services. IEICE Trans. Inf. Syst. **99**(7), 1949–1952 (2016)
11. ISO/IEC 23003–2:2010, MPEG-D (MPEG audio technologies), Part 2: Spatial audio object coding (2010)
12. Koo, K., Kim, K., Seo, J., Kang, K., Hahn, M.: Variable subband analysis for high quality spatial audio object coding. In: 2008 10th International Conference on Advanced Communication Technology, vol. 2, pp. 1205–1208. IEEE (2008)
13. Zheng, X., Ritz, C., Xi, J.: A psychoacoustic-based analysis-by-synthesis scheme for jointly encoding multiple audio objects into independent mixtures. In: 2013 IEEE International Conference on Acoustics, Speech and Signal Processing, pp. 281–285. IEEE (2013)
14. Jia, M., Yang, Z., Bao, C., Zheng, X., Ritz, C.: Encoding multiple audio objects using intra-object sparsity. IEEE/ACM Trans. Audio, Speech, Lang. Process. **23**(6), 1082–1095 (2015)

15. Jia, M., Zhang, J., Bao, C., Zheng, X.: A psychoacoustic-based multiple audio object coding approach via intra-object sparsity. Appl. Sci. **7**(12), 1301 (2017)
16. Villemoes, L., Hirvonen, T., Purnhagen, H.: Decorrelation for audio object coding. In: 2017 IEEE International Conference on Acoustics, Speech and Signal Processing (ICASSP), pp. 706–710. IEEE (2017)
17. Wu, T., Hu, R., Wang, X., Ke, S., Wang, J.: High quality audio object coding framework based on non-negative matrix factorization. China Commun. **14**(9), 32–41 (2017)
18. Zhang, S., Wu, X., Qu, T.: Sparse autoencoder based multiple audio objects coding method. In: Audio Engineering Society Convention 146. Audio Engineering Society (2019)
19. Wall, M.E., Rechtsteiner, A., Rocha, L.M.: Singular value decomposition and principal component analysis. A Practical Approach to Microarray Data Analysis, pp. 91–109. Springer, Boston (2003). https://doi.org/10.1007/0-306-47815-3_5
20. ADASP Homepage, QUASI database. http://www.tsi.telecom-paristech.fr/aao/en/2012/03/12/quasi/. Accessed 12 Mar 2012
21. Vincent, E., Gribonval, R., Févotte, C.: Performance measurement in blind audio source separation. IEEE Trans. Audio, Speech, Lang. Process. **14**(4), 1462–1469 (2006)
22. Recommendation ITU-R BS.1534-3. Method for the subjective assessment of intermediate quality level of coding systems (MUSHRA). In: Proceedings International Telecommunications Union, Switzerland (2015)

Thermal Face Recognition Based on Transformation by Residual U-Net and Pixel Shuffle Upsampling

Soumya Chatterjee[1,2] and Wei-Ta Chu[1,2](✉)

[1] Indian Institute of Technology Bombay, Mumbai, India
soumyac1999@gmail.com
[2] National Cheng Kung University, Tainan, Taiwan
wtchu@gs.ncku.edu.tw

Abstract. We present a thermal face recognition system that first transforms the given face in the thermal spectrum into the visible spectrum, and then recognizes the transformed face by matching it with the face gallery. To achieve high-fidelity transformation, the U-Net structure with a residual network backbone is developed for generating visible face images from thermal face images. Our work mainly improves upon previous works on the Nagoya University thermal face dataset. In the evaluation, we show that the rank-1 recognition accuracy can be improved by more than 10%. The improvement on visual quality of transformed faces is also measured in terms of PSNR (with 0.36 dB improvement) and SSIM (with 0.07 improvement).

Keywords: Thermal face recognition · Thermal-to-visible transformation · Thermal face verification

1 Introduction

Thermal face recognition has been attracting more and more attention in the recent years due to its broad application in many domains like night-time surveillance and access control. Face recognition has been mainly focused on the visible spectrum but this depends on external conditions like illumination. Imaging in the visible spectrum involves measuring the light reflected by the face. Hence, changes in lighting conditions can cause significant changes in visual appearance and degrade the performance of such systems. Thermal infrared images are captured by passive infrared sensors which measure the radiations emitted by the facial tissues, and hence are independent of the external lighting.

Infrared images are categorized according to the wavelengths sensed, including near infrared 'NIR' ($0.74\,\mu$–$1\,\mu$m), short-wave infrared 'SWIR' ($1\,\mu$–$3\,\mu$m), mid-wave infrared 'MWIR' ($3\,\mu$–$5\,\mu$m), and long-wave infrared 'LWIR' ($8\,\mu$–$14\,\mu$m). NIR and SWIR imaging are reflection based and visual appearance of objects and are similar to visible images. Prior studies on NIR or SWIR

Y. M. Ro et al. (Eds.): MMM 2020, LNCS 11961, pp. 679–689, 2020.
https://doi.org/10.1007/978-3-030-37731-1_55

images achieved promising recognition performance. On the contrary, MWIR and LWIR images measure material emissivity and temperature. Skin tissue has high emissivity in both the MWIR and LWIR spectrums. Because of this natural difference between the reflective visible spectrum and sensed emissivity in the thermal spectrum, images taken in the two modalities are very different and have a large modality gap. This hinders reliable face matching across the visible spectrum and the MSIR/LWIR spectrums. Currently some studies have focused on MWIR and LWIR face images, but only limited performance have been achieved [3,5,14]. In the following, we would call the MWIR/LWIR spectrums as *thermal spectrum*, and call face images captured in the thermal spectrum as *thermal faces*.

(a) Thermal Image (b) Visible Image

Fig. 1. Examples from NU dataset

The goal of thermal face recognition is to identify a person captured in the thermal spectrum by finding the most similar face images captured in visible spectrum. This task is thus a cross-modal matching problem, where we need a non-linear mapping from the thermal spectrum to the visible spectrum while preserving the identity information.

We present a deep convolutional neural network based on the U-Net [13] architecture for the thermal face recognition task. U-Nets have been widely used for various tasks including image segmentation [13], image feature extraction [2], etc. In our work, the U-Net is used to synthesize visible faces from given query thermal faces. The generated faces are used for matching against the gallery images. To improve upon visual quality of the generated visible face images, we propose a modified U-Net architecture using residual blocks instead of convolutional layers as the basic building components. It has been shown in [10] that the skip connections in residual networks [4] give rise to much smoother loss surfaces than similar networks without skip connections. Hence, they are easier to train and are able to find much better local optimums. In addition to this, we use pixel shuffle upsampling in the expansive part of our network in place of transposed convolutional layers. Pixel shuffle upsampling introduced in [15] achieves much better Peak Signal to Noise Ratio (PSNR) compared to other upsampling methods at a fraction of the computation cost.

In this paper, we evaluate the proposed networks on the thermal face dataset collected by Nagoya University [9] (which we will call the NU dataset). In the NU dataset, visible and thermal face pairs are available. In contrast to other thermal face dataset, visible faces and thermal faces were captured simultaneously by two closely located cameras. Therefore, the visible face and the thermal face of the same individual are well aligned. Such alignment is important for us to clearly study the performance of our models.

The rest of this paper is organized as follows. Section 2 describes related works of thermal face recognition. Section 3 presents details of the proposed method. Evaluation results are shown in Sect. 4, followed by concluding remarks in Sect. 5.

2 Related Works

Existing thermal to visible face recognition works can be roughly grouped into two categories: (1) transforming faces in the thermal spectrum into the visible spectrum, and then conducting recognition; (2) projecting thermal faces and visible faces into the common feature space and then achieving recognition.

Kresnaraman et al. [9] transformed the given thermal face into a visible face by utilizing the relationship between images in the thermal and visible spectra obtained by canonical correlation analysis. Given a polarimetric thermal face that is composed of three channels, Riggan et al. [12] proposed to extract features and then estimate the corresponding visible face based on a regression model. Both feature extraction and regression are developed based on convolutional neural networks. The same research team later proposed to improve quality of face synthesis by jointly considering global (entire face) and local regions (eyes, nose, and mouth) [11]. With a similar idea, Chen and Ross [1] proposed to develop a semantic-guided generative adversarial network to transform thermal faces into visible faces. The semantic labels obtained by a face parsing network provide important clues to improve synthesis.

One of the pioneering works in the second category is the deep perceptual mapping (DPM) [14]. Sarfraz and Stiefelhagen first extracted dense SIFT features from patches of thermal faces, and then transformed these features by an auto-encoder. The objective of this auto-encoder is to map the given features into that similar to the features extracted from the corresponding visible face. Iranmanesh et al. [7] proposed a coupled deep neural network architecture to make full use of the polarimetric thermal information. Taking VGG-16 network as the basic building component, polarimetric thermal faces and corresponding visible faces are fed to VGG-16 like networks to extract and embed features.

Our work falls into the first category, and we mainly focus on basic thermal faces rather than polarimetric thermal faces. In the evaluation, we would compare several proposed variants with one from the first category, i.e., [9], and one from the second category, i.e., [14].

3 Methods

The thermal face recognition problem is formulated as follows. Assume that we have a set $\mathcal{G}$ of visible faces called the gallery set. Given a thermal face x, called the probe, the visible face in $\mathcal{G}$ which corresponds to the same person as x needs to be found. For this, we design a mapping f from the domain of thermal face images $\mathcal{T}$ to visible face images $\mathcal{V}$. This mapping f is learnt from the training data using a deep convolutional neural network (CNN). Given a probe x, the visible face $\hat{y}$ is reconstructed using the learnt mapping function f, i.e., $\hat{y} = f(x)$. The Euclidean distance between $\hat{y}$ and each of the images in $\mathcal{G}$ is calculated, and the one with minimum distance to $\hat{y}$ is returned as the match y^*. That is,

$$y^* = \underset{t \in \mathcal{G}}{\operatorname{argmin}} \|t - f(x)\|_2 . \tag{1}$$

Alternatively, a pretrained face recognition network can be used to find the best match. In this case, the pretrained network can be thought of a mapping g from the domain of visible face images V to $\mathbb{R}^N$, i.e., given a visible face images, the network gives an encoding of the input as a vector of size N. The encodings are such that Euclidean distance between encodings of images of the same person is small while it is large for different people. For this,

$$y^* = \underset{t \in \mathcal{G}}{\operatorname{argmin}} \|g(t) - g(f(x))\|_2 . \tag{2}$$

3.1 U-Net Model for Face Recognition

The transformation function f that transforms a thermal face into a visible face is the most critical component in this work. We use a U-Net to develop the function f. Figure 2 shows the network structure. A U-Net has a contracting path and an expansive path. The contracting path is a conventional convolutional neural network, where the convolutional kernel is 3×3 with stride 2 and same padding; the activation function is ReLU, followed by a 2×2 max pooling for downsampling.

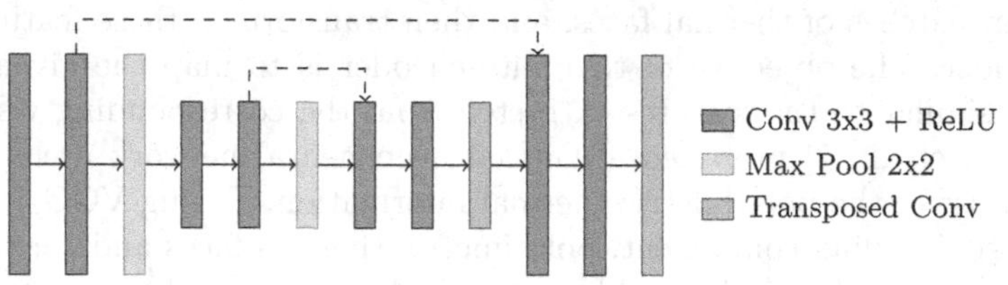

Fig. 2. The baseline network architecture. The dashed lines represent the skip connections in U-Net. Notice that the baseline encoder-decoder model does not have these connections.

Following [13], the number of feature channels are doubled at each downsampling step. In the expansive path we halve the number of feature channels at each upsampling step, by 2×2 transposed convolution. Every step in the expansive path contains upsampling, a concatenation with the corresponding feature map from the contracting path, and two convolutional layers similar to those in the contracting path. The last 1×1 convolution used in [13] has been omitted in our work, since we found that it gives better results. To demonstrate effectiveness of the skip connection in U-Net architecture, we will compare our architecture with a baseline model without these skip connections. Both the networks are trained using the same protocol based on a weighted combination of mean square error (MSE) loss and perceptual loss, which will be described later.

3.2 ResNet U-Net with Pixel Shuffle

The expansive part of the U-Net is implemented by deconvolution and conducts a sequence of upsampling. Given the feature maps generated by the contracting part, we can view the expansive part as a sequence of super-resolution processes, which upsample a low-resolution image into a high-resolution one. Shi et al. [15] proposed an efficient sub-pixel convolutional neural network to enable real-time super-resolution. Not only computational efficiency, the proposed sub-pixel CNN also yields better visual quality of high-resolution images.

In our work, we propose to view the expansive part of a U-Net as the process of super-resolution, and attempt to integrate sub-pixel CNNs to get performance improvement. This method is usually also called *pixel shuffle*, and we will take this term in the following. In addition, we further try to consider residual blocks [4] to improve visual quality of transformed faces.

Pixel Shuffle Upsampling: Upsampling by a factor r can be achieved by transposed convolution with a stride r or a fractionally strided convolution with a stride $\frac{1}{r}$ [15]. Pixel shuffle upsampling is an efficient implementation of the fractionally strided convolution. In this a $H \times W \times C \cdot r^2$ tensor is rearranged into a $rH \times rW \times C$ tensor thus achieving an upsampling by a factor r. Our network uses $r = 2$ to upsample tensors by a factor of 2 in the expansive part.

(a) Convolutional block (b) Residual block

Fig. 3. Illustration of convolutional blocks and residual blocks.

Residual Blocks: To further improve upon visual quality of the generated visible face images, we make the following modifications to our above network. The convolutional layers used are replaced by residual blocks each consisting of two convolutional blocks with a dropout [17] layer in between, as shown in Fig. 3b. Each convolutional block (Fig. 3a) is made up of a 3×3 convolutional layer, and a batch normalization layer [6] followed by ReLU activation. In the residual blocks, using ideas from [19], the number of input channels is first doubled and then halved such that the resultant tensor has the same shape as the input. We use 2×2 max pooling for downsampling but in the upsampling path, pixel shuffle upsampling [15] is used instead of transposed convolution. The number of channels are doubled and halved in the downsampling and upsampling, respectively, using 1×1 convolutional layers following each residual block. The final network architecture is shown in Fig. 4.

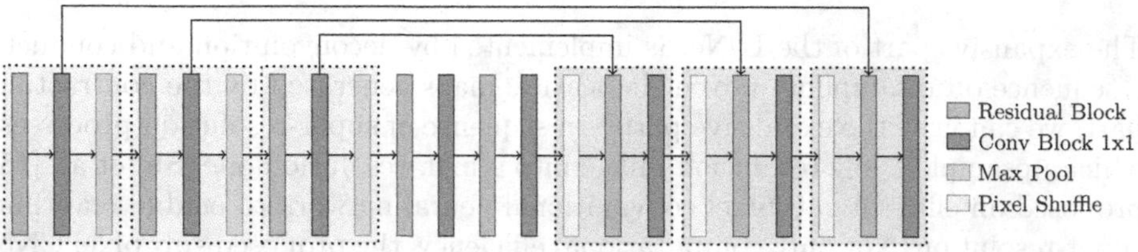

Fig. 4. The architecture of the proposed U-Net with residual blocks and pixel shuffle upsampling.

3.3 Losses

We use a weighted combination of two loss functions, namely mean squared error loss and perceptual loss to train our networks. These loss functions are described below.

Perceptual Loss proposed in [8] is used to measure the high-level semantic differences between transformed images and target images. It ensures that the transformed image is perceptually similar to the target. Given a transformed face $\hat{y}$ and a visible face y, a VGG-19 network [16] pretrained on the ImageNet dataset is used to extract features from them. The feature maps output by the last layer of each convolutional block are taken as the features. Let $\phi_j(\hat{y})$ and $\phi_j(y)$ denote the features extracted by the j considered convolutional layer, from the transformed face $\hat{y}$ and the visible face y, respectively. Perceptual loss between $\phi_j(\hat{y})$ and $\phi_j(y)$, both of shape $H_j \times W_j \times C_j$, is defined as

$$\mathcal{L}_j^{feat}(\hat{y}, y) = \frac{1}{H_j W_j C_j} \left\|\phi_j(\hat{y}) - \phi_j(y)\right\|_2^2, \tag{3}$$

where H_j and W_j denote height and width of a feature map $\phi_j(\hat{y})$ (or $\phi_j(y)$), and C_j denotes the number of channels (feature maps). Overall, the perceptual loss between an image and its reconstruction is the mean of $\mathcal{L}_j^{feat}$ over all j.

Mean Squared Error Loss ensures that the identity of the thermal face is preserved in the reconstructed visible face, i.e., ensuring fidelity between the thermal images and its transformation.

$$\mathcal{L}^{MSE}(\hat{y}, y) = \frac{1}{HW} \left\|\hat{y} - y\right\|_2^2. \tag{4}$$

For training, we linearly combine two losses:

$$\mathcal{L}(\hat{y}, y) = \mathcal{L}^{MSE}(\hat{y}, y) + \lambda \cdot \mathcal{L}^{feat}(\hat{y}, y), \tag{5}$$

where $\lambda = 0.01$.

4 Results

4.1 Evaluation Dataset

We evaluate the proposed networks on the thermal face dataset from Nagoya University, which consists of 180 Japanese subjects (169 males and 11 females). Five pairs of thermal faces and visible faces were captured for each individual. The ordinary camera capturing the visible spectrum and the thermal camera capturing LWIR images were mounted closely, and the same pair of thermal and visible faces were captured simultaneously, making the image pairs very well aligned. This characteristic is distinct to other thermal face datasets, and provides us a good foundation for the proposed study. There are thus 900 thermal images and 900 visible images in total. All of them are frontal faces with neutral expression. The thermal images were captured by the Advanced Thermo TVS-500EX camera, which senses wavelength ranging from 8 µm to 14 µm. The corresponding thermal and visible images were captured at the same time, and underwent the same preprocessing. After cropping, calibration, and resizing, resolution of both types of images is 56×64 pixels. Figure 1 shows a sample image pair from the NU database.

In the evaluation protocol of [9] and [3], 180 individuals are separated into two parts, i.e., 160 people and 20 people. The 160 people in the first part are equally divided into 16 groups, i.e., each group consists of 10 people. Among the 16 groups, 15 groups are selected as the training set. Thermal faces of the remaining group, consisting of 10 people, are taken as the probe image set (test data). In the gallery set, in addition to visible images corresponding to these 10 people, the 20 people in the second part separated at the beginning are also included in the gallery set to increase the number of candidate identities, i.e., increasing noise. These 20 people are also used as the validation set during training.

The models are trained with the Adam optimizer with learning rate of 0.01 for 150 epochs. A learning rate decay of 0.6 every 25 epochs is also used.

4.2 Face Recognition

First, we transform the thermal face images from the probe set to visible spectrum using the model illustrated in Fig. 4. The transformed images are then matched against the visible face images in the gallery set, and the one with the minimum Euclidean distance from the transformed probe is selected. The match is considered to be correct if the selected visible face and the query thermal face are of the same individual. We measure the rank-1 recognition accuracy which is averaged over 5 different splits of the dataset. The results of canonical correlation analysis (CCA) [9], deep perceptual model (DPM) [3] and the baseline encoder-decoder model (illustrated in Fig. 2) are compared with the proposed model (ResNet U-Net without/with Pixel Shuffle, illustrated in Fig. 4), as shown in Table 1. Please notice that all the methods but DPM in this table are developed for transforming thermal faces into visible faces. DPM uses a basic auto-encoder to transform features extracted from thermal faces into that similar to the corresponding visible faces. We take the auto-encoder part as the transformation, and do the same thing as other methods. Because this is not the original DPM, we denote this approach DPM* in Tables 1, 2, and Fig. 5.

Table 1. Rank-1 thermal face recognition accuracy.

Methods	Average accuracy (%)
CCA [9]	14.00
DPM* [3]	59.50
Baseline U-Net	67.60
ResNet U-Net (w/o PS)	68.80
ResNet U-Net (w. PS)	**69.60**

As can be seen, the baseline U-Net improves recognition accuracy over the basic auto-encoder from 59.50% to 67.60%. The proposed ResNet U-Net with pixel shuffle further provides performance over the baseline U-Net by 2%. This result shows effectiveness of taking residual blocks as the components in the U-Net over the baseline U-Net. The skip connections allow the model to infer finer details which may be lost in the downsampling part of the network.

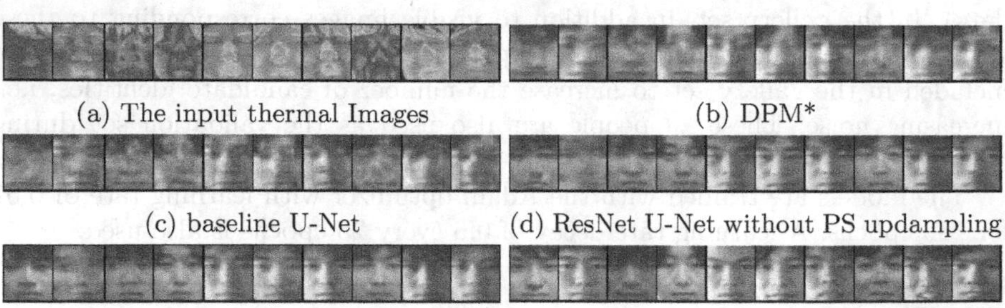

(a) The input thermal Images (b) DPM*

(c) baseline U-Net (d) ResNet U-Net without PS updampling

(e) ResNet U-Net with PS upsampling (f) Ground Truths

Fig. 5. Comparison of reconstructed visible images for all our models

4.3 Face Transformation

The main idea of this work is to transform thermal faces into visible faces, and then conduct face recognition in the visible domain. Therefore, we would like to evaluate the quality of transformed faces in the following.

We compare transformed faces by DPM [3], the baseline U-Net model, the ResNet U-Net model without pixel shuffle (PS) upsampling, and the ResNet U-Net model with PS upsampling. Figure 5 shows sample transformation results of different models. From these samples, we clearly can see that DPM and the baseline U-Net yield relatively blurry visible faces. On the other hand, comparing Fig. 5c with d, the ResNet U-Net model without PS upsampling yields much clearer faces, which shows the effectiveness of residual blocks. The ResNet U-Net model with PS upsampling further slightly improves visual quality.

Table 2. Visual quality comparison of different transformation methods.

Method	PSNR (dB)	SSIM
CCA [9]	20.260	0.730
DPM* [3]	19.709	0.705
Baseline U-Net	19.499	0.672
ResNet U-Net (w/o PS)	19.803	0.781
ResNet U-Net (w. PS)	**20.627**	**0.803**

To quantitatively evaluate different models, we calculate the average Peak Signal to Noise Ratio (PSNR) and Structural Similarity (SSIM) [18] values of transformed faces. Table 2 lists the values. Two observations can be made from this table. First, values of PSNR and SSIM may not always be consistent with human perception. For example, samples in Fig. 5d look much better than Fig. 5b, but in terms of PSNR, the ResNet U-Net model without PS upsampling (PSNR = 19.803) is just slightly better than the DPM (PSNR = 19.709). Second, our ResNet U-Net model with PS upsampling consistently performs better than all other methods on both the metrics. Also, the results with PS upsampling are better than those without it, which justifies the effectiveness of viewing a part of transformation as a super-resolution process.

5 Conclusion

We have presented a framework to reconstruct visible faces from thermal faces preserving identity of the subject. In the proposed network, a U-Net model with residual blocks as the building components are used. Using sub-pixel convolution and pixel shuffle upsampling, we are able to transform thermal faces into realistic visible faces. Based on the transformed faces, recognition performance better than the canonical deep perceptual model and other variants can be obtained.

In the future, more extensive experiments can be conducted. We would build a robust thermal face detection system so that these combined can be used for thermal face recognition in real-world situation.

Acknowledgement. This work was partially supported by the Ministry of Science and Technology under the grant 108-2221-E-006-227-MY3, 107-2221-E-006-239-MY2, 107-2923-E-194-003-MY3, 107-2627-H-155-001, and 107-2218-E-002-055.

References

1. Chen, C., Ross, A.: Matching thermal to visible face images using a semantic-guided generative adversarial network. In: Proceedings of IEEE International Conference on Automatic Face & Gesture Recognition (2019)
2. Chu, W.T., Liu, Y.H.: Thermal facial landmark detection by deep multi-task learning. In: Proceedings of IEEE International Workshop on Multimedia Signal Processing. IEEE (2019)
3. Chu, W.T., Wu, J.N.: A parametric study of deep perceptual model on visible to thermal face recognition. In: Proceedings of IEEE Visual Communications and Image Processing (2018)
4. He, K., Zhang, X., Ren, S., Sun, J.: Deep residual learning for image recognition. In: Proceedings of IEEE International Conference on Computer Vision and Pattern Recognition (2016)
5. Hu, S., Choi, J., Chan, A.L., Schwartz, W.R.: Thermal-to-visible face recognition using partial least squares. J. Opt. Soc. Am. A **32**(3), 431–442 (2015)
6. Ioffe, S., Szegedy, C.: Batch normalization: Accelerating deep network training by reducing internal covariate shift. In: Proceedings of International Conference on Machine Learning, pp. 448–456 (2015)
7. Iranmanesh, S.M., Dabouei, A., Kazemi, H., Nasrabadi, N.M.: Deep cross polarimetric thermal-to-visible face recognition. In: Proceedings of International Conference on Biometrics (2018)
8. Johnson, J., Alahi, A., Fei-Fei, L.: Perceptual losses for real-time style transfer and super-resolution. In: Leibe, B., Matas, J., Sebe, N., Welling, M. (eds.) ECCV 2016. LNCS, vol. 9906, pp. 694–711. Springer, Cham (2016). https://doi.org/10.1007/978-3-319-46475-6_43
9. Kresnaraman, B., Deguchi, D., Takahashi, T., Mekada, Y., Ide, I., Murase, H.: Reconstructing face image from the thermal infrared spectrum to the visible spectrum. Sensors **16**(4), 568 (2016)
10. Li, H., Xu, Z., Taylor, G., Studer, C., Goldstein, T.: Visualizing the loss landscape of neural nets. In: Proceedings of Advances in Neural Information Processing Systems (2018)
11. Riggan, B.S., Short, N.J., Hu, S.: Thermal to visible synthesis of face images using multiple regions. In: Proceedings of IEEE Winter Conference on Applications of Computer Vision (2018)
12. Riggan, B.S., Short, N.J., Hu, S., Kwon, H.: Estimation of visible spectrum faces from polarimetric thermal faces. In: Proceedings of IEEE International Conference on Biometrics Theory, Applications and Systems (2016)
13. Ronneberger, O., Fischer, P., Brox, T.: U-Net: convolutional networks for biomedical image segmentation. In: Navab, N., Hornegger, J., Wells, W.M., Frangi, A.F. (eds.) MICCAI 2015. LNCS, vol. 9351, pp. 234–241. Springer, Cham (2015). https://doi.org/10.1007/978-3-319-24574-4_28

14. Sarfraz, M.S., Stiefelhagen, R.: Deep perceptual mapping for thermal to visible face recognition. Int. J. Comput. Vis. **122**(3), 426–438 (2017)
15. Shi, W., et al.: Real-time single image and video super-resolution using an efficient sub-pixel convolutional neural network. In: Proceedings of IEEE International Conference on Computer Vision and Pattern Recognition (2016)
16. Simonyan, K., Zisserman, A.: Very deep convolutional networks for large-scale image recognition. In: Proceedings of International Conference on Learning Representations (2015)
17. Srivastava, N., Hinton, G., Krizhevsky, A., Sutskever, I., Salakhutdinov, R.: Dropout: a simple way to prevent neural networks from overfitting. J. Mach. Learn. Res. **15**, 1929–1958 (2014)
18. Wang, Z., Bovik, A.C., Sheikh, H.R., Simoncelli, E.P.: Image quality assessment: from error visibility to structural similarity. IEEE Trans. Image Process. **13**(4), 600–612 (2004)
19. Zagoruyko, S., Komodakis, N.: Wide residual networks. arXiv preprint arXiv:1605.07146 (2016)

K-SVD Based Point Cloud Coding for RGB-D Video Compression Using 3D Super-Point Clustering

Shyi-Chyi Cheng[1(✉)], Ting-Lan Lin[2], and Ping-Yuan Tseng[1]

[1] Department of Computer Science and Engineering, National Taiwan Ocean University, Keelung, Taiwan
csc@mail.ntou.edu.tw

[2] Department of Electronic Engineering, National Taipei University of Technology, Taipei, Taiwan

Abstract. In this paper, we present a novel 3D structure-awareness RGB-D video compression scheme, which applies the proposed 3D super-point clustering to partition the super-points in a colored point cloud, generated from an RGB-D image, into a centroid and a non-centroid super-point datasets. A super-point is a set of 3D points which are characterized with similar feature vectors. Input an RGB-D frame to the proposed scheme, the camera parameters are first used to generate a colored point cloud, which is segmented into multiple super-points using our multiple principal plane analysis (MPPA). These super-points are then grouped into multiple clusters, each of them characterized by a centroid super-point. Next, the median feature vectors of super-points are represented by the *K* singular value decomposition (*K*-SVD) based sparse codes. Given a super-point cluster, the sparse codes of the median feature vectors are very similar and thus the redundant information among them are easy to remove by the successive entropy coding. For each super-point, the residual super-point is computed by subtracting the feature vectors inside from the reconstructed median feature vector. These residual feature vectors are also collected and coded using the *K*-SVD based sparse coding to enhance the quality of the compressed point cloud. This process results in a multiple description coding scheme for 3D point cloud compression. Finally, the compressed point cloud is projected to the 2D image space to obtain the compressed RGB-D image. Experiments demonstrate the effectiveness of our approach which attains better performance than the current state-of-the-art point cloud compression methods.

Keywords: Point cloud coding · RGB-D video compression · Sparse representation · 3D motion estimation

1 Introduction

Multi-view videos captured by RGB-D sensors, such as Kinect [1] consist of sequences of synchronized color and depth images, fulfilling separate but complementary needs in

Y. M. Ro et al. (Eds.): MMM 2020, LNCS 11961, pp. 690–701, 2020.
https://doi.org/10.1007/978-3-030-37731-1_56

representing a real-world 3D scene. Thus, to capture multi-view video with an RGB-D sensor is a promising approach for reconstructing three-dimensional (3D) image-based models which are central to many video-based applications including simultaneous localization and mapping (SLAM), 3-D scene modeling, autonomous navigation, object detection and tracking [2]. In these applications, the depth images are used to reconstruct the shape of a static scene/object from different viewpoints, and the color images record the visual textures of the shape. These applications often generate enormous RGB-D data which usually result in long latency for network transmission and huge memory requirement for storage. To deal with these difficulties, in this paper, we present an efficient 3D point cloud coding algorithm which consists of two parts, i.e., the encoder and the decoder. The encoder compresses the input point cloud by generating the multiple description codes which can be transmitted through different communication channels. The multiple description coding scheme deals with the difficulty of transmitting a large point cloud in hash channel conditions. Bell Labs in the 1970 s proved that multiple description coding (MDC) can ensure the quality of the transmitted compressed bit streams through unreliable internet and wireless communication networks [3]. For image coding, many MDC methods have been presented in the literature [4, 5]. However, to our best knowledge, there are very few works on the design of MDC method for 3D model compression and transmission.

Recently, many new algorithms are developed to capture comprehensive shape models of static and dynamic scenes with RGB-D cameras in the research areas of computer graphics and computer vision [6, 7]. To combine the depth data and the camera parameters of each frame, the 3D point cloud consisting of a large amount of points is a common way to describe the shape model with color information or normal vectors of the shape. Octree structures have been proved to be efficient in compressing point clouds [8]. One of the obvious disadvantages in the octree-based methods is they introduce significant reconstruction errors and thus fail in generating high quality 3D models, especially when the compression ratio is high. Mekuria et al. [9] presented an octree-based approach to compress tele-immersive videos by partitioning the voxel space of an octree into macroblocks for inter-frame coding. Instead of using image prediction directly, Sun et al. [10] presented a point cloud clustering scheme which takes the correlation of the distance information of points into consideration to remove spatial redundancies.

In this paper, we present a novel 3D structure awareness RGB-D video compression scheme using the proposed super-point clustering which generates a set of centroid super-points for representing a simplified scene model. The algorithm starts from representing a point cloud with a set of super-points using our multiple principal plane analysis (MPPA) [11, 12]. In this work, a super-point is defined to be a small cluster of 3D points of similar feature vectors. To put all the super-points from the input point cloud together, the super-points are grouped into multiple clusters, each represented by a centroid super-point, by performing the proposed kernel-based clustering algorithm. Next, the median feature vectors of super-points are sparsely represented by the K singular value decomposition (K-SVD) [13]. Basically, the sparse codes of the median feature vectors in the same cluster are very similar and thus the redundant information among them are easy to remove by further entropy coding. To reconstruct the median feature vector of a super-point, the residual super-point defined by subtracting the feature vectors inside from the reconstructed median feature vector is computed. These residual feature vectors are also coded using the K-SVD based sparse representation to enhance the quality of the compressed point cloud. This results in a multiple description coding scheme for 3D point cloud compression. Every super-point in the point cloud is finally encoded with two description codes: the codes of the median feature vectors which reconstruct a simplified 3D model; the codes to encode the residual feature vectors of super-points. The multiple description coding enhances the reliability to transmit the compressed 3D point cloud when we transmit the codes in different channels of a less reliable communication network. To un-project the compressed point cloud into the 2D image space, the compressed RGB-D image is finally obtained (Fig. 1).

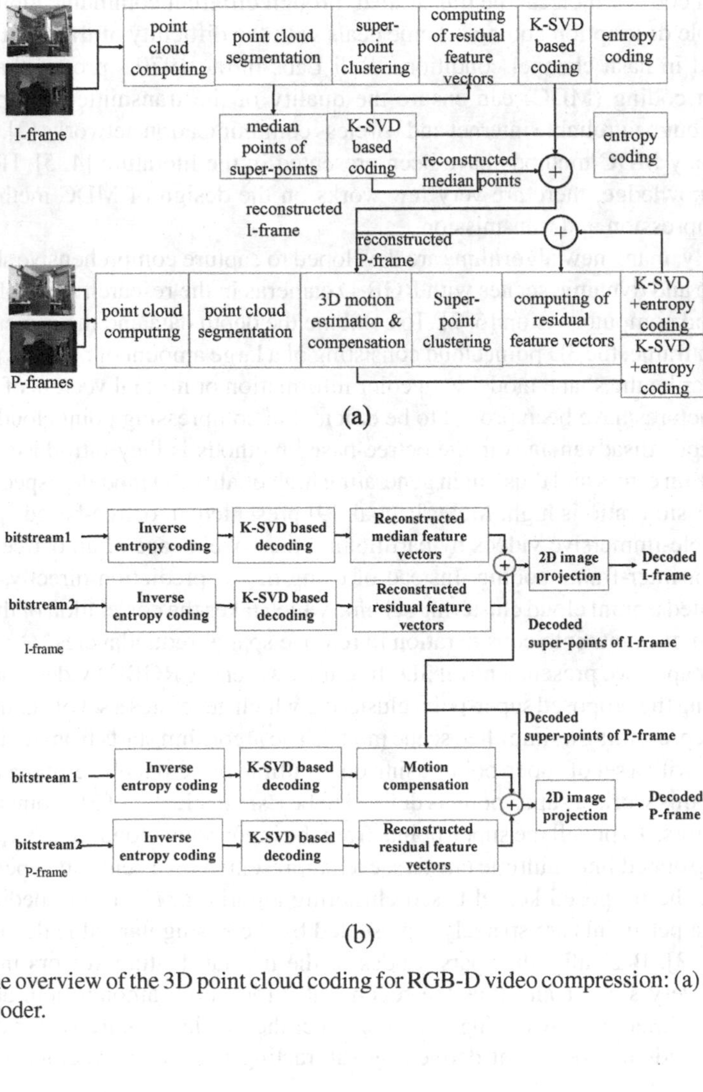

Fig. 1. The overview of the 3D point cloud coding for RGB-D video compression: (a) the encoder; (b) the decoder.

The contributions of our approach are listed as follows. Firstly, the proposed MPPA uses a binary tree to segment the input point cloud into a list of super-points, *i.e.*, the leave nodes of the tree. Secondly, to collect all the super-points in a point cloud, the kernel-based clustering algorithm generates super-point clusters with each of them represented by a centroid super-point. Thirdly, the 3D motion estimation and compression is proposed to compression the super-points of P-frames. Finally, we use traditional lossless entropy coding to complete the multiple description coding. Compared with the conventional octree-based point cloud compression methods, experiments demonstrate the effectiveness of our approach which attains a very high performance yielding significant compression ratios without sacrificing model quality.

2 The Point Cloud Segmentation Using the Multiple Principal Plane Analysis

Let $\mathrm{p}_E = [x_E, y_E, z_E, 1]^T$ be the homogeneous coordinates of a 3D point in Euclidean space. The pinhole camera model un-projects the 3D point into the pixel $\mathrm{p}_D = [u, v, 1]^T$ in a depth image D using the following equation:

$$\mathrm{p_D} = [u, v, 1] = \pi(\mathrm{p}_E) = \left(\frac{f_x x + c_x}{z(\mathrm{p_D})}, \frac{f_y y + c_y}{z(\mathrm{p_D})}, 1\right)^T \tag{1}$$

where f_x and f_y are the x and y direction focal length, respectively; c_x and c_y are the principal point offsets; $z(\mathrm{p_D})$ is the depth value of the 2D point p_D. Obviously, given the depth value $\mathrm{z}(\mathrm{p}_D)$, the inverse projection function $\pi^{-1}(\cdot)$ projects a 2D point p_D back to the 3D point p_E:

$$\mathrm{p}_E = [x_E, y_E, z_E, 1]^T = z(\mathrm{p}_D)\left(\frac{u - c_x}{f_x}, \frac{v - c_y}{f_y}, 1, \frac{1}{z(\mathrm{p}_D)}\right)^T \tag{2}$$

Based on the theory of three-dimensional special orthogonal (SO(3)) Lie group, the pose of the classical rigid body can be described by the camera motion model of six-degree-of-freedom (6-DOF) which constitutes an orthogonal rotation matrix $\mathrm{R}_{3\times3} \in \mathbb{R}^{3\times3}$ and a translation vector $\mathrm{t}_{3\times1} \in \mathbb{R}^3$. The 6-DOF camera motion model also defines the rigid body transformation in a 3D space $\mathbb{R}^3$ and is defined as a 4×4 matrix $\mathrm{M}_{4\times4}$ which consists of the rotation matrix $\mathrm{R}_{3\times3}$ and the translation vector $\mathrm{t}_{3\times1}$. Thus, a 3D point p_E in the camera coordinate system can be transformed into a 3D point $\mathrm{p}_W = [x, y, z, 1]^T$ in the world coordinate system by matrix left-multiplication: $\mathrm{p}_W = \psi(\mathrm{M}_{4\times4}, \mathrm{p}_E) = \mathrm{M}_{4\times4}\mathrm{p}_E$. Inversely, the inverse function $\psi^{-1}(\cdot)$ transformation p_W back to p_E:

$$\mathrm{p}_E = \begin{bmatrix} \mathrm{R}_{3\times3}^{-1} & -\mathrm{R}_{3\times3}^{-1}\mathrm{t}_{3\times1} \\ 0 & 1 \end{bmatrix} \begin{bmatrix} x \\ y \\ z \\ 1 \end{bmatrix}. \tag{3}$$

Researchers in 3D model reconstruction have shown that the colored point cloud representation [14] is an efficient and effective approach to define the visual appearance and shape of a scene. Accordingly, given the intrinsic and external parameters of an RGB-D camera, we first integrate the color and depth information of a frame to represent the geometry and texture of the corresponding viewpoint with a colored point cloud, which is a collection of points $\{p_i\}$, each consisting of a color vector and a depth value at a particular position in a 3D space. Thus, a point in the cloud may be represented as a feature tuple: $\mathbf{f}_i = (x_i, y_i, z_i, r_i, g_i, b_i)$, where x_i, y_i, and z_i describe the position of the point p_i in the 3D space; r_i, g_i, and b_i describe its color components. The depth value has been transformed into the value of z_i.

In our point cloud compression, the depth and color values of each pixel in the RGB-D image are used to calculate the corresponding 3D point using Eq. (2). This represents each frame as a colored local point cloud. Our MPPA-based tree partitioning scheme follows to recursively transform the local point cloud into a binary tree in which the leave nodes are flattened into a list of super-points using the depth-first-traversal process. Each super-point stores a small amount of points that basically are on a common 3D plane, *i.e.* the principal plane. Thus, the shape of the point cloud is finally represented as multiple principal planes (MPPs). The MPPA keeps a queue of non-leave nodes and removes each node in the queue one-by-one for further decomposition. Thus, the input point cloud is finally represented as a list of leave nodes (super-points) in which the shape of each super-point is modeled as its principal plane. The algorithm is summarized as follows.

Algorithm 1. Point Cloud Segmentation with the MPPA.
Input: A point cloud $P = \{f_j\}_{j=1}^{n} \in \mathbb{R}^{6\times n}$.
Output: A list of super-points $S = \{X_j\}_{j=1}^{m}$.
Method:
Step 1. Initially, let X = P and add X into the non-leave node list $L=\{X\}$; $S=\{\}$.
Step 2. **while** L is not empty **do**:
remove a non-leave node X from L: $L \leftarrow L-\{X\}$;
perform SVD to compute the eigenvalues λ_1, λ_2 and λ_3 and the corresponding eigenvectors v_1, v_2 and v_3;
annotate the type of X as a leave node if $\lambda_3 / \sum_{i=1,\ldots,3} \lambda_i < T_\lambda$ where T_λ is a threshold;
if X is not a leave node **do**:
decompose X into X_1 and X_2 using the principal plane with the normal vector v_3;
add new nodes into L: $L \leftarrow L \cup \{X_1, X_2\}$;
else: $S \leftarrow S \cup \{X\}$.
Step 3. **return** S.

3 The K-SVD Based 3D Point Cloud Coding

3.1 Level-1 Point Cloud Representation

As mentioned above, Algorithm 1 segments a point cloud into a set of super-points, each consisted of a small set of 3D points. The proposed compression scheme processes two input types: the I-frame and the P-frame. The super-points of each P-frame are basically reconstructed from the decoded super-points of the previous frame using the estimated motion vectors. To reduce the computational complexity of the 3D motion estimation, in this work, only the median feature vector of each super-point *SP* in the current frame is used to search the nearest neighbor *SP*' in the previous frame. Input the super-point pair (*SP*, *SP*') to a 3D registration algorithm, the 6-DOF motion vector is thus computed to reconstruct the feature vectors of *SP* using the corresponding ones in *SP*'. That is, the super-point in a P-frame is basically encoded with a 6-dimensional motion vector.

The median feature vectors (motion vectors) of super-points in an I-frame (P-frame) can be represented as a data matrix $\bar{X} \in \mathbb{R}^{m \times 6}$, where m is the number of super-points constituting the point cloud. The well-known K-SVD algorithm alternatively performs between sparse coding and dictionary updating to train a global dictionary D for data representation [30]. The K-SVD based sparse representation is summarized as follows.

Algorithm 2. The K-SVD based super-point coding.
Input: The median feature vectors of super-points $\bar{X} \in \mathbb{R}^{m\times 6}$.
Output: The dictionary D and sparse codes C of $\bar{X}$.
Method:
Step 1. Apply the K-SVD algorithm to train an over-complete dictionary D of size 6×*K*.
Step 2. Compute the transformation coefficients using the OMP pursuit algorithm: $C = D^{-1}\bar{X}$.
Step 3. Reconstruct the data matrix of median feature vectors: $\hat{X} = DC$.
Step 4. Return the dictionary D, the sparse codes C and the reconstructed data matrix $\hat{X}$.

3.2 The Kernel-Based Super-Point Clustering

Although Algorithm 2 has been used to encode the median feature vectors (motion vectors) of super-points, the residual parts of super-points should be carefully encoded to enhance the quality of the compressed point cloud. Let the set of feature vectors of super-point i in the input point cloud P be $X_i = \{f_j\}_{j=1}^{n_i} \in \mathbb{R}^{n_i \times 6}$. For P-frames, the feature vectors of a super-point are reconstructed from the previous frame using its motion vector. This is the so-called motion compensation process. Following similar concept proposed in [15], the structure vector $\hat{s}_i$ of super-point i in the kernel feature space can be represented as $\hat{s}_i = \sum_{j=1}^{n_i} \Phi(f_{ij})$, where Φ is a nonlinear mapping from the data space into some high, or even infinite-dimension feature space. Let $\hat{s}_j$ be the structure vector of super-point j which consists of n_j points. The dot product of $\hat{s}_i$ and $\hat{s}_j$ using kernel-trick [15] may be computed as $<\hat{s}_i, \hat{s}_j> = \sum_{k=1}^{n_i} \sum_{k'=1}^{n_j} \Psi(f_{ik}, f_{ik'})$, where $\Psi(f_{ik}, f_{ik'})$ is a kernel function. Polynomial, B_n-spline and Gaussian radial basis function (RBF) kernels are famous kernel functions. In this work, a Gaussian RBF $\Psi(f_{ik}, f_{ik'}) = \exp(-\beta \| f_{ik} - f_{ik'} \|_2^2)$ is chosen, where β is the regular parameter. In practice, we set $\beta = 2$. The inner product of two structure vectors can be used to measure the similarity between two super-points.

For each structure vector $\hat{s}$ that represents the structure of a super-point in a point cloud P, we divide the structure vector by its norm to form unit structure vector $\hat{\sigma}$. The unit eigenvectors of the sample autocorrelation matrix can be computed from Gram matrix G of which element at the ith row and jth column is $\langle \hat{\sigma}_i, \hat{\sigma}_j \rangle$: $\hat{h}_i = \sum_{j=1}^{m} \alpha_{ji}\hat{\sigma}_j \Big/ \sqrt{\lambda_i}$, $i = 1, 2, \ldots, n$, where m is the number of super-points in P, $\lambda_1 \geq \lambda_2 \geq \ldots \geq \lambda_m$ are the eigenvalues of G and $[\alpha_{1i}, \alpha_{2i}, \ldots, \alpha_{ni}]^T$ is the unit eigenvector associated with λ_i. The number of adopted eigenvectors is determined by the least l satisfying the formula: $(\lambda_1 + \lambda_2 + \cdots + \lambda_l / \lambda_1 + \lambda_2 + \cdots + \lambda_m) \geq \Delta E$, where ΔE is a predefined value such that the l eigenvectors can describe most of the structure vectors with certain accuracy. In practice, we set ΔE to be 0.99.

For each unit structure vector $\hat{\sigma}$ in P, we compute its normalized model parameters as $\hat{\mu} = [\mu_i]_{i=1}^{l}$, where $\mu_i = \left\langle \hat{\sigma}, \hat{h}_i \right\rangle$. Next, the standard k-means clustering algorithm is applied to group these vectors of normalized model parameters into K^* clusters. Let $C_k = \{X_i\}_{i=1}^{c_k}$ be the set of super-points with their structure vector assigned to cluster k. The median super-point defined as follows:

$$X_k = \arg\min_{k} \sum\nolimits_{j=1,\cdots,c_k} \|\hat{\mu}_j - \hat{\mu}_k\|_2^2 \tag{4}$$

is selected to the k-th centroid super-point. Thus, our super-point clustering algorithm partitions the super-points in P into the data matrix $\Gamma = \{[X_{k,i}]_{i=1}^{n_i}\}_{k=1}^{K^*}$, where K^* is the number of super-point clusters.

3.3 The Coding of Residual Super-Points

Algorithm 2 encodes the data matrix $\bar{X}$ as the sparse code matrix C, which is further quantized with a small quantization and coded by a traditional entropy coding to produce the encoded bit-stream for transmission. In the receiver end, with the dictionary D, these sparse codes are decoded to reconstruct the median feature vectors of super-points. For each feature vector f in a super-point, we subtract it from the corresponding reconstructed median feature vector to compute the residual feature vector $\tilde{f}$. This constructs the data matrix $\Gamma_r = \{[\tilde{f}_{k,i}]_{i=1}^{n_i}\}_{k=1}^{K^*}$ for compression. The encoder of these cluster-specific residual feature vectors with K-SVD based sparse representation is summarized as follows.

Algorithm 3. The encoder of residual super-points.
Input: The data sets of residual super-points $\Gamma_r = \{[\tilde{f}_{k,i}]_{i=1}^{n_i}\}_{k=1}^{K^*}$.
Output: encoded bit-streams B.
Method:

1. Initialize the bit-stream list B =[].
2. **for** each super-point cluster k **do**:
   - 2.1 Perform Algorithm 2 to encode the residual feature vector dataset $\Gamma_r(k) = [\tilde{f}_{k,i}]_{i=1}^{n_i}$ with sparse code C_k and dictionary D_k.
   - 2.2 Quantize the sparse codes C_k and input them to the arithmetic coding [16] for generating the bit-stream B_k: $B \leftarrow B \cup B_k$.
3. Transmit $[D_k]_{k=1}^{K^*}$ and B to the receiver.

The size of the global dictionary D, *i.e.* the value of K, is relatively larger than that of each cluster-specific dictionary D_k, $k = 1, \ldots, K^*$ since the residual feature vectors of super-points in a cluster would be similar with each other. In practice, for I-frames (P-frames), we set $K = 64$ ($K = 8$) and $K_k = 32$ for each cluster by considering the tradeoff between the compression ratio and the reconstruction error. The compression ratio (*CR*) of the proposed coding scheme is thus defined as follow

$$CR = \begin{cases} \frac{n\times6\times32}{[6K+6K*K_k]\times32+bits(code)\times n\times n_p}, & \text{for I - frames} \\ \frac{n\times6\times32}{6K*K_k\times32+6K\times8+bits(code)\times n\times n_p}, & \text{for P - frames} \end{cases} \quad (5)$$

where n and n_p are the number of points and the number of sparse codes to encode a feature vector, respectively; *bits(code)* is the number of bits to encode a sparse code. Basically, we assume each element of a feature vector in a point cloud is represented by a 32-bits floating point. To encode P-frames, each dimension of a motion vector is encoded with 8 bits since the elements of a motion vector are often small. In practice, the sparse codes can be further compressed by the entropy coding to achieve the goal of higher compression ratio. One of the significant contributions of the proposed approach is that the multiple description coding scene reduces the probability to fail in transmitting the 3D model to the receiver end using a wireless and internet communication channels. Also, the complexity of the proposed approach is low, this facilitates the construction of a real-time 3D application.

4 Experimental Results

The system is implemented on a PC with Intel Core i7 3.4 GHz CPU. The RGB-D benchmark datasets provided by the Technical University of Munich [17] are used to

Table 1. The compression results of test 3D mesh models [18] using the fusion of MPPA and the K-SVD based multiple description coding.

Models	Number of model points	Point cloud compression with the sparse representation			
Blast	882,954	196,076	40,731	28,596	No. of super-points
		3.0624	7.4089	8.3578	Compression ratio
		0.0449	0.6183	1.0332	Reconstruction Error
Dragon	437,645	108,630	24,279	13,656	No. of super-points
		2.8294	6.8829	8.4586	Compression ratio
		0.00009	0.0001	0.0003	Reconstruction Error
Angel	237,018	61,250	14,667	6,852	No. of super-points
		2.7409	6.5653	8.6437	Compression ratio
		0.00148	0.0190	0.0056	Reconstruction Error

verify the effectiveness of our approach in terms of the compression ratios and reconstruction error. In this benchmark, several datasets including aligned color and depth sequences captured with a single RGB-D moving camera are provided. The accurate ground-truth of each frame's camera pose is also provided, which is measured by an external motion capture system. This provides the ground-truth for computing the error between the original and reconstructed point clouds.

The first experiments demonstrate the effectiveness of our MPPA that represent 3D models [18] with multiple super-points. In this experiment, the residual feature vectors in each super-point are encoded with two sparse codes using a single pre-trained dictionary. In practice, the arithmetic coding can remove the redundancies existing in these sparse codes and leads to about 4 bits to encode the sparse codes of each residual feature vector. Table 1 shows the compression results of these models with each super-point as the basic coding unit. Notice that the reconstruction error of a super-point is small when the number of super-points is relative large. Figure 2 shows examples to compress point cloud using limited numbers of super-points.

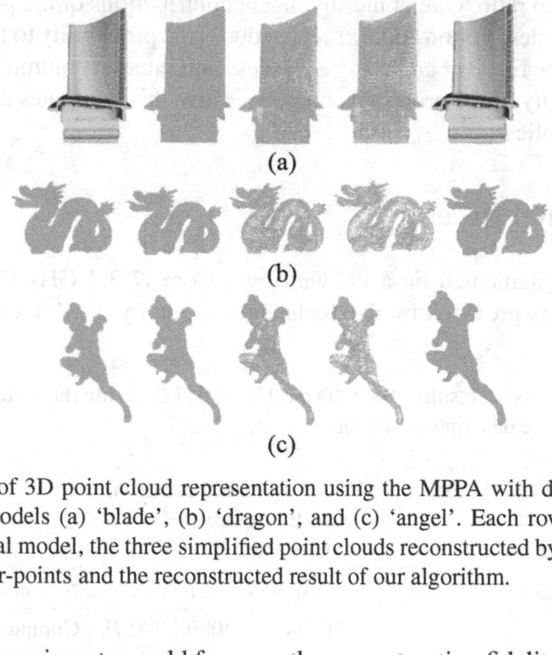

Fig. 2. Examples of 3D point cloud representation using the MPPA with different numbers of super-points for models (a) 'blade', (b) 'dragon', and (c) 'angel'. Each row from left to right contains the original model, the three simplified point clouds reconstructed by the median feature vectors of the super-points and the reconstructed result of our algorithm.

The second experiments would focus on the reconstruction fidelity over the RGB-D benchmark datasets [17]. We select "teddy," "room," "desk," "desk2," "360" and "plant" from the dataset collection "freiburg-1" for performance comparison. The compared methods include the octree based point cloud compression [19], the PCA coding and the artificial neural network (ANN) coding which is implemented by the auto-encoder [20]. For the octree based method, the maximal number of points allowed in any leave node of the octree representation are 10 and 100. The compressed point cloud in the octree based approach is only represented by the median feature vectors of super-points. For PCA coding, the numbers of principal components are 32, 64, and 128. The auto-encoder neural networks use sigmoid activation units and contain 4096, 512, d, 512, 4096 nodes, with d representing the number of dimensions of the descriptor. The number of sparse codes to encode each feature vector in our approach is 3. Table 2 shows the results of the performance comparison. The proposed approach has the best compression ratio without scarifying the quality of the reconstructed point cloud. It is noticed that the ANN approach cannot achieve the goal of reconstructing high quality 3D models. Although the compression ratio of the ANN with d dimensions of description is up to $4096/d$, the large amount of parameters, *i.e.* $4096*512*d$ to model the ANN should be learned and stored in advance. In Table 2, the compression ratios for the ANN approach are the results of representing each parameter with a 16-bit floating point.

Table 2. Average reconstruction results across all data sets; MSE is the mean squared error and σ is the standard derivation; for our approach, the size of the global dictionary $K = 64$ ($K = 8$) for I-frames (P-frames) and the size of the cluster dictionary K_k is 32.

Methods	Reconstruction error (MSE) $\pm\sigma$	Compression ratio (CR)	CR/MSE
PCA 32	42.8 ± 6.39	10.76	0.25
PCA 64	33.81± 3.88	5.38	0.15
PCA 128	26.88 ± 2.57	2.69	0.10
ANN 32	59.66 ± 7.17	7.33	0.12
ANN 64	49.18 ± 4.72	3.67	0.07
ANN 128	45.66 ± 4.25	1.83	0.04
Octree 10	102.27 ± 8.56	3.56	0.03
Octree 100	3964.10 ± 120.01	**34.32**	0.01
Proposed (Intra)	28.89 ± 6.06	12.45	0.43
Proposed (Intra+Inter)	**10.57**± 2.31	19.92	**1.88**

The last experiments verify the effectiveness of the proposed approach by un-project the reconstructed point cloud into the 2D space for generating the compressed RGB-D images. The peak-to-noise ratio (PSNR) is used to measure the quality of the compressed image. In this experiment, only the first frame is considered to be the I-frame. For our method, the PSNR values in some depth frames are not good since the 3D motion estimation and compensation cannot accurately predict the depth values across depth frames in the scene change areas. Figure 3 shows the results of the octree-based approaches and the proposed method. Although the octree based approaches can produce better RGB PSNR values based on the test RGB-D video 'plant', our approach does not generate artifacts in the compressed RGB images. Figure 4 shows an example to compare the quality of these compressed RGB images using the proposed approach and the octree based method. The proposed method outperforms the octree based method by subjective evaluation.

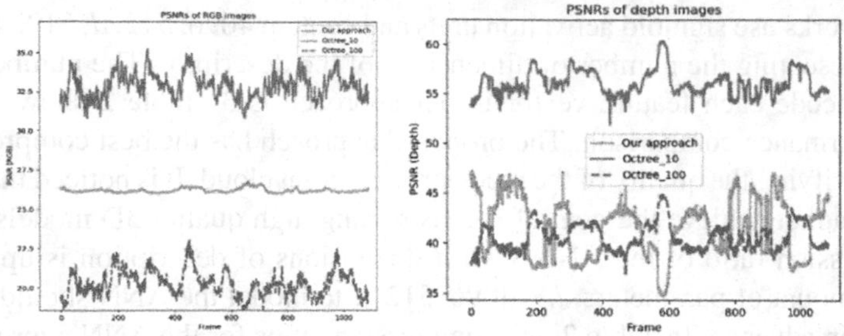

(a) (b)

Fig. 3. The performance comparison between the proposed method and the octree based approaches using the test video 'plant'; (a) the PSNR plots of the RGB images; (b) the PSNR plots of the depth images.

(a) (b) (c)

Fig. 4. Examples of the compressed RGB images using the proposed approach and the octree based approach; from top to bottom are (a) the original image, (b) the result of octree based approach and (c) the result of the proposed method.

5 Conclusions

In this paper, we have presented a novel 3D point cloud coding for RGB-D image compression. The contributions of the proposed method include (1) starting from the computation of the point cloud of an input RGB-D image, the MPPA automatically segments the point cloud into multiple super-points for reducing the coding complexity of the succeeding K-SVD based coding; (2) the proposed kernel-based super-point clustering algorithm partitions the super-points into multiple clusters; (3) the cluster-specific K-SVD based sparse representation can encode each super-point cluster with high compression ratio without degrading the quality of the reconstructed point cloud. In our experiments on publicly available datasets, we show that our approach gives better compression results on the whole and outperforms the state-of-the-art methods. In the next step of our research, we plan to expand the compression scheme to remove inter-frame redundancies in the input RGB-D video to achieve the goal of high quality 3D model reconstruction. Furthermore, based on the reconstructed models, we want to extend our approach to 3D object recognition, detection, segmentation, retrieval, and printing.

Acknowledgements. This work was supported in part by Minister of Science and Technology, Taiwan under grant numbers MOST 107-2221-E-019-033-MY2 and University System of Taipei Joint Research Program, under grand number USTP-NTUT-NTOU-108-03.

References

1. Han, J., Shao, L., Xu, D., Shotton, J.: Enhanced computer vision with Microsoft Kinect sensor: a review. IEEE Trans. Cybern. **43**(5), 1318–1334 (2013)
2. Zollhöfer, M., et al.: State of the art on 3D reconstruction with RGB-D cameras. EUROGRAPHICS **37**(2), 625–652 (2018)
3. Wolf, J.K., Wyner, A.D., Ziv, J.: Source coding for multiple descriptions. Bell Syst. Tech. J. **59**(8), 1417–1426 (1980)
4. Meng, L., Liang, J., Samarawickrama, U., Zhao, Y., Bai, H., Kaup, A.: Multiple description coding with randomly and uniformly offset quantizers. IEEE Trans. Image Process. **23**(2), 582–595 (2014)
5. Sun, G., Meng, L., Liu, L., Tan, Y., Zhang, J., Zhang, H.: KSVD-based multiple description coding. IEEE. Access **7**, 1962–1972 (2019)
6. Förster, E.-C., Löwe, T., Wenger, S., Magnor, M.: RGB-guided depth map compression via compressed sensing and sparse coding. In: Proceedings of the Picture Coding Symposium (PCS), pp. 1–4 (2015)
7. Wang, X., Şekercioğlu, Y.A., Drummond, T., Natalizio, E., Fantoni, I., Frémont, V.: Fast depth video compression for mobile RGB-D sensors. IEEE Trans. Circ. Syst. Video Technol. **26**(4), 673–686 (2016)
8. Thanou, D., Chou, P.A., Frossard, P.: Graph-based compression of dynamic 3D point cloud sequences. IEEE Trans. Image Process. **25**(4), 1765–1778 (2016)
9. Mekuria, R., Blom, K., Cesar, P.: Design, implementation and evaluation of a point cloud codec for tele-immersive video. IEEE Trans. Circ. Syst. Video Technol. **27**(4), 828–842 (2017)
10. Sun, X., Ma, H., Sun, Y., Liu, M.: A novel point cloud compression algorithm based on clustering. IEEE Robot. Autom. Lett. **4**(2), 2132–2139 (2019)
11. Cheng, S.-C., Kuo, C.-T., Wu, D.-C.: A novel 3D mesh compression using mesh segmentation with multiple principal plane analysis. Pattern Recogn. **43**(1), 267–279 (2010)
12. Su, R.-Y., Cheng, S.-C., Chang, C.-C., Chen, J.-M.: Model-based 3D pose estimation of a single RGB image using deep viewpoint classification neural network. Appl. Sci. **9**(12), 2478 (2019)
13. Aharon, M., Elad, M., Bruckstein, A.: K-SVD: an algorithm for designing overcomplete dictionaries for sparse representation. IEEE Trans. Signal Process. **54**(11), 4311–4322 (2006)
14. Kim, H., Lee, B.: Robust 3-D object reconstruction based on camera clustering with geodesic distance. IEEE/ASME Trans. Mechatron. **24**(2), 889–891 (2019)
15. Chang, C.-C.: Deformable shape finding with models based on kernel methods. IEEE Trans. Image Process. **15**(9), 2743–2754 (2006)
16. Howard, P.G., Vitter, J.S.: Arithmetic coding for data compression. Proc. IEEE **82**(6), 857–865 (1994)
17. Computer Vision Group—Dataset Download. https://vision.in.tum.de/data/datasets/rgbddataset/download. Accessed 9 June 2019
18. The Stanford 3D Scanning Repository. http://graphics.stanford.edu/data/3Dscanrep/. Accessed on 23 June 2019
19. Zeng, M., Zhao, F., Zheng, J., Liu, X.: A memory-efficient kinectfusion using octree. In: Hu, S.-M., Martin, R.R. (eds.) CVM 2012. LNCS, vol. 7633, pp. 234–241. Springer, Heidelberg (2012). https://doi.org/10.1007/978-3-642-34263-9_30
20. Canelhas, D.R., Schaffernicht, E., Stoyanov, T., Lilienthal, A.J., Davison, A.J.: Compressed voxel-based mapping using unsupervised learning. Robotics **6**(15), 1–13 (2017)

Resolution Booster: Global Structure Preserving Stitching Method for Ultra-High Resolution Image Translation

Siying Zhai(✉), Xiwei Hu(✉), Xuanhong Chen(✉), Bingbing Ni(✉), and Wenjun Zhang(✉)

Shanghai Jiao Tong University, Shanghai, China
{zzz2102015233326,huxiwei,chen19910528,nibingbing, zhangwenjun}@sjtu.edu.cn

Abstract. Current image translation networks (for instance image to image translation, style transfer *et al.*) have strict limitation on input image resolution due to high spatial complexity, which results in a wide gap to their usage in practice. In this paper we propose a novel patch-based auxiliary architecture, called Resolution Booster, to endow a trained image translation network ability to process ultra high resolution images. Different from previous methods which compute the results with the entire image, our network processes resized global image at low resolution as well as high-resolution local patches to save the memory. To increase the quality of generated image, we exploit the rough global information with global branch and high resolution information with local branch then combine the results with a designed reconstruction network. Then a joint global/local stitching result is produced. Our network is flexible to be deployed on any exiting image translation method to endow the new network to process larger images. Experimental results show the both capability of processing much higher resolution images while not decreasing the generating quality compared with baseline methods and generality of our model for flexible deployment.

Keywords: Image translation · Patch-based method · Style transfer

1 Introduction

Nowadays with the development of hardware for image capture almost all the images we encounter have high resolution (larger than 4M pixels). However, to the best of our knowledge, no methods in image translation field support ultra high resolution images yet. For instance, the most popular off-line style transfer model, fast neural style transfer [6], which is relatively small model, is only able to process 3M (2080 × 1560) pixels image on a single 12G memory Titan-X GPU. In contrast to this, with the deployment of our Resolution Booster we are aiming to achieve ultra high resolution image (up to 12M pixels) inference for style transfer on the same hardware condition.

Y. M. Ro et al. (Eds.): MMM 2020, LNCS 11961, pp. 702–713, 2020.
https://doi.org/10.1007/978-3-030-37731-1_57

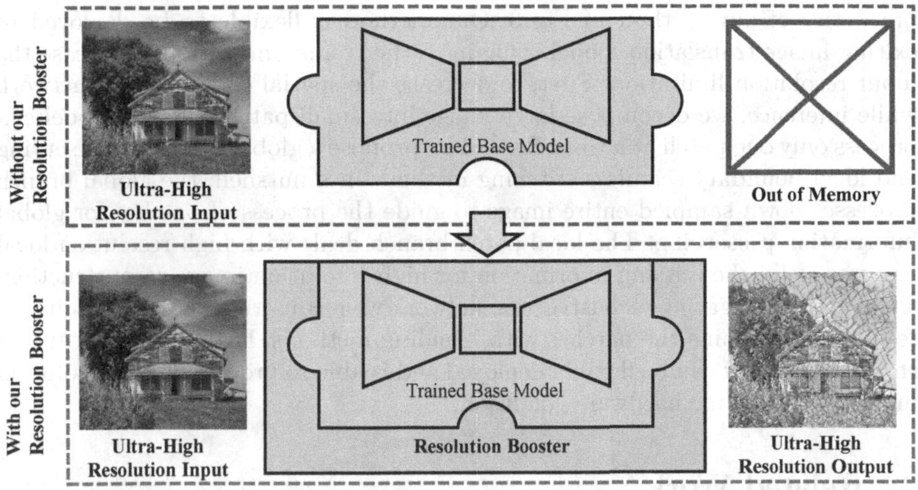

Fig. 1. Our method can be easily applied to a generation model and enlarge the input image resolution limitation.

Image translation is a popular research topic. Interesting works involve style transfer (introduced later), mask to image translation [5], unpaired image domains translation [16], low resolution to high resolution translation (super resolution) [9] *et al.* Despite the success of all these image translation methods, there exists one great common flaw in them: the input image resolution is strictly limited as the cost of memory is extremely high. The common processed image resolution in methods like mask to image translation [5] is 60 thousand pixels. For fast neural style transfer network usually 2 million pixels is the highest resolution for a single image to be processed. However, photos in real life taken by an ordinary phone these days reach at least 6 million resolution. This causes a deep gap to take these image processing methods in practice. Sanakoyeu *et al.* [12] simplify the generator of the style transfer model to reduce the memory usage but only achieve 1M pixels inference. Junginger *et al.* [7] explore patch-based method for ultra high resolution photographic style transfer. It only processes patches of high resolution image to save memory. It lacks global information to harmony all the patches so the implementation scenarios are limited. Wang *et al.* [14] propose an advanced method for mask to image translation to enlarge the input image resolution to 6 million pixels. However, it is not a general approach and consumes lots of extra memory (Fig. 1).

Most of the image translation models deal with entire images. When the input image has ultra high resolution, the cost memory of features flowing in the network will explode. Furthermore, generation of high resolution images suffers from conformity of long-term dependency and short-term integrity. In other words, We should consider that generated images globally compatible and keep integrity locally. In this paper we propose a general pipeline, Resolution Booster, to compose ultra high resolution images for base model. We show the general properties of our method in Fig. 3. Our method is flexible to be deployed to exiting image translation model (plug-in to the trained model) and increase the input resolution limitation. First, to decrease the spatial complexity of network while inference, we decompose large image into small patches so the model can process only one patch at a time. Second we propose a global structure preserving and local boundary seamless stitching method. In a nutshell, the global branch processes down sampled entire image to guide the process of patches for global information preserving. The local patch branch deals with high resolution local features to fill the missing information for high resolution image reconstruction. Then with aggregating reconstruction network we reconstruct the high resolution results and combine the patches with blending methods. Extensive experiments show our method can be flexibly deployed and is able to process higher resolution images on the same hardware condition.

2 Related Work

Here we briefly review some works involving patch-based method and memory efficiency of deep neural network.

Patch-based method is popular in some traditional tasks for instance texture synthesis. Liang *et al.* [8] propose generating texture by sampling patches from the source image. The patches are then stitched together with specific blending method. Efros *et al.* [4] propose Image Quilting, an algorithm to synthesis image appearance by stitching small patches using minimal boundary error cut, and extend it to texture transfer task. More recently, patch-based methods are also widely used in the area of deep learning. Chen *et al.* [1] share similar idea of exchange patches of two images as the above texture synthesis methods. The difference is that they manipulate the patches in the feature space. They exchange feature patches of style image and content image to transfer the style. PGGAN [3] proposes an additional patch-based discriminator for GAN to get more information of local areas of image for image inpainting.

There are a number of works related to memory efficiency in more developed vision area especially image segmentation. ICNet [15] uses multi-resolution input and cascades corresponding features in addition of filter pruning model compression method to achieve efficiency. ENet [11] applies encoder and decoder structure to support its early downsample operation. These works focus more on the term of time efficiency while we pay attention to the space efficiency. GLNet [2] has a similar global as well as local branches in the network and exchange information between two branches. They also process entire image of lower resolution in global branch and patches in local branch. The major difference from our work is that they directly interpolate the results at the end of network, which is not tolerable in generative tasks as the label contains much less information than a image. Instead we use a reconstruction network and a blending network to reach higher image quality.

3 Methodology

3.1 Problem Overview

To enable a network to process higher resolution image, a possible solution is to forward one patch of the entire image at one time and stitch the results together afterwards. It is flexible as the size of patches can be determined arbitrarily. In this way it is possible to process images with arbitrary resolution. It costs more time to use less memory. However, in this way it will cause the dilemma of conformity for long-term dependency and short-term integrity. The processed patches have no global information, as a result the neighbor patches do not synthesize related features on the boundaries. This leads to discontinuity at the edges of the patches.

In this work we focus on patch-based method and solve the discontinuity problem by proposing a pipeline composed by global and local branches, reconstruct network. We use down sampled entire image to provide rough global guidance for structure preserving, in the meantime, the local branch gives high resolution information to fill missing local details. With the concatenation of features in both branches, we can jointly reconstruct global structure preserving and local texture continuing high resolution images.

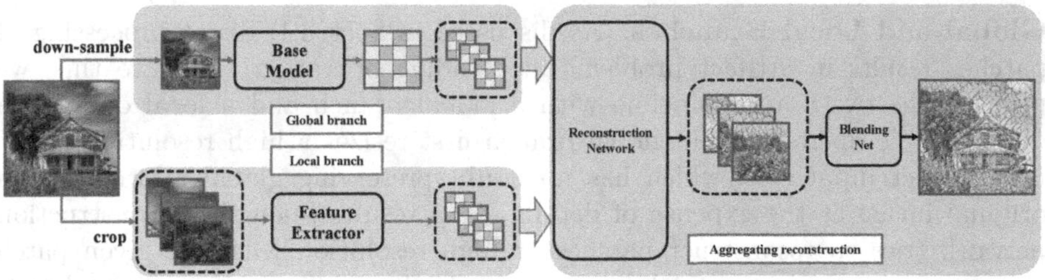

Fig. 2. Overview of pipeline. In global branch the high resolution image is down-sampled and processed, in local branch the cropped patches are processed. The results are concatenated and generated high resolution patches are reconstructed then stitched together.

3.2 Pipeline

Overview of Pipeline. Based on the analysis above, we propose our Resolution Booster pipeline as depicted in Fig. 2. The pipeline contains two main branches, a global branch gathering global features and a local branch grabbing local features of each patch. Given dataset of N high resolution images $D = \{I_i\}_{i=1}^{N}$ with $I_i \in \mathbb{R}^{H \times W}$, H the height of image and W the width, the global branch G first resizes input high resolution images as low-resolution ones $D_l = \{I_i^l\}_{i=1}^{N}$, where $I_i^l \in \mathbb{R}^{h \times w}$. Note that $h \times w$ is the desired image size for target base model for processing. Meanwhile, the local branch L crops input images into patches with desired size $D_p = \{\{I^p_{i,j}\}_{j=1}^{n_i}\}_{i=1}^N$ at the original resolution, where n_i represents the total number of patches of image I_i and $I^p_{i,j}$ indicates the jth patch of image I_i with $I^p_{i,j} \in \mathbb{R}^{h \times w}$.

With proper image size, D_l in global branch is fed to the given base model, for example a style transfer model, and D_p in local branch is processed by a feature extractor. Result features of global branch $R_l = \{I^l_i\}_{i=1}^N$ aggregates the global information after specific image processing, while results of local branch $R_p = \{\{I^p_{i,j}\}_{j=1}^{n_i}\}_{i=1}^N$ are considered as local feature maps. R_l is then cropped into patches and transferred to global feature maps R_{lp}. Note that global feature maps R_{lp} and local feature maps R_p are set at the same size, providing the precondition to aggregate the information together.

These two branches are later aggregated by concatenating their resulted feature maps and feeding them to a reconstruction network. Taking global information from the global branch and local information from the local one as input, the reconstruction network outputs patches $T_p = \{\{I^p_{i,j}\}_{j=1}^{n_i}\}_{i=1}^N$ of target images at high resolution. To stitch patches together, the blending net is applied to generate the final result image at desired resolution. The training method is based on the base model task. The specific loss can be calculated based on final results of our whole framework.

Global and Local Branches. As discussed in Sect. 3.1, direct processing of patches results in artifact problems in blending operation. To solve this, we propose the two-branch pipeline with a global branch and a local one. With down-sample operation, the global branch first resizes a high resolution image into correct input size, which has no doubt preserving global information of original image at the expense of details. As a result, when the reconstruction network tries to reconstruct patches at high resolution with the given patch feature maps after base model processing, it is often difficult to generate details that have been already lost. Therefore, a local branch is proposed to provide important details based on patches in original images with a light-weight feature extractor. Occupying only a small amount of memory, the supporting detail feature maps extracted by the local branch fill the missing information between global feature maps and high resolution patch results.

Different from GLNet [2] which applies also a two-branch framework, our pipeline collects the feature maps at the last layer of base model in global branch and feature extractor in local branch. Facing segmentation task in GLNet, the network in global branch is designed as the same as the one in local branch, and global and local information are exchanged at each layer of the network. Although this feature pyramid approach is often employed in segmentation problem, it commonly results in severe artifacts in image generation problem since extra features give too much useless information to image decoder and causes heavy artifacts.

Aggregating Reconstruction. To aggregate two branches, we propose a flexible reconstruction network to which the global feature maps and the local ones are fed. The design details of reconstruction network may differ in different circumstances. For example, for style transfer task, to decrease the artifacts, we need some down sample layers to remove abundant information. Relatively, for an easier task such as image reconstruction, the stack of one up-sampling layer and two convolutional layers are sufficient to obtain high quality results. Note that choosing a suitable design of reconstruction network is essential to improve final results when applying our general framework into a specific problem.

Outputs of reconstruction network are patches at high resolution with overlaps between each other. To generate the target image with its patches, we implement traditional blending methods by neural network. Note that previous two-branch feature extractors produce patches sharing global information between each other. As a result, edges of contiguous patches are relevant rather than independent, which offers possibility to simply blending them together. Our blending net is built by convolutional layers to realize Gaussian and Laplacian Pyramids with no need of training. As written as neural network, our blending net can be processed in GPU, which improves the efficiency of our framework while outputting high quality results.

Training Method. Our pipeline can be trained directly on the final output end to end with the loss of base model. For image reconstruction, with generated high resolution image $\hat{I}_i$ the smooth L1 loss L_{rec} is applied as

$$L_{rec} = \frac{\sum_{h,w,c} |\hat{I}_i| + s - I_i}{\sum_{h,w,c} \hat{I}_i + \sum_{h,w,c} I_i + s}, \quad (1)$$

where s is the smooth parameter, h, w and c are the height width and channel of the images, respectively.

For style transfer, with generated high resolution image $\hat{I}_i$ and $j_t h$ layer of VGG network [13] phi_j, we apply content loss L_{con} and style loss L_{style} as

$$\begin{aligned} L_{con} &= \frac{1}{hwc}||\phi_j(\hat{I}_i) - \phi_j(I_i)||_2^2, \\ L_{style} &= ||G_j^{\phi}(\hat{I}_i) - G_j^{\phi}(I_i)||_2^2, \end{aligned} \quad (2)$$

where $G_j^{\phi}(x) = \frac{1}{hwc} \sum_{h,w} \phi_j(x)_{h,w,c}\phi_j(x)_{h,w,c'}$ is Gram matrix.

4 Experiment

Our pipeline can be flexible deployed to a trained image translation model. For brevity of the paper, we choose two typical base models for testing our method: image reconstruction and style transfer. Image reconstruction is to rebuild the image with an encoder-decoder architecture. It is a suitable fundamental task to test our method. For style transfer, we use the fast neural style transfer [6] as the baseline method.

4.1 Image Reconstruction

Dataset and Implementation Details. To guarantee the diversity of the images, we use MS-COCO [10] dataset to evaluate our reconstruction model. It contains more than 118k training images and 1.5 million object instances over 80 semantic classes. The images are resized and cropped to 512 × 512 pixels for reconstruction training. We test the model on a test image set containing 100 novel images. The metric we use to evaluate the similarity of two images is Peak Signal to Noise Ratio (PSNR). We also directly test largest image that is able to be processed in two models on the same hardware condition.

The baseline model contains downsample encoder, several residual blocks and upsample decoder. So the global branch of our model has the same architecture. The local branch is small feature extractor composed by convolutional layers and residual blocks for memory efficiency. The reconstruction network is implemented by fully light-weighted convolutional layers and one upsample layer (Table 1).

Table 1. Major results of our method for image reconstruction. Baseline model is the model with the same architecture of our global branch but directly deals with the total resolution images. Blending method used here is linear blending. GPU memory is the used memory for single entire inference. The memory costs are evaluated on the patch branch for our method, the global branch costs the same memory (710 MB) for all patch sizes. As the two branch is processed separately during inference, total memory cost is the max of both.

Patch size (pixels)	40	80	120	160	200	240	Baseline
Patch number	49	16	9	4	4	4	–
PSNR (dB)	27.84	29.16	29.33	**29.37**	**29.37**	29.35	28.74
GPU memory (MB)	519	533	567	618	678	757	1392

Results. As a first step we test with quantitative evaluation whether our method can increase the input image size limitation while not decreasing the performance of the base model. The results are showed in Table 3. Basically results of most patch sizes have better performance than the baseline model and occupy much less memory. The performance of the model is highly related to the number of patches. The more patches are used, the lower accuracy of the results. This is as expected since increasing patches adds more noise. Even the largest patch size in the Table costs around half memory of the baseline model. The low memory usage is an base indicator that our method can process higher resolution image. More specifically, we test the highest resolution of images can be fed to both models on the same hardware condition. The largest image are 12M pixels for our method and 3M pixels for the baseline model, which is about 4 times of pixels. In this specific comparison, we test the models with images of different resolutions, from common HD (1M pixels) to ultra high resolution image (11M pixels). Results are showed in Table 2. As we increase the patch size with the resolution enlarging, the reconstruction error stay low. This shows the ability of enlarging input image resolution while preserving model quality of our model.

Table 2. Reconstruction results with different resolution images on the same hardware condition (Titan X Pascal 12 GB memory). When the number of pixels are larger than 3.6 million, baseline model is not able to process the image. Our model has much larger capacity of image resolution.

Total pixels (million)	0.7	1.9	3.6	5.0	7.5	11.1
Baseline	28.95	33.14	–	–	–	–
Ours	30.83	31.42	32.39	34.04	34.35	34.73

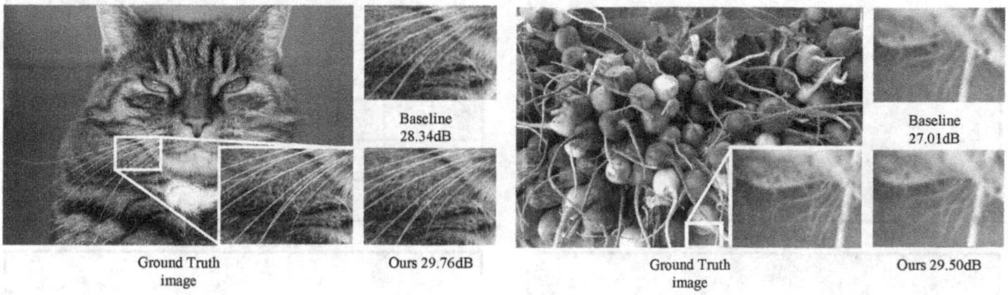

Fig. 3. Qualitative comparison of our method and baseline for image reconstruction.

Then the qualitative evaluation results are showed in Fig. 3. The patch size we use on this experiment is 200 (pixels). Our patch-based method has slightly better visual reconstruction results. The test images in the Figure have around 2M pixels.

Table 3. The ablation study for our pipeline (w/o means without). The results shows the effectiveness of our local, global branch, as well as blending net.

Experiment	Base model	w/o Local	w/o Global	w/o Blending	Ours
PSNR	28.74	25.12	22.56	29.24	**29.37**

Ablation Study. Finally in the additional experiments we show the necessity of the global branch, local branch and blending net for our pipeline. The global branch processes rough global information, it gives a lower but comparable result. The local branch is only a small feature extractor, it is not able to accomplish the image reconstruction task. However, the local branch provides more information of the high resolution image and rapidly increases the final results combined with global branch. The blending net also increases the final score of our pipeline.

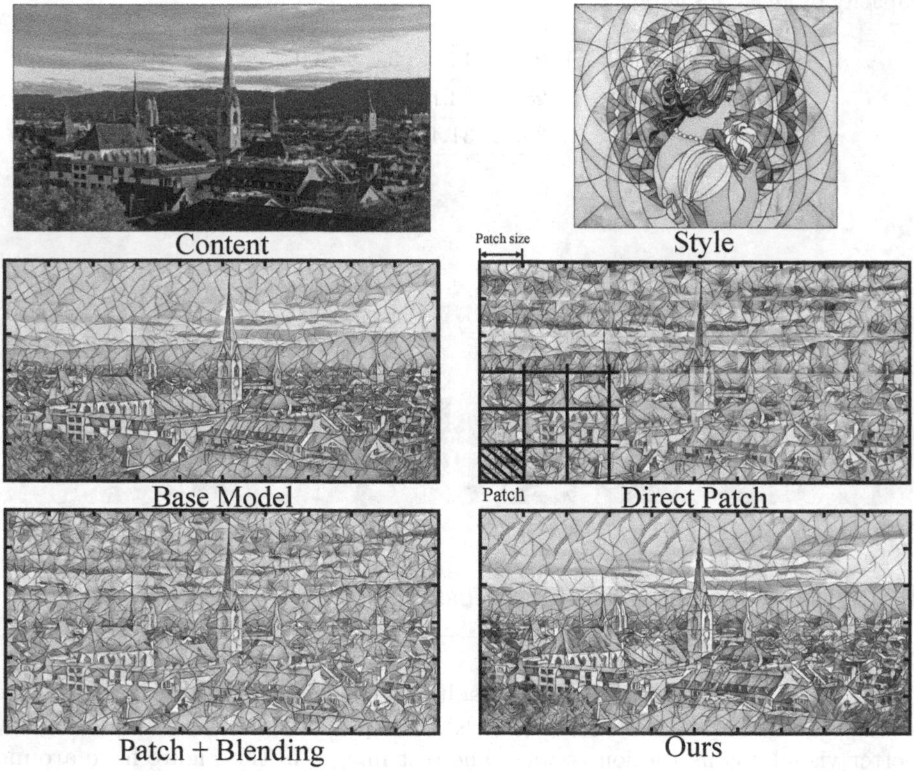

Fig. 4. Style transfer results. The baseline model is the fast neural style model from [6]. Direct patch is the model which directly processes patches and stitches them together. Patch plus blending model is the direct patch model with additional blending network. It shows blending is powerful to remove edges but lack of global information leads to dirty results. Only our full model gives as clear results as baseline model.

4.2 Style Transfer

Dataset and Implementation Details. To show the ability of flexible redeployment of our pipeline. We select a popular style transfer to test our method.

We follow the setup of the baseline model in [6]. It is trained on the MS-COCO [10]. We use pretrained VGG-16 [13] for perceptual loss calculation and the feature layer $relu1\_2, relu2\_2, relu3\_3, relu4\_3$ are selected as style layer and $relu2\_2$ is used as content layer. To evaluate the result of style transfer, we directly show the transferred result images and compare the visual results for evaluation. Different from the image reconstruction experiment, we add down-sample layers in the reconstruction network to decrease the artifacts.

Fig. 5. An ultra high resolution (11.4 million pixels) style transfer result. This image can be processed with 10G memory. For comparison with 10G memory the baseline model is only able to deal with image of less than 3 million pixels.

Results. First we show the effectiveness of our method. In Fig. 4 the basic qualitative results are showed. For a style transfer model, it is easy to tell that direct patch inference causes severe discontinuity on the edges. Due to the lack of global information, processed patches are not able to produce harmony colors and textures. Then we apply blending to the results and blending net can decrease these discontinuities, the edges are much smoother and not easy to distinguish. However, blending still does not provide global information for the patches, as a result the image is not clear and have diverse heavy colors all over the image.

With the global branch and local branch, our full method has enough global information and high resolution information for patches to express similar color and texture at edges of patches. As a result, our full model provides clear transfer results regardless of separate inferences of patches. Furthermore, compared with baseline model our model produces brighter and more clear results. For example, red color of the roof or blue for the mountain in our results have higher color saturation.

Most important property of our method is the ability to process ultra high resolution images. As in image reconstruction experiment, our model costs less GPU memory during inference. In Fig. 5 we show an example of the results. The content image contains 11.4 million pixels and is far too large to be processed by previous methods in such limited memory condition (single GPU with 12 GB memory). The result of our method is clear and well detailed, due to the large number of pixels, the textures of the image are detailed and all over the image.

5 Conclusion

In this paper we propose a novel auxiliary architecture that can enlarge the input image resolution limit for an image translation network. With the global and local branches and aggregating reconstruction net we are able to decrease the memory usage during inference while preserving the quality of generated image. We test our method on base image reconstruction net and more complex fast neural style transfer network. The results show the effectiveness of our method for enlarging the input image size limitation of base image translation network. Our method can be easily deployed on the trained model and be trained end to end.

References

1. Chen, T.Q., Schmidt, M.: Fast patch-based style transfer of arbitrary style. arXiv preprint arXiv:1612.04337 (2016)
2. Chen, W., Jiang, Z., Wang, Z., Cui, K., Qian, X.: Collaborative global-local networks for memory-efficient segmentation of ultra-high resolution images. In: Proceedings of the IEEE Conference on Computer Vision and Pattern Recognition, pp. 8924–8933 (2019)
3. Demir, U., Unal, G.: Patch-based image inpainting with generative adversarial networks. arXiv preprint arXiv:1803.07422 (2018)
4. Efros, A.A., Freeman, W.T.: Image quilting for texture synthesis and transfer. In: Proceedings of the 28th Annual Conference on Computer Graphics and Interactive Techniques, pp. 341–346. ACM (2001)
5. Isola, P., Zhu, J.Y., Zhou, T., Efros, A.A.: Image-to-image translation with conditional adversarial networks. In: Proceedings of the IEEE conference on Computer Vision and Pattern Recognition, pp. 1125–1134 (2017)
6. Johnson, J., Alahi, A., Fei-Fei, L.: Perceptual losses for real-time style transfer and super-resolution. In: Leibe, B., Matas, J., Sebe, N., Welling, M. (eds.) ECCV 2016. LNCS, vol. 9906, pp. 694–711. Springer, Cham (2016). https://doi.org/10.1007/978-3-319-46475-6_43

7. Junginger, A., Hanselmann, M., Strauss, T., Boblest, S., Buchner, J., Ulmer, H.: Unpaired high-resolution and scalable style transfer using generative adversarial networks. arXiv preprint arXiv:1810.05724 (2018)
8. Liang, L., Liu, C., Xu, Y.Q., Guo, B., Shum, H.Y.: Real-time texture synthesis by patch-based sampling. ACM Trans. Graph. (ToG) **20**(3), 127–150 (2001)
9. Lim, B., Son, S., Kim, H., Nah, S., Mu Lee, K.: Enhanced deep residual networks for single image super-resolution. In: Proceedings of the IEEE Conference on Computer Vision and Pattern Recognition Workshops, pp. 136–144 (2017)
10. Lin, T.-Y., et al.: Microsoft COCO: common objects in context. In: Fleet, D., Pajdla, T., Schiele, B., Tuytelaars, T. (eds.) ECCV 2014. LNCS, vol. 8693, pp. 740–755. Springer, Cham (2014). https://doi.org/10.1007/978-3-319-10602-1_48
11. Paszke, A., Chaurasia, A., Kim, S., Culurciello, E.: ENet: a deep neural network architecture for real-time semantic segmentation. arXiv preprint arXiv:1606.02147 (2016)
12. Sanakoyeu, A., Kotovenko, D., Lang, S., Ommer, B.: A style-aware content loss for real-time HD style transfer. In: Ferrari, V., Hebert, M., Sminchisescu, C., Weiss, Y. (eds.) ECCV 2018. LNCS, vol. 11212, pp. 715–731. Springer, Cham (2018). https://doi.org/10.1007/978-3-030-01237-3_43
13. Simonyan, K., Zisserman, A.: Very deep convolutional networks for large-scale image recognition. arXiv preprint arXiv:1409.1556 (2014)
14. Wang, T.C., Liu, M.Y., Zhu, J.Y., Tao, A., Kautz, J., Catanzaro, B.: High-resolution image synthesis and semantic manipulation with conditional GANs. In: Proceedings of the IEEE Conference on Computer Vision and Pattern Recognition, pp. 8798–8807 (2018)
15. Zhao, H., Qi, X., Shen, X., Shi, J., Jia, J.: ICNet for real-time semantic segmentation on high-resolution images. In: Ferrari, V., Hebert, M., Sminchisescu, C., Weiss, Y. (eds.) ECCV 2018. LNCS, vol. 11207, pp. 418–434. Springer, Cham (2018). https://doi.org/10.1007/978-3-030-01219-9_25
16. Zhu, J.Y., Park, T., Isola, P., Efros, A.A.: Unpaired image-to-image translation using cycle-consistent adversarial networks. In: Proceedings of the IEEE International Conference on Computer Vision, pp. 2223–2232 (2017)

Cross Fusion for Egocentric Interactive Action Recognition

Haiyu Jiang, Yan Song(✉), Jiang He, and Xiangbo Shu

Nanjing University of Science and Technology, Nanjing, China
songyan@njust.edu.cn

Abstract. The characteristics of egocentric interactive videos, which include heavy ego-motion, frequent viewpoint changes and multiple types of activities, hinder the action recognition methods of third-person vision from obtaining satisfactory results. In this paper, we introduce an effective architecture with two branches and a cross fusion method for action recognition in egocentric interactive vision. The two branches are responsible to model the information from observers and inter-actors respectively, and each branch is designed based on the multimodal multi-stream C3D networks. We leverage cross fusion to establish effective linkages between the two branches, which aims to reduce redundant information and fuse complementary features. Besides, we propose variable sampling to obtain discriminative snippets for training. Experimental results demonstrate that the proposed architecture achieves superior performance over several state-of-the-art methods on two benchmarks.

Keywords: Egocentric interactive videos · Action recognition · Cross fusion

1 Introduction

The egocentric vision has received considerable attention from the academic and community because of its potential applications, such as smart robot, auto pilot and so on. However, most of the first-person datasets focus on non-interactive activities, it still remains an open problem to construct a highly discriminative architecture for interaction recognition. In egocentric interactive videos, the interaction actors (abbreviated as inter-actors) typically appear in the center of the scene and create salient local motion, while the camera wearer (abbreviated as observer) behind the scene participates in the activities actively, which brings in global motion [1]. Previous studies have shown that the assumptions for action recognition in the first-person videos or even the third-person videos are ill-suited for this problem [2].

Most of the existing researches on egocentric interaction recognition combine the handcrafted spatiotemporal attributes with the image representations for appearance and dynamic description [3,4]. However, the low-level features are typically vulnerable to certain factors (e.g., camera motion, illumination

Y. M. Ro et al. (Eds.): MMM 2020, LNCS 11961, pp. 714–726, 2020.
https://doi.org/10.1007/978-3-030-37731-1_58

changes, etc.) and have poor generalization ability [5]. Some works resort to deep learning to obtain robust spatiotemporal representations [6,7], requiring no prior information regarding the data. It is capable of achieving high degree of generalization compared to hand-crafted features based approaches.

We analyze the characteristics of egocentric interactive videos and summarize the challenges as follows. Firstly, the egocentric interactive videos usually contain various action modes, including the self-motion from observers and the physical interaction (e.g., shaking), as well as the action from inter-actors. Secondly, although the rich heterogeneous features contain complementary clues, there are redundancies and noises which may bring about negative impact. Finally, consecutive frames are highly redundant in terms of temporal modeling. Considering the above issues, the main contributions of this paper are highlighted as follows: (1) we implement a framework based on multi-stream C3D with two branches, which aim at modeling the global information from observers and the local information from inter-actors; (2) we propose the cross fusion method to fuse pairs of heterogeneous and homogeneous streams, which establishes effective linkages between the two branches, then come to the conclusion that the fusion of global motion and local appearance performs best; (3) we propose the variable sampling to adaptively extend time span of snippets and adjust the overlap between consecutive snippets, which not only makes full use of limited data but also acquires more discriminative snippets.

2 Related Work

2.1 First-Person Vision Fields

According to diverse scenarios, first-person videos can be roughly divided into three types: indoor records, outdoor activities and egocentric interactions. Most of the indoor records happen in the kitchens or offices, which typically contain salient hand motion. So the exploration of this field concentrates on hand modeling, such as hand segmentation [8]. Compared with the first type, outdoor activity videos contain stronger ego-motion and more complex changes of background. Abebe *et al.* [9] used stacked spectrograms, which generated from the grid optical flow and the intensity centroid displacement, to capture global ego-motion information. The third type deals with the interactions and reactions of others to observers. One of the pioneering work in this area is recognizing interaction-level activities through the global and local motion descriptors [2]. Our work focuses on the third type of egocentric videos.

2.2 Recognition Methods for Egocentric Interactive Videos

These studies can be divided into handcrafted attributes based approaches and deep learning based approaches. Ryoo *et al.* [10] extracted five features that two global features were obtained from dense optical flow and local binary patterns, and three sparse spatiotemporal features were extracted as local features, based on a cuboid detector and a STIP detector, to represent different types of dog sports in the egocentric animal videos. Yudistira *et al.* [11] implemented pixel-level preprocessing through superpixels, which introduced motion superpixels in the motion space. Fa *et al.* designed a system, which contained global C3D branch and local C3D branch [7]. In addition, the recent advances for action recognition from non-interactive scenes, such as multiple modalities input [12] or multi-stream long short-term memory framework [13], motivated us to rethink the architecture for this task in egocentric interactive vision.

3 Algorithm

3.1 System Framework

We propose a framework for action recognition from egocentric interactive videos based on the insights of dealing with various kinds of motion, as shown in Fig. 1. This framework designs on a two-branch structure to learn the complementary motion representations. The global branch (the blue rectangle in Fig. 1(a)) can capture the global information, and the local branch (the red rectangle in Fig. 1(a)) focuses on the local information. In each branch, three kinds of modalities, i.e. RGB images, stacked optical flow [14], and warped optical flow [15], are adopted to encode spatiotemporal information.

Multimodal clues of different abstraction levels, i.e. fc6 features and logit scores, are integrated through two methods for single branch prediction. The first one concatenates multimodal information for neural network (NN) classification (the upper part of Fig. 1(b)). The second one feeds the summed multimodal logits into the softmax layer (the lower part of Fig. 1(b)). On the other hand, one component from each branch, either spatial or temporal, is fed into the cross fusion module for further NN classification.

3.2 Basic Network Structure

We adopt C3D [16] as the backbone for each stream. We replace the filling method of 3D Max-Pool layers with valid filling, making the convolution kernel only focus on the positions covering the entire kernel in frames, and the output pixel representation is more standard. Although C3D is designed with 3D kernels which seem unable to capture long temporal variations [17], optical flow is recurrent in some sense. Thereby it is import to have a temporal component (stacked optical flow and warped optical flow streams) configuration-with on.

3.3 Network Input

Global Branch Input. In global branch, RGB snippets are extracted from the original videos as the input of spatial component. The temporal component uses two kinds of optical flow, i.e. the stacked optical flow and the warped optical flow [12], both of which include the horizontal and vertical directions as two

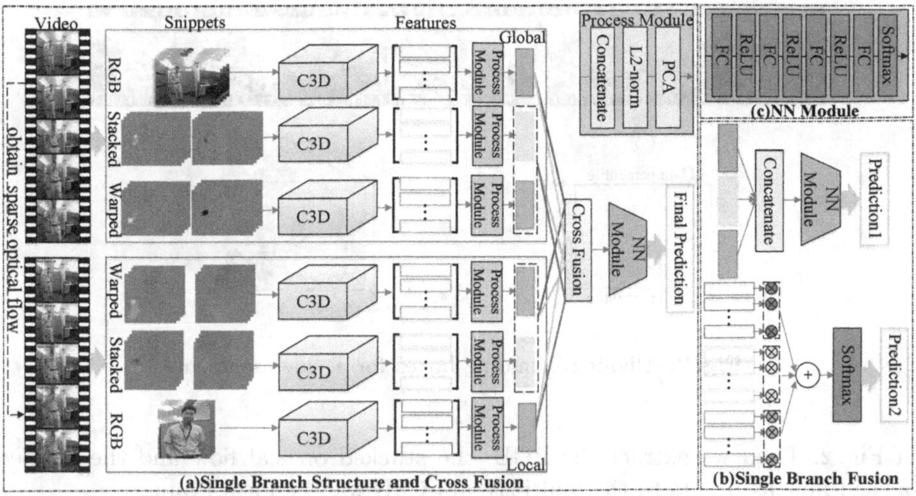

Fig. 1. Overview of the proposed system framework. (a) C3D is adopted as the backbone for both of global and local branches. Cross fusion is performed to establish the connection between them, then NN module is used to classify action. (b) To testify the performance of single branches, two methods are applied to fuse multimodal information following the backbone network structure. (c) A module of multilayer NN is composed of four fully connected (FC) layers, three ReLU layers located between them, and a softmax layer.

channels. The stacked optical flow performs pixels matching between frames, so the frame-wise motion information can be captured. The warped optical flow can suppress the impact of the camera motion and focus on the motion from actors.

Local Branch Input. Since the local branch concentrates on the inter-actors, we remove the noise of irrelevant motion by computing the sparse optical flow [18] from the original videos to match a limited number of corner points between adjacent frames. Observations show that the active areas of inter-actors contain larger displacement of corner points, so we choose the top 10 corner points with the largest displacement to determine the salient region [7].

As the 3D kernel blocks slide along video segments and the locations of salient regions may vary in different frames, the bounding boxes of local regions should be aligned. To achieve the alignment, the maximal region cropping which utilizes the union of the bounding boxes, still retains lots of irrelevant motion [7]. The minimal region cropping which keeps the intersection of the bounding boxes loses important regions. Thereby, we make a tradeoff to propose a cropping strategy based on the percentile. Specifically, we obtain the significant motion area by the percentile in the sets of the four corner coordinates. We select the 15-th percentile for the left and upper boundaries and 85-th percentile for the right and lower boundaries. The cropped region is marked with red arrows, as shown

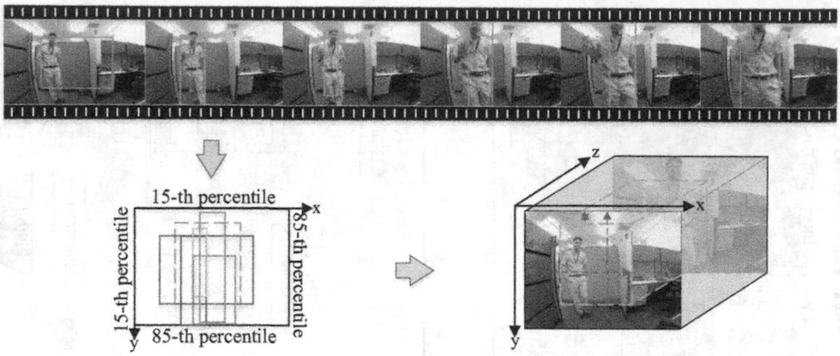

Fig. 2. Aligning bounding boxes for a video segment.

in Fig. 2. Then we extract the RGB, the stacked optical flow and the warped optical flow as inputs to the multi-stream C3D for the local branch.

3.4 Fusion Methods

The fusion of multiple modalities helps to characterize actions effectively in interaction videos. As mentioned above, we have two branches each of which takes three kinds of input in the proposed architecture. How to effectively mine the complementarity of them becomes an important issue.

Firstly, to evaluate each branch, we verify two methods, which respectively belong to the early fusion and the late fusion [19]. For the first one, we concatenate the feature vectors, then feed them into a NN module. The second one sums up the logits of snippets extracted from different modalities, then uses a softmax layer to predict the categories.

Secondly, to establish effective linkages between the two branches, we propose the cross fusion which adopts a class-wise manner to fuse pairs of heterogeneous and homogeneous streams, and each pair integrates the same or different feature representations from diverse aspects of motion. The stacked optical flow modality and the warped optical flow modality are grouped into one class. Then we get 4 fusion ways, which combine the RGB streams from both branches, the global RGB stream and the local optical flow streams, the global optical flow streams and the local RGB stream, and the optical flow streams from both branches. These representations are passed to a NN module which automatically explores the weights of the features.

Lastly, to obtain the video-level prediction from the clip-level prediction, we adopt the maximum-weighted-score voting that chooses the label with the highest weighted confidence score. Other voting methods are also compared with it (i.e., choosing the label with the highest confidence score and choosing the label which is predicted the most times [7]).

3.5 Variable Sampling

Usually, a 3D convolution network takes a snippet comprised of several frames as input with sampling methods. The traditional sampling methods, such as the fixed sampling method [7] which extracts non-overlap snippets, may obtain insufficient data. However, dense temporal sampling may result in highly similar snippets and destroy the space-time patterns for some specific action categories [20]. Here, we take two action categories (i.e., punch and throw) as an example, as illustrated in Fig. 3. The videos are sampled with the sampling interval of 6 and the extracted snippets are only parts of walking and raising hand, which may lead to a confusion.

Fig. 3. Similar sampled snippets from two different action categories.

Assume that a video has X frames and the collection of frames is represented as $\mathcal{F} = \{f_1, f_2, ..., f_X\}$. We use three parameters to control the range of the starting frames for the snippet, which are the snippets' length L, the sampling interval I and the stride S, constrained by $S < LI$. Each snippet overlaps with its adjacent snippets. As discussed above, the fixed sampling method probably extracts snippets which contain insufficient key action parts. In an extreme situation, when the frame number is less than $1 + (L - 1)I$, we are not able to extract valid snippets, leading to a waste of short videos for this category. Here, we propose a variable sampling method. It adaptively adjusts the sampling interval according to the video length as

$$I_v = max(1, \lfloor X/\alpha L \rfloor) \tag{1}$$

This method can ensure data balance to some extent, especially for short videos.

3.6 Class-Aware Batch Generation

Although variable sampling method ensures a certain number of snippets, the distribution of samples from different categories may still be uneven in simple random batch generation. This situation may be worse especially when the number of categories is larger than the batch size [21]. We propose a class-aware batch generation method, which makes the sampling probability even for each category. Assume the batch size is N_b and the number of categories is N_c, we randomly choose N_b classes and set the number of snippets per category to 1 when $N_b \leq N_c$; otherwise, we randomly select $\lfloor N_b/N_c \rfloor$ snippets from each category and select the rest randomly. This method helps reduce the bias towards the categories with more samples and helps the training converge faster.

4 Experiments and Results

4.1 Datasets

The experiment is carried out on JPL and DogCentric datasets, which respectively contain 84 and 209 videos with the frame resolution of 320×240.

JPL First-Person Interaction Dataset. The dataset is composed of human activity videos taken from first-person viewpoint and contains 7 types of activities, including positive interactions (e.g., shaking hands, etc.), negative interactions (e.g., punching the observer, etc.), and neutral interactions (e.g., pointing to the observer) [2].

DogCentric Activity Dataset. This dataset is composed of dog activity videos recorded from egocentric animal viewpoint. It contains 10 types of activities, including dogs' self-motion (e.g., body shaking, etc.), interactions between people and dogs (e.g., feeding, etc.), and activities recorded with other objects involved (e.g. waiting for a car to passed by, etc.) [10].

4.2 Data Preprocess

During the preprocessing of input snippets, the snippets are firstly scaled down to half of the original video resolution (i.e., 160×120). Then we perform 4 corners cropping and center cropping with the size of 120×120. The jittering and horizontal flipping operations are also applied. During the preprocessing of input features, we perform PCA dimensionality reduction (1024D) followed by L2-normalization.

4.3 Training Configuration

C3D Training. We train from scratch for the global branch, and do fine-tuning for the multi-stream networks of local branch. Each model is trained through 150 epochs with batch size of 28. We combine the step-decay schedule with Adam optimizer using cross entropy loss function. In each branch, the initial learning rates are set to 1×10^{-6}, 1×10^{-5} and 1.5×10^{-5} for the RGB, the stacked optical flow and the warped optical flow streams respectively. We adopt the dropout method with ratio of 0.1 and the early stopping mechanism to suppress over-fitting.

Fusion Module Training. The well-trained C3D models in the previous stage are used to extract each modal features which are fed into a NN module. We use SGD optimizer with Nesterov Momentum of 0.9, and train from scratch through 15000 epochs with the batch size of 512. The initial learning rate is set to 1×10^{-3} for single branch fusion and is set to 1×10^{-4} for the cross fusion. In addition to the two methods mentioned above for avoiding overfitting, L2 regularization is also used here.

4.4 Evaluation on the Sampling and Batch Generation Methods

Evaluation on the Variable Sampling. We compare the variable sampling with the fixed sampling method. The values of the fixed sampling method are set to 2, 4, 8, 12 in the global branch, and 4, 6, 8, 12 in the local branch. For the variable sampling, we found when $\alpha = 2$, that is, $I_v = max(1, \lfloor X/2L \rfloor)$, the effect is better. Each snippet is sampled 16 frames with stride of 1. The clip-level accuracy with varied sampling intervals for different input modalities in each branch are shown in Fig. 4. Because of the suitable temporal footprint, the variable sampling can achieve better performance for all the input modalities. It proves that the variable sampling is able to sample with suitable time span so as to improve the accuracy.

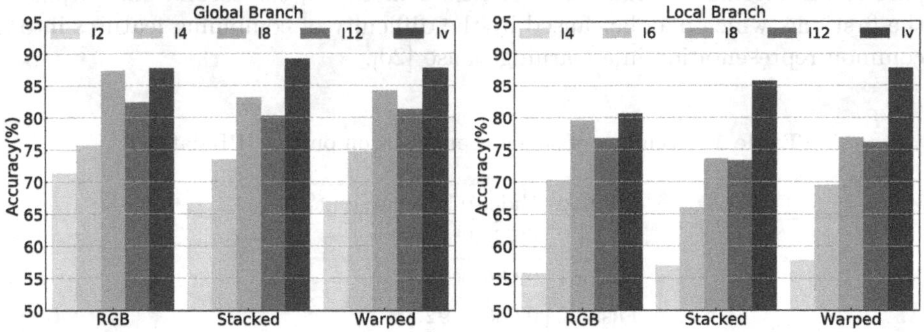

Fig. 4. Clip-level accuracy in each branch. In the legends, "Iv" represents variable sampling interval and the digits of the remaining notations represent the fixed sampling intervals.

Evaluation on the Class-Aware Batch Generation. We take the RGB stream of the global branch as an example to compare the class-aware batch generation with the random batch generation as shown in Fig. 5. The mean class precision of class-aware batch generation is 81.72%, which is 3.03% higher than the other one. The class-aware batch generation method still has good prediction for the classes with small snippet counts such as "waving" and "punching".

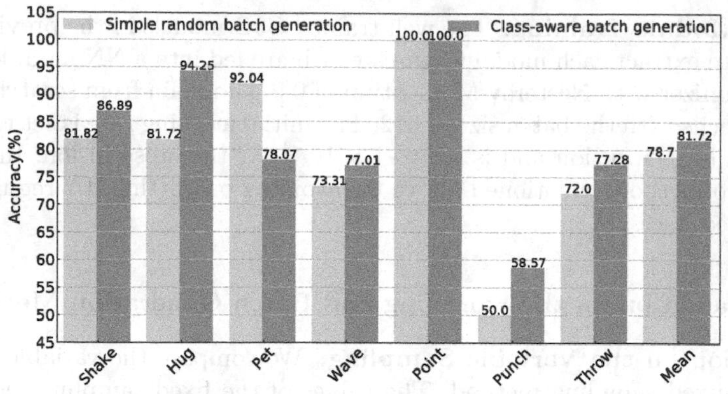

Fig. 5. Histogram of precisions on different batch generation methods.

4.5 Results of Fusion Methods

Single Branch Fusion. For each of the single branch, we perform two types of fusion methods to combine the multimodal information as described in Sect. 3.4, and the best results of the voting methods are listed in Table 1. Overall, the global branch performs better than the local one, because the latter discards a part of the original information. For fusion methods, the second one surpasses the first one, which may be caused by the difficulty of combining features into a common representation in a learning phase [20].

Table 1. Accuracy of single branch fusion on the JPL dataset.

Method	Video@1 Accuracy (%)	
	Global	Local
Fusion1	92.86	85.71
Fusion2	92.86	92.86

Cross Fusion. Table 2 shows the comparison results of cross fusion on the JPL dataset. We come to the conclusion that the performance ranking is GlobalFlow + LocalRGB, GlobalFlow + LocalFlow, GlobalRGB + LocalFlow, and GlobalRGB + LocalRGB. As there are lots of camera motion that comes from the observers' self motion and the physical interaction, the impact of GlobalFlow features is dominant in cross fusion. The results of GlobalFlow + LocalRGB are better than GlobalFlow + LocalFlow, which implies that the appearance is an important supplement to the dynamics. On the other hand, cross fusion outperforms single branch fusion in any case, which demonstrates the effectiveness of our framework.

Table 2. Accuracy of cross fusion on the JPL dataset.

Method	Video accuracy (%)		
	Max scores	Max weight	Most times
GlobalRGB + LocalRGB	50	64.29	57.14
GlobalRGB + LocalFlow	85.71	92.86	92.86
GlobalFlow + LocalRGB	92.86	100	100
GlobalFlow + LocalFlow	85.71	92.96	100

To evaluate the generalization ability of our framework, we also validate it on the datasets of egocentric animal viewpoint, as shown in Table 3. The ranking of cross fusion on the DogCentric dataset is consistent with that on the JPL. In terms of voting methods, the maximum-weighted-score voting is better than the others.

Table 3. Accuracy of cross fusion on the DogCentric dataset.

Method	Video accuracy (%)		
	Max scores	Max weight	Most times
GlobalRGB + LocalRGB	63.33	66.67	63.33
GlobalRGB + LocalFlow	73.33	80	76.67
GlobalFlow + LocalRGB	83.33	90	86.67
GlobalFlow + LocalFlow	80	83.33	83.33

Table 4. Result comparison on two benchmarks.

Dataset	Method	Global (%)	Local (%)	Global + Local (%)
JPL	Structure match [2]	–	83.10	89.60
	Global VRTD [22]	–	–	84
	Temporal motion superpixel [11]	–	88	–
	Rank pooling [6]	–	–	92.9
	C3D ensemble system [7]	78.57	85.71	92.96
	Proposed (ours)	**92.86**	**92.86**	**100**
DogCentric	Multi-channel χ^2 kernel [10]	–	–	60.5
	C3D (P$\triangle$) [23]	–	–	71.4
	Trajectory VRTD [22]	–	–	69.6
	Rank pooling [6]	–	–	75.2
	2SConv-LFP (G+SD+GS) w/ TP4 [24]	–	–	83
	Proposed (ours)	**86.67**	**83.33**	**90**

We also compare the proposed method with the state-of-the-art methods including both of the handcraft-feature based approaches and the deep-learning based approaches. Table 4 lists the video-level accuracy of each branch and the fusion. Our method outperforms around 7% on two datasets.

5 Conclusion

In this paper, we introduce a novel framework designed to classify activities in first-person interactive videos. On the basis of global-local branches, the multimodal multi-stream C3D networks are applied to each branch and the cross fusion is adopted to establish effective linkages between two branches. Besides, we also implement a series of good practices such as the variable sampling and the class-aware batch generation methods, which are utilized for keeping the space-time patterns of specific classes and the class balancing respectively. Our method outperforms around 7% than the state-of-art algorithms on both of the datasets. Action recognition on large-scale egocentric interactive datasets, such as EPIC-KITCHENS and EGTEA GAZE+, may require novel and deeper baselines for cross fusion, we leave it for future work.

Acknowledgments. This work was supported by the National Nature Science Foundation of China under Grants 61672285, U1611461, 61732007, and 61702265, Natural Science Foundation of Jiangsu Province (Grant No. BK20170856).

References

1. Tsutsui, S., Bambach, S., Crandall, D., Yu, C.: Estimating head motion from egocentric vision. In: Proceedings of the 20th ACM International Conference on Multimodal Interaction, ICMI 2018, pp. 342–346. ACM, New York (2018)
2. Ryoo, M.S., Matthies, L.: First-person activity recognition: what are they doing to me? In: 2013 IEEE Conference on Computer Vision and Pattern Recognition, pp. 2730–2737, June 2013
3. Xia, L., Gori, I., Aggarwal, J.K., Ryoo, M.S.: Robot-centric activity recognition from first-person RGB-D videos. In: 2015 IEEE Winter Conference on Applications of Computer Vision, pp. 357–364, January 2015
4. Mishra, S.R., Mishra, T.K., Sarkar, A., Sanyal, G.: PSO based combined kernel learning framework for recognition of first-person activity in a video. Evol. Intell. (2018)
5. Zhang, H.B., Zhang, Y.X., Zhong, B., Lei, Q., Yang, L., Du, J.X., Chen, D.S.: A comprehensive survey of vision-based human action recognition methods. Sensors **19**(5) (2019)
6. Zaki, H.F.M., Shafait, F., Mian, A.: Modeling sub-event dynamics in first-person action recognition. In: 2017 IEEE Conference on Computer Vision and Pattern Recognition (CVPR), pp. 1619–1628, July 2017
7. Fa, L., Song, Y., Shu, X.: Global and local C3D ensemble system for first person interactive action recognition. In: Schoeffmann, K., Chalidabhongse, T.H., Ngo, C.W., Aramvith, S., O'Connor, N.E., Ho, Y.-S., Gabbouj, M., Elgammal, A. (eds.) MMM 2018. LNCS, vol. 10705, pp. 153–164. Springer, Cham (2018). https://doi.org/10.1007/978-3-319-73600-6_14

8. Ma, M., Fan, H., Kitani, K.M.: Going deeper into first-person activity recognition. In: 2016 IEEE Conference on Computer Vision and Pattern Recognition (CVPR), pp. 1894–1903, June 2016
9. Abebe, G., Cavallaro, A.: A long short-term memory convolutional neural network for first-person vision activity recognition. In: 2017 IEEE International Conference on Computer Vision Workshops (ICCVW), pp. 1339–1346, October 2017
10. Iwashita, Y., Takamine, A., Kurazume, R., Ryoo, M.S.: First-person animal activity recognition from egocentric videos. In: 2014 22nd International Conference on Pattern Recognition, pp. 4310–4315, August 2014
11. Yudistira, N., Kurita, T.: Temporal evolution of motion superpixel for video classification. In: 2017 3rd IEEE International Conference on Cybernetics (CYBCONF), pp. 1–6, June 2017
12. Wang, L., Xiong, Y., Wang, Z., Qiao, Y., Lin, D., Tang, X., Van Gool, L.: Temporal segment networks: towards good practices for deep action recognition. In: Leibe, B., Matas, J., Sebe, N., Welling, M. (eds.) ECCV 2016. LNCS, vol. 9912, pp. 20–36. Springer, Cham (2016). https://doi.org/10.1007/978-3-319-46484-8_2
13. Song, S., Chandrasekhar, V., Mandal, B., Li, L., Lim, J., Babu, G.S., San, P.P., Cheung, N.: Multimodal multi-stream deep learning for egocentric activity recognition. In: 2016 IEEE Conference on Computer Vision and Pattern Recognition Workshops (CVPRW), pp. 378–385, June 2016
14. Simonyan, K., Zisserman, A.: Two-stream convolutional networks for action recognition in videos. In: Proceedings of the 27th International Conference on Neural Information Processing Systems, Cambridge, MA, USA, pp. 568–576 (2014)
15. Wang, H., Schmid, C.: Action recognition with improved trajectories. In: Proceedings of the 2013 IEEE International Conference on Computer Vision, ICCV 2013, pp. 3551–3558. IEEE Computer Society, Washington, DC (2013)
16. Tran, D., Bourdev, L., Fergus, R., Torresani, L., Paluri, M.: Learning spatiotemporal features with 3D convolutional networks. In: Proceedings of the 2015 IEEE International Conference on Computer Vision (ICCV), ICCV 2015, pp. 4489–4497. IEEE Computer Society, Washington, DC (2015)
17. Khong, V., Tran, T.: Improving human action recognition with two-stream 3D convolutional neural network. In: 2018 1st International Conference on Multimedia Analysis and Pattern Recognition (MAPR), pp. 1–6, April 2018
18. Poleg, Y., Ephrat, A., Peleg, S., Arora, C.: Compact CNN for indexing egocentric videos. In: 2016 IEEE Winter Conference on Applications of Computer Vision (WACV), pp. 1–9, March 2016
19. Lan, Z., Bao, L., Yu, S.-I., Liu, W., Hauptmann, A.G.: Double fusion for multimedia event detection. In: Schoeffmann, K., Merialdo, B., Hauptmann, A.G., Ngo, C.-W., Andreopoulos, Y., Breiteneder, C. (eds.) MMM 2012. LNCS, vol. 7131, pp. 173–185. Springer, Heidelberg (2012). https://doi.org/10.1007/978-3-642-27355-1_18
20. Varol, G., Laptev, I., Schmid, C.: Long-term temporal convolutions for action recognition. IEEE Trans. Pattern Anal. Mach. Intell. **40**(6), 1510–1517 (2018)
21. Shen, L., Lin, Z., Huang, Q.: Relay backpropagation for effective learning of deep convolutional neural networks. In: Leibe, B., Matas, J., Sebe, N., Welling, M. (eds.) ECCV 2016. LNCS, vol. 9911, pp. 467–482. Springer, Cham (2016). https://doi.org/10.1007/978-3-319-46478-7_29
22. Moreira, T.P., Menotti, D., Pedrini, H.: First-person action recognition through visual rhythm texture description. In: 2017 IEEE International Conference on Acoustics, Speech and Signal Processing (ICASSP), pp. 2627–2631, March 2017

23. Takamine, A., Iwashita, Y., Kurazume, R.: First-person activity recognition with C3D features from optical flow images. In: 2015 IEEE/SICE International Symposium on System Integration (SII), pp. 619–622, December 2015
24. Kwon, H., Kim, Y., Lee, J.S., Cho, M.: First person action recognition via two-stream convnet with long-term fusion pooling. Pattern Recogn. Lett. **112**, 161–167 (2018)

Improving Brain Tumor Segmentation with Dilated Pseudo-3D Convolution and Multi-direction Fusion

Sun'ao Liu[1], Hai Xu[1], Yizhi Liu[2], and Hongtao Xie[1(✉)]

[1] University of Science and Technology of China, Hefei, China
{lsa1997,keda2010}@mail.ustc.edu.cn, htxie@ustc.edu.cn
[2] Hunan University of Science and Technology, Xiangtan, China
yizhi_liu@sina.com

Abstract. Convolutional neural networks have shown their dominance in many computer vision tasks and been broadly used for medical image analysis. Unlike traditional image-based tasks, medical data is often in 3D form. 2D Networks designed for images shows poor performance and efficiency on these tasks. Although 3D networks work better, their computation and memory cost are rather high. To solve this problem, we decompose 3D convolution to decouple volumetric information, in the same way human experts treat volume data. Inspired by the concept of three medically-defined planes, we further propose a Multi-direction Fusion (MF) module, using three branches of this factorized 3D convolution in parallel to simultaneously extract features from three different directions and assemble them together. Moreover, we suggest introducing dilated convolution to preserve resolution and enlarge receptive field for segmentation. The network with proposed modules (MFNet) achieves competitive performance with other state-of-the-art methods on BraTS 2018 brain tumor segmentation task and is much more light-weight. We believe this is an effective and efficient way for volume-based medical segmentation.

Keywords: Brain tumor segmentation · 3D convolution · Multi-direction fusion

1 Introduction

Convolutional Neural Networks (CNN) have made significant progress in several computer vision tasks [14,28]. For semantic segmentation, a Fully Convolutional Network (FCN) [17] uses stacked convolution layers to form an encoder and a decoder. Given an input image, the encoder part extracts various image information and downsamples through pooling to construct feature maps from low-level to high-level. The decoder part integrates feature maps and recovers resolution through upsampling. FCN finally outputs a pixel-wise segmentation map with the same resolution as the input image.

Y. M. Ro et al. (Eds.): MMM 2020, LNCS 11961, pp. 727–738, 2020.
https://doi.org/10.1007/978-3-030-37731-1_59

Due to their success, more and more CNN-based algorithms are proposed for medical image analysis, of which medical image segmentation is an important part [15,16]. The Brain Tumor Segmentation Challenge (BraTS) [1–3,19] focuses on the segmentation of brain tumors, gliomas specifically. BraTS provides magnetic resonance imaging (MRI) scans with four modalities: T1, T1Gd, T2 and FLAIR. The participants are required to produce segmentation of three glioma sub-regions, which contains enhancing tumor (ET), tumor core (TC) and whole tumor (WT).

Unlike other segmentation tasks, medical datasets are much smaller and have serious class imbalance problems, which are harmful to network training. As for gliomas, their highly heterogeneous appearance and shapes make segmentation even harder. Another problem is that medical data is usually in 3D form with multiple modalities. General convolution networks are designed for 2D images and therefore show relatively poor performance and efficiency when processing this kind of data. Using 3D networks is a better solution, but leads to much higher computational cost. Considering the clinical relevance of medical image segmentation, there is a trade-off between efficiency and performance. It is not always a good choice to use much more parameters in exchange for a little bit performance improvement.

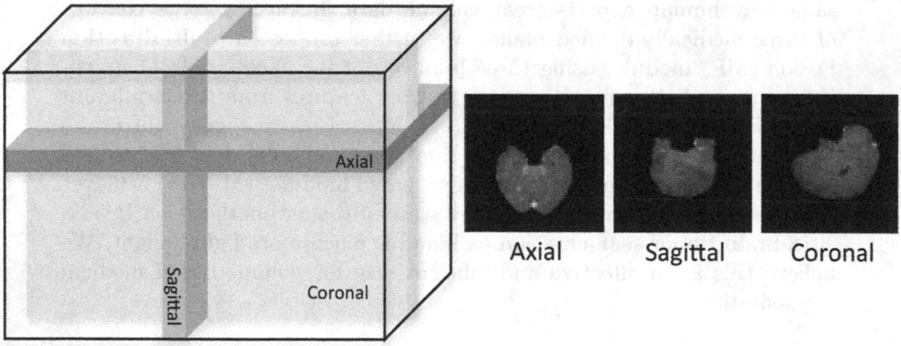

Fig. 1. Three planes of medical image.

In this paper, we combine the theories of deep learning and medical analysis and propose a light-weight yet effective network for glioma segmentation. We introduce pseudo-3D convolution rather than standard 3D convolution to reduce the number of parameters and decouple volumetric information. To retain spatial information for localization, dilated convolution is also used to enlarge receptive field and avoid undue resolution changes. Different information on three medically defined planes (i.e., sagittal, coronal and axial plane in Fig. 1) is considered simultaneously and integrated through the proposed Multi-direction Fusion module. We summarize our contribution as follows:

(1) We use dilated pseudo-3D convolution to construct the network structure, which decouples 3D information, dramatically reduces the number of parameters and retains spatial resolution.
(2) We propose Multi-direction Fusion (MF) module to extract and assemble features from multiple directions simultaneously.
(3) The network formed by proposed modules (MFNet) shows competitive performance on the BraTS 2018 online validation set and is much lighter than other state-of-the-art methods.

2 Related Work

2.1 Dilated Convolution

Convolutional blocks are often followed by a downsampling operation like maxpooling or stride convolution and then stacked together to build deep neural network and enlarge the receptive field. This inevitably causes resolution loss and is harmful to semantic segmentation which is a pixel-wise classification task and needs localization. Dilated convolution [30], also called atrous convolution [4], is proposed to enlarge receptive filed effectively without pooling layers. Dilated convolution can be considered as filter 'with holes'. With dilated rate r, it inserts $r - 1$ zeros between two adjacent weights and thus enlarges the kernel size from k to $k + (k - 1)(r - 1)$ without introducing extra parameters.

2.2 Pseudo-3D Convolution

General convolutional networks are designed for images. When inputs are in 3D form like videos or volumes, it is natural to expand convolution to three dimensions. But this way leads to an explosion of the number of parameters. To solve this problem, Pseudo-3D Convolution [23] is proposed to encode spatial-temporal information in videos. A Pseudo-3D block replaces a $3 \times 3 \times 3$ convolution with a $1 \times 3 \times 3$ convolution and a $3 \times 1 \times 1$ convolution in parallel or cascaded form. In this way P3D convolution decouples 3D convolutional filters into 2D convolutional filters on spatial domain and 1D filters on temporal domain. Meanwhile, it greatly reduces the number of parameters and doubles the nonlinearity. Another work is R(2+1)D convolution [25], which has similar structure to P3D-A block but is homogeneous and designed to match the number of parameters with the 3D convolutions.

Although medical volumetric data is essentially different from video, this factorization of 3D convolution is still beneficial. We can use pseudo-3D convolution to combine information from extra dimension after 2D filtering instead of standard convolution. The factorization also makes it possible to extract features in different directions, which will be shown later.

2.3 Brain Tumor Segmentation

In recent years, fully convolutional networks like U-Net [24] have been widely used for medical image segmentation. However, due to the difficulty of brain tumor segmentation, model ensemble or cascade is often necessary and leads to large number of parameters and long fine-tuning procedure. In BraTS 2017, Kamnitsas *et al.* [10] used Ensembles of Multiple Models and Architectures (EMMA) containing DeepMedic [11], FCN and U-Net. Wang *et al.* [26] used three cascaded networks to predict three tumor sub-regions separately. Similar to our method, they also decomposed 3D convolution, but only in one direction. Due to the constraint of their input size ($144 \times 144 \times 19$), they trained networks with data in axial, sagittal and coronal views respectively, and averaged the outputs of three views during testing time. This way of multi-view fusion is obviously inefficient, taking additional training and testing time.

In BraTS 2018, large 3D networks like 3D U-Net [5] became popular and performed well. Myronenko [21] used a large amount of 3D convolution with auto-encoder as regularization. Isensee *et al.* [9] used 3D U-Net architecture and extra data for co-training. 3D networks are often trained with large-size volumetric data and thus require huge computing resources. However, large models get quite limited improvement and are impractical for application. Xu *et al.* [29] proposed a compact model with cascaded attention mechanism. In this paper, we look for a light-weight but more general network without cascade.

3 Methods

3.1 Modified V-Net: A Strong Baseline

We modify V-Net [20], a U-Net-like 3D network, to get a strong baseline model. V-Net has encoder-decoder structure and skip-connection to combine semantic and texture features. Following previous works [9,21], we also divide the four-class segmentation task into three sub-tasks to simply distinguish background and foreground of three sub-regions respectively. So the network accepts multi-modal 3D volumetric data as input and outputs three segmentation maps. The modification details are shown in the following paragraphs.

Group Normalization. Batch Normalization (BN) [8] is an effective component in deep learning which can improve performance and accelerate training procedure. But the performance of BN is closely related to batch size and drops dramatically when batch size reduces [27]. In our experiment, each batch contains only one volume due to the limited memory and BN is inappropriate. Instead, Group Normalization (GN) [27] is used after a convolution layer, followed by a PReLU non-linearity [6]. GN divides features into G groups along channel axis and performs BN-like computation for each group of each sample. GN is independent of batch sizes and considers the potential dependency among feature channels. The number of groups G is a pre-defined hyper-parameter, we use $G = 16$ for all GN layers without selecting it carefully.

Hybrid Loss. The binary cross entropy loss shows poor performance when there are class imbalances. V-Net proposes Dice Loss as a solution:

$$L_{dice} = -\frac{2 * \sum_i p_i g_i + \epsilon}{\sum_i p_i + \sum_i g_i + \epsilon}, \tag{1}$$

where p_i, g_i are binary predicted label and ground truth respectively and ϵ is a smoothing constant. Dice loss indeed outperforms cross entropy loss but still has over-segmentation problem because it only focuses on those positive ground truth labels. So we suggest using Focal Loss [13] in addition:

$$L_{focal} = -\sum_{\boldsymbol{x} \in \Omega} (1 - p_{l(\boldsymbol{x})}(\boldsymbol{x}))^{\gamma} \log(p_{l(\boldsymbol{x})}(\boldsymbol{x})), \tag{2}$$

where $l(\cdot)$ is the true class and $p_{l(\cdot)}(\cdot)$ is the predicted probability of the true class for each pixel. Focal loss uses the factor γ ($\gamma = 2$ by default) to reduce the weights of easy examples and focuses on hard ones.

The proposed hybrid loss is weighted summation:

$$L_{hybrid} = L_{dice} + \omega L_{focal}. \tag{3}$$

In our experiments, ω is set to 1 for equal weights. The hybrid losses of three sub-tasks are then summed together as the final loss.

3.2 Multi-direction Fusion Module

There are several ways to deal with the three dimensions of medical volumetric data. The simplest way is to treat it as stacked slices and do per-image segmentation. Human experts often work in this way, partly because it is difficult for us to view voxels directly. But in practice, networks perform better when using 3D data. We think this is because slices of volumetric data differ significantly in different positions, however, the 2D network treats them equally. Though experienced experts labels pixels on each image, they can actually estimate the position of each slice in the whole brain and kinds of organs or tissues that might appear. In other words, information from three dimensions is decomposed.

Using 3D convolution is the most direct way to extract 3D features. But the exponential growth of the number of parameters does not bring a leap of performance, which means there are redundant parameters and indicates that we should reconsider the format of 3D convolution. Inspired by experts, we introduce the pseudo-3D-A [23] module to decompose 3D convolution. It uses a $1 \times 3 \times 3$ convolution to extract 2D features first and then a $3 \times 1 \times 1$ convolution for features from the third dimension. In this way the network can decouple information as human experts do.

Note that there are three different planes in a volume, defined as axial, sagittal and coronal planes for medical data. These planes view brain from three directions and contain different spatial information. Meanwhile, the direction

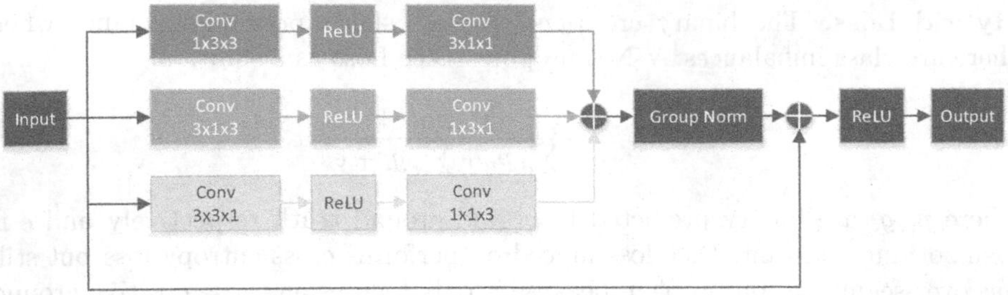

Fig. 2. Multi-direction Fusion Module. $1 \times 1 \times 1$ convolution is used to match dimensions for shortcut.

of convolutions in P3D can also be changed. Therefore we propose the Multi-direction Fusion (MF) module, which contains three different P3D convolutions in parallel. Each of them focuses on features from one direction and information from the third dimension in addition. The complete Multi-direction Fusion module (see Fig. 2) also contains residual connection [7] for better performance and quicker convergence.

3.3 Replace Pooling with Dilated Convolution

For semantic segmentation, local information is as important as global information to generate pixel-wise prediction. However, deep convolutional networks often use downsampling operations like max pooling or stride convolution to enlarge the receptive field and capture global information. Though we can use upsampling to recover resolution, it is inevitable to lose local spatial information during resolution changes. For example, the encoder of V-Net uses four stride convolution layers and can finally get a $194 \times 194 \times 194$ receptive field, while the size of feature maps shrinks from $128 \times 160 \times 160$ to $8 \times 10 \times 10$. We believe that this is harmful to brain tumor segmentation, which has very small tumor sub-regions like enhancing tumor and thus needs more reliable local information.

To avoid this problem, dilated convolution is applied in deep layers and the last stride convolution layer in V-Net is removed when we stack the proposed modules to form the MFNet (see Fig. 3). Note that dilated convolution is only applied to the 2D convolutions in our module, i.e., $1 \times 3 \times 3$, $3 \times 1 \times 3$ and $3 \times 3 \times 1$ convolutions. With dilated convolution, we extend the final receptive field from 78×78 to 158×158 and meanwhile keep the size of feature maps. Since our module uses branches in parallel, the receptive field is smaller than that of V-Net. But it can still cover the whole brain and is sufficient for brain tumor segmentation.

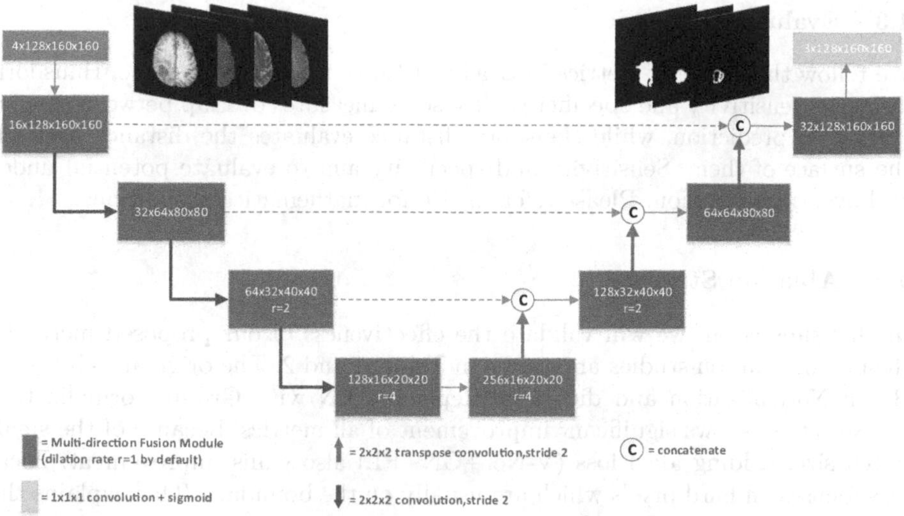

Fig. 3. Network with multi-direction fusion and dilated convolution (MFNet).

4 Experiments

4.1 Dataset

The training set of BraTS 2018 contains 210 high grade gliomas (HGG) and 75 low grade gliomas (LGG). In each sample there are four modalities and a segmentation map annotated by experts. All of them are co-registered to a common template, resampled to $1\,\text{mm}^3$ and skull-stripped, with the final size of $240 \times 240 \times 155$. 66 samples without grades and annotations are provided for validation. The results of validation set are evaluated by the online evaluation platform[1].

4.2 Implementation Details

All of our experiments are based on PyTorch [22] and trained on a single NVIDIA TITAN Xp for 150 epochs. We use Adam [12] optimizer with the initial learning rate 0.0003. The learning rate decreases 10% every 10 epochs and batch size is set to 1 due to limited memory.

During training, the grade of gliomas, i.e., HGG or LGG, is not distinguished. For data augmentation, we choose random rotation, random flip, random scaling and random noise. Input data is normalized based on non-zero voxels and randomly cropped to $160 \times 160 \times 128$. No additional data or post-processing method is used.

[1] https://ipp.cbica.upenn.edu/.

4.3 Evaluation Metrics

We follow the choice of metrics in BraTS 2018, containing Dice score, Hausdorff distance, sensitivity and specificity. Dice score measures overlap between ground truth and prediction, while Hausdorff distance evaluates the distance between the surface of them. Sensitivity and specificity aim to evaluate potential under and over segmentation. Please refer to [19] for mathematical definitions.

4.4 Ablation Studies

In this subsection, we will validate the effectiveness of our proposed methods. Results of ablation studies are shown in Tables 1 and 2. The original V-Net uses Batch Normalization and dice loss. Replacing BN with Group Normalization (V-Net+GN) shows significant improvement of all metrics, because of the small batch size. Adding focal loss (V-Net+GN+FL) also gains improvement. Focal loss focuses on hard pixels which are usually on the boundary. This explains the great improvement of Hausdorff distance.

Table 1. Ablation studies on BraTS 2018 validation set (Dice and HD95).

Model	Dice			HD95			Params
	WT	TC	ET	WT	TC	ET	
V-Net	0.8865	0.7304	0.7564	7.3429	22.8326	22.2509	14.70 M
V-Net+GN	0.8979	0.8175	0.7906	6.1963	10.0040	6.2502	14.70 M
V-Net+GN+FL	0.9019	0.8174	0.7958	5.0131	8.7624	2.7844	14.70 M
MFNet w/o dc	0.9079	0.8282	0.7988	4.7628	7.9966	2.7089	5.26 M
MFNet (proposed)	**0.9091**	**0.8408**	**0.8037**	**4.6872**	**7.4812**	**2.3884**	**3.82 M**

Table 2. Ablation studies on BraTS 2018 validation set (Se. and Sp.).

Model	Sensitivity			Specificity		
	WT	TC	ET	WT	TC	ET
V-Net	0.8944	0.7597	0.7746	0.9785	0.9806	0.9825
V-Net+GN	0.9079	0.8123	0.7976	0.9947	0.9979	0.9980
V-Net+GN+FL	0.9178	0.8230	0.7882	0.9946	0.9979	0.9985
MFNet w/o dc	0.9092	0.8107	0.7913	**0.9955**	**0.9984**	**0.9985**
MFNet (proposed)	**0.9182**	**0.8576**	**0.8193**	0.9950	0.9974	0.9979

Using the proposed Multi-direction Fusion module and dilated convolution (MFNet) improves the results, especially for tumor core. This might benefits from the extracted information from multiple directions and higher resolution of deep feature maps. Meanwhile, it reduces about 11 M parameters compared with V-Net. However, when removing dilated convolution and using 4 down and up sampling operations (MFNet w/o dc), the performance drops. We consider this is related to the size of receptive field. The parallel form of our module constraints its expansion, while dilated convolution can make up this shortcoming. But it still outperforms modified V-Net with less parameters.

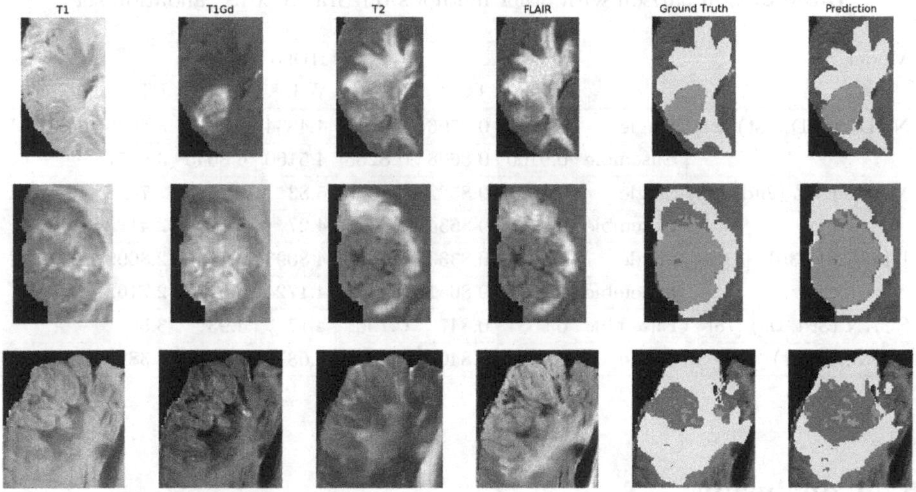

Fig. 4. Segmentation results on BraTS 2018 training set. Blue: enhancing tumor (ET). Red: necrotic and non-enhancing tumor core (NCR/NET). Yellow: peritumoral edema (ED). TC contains ET and NCR/NET, while WT covers TC and ED. (Color figure online)

Some segmentation samples are shown in Fig. 4. The top row is a precise segmentation map. Three sub-regions are segmented correctly, even on the irregular boundary. The result of sensitivity indicates that there is under-segmentation problem, as the middle row shows. Classifications of some regions can be ambiguous. However, all models show rather high performance on specificity. But we find this is because the great imbalance between the number of true negative and false positive samples. The former is much more and makes specificity abnormally high. Over-segmentation is still a tough problem for some samples like the bottom row.

4.5 Comparison with the State-of-the-Art

We further compare the metrics with participants of BraTS 2018, as Table 3 shows. Our single-model performance shows competitive results compared with these state-of-the-art methods.

It is noteworthy that our model reduces the number of parameters significantly. Calculating exactly for each reference model is difficult, since many details are not mentioned in their papers. We estimate these numbers mainly based on the convolution layers of networks if possible, which means the real number could be larger. We believe this is important for future applications and makes us to rethink the necessity of enlarging networks in exchange for better performance.

Table 3. Comparison with other methods on BraTS 2018 validation set.

Model		Dice			HD95			Params
		WT	TC	ET	WT	TC	ET	
NVDLMED (1st) [21]	Single	0.9042	0.8596	0.8145	4.4834	8.2777	3.8048	26.01 M
	Ensemble	0.9100	0.8668	0.8233	4.5160	6.8545	3.9257	–
MIC-DKFZ (2nd) [9]	Single	0.9092	0.8522	0.8066	5.83	7.20	2.74	14.61 M
	Ensemble	0.9126	0.8634	0.8087	4.27	6.52	2.41	–
DL_86_81 (3rd) [31]	Single	0.8948	0.8333	0.7925	4.8093	6.7755	2.8099	22.70 M
	Ensemble	0.9095	0.8651	0.8136	4.1724	6.5445	2.7162	–
SCAN (3rd, tie) [18]	Ensemble	0.903	0.847	0.796	4.17	4.93	3.55	–
MFNet (ours)	Single	0.9091	0.8408	0.8037	4.6872	7.4821	2.3884	3.82 M

5 Conclusion

In this paper, we propose a novel network for brain tumor segmentation. The most important part, Multi-direction Fusion module, uses three branches of dilated pseudo-3D convolution in parallel to extract and assemble features from three direction of a MRI volume data simultaneously as a replacement of standard 3D convolution block. The proposed network, MFNet, shows competitive results and brings significant parameter reduction compared with other state-of-the-art methods on the BraTS 2018 online validation set.

Since the concept of axial, sagittal and coronal planes is common for all medical data, we believe this method deserves further researches for not only brain tumor but also other medical image segmentation tasks, to achieve a better balance of effectiveness and efficiency.

Acknowledgements. This work is supported by the National Key Research and Development Program of China (2018YFB0804203), National Defense Science and Technology Fund for Distinguished Young Scholars (2017-JCJQ-ZQ-022), the National Nature Science Foundation of China (61525206, 61771468, 61976008), the Youth Innovation Promotion Association Chinese Academy of Sciences (2017209).

References

1. Bakas, S., et al.: Segmentation labels and radiomic features for the pre-operative scans of the tcga-gbm collection. the cancer imaging archive (2017)

2. Bakas, S., et al.: Segmentation labels and radiomic features for the pre-operative scans of the TCGA-LGG collection. The Cancer Imaging Archive **286** (2017)
3. Bakas, S., et al.: Advancing the cancer genome atlas glioma MRI collections with expert segmentation labels and radiomic features. Sci. Data **4**, 170117 (2017)
4. Chen, L.C., Papandreou, G., Kokkinos, I., Murphy, K., Yuille, A.L.: DeepLab: semantic image segmentation with deep convolutional nets, atrous convolution, and fully connected CRFs. IEEE Trans. Pattern Anal. Mach. Intell. **40**(4), 834–848 (2017)
5. Çiçek, Ö., Abdulkadir, A., Lienkamp, S.S., Brox, T., Ronneberger, O.: 3D U-Net: learning dense volumetric segmentation from sparse annotation. In: Ourselin, S., Joskowicz, L., Sabuncu, M.R., Unal, G., Wells, W. (eds.) MICCAI 2016. LNCS, vol. 9901, pp. 424–432. Springer, Cham (2016). https://doi.org/10.1007/978-3-319-46723-8_49
6. He, K., Zhang, X., Ren, S., Sun, J.: Delving deep into rectifiers: surpassing human-level performance on ImageNet classification. In: Proceedings of the IEEE International Conference on Computer Vision, pp. 1026–1034 (2015)
7. He, K., Zhang, X., Ren, S., Sun, J.: Deep residual learning for image recognition. In: Proceedings of the IEEE Conference on Computer Vision and Pattern Recognition, pp. 770–778 (2016)
8. Ioffe, S., Szegedy, C.: Batch normalization: accelerating deep network training by reducing internal covariate shift. arXiv preprint arXiv:1502.03167 (2015)
9. Isensee, F., Kickingereder, P., Wick, W., Bendszus, M., Maier-Hein, K.H.: No new-net. In: Crimi, A., Bakas, S., Kuijf, H., Keyvan, F., Reyes, M., van Walsum, T. (eds.) BrainLes 2018. LNCS, vol. 11384, pp. 234–244. Springer, Cham (2019). https://doi.org/10.1007/978-3-030-11726-9_21
10. Kamnitsas, K., et al.: Ensembles of multiple models and architectures for robust brain tumour segmentation. In: Crimi, A., Bakas, S., Kuijf, H., Menze, B., Reyes, M. (eds.) BrainLes 2017. LNCS, vol. 10670, pp. 450–462. Springer, Cham (2018). https://doi.org/10.1007/978-3-319-75238-9_38
11. Kamnitsas, K., et al.: DeepMedic for brain tumor segmentation. In: Crimi, A., Menze, B., Maier, O., Reyes, M., Winzeck, S., Handels, H. (eds.) BrainLes 2016. LNCS, pp. 138–149. Springer, Cham (2016). https://doi.org/10.1007/978-3-319-55524-9_14
12. Kingma, D.P., Ba, J.: Adam: a method for stochastic optimization. arXiv preprint arXiv:1412.6980 (2014)
13. Lin, T.Y., Goyal, P., Girshick, R., He, K., Dollár, P.: Focal loss for dense object detection. In: Proceedings of the IEEE International Conference on Computer Vision, pp. 2980–2988 (2017)
14. Liu, A.A., Su, Y.T., Nie, W.Z., Kankanhalli, M.: Hierarchical clustering multi-task learning for joint human action grouping and recognition. IEEE Trans. Pattern Anal. Mach. Intell. **39**(1), 102–114 (2016)
15. Liu, C., Xie, H., Liu, Y., Zha, Z., Lin, F., Zhang, Y.: Extract bone parts without human prior: end-to-end convolutional neural network for pediatric bone age assessment. In: Shen, D., et al. (eds.) MICCAI 2019. LNCS, vol. 11769, pp. 667–675. Springer, Cham (2019). https://doi.org/10.1007/978-3-030-32226-7_74
16. Liu, C., Xie, H., Zhang, S., Xu, J., Sun, J., Zhang, Y.: Misshapen pelvis landmark detection by spatial local correlation mining for diagnosing developmental dysplasia of the hip. In: Shen, D., et al. (eds.) MICCAI 2019. LNCS, vol. 11769, pp. 441–449. Springer, Cham (2019). https://doi.org/10.1007/978-3-030-32226-7_49

17. Long, J., Shelhamer, E., Darrell, T.: Fully convolutional networks for semantic segmentation. In: Proceedings of the IEEE Conference on Computer Vision and Pattern Recognition, pp. 3431–3440 (2015)
18. McKinley, R., Meier, R., Wiest, R.: Ensembles of densely-connected CNNs with label-uncertainty for brain tumor segmentation. In: Crimi, A., Bakas, S., Kuijf, H., Keyvan, F., Reyes, M., van Walsum, T. (eds.) BrainLes 2018. LNCS, vol. 11384, pp. 456–465. Springer, Cham (2019). https://doi.org/10.1007/978-3-030-11726-9_40
19. Menze, B.H., et al.: The multimodal brain tumor image segmentation benchmark (BRATS). IEEE Trans. Med. Imaging **34**(10), 1993–2024 (2014)
20. Milletari, F., Navab, N., Ahmadi, S.A.: V-net: fully convolutional neural networks for volumetric medical image segmentation. In: 2016 Fourth International Conference on 3D Vision (3DV), pp. 565–571. IEEE (2016)
21. Myronenko, A.: 3D MRI brain tumor segmentation using autoencoder regularization. In: Crimi, A., Bakas, S., Kuijf, H., Keyvan, F., Reyes, M., van Walsum, T. (eds.) BrainLes 2018. LNCS, vol. 11384, pp. 311–320. Springer, Cham (2019). https://doi.org/10.1007/978-3-030-11726-9_28
22. Paszke, A., et al.: Automatic differentiation in PyTorch (2017)
23. Qiu, Z., Yao, T., Mei, T.: Learning spatio-temporal representation with pseudo-3D residual networks. In: Proceedings of the IEEE International Conference on Computer Vision, pp. 5533–5541 (2017)
24. Ronneberger, O., Fischer, P., Brox, T.: U-Net: convolutional networks for biomedical image segmentation. In: Navab, N., Hornegger, J., Wells, W.M., Frangi, A.F. (eds.) MICCAI 2015. LNCS, vol. 9351, pp. 234–241. Springer, Cham (2015). https://doi.org/10.1007/978-3-319-24574-4_28
25. Tran, D., Wang, H., Torresani, L., Ray, J., LeCun, Y., Paluri, M.: A closer look at spatiotemporal convolutions for action recognition. In: Proceedings of the IEEE conference on Computer Vision and Pattern Recognition, pp. 6450–6459 (2018)
26. Wang, G., Li, W., Ourselin, S., Vercauteren, T.: Automatic brain tumor segmentation using cascaded anisotropic convolutional neural networks. In: Crimi, A., Bakas, S., Kuijf, H., Menze, B., Reyes, M. (eds.) BrainLes 2017. LNCS, vol. 10670, pp. 178–190. Springer, Cham (2018). https://doi.org/10.1007/978-3-319-75238-9_16
27. Wu, Y., He, K.: Group normalization. In: Ferrari, V., Hebert, M., Sminchisescu, C., Weiss, Y. (eds.) ECCV 2018. LNCS, vol. 11217, pp. 3–19. Springer, Cham (2018). https://doi.org/10.1007/978-3-030-01261-8_1
28. Xie, H., Yang, D., Sun, N., Chen, Z., Zhang, Y.: Automated pulmonary nodule detection in CT images using deep convolutional neural networks. Pattern Recogn. **85**, 109–119 (2019)
29. Xu, H., Xie, H., Liu, Y., Cheng, C., Niu, C., Zhang, Y.: Deep cascaded attention network for multi-task brain tumor segmentation. In: Shen, D., et al. (eds.) MICCAI 2019. LNCS, vol. 11766, pp. 420–428. Springer, Cham (2019). https://doi.org/10.1007/978-3-030-32248-9_47
30. Yu, F., Koltun, V.: Multi-scale context aggregation by dilated convolutions. arXiv preprint arXiv:1511.07122 (2015)
31. Zhou, C., Chen, S., Ding, C., Tao, D.: Learning contextual and attentive information for brain tumor segmentation. In: Crimi, A., Bakas, S., Kuijf, H., Keyvan, F., Reyes, M., van Walsum, T. (eds.) BrainLes 2018. LNCS, vol. 11384, pp. 497–507. Springer, Cham (2019). https://doi.org/10.1007/978-3-030-11726-9_44

Texture-Based Fast CU Size Decision and Intra Mode Decision Algorithm for VVC

Jian Cao[1], Na Tang[2], Jun Wang[1], and Fan Liang[1(✉)]

[1] School of Electronics and Information Technology, Sun Yat-Sen University, Guangzhou, China
isslf@mail.sysu.edu.cn

[2] School of Data and Computer Science, Sun Yat-Sen University, Guangzhou, China

Abstract. Versatile Video Coding (VVC) is the next generation video coding standard. Compared with HEVC/H.265, in order to improve coding efficiency, its complexity of intra coding increases significantly. Too much encoding time makes it difficult for real-time coding and hardware implementation. To tackle this urgent problem, a texture-based fast CU size decision and intra mode decision algorithm is proposed in this paper. The contributions of the proposed algorithm include two aspects. (1) Aiming at the latest adopted QTMT block partitioning scheme in VVC, some redundant splitting tree and direction are skipped according to texture characteristics and differences between sub-parts of CU. (2) A fast intra mode decision scheme is proposed which considers complexity and texture characteristics. Some hierarchical modifications are applied including reducing the number of checked Intra Prediction Modes (IPM) and candidate modes in Rough Modes Decision (RMD) and RD check stage respectively. Compared with the latest VVC reference software VTM-4.2, the proposed algorithm can achieve approximately 46% encoding time saving on average with only 0.91% BD-RATE increase or 0.046 BD-PSNR decrease.

Keywords: VVC · Intra coding · QTMT · IPM · Encoding complexity

1 Introduction

Versatile Video Coding (VVC), as the next generation video coding standard, is still under construction by Joint Video Experts Team (JVET). Compared with HEVC/H.265, many novel technologies have been introduced, such as Position Dependent Intra Prediction Combination (PDPC) [1], Affine Motion Compensated Prediction [2] and Intra Sub-Partitions (ISP) [3], etc. Those new coding tools contribute to improve coding efficiency significantly.

In the first draft of VVC [4], the block partitioning scheme by a quadtree with nested multi-type tree using binary and ternary splits (QTMT) is adopted. Figure 1 shows five splitting types in QTMT block partitioning scheme. As shown in Fig. 2, a Coding Tree Unit (CTU) can be split into one or more Coding Units (CU) using the mentioned QTMT block partitioning scheme.

Binary and ternary splitting make it possible for CU to have a rectangular shape, not just the square shape in HEVC. QTMT block partitioning scheme allows flexible

Y. M. Ro et al. (Eds.): MMM 2020, LNCS 11961, pp. 739–751, 2020.
https://doi.org/10.1007/978-3-030-37731-1_60

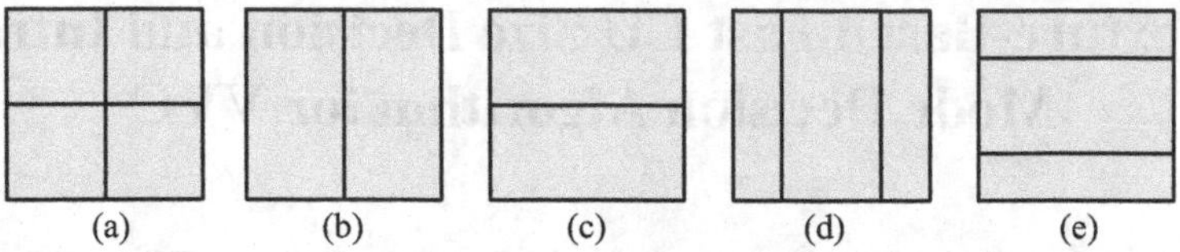

Fig. 1. Five splitting types in QTMT block partitioning scheme. (a) Quaternary splitting (b) Vertical binary splitting (c) Horizontal binary splitting (d) Vertical ternary splitting (e) Horizontal ternary splitting.

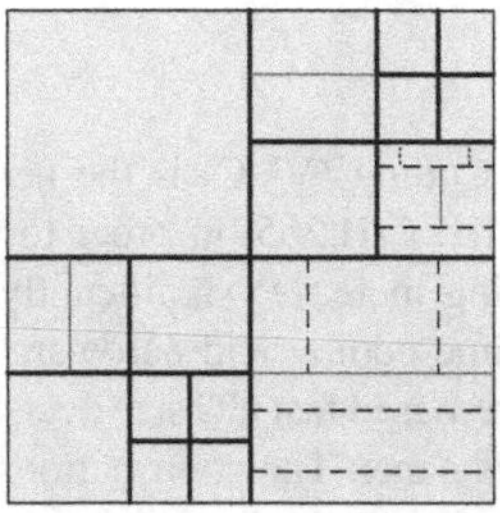

Fig. 2. Example of a CTU partition results using QTMT block partitioning scheme. Bold block edges represent quaternary splitting. Red block edges represent binary splitting. Dotted block edges represent ternary splitting.

adaptation to complex texture characteristics and enhances the performance significantly at the cost of huge increase of encoding time.

The number of intra directional prediction modes is extended from 33 in HEVC to 65 in VVC so that the arbitrary edge direction can be captured [5]. Intra directional prediction modes are shown in Fig. 3. Adding DC and Planar mode, the number of Intra Prediction Modes (IPM) has increased to 67. Although some fast mode decision methods [6] have been introduced in VVC, such as Rough Modes Decision (RMD), etc., there still exits improvements to save encoding time considering the high computational complexity caused by RD check, and it is the jumping-off point of the proposed fast intra mode decision method in this paper.

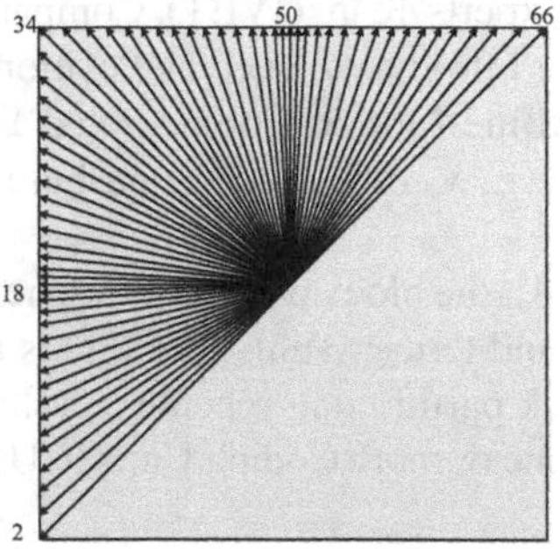

Fig. 3. 65 intra directional prediction modes in VVC.

In this paper, a texture-based fast CU size decision and intra mode decision algorithm is proposed. Two main methods are included to decrease encoding complexity.

- Aiming at the latest adopted QTMT block partitioning scheme in VVC, a fast CU size decision method is designed to skip redundant or unnecessary partition. Texture differences between two/three sub-parts of CU will be calculated. Then, whether to skip some splitting mode and direction will be judged based on the texture differences. The proposed method differs obviously from previous algorithms in HEVC due to the rectangular shape of CU. Previous algorithms in HEVC cease to be effective, which can only aim at quaternary splitting. However, the proposed method has taken it into account, so that encoding time can be reduced reasonably.
- A fast intra mode decision scheme is proposed which considers complexity and texture characteristics. Through the proposed method, the number of checked IPM and candidate modes can be further reduced in stage of RMD and RD check respectively. These hierarchical modifications reduce encoding time by making full use of texture characteristics.

The rest of this paper is organized as follows. In Sect. 2, related works are briefly introduced. In Sect. 3, the proposed texture-based fast CU size decision and intra mode decision algorithm is described in detail. In Sect. 4, the experimental results are shown and discussed. Finally, Sect. 5 draws the conclusion.

2 Related Works

2.1 Related Works in HEVC

For HEVC, there are many algorithms designed to simplify and accelerate the intra coding process. Most of them aim at fast CTU partitioning or fast IPM decision.

Öztekin and Erçelebi propose an early CU determination algorithm based on determining the strength of pixel variations [7]. Zhang, Lai, Liu, and An propose a fast CTU partitioning algorithm based on entropy and texture contrast [8]. Jamali and Coulombe use global and directional gradients to terminate the CU splitting procedure early and prevent processing of unnecessary depths [9]. Chang, Liu, Wang, and Li embed CNN into HEVC codec on efficiently performing the CU size decision and decreasing the amount of CU for full RDO process [10]. Ogata and Ichige restrict the number of mode candidates to be evaluated using outliers of DCT coefficients and neighboring block information [11]. Jamali and Coulombe propose a fast mode decision method based on the prediction of the RDO cost of intra modes [12].

Although approximately 45% encoding time saving can be achieved in [7], the BD-RATE loss increases up to 4.6%, which means the quality of video drops dramatically. What's worse, fast CTU partition algorithms in HEVC, including [7–11] mentioned above, cease to be effective because QTMT allows partitioning with direction in VVC, but HEVC only considers quaternary splitting (partitioning without direction). So these methods for HEVC must be improved vastly to be applied to horizontal/vertical binary tree and ternary tree splitting.

2.2 Related Works in VVC

For VVC, which is still under construction as the next generation video coding standard, a few researches have been done aiming at speed up the intra coding process, such as [13–16].

In [13], a fast CU depth decision method based on CNN is proposed, which aims at QTBT block partitioning scheme. In [14], spatial features for the binary and quaternary tree are employed for early splitting or termination of CU. In [15], a Machine Learning (ML) solution based on Random Forest (RF) classifiers is proposed to speed up the QTBT partitioning scheme. In [16], a fast intra coding algorithm consisting of CTU structure and intra mode decision is proposed and the algorithm is based on SVM and one-dimensional gradient descent.

However, horizontal/vertical ternary tree splitting has not been taken into consideration in [13–15], so that these algorithms need to be upgraded for the latest VVC Test Model (VTM). In [16], the decision tree and all classifiers are trained offline and the training time is not included in total time in experimental results. Actually, the training process must be carried out before encoding, which means training time and complexity should not be neglected. What's worse, it is difficult and time-consuming to train an accurate and satisfactory model.

3 Texture-Based Fast Intra Coding Algorithm

In this section, a texture-based fast intra coding algorithm consisting of fast CU size and intra mode decision method is proposed. The fast CU size decision method is designed aiming at the latest adopted QTMT block partitioning scheme in VVC. The fast intra mode decision method is designed considering the complexity and texture characteristics of CU. Some hierarchical modifications are applied including reducing the number of checked IPM and candidate modes in RMD and RD check stage.

3.1 Fast CU Size Decision Method

As shown in Fig. 1 above, partitioning with direction is allowed in VVC. After checking the coded stream, a connection is found between the partitioning result and texture characteristics. The connection is reflected in three aspects.

- As shown in area (a) of Fig. 4, flat or homogeneous regions tend to be treated as large blocks, which means non-splitting is more preferred. This feature in VVC is the same as that in HEVC.
- The direction of splitting is usually the same as the texture characteristics of the block, if the block has obvious horizontal/vertical texture characteristics. As shown in area (b) of Fig. 4, there is an obvious vertical texture between the background and the exhibition board, and the splitting direction nearby is also vertical.
- As shown in area (c) of Fig. 4, if there are obvious differences between two/three subparts in a block, corresponding splitting direction and splitting mode (binary splitting for two parts and ternary splitting for three parts) are preferred.

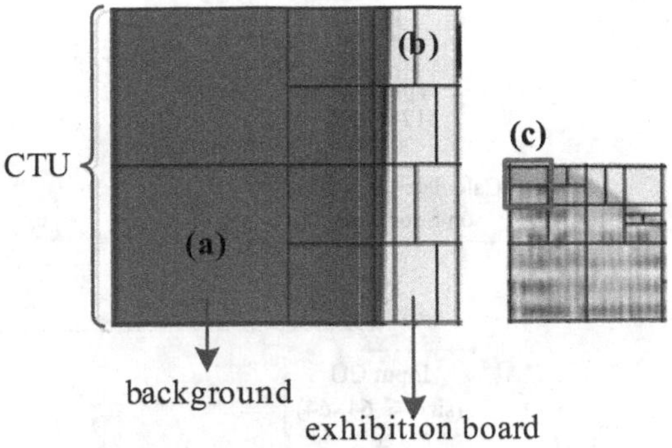

Fig. 4. Example of the connection between partitioning and texture (from sequence: *KristenAndSara*).

Aiming at the connection mentioned above, redundant or unnecessary partition can be skipped. The flowchart of the fast CU size decision method is shown in Fig. 5.

Step 1: Calculate texture based on Sobel operator for each CTU.

Use Sobel operator to calculate the gradient and texture characteristic of the current CTU. Horizontal gradient (G_{hor}) and vertical gradient (G_{ver}) can be calculated using a 3×3 Sobel convolution kernels:

$$G_{hor} = \begin{bmatrix} -1 & 0 & +1 \\ -2 & 0 & +2 \\ -1 & 0 & +1 \end{bmatrix} * \mathbf{P},\ G_{ver} = \begin{bmatrix} -1 & -2 & -1 \\ 0 & 0 & 0 \\ +1 & +2 & +1 \end{bmatrix} * \mathbf{P} \tag{1}$$

Where **P** presents the luminance pixel matrix of the CTU.

The texture value of each pixel G in the CTU can be calculated as:

$$G = |G_{hor}| + |G_{ver}| \tag{2}$$

Then, split CTU using quaternary splitting (QT) like the original process in VVC.

Step 2: Calculate texture differences between sub-parts of CU and judge whether to skip some splitting mode.

For each CU, calculate texture differences between two/three sub-parts.

An example of the calculating process is shown in Fig. 6. In the CU (size: w×h), a dot denotes texture value G of the pixel at the corresponding location. First, calculate the average value of G in three vertical sub-parts respectively by Eq. (3). Second, judge whether to skip vertical ternary splitting (TT_V) or horizontal ternary splitting (TT_H) for the current CU. The judging method is shown in Method 1. Last, add TT_V or TT_H to the candidate of splitting mode if *Skip_TTV* or *Skip_TTH* is 0.

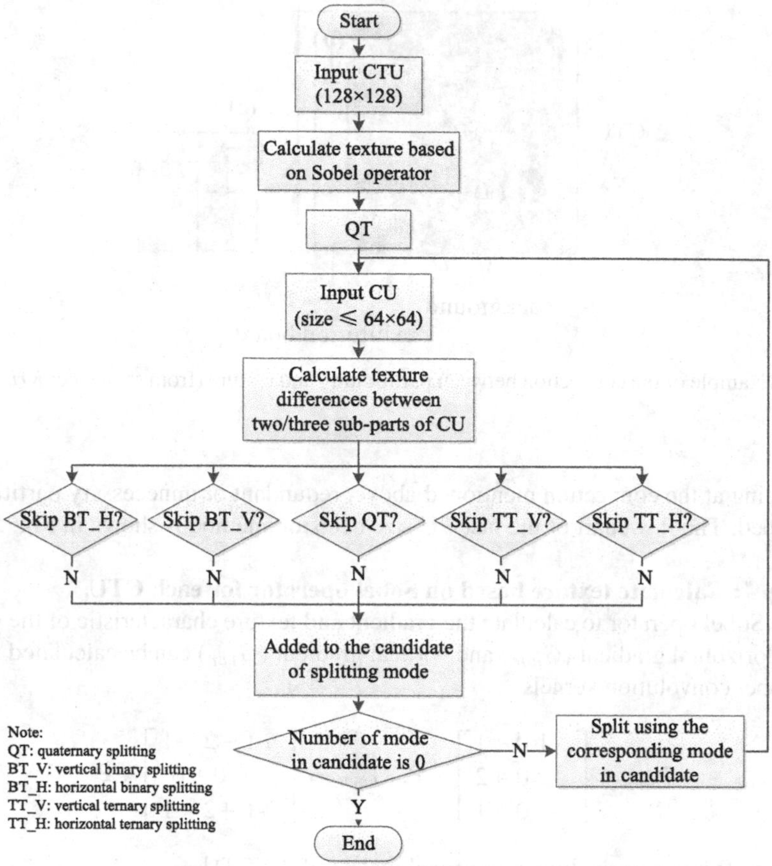

Fig. 5. The flowchart of the fast CU size decision method.

$$\begin{cases} G_{p1} = \sum_{x=0}^{w/4-1} \sum_{y=0}^{h-1} G(x, y)/(w/4 \times h) \\ G_{p2} = \sum_{x=w/4}^{3/4\times w-1} \sum_{y=0}^{h-1} G(x, y)/(w/2 \times h) \\ G_{p3} = \sum_{x=3/4\times w}^{w-1} \sum_{y=0}^{h-1} G(x, y)/(w/4 \times h) \end{cases} \quad (3)$$

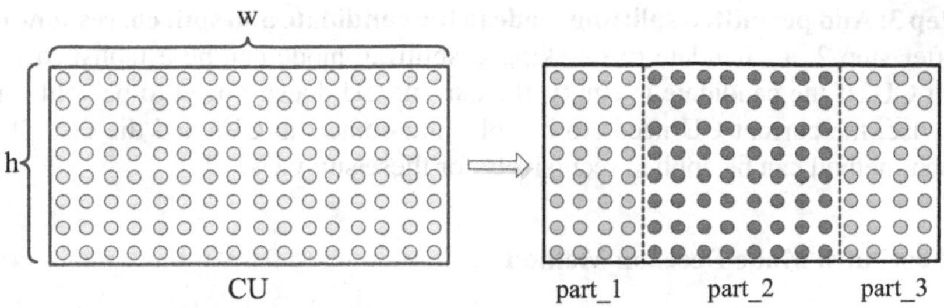

Fig. 6. Example of the calculating process in step 2.

Method 1. The judging method about whether to skip TT_V or TT_H.

Input:

G_{p1}, G_{p2}, and G_{p3}: the average texture value in the corresponding sub-parts.

Output:

Skip_TTV: a Boolean variable indicating whether to skip TT_V for CU.

Skip_TTH: a Boolean variable indicating whether to skip TT_H for CU.

(Note. Value 1 denotes that the corresponding splitting mode is skipped.)

```
Sort Gp1, Gp2: Gmax1, Gmin1;
Divide Gmax1 by Gmin1 and obtain the quotient: Q1;
Sort Gp2, Gp3: Gmax2, Gmin2;
Divide Gmax2 by Gmin2 and obtain the quotient: Q2;
if either Q1 or Q2 is bigger than threshold1,
  Set Skip_TTH 1. (Note. Judge there are obvious vertical differences or texture.)
else,
  Set Skip_TTH 0.
if all of Gp1, Gp2, and Gp3 are smaller than threshold2,
  if both Q1 and Q2 are smaller than threshold3,
    Set Skip_TTV 1. (Note. Judge that differences are small or it is a flat region.)
  else,
    Set Skip_TTV 0.
else,
  Set Skip_TTV 0.
Return Skip_TTV and Skip_TTH.
```

Calculating process for texture differences and judging methods for skipping other splitting modes are similar. As long as the calculation is performed according to the corresponding splitting tree and direction, it can be determined whether the corresponding splitting mode can be skipped.

Step 3: Add permitted splitting mode to the candidate and split correspondingly. After step 2, a candidate of un-skipped splitting mode can be established for the current CU. If the candidate is empty, the current CU doesn't need to be split further. Otherwise, the current CU needs to be split into some sub-CUs and the fast CU size decision method can be applied recursively for these sub-CUs.

3.2 Fast Intra Mode Decision Method

In the proposed fast intra mode decision method, based on complexity and texture characteristics of CU, some hierarchical modifications are applied, including reducing the number of checked IPM and candidate modes in RMD and RD check stage.

Besides the horizontal gradient (G_{hor}) and vertical gradient (G_{ver}) mentioned above, 45° gradient (G_{45}) and 135° gradient (G_{135}) can also reflect texture characteristics and they can be calculated as:

$$G_{45}=\begin{bmatrix}0 & -1 & -2\\ +1 & 0 & -1\\ +2 & +1 & 0\end{bmatrix}*\mathbf{P},\; G_{135}=\begin{bmatrix}-2 & -1 & 0\\ -1 & 0 & +1\\ 0 & +1 & +2\end{bmatrix}*\mathbf{P} \tag{4}$$

Where **P** presents the luminance pixel matrix of the CU.

The average directional gradients in the CU (size: w×h) can be calculated as:

$$\overline{G_{hor}}=\sum_{x=0}^{w-1}\sum_{y=0}^{h-1}G_{hor}(x,y)/(w\times h),\; \overline{G_{ver}}=\sum_{x=0}^{w-1}\sum_{y=0}^{h-1}G_{ver}(x,y)/(w\times h)$$
$$\overline{G_{45}}=\sum_{x=0}^{w-1}\sum_{y=0}^{h-1}G_{45}(x,y)/(w\times h),\; \overline{G_{135}}=\sum_{x=0}^{w-1}\sum_{y=0}^{h-1}G_{135}(x,y)/(w\times h) \tag{5}$$

The improved intra mode decision scheme is shown in Fig. 7.

First, judge whether the texture in the CU is simple. If simple, the number of candidate modes in RD check stage is reduced to 1. Under these circumstances, prediction error will increase little due to the homogeneous content, but the encoding complexity can be reduced significantly. An easy judging process is adopted as:

$$flag\_simple=\begin{cases}1, & \overline{G_{hor}}\le threshold4\ \&\&\ \overline{G_{ver}}\le threshold4\\ 0, & other\ cases\end{cases} \tag{6}$$

Second, judge whether to skip checking some IPM in RMD stage based on the average directional gradients. For example, as shown in Fig. 8, if there is an obvious vertical texture in the block, IPM around the horizontal direction will be skipped in RMD stage. The judging method is shown in Eq. (7). Methods for other directions are similar.

$$flag\_skip\_hor=\begin{cases}1, & \overline{G_{hor}}/\overline{G_{ver}}>=threshold5\\ 0, & other\ cases\end{cases} \tag{7}$$

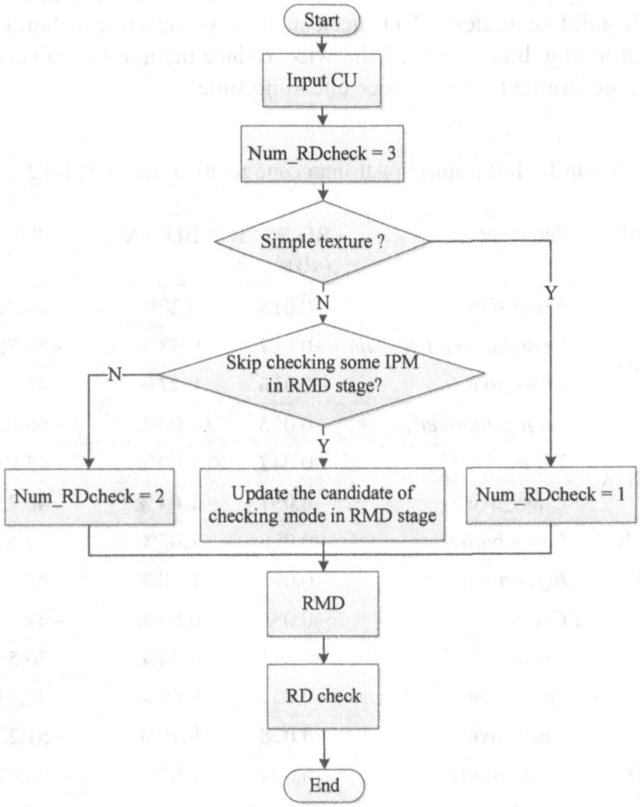

Fig. 7. The improved intra mode decision scheme.

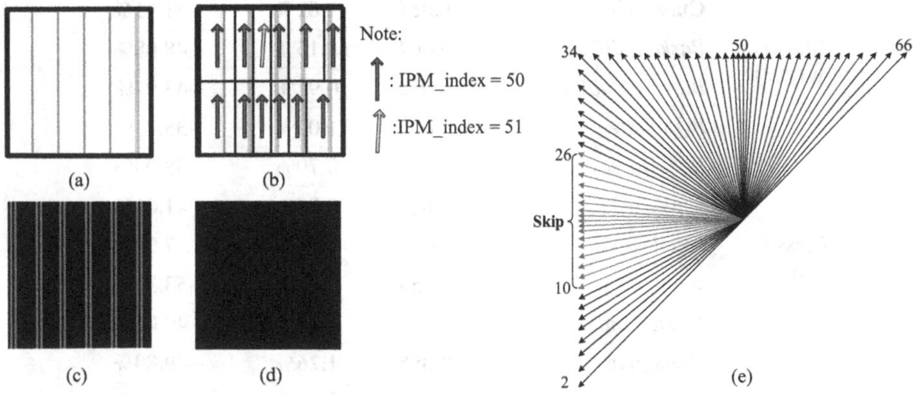

Fig. 8. Example of skip checking some IPM around the horizontal direction in RMD stage. (a) A block with obvious vertical texture. (b) The splitting result and IPM of each sub-block. (c) The horizontal gradient. (d) The vertical gradient. (e) The skipped IPM in RMD stage.

In RD check stage, if there is an obvious directional texture judged as stated before, the number of candidate modes in RD check stage stays the same as before to avoid the video quality dropping dramatically. Otherwise, reduce the number of candidate modes in RD check stage from 3 to 2, to reduce encoding time.

Table 1. Test results in All-Intra configuration over VTM-4.2

CLASS	Sequence	BD-PSNR (dB)	BD-RATE	ΔT
Class A 10bit WQXGA	*NebutaFestival*	−0.015	0.22%	−40.22%
	SteamLocomotiveTrain	−0.017	0.33%	−50.78%
	Class_ave	**−0.016**	**0.27%**	**−45.50%**
Class A 8bit WQXGA	*PeopleOnStreet*	−0.055	1.08%	−46.63%
	Traffic	−0.047	1.00%	−45.83%
	Class_ave	**−0.051**	**1.04%**	**−46.23%**
Class B 1080p	*BasketballDrive*	−0.026	1.07%	−59.62%
	BQTerrace	−0.048	1.00%	−43.18%
	Cactus	−0.030	0.89%	−49.29%
	Kimono	−0.011	0.34%	−56.56%
	ParkScene	−0.027	0.65%	−47.53%
	Class_ave	**−0.028**	**0.79%**	**−51.23%**
Class C WVGA	*BasketballDrill*	−0.084	1.87%	−46.61%
	BQMall	−0.053	0.96%	−42.94%
	PartyScene	−0.048	0.67%	−39.03%
	RaceHorses	−0.036	0.59%	−39.05%
	Class_ave	**−0.055**	**1.02%**	**−41.91%**
Class D WQVGA	*BasketballPass*	−0.064	1.15%	−48.08%
	BlowingBubbles	−0.052	0.92%	−43.97%
	BQSquare	−0.083	1.02%	−35.43%
	RaceHorses	−0.045	0.70%	−38.98%
	Class_ave	**−0.061**	**0.95%**	**−41.61%**
Class E 720p	*FourPeople*	−0.068	1.27%	−47.02%
	Johnny	−0.054	1.43%	−53.31%
	KristenAndSara	−0.051	1.08%	−49.06%
	Class_ave	**−0.058**	**1.26%**	**−49.80%**
Overall		**−0.046**	**0.91%**	**−46.16%**

4 Experimental Results

The proposed texture-based fast intra coding algorithm is implemented on VTM-4.2 [17] for experiment. Thresholds mentioned above are set as {1.5, 400, 3.0, 10, 5.0} based on multiple experiments and experience. VTM-4.2, published in April 2019, is chosen as the anchor, which is one of the latest VVC test models. QP values are chosen as {22, 27, 32, 37} in All-Intra configuration. All test sequences are encoded with 100 frames. The performance is evaluated by time-saving ΔT, BD-RATE and BD-PSNR metric [18]. ΔT can be calculated as:

$$\Delta T = \frac{\sum_{i=1}^{4} T_{pro}(QP_i) - \sum_{i=1}^{4} T_{anchor}(QP_i)}{\sum_{i=1}^{4} T_{anchor}(QP_i)} \tag{8}$$

All experiments run on *Intel^R Core^{TM} i7-8700 K CPU @ 3.70 GHz 32.0 GB RAM* platform. The test results are shown in Table 1.

As shown in Table 1, the proposed texture-based fast intra coding algorithm can save encoding time significantly for all test sequences. Approximately 46.16% encoding time can be saved on average with only 0.91% BD-RATE increase or 0.046 BD-PSNR decrease. In addition, the decreases of BD-PSNR for all test sequences are smaller than 0.1, which illustrates that redundant rather than necessary splitting and IPM are skipped. The results demonstrate that the proposed algorithm can make full use of the connection between splitting, intra prediction and texture characteristics.

What's more, the proposed algorithm performs particularly well with videos at high resolution, such as *SteamLocomotiveTrain* (2560 × 1600) and *Kimono* (1920 × 1080). Video quality drops little but encoding time decreases greatly. The proposed algorithm favors a great potential with the rapid development of HD video.

Compared to the method based on SVM and one-dimensional gradient descent in [16], the proposed method strikes a better balance between encoding complexity and efficiency. The increase of BD-RATE and decrease of encoding time are up to about 2% and 62% in [16], but less than 1% and about 46% in this paper. In addition, in [16], the decision tree and all classifiers are trained offline and the training time is not included in total time in experimental results. Considering that the training process must be carried out before encoding, training time and complexity should not be neglected, which means 62% time saving in [16] cannot be achieved actually. However, judging method of the proposed algorithm is completely embedded into the coding process, so that the saved encoding time can fully reflect the excellent performance.

5 Conclusions

In this paper, a texture-based fast intra coding algorithm consisting of fast CU size and intra mode decision method is proposed. The fast CU size decision method is designed aiming at the latest QTMT block partitioning scheme in VVC. The fast intra mode decision method is developed to further reduce the number of checked IPM and candidate modes in RMD and RD check stage respectively. Approximately 46% encoding time saving can be achieved on average with only 0.91% BD-RATE increase or 0.046 BD-PSNR decrease. What's more, the proposed algorithm has a great potential in the future due to its excellent performance in high-definition video.

Acknowledgments. This work is supported by Key R&D Program of Guangdong Province (No. 2019B010135002).

References

1. Van der Auwera, G., Seregin, V., Said, A., Ramasubramonian, A.K., Karczewicz, M.: CE3: simplified PDPC (Test 2.4.1), document JVET-K0063. In: Proceedings of 11th JVET Meeting, Ljubljana, SI, July 2018
2. Chen, H., Yang, H., Chen, J.: CE4: affine motion compensation with fixed sub-block size (Test 1.1), document JVET-K0184. In: Proceedings of 11th JVET Meeting, Ljubljana, SI, July 2018
3. De-Luxán-Hernández, S., et al.: CE3: Intra sub-partitions coding mode (Tests 1.1.1 and 1.1.2), document JVET -M0102. In: Proceedings of 13th JVET Meeting, Marrakech, MA, Jan 2019
4. Bross, B.: Versatile video coding (Draft 1), document JVET-J1001. In: Proceedings of 10th JVET Meeting, San Diego, US, Apr 2018
5. Choi, N., Piao, Y., Choi, K., Kim, C.: CE3.3 related: intra 67 modes coding with 3MPM, document JVET-K0529, JVET-K0368. In: Proceedings of 11th JVET meeting, Ljubljana, SI, July 2018
6. Chen, J., et al.: Coding tools investigation for next generation video coding, ITU-T SG16 Doc. COM16CC806, Feb 2015
7. Öztekin, A., Erçelebi, E.: An early split and skip algorithm for fast intra CU selection in HEVC. J. Real-Time Image Process. **12**, 273–283 (2016)
8. Zhang, M., Lai, D., Liu, Z., An, C.: A novel adaptive fast partition algorithm based on CU complexity analysis in HEVC. Multimedia Tools Appl. **78**, 1035–1051 (2019)
9. Jamali, M., Coulombe, S.: Coding unit splitting early termination for fast HEVC intra coding based on global and directional gradients. In: 2016 IEEE 18th International Workshop on Multimedia Signal Processing (MMSP), pp. 1–5 (2016)
10. Chang, L., Liu, Z., Wang, L., Li, X: Enhance the HEVC fast intra CU mode decision based on convolutional neural network by corner power estimation. In: 2018 Data Compression Conference (DCC), p. 400 (2018)
11. Ogata, J., Ichige, K.: Fast intra mode decision method based on outliers of DCT coefficients and neighboring block information for H. 265/HEVC. In: 2018 IEEE International Symposium on Circuits and Systems (ISCAS), pp. 1–5 (2018)
12. Jamali, M., Coulombe, S.: Fast HEVC intra mode decision based on RDO cost prediction. IEEE Trans. Broadcast. **65**(1), 109–122 (2019)
13. Jin, Z., An, P., Shen, L.: Fast QTBT partition algorithm for JVET intra coding based on CNN. In: Pacific Rim Conference on Multimedia (PCM), pp. 59–69 (2017)
14. Lin, T., Jiang, H., Huang, J., Chang, P.: Fast intra coding unit partition decision in H. 266/FVC based on spatial features. J. Real-Time Image Process. 1–18 (2018)
15. Amestoy, T., Mercat, A., Hamidouche, W., Bergeron, C., Menard, D.: Random forest oriented fast QTBT frame partitioning. In: 2019 IEEE International Conference on Acoustics, Speech and Signal Processing (ICASSP), pp. 1837–1841 (2019)

16. Yang, H., Shen, L., Dong, X., Ding, Q., An, P., Jiang, G.: Low complexity CTU partition structure decision and fast intra mode decision for Versatile video coding. In: IEEE Transactions on Circuits and Systems for Video Technology (2019)
17. VTM-4.2. https://vcgit.hhi.fraunhofer.de/jvet/VVCSoftware_VTM/tree/VTM-4.2
18. Bjontegaard, G.: Calculation of average PSNR differences between RD curves, document VCEG-M33. Texas, USA (2001)

An Efficient Hierarchical Near-Duplicate Video Detection Algorithm Based on Deep Semantic Features

Siying Liang and Ping Wang(✉)

School of Electronic and Information Engineering, Xi'an Jiaotong University, Xi'an 710049, China
ping.fu@xjtu.edu.cn

Abstract. With the rapid development of the Internet and multimedia technology, the amount of multimedia data on the Internet is escalating exponentially, which has attracted much research attention in the field of Near-Duplicate Video Detection (NDVD). Motivated by the excellent performance of Convolutional Neural Networks (CNNs) in image classification, we bring the powerful discrimination ability of the CNN model to the NDVD system and propose a hierarchical detection method based on the derived deep semantic features from the CNN models. The original CNN features are firstly extracted from the video frames, and then a semantic descriptor and a labels descriptor are obtained respectively based on the basic content unit. Finally, a hierarchical matching scheme is proposed to promote fast near-duplicate video detection. The proposed approach has been tested on the widely used CC_WEB_VIDEO dataset, and has achieved state-of-the-art results with the mean Average Precision (mAP) of 0.977.

Keywords: Near-Duplicate Video Detection · Convolutional Neural Network · Semantic descriptor · Labels descriptor · Hierarchical matching

1 Introduction

With the development of digital media, video sharing and propagation become more and more convenient. Due to the openness of video sharing websites and the emergence of various video editing software, users can easily edit and upload the video. It is reported that about 500 h of video are uploaded to YouTube every minute and the total number of videos on YouTube is more than 5 billion[1]. However, there exist large numbers of duplicate and near-duplicate videos among these huge volumes of videos. Wu et al. [1] searched on three video sharing websites (YouTube, Google Video and Yahoo! Video) with 24 popular queries and finally collected 12,790 video segments. In the search result, on average 27% of the videos are duplicates or near-duplicates.

Near-duplicate videos (NDVs) are considered to be identical or close to the exact duplicate videos, but different in terms of the file format, encoding parameters,

[1] https://www.omnicoreagency.com/youtube-statistics/.

Y. M. Ro et al. (Eds.): MMM 2020, LNCS 11961, pp. 752–763, 2020.
https://doi.org/10.1007/978-3-030-37731-1_61

photometric variations (colour, lighting changes), editing operations (caption, logo and border insertion), lengths, and other modifications [1]. The existence of a large number of near-duplicate videos not only reduces user experience but also brings great challenges to video storage, management, copyright protection and other issues. Therefore, fast and effective approaches are urgently needed to detect the NDVs.

At present, many effective content-based detection methods have been proposed. The video frame features have a significant influence on the retrieval accuracy. In the existing methods, the frame features can broadly be divided into two types: the global features and the local features. Typical global features are based on the statistical information of the frames; the local features mainly refer to the key-point based descriptors. However, both types of features give a relatively low-level visual representation while limited research attention has been given to investigate some high-level semantic feature representations for the NDVD.

The Convolutional neural network (CNN) is a popular machine learning method and has achieved great success in the fields of computer vision. Because of its excellent ability in feature extraction and representation, it has been widely used in many fields. In the last few years, CNN based algorithms have achieved significantly better performance than traditional methods, and many excellent CNN models have been proposed, such as AlexNet [2], VGG [3], GoogLeNet [4], etc. In ILSVRC 2017, the top-5 error was reduced to 2.251% [5].

In this paper, an efficient hierarchical near-duplicate video detection algorithm is proposed. Firstly, all frames of video are fed into the CNN model to extract the original dense features which are the output of a fully-connected layer. Then the original features are further abstracted based on the basic "content unit" to obtain the video-level semantic representation. Additionally, the output of the softmax layer is processed to obtain the high-level semantic labels feature based on the classification results of CNN. Finally, a hierarchical algorithm combining the two kinds of semantic descriptors are used to identify NDVs.

The performance of the proposed approach has been evaluated through extensive experiments on a popular NDVD dataset (CC_WEB_VIDEO [1]). The experiment results have shown the effectiveness and applicability of the proposed method. The best performance of our approach achieves a mean Average Precision (mAP) of 0.977, which is superior than the state-of-the-art approach. More importantly, with the compact and low-dimensional semantic features, the proposed method will help to perform the video retrieval more efficiently and at a lower cost.

2 Related Work

Near-duplicate video detection has attracted increasing research interests in recent years. Although the research results and technical details are different from each other, the NDVD methods can still be roughly divided into three steps: extracting features for sampled frames, building an index for video features, retrieving and calculating similarity.

The stable and high discriminating video frame features can improve retrieval accuracy. Therefore, the feature extraction becomes the most crucial task in NDVD. The frame features can generally be divided into two categories: global feature and local feature.

Cai et al. [6] extracted colour correlogram features for each uniform sampling frames, then quantized these features into visual words using K-means algorithm and represent the whole video as a bag of words. Paisitkriangkrai et al. [7] used an extension of ordinal measures as video features based on video clips instead of video frames. Global features are very efficient in extracting and matching, but they cannot cope with complex video changes very well.

Douze et al. [8] extracted the SIFT and CS-LBP descriptors for a subsample of frames. Then those local features were clustered into visual words and mapped into binary signatures by hamming embedding. Law-To et al. [9] employed Harris detector [10] associated to a local description of the point to extract interest points for frames, then described the geometric and kinematic behaviour of the interest points along its trajectory and labelled some interest points by different motion. The calculation of local features is massive, and the relevant algorithms are complex. However, compared with global features, local features are more robust to distortion, such as photometric changing, geometric transformation, complex editing and post-processing.

Due to the limitations of using only local features or global features, some researchers also combine these two features to complement each other. Wu et al. [1] proposed a hierarchical method. A global feature from colour histograms was first used to detect the near-duplicate videos with high confidence and filter out very different videos. Then the local features PCA-SIFT [11] was used to detect near-duplicate keyframes for the rest videos. Song et al. [12] proposed a novel Multiple Feature Hashing (MFH) algorithm, which preserved the local structural information of each feature and also globally considered the local structures for all the features.

Building index aims to improve retrieval efficiency. The ideal index structure should not only improve the retrieval speed but also minimize the quantitative error caused by the establishment of the index. At present, many tree index structures have been proposed, a structure called "Gauss-Tree" [13] achieved not only efficient retrieval but also preserved much visual information. Besides, existing widely used algorithms also include vector approximation file [14, 15], locality-sensitive hash structure [16], multiple feature hashing [12], etc.

Distance measurement is commonly used in feature matching, and the common distance measurement functions include Euclidean distance [18] and cosine distance [17]. The process of feature matching also gives the score of similarity. Besides, other measures are also used for some particular types of features, such as the earth mover's distance [19] and the edit distance [20]. Videos with a score higher than a certain threshold are usually taken as near-duplicate videos, and the threshold is generally determined according to the specific application situation.

3 Approach Overview

We propose an efficient hierarchical near-duplicate video detection approach based on semantic features, as shown in Fig. 1. Firstly, all frames of video are fed into the CNN model to extract original features, which include a fully-connected layer output and the softmax layer output. Then two different types of low dimensional compact semantic descriptors are generated. Finally, these two descriptors are combined in a hierarchical strategy to achieve near-duplicate video detection.

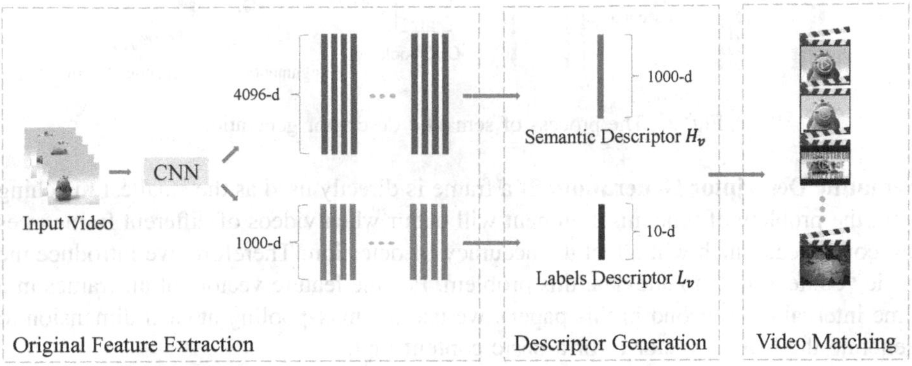

Fig. 1. The outline of the proposed near-duplicate video detection system.

3.1 Feature Extraction

In order to balance the efficiency and accuracy of detection, most work usually sparsely sample keyframes from videos, such as sampling one to two frames per second or one to two frames per shot. However, some useful information may be lost due to keyframe extraction. Thus, our approach firstly extracts features for all frames in the video to get a dense description of video content.

All frames of video are fed into the CNN model to extract original features. Although the number of frames is far more than that of sparse sampling frames, it will not waste much time in feature extraction, which is because the GPU and parallelize networks can allow simultaneous processing of images, and it is possible to process many frames in a batch which reduces the per-frame time to a few milliseconds. We utilize the Caffe [21] toolkit to implement the deep learning algorithm on the video frames. We experiment with AlexNet model, which is pre-trained on ImageNet dataset and is provided by Caffe[2]. For AlexNet model, we extract the 4096-d feature of the fc7 layer and 1000-d feature of the softmax layer.

[2] https://github.com/BVLC/caffe/wiki/Model-Zoo.

3.2 Semantic Descriptor

In this section, we introduce the process of generating semantic descriptor based on the output of the fully-connected layer, as shown in Fig. 2. Since the features for all video frames are extracted, and the dimension of the features from the fully-connected layer is too high, such a large corpus of features is not suitable for direct matching. Therefore, we need to process the original features further to generate low-dimensional descriptors.

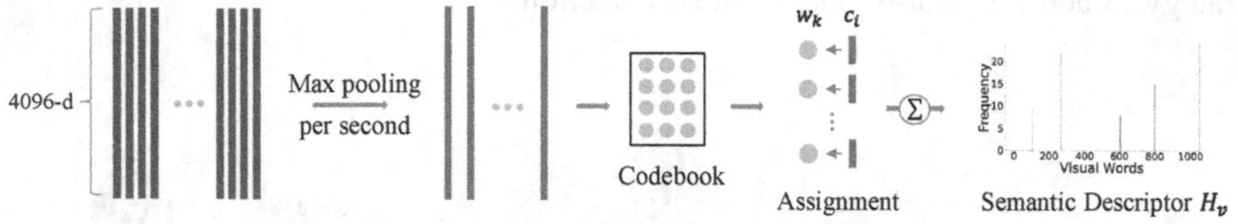

Fig. 2. The process of semantic descriptor generation.

Semantic Descriptor Generation. If a frame is directly used as the smallest matching unit, the problem of time misalignment will occur when videos of different frame rates are compared, which will affect the accuracy of detection. Therefore, we introduce the basic "content unit" to alleviate this problem. For the feature vectors of all frames in a time interval (one second in this paper), we use the max-pooling at each dimension to generate the feature vector c for a basic content unit.

$$c^m = f^m, \forall m \in M \tag{1}$$

$$f^m = \max_i f_i^m, i = 1, 2, \cdots, n \tag{2}$$

where c is the feature vector of basic content unit and f is the feature vector of a frame, both the two features are with M dimension which is the dimension of fully-connected layer feature vector, i.e. $M = 4096$, m is the $m-th$ dimension, i is the feature vector of the $i-th$ frame in one second, and n is the total number of frames in one second.

A bag-of-words scheme is applied to the feature vector c to generate a codebook of K visual words, denoted as $W_K = \{w_1, w_2, \cdots, w_K\}$. After the visual codebook is generated, the feature vector of every basic content unit is assigned to the nearest visual word. The final semantic descriptor H_v for the video is generated by aggregating the number of visual words of all basic content units. Obviously, H_v is a histogram with K dimension representing the frequency of each visual word.

Semantic Descriptor Matching. For the matching of the semantic descriptors of two videos, we use cosine distance to measure their similarity, as described by the following equation:

$$S_S(v_1, v_2) = \frac{\sum_{i=1}^{K} H_{v_1}^i H_{v_2}^i}{\sqrt{\sum_{i=1}^{K} (H_{v_1}^i)^2} \sqrt{\sum_{i=1}^{K} (H_{v_2}^i)^2}} \tag{3}$$

$S_S \in [0, 1]$, the higher S_S indicates a higher similarity between the two videos.

3.3 Labels Descriptor

Here, we introduce the process of generating another semantic descriptor called labels descriptor using the feature of the softmax layer, as shown in Fig. 3.

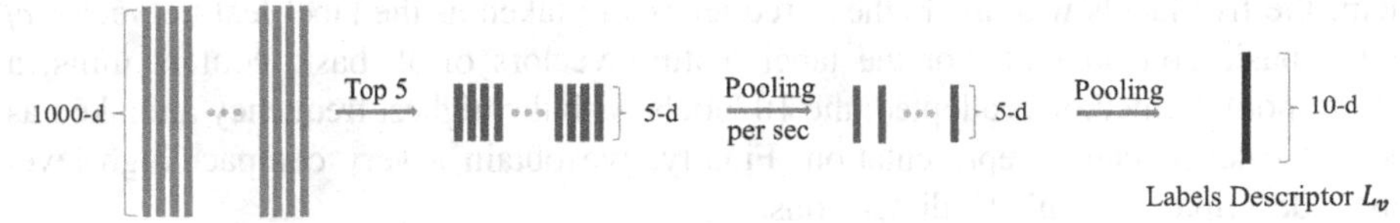

Fig. 3. The process of labels descriptor generation.

Labels Descriptor Generation. The output of the softmax layer is a probability distribution among N categories (for AlexNet, $N = 1000$). The higher the probability value, the higher the probability that the input image is classified into the corresponding category. In this paper, we choose the five categories with the highest probabilities as the labels of the frame. As shown in Table 1, these labels can describe the contents of the frame well. Because the labels are described by words, which are not convenient for subsequent steps, we replace these words with IDs, which is the ordinal number of every probability value in the original vector. Thus, each frame can be represented by a 5-dimensional real vector $f_i = [l_i^1, l_i^2, l_i^3, l_i^4, l_i^5]$. Several near-duplicate keyframes examples from CC_WEB_VIDEO are illustrated in Table 2, and their label IDs are also shown. It can be shown that the original keyframe and the near-duplicate keyframes share the same labels. From this point of view, these labels can be considered for near-duplicate video detection.

Table 1. Semantic labels and their IDs of three example images extracted by AlexNet.

Image	Semantic labels	ID
	African elephant, Loxodonta africana	387
	Tusker	102
	Indian elephant, Elephas maximus	386
	Warthog	344
	Water buffalo, Water ox, Asiatic buffalo	347
	Tabby, Tabby cat	282
	Egyptian cat	286
	Red fox, Vulpes	278
	Tiger cat	283
	Lynx, Catamount	288
	Minivan	657
	Cab, Hack, Taxi, Taxicab	469
	Sports car	818
	Beach wagon, Station wagon, Estate car	437
	Limousine, limo	628

When using labels to compare the similarity of video content, the frame-by-frame comparison is also sufficient, and there is also much redundant information. Similar to the generation of the semantic descriptor, the basic content unit is introduced to gradually abstract frame-level features into a higher video-level feature representation. As shown in Fig. 3, for the label vectors in one content unit, we adopt "pooling" on them: the five labels with the highest frequency are taken as the label feature vector c_i of the basic content unit. For the label feature vectors of all basic content units, a similar pooling method is adopted: the 10 labels with the highest frequency are taken as the video-level feature representation. Finally, we obtain a very compact high-level labels descriptor L_v with 10 dimensions.

Table 2. IDs of labels for a query frame and its near-duplicate frames. (These keyframes come from CC_WEB_VIDEO dataset, and they contain several variations, which include rotation, mirror, lighting change, caption and stretch.)

Query frame	Near-duplicate frames			
	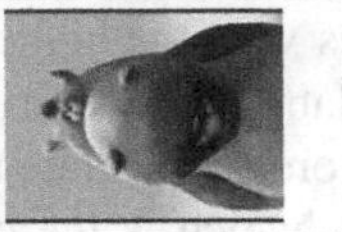			
685	720	685	147	685
720	692	720	685	147
147	685	172	151	151
151	837	254	720	720
172	393	678	147	681

Labels Descriptor Matching. For labels descriptors of two videos, the general distance measurements are no longer applicable. Since we focus on whether they have common semantic labels, a specific similarity metric is defined

$$S_L(v_1, v_2) = \frac{|L_{v_1} \cap L_{v_2}|}{|L_{v_1} \cup L_{v_2}|} \tag{4}$$

where $|L_{v_1} \cap L_{v_2}|$ represents the number of label shared by both descriptors, $|L_{v_1} \cup L_{v_2}|$ represents the number of label in the union of the two descriptors. $S_L \in [0, 1]$, the higher S_L indicates a higher similarity between the two videos.

3.4 Hierarchical Matching

After the semantic descriptor and labels descriptor mentioned above are both obtained, a hierarchical matching strategy is introduced to perform the matching process. Since the labels descriptor has a lower dimension than that of the semantic descriptor, and it represents the video content in a more abstract way, the labels descriptor is first utilized to filter out the videos that are entirely different from the query video and the video that are semantically identical to the query video. So that a candidate video set is obtained. In this step, two videos are considered to hold the same semantic content when S_L equals to 1 and are entirely irrelevant when S_L equals to 0. Then the semantic descriptor is further used to identify the near-duplicate videos from the candidate video set.

4 Experimental Results

4.1 Dataset

To test the performance of the proposed approach, all experiments were performed on the CC_WEB_VIDEO dataset. The dataset includes samples of video retrieved using 24 popular text queries on popular video sharing websites (YouTube, Google and Yahoo!). The final dataset contains 12,790 video segments. For each query in the dataset, the most popular video was regarded as the seed video (query), then other videos were manually labelled based on their relationship with the query video.

4.2 Evaluation Metrics

We use the Precision-Recall (PR) curve and the mean average precision (mAP) to evaluate the performance. Precision and Recall are defined as follows:

$$Precision = \frac{|G \cap D|}{|D|} \qquad Recall = \frac{|G \cap D|}{|G|} \tag{5}$$

where $\boldsymbol{G}$ is the set of near-duplicate videos in the ground truth, and $\boldsymbol{D}$ is the set of detected ones.

With the returned results generated by the algorithm in the j-th query Q_j, the average precision (AP) is defined as:

$$AP(j) = \frac{1}{n}\sum\nolimits_{i=0}^{n} \frac{i}{r_i} \tag{6}$$

where n is the number of related videos to the query video and r_i is the rank of the i-th retrieved relevant video. The mAP is the mean of AP and is calculated as:

$$mAP = \frac{1}{Q}\sum\nolimits_{j=1}^{Q} AP(j) \tag{7}$$

where Q is the number of queries.

4.3 Impact of Codebook Size

To evaluate the impact of codebook size K on the detection performance, we implement corresponding experiments with $K = 100$, $K = 1000$ and $K = 10000$. Figure 4 illustrates the PR curves of the different size K. The precision of $K = 1000$ is always higher than the other two at all levels of recall. It illustrates that the proposed method achieves the best performance when the codebook size $K = 1000$. When K is small, the dissimilar basic content units might be assigned to the same visual word; while the similar basic content units may be assigned to the different visual word when K is too large. These two cases both result in poor performance.

The same conclusion can be obtained by analyzing the mAP, as shown in Table 3. When $K = 1000$, the proposed approach achieves the best performance with a mAP of 0.977. Therefore, in the following experiments, the codebook size K is 1000.

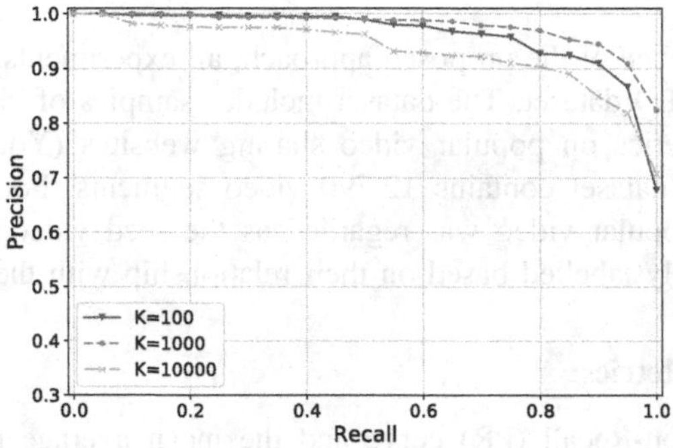

Fig. 4. The PR curves of different codebook sizes.

Table 3. The mAP of different codebook size.

Codebook size	$K = 100$	$K = 1000$	$K = 10000$
mAP	0.963	0.977	0.935

4.4 Performance of Different Feature Descriptors

In this section, the performance of two kinds of semantic descriptors mentioned above will be discussed. Table 4 shows the mAP and mean processing time (mPT) for all videos during querying in the three cases, which are using the semantic descriptor only, using the labels descriptor only and combining these two descriptors in the hierarchical approach. Compared with the hierarchical matching, using the semantic descriptor only achieves almost the same mAP performance, but using the labels descriptor only has a slight drop. However, in terms of mPT, the labels descriptor is superior to the semantic descriptor due to its lower dimension, which also greatly reduces the processing time of the hierarchical matching method. Table 5 shows the proportion of video filtered by labels descriptor for each query set, averaging 38%. Therefore, the proposed hierarchical method combining these two descriptors greatly improves the detection efficiency with excellent precision performance.

Table 4. The mAP and mPT of using different feature descriptors.

Descriptor	*mAP*	*mPT(s)*
Semantic descriptor	0.978	$2.98e^{-3}$
Labels descriptor	0.952	$5.19e^{-4}$
Hierarchical matching	0.977	$1.15e^{-3}$

Table 5. The proportion of videos filtered by labels descriptor over each query set.

Query ID	1	2	3	4	5	6	7	8
Proportion	0.57	0.41	0.34	0.39	0.66	0.35	0.31	0.33
Query ID	**9**	**10**	**11**	**12**	**13**	**14**	**15**	**16**
Proportion	0.37	0.37	0.48	0.26	0.38	0.42	0.20	0.27
Query ID	**17**	**18**	**19**	**20**	**21**	**22**	**23**	**24**
Proportion	0.21	0.65	0.31	0.45	0.36	0.23	0.32	0.52

4.5 Comparison with Existing NDVD Approaches

The proposed approach will be compared with four popular NDVD approaches, including color histogram features based approach (CH) [1], auto-color correlograms with bag-of-words scheme based approach (ACC) [6], the approach which used pattern-based indexing tree, m-pattern-based dynamic programming and time-shift m-pattern similarity (PPT) [21], and the approach which leveraged intermediate CNN features in a global video representation by means of a vector-based feature aggregation scheme (I-CNN-V) and a layer-based feature aggregation scheme (I-CNN-L) [22]. For the I-CNN-L and I-CNN-V approaches, we also use the AlexNet model.

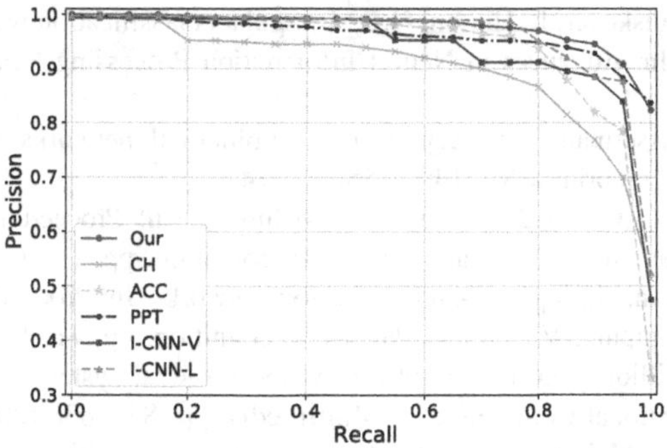

Fig. 5. The PR curves of the proposed approach and five existing approaches.

Figure 5 illustrates the PR curves of the five approaches. The proposed approach is consistently superior to the other five approaches up to 0.9 of recall. The precision of I-CNN-L is slightly better than the proposed approach when the recall is between 0.65 and 0.75. Our approach can maintain a high precision at a high-level recall (greater than

0.9), while the precision of the other four approaches (CH, ACC, I-CNN-L and I-CNN-V) decreases significantly. As shown in Table 6, the proposed approach achieves the best performance with mAP of 0.977.

Table 6. The mAP of the proposed approach and five existing approaches.

Method	CH	ACC	PPT	I-CNN-V	I-CNN-L	Our
mAP	0.892	0.944	0.958	0.951	0.969	0.977

5 Conclusion

In this paper, we have proposed a hierarchical approach for NDVD, which uses semantic features generated from CNN. Two kinds of global video descriptors are introduced, one is from the fully-connected layer with the bag-of-words scheme, and the other uses the classification labels from the softmax layer. Experimental results on the CC_WEB_VIDEO dataset show that the proposed approach is superior to four existing NDVD approaches. Meanwhile, the proposed global semantic descriptors are compact and have low-dimension, especially labels descriptor, which results in less processing time and feature storage. Therefore, the proposed approach is feasible and effective.

References

1. Wu, X., Hauptmann, A.G., Ngo, C.W.: Practical elimination of near-duplicates from web video search. In: Proceedings of the 15th International Conference on Multimedia, pp. 218–227 (2007)
2. Krizhevsky, A., Sutskever, I., Hinton, G.E.: ImageNet classification with deep convolutional neural networks. In: Advances in Neural Information Processing Systems, pp. 1097–1105 (2012)
3. Simonyan, K., Zisserman, A.: Very deep convolutional networks for large-scale image recognition. arXiv preprint arXiv:1409.1556 (2014)
4. Szegedy, C., et al.: Going deeper with convolutions. In: Proceedings of the 28th IEEE Conference on Computer Vision and Pattern Recognition, pp. 1–9 (2015)
5. Hu, J., Shen, L., Sun, G.: Squeeze-and-excitation networks. In: Proceedings of the 31st IEEE Conference on Computer Vision and Pattern Recognition, pp. 7132–7141 (2018)
6. Cai, Y., et al.: Million-scale near-duplicate video retrieval system. In: Proceedings of the 19th ACM International Conference on Multimedia, pp. 837–838 (2011)
7. Paisitkriangkrai, S., Mei, T., Zhang, J., Hua, X.S.: Clip-based hierarchical representation of near-duplicate video detection. Int. J. Comput. Math. **88**(18), 3817–3833 (2011)
8. Douze, M., Jegou, H., Schmid, C.: An image-based approach to video copy detection with spatio-temporal post-filtering. IEEE Trans. Multimed. **12**(4), 257–266 (2010)
9. Law-To, J., Buisson, O., Gouet-Brunet, V., Boujemaa, N.: Robust voting algorithm based on labels of behavior for video copy detection. In: Proceedings of the 14th ACM International Conference on Multimedia, pp. 835–844 (2006)

10. Harris, C., Stevens, M.: A combined corner and edge detector. In: 4th Alvey Vision Conference, pp. 153–158 (1988)
11. Ke, Y., Sukthankar, R., Huston, L.: An efficient parts-based near-duplicate and sub-image retrieval system. In: Proceedings of the 12th ACM International Conference on Multimedia, pp. 869–876 (2004)
12. Song, J., Yang, Y., Huang, Z., Shen, H.T., Hong, R.: Multiple feature hashing for real-time large scale near-duplicate video retrieval. In: Proceedings of the 19th International Conference on Multimedea, pp. 423–432 (2011)
13. Bohm, C., Pryakhin, A., Schubert, M., Gruber, M., Kunath, P.: ProVeR: probabilistic video retrieval using the Gauss-Tree. In: Proceedings of the 23rd IEEE International Conference on Data Engineering, pp. 1521–1522 (2007)
14. Weber, R., Sehek, H.J., Blott, S.: A quantitative analysis and performance study for similarity-search methods in high-dimensional spaces. In: Proceedings of the 24th International Conference on Very Large Data Bases, pp. 194–205 (1998)
15. Weber, R., Böhm, K.: Trading quality for time with nearest-neighbor search. In: Zaniolo, C., Lockemann, Peter C., Scholl, Marc H., Grust, T. (eds.) EDBT 2000. LNCS, vol. 1777, pp. 21–35. Springer, Heidelberg (2000). https://doi.org/10.1007/3-540-46439-5_2
16. Datar, M., Immorlica, N., Indyk, P., Mirrokni, V.S.: Locality-sensitive hashing scheme based on p-stable distributions. In: Proceedings of the 20th Annual Symposium on Computational Geometry, pp. 253–262 (2004)
17. Jiang, Y.G., Wang, J.: Partial copy detection in videos: a benchmark and an evaluation of popular methods. IEEE Trans. Big Data **2**, 32–42 (2016)
18. Wang, L., Bao, Yu., Li, H., Fan, X., Luo, Z.: Compact CNN based video representation for efficient video copy detection. In: Amsaleg, L., Guðmundsson, G.Þ., Gurrin, C., Jónsson, B.Þ., Satoh, S. (eds.) MMM 2017. LNCS, vol. 10132, pp. 576–587. Springer, Cham (2017). https://doi.org/10.1007/978-3-319-51811-4_47
19. Jiang, Y.G., Ngo, C.W.: Visual word proximity and linguistics for semantic video indexing and near-duplicate retrieval. Comput. Vis. Image Underst. **3**(3), 405–414 (2009)
20. Huang, Z., Shen, H.T., Shao, J., Cui, B., Zhou, X.: Practical online near-duplicate subsequence detection for continuous video streams. IEEE Trans. Multimed. **12**(5), 386–398 (2010)
21. Chou, C.L., Chen, H.T., Lee, S.Y.: Pattern-based near-duplicate video retrieval and localization on web-scale videos. IEEE Trans. Multimed. **17**(3), 382–395 (2015)
22. Kordopatis-Zilos, G., Papadopoulos, S., Patras, I., Kompatsiaris, Y.: Near-Duplicate video retrieval by aggregating intermediate CNN layers. In: Amsaleg, L., Guðmundsson, G.Þ., Gurrin, C., Jónsson, B.Þ., Satoh, S. (eds.) MMM 2017. LNCS, vol. 10132, pp. 251–263. Springer, Cham (2017). https://doi.org/10.1007/978-3-319-51811-4_21

Meta Transfer Learning for Adaptive Vehicle Tracking in UAV Videos

Wenfeng Song[1], Shuai Li[1,2](✉), Yuting Guo[1,2], Shaoqi Li[1], Aimin Hao[1], Hong Qin[3](✉), and Qinping Zhao[1]

[1] The State Key Laboratory of Virtual Reality Technology and Systems, Beihang University, Beijing, China
{songwenfeng,lishuai}@buaa.edu.cn

[2] Qingdao Research Institute, Beihang University, Qingdao, China

[3] Department of Computer Science, State University of New York at Stony Brook, Stony Brook, USA
qin@cs.stonybrook.edu

Abstract. The vehicle tracking in UAV videos is still under-explored with the deep learning methods due to the lack of well labeled datasets. The challenges mainly come from the fact that the UAV view has much wider and changeable landscapes, which hinders the labeling task. In this paper, we propose a meta transfer learning method for adaptive vehicle tracking in UAV videos (MTAVT), which transfers the common features across landscapes, so that it can avoid over-fitting with the limited scale of dataset. Our MTAVT consists of two critical components: a meta learner and a transfer learner. Specifically, meta-learner is employed to adaptively learn the models to extract the sharing features between ground and drone views. The transfer learner is used to learn the domain-shifted features from ground-view to drone-view datasets by optimizing the ground-view models. We further seamlessly incorporate an exemplar-memory curriculum into meta learning by leveraging the memorized models, which serves as the training guidance for sequential sampling. Hence, this curriculum can enforce the meta learner to adapt to the new sequences in the drone-view datasets without losing the previous learned knowledge. Meanwhile, we simplify and stabilize the higher-order gradient training criteria for meta learning by exploring curriculum learning in multiple stages with various domains. We conduct extensive experiments and ablation studies on four public benchmarks and an evaluation dataset from YouTube (to release soon). All the experiments demonstrate that, our MTAVT has superior advantages over state-of-the-art methods in terms of accuracy, robustness, and versatility.

Keywords: Meta learner · Transfer learner · Exemplar-memory curriculum · UAV tracking

---

Electronic supplementary material The online version of this chapter (https://doi.org/10.1007/978-3-030-37731-1_62) contains supplementary material, which is available to authorized users.

Y. M. Ro et al. (Eds.): MMM 2020, LNCS 11961, pp. 764–777, 2020.
https://doi.org/10.1007/978-3-030-37731-1_62

1 Introduction

With the built-in advantages of high mobility and flexibility, Unmanned Aerial Vehicles (UAV) based techniques are becoming more and more prominent in security surveillance and rescue-relevant applications in recent years [1]. UAV videos can capture large-scale scene information more efficiently and conveniently than what ground-view cameras could accommodate, wherein, UAV tracking aims to continuously identify and locate the targeted vehicles in drone view. The main difficulty is that the datasets are far from sufficient for arbitrary scenery to track the fine-grained objects (e.g., vehicles identities). The drone-view objects are hard to label due to clutter background, largely-deformed appearance, and densely-crowded objects. Previous works [9,15,27] obtained impressive achievements in tracking algorithms/techniques, especially for ground view tracking tasks. However, it remains challenging to train a ground-view tracking model in prior that can generalize well in UAV videos. We address the problem of improving the generalization performance of the tracking models when transferring from ground view to drone view, since there are more labeled data in ground view. In fact, the datasets from the two views usually share similar appearance features to some extend. Our goal is to train a tracking network to accumulate proper experience from the ground view.

Existing works [4,10,14,23,25,29] perform badly in the cross-view tracking tasks. Their performance considerably decreases when training data is scarce or when they need to be adapted to new tasks. Some existing works [13,18] attempt to use 'tracking-by-detection' method [13] with two stages of models: an offline model to learn the common knowledge across sequences, and an online model to adapt to the specific sequences. However, these works still cannot satisfy the task in an unknown view, which involves largely-different appearances w.r.t the datasets used in offline model due to the heterogeneous distributions of datasets. Additionally, during online tracking, the convolutional neural network (CNN) architectures mostly suffer from catastrophic forgetting [3] problem, which is rarely considered in conventional methods.

To cope with the aforementioned difficulties, we propose a meta transfer learning based framework to accumulate the experience from the well-trained ground-view models and to quickly adapt it to new sequences in drone view, instead of transferring the targeted objects from ground view to UAV view directly use the pre-trained CNN model. We observe that, even though the object scales and camera views are totally different in datasets containing different views (e.g., VisDrone2018 [30] and VID), the involved vehicle structure appears to be stable in datasets containing different views. Consequently, the meta learner can optimize the models with the most common clues, which are important for the tracking task in drone view.

Meanwhile, human eye needs only a few samples to recognize new concepts. Mimicking the learning capability of human vision mechanism, we design a curriculum to accumulate the prior experience learned from the pre-trained model, so that it could learn new categories while not sacrificing any performance on the initial tracking targets. This attributes to the easy to complex learning mechanism of curriculum. Moreover, the curriculum learning [26] process from simple samples to difficult samples can satisfy the non-convex optimization [8], which is challenging due to the higher-order gradient in the loss criteria of meta learning.

We explicitly take into account the view-invariant features and view-sensitive features. Concretely, we firstly learn the view-invariant features, such as the structure of the vehicles, color, and even the accessories. Hence, our meta learner is designed to optimally explore the common knowledge, which searches the boundary distributions of CNN weights for view-invariant features. Afterwards, we consider the differences between the two views, such as the appearance deformation due to view changes, occlusions, and different backgrounds. Our transfer learner is developed as an online model, which preserves the strong discriminative ability of the meta learner, and iterates a few times to fit for the UAV videos. Specifically, the salient contributions of this paper can be summarized as follows.

- We propose a meta transfer learning based tracking method to transfer the knowledge from the sufficiently-trained ground-view CNN model to drone-view model, which consists of a novel meta-learner and a transfer learner to maximally learn the common features across views, and thus is suitable for the UAV videos with low shot of samples.
- We propose an exemplar-memory curriculum, which stores the learned ground-view models. On that basis, we can optimize the drone-view model in auxiliary with the previous models. Specifically, the exemplar-memory curriculum samples are ranked according to the performance of the prior trained models, so that it can bias to the newly-appearing difficult samples in drone view in an efficient way.

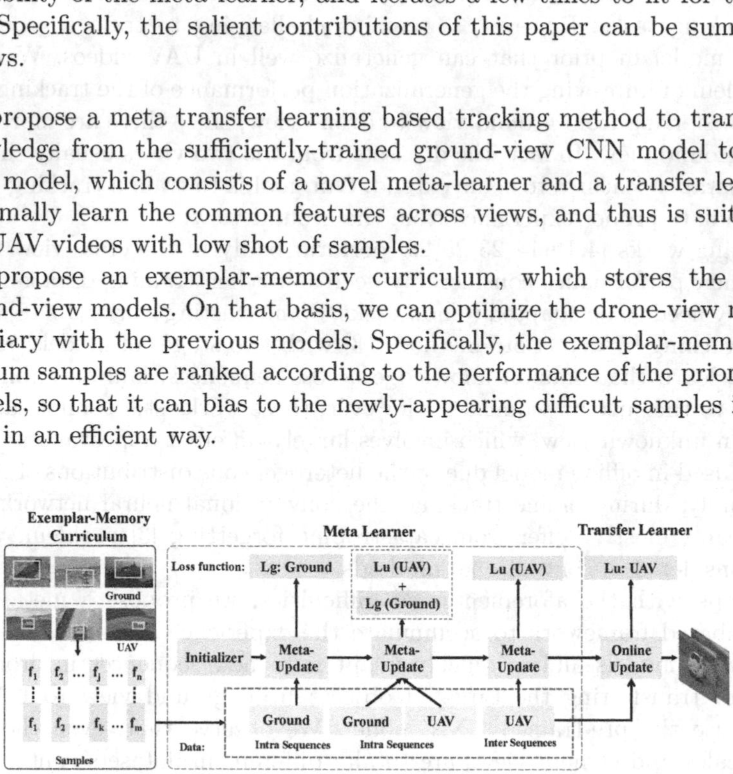

Fig. 1. The architecture of our MTAVT (Components with blue backgrounds indicate our contributions). It includes two components: (1) meta learner and (2) transfer learner, wherein the exemplar-memory curriculum accelerates the meta learning process to improve the robustness on cross-view datasets. Meta learner is offline trained with sufficient well-labeled dataset from ground view and drone view of the exemplar-memory curriculum. On that basis, the transfer learner further refines the models towards online target tracking. (Color figure online)

– We conduct extensive experiments to verify the efficiency and superiority of our method. It has high performance and fast convergence on both existing benchmark datasets and arbitrarily-collected UAV videos from YouTube.

2 Related Works

Few Shot Based Tracking Methods. Visual tracking has undergone extensive research on how to represent and localize a target in video sequences. The online tracking is usually considered as a few-shot learning problem [20], which aims at improving the discriminative ability with limited training dataset. As one of the most representative works, Nam et al. [13] proposed to extract general features offline and fine-tune the model over online sequences with a multiple fully-connected deep network. On that basis, many deeper neural networks were proposed to enhance the discriminative ability of offline model to delineate appearance features, such as SiamFC [23], SiamRPN [23], and DasiamRPN [31]. Other extensions include (but are not limited to) data augmentation [18], multiple kernel [22], reinforcement learning [4], multi-expert ensemble trackers [25]. Alternatively, to leverage the temporal clues underlying the limited training datasets, Li et al. [10], and Sun et al. [19] respectively proposed to learn spatial-temporal clues regularized correlation filters for visual tracking. However, these methods failed to capture the view-invariant features when given limited scale of datasets.

Meta/Curriculum Learning Based Tracking Methods. Meta learning is a very promising topic along with the success of deep learning, which aims at being aware of and taking control of the models' learning process to get the ability of learning to learn. Some works [5,6,20] utilized meta learning mechanism to complement the cross-domain tracking, and achieved very impressive results. For example, Park et al. [14] were among the first to dynamically conduct target tracking based on the classic meta learning method MAML [8]. Alternatively, some works [16,21] attempted to find the hyper-parameters with meta-learned deep networks. Recently, Wang et al. [24] proposed unsupervised tracking, which explored the temporal clues and could fit for arbitrary domains. These methods verified that, meta learning can boost the tacking performance with limited training sequences. Meanwhile, curriculum learning was proposed by Bengio et al. [2], which was widely used for multi-task learning. They verified that task-driven samples could give rise to faster convergence and better generalization. Recently, Weinshall et al. [26] further proposed curriculum transfer learning.

Motivated by the meta learning and curriculum learning ideas, we propose to dynamically train a meta learner with curriculum learning, which should flexibly handle the new sequences in few shot. Different from previous works, our method train the offline model with the ability of meta learning to adapt for new sequences with fewer iterations during online tracking, so that the adaption could be more efficiently generalized to new sequences.

3 Method

There are sufficient annotated ground view datasets with labels, each sequence x_g is associated with an identity y_g, while only a low shot of target sequences x_u with y_u in drone view are provided, containing n_u vehicle sequences. It means that the identity annotation of the target sequences has much smaller scale compared with ground view cases[1]. Namely, to leverage meta transfer learning for adaptive vehicle tracking in UAV videos, there are two main challenges: (1) in the first stage offline training process, few annotations are available in training datasets, and (2) one shot online tracking frame, that means the online training process relies on the only frame which is obtained by initialized object box. Hence, our goal is to learn a transferable tracking model using both ground and drone view datasets, which should generalize well in the drone view.

Overall Architecture of MTAVT. To obtain the fundamental experience in prior trained models for extracting the general features, the meta learner is firstly pre-trained on large-scale datasets (e.g., VID [17]), which provides sufficient kinds of common objects. Afterwards, this meta learner is updated to accommodate the drone view sequences via an optimization process. This process aims at updating the meta learner with the domain-shifted (e.g., view-sensitive) samples (sampling on CNN models instead of the videos) across the two views (detailed in Sect. 3.1). Furthermore, based on the meta-learner, we propose a domain-shifting transfer learner which learns the UAV-related semantic features (detailed in Sect. 3.1). However, the heterogeneous distributions of datasets may lead to computation instability. To alleviate, the exemplar-memory learning curriculum is employed to guide the learning process of the two learners, as shown in Fig. 1 (detailed in Sect. 3.2).

3.1 Meta Adaptive Tracker

The eventual goal of the our tracker is to predict the target locations in drone view. Considering a large amount of training datasets are only available in ground view while the scale of UAV dataset is limited, our MTAVT follows the classical 'tracking-by-detection' idea, which consists of offline and online training phases. A key motivation is to incorporate a carefully-designed meta learner for the offline training in a transfer learner for the online training. Meta learner is to extract the common features across the two views, and it facilitates avoiding over-fitting on the source datasets, because this learner can be trained sufficiently on a large-scale datasets. Thus, it would be desirable to learn a CNN model that can extract discriminative features for the specific targets. As for the transfer learner, it is designed for the online updating via only a few iterations when tracking certain target.

---
[1] The subscript of g/u stands for the parameters from ground/drone view.

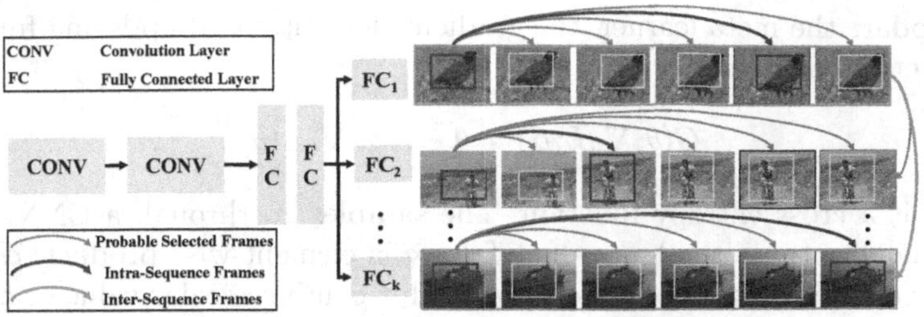

Fig. 2. Illustration for the updating process of the adaptive meta tracker. It extracts the features from the offline meta learner, and then updates the patches (red) ahead of the current frame or cross-view sequences (blue), which is robust to appearance and view changes. (Color figure online)

Meta Learner. This section describes the meta learner's construction and updating process (simplified as 'meta-update' in Fig. 1). Our meta learner has two goals. One is to provide an initializer for the tracker, which can be performed by starting with a pre-trained model θ_0 and performing one/a very small number of iterations on an update function $G(x)$. Another goal is to promote the robustness of tracker to adapt for the later frames in the same sequences and even in different view sequences.

To achieve the first goal, the meta learner is to learn a general CNN with discriminative ability based on the sufficient ground-view sequences. Concretely, we develop multiple domain-oriented branches by alternatively training the last layer of the fully connected (FC) layers, and this layer is trained separately with different sequences in a meta-update manner, motivated by the design of MDNET [13]. Furthermore, a curriculum learning strategy is to provide sufficient training samples while learning the cross-view features efficiently. Thus, we can get a meta learner, which gives rise to a common model to quickly adapt to the new tasks.

The second goal is achieved via specially-designed sample-generating strategy. For intra (same) sequences updating, the learner generates samples from the single sequence x to capture the feature of the same identity y_i. Concretely, this model is initialized with the random frame $f_i \in x$, and then is updated by selected frame from the intra sequences, shown in Fig. 2. The loss aims to refine the later selected frame. This meta learning process can avoid over-fitting and generalize well to form a robust feature extraction model. Namely, it can extract discriminative features for the two frames, considering the deformation and appearance changes. The model parameters are trained by optimizing the performance of the trackers θ corresponding to the tasks (trackers on various domains) sampled from the tasks' distribution $p(T)$. More concretely, the meta-objective is $\min_\theta \sum_{T_i \in p(T)} L_T(G(\theta))$. Meanwhile, the sequences from different views are used for the generalization via curriculum learning (B in Sect. 3).

To update the meta learner, the gradient-descent based updating function G is parameterized by α,

$$G(\theta, \nabla_\theta L; \alpha) = \theta - \alpha \otimes \nabla_\theta L(\theta), \tag{1}$$

where L is a cross entropy function. The samples go through a CNN classifier which finally outputs the loss value of L. $\otimes$ is element-wise product. α has the same size as the tracker's parameters θ, and it can be a scalar value or a matrix, whose value is mostly to be determined in either learnable or manually-fixed way. We set α as the parameter of the tracking network, as suggested in [8]. Based on curriculum learning, we explore different definitions in Sect. 3.2 to satisfy the different meta learning phases.

From the perspective of the whole learning process, our meta learner is to find a good common feature extractor θ and α by repeatedly sampling the videos, performing initialization, applying the learned initial model to a new frame in the same sequence or a new video from a drone-view dataset, and then back-propagating to update θ and α. Applying the initial model to the drone-view sequence has two advantages, the model should be robust enough to handle more appearance deformation in view variation, and this makes the updating process converge in fewer iteration times. Besides, this sampling way optimizes the non-convex problem from the easy to complex step by step for the meta learning process more stable converge with low shot samples.

Transfer Learner. Transfer learner is proposed to quickly adapt to the changes of specific online tracking target. It is designed to avoid model forgetting via ground-view and drone-view mixed learning. The main challenge in transfer learner is that the network for tracking tasks needs much more datasets and iteration times than that of the conventional meta learning networks. This is because the tracking sequences vary severely in the same datasets. To alleviate this, we simplify this transfer learner as follows. It employs the meta learner as the initialization model F_0, and performs one or a very small number of iterations to update the function F (parameterized by α), follows the α in Eq. 1. It automatically generates the boxes overlapped with the target in drone view, and updates the classifier when the tracking score is good enough. The input image patches are sampled from a frame $f_i \in x_j$ (and $y_j \in \{0,1\}^N$ donates the corresponding labels for the patches), where N is the number of patches. Based on this, it updates the meta learner from ground-view videos towards the drone-view videos regularly to adjust to new examples collected by the curriculum during tracking. This process is formulated as,

$$G(\theta_j, F_u) = G(\theta_{j-1}, F_g) - \alpha \otimes \nabla_{\theta_{j-1}} L. \tag{2}$$

Here, F_g is the ground-view tracker, and the drone-view tracker is denoted as F_u. L denotes the loss function of the classifier, which is cross entropy loss $-\sum_{i=1}^{N} y_i log(F_u(x_i;\theta))$. The patches will be fed into the initialized model F_0, after that, this model will output the cross entropy loss, which will be back-propagated via Stochastic Gradient Descent optimization.

3.2 Memory-Exemplar Curriculum

In this section, we focus on the sampling process of the meta adaptive tracker. Based on the meta learner and the transfer learner, this process is designed to train the trackers with sufficient ground-view videos and certain specific drone-view videos via three sequential stages (A, B, C in Fig. 3). The curriculum is generated based on the three stages as A, B, and C. To be specific, the strategy of our curriculum learning is to firstly train the tracker with samples from ground-view datasets, and then we update it with the samples from the two views, finally, this tracker is trained with the samples from the drone-view datasets.

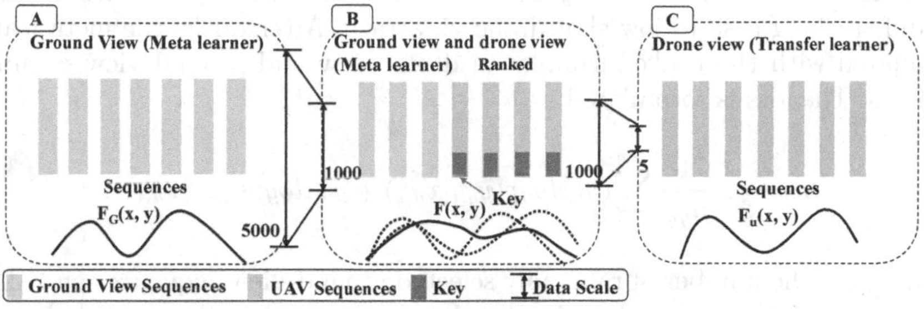

Fig. 3. Three stages of the exemplar-memory curriculum. A: Training the meta learner with the samples from ground-view sequences, B: Updating the meta learner partially with the samples from ground-view and the drone-view sequences ranked by the meta learner, C: Training the transfer learner the samples from drone-view sequences.

Specifically, the first stage is to learn the common and basic knowledge from the large scale of ground-view datasets (A in Fig. 3), which is trained by updating the initialized model with different sequences in offline manner. Wherein, the training samples are randomly generated and cropped based on the distributions of the ground-view datasets, the training loss is formulated as,

$$L_g = -\frac{1}{n_g}\sum_{i=1}^{n_g} y_{g,i} logp(y_{g,i}|x_{g,i}), \tag{3}$$

where n_g is the number of ground-view images in a training batch. $p(y_{g,i}|x_{g,i})$ is the predicted probability that the ground-view sequences $x_{g,i}$ belong to identity $y_{g,i}$ which is obtained by the classification layer in tracking networks (e.g., Softmax).

Furthermore, we aim to transfer the model trained from the ground-view datasets to the combined ground and drone view (B in Fig. 3) datasets. The previous works try to model the common knowledge while ignoring the domain-shifted feature in drone-view datasets. On the other hand, we try to update the meta-learner with drone-view features by the limited scales of training sequences. To preserve the discriminative feature-extracting ability of the previous models, which is learned in exemplar sequences sampled from ground-view dataset, we construct a memory-exemplar curriculum to handle the easily-forgotten parameters. In detail, the memory-exemplar curriculum consists of two branches, one is to sample from ground view dataset for meta learner, which preserves the distribution of the original source datasets. The other branch focuses on the target domain, which firstly extracts the features with the offline pre-trained MDNET [13], then ranks the sequences according to the tracking scores produced by the pre-trained model. The ranking order of the sequences serves as the key of the sequences, following the key-value structure [28]. The key of the curriculum is to make correspondence with the tracking performance of the meta tracker in stage A. Hence, the hard level which is measured by the confidence for tracking the target is in association with the exemplar curriculum. Accordingly, the curriculum could drive the learning process from easy samples to hard samples (the samples are ranked by the confidence in trackers), and from general ground tracking task to low shot drone view task. Afterwards, the meta-learner is updated with the ranked samples in drone view and ground view combined datasets. The loss is formulated,

$$L_{gu} = -\frac{1}{n_{gu}} \sum_{i=1}^{n_{gu}} (y_{g,i} logp(y_{g,i}|x_{g,i}) + y_{u,i} logp(y_{u,i}|x_{u,i})), \quad (4)$$

where n_{gu} is the number of randomly selected ground-view sequences and all the drone-view sequences in a training batch. $p(y_{gu,i}|x_{gu,i})$ is the predicted probability that the source image $x_{gu,i}$ belongs to identity $y_{gu,i}$.

Finally, the transfer learner updates the parameters α and θ in meta learner towards the drone view (C in Fig. 3). Hence, the loss in the optimization process (Eq. 2) is as follows.

$$L_u = -\frac{1}{n_u} \sum_{i=1}^{n_u} y_{u,i} logp(y_{u,i}|x_{u,i}), \quad (5)$$

where n_u (mostly is one) is the number of ground-view sequences in a training batch. $p(y_{u,i}|x_{u,i})$ is the predicted probability that the ground-view sequences $x_{u,i}$ belong to identity $y_{u,i}$, which is obtained from the online updating module. Then, we finely-tune the domain-specific layer (2nd fully-connected layer in MDNET [13]) and the fully-connected layers in the shared network online at the same time. The meta learning in this curriculum facilitates the convergence of the offline and online models. These models' learned weights are based on the statistic theory that the sufficient large scale of datasets is close to the distribution of the real dataset un-biased.

4 Experiments and Evaluations

We conduct extensive experiments to demonstrate the effectiveness of our MTAVT, and compare it with state-of-the-art trackers on the vehicle sequences in VisDrone2018 [30], UAV123 [12], Drone Tracking Benchmark (DTB) [11] and the large-scale UAV-Vehicle [7] dataset. We further collect a generalized evaluation dataset from YouTube (YTB). All the experiments on the four datasets are trained with small scale (<32 sequences for training) datasets. The datasets are split as 8:2 (120 and 30 sequences) in VisDrone2018, UAV123, DTB, UAV-Vehicles, whereas YTB dataset (27 sequences) is totally used for testing due to its challenging appearance and scenario changes (more results are provided in supplementary material).

Implementation Details and Experiment Settings. Our MTAVT is implemented using the Pytorch library of MAML [8], and we initialize the tracking network with a pre-trained CNN network on VID [17]. We follow the standard evaluation approaches. In the VisDrone2018, UAV123, DTB, UAV-Vehicle and YTB datasets, we use the one-pass evaluation (OPE) with 'precision' and 'success plots' metrics. The 'precision' metric measures the target location rate, within a certain threshold distance w.r.t ground truth location. The error threshold of 20 pixels is used for ranking. The 'success plots' metric is used to measure the overlapping ratio between the predicted bounding box and the ground truth.

Meta Learner: during the offline training phase, we integrate the VID dataset and the training parts of the drone-view datasets to train the meta learner. For the parameter α, it is initialized to 10^{-3}, and then it is decayed to 10^{-6} after 10,000 iterations, wherein Adam is used with learning rate 10^{-5}. We employ the first three convolution layers from pre-trained VGG16 as feature extractors and set mini-batch size to be 8. For the 'meta-update', to make a trade off between the computation complexity and the performance, it is iterated only one time.

Transfer Learner: the tracking network, extended from the network structure of MDNET [13], is trained in meta learning manner, wherein the parameters are same with the meta learner. During online tracking, we finely tune the meta learner with the annotation of the first frame, and conduct tracking in the subsequential frames.

Table 1. Comparisons with State-of-the-Art methods on YTB dataset. (AUC score (OPE))

Model	ACT	ADNet	DasiamRPN	MCCT	Meta-SDNET	Meta-CREST	MDNET	SiamFC	SiamRPN	STRCF	MTVAT
Score	65.6	64.2	73.2	65.6	62.6	60.4	51.3	69.7	72.8	64.9	**75.7**

Comparisons with State-of-the-Art Methods. We compare our MTAVT with ten state-of-the-art trackers, including MDNET [13], DasiamRPN [31], ACT [4], ADNet [29], STRCF [10], Meta-CREST and Meta-SDNET [14], SiamFC [23], SiamRPN [23], and MCCT [25]. We evaluate all the trackers on 57 video sequences from the drone-view datasets with 'precision' and 'success plots' metrics. Figure 4 shows that our MTAVT outperforms other methods in 'precision' and 'success plots' on VisDrone2018, DTB, UAV123, UAV-Vehicle datasets (30 sequences in total for testing). We merge the vehicle sequences in the four public datasets (train/test on four datasets respectively) to simplify the performance evaluation. DasiamRPN [31] employs a much deeper backbone network for tracking, which performs slightly better in 'success rate', however, our precision is much more better. Meanwhile, Table 1 shows our MTAVT also performs well on the challenging YTB datasets. Compared with the representative 'tracking-by-detection' trackers (MDNET and Meta-SDNET), we attribute our performance improvements to the meta learning and exemplar-memory curriculum, which gives rise to robust performance for cross-view datasets. For most of the limited-scale drone-view training sequences, other trackers fail to locate the target objects and to estimate the scale correctly. Our MTAVT ameliorates such problems, and bridges the gap between ground-view training datasets and the learned drone-view tracking.

Besides, our MTAVT network is more efficient w.r.t the corresponding baseline trackers. The performance and efficiency comparisons are documented in Fig. 5.

Ablation Studies. To verify the contribution of each component in our method, we evaluate different configurations of our approach. The effectiveness of the three critical elements (meta learner, transfer learner, and exemplar-memory curriculum) in our MTAVT framework are evaluated on the four datasets, and the results are listed in Table 2. The performance is shown in Fig. 4.

The performances of all the incomplete configurations are not as good as the complete configuration of our MTAVT, and each component in our tracking algorithm boosts the performance. The meta learner process contributes most, which improves MTAVT from 71.2 to 75 in precision plots, because our meta learner tends to flexibly preserve more sharing features provided in ground view. It can be concluded that, our MTAVT can accumulate experience in meta learning process, which can well benefit the drone-view tracking task.

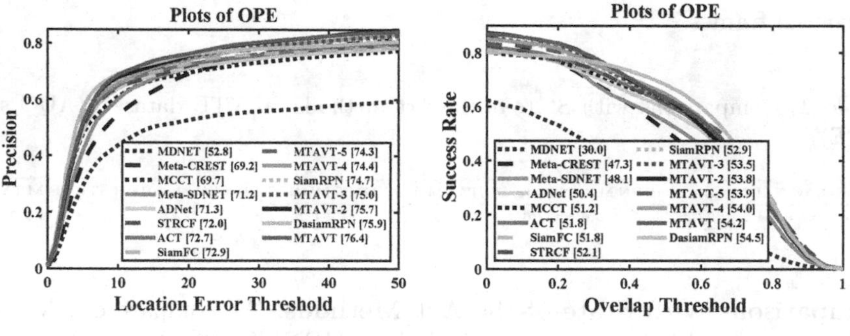

Fig. 4. Comparisons and ablation studies on VisDrone2018, UAV123, DTB70 and UAV-Vehicle datasets, wherein the ablation settings are listed in Table 2.

Convergence and Efficiency Analysis. To verify the convergence of our MTAVT, we compare our loss with the baseline Meta-SDNET [14], which is similar to the meta learner's intra-sequence updating process. The results in Fig. 5 demonstrate that, our MTAVT performs better and converges faster than Meta-SDNET [14]. As for efficiency, our MTAVT tends to be the most efficient, compared with the 'tracking-by-detection' trackers or the trackers with similar performance.

Table 2. The setting of ablation studies.

ID	Meta learner	Transfer learner	Exemplar-memory curriculum	Model	Name
1	✓	✓	✓	MTAVT	MTAVT
2		✓	✓	Transfer learner	MTAVT-2
3	✓		✓	Meta learner	MTAVT-3
4			✓	Baseline (MDNET)	MTAVT-4
5			✓	Baseline (Meta-SDNET)	MTAVT-5

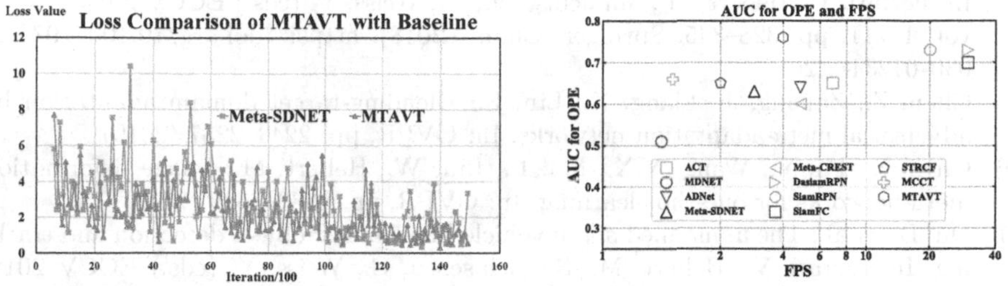

Fig. 5. Left: Loss curve comparisons. Right: FPS (Frames per second) of the state-of-the-art trackers on YTB.

5 Conclusions

In this paper, we propose a novel meta learning based method (MTAVT) to leverage the ground-view dataset to augment the drone-view tracking, which can reduce the dependence on large-scale well-labeled training dataset. Our MTAVT consists of three critical components: a meta learner, transfer learner, and an exemplar-memory scheme. Our MTAVT smartly complements the limited drone-view training datasets with sufficient ground-view training datasets. Extensive experiments on various benchmarks demonstrate that our MTAVT outperforms state-of-the-art trackers.

However, when the vehicles are different from the those scarcely appearing in the ground-view datasets, our MTAVT may tend to locate wrong target or lose the target, thus, we should add temporal constraints to improve the performance in future. Besides, we will extend our MTAVT for more cross-view transferring tasks, such as vehicle related Re-ID, semantic event recognition, etc.

Acknowledgement. This research is supported in part by National Key R&D Program of China (No. 2017YFB1002602), National Key R&D Program of China (No. 2017YFF0106407), National Natural Science Foundation of China (No. 61672077 and 61532002), Applied Basic Research Program of Qingdao (No. 161013xx), National Science Foundation of USA (No. IIS-0949467, IIS-1047715, IIS-1715985, and IIS-1049448), capital health research and development of special 2016-1-4011, Fundamental Research Funds for the Central Universities, and Beijing Natural Science Foundation-Haidian Primitive Innovation Joint Fund (L182016).

References

1. Arandjelović, O.: Automatic vehicle tracking and recognition from aerial image sequences. In: AVSS, pp. 1–6 (2015)
2. Bengio, Y., Louradour, J., Collobert, R., Weston, J.: Curriculum learning. In: ICML, pp. 41–48 (2009)
3. Castro, F.M., Marín-Jiménez, M.J., Guil, N., Schmid, C., Alahari, K.: End-to-end incremental learning. In: Ferrari, V., Hebert, M., Sminchisescu, C., Weiss, Y. (eds.) ECCV 2018. LNCS, vol. 11216, pp. 241–257. Springer, Cham (2018). https://doi.org/10.1007/978-3-030-01258-8_15
4. Chen, B., Wang, D., Li, P., Wang, S., Lu, H.: Real-time 'Actor-Critic' tracking. In: Ferrari, V., Hebert, M., Sminchisescu, C., Weiss, Y. (eds.) ECCV 2018. LNCS, vol. 11211, pp. 328–345. Springer, Cham (2018). https://doi.org/10.1007/978-3-030-01234-2_20
5. Chen, Z., Zhuang, J., Liang, X., Lin, L.: Blending-target domain adaptation by adversarial meta-adaptation networks. In: CVPR, pp. 2248–2257 (2019)
6. Chen, Z., Fu, Y., Wang, Y.X., Ma, L., Liu, W., Hebert, M.: Image deformation meta-networks for one-shot learning. In: CVPR, pp. 8680–8689 (2019)
7. Du, D., et al.: The unmanned aerial vehicle benchmark: object detection and tracking. In: Ferrari, V., Hebert, M., Sminchisescu, C., Weiss, Y. (eds.) ECCV 2018. LNCS, vol. 11214, pp. 375–391. Springer, Cham (2018). https://doi.org/10.1007/978-3-030-01249-6_23
8. Finn, C., Abbeel, P., Levine, S.: Model-agnostic meta-learning for fast adaptation of deep networks. In: ICML, pp. 1126–1135 (2017)
9. Li, B., et al.: SiamRPN++: evolution of siamese visual tracking with very deep networks. In: CVPR, pp. 4282–4291 (2019)
10. Li, F., Tian, C., Zuo, W., Zhang, L., Yang, M.H.: Learning spatial-temporal regularized correlation filters for visual tracking. In: CVPR, pp. 4904–4913 (2018)
11. Li, S., Yeung, D.Y.: Visual object tracking for unmanned aerial vehicles: a benchmark and new motion models. In: AAAI, pp. 4140–4146 (2017)
12. Mueller, M., Smith, N., Ghanem, B.: A benchmark and simulator for UAV tracking. In: Leibe, B., Matas, J., Sebe, N., Welling, M. (eds.) ECCV 2016. LNCS, vol. 9905, pp. 445–461. Springer, Cham (2016). https://doi.org/10.1007/978-3-319-46448-0_27
13. Nam, H., Han, B.: Learning multi-domain convolutional neural networks for visual tracking. In: CVPR, pp. 4293–4302 (2016)
14. Park, E., Berg, A.C.: Meta-tracker: fast and robust online adaptation for visual object trackers. In: Ferrari, V., Hebert, M., Sminchisescu, C., Weiss, Y. (eds.) ECCV 2018. LNCS, vol. 11207, pp. 587–604. Springer, Cham (2018). https://doi.org/10.1007/978-3-030-01219-9_35
15. Ran, N., Kong, L., Wang, Y., Liu, Q.: A robust multi-athlete tracking algorithm by exploiting discriminant features and long-term dependencies. In: Kompatsiaris, I., Huet, B., Mezaris, V., Gurrin, C., Cheng, W.H., Vrochidis, S. (eds.) MMM 2019. LNCS, vol. 11295, pp. 411–423. Springer, Cham (2019). https://doi.org/10.1007/978-3-030-05710-7_34
16. Ravi, S., Larochelle, H.: Optimization as a model for few-shot learning. In: ICLR (2017)
17. Russakovsky, O., et al.: ImageNet large scale visual recognition challenge. IJCV **115**(3), 211–252 (2015)

18. Song, Y., et al.: Vital: visual tracking via adversarial learning. In: CVPR, pp. 8990–8999 (2018)
19. Sun, C., Wang, D., Lu, H., Yang, M.H.: Learning spatial-aware regressions for visual tracking. In: CVPR, pp. 8962–8970 (2018)
20. Sun, Q., Liu, Y., Chua, T.S., Schiele, B.: Meta-transfer learning for few-shot learning. In: CVPR, pp. 403–412 (2019)
21. Sung, F., Yang, Y., Zhang, L., Xiang, T., Torr, P.H.S., Hospedales, T.M.: Learning to compare: relation network for few-shot learning. In: CVPR, pp. 1199–1208 (2018)
22. Tang, M., Yu, B., Zhang, F., Wang, J.: High-speed tracking with multi-kernel correlation filters. In: CVPR, pp. 4874–4883 (2018)
23. Valmadre, J., Bertinetto, L., Henriques, J., Vedaldi, A., Torr, P.H.S.: End-to-end representation learning for correlation filter based tracking. In: CVPR, pp. 2805–2813 (2017)
24. Wang, N., Song, Y., Ma, C., Zhou, W., Liu, W., Li, H.: Unsupervised deep tracking. In: CVPR, pp. 1308–1317 (2019)
25. Wang, N., Zhou, W., Tian, Q., Hong, R., Wang, M., Li, H.: Multi-cue correlation filters for robust visual tracking. In: CVPR, pp. 4844–4853 (2018)
26. Weinshall, D., Cohen, G., Amir, D.: Curriculum learning by transfer learning: theory and experiments with deep networks. arXiv preprint arXiv:1802.03796 (2018)
27. Wu, P., Huang, D., Wang, Y.: REVT: robust and efficient visual tracking by region-convolutional regression network. In: Schoeffmann, K., et al. (eds.) MMM 2018. LNCS, vol. 10704, pp. 440–452. Springer, Cham (2018). https://doi.org/10.1007/978-3-319-73603-7_36
28. Xiao, T., Li, S., Wang, B., Lin, L., Wang, X.: Joint detection and identification feature learning for person search. In: CVPR, pp. 3415–3424 (2017)
29. Yun, S., et al.: Action-decision networks for visual tracking with deep reinforcement learning. In: CVPR, pp. 2711–2720 (2017)
30. Zhu, P., Wen, L., Bian, X., Haibin, L., Hu, Q.: Vision meets drones: a challenge. arXiv preprint arXiv:1804.07437 (2018)
31. Zhu, Z., Wang, Q., Li, B., Wu, W., Yan, J., Hu, W.: Distractor-aware siamese networks for visual object tracking. In: Ferrari, V., Hebert, M., Sminchisescu, C., Weiss, Y. (eds.) ECCV 2018. LNCS, vol. 11213, pp. 103–119. Springer, Cham (2018). https://doi.org/10.1007/978-3-030-01240-3_7

Adversarial Query-by-Image Video Retrieval Based on Attention Mechanism

Ruicong Xu, Li Niu(✉), and Liqing Zhang

Department of Computer Science and Engineering, Key Laboratory of Shanghai Education Commission for Intelligent Interaction and Cognitive Engineering, Shanghai Jiao Tong University, Shanghai, China
{ranranxu,utscnewly,zhang-lq}@sjtu.edu.cn

Abstract. The query-by-image video retrieval (QBIVR) is a difficult feature matching task across different modalities. More and more retrieval tasks require indexing the videos containing the activities in the image, which makes extracting meaningful spatio-temporal video features crucial. In this paper, we propose an approach based on adversarial learning, termed *Adversarial Image-to-Video* (*AIV*) approach. To capture the temporal pattern of videos, we utilize temporal regions likely to contain activities via fully-convolutional 3D ConvNet features, and then obtain the video bag features by 3D RoI Pooling. To solve mismatch issue with image vector features and identify the importances of information for videos, we add a Multiple Instance Learning (*MIL*) module to assign different weights to each temporal information in video bags. Moreover, we utilize the triplet loss to distinguish different semantic categorites and support intraclass variability of images and videos. Specially, our *AIV* proposes modality loss as an adversary to the triplet loss in the adversarial learning. The interplay between two losses jointly bridges the domain gap across different modalities. Extensive experiments on two widely used datasets verify the effectiveness of our proposed methods as compared with other methods.

Keywords: Spatio-temporal features · Triplet loss · Modality loss · Adversarial learning

1 Introduction

Nowadays, people can not be satisfied with the single-modality information requirement, cross-modal retrieval tasks have received widespread attention. As video applications in daily life are rapidly growing, query-by-image video retrieval (QBIVR) undoubtedly draws considerable interests in retrieval fields. Specially, QBIVR task, which focuses on retrieving the videos with the relevant activity as the image, faces big challenge in representing video information. Even though there are several methods target at cross-modal retrieval, few methods are considered to utilize temporal information of videos for video retrieval. A number of solutions [4,12,13] to cross-modal task only focus on modality gap

Y. M. Ro et al. (Eds.): MMM 2020, LNCS 11961, pp. 778–789, 2020.
https://doi.org/10.1007/978-3-030-37731-1_63

caused by inconsistent distribution of modalities. However, the task also demands more on capturing video temporal information of activity for retrieval. Thus, it is very important to preserve activity information in video representations.

Traditional descriptor aggragation schemes for video clips [7,20,21] ignore the correlations among video frames, resulting in the loss of structural properties, such as viewpoint, spatial transformation. Therefore, large numbers of endeavors have been dedicated to constructing subspace representations of videos for its amply expression of the whole video. Even though, subspace representations, such as mixture of linear subspaces, affine subspace and covariance matrix, preserve more structural information than the vector representations, they lose temporal consistency for activity, which motivates us to explore suitable video representations for the cross-modal task further. C3D [9] is a three-dimensional fully convolutional network which extracts meaningful spatio-temporal features. Based on a sequence of video frames with dimension $\mathbb{R}^{3\times L\times H\times W}$, we use $F_{conv5b} \in \mathbb{R}^{512\times \frac{L}{8}\times \frac{H}{16}\times \frac{W}{16}}$ featuremap of C3D and utilize candidate temporal regions containig activities by a 3D-RoI Pooling to obtain the superior representations. Therefore, we can represesnt video as a bag feature of spatio-temporal information, different from the prior work.

Even though spatio-temporal video representations provide rich information to retrieve, there still exist two main challenges to overcome in our task. Firstly, structure mismatch issue arises when video features are structured as spatio-temporal information bags and cannot be compared with image vector features directly. Secondly, cross-modal retrieval exists modality gap caused by inconsistent distributions of different modalities. To solve the above two issues, we propose a new framework as illustrated in Fig. 1. Images, videos from the same category (positive videos) and videos from the different category (negative videos) constitute tuples as our network inputs. The image features and video bag features are extracted by VGG and C3D + 3D-RoI Pooling models respectively, and then projected into a common feature space, in which images and videos can be compared without domain gap. We exploit Multiple Instance Learning (MIL) module to recognize the contributions of information in the video bag and vectorize the video representations by different weights. Then the video expression can be enhanced and structure issue between video and image can be eliminated. Meanwhile, to minimize the modality gap of feature representations, we utilize the triplet loss to gather the image and its positive videos together and push the image and its negative videos apart. It not only distinguishes different semantic categorites, but also supports intraclass variability across different modalities. In addition, adversarial learning is employed in our framework as a minimax game by discriminating and intergrating modalities of images and videos. The interplay between modality loss and triplet loss jointly minimizes the modality gap further, which improves the performance greatly. The main contributions are summarized as follows:

- For query-by-image video retrieval task, we use C3D + 3D RoI Pooling model to capture spatio-temporal information of videos as bag features and utilize

Multiple Instance Learning module to solve structure issue between image and video representations.
- Triplet loss in our framework is used to supports intraclass variability by images and the corresponding positive videos and distinguish different semantic categorites by images and the corresponding negative videos.
- The framework implements adversarial learning as an interplay between triplet loss and modality loss to further bridge the feature domain gap across different modalities.

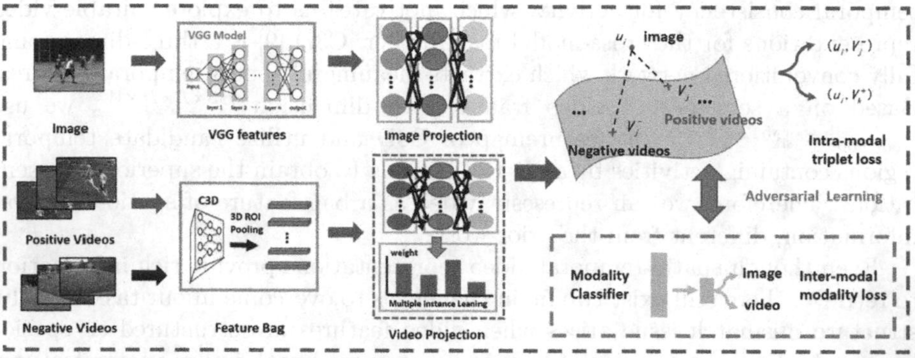

Fig. 1. The flowchart of our proposed approach. The image features and video bag features are projected into a common feature space. Intra-modal triplet loss and Inter-modal modality loss are implemented as an interplay to minimize the modality gap jointly in the common feature space.

2 Related Work

Query-by-image video retrieval (QBIVR) task plays an important role in the retrieval task. Action-oriented and event-oriented are two common tasks in query-by-image video retrieval, which are affected by representation learning and the feature extraction greatly.

Representation learning falls into two major categories, i.e., real-valued and binary representation learning. Retrieval problem has made great progress in binary representation, such as supervised hashing CBE-opt [17], SKLSH [11], semi-supervised hashing FastH [10], and unsupervised hashing ITQ [5], SpH [8]. Multi-modalities hashing, which maps the items of different modalities into a common binary Hamming space, such as MFH [15], SCM [19], to achieve the retrieval efficiency. For real-value based retrieval methods, JRL [18], JFSSL [12], and Corr-AE [4] are all effective for retrieval task.

Considering the different modalities in QBIVR task, efficient feature extraction is a critical step to guarantee retrieval accuracy. In general, shots indexing, sets aggregation and global signature representations are three main ways for video features. Araujo et al. [1] is proposed for less retrieval latency and memory requirements, but is not suitable for preservation of temporal information. Thus, different from the prior work, we employ spatio-temporal representations to reserve pretty rich inter-frame and intra-frame relationships. Specially, Jiang et al. [9] proposes a network for temporal activity detection, termed R-C3D model, which inspires us to take full advantage of their spatio-temporal features into other tasks. And 3D-RoI Pooling can further extract temporal regions features for locating video activities and finally we obtain video bags as representations.

Video bags of rich temporal information also affect retrieval accuracy. To solve this issue, we use attention mechanism, which is widely studied in distinguishing importance of information. Bahdanau et al. [2] introduced a novel attention mechanism that allows neural networks to assign different weights to their inputs. You et al. [16] proposed a bilinear attention model to identify the correlations between words and image regions. And meanwhile, to attain effective features, we utilize adversarial learning inspired by GAN [6]. Through the convergence of this minimax process, our feature space would be optimal for cross-modal retrieval. Compared with the prior work, in this paper, we firstly utilize spatio-temporal representations as video bags, and then combine attention mechanism and concept of GAN to utilize Multiple Instance Learning (MIL) module and adversarial learning in our framework. The improved results verify the effectiveness of our network.

3 Our Approach

3.1 Problem Formulation

For concise mathematical expression, we denote a matrix/vector by using a uppercase/lowercase letter in boldface respectively, and a lowercase letter denotes a scalar, *e.g.*, $\mathbf{A}$ denotes a matrix, $\mathbf{a}$ denotes a vector and a denotes a scalar. We use $\mathbf{A}^T$ to denote the transpose of $\mathbf{A}$.

In the query-by-image video retrieval task, given an image query $I \in \mathbb{R}^{d_2 \times 1}$, we aim to find the relevent video from video database. The objective can be formulated as below:

$$\boldsymbol{V}^* = \mathop{\mathbf{argmin}}_{\boldsymbol{V}_j} d(\boldsymbol{I}, \boldsymbol{V}_j). \tag{1}$$

Obviously, we need a common feature space for images and videos to compare directly and retrieve the video with the shortest distance from the image query. In our network, the inputs of the framework are tuples of images and videos, i.e., $\{(\boldsymbol{I}_k, \boldsymbol{V}_k^+, \boldsymbol{V}_k^-)\}_{k=1}^n$, where $\boldsymbol{I}_k \in \mathbb{R}^{d_2 \times 1}$ is an image vector feature and $\boldsymbol{V}_k = \{\boldsymbol{s}_1, \boldsymbol{s}_2, ..., \boldsymbol{s}_j\}$ with $\boldsymbol{s}_j \in \mathbb{R}^{d_1 \times 1}$ is a video bag representation of spatio-temporal information. $\boldsymbol{V}_k^+$ is the positive video in the same category as k-th image query $\boldsymbol{I}_k$, and $\boldsymbol{V}_k^-$ is the negative video in the different categories. The goal of the whole framework is to learn better embedding features in the common feature space for cross-modal data.

3.2 Attention-Based Feature

As the different statistical properties and data distribution of videos and images, we project video and image features into a common embedding space with mapping function f_v and f_i respectively. We define the mapping functions as:

$$\begin{aligned} f_v(\boldsymbol{V}) &= \{\bar{\boldsymbol{s}}_1, \bar{\boldsymbol{s}}_2, ..., \bar{\boldsymbol{s}}_j\} = \bar{\boldsymbol{V}}, \\ f_i(\boldsymbol{I}) &= \bar{\boldsymbol{I}}, \end{aligned} \tag{2}$$

where $f_v : \mathbb{R}^{d_1 \times j} \rightarrow \mathbb{R}^{r \times j}, f_i : \mathbb{R}^{d_2 \times 1} \rightarrow \mathbb{R}^{r \times 1}$, we project the image and video representations into the same dimensionality, i.e., $r = 64$ in our framework. To learn abundant information of videos and images, the mapping functions f_v and f_i are 2-fully-connected layers with enough parameters to ensure the effective expressions.

Multiple Instance Learning Module. Although video bag features are abundant in spatio-temporal information, the redundant information interference can also have an impact on retrieval. Besides, video bag features are different from image vector features in structure, which leads to structure mismatch issue. Thus, we propose a Multiple Instance Learning (MIL) module to automatically distinguish the importance of information in video bag. Our MIL module learns the different impact of spatio-temporal information and assign suitable weights to them. Finally, the integrated feature of video bag is capable to represent video activity well. The datails are as follows

$$a_j = \frac{exp\{\boldsymbol{w}^T tanh(\boldsymbol{L}\bar{\boldsymbol{s}}_j^T)\}}{\sum\sum exp\{\boldsymbol{w}^T tanh(\boldsymbol{L}\bar{\boldsymbol{s}}_j^T)\}}, \tag{3}$$

then,

$$Z(\bar{\boldsymbol{V}}) = \sum a_j \bar{\boldsymbol{s}}_j. \tag{4}$$

Where $\boldsymbol{w} \in \mathbb{R}^{r' \times 1}$, $\boldsymbol{L} \in \mathbb{R}^{r' \times r}$. We apply a fully-connected layer with nonlinear operation $tanh(\cdot)$ to measure the contribution of $\bar{\boldsymbol{s}}_j$ in the video bags. And the normalized weight a_j is calculated by a softmax function. Based on a_j, $Z(\bar{\boldsymbol{V}})$ is obtained by a weighted sum of $\bar{\boldsymbol{s}}_j$. The process is illustrated in Fig. 2. Normalized video features not only indicate the importances of different spatio-temporal information, but also can be compared with image vectors directly without structure issue in the common feature space.

3.3 Objective Function

Based on the projected features $\bar{\boldsymbol{I}}$ and $Z(\bar{\boldsymbol{V}})$, we employ triplet loss and modality loss in an adversarial learning way. On the one hand, the triplet loss preserves intraclass invariance and distinguish different semantic categories across modalities. On the other hand, the modality loss generates modality-agnostic representations to confuse the modality classifier. In summary, the two losses are applied in a minimax game to further reduce the modality gap in the common feature space.

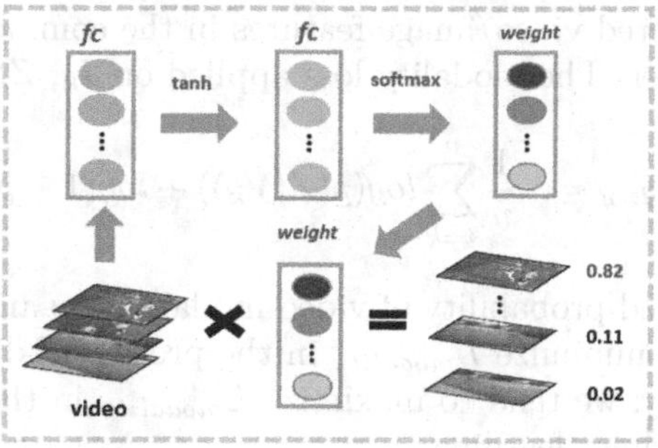

Fig. 2. Illustration of Multiple Instance Learning module in our framework.

Triplet Loss. In cross-modal retrieval, modality gap is a major challenge to solve. We need to ensure preservation of inter-modal invariance and meanwhile distinguish semantically different items across modalities. Triplet loss is widely used in feature learning with triplets, in this section, we use triplet loss to learn the semantic relevance across different modalities of images and videos. Our goal is to optimize the embedding features with the same identity are closer to each other than those with different identities. Following the definition in triplet loss, we set projected image vector $\bar{\boldsymbol{I}}$ as an anchor, and the video with the same label $Z(\bar{\boldsymbol{V}}^+)$ as positive sample, the video with different label $Z(\bar{\boldsymbol{V}}^-)$ as negative sample. Based on tuple $(\bar{\boldsymbol{I}}, Z(\bar{\boldsymbol{V}}^+), Z(\bar{\boldsymbol{V}}^-)$, we enforce the distance between $\bar{\boldsymbol{I}}$ and $Z(\bar{\boldsymbol{V}}^+)$ is smaller than that between $\bar{\boldsymbol{I}}$ and $Z(\bar{\boldsymbol{V}}^-)$. Then our triplet loss is formulated as

$$L_{triplet} = \sum_k \mid d(\bar{\boldsymbol{I}}_k, Z(\bar{\boldsymbol{V}}_k^+)) - d(\bar{\boldsymbol{I}}_k, Z(\bar{\boldsymbol{V}}_k^-)) + margin \mid_+, \tag{5}$$

where,

$$d(\bar{\boldsymbol{I}}, Z(\bar{\boldsymbol{V}})) = \|f_i(\boldsymbol{I}) - Z(f_v(\boldsymbol{V}))\|_2 . \tag{6}$$

We choose l_2 norm to measure the similarities between images and videos. $margin$ in our experiment is set to 0.1, and $|a|_+ = a$ if $a > 0$ and 0 otherwise. Then, the intraclass variability and semantic differences can be well balanced by triplet loss across modalities.

Modality Loss. The core concept of our framework is the interplay between triplet learning and modality learning, conducted as a minimax game. The triplet learning aims to optimize semantic representations across different modalities, but modality learning focuses on confusing classifier about image and video modalities. The interplay between two processes makes representations in the common space more optimal for cross-modal retrieval. In our framework, adversarial learning can further minimize the modality gap between images and videos.

The modality classifier is implemented as a binary classifier, in which the label of video modality is 1 and the label of image modality is 0. As an adversary role, we expect the projected video/image features in the common space can confuse the modality classifier. The modality loss applied on $\bar{\boldsymbol{I}}_k$, $Z(\bar{\boldsymbol{V}}_k)$ is defined as

$$L_{modality} = -\frac{1}{n}\sum_{i=k}^{n} log(p(Z(\bar{\boldsymbol{V}}_k)) + log(1 - p(\bar{\boldsymbol{I}}_k)), \tag{7}$$

where $p(\cdot)$ is predicted probability of video modality. As an adversarial learning network, we tend to minimize $L_{modality}$ in the process of discriminating modalities, on the contrary, we tend to maximize $L_{modality}$ in the process of learning representations in triplet learning.

3.4 Adversarial Algorithm

The process of learning the optimal feature representation is conducted by jointly minimizing the triplet loss and modality loss, as obtained in Eqs. 5 and 7, respectively. Then the optimization runs as a minimax game of two objective functions, and the two opposite sub-processes are written as follows

$$\begin{aligned} \theta_{triplet} &= \underset{\theta_{triplet}}{\mathbf{argmin}}\,(L_{triplet} - L_{modality}), \\ \theta_{modality} &= \underset{\theta_{modality}}{\mathbf{argmax}}\,(L_{triplet} - L_{modality}) \end{aligned} \tag{8}$$

where $\theta_{triplet}, \theta_{modality}$ are parameters in triplet loss and modality loss. The adversarial learning process is implemented as a minimax game by generating representations and discriminating modalities alternatingly. The training details are shown in the Algorithm 1.

4 Experiment

The paper evaluates the proposed approach on one activity detection datasets, i.e., THUMOS'14, and one event detection dataset, i.e., MED2017. Specially, we compare the performance of our approach with several advanced methods including single modality hashing methods, multiple modalities hashing methods and cross-modal methods. Specifically, we analyze the effects of the Multiple Instance Learning module and adversarial learning in our network. Superior experiment results on two datasets demonstrate the effectiveness of our approach.

4.1 Experimental Settings

Our experiment has two steps for data processing, i.e., video step and image step. In the video step, as datasets may have some long videos and multiple activity instances, based on annotations, we clip the video to several smaller segmentations to make sure every clip has one category. We first adopted the FFmpeg to sample the input videos as the keyframes and then input the buffers of fixed number keyframes, which is long enough to cover at least one activity

Algorithm 1. The training process of *AIV* approach.

Input: image-video tuples $\{(\boldsymbol{I}_k, \boldsymbol{V}_k^+, \boldsymbol{V}_k^-)|_{k=1}^n\}$. The number of steps m, learning rate λ, μ, and module parameters $\theta_{triplet}, \theta_{modality}$.

update until convergence:

1: **for** m steps **do**

2: update $\boldsymbol{\theta}_{triplet}$ by **descending** stochastic gradients:
$\boldsymbol{\theta}_{triplet} \leftarrow \boldsymbol{\theta}_{triplet} - \lambda \cdot \nabla \boldsymbol{\theta}_{triplet}(L_{triplet} - L_{modality})$.

3: **end for**

4: update parameter $\boldsymbol{\theta}_{modality}$ by **ascending** stochastic gradients:
$\boldsymbol{\theta}_{modality} \leftarrow \boldsymbol{\theta}_{modality} + \mu \cdot \nabla \boldsymbol{\theta}_{modality}(L_{triplet} - L_{modality})$.

5: **return** the projected features $\bar{\boldsymbol{I}}, \bar{\boldsymbol{V}}^+, \bar{\boldsymbol{V}}^-$. ,

instance, into the C3D model. We compute fully-convolutional 3D ConvNet features and propose temporal regions likely to contain activities, then pool these features within these regions as our video bag representations.

In the image step, we firstly locate the activity intervals according to the video annotations, which can ensure that there exist actions in the images. And then, for the ease of the memory and computation, we reduce VGG fc7 layer dimension to 128-dim by PCA to extract the features of the interval keyframes as image queries. Based on annotation, we set the videos with the same label as positive videos and randomly select videos of other category as negative videos. At last, we get image-video tuples from each category as our inputs of network.

Results are shown in terms of mean Average Precision(mAP)@k where k denotes the top-ranked retrieved number in the cross-modal retrieval task. For a given image query, the average precision is defined as $AP = \frac{1}{M}\sum_{r=1}^{k} \frac{M_r}{r} \cdot \delta(r)$, where M denotes the number of relevant videos to the query in the testing set, M_r is the number of relevant videos in top r results and $\delta(r) = 1$ if rth video is relevant to the query and $\delta(r) = 0$ otherwise. Then, mAP@k is calculated by averaging the AP values over all queries in the query set.

4.2 Datasets

THUMOS'14 Dataset. The THUMOS14 activity detection dataset contains over 24 h of video from 20 different sport activities. It consists of 2765 trimmed training videos and 200 untrimmed validation videos. For the video step, we use 200 untrimmed validation videos as our training and testing datasets. We input video clips as buffers of 768 frames at 5 frames per second (fps), which contains approximately 154 s for a video clip to make sure one activity in. We slide from the beginning to the end and also from the end to the beginning of the video to create various buffers with a fixed stride. Following [14], these buffers of frames are put into the C3D model pretrained on Sports-1M dataset, and we obtain the spatio-temporal video bags by 3D RoI Pooling as our video representations at last. For the image step, we randomly sample the keyframes from videos action intervals and extract the images by VGG model. Finally, we randomly choose

Table 1. Performance of different methods in terms of mAP@k on the THUMOS'14 Dataset. Best results are denoted in boldface.

Method		mean Average Precision			
		@10	@20	@50	@100
Single modality hashing methods	ITQ	0.1817	0.1782	0.1731	0.1688
	SpH	0.1786	0.1732	0.1667	0.1591
	SKLSH	0.1689	0.1557	0.1507	0.1477
Multi-modalities hashing methods	MFH	0.2075	0.1978	0.1903	0.1893
	SCM	0.2165	0.2080	0.1966	0.1931
	CMFH	0.2124	0.2078	0.1988	0.1955
Cross-modal methods	JFSSL	0.2276	0.2131	0.2087	0.1904
	Corr-AE	0.2011	0.1988	0.1932	0.1877
Our method	*AIV*	**0.2378**	**0.2203**	**0.2015**	**0.1895**

1,500 image-video tuples as training samples and the remaining 200 images as test samples.

MED2017 Event Dataset. The Multimedia Event Detection (MED) launched by TRECVID aims to encourage new technologies for detecting more complicated events. MED2017 resources were assembled from previous evaluations, the Omnibus MED text data release and the YFCC100M dataset. We use the resources for the Pre-Specified Event portion of the MED2017 evaluation. The dataset has total 10 categories and 200 clipped videos whose durations between 30 s and 3 min. Video scenes vary from indoors to outdoors and each clip is only classified to one category. All the buffers are of 768 frames at 5 fps which can totally cover 97% training videos. We conduct the same data processing as THUMOS'14 dataset to the MED2017 Event dataset, the training and testing samples are divided into 2000 and 400 in the experiment.

4.3 Results Analysis

Results on THUMOS'14 Dataset. We test our approaches on the THUMOS'14 Dataset with several popular methods including single modality hashing methods ITQ [5], SKLSH [11], SpH [8], multiple modalities hashing methods MFH [15], SCM [19], CMFH [3], and cross-modal retrieval methods, Corr-AE [4], JFSSL [12]. The results in Table 1 show that our proposed approach outperforms the effective hashing methods on mAP in all scope of k. We can also observe that cross-modal methods are not suitable for the image-video retrieval even though they are very successful in text-image task. And moreover, our approach can overcome the limitation of modalities by optimizing the triplet loss between images and videos in the common feature space. The subsequent experiments on the event datasets will further prove that our approach can also be effective in event-based scene.

Table 2. Performance of different methods in terms of mAP@k on the MED2017 Event Dataset. Best results are denoted in boldface.

Method		mean Average Precision			
		@10	@20	@50	@100
Single modality hashing methods	ITQ	0.1651	0.1562	0.1513	0.1218
	SpH	0.1686	0.1543	0.1417	0.1259
	SKLSH	0.1438	0.1395	0.1257	0.1174
Multi-modalities hashing methods	MFH	0.1885	0.1768	0.1737	0.1694
	SCM	0.1985	0.1950	0.1906	0.1872
	CMFH	0.2034	0.1988	0.1895	0.1852
Cross-modal methods	JFSSL	0.2146	0.2067	0.1908	0.1879
	Corr-AE	0.2124	0.1992	0.1934	0.1894
Our method	*AIV*	**0.2218**	**0.2183**	**0.2035**	**0.1988**

Results on MED2017 Event Dataset. To further demonstrate the effectiveness of our approach, we also test the proposed approach on the event-based dataset, i.e., MED2017 Event Dataset. Table 2 shows the performance of our approach and different compared methods. Obviously, even for an event-based dataset with shorter-time videos, the performance on mAP@k is also satisfactory. In summary, our approach can achieve superior improvement over other methods in all scope of k on both action-based and event-based datasets.

4.4 Ablation Analysis

In order to explore the effect of different components in our approach, we investigate some special cases of our approach. Specifically, we study the contributions of Multiple Instance Learning (MIL) module and adversarial learning in our framework. The performance of ablation experiments are presented in Table 3 and analysis is as follows.

Multiple Instance Learning Module. MIL in our framework aims to learn different contributions of spatio-temporal information in video bag. To verify the effectiveness of our Multiple Instance Learning (MIL) module, we assign uniform weights to each information instead of learning weights using attention module. We formulate it as $Z(\bar{\boldsymbol{V}}) = \frac{1}{n}\sum_{j=1}^{n} \bar{\boldsymbol{s}}_j$, and refer to this case as AIV/mil. As shown in Table 3, the average of video bag has worse performance than that of MIL, which proves the effectiveness of MIL module. MIL module can take advantage of the relationship among information and learn the importances of each features in the video bag, which improves the expressiveness of videos.

Table 3. mAP@k of AIV approach and our special cases on the THUMOS'14 Dataset.

Method	mean Average Precision			
	@10	@20	@50	@100
AIV/mil	0.2036	0.1956	0.1906	0.1875
AIV/mod	0.1587	0.1451	0.1367	0.1245
Full *AIV*	**0.2378**	**0.2203**	**0.2015**	**0.1895**

Adversarial Learning. Modality loss plays an adversary role in the framework to the triplet loss. Modality loss is involved in a minimax game by discriminating two modalities with a modality classifier, which aims to further reduce the modality gap. In order to evaluate the adversarial learning in our framework, we present a case without modality loss, and name the case as *AIV/mod*. Experimental results in Table 3 show that performance without modality loss is inferior to our *AIV* approach, which indicates that adversarial learning plays an essential role to our cross-modal framework.

5 Conclusion

In this paper, we proposed an adversarial *AIV* approach, which utilizes a minimax game by discriminating and intergrating modalities of images and videos. Triplet loss in our framework is designed to preserve intraclass variability and meanwhile distinguish different semantic categories. As an adversary, modality loss further minimizes the domain gap by interacting with triplet loss. Furthermore, we use spatio-temporal video bag features to preserve abundent information and address the structure mismatch issue by a Multiple Instance Learning module, which improves the expression of videos. Experiments on two datasets have demonstrated the superiority of our approach compared to other methods.

Acknowledgement. The work was supported in part by the National Basic Research Program of China (2015CB856004), the Key Basic Research Program of Shanghai Municipality, China (16JC1402800), Shanghai Sailing Program (BI0300271) and Startup Fund for Youngman Research at SJTU (WF220403041).

References

1. de Araújo, A.F., Chaves, J., Angst, R., Girod, B.: Temporal aggregation for large-scale query-by-image video retrieval. In: ICIP (2015)
2. Bahdanau, D., Cho, K., Bengio, Y.: Neural machine translation by jointly learning to align and translate. In: ICLR (2015)
3. Ding, G., Guo, Y., Zhou, J.: Collective matrix factorization hashing for multimodal data. In: CVPR (2014)
4. Feng, F., Wang, X., Li, R.: Cross-modal retrieval with correspondence autoencoder. In: MM (2014)

5. Gong, Y., Lazebnik, S.: Iterative quantization: a procrustean approach to learning binary codes. In: CVPR, pp. 817–824 (2011)
6. Goodfellow, I.J., et al.: Generative adversarial networks. CoRR abs/1406.2661 (2014)
7. Gorisse, D., et al.: IRIM at TRECVID 2010: semantic indexing and instance search. In: TRECVID (2010)
8. Heo, J., Lee, Y., He, J., Chang, S., Yoon, S.: Spherical hashing. In: CVPR (2012)
9. Jiang, Z., Rozgic, V., Adali, S.: Learning spatiotemporal features for infrared action recognition with 3D convolutional neural networks. In: CVPR, pp. 309–317 (2017)
10. Lin, G., Shen, C., van den Hengel, A.: Supervised hashing using graph cuts and boosted decision trees. CoRR abs/1408.5574 (2014)
11. Raginsky, M., Lazebnik, S.: Locality-sensitive binary codes from shift-invariant kernels. In: NIPS (2009)
12. Wang, K., He, R., Wang, L., Wang, W., Tan, T.: Joint feature selection and subspace learning for cross-modal retrieval. IEEE Trans. Pattern Anal. Mach. Intell. **38**(10), 2010–2023 (2016)
13. Wang, K., He, R., Wang, W., Wang, L., Tan, T.: Learning coupled feature spaces for cross-modal matching. In: ICCV (2013)
14. Xu, H., Das, A., Saenko, K.: R-C3D: region convolutional 3d network for temporal activity detection. In: ICCV (2017)
15. Ye, D., Li, Y., Tao, C., Xie, X., Wang, X.: Multiple feature hashing learning for large-scale remote sensing image retrieval. ISPRS Int. J. Geo-Inf. **6**(11), 364 (2017)
16. You, Q., Cao, L., Jin, H., Luo, J.: Robust visual-textual sentiment analysis: when attention meets tree-structured recursive neural networks. In: Proceedings of the 2016 ACM Conference on Multimedia Conference, MM, pp. 1008–1017 (2016)
17. Yu, F.X., Kumar, S., Gong, Y., Chang, S.: Circulant binary embedding. In: ICML (2014)
18. Zhai, X., Peng, Y., Xiao, J.: Learning cross-media joint representation with sparse and semisupervised regularization. IEEE Trans. Circ. Syst. Video Techn. **24**(6), 965–978 (2014)
19. Zhang, D., Li, W.: Large-scale supervised multimodal hashing with semantic correlation maximization. In: AAAI (2014)
20. Zhu, C., Huang, Y., Satoh, S.: Multi-image aggregation for better visual object retrieval. In: ICASSP (2014)
21. Zhu, C., Satoh, S.: Large vocabulary quantization for searching instances from videos. In: ICMR (2012)

Joint Sketch-Attribute Learning for Fine-Grained Face Synthesis

Binxin Yang[1], Xuejin Chen[1(✉)], Richang Hong[2], Zihan Chen[1], Yuhang Li[1], and Zheng-Jun Zha[1]

[1] University of Science and Technology of China, Hefei, China
{tennyson,zhchen25,lyh9001}@mail.ustc.edu.cn,
{xjchen99,zhazj}@ustc.edu.cn
[2] Hefei University of Technology, Hefei, China
hongrc@hfut.edu.cn

Abstract. The photorealism of synthetic face images has been significantly improved by generative adversarial networks (GANs). Besides of the realism, more accurate control on the properties of face images. While sketches convey the desired shapes, attributes describe appearance. However, it remains challenging to jointly exploit sketches and attributes, which are in different modalities, to generate high-resolution photorealistic face images. In this paper, we propose a novel joint sketch-attribute learning approach to synthesize photo-realistic face images with conditional GANs. A hybrid generator is proposed to learn a unified embedding of shape from sketches and appearance from attributes for synthesizing images. We propose an attribute modulation module, which transfers user-preferred attributes to reinforce sketch representation with appearance details. Using the proposed approach, users could flexibly manipulate the desired shape and appearance of synthesized face images with fine-grained control. We conducted extensive experiments on the CelebA-HQ dataset [16]. The experimental results have demonstrated the effectiveness of the proposed approach.

Keywords: Conditional GANs · Sketch · Face attributes · Image synthesis · Joint learning

1 Introduction

Realistic image synthesis has been a hot topic in multimedia and computer graphics for decades. It is crucial for a wide range of applications, such as data enhancement, content creation, intelligent editing, etc. Traditional approaches rely on annotated face photos and synthesize new face images by image retrieval and fusion. However, due to the scarcity of annotated data and limited capability of image fusion of low-level signals, these approaches suffer from inconsistent lighting, texture, and scales.

Y. M. Ro et al. (Eds.): MMM 2020, LNCS 11961, pp. 790–801, 2020.
https://doi.org/10.1007/978-3-030-37731-1_64

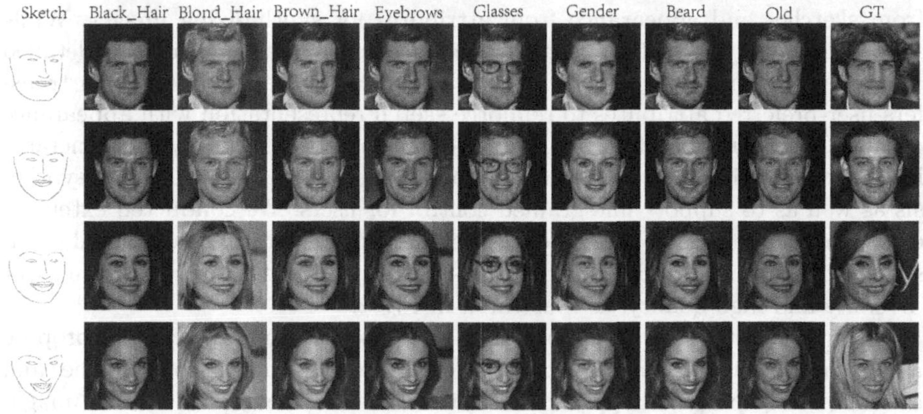

Fig. 1. By joint modeling sketches and attributes, our method provides a flexible tool for users to synthesize high-resolution photo-realistic face images with fine-grained control on the face shape and appearance.

Generative Adversarial Networks (GANs) bring a new and promising mechanism for image generation [4,7,10,28,30]. Utilizing the minimax strategy to train a discriminator and a generator such that the fake images are indistinguishable from real ones, GANs synthesize virtual images from a noise vector in an embedded space. However, these methods cannot take any specific preference of users as input to generate face images with desired characteristics, such as hair color, age, gender, etc. Instead of using noise vectors, Conditional Generative Adversarial Networks (CGANs) control the generation of images with conditions, which could be texts [23,26,29], class labels [3,8,19,25], images from another domain [13,15,17,18,21,22], and so on. CGANs trained in supervised manner is able to model the distribution of conditional information. Existing CGAN-based methods have shown effectiveness in generating visually plausible images with specific conditions.

However, existing CGAN-based methods only exploit one modality of condition. These networks are trained to encode one specific type of condition and the generators learn to decode an embedded vector to synthesize images based on the condition. However, when creating a new face image, users may prefer different ways to describe the desired characteristics. Sketching is a natural way for users to describe the geometric pattern of a face, including the shape of facial features, the layout, as well as facial expressions. However, it is non-trivial to sketch appearance details. On the other hand, users prefer to describe the desired appearance with attributes, such as "black hair", "young", "gender", etc. There is a great demand for synthesizing photo-realistic face images by jointly exploiting sketches and attributes.

Motivated by the above observations, we propose a novel joint sketch-attribute learning approach for face image synthesis based on conditional GANs. We design a hybrid generator to learn a unified embedding of the geometric shape from sketches and appearance from attributes for synthesizing images. While sketches provide abstraction of the desired face shape, attributes convey detailed appearance. Hence, we propose an attribute modulation module, which transfers user-preferred attributes to reinforce sketch representation with appearance details. Together with the attribute modulation module, the hybrid generator is able to effectively exploit geometry and appearance for face image synthesis as well as to support fine-grained control for users. We conducted extensive experiments on the CelebA-HQ dataset. The experimental results have demonstrated that our approach can support users to create new face images in a great diversity and high quality, as illustrated in Fig. 1.

In summary, the main contribution of this paper is two-fold. First, we propose a novel approach which synthesizes photo-realistic face images from sketches and attributes. The proposed approach is flexible and effective to produce face images with fine-grained control on both shape and appearance. Secondly, we propose a novel joint sketch-attribute learning method to simultaneously exploit the user-preferred conditions in two modalities.

2 Related Work

Generative Adversarial Networks (GANs) have made breakthrough progress in generating photorealistic images. Many variants of GANs have been developed according to different type of sources, including noise vectors, class labels, attributes, or images. We will review some representative works in this field.

Generative Adversarial Networks. Since the generative adversarial networks [7] was first proposed, this new framework has drawn tremendous attention in the image synthesis field. The GAN framework significantly increases the photorealism of the synthesized images compared with traditional methods. Built upon GANs, a series of approaches have been proposed to progressively improve the resolution and photorealism of synthesized images by using coarse-to-fine schemes [4,10,26,27]. All these methods transform a noise vector that is randomly sampled from a prior distribution to a synthetic image. While they inspire the generator design in many applications, user control is not supported to generate the desired appearance in the synthesized images.

Attribute-based Face Generation and Editing. Recent works have achieved impressive results in attribute-based face generation and editing [3, 8,13,15,22,25]. The attributes are typically given by a class label or an example image. StarGAN [3] is a multi-domain image-to-image translation model which edits different attributes within a single network. In order to only alter the attribute-specific region and keep the rest unchanged, SaGAN [25] employs spatial attention mechanism in GAN framework. ELEGANT [22] applies face attribute editing with multiple attributes from an example face image by exchanging disentangled latent embeddings. [17] generates high-resolution face images with specific attributes from low-resolution face images. AttGAN [8] is able to generate face images with novel expressions in a continuum by controlling the magnitude of activation of action units. Cycle consistency is applied so that this model is capable to be trained in an unsupervised manner. CollaGAN [13] focuses on the task of multi-domain images-to-image translation, proposing a model to generate face images with a specific attribute from multiple images. Unlike previous works of which the input information comes from class labels or example images, our method takes both a sketch and a class label as input.

Image-to-Image Translation with CGANs. Image-to-image transformation, as a specific application of conditional GANs, has attracted widespread attentions in recent years. Its purpose is to apply a conditional image in one domain and generate a corresponding target image in another domain. The shared concept, such as object or scene, should be preserved in both images. Pix2pix [9], the pioneering work, firstly introduces the concept of image-to-image translation. Subsequent works are committed to improving the visual quality and resolution of the synthesized images in different ways. Pix2pixHD [20] proposes multi-scale generators and discriminators to increase the resolution of synthesized images. It also introduces a novel perceptual loss, to significantly improve the visual quality of generated images. One vital limitation of these supervised methods is the lack of paired training examples in two domains. Techniques for image-to-image transformation with unpaired samples have been extensively studied. An unsupervised image-to-image transformation (UNIT) framework is proposed assuming a shared-latent space between two domains [14]. The share-latent space assumption is implemented using a weight sharing constraint in the two branches of a coupled GAN. CycleGAN [31], DiscoGAN [11], and DualGAN [24] employ similar architectures to transform unpaired images. In order to facilitate the mapping of input images in one domain to generated images in another domain, these three methods learn two mappings during the confrontation training process. However, the images translated in UNIT methods are all nature images that contain rich texture details. In comparison, our goal is to complement facial textures and details to a binary sketch with discrete attribute labels.

Generating Images From Sketches. It is significantly challenging to generate realistic images with sketches, which are spatially sparse. No appearance detail is carried in sketches. Traditional techniques of image generation from sketches, such as Sketch2photo [1] and PhotoSketcher [6], are mainly based on image retrieval technique. These methods design hand-crafted features to fill the gap between sketches and photos. Complex post-processing techniques are also required to eliminate appearance inconsistency in the composed images caused by various lighting, object scale, and so on. Benefited from the recent progress of deep learning technique, SketchyGAN [2] is proposed to generate images from sketches for 50 object categories. However, the visual quality of the results is unsatisfactory, due to insufficient sketch-image training examples. While sketches only depict desired shapes, we propose to integrate sketches with attribute labels to support fine-grained control on the synthesized images.

3 Our Method

In our system, the input is a black-white sketch $\mathbf{s}$ to depict the desired face shape on a canvas with single-pixel width strokes. We provide a five-point landmark as reference for the user to draw a sketch on a $N \times N$ canvas so that the input sketches drawn by different users are on a consistent scale. While sketching is a natural way to depict face shapes, it is unrealistic to derive appearance details from the sparse strokes. In contrast, it is easier for common users to describe the desired face appearance through a few attributes. To specify the expected face appearance, the user selects one or more attribute labels from a pre-defined list. We represent the specified attribute as a K dimensional binary vector $\mathbf{a}$, where K is the number of all possible attributes in our system. When $\mathbf{a}_i = 1$, it indicates that the ith attribute is desired in the synthesized image.

According to the input sketch and attributes, our system generates high-resolution photo-realistic face images. Our method integrates the inputs in two modalities and jointly learns the embedding of sketches and attributes, in a conditional GAN framework, as shown Fig. 2. A conditional GAN typically consists of a generator G and a discriminator D and are optimized by the following minimax game

$$\min_G \max_D \mathcal{L}_{GAN}(G, D). \tag{1}$$

Our network is built on the image-to-image translation network, pix2pix-HD [20]. We design a new generator and discriminator to integrate attribute vectors and sketch images into the image-to-image translation network.

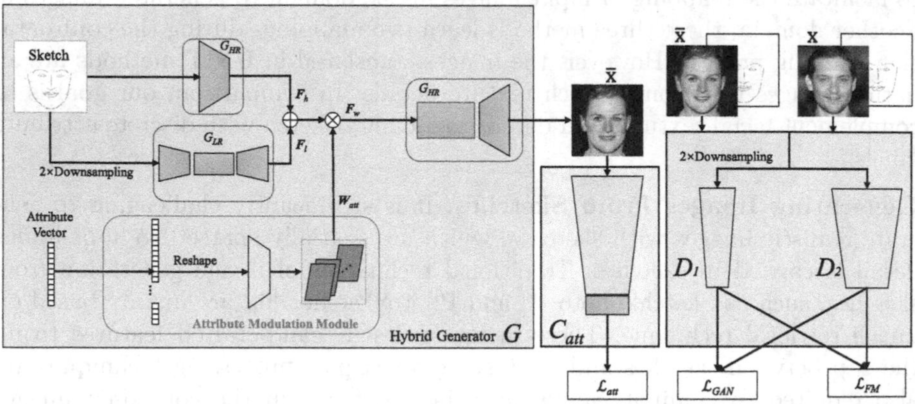

Fig. 2. The architecture of our face synthesis network. Taking a sketch image and an attribute vector as input, two generators G_{LR} and G_{HR} are integrated to produce high-resolution face images. The input sketch and attribute vector in distinct modalities are fused by embedding the attribute vector into weight maps to modulate the feature maps. Thus, both shape and appearance features are conveyed in the hybrid generator.

3.1 Hybrid Generator

The coarse-to-fine scheme is widely used in state-of-the-art image-to-image translation networks to improve the resolution and photorealism of the synthesized images. We also employ a low-resolution generator G_{LR} based on the downsampled sketch and a high-resolution generator G_{HR} to synthesize a high-resolution face image. Most importantly, to integrate the shape from the sketch and appearance from the specified attribute vector, we propose an attribute modulation module to compose a hybrid generator.

Low-Resolution Generator. The low-resolution generator G_{LR} takes the $2\times$ down-sampled sketch image $\mathbf{s}_l$ as input and generates low-resolution feature maps $\mathbf{F}_l$ using the encoder-residual-decoder architecture. This generator aims to provide coarse feature maps that mainly carry the geometric shape and structure delivered by the input sketch. Since sketches are very sparse and plain, the synthesized low-resolution feature maps do not carry fine-grained appearance details, such as expressions, decorations and so on. Next, we exploit fine-grained features that were extracted from the sketch and attributes.

High-Resolution Generator. The high-resolution generator G_{HR} consists of three main components: a convolutional front end to embed the input sketch in to feature maps $\mathbf{F}_h$, a set of residual blocks taking the element-wise sum of the global feature maps $\mathbf{F}_l$ and $\mathbf{F}_h$ as input, and a transposed convolutional back end, shown as the green blocks in Fig. 2 in G_{HR}. Sketches are not the only input to our generator. The specified attribute is represented in a binary vector and fed into our network as well. To exploit the complementarity between multiple modalities, we propose an attribute modulation module to transfer the binary attribute vector into a weight map $\mathbf{W}_{att}$ to modulate the sketch feature maps. The modulated feature maps $\mathbf{F}_w$ are fed into the residual blocks and the back end of G_{HR} to produce a high-resolution image $\hat{\mathbf{x}}$.

Attribute Modulation Module. To combine the dense feature maps extracted from sketch images and the sparse binary attribute vector, we transfer the attribute vector into dense weight maps to modulate the feature maps decoded from the input sketch. A K-D binary vector $\mathbf{a}$ is firstly embedded into a H-D vector using H multilayer perceptrons (MLPs), where $H = N \times N$. The high-dimensional vector is reshaped into a $N \times N \times 1$ map, which is subsequently fed into a convolution layer to produce weight maps $\mathbf{W}$ to modulate the feature maps decoded from the input sketch.

We fuse the three maps, including $\mathbf{F}_l$ from the last layer of the low resolution generator, the feature maps $\mathbf{F}_s$ extracted from the sketch in the original resolution, and the weight map $\mathbf{W}_{att}$ derived from the user-specified attributes to obtain a modulated feature map $\mathbf{F}_w$ as

$$\mathbf{F}_w = \mathbf{W}_{att} \otimes (\mathbf{F}_s \oplus \mathbf{F}_l), \tag{2}$$

where $\otimes$ denotes the element-wise product of two matrices, and $\oplus$ denotes the element-wise sum of two matrices.

3.2 Adversarial Loss Function

A GAN loss used in Eq. 1 to train a generator G and a discriminator D in image-to-image translation networks is defined as

$$\mathcal{L}_{GAN}(G, D) = \mathbb{E}_{(\mathbf{s},\mathbf{x})}\left[\log D(\mathbf{s},\mathbf{x})\right] + \mathbb{E}_{\mathbf{s}}\left[\log\left(1 - D(\mathbf{s}, G(\mathbf{s}))\right)\right]. \quad (3)$$

While pix2pixHD [20] uses three discriminators in three scales, we use two discriminators D_1 and D_2 with a similar architecture to save the memory cost.

We employ feature matching loss $\mathcal{L}_{FM}$ in our network training, same as [12,20], to improve the realism of synthesized images. Denoting the ith-layer feature extractor of a discriminator D_k as $D_k^{(i)}$ ($k = 1, 2$ in our case), the feature matching loss $\mathcal{L}_{FM}(G, D_k)$ is defined as:

$$\mathcal{L}_{FM}(G, D_k) = \mathbb{E}_{(\mathbf{s},\mathbf{x})} \sum\nolimits_{i=1}^{T} \frac{1}{N_i}\left[\|D_k^{(i)}(\mathbf{s},\mathbf{x}) - D_k^{(i)}(\mathbf{s}, G(\mathbf{s}))\|_1\right], \quad (4)$$

where T is the total number of layers of the discriminator and N_i denotes the number of elements in the feature maps of each layer.

Attribute Classification Loss. In order to force the hybrid generator to precisely convey the desired face attributes, we employ an attribute classifier C_{att} to predict the attributes of the generated face images. Our attribute classifier contains six convolutional layers, two fully connected layers and a sigmoid layer at the end. The attribute classifier C_{att} is a multi-label classifier that predicts the K-D probability vector $\mathbf{y} = C_{att}(\mathbf{x})$ of a face image $\mathbf{x}$. $\mathbf{y}_i$ indicates the probability of the face image with the ith attribute. To train our generator G, we minimize the attribute classification loss given by

$$\mathcal{L}_{att}(G, C_{att}) = \mathbb{E}_{(\mathbf{s},\mathbf{a})}\left[f_{bce}\left(\mathbf{a}, C_{att}\left(G(\mathbf{s},\mathbf{a})\right)\right)\right], \quad (5)$$

where f_{bce} calculates the binary cross entropy of two vectors $\mathbf{a}$ and $\mathbf{y}$ given an attribute classifier C_{att} which is pretrained on real images:

$$f(\mathbf{a},\mathbf{y}) = -\frac{1}{K}\sum_i \mathbf{a}_i \log \mathbf{y}_i + (1 - \mathbf{a}_i)\log(1 - \mathbf{y}_i). \quad (6)$$

The entire objective function combines the GAN loss with two discriminators, the feature matching loss and the attribute classification loss as:

$$\min_G \left(\left(\max_{D_1,D_2} \sum_{k=1,2} \mathcal{L}_{GAN}(G, D_k)\right) + \lambda \sum_{k=1,2} \mathcal{L}_{\mathcal{FM}}(G, D_k) + \beta\mathcal{L}_{att}(G, C_{att})\right), \quad (7)$$

where λ and β control the importance of the feature matching loss and attribute classification loss, respectively. Note that the two discriminators D_1 and D_2 are only trained to maximize the GAN loss $\mathcal{L}_{GAN}$. D_1 and D_2 serve as feature extractors when calculating L_{FM}.

4 Results and Discussion

Dataset and Experiment Settings. To train our network, we use the CelebA-HQ dataset [16], which contains 30 K high-resolution celebrity images and each image is annotated with 40 attributes being true or false. To generate sketch samples, we use the style aggregated network [5] to extract 68 face landmarks from each image in the CelebA-HQ dataset. The extracted landmarks are connected with single-pixel-width lines to generate a sketch, as shown in Fig. 3. However, the network sometimes fails to produce reasonable sketches if the real image lacks of some face landmarks. We selected 19,965 visually reasonable sketches and their corresponding face images as our training dataset. Among them, 14,973 sketch-image pairs are randomly selected for training and 4,992 sketch-image pairs for testing. All the images and sketches are resized to 512×512 in our experiments. There are 40 attributes in the CelebA-HQ dataset. However, some attributes, such as "Oval Face", "Pointly Nose", are shape-related. Therefore, we choose 13 attributes that are appearance-related to test our hybrid generator. These 13 attributes are Bald, Bangs, Black Hair, Blond Hair, Brown Hair, Bushy Eyebrow, Eyeglasses, Gender (1 for male, and 0 for female), No Beard, Smiling, Straight Hair, Wavy Hair, and Young. At the test stage, we use a default attribute vector as $(0, 0, 0, 0, 0, 0, 0, 0, 1, 0, 0, 0, 1)$ to modulate the sketch feature maps for face image synthesis. Image flipping is conducted to augment our training set. All our experiments were conducted in PyTorch on a computer with an NVIDIA Tesla V100. The parameters in Eq. 7 are fixed at $\beta = 0.5$ and $\lambda = 1$.

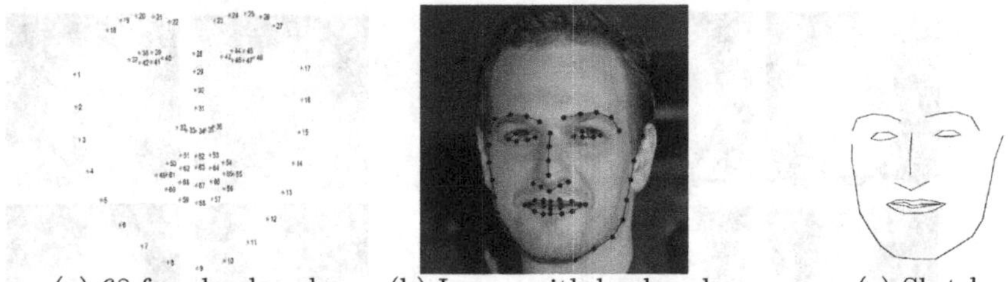

(a) 68 face landmarks (b) Image with landmarks (c) Sketch

Fig. 3. Sketch generation from a face image.

Fine-Grained Face Synthesis. We evaluate our face generation network on a large variety of combinations of sketches and attributes. Fig. 1 shows four groups of synthesized face images from four sketches combined with various attributes. Each row shows the synthetic face images from the same sketch but different attributes. We can see that the input sketches effectively describe the desired geometric attributes, such as contour shape, pose, the layout of facial features and so on. When one of the 13 attributes is set as true, the generated face images show the desired appearance, such as glasses, black hair and so on. Two more groups of results are shown in Fig. 4. From various sketches and the attribute "Glasses" or "Blond Hair", our method synthesizes photorealistic face images with the desired features.

Fig. 4. Two groups of results generated from various sketches with two attributes.

Correlation Between Attributes. It is interesting that the attribute "Beard" produces a distinct effect on females compared with males. Figure 5 shows four pairs of generated images with and without beard. When "Beard" is selected for males, as shown on the left, the synthesized male faces have apparent beard. In comparison, when "Beard" is selected for females, as shown on the right, it makes weak effect on the synthesized female face images. This indicates that our approach well models the correlation between attributes, and thus generates reasonable face images. Moreover, with regard to different sketches, the synthesized beards are well aligned with the face shapes. This further demonstrates that our approach effectively integrates the attributes and sketches.

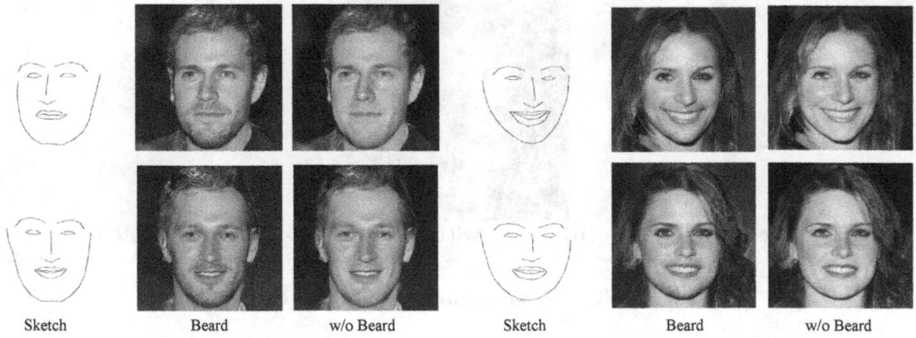

Fig. 5. Correlation between two attributes "beard" and "gender".

Comparison with Pix2PixHD. To the best of our knowledge, our system is the first one which supports both sketches and attribute labels as input. We compare with pix2pixHD which only supports sketch-to-face to demonstrate the effectiveness and flexibility of our method. As shown in Fig. 6, both pix2pixHD and our method synthesizes photo-realistic face images. However, by integrating attributes with sketches, our method generates more face images with diverse appearances from the same sketch.

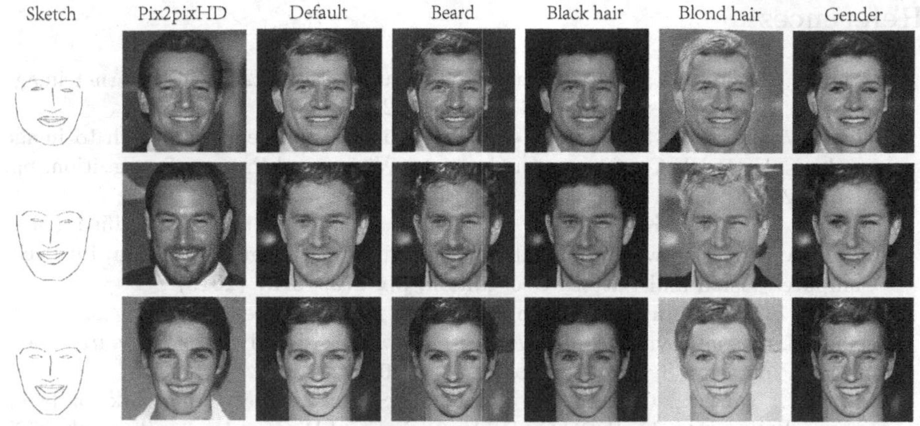

Fig. 6. Comparison with pix2pixHD [20]. Left to right: input sketches, results of pix2pixHD, and our results with different attributes.

5 Conclusion

In this paper, we introduced a novel approach for joint learning of sketches and attributes based on conditional GANs to synthesize high-resolution photo-realistic face images. To integrate the desired shape and appearance derived from a 2D sketch and attributes respectively, a hybrid generator is proposed to learn a unified embedding of shape and appearance. The photorealism of the synthesized images is significantly reinforced by integrating sketch and attributes. Our approach is flexible and effective for users to generate face images with fine-grained control on both face shape and appearance. We show a large variety of face images generated by our approach with various shapes and attributes, demonstrating the effectiveness of the joint sketch-attribute representation in generating photo-realistic face images.

However, there are still some limitations in our work. The input sketch should be consistent with the data distribution of training examples. Our method fails to synthesize realistic images when the input sketch presents large distortions. A future direction is to utilize transfer-learning in order to support greater diversity of hand-drawn sketches.

Acknowledgements. This work was supported by the National Key Research & Development Plan of China under Grant 2016YFB1001402, the National Natural Science Foundation of China (NSFC) under Grants 61632006, 61622211, and 61620106009, as well as the Fundamental Re-search Funds for the Central Universities under Grants WK3490000003 and WK2100100030.

References

1. Chen, T., Cheng, M., Tan, P., Shamir, A., Hu, S.: Sketch2Photo: Internet image montage. ACM Trans. Graph. **28**(5), 124:1–124:10 (2009)
2. Chen, W., Hays, J.: SketchyGAN: towards diverse and realistic sketch to image synthesis. In: IEEE Conference on Computer Vision and Pattern Recognition, pp. 9416–9425 (2018)
3. Choi, Y., Choi, M., Kim, M., Ha, J., Kim, S., Choo, J.: StarGAN: unified generative adversarial networks for multi-domain image-to-image translation. In: IEEE Computer Vision and Pattern Recognition, pp. 8789–8797 (2018)
4. Denton, E.L., Chintala, S., Szlam, A., Fergus, R.: Deep generative image models using a Laplacian pyramid of adversarial networks. In: Advances in Neural Information Processing Systems, pp. 1486–1494 (2015)
5. Dong, X., Yan, Y., Ouyang, W., Yang, Y.: Style aggregated network for facial landmark detection. In: IEEE Computer Vision and Pattern Recognition, pp. 379–388 (2018)
6. Eitz, M., Richter, R., Hildebrand, K., Boubekeur, T., Alexa, M.: Photosketcher: Interactive sketch-based image synthesis. IEEE Comput. Graph. Appl. **31**(6), 56–66 (2011)
7. Goodfellow, I.J., et al.: Generative adversarial nets. In: Advances in Annual Conference on Neural Information Processing Systems 2014, pp. 2672–2680 (2014)
8. He, Z., Zuo, W., Kan, M., Shan, S., Chen, X.: AttGAN: facial attribute editing by only changing what you want. IEEE Trans. Image Process. **28**(11), 5464–5478 (2019)
9. Isola, P., Zhu, J.Y., Zhou, T., Efros, A.A.: Image-to-image translation with conditional adversarial networks. In: IEEE Conference on Computer Vision and Pattern Recognition, pp. 5967–5976 (2017)
10. Karras, T., Aila, T., Laine, S., Lehtinen, J.: Progressive growing of GANs for improved quality, stability, and variation. In: International Conference on Learning Representations (2018)
11. Kim, T., Cha, M., Kim, H., Lee, J.K., Kim, J.: Learning to discover cross-domain relations with generative adversarial networks. In: Proceedings of the 34th International Conference on Machine Learning, vol. 70, pp. 1857–1865 (2017)
12. Ledig, C., et al.: Photo-realistic single image super-resolution using a generative adversarial network. In: IEEE Conference on Computer Vision and Pattern Recognition, pp. 105–114 (2017)
13. Lee, D., Kim, J., Moon, W.J., Ye, J.C.: CollaGAN: collaborative GAN for missing image data imputation. In: IEEE Conference on Computer Vision and Pattern Recognition, pp. 2487–2496 (2019)
14. Liu, M.Y., Breuel, T., Kautz, J.: Unsupervised image-to-image translation networks. In: Advances in Neural Information Processing Systems, pp. 700–708 (2017)
15. Liu, S., et al.: Face aging with contextual generative adversarial nets. In: ACM International Conference on Multimedia, pp. 82–90 (2018)
16. Liu, Z., Luo, P., Wang, X., Tang, X.: Deep learning face attributes in the wild. In: IEEE International Conference on Computer Vision, pp. 3730–3738 (2015)
17. Lu, Y., Tai, Y., Tang, C.: Attribute-guided face generation using conditional CycleGAN. In: ECCV, pp. 293–308 (2018)
18. Park, M., Kim, H.G., Ro, Y.M.: Photo-realistic facial emotion synthesis using multi-level critic networks with multi-level generative model. In: MultiMedia Modeling, pp. 3–15 (2019)

19. Pumarola, A., Agudo, A., Martínez, A.M., Sanfeliu, A., Moreno-Noguer, F.: GANimation: anatomically-aware facial animation from a single image. In: ECCV, pp. 835–851 (2018)
20. Wang, T., Liu, M., Zhu, J., Tao, A., Kautz, J., Catanzaro, B.: High-resolution image synthesis and semantic manipulation with conditional GANs. In: IEEE Conference on Computer Vision and Pattern Recognition, pp. 8798–8807 (2018)
21. Wang, X., Li, W., Mu, G., Huang, D., Wang, Y.: Facial expression synthesis by u-net conditional generative adversarial networks. In: ACM International Conference on Multimedia Retrieval, pp. 283–290 (2018)
22. Xiao, T., Hong, J., Ma, J.: ELEGANT: exchanging latent encodings with GAN for transferring multiple face attributes. In: ECCV, pp. 172–187 (2018)
23. Xu, T., et al.: AttnGAN: fine-grained text to image generation with attentional generative adversarial networks. In: IEEE Conference on Computer Vision and Pattern Recognition, pp. 1316–1324 (2018)
24. Yi, Z., Zhang, H., Tan, P., Gong, M.: DualGAN: unsupervised dual learning for image-to-image translation. In: IEEE International Conference on Computer Vision, pp. 2868–2876 (2017)
25. Zhang, G., Kan, M., Shan, S., Chen, X.: Generative adversarial network with spatial attention for face attribute editing. In: ECCV, pp. 422–437 (2018)
26. Zhang, H., Xu, T., Li, H.: StackGAN: text to photo-realistic image synthesis with stacked generative adversarial networks. In: IEEE International Conference on Computer Vision, pp. 5908–5916 (2017)
27. Zhang, H., et al.: StackGAN++: realistic image synthesis with stacked generative adversarial networks. IEEE Trans. Pattern Anal. Mach. Intell. **41**(8), 1947–1962 (2019)
28. Zhang, R., et al.: Style separation and synthesis via generative adversarial networks. In: ACM International Conference on Multimedia, pp. 183–191 (2018)
29. Zhang, Z., Xie, Y., Yang, L.: Photographic text-to-image synthesis with a hierarchically-nested adversarial network. In: IEEE Conference on Computer Vision and Pattern Recognition, pp. 6199–6208 (2018)
30. Zhao, Y., Deng, B., Huang, J., Lu, H., Hua, X.S.: Stylized adversarial autoencoder for image generation. In: ACM International Conference on Multimedia, pp. 244–251 (2017)
31. Zhu, J.Y., Park, T., Isola, P., Efros, A.A.: Unpaired image-to-image translation using cycle-consistent adversarial networks. In: IEEE International Conference on Computer Vision, pp. 2242–2251 (2017)

High Accuracy Perceptual Video Hashing via Low-Rank Decomposition and DWT

Lv Chen(✉), Dengpan Ye, and Shunzhi Jiang

Key Laboratory of Aerospace Information Security and Trusted Computing, Ministry of Education, School of Cyber Science and Engineering, Wuhan University, Wuhan 430072, Hubei, China
Lv.chen@whu.edu.cn

Abstract. In this work, we propose a novel robust video hashing algorithm with High Accuracy. The proposed algorithm generates a fix-up hash via low-rank and sparse decomposition and discrete wavelet transform (DWT). Specifically, input video is converted to randomly normalized video with logistic map, and then content-based feature matrices extract from a randomly normalized video with low-rank and sparse decomposition. Finally, data compression with 2D-DWT of LL sub-band is applied to feature matrices and statistic properties of DWT coefficients are quantized to derive a compact video hash. Experiments with 4760 videos are carried out to validate efficiency of the proposed video hashing. The results show that the proposed video hashing is robust to many digital operations and reaches good discrimination. Receiver operating characteristic (ROC) curve comparisons indicate that the proposed video hashing more desirable performance than some algorithms in classification between robustness and discrimination.

Keywords: Video hashing · Low-rank and sparse decomposition · Discreate wavelet transform · Copy detection

1 Introduction

The rapid development of social networks has entered people's daily work and life. Many people would like to share personal digital videos through the social networks. Plenty of digital videos are uploaded to social websites (e.g., Facebook and YouTube). Consequently, it is necessary to find an efficient technology to manage large-scale digital videos. Perceptual robust video hashing is a useful technique, which map a digital video with any size into a content-based and short string. Actually, it has been widely apply to many applications [1] (e.g., video indexing, video authentication and video copy detection). Generally, two essential properties should be satisfied for a video hashing which called robustness and discrimination. The robustness means that two visually similar videos should be generated very similar hashes. In other words, two visually different

Y. M. Ro et al. (Eds.): MMM 2020, LNCS 11961, pp. 802–812, 2020.
https://doi.org/10.1007/978-3-030-37731-1_65

videos should be generated different hashes. Certainly, in addition to two essential properties, video hashing should be key-dependent for some secure applications [2–4] such as authentication and thus avoid forgery in process of hash generated.

Recently, Yang et al. [5] combines speeded up robust feature (SURF) and ordinal measure (OM) to form hash. The SURF-OM hashing can resist many content-based operations and has good performance applied to video copy detection, but its discrimination not desirable enough. Li and Monga [6] modeled a video as a three-order tensor and exploited low-rank tensor approximations (LRTA) to calculate video hash. The LRTA hashing is robust against some common combined attack operations. Saikia [7] extracted spatio-temporal low-pass (STLP) band by three dimension discrete wavelet transform (3D-DWT) and selected DCT coefficients from STLP band to derive hash. The DWT-DCT hashing is robust to frame dropping and MPEG compression. Setyawan and Timotius [8] exploited gradient edge histogram (EOH) of each frame and compressed it to form a short hash by a temporal DCT. The EOH-DCT hashing can resist frame resizing and frame dropping. Chen et al. [9] applied 3D-DWT to video of normalization and extracted polar complex exponential transform (PCET) moments from low-pass sub-band of 3D-DWT to construct hash. This method has been successful applied to temper detection and achieved good results. In another work, Nie et al. [10] extracted spherical tori (ST) information to form feature matrices and reduced them with non-negative matrix factorization (NMF) to construct hash. The ST-NMF hashing is resilient to some content-preserving operations, such as blurring and noise attack, but its discrimination should be improvement. Sandeep et al. [11] viewed video as a three tensor and using 3D-radial projection technique extracted feature vectors. Then hash was constructed by DCT applied to feature vectors. This hashing can resist small angle of rotation, but discrimination should be improved. Tang et al. [12] designed a hashing via dominant DCT coefficients and NMF, This method is effective in resisting scale adjustment and noise attack, but it is vulnerable to operation of rotation.

From above analysis, it is clear that still existing some problem in video hashing derive. In this work, we design a novel video hashing with low-rank decomposition and DWT. Our hashing showed good trade off between robustness and discrimination, and many experiments carried out that our performance comparison with other some popular video hashing algorithms which republish in famous journals and conferences. Receiver operating characteristics (ROC) curve comparisons indicated that our video hashing has better performance than many advanced video hashing algorithms in classification between robustness and discrimination. The remainder of this work is organized as follows: Sect. 2 introduce the proposed video hashing algorithm. Section 3 presents our experimental results and performance comparisons. Finally, conclusions are given in Sect. 4.

2 Proposed Video Hashing

Our work contained three parts as shown in Fig. 1. The first step is Preprocessing, which converted an input video to a randomly normalized video. Then extract content-based feature matrices from randomly normalized video via low-rank and sparse decomposition. Finally, a short hash was compressed by 2D-DWT from the feature matrices. The detail of process in the following sections.

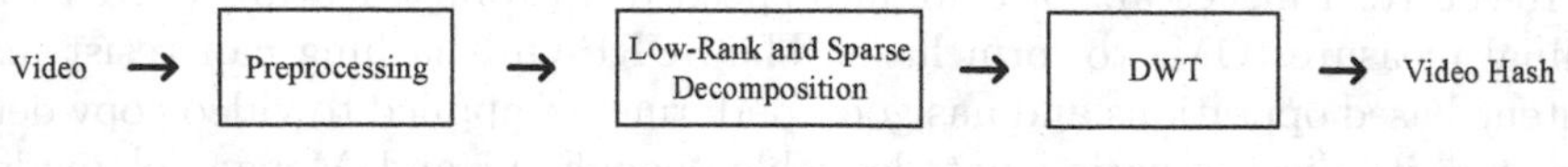

Fig. 1. Block diagram of the proposed video hashing.

2.1 Preprocessing

To make a normalized video, some operations applied to the input video. Color video is firstly should be converted to grayscale video. Then two resampling operations are used to ensure output hash with same length. It means input video is mapped to normalized video with the same resolutions and frames by two resampling operations. The first operation is temporal resampling, which map video of different frames to the same number of frames. Specifically, the pixels of all frames at the same position can be viewed as orderly tubes. Next the linear interpolation applied to resize the pixel of tube to a properly length M and smoothed by a Gaussian low-pass filter with kernel size $1 \times f$. The second operation is spatio resampling, which resize videos of different size to the same resolution. Each frame converted to a square size $M \times M$ by the bi-cubic linear interpolation. After this operation of process, a normalized video $\mathbf{V}_{\mathbf{norm}}^{M\times M\times M}$ of M frames with size $M \times M$ is obtained.

To ensure security of hash generated, a useful technique logistic map [13] applied to construct a randomly normalized video. Logistic map is a well-known chaotic system, it can be define as following equation:

$$x_{i+1} = rx_i(1 - x_i), \tag{1}$$

where r and x_0 are control parameters. When $r \in (3.57, 4)$ and $x_0 \in (0, 1)$, the logistic map can reach a chaotic state. In our work, we select $r = 3.85$ and take the initial value x_0 as a key. A randomly initial sequence $\mathbf{x} = \{x_1, x_2, \dots x_M\}$ is obtained by use a pseudo-random generator controlled with a key k_1 and a randomly iteratively times sequence $\mathbf{y} = \{y_1, y_2, \dots y_M\}$ is conducted by use a pseudo-random generator controlled with a key k_2. Then a chaotic sequence $\mathbf{u} = \{u_1, u_2, \dots u_M\}$ with M numbers are generated, u_i is calculated by x_i iteration y_i times. Next, the sequence $\mathbf{u}$ is further map to a new sequence $\mathbf{g}$, which according to relative positional of sequence $\mathbf{u}$ by there element values orders. For example, the minimum element in $\mathbf{u}$ corresponds to the relative position 1 and maximum element in $\mathbf{u}$ corresponds to the relative position M.

$$\mathbf{g} = \{g_1, g_2, \cdots g_M\}. \tag{2}$$

It observed that the generated sequence $\mathbf{g}$ is random. Finally, a randomly normalized video $\mathbf{V}_{\mathbf{rand}}^{M\times M\times M}$ is rearranged from $\mathbf{V}_{\mathbf{norm}}^{M\times M\times M}$ by using relative positional sequence. Note that, $\mathbf{g}$ is a chaotic sequence, it difficult to guess the correctly number of $\mathbf{g}$ without knowledge the key values k_1 and k_2. Key dependence will be validated in experimental phase.

2.2 Low-Rank and Sparse Decomposition

Low-rank and sparse decomposition is a well-known image representation method [14]. In past decades, it has been used in many image fields (e.g., Biomedical image and Remote sensing satellite image) and successful applied to many applications [15] such as image classification, image denoising and so on. $\mathbf{I} \in \mathbb{R}^{M\times M}$ represented an image with size $M \times M$. Low-rank and sparse decomposition results of $\mathbf{I}$ are two matrices $\mathbf{L} \in \mathbb{R}^{M\times M}$ and $\mathbf{S} \in \mathbb{R}^{M\times M}$. Figure 2 illustrates a sample frame of video with low-rank and decomposition. Figure 2(a) is the low-rank component which reflected the principle structures of $\mathbf{I}$ and Fig. 2(b) is the sparse component which represented salient components of $\mathbf{I}$. They can be used represent $\mathbf{I}$ as following:

$$\begin{aligned} &\min_{\mathbf{L},\mathbf{S}} \mathbf{Rank}(\mathbf{L}) + \lambda \left\| \mathbf{S} \right\|_0 \\ &s.t.\ \mathbf{I} = \mathbf{L} + \mathbf{S}, \end{aligned} \tag{3}$$

where $\left\|\cdot\right\|_0$ denotes the l_0 norm of a matrix and λ denotes a consist. This constrained convex minimization problem can be solved [16] by a well-known method called inexact augmented Lagrange multipliers (IALM).

In this work, feature extracted can be viewed as mining content-based data from a randomly normalized video. Low-rank matrix $\mathbf{L}$ is selected as a content-based feature matrix, and video hash is constructed by using these feature matrices. As the low-rank matrix $\mathbf{L}$ can reflect the principle structures of original image $\mathbf{I}$, we exploits each frame of $\mathbf{V}_{\mathbf{rand}}^{M\times M\times M}$ to construct hash, thus good discrimination is achieved.

(a)low-rank component (b)sparse component

Fig. 2. A sample frame of video with low-rank and sparse decomposition.

2.3 DWT

DWT is a useful technique [17] of image processing and a single-level 2-D DWT can decompose an input image into four sub-bands as Fig. 3 LL sub-band, LH sub-band, HL sub-band and HH sub-band, where LL sub-band is a low frequency sub-band and other three sub-bands are high frequency sub-bands. In this work, we select LL sub-band for representation to derive a short code based on next two considerations: the first consideration is that some content-preserving operations, such as low-pass filtering and noise contamination, have slight influence on the low frequency sub-band coefficients; The other consideration is that DWT coefficients in the LL sub-band are approximation coefficients of the feature matrix and only reserved a quarter coefficients. This two good properties are advanced our hash more robustness and help our hash derive to a short code with content-based features.

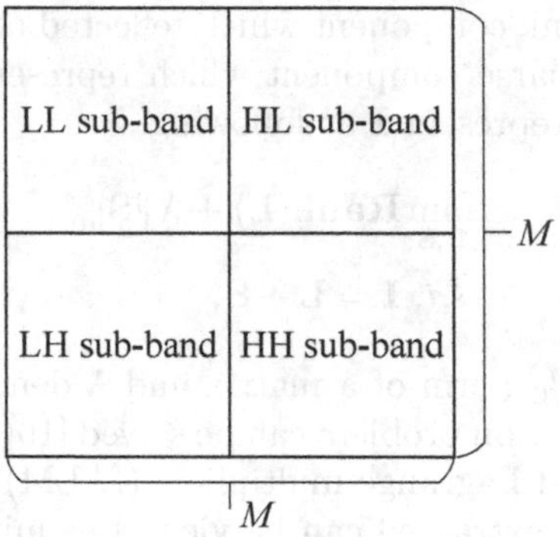

Fig. 3. Schematic diagram of 2D-DWT.

2.4 Illustrating Our Algorithm

Step1: An input video is first converted to a normalized video $\mathbf{V}_{\mathbf{norm}}^{M\times M\times M}$ with twice resampling operations, and then further generated to a $\mathbf{V}_{\mathbf{rand}}^{M\times M\times M}$ by using relative position sequence which reference to a chaotic sequence **g**.
Step2: Apply low-rank and sparse decomposition to each frame of $\mathbf{V}_{\mathbf{rand}}^{M\times M\times M}$, extract low-rank matrix **L** as the content-based feature matrices for each frame.
Step3: Apply 2D-DWT for each frame of video, and collect the mean of all LL sub-band coefficients to form a compact short string **s**. Clearly, the **s** has M elements in total. Next, the elements of **s** is quantized by the below rule:

$$h(i) = \begin{cases} 1 & \text{If s(i) < s(i+1)} \\ 0 & \text{Otherwise,} \end{cases} \qquad i = 1, 2, ..., M, \tag{4}$$

where s(i) is the i-th elements of $\mathbf{s}$. Consequently, our hash is generated as follows:

$$\mathbf{h} = [h(1), h(2), ..., h(M)]. \tag{5}$$

2.5 Hash Similarity

Since our hash is bit string, the Hamming distance [18] is taken to evaluate the degree of similar between two hashes. Suppose $\mathbf{V}_1$ and $\mathbf{V}_2$ represents two different videos and $\mathbf{h}_1$ and $\mathbf{h}_2$ represents their corresponding two hashes respectively. Hamming distance between two hashes can be computed as following equation:

$$d_{\mathbf{H}}(\mathbf{h}_1, \mathbf{h}_2) = \sum_{i=1}^{M} |h_1(i) - h_2(i)|. \tag{6}$$

Where the i-th element of the $\mathbf{h}_1$ and $\mathbf{h}_2$ are h_1(i) and h_2(i) respectively, and M represents the length of hash. Obviously, the smaller Hamming distance between two hashes, their corresponding video are more similar. A pre-determined threshold T can be used to evaluate the similarity of two videos. In other word, two videos can be judged as visually similar video when $d_{\mathbf{H}} \leq T$. Otherwise two videos can be considered as visually different videos.

3 Experimental Results

In the following experiments, the used parameters of our hashing are as follows: The randomly normalized video is 128×128×128; A Gaussian low-pass filter with kernel size is 1×20; Therefore, the length of our hash is 128 bits. The remainder of section is that robustness experiment is conducted in Sect. 3.1 and discrimination discussed in Sect. 3.2; Key dependence and performance comparison validated in Sects. 3.3 and 3.4.

3.1 Robustness

Video dataset from The open video project [19], 76 videos from the item called "University of Maryland HCIL Open House Video Reports". Attacked these videos by normal content-preserving operations with different parameters, and calculated similarities between hashes of the original and their attacked videos. Some typical test videos selected open databases [19,20] represented as Fig. 4. Detail of these operations setting as following: Brightness adjustment with Photoshop's scale are $-20, -15, ..., 20$; 3×3 Gaussian low-pass filtering with Standard deviation are $0.1, 0.2, ..., 1$; Salt and pepper noise of Density are $0.001, 0.002, ..., 0.01$; AWGN of signal noise ratio are $1, 2, ..., 6$; Bit rate for MPEG-2 are $100, 200, ..., 1000$; The number of frame dropping are $5, 10, ..., 20$; Ratio of frame scaling are $0.8, 0.85, ..., 1.2$ and rotation angle are $-2, -1, .., 2$. For each attack, different parameters are used and thus every original video has 60 similar videos. Figure 5 presents the mean Hamming distance under different

Fig. 4. Some typical test videos selected open databases.

attacks, where the x-axis is the used parameter and the y-axis is the Hamming distance. It is observed that most mean value smaller than 6 except operation of Rotation and mean value of Rotation is not more than 15. This imply that the threshold is selected as $T = 15$, our hash is robust to most digital operations in Fig. 5.

3.2 Discrimination

To validate the discrimination, 200 different videos were collected from Free Reef Video Clip Database [20]. We extracted hashes for each video, calculate Hamming distances between its original hash and the hashes of other 199 videos. Thus, the pair of $200 \times 199/2 = 19900$ Hamming distances are obtained. Figure 6 showed the minimum Hamming distance between two different videos are 16 and the maximum are 89. In addition, the mean and standard deviation are 38.52 and 8.06, respectively. If we set the threshold as 35, there are 0.003% pairs of different videos are falsely considered as visually similar videos.

3.3 Key Dependence

To validate our hash security, we also take the videos of robustness and discrimination test database as test videos. Set different secret key groups k_1 and k_2 of logistic map to generate hashes of every test video and calculate Hamming distance between the hashes of test video. It is observed that all Hamming distance are big. For space limitation, a typical example is illustrated. Figure 7 presents Hamming distances between hashes of the test video controlled by 1000 different key groups (k_1, k_2), where the x-axis is the index of the wrong keys and the y-axis is the Hamming distance. Clearly, the Hamming distance of wrong keys distributed from 17 to 89. Which is bigger than the above-mentioned threshold $T = 15$. This results illustrated that our hashing is key-dependent.

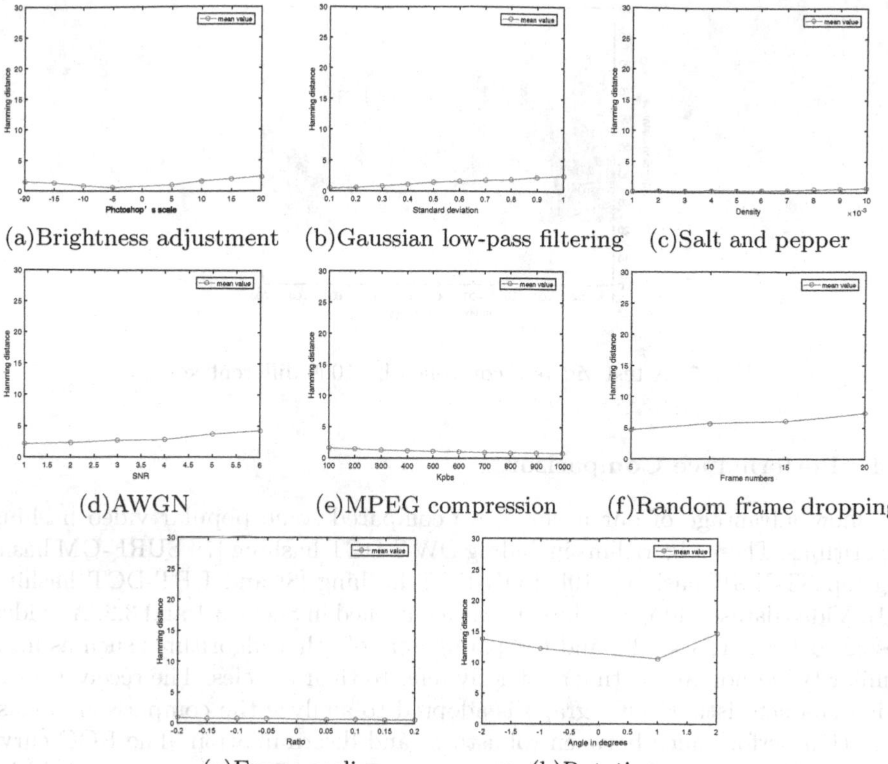

(a)Brightness adjustment (b)Gaussian low-pass filtering (c)Salt and pepper

(d)AWGN (e)MPEG compression (f)Random frame dropping

(g)Frame scaling (h)Rotation

Fig. 5. Robustness test under different attacks.

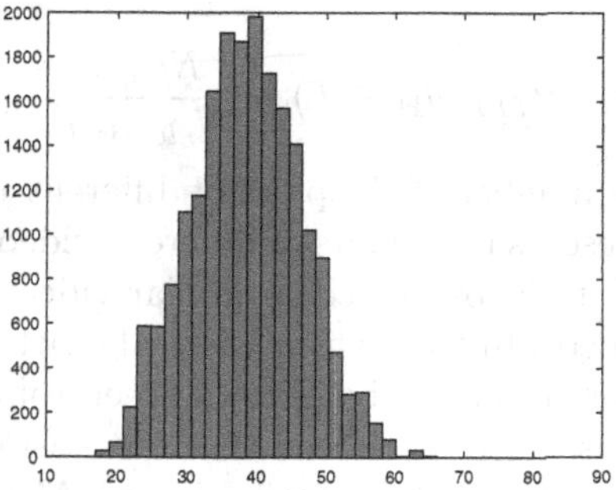

Fig. 6. Hash distance distribution of different videos.

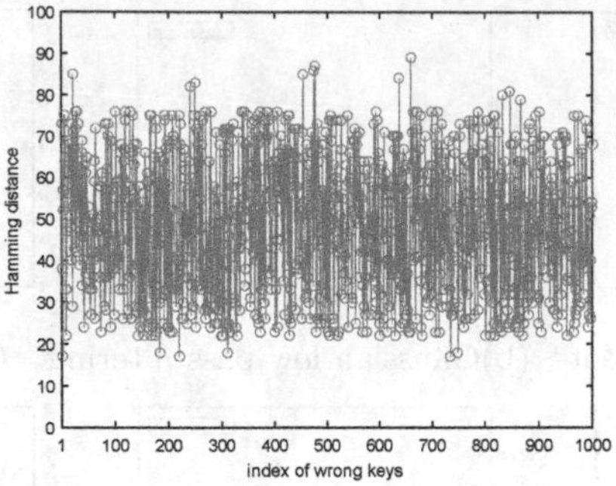

Fig. 7. A test video of controlled by 1000 different keys.

3.4 Performance Comparison

To show advantage of our hashing, we compared some popular video hashing algorithms. These algorithms including DWT-DCT hashing [7], SURF-OM hashing [5], ST-NMF hashing [10], EOH-DCT hashing [8] and RPT-DCT hashing [11]. Video dataset adopted the same as mentioned in Sects. 3.1 and 3.2. All video resize to $128 \times 128 \times 128$, and the parameters of other algorithms such as hash similarity method are setting as strictly refer to their articles. The receiver operating characteristic (ROC) graph is adopted to analyze the comparison of classification performance between robustness and discrimination. The ROC curve is formed by a set of point pairs P_{FPR} and P_{TPR}. P_{FPR} represents the false positive rate (FPR) and P_{TPR} represents the true positive rate (TPR).

$$P_{FPR}(d_{\mathbf{H}} \leq T) = \frac{N_{similar}}{N_{different}} \tag{7}$$

$$P_{TPR}(d_{\mathbf{H}} \leq T) = \frac{N_{same}}{N_{identical}}, \tag{8}$$

where $N_{similar}$ presents number of the pairs of different videos judged as similar videos and $N_{different}$ presents total pairs of different videos; N_{same} presents number of the pairs of similar videos judged as similar videos and $N_{identical}$ presents total pairs of similar videos; In fact, which video algorithm of ROC much nearby the left-top indicate more desirable balance between robustness and discrimination. The results show as Fig. 8, it cleared that our hashing is more closed ROC of left-top. The range of AUC is [0, 1], and a bigger AUC means a better classification performance. Here, the AUCs of five hashing was calculated as follows: DWT-DCT hashing is 0.95141; SURF-OM hashing is 0.90329; ST-NMF hashing is 0.97136; EOH-DCT hashing is 0.9686; RPT-DCT is 0.97173 and our hashing is 0.99546. The results illustrated that our hashing more desirable classification between robustness and discrimination than the other five algorithms.

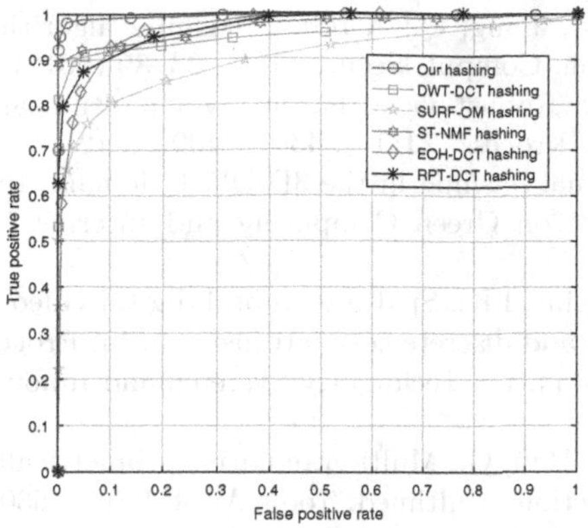

Fig. 8. ROC curve among comparison algorithms.

4 Conclusions

We have designed a novel video hashing algorithm with low-rank decomposition and DWT with high accuracy which achieve a desirable balance between robustness and discrimination. The main innovation of our work is use of low-rank decomposition and DWT to derived a video hash. Logistic map applied to constructed a randomly normalized video, which ensure the security of hash generated. Content-based feature matrices extract from a randomly normalized video with low-rank and sparse decomposition. Since low-rank component can reflect the principle structures of original content, which provides our hash good discrimination. Then feature matrices compressed with 2D-DWT of LL sub-band also provides our hash desirable robustness and derive to a short compact code. Experiments conducted our hashing is robust against many content-based operations and outperform some popular video algorithms.

Acknowledgements. This work was partially supported by the National Natural Science Foundation of China NSFC (U1636101, U1736211, U1636219), the National Key Research Development Program of China (2016QY01W0200).

References

1. Ye, D., et al.: Improved ordinary measure and image entropy theory based intelligent copy detection method. Int. J. Comput. Intell. Syst. **4**(5), 777–787 (2011)
2. Qin, C., Chang, C., Chiu, Y.: A novel joint data-hiding and compression scheme based on SMVQ and image inpainting. IEEE Trans. Image Process. **23**(3), 969–978 (2014)
3. Ye, D., et al.: Scalable content authentication in H.264/SVC video using perceptual hashing based on Dempster-Shafer theory. Int. J. Comput. Intell. Syst. **5**(5), 953–963 (2012)
4. Qin, C., et al.: Separable reversible data hiding in encrypted images via adaptive embedding strategy with block selection. Sig. Process. **153**, 109–122 (2018)

5. Yang, G., Chen, N., Jiang, Q.: A robust hashing algorithm based on SURF for video copy detection. Comput. Secur. **31**(1), 33–39 (2012)
6. Li, M., Monga, V.: Robust video hashing via multilinear subspace projections. IEEE Trans. Image Process. **21**(10), 4397–4409 (2012)
7. Saikia, N.: Perceptual hashing in the 3D-DWT domain. In: Proceedings of International Conference on Green Computing and Internet of Things, pp. 694–698 (2015)
8. Setyawan, I., Timotius, I.K.: Spatio-temporal digital video hashing using edge orientation histogram and discrete cosine transform. In: Proceedings of International Conference on Information Technology Systems and Innovation (ICITSI), pp. 24–27 (2015)
9. Chen, H., Yan, W., Han, G.: Multi-granularity geometrically robust video hashing for tampering detection. Multimed. Tools Appl. **77**(5), 5303–5321 (2017)
10. Nie, X., et al.: Spherical torus-based video hashing for near-duplicate video detection. Sci. China Inf. Sci. **59**(5), 1–3 (2016)
11. Sandeep, R., Saksham, S., Prabin, K.B.: Perceptual video hashing using 3D-radial projection technique. In: Proceedings of International Conference on Signal Processing, Communication and Networking, pp. 1–6 (2017)
12. Tang, Z., et al.: Video hashing with DCT and NMF. Comput. J., Oxford (2019). https://doi.org/10.1093/comjnl/bxz060
13. Pareek, N.K., Patidar, V., Sud, K.K.: Image encryption using chaotic logistic map. Image Vis. Comput. **24**(9), 926–934 (2006)
14. Liu, Y., et al.: Structure-constrained low-rank and partial sparse representation for image classification. In: Proceedings of International Conference on Image Processing, Communication and Networking, pp. 5222–5226 (2014)
15. Xiong, F., Zhou, J., Qian, Y.: Hyperspectral imagery denoising via reweighed sparse low-rank nonnegative tensor factorization. In: Proceedings of International Conference on Image Processing, pp. 3219–3223 (2018)
16. Lin, Z., et al.: The augmented Lagrange multiplier method for exact recovery of corrupted low-rank matrices. UIUC, UILUENG-09-2215 (2009)
17. Tang, Z., et al.: Perceptual image hashing with weighted DWT features for reduced-reference image quality assessment. Comput. J. **61**(11), 1695–1709 (2018)
18. Tang, Z., et al.: Robust image hashing with tensor decomposition. IEEE Trans. Knowl. Data Eng. **31**(3), 549–560 (2019)
19. The open video project. http://www.open-video.org/. Accessed 12 May 2018
20. ReefVid: Free Reef Video Clip Database. http://www.reefvid.org/. Accessed 16 July 2018

HMM-Based Person Re-identification in Large-Scale Open Scenario

Dongyang Li[1,2], Ruimin Hu[1,2], Wenxin Huang[1,2], Xiaochen Wang[1,2](✉), Dengshi Li[1,3], and Fei Zheng[4]

[1] National Engineering Research Center for Multimedia Software, School of Computer Science, Wuhan University, Wuhan, China
{dongyang.li,hrm,wenxin.huang,clowang}@whu.edu.cn
[2] Hubei Key Laboratory of Multimedia and Network Communication Engineering, Wuhan University, Wuhan, China
[3] School of Mathematics and Computer, Jianghan University, Wuhan, China
reallds@126.com
[4] China General Technology Research Institute, Beijing, China
lyzhengfei@163.com

Abstract. This paper aims to tackle person re-identification (person re-ID) in large-scale open scenario, which differs from the conventional person re-ID tasks but is significant for some real suspect investigation cases. In the large-scale open scenario, the image background and person appearance may change immensely. There are a large number of irrelevant pedestrians appearing in the urban surveillance systems, some of which may have very similar appearance with the target person. Existing methods utilize only surveillance video information, which can not solve the problem well due to above challenges. In this paper, we explore that pedestrians' paths from multiple spaces (such as surveillance space and geospatial space) are matched due to temporal-spatial consistency. Moreover, people have their unique behavior path due to the differences of individual behavioral. Inspired by these two observations, we propose to use the association relationship of paths from surveillance space and geospatial space to solve the person re-ID in large-scale open scenario. A Hidden Markov Model based Path Association(HMM-PA) framework is presented to jointly analyze image path and geospatial path. In addition, according to our research scenario, we manually annotate path description on two large-scale public re-ID datasets, termed as Duke-PDD and Market-PDD. Comprehensive experiments on these two datasets show proposed HMM-PA outperforms the state-of-art methods.

Keywords: Person re-identification · Path Association · Hidden Markov Model · Dynamic programming

1 Introduction

Person re-identification (re-ID) aims to retrieve the same person across non-overlapping camera views, which plays an important role in public security applications [1–3]. In some real criminal cases, retrieving target person in a large-scale

Y. M. Ro et al. (Eds.): MMM 2020, LNCS 11961, pp. 813–825, 2020.
https://doi.org/10.1007/978-3-030-37731-1_66

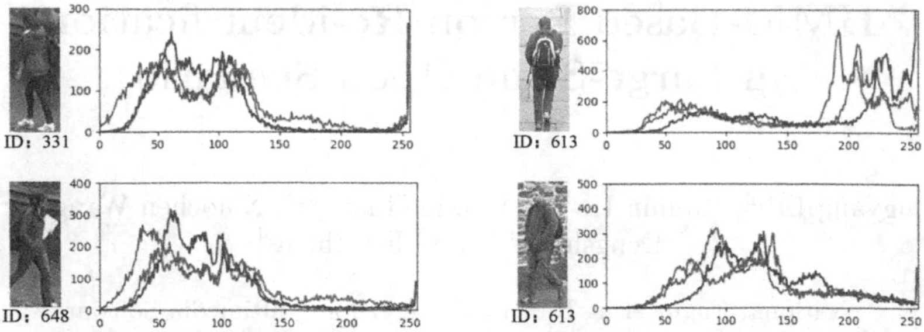

Fig. 1. Challenges of appearance based approaches. (a) shows different persons may have very similar appearance due to the similar clothes; (b) shows the same person may have different appearance features due to background clutter and posture variance.

search open scenario is demanded. Such large-scale open scenario has at least the following characteristics: (i) The surveillance camera network has a wide coverage, which causes the great change of the image background; (ii) Surveillance video has a long time span, and the appearance of persons changes greatly due to clothing and posture variance; (iii) The search scenario contains a large number of irrelevant persons, some of which may have very similar appearance with the target person. Therefore, person re-ID in a large-scale open scenario is extremely challenging, which strongly motivates us to solve this problem in this paper.

The majority of current person re-ID methods only utilize surveillance video, consisting of appearance based methods and temporal-spatial based methods. Appearance based methods [4–9] search for the target person according to the similarity ranking of visual features. As Fig. 1 shows, different persons may have very similar features due to the similar clothes, while the same person in different environments may have various appearance features. Therefore, methods that only focus on appearance features can not solve person re-ID problem well due to illumination, background clutter, posture variance, etc. Other temporal-spatial based methods [10–13] focus on the transition patterns between pairs of cameras, neglecting the strong connection of temporal-spatial data and visual data. In addition, in the case of a long time span, the same person may repeatedly appear under the same camera, which leads to a large error in expression of temporal-spatial transition pattern.

In real environment, people have multiple identity paths (such as image path and geospatial path) in multiple spaces, and their multiple identity paths complement each other in multiple spaces due to temporal-spatial consistency. As shown in Fig. 2, the target person's geospatial path captured by mobile device matches image path captured by the camera network. On the other hand, each person has a unique behavioral path due to the differences in human behavior. As Fig. 2(a) shows, each person has own geospatial due to their behavior differences. Based on these two observations, we propose to use the association

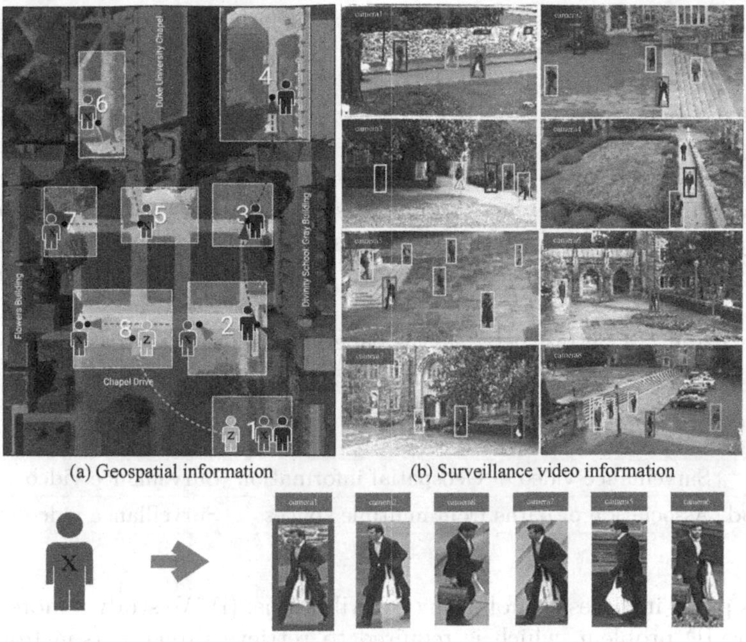

(a) Geospatial information (b) Surveillance video information

(c) Retrieved image sequence

Fig. 2. An sample of person re-ID in large-scale open scenario. (a) shows there are 3 possible suspects in the crime scene, and only one is the target person. Each person's geospatial path is recorded by the mobile device and the geospatial path of the target person is already known (the red dotted line). (b) shows the surveillance video information, including all pedestrian images of both the target person and irrelevant persons. (c) shows the images which are retrieved by combining surveillance video information and geospatial information. (Color figure online)

relationship between geospatial path and image path to solve the person re-ID in large-scale open scenario. This paper mainly focuses on the study of finding image path of the target person on a known geospatial path. Since the irrelevant people may have higher association probability (local probability) than target person under a certain monitoring, we calculate the global probability over the entire geospatial path to search image path of the target person. Specifically, a Hidden Markov Model based Path Association (HMM-PA) framework is proposed. As shown in Fig. 3, an appearance network is firstly pretrained for visual feature representation. Then Hidden Markov Model of image path on the known geospatial path is established with the trained network. Finally, the idea of dynamic programming is used to retrieve images of the target person under each camera on the known geospatial path and identify the target person at the beginning of the geospatial path.

The differences of this paper and conventional researches are summarized in Table 1, and further explanations are as follows: (i) Previous researches only focus on matching target person in small-scale search scenario, while we concentrate on a large-scale open scenario, under which the gallery set consists a large number of irrelevant people, and the image background and person posture may change extremely; (ii) Previous researches only utilize surveillance video while we exploit geospatial information besides surveillance video; (iii) Traditional person re-ID methods [3,9,14,15] regard person re-ID as a ranking problem and solve it by measuring the differences among visual features. We exploit association relationship of paths from multiple spaces, and retrieve the target person by measuring the similarity of the image path and geospatial path from two spaces.

Table 1. Contrast between this paper and conventional researches

	Our framework	Conventional researches
Scene	Large-scale	Small-scale
Data	Surveillance video + Geospatial information	Surveillance video
Method	Association of paths from multiple spaces	Surveillance video analysis

This paper includes the following contributions: (i) We study a more realistic person re-ID problem, which is required to retrieve target person from large-scale open scenario; (ii) To support this research, we manually annotate path description on two large-scale public person re-ID datasets according to their spatial and temporal label; (iii) We propose a Hidden Markov Model based Path Association (HMM-PA) framework to establish association of image path and geospatial path from multiple spaces, and massive experiments show the effectiveness of our method on these two annotated datasets.

2 Related Work

Appearance Based. Deep learning methods [4–9] based on appearance are proposed recent years. Xiao *et al.* [16] conducted Domain Guided Dropout to train the classification model from multiple domains. Huang *et al.* [5] developed Dense Convolutional Network (DenseNet) to connect any two layers in a block, which enhanced transmission and utilization of features outputted from each layer. Zhang *et al.* [17] developed AlignedReID to find optimal matching of local features by dynamic programming when the global feature can not accurately distinguish persons. Qian *et al.* [18] proposed Multi-scale Deep Learning Architectures to learn feature representation from different image scales. Sun *et al.* [19] conducted Part-based Convolutional Baseline (PCB) to learn part-level features and then discuss better way to combine each part.

Temporal-Spatial Based. Recent researches utilized new elements [20–22] besides visual information such as temporal-spatial information [10–13] in person re-ID. Specifically, Lian *et al.* [10] formulated a temporal-spatial probabilistic model consists the matched between the exit field view (FOV) of a camera and the entry FOV of another camera. Huang *et al.* [11] utilized camera relations and temporal-spatial gaps between two cameras to narrow the search space and optimize the result of visual classifier. Lv *et al.* [13] combined transition pattern with visual classifier to conduct an iterative co-train procedure to promote each other. In large-scale open scenario, it is difficult to obtain the temporal-spatial transition pattern due to the large time span and the dependence on visual information. Therefore, these kind of approaches can not solve our problem.

3 The Proposed Method

See Fig. 3.

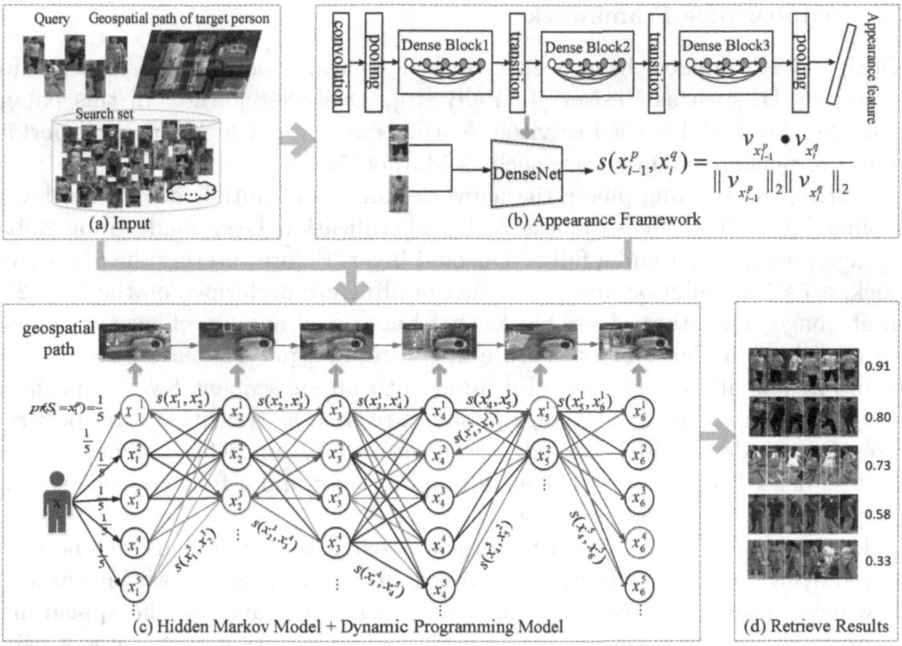

Fig. 3. Framework of proposed HMM-PA. (a) shows the input information; (b) shows the appearance framework; (c) shows hidden markov model and dynamic programming model; (d) shows the retrieve results.

3.1 Problem Definition

This section gives a brief definition of person re-ID in large-scale open scenario. We consider a geospatial path set $T = \{T_k | 1 \leq k \leq M\}$ and a camera network $C = \{c_j | 1 \leq j \leq N\}$. Here M is the number of geospatial paths and N represents the number of cameras in the camera network.

For each geospatial path $T_k \in T$, we have $T_k = \{i - c_j | 1 \leq i \leq n, 1 \leq j \leq N\}$. Here $1 - c_j$ denotes the camera at the beginning of the path, and the n

elements represent all cameras on T_k. For each element $i - c_j \in T_k$, we have $i - c_j = \{x_i^p | 1 \leq p \leq u\}$. Here x_i^p is image of the $p - th$ object captured by the $i - th$ camera on T_k, and u denotes the number of objects captured by $i - c_j$. Then the problem can be described as following equation:

$$\{x_i^\theta | 1 \leq i \leq n\} :\rightarrow F(T_\sigma, C) \tag{1}$$

Equation (1) indicates when given the geospatial path of target person and all images of the camera network, we will retrieve the images of the target person under each camera on the geospatial path. Figure 2 shows a sample of this research.

3.2 Appearance Framework

Multiple CNN models have been proposed to learn visual representation for person re-ID, such as ResNet [4], PCB [19], DenseNet [5] etc. In this paper, DenseNet [5] model is used as visual feature extractor, which has good performance in person re-ID datasets such as Market1501.

During the training phase, the network consists of initial convolution layer, pooling layer, three dense blocks and a classification layer made by a global average pooling layer and a fully-connected layer. Before entering the first dense block, a $7 * 7$ convolution and a $3 * 3$ max pooling are performed on the $224 * 224$ input image. Then three dense blocks that have equal number of layers are used. For each layer in dense block, feature-maps from all previous layers are used as its input, and its feature-map also input into all subsequent layers. Specially, $1 * 1$ convolution and $2 * 2$ average pooling are used as transition layer between two adjacent dense blocks to reduce the number of input feature-maps. After the last dense block, a global average pooling layer and a fully connected layer are performed to achieve classification.

In the testing phase, visual features are extracted from DenseNet network by removing its fully-connected. As shown in Fig. 3(b), given two images x_{i-1}^p x_i^q which represent different persons' image from two cameras, the appearance framework extracts their visual features vectors, denoting $\boldsymbol{v}_{x_{i-1}^p}$, $\boldsymbol{v}_{x_i^q}$. Cosine distance is used as similarity score between two images:

$$s(\boldsymbol{v}_{x_{i-1}^p}, \boldsymbol{v}_{x_i^q}) = \frac{\boldsymbol{v}_{x_{i-1}^p} \cdot \boldsymbol{v}_{x_i^q}}{\left\| \boldsymbol{v}_{x_{i-1}^p} \right\|_2 \left\| \boldsymbol{v}_{x_i^q} \right\|_2} \tag{2}$$

3.3 Hidden Markov Model of Image Path

HMM is a probabilistic model about time series, which describes the process of generating unobservable state random sequence from Markov chain and regenerating observable random sequence from state sequence. In this paper, the essence of this problem is to find hidden image path under the observable geospatial path, which motivates us to consider that person re-ID in large-scale open scenario is a decoding problem in HMM.

Formally, the HMM of images can be denoted by triples:

$$\lambda = (A, B, \pi) \tag{3}$$

Here A is the set of transition probability matrices, B represents the observation probability matrix, and π means initial probability vector.

A in Eq. (3) is denoted by the following formula:

$$A = \{[a_{pq}]_\gamma | 1 \leq \gamma \leq n - 1\} \tag{4}$$

Here A is composed of $n - 1$ transition probability matrices, which reflects the probability of transmission between any image pairs under two adjacent cameras. γ means the number of adjacent camera pairs, and p, q represent index of two images from two cameras. Here a_{pq} can be computed via the following equation:

$$a_{pq} = pr(S_i = x_i^q | S_{i-1} = x_{i-1}^p) \tag{5}$$

Equation (5) indicates the transition probability which means the current image is x_i^q on condition that the last image is x_{x-1}^p. Here the transfer probability is expressed by similarity score between images, which can be calculated with the base network introduced in Sect. 3.2. In other words, Eq. (5) also means the similarity score between $p - th$ image in $(i + 1) - c_j$ and $q - th$ image in $i - c_j$ on the geospatial path.

B in Eq. (3) is expressed by the following formula:

$$B = [Pr(i - c_j | S_i = x_i^q)] \tag{6}$$

$$Pr(i - c_j | S_i = x_i^q) = \begin{cases} 1, if\ x_i^q\ is\ captured\ by\ c_j \\ 0, otherwise \end{cases} \tag{7}$$

Equation (6) indicates the probability of generating the observation point $i - c_j$ on condition that the current image is x_i^q. As illustrated in Eq. (7), if image x_i^q is captured by c_j, $Pr(i - c_j | S_i = x_i^q)$ is equal to 1, otherwise $Pr(i - c_j | S_i = x_i^q)$ is equal to 0.

π in Eq. (3) is a denoted as $\pi = \{\pi_t | 1 \leq t \leq m\}$, which contains the initial probability of each image at the first camera. Here m is the number of objects in the first camera. The initial probability of each object is the same before computing, denoted as $\pi_t = \frac{1}{m}$.

3.4 Dynamic Programming Model

As represented in the last section, the HMM model of image path $\lambda = (A, B, \pi)$ is established with the appearance framework. To find the optimal image path, dynamic programming model is used in this step.

Formally, images to be retrieved can be denoted as following:

$$\{x_i^\theta | 1 \leq i \leq n\} :\rightarrow V(\lambda = (A, B, \pi), T_k) \tag{8}$$

Here $\lambda = (A, B, \pi)$ represent HMM established in Sect. 3.3. T_k is the geospatial path of target person. $\{x_i^{\theta}|1 \leq i \leq n\}$ represent images of the target person under each camera on the geospatial path.

From the second camera, the maximum probability of each image until current camera can be calculated recursively via Eqs. (9) and (10).

$$\delta_i(q) = \max_{1 \leq p \leq u} [\delta_{i-1}(p) a_{x_{i-1}^p x_i^q}] Pr(i - c_j | S_i = x_i^q), 1 \leq q \leq v \tag{9}$$

$$\phi_i(q) = \underset{1 \leq p \leq u}{argmax} [\delta_{i-1}(p) a_{x_{i-1}^p x_i^q}], 1 \leq q \leq v \tag{10}$$

Here $\delta_i(q)$ represents the maximum probability of the image path up to the image x_i^q, and $\phi_i(q)$ represents the image index of this maximum probability path under the last camera. p, q mean image index in $(i-1)-th$ camera and $i-th$ camera. Specially, at the first camera, we have $\delta_1(q) = \frac{1}{m} Pr(1 - c_j | S_1 = x_1^q)$ and $\phi_1(q) = 0$.

After traversing the whole path, the optimal image path is got by backtracking.

$$index_i = \phi_{i+1}(index_{i+1}), i = n-1, n-2, ..., 1 \tag{11}$$

$$\{x_i^{\theta}|1 \leq i \leq n\} = \{x_i^{index_i}|1 \leq i \leq n\} \tag{12}$$

Where $index_i$ represents image index under each camera, and x_i^{θ} is the images retrieved. Specially, $index_n = argmax[\delta_n(q)]$.

4 Experiment

4.1 Experimental Settings

Datasets. Since there is no existing person re-ID datasets with both surveillance video information and geospatial information, we manually annotate path

(a)An sample of Duke-TDD

(b) An sample of Market-TDD

Fig. 4. Samples of Duke-PDD and Market-PDD. (a) shows an example of a Duke-PDD dataset and (b) shows an sample of Market-PDD dataset. Each row illustrates images which are captured by 4 cameras. Images in the same blue bounding box are captured by the same camera in the time range of target people's geospatial path. The person in red bounding box is the target object. (Color figure online) description on two large-scale datasets (DukeMTMC-reID [23] and Market1501 [24]). We first select objects who pass through more than 3 cameras in surveillance system. Each object satisfying the condition is regarded as a target person and the connection of the cameras which they pass through is regarded as their geospatial path. For each target person, we annotate image information in corresponding large-scale open scenario. In the whole surveillance system, all images captured in the time range of target person's path are selected to make up the gallery set of corresponding open scenario. We rename these two datasets as Duke Path Description Dataset (Duke-PDD) and Market1501 Path Description Dataset (Market-PDD). Samples of these two datasets are shown in Fig. 4.

Duke-PDD contains 16 geospatial paths and 624 images of 357 identities captured by 8 cameras. The training set contains 347 images of 194 identities appearing on 8 geospatial paths. The test set is divided into 8 groups according to the number of target persons. Each group contains the geospatial path of the target person and all the images in camera network. The entire test set shared 277 images of 163 identities appearing on 8 geographic paths.

Market-PDD contains 147 geospatial paths and 12,722 images of 641 identities captured by 6 cameras. All images are automatically detected with the Deformable Part Model (DPM) [25]. Training set contains 5,653 images of 384 identities from 71 geospatial paths. Testing set is divided into 76 groups, containing 7,069 images of 257 identities and geospatial paths.

Evaluation Metrics. Cumulative Matching Characteristic (CMC) is extensively used to evaluate the performance of person re-ID algorithm. The rank-n hit rate in CMC curve indicates the probability of correct result in the top-n position of search ranking. The other evaluation metric is the mean average precision (mAP), which measures the performance of our approach in all categories.

4.2 Comparison to the State-of-Art

We compare our approach with the state-of-art methods on the Duke-PDD and Market-PDD, and discuss the performance of our approach with different appearance framework on these two datasets. PCB [19], ResNet [4], DenseNet [5] are methods utilizing only surveillance video. They select the most similar images

Table 2. Performance comparisons to the state-of-art methods on Duke-PDD

Data source	Method	Rank-1	Rank-5	mAP
Surveillance video	PCB	25.00	–	30.00
	ResNet	0.00	–	32.50
	DenseNet	25.00	–	22.50
Multiple spaces	HMM-PA (PCB)	37.50	37.50	42.50
	HMM-PA (ResNet)	37.50	50.00	70.00
	HMM-PA (DenseNet)	**50.00**	**62.50**	**65.00**

Table 3. Performance comparisons to the state-of-art methods on Market-PDD

Data source	Method	Rank-1	Rank-5	mAP
Surveillance video	PCB	28.95	67.11	35.11
	ResNet	23.68	71.05	23.68
	DenseNet	31.58	69.74	34.78
Multiple spaces	HMM-PA (PCB)	51.32	59.21	58.90
	HMM-PA (ResNet)	56.58	64.47	67.67
	HMM-PA (DenseNet)	**60.53**	**67.11**	**68.97**

according to the similarity ranking, then connect the image path according to the time information of these images. They retrieve the target person by measuring the number of matching cameras between the image path and the geospatial path. Tables 2 and 3 illustrate re-ID results.

We discuss the results as follows: Due to the limited data of the Duke-PDD, the obtained results on the Duke-PDD is very neat. As the results show, our proposed HMM-PA achieves best performance in terms of Rank-1 recognition rate and mAP on both Duke-PDD and Market-PDD, which proves the effectiveness of the proposed approach. Since we consider the association relationship of image path and geospatial path from two different spaces, the HMM-PA (DenseNet) obtains 25% improvement in Rank-1 recognition rate and 42.5% improvement in mAP score on Duke-PDD compared with DenseNet [5] which gets best performance considering only surveillance video information. On Market-PDD, HMM-PA (DenseNet) obtains 28.95% improvement in Rank-1 recognition rate and 34.19% improvement in mAP score compared DenseNet [5]. In real investigative scenarios, the appearance of the target person may be very similar to some of irrelevant persons, causing methods only focus on surveillance video can not identify a person accurately, while HMM-PA utilizes geospatial information besides surveillance video information to overcome the problem of similar appearance

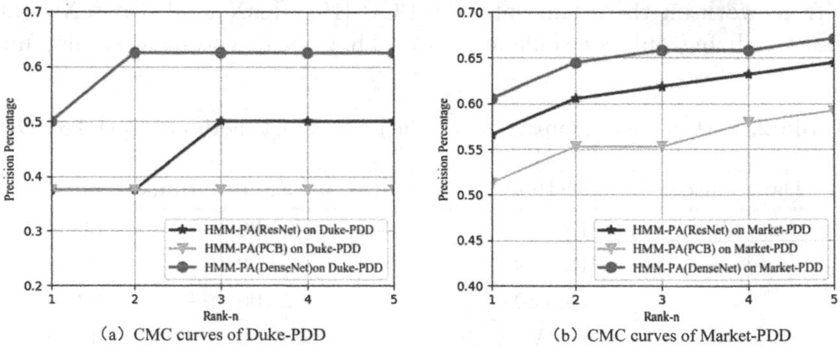

Fig. 5. CMC curves of HMM-PA (ResNet), HMM-PA (PCB) and HMM-PA (DenseNet).

between different people. Although the improvement on Rank-5 recognition rate is not obvious, HMM-PA outperforms methods which focus on only surveillance video by a large margin on Rank-1 recognition rate and mAP score. On the other hand, HMM-PA (PCB), HMM-PA (ResNet), HMM-PA (DenseNet) are both methods considering multi-spaces information. They use PCB [19], ResNet [4] and DenseNet [5] as appearance network respectively. As Fig. 5 shows, using DenseNet [5] as appearance network gets the best performance on both two datasets. Though HMM-PA (ResNet) gets higher mAP score on Duke-PDD shown in Table 2, HMM-PA (DenseNet) gets highest mAP score on Market-PDD. This suggests us that DenseNet [5] should be used as appearance network in real deployment of HMM-PA.

5 Conclusion

This paper aims to tackle person re-ID in a large-scale open scenario. Two observations are explored: Person's image path captured in surveillance video matches the geospatial path captured in geospatial. People have unique behavior path due to the individual behavior differences. On this basis, association relationship of paths from multiple spaces is utilized in this paper. In order to solve the path association from a global perspective, a Hidden Markov Model based Path Association (HMM-PA) framework is presented. In addition, two large-scale person re-ID datasets are annotated to support this research. Massive experiments conducted on these two datasets show significant improvement in accuracy compared with the state-of-art. In the future, we will conduct research on searching images multiple target people simultaneously on multiple geospatial paths.

Acknowledgement. This work was supported by National Key R&D Program of China (No. 2017YFB1002803) and National Nature Science Foundation of China (No. U1736206, No. 61701194).

References

1. Li, Z., Zhang, J., Zhang, K., Li, Z.: Visual tracking with weighted adaptive local sparse appearance model via spatio-temporal context learning. IEEE Trans. Image Process. **27**(9), 4478–4489 (2018)
2. Liu, J., Zha, Z.J., Chen, X., Wang, Z., Zhang, Y.: Dense 3D-convolutional neural network for person re-identification in videos. ACM Trans. Multimedia Comput. Commun. Appl. (TOMM) **15**(1s), 8 (2019)
3. Liu, J., et al.: Multi-scale triplet CNN for person re-identification. In: Proceedings of the 24th ACM International Conference on Multimedia, pp. 192–196. ACM (2016)
4. He, K., Zhang, X., Ren, S., Sun, J.: Deep residual learning for image recognition. In: Proceedings of the IEEE Conference on Computer Vision and Pattern Recognition, pp. 770–778 (2016)
5. Huang, G., Liu, Z., Van Der Maaten, L., Weinberger, K.Q.: Densely connected convolutional networks. In: Proceedings of the IEEE Conference on Computer Vision and Pattern Recognition, pp. 4700–4708 (2017)

6. Li, D., Chen, X., Zhang, Z., Huang, K.: Learning deep context-aware features over body and latent parts for person re-identification. In: Proceedings of the IEEE Conference on Computer Vision and Pattern Recognition, pp. 384–393 (2017)
7. Song, C., Huang, Y., Ouyang, W., Wang, L.: Mask-guided contrastive attention model for person re-identification. In: Proceedings of the IEEE Conference on Computer Vision and Pattern Recognition, pp. 1179–1188 (2018)
8. Zheng, Z., Zheng, L., Yang, Y.: A discriminatively learned CNN embedding for person reidentification. ACM Trans. Multimedia Comput. Commun. Appl. (TOMM) **14**(1), 13 (2018)
9. Wu, Y., Lin, Y., Dong, X., Yan, Y., Bian, W., Yang, Y.: Progressive learning for person re-identification with one example. IEEE Trans. Image Process. **28**(6), 2872–2881 (2019)
10. Lian, G., Lai, J., Zheng, W.S.: Spatial-temporal consistent labeling of tracked pedestrians across non-overlapping camera views. Pattern Recogn. **44**(5), 1121–1136 (2011)
11. Huang, W., et al.: Camera network based person re-identification by leveraging spatial-temporal constraint and multiple cameras relations. In: Tian, Q., Sebe, N., Qi, G.-J., Huet, B., Hong, R., Liu, X. (eds.) MMM 2016. LNCS, vol. 9516, pp. 174–186. Springer, Cham (2016). https://doi.org/10.1007/978-3-319-27671-7_15
12. Martinel, N., Foresti, G.L., Micheloni, C.: Person reidentification in a distributed camera network framework. IEEE Trans. Cybern. **47**(11), 3530–3541 (2016)
13. Lv, J., Chen, W., Li, Q., Yang, C.: Unsupervised cross-dataset person re-identification by transfer learning of spatial-temporal patterns. In: Proceedings of the IEEE Conference on Computer Vision and Pattern Recognition, pp. 7948–7956 (2018)
14. Bai, S., Tang, P., Torr, P.H., Latecki, L.J.: Re-ranking via metric fusion for object retrieval and person re-identification. In: The IEEE Conference on Computer Vision and Pattern Recognition (CVPR), June 2019
15. Li, M., Zhu, X., Gong, S.: Unsupervised tracklet person re-identification. IEEE Trans. Pattern Anal. Mach. Intell. (2019)
16. Xiao, T., Li, H., Ouyang, W., Wang, X.: Learning deep feature representations with domain guided dropout for person re-identification. In: Proceedings of the IEEE Conference on Computer Vision and Pattern Recognition, pp. 1249–1258 (2016)
17. Zhang, X., et al.: AlignedReID: surpassing human-level performance in person re-identification. arXiv preprint arXiv:1711.08184 (2017)
18. Qian, X., Fu, Y., Jiang, Y.G., Xiang, T., Xue, X.: Multi-scale deep learning architectures for person re-identification. In: Proceedings of the IEEE International Conference on Computer Vision, pp. 5399–5408 (2017)
19. Sun, Y., Zheng, L., Yang, Y., Tian, Q., Wang, S.: Beyond part models: person retrieval with refined part pooling (and a strong convolutional baseline). In: Ferrari, V., Hebert, M., Sminchisescu, C., Weiss, Y. (eds.) ECCV 2018. LNCS, vol. 11208, pp. 501–518. Springer, Cham (2018). https://doi.org/10.1007/978-3-030-01225-0_30
20. Lv, J., Lin, H., Yang, C., Yu, Z., Chen, Y., Deng, M.: Identify and trace criminal suspects in the crowd aided by fast trajectories retrieval. In: Bhowmick, S.S., Dyreson, C.E., Jensen, C.S., Lee, M.L., Muliantara, A., Thalheim, B. (eds.) DASFAA 2014. LNCS, vol. 8422, pp. 16–30. Springer, Cham (2014). https://doi.org/10.1007/978-3-319-05813-9_2

21. Li, S., Xiao, T., Li, H., Zhou, B., Yue, D., Wang, X.: Person search with natural language description. In: Proceedings of the IEEE Conference on Computer Vision and Pattern Recognition, pp. 1970–1979 (2017)
22. Niu, K., Huang, Y., Ouyang, W., Wang, L.: Improving description-based person re-identification by multi-granularity image-text alignments. arXiv preprint arXiv:1906.09610 (2019)
23. Zheng, Z., Zheng, L., Yang, Y.: Unlabeled samples generated by GAN improve the person re-identification baseline in vitro. In: Proceedings of the IEEE International Conference on Computer Vision, pp. 3754–3762 (2017)
24. Zheng, L., Shen, L., Tian, L., Wang, S., Wang, J., Tian, Q.: Scalable person re-identification: a benchmark. In: Proceedings of the IEEE International Conference on Computer Vision, pp. 1116–1124 (2015)
25. Felzenszwalb, P.F., McAllester, D.A., Ramanan, D., et al.: A discriminatively trained, multiscale, deformable part model. In: CVPR, vol. 2, p. 7 (2008)

No Reference Image Quality Assessment by Information Decomposition

Junchen Deng[2], Ci Wang[1](✉), and Shiqi Liu[2]

[1] School of Communication and Electronic Engineering, East China Normal University, Shanghai, China
cwang@cs.ecnu.edu.cn

[2] School of Computer Science and Technology, East China Normal University, Shanghai, China
juncn.deng@gmail.com

Abstract. No reference (NR) image quality assessment (IQA) is to automatically assess image quality as would be perceived by human without reference images. Currently, almost all state-of-the-art NR IQA approaches are trained and tested on the databases of synthetically distorted images. The synthetically distorted images are usually produced by superimposing one or several common distortions on the clean image, but the authentically distorted images are often simultaneously contaminated by several unknown distortions. Therefore, most IQA performances will greatly drop on the authentically distorted images. Recent researches on the human brain demonstrate that the human visual system (HVS) perceives image scenes by predicting the primary information and avoiding residual uncertainty. According to this theory, a new and robust NR IQA approach is proposed in this paper. By the proposed approach, the distorted image is decomposed into the orderly part and disorderly part to be separately processed as its primary information and uncertainty information. Global features of the distorted image are also calculated to describe the overall image contents. Experimental results on the synthetically and authentically image databases demonstrate that the proposed approach makes great progress in IQA performance.

Keywords: No reference · Image quality assessment · Internal generative mechanism · Authentically distorted images · Salient map · Local binary pattern

1 Introduction

NR IQA approaches assume that pristine images contain certain natural statistical characteristics that will be altered by the introduced distortions. If these statistical properties are properly abstracted as the quality-related features to reflect the statistical changes caused by different types and degrees of distortions, image quality can be inferred through these features. Many NR IQA approaches have been developed in the past decades, but most of them focus on assessing the

Y. M. Ro et al. (Eds.): MMM 2020, LNCS 11961, pp. 826–838, 2020.
https://doi.org/10.1007/978-3-030-37731-1_67

quality of images with single distortion. As for the authentically distorted images, they are often contaminated by multiply distortions, and their IQA research is still in infancy due to the difficulty of multiply-distorted description. Most IQA approaches cannot keep high performance when evaluating multiply-distorted images as that done on single-distorted images.

Several new models are developed recently to assess multiply-distorted images. In [1], Gu et al. propose a six-step blind IQA (BIQA) approach by simulating three stages of image degradation, where the intensities of Noise, Blur, and JPEG distortion are separately calculated and the free energy theory is used to account for their joint effects. Li et al. [2] encode the micro-structures by accumulating the pixel values with the same local binary pattern (LBP) in the gradient domain to capture the structure degradation. This approach is extended to the macro-structures by Tao et al. [3]. They encode the high-order structures from the globally normalized image by a new generalized center-symmetric LBP operator. Though these approaches have high efficiency in assessing the synthetically multiply-distorted images, their performances are greatly reduced when evaluating the authentically distorted images [4]. The authentically distorted images contain randomly mixed distortions with diverse characteristics, which makes their evaluation still an intractable problem. Ghadiyaram and Bovik develop an efficient NR IQA approach, named FRIQUEE [5], by extracting a bag of natural scene statistics (NSS) features in different color spaces and transform domains. Although FRIQUEE's performance on the authentically distorted images exceeds all NR approaches before, it has a rather high time complexity which limits its application.

According to the Bayesian brain theory [6] and the free-energy principle [7], human brains have an internal generative mechanism (IGM) for outward scene understanding. Brains work as an inference system by proactively predicting the primary information of the input scenes and minimizing the predicting error. For IGM-based IQA approaches, the distorted image is usually decomposed into the orderly part and the disorderly part to separately describe primary information and residual uncertainty. In [8], Wu et al. calculate the probability distribution of the luminance contrast map for the orderly part and the intensity energy for the disorderly part, and they employ Shannon Entropy to quantify the information fidelity of these two parts. In their other work [9], the edge and structure similarities of the orderly part are measured to capture the degradation of the primary information, while peak signal-to-noise ratio (PSNR) of the disorderly part is computed to describe the uncomfortable sensation. These two successful IQA approaches prove that it is reasonable to develop an IQA approach based on the IGM model. However, they need the pristine reference image, which makes them incapable of evaluating the authentically distorted images. Recently, Qian et al. [10] propose an NR IQA approach based on IGM theory by calculating the gradient features of the orderly part and the LBP features of the disorderly part. Although their approach works well, there is still room for improvement in describing the different characteristics of the orderly part and the disorderly part.

Motivated by the success of IGM-based IQA works, we propose a novel NR IQA approach in this paper for the authentically distorted images. The main innovations of our work are the proposed feature extraction and the additional description of image contents. According to the distortion influence on image structures, the LBP operator with rotation-invariance and uniform patterns is employed to extract the quality-related features. The visual attention mechanism of HVS is taken into account in the proposed feature extraction by fusing the saliency map (SM) and local binary patterns. For the orderly part, local binary patterns are calculated on its gradient magnitudes (GLBP), and then SM weighted GLBP histograms are proposed as the orderly features to describe the primary structure degradation. For the disorderly part, local binary patterns are calculated on its spatial pixels (SLBP), and then SLBP histograms are encoded as the disorderly features to capture distortions of the uncertainty information. Besides, the SM weighted SLBP histograms and color-related features of the original distorted image are also calculated as the global features to describe the overall image contents. Experimental results demonstrate that the proposed approach not only efficiently evaluates the quality of synthetically distorted images but also has a strong robustness to the authentically distorted images.

2 The Proposed NR IQA Approach

2.1 Image Information Decomposition

The sensory uncertainty determines the optimal weighting scheme of the brain to combine perceptual cues for the prediction of primary information [6]. Inspired by this process, the original distorted image is decomposed into the orderly part and disorderly part for the separate processing of the primary information and uncertainty information. The decomposition method used in this work is low-pass filtering according to the sensitivities of HVS to different image frequencies. Low-frequency components dominate the visual perception of global information. The primary scenes of one image are first inferred by HVS through the low-frequency stimuli and then the local details are perceived through the high-frequency stimuli [11]. For a given image I, its orderly part I_f and disorderly part I_n are defined as

$$I_f = f\left(I_d\right), I_n = I_d - I_f \tag{1}$$

where $f(\cdot)$ is the low-pass filtering and I_d is the grayscale image of I.

BM3D [12] is employed in the proposed approach to perform low-pass filtering. Figure 1 gives us an example of decomposition. Figure 1(a) and (d) are two multiply-distorted images from [1]. Figure 1(a) is mainly contaminated by Noise and JPEG, while Fig. 1(d) is mainly contaminated by Blur and JPEG. As shown in Fig. 1, the different Blur degrees of Fig. 1(a) and (d) result in the different blurring artifacts on their orderly parts, i.e. Fig. 1(b) and (e). For the disorderly part, Fig. 1(c) is more chaotic than Fig. 1(f) due to the heavier noise on Fig. 1(a).

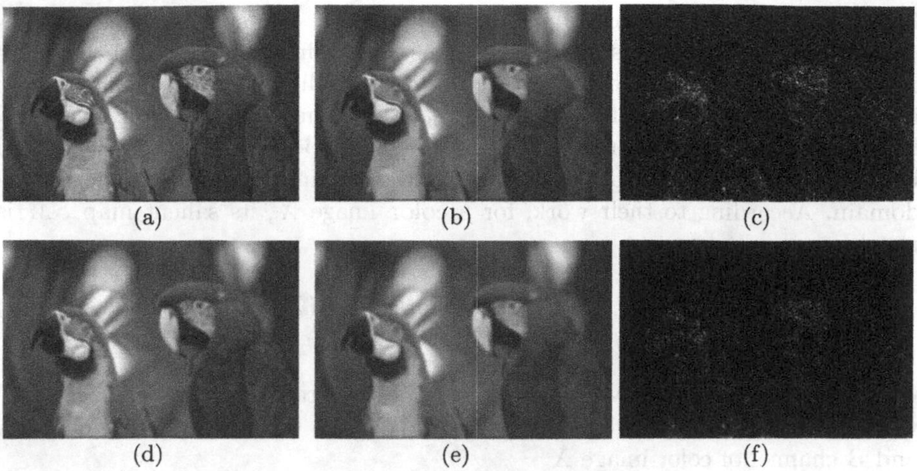

Fig. 1. Two distorted versions of parrots.png from [1], i.e. (a) and (d). The orderly part and disorderly part of (a), i.e. (b) and (c), and (d), i.e. (e) and (f). For good display, the pixel values of the disorderly part are scaled.

2.2 Preliminary Knowledge for Feature Extraction

Quality-related features are extracted from the orderly part, the disorderly part, and the original distorted image. Before discussing feature extraction strategies, we first briefly introduce rotation-invariant LBP operator with uniform patterns ($LBP_{P,R}^{riu2}$) and salient map in this subsection, which are the preliminary knowledge to extract the quality-related features.

The $LBP_{P,R}^{riu2}$ Operator. The $LBP_{P,R}^{riu2}$ operator reflects the relationship between the intermediate pixel and surrounding pixels, which was first proposed in [13] with the purpose of texture classification. The subscript R is the distance between the intermediate pixel and surrounding pixels, and P is the total number of surrounding pixels. The superscript ^{riu2} denotes the "uniform" patterns with rotation invariance. For the pixel i in an image, its $LBP_{P,R}^{riu2}$ value is deduced by

$$LBP_{P,R}^{riu2}(i) = \begin{cases} \sum_{k=0}^{P-1} s\left(g_k - g_i\right) & \text{if } U\left(g_i\right) \leq 2, \\ P+1 & \text{otherwise.} \end{cases} \tag{2}$$

where g_i is the value of pixel i and g_k is its neighboring pixel value with radius R. $s(t)$ equals 1 for $t \geq 0$ and is 0 for other cases. $U\left(g_i\right)$ is the number of bitwise transitions and is defined as

$$U\left(g_i\right) = \left|s\left(g_{P-1} - g_i\right) - s\left(g_0 - g_i\right)\right| + \sum_{k=1}^{P-1} \left|s\left(g_k - g_i\right) - s\left(g_{k-1} - g_i\right)\right| \tag{3}$$

Salient Map. The visual attention mechanism explains the sensitivities of HVS to distinguishable image structures. Human eyes always track significant objects by automatically filtering unimportant image scenes. When an image is contaminated by homogeneous distortions, the conspicuous image areas which are more eye-catching could more affect the overall image quality. Thus, the saliency map is used in this work to reflect the visual attention mechanism. Hou et al. [14] have proved that the salient areas of an image can be approximately separated by taking the signs of DCT coefficients and reversing it back into the spatial domain. According to their work, for a color image X, its salient map SM is roughly computed as

$$SM = \sum_{n=r,g,b} \left[IDCT\left(sign\left(DCT\left(X_n\right)\right)\right)\right]^2 . \quad (4)$$

where $sign(\cdot)$ is the entry-wise sign operator to determine whether each pixel value is positive, negative or 0. X_r, X_g, and X_b are the R channel, G channel, and B channel of color image X.

2.3 Feature Extraction Strategies

For one pristine image, there is a strong dependence among spatially proximate pixels, whose relationship reflects local structures of the image [15]. Image quality degradation essentially results from the alterations in structural correlations among pixels by distortions, which inspires us to use the $LBP_{P,R}^{riu2}$ operator to encode quality-related features. In this subsection, we introduce three types of features, i.e. orderly features of the orderly part, disorderly features of the disorderly part, and global features of the original distorted image. The saliency map computed by (4) is used for the orderly features and global features to reflect the visual attention mechanism of HVS. Distortions on the disorderly part mainly make the HVS feel uncomfortable but have little impact on the understanding of the primary image contents [9]. Thus, the saliency map is not used for the disorderly features.

Local binary patterns computed on the gradient magnitudes and the spatial pixels are respectively denoted as GLBP (gradient LBP) and SLBP (spatial LBP). GLBP map of the orderly part and SLBP map of the disorderly part are used to encode structural features. Figure 2 shows us an example to explain the rationality. Figure 2(a) and (b) are two multiply-distorted images contaminated by Blur and Noise with different degrees. Structural features computed from their orderly parts and disorderly parts are shown in Fig. 2(c)–(f). The significantly changed bins in Fig. 2(c)–(f) are marked with red ellipses. For the good IQA features, the features of Fig. 2(a) and (b) should be easily distinguished from each other. Although both blue bins and cyan bins are varied for these two images, the blue bins change much obviously in the orderly parts, i.e. Fig. 2(c) and (d). Meanwhile, the cyan bins change larger than blue bins in the disorderly parts, i.e. Fig. 2(e) and (f). The features that most effectively reflect quality changes are chosen in this work to reduce the feature dimension and IQA time complexity.

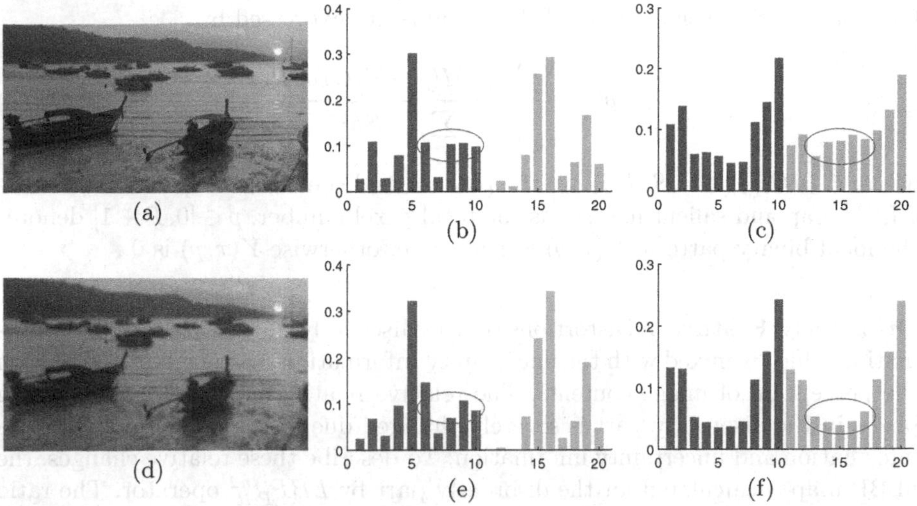

Fig. 2. Two distorted versions of sunrise.bmp from [16], i.e. (a) and (d). Structural features computed from GLBP map (blue bins) and SLBP map (cyan bins) of the orderly part and disorderly part of (a), i.e. (b) and (c), and (d), i.e. (e) and (f). The abscissas are different GLBP and SLBP patterns. The ordinates are the values of GLBP and SLBP histograms. The histograms of (b) and (e) are weighted by SM, which is described by Eq. (6). (Color figure online)

Orderly Features. GLBP map is computed for the orderly part to extract structural features that reflect the primary structure degradation. For the orderly part I_f, its GLBP map is computed by applying the $LBP_{P,R}^{riu2}$ operator on its gradient magnitudes map (∇I_f). ∇I_f is calculated by (5).

$$\nabla I_f = \sqrt{(I_f \otimes P_x)^2 + (I_f \otimes P_y)^2}. \tag{5}$$

where $\otimes$ denotes the convolution operation. P_x and P_y are the Prewitt filters along two perpendicular directions.

GLBP reflects the interpixel associations in the local areas and encodes diverse microstructures into a fixed number of patterns. Multitudinous local structure modes are uniformly represented by GLBP patterns whose statistical changes effectively describe the alterations of microstructures from various distortions [2]. However, GLBP only encodes relative information of the gradient magnitudes and cannot reflect the different visual importance of image contents. To make up for this shortcoming, we fuse the GLBP patterns and the saliency map obtained by (4). Specifically, the salient coefficients at positions with the same GLBP pattern are accumulated to form the SM weighted GLBP histograms which are taken as the orderly features. By combining relative changes in structure information with salient weights, the conspicuous image regions are emphasized and the extracted features reflect human perceived quality better. The formation of SM weighted GLBP histograms are expressed by

$$H_{GLBP}(p) = \frac{\sum_{j=1}^{N} SM(j) \cdot Y(GLBP(j), p)}{\sum_{j=1}^{N} SM(j)} \tag{6}$$

where $GLBP(j)$ and $SM(j)$ are the pattern and coefficient at position j on the GLBP map and salient map. N is the total pixel number. $p \in [0, P+1]$ denotes the local binary pattern. $Y(x,p)$ is 1 if $x = p$, otherwise $Y(x,p)$ is 0.

Disorderly Features. Distortions on the disorderly part bring spurious information which is mixed with the uncertainty information, thereby interfering with the perception of image contents. The relative relationship among neighboring pixels in the disorderly part is severely changed due to the mixture of spurious information and uncertainty information. To describe these relative changes, the SLBP map is calculated for the disorderly part by $LBP_{P,R}^{riu2}$ operator. The ratio of the number of pixels with the same pattern to the total pixel number is calculated, which is the formation of SLBP histogram described by (7). The resulted SLBP histograms centrally reflect distortion influences and are treated as the disorderly features.

$$H_{SLBP}(p) = \frac{1}{N} \sum_{j=1}^{N} Y(SLBP(j), p) \tag{7}$$

where $SLBP(j)$ is the pattern at position j on SLBP map of the disorderly part.

Global Features. For some image scenes, quality degradation is imperceptible when the distortion below a certain threshold, while the same distortion on other scenes may be quite visible [17]. In fact, there is an approximately parabolic relationship between the perceptibility thresholds of distortions and gray levels [18]. When images with distinguished contents are contaminated by the same distortion, human may perceive different qualities due to disparate distortion immunity of different images. Therefore, image contents is a very important factor for IQA modeling. The SM weighted SLBP histograms and color-related features of the original distorted image are calculated as the global features to describe the overall image contents. The calculation of SM weighted SLBP histograms is the same as (6) except that GLBP map is replaced with SLBP map of the grayscale image. Color-related features are extracted on the HSI color space such as the arithmetic mean and standard deviation of its three channels, i.e. hue, saturation, and intensity.

2.4 Feature Pooling and Quality Prediction

The $LBP_{P,R}^{riu2}$ operator described by (2) produces P + 2 patterns [13]. P = 8 and R = 1 are set for $LBP_{P,R}^{riu2}$ operator in this work, which means that (6) and (7) can form 10 histograms respectively. The HVS perceives and understands image scenes from low resolution to high resolution [11], hence that the proposed features are also calculated on multi-scales. Besides original scale, two coarser layers are calculated to simulate human perception. The coarser layer is computed by down-sampling the current scale into its half size. Therefore, the orderly part and the disorderly part each produce 30 features (3 scales with 10 features respectively). Besides, 36 global features are calculated from the original distorted image to characterize the image contents, which contain 30 SW weighted SLBP histograms and 6 color-related features. A total of 96 features are extracted and these features are pooled together to learn the quality prediction model.

Support vector regressor (SVR) with a radial basis kernel function (RBF) [19] is employed in this work to learn the relationship between quality-related features and objective quality scores. The LIBSVM [20] package is selected to implement SVR for training and testing, and the parameters of SVR are set by the grid regression optimization proposed in [20]. Image quality to be evaluated can be obtained through above learning.

3 Experiment Results and Discussions

3.1 Evaluation Criteria and Database Selection

The IQA performance is usually tested on some standard image databases with subjective quality scores given by human. For a good IQA approach, the predicted scores should have a strong linear correlation with subject scores. In this paper, Spearman's rank-order correlation coefficient (SROCC) and Pearson's linear correlation coefficient (PLCC) between the predicted scores and subjective scores are chosen to measure this linear correlation. Besides, the root-mean-squared error (RMSE) is chosen to measure the prediction deviation. The predicted scores are processed by the monotonic mapping [21] before computing PLCC and RMSE. For high IQA performance, SROCC and PLCC should approach 1 and RMSE should be as small as possible.

The benchmark databases chosen here are MLIVE [16], MDID2013 [1], and LIVE Challenge [4]. MLIVE contains 135 single-distortion images and 270 multiply-distorted images. The multiply-distorted images in MLIVE are chosen for performance testing, and their distortion types are Blur followed by Noise and Blur followed by JPEG. MDID2013 contains 324 multiply-distorted images that are simultaneously contaminated by Noise, Blur, and JPEG with different degrees. LIVE Challenge consists of 1169 distorted images with diverse authentic distortions. The subjective image quality scores are scaled to [0, 5] for all databases. 80% of images in each database are selected randomly for SVR learning and the remaining 20% of images are used for testing. This random training-testing experiment is repeated 1000 times and the median performance is reported. For comparison fairness, the methods without training are tested on the randomly selected 20% images from each database.

3.2 Performance Evaluation and Comparison

The proposed approach is named as NIIFD to represent NR IQA by information decomposition. In order to show the progress of this work, we compare NIIFD with 12 state-of-the-art NR IQA approaches and 6 full reference (FR) IQA approaches. The performances of these approaches are tabulated and the best two results for all databases are highlighted by the bolded font.

Table 1. Performance comparisons with NR approaches and FR approaches on MLIVE and MDID2013.

IQA approaches	MLIVE (270 images)			MDID2013 (324 images)		
	SROCC	PLCC	RMSE	SROCC	PLCC	RMSE
*W*u's [9]	0.712	0.695	0.821	0.817	0.821	0.692
*S*SIM [15]	0.738	0.705	0.728	0.487	0.525	0.928
*V*IF [22]	0.775	0.797	0.691	0.839	0.845	0.654
*P*SIM [23]	0.718	0.715	0.804	0.855	0.858	0.625
*M*AD [24]	0.755	0.771	0.727	0.746	0.766	0.785
*G*MSD [25]	0.710	0.739	0.778	0.840	0.857	0.660
NIQE [26]	0.551	0.606	0.916	0.560	0.586	0.987
ILNIQE [27]	0.768	0.787	0.706	0.515	0.540	1.022
DIIVINE [28]	0.832	0.851	0.534	0.896	0.908	0.459
BLIINDS2 [29]	0.853	0.867	0.507	0.897	0.907	0.461
BRISQUE [30]	0.834	0.859	0.523	0.893	0.905	0.464
C-DIIVINE [31]	0.915	0.924	0.383	0.939	0.947	0.355
GMLOG [32]	0.767	0.788	0.625	0.798	0.813	0.635
CurveletQA [33]	0.842	0.857	0.525	0.894	0.904	0.473
SISBLM [1]	0.783	0.802	0.685	0.806	0.827	0.686
GWH-GLBP [2]	**0.949**	**0.955**	**0.293**	**0.948**	**0.955**	**0.323**
FRIQUEE [5]	0.940	0.950	0.317	0.942	0.950	0.341
Qian's [10]	0.869	0.880	0.480	0.824	0.844	0.588
NIIFD	**0.946**	**0.954**	**0.304**	**0.947**	**0.953**	**0.336**

Experimental results tested on MLIVE and MDID2013 are listed in Table 1. FR approaches are displayed in italics. It can be found from Table 1 that GWH-GLBP and NIIFD have the best testing results on these two databases, which illustrates that NIIFD's performance can keep pace with the highest performance in the IQA field. Although GWH-GLBP works slightly better than NIIFD, it cannot be concluded that NIIFD is inferior to GWH-GLBP because images in these two databases only contain limited synthetic distortions. Synthetic distortions are deterministic and controllable, while authentic distortions are random and unpredictable. Thus, experimental results on MLIVE and MDID2013 are insufficient to fully explain the performances of IQA approaches.

To more comprehensively demonstrate the progress of NIIFD in evaluating distorted images, NR approaches are tested on LIVE Challenge. FR approaches are not tested due to the unavailability of reference images in this database. The experiments on LIVE Challenge can better examine the robustness and practicability of an IQA approach because this database contains various authentically distorted images. The testing results are listed in Table 2, where it can be seen that the performances of all NR approaches for the authentically distorted images drop a lot due to the difficulty of describing so many authentic distortions. FRIQUEE and NIIFD are two top-performing approaches and are significantly ahead of other approaches in terms of SROCC, PLCC, and RMSE. FRIQUEE uses 562 features to train the quality prediction model, while NIIFD only uses 96 features, hence that feature dimension and time complexity of NIIFD are much lower than that of FRIQUEE. Besides, although GWH-GLBP has the comparative performance with NIIFD on MLIVE and MDID2013, its performance on LIVE Challenge is much lower than NIIFD, which means that GWH-GLBP has weaker robustness than NIIFD.

Table 2. Performance comparisons with NR approaches on LIVE Challenge.

NR approaches	LIVE Challenge (1169 images)			Time (s)
	SROCC	PLCC	RMSE	
NIQE	0.450	0.504	1.019	0.168
ILNIQE	0.440	0.525	10.274	5.471
DIIVINE	0.591	0.629	0.885	10.675
BLIINDS2	0.497	0.549	0.949	20.476
BRISQUE	0.605	0.641	0.871	**0.074**
C-DIIVINE	0.661	0.691	0.825	5.669
GMLOG	0.594	0.626	0.889	**0.063**
CurveletQA	0.609	0.630	0.886	0.701
SISBLM	0.482	0.528	0.999	3.464
GWH-GLBP	0.570	0.615	0.898	0.109
FRIQUEE	**0.682**	**0.716**	**0.797**	24.524
Qian's	0.548	0.574	0.928	9.496
NIIFD	**0.697**	**0.726**	**0.785**	0.742

To verify statistically significant advantages of NIIFD over the compared NR approaches, one-sided t-test [34] with 95% confidence is performed on SROCC and PLCC values obtained from 1000 train-test trials on LIVE Challenge database. Testing results show that NIIFD is statistically better than all compared approaches. Besides, the time required to test an image with resolution 500*500 for those NR approaches is also listed in the last column of Table 2. The test is performed on the computer with Intel(R) Core(TM) i5-7400 CPU @ 3.00 GHz and RAM 8.00 GB using Matlab 2017a software. Among all the competing approaches, NIIFD achieves the highest performance on LIVE Challenge database while keeping low time complexity.

4 Conclusion

Based on the IGM theory, a novel NR IQA approach is proposed in this paper. To describe the primary information and uncertainty information, the distorted image is decomposed into the orderly part and disorderly part by low-pass filtering. The SM weighted GLBP histograms are proposed for the orderly part to describe quality degradation of the primary information. The SLBP histograms are calculated for the disorderly part to capture distortions of the uncertain information. Besides, the distortion tolerance of image contents is also considered by calculating the SM weighted SLBP histograms and color-related features of the original distorted image. The performance comparisons verify that NIIFD achieves significant improvement of IQA performance in terms of robustness and implementation speed.

References

1. Gu, K., Zhai, G., Yang, X., Zhang, W.: Hybrid no-reference quality metric for singly and multiply distorted images. IEEE Trans. Broadcast. **60**(3), 555–567 (2014)
2. Li, Q., Lin, W., Fang, Y.: No-reference quality assessment for multiply-distorted images in gradient domain. IEEE Sig. Process. Lett. **23**(4), 541–545 (2016)
3. Dai, T., Gu, K., Xu, Z., Tang, Q.: Blind quality assessment of multiply-distorted images based on structural degradation. In: 2017 IEEE International Conference on Image Processing (ICIP), pp. 171–175. IEEE (2017)
4. Ghadiyaram, D., Bovik, A.C.: Massive online crowdsourced study of subjective and objective picture quality. IEEE Trans. Image Process. **25**(1), 372–387 (2015)
5. Ghadiyaram, D., Bovik, A.C.: Perceptual quality prediction on authentically distorted images using a bag of features approach. J. Vis. **17**(1), 32–32 (2017)
6. Knill, D.C., Pouget, A.: The Bayesian brain: the role of uncertainty in neural coding and computation. Trends Neurosci. **27**(12), 712–719 (2004)
7. Friston, K.: The free-energy principle: a unified brain theory? Nat. Rev. Neurosci. **11**(2), 127–138 (2010)
8. Wu, J., Lin, W., Shi, G., Liu, A.: Reduced-reference image quality assessment with visual information fidelity. IEEE Trans. Multimed. **15**(7), 1700–1705 (2013)
9. Wu, J., Lin, W., Shi, G., Liu, A.: Perceptual quality metric with internal generative mechanism. IEEE Trans. Image Process. **22**(1), 43–54 (2013)
10. Qian, X., Zhou, W., Li, H.: No-reference image quality assessment based on internal generative mechanism. In: Amsaleg, L., Guðmundsson, G.Þ., Gurrin, C., Jónsson, B.Þ., Satoh, S. (eds.) MMM 2017. LNCS, vol. 10132, pp. 264–276. Springer, Cham (2017). https://doi.org/10.1007/978-3-319-51811-4_22

11. Hughes, H.C., Nozawa, G., Kitterle, F.: Global precedence, spatial frequency channels, and the statistics of natural images. J. Cogn. Neurosci. **8**(3), 197–230 (1996)
12. Dabov, K., Foi, A., Katkovnik, V., Egiazarian, K.: Image denoising by sparse 3-D transform-domain collaborative filtering. IEEE Trans. Image Process. **16**(8), 2080–2095 (2007)
13. Ojala, T., Pietikainen, M., Maenpaa, T.: Multiresolution gray-scale and rotation invariant texture classification with local binary patterns. IEEE Trans. Pattern Anal. Mach. Intell. **24**(7), 971–987 (2002)
14. Hou, X., Harel, J., Koch, C.: Image signature: highlighting sparse salient regions. IEEE Trans. Pattern Anal. Mach. Intell. **34**(1), 194–201 (2011)
15. Wang, Z., Bovik, A.C., Sheikh, H.R., Simoncelli, E.P.: Image quality assessment: from error visibility to structural similarity. IEEE Trans. Image Process. **13**(4), 600–612 (2004)
16. Jayaraman, D., Mittal, A., Moorthy, A.K., Bovik, A.C.: Objective quality assessment of multiply distorted images. In: 2012 Conference Record of 46th Asilomar Conference on Signals, Systems and Computers (ASILOMAR), pp. 1693–1697, November 2012
17. Jayant, N., Johnston, J., Safranek, R.: Signal compression based on models of human perception. In: Proceedings of the IEEE, pp. 1385–1422. IEEE, October 1993
18. Zhang, X.H., Lin, W.S., Xue, P.: Improved estimation for just-noticeable visual distortion. Signal Process. **85**(4), 795–808 (2005)
19. Schölkopf, B., Smola, A.J., Williamson, R.C., Bartlett, P.L.: New support vector algorithms. Neural Comput. **12**(5), 1207–1245 (2000)
20. Chang, C.C., Lin, C.J.: LIBSVM: a library for support vector machines. ACM Trans. Intell. Syst. Tech. **2**(3), 27 (2011). https://www.csie.ntu.edu.tw/~cjlin/libsvm/
21. Video Quality Experts Group: Final report from the video quality experts group on the validation of objective models of video quality assessment, VQEG, March 2000
22. Sheikh, H.R., Bovik, A.C.: Image information and visual quality. IEEE Trans. Image Process. **15**(2), 430–444 (2006)
23. Gu, K., Li, L., Lu, H., Lin, W.: A fast reliable image quality predictor by fusing micro-and macro-structures. IEEE Trans. Ind. Electron. **64**(5), 3903–3912 (2017)
24. Larson, E.C., Chandler, D.M.: Most apparent distortion: full-reference image quality assessment and the role of strategy. J. Electron. Imaging **19**(1), 011006 (2010)
25. Xue, W., Zhang, L., Mou, X., Bovik, A.C.: Gradient magnitude similarity deviation: a highly efficient perceptual image quality index. IEEE Trans. Image Process. **23**(2), 684–695 (2013)
26. Mittal, A., Soundararajan, R., Bovik, A.C.: Making a completely blind image quality analyzer. IEEE Signal Process. Lett. **20**(3), 209–212 (2013)
27. Zhang, L., Zhang, L., Bovik, A.C.: A feature-enriched completely blind image quality evaluator. IEEE Trans. Image Process. **24**(8), 2579–2591 (2015)
28. Saad, M.A., Bovik, A.C., Charrier, C.: Blind image quality assessment: a natural scene statistics approach in the DCT domain. IEEE Trans. Image Process. **21**(8), 3339–3352 (2012)
29. Moorthy, A.K., Bovik, A.C.: Blind image quality assessment: from natural scene statistics to perceptual quality. IEEE Trans. Image Process. **20**(12), 3350–3364 (2011)
30. Mittal, A., Moorthy, A.K., Bovik, A.C.: No-reference image quality assessment in the spatial domain. IEEE Trans. Image Process. **21**(12), 4695–4708 (2012)

31. Zhang, Y., Moorthy, A.K., Chandler, D.M., Bovik, A.C.: C-DIIVINE: no-reference image quality assessment based on local magnitude and phase statistics of natural scenes. Signal Process.: Image Commun. **29**(7), 725–747 (2014)
32. Xue, W., Mou, X., Zhang, L., Bovik, A.C., Feng, X.: Blind image quality assessment using joint statistics of gradient magnitude and Laplacian features. IEEE Trans. Image Process. **23**(11), 4850–4862 (2014)
33. Liu, L., Dong, H., Huang, H., Bovik, A.C.: No-reference image quality assessment in curvelet domain. Sig. Process.: Image Commun. **29**(4), 494–505 (2014)
34. Sheskin, D.J.: Handbook of Parametric and Nonparametric Statistical Procedures, 3rd edn. Chapman and Hall/CRC, New York (2003)

Correction to: MultiMedia Modeling

Yong Man Ro, Wen-Huang Cheng, Junmo Kim, Wei-Ta Chu,
Peng Cui, Jung-Woo Choi, Min-Chun Hu, and Wesley De Neve

Correction to: Y. M. Ro et al. (Eds.): *MultiMedia Modeling*, LNCS 11961, https://doi.org/10.1007/978-3-030-37731-1

The original version of this book was revised. Due to a technical error, the first volume editor did not appear in the volumes of the MMM 2020 proceedings. This was corrected and the first volume editor was added.

The updated version of the book can be found at
https://doi.org/10.1007/978-3-030-37731-1

Y. M. Ro et al. (Eds.): MMM 2020, LNCS 11961, p. C1, 2020.
https://doi.org/10.1007/978-3-030-37731-1_68

Author Index

Printed in the United States
By Bookmasters